W9-ATC-958

Microsoft®

3

Third Edition

PROGRAMMING MICROSOFT® OUTLOOK® AND MICROSOFT EXCHANGE 2003

Microsoft® .net

Thomas Rizzo

PUBLISHED BY
Microsoft Press
A Division of Microsoft Corporation
One Microsoft Way
Redmond, Washington 98052-6399

Library of Congress Cataloging-in-Publication Data
Rizzo, Thomas, 1972-

Programming Microsoft Outlook and Microsoft Exchange 2003, Third Edition / Thomas Rizzo.--3rd ed.

p. cm.

Includes index.

ISBN 0-7356-1464-4

1. Application software--Development. 2. Microsoft Outlook. 3. Microsoft Exchange. I. Title.

QA76.76.A65R59 2003
005.369--dc21 2003046497

Printed and bound in the United States of America.

1 2 3 4 5 6 7 8 9 QWT 8 7 6 5 4 3

Distributed in Canada by H.B. Fenn and Company Ltd.

A CIP catalogue record for this book is available from the British Library.

Microsoft Press books are available through booksellers and distributors worldwide. For further information about international editions, contact your local Microsoft Corporation office or contact Microsoft Press International directly at fax (425) 936-7329. Visit our Web site at www.microsoft.com/mspress. Send comments to *mspinput@microsoft.com*.

Acquisitions Editor: Anne Hamilton
Project Editor: Barbara Moreland
Technical Editor: Jerry Camel

Body Part No. X08-24435

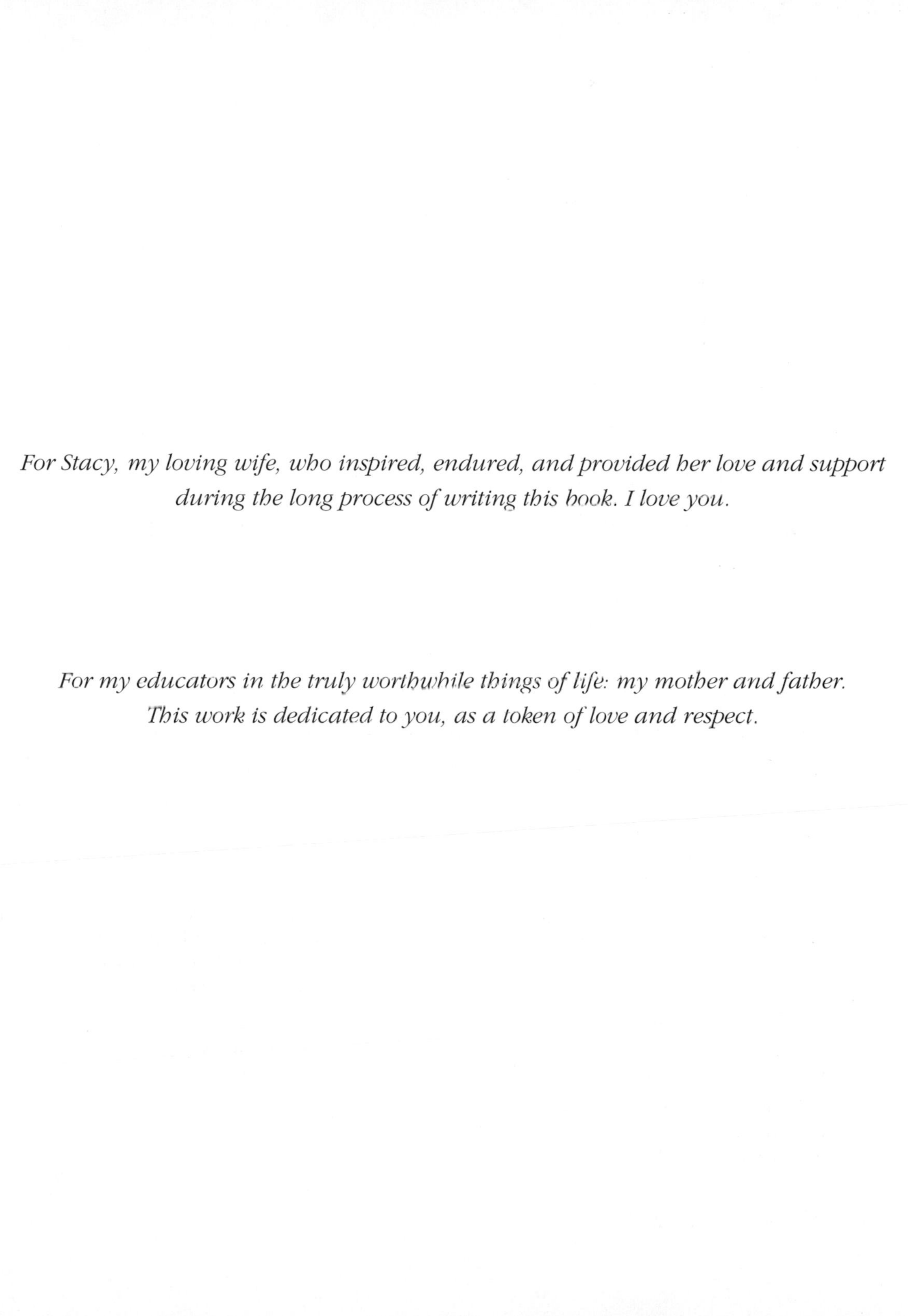

For Stacy, my loving wife, who inspired, endured, and provided her love and support during the long process of writing this book. I love you.

For my educators in the truly worthwhile things of life: my mother and father. This work is dedicated to you, as a token of love and respect.

Table of Contents

Acknowledgments

Writing a book is never a one person job. It always involves help from other people either reviewing your work or teaching you things that you never knew before. The first people to thank are the folks at Microsoft Press, especially Barbara Moreland, John Pierce, Anne Hamilton, Jerry Camel, Kay Unkroth, Ina Chang, and Seth Maslin. Their hard work is greatly appreciated.

Thanks are owed to a number of people throughout Microsoft who helped in one way or another with this endeavor. First and foremost, thanks must go to the members of the Exchange and Outlook teams who contributed to my knowledge of both products. Among those who helped me were members of the OWA team, specifically Jim Van Eaton and Bob Gering, who lent their expertise of XML, XSL, WebDAV, and OWA to the Training application in the Exchange chapters. Unfortunately, Bob passed away during the writing of this book. Bob was always willing to help both Microsoft and non-Microsoft developers with the questions they had and always gave a helping hand figuring out hard coding problems. The information that Bob provided and the help he gave me on the code in this book are a testament to the good person that Bob was. Bob, you'll be missed.

Thanks go to people who were on the Exchange Development team when this book was being written including Nat Ballou, Andrew Sinclair, Naveen Kachroo, Jamie Cool, Alex Hopmann, Jim Reitz, Chuck Daniel, and Dana Birkby, who filled me in on the latest and greatest about the Exchange technologies. Another debt of gratitude must go to the Exchange management team including Gord Mangione and Stan Sorensen because I stole away the time of their valuable people to answer my questions during the two years this book was written.

I also have to thank the SharePoint team. Their enthusiasm for helping me get my questions answered and getting the best information out to their developer community really shows in the SharePoint chapters. Thanks to SharePoint management, especially Jeff Teper and Jon Kauffman, who allowed their people to help me whenever I needed it. A special thanks goes to Viki Selca, Clint Covington, Brian Murphy, Suraj Poozhiyil, and Nilly Banerjee, who reviewed my SharePoint chapters, provided great feedback, and offered their time unselflessly.

Special thanks also go to Jeff Wierer and Lyle Curry, who helped throughout the process of this book. They provided some great ideas for the sample applications for the book.

Introduction

This book is the culmination of two years of work while I was waiting for Microsoft Outlook 2003 and Microsoft Exchange 2003 to be released to the public. You will find in-depth information on how to build collaborative applications on the Microsoft platform using technologies such as Outlook, Exchange Server, Microsoft SharePoint, smart documents, smart tags, and Microsoft Office Live Communications Server. All of the relevant content could not fit into a single printed book, however, so you will find chapters on some of the technologies available for download from the Microsoft Press Web site. The Web site also includes all the book's sample applications and sample files, including SharePoint 2.0 Web parts and Outlook and Exchange samples. (See "Installing and Using the Sample Files and Supplemental Chapters" for the location of this matetrial.)

Who This Book Is For

This book is targeted at all levels of developers. I've tried to make the book approachable for beginners while also providing the in-depth information and advanced tips and tricks that readers of the previous two editions have come to expect. Many of the samples are written both for native code and Microsoft .NET. Users of native code will find samples that show how to build collaborative applications with tools they are used to, such as Microsoft Visual Basic 6 and Microsoft Active Server Pages (ASP). You will even learn how to build Exchange Web services with Visual Basic 6 and the SOAP Toolkit. Most samples have a .NET version as well. They show how to use Microsoft's collaborative technologies in the .NET environment. I have also tried to provide the code in more than one language throughout the book so that Visual Basic and Visual C# developers can benefit from the samples.

How the Book Is Organized

Part I of the book offers useful background information about collaborative systems and Exchange Server as a platform for collaboration.

Part II is for the Office developer, specifically the Outlook developer. I start with the basics in Outlook, such as creating forms, fields, and views. Then we quickly progress to building advanced forms and COM add-ins, in both native and .NET-compatible code, for Outlook. Part II also covers the security changes in Outlook that affect (and sometime irritate) Outlook developers. I also include advanced information on smart tags and smart documents in Office 2003. As an Outlook developer, you will probably want to understand how to use all these technologies in your applications.

Part III covers the server side, specifically Exchange Server and Live Communications Server, which provide instant messaging and collaboration capabilities. I cover all the APIs that are available for programming with Exchange, including Collaboration Data Objects (CDO) 1.21, CDO for Exchange, CDO for Exchange Management, and Web Distributed Authoring and Versioning (WebDAV). We also look at advanced features such as Active Directory Services Interfaces (ADSI), server events, workflow, Web services, and programming Exchange in .NET.

The additional chapters on the Web site cover in greater detail some areas that are covered briefly in the book, such as the Rules and ACL components (which were covered in the second edition and have been updated for .NET) as well as how to build collaborative applications on SharePoint. These chapters show you how to program SharePoint Portal Server (SPS) 2001, Windows SharePoint Services, and SPS 2.0.

Author Contact

I hope you enjoy reading this book as much as I enjoyed writing it. I also hope you will find it a useful reference when you're building collaborative applications and need help understanding how to use Microsoft's collaborative tools. I provide a large number of code samples so that you'll always have a sample showing how to implement the functionality you want from the many collaborative technologies that Microsoft provides.

Enjoy the book! If you ever have any comments or questions about developing on the Microsoft collaborative platform, do not hesitate to shoot me an e-mail message using my favorite e-mail client, Microsoft Outlook. You can reach me at thomriz@microsoft.com.

Installing and Using the Sample Files and Supplemental Chapters

You can download the sample files and additional chapters from the Web by connecting to

http://www.microsoft.com/mspress/books/5517.asp

To access the sample files and the links to other resources we've provided, click Companion Content in the More Information menu box on the right side of the page. This will load the Companion Content Web page, which includes links for downloading the sample files and additional chapters and for connecting to Microsoft Press Support. Each download link on the page opens an InstallShield executable file containing a license agreement. To copy the sample files or additional chapters onto your hard disk, click the link to run the executable and then accept the license agreement that is presented. By default, the files will be copied to [My Documents]\Microsoft Press\Programming Outlook and Exchange. (During the installation process, you'll be given the option of changing that destination folder.)

System Requirements

The sample code is this book will run on a system with the following minimum requirements.

Microsoft Windows Server

- Microsoft Windows 2000 Server or later. Windows 2003 is preferred.
- Internet Information Services enabled on the Windows Server.
- Microsoft Exchange 2000 or later. Exchange 2003 is preferred
- Microsoft Visual Studio 6 or later. Visual Studio .NET is preferred

Microsoft Windows Client

- Microsoft Windows 2000 or later operating system. Microsoft Windows XP is preferred.
- Microsoft Office XP or later. Microsoft Office 2003 is preferred.
- Internet Explorer 5 or later.

Support Information

Every effort has been made to ensure the accuracy of this book and the companion content. Microsoft Press provides corrections for books through the World Wide Web at

http://www.microsoft.com/mspress/support/

To connect directly to the Microsoft Press Knowledge Base and enter a query regarding a question or issue that you may have, go to

http://www.microsoft.com/mspress/support/search.asp

If you have comments, questions, or ideas regarding the book or its companion content, please send them to Microsoft Press via e-mail to:

MSPInput@microsoft.com

or via postal mail to:

Microsoft Press
Attn: Programming Microsoft Outlook and Microsoft Exchange 2003, 3rd ed., Editor
One Microsoft Way
Redmond, WA 98052-6399

Please note that product support is not offered through the preceding addresses.

Part I

Introduction to Collaborative Systems

1

A Broader Definition of Collaboration

If you asked 10 people to define collaboration in a computing environment, you would receive a variety of answers. Some would say collaboration is e-mail. Others would mention video teleconferencing or the World Wide Web. You might even hear Internet chat as an answer. People struggle to define collaboration because so many technologies are related to the concept, and its definition today is broad. Really, all of these answers are correct. Collaboration—at least in part—is the integration of many technologies into a single application or environment to facilitate information sharing and information management.

Integrated technology, however, is only one aspect of collaboration as I'm defining it. Timing is another. We're all familiar with the kind of real-time collaboration in which teams gather and work together, taking turns communicating ideas. But new technology offers an entirely different form of collaboration—asynchronous collaboration—in which you don't have to be present to participate. Asynchronous collaboration allows you, at your convenience, to collaborate with other people at their convenience. E-mail, public databases, the Internet, and intranets are all forms of asynchronous communication.

Collaborative technology provides these key benefits to businesses and organizations:

- **Extensive, secure communication** Collaborative technologies enable extensive communication through many mediums and secure communication through encryption and digital signature technology—critical features for business transactions conducted over the Internet.

- **Storing information in a central location** Information is placed in a central repository, or database, so individuals inside and outside a corporation can access it.
- **Showing information in a threaded view** Information can be shown in a threaded view so its history is accessible and new information can be added to it.
- **Ability to extend technologies with new functionality and bridge islands of information** Collaborative systems connect disparate systems and facilitate finding and sharing information stored in formats used by existing technologies. Essentially, they bridge islands of information.

How does a collaborative system provide these benefits to organizations? In terms of its architecture, a collaborative system must have several characteristics. First, it must have a robust, easily replicated object database that can store many types of information, such as Web pages, Microsoft Office documents, and e-mail messages. The system must support replication from server to server and from server to client. Replication allows information to be accessed by individuals who are dispersed geographically. For users to work with the data, the database must allow connections from many different clients, from Web browsers to industry-specific applications.

Second, a collaborative system must support the Internet and industry standards. The days of stovepipe computing are over. Technologies now connect disparate networks to form one global, cohesive network. A collaborative system must be able to interoperate with networks over the Internet, and it must follow industry standards that open it to a large number of external systems as well as guarantee the integrity of the data.

Third, a collaborative system must offer development tools and technologies and be easily programmable. The environment must be open so developers can use any tool to develop solutions and users can access and customize the user interface.

Tools for Building Collaborative Systems

Microsoft offers a number of products and tools that help developers make use of the technologies in which a company is currently invested and add new functionality to them. These tools fall into three key product types:

- **Client products** Microsoft Office, especially Microsoft Outlook, Microsoft Internet Explorer, and MSN Messenger

- **Server products** Microsoft Exchange Server, Microsoft SQL Server, Microsoft Internet Information Services (IIS), and the SharePoint family of products
- **Development products** Microsoft Visual Studio .NET, which encompasses Microsoft Visual Basic, Microsoft Visual C#, Microsoft Visual C++, and the Microsoft .NET Framework

The two tools you will mainly want to learn about are Outlook and Exchange Server. Both provide a robust infrastructure with which corporations can run mission-critical services. Combine this infrastructure with the rich development capabilities provided by both products and you have a powerful platform on which to build solutions ranging from simple forms to complex applications. Next we'll take a quick look at some of the products and tools available from Microsoft for building collaborative solutions.

Outlook 2003

Outlook is Microsoft's premier client that has the ability to manage information (e-mail messages, appointments, contacts, and tasks) and share it throughout an organization. Outlook also includes a development environment in which you can write collaborative applications quickly. Part II of this book is dedicated to Outlook and its development environment. Chapters 4, 5, and 6 in particular describe and illustrate the features of Outlook that will enable you to extend it.

Before diving into how to build applications in the Outlook environment, I'll give you an overview of enhancements in Outlook 2003. I'll cover both developer and end user enhancements because the end user enhancements often have developer counterparts. I'll assume that you already know many of the features in Outlook 2002 and earlier.

End User Features

This section describes some of the new end user features in Outlook. These features fall into two main categories, information management enhancements and better replication technologies in Outlook.

Better Network Performance

Two of the major requests for improvements that Outlook users make is in latency and network utilization. When you use Outlook 2003 with servers running Exchange Server 2003, you can have Outlook use a cached copy of your mailbox to work continuously off line while synchronizing with the server in the background. In this new offline mode, you can look up free/busy information and work directly with the Global Address List (GAL)—something you couldn't do in previous versions. Outlook also displays the status of your folders (such as whether they are up-to-date or whether they need to be synchronized with the server).

MAPI over HTTP

When you work from home or via a dial-up connection, you often need to establish a VPN connection to your corporate network before you can launch Outlook. Outlook now supports sending MAPI calls over HTTP, which means you don't have to create a VPN to your corporate network. Instead, if your Exchange servers are enabled for this technology, you can tunnel into your Exchange servers from Outlook over HTTP. In addition, to provide security all the interaction can be performed over HTTPS so that the network traffic is protected by encryption. This approach is similar to the way you work with Outlook Web Access (OWA).

Reading Pane

You can now reposition the reading pane (formerly the preview pane) to one of several places on your screen. You can also move the preview pane from the bottom of the screen to the right side or to the top of the screen. Figure 1-1 shows the preview pane on the right side of the Outlook window.

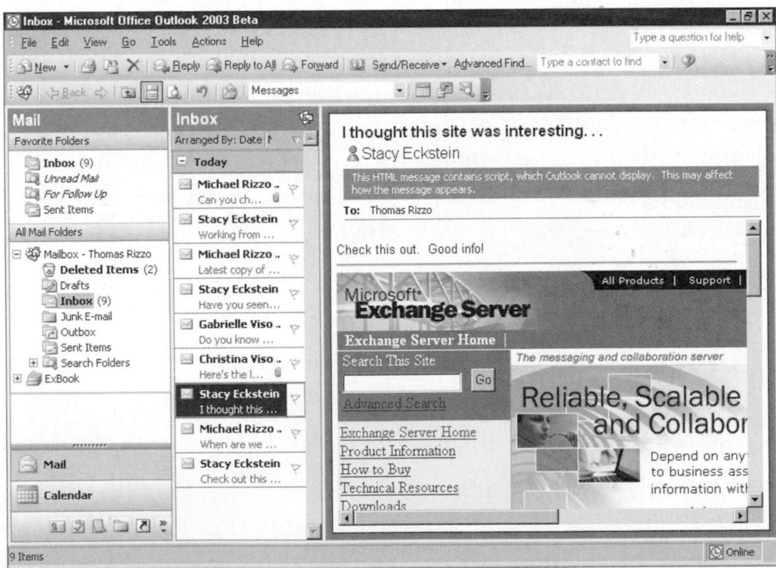

Figure 1-1 The new reading pane in Outlook 2003

Switching Between Online and Offline Mode

One of the biggest hassles with Outlook is switching between working on line and working off line and having to restart Outlook. Now you can switch from online to offline mode in Outlook without having to restart it. With Outlook 2003, if you suddenly lose connectivity to your server, you can quickly switch to offline mode.

Better Notifications via Desktop Alerts

Taking a page from Windows Messenger and its pop-up alerts, Outlook can now display your new e-mail messages and alerts using a transparent pop-up on your desktop. Figure 1-2 shows the new Desktop Alert feature in Outlook.

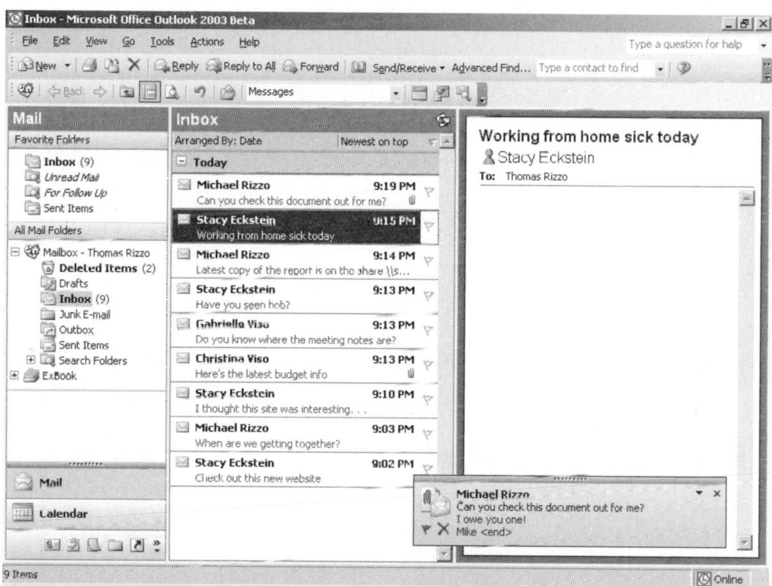

Figure 1-2 The new Desktop Alert feature in Outlook 2003; note the small alert window at the bottom right of the screen.

Search Folders

When you work in Outlook, you often need to perform a search for the same items multiple times. For example, you might search for all flagged items in your inbox. To help you better organize your e-mail, Outlook 2003 introduces *search folders*. Search folders contain a query, and Outlook dynamically updates the folders with new items that meet the query's criteria. You will learn about search folders in Exchange Server 2003 in Chapter 16. Figure 1-3 shows a search folder in Outlook.

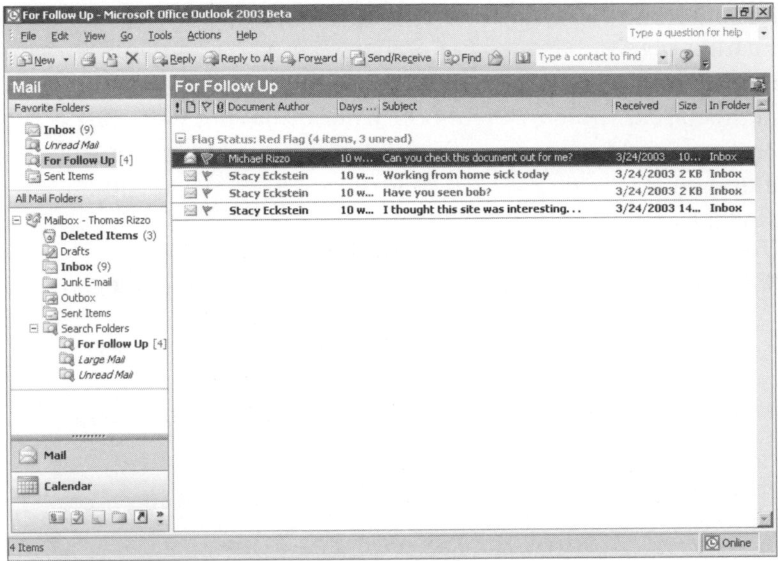

Figure 1-3 Search folders in Outlook 2003

Quick Flagging

The Quick Flag feature in Outlook 2003 allows you to quickly flag an item. Using a column in your view, you can click on the flag and add different color flags to a message. Combined with search folders, quick flags let you organize information efficiently in Outlook. Figure 1-4 shows the Quick Flag feature in Outlook.

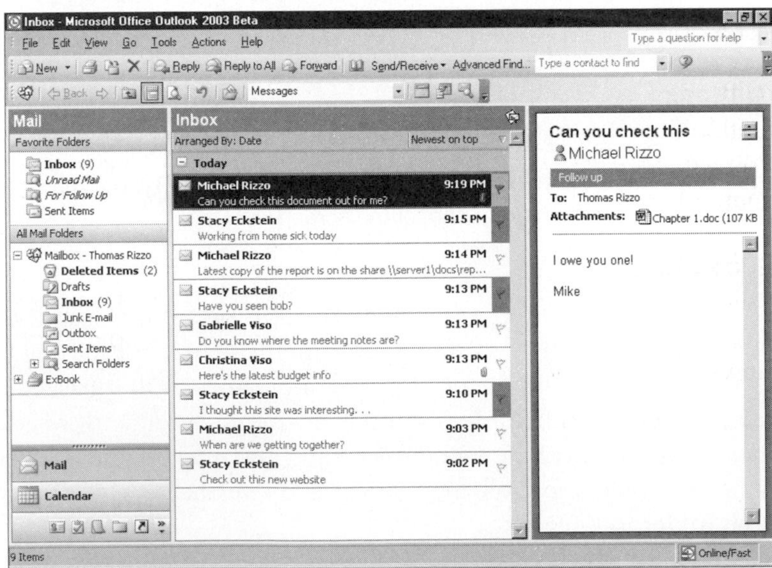

Figure 1-4 Quick flagging in Outlook 2003; note the flag icons on the right side of the *Inbox* pane.

Distribution List Expansion in E-Mail Messages

With earlier versions of Outlook, when you view free/busy information in a meeting request, you can expand distribution lists (DLs) to display their individual members, but you cannot do this in an e-mail message. With Outlook 2003, you can expand DLs in e-mail messages by clicking the plus sign next to the DL name. Figure 1-5 shows a message addressed to a DL in Outlook 2003. Note the small plus sign next to the DL name.

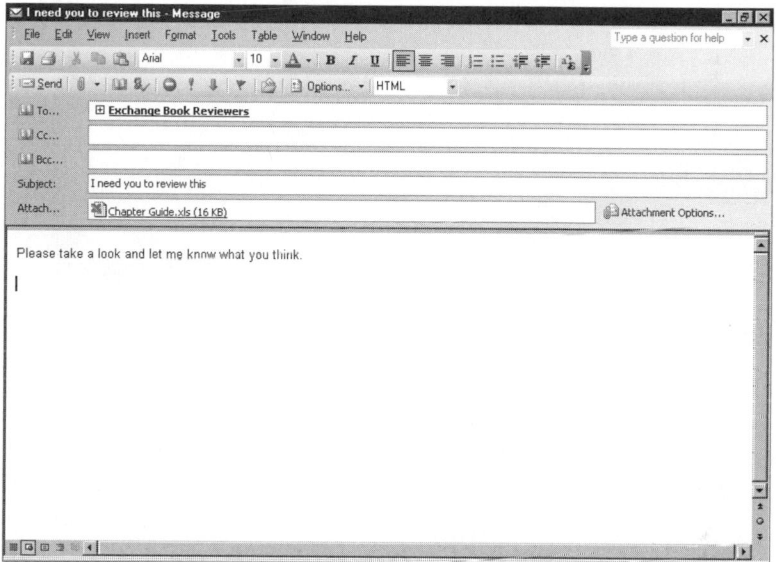

Figure 1-5 Distribution list expansion in Outlook 2003

New Outlook Bar

The Outlook bar in Outlook 2003 combines the folder list and the old Outlook bar. You can even add your view list to the Outlook bar. Figure 1-6 shows the new Outlook bar.

Rules Wizard Enhancements

The Rules Wizard has new functionality in Outlook 2003. It has a new user interface, and mobile and desktop alerts are integrated into the wizard. Figure 1-7 shows the new Rules Wizard.

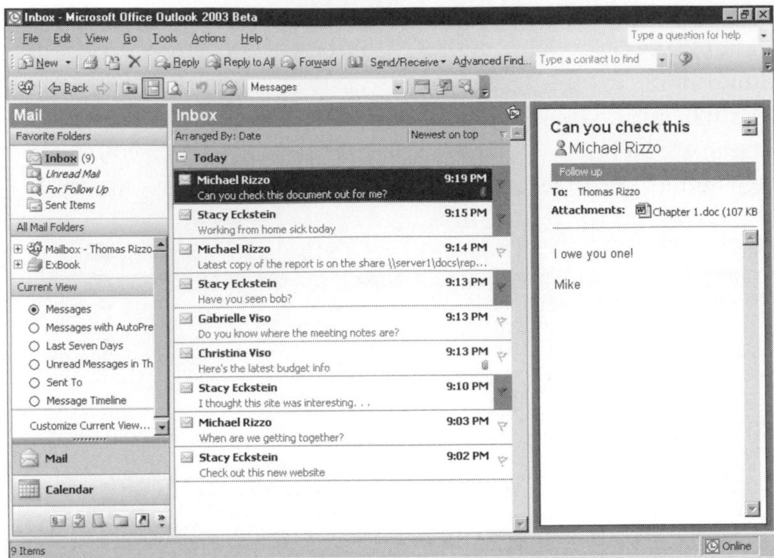

Figure 1-6 The Outlook bar, on the left of the screen, displaying the Mail tab in Outlook 2003

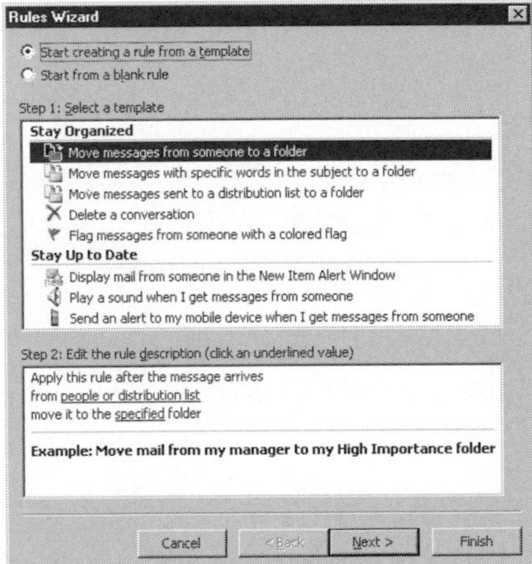

Figure 1-7 The Rules Wizard in Outlook 2003

Automatic Conflict Resolution

With the new offline-only mode in Outlook 2003, conflicts might occur more regularly because the offline and online copies of items might change at the same time. For example, say you're working off line in Outlook and you flag an item for follow-up. You then open OWA and do the same thing, forgetting that you already flagged the item when you were working off line. When you synchronize Outlook, you'll have a conflict. Another example is a case in which you dismiss a reminder in Outlook when you're working off line, dismiss it again in OWA, and then synchronize Outlook. Another conflict will occur. Outlook automatically resolves conflicts that it can safely resolve without losing data. It has also added a new Conflicts folder and conflict cleanup to its user interface. Figure 1-8 shows the Conflicts folder. Figure 1-9 shows the conflict InfoBar when a conflict has occurred in Outlook.

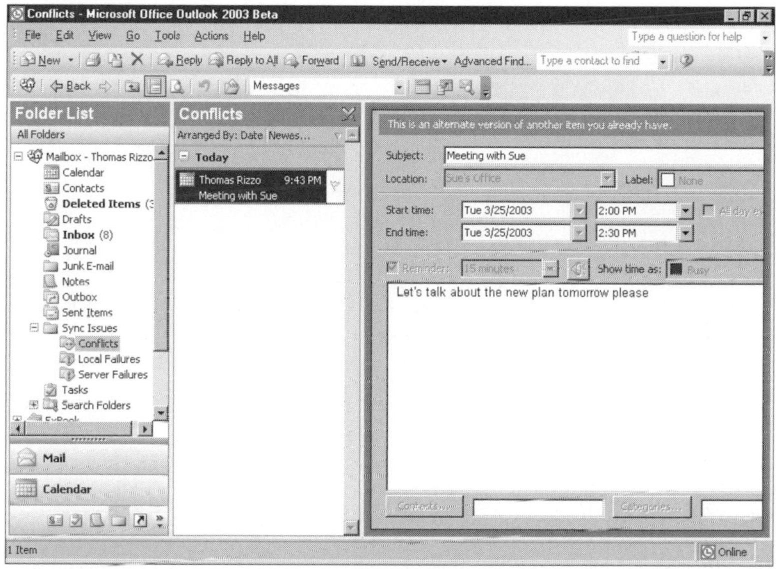

Figure 1-8 The Conflicts folder in Outlook

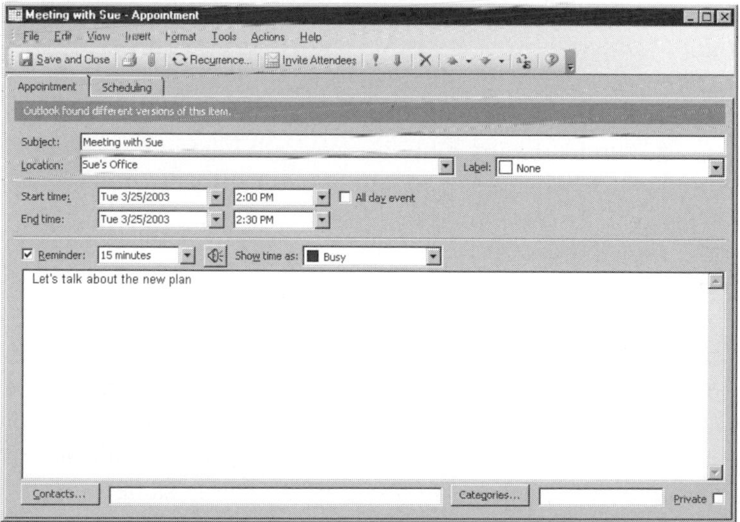

Figure 1-9 An item in conflict in Outlook

Multiple Calendars Side by Side

One of the most requested calendar features has been the ability to view multiple calendars side by side. With Outlook 2003, you can view your calendar, another person's calendar, public folder calendars, and even Windows SharePoint Services (WSS) calendars side by side. Figure 1-10 shows a personal folder, a public folder, and a WSS calendar in Outlook.

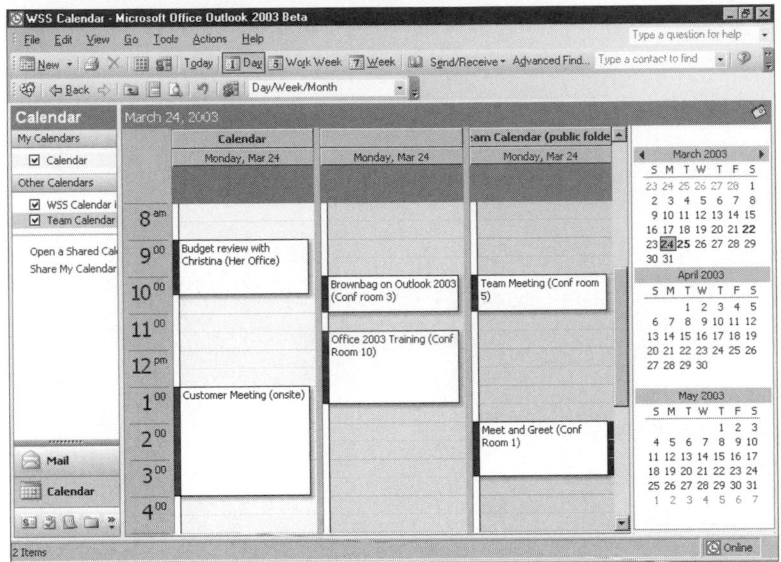

Figure 1-10 Multiple calendars in a single view in Outlook 2003

Integration with WSS

Tight integration with WSS is a new feature in Outlook 2003. From Outlook, you can replicate your WSS calendars and contacts into the Outlook environment. Plus, you can create WSS document workspaces from Outlook so that instead of e-mailing a document back and forth between users as a form of collaboration, you can create a workspace in which to collaborate on the document. Finally, you can integrate WSS alerts with your Outlook alerts. Figure 1-11 shows WSS folders listed in the folder list in the Outlook user interface.

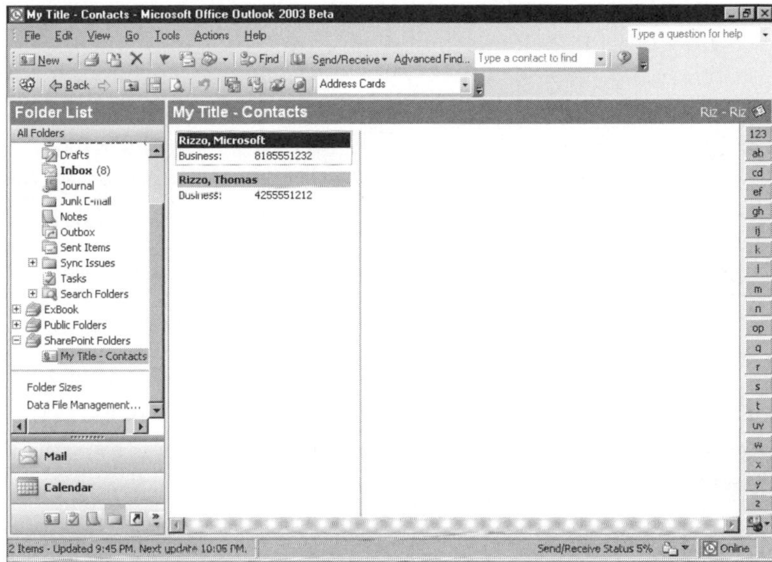

Figure 1-11 SharePoint folders linked in the user interface in Outlook

Contact Pictures

In Outlook 2003, you can store a picture of the contact with the contact item. Figure 1-12 shows the new picture capabilities of Outlook contacts.

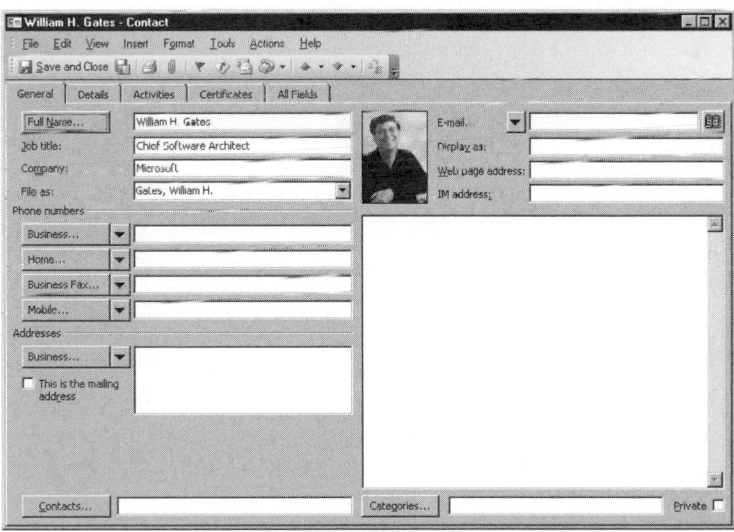

Figure 1-12 Picture support for contacts in Outlook

Calendar Color Coding (Automatic Formatting)

If you are an e-mail power user, you have used the automatic formatting feature in views in Outlook 2000. This feature allows you to specify different fonts and colors for items that meet a particular condition. For example, you can make all the e-mail from your boss appear in green, bold, 16-point Arial font. However, automatic formatting is supported only in table views in Outlook 2002. With Outlook 2003, you can use automatic formatting in the calendar view as well. This means you can specify that appointments meeting certain criteria appear in different colors in the calendar. For example, you can make your personal appointments green, your business appointments blue, appointments where your boss will be attending red, and your golf tee times yellow. Figure 1-13 shows automatic formatting inside a calendar view.

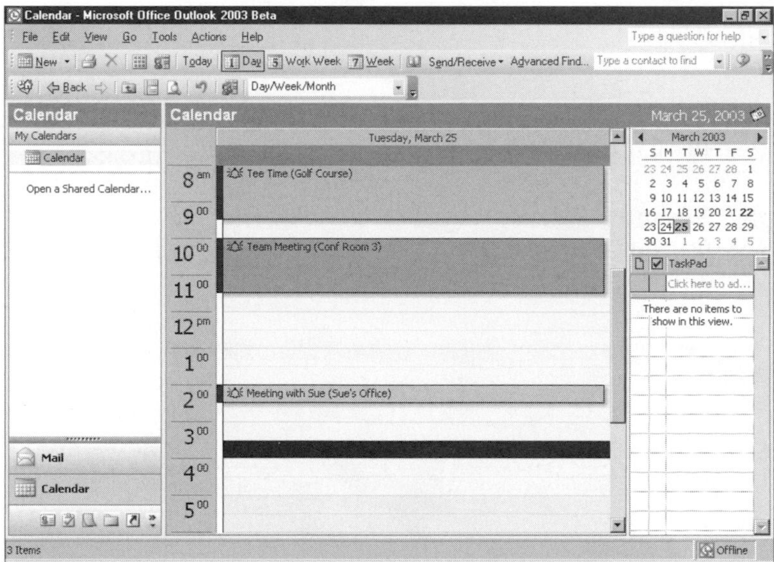

Figure 1-13 Automatic formatting in a calendar view

Developer Features

As you'll see throughout this book, Outlook provides a rich way to build collaborative applications. Following is a quick overview of some of these technologies.

Custom Forms, Fields, and Views

Using custom forms, fields, and views, you can build rich applications that leverage the features of Outlook. You can customize built-in Outlook forms to add new functionality, or you can just add new fields to an Outlook folder to track new information.

Folder Home Pages

Folder home pages allow you to view Web information directly within Outlook. You can combine the folder home page with the Outlook View control to view Web content and Outlook content together in a single view.

Outlook View Control

The Outlook View control is an ActiveX control that wraps the Outlook view pane. This control is programmable—you can modify it using its properties, methods, and events.

Outlook Object Model

Outlook provides a rich object model that you can write your Outlook applications to. This object model exposes much of the functionality that you see in the Outlook user interface and also provides extensibility for that interface. This object model is the main way in which you will interact with Outlook in your code.

Smart Tags

Smart tags are supported by most of the Office applications. Smart tags allow you to recognize key terms in your documents and add custom functionality to those terms. For example, if a stock symbol is entered into a Word document, your smart tag can offer the ability to look up the current stock price from the Web for the user.

COM Add-ins

COM add-ins provide an extensibility model for customizing Office applications using COM components that you write in Visual Basic, C++, or even .NET. This is a key technology that you will learn about in Part 2 of this book.

Internet Explorer

Browser technology is an important component of collaborative systems. Internet Explorer, with its support for Dynamic HTML (DHTML), XML, scripting, and security, is an ideal client interface for your applications.

Exchange Server

Exchange Server is the linchpin for any collaborative system because it supports communication, information sharing, and workflow services that use Internet standards and protocols. Chapter 2 introduces the features of Exchange Server.

SQL Server

SQL Server, a high-powered relational database system, includes built-in data replication, sophisticated management tools, Internet integration, and open system architecture. These key features, and the ease with which you can use SQL Server to store and retrieve information, allow you to integrate SQL Server into existing environments in a cost-effective way.

Internet Information Services

IIS is a Web server that's included with Microsoft Windows 2000 and Windows Server 2003. IIS provides a way to publish and share information securely over corporate intranets and the Internet through HTML documents. The power of IIS is demonstrated when Web applications are written using its built-in server-side script technology, called Microsoft Active Server Pages (ASP), or the newer ASP.NET. ASP allows developers to write applications by using any ActiveX scripting language, such as JScript or Microsoft Visual Basic Scripting Edition (VBScript). These scripts execute on IIS and can access different data such as that provided by Exchange Server or SQL Server. ASP.NET allows you to write code in Visual Basic .NET or Visual C# .NET. The information returned from the server-side script is in HTML, making these applications compatible with any standard HTML Web browser (such as Internet Explorer). Chapter 10 introduces ASP and ASP.NET and their programming models.

Visual Studio

Visual Studio is an integrated and comprehensive suite of development tools for building Web-based or Windows-based applications. You can use Visual Studio to build collaborative solutions that take advantage of the Windows Server System family of products (which includes Exchange Server and SQL Server) because Visual Studio and the Windows Server System are integrated.

Visual Studio .NET is the development tool for the .NET Framework; we'll discuss it in detail later in this chapter. Visual Studio .NET provides native support for creating and consuming XML Web services, the common language runtime (CLR), the .NET Framework, and .NET programming languages. Many of the examples in this book will be built with Visual Studio .NET.

SharePoint Portal Server

SharePoint Portal Server (SPS), introduced by Microsoft in Spring 2001, is designed for managing information. It provides a customizable portal using the Digital Dashboard framework and enterprise search capabilities. SPS is also a document management server that is integrated with the clients that almost everyone uses, including browsers, Office, and Windows. Finally, SPS provides a departmental version of the Exchange development platform, specifically the Web Storage System, which is called the document store in SharePoint. You can deploy collaborative applications without the infrastructure requirements of Exchange. SPS does not require Active Directory, and it can work in a Windows NT 4.0 environment. We'll discuss the differences between SPS and Exchange in the additional chapter found on this book's Web site.

Windows SharePoint Services

While SPS provides collaborative services for portal and document management, Windows SharePoint Services (WSS) provides out-of-the-box functionality for project teams, including event calendars, discussions, document libraries (without the level of document management that SPS provides), and surveys The nice thing about WSS is that users can easily modify a site by using Microsoft FrontPage. You can integrate WSS with SPS through the Digital Dashboard or through the search capabilities in SPS. With SPS 2.0, which is scheduled for release in late 2003, SPS and WSS are more tightly integrated.

Mobile Information Server

With the explosive growth of wireless communications, collaborative applications must be designed to be accessible on mobile devices. The product that helps facilitate this access is Microsoft Mobile Information Server (MIS). MIS provides a server environment that you can connect to in order to browse through information with Outlook Mobile Access. Outlook Mobile Access is to mobile browsers what OWA is to a Web browser. Outlook Mobile Access allows client access to your inbox, calendar, contacts, and tasks through any browser that supports Wireless Access Protocol (WAP) and Wireless Markup Language (WML).

MIS also supports notifications to mobile devices. For example, you can use MIS to send an alert to your cell phone when you receive an e-mail message or a meeting request. Beyond its basic functionality, MIS also provides an extensible platform on which you can build wireless applications. The .NET Mobile Software Developers Kit (SDK), in conjunction with MIS, provides the means to build applications that work in a regular or a mobile browser with little or no modification of your code. Visual Studio .NET 2003 incorporates all the features of the .NET Mobile SDK so you can just use Visual Studio .NET 2003 to build robust mobile applications.

With the release of Exchange 2003, MIS has mostly become part of Exchange. The only piece that is not part of Exchange is the mobile gateway technology that is part of Internet Security and Acceleration (ISA) Server.

Examples of Collaborative Solutions

Now that you have a better understanding of collaboration and collaborative technologies, let's look briefly at the systems you can create. With Exchange Server, you can build many types of open and extensible applications, all of which can take advantage of information stored inside or outside Exchange Server. You can make use of other data sources in your organization, such as SQL Server databases. This allows you to pick the best database for storing the application's information without compromising the consistency of the user interface.

The types of collaborative applications you can build can be broken down into five categories: messaging, tracking, workflow, real-time, and knowledge management. These categories are not mutually exclusive—for example, a workflow application can take advantage of messaging services. These categories simply define the primary function of a particular application. Throughout this book, we'll explore sample applications that fall into these categories.

Messaging Applications

Messaging applications primarily use the messaging infrastructure of Exchange Server. E-mail is the best known of these, but you can build many other types, such as discussion group applications. Exchange Server supports threaded discussions; you can make any folder in Exchange Server a threaded discussion folder by changing the view of the messages inside that folder. These discussions can be replicated to and from Internet newsgroups and can be moderated for appropriate content.

Another example of an application built on the messaging infrastructure is a mailbox agent. A mailbox agent can perform many types of functions, depending on how it's programmed. For example, suppose a sales force needs to run certain queries against a database of sales information. You could write a Microsoft Access application that queries the database and returns the results, but with such a solution a salesperson wouldn't be able to work on other tasks until the database had processed the request and returned the data set to the

Access user interface. This means that users would have to check the Access application continually to see whether the data is available. With a mailbox agent or a server event, a salesperson can use a form to specify the type of information she needs and then e-mail the form to the agent. The agent can process the form and run the query on the salesperson's behalf. Once the database processes the query, the agent can e-mail the data set to the salesperson. Then the salesperson will receive notification containing the requested data set.

A mailing list server is a messaging agent that forwards all messages it receives to its registered recipients and allows users to add and remove themselves from the list of recipients via e-mail. A document library, another example of a messaging application, lets users submit documents to a library by dragging and dropping them, e-mailing them, or sending them through a Web browser. Because these libraries are stored in a central location, many users have access to the documents. A developer can add intelligence to the library by creating a mailbox agent that notifies users when new documents are available. Custom views are available on a folder so users can quickly find the documents they want. Comments about the documents can be placed in the folder, and interested users can gauge their relative value.

One popular example of a document library is a library of Web favorites. You can drag and drop Internet shortcuts into this library to make a user's personal favorites become corporate favorites. Users also gain the benefit of being able to create custom fields and views that describe and categorize the favorites in the folder.

Tracking Applications

Tracking applications manage and track information, such as a list of tasks, from its creation to its deletion or "completion." Tracking applications usually require the integration of many different data sources because the information usually resides in more than one location.

One example of a tracking application is a job candidate application that enables a human resource department and other employees to track a prospective employee from the moment he submits a resume through the interview process and the decision to hire or reject. The candidate's status is always available for review. Figure 1-14 shows an example of a hypothetical job candidate tracking application that uses Outlook and Exchange Server to follow prospective candidates.

You could also create an account tracking application that includes tracking for contacts, revenue, and tasks. Figure 1-15 shows the Account Tracking application we'll build in Chapter 8.

Help desks also make use of tracking applications. In a help desk application, trouble tickets that specify technical problems are submitted to the help desk by users. Problems are assigned to technicians on the basis of the ticket type. Audit trails are established for each ticket so the technicians have historical information that helps them work on the problems. After fixing a problem, the technician adds the ticket and its resolution to a log of frequently asked questions, which users can query.

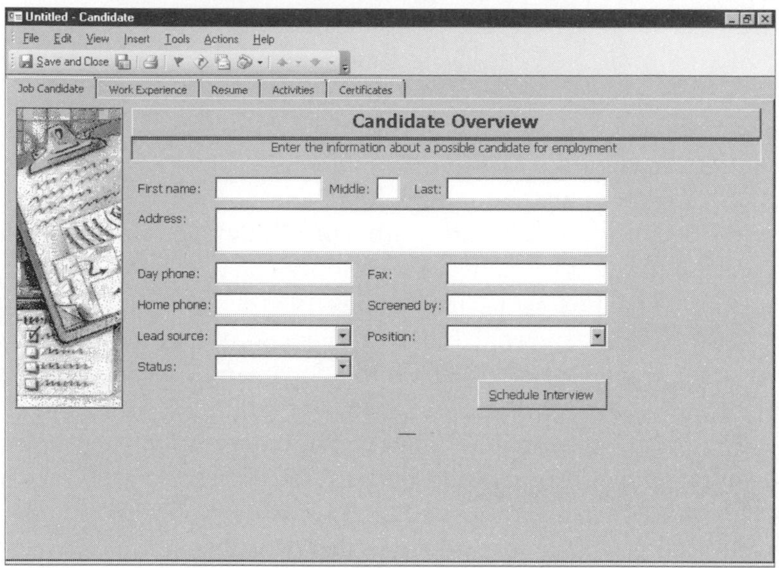

Figure 1-14 A hypothetical job candidate tracking application in Outlook

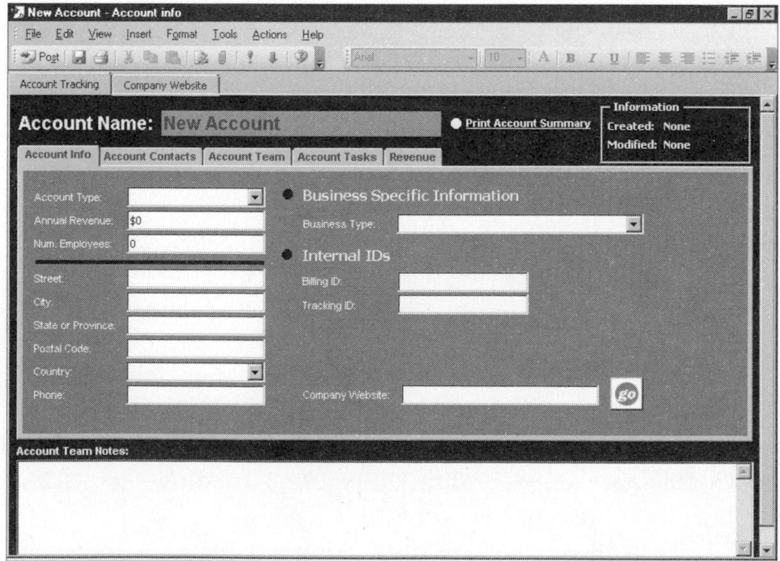

Figure 1-15 The Account Tracking application from Chapter 8

A help desk might make use of tracking applications for other purposes as well, such as inventory management. For example, if a technician has to request a new machine for a user, an inventory management program can inform the technician whether a new machine is in stock. By adding a workflow application to the help desk application, the technician can obtain approval for the machine from the user's manager and the help desk manager. Figure 1-16 shows the Help desk application we'll build in Chapter 11.

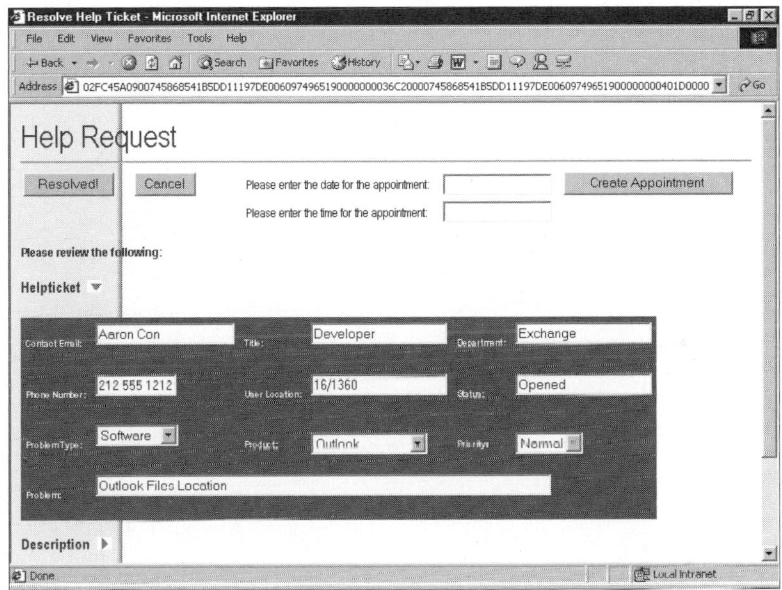

Figure 1-16 The Web-based Help desk application from Chapter 11

One last example of a tracking application you might build is a class registration system that tracks information about a class and its participants. It informs users when classes they want to take are available, reminds them at least one day in advance which classes they are registered for, and notifies them of any updated materials the teacher has made available. When the class is completed, class notes and a survey can be distributed to class members. Chapter 15 shows how to build this type of tracking application.

Workflow Applications

Workflow applications are primarily constructed around the concept of the three R's: roles, routes, and rules:

- **Roles** A role is the logical representation of a person or an application in a workflow process. For example, the expense report approver role can change dynamically depending on who is involved in the particular workflow process. A role allows you to easily abstract the different functions people perform in a workflow process.

- **Routes** A route defines what information will be routed and who will receive it. A route can be sequential, parallel, conditional, or any combination of these. Figure 1-17 illustrates three types of routes.
- **Rules** A rule is conditional logic that assesses the status of the workflow process and determines the next steps. Here's an example of a rule: *if the manager approves the expense report, route the report to accounting; otherwise, send the expense report back to the submitter.* A rule can be based on the properties of a message or some other data source.

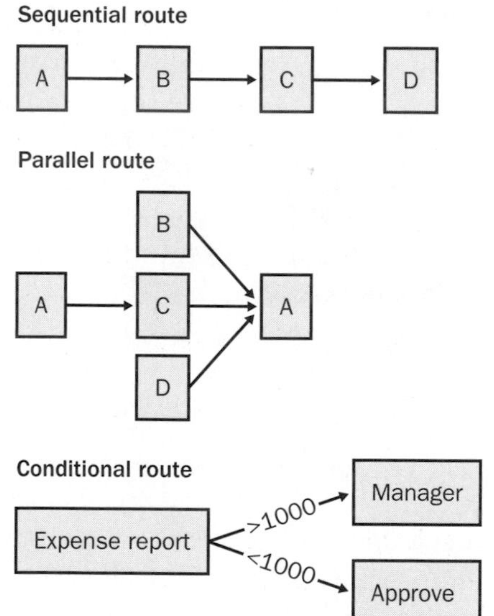

Figure 1-17 Sequential, parallel, and conditional routing types

Let's take a brief look at a few workflow samples. Expense reports are one example of a workflow application that you can build with Exchange Server. Here's how such a workflow application might function: A user submits expense reports from a Web application, and depending on the total amount of the expense reports, a particular workflow process is started. If the expense is under $1,000, the expense report is automatically approved; if the expense is $1,000 or more, the report is routed to the user's manager for approval. The manager either approves or rejects the expense report. Based on the manager's decision, another workflow process is initiated to either pay the expense report or inform the user that the expense report has been denied. Finally, if the manager does not approve or reject the expense report in a certain period of time, the workflow application routes the expense report to the manager's manager for approval.

Another example of a workflow application is a document routing application in which a document to be reviewed is routed to users in parallel, user feedback is collected within a certain period of time and consolidated into a single message, and the message is sent to the author of the document. You can build this type of application using server events in Exchange 2003.

Real-Time Applications

Real-time collaborative applications are the newest category of Exchange Server applications. Real-time applications have the potential to enable instantaneous collaboration (as compared to the "delayed" collaboration of messaging-based applications). The challenge, of course, is to connect geographically dispersed users in real time. When you combine real-time and messaging technologies, you can build applications that leverage the strengths of both.

One example of a real-time application that you can build with Exchange Server is a class registration system that schedules virtual classes by sending Microsoft NetMeeting requests. NetMeeting allows individuals to collaborate over the Internet using video, audio, whiteboards, and application-sharing technology, as shown in Figure 1-18. In Chapter 8, we'll examine an Account Tracking sample that demonstrates how to integrate NetMeeting into your own application.

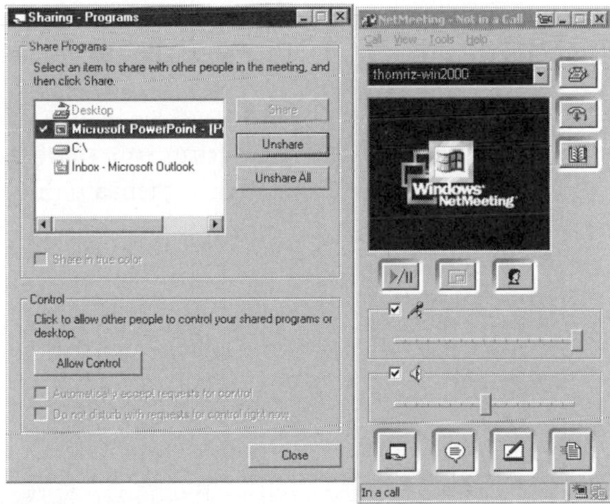

Figure 1-18 NetMeeting allows you to collaborate with other people in real time.

Another real-time application that will interest Exchange Server developers is instant messaging (IM). IM allows users to monitor when other users are on line so they can collaborate with one another. It allows two different organizations to create virtual "buddies," or business partners. IM is like a virtual water cooler!

As you will see with the real-time communication server that works on Windows Server 2003, IM is becoming a crucial part of collaborative applications because of IM's ability to view presence information and also provide rich communication and collaboration capabilities such as whiteboarding, file transfer, and video teleconferencing. In Chapter 19, I will cover how to programmatically add IM capabilities to your collaborative applications.

Chat and Real-Time Collaboration

Chat, a popular service on the Internet, is one example of a real-time application. Chat enables real-time conversation by allowing a participant to type messages that appear instantly on another participant's computer. Chat can greatly enhance functionality for users when it's added to collaborative applications. For example, you can extend a help desk application with chat services so the help desk technicians can hold "office hours" during which they conduct real-time question-and-answer sessions. Those chat transcripts can be posted to a discussion group so other users can troubleshoot problems based on the transcript.

Knowledge Management Applications

Knowledge management refers to the use of collaborative technology to implement structured processes for finding and gathering information—in other words, it is a strategy for moving information from an individual to a larger group or a corporation. Knowledge management applications make available all kinds of information, from individual experiences to best practices to detailed technical data. The effective sharing of knowledge brings to a company three primary advantages: more effective use of existing intellectual assets, competitive advantage through the pooling of resources and greater accessibility of important information, and new opportunities through more focused innovation.

You can use collaborative technology such as Exchange Server to employ a knowledge management strategy, but collaborative technology is not synonymous with knowledge management. That is, corporations must establish processes not only for collaboration but also for gathering and making accessible information that is current, relevant, and tested.

One type of application you can build with Exchange Server to implement knowledge management is a search application for searching discussion groups and contacts in Exchange Server as well as searching in SQL Server databases and Web sites. With this powerful search capability, users do not have to change the way they collaborate because the search engine crawls through the necessary data sources to retrieve the relevant information.

Another type of application that facilitates knowledge management is a knowledge base. By developing knowledge bases with Exchange Server, you can enhance conventional collaborative methods. Typically, knowledge bases are used by corporate users who post free-form, unmoderated messages to a common folder. Users who want specific information, such as text in a message, query the knowledge base in a general way and then cull the returned information that meets their criteria.

Because of the general nature of the queries and the unstructured way information is posted, many of the results are irrelevant or invalid. Imagine how a more structured method of entering and searching for information in a knowledge base could facilitate collaboration and knowledge management. Suppose users who post information to a knowledge base had to fill out a form that asked them to categorize their information, indicate how long it would be valid, and rate its usefulness if it originated from external sources. Users would be able to query by using categories and ratings and would receive only current and relevant information. By supplying just a little extra information, users can make the data stored in the knowledge base infinitely more useful. And if you were to add smart agent technology to the application, you could program the knowledge base to e-mail links to relevant information that meets the users' predefined criteria.

Summary

Now that you've seen an overview of the entire collaborative environment and a sneak peek at the client-side portion of that environment, including Office and IM, in the next chapter we'll turn our focus to the main collaboration services on the server side.

2

Exchange Server as a Platform for Collaboration

A builder is only as good as his tools. This adage holds true for software developers as much as for carpenters. Microsoft Exchange Server is one of the most solid tools you can use. It provides robust messaging functionality, an industrial-strength object database, support for Internet protocols, and an open directory structure. These capabilities, which I'll cover in this chapter, make it an ideal platform for your collaborative applications.

Exchange 2003 also has development features such as ADO/OLEDB and WebDAV support, new event architecture, a new workflow engine and designer, Microsoft FrontPage development tools, enhanced real-time collaboration (including a conferencing server) and a new version of the Collaboration Data Objects (CDO) model. We'll look at all the new features in Exchange 2003 in detail in Part III of this book.

Exchange Messaging Infrastructure

The Exchange Server messaging infrastructure provides certain core services that enable you to focus on developing value-added services rather than essential ones. This infrastructure complements current network topologies and protocols and, as you'll see, guarantees that every message gets through to its destination. The following sections discuss some of the advantages of the Exchange Server messaging infrastructure.

Least-Cost Routing, Load Balancing, and Failover

Technologies in the Exchange Server messaging engine allow organizations to define different communication routes between Exchange servers. Costs can be assigned to these different routes, and the least costly route is always attempted first by the Exchange server. If this route is not available, Exchange Server will fail over to the next least costly route. If you assign the same cost to two routes, Exchange Server will distribute the communications traffic evenly over both routes, thereby load balancing the connections.

Let's look at an example. Imagine a network with three routes between an Exchange server in New York and an Exchange server in California. One route communicates over a wide area network (WAN), the second over a dial-up 28.8 modem, and the third over a satellite link. The administrator of the Exchange Server system assigns costs to each of these routes: the WAN route is assigned a cost of 20, the modem route a cost of 50, and the satellite route a cost of 70. Based on the cost of the routes, the Exchange Server system will always attempt the WAN route first. If this route is down, Exchange Server will fail over to the next least-costly route, the modem; if that route is unavailable, it will attempt to connect over the satellite.

This is just a simple example; Exchange Server supports very complex routing tables with associated costs that it automatically calculates. For example, consider a message that has to be routed through seven Exchange servers until it reaches its final destination. Each Exchange server has three unique routes to the next server. Exchange Server automatically finds the least costly route among all the routes supplied.

Delivery and Read Receipts

Exchange Server supports both delivery and read receipts when delivering information through an Exchange Server system. Delivery receipts are returned to an individual user or an application when an item has been delivered to its final destination. This destination can be another Exchange server or a messaging server over the Internet. A delivery receipt also reports the time and date that an item was received by a particular system. You can use delivery receipts in your applications to trigger events when they are returned. For example, a workflow application can consolidate delivery receipts to track the status of message delivery to workflow participants. Figure 2-1 shows an example of a delivery receipt.

Read receipts, which are similar to delivery receipts, are sent to a user or an application when the recipient actually opens the item. You might use read receipts in your application for time-sensitive items sent through the Exchange

Server system. The application can track when an item is read, and if no action is taken after a certain amount of time, it can reroute the item to a different user or application. Figure 2-2 shows an example of a read receipt.

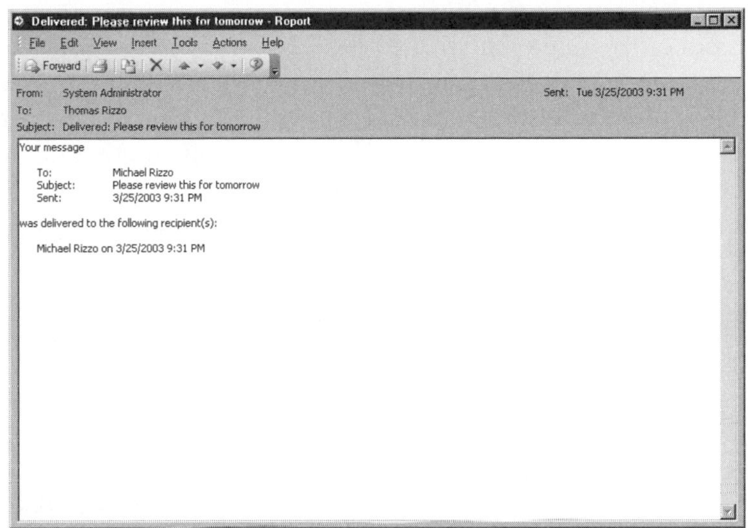

Figure 2-1 A delivery receipt sent back to a user

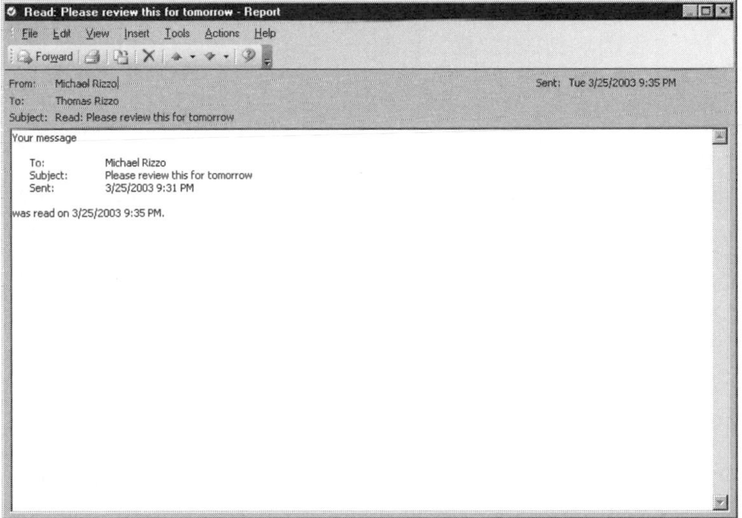

Figure 2-2 Applications using read receipts to track when users open items sent by the application

Message Tracking

Exchange Server supports more than delivery and read receipts. When message tracking is enabled, Exchange Server keeps logs of the items that have entered the Exchange Server system from other systems. You can trace any item in your application to determine if it reached its destination.

Exchange Server also logs where items were routed, which Exchange Server components routed them, and when the items were delivered to their final destination. Message tracking enables you to find an item's route based on criteria such as the sender of the item, the intended recipient, or even the component of Exchange Server that handled the message. Figure 2-3 shows the Exchange Server Message Tracking Center interface.

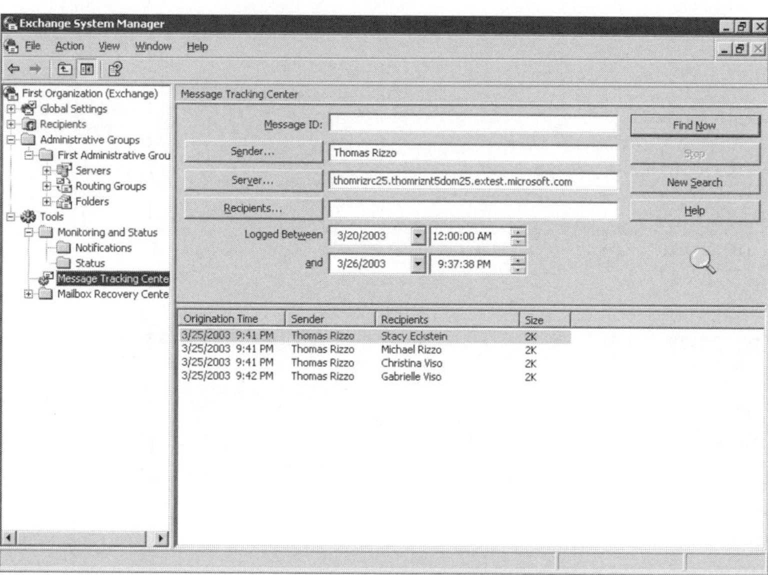

Figure 2-3 Tracking items from Thomas Rizzo across the Exchange Server system

An Industrial-Strength Object Database

At its core, Exchange Server is an object database. This object database is highly scalable, can be replicated, is built for 24/7 availability, and can hold many different types of objects, including messages, Microsoft Office documents, video files, voicemail, faxes, hyperlinks, text documents, custom forms, and executable files. You can store all of your application's data in the database and replicate the information to other locations so the application and its relevant information are available anywhere at any time. We'll look at key features of the Exchange Server database next.

Huge Storage Capacity

Many collaborative applications require that large amounts of data be continuously available. Exchange Server makes an excellent repository for this data because it can handle large amounts of information and ensure the reliability and availability of that information. Exchange Server supports very large databases—up to 16 terabytes (16,000 gigabytes). That's a lot of information—consider that if you compiled every Wall Street transaction in history, you'd have only a little more than 1 terabyte. The only factor that really limits the size of your database is the hardware you run Exchange Server on. The database can run continuously because it has online defragmentation and allows backup programs to work with the database, even when users are logged on.

Exchange Server can store many types of objects and their associated data in the same database. These different types of objects can even be in the same table, or folder (as tables are called in Exchange Server). Users simply drag and drop objects into these folders, and Exchange Server adds them to the database. This flexibility gives you a distinct advantage when you develop applications. Figure 2-4 shows a folder in Microsoft Outlook with many different objects.

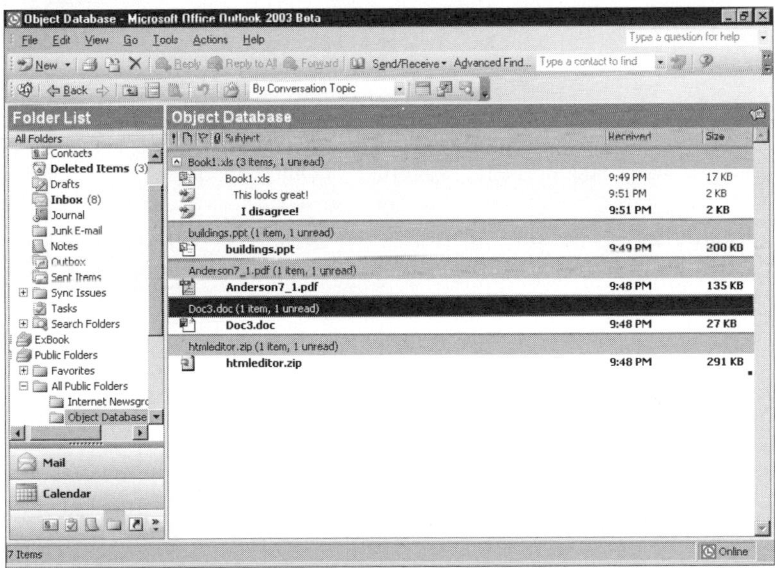

Figure 2-4 The Exchange Server database with many types of objects in a single folder

Multiple Views

The Exchange Server database not only supports multiple objects in a single folder but also multiple views of those objects. You can create views of the objects stored in the folder by sorting, grouping, and filtering the objects using any combination of their properties. For example, you can customize the view of an Exchange Server folder containing Office documents by specifying Office properties, as shown in Figure 2-5. Properties you define can be included as columns in a view, and you can use them to sort and group items in the view.

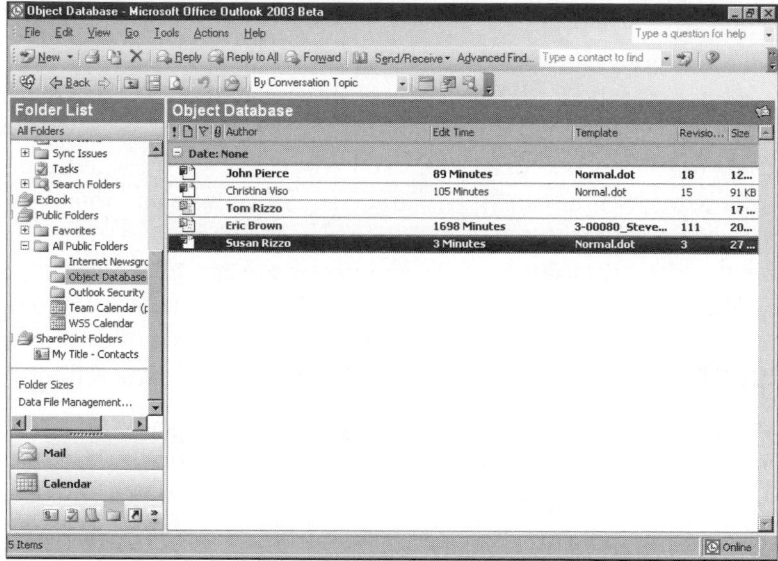

Figure 2-5 Views support using properties of Office documents

Exchange Server also supports "per-user" views that allow individual users to create views. Exchange Server actually maintains, for each user, the initial view of the folder, the status of read and unread items, and whether a particular grouping is expanded in the view. Figure 2-6 shows the same view as Figure 2-5, but for a different user. Notice how different the screen shots look in terms of read and unread items. Certain items are marked as read and stored per-user so that the system can track individual read and unread messages for each user. Views can also be replicated off line by using Exchange Server's built-in replication features.

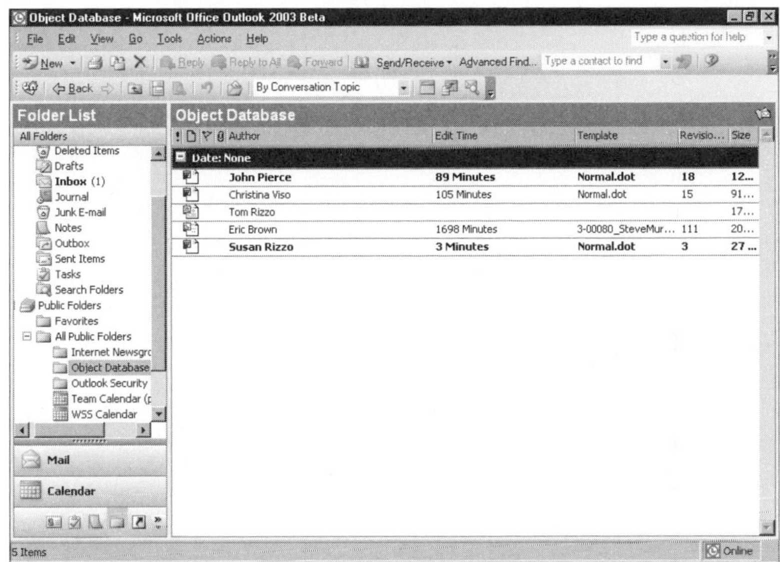

Figure 2-6 The initial view of the same discussion folder for a different user

Built-In Replication

The Exchange Server database can be replicated from one instance of Exchange Server to another and from Exchange Server to Outlook on a client machine. Exchange Server even supports filtered replication between the server and the client.

Replication in Exchange is not the same as simple duplication. Exchange Server replication is more similar to synchronization in that only the changes are sent to replicas in the system. Sending only changes, as opposed to copying an entire folder in each replication cycle, saves time and network bandwidth.

To set up server-to-server replication with Exchange Server, an administrator simply selects the folder to be replicated and then selects the server to replicate the folder to. The settings that enable server-to-server replication in the Microsoft Exchange System Manager program are shown in Figure 2-7. Once these settings are in place, the actual replication messages are sent over the Exchange Server messaging infrastructure. This allows the replication messages to leverage Exchange Server's load balancing, least-cost routing, and failover capabilities. Exchange Server also supports setting the time and size limits of the replication messages.

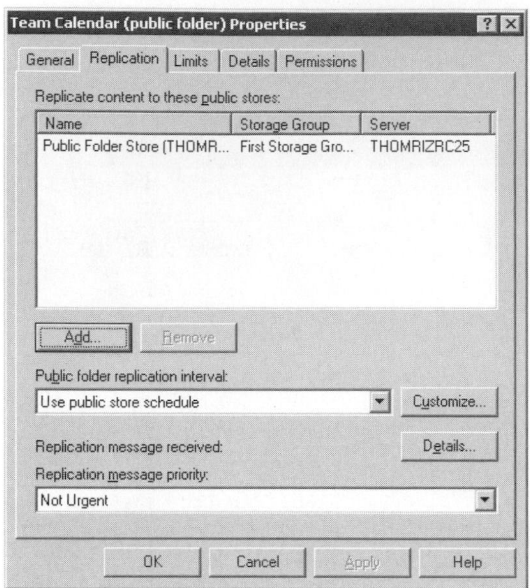

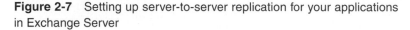

Figure 2-7 Setting up server-to-server replication for your applications in Exchange Server

The Exchange Server replication feature has built-in conflict management capabilities that enable different users to edit the same information at the same time in the same folder or even in replicas of a folder in different locations. To determine which item to accept as the newest, Exchange Server implements "last saved wins," the process of querying the time an item was saved and retaining the most recently saved version. You can also set an option that alerts users via e-mail when items are in conflict. Both versions of the item are sent to these users, and they decide which item is the most up-to-date. Exchange Server keeps the item they select.

For server-to-client replication, Exchange Server and Outlook support bidirectional synchronization of changes to information in Exchange Server folders. This synchronization occurs in Outlook as a background process so users can continue working in Outlook. Synchronization can be scheduled at certain intervals. For example, a user can configure Outlook replication so that every 30 minutes the Outlook client synchronizes its local database with new information from Exchange Server.

Outlook also supports filtered replication, in which only a subset of information is synchronized with the local database. Filtered replication is most useful to users when they want to take only a subset of the large amount of data in the Exchange Server database off line. For example, imagine an Exchange Server folder with 50,000 sales contacts. A typical user cannot accommodate the entire folder on her local hard disk, so she can set the replication criterion to only the contacts for whom she is the sales representative. Instead of 50,000 contacts, the filtered subset is 1000 contacts. Figure 2-8 shows the dialog box in Outlook in which users set criteria for filtered replication.

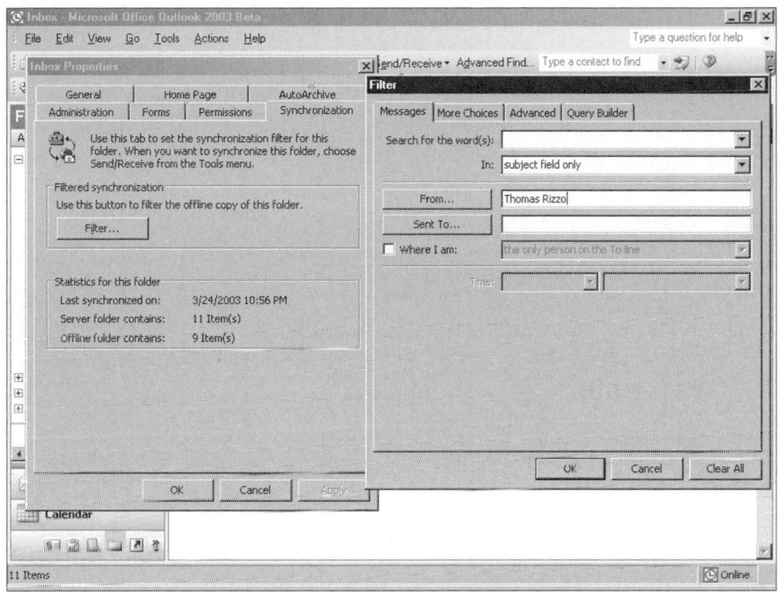

Figure 2-8 Setting up filtered replication in Outlook

Schema Flexibility

When you begin work on an application that connects to a database, you are usually forced to plan your schema for the database before you start writing your application. If the application's requirements change and a new field has to be added to the database, the schema might not be flexible enough to support the addition and you might have to drop your database and create a new one.

With the Exchange Server database, however, you can add new fields at any point in development, which means you can accommodate the changing requirements of an application. New fields are automatically available for users to include in custom views.

Transaction Logging

A *transaction* is a unit of work—for example, adding an item to an Exchange Server database. Before any item is committed to the Exchange Server database, the transaction is written to a transaction log file. This process is called *write-ahead transaction logging*, and it guarantees that no item will be lost.

Transaction logs allow Exchange Server to recover the database after a failure such as a power loss. In this scenario, once power is restored and the server rebooted, Exchange Server automatically recovers the database using checkpoints in the transaction logs, to replay any transactions that were not committed to the database before the power failure.

The transaction log is an inherent feature of the Exchange Server database, so any application you develop on Exchange Server can take advantage of it. Any items your application sends or stores in the Exchange Server system will be delivered or committed, even in the event of certain failures in the computer system or network.

Multiple Databases

Exchange supports multiple databases on a single server. This support provides administrative flexibility because you can break out multiple mailbox databases on a single server and do a backup/restore on each of these mailbox databases individually. Multiple databases also give developers the flexibility of having multiple application databases on a single server.

Integration with Active Directory

To collaborate effectively, users must be able to find other users and information easily. Exchange Server is integrated with the Active Directory directory service for this purpose. Active Directory holds an organization's critical information, and it can meet the needs of both large and small organizations because it's scalable and easy to manage. Some of the most important features of Active Directory are described in the following sections.

Reliable Database Engine

The Active Directory directory service has the same database technology as the Exchange Server messaging infrastructure, so the database engine's reliability is high. This reliability ensures that the directory will always be available to your applications.

Multimaster and Replication Capabilities

Active Directory is a multimaster, replicated directory. An administrator can make changes to it on any Active Directory server in the organization, and the changes are replicated to the other directory servers by the Active Directory server on which the changes were made.

Directory replication in the Active Directory system is not limited to server-to-server replication. With the help of Exchange Server, Active Directory also supports server-to-client directory replication. By using a feature called the Offline Address Book, Outlook can replicate certain Active Directory information or a subset of it to a user's local machine. This allows a user of your application to address items to other users and to look up detailed directory information even when the user is working off line.

Customizable Attributes and White Pages

Active Directory exposes a number of attributes in the directory that you can customize and replicate. For example, you can customize Active Directory with a field named Cost Center and set up a supplies requisition program that dynamically queries the directory for users who are ordering supplies. Depending on the information in the Cost Center field, the application will have the accounting system use that cost center so the cost of supplies is deducted from that cost center. Figure 2-9 shows where you can customize Active Directory.

Active Directory has some additional built-in features, such as the ability to store all types of information about an organization, including users' office locations, phone numbers, department names, and titles—and even a user's manager and direct reports. Active Directory provides an ideal "white pages" directory.

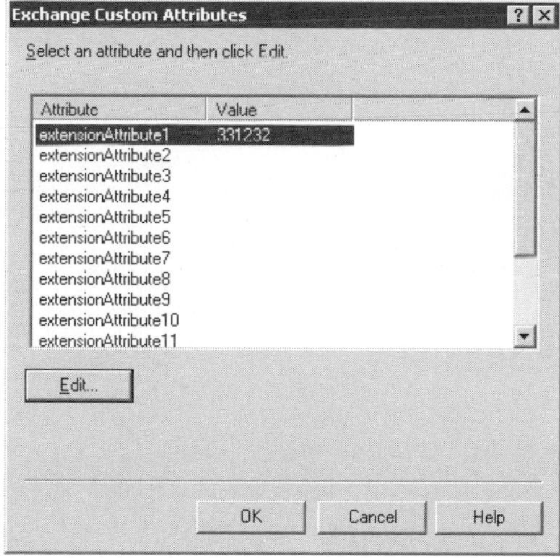

Figure 2-9 Customizing attributes in the directory

For workflow applications, a central, hierarchical directory of this kind is crucial. Workflow applications must be able to route items based on an organization's staff structure, which is dynamic. If names of individuals are hardcoded in an application, staffing changes will require the application to be rewritten. With Active Directory, you can query and dynamically generate employee information.

Extensibility and Security

Active Directory is not limited to storing information for only one organization. Through the use of contacts (formerly called custom recipients), Active Directory can also hold address and organizational information for users from other organizations. Active Directory exposes the same functionality to these directory objects as it does to its standard directory objects. Figure 2-10 shows an example of a contact in Active Directory.

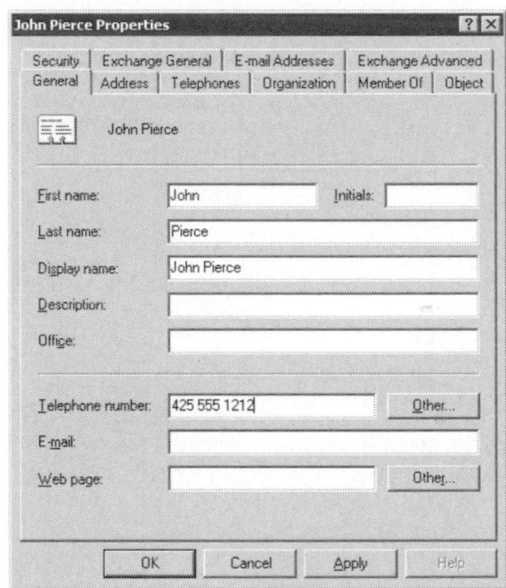

Figure 2-10 A custom contact in Active Directory

Internet and Industry Standards Support

Active Directory supports Internet standards such as Lightweight Directory Access Protocol (LDAP) 3.0. LDAP is an adapted subset of the X.500 standard that specifies a common protocol for directory access over TCP/IP. The key benefit of LDAP support in Active Directory is that any LDAP-compliant client or application can query Active Directory. LDAP 3.0 as implemented in Active Directory enables you to chain directories together through *referrals*, which tell Active Directory where to look for information that a user is querying for if it is not in the directory itself. For an application, referrals are crucial because one directory might not contain all the necessary information about users and services. The information might be in many different directories, which might be hosted on servers in different locations or even in different organizations.

Active Directory supports Active Directory Services Interface (ADSI), an API that enables you to modify many different directories using standard protocols. The directories that ADSI supports are Active Directory in Microsoft Windows 2000 and Windows Server 2003, the Windows NT 4.0 domain-based directory, any LDAP-compliant directory, Novell NetWare's NDS Directory, and Novell NetWare Bindery. The ADSI interface abstracts the low-level functions of these directories and exposes a number of objects you can use to write applications. Because ADSI provides COM and .NET interfaces that give every directory element a common set of properties, the application can use the same API to connect to directory elements in several directory services.

Figure 2-11 shows a diagram of ADSI and some of the directory services it can access. ADSI is an important technology because it ties together all of these disparate directories with a common programming model and because it is Microsoft's strategic directory programming interface. Chapter 13 shows how to program Active Directory using ADSI.

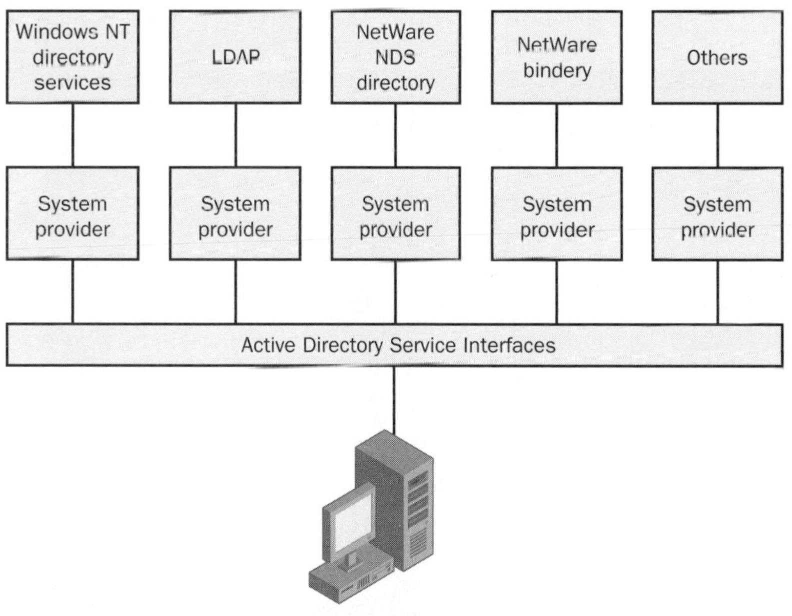

Figure 2-11 ADSI, which allows you to talk to many different directories, including Active Directory, using the same interfaces

Public Folders

The mainstay of Exchange Server's collaborative technologies is *public folders*, which are repositories for all kinds of information that users share. They can be accessed by many types of clients, using various protocols. Public folders can contain custom forms for contributing or reviewing information in the folder, and users can create their own views for organizing and filtering the information in the folder. Public folders and private mailboxes are built on the Exchange Server object database. They take advantage of its architecture and enjoy the benefits of a flexible database schema and server-to-server, server-to-client, and filtered replication. The main features of public folders for developers are described in the following sections.

Folder and Application Accessibility

Public folders in Outlook are arranged in a hierarchical tree view, as shown in the Folder List pane in Figure 2-12. This arrangement makes it easy for users to scroll and find information. This hierarchy is actually a virtual view of public folder replicas in the Exchange Server system; users don't have to know which server a public folder is actually on.

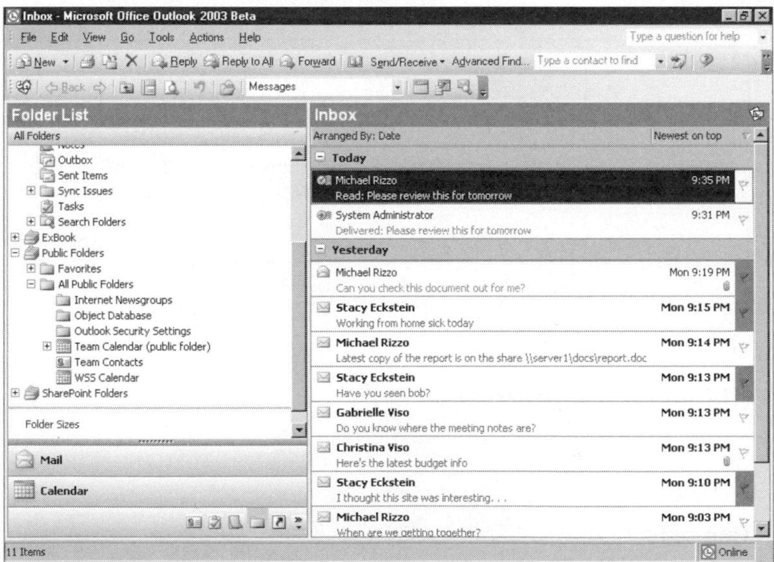

Figure 2-12 The hierarchical tree view of a public folder

Exchange Server can assign costs to different sites so users connecting to a public folder with no local replica are directed to a replica in the remote site using the least costly route. The assignment of costs to remote connections for public folders is called *public folder affinity*. Figure 2-13 shows the administrative interface for routing groups, which provide public folder affinity. If you set up routing groups, users of your application will access one replica of the Public Folder database over another depending on their location on the network.

Public folders are not limited to holding data for an application; they can also hold custom forms associated with the application. Users can select the associated form directly in the public folder rather than having to search for the form in a global forms list.

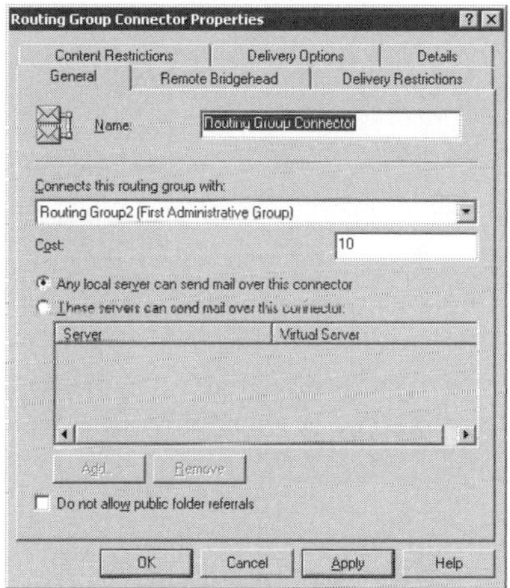

Figure 2-13 Administrative interface for routing groups

Security and Content Control

Security control is built into each public folder. Three levels of permissions are possible for public folders:

- **Global** The default permissions for everyone in the organization and for anonymous users
- **Group** Permissions for a specific list of users
- **Per-user** Individual permissions for a particular folder

All of these permission levels can be combined for a particular folder or set of users. Assigning permissions is straightforward, as shown in Figure 2-14.

Notice that the Permissions tab supports built-in roles for users; you can use these to quickly set permissions for a folder.

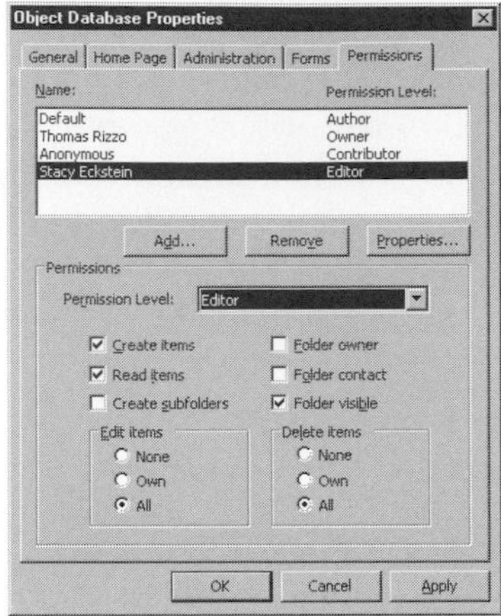

Figure 2-14 Setting permissions for a public folder

In addition to roles-based permissions, public folders have built-in moderation capabilities. A moderated public folder allows you to control what content is posted to a folder and who has permission to approve this content. Before any item is posted to a folder, the item is mailed to the selected moderators, who approve or reject the content. You can quickly set up a moderated public folder in the folder properties.

Public folders support the e-mailing of items to a public folder, which makes information available to many users, cuts down on e-mail traffic, and saves disk space. Public folders can be exposed in the Active Directory as recipients just like regular mail users. Mailing-list server applications and distribution list applications can really take advantage of public folders. By default, the e-mail address of the public folder is hidden from the address book, but the public folder can be exposed in the address book so that users can browse for its e-mail address.

Internet Standards Support

By using Exchange Server public folders as a central location for information, organizations can expose information to any standard Internet client that supports Network News Transfer Protocol (NNTP), Internet Mail Access Protocol version 4 (IMAP4), or HTTP. Internet clients that support these protocols can post and read information securely from a public folder. More important, these protocols allow users who do not have Outlook on their machines to use the functionality of an Exchange Server public folder. For example, an organization can implement a public folder for customer service that internal users can view with Outlook and external users can view by choosing from several clients, including Outlook, an NNTP newsreader such as Outlook Express, a standard Web browser, or even an IMAP4 client such as Netscape Communicator. Let's look more closely at the Internet protocols supported in Exchange Server.

Network News Transfer Protocol

NNTP is an Internet standard that defines server-to-server replication of data in the form of articles. These articles exist in a hierarchy of newsgroups, which are similar to discussion folders in Exchange Server. Users can replicate the articles off line, and the articles are presented in a threaded view so users can view their history. Exchange Server supports both NNTP server-to-server replication and the ability of any standard NNTP client to read information in Exchange Server public folders. Any public folder in Exchange Server can therefore be replicated to another NNTP server or be read by an NNTP client. Organizations can use this feature to expose public folders and their information to their customers. Figure 2-15 shows an example of a newsreader using NNTP to access an Exchange Server public folder.

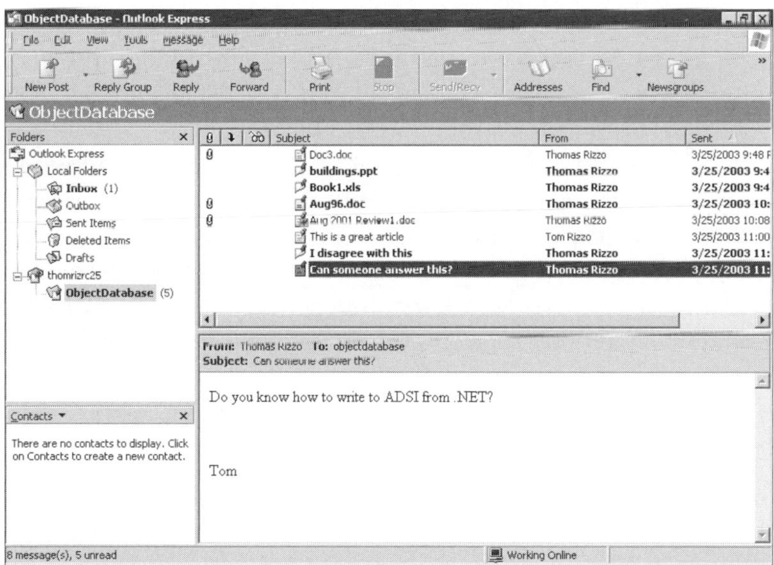

Figure 2-15 A public folder being viewed by Outlook Express, an NNTP newsreader

Internet Mail Access Protocol Version 4

IMAP4 is an Internet standard that defines a way for clients to access messaging information on a server. Exchange Server is an IMAP4-compliant messaging server, so any standard IMAP4 client can access the messaging services of Exchange Server. Some of these services include sending and receiving e-mail, synchronizing e-mail to offline storage, and accessing public folders. Accessing public folders with IMAP4 extends the power of public folders to any standard IMAP4 client.

Hypertext Transfer Protocol

HTTP is the primary protocol used to distribute information on the Web—that is, to transmit graphics and documents from a Web server to a Web browser. HTTP is a client-to-server protocol, which means that a client running on the user's machine sends a request for data to a server, and the server receives the request and sends the relevant information back to the client. HTTP servers can do more than just send back simple data. Scripts that access other back-end services on the network can run on the HTTP server. These services can be databases, collaboration servers such as Exchange Server, or custom-built applications.

After Exchange 5.5, the Outlook Web Access (OWA) architecture changed significantly. Instead of leveraging ASP, Exchange 2000 and 2003 use compiled code in an ISAPI DLL and some helper files to display OWA. This change removes some of the ways in which OWA can be customized, but it increases its scalability. For this reason, if you want to customize OWA, you should learn how OWA uses URLs. Also, you should learn how to use Windows SharePoint Services (WSS) Forms because you can replace any OWA standard form with a WSS Form. All these topics are discussed in Chapter 20. For accessing your Exchange Server, OWA uses WebDAV and CDO with Internet Explorer 5.0 and later and uses standard HTML for the clients that don't support DHTML and XML, such as Internet Explorer 4.0 and Netscape Navigator.

Integrated, Internet Standards–Based Security

Corporations whose systems are connected to the Internet expose their networks to millions of Internet users, so security is a significant concern. Most users of the Internet are not lurking, waiting to break into corporate networks, but some are. Exchange Server prevents malicious users from accessing privileged information by implementing Internet standards–based security in an integrated way.

Windows Security

Exchange Server integrates with Windows security in two ways. First, users have to be authenticated using a Windows account before gaining access to any Exchange Server resource that requires authenticated access. Administrators can set up a Windows security infrastructure, and Exchange Server uses that infrastructure for its own security and access permissions. This enables users to log on only once to access both the network and Exchange Server services.

Second, Exchange Server uses the built-in auditing capabilities of Windows. This integration allows an administrator to detect security breaches by tracking events across Windows and Exchange Server that occur within a system. All the events can be viewed in one window using the Windows event log.

Secure Messaging

Many corporations today use the Internet as a backbone for their corporate communications system. While this setup is cheaper than leasing lines between servers, it opens a world of security concerns. Exchange Server alleviates these concerns by implementing features that allow corporations to use the Internet securely. For securely sending messages between servers, Exchange Server supports Secure Sockets Layer (SSL) in combination with Simple Mail Transfer Protocol (SMTP). SMTP is the primary protocol that different mail systems use to communicate over the Internet and Exchange uses to talk with other Exchange servers. SSL allows systems to encrypt data sent from one system to another. By implementing SSL with SMTP, an organization can encrypt the data sent from one Exchange Server to another when it sends the data over the Internet.

Secure Applications

SSL is also used with other Internet protocols that Exchange Server supports. By using SSL, OWA can encrypt any traffic between a user's Web browser and Web server. This secures any HTML documents that OWA is sending to the user. You can also take advantage of SSL when you use custom Web forms with Exchange Server.

S/MIME Support

Exchange Server supports encryption and digital signatures by using Secure Multipurpose Internet Mail Extensions (S/MIME). An Internet standard, S/MIME is a method of digitally signing and encrypting messages sent between users on the same vendor's system or between users on different vendors' systems.

S/MIME is built on X.509 version 3 certificates. These certificates are generated by a certificate authority such as VeriSign or Certificate Server (which is included with Windows 2000 Server). Because Exchange Server supports X.509 version 3 certificates, it can accept the certificates from other certificate authorities. Similarly, clients can trust certificates from other authorities through the use of Certificate Trust Lists.

Exchange Server also supports the revocation of security certificates. Revoking certificates is useful when a user thinks that her security has been compromised and someone else is signing messages on her behalf. After revoking a certificate, the administrator can issue a new certificate to the user. Also, when a user leaves an organization, you might want to revoke his certificate to be sure that all messages sent by him are marked as invalid. When an administrator revokes the certificates for a user, any encrypted messages previously sent by the revoked user will appear as invalid messages.

As a developer, you can take advantage of the advanced security features of Exchange Server. By basing your applications on the standard Outlook e-mail message, you automatically inherit the advanced security functionality in Outlook. This allows you to digitally sign and encrypt your custom forms before the user sends or posts forms.

Multitier, Replicated, Secure Forms Library

Users might have difficulty locating a new application in an organization if the application is on one of many servers. Intranets have made finding applications easier, but users still have to find the site with explicit links to the information they want. And once users find the Web server that has the application, that server might be halfway around the globe, making connection speeds to that application very slow.

Exchange Server's multitier, replicated, secure forms library makes locating applications easier. The Exchange Server forms library has four main components: an Organizational Forms Library, the folder forms libraries, a Personal Forms Library, and a Web forms library. Some of these libraries can be synchronized offline, so users can work with the applications even when they are disconnected from the network. You can choose which of these libraries is best for your application.

Organizational Forms Library

The Organizational Forms Library usually contains forms that everyone in an organization needs access to, such as vacation requests, business card order forms, and travel expense reports. The Organizational Forms Library is on the

Exchange server and can be replicated to other Exchange servers throughout your network, enabling quick access to these forms. It lists all the available forms throughout an organization. Figure 2-16 shows the Organizational Forms Library in Outlook.

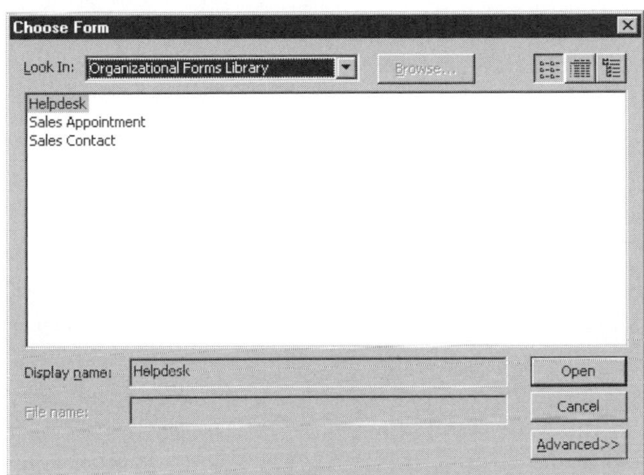

Figure 2-16 The Organizational Forms Library

The Organizational Forms Library is secure, allowing administrators to set which users have permissions to publish or edit information in the library. It is also multilingual; Exchange Server presents the server-based forms library that corresponds to the language of the client program accessing the forms library. For example, when a Japanese client requests a list of forms in the Organizational Forms Library, Exchange Server displays all the corresponding Japanese forms. This multilingual capability allows you to customize and deploy your applications without having to write any code to detect the language of the client.

Folder Forms Library

The folder forms library is for folder-specific forms. The folder forms library is more secure than the Organizational Forms Library. You post forms that you do not want to share globally in the folder forms library. The forms stored in a personal folder forms library are shared only with the users to whom you give access. The forms stored in a public folder forms library can be shared with any user who has the correct permissions on that public folder. Using the synchronization capabilities of Exchange Server, users can replicate public folders (including their data and forms) off line.

Personal Forms Library

The Personal Forms Library is the most restrictive library in terms of sharing its forms with other users. It "belongs" to a particular user and cannot be shared with any other users in the organization. All forms in the Personal Forms Library can be used both on and off the network. Users can test forms in the Personal Forms Library before publishing them to the Organizational Forms Library or folder forms library.

Web Forms Library

The Web forms library is a hierarchy of folders stored in the Windows file system where your Web server (IIS) runs OWA. Exchange Server supports HTML forms as a development environment, so OWA has an easy and automatic way for Web developers to publish custom forms in the Web forms library. To create an HTML-based application, you simply create a subdirectory in the file system where OWA is stored and copy your HTML files to it. The new form will appear in the Launch Custom Forms window of OWA. Users can then start working with the application from the Web forms library. Figure 2-17 shows forms in the Web forms library.

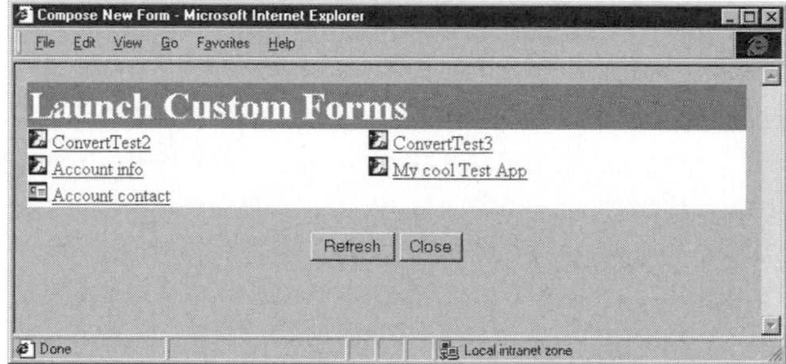

Figure 2-17 The Web forms library, which holds HTML applications that you develop

Starting with Exchange 2000, the Web forms library has been replaced by WSS Forms and the WSS Forms Registry. Existing Web forms will still work on Exchange Server 5.5, but not on Exchange Server 2000 and later. For this reason, if you are using the Web forms library, you should keep at least one OWA 5.5 server in your organization.

Built-in Information Management Tools

Managing information in applications can be one of the most tedious tasks for a developer. But public folders, with their built-in and configurable services, will handle this for you automatically. You can set the expiration time for information in public folders, thereby preventing the folders from becoming inundated with megabytes of outdated and useless information. The conflict management features in public folders prevent two users from unintentionally saving two versions of the same document. If two users edit the same document stored in a public folder and then try to save their changes, Exchange Server will send a message about the conflict to both users and to any folder contacts defined on the public folder. The users can then decide whether to keep one of the two items or both. Figure 2-18 shows the Conflict Message dialog box.

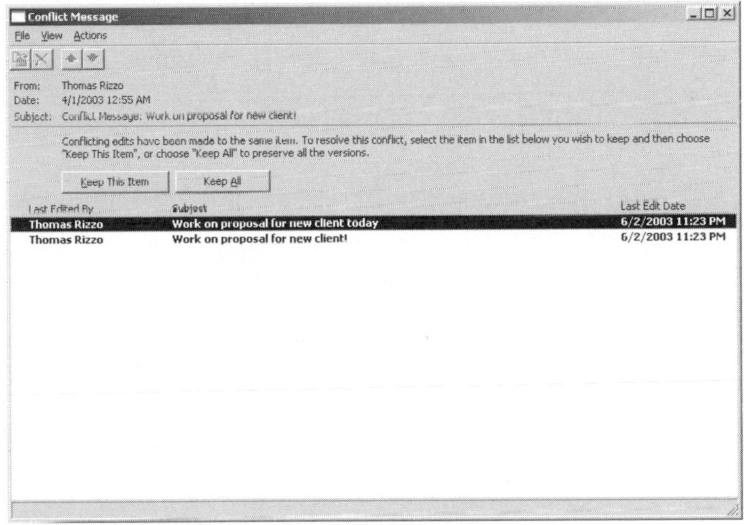

Figure 2-18 Conflict Message dialog box

Rules

Exchange Server uses rules to help manage the massive amount of information received by an organization. Although many other collaborative systems have this functionality in some form, a user generally must be logged on to the system before rules can be processed. Also, other systems don't allow rules in folders other than a user's personal folders. With Exchange Server, rules are supported for both personal folders (such as an inbox) and for public folders.

By setting rules in your public folder application, you can to some extent control the flow of information into and out of the folder. Public folder rules are configurable by the owner of the public folder and are set up on the server, which means no client has to be logged on for the rules to fire. Instead, the server fires the rules.

The types of rules you can create range from simple rules, such as "send a thank you e-mail to anyone who sends a message to the public folder," to very complex rules. Complex rules can entail checking multiple fields on an item and taking a specific action based on those fields.

Server Events

With Exchange 2000 and 2003, the Exchange 5.5 event scripting agent applications still work, but you must enable the event service (which is disabled by default in Exchange 2000 and 2003). Also, new and more powerful server events are available. Chapter 17 covers events in more detail, but you can use the full power of COM or .NET applications to capture server-side events such as items being created or deleted and perform your own business logic on these items.

Connectivity and Migration Tools

Information is stored in various places within a corporation. For employees, business partners, and customers to collaborate effectively, these islands of information must be connected and made accessible. To enable this, Exchange Server has a number of built-in migration and coexistence tools.

A series of connectors enables an Exchange Server system to coexist with other types of collaborative systems. These connectors ensure the reliable delivery of messages between Exchange Server and these other systems, but the connector's capabilities do not stop there. These connectors, such as the Lotus Notes connector, can also provide directory synchronization between two systems. Directory synchronization gives clients on both systems the ability to query the directory for users on another system. This global, unified directory in the Exchange Server system makes building collaborative applications easier because it centralizes information. The systems that Exchange Server can connect to, send messages from, and synchronize directories with include Microsoft Mail, Lotus cc:Mail, and Lotus Notes. Exchange Server can transfer messages with host-based systems such as OfficeVision VM (PROFS) and System Network

Architecture Distribution Services (SNADS) systems such as IBM OfficeVision/MVS and Fisher TAO.

Sometimes corporations find it more cost-effective to have only one collaborative system rather than several. To help organizations move to Exchange Server, migration tools for a large number of systems are included in the product. These tools make it easier for organizations to transfer their users and information into the Exchange Server system. The products supported by these migration tools are Microsoft Mail, Lotus cc:Mail, Novell Groupwise, and Lotus Notes.

SharePoint Portal Server

SharePoint Portal Server (SPS) 1.0 shares most of the same underlying technology as Exchange 2000, with a few key differences. Because SPS has the same fundamental architecture as Exchange, many of the development options we've looked at in this chapter also work on SPS. For example, SPS ships with CDO for Exchange 2000 and with OWA. This means you can build rich collaborative applications on SPS that are similar to the types of applications you can build on Exchange and also take advantage of the SPS feature set, such as the portal, document management, and search capabilities. Furthermore, SPS 2.0 provides even more functionality than version 1.0 and ties in well with your Exchange environment. You'll find a wealth of information about SharePoint in the companion material for this book, which is posted on the book's Web site.

Exchange Server 2003 Enhancements

Exchange Server 2003 builds on the extensive collaborative features introduced in Exchange Server 5.5. It comes with enhancements across the entire product—enhancements that affect administrators, developers, and end users. When coupled with Outlook 2003, Exchange Server 2003 offers a compelling information management server and client. We'll look next at the major changes to the developer capabilities on the server; we'll take only a cursory look at IT advancements.

Outlook Web Access Enhancements

The new OWA provides many features that you are already familiar with in Outlook:

- **Logon enhancements** OWA provides a new logon page in which users can select the version of OWA they want to use. As part of this new logon, a cookie is stored on your client for authentication purposes. This cookie is automatically deleted when a user logs off or after a specified period of user inactivity, by default, 30 minutes. Figure 2-19 shows the new OWA logon page.

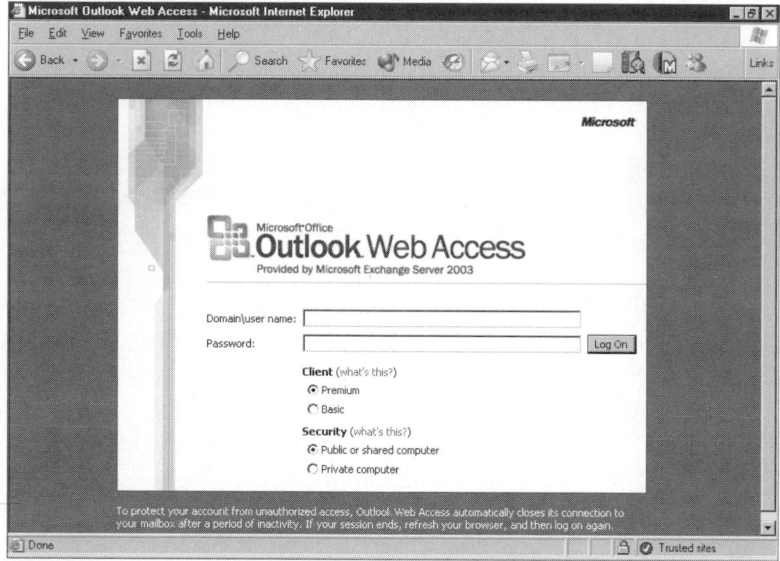

Figure 2-19 Outlook Web Access logon page, which allows you to select the version of OWA to use

- **New user interface** To make OWA look more like Outlook, the OWA interface (shown in Figure 2-20) has been revamped. Users no longer have to learn how to navigate separate user experiences.
- **Shortcut menus** The Exchange 2000 version of OWA supports some shortcut menus on folders. But when you right-click on a message, you see the standard browser menu, unlike in Outlook, where you're presented with the menu commands for an e-mail message. The new OWA provides content-sensitive menus for folders and messages so the experience is similar in Outlook and in OWA (as shown in Figure 2-21).

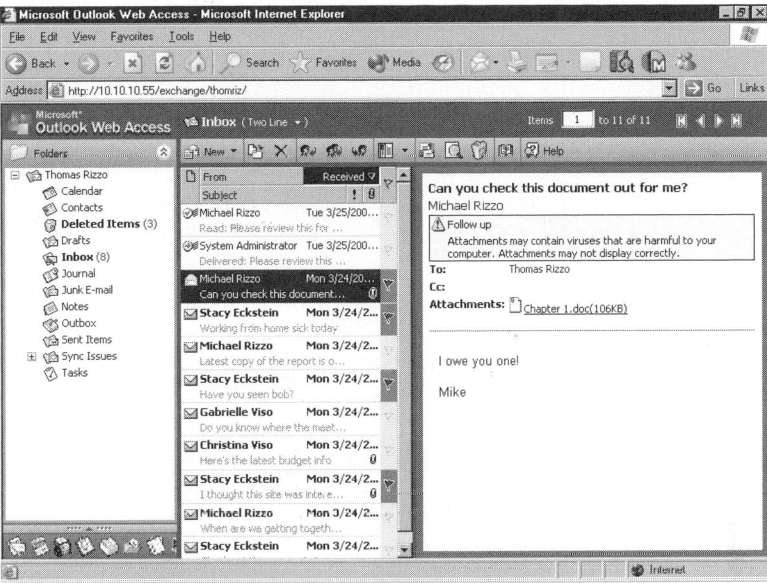

Figure 2-20 The new OWA interface

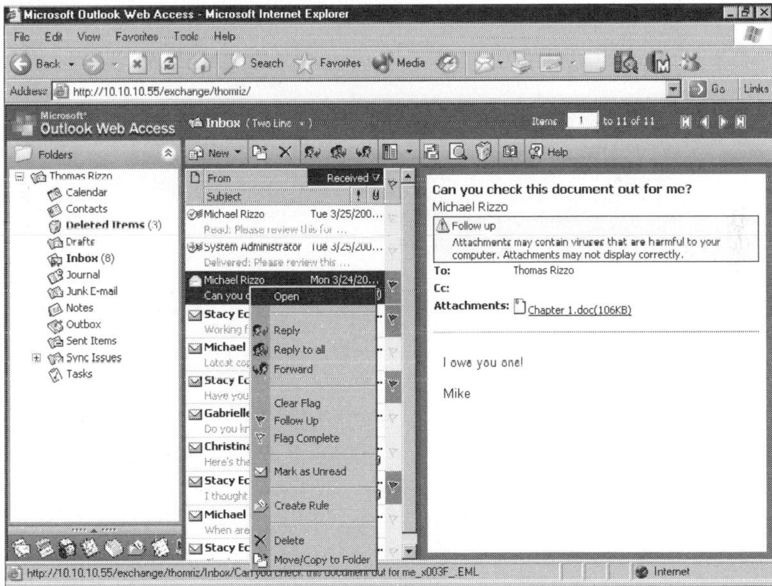

Figure 2-21 Shortcut menu support for messages in OWA

- **Quick flagging** Another Outlook feature that's now implemented in OWA is quick flags. You can now quickly flag a message on the right side of the message list in your browser interface.

- **Search folder support** OWA exposes the search folder capabilities of Outlook. Search folders, as you will see in Chapter 16, are dynamically populated by the server based on a query you specify through the Outlook user interface or through code.
- **Spelling checker** You can check the spelling of your messages before sending them. OWA implements a server-side, multilingual spelling checker (as shown in Figure 2-22). With this feature on the server side, the user doesn't need to download any controls or software to the client to check spelling.

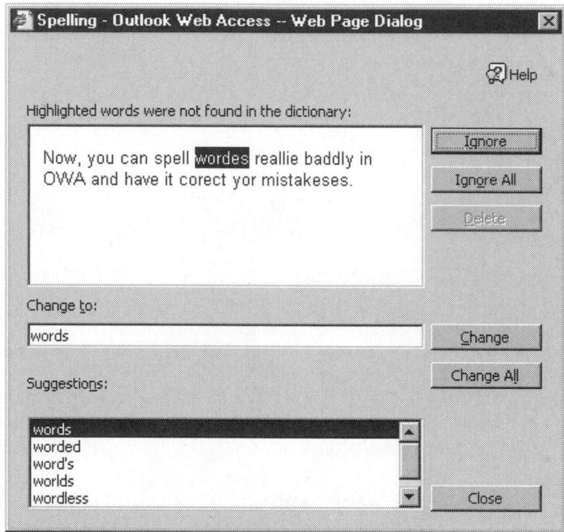

Figure 2-22 The new OWA spelling checker

- **E-mail signature support** Instead of having to type your e-mail signature on every message, OWA now supports signatures, just like Outlook does.
- **Signed and encrypted messages** To help lessen the gap between OWA and Outlook, OWA can now send and receive signed and encrypted e-mail messages. To perform this functionality, you need to download an ActiveX control to your machine. Also, you need to have a valid digital certificate for this feature to work.
- **Rules support** You can now view and create rules that are interoperable with Outlook. This is a powerful feature because sometimes you might want to turn off a rule or create a rule but you don't have access to the full Outlook client. Figure 2-23 shows the new rules interface in OWA.

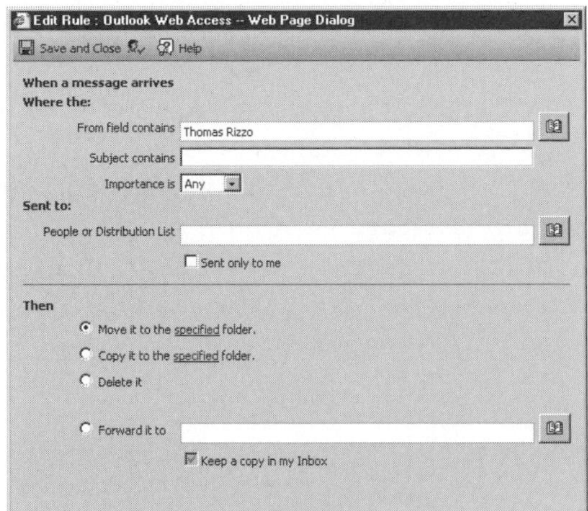

Figure 2-23 The new OWA rules interface

- **Tasks support** To improve interoperability with Outlook, OWA supports personal tasks. The task support is basic, however. It does not include task assignment or deletion of individual tasks in recurring tasks, for example. Figure 2-24 shows the new task interface in OWA.

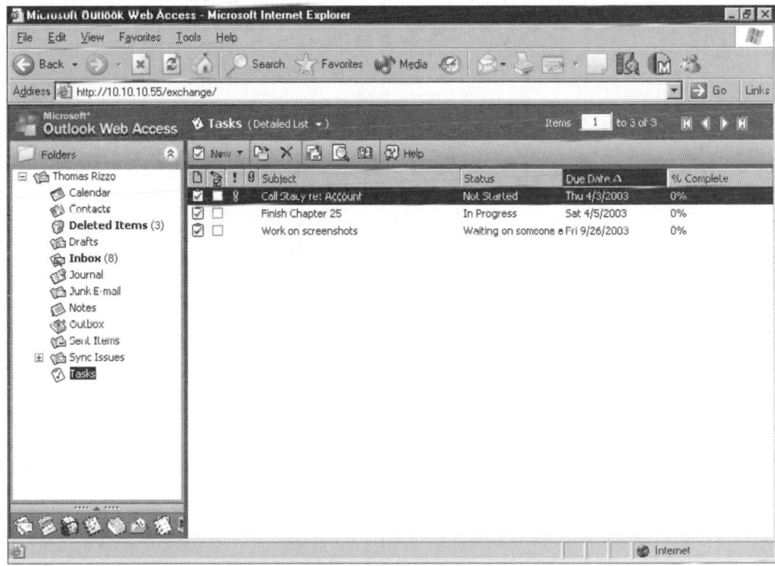

Figure 2-24 The new OWA task interface

Mobility Enhancements

With Exchange Server 2003, the features of Mobile Information Server are directly integrated into Exchange Server. Outlook Mobile Access, the mobile version of OWA, is installed with Exchange by default. When a mobile device hits an Exchange server, Exchange detects that the client is a mobile device and renders a Wireless Markup Language (WML) version of OWA to the client. Figure 2-25 shows an example of using a phone simulator to browse Exchange information using Outlook Mobile Access.

Figure 2-25 The Outlook Mobile Access interface

The sample Exchange application covered in Chapter 15, the Training application, also has a mobile Web browser interface and can detect when a mobile browser is hitting the application. Figure 2-26 shows the mobile interface for the Training application.

Figure 2-26 Mobile interface for the Training application

Developer Enhancements

Following are some of the most significant Exchange Server developer enhancements:

- OLE DB and Microsoft ActiveX Data Objects (ADO) support
- Friendly URL access to every item in the Exchange Server database—no more globally unique identifiers (GUIDs)
- XML support
- A richer events model in terms of types of events supported and the programming of events
- A new version of CDO
- A new version of OWA that's much easier to reuse
- An enhanced platform for real-time collaboration development
- A greatly improved and built-in workflow engine for building workflow applications

The Web Storage System

You might have heard of the Web Storage System, but you might not know what this technology means for the developer. For the past few years, Microsoft's Exchange Server group has been developing a great data storage technology, but until now it has shipped only with Exchange Server. Microsoft has renamed this database technology Web Storage System and ripped it out of Exchange Server. Not only is this technology now identifiable by name, but it can also be embedded into other Microsoft products. This means that you can use the Web Storage System in situations that require a rich, semistructured, Web-aware database that you can access from a number of client access methods. Furthermore, the Web Storage System technology provides a rich set of development services.

Exchange Server 2000 was the first Microsoft product to ship with the Web Storage System technology. Then SPS 2001 shipped with the Web Storage System. You might see the Web Storage System referred to as the *Exchange store* in Exchange Server and as the *document store* in SharePoint. It's pretty much the same technology despite the different names.

Enough background. Let's talk about the core features of the Web Storage System technology. They fall into three main areas: data access, programmability, and security.

Data Access Features

One of the major new data access features of the Web Storage System is a native OLE DB 2.5 provider. This provider allows developers to write directly to OLE DB interfaces to get or set information contained in the Web Storage System. It also allows developers who are familiar with ADO to write ADO applications using the Web Storage System as the data store. We'll look closely at the ADO 2.5 support provided by the Web Storage System later in this chapter.

Another data access feature is Web Distributed Authoring and Versioning (WebDAV) support. The Web Storage System is tightly integrated with IIS, so it can provide rich access to data over Web protocols such as HTTP. However, standard HTTP commands, such as GET and POST, do not provide a rich enough set of features to build collaborative applications. For this reason, the Internet Engineering Task Force (IETF) came up with WebDAV—extensions to HTTP 1.1 that allow you to move, copy, query, and delete resources. For example, with WebDAV, you can create a new folder in the Web Storage System, create a new item in that folder, and then query for the new item using requests formatted in a specific XML format that WebDAV understands. You'll see some examples of using WebDAV in Chapter 16.

The final way—and in my opinion, one of the most interesting ways—to get data from the Web Storage System is by using its Installable File System (IFS) provider. The IFS provider allows you to provide access to your data in the Web Storage System using standard file system programs or interfaces. For example, you can make the documents you create in the Web Storage System available to your application users through Windows Explorer. And without having to write a single line of code, you can turn any file system–aware application into an interface for your application's data. The Training application we'll look at in Chapter 15 will show some ways you can use the IFS provider in your applications.

Programmability Features

The Web Storage System gives Web and Windows developers a great amount of flexibility in their programming. Programmability features fall into five key areas: schema, form, event, workflow, and XML support. The upcoming sections will give you an overview of each of these areas; you'll see more in-depth coverage when we look at the Training application in Chapter 15.

Schema Support

Built directly into the Web Storage System is an extensive array of schema support. By being able to create a schema, developers can define sets of properties that are common to a certain type of item in the Web Storage System. Such support is similar to object support for certain properties. The Web Storage System defines some built-in schemas, such as a schema for an object or an item. Exchange Server 2003 specifically defines a schema for messages, appointments, and contacts.

One great thing about the Web Storage System schema support is that schemas are inheritable. This means you can inherit schema properties from another schema collection and extend the inherited properties with your own properties. For example, suppose I want to create a customer schema definition that includes properties similar to those of the built-in contact schema as well as some custom properties for my application. I simply tell the Web Storage System that I want to inherit the properties from the built-in contact schema and extend it with my own properties.

By creating a custom schema, you are guaranteed that all of the properties will be returned when you submit searches using the SQL SELECT * syntax. This allows other application developers to traverse the ADO *fields* collection instead of having to know the actual names of your properties. (For performance reasons, however, you might not want applications that use SELECT * because the Web Storage System must return all the properties on the items contained in your search. For most Web Storage System items, this can be in excess of 100 properties for each item!)

Even though you're not required to use schemas to build applications on the Web Storage System, I highly recommend that you do, when appropriate—and most of the time, using schemas will be appropriate. However, using a schema might not make sense if you're only creating a one-off, single-use item for which you don't care whether the properties are reused on other items or for which the property definitions will be lost if the item is deleted. Furthermore, you might find that creating a schema is more tedious than simply appending new fields onto the item using ADO. This is the case in the code for the workflow process in the Training application in Chapter 15; it is easier to append items onto the process instance in the workflow than to create a full-fledged schema definition for the process instance itself. However, you'll see other code samples in this book in which schema and their definitions play an important role.

Web Storage System Forms

The Web Storage System supports an HTML-based forms technology. This technology has three key components: HTML markup for the forms, a server-side Internet Server API (ISAPI) filter, and a forms registry.

To create Web Storage System forms, you must add some special markup to your HTML-based forms that indicate to the Web Storage System that the fields you're requesting in your form should be pulled from your Web Storage System application. You'll see what this markup actually consists of when we look at the Web Storage System form used in the Training application in Chapter 15.

Beyond client-side markup, the Web Storage System forms technology also includes a server-side ISAPI extension. This extension captures requests sent to your Web server and checks to see whether the Web browser is requesting an item that has an associated Web Storage System form. If the item does have an associated Web Storage System form, the ISAPI extension finds that form and returns the form to the Web browser. Web Storage System forms support both standard HTML 3.2 browsers and XML-aware browsers, so data binding can occur in one of two places: on the server or on the client. For HTML 3.2 clients, you should perform data binding on the server, which forces the Web Storage System to pull the values for the fields in the form, and return only the form's HTML 3.2 representation to the client.

For XML-aware browsers, such as Internet Explorer 5.0 and 6.0, you can perform server-side or client-side data binding. If you perform client-side data binding, the forms engine will return the form and you can perform the data binding on the client. This allows you to provide easier manipulation of the data without having to make an extra round-trip to the server each time the form needs to be updated. For example, you can re-sort or change the format of the data representation to suit your application's needs without incurring the cost of returning to the server to do this.

The final component of the Web Storage System forms technology is the Web Storage System forms registry. By allowing you to specify which forms should appear for specific items, the Web Storage System enables you to customize the default renderings of items. Each built-in item has some default forms that will be rendered for it. Because the forms registry is flexible, you can register forms based on the browser type requesting the item, the language of the browser client, or the type of item that the user requests from the Web Storage System. You can thus build different forms for different clients. For example, you can create a microbrowser form for cell phone clients that browse your application using the Microsoft microbrowser technology. We'll look at the forms registry in more detail when we examine the Training application in Chapter 15.

Web Storage System Events

Exchange Server 5.5 introduced an event mechanism that allows application developers to write code to handle events occurring in the Exchange Server database. The Web Storage System improves on this concept. In Exchange Server 5.5, events are asynchronous, which means that the event fires after the item is committed to the database. The Web Storage System supports asynchronous events, but it also supports synchronous and system events. Synchronous events fire before the item is committed to the database, enabling your application to decide whether the item should be committed or aborted (in which case the item won't be saved). Synchronous events guarantee that the application is the only process making this decision for the item. Users or other processes are blocked until the application finishes processing. The system events notify the applications about key occurrences in the Web Storage System—for example, a system event might fire after the Web Storage System starts up. Developers can write code to either begin replication or start processing their custom application when this event occurs. These two new classes of events allow you to build even richer applications on the Web Storage System.

Workflow Support

A workflow application is an excellent example of an application you can build with Web Storage System events. The Web Storage System ships with a built-in workflow engine that uses synchronous and system events to perform its functionality. This built-in workflow support enables developers to start writing workflow applications as soon as they obtain a product containing the Web Storage System.

XML Support

The Web Storage System is very Web-centric, which explains how it got its name. The Web Storage System natively supports XML which you can use to retrieve and set data. We'll look at the XML support of the Web Storage System more closely in Chapter 20.

Security Features

Information security is always a major concern for developers and users, so the Web Storage System supports securing data at both the item level and the property level. This allows you to select which users or groups of users can access data contained in the Web Storage System. Furthermore, you can query or modify this access programmatically.

Additional Features

Besides the standard Web Storage System features, Exchange Server 2003 provides some additional features in its implementation of the Web Storage System technology. These features include Messaging Application Programming Interface (MAPI) support, multiple top-level hierarchies (TLHs), and a set of management objects that allow you to programmatically manage information in Active Directory and the Exchange Server 2003 Web Storage System. Let's take a look at each of these features.

MAPI Support

Exchange Server 2003 continues to fully support the MAPI interfaces. This means clients that use MAPI (such as Outlook) run against the Web Storage System without modification. The applications you have written to MAPI will continue to work, but you should test your applications to ensure that all functionality continues to behave as expected.

Multiple Top-Level Hierarchies

A TLH is simply a tree of folders with a top-level root folder. For example, the Public Folder hierarchy that starts with Public Folders and continues to All Public Folders is a top-level hierarchy. To make application development easier, Exchange Server 2003 lets you have TLHs other than the Public Folder hierarchy. You can thus break your applications into multiple hierarchies so users can avoid crawling through the Public Folder tree to find the application they need. This change also makes it easier for administrators to manage your applications because they can separate the applications into independent TLHs. You should, when possible, place your applications in a top-level hierarchy other than the Public Folders hierarchy because other top-level hierarchies provide more functionality. However, if you require Outlook access to your application, you must keep your application in the Public Folder hierarchy. Outlook cannot view hierarchies other than the Public Folder hierarchy.

Figure 2-27 shows the Exchange System Manager (which replaces the Exchange 5.5 Administration program) displaying multiple TLHs on a single Exchange server. Notice that the multiple TLHs also allow developers to place applications into different naming contexts.

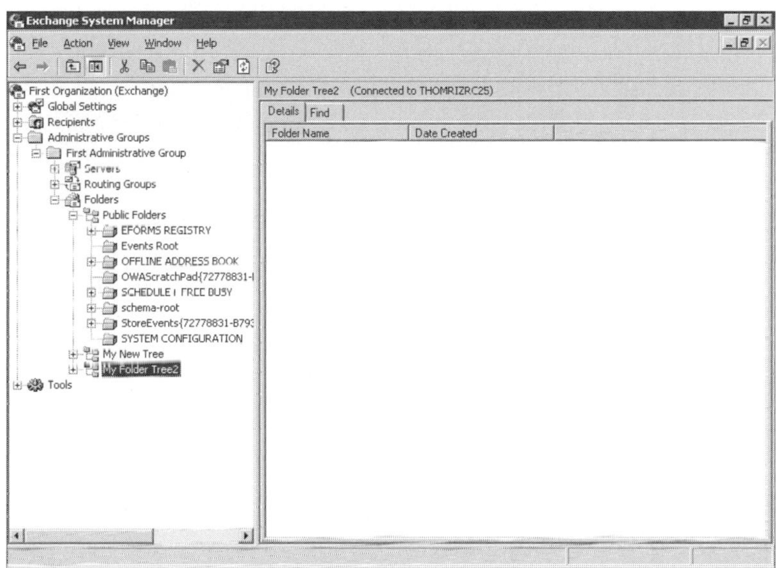

Figure 2-27 The Exchange System Manager with multiple-TLH support

CDO for Exchange Management

To provide a programmatic way for developers to manage recipients and servers, CDO in Exchange Server 2000 and later contains an extended set of management objects called CDO for Exchange Management Objects (EMO, or CDOEXM). With EMO, you can create, modify, or delete recipients or groups of recipients, and you can manage the structure of the information stored in Exchange. Notice that I said *structure* and not *content*. EMO doesn't give you the ability to create items, change properties, or perform other such content-related tasks. You must use CDO and ADO to attain such functionality. EMO is there to help you create storage groups and folder hierarchies, as well as change storage quotas and deleted-item recovery periods.

If you plan to write any administration components for Exchange Server, such as Microsoft Management Console (MMC) snap-ins, you'll need to learn about and use the EMO object model. The Training application makes heavy use of EMO when working with Exchange Server to allow you to create new storage groups, folder databases, hierarchies, and virtual roots. We'll look at CDO for Exchange Management in Chapter 18.

Exchange Server Web Services Support

Exchange Server Objects (XSO) is the next generation of programming interfaces for Exchange built using XML Web services technology. The technology under XSO is actually a higher-level object model on WebDAV. In Chapter 14, we will look at wrapping Exchange Server object models with your own Web services interfaces so you do not have to wait for XSO and can start writing applications that leverage Web services against Exchange today.

Changes from Exchange Server 2000

We'll look next at the differences between Exchange Server 2000 and Exchange Server 2003—specifically, the technologies that have been removed or are no longer supported in Exchange Server 2003.

M: Drive Removed

The M: drive is disabled by default. However, you can turn it back on through registry settings. The training application in Chapter 15 does that so that it can copy files using file copy to the drive if necessary. However, you should not use the M: drive to perform administrative work on Exchange. The following is the code from the sample that enables the M: drive. You must recycle the Exchange store in order for the changes to take effect.

```
Sub EnableWSSDrive()
'Enable the M Drive
   Dim strWSSDrive As String
   strWSSDrive = "M"
   SetKeyValue "SYSTEM\CurrentControlSet\Services\EXIFS\Parameters", _
            "DriveLetter", strWSSDrive, REG_SZ
   Shell App.Path & "\cycle.bat", vbNormalFocus
   MsgBox "The application is now stopping and restarting SharePoint " & _
          "Portal Server for the change to take effect. Please click " & _
          "ok when the services are done restarting.", _
          vbInformation + vbOKOnly, App.Title
End Sub
```

Instant Messaging Removed

The IM server support has been removed from Exchanger Server 2003. Instead, you should use the real-time collaboration capabilities in Windows Server 2003. Exchange IM is based on the Rendezvous RVP protocol. The new Windows Server IM server is based on Session Initiation Protocol (SIP). In Chapter 19, I'll cover the IM controls included with the Exchange SDK, which use RVP, as well as programming Windows Messenger, which supports SIP.

Create Index No Longer Supported

In Exchange Server 2000, you can create indexes programmatically. In Exchange Server 2003, this capability is removed. As a result, the *Create Index* function, which is part of the ADO commands you can send to Exchange, is no longer supported.

CDOHTML Removed

If you install a clean build of Exchange Server 2003, you will not find the CDO 1.21 Rendering Library (CDOHTML) on the server. CDOHTML does not ship with Exchange Server 2003. This means you have to install Outlook Web Access 5.5 to get CDOHTML. You cannot install OWA 5.5 on an Exchange Server 2003 server, so if you want to use CDOHTML, it must be on a server that isn't running Exchange Server 2003. The only time you will use CDOHTML is in ASP or ASP .NET for authorization impersonation and rendering. Using CDOHTML for rendering is the least common usage.

FrontPage WSS Form Authoring Tool No Longer Supported

The FrontPage tools to build WSS forms are no longer supported because they built on the M: drive capabilities of Exchange. WSS forms are still supported—just not this authoring tool.

Anonymous Access to Metabase Removed

Starting with Service Pack 3 of Exchange 2000 and Exchange Server 2003, CDO can no longer access the metabase using an anonymous account. Therefore, when you attempt to send messages in CDO without setting the way to send the message—for example, using the IIS pickup directory or by using a SMTP port—CDO will fail. You must explicitly designate the CDO configuration object, which we will look at in Chapter 15, as the way to send messages via CDO.

What About Exchange Server 5.5 Applications?

You might wonder what will happen to the Exchange Server 5.5 applications you've written using MAPI, CDO, ADSI, or even the Event Scripting Agent. Have no fear—those applications should continue to run without modification, except for some cases that I'll describe here.

MAPI, CDO 1.21, and the Event Scripting Agent are all supported by Exchange Server 2000. Event Scripting Agents are not supported by Exchange 2003. CDO 1.21 is supported against Exchange 2003 servers. Outlook 2003 uses MAPI, so you know that MAPI continues to work well against Exchange because Outlook continues to work well against Exchange.

If you've written applications that use the Directory API (DAPI), you must rewrite your code to use ADSI because Active Directory replaces the Exchange Server directory. If you've written administration extensions to the Exchange Server administration program, you must rewrite these extensions to the MMC because this is the way you administer Exchange servers.

The major hurdle of moving your Exchange Server 5.5 applications to Exchange Server 2003 is the conceptual differences between the two versions of Exchange Server. You can continue to run your Exchange Server 5.5 applications as is on Exchange Server 2003, but you should at least look at the features of Exchange Server 2000 and 2003 to see where you can enhance your existing applications. For example, if you have an Outlook forms-based application, you might want to extend it using the new server events in Exchange Server to add workflow or other functionality.

Summary

In this chapter, you've learned about the server-side infrastructure for collaboration. When you combine Exchange Server with the other Microsoft servers as well as the Microsoft Office system, you get one of the best environments available for creating collaboration solutions. In Part 2 we will drill into using Microsoft Outlook as the client with which to build rich solutions. In Part 3 we will turn our attention to using Microsoft Exchange in the server-side development environment.

Part II

Building Outlook Applications

3

Folders, Fields, and Views

The first step in developing any application is planning it. Without proper planning, you might dive too quickly into development, only to realize that you need more resources than you expected or the application does not meet the requirements of your users. Planning an application begins with assessing why the application is needed—the business purpose of the application. This step sounds obvious, but it helps you focus your development efforts and define how complex or simple the application should be.

After deciding why to build the application, you need to figure out who the users of the application will be. If the users will be technically savvy, for example, you might want to include advanced functionality. If you are developing an expense report application that everyone in an organization will use, you should keep the design of the application simple enough to accommodate users with a wide range of technical skills.

In addition to considering the technical skills of your users, you have to think about the hardware on which the application will run. If laptop users will use your application while traveling and will be disconnected from the network, you need to plan for offline support. If remote users will be the principal users of your application, you should make the application small and fast because your users will have low-bandwidth connectivity.

To develop applications, you need software building blocks. In the same way that brick, wood, and concrete are the materials that contractors need to build a house, software building blocks are the materials you need to build an application. Microsoft Outlook provides five key building blocks for developing collaborative applications: folders, fields, views, forms, and actions. This chapter will show you how to take advantage of the first three. In the next chapter, you will learn how to use forms and actions. Specifically, this chapter will cover how to do the following:

- Create folders and set properties for a folder, including setting the permissions on a folder, setting the replication properties of a folder, and creating custom rules in a folder.
- Create custom fields, such as combination and formula fields, which allow your application to hold custom data. You will also learn how to use these fields in setting properties for filtered replication in Outlook.
- Create your own views by using the five default view types in Outlook, custom fields, and Microsoft Office document properties.

Outlook Development Tips

Here are a few tips for developing applications with Outlook. As you read through this chapter and Chapters 4 and 5, keep these issues in mind.

If possible, develop and test your application in a personal folder before deploying it in a public folder. If you have to develop your application in a public folder, restrict access. Personal folders lack some public folder functionality such as permissions and rules, so if your application requires complex permissions or rules, you might want to build your application in a public folder. To limit access to this folder while you build the application, set an option in the folder to allow access by only owners of the folder. I'll talk more about this feature later in this chapter.

Always save a backup copy of a custom form before testing it. Certain logic errors on your form can freeze Outlook and force you to kill the Outlook process. For example, a simple oversight in your VBScript code might cause an infinite loop in your application. The only way to end the loop is to kill the Outlook process. If you did not save a backup copy of the form, you will lose all the changes since the last backup.

As obvious as it sounds, you should test your application thoroughly before deploying it. Your testing should involve trying all the permissions, views, rules, forms, actions, and custom code in the application. If you deploy an application and later realize you need to make changes, make a backup copy of the original application in your personal folders, modify the application backup in your personal folders, and retest and deploy the new application. This method provides the least disruption to current users of the application.

Folders

Folders are the focal point of any Outlook application. They hold data, defined views for that data, forms, agents, and rules. They provide users with a storage location for information and a hierarchical structure that makes finding information easy.

In Outlook, you can create folders in three places: in a mailbox stored on an Exchange server, in personal folders stored on your computer's hard disk, and in public folders. Each location has advantages and disadvantages. For example, if you create a new folder in your personal folders, you cannot easily share it with other users in your organization. You also cannot set permissions on it. (In this book, the examples use public folders for storing application data.) Many of the properties you can set on public folders are applicable to the other two types of folders.

Note Some of the examples and figures in this chapter assume that you have permission to create public folders. If you right-click on a public folder and can choose New Folder, you have permission to create a subfolder within that folder. If you are unable to create a public folder, contact your Exchange Server administrator to see whether a public folder is available to you that will allow you to create folders. If no public folder is available to you, ask your Exchange Server administrator for the proper permission.

Creating Public Folders

To help you work through the rest of the chapter, I'll describe three simple applications that use the building blocks of Outlook: a threaded discussion application, an account tracking system, and a document library application. Each of these applications needs its own separate public folder to store its data.

To create a public folder for each application, follow these steps:

1. In Outlook, select the Folder List shortcut on the Outlook bar. In the Folder List, select the public folder in which you want to create subfolders for the sample application, or select All Public Folders to create the applications in the root of the public folder tree. Then, from the File menu choose New and then Folder. The Create New Folder dialog box will appear.

2. In the Name box, type a name for the folder. For the threaded discussion application, type **Outlook Discussion Group**.
3. Keep the default selection in the Folder Contains drop-down list, which is Mail And Post Items.

> **Note** Outlook allows you to set the default type of item contained in the folder. When you create a public folder of task items, you select Task Items from the drop-down list, although the folder can hold other types of items besides the default item you select.

4. Outlook might ask you whether you want to add a shortcut to this folder to your Outlook bar. Click No.
5. Repeat these steps to create a public folder named Account Tracking and one named Document Library.

Customizing Folder Properties

After creating the folders, you need to customize their properties to fit the needs of your application. Outlook automatically creates and sets certain properties of the folder for you. For example, Outlook defines a default set of views for a folder based on the content type you select when creating the folder. For a calendar folder, Outlook creates calendar views such as day/week/month and active appointments; for a contacts folder, Outlook creates default contact views. You can change the default properties for a folder in the folder's Properties dialog box: right-click on a folder in the folder list and then choose Properties. Figure 3-1 shows the Properties dialog box for a folder named Job Candidates.

General Tab

On the General tab of the Properties dialog box, you can modify the general properties of a folder. In addition to specifying the folder name and describing the folder, you can perform the following tasks:

- **Specify the default form for posting items to the folder** You can set which default or custom form a user should use when submitting an item to the folder. As you will see with our sample applications, you'll want to modify this property after you develop custom forms for the folder.

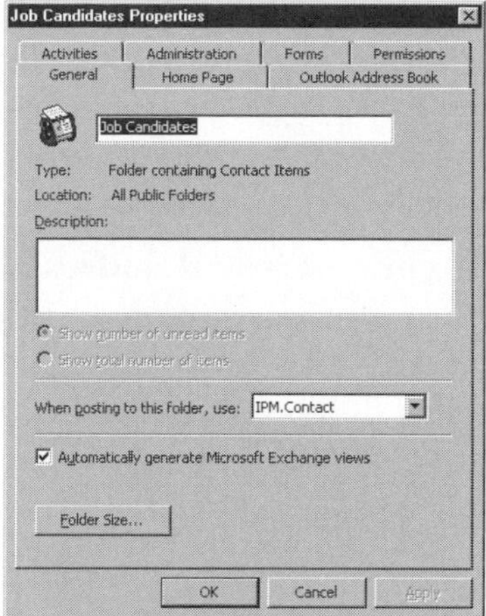

Figure 3-1 The Properties dialog box for a folder named Job Candidates

- **Automatically generate Outlook views for users of the Exchange client** When the Automatically Generate Microsoft Exchange Views option is selected, Outlook automatically creates all views for the folder so users on the Exchange client can use them. This property must be set if you want your custom Outlook views to be available in the Outlook Web Access (OWA) client or available to your Collaboration Data Objects (CDO) applications. By default, Outlook enables this property.
- **Check the size of the folder** Click the Folder Size button to check how much space the folder is using to store its items and any subfolders. Tracking this information can help with planning your local and server disk space requirements.

Administration Tab

The Administration tab of the Properties dialog box allows you to perform common administrative tasks:

- **Set the initial view for the folder** The initial view can be a built-in Outlook view or a custom view. OWA respects this initial view property; when a user browses this folder in OWA, the view you set will be the initial view.
- **Set how Outlook posts items dragged into your folder** The Drag/Drop Posting drop-down list has two settings: Move/Copy and Forward. Move/Copy specifies that when an item is dragged into the folder, the item will appear exactly as it appears in its original location. The user who drags the item to the folder is not indicated, and

the person who originally posted the item is retained as the owner of the item. The Forward setting, in contrast, identifies the user who dragged the item to the folder as the user who forwarded the item. Outlook modifies the original text of the item to indicate that the item was forwarded.

- **Save the folder address to your personal address book** You use the Add Folder Address To Contacts button to save a folder's address so you can later preaddress any custom forms that you want Outlook to send to the folder. The administrator can also include the folder in the Global Address List. The folder will appear as just another recipient, which you can select in the address fields on your form.
- **Set the current availability of the folder** By default, the This Folder Is Available To option is set to All Users With Access Permissions. When you design your application in a folder, you can set this property to Owners Only so users cannot access the folder. This property affects only the current folder, so users still can access and continue working with subfolders under the parent folder. If a user tries to submit items to the parent folder while you have it disabled, Outlook will return the items with a note explaining that the folder and its contents are currently available only to owners. After the application is complete, you can reset this option so all users with proper permissions can access the folders.
- **Create rules for the folder** You use the Folder Assistant button to set rules for the folder. These rules can control information flow in a public folder and check specific properties of items as they are submitted to the folder. For more information on designing rules, see the section titled "Creating Public Folder Rules" later in this chapter.
- **Moderate folder content** The Moderated Folder button gives you access to settings that automatically moderate all the content in a folder before a user can post information. You can enable moderation on any public folder. For information on how to set up a moderated folder, see the section titled "Setting Up Moderated Folders" later in this chapter.
- **Show the folder path** The Folder Path text box shows the location of the folder in the public folder hierarchy. By using this folder path in your applications and also e-mailing these links, it enables users to quickly open a folder without having to search through the public folder tree.

Forms Tab

On the Forms tab of the Properties dialog box, you can specify which forms are associated with a folder. You can also restrict which forms users can post to the folder. Clicking the Manage button displays the Forms Manager dialog box, shown in Figure 3-2. Here you can copy custom forms from other folders or forms libraries into the current folder. You can also update or delete forms.

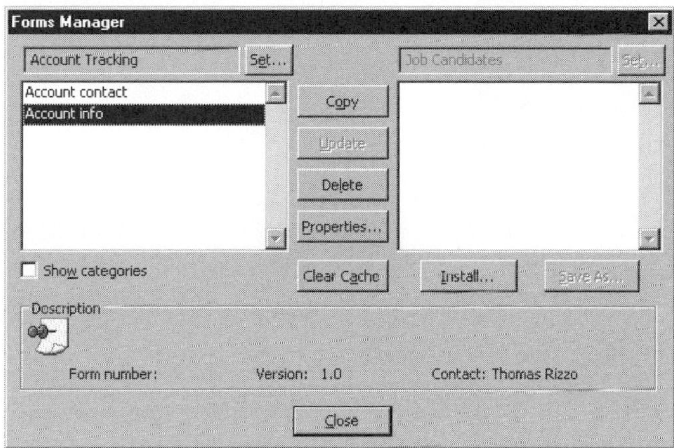

Figure 3-2 The Forms Manager dialog box

Permissions Tab

The Permissions tab of the Properties dialog box, shown in Figure 3-3, allows you to set user and group permissions for your folder and its items so that only the features you want your users to access are exposed. To modify these permissions, you must be an owner of the folder. When you create a folder, Outlook gives you owner rights by default. This means you have the full range of permissions to create, edit, or delete items in the folder. You can also change the permissions of other users in the folder.

When you first click on the tab, the default role for authenticated users is set to Author. This role corresponds to a set of permissions on the folder: users have the ability to view the folder, create and open items in it, and delete and edit their own items.

To learn how to set permissions for our Document Library and Account Tracking applications, follow the next set of steps. We'll limit who can create and edit documents in the folder to users in our division, but we'll enable all users to at least read the information in our Document Library application.

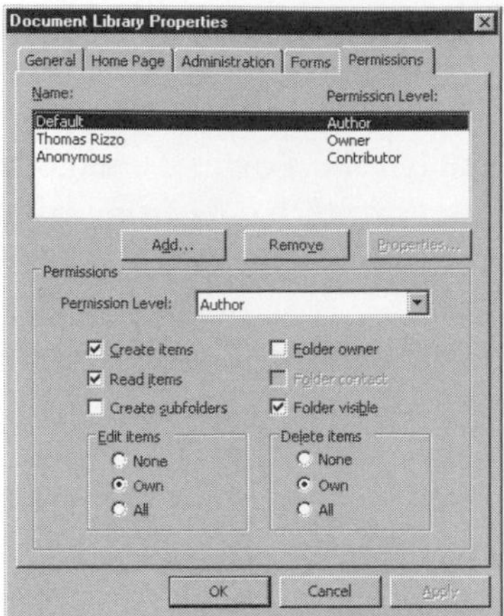

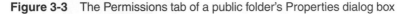

Figure 3-3 The Permissions tab of a public folder's Properties dialog box

1. In the folder list, right-click on the Document Library folder you created earlier and choose Properties.
2. Click on the Permissions tab.
3. In the Name box, select Default. In the Permissions area, select Reviewer from the Roles drop-down list.
4. Click Add, and then select several coworkers from the address list in the Add Users dialog box. (Outlook also allows you to select and assign permissions to distribution lists. This capability makes it easier to set permissions for a large number of users.) Click OK.
5. In the Name box, select one of the names you added in the preceding step. In the Roles drop-down list, select Publishing Author. This role will allow your coworkers to create, read, and edit their own items in the folder. Your Permissions tab should look similar to Figure 3-4.

Follow the same steps for the Account Tracking application, with these exceptions:

- Set the default permissions to None because we do not want anyone in our organization besides sales representatives accessing the application.
- Set the default permissions for the anonymous user to None because we do not want anyone outside the organization or who is logged on anonymously to access the application.

- Hide the folder from Default and Anonymous users by deselecting the Folder Visible check box for each of those names. Remember to give your salespeople the Folder Visible permission on the folder—otherwise, they won't be able to see it either!

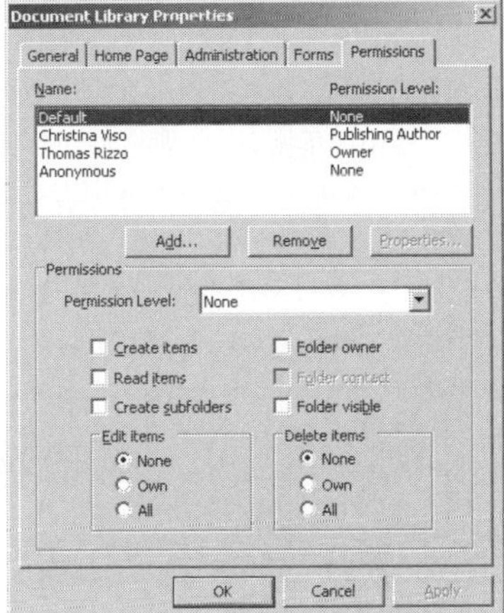

Figure 3-4 Permissions for the Document Library application

Figure 3-5 shows an Outlook user browsing the public folder hierarchy. Notice that the Account Tracking folder is not visible to this user because he does not have the Folder Visible permission.

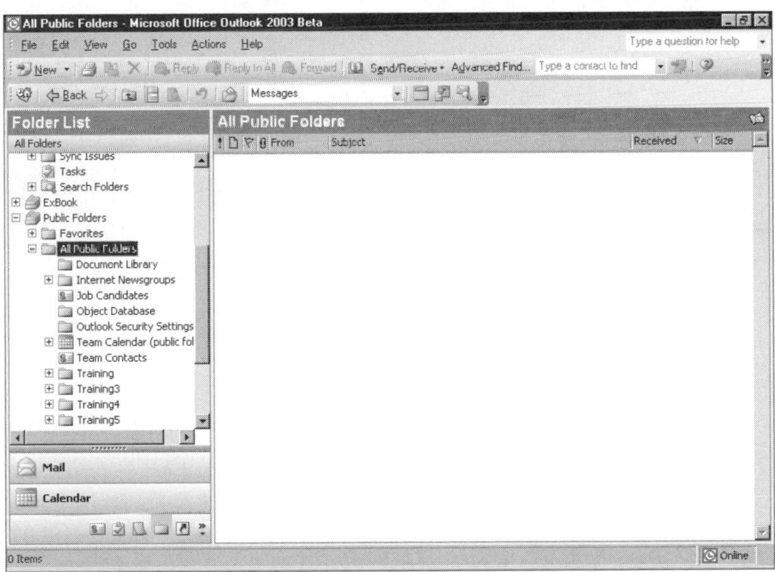

Figure 3-5 A user browsing the public folder hierarchy

Individual Permissions vs. Roles

Outlook provides roles with associated permissions so you do not have to select each permission individually. If you want to create a custom role, you can select the permissions individually, and Outlook will apply these permissions to any type of item in the folder. For example, try dragging and dropping some Microsoft Word documents into the Document Library folder. Log on to Outlook as a different user. This user will be assigned the default permissions for the folder, which means that all documents in the folder will be read-only. Now double-click on one of the Word documents. You should see Word open but with Read-Only at the top of the document. This indicates that Outlook is maintaining the permissions you set on the items in the folder even though the Word document is not a default Outlook item type.

Synchronization Tab

Outlook supports synchronizing folders and forms for offline use. Now let's set up two of our applications to handle offline synchronization:

1. To enable offline synchronization for public folders, you add the folders to your public folder favorites. Open the folder list in Outlook. Expand the Public Folders tree to display Favorites and All Public Folders. Drag and drop the Document Library folder and the Account Tracking folder into the Favorites folder.
2. To set synchronization, choose Options from the Tools menu, click on the Mail Setup tab, and click the Send/Receive button. Click New to add a new Send/Receive Group. Name the group App Folders and click OK. The Send/Receive Settings dialog for the App Folders group is displayed.
3. Select the Include The Selected Account In This Group check box.
4. In the Account Options section, select the Synchronize Forms check box to make sure the most current versions of forms are available off line.
5. In the Folder Options section, expand the folder tree until you can see the folder shortcuts you created previously in Public Folder Favorites. Select the check boxes for the Document Library folder and the Account Tracking folder. Click OK. Click Close. Click OK.

6. In your Favorites folder, select the Account Tracking folder. Click the Send/Receive toolbar button. The Account Tracking and Document Library folders should synchronize their contents off line.

Setting Up Moderated Folders

One of the most requested features of applications that distribute information to many users is the ability to moderate content before it is posted. Moderation allows folder owners to decide which content is appropriate for the application and to select a group of people who can approve the content. It also discourages people from posting random information to the application. By using public folders, you can supply this functionality to your users without having to write any code yourself. The ability to moderate content is a built-in feature of public folders. To show you how moderated public folders work, let's enable moderation for the Outlook Discussion Group application. Take a look at Figure 3-6 as you follow these steps:

1. Find the Outlook Discussion Group folder you created in the public folder list, right-click on it, and choose Properties.
2. In the Properties dialog box, click on the Administration tab.
3. Click the Moderated Folder button to open the Moderated Folder dialog box.

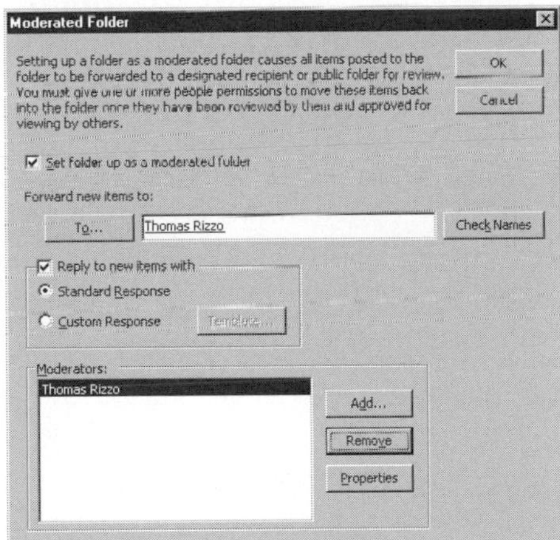

Figure 3-6 The Moderated Folder dialog box

4. Select the Set Folder Up As A Moderated Folder option to make the discussion folder a moderated folder.

5. In the Forward New Items To box, either type the names of people who are moderators or enter the address of another public folder to which Outlook should forward the items.

6. Select the Reply To New Items With option so that every user who mails or posts items in the folder will receive a reply note from Outlook.

7. Select Standard Response as the response type. Users will receive an e-mail in their Inbox thanking them for their submission and explaining that a pending review by other users might delay the item's availability in the folder. You can also send a custom response if the standard response does not meet your needs.

8. In the Moderators area, click the Add button to open the Select Additional Moderators dialog box. Select users or distribution lists to be moderators of content placed in the folder, and then click OK.

More About Moderators and Forwarding Items

Moderators are individual users or distribution lists that are allowed to approve content. When a moderator posts an item to a folder, the item is not forwarded for review—it is left in the folder. If the owner of the folder is not listed as a moderator, the item she posts to a folder will be forwarded for review. The owner cannot drag and drop the item back into the folder; Outlook automatically forwards the item for review again until a moderator drags and drops the item back into the folder. If you are going to use a moderated folder, add the folder owners as moderators.

Creating Public Folder Rules

Sometimes the built-in moderation features make it a burden to manage all the posts that are flowing into the system. Instead of using moderated public folders, you can design custom rules for your application. These rules automatically process new items as they arrive.

Rules consist of conditions and actions. As you might guess, if the conditions of a rule are met by an item, the associated action occurs. Outlook provides an easy way to create custom rules through the Folder Assistant. The Folder Assistant (shown in Figure 3-7) allows you to create, edit, delete, enable, disable, and order rules. We will step through an example shortly.

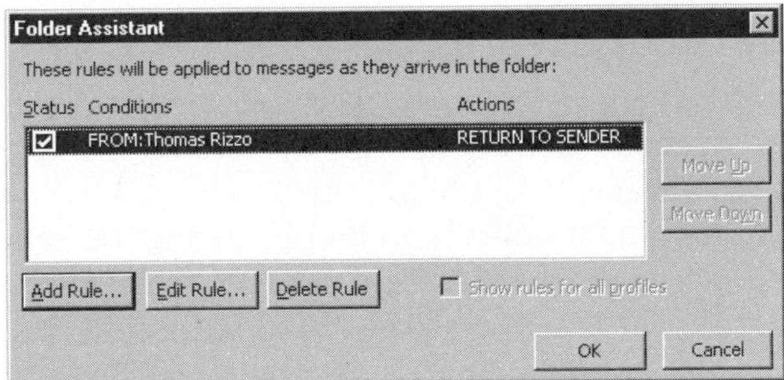

Figure 3-7 The Outlook Folder Assistant

Setting the Conditions for a Rule

The conditions for a rule can range from very simple—for example, checking who the item is from—to very complex, such as checking who the item is from and also searching the subject and text for specific phrases or text strings.

The Folder Assistant allows you to specify multiple conditions as well as multiple arguments within a single condition. Multiple arguments in a condition are separated by semicolons. Exchange Server uses an OR operation on the arguments when processing incoming items for a rule. If the item meets one of the arguments, the associated action occurs. For example, you can create a single rule that checks whether an incoming item is from any of the people you have specified. To do this, you use the From condition and separate each name with a semicolon, as in *FROM:Michael Rizzo; Jo Brown*. If the item is from either Michael Rizzo or Jo Brown, the action for the rule will occur.

If you specify multiple conditions on different items within a rule, Exchange Server will use an AND operation on the conditions. All conditions must return true for the action to occur. For example, if you specify the From condition as *FROM:Jo Brown* and the Subject condition as *SUBJECT:New sales quote*, the item must be from Jo Brown *and* have a subject of *New sales quote* for the action to occur.

You can combine the two techniques to make more complex conditions with multiple arguments. For example, within a discussion database, you can set the message Body condition to *BODY:help;problem* and the From condition to *FROM:CEO;CIO*. If a message is submitted to the folder from either the CEO or CIO and has either *help* or *problem* in the message body, your rule's action will occur. My recommendation for the action for this rule is to forward it to the help desk as a high-priority message!

The Folder Assistant also allows you to set up what are called *advanced conditions*. Examples of advanced conditions include the size of the item, date ranges, and the presence of attachments. You can even specify advanced conditions that check user-defined fields on forms, folders, and custom Office document properties.

One other advanced feature is the ability to create rules that fire when the conditions you specify are *not* met. For example, you can create a rule that fires for items that are from anyone except John Hand. To do this, you specify *John Hand* in the From condition and then specify processing the rule only if the condition is *not* met. This type of rule comes in handy when an inclusive condition, such as every user in an address book, is impractical to specify.

Finally, you can set an option in the Folder Assistant that stops the rules engine from processing any subsequent rules after the current rule fires. You can use this condition when you have multiple rules in your folder and you want the current rule to be the last one applied.

Setting the Actions for a Rule

If the conditions of a rule are met, Exchange Server applies the rule's action(s) to the item. Outlook offers four response actions for a rule (as shown in Figure 3-8):

- **Return To Sender** This action sends any item e-mailed to a folder back to the sender. Outlook does not allow the user to post the item. Instead, it returns notification that the user does not have permission to add this item into the folder.
- **Delete** This action deletes the item immediately. By setting this action, you disable other possible actions in the rule, such as Return To Sender, and you automatically enable the Do Not Process Subsequent Rules condition.
- **Reply With** This action sends an automatic reply to the sender. You can customize the reply message by clicking the Template button, which opens a new message form. You can add recipients to the reply, enter custom message text, or insert any attachments that you want to include for the user. To save and close your reply template, choose Save & Close from the File menu.
- **Forward** This action forwards all messages not marked as private to a specified recipient. You can specify the method that Outlook will use to forward the item: Standard, Leave Message Intact, or Insert Message As An Attachment.

Applying Rules

Exchange Server processes multiple rules in the order that they appear in the Folder Assistant, from top to bottom. To change the order in which rules are applied, use the Move Up or Move Down button to move a rule higher or lower in the list.

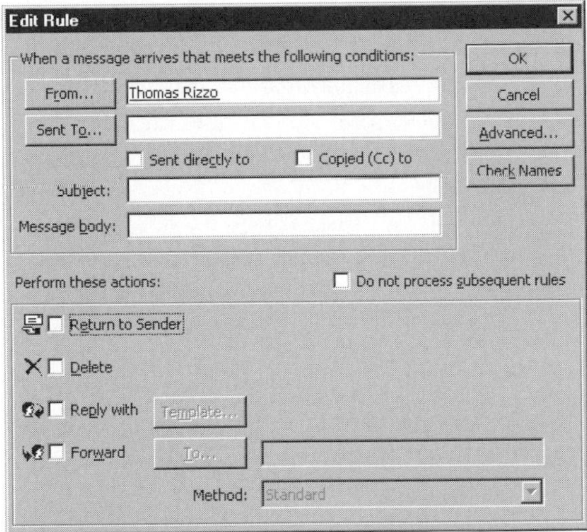

Figure 3-8 The Edit Rule dialog box

Implementing Public Folder Rules

To help you understand how to implement public folder rules, we'll create rules for the Account Tracking and Document Library applications. For the Account Tracking application, we'll add a reply for the user who submits an item. This reply will state that the folder has received the new item. Follow these steps:

1. Find the Account Tracking folder in the folder list, right-click on it, and choose Properties. Don't use the folder from your Favorites, you will have to find the folder in the All Public Folders tree.
2. On the Administration tab of the Properties dialog box, click the Folder Assistant button.
3. Click the Add Rule button.
4. Select the Reply With option.
5. Click the Template button to display the reply template.
6. In the reply template, type the following in the Subject field: **Your item has been received.** In the message body, type **Thank you for submitting your item to the Account Tracking application. Your item should be available immediately for other people in the organization to use.**
7. From the File menu, choose Save & Close.
8. Click OK in the Edit Rule dialog box. Outlook will inform you that this rule will fire for all incoming messages. Click Yes.

9. Click OK in the Folder Assistant dialog box. (If a message box appears indicating that you do not have Send As permission, check with your Exchange Server administrator to ensure that you have Send As permission on the public Account Tracking folder. See Microsoft Knowledge Base article 152113 for more information.)

You should see your new rule in the Folder Assistant. Try posting a new message to the Account Tracking application to test your rule.

For the Document Library application, we'll add an advanced rule that checks the Author property of the Office document. If the author is not a member of our team, the item will be returned to the sender. To add this rule, follow these steps:

1. Follow steps 1 through 3 from the preceding procedure, but use the Document Library folder instead.
2. In the Edit Rule dialog box, click the Advanced button. In the Show Properties Of area, select the Document option.

> **Note** On some configurations, the properties are not displayed when you select the Document option. Please see Microsoft Knowledge Base article Q292963 for an explanation of the issue.

3. Enable the Author property in the Show Properties Of section. For the values, type the names of people on your team; separate the names with semicolons.
4. Select the Only Items That Do Not Match These Conditions option. Click OK.
5. Select the Return To Sender option.
6. Click OK three times.

Fields

Fields are named variables in which Outlook stores the data for your application. A number of built-in fields store default information. These built-in fields are associated with folders and their default content type. For example, in a Contacts folder, built-in fields include First Name, Last Name, Mailing Address, and Primary Phone. In your Inbox, built-in fields include From, To, Subject, and

Message. Outlook also supports Office document properties as fields. For more information on using Office document properties as fields, see the section titled "Extending Functionality with Office Documents" in Chapter 4.

Outlook provides a large number of built-in fields, but you'll often need to add custom fields for your application. Outlook allows you to add fields to any folder. Your custom fields can range from a simple data type, such as a text field, to a complex data type, such as a field that holds the result of a formula that calculates a value using data from other Outlook fields.

Creating Custom Fields

The easiest way to create and delete custom fields in Outlook is to use the Field Chooser. The Field Chooser allows you to see both the built-in Outlook fields and your own fields. To view the Field Chooser, select a table view in your folder (any of the default Outlook views that begin with the word *By*—for example, in your calendar you can switch your view to the By Category view). After selecting a table view, right-click on the column headings and choose Field Chooser, as shown in Figure 3-9.

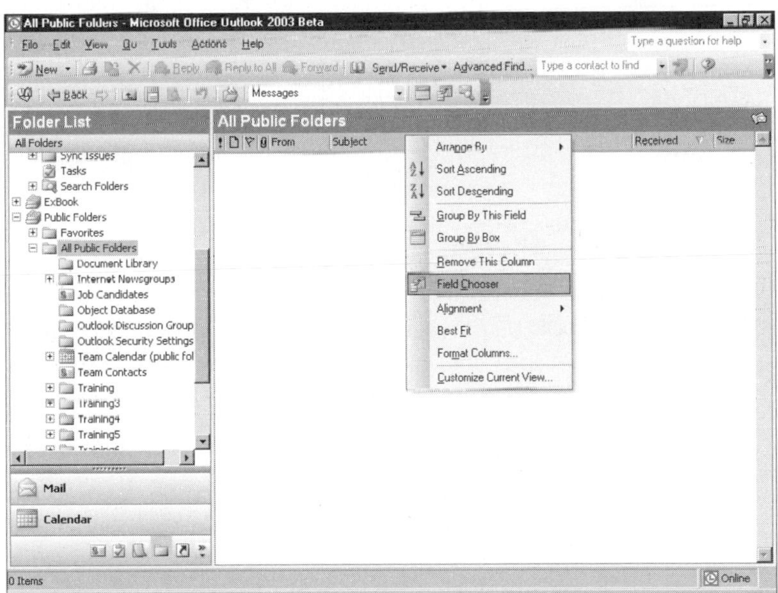

Figure 3-9 Selecting the Field Chooser from the shortcut menu

To create a new field, click the New button, enter a name and data type for the field, and then select the appropriate format. Following is a list of possible data types for fields in Outlook and the type of formatting these fields support:

- **Text** This field type can hold text strings or a combination of text strings and numbers, such as in a mailing address. It can hold up to 255 characters.
- **Number** This field type is for numeric data (except numbers that represent currency) and for mathematical calculations. You can format this field with one of nine different formats, such as a scientific notation format (125.3E+03).
- **Percent** This field type stores numeric data that is a percentage. You can choose from four formats. For example, you can set how many decimal places to show in the percentage.
- **Currency** This field type stores numeric data that represents a currency value. You can format this data type to show or hide the cents portion of the currency—for example, $5,232 or $5,232.10.
- **Yes/No** This field stores data that holds one of two values in a pair of values. You can select Yes/No, True/False, On/Off, or a check box icon in your Outlook view.
- **Date/Time** This field stores date and time data. You can format this field using a number of standard formats, as in these examples: Monday, May 05, 2003 7:00 AM; 5/5/03 7:00 AM; May 5, 2003; or Mon 5/5/2003.
- **Duration** This field is for numeric time data that represents an elapsed time value. You can expose the data in several formats, such as 12h or 12 hours. The value in this field is automatically calculated when the data should be displayed as days, hours, or minutes. For example, if you set the format for this field as "12 hours" and you enter *.25*, Outlook displays 15 minutes. You can also set the format so Outlook takes into account only working hours. (By default, this means an 8-hour day, but you can customize the default.)
- **Keywords** This data type holds multiple text values (which are separated by commas) and is similar to the Categories field in Outlook. When you create custom views, you can use keywords to filter the items displayed.
- **Combination** This data type holds a combination of fields and literal text. You can show each field or only the first nonempty field. The fields created with this data type are read-only in Outlook. For more information on creating combination fields, see the next section, "Creating Combination Fields."

- **Formula** This data type holds the results of formulas you create. You can use the Microsoft Visual Basic expression service that is built into Outlook to create functions and operators for your formula. The fields created with this data type are read-only in Outlook. For more information on creating formula fields, see the section titled "Creating Formula Fields" later in this chapter.
- **Integer** This data type holds nondecimal numeric information. You can customize the format to be only numbers, such as 3,332, or to be "computer" numbers formatted as kilobytes, megabytes, and gigabytes.

Creating Combination Fields

You can create a combined value, or *combination field*, by concatenating literal strings and the values from one or more Outlook fields. Combination fields are useful when you have many types of fields and want to create a single field that combines them. You can also use a combination field when you have multiple fields that hold conflicting data and you want to display only one of the fields in your form. Here's how you create a combination field from two fields and a text fragment:

1. In your Inbox, right-click on a column in your view, choose Field Chooser, and click New. (If the Inbox pane is not wide enough to show multiple columns, you might not see the Field Chooser in the shortcut menu.)
2. Enter a name for the field, such as *My Follow-Up Field*, and select Combination as the type of field.
3. Click Edit.
4. You have the choice to join fields and text fragments to create a combination field or show only the first nonempty field and ignore all the subsequent fields. Select the Joining Fields And Any Text Fragments To Each Other option.
5. In the Formula text box, type **Need**.
6. Click the Field button, point to Frequently-Used Fields, and then click Follow Up Flag.
7. In the Formula text box, type **By**.
8. Click the Field button, point to Frequently-Used Fields, and then click Due By.

9. Click OK twice.

10. Drag and drop this new field from the Field Chooser onto your Inbox column headings. You should see something similar to Figure 3-10.

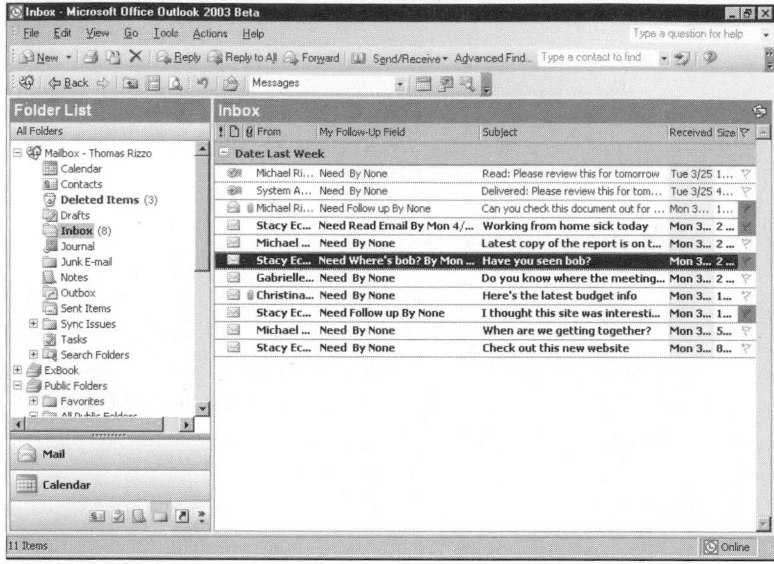

Figure 3-10 Two fields combined with string literals to create a single combination field

Use a combination field when you want to expose a primary value for a specific field but also need the option to expose a field that holds a secondary value if the primary value is not available. For example, in our Document Library application, users can drag and drop Office documents into the public folder. Outlook can expose the properties of these Office documents as fields. In the Outlook view, we want to expose the document author, but because users are not required to fill in this property when designing or saving the document, the Author property can be left blank. If the Author property is left blank, we want to use the From field in Outlook to display the name of the user who dragged and dropped the document into the folder.

Follow these steps to create the combination field that shows the first nonempty field:

1. Go to the Document Library folder you created, and open the Field Chooser.

2. Click New.

3. Type a name for the field, such as *Document Author*.
4. Select Combination as the field type.
5. Click Edit.
6. Select the option named Showing Only The First Non-Empty Field, Ignoring Subsequent Ones.
7. Click the Field button, point to All Document Fields, and then click Author.
8. Click the Field button, point to All Mail Fields, and then click From.
9. Click OK twice.
10. Drag and drop your new field from the Field Chooser onto the view column headings. You should see a view similar to the one shown in Figure 3-11.

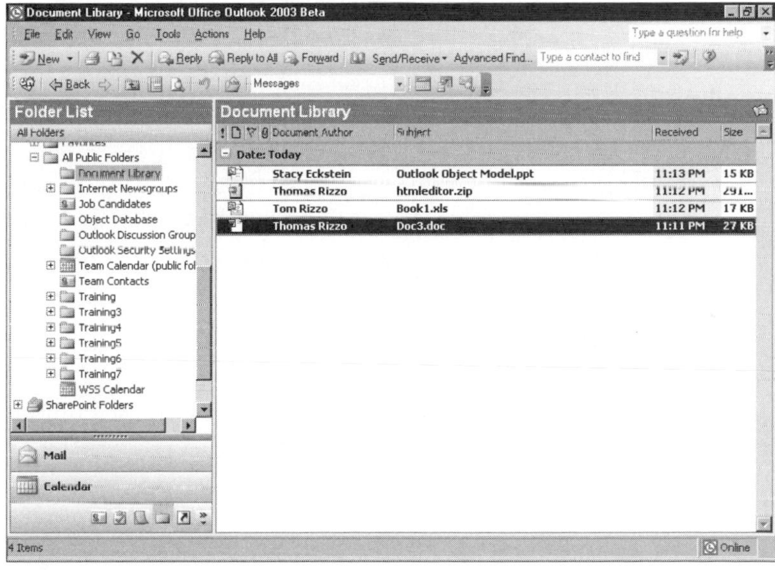

Figure 3-11 Combination fields that show the first nonempty value from multiple Outlook fields

Creating Formula Fields

In formula fields, you use functions to calculate values from both standard and custom fields. These values are then stored inside the formula field. For example, you can use a formula field to calculate the total of an expense report or a person's wage based on the number of hours worked multiplied by his hourly rate. Outlook makes creating formula fields quite easy by offering a simple interface for field selection and by displaying a list of all possible formulas and required inputs. You can use the Field and Function buttons to select the fields and functions you want to use in your formula. Outlook parses your formula and checks it for syntactical errors.

Formula fields do have a few performance implications. First, Outlook has to process formula fields whenever values change in the application. The more complex you make your formulas, the longer Outlook takes to process them. Second, Outlook recalculates formula fields whenever the current view changes. Third, Outlook does not allow you to sort, group, or filter views by using formula fields.

Follow these steps to create a formula field that displays the amount of time elapsed since an item was received. Figure 3-12 shows a custom formula field.

1. In the Field Chooser, click New.
2. Type a name for your new field, such as *Days since received.*
3. Select Formula from the Type drop-down list.
4. Click the Edit button.
5. In the Formula box, type all of the following on the same line:

```
IIF(DateDiff("d",[Received],Now())>=7,
DateDiff("w",[Received],Now()) & " week(s) ago",
DateDiff("d",[Received],Now()) & " day(s) ago")
```

6. Click OK twice.
7. Drag and drop the new field onto your view column headings. You should see the field calculate automatically. If the item was received within one week, the field will display the amount in days. If the item was received more than a week ago, the field will display the amount in weeks.

Using Custom Fields in Filtered Replication

As you learned in Part I of this book, Outlook and Exchange Server support synchronizing items with an offline store. By default, Outlook synchronizes all items between the server and your offline database. But what if you don't want to synchronize all the items? Outlook offers the ability to synchronize subsets of information—a process known as *filtered replication*. You select the parameters—based on either built-in or custom fields—that Outlook will use to filter the synchronized items.

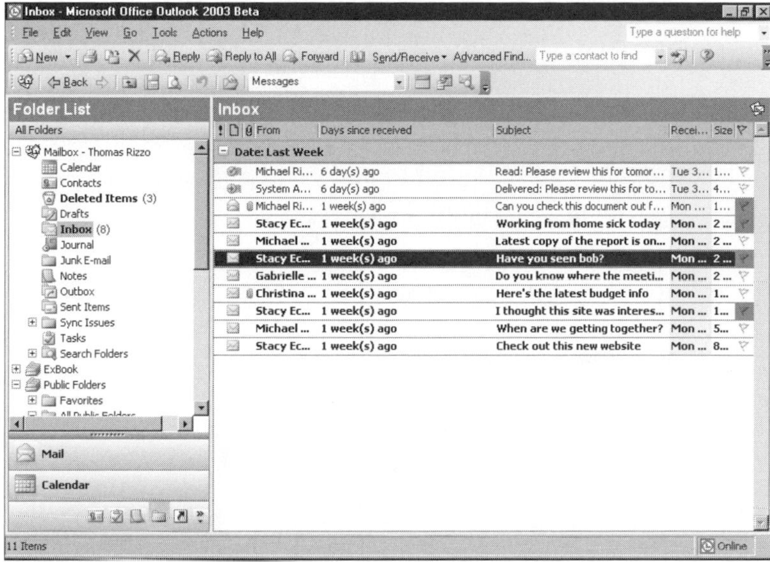

Figure 3-12 A custom formula field in an Outlook view

Follow these steps to set up filtered replication for the Account Tracking application:

1. To create the filter criterion, add a custom property to the Account Tracking application. Select the Account Tracking folder within the Favorites folder, right click on the column headers, and select the Field Chooser.
2. In the Field Chooser, click New.
3. In the Name text box, type **txtAccountSalesRep**, and then select Text as the type.
4. Click OK.
5. From the File menu, select Folder and then Properties For Account Tracking.
6. Click on the Synchronization tab.
7. Click the Filter button. If the filter button is not enabled, set the folder as an offline folder by using the Send/Receive settings.
8. In the Filter dialog box, click on the Advanced tab.

9. Click the Field button, point to User-Defined Fields In Folder, and click txtAccountSalesRep.
10. From the Condition drop-down list, select Is (Exactly). In the Value text box, type the name of a user of the Account Tracking application.
11. Click the Add To List button to add your criteria. Your screen should look something like Figure 3-13.

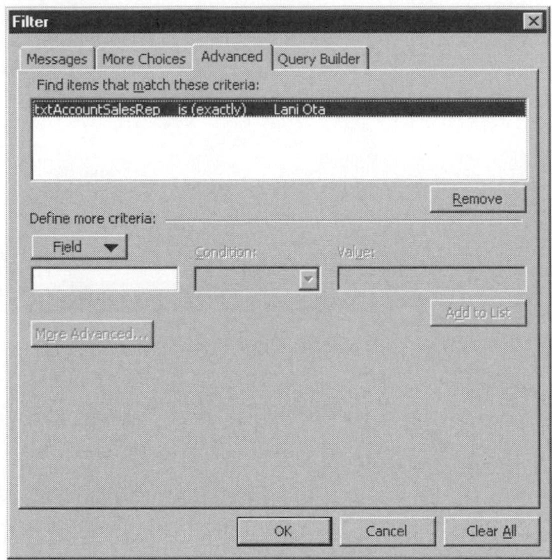

Figure 3-13 The Filter dialog box, showing synchronization criteria for the Account Tracking application

12. Click OK to close the filter dialog, click OK to acknowledge the message regarding the next synchronization and, finally, click OK to close the folder properties sheet. Now only the items meeting your criteria will be synchronized with your offline database.

Figures 3-14 shows the Account Tracking folder before filtered replication is set. Figure 3-15 shows the same folder after filtered replication. As you can see, only a subset of the information in the folder is available to the client off line.

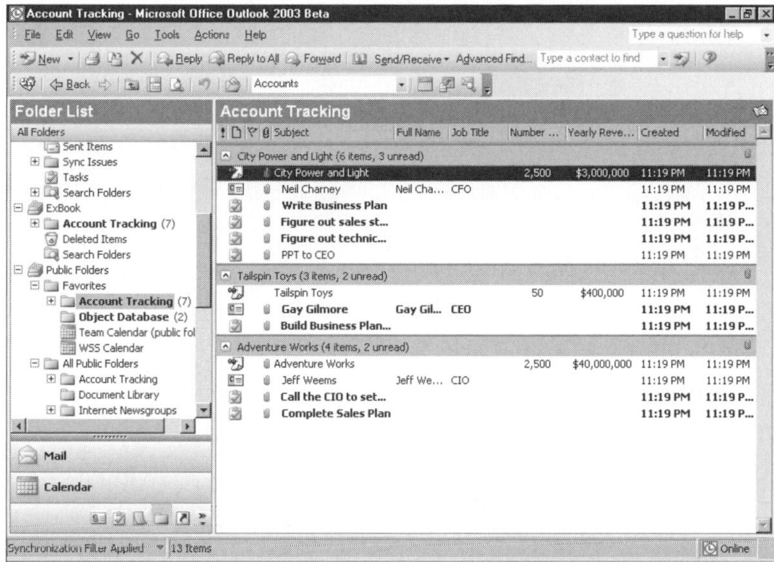

Figure 3-14 The Account Tracking folder before filtered replication

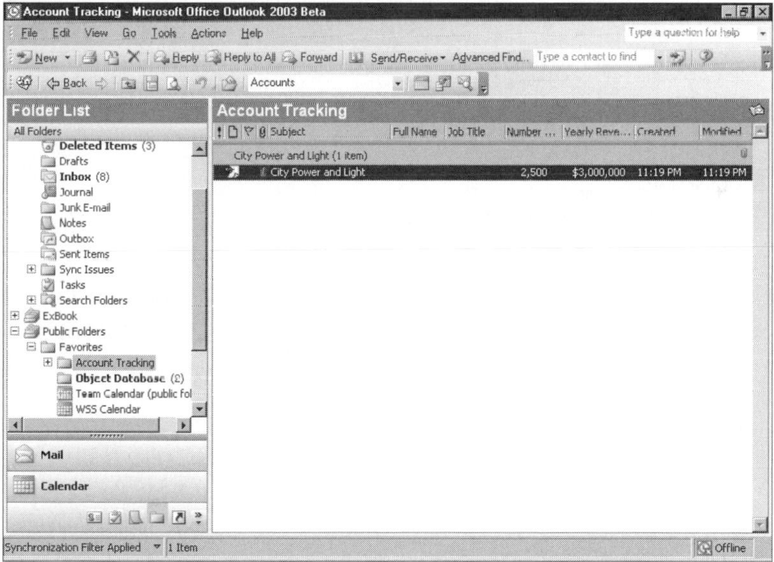

Figure 3-15 The Account Tracking folder after filtered replication

Views

Outlook supports a variety of folder views, including custom views, to give you and your users flexibility in the presentation and organization of information. These views can be used in any type of Outlook folder. Outlook allows you to set the initial view for a folder, and it remembers the state of the view for each user. Outlook supports five types of views:

- **Table view** The most commonly used Outlook view. The table view consists of rows and columns that display the information in the folder.
- **Timeline view** Shows the chronological order of the items in the folder as icons.
- **Card view** Shows the items in the folder as individual cards, similar to a business card file.
- **Day/Week/Month view** Shows items arranged in a calendar. This view is best used for applications that have a date and time field as one of the application's primary fields.
- **Icon view** Shows all items in the folder as individual icons on an invisible grid. The icon view is best used in folders in which displaying details of the items are not important.

Creating New Views

You can create new views in Outlook in two ways: by defining a new view in the Define Views dialog box or by adding the Current View box to your Outlook toolbar. The second option is the easiest and is the one you will probably use more often. To add the Current View box to your Outlook toolbar, follow these steps:

1. Right-click on the Outlook toolbar, and then choose Customize.
2. On the Commands tab, select Advanced from the Categories list.
3. In the Commands list, scroll down until you find the Current View drop-down list.
4. Drag and drop the Current View drop-down list onto your toolbar. Close the Customize window by clicking Close. You should see Outlook fill in the Current View drop-down list with the name of the current view of the folder. You can now use the Current View drop-down list to create new views by typing over the name in the box.

When you attempt to save your views, Outlook prompts you to indicate what type of view will be used. For example, if you type a new name for a view in the Current View drop-down list, Outlook will ask you how the view should be used. You can apply your views in Outlook in three primary ways:

- **This Folder, Visible To Everyone** This option enables the view to be used on the current folder and to be visible to everyone. Any person with permission to open the folder can select this view from the drop-down list of current views. As a developer, you can create the views for your Outlook application and then save them so that all your users can use them.
- **This Folder, Visible Only To Me** If you select this option, the view is for the current folder but is visible only to the current user. You can use this view to show specialized information (such as debugging information) to only certain users of your application.
- **All Folders** This option enables the view to be used in all folders that have the same item type as the current folder. This allows you to share your favorite views across folders of the same type.

So far, our Document Library application is only a folder into which users can drag and drop documents to share with other users. By using views, we can transform our simple Document Library application into a more useful application for our users. The first view we'll create is an icon view so that our application looks more like a network file share than an Outlook folder. Adding this view will make navigating among the files in the folder easier for our users. To create the icon view for the Document Library application, follow these steps:

1. Select the Document Library folder in Outlook.
2. From the View menu, choose Arrange By, and then Current View, and then click Define Views.
3. Click the New button, and then type a name for your view, such as *As Icon*.
4. In the Type Of View list box, select Icon.
5. In the Can Be Used On area, select This Folder, Visible To Everyone.
6. Click OK. The Customize View: <View Name> dialog box will appear.
7. Click the Other Settings button, and then select the type of icon you want to use: Large Icon, Small Icon, or Icon List.

8. Click OK twice.
9. Click Apply View. You now have an icon view for our Document Library application. Your view should be similar to the one shown in Figure 3-16.

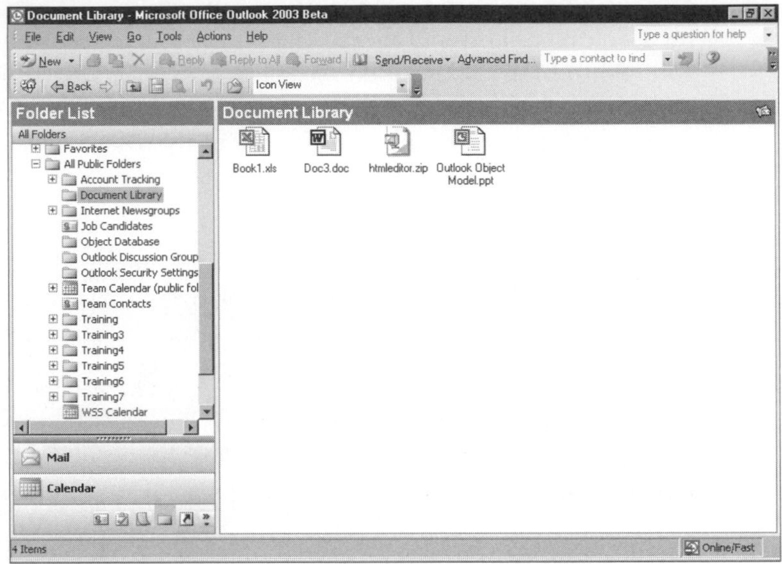

Figure 3-16 A Large Icon view of the information in the Document Library application

The second view we'll create is a timeline view. This view will enable our users to quickly see the last time a document was saved and how much time has elapsed between when the document was created and when it was last edited and saved. By implementing this feature, users can discard older versions of the document and ensure that they are using the most recent version. As you will see in Chapter 4, you can customize your views by using custom properties directly from Office documents.

To create the timeline view for the Document Library application, follow these steps:

1. Select the Document Library folder in Outlook.
2. From the View menu, choose Arrange By, and then Current View, and then click Define Views.
3. Click the New button, and then type a name for your view, such as *Document Timeline*.

4. In the Type Of View list box, select Timeline.
5. In the Can Be Used On area, select This Folder, Visible To Everyone.
6. Click OK. The Customize View: <View Name> dialog box will appear.
7. Click the Fields button to open the Date/Time Fields dialog box.
8. In the Available Date/Time Fields list, select the Created field as the starting time for the document in the view and then click the Start button.
9. In the Select Available Fields From drop-down list, select All Document Fields.
10. In the Available Date/Time Fields list, select Last Saved Time and then click the End button to make the time the document was last saved the ending time for the document in the view.
11. Click OK twice. Click Apply View. The view of your documents folder should be similar to Figure 3-17. Outlook automatically draws a line indicating the amount of time that has elapsed between the creation time and the time the document was last saved.

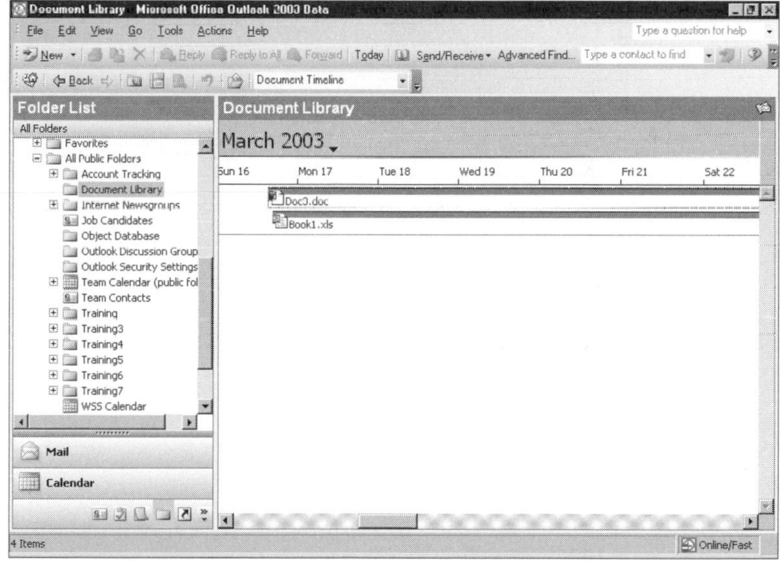

Figure 3-17 A timeline view of the Document Library application

Customizing the Current View

You can customize the current view by using the Field Chooser to drag and drop new columns. After you add a new column, the view is automatically updated. You can also add complex data types such as combination or formula fields to the view. Many people find customizing a view easier using the drag-and-drop capabilities of the Field Chooser than by selecting available columns from a drop-down list as in the Customize View dialog.

To add new columns to the Document Library view, follow these steps:

1. In the Document Library application, create a new table view and name it *Document Properties*.
2. Right-click on any column heading in the Document Properties view, and then choose Field Chooser.
3. Select All Document Fields from the drop-down list.
4. Drag and drop Author, Revision Number, and Last Saved Time from the Field Chooser to an area next to one of the columns in the view. (Outlook displays red arrows in the column header bar to indicate where the field will be inserted.)
5. To remove a column, select the column heading and then drag it off the column heading row.

> **Note** You can remove columns from your view by dragging the columns until a large X appears. After you release the mouse button, the column disappears from the view.

Formatting the Columns in a View

Notice that when you drag and drop columns from the Field Chooser, by default Outlook gives the column heading the same name as the field on which the column is based. Also notice that Outlook applies default formatting for the columns. For example, Outlook formats the Last Saved Time column with the day, the date, the year, and the time the document was last saved. Most users won't need this much detail about the last-saved time for the document. To make views more intuitive for your users, Outlook allows you to change the name of the column heading without changing the name of the underlying field. You can also change the default format of values for a specific column in the view. For example, you can change the format of the Last Saved Time column heading so that it displays only the date the document was last saved rather than the date and the time, as you saw earlier. Note, however, that changing the format of the column does not modify the format of the field on which the column is based. To modify the format of the field, you must use the Field Chooser.

To change the format of a column in the Document Library application, follow these steps:

1. Right-click on the Last Saved Time column heading in the Document Properties view, and then choose Format Columns.
2. In the Format drop-down list, select the option that shows only the month, the day, and the year (such as April 07, 2003).
3. In the Label box, type **Last Edit Time**.
4. Click OK. Your date/time column should look similar to the one shown in Figure 3-18.

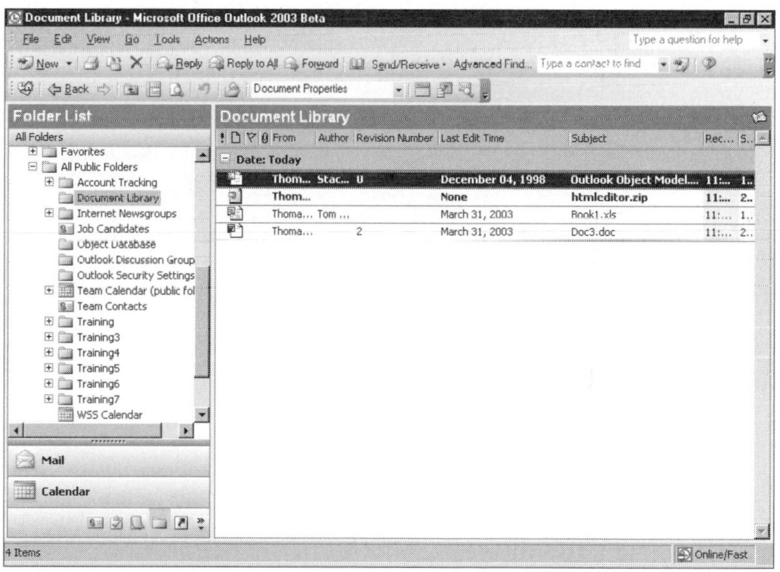

Figure 3-18 The new Document Properties view after we change the format and label of the date/time column

Grouping Items in a View

Grouping items in an Outlook view makes it easy for users to find items that are related. Outlook supports up to four levels of grouping in a single view. You can group items in a view in one of two ways:

- **Using the Group By box** This method is the easiest because it allows you to use drag-and-drop functionality to select the column as the grouping. If you drag and drop more than one field into the Group By box, Outlook graphically draws the relationship between the fields as primary groups and subgroups.
- **Customizing the Current View option** This method gives you a few more options when you set the grouping for a view, but it isn't as easy as using the Group By box.

To group items by Author using the Group By box, follow these steps:

1. Right-click on a column for the Document Library application, and then choose Group By box to display the Group By box above the column headings.
2. To remove the Date field, from the View menu choose Arrange By, and then Show In Groups. (Show In Groups is a toggle menu item. If a check mark is next to the menu item, it is on and will be turned off the next time you choose it.) Drag and drop the Author column into the Group By box, or drag items from the Field Chooser into the Group By box.
3. If you want to group by more than one field, drag and drop a second field into the Group By box. For our purposes, just drag the Category field from the Field Chooser in the All Document Properties section to the Group By box. Notice that Outlook draws a line from the Author field to the Category field to indicate that the view is grouped first by author and then by category. If you click on the field in the Group By box, you can also change the sorting of the field as part of the grouped view. Take a look at Figure 3-19.

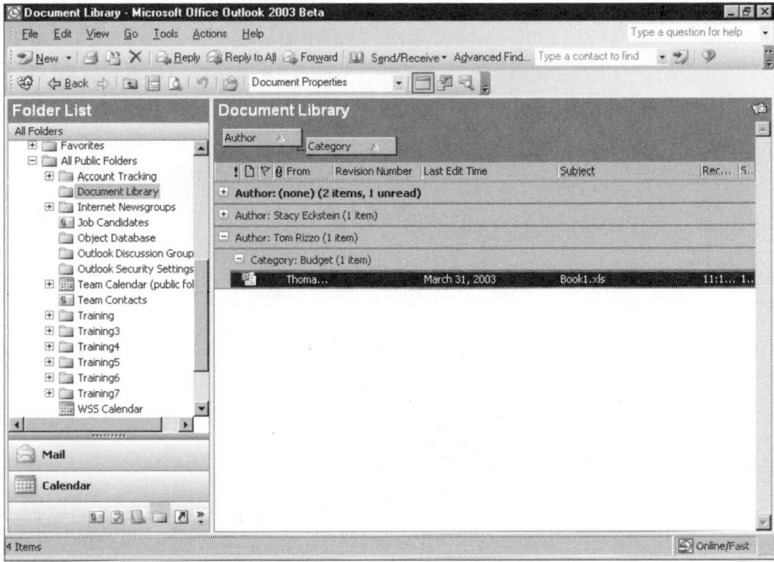

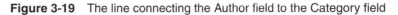

Figure 3-19 The line connecting the Author field to the Category field

4. Close the Group By box by right-clicking on a column heading and selecting Group By box.

To create the same grouping using the Current View option, follow these steps:

1. From the View menu, choose Arrange By, and then Current View, and then click Customize Current View.
2. Click the Group By button to display the Group By dialog box.
3. In the Select Available Fields From drop-down list, select All Documents Fields.
4. In the Group Items By area, select the Author field. You can also show the field in the view by selecting the Show Field In View option. If you drag and drop the field into the column headings, you will lose it from the Group By box.
5. In the Select Available Fields From drop-down list, select Frequently-Used Fields. In the first Then By area, select the Categories field. Figure 3-20 shows the completed Group By dialog box.
6. Click OK twice.

The only difference between the two methods we've used to create the same view is that in the Group By dialog box that appears when you choose Customize Current View from the menu, you can specify whether the groups are expanded or collapsed by default.

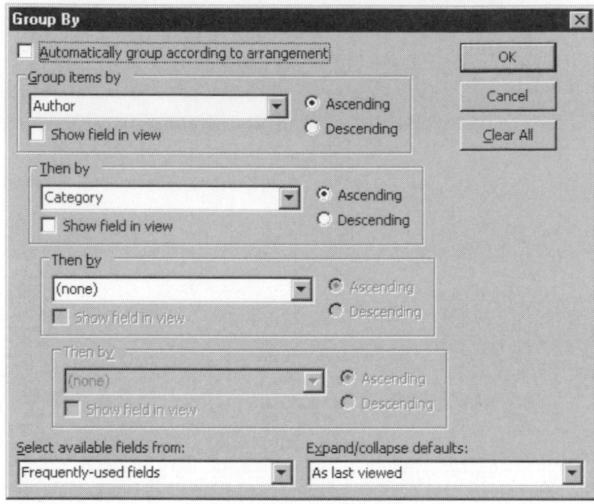

Figure 3-20 The Group By dialog box

Sorting Items in a View

Outlook also supports sorting items in a view in either ascending or descending order. When you combine sorting with grouping, you get the best combination of features for making your information available to users in a view. For example, instead of just grouping our Document Library items by author, we can also sort the items so the most recently saved documents appear at the top of each grouping.

To create a sorted list, you can click on the column heading or use the Sort dialog box. To create a sorted view by using the Sort dialog box, follow these steps:

1. From the View menu, choose Arrange By, and then Current View, and then click Customize Current View.
2. Click the Sort button to display the Sort dialog box (shown in Figure 3-21). In the Select Available Fields From drop-down list, select the subset category of the fields from which you want to choose the sort criterion.
3. In the Sort Items By area, select the field you want to use as your sort criterion.

4. To select further sorting subsets, select the next field you want to sort by in the Then By area.
5. Click OK twice.

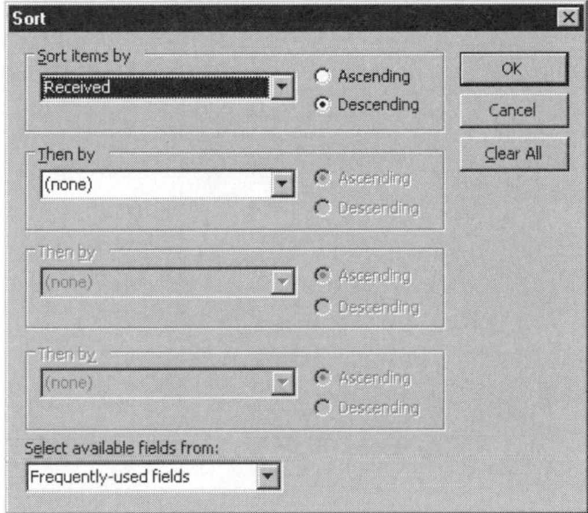

Figure 3-21 The Sort dialog box

Filtering Information in Views

Filtering allows you to create views in which only certain items are visible to users. The criteria you set can be based on built-in Outlook fields or custom fields. Filters can be simple, with only one or two conditions, or they can be more complex, using multiple conditions or the advanced filtering features. When you set multiple conditions on a filter, Outlook ANDs them together. When you set multiple arguments in a single condition, Outlook ORs these arguments so that if only some meet the condition, the item appears in the view.

To create a simple filter for the Document Library application, follow these steps:

1. From the View menu, choose Arrange By, and then Current View, and then click Customize Current View.
2. Click the Filter button.
3. Click on the More Choices tab.
4. In the Categories box, type **Outlook; Exchange**, as shown in Figure 3-22.
5. Click OK twice.

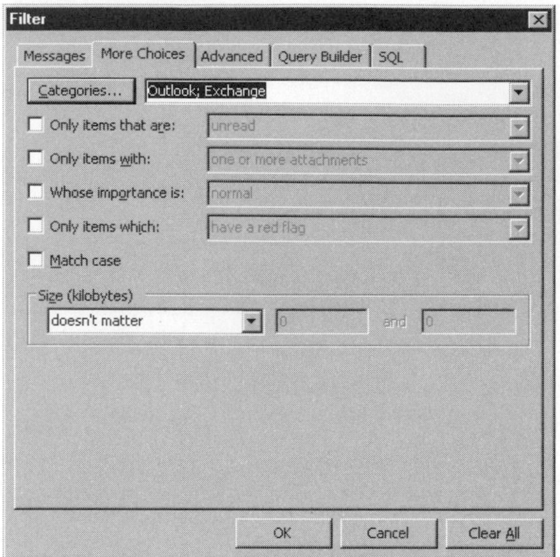

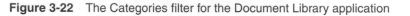

Figure 3-22 The Categories filter for the Document Library application

Here's how to create a complex filter for the Document Library application:

1. From the View menu, choose Arrange By, and then Current View, and then click Customize Current View.
2. Click the Filter button.
3. Click on the Advanced tab.
4. Click Field, point to All Document Fields, and then click the Last Saved Time field.
5. In the Condition drop-down list, select Last Month.
6. Click Add To List.
7. Click Field again, point to All Document Fields, and then click the Author field.
8. In the Condition drop-down list, select Is Not Empty. Click Add To List.
9. Click Field again, point to All Mail Fields, and then click the Message Class field.
10. In the Condition drop-down list, select Contains and type **IPM.Document.Word.Document** in the Value box. Click Add To List.

11. Click OK twice. You might find that you have no items in your folder after doing this. If you do not have documents with the Author field set, you will not meet the filter criteria.

Editing View Settings

You can customize the formatting of your views at a more detailed level by using the Other Settings dialog box. The type of view you create determines which settings are available for you to edit. For example, if you are editing a table view, you can set the font size, enable in-cell editing, enable autopreview, create gridlines, and enable the preview pane. If you are editing an icon view, you can set the view type (such as Large Icons, Small Icons, or Icon List), and you can specify whether Outlook should automatically arrange and sort the icons in your view.

In-Cell Editing

The in-cell editing option for customizing a table view allows users to quickly add new items to a folder or change the properties of current items in the folder without opening a form. All of the changes to the item can be typed directly into the view. This capability helps speed up applications that require a lot of data entry, such as customer contact lists or surveys.

If you enable in-cell editing in a folder that contains Office documents, you cannot modify the properties of the documents directly in the view. These properties are read-only inside Outlook. You must modify these properties using the Office program that originally created the document.

Conditional Formatting

If your custom view is a table view, you can use the conditional formatting capabilities of Outlook. Conditional formatting lets you apply custom formatting to items that meet certain conditions. For example, you can set a condition in the Document Library application so that all Word documents appear in 12-point, red Arial font. Outlook automatically sets some default formats for the most common conditions, such as unread, expired, and overdue e-mail. You can customize the settings for these default conditions or create your own conditions.

To set conditional formatting, follow these steps:

1. From the View menu, choose Arrange By, and then Current View, and then click Customize Current View.
2. Click the Automatic Formatting button.
3. Click Add, and then type a name for the formatting rule in the Name box; for this example, type **Word Documents**.
4. Click the Font button, and then select 12-point Arial as the font and red as the font color. Click OK.
5. Click the Condition button. As you can see, the dialog box is the same as the Filter dialog box shown earlier in Figure 3-22.
6. Click on the Advanced tab.
7. Click Field, point to All Document Fields, and then click Author.
8. From the Condition drop-down list, select Is Empty.
9. Click Add To List.
10. Click Field, point to All Mail Fields, and click Message Class.
11. From the Condition drop-down list, select Contains.
12. In the Value text box type, **IPM.Document.Word**. Click Add To List.
13. Click OK two more times.

Limiting Views to Those Created for the Folder

Outlook provides several standard views in a folder by default. These views depend on the folder's default content type, and in many cases they are not relevant to your application, so you will not want them to appear in the Outlook view list. Outlook allows you to hide the default views and show only custom views created for the current folder by selecting the Only Show Views Created For This Folder option in the Define Views dialog box.

Implementing Threaded Views

You'll often want to display the information in a folder as a threaded view so users can see the history of responses to an item. These responses are indented in the view to make it easier to follow the flow of information specific to the item. In a folder based on e-mail items, Outlook provides a default view called By Conversation Topic, which provides this threading capability. But suppose you don't build your application using e-mail items, and you use task items instead. To create threaded views in a folder such as this, Outlook supports two unique properties, called Conversation and Conversation Index.

Disabling Default Views in OWA

If you use OWA as one of the clients for your application, the Only Show Views Created For This Folder property will not disable the default views in OWA. To disable the default views in OWA, you must customize the Active Server Pages of OWA for Exchange 5.5 to hide the default views for your folder. Any custom table views that you create in the Outlook client will automatically be available to the OWA client as long as the Automatically Generate Microsoft Exchange Views check box is selected. OWA for Exchange 2003 will only show custom views if this option is selected.

The Conversation field is based on the message's Subject field. When you create a new item in a folder, the Conversation field is automatically filled in with the content of the item's Subject field. Any replies inherit the Conversation field from the original item.

The Conversation Index is a unique identifier used by Outlook to track the series of responses to an item. This index allows Outlook to know which item in the thread the user is responding to and where the response should be placed in the threaded view.

To implement threaded views for any of your Outlook folders, you must group by the Conversation field and sort in ascending order by the Conversation Index. Most developers forget about the step of sorting by the Conversation Index when they try to implement threading. Without it, your view will be grouped only by the Conversation Index and will have no indented text indicating responses to items.

To implement threaded views in Outlook folders, follow these steps:

1. From the View menu, choose Arrange By, and then Current View, and then click Customize Current View.
2. Click the Group By button. Be sure the Automatically Group According To Arrangement check box is not selected.
3. In the Group Items By area, select Conversation and then click OK.
4. Click the Sort button.
5. In the Sort Items By area, select Conversation Index. To see this property, you might have to select All Mail Fields from the Select Available Fields From drop-down list.
6. Click OK twice.

Figure 3-23 shows a threaded view.

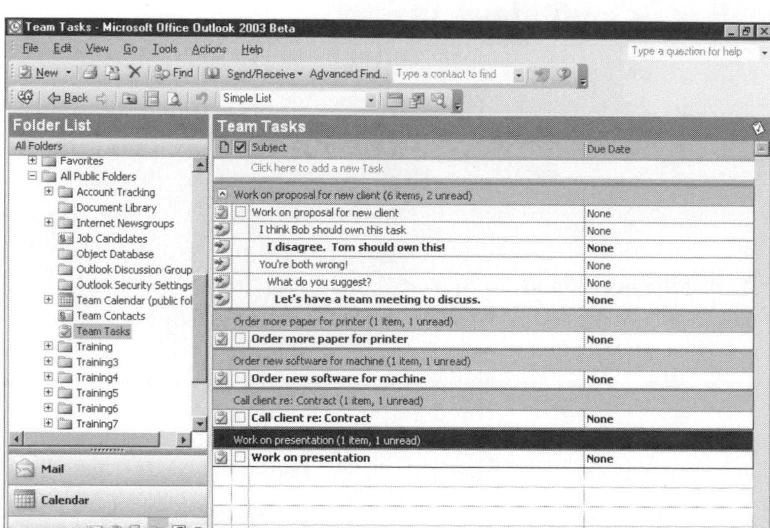

Figure 3-23 A threaded view of a Team Tasks public folder

> **Note** In all folders except those based on e-mail items, Outlook does not automatically make the Post Reply To This Folder menu command available. This command allows you to post replies in a folder that automatically inherit the conversation property from the original item. To enable this command, you can add it to the Outlook menu or toolbar.

Summary

In this chapter, you've seen the power of Outlook folders, fields, and views. These technologies will be the basis for your applications in Outlook. However, once you create your folders, fields, and views, you might want to create forms that you can use with these technologies. In the next chapter, we will combine what we learned in this chapter with the Outlook forms environment to create richer collaboration applications.

4

Customized Forms

You are already familiar with the capabilities of Microsoft Outlook forms because every item you view or use in Outlook is based on one. By customizing these forms, you can enhance the way you distribute and collect information electronically both inside and outside your organization.

Outlook allows you to build custom forms based on default Outlook items. When you customize built-in forms, your application inherits default capabilities. You can extend the functionality of these forms using custom controls and Microsoft Visual Basic Scripting Edition (VBScript). We'll look at VBScript in more detail in Chapter 5.

Outlook also allows you to base your forms on Microsoft Office documents, which prevents you from having to re-create existing functionality. For example, if you are building an expense reporting application, you can base your Outlook expense reporting form on a Microsoft Excel document, giving you the full power of Excel inside your application. You can then further extend your application using Microsoft Visual Basic for Applications (VBA) inside the Excel document. You can also use custom Excel properties inside your Outlook views to sort and group items.

Outlook Form Types

Before we look at the types of applications you can develop and when to customize certain forms in the Outlook environment, you need to know what the form types are and how they can be extended.

Message Forms

You use the Message form for applications in which users have to send information to other users, to a folder, or to another application for processing. You inherit all built-in capabilities of the form, such as automatic name resolution and nickname support, and you can customize any fields on the form. Figure 4-1 shows an example of a Message form in design mode. You can display different pages of the form by clicking on the appropriate tab.

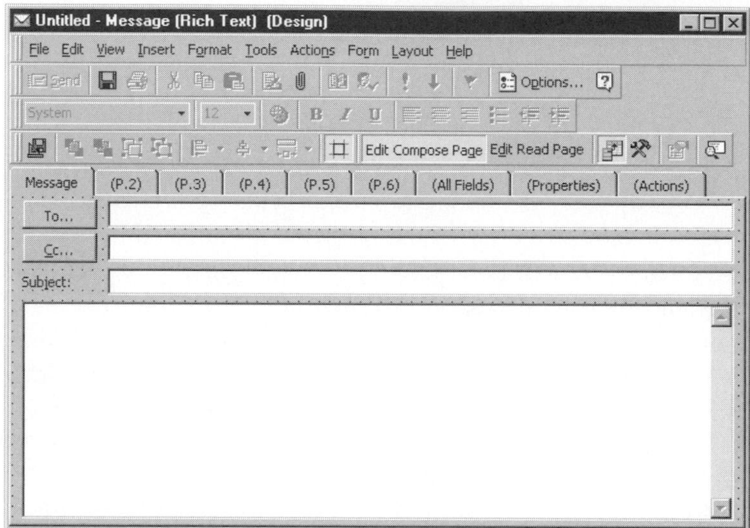

Figure 4-1 The Message form in design mode

Post Forms

The Post form is best used in applications that post or retrieve messages in an Outlook folder. When you customize a Post form, Outlook automatically assigns the currently open Outlook folder to the In Folder field. For example, if you customize a Post form in a helpdesk public folder, Outlook automatically assigns the helpdesk public folder to the In Folder field. This automatic assignment means that even though the user can install, or publish, the Post form in any folder, any items the user creates with the form will be posted to the helpdesk public folder. Figure 4-2 shows the Post form.

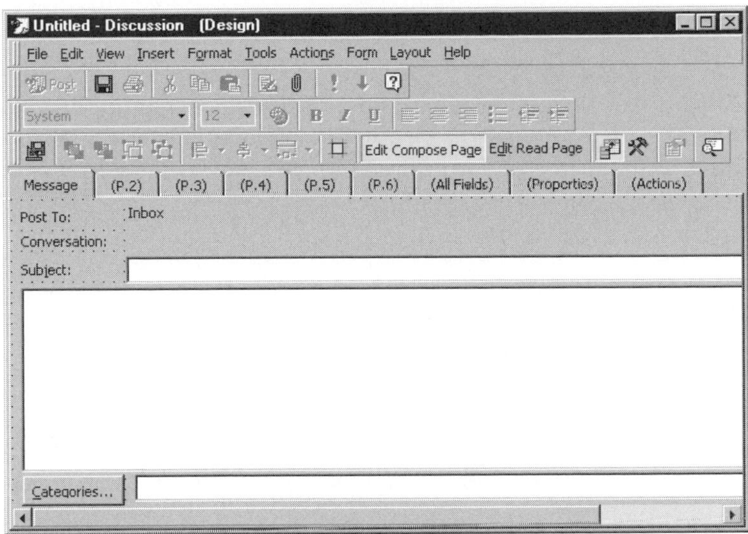

Figure 4-2 The Post form in design mode

Contact Forms

Use the Contact form in applications that track address or customer information. You can customize the first page of the Contact form; you thereby inherit the form's journaling, mapping, Microsoft NetMeeting, and address resolution capabilities. The other default pages in the form are not customizable but can be hidden. Figure 4-3 shows the Contact form.

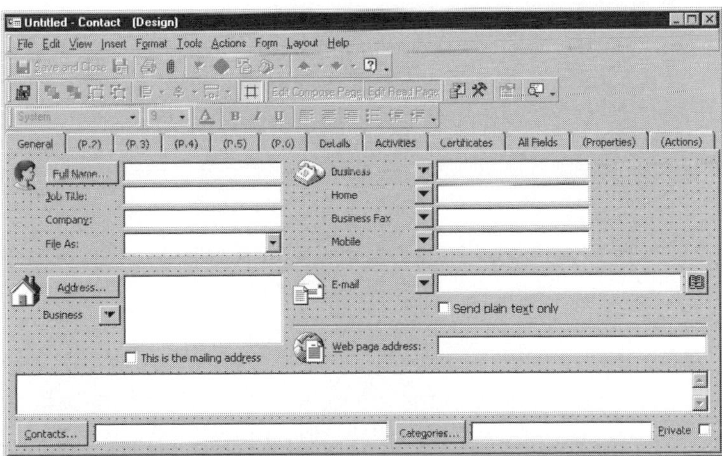

Figure 4-3 The Contact form in design mode

Note You can customize a number of other Outlook forms, including the Appointment, Task, and Journal forms, by hiding them or adding new pages to them. However, you cannot customize any of the built-in pages of these forms. Also, any custom applications you develop using the Journal form will post information to a user's personal journal.

Office Document Forms

Outlook supports embedding Microsoft Word, Excel, and PowerPoint documents directly into a form, so you can send these documents to a user or post them to a folder. These types of forms are best used when you want the advanced replication and forms library support of Outlook but you also want the functionality of other Office applications. Outlook places a wrapper around the Office application you use to design the form, so you cannot add custom tabs to the form. You can, however, customize the application by using the built-in capabilities and tools provided by the specific Office application. For example, you can use VBA to customize an Outlook Office document form. Figure 4-4 shows an Excel Office document form.

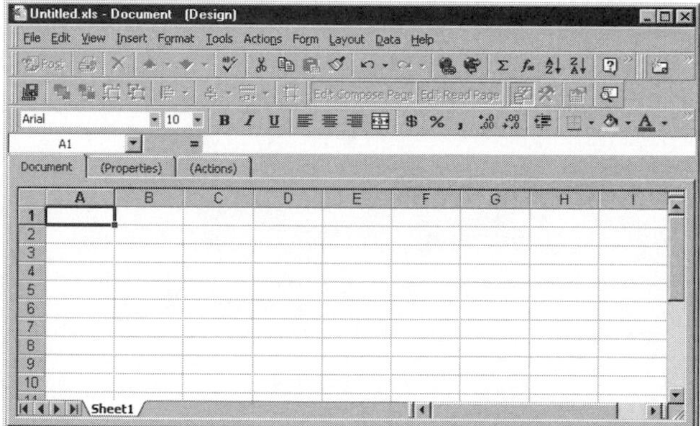

Figure 4-4 An Excel Office document form in design mode

Note Office document forms are no longer available in Outlook 2002 and later. If you want to build Office document forms, you have to use a previous version of Outlook, such as Outlook 2000. Any Office document forms you build will run in Outlook 2002 and Outlook 2003.

How Forms Work

Before we dive into building forms, let's step back and take a look at how forms work inside the Outlook and Microsoft Exchange Server environments. When you double-click on an Outlook item to open it, Outlook queries a property on the item named *Message Class*. The message class uniquely identifies the form that the item is based on. For example, when you create a new e-mail message, you are creating a form with the message class *IPM.Note*. (IPM stands for *interpersonal message*.) When you send the message to another user, the message class travels with the item as a property. You can see all the different message types by simply adding the message class property to your views. These message classes are extensible, so you can create your own types of forms with unique message classes.

When you work with forms in the Outlook development environment, you have to base them on built-in forms. You cannot start with a blank slate, as you can with Visual Basic forms. After you customize your form, you can publish it. This is where you can customize the message class. For example, if you modify the standard Outlook Appointment form to make it a class registration system, you can publish the form with its own unique message class, such as *IPM.Appointment.Class Registration Form*. There are numerous message classes; Table 4-1 lists the message classes for the built-in Outlook forms.

Table 4-1 Message Classes for Built-in Outlook Forms

Form	Message Class
Appointment	*IPM.Appointment*
Contact	*IPM.Contact*
Distribution List	*IPM.DistList*
Journal	*IPM.Activity*
Message	*IPM.Note*
Post	*IPM.Post*
Task	*IPM.Task*

These message classes work in conjunction with the different forms libraries in Outlook. For example, when a user launches a form, Outlook first checks to see whether the item is a standard form, such as the Note form or a Post form. If the item is not a standard form, Outlook checks the forms cache on the local machine. The forms cache is a folder located on the user's local machine; by default, Outlook caches all custom forms in this folder to improve performance. If the form is not in the cache or a newer version of the form is available, Outlook downloads the form's definition into the cache. This automatic update feature ensures that your users will always use the most recent version of the application even after you've modified your forms. The user can change the size of the cache in Outlook by choosing Options from the Tools menu, clicking on the Other tab, clicking the Advanced Options button, and then clicking the Custom Forms button.

If the form is not in the cache, Outlook will search the forms library of the current folder. If the form is not in the current folder, Outlook searches the user's Personal Forms Library and the Organizational Forms Library. If the user has Web services enabled in Outlook, Outlook will search the Web forms library in Outlook Web Access (OWA). Note that this works only with Exchange 5.5 OWA, not Exchange 2000 or 2003.

If Outlook cannot find the form in any of the forms libraries, Outlook will use the standard form on which the custom application is based. For example, if a user receives an appointment item with a message class of *IPM.Appointment.Job Interview* and the form does not exist in any of the forms libraries, Outlook will use the standard Appointment form to open the message.

Outlook allows you to save the form definition directly with an item, so when a user does not have a copy of your custom form installed in any of her forms libraries or the user is in a different organization, she can still receive your item and view it. Because the form definition is saved with the message, the size of the message you send to the user increases slightly. You'll learn how to save the form definition with an item later in this chapter.

Data Binding

To retrieve and set the underlying properties of the form, Outlook uses data binding. If you are new to developing with Outlook, it is important that you understand data binding; otherwise, you can easily run into early design problems.

The layout of the form, or *form definition*, is separate from the data of the form. Form definitions do not store any application data—they store data bindings. At run time, Outlook finds the field that the control on the form is bound to, and it retrieves and sets the value of the control. The most common mistake new developers make is to add a new control on a form without setting its data binding. If the control is not bound to any field, Outlook does not maintain the data in the Exchange Server database. You will learn how to implement data binding later in this chapter.

Designing Forms

Once you determine the purpose of your form and which form to modify, you have to open the form in design mode and make decisions about a variety of issues.

Outlook provides an environment for creating and editing forms, which is sometimes referred to as the forms designer. The forms designer is automatically installed with Outlook.

Opening a Form in Design Mode

Opening a form in design mode is easy. If the form is not based on an Office document, you can use one of two approaches: open a standard form of the type you want to modify and enter design mode by choosing Forms, Design This Form from the Tools menu; or select a form from a list of available forms, which automatically opens the form in design mode. To use the second approach, follow these steps:

1. From the Tools menu, choose Forms, Design A Form. The Design Form dialog box (shown in Figure 4-5) will open.
2. In the Look In drop-down list, find the location of the form you want to modify or use as a template. You can select forms from any forms library as well as from templates in the file system.
3. Click the Details button to display the properties of the currently selected form, which include the icon, description, contact, version, and message class of the form.
4. Click Open to open the selected form in design mode.

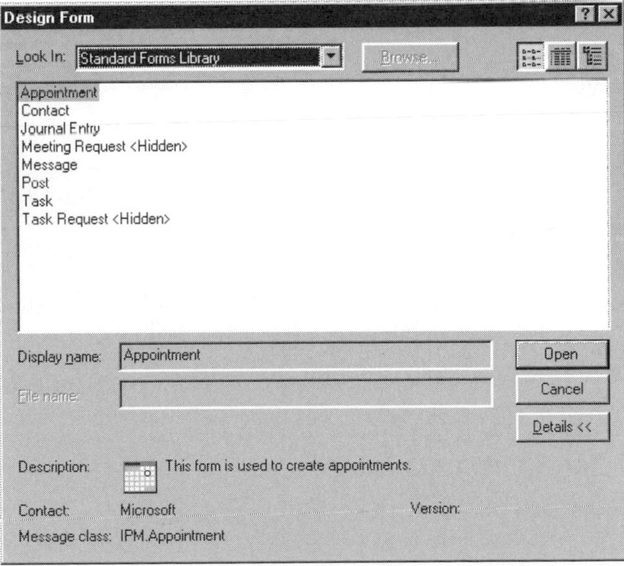

Figure 4-5 The Design Form dialog box in Outlook

Choosing Display Properties

When you design an Outlook application, you must decide whether to display, rename, or hide the default pages on the form. Your decision will be based on what the forms are for. For example, if you want to preaddress an item sent to users to prevent them from modifying the values in the address field or knowing where the item is being sent, you can fill in the address information on the message and then hide the default pages. To change the display properties for a form page or to rename a default or custom page, enter design mode, click on the desired page, and then select the appropriate option from the Form menu. You can quickly see the display status of a form page in design mode because Outlook places parentheses around the name of any page that will be hidden at run time.

Separating the Read Layout from the Compose Layout

Outlook supports having separate layouts for compose and read form pages. The compose page appears when a user opens a form to compose a new item. The read page appears when a user double-clicks on an item to view it. The standard e-mail message is a great example of a form that effectively uses compose and read pages.

Outlook enables you to separate the compose and read pages for a form so that you can add custom functionality to each of these user modes. Outlook supports compose and read pages on every customizable forms page. By default, the Message page on an Outlook Post form and on a Message form have the Separate Read Layout option enabled. However, your custom pages, by default, do not. To enable Separate Read Layout, in design mode, select the form page where you want separate compose and read layouts. On the Form menu, be sure there is a check mark next to Separate Read Layout. Outlook automatically copies the layout from the compose page to the read page. You can then select the layout you want to modify by selecting the appropriate edit option from the Form menu.

If you find that you are making extensive changes to the compose page and you want to discard your read page and re-create it with the layout of the compose page, you can disable the Separate Read Layout option and then re-enable it. Outlook will copy the layout of the compose page to the new read page.

Using the Field Chooser to Drag and Drop Fields

The Field Chooser provides a simple way to drag and drop built-in and custom fields onto your form. When you drag and drop a field from the Field Chooser onto the form, Outlook creates the appropriate controls. If the AutoLayout option is enabled on the Layout menu, Outlook automatically positions your controls on the form. The controls that Outlook creates are based on the data type of the associated field. For example, if you drag and drop a field with a data type of *text*, Outlook will automatically create a text box control and typically a label control with the name of the field. If you drag and drop a field with a data type of *Yes/No*, Outlook will create a check box control with the *Caption* property set to the name of the field. Figure 4-6 shows a Post form with the controls for the Attachment, Categories, From, Icon, and Importance fields added by using the Field Chooser.

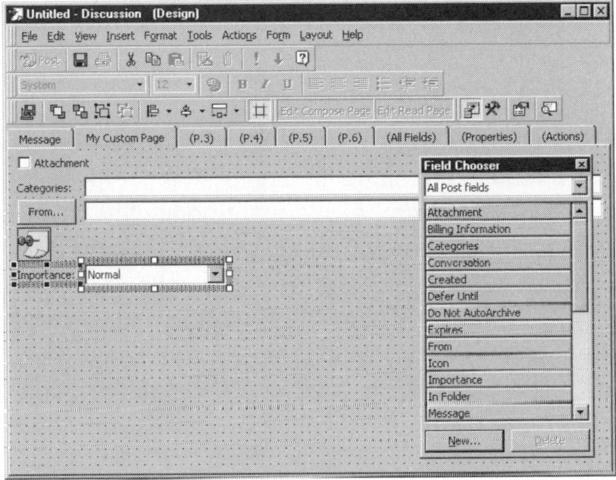

Figure 4-6 Dragging fields from the Field Chooser to an Outlook form

Important Default Fields

Outlook includes some important default fields, such as the address fields, that you should take advantage of when you design an application. We'll briefly discuss the address fields, the Subject field, and the Message field next.

Address Fields

The address fields include From, To, Cc, and Bcc. The address fields enable you to preaddress your form to individual users or distribution lists by typing an address at design time or by setting the initial value of the fields. (You will see how to set initial values later in this chapter.) You can enable these fields if you want to allow the user to change the address, but most likely you will want to disable the To field and just expose the Cc field so a user can send a copy of the form to another user. By default, the To field is exposed only on a Message form, but you can use the Field Chooser to drag and drop the To field or any other address field onto another type of Outlook form and set its initial value. This ensures that if the user forwards the form, the address you have supplied will automatically appear in the displayed Message form.

To preaddress a form to a folder (as opposed to a user), either the folder has to be exposed in the Global Address List (GAL) or you have to copy the folder address into your personal address book. To expose the folder in the GAL, you must have administrator rights on the Exchange Server system. You launch the Microsoft Exchange System Manager program and expand the folder trees to find the folder you want to expose. Right click on it and choose Properties. On the Exchange Advanced tab, deselect the Hide From Exchange Address Lists check box, and click OK.

> **Note** Outlook supports shared fields in an item. Shared fields are controls that are bound to the same field on both a compose page and a read page of a particular form. A user can modify the field on either page, and the changes will be available universally. Shared fields can be used between Outlook forms—for example, when you respond to an item in a folder using a custom form, Outlook copies the values from the shared fields in the open item to the same field in the response item.

Subject Field

The Subject field is important for two reasons. First, the text in the Subject field is the caption that appears at the top of a form. Second, the Subject field typically takes its value from the Conversation field. This point is important if you want to have a threaded view of the items in your application.

The value of the Subject field can also be determined by formulas. For example, you can create a formula that sets the value of the Subject field by combining two other fields on your form.

Message Field

The Message field is the only field for which text formatting, attachments, hyperlinks, and objects are supported. This extensive support allows you to embed instructions or other important material as an attachment, or to add shortcuts to Web sites, files, or other Outlook items. To add an attachment to the Message field, open the item you want to modify in run mode. From the Insert menu, choose File, and then find the file you want to insert.

Note that if you are using HTML as your default mail format in Outlook, you can insert files only as attachments or text. If you are using the Outlook Rich Text mail format, you can insert files as attachments, shortcuts, text, or embedded objects. To simulate file shortcuts using the HTML mail format, you have to add hyperlinks in the Message field that point to your files.

Outlook supports many protocols that you can place in the Message field as hyperlinks. The most useful protocols are:

- ***file://*** For adding hyperlink shortcuts to any file stored on a file server that your computer can access. Examples include:
  - ***file://c:\temp*** For linking to files or directories on your own file system and for pointing at files that are unique to each user's system.
  - ***file://docserver/docs/earning statements*** For linking to files or directories on other servers. This format is useful for sending users shortcuts to shared files or directories. Notice that the hyperlink should be placed in brackets—this is required if the hyperlink contains any spaces.
- ***http:// or https://*** For adding hyperlink shortcuts to Internet and intranet Web sites. The difference between the protocols is that Hypertext Transfer Protocol Secure (HTTPS) is a secure version of Hypertext Transfer Protocol (HTTP). HTTPS uses Secure Sockets Layer (SSL) to encrypt the traffic between the Web browser and the Web server. Here are two examples that use the HTTP protocol:
  - ***http://www.microsoft.com/exchange*** For linking quickly to external sites.
  - ***http://finance/earnings.htm*** For linking to internal sites. These internal sites can be individual servers that users set up or can be part of your organization's intranet.
- ***mailto:*** For adding shortcuts that allow the user to automatically address a message to the specified location, even if the user is not using Outlook but needs to respond to messages automatically sent by Outlook. Here are a few examples of mailto hyperlinks:
  - ***mailto:thomriz*** Use this format if the default mail program of your users is Outlook, which enables you to use the user's simple address. Outlook automatically resolves the name by using an address book.

- ***mailto:thomriz@microsoft.com*** Use this format when you cannot guarantee that the user of the mailto hyperlink is an Outlook client.
- ***mailto:thomriz@microsoft.com?subject=Great Book&body=I loved every minute*** Use this format to pass additional information after the address of the item. The formatting of the information is exactly the same as when you pass variables along an HTTP query string. This mailto hyperlink automatically fills in the message subject and text.

- ***Outlook:*** For creating a hyperlink directly to Outlook information. This protocol is supported only if Outlook is installed on the local machine. Here are some examples:
    - ***Outlook:Inbox\Subfolder*** For linking to Outlook folders. In this example, the Subfolder folder of the Inbox will appear on the machine of the user. You can replace *Inbox* with the name of another Outlook folder, such as Tasks, Contacts, Calendar, or Journal.
    - ***Outlook:Contacts/~Thomas Rizzo*** For linking to a specific item in the folder. This example opens the Thomas Rizzo contact in the Contacts folder of the current user. Remember to place the hyperlink in angle brackets if it contains spaces.
    - ***<Outlook:\\Public Folders\All Public Folders\Discussion>*** For linking to a public folder. This example opens the Discussion public folder. You can use a similar syntax to open only the public folder tree or to access a user's favorite folders stored in Public Folders\Favorites.
    - ***Outlook:EntryID*** For linking to items in the Outlook environment by using the EntryID. This is useful if you are generating mail messages using the Microsoft Event Scripting Agent or the Microsoft Workflow Engine and you need to send a link to an item in a public folder. Collaboration Data Objects (CDO) does not currently provide this functionality, but using *Outlook:EntryID* is a great workaround. The only problem is that the Outlook protocol requires Outlook on the local machine. Also, if you try to access an item in a public folder and the user has not yet accessed the Public Folder hierarchy, this type of link will fail. Here is an example of this protocol:

Outlook:EF000000D4B32904495CD111921D08002BE4F322646C2700

This is a short-term EntryID. You can also use long-term EntryIDs. Long-term EntryIDs are valid between Outlook sessions and should not start with *EF*. Short-term EntryIDs are valid only in the current session, so do not save them off to permanent storage and attempt to use them as a long-term identifier for the item or folder.

You can also express spaces in any of these protocols by using the characters *%20*. For example, to link to a specific message in your Inbox with the subject *Earnings reports*, you use the following syntax for the Outlook protocol: *Outlook:Inbox/~Earnings%20reports*.

The Message control, which is inserted in your form when you insert a Message field, and its underlying field, the Message field, provide extensive functionality to your applications. However, there are some restrictions on the use of the Message control inside an Outlook form.

First, you should create only one Message control on an Outlook form. The Message control is automatically bound to the Message field, so more than one control will cause a conflict over which content should be saved to the Message field. For example, if you have three Message controls on different pages in the Outlook form and a user writes a different value to each control, Outlook will save the contents of only one of those controls. This means that only one value of the Message field will be displayed in all three Message controls.

Note Outlook automatically displays a warning message if you attempt to place multiple Message controls on a form. If you need to sidestep this restriction because your application needs to span multiple pages with Message controls across each page, you should use a MultiPage control and keep only one Message control at the bottom of the form. For more information on how to use MultiPage controls, see the next section.

Second, only the Message control accepts attachments or the hyperlinks we looked at earlier. The other controls in Outlook do not understand hyperlinks and will not automatically display and link information.

Third, the Message control is always bound to the Message field, and Outlook automatically establishes this binding. You cannot change it, nor can you set initial values of the Message control in design mode. You must either insert your hyperlinks, text, or attachments before designing the form or insert them programmatically.

Using Controls

You've learned how to use the Field Chooser to add controls to a form. The Field Chooser automatically binds the control to the appropriate field. You can also add controls to your form manually.

You can set properties for the controls you use on forms—for example, you can change the name, change the display properties, or bind the control to an Outlook field. You access the properties for a control via the Properties dialog box. In design mode, right-click on the control and choose Properties. In the Properties dialog box (shown in Figure 4-7), you can select options that control the behavior and appearance of the different Outlook controls. The following sections describe some of the Outlook controls and how to manipulate some of their properties.

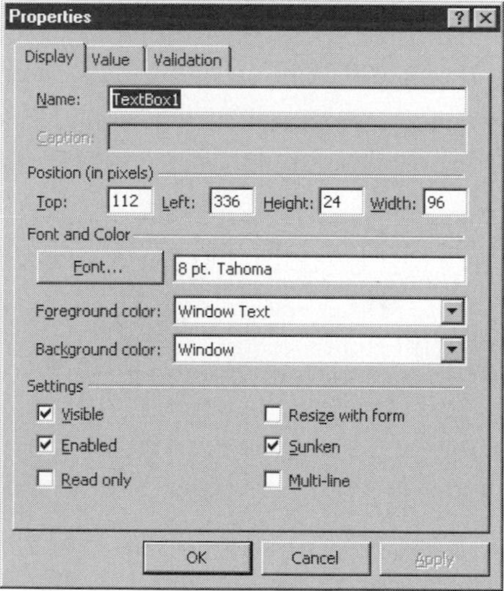

Figure 4-7 The Properties dialog box

Accessing Controls from the Control Toolbox

The Control Toolbox, shown in Figure 4-8, provides an easy way for you to select controls when you design your forms. To launch the Control Toolbox in Outlook, enter design mode and choose Control Toolbox from the Form menu. You can also customize the Control Toolbox. For example, you can add the controls that you use most often to the toolbox. You can customize the Control Toolbox in the following ways:

- Add pages to the toolbox
- Rename the pages
- Move controls from one page to another
- Add other controls, such as ActiveX controls
- Copy modified controls or groups of controls from your custom forms to the toolbox for use on other forms

To add controls to the toolbox from an Outlook form, select the controls that you want to add and drag and drop them onto the toolbox. You can select individual controls or groups of controls.

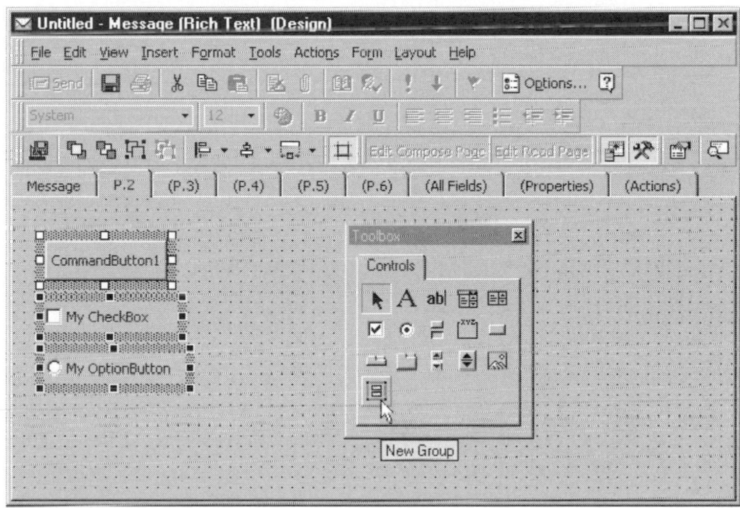

Figure 4-8 The Control Toolbox and a group of controls that have been dragged and dropped on the form

Renaming Controls

By default, when you add a control to an Outlook form, Outlook assigns a name to it—for example, Outlook would assign the name *TextBox1* to a new TextBox control. However, it is good practice to change the name to one that better describes the control's function. Just be sure the name you choose is different from the name of the field the control is bound to. By giving the control and the field different names, you can avoid some confusion when writing your applications. You should also place an abbreviation at the beginning of the control to identify the content type. For example, if you add a TextBox control that holds the job status information for a potential job candidate, you might want to precede the control name with *txt* to indicate the control type—for example, *txtJobStatus*. When you extend your form with VBScript, you must use the name of the control inside your script.

Assigning Captions

The *Caption* property is available for only some of the Outlook controls: the CheckBox, CommandButton, Frame, Label, OptionButton, MultiPage, and ToggleButton controls. You set the *Caption* property via the Properties page. This property has a different effect for each control. For the Label and CommandButton controls, the *Caption* property specifies the text that appears in the control. For the MultiPage control, the *Caption* property applies to each page of the control and specifies the text that appears as the tab name.

You can use the *Caption* property to set up accelerator keys (single-character shortcuts) for your controls. For example, you might assign the ALT-A accelerator key combination to a CommandButton control named *Automatically Populate Fields*. To turn any letter in the text of the caption into an accelerator key, place an ampersand (&) before the letter. Try to avoid duplicating existing shortcuts, such as ALT-F; otherwise, the accelerator will not perform as expected.

For the Outlook controls that do not support captions, such as the TextBox control, you can create individual Label controls for identification. For example, suppose you create a TextBox control that takes the name of a user as input. You can create a label control with the text *User Name:* and position it to appear before the TextBox control. Be sure to adjust the tab order (as shown later in this chapter) so your label and the data entry control that it describes are in the correct order.

Setting the Font and Color

Outlook allows you to set the font and color of your controls. The colors you set for controls can be relative to the colors your users have set for their system. For example, you can set the background color for a control to be the same as the system window color, which the user establishes.

You can use different properties for a control to create unique effects in your application. For example, to create shading, you can set the background color of a label control and then layer it behind other controls on your form. This effect is shown in Figure 4-9.

Note If you want to provide shading for a whole page of your form, use the Advanced Properties window of the form to set the *BackColor* property of the form itself, rather than adding a label that stretches across the entire page. To learn how to set the advanced properties for a control or a page, see the section titled "Setting Advanced Control Properties" later in this chapter.

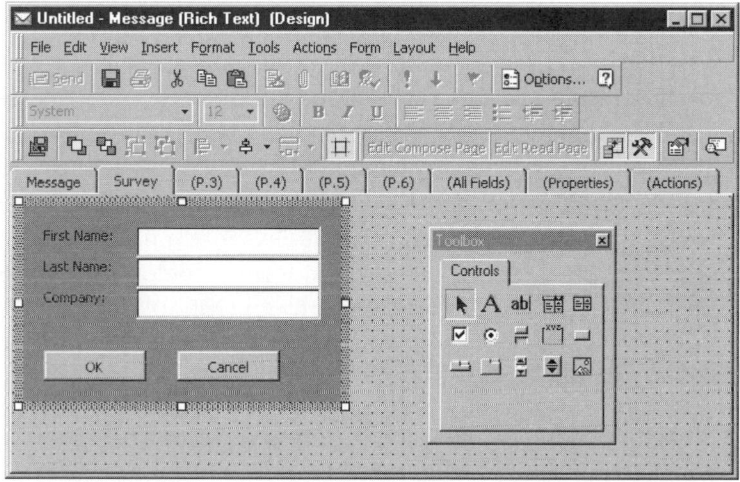

Figure 4-9 Setting the background color of a Label control to provide shading on a certain portion of the form

Establishing Display Settings

Outlook provides six settings for the display of a control:

- *Visible*
- *Enabled*
- *Read Only*
- *Resize with Form*
- *Sunken*
- *MultiLine*

With the first three of these properties, you can make your controls behave differently depending on the user who accesses the form.

Binding Controls

When you create a new control, you might want to bind it to an existing field rather than create a new field. To do so, in design mode, right-click on the control, choose Properties, click on the Value tab, and click Choose Field. In the drop-down list, select the field you want to bind to your control. Because this control is bound to a field, any changes made to the information in the control will be automatically reflected in the field.

Setting Initial Values

You can set initial values for the controls on your form that are either static or calculated via the Value tab of the Properties dialog box, as shown in Figure 4-10. You can also specify whether Outlook should use your initial value only when a user is composing an item based on the form, or automatically whenever any of the values used to calculate the initial value change or a user opens the form. For example, you can set Outlook to automatically set the due date for a new item to a week from the current day. When calculating initial values, you can use the same functionality used in formula fields. To take advantage of initial values, you must bind your control to an Outlook field.

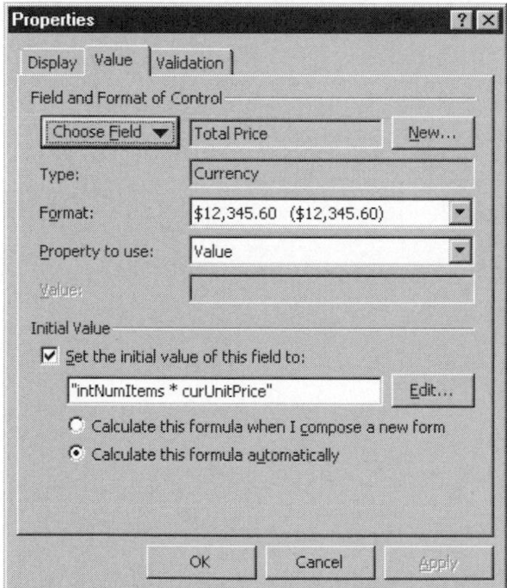

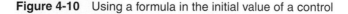

Figure 4-10 Using a formula in the initial value of a control

Requiring and Validating Information in Fields

You can require that any field or any control bound to a field have a value. If the user does not enter any information in the field and attempts to close, save, or send the form, Outlook will return an error message that tells the user a value is required.

Outlook can also compare the value the user has entered to the validation criteria you specify. These criteria can range from simple text to complex formulas. If the validation fails, you can specify the message that will appear. This message should tell the user what the accepted values are for the field. For example, if you create a TextBox control on your form that should contain a number value greater than 0, you can use a validation formula to make sure the user does not enter a negative number in the field. If the user attempts to enter a negative number, your custom message can ask the user to enter a positive number in the field. You set these properties on the Validation tab of the Properties dialog box.

Built-in Outlook Controls

Outlook provides 14 built-in controls that you can add to your forms, each of which provides unique functionality. The following sections introduce these built-in controls.

> **Note** In addition to the 14 built-in controls, you can also use ActiveX controls. We'll discuss ActiveX controls in the section titled "Using Custom or Third-Party Controls" later in the chapter.

Label Control

You use a Label control to display descriptive text such as titles, captions, or company logos. For example, you use a Label control to identify a text box or to display read-only information. The only time you typically bind a Label control to a field is when you want to display just a field value. Figure 4-11 shows a timecard application in which a user enters the number of hours worked each day. The Label control displays the total number of hours worked.

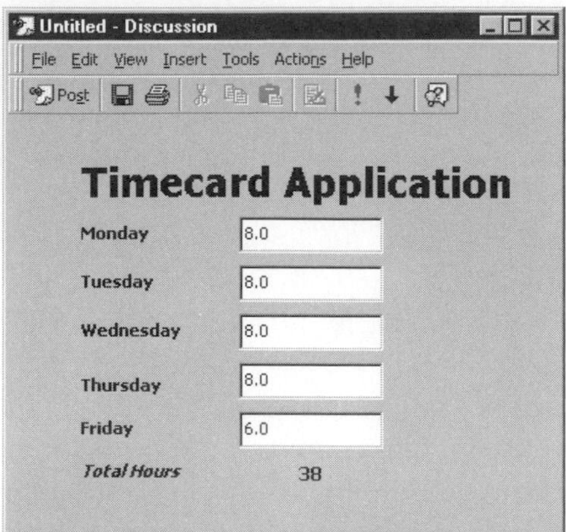

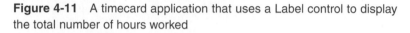

Figure 4-11 A timecard application that uses a Label control to display the total number of hours worked

> **Note** You can display pictures inside Label controls by using the Advanced Properties of the control. However, you cannot crop or size the picture unless you use an Image control, which is described later in this chapter.

TextBox Control

You use a TextBox control to display or gather information from a user—generally the latter. You can use a TextBox control on a customer survey form to gather comments. If you bind the TextBox control to a field, the information entered by the user is saved in that field. Figure 4-12 shows some TextBox controls on a form. These TextBox controls are combined with Label controls to let users know what type of information they are expected to enter.

The TextBox control is highly customizable. You can govern its functionality by setting specific properties on it. For example, you can make a TextBox control automatically adjust its size to fit text entered by the user. You can also add multiline functionality so users can enter more than one line of text in the TextBox control. You can enable or disable the *AutoSize*, *MultiLine*, and *WordWrap* properties for a specific TextBox control by right-clicking on it and choosing Advanced Properties.

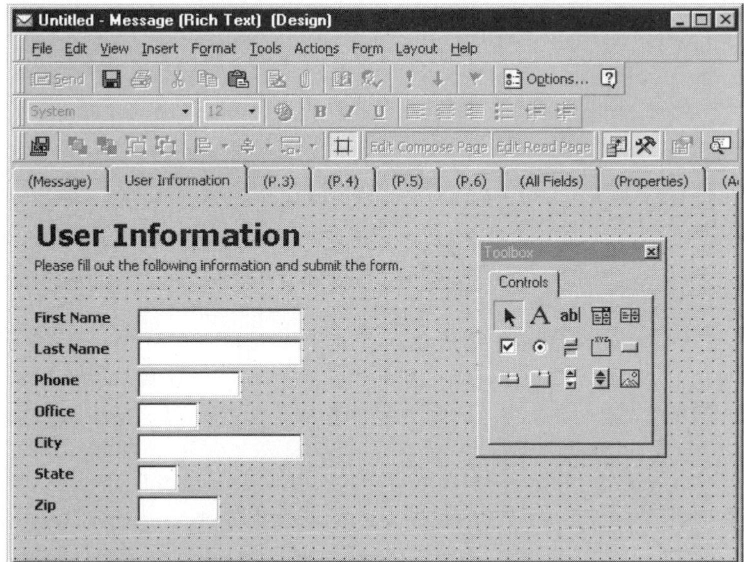

Figure 4-12 TextBox controls on an Outlook form

> **Caution** Avoid using the *AutoSize* property when you use a TextBox control that already has *WordWrap* and *MultiLine* enabled. If you use this property, when the TextBox control is empty, the size of the control will appear only 1 character wide and 1 character high. Further, when the user adds text to the control, the control will automatically resize itself to one long line of text rather than having text on multiple lines.

ListBox Control

The ListBox control displays multiple values, of which users can select one or more. A ListBox control offers two presentation styles:

- Each item in the ListBox appearing on a separate row. The user can select items by highlighting one or more rows.
- Items presented as option buttons or check boxes. For this to work, the ListBox control must be bound to a Keywords field type. Set the *MultiSelect* property to *single* for option buttons, and set it to *multi* for check boxes.

If you set the *MultiSelect* property for the ListBox control in the Advanced Properties window to *1 - Multi*, the user can select multiple items in the ListBox. When a user selects multiple items in the ListBox, the selections are entered in the field as comma-separated values. You can create views that group or sort by these values.

You create a list of values in a ListBox control in two ways:

- Right-click on the ListBox control that is placed on the form, choose Properties, and click on the Value tab. Click the New button, and create a new field that has a type of *Keywords*. Enter the desired values in the Possible Values box. You must separate the values with a comma or semicolon. Do not surround your text with quotes unless you want these quotes to appear in the ListBox control. Figure 4-13 shows where to set values for a ListBox control. You can see the check boxes that appear when the ListBox control is bound to a *Keywords* field and the *MultiSelect* property is set to *1 – Multi* and *ListStyle* set to *1 - Option*.
- Establish the values programmatically at run time.

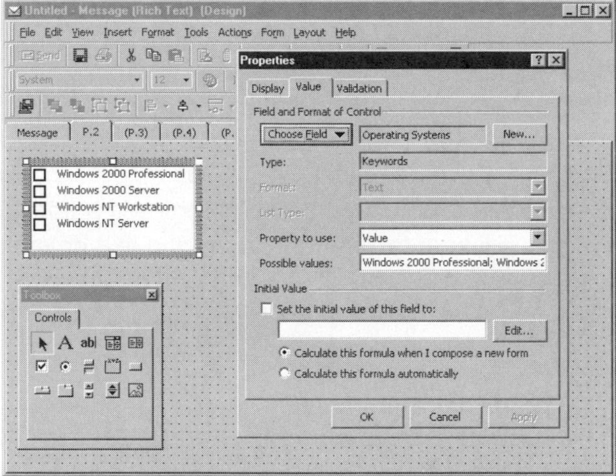

Figure 4-13 Setting values for a ListBox control

ComboBox Control

A ComboBox control combines the features of a ListBox control and a TextBox control—it enables you to provide a list from which the user can select an item and a text box into which a user can type information.

You add values to the drop-down list of a ComboBox control in the same way you add them for the ListBox control. You can specify the list type on the Value tab of the Properties dialog box, in the List Type drop-down list. Here are the List Type options:

- ***Dropdown*** Allows the user to type new text in the TextBox portion of the control or select a value from the drop-down portion of the control
- ***Droplist*** Forces the user to select a value from the drop-down list

Figure 4-14 shows how to set properties for a ComboBox control.

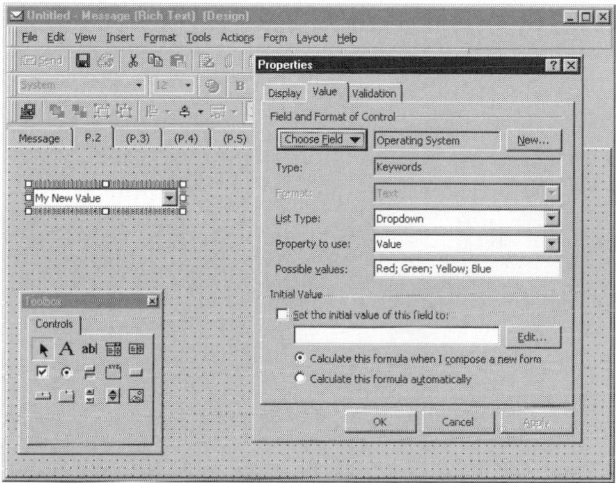

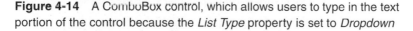

Figure 4-14 A ComboBox control, which allows users to type in the text portion of the control because the *List Type* property is set to *Dropdown*

CheckBox and ToggleButton Controls

You use the CheckBox and ToggleButton controls to give the user a choice between two values, such as on or off, yes or no, or true or false. You should bind the CheckBox or ToggleButton controls to a *Yes/No* field type for the control to work properly.

OptionButton Control

The OptionButton control also gives the user multiple choices, but it differs from the CheckBox and ToggleButton controls in that multiple OptionButton controls in a group are mutually exclusive. For example, on a helpdesk form, you can associate OptionButton controls with operating systems that users might be running, such as Microsoft Windows 2000 Professional, Windows 2000 Server, or Windows NT, as shown in Figure 4-15. You can bind all of the OptionButton controls to the same field—for example, the *txtUserOS* field. The value of the *txtUserOS* field will be the value of the currently selected OptionButton control. You set the value for an OptionButton control on the Value tab of the Properties dialog box.

You can group OptionButton controls together using containers, such as a Frame control or a MultiPage control. Figure 4-15 shows a Frame control being used to group the OptionButton controls. When you bind one of the OptionButton controls in the group to a particular field, the other controls automatically bind to that same field. Be careful to drag and drop the OptionButton controls onto a container on your form, not onto the form page—Outlook automatically groups together all OptionButton controls on the form page, which might not produce the desired functionality.

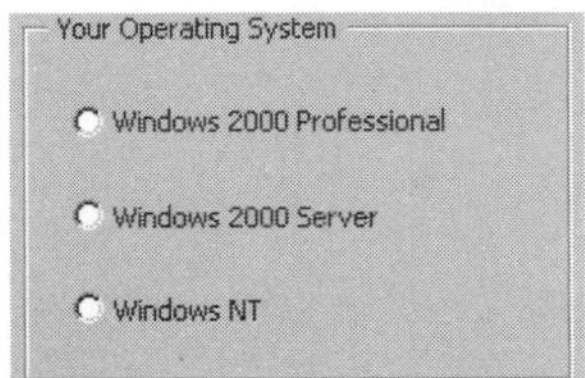

Figure 4-15 A set of OptionButton controls grouped together with a Frame control

You can also group your OptionButton controls by using the *GroupName* property, which identifies related OptionButton controls on a form. To set the *GroupName* property for an OptionButton control, in design mode, right-click on the OptionButton control that you want to modify and choose Advanced Properties. Double-click on the *GroupName* property, and type a unique name for the group. Click Apply, and repeat the steps for all the other OptionButton controls in your group.

> **Note** Some controls, such as the TabStrip control, appear to contain other controls but actually do not. If you want to create a group of OptionButton controls on a TabStrip control (described later), you must use the *GroupName* property to distinguish which controls are "on" the TabStrip and which are just on the form.

Frame Control

Frame controls are used to create groups of related controls. You've seen that a frame can hold a group of mutually exclusive OptionButton controls, but it can hold other types of controls as well. You add controls to and remove controls from a frame by dragging and dropping them. When you move the frame on the form, all of the controls within the frame move with it. Be aware that when you delete a frame, all of the controls within the frame are deleted as well. You can also cut and paste controls from the form into the Frame control and vice-versa.

CommandButton Control

A CommandButton control provides custom functionality when a user clicks it. You write the script that responds to the control's click event. The click event is the only event for the CommandButton control. For information on writing scripts in Outlook forms, see Chapter 5.

MultiPage and TabStrip Controls

The MultiPage and TabStrip controls are similar in that they offer multiple pages, or tabs, for holding information. The difference is that every page in a MultiPage control is its own form, so you can customize the layout and background colors of each page as well as place unique controls on them; the TabStrip control must contain the same controls on every page, so you do not have flexibility with layout. The TabStrip control is appropriate if you want a single layout for your data that you can map a unique set of data to. Figure 4-16 shows how the MultiPage control is used for the Account Tracking application we'll look at in Chapter 8.

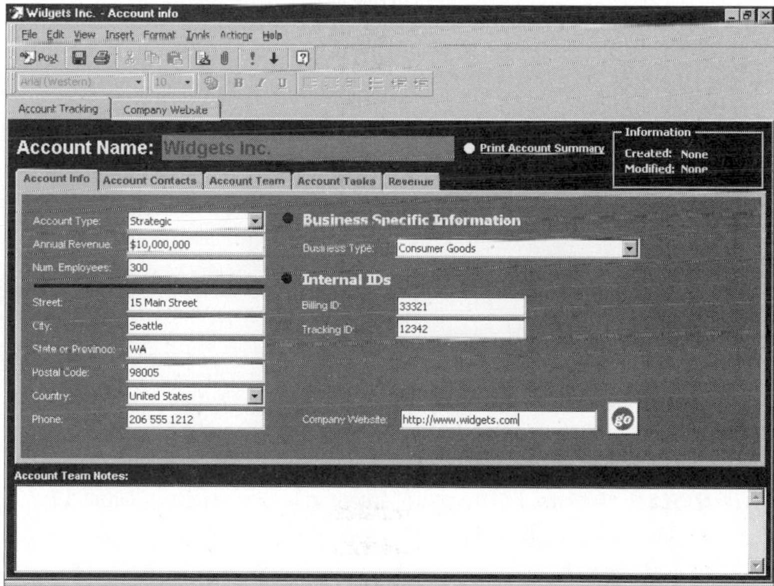

Figure 4-16 The MultiPage control for the Account Tracking application provides several pages of information

To add controls to and remove controls from a MultiPage or TabStrip control, you drag and drop them into the control. To customize a page of a MultiPage control, enter design mode, right-click on the desired tab, and choose Insert, Delete, Rename, or Move. The Insert command always places the page as the last tab, so to position the tab correctly after you've added it, use the Move command.

SpinButton Control

The SpinButton control has arrows that allow you to increment or decrement a number. It accepts custom script—you decide whether to write it. If you want to use the SpinButton control to increment and decrement values in another control, such as a TextBox control, rather than write script, you simply bind the data to the same field for both controls. Figure 4-17 shows a SpinButton control and a TextBox control bound to the same field. The user can use the SpinButton to increment and decrement the value in the TextBox control.

Figure 4-17 A SpinButton control and a TextBox control are bound to the same field

Image Control

The Image control displays an image on your form, as shown in Figure 4-18. The Image control supports the following file formats:

- .bmp
- .cur
- .gif
- .ico
- .jpg
- .wmf

Here are some of the properties you can set in the Advanced Properties window for the Image control:

- ***AutoSize*** Control automatically grows or shrinks based on the size of its associated graphic.
- ***Picture*** Specifies the picture to display.
- ***PictureAlignment*** Determines where the image appears in the control if the height and width of the Image control is greater than the size of the image.

- ***PictureSizeMode*** Lets you clip, stretch, or zoom the image.
- ***PictureTiling*** Creates picture tiles that fill all available space in the Image control.

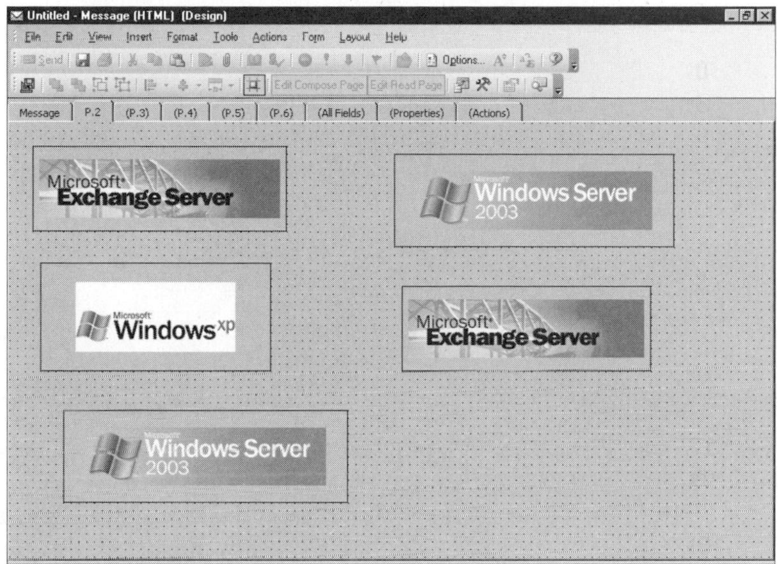

Figure 4-18 Image controls on an Outlook form displaying pictures

You can also set the *Picture* property for the Image control by using VBScript in your Outlook form. You'll learn about writing script for Outlook in the next chapter. By setting the *Picture* property programmatically, you can dynamically change the graphic contained in the Image control.

ScrollBar Control

You can use the ScrollBar to allow users to scroll through text or to increment or decrement integer values. The ScrollBar requires coding because it does not automatically associate itself with any other control on the form.

Using Custom or Third-Party Controls

Sometimes the built-in controls in Outlook might not meet the requirements of your application. In these cases, you can extend the Outlook forms environment by adding controls, such as ActiveX controls. You can create these controls by using development tools such as Microsoft Visual Basic or Microsoft Visual C++, or you can use controls developed by third-party companies. Figure 4-19 shows three ActiveX controls placed on an Outlook form.

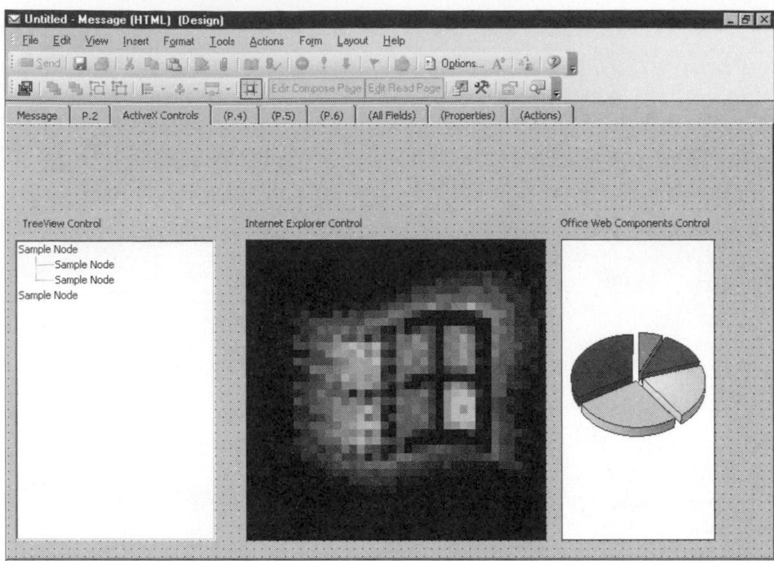

Figure 4-19 ActiveX controls on an Outlook form

To add custom controls to your Control Toolbox, in design mode, right-click on the Control Toolbox and choose Custom Controls. In the Additional Controls dialog box, select the custom controls you want to add and click OK.

> **Note** For the controls placed on your form to work correctly, they must be available on the computers of your users. Outlook does not automatically distribute ActiveX controls with the form. One way to distribute the controls is to make a Web page download for the control and automatically redirect the Web browser or an embedded Web browser control on the form to that Web page. Another approach is to package your ActiveX control as a self-installing program and provide it to your users.

When you add one of these controls to your form, you can take advantage of its unique functionality by binding specific properties of the control to Outlook fields, by setting the advanced properties for the control, or by automating the control through VBScript. For example, you can place the TreeView control included with Visual Basic on your form and then bind the selected node of the tree to your custom text field in Outlook so you can track which node the user has selected. (You can also capture this information by using a click event handler to place the value in your custom field. You'll learn how to do this in the next chapter.)

Usually, when you bind a control to an Outlook field, it's the default property of the control, typically the value of the control, that you bind. However, sometimes you might want to bind to other properties in the control. To bind a custom control property to an Outlook field, on the Value tab of the Properties dialog box, select the desired field from the Choose Field drop-down list, and in the Property To Use drop-down list, select the custom property of the control you want to bind the field to.

Different controls support different properties. To learn about the properties of a control, access the help file included with the control or use an object browser, such as the VBA Object Browser, to browse the properties of the control. The Object Browser is discussed in Chapter 5.

Setting Advanced Control Properties

You'll often need to change the advanced properties of a control on your form, such as the background color of the control or the way the control lists the values contained in it. Here are some of the properties for controls displayed only in the Advanced Properties window:

- ***ForeColor*** This property determines the foreground color of the control, which in turn affects any text associated with the control. This text can be inside the control or the caption of the control. You can use selected system colors or create your own color scheme for this property.
- ***BackColor* and *BackStyle*** These properties determine the background of the control. *BackColor* specifies the background color. *BackStyle* determines whether a control is transparent. For this property, you can use selected system colors or create your own color scheme.
- ***BorderColor*, *BorderStyle*, and *SpecialEffect*** These properties apply to the border of the control. You can use the *BorderColor* property to specify whether a control has a unique color around its border, and you can use *BorderStyle* and *SpecialEffect* to specify whether it looks sunken into the form or raised off the form, respectively. *BorderStyle* and *SpecialEffect* are mutually exclusive; when you assign a value to one of these properties, Outlook automatically resets the other.
- ***Picture*** This property specifies the picture on the control. You can set this property for many Outlook controls.
- ***ControlTipText*** This property specifies the short, descriptive text that appears when a user holds the mouse over the control.
- ***MousePointer* and *MouseIcon*** These properties together determine the icon used when the mouse passes over the control. You

can set the *MousePointer* property to one of 16 built-in icons, such as the hourglass icon or the arrow-and-question mark icon. When you set the *MousePointer* property to *99 – Custom*, the *MouseIcon* property is used to determine which icon to use. You can specify your own icons in the *MouseIcon* property.

- ***PasswordChar*** This property specifies the placeholder character that is displayed in the control in place of the real characters. This property is available only for TextBox controls. You can use it to provide some protection when users enter sensitive information into the form. An asterisk (*) is a common *PasswordChar* property value.

Setting the Tab Order

The tab order determines which control the focus moves to when the user presses the Tab key or presses Shift-Tab. Setting up a logical tab order for your form makes it easier for users to quickly enter information in the controls. To set the tab order, right-click on the desired page on the form (being careful not to click on the controls) and then select Tab Order. In the Tab Order dialog box, select controls from the list box and click the Move Up button or Move Down button to adjust the order. You can select more than one control at a time by holding down the Ctrl key while clicking controls.

> **Note** Label controls are included in the Tab Order dialog box. However, at run time, these controls are not included in the tab order—they automatically forward their tab focus to the next control.

Layering Controls on a Form

By using the layering capabilities of Outlook forms, you can create dynamic visual effects. For example, you can shade different areas of the forms by creating colored label controls that serve as the background for other controls on the form. Outlook layers controls by using the z-order (depth) axis, which determines whether controls are in front of or behind other controls. To layer the controls on your Outlook form, in design mode, select the control or controls whose order you want to adjust. From the Layout menu, choose Order, and then select the desired placement option.

Setting Form Properties

Before you publish your forms, you should set various form properties. These properties can be default or advanced.

Default Form Properties

Default form properties include the name of the form, the form description, and icons for the form. You set these properties on the Properties page, as shown in Figure 4-20.

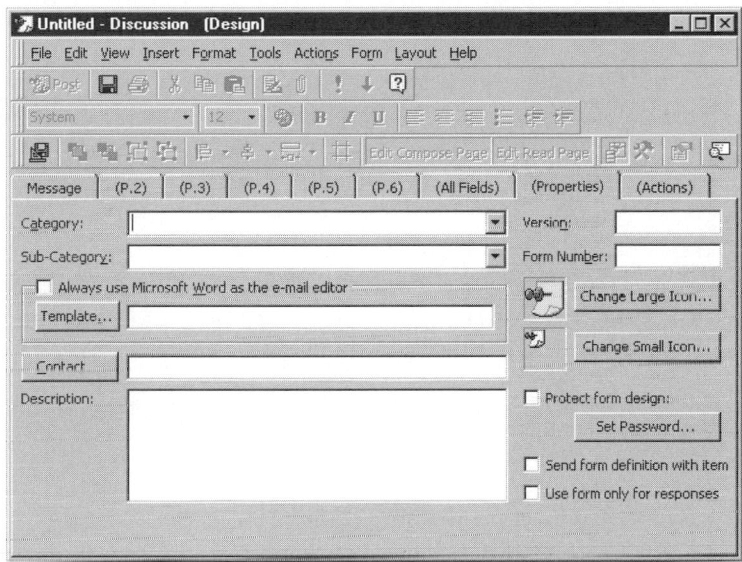

Figure 4-20 The Properties page in an Outlook form

Following are the properties you can set on the Properties page:

- ***Category*** Specifies a category name for your form, which will ultimately appear in the Choose Form dialog box. Use category names to group similar forms.
- ***Sub-Category*** Specifies a subcategory for your form so you can divide your forms into subgroups. For example, a marketing forms category can be divided into advertising, events, pricing, and promotions.
- ***Always Use Microsoft Word As The E-Mail Editor*** Specifies Word as the editor for the Message control of the form. By selecting this property, users can take advantage of the advanced features of Word.

- ***Template*** Specifies which Word template to use for the Message control on your form.
- ***Contact*** Specifies the contact responsible for the form. This name appears in the Choose Form dialog box if the user views the details about the form, and in the About dialog box for this form when the user chooses About This Form from the Help menu. (The About This Form command is not available if you send the form definition with the item.)
- ***Description*** Allows you to enter the form description, which will appear in the Choose Form dialog box if the user views the details about the form, and in the About dialog box for this form.
- ***Version*** Specifies a version number for the form. This version number will appear in the Choose Form dialog box and in the About dialog box for this form.
- ***Form Number*** Specifies a number for the form, which will appear in the About dialog box for this form.
- ***Change Large Icon*** Specifies the large icon that will be used when a user selects a large icon view for any folder containing this custom form.
- ***Change Small Icon*** Specifies the small icon that will appear in the default, custom table, timeline, or icon view of the form.
- ***Protect Form Design*** Specifies a password to protect the design of your form after you publish it. You should specify a password for all of your custom forms unless you want users to be able to modify or customize your form. For example, you should not password-protect business form templates, such as a joint marketing agreement form, that users will have to modify to meet their specific needs.
- ***Send Form Definition With Item*** Allows you to save the form layout with the item. Use this feature if you are not going to publish the form in a forms library. When you save the form definition with the item, Outlook considers these forms to be one-off forms—if you modify the form later and publish it to the forms library, any older items will continue to use the form definition saved inside of the item. This feature is useful for sending forms to users who are not in your organization or who do not have a copy of the Outlook form. For example, you can use this property to create an event registration form that users both inside and outside of your organization can

use. This form will not be useful beyond the event, so you would not publish it into a forms library. Note that when you save the form definition with the item, Outlook displays a security warning if the form contains VBScript and is not published anywhere in the user's Outlook system. With Outlook 2002 and 2003, you do not get the warning dialog box. Instead, Outlook just doesn't run any script behind a form that has a form definition attached.

- ***Use Form Only For Responses*** Makes your form available only as a response to other forms, so users cannot create your form directly from the Choose Form dialog box. Instead, they must open the parent form and use the methods provided in the parent to create the form. This option is useful if you want to create hidden forms for your application. (Outlook uses this feature to implement meeting responses.)

Advanced Form Properties

The advanced form properties help you create visually appealing forms. These properties allow you to specify the individual background colors or images for the pages of your forms and also the default mouse pointers. To set the advanced properties of your forms, in design mode, right-click on the desired page and choose Advanced Properties. (Be sure to click on the page, not on a control.) In the Advanced Properties window, select the options you want to modify. Figure 4-21 shows the Advanced Properties window.

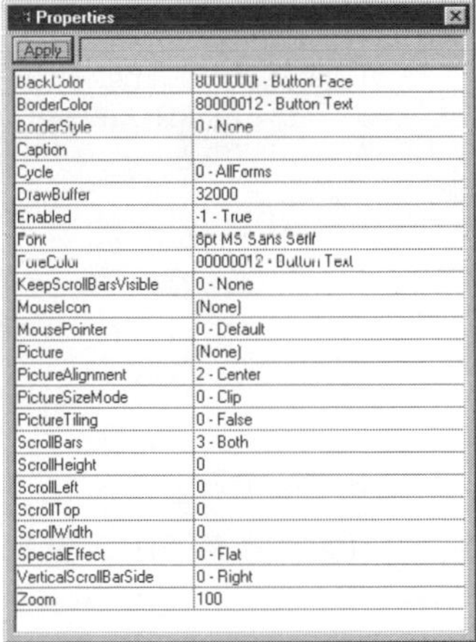

Properties
Apply
BorderColor 80000012 - Button Text
BorderStyle 0 - None
Caption
Cycle 0 - AllForms
DrawBuffer 32000
Enabled -1 - True
Font 8pt MS Sans Serif
KeepScrollBarsVisible 0 - None
MouseIcon (None)
MousePointer 0 - Default
Picture (None)
PictureAlignment 2 - Center
PictureSizeMode 0 - Clip
PictureTiling 0 - False
ScrollBars 3 - Both
ScrollHeight 0
ScrollLeft 0
ScrollTop 0
ScrollWidth 0
SpecialEffect 0 - Flat
VerticalScrollBarSide 0 - Right
Zoom 100

Figure 4-21 The Advanced Properties window for a page on an Outlook form

Testing Forms

Outlook enables you to test your forms as you develop them. Because the design and run environment are built into Outlook, you do not have to compile or save your forms before testing them. You can start a separate run mode so you can test the form's functionality while making changes to it in design mode. You can also enable multiple instances of your forms in run mode, which can be useful if you want to try different versions of the form and test different areas of functionality. To test your forms in run mode, enter design mode and choose Run This Form from the Form menu. Outlook automatically creates a new instance of your form in run mode. To get back to design mode, just close the running instance of the form. Figure 4-22 shows an Outlook form in both design mode and run mode. These separate modes make it easier to test your Outlook applications.

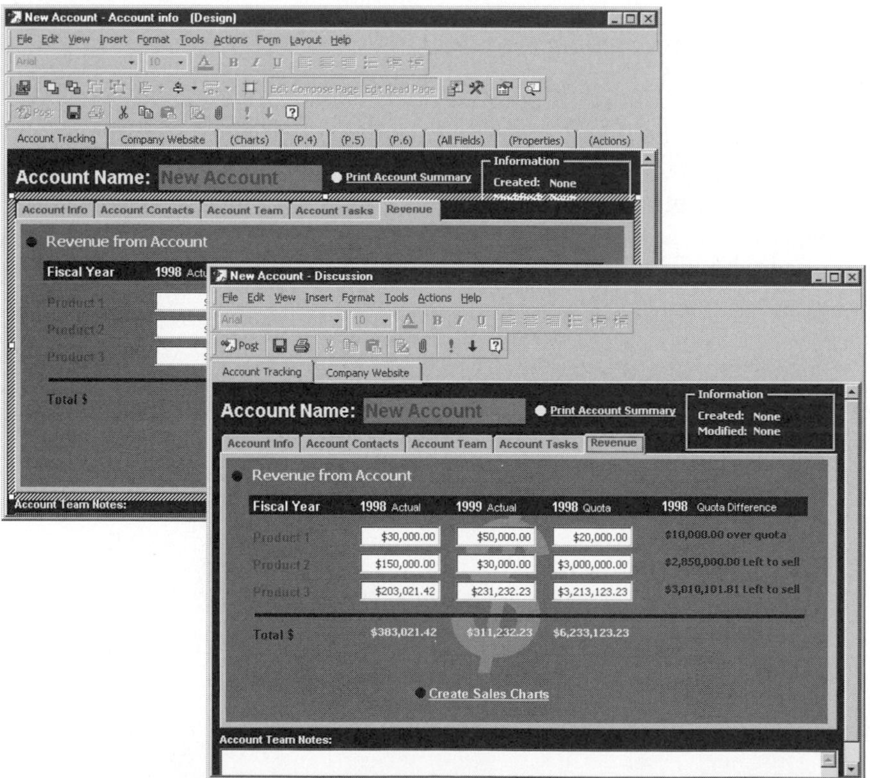

Figure 4-22 An Outlook form in both design mode and run mode

Publishing Forms

After customizing your forms, you need to make them available to your users. You can distribute your forms to users in three ways:

- **Publish the form in a forms library** The forms library can be the Organizational Forms Library, a folder forms library, your Personal Forms Library, or a Web forms library. Publishing the form to a library is the most common distribution method.
- **Save the form definition with the item, and send the item to your users** This approach is best suited for one-off forms that users will use only once.
- **Save the form to the file system as an .oft file and attach it to an e-mail that you send to your users** Users can then use the form from their file systems or publish the form in their Personal Forms Library.

The following sections describe each of these methods in detail.

Publishing a Form in a Forms Library

As you learned in Chapter 2, Outlook supports four types of forms libraries, and each type meets a specific need for forms publishing:

- **Organizational Forms Library** Use this library to publish public forms that should be available to the entire company.
- **Folder Forms Library** Use this library to publish forms in specific folders. To compose a form from this library, users must click on the folder in the Choose Form dialog box or open the folder and launch the form from the Actions menu. Any user can create forms in her own personal folders, and users with editor, publishing editor, or owner permissions can create forms in a public folder.
- **Personal Forms Library** Use this library to publish personal forms. This library, which is stored on the local machine, cannot be shared with other users in the organization. Publish personal templates and forms to this library, and test your forms there before deploying them to your users.
- **Web Forms Library** A Web forms library is stored using OWA. It can contain Outlook forms that were converted to HTML or forms that you created using HTML.

Note that Outlook also allows you to create personal folder (.pst) files. These files implement the same functionality as your personal mail folders, so you can create new folders in these personal store files and publish forms to the folders in your PST. Because you can save the forms to your local hard disk, you can e-mail or copy them to a floppy disk for distribution.

To publish your forms to a forms library, follow these steps:

1. In design mode, from the Tools menu, choose Forms and then Publish Form As.
2. In the Look In drop-down list, select the forms library where you want to publish the form.
3. In the Display Name box, type the friendly name of your form. Outlook automatically fills in the Form Name box. (Note that this name will appear in the caption at the top of the form.) If you want to use a form name that is different from the display name, type a name in the Form Name box.
4. Click Publish.

Saving the Form Definition with the Item

As you learned earlier in this chapter, you should save the form definition with an item when you know that users will not have the form anywhere in their systems. If the definition is saved with the item, Outlook will use the saved version of the form, which is the most current. If the definition is not saved with the item, Outlook will look for the form definition in other locations. To save the form definition with the form, in design mode, click on the form's Properties tab. Select the Send Form Definition With The Item check box.

You must keep two issues in mind when you consider whether to save the form definition with the item. The first issue is security—particularly when VBScript is used to customize the form. To alleviate security concerns, Outlook provides a security measure when users receive an item with a form containing VBScript. Because Outlook supports customizing forms with VBScript, this is a necessary precaution. Without it, users could send malicious forms containing VBScript that could, for example, delete data on your hard drive. This security measure displays a warning message box, as shown in Figure 4-23, that allows the user to enable or disable the VBScript in the form. This security warning appears only if the form has the definition saved with it, is not published in any of the forms libraries, and has VBScript included with it. Outlook 2003 does not even display the warning dialog box—it simply disables all VBScript behind forms that are not published.

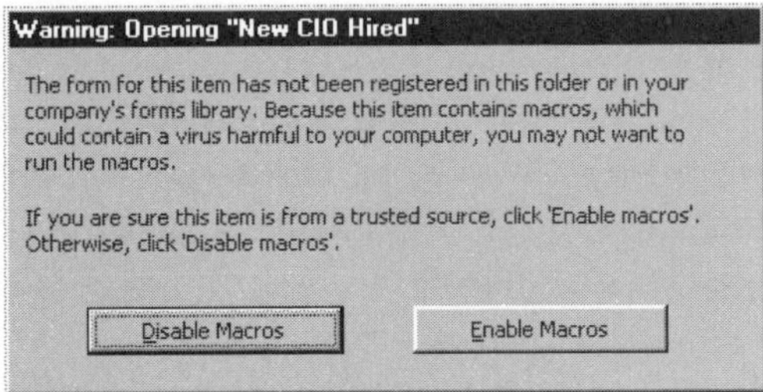
Warning: Opening "New CIO Hired"

The form for this item has not been registered in this folder or in your company's forms library. Because this item contains macros, which could contain a virus harmful to your computer, you may not want to run the macros.

If you are sure this item is from a trusted source, click 'Enable macros'. Otherwise, click 'Disable macros'.

Disable Macros | Enable Macros

Figure 4-23 The warning message that is displayed when a form has the definition saved with the item and also contains VBScript

The second issue is that when you save the form definition with the item, you cannot take advantage of the automatic update capabilities of Outlook forms. For example, if you change the form, the new version of the form will be included only with new items you create based on it. Any old items will use whatever form definition was originally saved with the item.

Saving the Form as an .oft File

Outlook allows you to save your forms as Outlook templates, or .oft files. This enables you to embed the form in a mail message and send it to users inside and outside the organization. Your users open the form using the attachment, and they either return the form completed or publish the form in a forms library. Saving your custom forms as .oft files is one way to create backups of your custom forms. To save a form as an .oft file, in design mode, choose Save As from the File menu. In the Save In box, select the location to which you want to save your file. In the File Name box, type a name for your file.

Enhancing Forms

You can enhance your forms and applications by taking advantage of additional features available in Outlook such as custom actions and voting buttons. If you have any Office products installed, you can tie into some of their capabilities. You can also add actions to your forms by customizing Reply and Forward forms and by using voting buttons. We'll take a look at these features next.

Extending Functionality with Office Documents

Outlook is part of Office, so you can tie together Outlook and the other Office programs. The main way you do this is by creating custom properties of Office documents that you can use in your Outlook views. For example, an Excel expense reporting form can use its cell values as properties in an Outlook view. You implement this sharing of properties by creating custom properties in the Office application. Following is a description of how to create custom properties in Excel. (You create custom properties in Word and PowerPoint in the same way, except that in Word, the custom properties link to custom bookmarks, and in PowerPoint, the custom properties link to objects in the presentation.)

1. Start Excel, type a value (such as *100*) in a cell, and select that cell.
2. From the Insert menu, choose Name and then Define.
3. In the Names In Workbook box, type the custom name you want for the cell, such as *Total*, and click Add. Click Close.
4. From the File menu, choose Properties.
5. Click on the Custom tab. In the Name box, type the name for your custom property. This can be the same name you selected for the cell.
6. In the Type drop-down list, select the type that corresponds to the values contained in the cell. For example, for a *Total* field, you should select Number.
7. Select the Link To Content check box. In the Source drop-down list, select the custom cell name you created in step 3.
8. Click Add. In the Properties box, you should see the name, value, and type of the property you just added.
9. Click OK.

After you create a custom property to hold the value from the Office document, you can add it to your Outlook view. To do this, save the Office document and drag and drop it into an Outlook folder. Right-click on the column headings for the view, and choose Field Chooser. In the Field Chooser, in the drop-down list, select User-Defined Fields In Folder. The *Total* field should be listed. You can use this property to group, sort, and filter your view. The only restriction on using this property is that you cannot edit it using in-cell editing in Outlook. The properties are read-only within Outlook, and you must use the Office document form to edit the properties. Figure 4-24 shows a view of expense reports inside an Outlook folder. The properties in the view are actually values from the Excel documents.

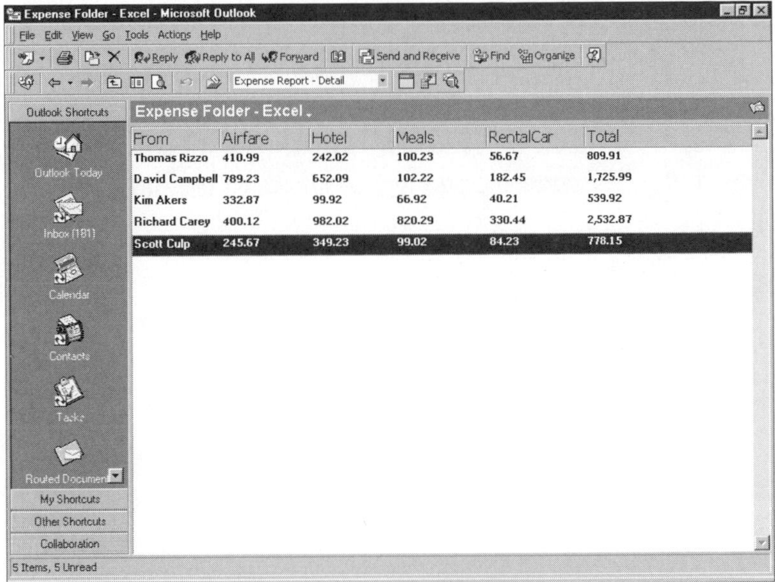

Figure 4-24 A view of expense reports inside an Outlook folder

Creating Actions

Actions are built-in or custom responses to a particular item on a form. They add dynamic functionality to your application without requiring you to do any coding. For example, in the Account Tracking application we'll look at in Chapter 8, individual contacts for the company can be created off the master company contact information. In a threaded discussion application, new items can be created as responses to posted items. We'll look at how to create actions for Outlook items and associate those actions with custom forms, and we'll examine some strategies for using actions in your applications.

By default, Outlook provides you with four built-in actions for items: Reply, Reply To All, Forward, and Reply To Folder. In many cases, you'll want to customize these actions or create your own. Figure 4-25 shows the Actions page, in which you create actions.

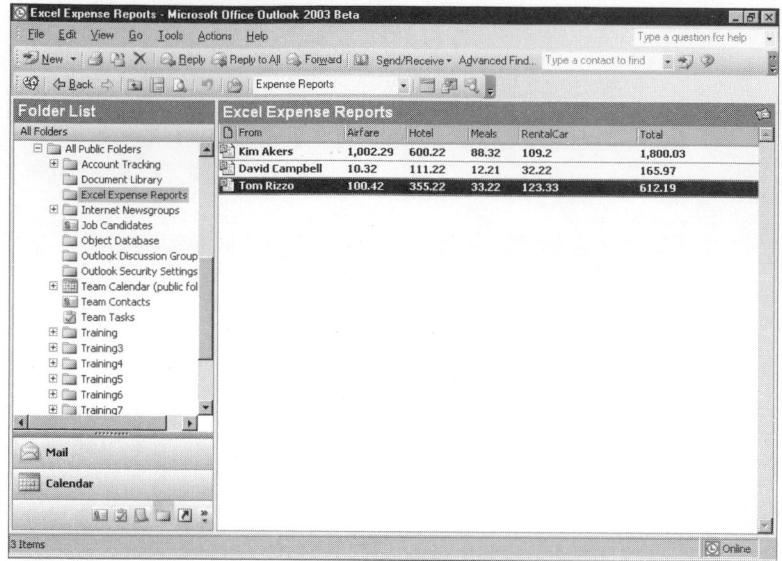

Figure 4-25 The Actions page of a form

To create a new action, follow these steps:

1. In design mode, click on the Actions tab.
2. Click the New button at the bottom of the form.
3. In the Action Name text box, type the name of your custom action. Outlook uses this name to display your custom action on the form or menu.
4. In the Form Name drop-down list, select a custom form. By default, Outlook displays the custom forms in the active folder. If the form you want is not in the active folder, you can locate it in one of two ways:
    - From the Forms menu, choose the Choose Form command. You can then select any forms in the forms libraries.
    - Type the name of a form in the drop-down list. Outlook will automatically enter its message class in the Message Class box.
5. In the When Responding drop-down list, select a method for copying the contents of the original item to the new form:
    - **Do Not Include Original Message** Outlook will not include the original item in the action.
    - **Attach Original Message** Outlook will attach the original message as an icon in the message body or in a separate window at the bottom of the message. The mail format of the attached message will be based on the user's settings.

- **Include Original Message Text** Outlook will include the original message text and some carriage returns before the text in the message body of the form.
- **Include And Indent Original Message Text** Outlook will include the original message text, indented in the message body of the form.
- **Prefix Each Line Of The Original Message** Outlook will prefix each line of the message with the default prefix character that the user selected from the Options/E-mail Options dialog box. By default, the character is a greater-than sign (>).
- **Attach Link To Original Message** Outlook will attach a shortcut to the original message. This functionality is useful when the reply item is a message form that is sent to the user and the original item is posted in a public folder. It allows the user to double-click on the reply item and quickly find the original item without having to search the public folder tree for the folder.
- **Respect User's Default** Outlook will use the settings for replying and forwarding messages that the user selected from the Options/E-mail Options dialog box.

6. In the Address Form Like A drop-down list, select how you want to address the form:
   - **Reply** Outlook will copy the contents of the original From field to the To field in the reply form. No Cc and Bcc information will be copied. The Subject field contains the text from the original item.
   - **Reply To All** Outlook will copy the contents of the original From field to the To field in the reply form as well as Cc information. The Subject field contains the text from the original item.
   - **Forward** Outlook will clear the address information in the reply form so the To, Cc, and Bcc fields will be empty. However, Outlook will copy the subject of the message to the reply form.
   - **Reply To Folder** Outlook will place in the Post To field the active folder so the reply automatically posts to the folder. Outlook will also copy the subject of the message to the Conversation field and clear the Subject field. This will allow you to create threaded views of your items.

- ❑ **Response** This option is used only with voting buttons.

7. Select the Show Action On check box to make your custom action appear on both the Actions menu and the toolbar or on just the Actions menu.

> **Note** Sometimes you will want only the action to appear on the menu. For example, if you create a CommandButton control on your form and program the control to execute the action when clicked, you might not want the action to also appear in the toolbar. In other cases, you might not want the action to appear on either the toolbar or the menu—for example, when the action is used in an event such as the close event for an Outlook form. In this situation, you do not want users to be able to launch this action—only your application.

8. Select an option in the This Action Will area. The default option, Open The Form, is the one you'll probably use most often. You can also select options to send the form immediately or to prompt the user about whether to send the form or open it for modification.
9. In the Subject Prefix text box, type the characters that should precede the Subject in the reply form. Outlook will automatically place a colon after the characters.
10. Click OK.

That's it. Now you have custom functionality on your form without writing a single line of code.

Modifying and Disabling Actions

Outlook allows you to modify and disable built-in and custom actions so you can control which actions are available to the user. When you disable a built-in action such as Reply All, you can replace it with your own. Disabling doesn't actually delete the action, so you can reenable it. You can also modify a built-in action so that its functionality is consistent with the functionality of your application.

You modify, disable, and delete built-in actions on the Actions page. To modify or disable the action, select the action on the Actions page and click the Properties button to open the Form Action Properties dialog box. To delete an action, select the action and click the Delete button. Once you delete an action, you must re-create it to get it back. If there is any chance you will need the action in the future, you're better off disabling it.

Actions and Hidden Forms

Actions can take advantage of hidden forms in your applications. Remember that selecting the Use Form Only For Responses check box on the form's Properties page hides the form from the user when the user selects a form to compose. Suppose you are writing a helpdesk application and on your form you want to include an action called Resolved. This action launches a new form, which the technician fills out to mark a ticket as resolved. Suppose also that you do not want users creating their own resolved forms. You can hide the resolved form from users by marking it as a response form and then setting permissions on the folder that holds the resolved forms that will prevent users from reading the items posted there. Technicians can open the items and click the resolved action to resolve the ticket, but users will not see the resolved form in the Choose Forms dialog box.

The Forms Cache

No Outlook discussion would be complete without mention of the dreaded forms cache. If you have never run into the issue I am about to describe, you will. Sometimes when your users attempt to open your form, they will get a message stating that the form could not be opened and that Outlook will use the standard form for that type of message instead. Most times, this problem is caused by forms cache corruption.

The forms cache is a local file system folder that, as its name implies, caches forms. Outlook uses the forms cache to minimize round-trips to the server if the form has not changed. The nice thing about the forms cache is that it automatically updates itself with the latest version of a form. You can usually find the physical folder in your file system that contains the forms cache by searching for the file frmcache.dat. This file is included in the folder to prevent multiple instances of a form from being cached.

This is one of the problems with the forms cache. Only single versions of the form can be cached. So if you publish your form to multiple form libraries, such as a folder form library and the Organizational Forms Library, the forms cache can easily get corrupted. You should therefore avoid publishing the same form to multiple forms libraries.

The second problem with the forms cache is that by default, the size for the cache is 2048 KB. This means that if you have a huge form (and I hope you do not build forms that big), Outlook will not be able to cache the form.

If you do run into weird errors in Outlook with your forms, you should clear the forms cache. You can delete all the files except frmcache.dat in the file folder, and Outlook will automatically download new copies of the forms. However, Outlook 2002 offers an even easier way to clear the forms cache: directly in the Custom Forms dialog box. From the Tools menu, choose Options. In the Options dialog box, click on the Other tab and then click the Advanced Options button. In the Advanced Options dialog box, click the Custom Forms button. In the resulting dialog box, click the Manage Forms button. In the Manage Forms dialog box, click the Clear Cache button. Exit and restart Outlook. Clearing the cache will solve most of your form corruption problems.

However, if your problem was not solved and you were saving backups of your form as an .oft file, you can delete the form from the Exchange Server and then republish it. This should remove any corruption from the form. If this does not clear the corruption, you probably have bigger problems than just forms in your Outlook client.

One-Off Forms

One other gotcha that you might run into when you use Outlook to build solutions is one-offing of a form. As discussed earlier, one-off forms are forms that contain their form definition directly in the item itself rather than querying or pulling from a forms library. A form can become a one-off form in Outlook in many ways. For example, if you hide or show a control on an Outlook form at run time, this will immediately one-off the form. Any sort of adding, hiding, or showing of controls on an Outlook form will one-off the form when the form is running in nondesign mode. This means that any future updates to the form definition will not be applied because Outlook will immediately save the form definition on the item and never check any form library for a new form definition.

You can identify a one-off form that you did not intend to one-off. One way is to look at the message class. One-off forms always have the default message class for that type of item but usually display a custom form. For example, if your custom form has a message class of *IPM.Note.MyCustomForm* and after running your form the message class of a saved item that uses the form appears to be *IPM.Note*, you have a one-off form problem.

Another way to identify a one-off form is to look at the size of the item. Because the form definition is saved on the item, the size of the item should increase.

The final way is to look at the icon for the item. If you are using custom icons, you will see that the icon will revert back to the standard icon for that type of item. This happens because the message class has reverted back to the standard message class for the type of item.

In a nutshell, avoid having your forms become one-off forms by avoiding the methods that one-off your forms and by quickly detecting when you are forcing Outlook to one-off your form via code.

Summary

In this chapter, we took the first step toward creating Outlook applications. The forms environment in Outlook is powerful but will probably meet only some of your needs. In some situations, you might want to extend forms with code that automates Outlook or other applications from your forms. In the next chapter, you will learn about the Outlook object model and how to leverage this technology in your applications.

5

Programming Outlook Using VBScript

In Chapters 3 and 4, you learned about folders and the form design tools that can assist you in developing collaborative applications in Microsoft Outlook. Outlook also provides a built-in development environment that uses the Microsoft Visual Basic Scripting Edition (VBScript) programming language. Using VBScript, you can write procedures to manipulate items, folders, controls, and the other objects in the Outlook object library. VBScript also lets you automate applications, such as Microsoft Excel, inside your own application so you can take advantage of their functionality.

The examples in this chapter are VBScript examples, as are many other examples in the book. Chapters 11 and 12, on Collaboration Data Objects (CDO), and Chapter 13, on Active Directory Services Interfaces (ADSI), are both interlaced with VBScript examples. By using VBScript, you can easily use the tools and APIs provided by Microsoft Exchange Server and Outlook. This is the power of the Windows platform: you need to learn only one language to develop applications in many different contexts.

This chapter is not an extensive tutorial on VBScript, but it does provide you with enough information on the language to work through the examples in this book. For more information, check out the VBScript help file included with the book's companion content. It has a language reference section and a simple tutorial. Many great books published by Microsoft Press also cover VBScript in more detail, as do a number of Web sites, such as *http://msdn.microsoft.com/scripting*, which has up-to-date information on VBScript and offers VBScript-related files for downloading.

You can, of course, use other development languages to create solutions that take advantage of Outlook, CDO, and the other Exchange Server tools. However, VBScript is integrated with the Outlook environment, and Outlook provides a number of great tools that take advantage of this integration.

The Outlook Script Editor

While creating forms and actions in the two previous chapters, you might have wondered what the View Code command on the Form menu does. When you choose this command, the Outlook Script Editor appears, showing you how VBScript is integrated with Outlook. Figure 5-1 shows the Script Editor displaying code from a sample application.

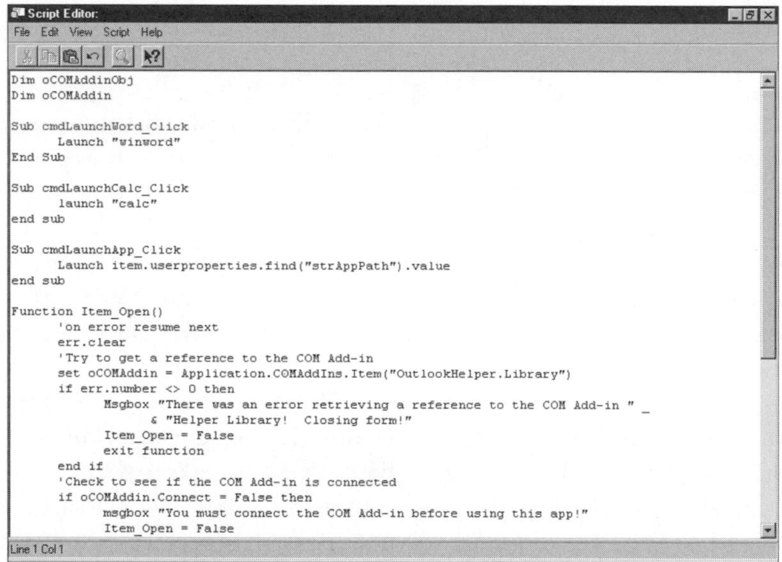

Figure 5-1 The integrated Outlook Script Editor

Using the Script Editor, you can add VBScript procedures and variables to your Outlook applications, use Outlook objects in your applications, and write VBScript to handle Outlook events. The Script Editor provides the Insert Event Handler dialog box, in which you select the event you want to write a handler for. We'll discuss Outlook events in more detail in Chapter 17.

The Script Editor also makes it easy to debug errant code in your application. Outlook provides line numbers when reporting errors; you can jump to a specific line of code by choosing Go To from the Edit menu, specifying the line number, and clicking OK.

VBScript Fundamentals

VBScript should be familiar to any developer who has experience with Microsoft Visual Basic or Microsoft Visual Basic for Applications (VBA) because VBScript is a subset of those languages. Version 5.6 of VBScript, which includes many enhancements over previous versions, ships with Outlook. As you would expect, you write VBScript applications in the same way you write applications in other programming languages—by using variables, procedures, and objects.

Working with Variables

Variables in VBScript correspond to locations in memory where you can store information while your application is running. Variable names consist of easily identifiable words or phrases, as in *myColor*, *myObject*, and *myTotal*. You are restricted in how you can name variables in the VBScript environment, however. The restrictions include the following:

- The variable name must begin with an alphabetic character. For example, *myTotal* is a legal variable name, but *$Total* is not.
- The variable name cannot contain an embedded period. For example, *this.total* is not a valid variable name.
- The variable name cannot contain more than 255 characters.
- The variable name must be in a unique scope when declared. (We'll discuss scope shortly.)

Declaring Variables

To make a variable available to your application, you must either explicitly declare it or have the VBScript language implicitly declare it for you. The easiest way to declare a new variable is to use the *Dim* statement in your VBScript code. For example, to declare three new variables, you can write either of the following code fragments:

```
'Declaring variables using separate lines
Dim myColor
Dim myObject
Dim Total

'Declaring variables on one line, separating the names with commas
Dim myColor, myObject, Total
```

VBScript does not require you to explicitly declare variables. If you do not declare a variable and you use that variable in your code, VBScript will automatically save storage space for your data and use your variable as the friendly name for that storage space. However, if you accidentally misspell a variable in your code, errors will likely occur in your application. These errors are particularly hard to track down because the VBScript interpreter does not know that a variable has been misspelled. To make these types of errors more manageable, VBScript provides the *Option Explicit* statement. If you use this statement, you must explicitly declare all VBScript variables or VBScript will display an error. The *Option Explicit* statement must appear before any procedures and is typically the first statement in your code.

Scope and Lifetime of a Variable

A variable's lifetime—how long it exists—is determined by the scope in which the variable is declared. A variable can have one of two levels of scope in VBScript: global (script-level) scope or local (procedure-level) scope.

Global variables can be called from any procedure within the running script. To create a global variable, you simply declare that variable outside any procedure in your script. It is best to group all global variables at the top of your script instead of scattering them throughout your code.

Local variables are declared within procedures and can be accessed only by the code in that procedure. If you attempt to call one of these variables from other procedures, VBScript will display an error. Also, procedure-level variables in different procedures can have the same name.

The next code snippet shows declarations for both script-level and procedure-level variables. You first create a new Message form in Outlook and enter design mode. Drag and drop a CommandButton control onto the second tab of the Outlook form. This control is automatically named CommandButton1. Display the Script Editor by choosing View Code from the Form menu. Type the following code in the Script Editor. When you finish, try running the form by choosing Run This Form from the Form menu and then clicking the button on the second tab.

```
'Make sure to enforce variable declarations
Option Explicit

'Global/script-level variables
Dim strName
strName = "Joe User"

Sub CommandButton1_Click
    'Procedure-level variable
    Dim strLocation

    strLocation = "Seattle, Washington"
    MsgBox strName & " is located in " & strLocation
End Sub
```

The scope in which the variable is declared affects the lifetime of the variable. For example, if a variable is declared with script-level scope, it will exist the entire time the script is running. If the variable is declared with procedure-level scope, it will be created when the procedure begins and destroyed when the procedure ends. This is why procedure-level variables are useful as temporary storage space inside your VBScript procedures. Some restrictions apply to VBScript variables and their lifetimes:

- You can have up to 127 procedure-level variables. Arrays count as only one variable.
- You can have up to 127 script-level variables.

To demonstrate variable lifetime, let's add a second CommandButton (automatically named CommandButton2) to the form and modify the script to look like the following:

```
'Make sure to enforce variable declarations
Option Explicit
'Global/script-level variables
Dim strName
strName = "Joe User"

Sub CommandButton1_Click
    'Procedure-level variable
    Dim strLocation

    strLocation = "Seattle, Washington"
    MsgBox strName & " is located in " & strLocation
End Sub

Sub CommandButton2_Click
   'Attempt to use variable from the previous procedure
   MsgBox strLocation
End Sub
```

When you run this code, click CommandButton1 and then click CommandButton2. If you do not have JIT debugging enabled, you will receive a "Variable is undefined: strLocation" error message from Outlook because the variable *strLocation* is a procedure-level variable and is destroyed after the *CommandButton1_Click* procedure is complete.

Data Types in VBScript

If you're a Visual Basic or VBA programmer, you've probably been wondering how to explicitly declare variables as different data types in VBScript. Well, you can't because VBScript supports only one data type, *Variant*. This data type is special in that it can hold many categories of information, such as text, numbers, dates, times, floating-point numbers, and objects. These categories of the

Variant data type are called *subtypes*. The *Variant* data type works in such a way that VBScript can figure out what subtype to use based on the information the variable holds; for example, if you place a number in a VBScript variable, VBScript will assume that the subtype is numeric and will treat it as a number.

By using the built-in conversion functions of VBScript, you can turn any variable into a different subtype. For example, by using the *CStr* function, you can convert an expression into a string. By using the *VarType* function, you can obtain the current subtype for a variable.

Working with Objects

You work with objects in VBScript in the same way you work with variables, but with one difference: when you work with objects, you use the *Set* statement to set the variable to point to the object. When you work with variables, you do not use the *Set* statement. To see why, consider the previous code example in which we set the *strName* variable to the string *"Joe User"* by using the following statement:

```
strName = "Joe User"
```

For an object, the syntax is different. Let's look at an example in which a hypothetical object named *Information* has a property named *UserName*. To access this object in VBScript, you must first set a variable to the object and then use the dot (.) operator to access the specific object property. You can also use the dot operator to access a specific method on the object. Following is a code snippet that shows the variable *myInformation* being set to the *Information* object. Using the *myInformation* variable, you can access properties and methods by using the dot notation.

```
'The variable that will hold the Information object
Dim myInformation

'Set a variable to the Information object
Set myInformation = Information
'Initialize the UserName property of the Information object
myInformation.UserName = "Michael Dunn"
'Get the UserName property of the Information object
msgbox "Current User is " & myInformation.UserName
'Call the Print method of the Information object
myInformation.Print
```

Early Binding vs. Late Binding

Binding describes the association of a variable with an object. In Visual Basic, binding for a particular variable can occur at compile time or at run time. Binding that occurs at compile time is called *early binding*. The advantage of early binding is that the compiler can perform some data-type and function-name checking. Binding at run time, or *late binding,* provides flexibility because the object does not have to be explicitly specified at compile time. The disadvantage of late binding, however, is that it requires additional code, which makes it slower than early binding. Because all variables in VBScript are declared as *Variant* data types, you cannot take advantage of early binding in your code. VBScript uses only late binding.

Constants in VBScript

When you use VBScript in Outlook, you must sometimes refer to predefined constants, such as *olMailItem*. You can't use the constant by name; instead, you must use its numeric value. For example, if you want to use the constant *olMailItem* in your code, you must use the value 0. VBScript does support user-defined constants and some intrinsic constants, but if the constants are defined in another file, you must either use the constant's numeric value or explicitly declare the constants in your code. You can find a list of all the constants and their values in the Outlook help file, or you can look up a particular constant in the Outlook Object Browser. The Object Browser is discussed later in this chapter.

Error Handling

The VBScript engine provides very basic error-handling functionality. For example, if a run-time error occurs, VBScript will display a message and stop execution. You'll probably want to override the default error handler because it returns messages that are not properly formatted for the user—they're really more for the developer. To override it, you must perform two steps in your VBScript code.

First you tell VBScript how to proceed when an error occurs. By default, all run-time errors in VBScript are considered fatal errors, which means that an error message appears and the script stops running. To override the built-in error message in your code, add the *On Error Resume Next* statement in each procedure in which you want custom error handling. This statement informs VBScript to continue executing, beginning at the line following the code that caused the error.

Second you need to figure out what the error was and what the application should do about it. VBScript provides a global object, *Err*, that has properties you can check to get information about the error. These properties include a number that identifies the error and descriptive text about the error. Typically, you check the error number property to see whether it is a number other than 0. If the property is 0, no error has occurred. The following code shows how to check the error number using VBScript:

```
If Err.Number <> 0 Then
    'Put your error-handling code here, and exit the procedure
    Exit Sub
End if
```

VBScript lets you clear the *Err* object after an error has been raised so that other error-handling routines in your application do not reprocess the error. VBScript also automatically clears the *Err* object for you after it encounters the *On Error Resume Next*, *Exit Sub*, or *Exit Function* statement. The following code snippet demonstrates how to display more detailed error messages by using the properties of the *Err* object:

```
Dim strMessage
strMessage = "The following error, " & Err.Description & _
             ", has occurred in the " & Err.Source & " application. " & _
             "The error number was " & Err.Number & ". " & _
             "Please report this error to the help desk."
MsgBox strMessage, 16, "Run-time Error #" & Err.Number
```

When determining what action to take in your error-handling code, you should consider whether to exit the procedure or just continue executing the code in the procedure. If the error is nonfatal, you should display a dialog box to inform the user of the error and continue executing. If the error is fatal, gracefully exit the procedure and continue the application if possible.

The Script Debugger

Using the Microsoft Script Debugger, shown in Figure 5-2, you can debug the VBScript code you add to an Outlook application.

To use the Script Debugger, you must first install it. It's best to get the latest version from *http://msdn.microsoft.com/scripting/*. The Script Debugger is also installed as part of Microsoft Office. If you do not already have the debugger, Office will automatically install it when you attempt to use it from Outlook.

You can launch the Script Debugger in three ways. The first way is to insert a *Stop* statement in your VBScript. When you run your form and the *Stop* statement is executed, the Script Debugger should automatically be launched. The second way is to launch it manually from a form that contains VBScript and is in run mode by choosing Forms, Script Debugger from the Tools menu. The final way is to enable JIT debugging; when you hit an error, the debugger is automatically launched.

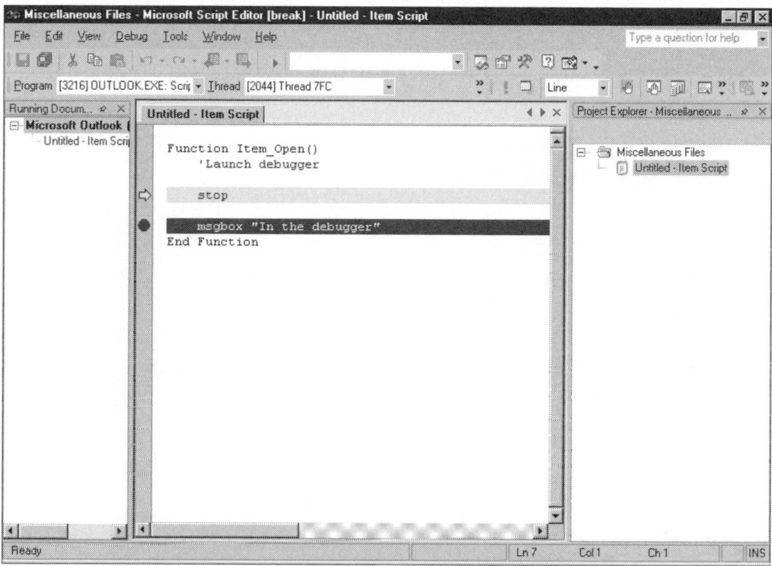

Figure 5-2 The Microsoft Script Debugger

Here are some common tasks you can perform with the Script Debugger:

- **Set a breakpoint** To set a breakpoint, insert a *Stop* statement in your VBScript code. When the *Stop* statement is encountered, the Script Debugger is launched automatically.
- **Control script execution** Once you're working with the Script Debugger, you can control the execution of the script. You can either step through a procedure line by line or step over procedures to have it run without having to step line by line. You can also cause the script to continue executing normally after it has been stopped.
- **View and change values at run time** Using the Command window of the Script Debugger, you can view and change the values for specific variables in your application. These changes are preserved

only in the context of the current script. For example, you can print to the Command window the value of a variable—such as the *Subject* property of the current item—by using the *Item.Subject* command. You can also change the value by typing an assignment statement such as *Item.Subject = My Debugged Script*. You can execute methods inside your script by calling them directly.

- **Trace the call stack** The Script Debugger includes all the currently running procedures in your script. This allows you to see how a particular procedure was called, which is especially helpful when that procedure is a part of a group of nested procedure calls. (You can view the source of your script in the Script Debugger, but it's read-only; to make changes to your script, you must go back to the Outlook Script Editor.)

Client Security

Before diving into the Outlook object model in the next chapter, we first need to look at some of the security features in Outlook that will affect your programming. You have probably heard of the Melissa, ILoveYou, and Funlove viruses that spread like wildfire across the Internet. Because Outlook's flexibility enables such viruses and worms to spread quickly by unsuspecting users clicking on items, Outlook restricts access to particular objects, methods, and properties in its object model. Outlook also restricts the file types that users can click on and open.

The Outlook Security Update

Outlook provides a powerful programming environment, but without safeguards, malicious code can use the extensible environment of Outlook to facilitate the creation and spread of computer viruses. Microsoft developed the Outlook Security Update to limit the exposure of typical end users to computer viruses and to help protect them from spreading viruses inadvertently.

The security update is available for Outlook 98, Outlook 2000, and Outlook 2002. It limits not only Outlook but CDO 1.21. It is automatically included with Outlook 2002 and 2003. For earlier versions of Outlook, you must download the security update and install it on your client.

The security update includes attachment precautions and object model guards, and it allows the administrator of a system to force end users to respect a certain level of security in their Outlook clients. The only issue with this level of control, as you'll see shortly, is that it is available only when Outlook users connect to Exchange Server and their messages are delivered to a server mailbox and not a PST. (An offline store (.ost) behaves like a server mailbox because the security settings folder is automatically synchronized with the offline store in Outlook.)

> **More Info** The book's companion content contains links to Microsoft Knowledge Base articles and tools to help you better understand and administer the new security model.

Attachment Security

E-mail viruses spread on the Internet mainly by users double-clicking on executables or scripts that they receive in e-mail. To counter this, the Outlook Security Update implements stringent attachment handling. Outlook uses levels to rank attachment types. It blocks Level 1 attachment types from the user interface, as shown in Figure 5-3. It also blocks programmatic access to Level 1 attachments. These attachments are still stored in Exchange and can be accessed by non-Outlook clients such as Outlook Web Access (OWA). However, Microsoft is working to secure OWA with the same security that you find in Outlook. (Note that custom forms do not support the Infobar shown in Figure 5-3; this means your users will not know that an unsafe attachment was included in the message or, for that matter, that the item had any attachment at all.)

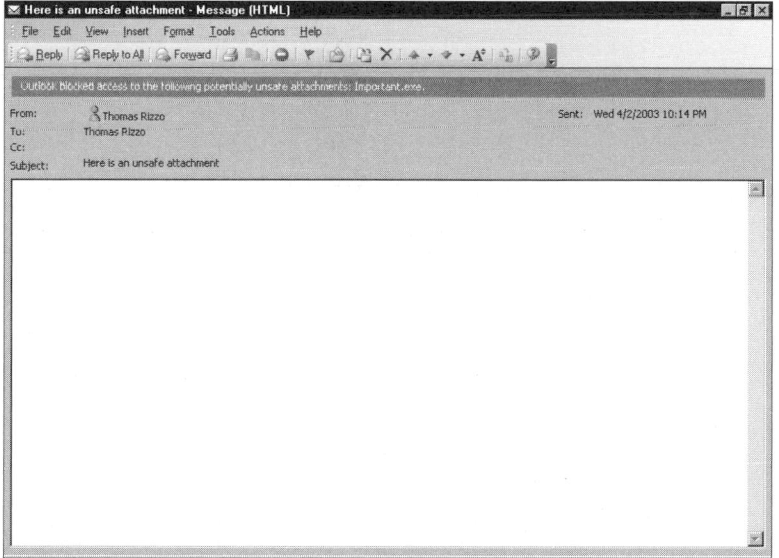

Figure 5-3 Outlook blocks potentially dangerous attachments.

Level 2 attachments must be saved to disk before being opened. This extra step encourages users to think about the attachment before simply double-clicking on it to run it. Figure 5-4 shows the interface for saving an attachment to disk.

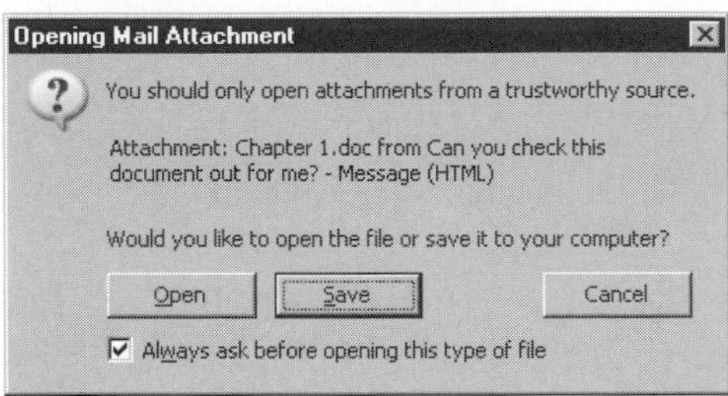

Figure 5-4 Saving an attachment to disk

In addition to blocking attachments, Outlook displays a warning to users if they attempt to send a message with what might be an unsafe attachment (as shown in Figure 5-5). As a result, users might think twice before sending potentially unsafe materials, and they will know that if a virus somehow got through the safeguards in Outlook, they might be unintentionally sending something harmful.

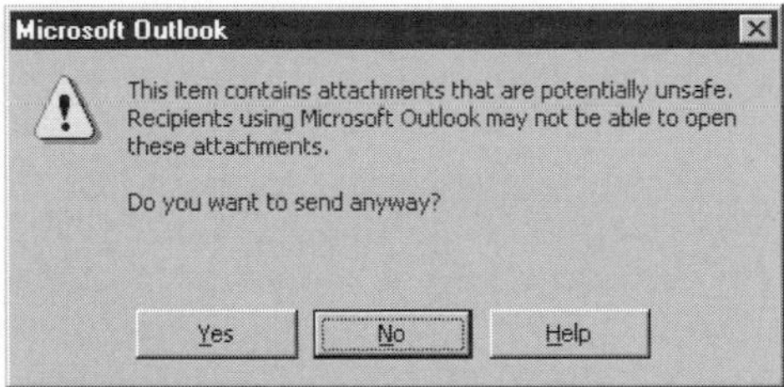

Figure 5-5 Outlook displaying a dialog box warning users about sending potentially unsafe attachments

Outlook also blocks in-place activation of embedded OLE objects. For example, if you insert an Excel spreadsheet in a rich-text message and send the message, the object will be received as read-only; the user cannot activate the object within the message window.

The book's companion content lists the attachment file extensions defined as Level 1 and Level 2. Many of the extensions that are blocked are obvious, such as .exe, .vbs, .bat, .cmd, and .com. Others aren't as familiar, such as .shs, .scr, .mst, and .mdz.

Object Model Security

Virus writers need a way to automate the distribution of their viruses—their intent is not to infect only a single machine. To achieve the greatest distribution with the least amount of suspicion, virus writers sometimes programmatically check each recipient's Outlook address book and send the virus to the first 50 recipients found. The recipient sees a message from a contact or a fellow employee, with some friendly text in the subject line, and opens the attachment. The virus then looks up another 50 addresses and continues replicating. You can see the snowball effect this mechanism has.

Virus writers can accomplish all this because of the robust object model in Outlook. To safeguard against this type of access, Outlook, CDO, and Simple MAPI have been beefed up with security features. The Outlook object model, and Outlook itself, communicates with Exchange Server through MAPI—specifically, Extended MAPI, the C++ programming interface for MAPI. Extended MAPI does not have security features built in because most virus writers are not C++ developers—they use script or Visual Basic instead. If you need to "get around" the security features in Outlook, you can write directly to Extended MAPI. Simple MAPI is a simplified version of MAPI that Outlook Express and the Office applications use when you send an e-mail message through those applications.

Chapters 11 and 12 cover CDO in detail. However, just so you know, the secure version of CDO is labeled CDO 1.21s, and the unsecured version is simply CDO 1.21. Only the security update has the secured version; Exchange Server does not install the secured version on the server.

Any application you develop that uses either of these object models is restricted. Outlook forms, COM add-ins, VBA code, folder home pages, and other programs must take into account the security restrictions. Table 5-1 lists the Outlook object model objects and the properties and methods of those objects that trigger the security restrictions and prompt the user to continue or cancel.

Table 5-1 Restricted Properties and Methods in Outlook

Object	Properties	Methods
Action		*Execute*
AddressEntries	All	All
AddressEntry	All	All

Table 5-1 Restricted Properties and Methods in Outlook

Object	Properties	Methods
AppointmentItem	*Body*	*Respond*
	Organizer	*SaveAs*
	RequiredAttendees	*Send*
	OptionalAttendees	
	Resources	
	NetMeetingOrganizerAlias	
ContactItem	*Body* (2003 only)	*SaveAs*
	Email1.Address	
	Email1.AddressType Email1.DisplayName	
	Email1.EntryID	
	Email2.Address	
	Email2.AddressType Email2.DisplayName	
	Email2.EntryID	
	Email3.Address	
	Email3.AddressType Email3.DisplayName	
	Email3.EntryID	
	HTMLBody	
	IMAddress	
	NetMeetingAlias	
	ReferredBy	
DocumentItem	*Body*	
DistListItem		*GetMember*
		SaveAs
ItemProperties	Any restricted properties mentioned in this table since *ItemProperties* lists all properties on a particular item. For example, the *To*, *CC*, and *SenderName* properties are restricted directly on the *MailItem* object and through the *MailItem* object's *ItemProperties* collection.	
JournalItem	*Body*	*SaveAs*
	ContactNames	

Table 5-1 Restricted Properties and Methods in Outlook

Object	Properties	Methods
MailItem	*Body*	*SaveAs*
	HTMLBody	*Send*
	ReceivedByName	
	ReceivedOnBehalfOfName	
	ReplyRecipientNames	
	SentOnBehalfOfName	
	SenderName	
	To	
	Cc	
	Bcc	
MeetingItem	*Body*	*SaveAs*
	SenderName	
Namespace	*CurrentUser*	
	GetRecipientFromID	
NoteItem	*Body*	
PostItem	*Body*	*SaveAs*
	HTMLBody	
	SenderName	
Recipient	All	All
Recipients	All	All
RemoteItem	*Body*	
ReportItem	*Body*	
TaskItem	*Body*	*SaveAs*
	ContactNames	*Send*
	Contacts	
	Delegator	
	Owner	
	StatusUpdateRecipients	
	StatusOnCompletionRecipients	
TaskRequestItem *TaskRequestAcceptItem* *TaskRequestDeclineItem* *TaskRequestUpdateItem*	*Body*	

Table 5-1 Restricted Properties and Methods in Outlook

Object	Properties	Methods
UserProperties		*Find*
UserProperty	*Formula*	

If you attempt to use a restricted method, Outlook will display a warning dialog box. For example, if you attempt to look up a recipient and then attempt to call the *Send* method of an e-mail item programmatically, you will receive the e-mail address dialog box shown in Figure 5-6 and then the Send dialog box shown in Figure 5-7.

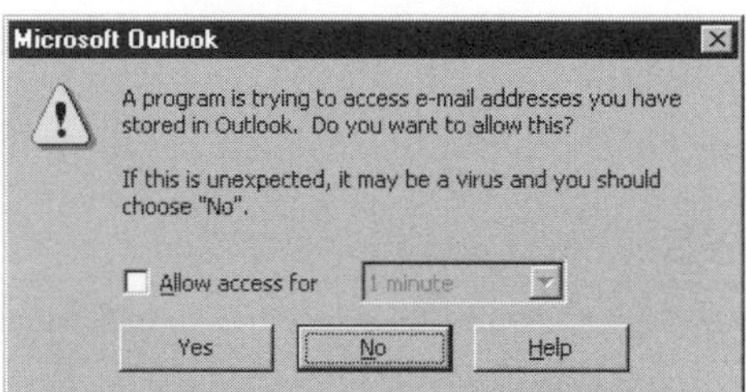

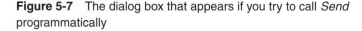

Figure 5-6 The address access dialog box

Figure 5-7 The dialog box that appears if you try to call *Send* programmatically

Because a user can click No in either of these dialog boxes, you must program defensively to make sure your code can handle the user's rejection and not fail or crash. We will look at how to program for the security update later in this chapter.

> **Note** You can use the *WordEditor* property of an *Outlook Inspector* object to trigger security warnings.

CDO Security

In addition to protecting the Outlook object model, the security update also protects CDO. The new version of CDO, CDO 1.21s, has safeguards in its object model to protect against virus writers. Unfortunately, if you programmatically query the version using the CDO *Session* object, you will still get CDO 1.21. If you look at the DLL itself, however, you can see that the version is CDO 1.21s. Furthermore, the CDO update is only for clients. Do not attempt to change the version of CDO on your Exchange servers until the appropriate server patch comes out.

Table 5-2 lists the objects, methods, and properties that are restricted in CDO.

Table 5-2 Restricted Properties and Methods in CDO

Object	Properties	Methods
AddressEntries	*Item*	*Add*
		GetFirst
		GetLast
		GetNext
		GetPrevious
AppointmentItem	Field properties listed under *Fields*	
Fields	*PR_SENT_REPRESENTING_ENTRYID*	
	PR_SENT_REPRESENTING_SEARCH_KEY	
	PR_SENT_REPRESENTING_NAME	
	PR_SENT_REPRESENTING_ADDRTYPE	
	PR_SENT_REPRESENTING_EMAIL_ADDRESS	
	PR_SENDER_ENTRYID	
	PR_SENDER_SEARCH_KEY	
	PR_SENDER_NAME	
	PR_SENDER_ADDRTYPE	
	PR_SENDER_EMAIL_ADDRESS	
	PR_DISPLAY_TO	
	PR_DISPLAY_CC	
	PR_DISPLAY_BCC	
	PR_ORIGINAL_DISPLAY_TO	
	PR_ORIGINAL_DISPLAY_CC	
	PR_ORIGINAL_DISPLAY_BCC	

Table 5-2 Restricted Properties and Methods in CDO

Object	Properties	Methods
Folder	Messages (folder containing contact items only)	
Message	Field properties listed under *Fields* *Sender*	*Send* (when the *ShowDialog* parameter is set to *False*)
Recipients	*Item*	*Add* *AddMultiple* *GetFirstUnresolved* *GetNextUnresolved* *Resolve*
Session	*CurrentUser*	*GetAddressEntry* *GetRecipientFromID*

As with Outlook, in CDO you must program defensively when you use these methods or properties because the user can click No in any of the popup dialog boxes. If the user does click No, CDO will return the error *E_ACCESSDENIED*, which is *&H80070005*.

Furthermore, as in Outlook, CDO does not allow you to programmatically access Level 1 attachments. The attachment count will return 0 if only unsafe attachments are in the collection.

Other Limitations

The Outlook Security Update also limits a number of developer features:

- **One-off forms no longer run scripts.** Outlook allows you to save the form definition and code with an item and send that item to others. If you do this in versions of Outlook previous to Outlook 2002, the user is prompted to choose whether to run any VBScript behind the one-off item. In Outlook 2002 and later, the VBScript behind all one-off items is disabled. The only way around this limitation is to publish the form to a trusted forms library, such as the personal, folder, or organizational forms library, or to change the default security settings by using the administrative security package described later in this chapter.
- **You can no longer use the *Execute* method to programmatically click the Send button on the Outlook toolbar.** Although most solutions don't use this approach—they use the *Send* method

instead—this change was made to stop anyone from trying to hack around the security update.

- **Use of the *SendKeys* method is restricted.** Visual Basic and VBA allow you to send keyboard commands to running applications by using the *SendKeys* method. Outlook displays warning dialog boxes if a program attempts to use *SendKeys* to perform restricted functions. Also, Outlook does not support using *SendKeys* to dismiss the warning dialog boxes; this prevents virus writers from programmatically bypassing these warnings from being displayed to the user.
- **Macro security for all Office applications except Access is set to High.** All Office applications except Access, which does not support macro security settings, have their macro security settings set to High by default. This setting means that you must either lower your settings to run VBA code in Outlook or move your VBA code to a COM add-in. (The fact that Access does not support macro security settings is the reason that all Access file extensions are included in the blocked attachments list.)
- **HTML mail is restricted.** By default, Outlook uses the Restricted Sites security zone in Microsoft Internet Explorer to display HTML mail. This setting stops scripts in HTML mail from running and ActiveX controls from being enabled.

Programming with the Security Update in Mind

In light of all the changes to Outlook described in the previous sections, your programs must be ready to respond to failed calls and to users clicking No in security warning dialog boxes. The easiest way to program your collaborative applications with the new security restrictions in mind is to leverage the built-in error trapping mechanism of the language you're using. For example, in Visual Basic or VBScript, you can make use of the built-in error handling capabilities. If a user clicks No in a dialog box, Outlook will return an error. Depending on how you want to handle the error in your program, you can either attempt the call again after informing the user what your program is doing or simply abort the action of your program.

The following code triggers the dialog box for sending a message. If the user responds negatively to the request to send, the program will display a message directing the user to an internal Web site that explains what the program is doing.

```
Dim oApp As New Outlook.Application
Dim oMailItem As Outlook.MailItem

Set oMailItem = oApp.CreateItem(olMailItem)
oMailItem.To = "thomriz@microsoft.com"
oMailItem.Subject = "New Message for you!"
On Error Resume Next
oMailItem.Send
If Err.Number = 287 Then
   'User said no!
   MsgBox "This application, written by your IT department, " & _
          "sends mail on your behalf.  To see the functionality " & _
          "that this mail performs, please visit our internal help " & _
          "at http://mycompany/app/myapp."
   Err.Clear
   oMailItem.Send
   If Err.Number = 287 Then
      MsgBox "The application cannot continue due to the user " & _
             "canceling the Send action."
    End If
End If
```

Customizing the Security Update

Although Outlook defaults to very stringent security controls out of the box, you can customize the security update for your environment. You can ease some of the restrictions by using the Administrative Security Package, which is included with the book's companion content. Rather than describe every aspect of the package, I'll simply highlight some of the features; see the book's sample files and the documentation for the package for complete details.

The Administrative Security Package

The administrative security package includes a number of tools to help you administer the Outlook Security Update:

- **OutlookSecurity.oft** This Outlook template, when used with the security public folder (described in the next section), allows you to customize the security settings for your Outlook user base.
- **Hashctl.dll** This DLL is used by the security settings template to specify trusted COM add-ins.
- **Comdlg32.ocx** This is the ActiveX control for common dialog boxes that allows the security settings template to show the File dialog boxes in which you can select a trusted COM add-in.
- **Readme.doc** You should read this document before you attempt to modify any of the security settings in Outlook. It describes the security settings you can manipulate with the administrative security package.

Public Folder for Security Settings

Before you can modify any security setting, you must create a public folder on your Exchange Server. This public folder must be named either Outlook Security Settings or Outlook 10 Security Settings, and it must be created in the root of your public folder tree. You should then modify the security settings on the folder so that only administrators can modify the items within it and all users have only read permission for the folder. This folder is used to store the security template and any security overrides that you set. In addition, Outlook automatically synchronizes this folder with the offline store of any Outlook user who uses an .ost file.

Outlook Security Form

After you set up your public folder, you can use the OutlookSecurity.oft file to set your security settings. You should first publish this form to the public folder you created. One convenient feature of the administrative security package is that you can set custom security settings for all users or you can make individual settings for a group of users. The readme file included with the administrative package has all the information you need to set up custom security. Figures 5-8 and 5-9 show the first two tabs of the Outlook form that you use to customize your security settings.

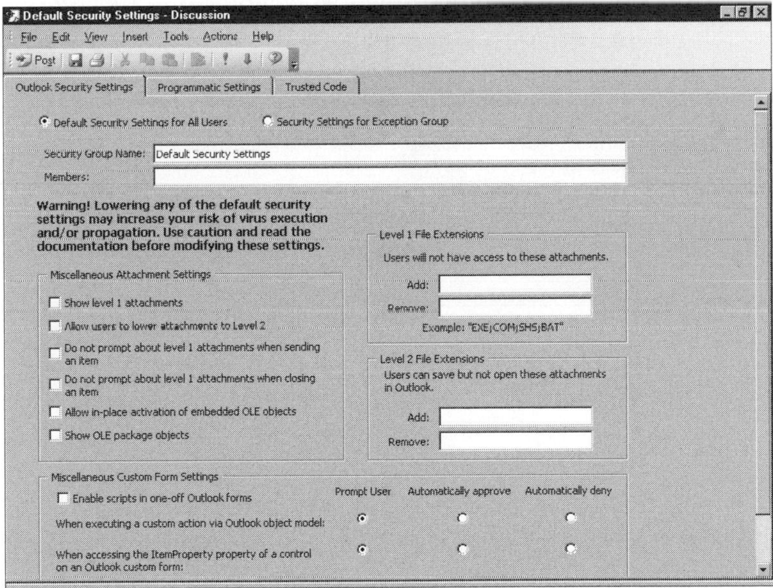

Figure 5-8 The Outlook Security Settings tab of the Outlook custom security form

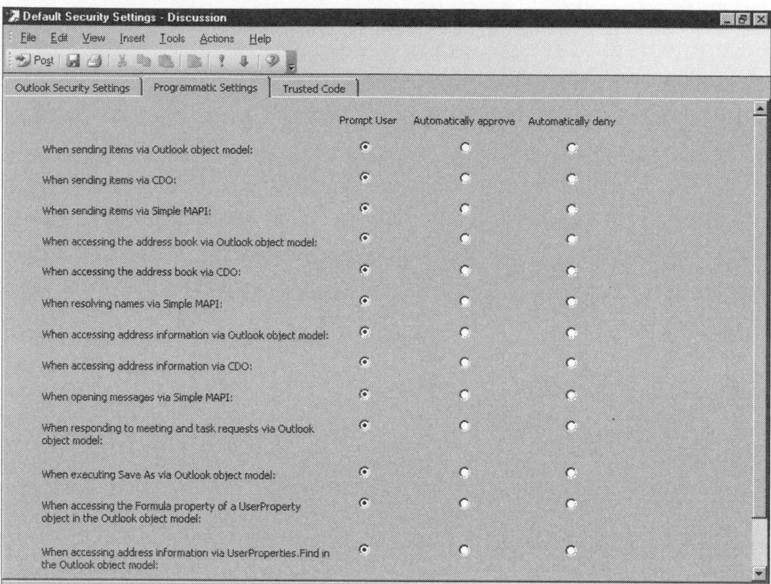

Figure 5-9 The Programmatic Settings tab of the Outlook custom security form

The last tab of the custom Outlook security form, the Trusted Code tab (shown in Figure 5-10), lets you specify which COM add-ins will be trusted.

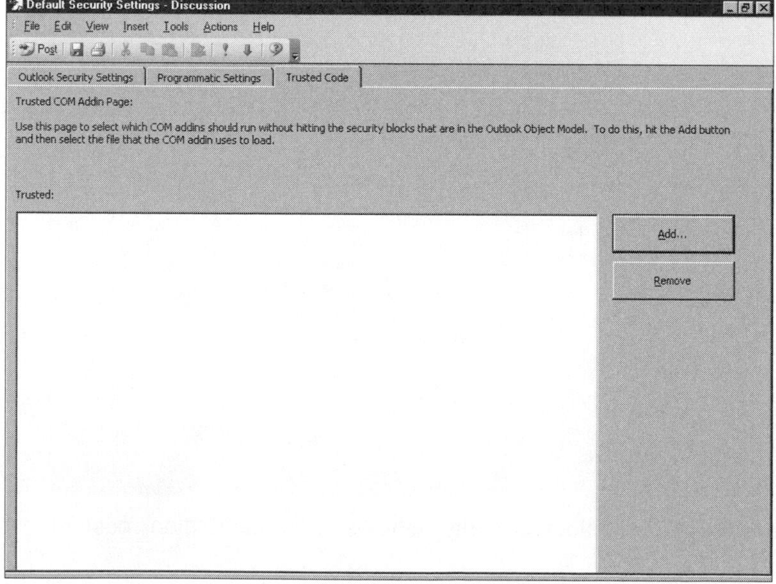

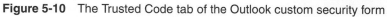

Figure 5-10 The Trusted Code tab of the Outlook custom security form

Outlook 2002 and 2003 support trusted COM add-ins. Outlook 2000 does not differentiate among COM add-ins, which means that every COM add-in in Outlook 2000 is trusted. When an add-in is trusted, it has full access to the Outlook object model. Calls from the COM add-in to the restricted properties or methods in the object model will not display prompts to the user.

This trust mechanism is powerful, but it does have some limitations. First and foremost, only a certain version of a COM add-in is trusted. Outlook takes a hash of the add-in DLL at the time you trust it and stores that hash in the form. Recompiling the add-in changes the value stored in the hash and the hash value that Outlook determines at run time for your COM add-in. So if you recompile your add-in after designating it as a trusted add-in on the custom security form, you will have to remove the add-in and then add it back to the trusted COM add-in list before deploying the add-in again.

Even though you can trust COM add-ins to have unrestricted access to the Outlook object model, this trust mechanism does not extend to CDO. If your trusted COM add-in calls any restricted CDO object model properties or methods, you must enable the security access for that CDO call on the Programmatic Settings tab of the Outlook custom security form. If you don't care whether users are prompted for that portion of the code in your add-in, you don't have to perform this step. However, opening CDO calls such as these to your users also opens the calls to virus writers. You should carefully weigh the risks of lowering your security settings against your ability to block viruses from entering your system as a result of lowered security settings.

Keep in mind that your COM add-in is passed an Outlook *Application* object as part of its *OnConnection* event. This *Application* object and all of its child objects are trusted. This means that calls from this object to restricted methods do not display warnings. However, if you create new Outlook objects programmatically by using *GetObject* or *CreateObject*, these new objects will not be trusted and will force warnings to appear to the users of your application.

> **Note** One good security change in Outlook 2003 is that if a form that sends mail or normally would trigger the security dialog boxes is published, it will not trigger the security update. This change is currently for Outlook 2003 only and has not been back-ported to previous versions of Outlook.

Summary

In this chapter, we looked at the fundamentals of programming Outlook, including scripting and security. When you combine these technologies with the power of the Outlook Object Model, Outlook forms, COM add-ins, and CDO, you can build some great collaboration applications. In the next chapters, you'll see some of these technologies in action in Outlook.

6

The Outlook Object Model

Two object libraries are available to you for creating Outlook applications: the Microsoft Forms 2.0 object library and the Microsoft Outlook object library. The Microsoft Forms 2.0 object library contains all the built-in controls for creating Outlook forms (discussed in Chapter 4), including text boxes, list boxes, and multipage controls. It is in the file called Fm20.dll. If you've developed Microsoft Office applications, you'll be familiar with these controls—they are the same controls you use to create forms in the other Office applications.

The Microsoft Outlook object library is in the file Msoutl.olb. It contains the objects you can use to develop custom Outlook solutions. It is not necessary to have a reference to either of these two libraries in your Outlook forms. Outlook automatically references the libraries so you can start taking advantage of their powerful features.

Getting Help with Outlook Objects

The documentation provided by Outlook can be very helpful when you create applications. The documentation file is Vbaol11.chm. (For Outlook 2002, the file is called VBAOL10.chm.) These files are normally stored in Program Files\Microsoft Office\... folder hierarchy, and you can also find both of these files on the book's companion Web site. The help file includes information about the Outlook object library and the Forms object library (as shown in Figure 6-1). Note that you must select the option to install VBA help in the custom settings for Office setup to have these files loaded onto your computer.

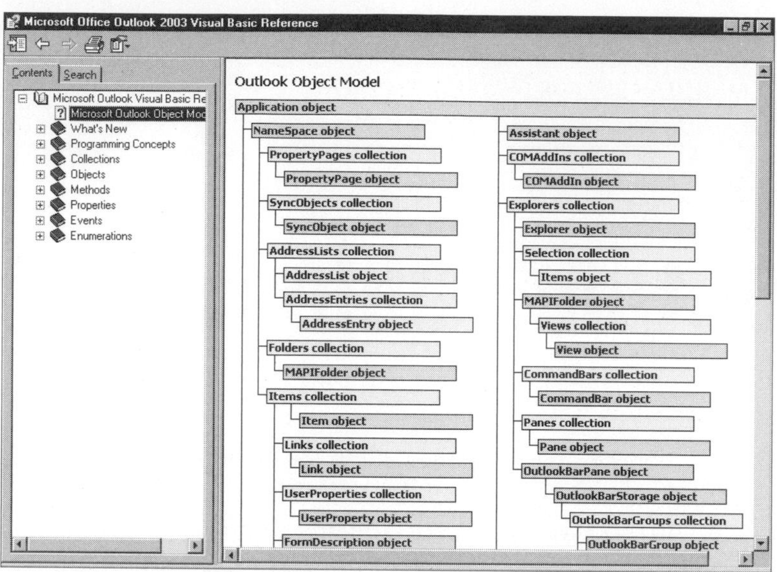

Figure 6-1 The Outlook Object Model hierarchy from the Outlook help file.

These help files include not only detailed information about the Outlook objects and controls in the libraries but also code samples to help you get started with the objects. This documentation is a great reference tool to use in conjunction with this book: the documentation outlines the objects and their properties, methods, and events, and this book shows you how to implement those objects to create complete solutions.

To access the Outlook object help file in Outlook, open a form in design mode. From the Form menu, choose View Code. From the Help menu, choose Microsoft Outlook Object Library Help.

The Outlook object library contains many objects. Because of the sheer volume and scope of functionality of these objects, I won't cover all of the objects in detail in this chapter. Instead, you should refer to the Outlook help file and MSDN to get the necessary base information about the Outlook objects. We will focus more on how to use the objects.

The Outlook Object Browser

To make finding objects in the Outlook object model easier, Outlook provides an object browser, shown in Figure 6-2. The Object Browser lists the available Outlook objects with their methods and properties. You can add an object to your code by clicking the Insert button. Clicking Object Help opens the Outlook object library help file.

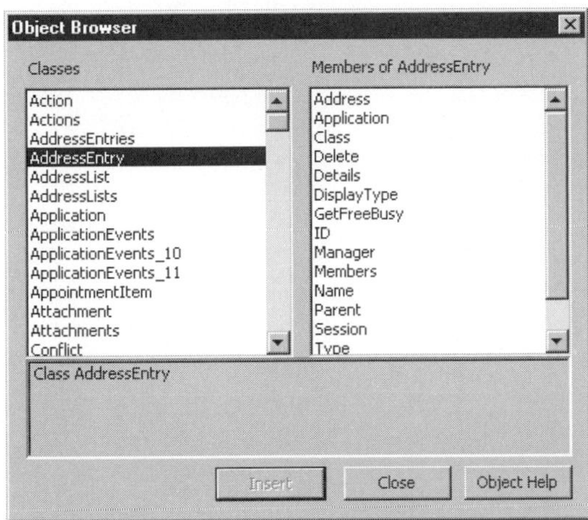

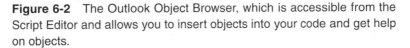

Figure 6-2 The Outlook Object Browser, which is accessible from the Script Editor and allows you to insert objects into your code and get help on objects.

Outlook provides an object browser only for the Outlook object library, not for the Microsoft Forms 2.0 object library. To browse the objects contained in this library, you must use the VBA Object Browser from another product or within Outlook. Also, because the Microsoft Forms 2.0 object library is shared across the Office applications, you do not need to add a reference to this library in the Object Browser: the library is added by default to the VBA Object Browser. The following steps explain how to view the Microsoft Forms 2.0 object library from Outlook. You can use the same steps in other Office applications.

1. From the Tools menu, choose Macro and then Visual Basic Editor.
2. From the View menu, choose Object Browser.
3. To view the Microsoft Forms 2.0 object library, select MSForms from the Project/Library drop-down list, as shown in Figure 6-3. (If you don't see MSForms in your drop-down list, add it to your references, as explained in the next step.)

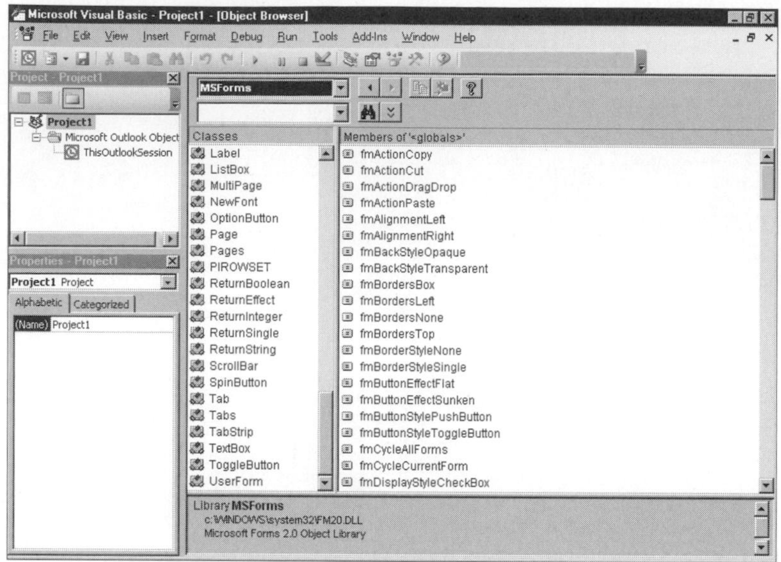

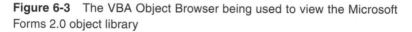

Figure 6-3 The VBA Object Browser being used to view the Microsoft Forms 2.0 object library

4. To view other object libraries, such as the Outlook object library, you must add a reference to the library: from the Visual Basic Editor Tools menu, choose References. Select the library you want to add as a reference. For Outlook, select Microsoft Outlook 11.0 Object Library and then click OK. For Forms 2.0, you can browse to c:\windows\system32\fm20.dll.

5. In the Project/Library drop-down list, select Outlook to view only the Outlook object library.

The Outlook Object Hierarchy

Let's look at the Outlook object hierarchy so you can gain an understanding of how you can use these objects. In Chapter 8, we will bring together a lot of the concepts you've learned when we build an account tracking application.

The Outlook object library is a hierarchy of unique objects, as shown in Figure 6-4. To create or edit certain instances of the objects, you must traverse the hierarchy.

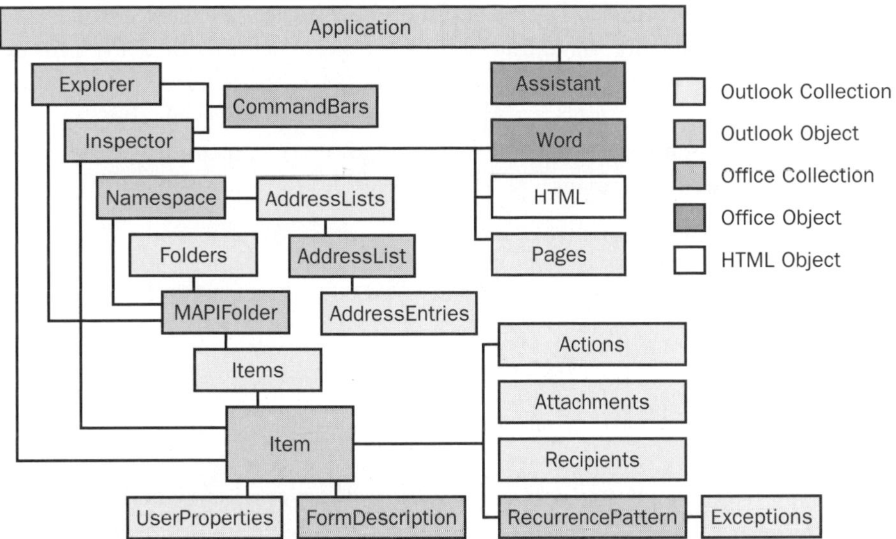

Figure 6-4 The Outlook object hierarchy

In the Outlook object library, user interface objects are separated from data objects. This separation allows you to change the controls on your forms without having to modify the underlying data, and it gives you great flexibility in controlling the user interface you present to your users.

The Outlook object library also includes items and collections. An item is a distinct object, such as the *ContactItem* object, the *TaskItem* object, or the *PostItem* object. A collection is a group of related objects. For example, the *Items* collection is a container for Outlook items.

In Outlook, you can access the specific items in a collection in two ways. The first way is to use the *Items* collection with an index that references the specific item you want to access. The following code illustrates this approach. It shows how you can use the *Items* collection to retrieve the items in your Inbox and display the message text:

```
Sub CommandButton1_Click
    'Open the Inbox using the GetDefaultFolder method
    Set oInbox = Application.GetNameSpace("MAPI").GetDefaultFolder(6)
    Set oItems = oInbox.Items
    'Notice how you can get the count
    MsgBox "Number of items in your Inbox: " & oItems.Count
    For counter = 1 to 3
        MsgBox oItems(counter).Subject
    Next
End Sub
```

The second way to access a specific item in a collection is by using a named argument. Instead of calling the *Items* collection with an index, you pass in a name that corresponds to the default property of the item and uniquely identifies the item. For example, the *Subject* property is the default property for the *MailItem* object. Therefore, you can pass in a unique subject name to identify a specific message. The following code shows how:

```
Sub CommandButton1_Click
    'Open the Inbox using the GetDefaultFolder method
    Set oInbox = Application.GetNameSpace("MAPI").GetDefaultFolder(6)
    'Point to the Inbox Items collection
    Set oItems = oInbox.Items
    'Display the body of the message that has the Subject
    'My Unique Subject
    MsgBox oItems("My Unique Subject").Body
End Sub
```

The topmost object in the Outlook object library is the *Application* object. All other Outlook objects are created from the *Application* object or from a child object of the *Application* object. The *Application* object provides four key functions that you can implement in your applications. First, the *Application* object provides one-step creation of any of the built-in Outlook types, such as the Contact, Task, or Message item. Second, the *Application* object allows you to obtain a reference to the currently active user interface elements, such as the Outlook window the user is displaying and the Outlook window that contains the folder the user is viewing. Third, the *Application* object provides an entry point for you to access the data that is stored inside Exchange Server by using the Outlook objects. Fourth, the *Application* object, because it is the topmost object, enables you to create or reference the other Outlook objects in your application. When you write code, you'll use the Outlook *Application* object extensively.

The code you write in Outlook forms is automatically passed an *Application* object and an *Item* object. The *Application* object corresponds to the currently active instance of Outlook, and the *Item* object corresponds to the currently active instance of the form. This frees you from having to write code that creates both of these objects in your application. In fact, I strongly recommend that you do not attempt to use the *CreateObject* function in Outlook to create another instance of Outlook. Instead, you should use the *Application* object that is available in your VBScript code.

Because the *Application* and *Item* objects are already created for your application, you can use their methods and properties immediately. For example, you can change the subject or body of the currently displayed item without having to search the current folder for the item, as shown in the following code:

```
Sub CommandButton1_Click
    Item.Subject = "This is using the built-in Item object"
```

```
    Item.Body = "This can make writing code easier"
    Importance = 2'High
    'Notice how you do not have to include the Item keyword.
    'However, it's a good practice to include the explicit Item
    'keyword to make your code more readable.
End Sub
```

> **Note** This implicit *Item* object and its methods and properties correspond to the type of Outlook item the form is based on. For example, the properties and methods for an implicit *Item* in a Contact form are different from those for a Message form. You need to be aware of this when you develop your applications.

As you saw with the *Item* object, the *Application* object is also automatically available to you in your VBScript code. The following code shows how to use some of the properties of the built-in *Application* object. Note that unlike the *Item* object, the built-in *Application* object requires you to explicitly place the word *Application* before any of its methods or properties.

```
Sub CommandButton1_Click
    MsgBox Application.Version
    Application.Quit 'Quits Outlook
End Sub
```

Outlook Objects in Detail

In this section, I'll describe some of the objects, methods, properties, and events in Outlook that you can use in your own applications. Most of these objects are supported in Outlook 2002 and later. I'll cover new objects in Outlook 2003 later in the chapter. I'll assume that you have basic knowledge of the standard Outlook objects, such as the *Application*, *Namespace*, and *MAPIFolder* objects. (You can look at the sample applications included with this book to understand how to use these basic Outlook objects in an application.)

Outlook Events

Outlook supports 11 events that are called when users of an Outlook application use some of the built-in capabilities of Outlook. You can write code to handle these events as well as disable these events. We'll look next at how to add event-handling code to your application.

> **Note** The events discussed in this section are not available in VBScript. You must use VBA, Visual Basic, Visual C#, or Visual C++ to use these events. In addition, some of the methods and properties trigger security dialog boxes. See Chapter 5 for more information on the security update for Outlook.

Writing Event Handlers

The Outlook Script Editor makes adding event handlers to your VBScript code quite easy. In the Script Editor, choose Event Handler from the Script menu. Select the event you want to write a handler for, and then click Add. Outlook automatically adds a skeleton function with the correct parameters. All you need to do is fill in your specific code to handle the event. The Script Editor does not, however, provide the option to add skeleton code to handle the events your controls support. In this case, you must write your event handlers from scratch. In Outlook, the event names are preceded with the word *Item*. For example, the open event handler is named *Item_Open*.

Disabling Events

You can prevent events and their default behavior from occurring by setting the function value, or the name of the event, to *False*. You can then place your own code inside the event handler to replace the standard behavior. For example, if you write a custom Contact form that synchronizes contact information with a database, you can disable the *Write* event when the database is not available, preventing Outlook from saving the item and also preventing the two data sources, Outlook and the database, from being out of sync. The following code sample shows an example of this:

```
Function Item_Write()
   'Call the CheckDatabase function
   boolIsOnline = CheckDatabase()
   If boolIsOnline = False Then
      'No database. Do not save the item.
      Item_Write = False
      MsgBox "The database is offline"
   End If
End Function

Function CheckDatabase
   'You would put your database connection code here
   CheckDatabase = False
End Function
```

Events in Outlook Forms

Here is a list of the built-in Outlook events:

- *Item_AttachmentAdd*
- *Item_AttachmentRead*
- *Item_BeforeAttachmentSave*
- *Item_BeforeCheckNames*
- *Item_BeforeDelete*
- *Item_Close*
- *Item_CustomAction*
- *Item_CustomPropertyChange*
- *Item_Forward*
- *Item_Open*
- *Item_PropertyChange*
- *Item_Read*
- *Item_Reply*
- *Item_ReplyAll*
- *Item_Send*
- *Item_Write*

Outlook also includes another event, named *Click*, that you can use with your custom controls. The *Click* event is the only control event supported in Outlook. The following list describes the sequence of some of these events when you perform common Outlook tasks:

- **Creating a new item using a form or in-cell editing** When a user attempts to create a new item in Outlook either by clicking the new mail icon to open a form or by starting to type information into a new item row in a view with in-cell editing enabled, Outlook fires the *Item_Open* event.
- **Sending an item** When a user attempts to send an item in Outlook, the *Item_Send* event is fired first, followed by the *Item_Write* event and then the *Item_Close* event. If you disable any event in the sequence, the remaining events in that sequence will not fire.

> **Note** Sometimes you'll want to open your Outlook form without executing the VBScript code contained in the form. To do this, hold down the Shift key while opening the form. This method of opening forms is useful while you're designing your applications because it prevents VBScript functions from adding undesired data into the form.

- **Posting an item** When a user attempts to post an item, the *Item_Write* event is fired and then the *Item_Close* event is fired. If you disable any event in the sequence, the subsequent events in that sequence will not fire.
- **Saving an item** When a user tries to save an item, the *Item_Write* event is fired.
- **Opening an item** When a user opens an item, the *Item_Read* event is fired, followed by the *Item_Open* event.
- **Closing an item** When a user attempts to close an item, the *Item_Close* event is fired.

Objects and Collections

Outlook contains some collections and objects that consist of item types that you can create, such as distribution lists, as well as user interface controls, such as custom property pages.

DistListItem Object

The *DistListItem* object represents a distribution list in a Contacts folder. A distribution list allows your users to do away with personal address books. The *DistListItem* object can hold multiple recipients, both those from the address list in Exchange Server as well as one-off addresses.

You can use the *CreateItem* method on the *Application* object to create a new *DistListItem* object, or you can add the *DistListItem* object to a Contacts folder by using the *Add* method of the *Items* collection for the folder. The following code shows how to use both methods to create a *DistListItem* object:

```
Dim oApp As Outlook.Application
Dim oNS As Outlook.NameSpace
Dim oExplorer As Outlook.Explorer
Dim oContact As Outlook.MAPIFolder
Dim oItems As Outlook.Items
Dim oDistList As Outlook.DistListItem
Dim oDistList2 As Outlook.DistListItem
```

```
Set oApp = CreateObject("Outlook.Application")
Set oNS = oApp.GetNamespace("MAPI")
Set oExplorer = oApp.ActiveExplorer
Set oContact = oNS.GetDefaultFolder(olFolderContacts)
Set oItems = oContact.Items
Set oDistList = oItems.Add(olDistributionListItem)
oDistList.DLName = "My new distribution list"
oDistList.Save
Set oDistList2 = oApp.CreateItem(olDistributionListItem)
oDistList2.DLName = "My other new distribution list"
oDistList2.Save
```

The *DistListItem* object inherits many of the same methods and properties that other Outlook items inherit, but it also has some methods and properties of its own, which I'll describe in the following sections.

Adding new members to the distribution list To add new members to your *DistListItem* object, you use the *AddMembers* method. Before you call this method, however, you must create a new *Recipients* collection to hold the names of the members you want to add to the distribution list. The easiest way to create a *Recipients* collection is to create a new mail item and use the *Recipients* collection available on the mail item. You can then populate the collection and create the new *DistListItem* object as shown here:

```
Dim oDistList As Outlook.DistListItem
Dim oTempMail As Outlook.MailItem
Dim oTempRecips As Outlook.Recipients

Set oDistList = oItems("My new distribution list")
Set oTempMail = oApp.CreateItem(olMailItem)
Set oTempRecips = oTempMail.Recipients
oTempRecips.Add "Thomas Rizzo"
oTempRecips.Add "Aaron Con"
oDistList.AddMembers oTempRecips
oDistList.Display
```

If you would rather add a single user to the distribution list, you should use the *AddMember* method (which is supported only in Outlook 2002 and later). This method takes the *Recipient* object of the user you want to add. It is different from the *AddMembers* method, which takes a *Recipients* collection object.

Removing members from a distribution list To remove members from your *DistListItem* object, use the *RemoveMembers* method. This method is similar to the *AddMembers* method; you must pass it to a valid *Recipients* collection object that contains the members you want to remove. The following code shows how to use this method:

```
Dim oDistList As Outlook.DistListItem
Dim oTempMail As Outlook.MailItem
Dim oTempRecips As Outlook.Recipients
```

```
Set oDistList = oItems("My new distribution list")
Set oTempMail = oApp.CreateItem(olMailItem)
Set oTempRecips = oTempMail.Recipients
oTempRecips.Add "Thomas Rizzo"
oTempRecips.Add "Aaron Con"
oDistList.RemoveMembers oTempRecips
oDistList.Display
```

If you would rather remove a single user from a distribution list, you should use the *RemoveMember* method (which is supported only in Outlook 2002 and later), which removes the specified *Recipient* object from a distribution list.

Retrieving the name of the distribution list The *DistListItem* object contains a property named *DLName* that you can use to set or return the name of the distribution list. The following code finds all the distribution lists in your Contacts folder and returns their names in a message box:

```
Dim oItem As Outlook.DistListItem

RestrictString = "[Message Class] = 'IPM.DistList'"
Set oRestrictedItems = oItems.Restrict(RestrictString)
For Each oItem In oRestrictedItems
    strDLs = strDLs & vbLf & oItem.DLName
Next
MsgBox "You have " & oRestrictedItems.Count & " DL(s) in your " _
   & "contacts folder.  Names: " & strDLs
```

Counting the number of users in a distribution list Sometimes you'll want to know how many users a distribution list contains before you send items to it. To retrieve the count of the number of users on a distribution list, you must use the *MemberCount* property. Note that this count does not include the member count for distribution lists nested in the original list. For example, if you have a distribution list with 20 members and one of those members is a distribution list with 50 members, the *MemberCount* property will return 20, not 70. The following code finds all the distribution lists in your Contacts folder and returns a sum of all the *MemberCount* properties:

```
RestrictString = "[Message Class] = 'IPM.DistList'"
Set oRestrictedItems = oItems.Restrict(RestrictString)
For Each oItem In oRestrictedItems
    intCount = intCount + oItem.MemberCount
Next
MsgBox "Member count for all DLs is: " & intCount
```

SyncObject Object and *SyncObjects* Collection

Outlook allows users to set up quick synchronization folder groups. These synchronization groups, or profiles, allow users to configure different synchronization scenarios, such as which folders are synchronized off line and which filters apply to those folders. Users can then select the proper profile for their connection speed or synchronization preferences.

The Outlook *SyncObjects* collection contains the synchronization profiles set up for the current user. Your program can start or stop any of these synchronization profiles by using the methods of the *SyncObject* object. You can also monitor the progress of the synchronization by hooking into the events provided by the *SyncObject* object. These events are *SyncStart*, *Progress*, *OnError*, and *SyncEnd*. We'll look at how to use the *SyncObjects* collection and the *SyncObject* object next.

Finding a *SyncObject* in the *SyncObjects* collection The *SyncObjects* collection contains one property, named *Count*, and one method, named *Item*, that you can use to discover more information about the *SyncObject* objects in the collection. The *Count* property returns the number of *SyncObject* objects contained in the collection. The *Item* method allows you to identify an object in the collection by specifying a numeric or named index. By using the *Item* method, you can quickly retrieve a *SyncObject* object.

The next code example shows you how to use the *Item* method and the *Count* property. First the code finds a *SyncObject* object named *slow modem*, and then it displays the number of synchronization profiles the user has set up. You cannot create or delete *SyncObject* objects programmatically. Only the user can do this through the Outlook user interface.

```
Dim oSyncObjects As Outlook.SyncObjects
Dim oSyncObject As Outlook.SyncObject

Set oSyncObjects = oNS.SyncObjects
Set oSyncObject = oSyncObjects("slow modem")
MsgBox "You have " & oSyncObjects.Count & " SyncObjects!"
strNames = vbLf
For Each oSyncObject In oSyncObjects
    strNames = strNames & vbLf & oSyncObject.Name
Next
MsgBox "Names: " & strNames
```

Starting and stopping synchronization After you find a *SyncObject* object, you might want to start or stop the synchronization process. You can do this by using the *Start* and *Stop* methods of the *SyncObject* object, respectively, as shown here:

```
Set oSyncObjects = oNS.SyncObjects
Set oSyncObject = oSyncObjects("slow modem")
oSyncObject.Start
```

Monitoring the progress of synchronization In Visual Basic, to implement the events the *SyncObject* provides, you must first declare a *SyncObject* variable with the *WithEvents* keyword. The *SyncStart* event is fired when Outlook starts synchronizing using a particular *SyncObject*. The *SyncEnd* event is fired immediately after Outlook finishes synchronizing. The *OnError* event is fired if Outlook encounters an error when synchronizing. The *OnError* event procedure is passed both the error code and the description of the error as a string.

The final event, *Progress*, is fired periodically by Outlook to report on the progress of synchronization. Four parameters are passed to the *Progress* event procedure: *State*, *Description*, *Value*, and *Max*:

- *State* is a *Long* data type that indicates the status of the synchronization. *State* can have the value *olSyncStopped (0)* or *olSyncStarted (1)*.
- *Description* is a string that describes the current state of synchronization.
- *Value* is a variable of the *Long* data type that indicates the current value in the synchronization process. *Value* can be the number of items synchronized in the folder.
- *Max* is a *Long* parameter that indicates the maximum value for the third parameter. The ratio of the third parameter (the value) to the fourth parameter (the maximum) is the percentage of the synchronization process that is complete.

```
Private Sub oSyncObject_Progress( _
    ByVal State As Outlook.OlSyncState, _
    ByVal Description As String, ByVal Value As Long, _
    ByVal Max As Long)

    strPercent = Description & Str(State / Max * 100) & "% "
    MsgBox strPercent & vbLf & "State: " & State & vbLf & _
        "Max: " & Max
End Sub
```

Outlook 2002 Objects

The objects described in the following sections are supported in Outlook 2002 and later.

ItemProperties Collection and the *ItemProperty* Object

The *ItemProperties* object is related to the *UserProperties* collection in that it contains all the items in the *UserProperties* collection in addition to the built-in Outlook properties. *UserProperties* returns only custom properties. The *ItemProperties* collection returns a collection of *ItemProperty* objects. When you use the *Add* or *Remove* method on the collection, you can add or remove custom properties only. The main purpose of the *ItemProperties* collection is to provide an easy way for your application to scroll through the properties on an Outlook item as a collection and not have to call each property individually by name.

The *ItemProperty* object has properties and methods that are quite similar to those of *UserProperty*. The main difference is that the *ItemProperty* object has the *IsUserProperty* property—a Boolean that specifies whether the property is a custom property. Unfortunately, these objects do not solve the problem of gaining access to MAPI properties on items that might not be part of the built-in properties that Outlook returns or properties that you created. Also, these objects are not supported on *AddressEntry* objects, which means you still have to use Collaboration Data Objects (CDO) to access more detailed item and user information. The following code shows how to use these objects:

```
'Item Properties example
Dim oApp As New Outlook.Application
Dim oNS As Outlook.NameSpace
Set oNS = oApp.GetNamespace("MAPI")

'Retrieve an Item that has custom and built-in properties
Dim oFolder As Outlook.MAPIFolder
Set oMailbox = oNS.Folders.Item("Mailbox - Thomas Rizzo")
Set oFolder = oMailbox.Folders("SPS Sync")

Dim oItem As Outlook.PostItem
Set oItem = oFolder.Items.GetFirst
'ItemProperties is zero based
Dim oItemProperties As Outlook.ItemProperties

Set oItemProperties = oItem.ItemProperties
Dim oItemProperty As Outlook.ItemProperty

Debug.Print "There are " & oItemProperties.Count & _
    " properties in the collection."

'Certain Address properties WILL trigger the security dialog box

For x = 0 To oItemProperties.Count - 1
    Set oItemProperty = oItemProperties.Item(x)
    On Error Resume Next
    Debug.Print oItemProperties(x).Name & " " & " " & _
    oItemProperties(x).Type & " " & oItemProperties(x).Value & _
    " " & oItemProperties(i).IsUserProperty
Next
```

Reminders Collection and *Reminder* Object

The *Reminders* collection is made up of *Reminder* objects. These objects were introduced in Outlook 2002 and provide a better means of working with reminders than that provided in earlier versions of Outlook. The key point about the *Reminders* collection and *Reminder* object is that the collection supports a number of events that you can use to track when reminders are fired, dismissed, snoozed, added, deleted, or changed. The *Reminders* collection is a property of the Outlook *Application* object. Table 6-1 lists the events that the *Reminders* collection supports.

Table 6-1 Events for the *Reminders* Collection

Event	Description
BeforeReminderShow	Fires before the new reminder dialog box is displayed in the user interface. This event can be canceled so that you can display your own user interface for reminders.
ReminderAdd	Fires when a new reminder is added to the collection. You are passed the reminder as a *Reminder* object.
ReminderChange	Fires when a reminder is changed. You are passed the reminder as a *Reminder* object.
ReminderFire	Fires just before a reminder is fired. You are passed the reminder as a *Reminder* object. You can use this event to forward the reminder to a cell phone or other device.
ReminderRemove	Fires when a reminder is removed from the collection—for example, by a call to the *Remove* method on the *Reminders* collection, dismissal of a reminder programmatically or through the user interface, turning off of a meeting reminder, or deletion of an item with a reminder on it. You are not passed the reminder that is removed, so you must store the original reminders and then compare the original list to the list with the reminder removed.
Snooze	Fires when you call the *Snooze* method or a user clicks Snooze in the user interface. You are passed the reminder that is being snoozed as a *Reminder* object.

The following example shows how to use these events. Notice that the *Reminders* collection is declared using the *WithEvents* keyword.

```
Dim WithEvents oReminders As Outlook.Reminders

Private Sub Command2_Click()
    'Outlook Reminders Example
    Dim oApp As New Outlook.Application
    Dim oNS As Outlook.NameSpace
    Set oNS = oApp.GetNamespace("MAPI")
    Set oReminders = oApp.Reminders
End Sub

Private Sub oReminders_BeforeReminderShow(Cancel As Boolean)
    'You can add custom code to display your own reminder dialog box here
    'by setting Cancel = True
End Sub
```

```
Private Sub oReminders_ReminderAdd( _
    ByVal ReminderObject As Outlook.Reminder)
    'Fired after a reminder is added to the collection

    MsgBox "You added a reminder to an item called " & _
           ReminderObject.Item.Subject & _
           " and the reminder will fire " & _
           ReminderObject.NextReminderDate
End Sub

Private Sub oReminders_ReminderChange( _
    ByVal ReminderObject As Outlook.Reminder)
    'Fired after you change a reminder

    MsgBox "You changed a reminder on the item called " & _
        ReminderObject.Item.Subject & _
        " and the reminder will fire " & _
        ReminderObject.NextReminderDate
End Sub

Private Sub oReminders_ReminderFire( _
    ByVal ReminderObject As Outlook.Reminder)
    'Fired when the reminder fires
End Sub

Private Sub oReminders_ReminderRemove()
    'Fired when a reminder is removed
    'You do not know which reminder was removed
    'unless you scroll through the collection

    'On startup you can set a variable to the reminders collection and
    'then compare the original variable to the current reminders collection
    'to see which one was removed
End Sub

Private Sub oReminders_Snooze(ByVal ReminderObject As Outlook.Reminder)
    'Fired when snoozed

    MsgBox "You snoozed a reminder on the item called " & _
        ReminderObject.Item.Subject & _
        " and the reminder will fire " & _
        ReminderObject.NextReminderDate
End Sub
```

The *Reminder* object has some unique methods and properties, which are listed in Table 6-2.

Table 6-2 Unique Methods and Properties of the *Reminder* Object

Method or Property	Description
IsVisible	A Boolean that indicates whether the reminder is visible in the user interface and has not been dismissed or snoozed.
Item	Returns the Outlook item that the reminder is reminding the user about.
NextReminderDate	Contains the date when the reminder will fire again.
OriginalReminderDate	Returns the date the reminder was scheduled to fire (before the *Snooze* method is called or the user hits the Snooze button).

Search Object

The *Search* object allows you to perform programmatic searches through your Outlook information. This object works hand in hand with the *Results* object, which allows you to scroll through and sort the results of your searches. The capabilities of the *Search* object correspond most closely to those of the Advanced Find feature. You can perform asynchronous or synchronous searches of multiple folders using the same SQL syntax that you use when querying Exchange or SharePoint Portal Server (SPS). The *Search* object has some unique properties and methods. You can also use this object in conjunction with the *AdvancedSearch* method on the *Application* object.

Most often, you will create a programmatic search of your Outlook data by first calling the *AdvancedSearch* method, which returns a *Search* object that contains a *Results* object. The *AdvancedSearch* method takes four parameters. The first parameter is the scope of the search; it uses the same scope qualifiers you create for Exchange or SPS searches, such as shallow traversal or *http://server/folder*. The difference here, however, is that instead of using http or file paths for scope, you use Outlook folder paths such as \\Mailbox – UserName\Folder. Deep traversals are supported only in mailbox folders, not in public folders.

The second parameter, which is optional, is the SQL WHERE clause that you want to specify for your filter but without the WHERE keyword. This WHERE clause can be any clause supported by the standard Exchange query syntax. In this situation, you should take advantage of the query builder tab feature. This feature shows the SQL statement that is passed to Outlook to create filters for your views; you can copy and paste this statement to use as the filter for your searches. The key differences between the Exchange syntax and the Outlook search syntax are listed here:

- No full-text indexing support. You can use the *CONTAINS* keyword, but Outlook converts the search text under the covers to a *LIKE %searchterm%* query. The *FREETEXT* predicate is not supported at all.
- No need to *CAST* your non-string or non-Boolean variables, such as dates. Outlook can interpret these values automatically. The following query example shows how to query the multivalue *Categories* property:

```
(("urn:schemas-microsoft-com:office:office#Keywords"
LIKE '%Outlook%' OR "urn:schemas-microsoft-com:office:office#Key-
words" LIKE '%Exchange%'))
```

- Outlook supports relative values in date fields, such as *yesterday*, *today*, *this week*, *next week*, *next month*, and *this month*. To implement these relative values in your queries, you must use a special format query. The following queries demonstrate how to use the relative date formats. The queries search for any items received within the relative date.

```
yesterday - (%yesterday("urn:schemas:httpmail:datereceived")%)
today - (%today("urn:schemas:httpmail:datereceived")%)
tomorrow - (%tomorrow("urn:schemas:httpmail:datereceived")%)
last 7 - (%last7days("urn:schemas:httpmail:datereceived")%)
next 7 - (%next7days("urn:schemas:httpmail:datereceived")%)
last week - (%lastweek("urn:schemas:httpmail:datereceived")%)
this week - (%thisweek("urn:schemas:httpmail:datereceived")%)
next week - (%nextweek("urn:schemas:httpmail:datereceived")%)
last month - (%lastmonth("urn:schemas:httpmail:datereceived")%)
this month - (%thismonth("urn:schemas:httpmail:datereceived")%)
next month - (%nextmonth("urn:schemas:httpmail:datereceived")%)
on - ("urn:schemas:httpmail:datereceived" = '10/15/01')
on or after - ("urn:schemas:httpmail:datereceived" >= '10/15/01')
```

- When you enter scopes into Outlook without the full *SCOPE* predicate—for example, *SCOPE('DEEP TRAVERSAL OF ""FolderPath""')*—you must enter any folder paths that have spaces, such as My Folder, using single quotes, as in 'My Folder'. Otherwise, you will receive an error.

- Outlook can query MAPI and Exchange properties using the Exchange schema syntax. The following query searches for a Boolean property indicating whether the user requested a delivery receipt and whether the Do Not Archive flag is set on the item:

```
(("http://schemas.microsoft.com/exchange/deliveryreportrequested"
= 0 AND "http://schemas.microsoft.com/mapi/id/{00062008-0000-0000-
C000-000000000046}/850e000b" = 0))
```

- You can specify multiple folders by using the *DEEP* traversal *SCOPE* parameter or by specifying multiple folders separated by commas, as in *'Inbox', 'Calendar', 'Tasks'*. Outlook supports multiple folder and subfolder searching only in an individual person's mailbox.

The third optional parameter is a Boolean that specifies whether to search subfolders. You can search subfolders only in your mailbox and not in public folders. Do not specify a *DEEP* traversal scope, which means you want to search subfolders, and then use *False* for this parameter.

The final optional parameter is a string that is a unique tag for the search. Because you can have as many as 99 simultaneous searches in Outlook, this tag provides a way to uniquely identify your search when the event fires after the search is complete.

Once you define your parameters for the *AdvancedSearch* method and call that method, you should implement the *AdvancedSearchComplete* and *AdvancedSearchStop* events. These events are fired when the search is complete or when you programmatically stop the search. Their timing allows you to leverage asynchronous searches, which means that Outlook does not wait for the search results to return before continuing. This situation is unlike those in which you use the *Find* and *Restrict* methods in Outlook. Both of these methods are synchronous and must finish before your application can continue to run. Both events return a *Search* object that is the search that completed or was stopped. Both events are implemented by the *Application* object.

When you do an advanced search using the object model, what really happens behind the covers is that a new search folder is created in Outlook. The key point is that search folders support notifications so that as new items are added to the scope you specify, your search results are updated with these new results. As results are changed or deleted, your search results are updated as well.

The *Search* object includes a couple of new properties and a single method, as listed in Table 6-3.

Table 6-3 Properties and Methods of the *Search* Object

Property	Description
Filter	A read-only property that returns the filter used for the search.
IsSearchSynchronous	A property that returns a Boolean that specifies whether the search was synchronous or asynchronous. Synchronous searches are required only for public folders. You can still use the event notification technique with synchronous searches.
Results	Returns the *Results* object that contains any results obtained by the search.
Scope	A read-only property that returns the scope specified for the search.
SearchSubFolders	A Boolean property that returns whether subfolders were searched as part of the search.
Tag	A string property that allows you to tag your searches so that when *AdvancedSearchComplete* or *AdvancedSearch-Stopped* is fired, you can identify which search was completed or stopped.

Method	Description
Stop	Stops searching for an asynchronous search. Calling this method on a synchronous search does nothing.

The following code shows how to use the *Search* object and events:

```
⋮
Dim WithEvents oAppl As Outlook.Application
Set oAppl = CreateObject("Outlook.Application")
Dim oNS As Outlook.NameSpace
Set oNS = oAppl.GetNamespace("MAPI")

Dim oSearch As Outlook.Search

'Single quote your search paths
strScope = "'SPS Sync'"

'To search public folders you can use this path
'strScope = "'\\Public Folders\All Public Folders\My Folder'"
'If you want to use a real scope statement you can, such as
'strScope = _
'"SCOPE ('DEEP TRAVERSAL OF ""\\Mailbox - Thomas Rizzo\Add Subs\""')"

oAppl.AdvancedSearch strScope, _
    "(%today(""urn:schemas:httpmail:datereceived"")%)", , "My Search"
⋮
```

```
Private Sub oAppl_AdvancedSearchComplete( _
    ByVal SearchObject As Outlook.Search)

    MsgBox "The search called " & SearchObject.Tag & _
         " with the scope " & SearchObject.Filter & _
         " and the Scope " & SearchObject.Scope & " was completed."
    MsgBox "The search returned " & SearchObject.Results.Count & " results."
End Sub

Private Sub oAppl_AdvancedSearchStopped( _
    ByVal SearchObject As Outlook.Search)

    MsgBox "The search called " & SearchObject.Tag & _
        " with the scope " & SearchObject.Filter & _
        " and the Scope " &  SearchObject.Scope & " was stopped."
End Sub
```

Results Collection Object

The *Results* collection object is used in conjunction with the *Search* object described in the previous section. The *Results* collection is simply a view into the search folder that is created by Outlook when you perform a search. This collection has some unique methods and properties as well as some events that you will want to make use of. Because the only interesting property on the object is the *Count* property, I won't describe the properties in detail. As you can guess, the *Count* property returns the number of items in the folder, which are the results of the search. Table 6-4 lists the unique methods for the *Results* collection.

Table 6-4 Methods of the *Results* Collection

Method	Description
GetFirst	Gets the first item in the folder. The *Results* collection is dynamic; you can add new items to it.
GetLast	Gets the last item in the results.
GetNext	Gets the next item, if there is a next item.
GetPrevious	Gets the previous item, if it exists.
ResetColumns	Resets the columns that are cached with the *SetColumns* method.
SetColumns	Caches columns to make Outlook data access performance faster. You pass the set of columns, separated by commas, to this method. Outlook does not retrieve any other columns on the item except the ones specified.
Sort	Allows you to sort the results returned by a particular column, which you specify in either ascending or descending order.

Table 6-5 lists the events implemented by the *Results* collection. You can use these events to determine when new items are added to the results, changed, or removed. These events are useful if you want your application to always be running a search and want to be notified when new items of interest meet your criteria. All of these events are fired after their counterpart events on the folder they live in are fired.

Table 6-5 Events for the *Results* Collection

Event	Description
ItemAdd	Fires when a new item is added to the collection. This event passes the item as part of the event.
ItemChange	Fires when the item changes. This event passes the item as part of the event.
ItemRemove	Fires when an item is removed. Because the item is not passed to the event, you must figure out which item was removed. The sample application (found in this book's companion content on the Web) that provides an example of SPS offline synchronization shows a technique for figuring out which item was removed from a folder with this event.

Views Object

One of the first items you'll want to enable on either Outlook 2000 or Outlook 2002 is the *querybuilder* registry key. This key offers an unsupported but powerful way to work with views in Outlook. In addition, the *querybuilder* interface allows you to build views more intuitively and logically and see the actual query that is sent to the server to generate the view. Figure 6-5 shows the *querybuilder* interface in Outlook. The following steps show you how to enable the *querybuilder* in Outlook:

1. Open the Windows Registry Editor by entering Regedit in the Run dialog box.
2. In the Registry tree, navigate to HKEY_CURRENT_USER\Software\Microsoft\Office\11.0\Outlook. (If you are running Outlook 2002, replace 11.0 with 10.0.)
3. Choose New from the Edit menu, and then select Key.
4. Name the key QueryBuilder.

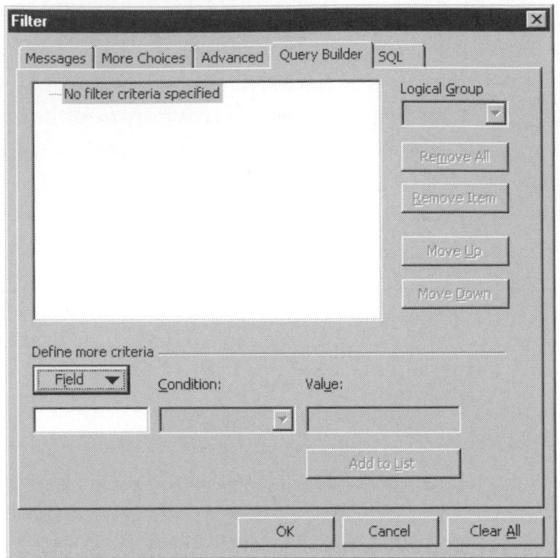

Figure 6-5 The *QueryBuilder* interface in Outlook

The *Views* collection, which is a collection of the *MAPIFolder* object, provides *View* objects that you can use to enumerate, add, change, or remove Outlook views programmatically. In previous versions of Outlook, there is no way to work with views cleanly. You can use CDO to access views because views are stored as hidden messages in a folder. But CDO cannot create new views because Outlook uses a proprietary format for its views.

The *Views* collection has two interesting methods and two interesting events. The methods are named *Add* and *Remove*. The *Add* method takes two required parameters and one optional parameter. The first required parameter is the name of the view, which must be a unique name. The second parameter is the view type. You can use one of five constants: *olCalendarView*, *olCardView*, *olIconView*, *olTableView*, and *olTimelineView*. The optional parameter specifies the save options for the view. You can have three constants for this parameter, such as *olViewSaveOptionAllFoldersOfType*, *olViewSaveOptionThisFolderEveryOne*, and *olViewSaveOptionThisFolderOnlyMe*. The names of these constants are self-explanatory.

The *Remove* method takes the index of the view that you want to remove. You can use this method to remove any views that you no longer need on the folder.

The two events are *ViewAdd* and *ViewRemove*. The *ViewAdd* event is called when a new view is added to the collection. This event passes the new view as a *View* object as part of the event.

The *ViewRemove* event is called when you remove a view from the collection. This event passes the view as a *View* object as part of the event.

The following code shows how to use the events. The methods of the *Views* collection are shown in the sample code for the *View* object, which we'll look at shortly. Keep in mind that if you make any changes to the *View* object passed to you, you should call the *Save* method to save your changes.

```
Dim WithEvents oViews As Outlook.Views
Private Sub Command4_Click()
    'View Example
    Dim oApp As New Outlook.Application
    Dim oNS As Outlook.NameSpace
    Set oNS = oApp.GetNamespace("MAPI")

    'Get the views collection for a folder
    Dim oFolder As Outlook.MAPIFolder
    Set oMailbox = oNS.Folders.Item("Mailbox - Thomas Rizzo")
    Set oFolder = oMailbox.Folders("SPS Sync")
    Set oViews = oFolder.Views
End Sub

Private Sub oViews_ViewAdd(ByVal View As Outlook.View)
    MsgBox "You added the view called " & View.Name & _
        " and the XML for the view is " & View.XML
End Sub

Private Sub oViews_ViewRemove(ByVal View As Outlook.View)
    MsgBox "You removed the view called " & View.Name
End Sub
```

View Object

The *View* object is the real meat of view creation. This is the object in which you actually specify the XML that makes up your view. The *View* object exposes the methods that allow you to copy, reset, and change your views. Table 6-6 lists the unique properties of the *View* object.

Table 6-6 Properties of the *View* Object

Property	Description
Language	A string value that returns the language that the view should be used in, such as EN-US. If this property is blank or you set it to blank, the view should be used for all languages.
LockUserChanges	A Boolean read/write property that specifies whether the user can modify the settings contained in the view. You can use this property to lock your views. However, if users go to another version of Outlook or use CDO, they can get around this setting.
Name	Specifies the name of the view.

Table 6-6 Properties of the *View* Object

Property	Description
SaveOption	Returns the save option specified for the view. The following constants are the possible values for this read-only property: *olViewSaveOptionAllFoldersOfType* *olViewSaveOptionThisFolderEveryone* *olViewSaveOptionThisFolderOnlyMe*
Standard	A Boolean that returns *True* if this view is a standard, built-in Outlook view such as Messages, or *False* if the view is a custom view.
ViewType	Returns the type of view, using the constants *olCalendarView*, *olCardView*, *olIconView*, *olTableView*, and *olTimelineView*.
XML	Returns or sets the XML view descriptor for the view. This view descriptor maps to the WSS Forms view descriptor and adds some custom tags for Outlook. Included on the companion Web site is a white paper that lists all the XML tags that you can use in your Outlook views.

Table 6-7 lists the methods of the *View* object.

Table 6-7 Methods of the *View* Object

Method	Description
Apply	Changes the view in the user interface to the current *View* object.
Copy	Copies a view into a new *View* object so you can modify the original view and save a new copy. This method does not copy views between folders. You can add code that leverages MAPI (a sample is provided on the companion Web site) to copy views between folders.
Delete	Deletes the view.
GoToDate	Takes a date and jumps a calendar view to the date you specify. You should not use this method if your Outlook objects are late-bound. This method is known to hang Outlook in this situation.
Reset	Only for built-in Outlook views. This method resets the view to its original configuration.
Save	Saves the current view.

The following code, used in the SPS Offline Synchronization application, shows how to create views. The code generates the XML string needed to describe the view and then adds the view to the folder. (The XML strings in the listing are long strings so the code is formatted for readability.)

```
Private Sub cmdFinish_Click()
    On Error Resume Next
    Err.Clear

    strViewHeaderText = _
"<?xml version=""1.0""?>" & _
  "<view type=""table"">" & _
    "<viewname>%%!!--ViewName--!!%%</viewname>" & _
    "<viewstyle>table-layout:fixed;width:100%;" & _
      "font-family:Tahoma;font-style:normal;" & _
      "font-weight:normal;font-size:8pt;color:Black" & _
    "</viewstyle>" & _
    "<viewtime>210703620</viewtime>" & _
    "<linecolor>8421504</linecolor>" & _
    "<linestyle>0</linestyle>" & _
    "<collapsestate></collapsestate>" & _
    "<rowstyle>background-color:#ffffff</rowstyle>" & _
    "<headerstyle>background-color:#d3d3d3</headerstyle>" & _
    "<previewstyle>color:Blue</previewstyle>"

    strDAVHrefText = _
    "<column>" & _
      "<name>HREF</name>" & _
      "<prop>DAV:href</prop>" & _
      "<checkbox>1</checkbox>" & _
    "</column>"

    strIconText = _
    "<column>" & _
      "<heading>Icon</heading>" & _
      "<prop>" & _
        "http://schemas.microsoft.com/mapi/proptag/0x0fff0102" & _
      "</prop>" & _
      "<bitmap>1</bitmap>" & _
      "<width>18</width>" & _
      "<style>padding-left:3px;;text-align:center</style>" & _
    "</column>"

    strFromText = _
    "<column>" & _
      "<heading>From</heading>" & _
      "<prop>urn:schemas:httpmail:fromname</prop>" & _
      "<type>string</type>" & _
      "<width>25</width>" & _
      "<style>padding-left:3px;;text-align:left</style>" & _
      "<displayformat>1</displayformat>" & _
    "</column>"

    strSubjectText = _
    "<column>" & _
      "<heading>Subject</heading>" & _
      "<prop>urn:schemas:httpmail:subject</prop>" & _
      "<type>string</type>" & _
```

```
    "<width>120</width>" & _
    "<style>padding-left:3px;;text-align:left</style>" & _
  "</column>"

  strApproversText = _
  "<column>" & _
    "<heading>SPSApprovers</heading>" & _
    "<prop>" & _
      "http://schemas.microsoft.com/mapi/string/" & _
      "{00020329-0000-0000-C000-000000000046}/SPSApprovers" & _
    "</prop>" & _
    "<width>50</width>" & _
    "<sortable>0</sortable>" & _
    "<style>padding-left:3px;;text-align:left</style>" & _
    "<userheading>Approvers</userheading>" & _
  "</column>"

  strApproversLeftText = _
  "<column>" & _
    "<heading>SPSApproversLeft</heading>" & _
    "<prop>" & _
      "http://schemas.microsoft.com/mapi/string/" & _
      "{00020329-0000-0000-C000-000000000046}/SPSApproversLeft" & _
    "</prop>" & _
    "<width>50</width>" & _
    "<sortable>0</sortable>" & _
    "<style>padding-left:3px;;text-align:left</style>" & _
    "<userheading>Approvers Left</userheading>" & _
  "</column>"

  strAuthorText = _
  "<column>" & _
    "<heading>Author</heading>" & _
    "<prop>" & _
      "http://schemas.microsoft.com/mapi/string/" & _
      "{00020329-0000-0000-C000-000000000046}/SPSAuthor" & _
    "</prop>" & _
    "<type>string</type>" & _
    "<width>50</width>" & _
    "<style>padding-left:3px;;text-align:left</style>" & _
    "<userheading>Author</userheading>" & _
  "</column>"

  strCategoriesText = _
  "<column>" & _
    "<heading>SPSCategories</heading>" & _
    "<prop>" & _
      "http://schemas.microsoft.com/mapi/string/" & _
      "{00020329-0000-0000-C000-000000000046}/SPSCategories" & _
    "</prop>" & _
    "<width>50</width>" & _
    "<sortable>0</sortable>" & _
    "<style>padding-left:3px;;text-align:left</style>" & _
    "<userheading>Categories</userheading>" & _
  "</column>"
```

```
strCheckedOutText = _
"<column>" & _
  "<format>boolicon</format>" & _
  "<heading>Checked Out</heading>" & _
  "<prop>" & _
    "http://schemas.microsoft.com/mapi/string/" & _
    "{00020329-0000-0000-C000-000000000046}/SPSCheckedOut" & _
  "</prop>" & _
  "<type>boolean</type>" & _
  "<width>50</width>" & _
  "<style>padding-left:3px;;text-align:center</style>" & _
  "<displayformat>3</displayformat>" & _
  "<userheading>Checked Out</userheading>" & _
"</column>"

strCheckedOutByText = _
"<column>" & _
  "<heading>Checked Out By</heading>" & _
  "<prop>" & _
    "http://schemas.microsoft.com/mapi/string/" & _
    "{00020329-0000-0000-C000-000000000046}/SPSCheckedOutBy" & _
  "</prop>" & _
  "<type>string</type>" & _
  "<width>50</width>" & _
  "<style>padding-left:3px;;text-align:left</style>" & _
  "<userheading>Checked Out By</userheading>" & _
"</column>"

strCurrentApproversText = _
"<column>" & _
  "<heading>SPSCurrentApprovers</heading>" & _
  "<prop>" & _
    "http://schemas.microsoft.com/mapi/string/" & _
    "{00020329-0000-0000-C000-000000000046}/SPSCurrentApprovers" & _
  "</prop>" & _
  "<width>50</width>" & _
  "<sortable>0</sortable>" & _
  "<style>padding-left:3px;;text-align:left</style>" & _
  "<userheading>Current Approvers</userheading>" & _
"</column>"

strDescriptionText = _
"<column>" & _
  "<heading>Description</heading>" & _
  "<prop>" & _
    "http://schemas.microsoft.com/mapi/string/" & _
    "{00020329-0000-0000-C000-000000000046}/SPSDescription" & _
  "</prop>" & _
  "<type>string</type>" & _
  "<width>50</width>" & _
  "<style>padding-left:3px;;text-align:left</style>" & _
  "<userheading>Description</userheading>" & _
"</column>"
```

```
strDocProfileText = _
"<column>" & _
  "<heading>Doc Profile</heading>" & _
  "<prop>" & _
    "http://schemas.microsoft.com/mapi/string/" & _
    "{00020329-0000-0000-C000-000000000046}/SPSDocProfile" & _
  "</prop>" & _
  "<type>string</type>" & _
  "<width>50</width>" & _
  "<style>padding-left:3px;;text-align:left</style>" & _
  "<userheading>Doc Profile</userheading>" & _
"</column>"

strKeywordsText = _
"<column>" & _
  "<heading>SPSKeywords</heading>" & _
  "<prop>" & _
    "http://schemas.microsoft.com/mapi/string/" & _
    "{00020329-0000-0000-C000-000000000046}/SPSKeywords" & _
  "</prop>" & _
  "<width>50</width>" & _
  "<sortable>0</sortable>" & _
  "<style>padding-left:3px;;text-align:left</style>" & _
  "<userheading>Keywords</userheading>" & _
"</column>"

strLastModifiedText = _
"<column>" & _
  "<heading>Last Modified</heading>" & _
  "<prop>" & _
    "http://schemas.microsoft.com/mapi/string/" & _
    "{00020329-0000-0000-C000-000000000046}/SPSLastModified" & _
  "</prop>" & _
  "<type>datetime</type>" & _
  "<width>50</width>" & _
  "<style>padding-left:3px;;text-align:left</style>" & _
  "<format>M/d/yyyy||h:mm tt</format>" & _
  "<displayformat>2</displayformat>" & _
  "<userheading>Last Modified</userheading>" & _
"</column>"

strTitleText = _
"<column>" & _
  "<heading>Title</heading>" & _
  "<prop>" & _
    "http://schemas.microsoft.com/mapi/string/" & _
    "{00020329-0000-0000-C000-000000000046}/SPSTitle" & _
  "</prop>" & _
  "<type>string</type>" & _
  "<width>50</width>" & _
  "<style>padding-left:3px;;text-align:left</style>" & _
  "<userheading>Title</userheading>" & _
"</column>"
```

```
  strReceivedText = _
  "<column>" & _
    "<heading>Received</heading>" & _
    "<prop>urn:schemas:httpmail:datereceived</prop>" & _
    "<type>datetime</type>" & _
    "<width>30</width>" & _
    "<style>padding-left:3px;;text-align:left</style>" & _
    "<format>M/d/yyyy||h:mm tt</format>" & _
    "<displayformat>2</displayformat>" & _
  "</column>"

  strSizeText = _
  "<column>" & _
    "<heading>Size</heading>" & _
    "<prop>" & _
      "http://schemas.microsoft.com/mapi/id/" & _
      "{00020328-0000-0000-C000-000000000046}/8ff00003" & _
    "</prop>" & _
    "<type>i4</type>" & _
    "<width>15</width>" & _
    "<style>padding-left:3px;;text-align:left</style>" & _
    "<displayformat>3</displayformat>" & _
  "</column>"

  strFooterText = _
  "<orderby>" & _
    "<order>" & _
      "<heading>Subject</heading>" & _
      "<prop>urn:schemas:httpmail:subject</prop>" & _
      "<type>string</type>" & _
      "<sort>asc</sort>" & _
    "</order>" & _
  "</orderby>" & _
  "<groupbydefault>2</groupbydefault>" & _
  "<previewpane>" & _
    "<markasread>0</markasread>" & _
    "<previewwidth>0</previewwidth>" & _
    "<previewheight>500</previewheight>" & _
  "</previewpane>" & _
"</view>"

  'Check to make sure they put a name
  If txtViewName = "" Then
      MsgBox "You must enter a name for the view before continuing.", _
          vbExclamation + vbOKOnly
      Exit Sub
  End If
  'See if the view name already exists
  Dim otmpViews As Outlook.Views
  Set otmpFolder = oVWApp.ActiveExplorer.CurrentFolder
  Set otmpViews = otmpFolder.Views
  Dim oView As Outlook.View
  For Each oView In otmpViews
```

```
        If oView.Name = txtViewName.Text Then
            MsgBox "This view already exists in the folder. " & _
                    "Please select a different view name.", _
                    vbExclamation + vbOKOnly
            Exit Sub
            Exit For
        End If
    Next
    'View doesn't exists, create it
    Dim oNewView As Outlook.View
    Set oNewView = otmpViews.Add(txtViewName.Text, olTableView, _
                                 olViewSaveOptionThisFolderEveryone)
    If Err.Number = 0 Then
        'Modify the view settings
        'Add the fields to the view
        strViewXML = ""
        'Find the view name in the view header and
        'replace with the real name
        strViewHeaderText = Replace(strViewHeaderText, _
                            "%%!!--ViewName--!!%%", txtViewName.Text)
        strViewXML = strViewHeaderText
        'See what properties they selected.
        'Icon, Subject and received are always included.
        strViewXML = strViewXML & strDAVHrefText
        strViewXML = strViewXML & strIconText

        If checkAuthor.Value = vbChecked Then
            strViewXML = strViewXML & strAuthorText
        End If

        'strViewXML = strViewXML & strFromText

        strViewXML = strViewXML & strSubjectText

        If checkApprovers.Value = vbChecked Then
            strViewXML = strViewXML & strApproversText
        End If

        If checkApproversLeft.Value = vbChecked Then
            strViewXML = strViewXML & strApproversLeftText
        End If

        If checkCategories.Value = vbChecked Then
            strViewXML = strViewXML & strCategoriesText
        End If

        If checkCheckedout.Value = vbChecked Then
            strViewXML = strViewXML & strCheckedOutText
        End If

        If checkCheckedOutBy.Value = vbChecked Then
            strViewXML = strViewXML & strCheckedOutByText
        End If
```

```
        If checkCurrentApprovers.Value = vbChecked Then
            strViewXML = strViewXML & strCurrentApproversText
        End If

        If checkDescription.Value = vbChecked Then
            strViewXML = strViewXML & strDescriptionText
        End If

        If checkDocProfile.Value = vbChecked Then
            strViewXML = strViewXML & strDocProfileText
        End If

        If checkKeywords.Value = vbChecked Then
            strViewXML = strViewXML & strKeywordsText
        End If

         If checkLastModified.Value = vbChecked Then
            strViewXML = strViewXML & strLastModifiedText
        End If

         If checkTitle.Value = vbChecked Then
            strViewXML = strViewXML & strTitleText
        End If

        strViewXML = strViewXML & strReceivedText

        If checkSize.Value = vbChecked Then
            strViewXML = strViewXML & strSizeText
        End If

        strViewXML = strViewXML & strFooterText
        oNewView.XML = strViewXML
        oNewView.Save
        iResponse = MsgBox("Your view - " & txtViewName.Text & _
                           " - was successfully created. " & _
                           "Would you like to switch to " & _
                           "this view right now?", vbYesNo + vbQuestion)
        If iResponse = vbYes Then
            'Change the folder's view to the new view
            bChangeView = True
            strSwitchViewName = txtViewName.Text
        End If
    Else
        MsgBox "There was an error creating your new view. " & _
               "Please try again later.", vbExclamation + vbOKOnly
    End If
    Unload Me
End Sub
```

Outlook Bar Object Model

Some of the most significant elements in the Outlook object model are the Outlook Bar objects, which allow you to manipulate the Outlook Bar shortcuts as well as the user interface. Outlook Bar shortcuts hold not only file and folder shortcuts but also URL shortcuts to Web pages. Let's take a look at the objects and collections for the Outlook Bar object model. Figure 6-6 shows how the objects in the Outlook Bar object model work together. Except for the *SetIcon* method, these objects are all supported by Outlook 2000 and later.

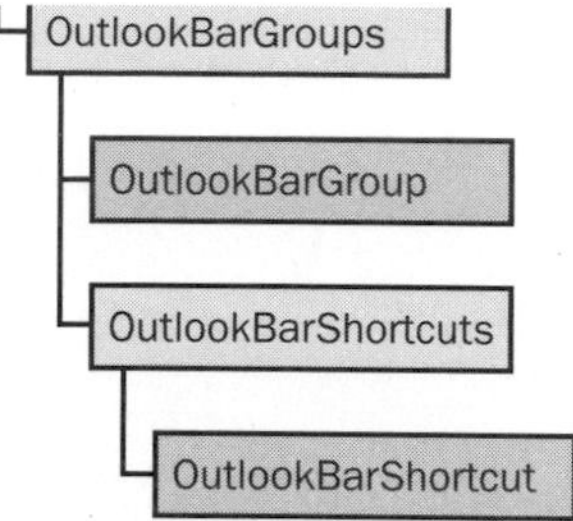

Figure 6-6 The relationship between the objects and collections in the Outlook Bar object model

Panes Collection

The *Panes* collection enables developers to access the available Outlook application window panes. Outlook supports three panes—the *OutlookBar*, the FolderList, and the Preview pane—but only the *OutlookBar* pane is accessible as an object in the *Panes* collection. If you try to access either of the other two panes, you will receive an error.

You retrieve the *Panes* collection from an *Explorer* object by using the new *Pane* property on that object. You can then use the *Item* method of the *Pane* object and pass in either the numeric index or the name of the *Pane* object you want. To retrieve the *OutlookBarPane* object, you should pass in the text *OutlookBar* to the *Item* method.

The *Panes* collection also supports the *Count* property, which you can use to retrieve the number of *Pane* objects in the collection.

OutlookBarPane Object

After you pass the text *OutlookBar* to the *Item* method of the *Panes* collection, Outlook returns an *OutlookBarPane* object. This object contains events and properties that let you control and monitor the Outlook Bar. Here are the four properties you will use:

- ***Contents*** A read-only property that returns the *OutlookBarStorage* object for the current *OutlookBarPane* object. From the object returned, you can retrieve the shortcuts and groups for the Outlook Bar.
- ***CurrentGroup*** Returns or sets the current group displayed in the Outlook Bar. You must pass a valid *OutlookBarGroup* object as the value for this property.
- ***Name*** A read-only property that returns a string indicating the name of the current *OutlookBarPane* object.
- ***Visible*** Returns or sets the visibility of the *OutlookBarPane* object. *Visible* takes a Boolean value that specifies whether you want to show the Outlook Bar in the user interface.

The following code shows how to use the *OutlookBarPane* object:

```
Dim oPanes As Outlook.Panes
Dim oOutlookBarPane As Outlook.OutlookBarPane

Set oPanes = oExplorer.Panes
Set oOutlookBarPane = oPanes("OutlookBar")
'Flip whether the pane is visible
oOutlookBarPane.Visible = Not (oOutlookBarPane.Visible)
```

The *OutlookBarPane* object also provides two events that you can capture when users work with the Outlook Bar: *BeforeGroupSwitch* and *BeforeNavigate*. The *BeforeGroupSwitch* event is fired when the user or object model attempts to switch to a new visible group. The *BeforeGroupSwitch* event procedure takes two parameters, *Group* and *Cancel*. If you set the *Cancel* parameter to *True*, the switch is canceled. The *Group* parameter is an *OutlookBarGroup* object containing the Outlook group that the user is trying to navigate to. The following code shows how to use *BeforeGroupSwitch* and cancel it when a user tries to navigate to a specific Outlook group:

```
Dim WithEvents oOutlookBarPane As Outlook.OutlookBarPane
Private Sub oOutlookBarPane_BeforeGroupSwitch( _
            ByVal ToGroup As Outlook.OutlookBarGroup, _
            Cancel As Boolean)
    If ToGroup.Name = "My Shortcuts" Then
        MsgBox "You cannot switch to the My Shortcuts group!"
        Cancel = True
    Else
        MsgBox "Now switching to the " & ToGroup.Name & " group."
    End If
End Sub
```

The *BeforeNavigate* event fires when the user attempts to click on an Outlook Bar shortcut. The *BeforeNavigate* event procedure takes two parameters, *Shortcut* and *Cancel*. *Shortcut* is an *OutlookBarShortcut* object that is the Outlook Bar shortcut the user is trying to navigate to. *Cancel* is a Boolean that you can set to *True* to cancel the navigation. The following code example shows how to use *BeforeNavigate*:

```
Dim WithEvents oOutlookBarPane As Outlook.OutlookBarPane
Private Sub oOutlookBarPane_BeforeNavigate( _
            ByVal Shortcut As Outlook.OutlookBarShortcut, _
            Cancel As Boolean)
    On Error Resume Next
    'Need to watch out for file shortcuts!
    Err.Clear
    Set oTempFolder = Shortcut.Target
    strName = oTempFolder.Name
    If Err.Number = 0 Then
        If strName = "Inbox" Then
            MsgBox "Sorry, you can't switch to your Inbox."
            Cancel = True
        Else
            MsgBox "Now switching to the " & Shortcut.Name & " shortcut."
        End If
    End If
End Sub
```

OutlookBarStorage Object

The *OutlookBarStorage* object is a container for the objects in an *OutlookBarPane* object. This object contains only one property—the *Groups* property—that you will use in your applications. The *Groups* property returns an *OutlookBarGroups* collection, which enables you to scroll through the groups on the Outlook Bar. The following code shows how to use the *Groups* property to retrieve the *OutlookBarGroups* collection and then scroll through each group in the collection:

```
Dim oOutlookBarStorage As Outlook.OutlookBarStorage
Dim oOutlookBarGroups As Outlook.OutlookBarGroups
Dim oOutlookBarGroup As Outlook.OutlookBarGroup

Set oPanes = oExplorer.Panes
Set oOutlookBarPane = oPanes("OutlookBar")
Set oOutlookBarStorage = oOutlookBarPane.Contents
Set oOutlookBarGroups = oOutlookBarStorage.Groups
strGroups = vbLf
For Each oOutlookBarGroup In oOutlookBarGroups
    strGroups = strGroups & vbLf & oOutlookBarGroup.Name
Next
MsgBox "The names of the groups on your Outlook Bar: " _
    & strGroups
```

OutlookBarGroups Collection

The *OutlookBarGroups* collection contains *OutlookBarGroup* objects that represent all the Outlook groups on your Outlook Bar. You use this collection to count and add new groups to the Outlook Bar. This collection supports one property, *Count*, which you can use to retrieve the number of groups in the collection, as shown in the following code:

```
Set oPanes = oExplorer.Panes
Set oOutlookBarPane = oPanes("OutlookBar")
Set oOutlookBarStorage = oOutlookBarPane.Contents
Set oOutlookBarGroups = oOutlookBarStorage.Groups
MsgBox "The number of Outlook groups on your Outlook Bar is: " _
    & oOutlookBarGroups.Count
```

This collection also supports three methods—*Add*, *Item*, and *Remove*. The *Add* method adds an empty *OutlookBarGroup* object to the collection and returns a reference to this new *OutlookBarGroup* object. The *Add* method takes two parameters: the first is a string that specifies the name of the group to add; the second is optional and specifies a number indicating the insertion position for the new Outlook group. The top of the bar is at position 1.

The *Item* method allows you to retrieve an *OutlookBarGroup* object by name or by index. The *Remove* method allows you to delete an *OutlookBarGroup* object by specifying the index of the object you want to remove.

The following example uses all three of these methods. It creates a new *OutlookBarGroup* object, finds the object by using the *Item* method, and then deletes the object by using the *Remove* method.

```
'Create the new group at the top of the bar
Set oNewOLBarGroup = oOutlookBarGroups.Add(""My New Group", 1)
MsgBox "Added Group"
Set oTempOLBarGroup = oOutlookBarGroups("My New Group")
MsgBox "Got Group Named: " & oTempOLBarGroup.Name
'Since you have to remove a group by numeric index, we can loop
'through the collection, find the OutlookBarGroup by name, and
'get the corresponding index
intCounter = 0
boolFound = 0
For Each oOutlookBarGroup In oOutlookBarGroups
    intCounter = intCounter + 1
    If oOutlookBarGroup.Name = "My New Group" Then
        boolFound = intCounter
    End If
Next
If boolFound <> 0 Then
    oOutlookBarGroups.Remove boolFound
    MsgBox "Deleted Group"
End If
```

The *OutlookBarGroups* collection is interesting because it supports three events that you can hook into: *BeforeGroupAdd*, *BeforeGroupRemove*, and *GroupAdd*. These events enable you to trace when users try to add or remove certain Outlook groups and, if you want, cancel the user's action.

The *BeforeGroupAdd* event is fired before a new group is added to the Outlook Bar through the user interface or code. The *BeforeGroupAdd* event procedure is passed a Boolean parameter named *Cancel* that, if set to *True*, programmatically cancels the action, and prevents the group from being added to the Outlook Bar. The next code snippet shows how to use the *BeforeGroupAdd* event to cancel a user's attempt to add an Outlook group. Notice that because the group hasn't been created yet, a reference to the new group is not passed the *BeforeGroupAdd* event procedure, so you have no way of knowing which group the user is trying to add. However, because the *GroupAdd* event passes the group the user added, you can write code in that event procedure to remove the group if the user is not allowed to add it.

```
Dim WithEvents oOutlookBarGroups As Outlook.OutlookBarGroups

Private Sub oOutlookBarGroups_BeforeGroupAdd(Cancel As Boolean)
   MsgBox "You are not allowed to add groups to your Outlook Bar!"
   Cancel = True
End Sub
```

The *BeforeGroupRemove* event is fired before a group is removed from an Outlook Bar. You can hook into this event with your applications to prevent users from deleting Outlook groups you created programmatically. The *BeforeGroupRemove* event procedure is passed two parameters. The first is an *OutlookBarGroup* object that corresponds to the Outlook group that a program or user is trying to remove. The second is the *Cancel* Boolean parameter, which you can set to *True* to cancel the removal of the Outlook group. The following code checks to see whether the user is trying to remove her Outlook Shortcuts group. If she is, it cancels the action.

```
Private Sub oOutlookBarGroups_BeforeGroupRemove( _
            ByVal Group As Outlook.OutlookBarGroup, _
            Cancel As Boolean)
    If Group.Name = "Outlook Shortcuts" Then
        MsgBox "You cannot remove this group!"
        Cancel = True
    End If
End Sub
```

The *GroupAdd* event fires when a new group has been added successfully to the Outlook Bar. The *GroupAdd* event procedure is passed an *OutlookBarGroup* object so that you know which group has been added. If the user adds the new group by using the Outlook user interface, the group will be named

New Group because this name is the default for newly created Outlook groups. The following code displays a message box that shows the name of the Outlook group you added:

```
Private Sub oOutlookBarGroups_GroupAdd( _
            ByVal NewGroup As Outlook.OutlookBarGroup)
    MsgBox "You added the " & NewGroup.Name & " group!"
End Sub
```

OutlookBarGroup Object

The *OutlookBarGroup* object represents a group on your Outlook Bar. The *OutlookBarGroup* object supports three properties but no methods. You use these three properties to access information about the Outlook group and the shortcuts inside the Outlook group:

- ***Name*** Returns or sets the name of the *OutlookBarGroup* by using a string.
- ***Shortcuts*** Returns the set of Outlook shortcuts contained in the group as an *OutlookBarShortcuts* collection.
- ***ViewType*** Returns or sets the way icons are displayed on the Outlook Bar. This property can have the value *olLargeIcon (1)* or *olSmallIcon (2)*.

The following example shows how to use these properties. It loops through the *OutlookBarGroups* collection and then retrieves each *OutlookBarGroup* object and displays information about it.

```
For Each oOutlookBarGroup In oOutlookBarGroups
    strName = oOutlookBarGroup.Name
    Set oOutlookBarShortcuts = oOutlookBarGroup.Shortcuts
    intShortcutCount = oOutlookBarShortcuts.Count
    strNames = vbLf

    For Each oOutlookBarShortcut In oOutlookBarShortcuts
        strNames = strNames & vbLf & oOutlookBarShortcut.Name
    Next

    Select Case oOutlookBarGroup.ViewType
        Case olLargeIcon:
            strViewType = "Large Icons"
        Case olSmallIcon:
            strViewType = "Small Icons"
    End Select

    MsgBox "The following information is for the " & strName & _
        " group." & vbLf & "The ViewType is: " & strViewType & _
        "vbLf & "The number of shortcuts in the group" & _
        " is: " & intShortcutCount & vbLf & _
        "The shortcuts are named:" & strNames & vbLf
Next
```

OutlookBarShortcuts Collection

The *OutlookBarShortcuts* collection contains a set of *OutlookBarShortcut* objects and represents the shortcuts in an *OutlookBarGroup* object. This collection supports the *Count* property, which returns the number of *OutlookBarShortcut* objects in the collection.

This collection also supports three methods: *Add*, *Item*, and *Remove*. *Add* allows you to create a new shortcut in your Outlook group. The return value for *Add* is the new *OutlookShortcut* object. This method takes three parameters. The first parameter is a *Variant* that is the target for the shortcut. The target can be either a *MAPIFolder* object or a string that specifies a URL. Outlook supports placing URL shortcuts on your Outlook Bar. The second parameter is a string that specifies the name of the shortcut you are creating. The final parameter is optional; it specifies the position at which the new shortcut should be inserted. A value of 0 indicates that the shortcut should be inserted at the top of the Outlook group. The following code adds a folder and a URL shortcut to a newly created Outlook group using the *Add* method:

```
'Create the new group at the top of the bar
Set oNewOLBarGroup = oOutlookBarGroups.Add("My New Group", 1)
'Get the shortcuts in the new group
Set oOutlookBarShortcuts = oNewOLBarGroup.Shortcuts
'Now add a shortcut that points to a folder
Set oFolder = oNS.GetDefaultFolder(olFolderInbox)
'Optionally, we can set a variable to retrieve the
'new shortcut. 0 at the end means add it to the
'top of the group.
Set oNewShortcut = oOutlookBarShortcuts.Add(oFolder, "My Inbox", 0)
'Now let's create a new shortcut to a Web page
strEXHTTP = "http://www.microsoft.com/exchange"
oOutlookBarShortcuts.Add strEXHTTP, "Exchange Web site"
```

You use the second method, *Item*, to specify the index number or the name of the shortcut you want to retrieve from the collection. The third method, *Remove*, takes the index of the *OutlookBarShortcut* object you want to remove from the collection. The following code shows how to find and remove all shortcuts that point to the Inbox:

```
On Error Resume Next
For Each oOutlookBarGroup In oOutlookBarGroups
    Set oOutlookShortcuts = oOutlookBarGroup.Shortcuts
    intCounter = 1
    For Each oOutlookShortcut In oOutlookShortcuts
        'Watch out for File System shortcuts
        Err.Clear
        If oOutlookShortcut.Target.Name = "Inbox" Then
            If Err.Number = 0 Then
                oOutlookShortcuts.Remove intCounter
            End If
        End If
```

```
        intCounter = intCounter + 1
    Next
Next
```

The *OutlookBarShortcuts* collection supports the *BeforeShortcutAdd*, *BeforeShorcutRemove*, and *ShortcutAdd* events. The *BeforeShortcutAdd* event, which fires before a new shortcut is added to the Outlook Bar, is passed a parameter named *Cancel* that you can set to *True* to cancel the attempt to add the shortcut. The following code shows how to hook into this event and cancel the action of a user trying to add a new shortcut to her Outlook Shortcuts group. Notice that you are not passed the new Outlook shortcut object because the event is fired before the new shortcut is created.

```
⋮
Dim WithEvents oOutlookShortcuts As OutlookBarShortcuts

'The oOutlookShortcuts variable must be set before the event
'will fire
Set oOutlookBarGroup = oOutlookBarGroups("Outlook Shortcuts")
Set oOutlookShortcuts = oOutlookBarGroup.Shortcuts
⋮

Private Sub oOutlookShortcuts_BeforeShortcutAdd(Cancel As Boolean)
    On Error Resume Next
    MsgBox "You are not allowed to add shortcuts!"
    Cancel = True
End Sub
```

The second event supported by the *OutlookBarShortcuts* collection is the *BeforeShortcutRemove* event, which fires before a shortcut is removed from a group in the Outlook Bar. The *BeforeShortcutRemove* event procedure is passed two parameters: an *OutlookBarShortcut* object that corresponds to the shortcut the user or program is trying to remove, and *Cancel*, which is a Boolean parameter that you can set to *True* to cancel the removal. The following code shows how to use this event to prevent a user from removing the Calendar shortcut from the Outlook Shortcuts group:

```
⋮
Dim WithEvents oOutlookShortcuts As OutlookBarShortcuts

'The oOutlookShortcuts variable must be set before the event
'will fire
Set oOutlookBarGroup = oOutlookBarGroups("Outlook Shortcuts")
Set oOutlookShortcuts = oOutlookBarGroup.Shortcuts
⋮

Private Sub oOutlookShortcuts_BeforeShortcutRemove( _
            ByVal Shortcut As Outlook.OutlookBarShortcut, _
            Cancel As Boolean)
    On Error Resume Next
    If Shortcut.Target.Name = "Calendar" Then
        MsgBox "You can't remove the shortcut to your calendar!"
```

```
        Cancel = True
    End If
End Sub
```

The third event supported by the *OutlookBarShortcuts* collection is *ShortcutAdd*. This event fires after a new Outlook shortcut has been added to the Outlook Bar. This event passes the newly added shortcut as an *OutlookBarShortcut* object. The following example shows how to hook into this event:

```
⋮
Dim WithEvents oOutlookShortcuts As OutlookBarShortcuts
'The oOutlookShortcuts variable must be set before the event
'will fire
Set oOutlookBarGroup = oOutlookBarGroups("Outlook Shortcuts")
Set oOutlookShortcuts = oOutlookBarGroup.Shortcuts
⋮

Private Sub oOutlookShortcuts_ShortcutAdd( _
            ByVal NewShortcut As Outlook.OutlookBarShortcut)
    MsgBox "You added the " & NewShortcut.Name & " shortcut!"
End Sub
```

OutlookBarShortcut Object

The *OutlookBarShortcut* object represents an Outlook shortcut on your Outlook Bar. You use this object to inquire about the target that a shortcut points to. You make the inquiry by using the object's *Target* property, which returns a *Variant* object. The data type of this *Variant* is determined by the target for the shortcut. If the shortcut points to a folder, the data type is *MAPIFolder*. If the shortcut points to a file system folder, the data type is *Object*. If the shortcut points to a URL or a file system path, the data type is *String*. If you want to change the icon used by the shortcut, use the *SetIcon* method. This method replaces the icon in the shortcut with the icon that you specify to the method as a path to the icon file—for example, c:\icons\myicon.ico. You can see how to use this object in the Account Tracking application in Chapter 8.

Selection Collection Object

To enable your applications to identify what the user has selected in an Explorer window in Outlook, the Outlook object model includes the *Selection* collection object, which contains the set of items that a user has selected in the user interface. For example, you can use this collection to validate that the user has selected the item required for your application to continue. You can also use it to dynamically add menu commands and toolbar buttons when a user selects a certain item.

You must use the *Item* method with the object's index as a parameter to retrieve a specific object in the collection. The object is returned to you as an *Object* variable, which means that if you want to call a specific method or property on the object, you should first cast the object to a specific data type.

This collection supports the *Count* property, which returns the number of items selected in a collection. You can use the *Count* property to determine the number of items the user has currently selected.

> **Note** To see the *Selection* collection in action, see the Account Tracking application in Chapter 8.

Explorers Collection

An *Explorer* object represents the window in which the contents of a folder are displayed. To make accessing these Explorer windows in your application easier, Outlook provides an *Explorers* collection below the *Application* object. The *Explorers* collection contains all the *Explorer* objects in your application, even those that are not visible.

The *Explorers* collection also contains a *Count* property, which you can use to determine how many *Explorer* objects are in the collection. You can use the *Count* property to identify open *Explorer* objects that need to be closed before your application exits. Making this determination is important because Outlook cannot terminate properly when *Explorer* objects are running.

The *Explorers* collection contains two methods, *Add* and *Item*. You can use the *Add* method to create a new *Explorer* object and specify the folder to display in that *Explorer* object's window. The *Add* method takes two parameters. The first parameter is either a *MAPIFolder* object or a string containing a path to the folder. The second parameter is an optional *Long* data type that specifies the display mode for the folder. This value can be *olFolderDisplayNormal (0)*, *olFolderDisplayFolderOnly (1)*, or *olFolderDisplayNoNavigation (2)*. The *Add* method returns the newly created *Explorer* object. This new *Explorer* object is initially hidden; you must call the *Display* method to reveal it. The following code shows how to use the *Add* method:

```
Dim oExplorers As Outlook.Explorers
Dim oExplorer As Outlook.Explorer

Set oFolder = oNS.GetDefaultFolder(olFolderContacts)
Set oExplorers = oApp.Explorers
Set oExplorer = oExplorers.Add(oFolder, olDisplayNormal)
oExplorer.Display
```

By passing an individual *Explorer* object's index, you can use the *Item* method of the *Explorers* collection to access that object in the collection. The following example shows how to do this:

```
Set oFolder = oNS.GetDefaultFolder(olFolderContacts)
Set oExplorers = oApp.Explorers
Set oExplorer = oExplorers.Item(1)
MsgBox oExplorer.Caption
```

The *Explorers* collection includes a single event, *NewExplorer*, which you can use to track a newly created *Explorer* object that has not yet been made visible. This event passes an *Explorer* object that is being opened or created. The following code shows how to use the *NewExplorer* event:

```
Dim WithEvents oExplorers As Outlook.Explorers

Set oExplorers = oApp.Explorers
Private Sub oExplorers_NewExplorer( _
ByVal Explorer As Outlook.Explorer)
    MsgBox "You opened or added a new Explorer with the caption: " & _
           Explorer.Caption
End Sub
```

Inspectors Collection

An *Inspector* object represents the window in which an Outlook item is displayed. To make it easier for you to find out which *Inspector* objects are available in your application, the Outlook object model includes an *Inspectors* collection, which contains *Inspector* objects that are not currently visible to the user as well as *Inspector* objects that are. The *Inspectors* collection is accessed from the *Application* object in Outlook.

The *Inspectors* collection contains one property, *Count*, which returns the number of *Inspector* objects in the collection.

The *Inspectors* collection also contains two methods, *Add* and *Item*. The *Add* method takes one parameter—a valid Outlook *Item* object—to display in the new *Inspector*. This method returns an *Inspector* object. You must call the *Display* method on the *Inspector* object that's returned in order to display the item. The following code shows how to use this method:

```
Set oFolder = oNS.GetDefaultFolder(olFolderTasks)
Set oItem = oFolder.Items.GetFirst
Set oInspectors = oApp.Inspectors
Set oInspector = oInspectors.Add(oItem)
oInspector.Display
```

The *Item* method allows you to access an *Inspector* object in the collection. You must pass the numeric index of the *Inspector* object you want to retrieve.

Links Collection and *Link* Object

To make group tracking activities possible, Outlook supports a feature named Activity Tracking. You use Activity Tracking to associate items and documents with a contact so Outlook can search folders that you specify for any linked items. To enable Activity Tracking, open a contact and click on the Activities tab. A sample Activities contact is shown in Figure 6-7.

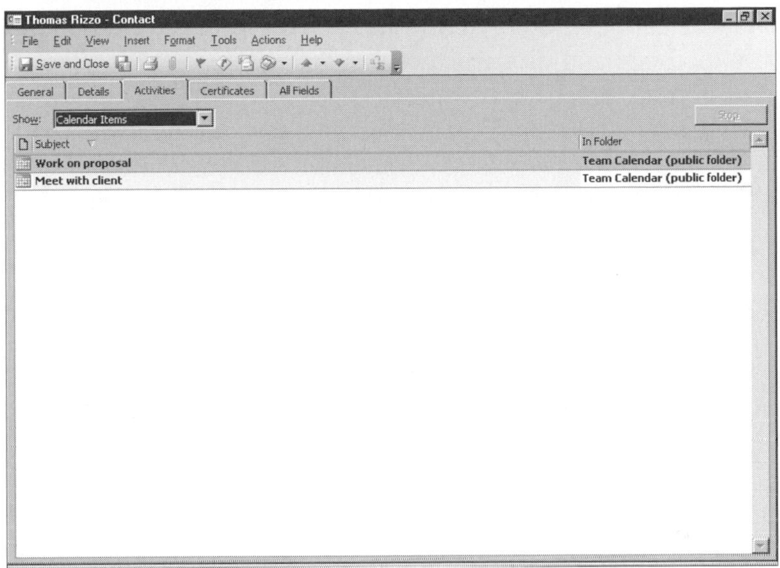

Figure 6-7 The Activities tab for a specific contact

Outlook can search both private and public folders. To specify which folders Outlook should search, right-click on the Contacts folder and choose Properties. In the Contact Properties dialog box, click on the Activities tab. On this tab, you'll see a list of searchable folders you specified. You can also add new folders to the search criteria, as shown in Figure 6-8.

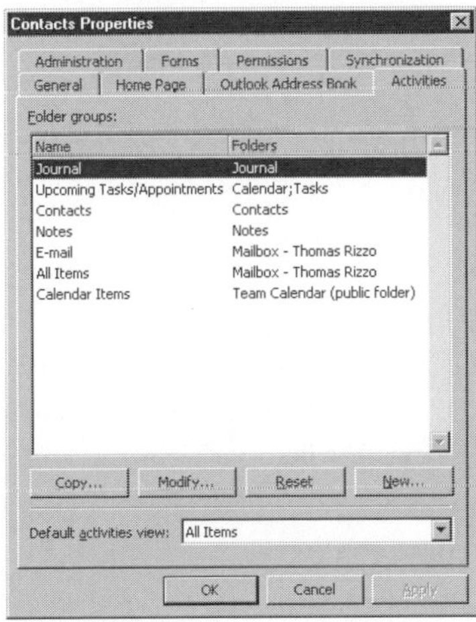

Figure 6-8 On the Activities tab for a folder, you can add new folders to the search criteria.

The use of Activity Tracking would be limited if the Outlook object model didn't support working with these links programmatically. The model includes a *Links* collection and a *Link* object. The *Links* collection contains a set of *Link* objects that comprise other items linked to a particular Outlook item. You can use the methods and properties of this collection to add, delete, or count the number of links to a particular item.

The *Links* collection contains three methods: *Add*, *Item*, and *Remove*. *Add* creates a new *Link* object in the collection. You must pass to this method the object you want to link to. Currently that object must be an Outlook Contact object. You use the *Links* collection and the *Add* method on message items, task items, and other types of Outlook items. The following example shows how to use the *Add* method:

```
Dim oLinks As Outlook.Links
Dim oLink As Outlook.Link
Dim oContact As Outlook.ContactItem

Set oFolder = oNS.GetDefaultFolder(olFolderInbox)
Set oMailItem = oFolder.Items.Find("[Message Class] = 'IPM.Note'")
Set oLinks = oMailItem.Links
Set oContactFldr = oNS.GetDefaultFolder(olFolderContacts)
Set oItems = oContactFldr.Items
Set oContact = oItems.GetFirst

oLinks.Add oContact
MsgBox "Added a link to the " & oContact.FullName & " contact on " & _
       "the item " & oMailItem.Subject
```

The *Item* method allows you to retrieve an item in the collection by using its index or its name. The following code shows how to retrieve a *Link* object in the collection by using the name of the contact that the link refers to:

```
Set oFolder = oNS.GetDefaultFolder(olFolderInbox)
Set oMailItem = oFolder.Items.Find("[Message Class] = 'IPM.Note'")
Set oLinks = oMailItem.Links
Set oLink = oLinks.Item("Don Hall")
MsgBox "The link refers to the " & oLink.Name & " contact on " & _
       "the item " & oMailItem.Subject
```

The third method supported in the *Links* collection is *Remove*, which you use to remove a link from the collection by specifying the index of the *Link* object to remove. The next bit of code shows how to find and remove a specific *Link* object in the collection. Keep in mind that a user or an application can associate an Outlook item with multiple contact items. This means that a single task can be linked to more than one contact.

```
Set oFolder = oNS.GetDefaultFolder(olFolderInbox)
Set oMailItem = oFolder.Items.Find("[Message Class] = 'IPM.Note'")
```

```
Set oLinks = oMailItem.Links
Counter = 1
For Each oLink In oLinks
    If oLink.Name = "Don Hall" Then
       oLinks.Remove Counter
       oMailItem.Save
    End If
    Counter = Counter + 1
Next

MsgBox "Removed the Don Hall link object."
```

The *Link* object contains properties but no methods. Of all the properties, you will probably use only three in your applications: *Item*, *Name*, and *Type*. The *Item* property returns the Outlook item represented by the *Link* object. For Outlook, this property always returns an Outlook Contact item, which you can then manipulate in your code. The following example shows how to use the *Item* property:

```
Set oFolder = oNS.GetDefaultFolder(olFolderInbox)
Set oMailItem = oFolder.Items.Find("[Message Class] = 'IPM.Note'")
Set oLinks = oMailItem.Links
Set oLink = oLinks.Item(1)
Set oContact = oLink.Item
MsgBox "The contact name is " & oContact.FullName
```

The *Name* property returns the name of the contact that the *Link* object represents. This name is the display name for the contact. The *Type* property returns the Outlook item type represented by the *Link* object. As of this writing, the only valid type is *olContact*.

> **Note** For information on the *PropertyPages* collection, the *PropertyPage* object, and the *PropertyPageSite* object, see the discussion of the Account Tracking application in Chapter 8.

Methods, Properties, and Events

Next we'll look at methods and properties of other Outlook objects as well as a host of events that your applications can use to receive notifications from Outlook.

Application Object

Recall that the *Application* object is the topmost object in the Outlook object model. You must create an *Application* object before you create any other objects. Let's take a look at some of the methods, properties, and events of the *Application* object.

ActiveWindow Method

The *ActiveWindow* method returns the object that represents the topmost Outlook window on the desktop. The return type for this object can be an *Explorer* object or an *Inspector* object. If no *Explorer* or *Inspector* object is open, this method returns *Nothing*. You use this method to determine which object the current user is viewing and, if necessary, to change the state of that object. The following code shows how to use the *ActiveWindow* method:

```
Set oWindow = oApp.ActiveWindow
If Not (oWindow Is Nothing) Then
    If oWindow.Class = olExplorer Then
        strTop = "Explorer"
    ElseIf oWindow.Class = olInspector Then
        strTop = "Inspector"
    End If
    MsgBox "The topmost object is a(n) " & strTop & " object."
End If
```

AnswerWizard Property

The *AnswerWizard* property returns an *AnswerWizard* object for the application. For more information about the *AnswerWizard* object model, see the Office documentation.

COMAddIns Property

The *COMAddIns* property returns a *COMAddIns* collection that represents all COM add-ins currently loaded and connected in Outlook. You can use this collection to quickly access COM add-ins and their exposed objects. The following example shows how to use the *COMAddIns* property:

```
Dim oCOMAddins As Office.COMAddIns
Dim oCOMAddin As Office.COMAddIn

Set oCOMAddins = oApp.COMAddIns
strName = vbLf
For Each oCOMAddin In oCOMAddins
    strName = strName & vbLf & oCOMAddin.ProgId
Next
MsgBox "The COM Add-Ins ProgIDs in Outlook are: " & _
       strNameExplorers
```

CopyFile Method

The *CopyFile* method copies a file from the file system to a folder you specify in Outlook. The first parameter you must specify is the path to the file you want to copy. The second parameter is the Outlook path to the folder you want to copy the item to. The path defaults to the mailbox of the user, so entering *Inbox\Test* for this parameter copies the item to the Test folder under the Inbox. To copy the item to a public folder, use *\\Public Folders\All Public Folders\<Folder>*.

Explorers and *Inspectors* Properties

The *Explorers* property returns the *Explorers* collection. The *Inspectors* property returns the *Inspectors* collection. We covered these collections earlier in this chapter.

LanguageSettings Property

The *LanguageSettings* property returns a *LanguageSettings* object that you can use to retrieve language-related information about Outlook. For example, you can retrieve the install language, the user interface language, and the help language for Outlook. You can use this information in COM add-ins to load the proper resource string for a user interface, based on the information you obtain from the LanguageSettings object.

ProductCode Property

The *ProductCode* property returns a string that is the globally unique identifier (GUID) for the Outlook product. If you need to identify Outlook in your COM add-ins or applications, you can use this GUID to identify it.

ItemSend Event

The *ItemSend* event fires when a user or an application uses Outlook to attempt to send an item. This event returns an object for the item and a Boolean named *Cancel*. If you set *Cancel* to *True*, Outlook will stop the send action and leave the *Inspector* open for the user. If you do cancel the send, you should display an explanation in a message box so users will know what they need to add or delete to successfully send the item. The following code checks to see whether a user added a subject and a category to his message. Note that the *ItemSend* event does not fire when a user posts an item to a folder. In this case, you should monitor the folder for the *ItemAdd* event.

```
Dim WithEvents oApp As Outlook.Application

Private Sub oApp_ItemSend(ByVal Item As Object, Cancel As Boolean)
    If Item.Subject = "" Then
        MsgBox "You must add a subject!"
        Cancel = True
```

```
    ElseIf Item.Categories = "" Then
        MsgBox "You must have a category!"
        Cancel = True
    End If
End Sub
```

MAPILogonComplete Event

The *MAPILogonComplete* event fires after the *OnStartupComplete* event and guarantees that you have a valid MAPI session with the server so that all properties and methods are available across the Outlook object model.

NewMail Event

The *NewMail* event fires when a new item is received in the Inbox of the current user. This event does not pass any parameters, nor is there any one-to-one correspondence between the number of arriving messages and the number of times this event fires; even if the Inbox receives many new messages, Outlook might fire this event only once. The following code shows how to use the *NewMail* event:

```
Private Sub oApp_NewMail()
    MsgBox "You have received new mail!"
End Sub
```

OptionsPagesAdd Event

For information about the *OptionsPagesAdd* event, see the Account Tracking application in Chapter 8.

Quit Event

The *Quit* event is fired when Outlook begins to close. Using this event, you can persist any settings or other information as well as destroy any objects that are left open by your application.

Reminder Event

The *Reminder* event is fired immediately before a reminder is displayed. This event passes one parameter, which is an object that corresponds to the item firing the reminder. There is no *Cancel* parameter for this event, so you cannot keep the reminder from appearing, but this event allows you to take other actions based on the reminder. The following example shows how to use the *Reminder* event:

```
Private Sub oApp_Reminder(ByVal Item As Object)
    MsgBox "The following item " & Item.Subject & " has " & _
        "fired a reminder."
End Sub
```

Startup Event

The *Startup* event is fired after Outlook and any of its COM add-ins have been loaded. You can use this event to initialize VBA programs that you created with Outlook.

NameSpace Object

The *NameSpace* object has been enhanced incrementally through successive versions of Outlook. The features you are mostly likely to use in your applications are the ability to dynamically add a .pst file to the *NameSpace* object and the ability to create custom property pages for folders. Let's examine more closely these aspects of the *NameSpace* object.

SyncObjects Property

The *SyncObjects* property returns the *SyncObjects* collection for the *NameSpace* object. We covered the *SyncObjects* collection earlier in the chapter.

AddStore Method

The *AddStore* method allows you to dynamically connect an existing .pst file to Outlook and to create a new .pst file. This method takes one parameter, which is a path to the .pst file you want to access or create. If you pass in a path for the .pst file and the .pst file doesn't exist, Outlook will create the file. You can then retrieve the information in the .pst file by using the Outlook object model. The following example shows how to use the *AddStore* method to access an existing .pst file:

```
oNS.AddStore "c:\my new store.pst"

'Retrieve a folder from the newly connected store
Set oFolder = oNS.Folders("Personal Folders").Folders("My Folder")

'Display the folder
oFolder.Display
```

Dial Method

The Dial method is a new method. Outlook allows you to dial a contact's phone number directly, just as you can do from the contact item itself. You can optionally pass a *Contact* object as a parameter, which populates the Dial dialog box with the contact's information. If you do not specify a contact, a blank dial screen will be displayed.

Offline Property

The *Offline* property is a Boolean property that returns whether the user is working on line or off line. You no longer have to use CDO to determine this status.

OptionsPagesAdd Event

For more information about this event, see the Account Tracking application in Chapter 8.

RemoveStore Method

The *RemoveStore* method removes the store that you pass as a *MAPIFolder* object from Outlook. It does not delete the store, and you cannot remove the standard mailbox store. This operation is the same as right-clicking on the root folder of a store and choosing Close StoreName.

Explorer Object

Outlook developers have often requested more granular control over how *Explorers* and *Inspectors* are displayed on the screen. With Outlook 2003, you can control the location of your Explorer and Inspector windows and also receive events from these objects that indicate what the user is doing in the user interface. In addition, the *Explorer* object adds a number of new events. Let's take a look at the recent additions to the *Explorer* object.

Caption Property

The *Caption* property returns the string for the Explorer window text. This property is read-only.

CurrentView Property

The *CurrentView* property returns or sets the view for the *Explorer*. When you set this property, you cause the *BeforeViewSwitch* and *ViewSwitch* events to fire on the *Explorer* object. Because Outlook supports only a single initial view of a folder, you can use this property to customize per-user settings for the initial view. To do this, you use the *FolderSwitch* event for the *Explorer* object. When this event fires, you check the current folder and current user and then set the *CurrentView* property appropriately. The following code snippet shows an example of this functionality:

```
Dim WithEvents oExplorer As Outlook.Explorer
Private Sub oExplorer_FolderSwitch()
On Error Resume Next
    If oExplorer.CurrentFolder.Class = olFolder Then
        If oExplorer.CurrentFolder.Name = "Contacts" Then
```

```
            If oNS.CurrentUser.Name = "Thomas Rizzo" Then
                oExplorer.CurrentView = "By Category"
            End If
        End If
    End If
End Sub
```

Height Property

The *Height* property returns or sets the height of the Explorer window in pixels. You can use this property to change the height of your Explorer window.

HTMLDocument Property

The *HTMLDocument* property returns the HTML document for the home page for the current folder in the *Explorer* object. You can then script the HTML document object model to implement your functionality.

Left Property

The *Left* property returns or sets the distance, in pixels, from the left edge of the screen to the left edge of the Explorer window.

Panes Property

The *Panes* property returns the *Panes* collection for the *Explorer* object. We covered the *Panes* collection earlier in the chapter.

Selection Property

The *Selection* property returns a *Selection* collection, which enables you to access the items currently selected by the user. We covered the *Selection* collection earlier in the chapter.

Top Property

The *Top* property returns or sets the distance, in pixels, from the top edge of the screen to the top edge of the Explorer window.

Width Property

The *Width* property returns or sets the width of the Explorer window in pixels.

WindowState Property

The *WindowState* property returns or sets the window state. The possible values for this property include *olMaximized (1)*, *olMinimized (2)*, and *olNormalWindow (3)*. The next code sample uses the *Top*, *Width*, *Left*, and *Height* properties to move an Explorer window around the screen. Notice that the code first sets the *WindowState* property to *olNormalWindow*. Outlook will return an error if the window is already maximized or minimized when you try to set these properties.

```
oExplorer.WindowState = olNormalWindow
oExplorer.Top = 100
oExplorer.Width = 200
oExplorer.Left = 300
oExplorer.Height = 100
```

Activate Method

The *Activate* method activates an *Explorer* object by bringing it to the foreground and giving it keyboard focus. You can use this method to highlight a specific Explorer or Inspector window for your application.

IsPaneVisible Method

The *IsPaneVisible* method returns a Boolean that specifies whether a particular pane is visible in the Explorer window. You pass the desired pane as a parameter to this method. The possible values you can pass are *olOutlookBar (1)*, *olFolderList (2)*, and *olPreview (3)*. You use the *IsPaneVisible* method in conjunction with the *ShowPane* method, which is described next.

ShowPane Method

The *ShowPane* method hides or displays a specific pane in your Explorer window. You must pass to this method the pane you are interested in as well as a Boolean parameter that is set to *True* to display the pane or *False* to hide the pane. The following code shows how to use the *IsPaneVisible* method with the *ShowPane* method to hide and display panes in an Explorer window:

```
'Flip the settings that the user already has
boolFolderList = oExplorer.IsPaneVisible(olFolderList)
boolOutlookBar = oExplorer.IsPaneVisible(olOutlookBar)
boolPreviewPane = oExplorer.IsPaneVisible(olPreview)

oExplorer.ShowPane olFolderList, Not (boolFolderList)
oExplorer.ShowPane olOutlookBar, Not (boolOutlookBar)
oExplorer.ShowPane olPreview, Not (boolPreviewPane)
```

Activate Event

The *Activate* event is fired when an Explorer window or an Inspector window becomes the active window. You can use this event to determine whether a specific Explorer or Inspector window becomes the active window and then customize the toolbar for that window. The following code shows how to use this event:

```
Dim WithEvents oExplorer as Outlook.Explorer

Private Sub oExplorer_Activate()
   MsgBox "This Explorer window has become active!"
End Sub
```

BeforeFolderSwitch Event

The *BeforeFolderSwitch* event occurs before the *Explorer* navigates to the new folder. This event passes an object that represents the folder the user is trying to navigate to and also a Boolean parameter named *Cancel*. To keep the current folder active and prevent the user from navigating to the new folder, set *Cancel* to *True*. If the user navigates to a folder in the file system, the *BeforeFolderSwitch* event will not pass an object for that folder. For an example of this event in action, see the Account Tracking application in Chapter 8.

BeforeItemCopy Event

The *BeforeItemCopy* event fires before an item is copied to the Clipboard. This event is cancelable.

BeforeItemCut Event

The *BeforeItemCut* event fires before an item is cut and moved to the Clipboard. This event is cancelable.

BeforeItemPaste Event

The *BeforeItemPaste* event fires before a user pastes an item from the Clipboard or when a user drags and drops an item from one folder to another. This event is cancelable and passes the Clipboard contents and the target folder for the paste operation.

BeforeMaximize Event

The *BeforeMaximize* event fires before the Explorer window is maximized. This event is cancelable.

BeforeMinimize Event

The *BeforeMinimize* event fires before the Explorer window is minimized. This event is cancelable.

BeforeMove Event

The *BeforeMove* event fires before the Explorer window is moved to a different location. This event is cancelable.

BeforeSize Event

The *BeforeSize* event fires before a window is resized but not before a window is restored. This event is cancelable.

BeforeViewSwitch Event

The *BeforeViewSwitch* event fires when a user tries to switch views. This event passes the name of the view the user is trying to switch to as well as the Boolean variable *Cancel*. To cancel the change in views and maintain the user's current view, set *Cancel* to *True*. The following code shows how to use the *BeforeViewSwitch* event:

```
Private Sub oExplorer_BeforeViewSwitch(ByVal NewView As Variant, _
                                       Cancel As Boolean)
    If NewView = "By Category" Then
        Cancel = True
    End If
End Sub
```

Close Event

The *Close* event fires when the Explorer window is being closed. You will generally listen for this event only when you're developing COM add-ins that need to correctly destroy *Explorer* objects or the variables that reference them.

Deactivate Event

The *Deactivate* event fires when the Explorer or Inspector window is no longer the active window. This event does not pass any parameters.

FolderSwitch Event

The *FolderSwitch* event fires after a user successfully switches folders. This event does not pass any parameters.

SelectionChange Event

The *SelectionChange* event fires after the user selects a different item in the current view. This event does not pass any parameters. The following code shows how to use this event with the *Selection* collection:

```
Private Sub oExplorer_SelectionChange()
    On Error Resume Next
    Set oSelection = oExplorer.Selection
    strName = vbLf
    For Each oItem In oSelection
        strName = strName & vbLf & oItem.Subject
    Next
    MsgBox "New Selection: " & strName
End Sub
```

ViewSwitch Event

The *ViewSwitch* event fires when the user successfully changes the view in the Explorer window. This event does not pass any parameters.

Sample Code for Events

The following code shows you how to use a number of the events just described:

```
⋮
Dim WithEvents oExplorer As Outlook.Explorer
Dim oApp As New Outlook.Application
Set oExplorer = oApp.ActiveExplorer
⋮

Private Sub oExplorer_BeforeItemCopy(Cancel As Boolean)
    If oExplorer.Selection.Count = 1 Then
        MsgBox "You are copying 1 item called " & _
                oExplorer.Selection.Item(1).Subject
    Else
        MsgBox "You are copying " & oExplorer.Selection.Count & " items."
        Dim oSelection As Outlook.Selection
        For x = 1 To oExplorer.Selection.Count
            MsgBox "Item Name: " & oExplorer.Selection.Item(x).Subject
        Next
    End If
End Sub

Private Sub oExplorer_BeforeItemCut(Cancel As Boolean)
    If oExplorer.Selection.Count = 1 Then
        MsgBox "You are copying 1 item called " & _
                oExplorer.Selection.Item(1).Subject
    Else
        MsgBox "You are copying " & oExplorer.Selection.Count & " items."
        Dim oSelection As Outlook.Selection
        For x = 1 To oExplorer.Selection.Count
            MsgBox "Item Name: " & oExplorer.Selection.Item(x).Subject
        Next
    End If
End Sub

Private Sub oExplorer_BeforeItemPaste(ClipboardContent As Variant, _
            ByVal Target As Outlook.MAPIFolder, Cancel As Boolean)
    'See what they are trying to paste
    If TypeOf ClipboardContent Is Selection Then
        'Scroll through the selection to make sure we will allow the paste
        For x = 1 To ClipboardContent.Count
            'check some variable
            If ClipboardContent.Item(x).Subject = "No Paste" Then
                Cancel = True
            End If
        Next
    End If
End Sub

Private Sub oExplorer_BeforeMaximize(Cancel As Boolean)
    MsgBox "Maximizing!"
End Sub

Private Sub oExplorer_BeforeMinimize(Cancel As Boolean)
    MsgBox "Minimizing!"
End Sub
```

```
Private Sub oExplorer_BeforeMove(Cancel As Boolean)
    MsgBox "Moving!"
End Sub

Private Sub oExplorer_BeforeSize(Cancel As Boolean)
    MsgBox "Sizing!"
End Sub
```

Inspector Object

The properties, methods, and events of the *Inspector* object are the same as their *Explorer* object counterparts that I've described, so I'll simply list them. For details, you can refer back to the descriptions provided earlier.

- *Caption* property
- *Height* property
- *Top* property
- *Width* property
- *WindowState* property
- *Activate* method
- *Activate* event
- *BeforeMaximize* event
- *BeforeMinimize* event
- *BeforeMove* event
- *BeforeSize* event
- *Deactivate* event
- *Close* event

Folders Collection

The *Folders* collection contains three new events: *FolderAdd*, *FolderChange*, and *FolderRemove*.

FolderAdd Event

The *FolderAdd* event fires when a folder is added to the *Folders* collection. This event passes the added folder as a *MAPIFolder* object. You cannot cancel this event. You might want to hook into this event to prompt the user to add a folder to a specific group on the Outlook Bar. The following code shows how to use the *FolderAdd* event:

```
:
Dim WithEvents oFolders As Outlook.Folders
Set oFolders = oNS.Folders("Mailbox - Thomas Rizzo").Folders
:

Private Sub oFolders_FolderAdd(ByVal Folder As Outlook.MAPIFolder)
    MsgBox "You have added the " & Folder.Name & " folder!"
End Sub
```

FolderChange Event

The *FolderChange* event fires when some property of the specified *Folders* collection—such as all the items in the folder—are deleted. This event passes the changed folder as a *MAPIFolder* object, but it does not pass the actual folder property that was changed. You must figure out programmatically which property was changed. You can't cancel this event. The following code shows how to use the *FolderChange* event:

```
Private Sub oFolders_FolderChange(ByVal Folder As Outlook.MAPIFolder)
    MsgBox "You changed the " & Folder.Name & " folder!"
End Sub
```

FolderRemove Event

The *FolderRemove* event fires when a folder is removed from the collection. It does not pass any parameters, so if you need to know which folder was removed, your code has to figure that out. Outlook notifies you only that some folder was removed. You can't cancel the *FolderRemove* event.

MAPIFolder Object

The *MAPIFolder* object provides three interesting properties that are described in Chapter 8: *WebViewAllowNavigation*, *WebViewOn*, and *WebViewURL*. The other properties, methods, and events of the *MAPIFolder* object are described next.

AddressBookName Property

The *AddressBookName* property is a string property that can get or set the name to use when you display the Contact address book in the address book selection interface.

AddToFavorites Method

The *AddToFavorites* method adds the current folder to the favorites list in Microsoft Internet Explorer. It takes two optional parameters. The first is a Boolean that specifies whether to display the standard user interface for naming the folder and selecting the location. If you specify *True* for this parameter, the second parameter will be the name of the folder.

AddToPFFavorites Method

The *AddToPFFavorites* method adds the current folder to the Public Folder Favorites folder. You can add only public folders to the Public Folder Favorites folder.

CustomViewsOnly Property

The *CustomViewsOnly* property is a Boolean property that you can use to specify whether to display only custom views for the folder.

FolderPath Property

The *FolderPath* property returns a string indicating the path to the current folder, such as *\\Public Folders\All Public Folders\My Folder*.

InAppFolderFolderSyncObject Property

The *InAppFolderFolderSyncObject* property is a Boolean property that gets or sets whether the current folder is in the Application Folders Send/Receive group. You can then programmatically synchronize the Application Folders group that contains the folder.

ShowAsOutlookAB Property

The *ShowAsOutlookAB* property is a Boolean property that specifies whether to show the current folder as an Outlook address book so users can browse and resolve names against the folder. This method works only with contact folders.

Views Collection

Returns the *Views* collection for the folder. We covered the *Views* collection earlier in the chapter.

Items Collection

Recall that the Outlook *Items* collection is a collection of objects in a particular folder. The type of object the *Items* collection contains depends on the items in the folder. For example, in your Calendar folder, the *Items* collection will most likely contain *AppointmentItem* objects. We'll look at the enhancements to the *Items* collection next.

ItemAdd Event

The *ItemAdd* event fires when a new item is added to the folder. This event returns an object for the item added to the folder's collection. Remember that before you attempt to call methods or properties on a returned object, you should check which type of object was returned. It might not be the type you expected and might cause unwanted behavior in your application. For an example of how to use this event, see the Account Tracking application in Chapter 8.

ItemChange Event

The *ItemChange* event fires when an item in the collection is changed in any way. The event passes an object for the item that was changed; it does not pass the changed property. This means you must use your code to determine what was changed on the item. For an example of using this event, see the Account Tracking application in Chapter 8.

ItemRemove Event

The *ItemRemove* event fires when an item is removed or deleted from the collection. This event does not pass any parameters, so your code must figure out which items were deleted from the collection.

Characteristics of Item Types

We'll look next at some characteristics of all the item types in Outlook, such as the *PostItem*, the *MailItem*, and the *AppointmentItem* objects. The events I'll discuss can be used with Visual Basic, VBA, and VBScript. The examples are written using VBScript.

Links Property

The *Links* property returns the *Links* collection for the object. We covered the *Links* collection earlier in the chapter.

AttachmentAdd Event

The *AttachmentAdd* event fires after an attachment has been added to an Outlook item. This event passes the attachment as an *Attachment* object. Once the object is passed, you can perform tasks such as checking the attachment for viruses before the user sends the item. You cannot, however, cancel or stop the user from adding an attachment to the item. The following VBScript example shows how to use this event:

```
Sub Item_AttachmentAdd(ByVal NewAttachment)
    If NewAttachment.Type = 1 Then
        Item.Save
        If Item.Size > 10000 then
            MsgBox "Sending a message with an attachment this large" & _
                    " may take a long time."
        End If
    End If
End Sub
```

AttachmentRead Event

The *AttachmentRead* event fires after an attachment has been opened for reading; it passes the attachment as an *Attachment* object. You can use this event to perform certain actions when the user opens the attachment, such as making a backup copy of the attachment or marking this attachment as checked out for a document management solution. The following example shows how to prompt the user to save changes when the user opens an attachment to read it:

```
Sub Item_AttachmentRead(ByVal ReadAttachment)
    If ReadAttachment.Type = 1 Then
        MsgBox "Make sure to save any changes that " & _
               "you make to the attachment."
    End If
End Sub
```

BeforeAttachmentSave Event

The *BeforeAttachmentSave* event fires before an attachment is saved with the item. This event is supported in VBScript, Visual Basic, and VBA, so you must follow the appropriate syntax. When you use this event in VBScript that's automating an Outlook form, the *BeforeAttachmentSave* event passes the attachment that is trying to be saved as an *Attachment* object. If you're using Visual Basic or VBA, this event passes both the attachment and a Boolean parameter named *Cancel*. To abort the save, set *Cancel* to *True*. The next two code examples show a VBScript version and a Visual Basic/VBA version of this event, respectively. Notice that the VBScript version is a function and the Visual Basic/VBA version is a subroutine.

```
Function Item_BeforeAttachmentSave(ByVal SaveAttachment)
    If SaveAttachment.Type = 1 then
        If SaveAttachment.FileName = "sales.mdb" Then
            MsgBox "You cannot save this file!"
            Item_BeforeAttachmentSave = False
        End If
    End if
End Function

Private Sub oMailItem_BeforeAttachmentSave( _
            ByVal Attachment As Outlook.Attachment, Cancel As Boolean)
    If Attachment.Type = 1 then
        If Attachment.FileName = "sales.mdb" Then
            MsgBox "You cannot save this file!"
            Cancel = True
        End If
    End if
End Sub
```

BeforeCheckNames Event

The *BeforeCheckNames* event fires before Outlook starts resolving names for the recipients of an item. You can use this event to check the names of the recipients from a data source such as a database. This event, like the *BeforeAttachmentSave* event, uses different syntax depending on whether you call the event from VBScript or Visual Basic/VBA. In VBScript, this event is implemented as a function that you can cancel by setting the name of the function to *False*. In Visual Basic/VBA, you are passed a Boolean parameter named *Cancel*. To cancel the name resolution, you set *Cancel* to *True*. Here are examples that show the VBScript version and the Visual Basic/VBA version:

```
Function Item_BeforeCheckNames()
    'You can use this event to cancel Outlook's resolution
    'And put your own resolution in
    Item_BeforeCheckNames = False
End Function

Private Sub oMailItem_BeforeCheckNames(Cancel As Boolean)
    'You can use this event to cancel Outlook's resolution
    'And put your own resolution in
    Cancel = True
End Sub
```

SyncObjects Collection

The *SyncObjects* collection has been enhanced to support Application Folders. These are folders that a user or developer can add to a particular synchronization group called AppFolders. When synchronization occurs, the application folder is synchronized off line.

AppFolders Property

The *AppFolders* property returns the Application Folders' SyncObject. This SyncObject contains all Application Folders that you add programmatically to the application folders group using the *InAppFolderSyncObject* property.

ContactItem Enhancements

Two enhancements have been added to *ContactItem*, the *IMAddress* property and the *LastFirstNoSpaceandSuffix* property.

IMAddress Property

The *ContactItem* property gets or sets the Instant Messaging (IM) address for the contact.

LastFirstNoSpaceandSuffix Property

The *LastFirstNoSpaceandSuffix* property is used only when the first name, last name, or suffix field contains Asian (double-byte) characters.

Other Methods

Table 6-8 lists methods not covered elsewhere in this chapter. These methods work only in Outlook 2002.

Table 6-8 Additional Important Methods of Outlook Objects

Method	Object	Description
SaveAs	Multiple item types	This method is not new, but there are new *SaveAs* types. You can now save contacts as vCards by passing in *olVCard*, or you can save appointments as *iCal* appointments by passing in *olICal*.
ShowCategoriesDialog	Any Outlook item object	Displays the Categories dialog box for the item.

Other Properties

Table 6-9 describes properties that have not been covered elsewhere in the chapter.

Table 6-9 Additional Important Properties of Outlook Objects

Property	Object	Description
BodyFormat	*MailItem*, *PostItem*	Returns or sets the format for the body of a message. The constants you can use with this property are: ■ *olFormatHTML* ■ *olFormatPlain* ■ *olFormatRichText* ■ *olFormatUnspecified*
DownloadState	All Outlook items	Returns or sets the download state for an item. You can use the following constants: ■ *olFullItem* ■ *olHeaderOnly*

Table 6-9 Additional Important Properties of Outlook Objects

Property	Object	Description
InternetCodepage	*AppointmentItem, MailItem, PostItem, TaskItem*	Returns a *Long* value that is the Internet code page used by the item. For example, US English is hex value *4E9F*.
IsConflict	All Outlook items	A Boolean property that indicates whether the current item is in conflict. You can then access the attachments collection to get the different versions of the conflicted message.
MarkForDownload	All Outlook items	Determines the status of an item after you have received the item. You can use the following constants with this property: ■ *olMarkedForCopy* ■ *olMarkedForDelete* ■ *olMarkedForDownload* ■ *olRemoteStatusNone* ■ *olUnMarked*

Other Events

Table 6-10 describes events added to Outlook 2002 that have not been described elsewhere in the chapter.

Table 6-10 Additional Important Events for Outlook Objects

Event	Object	Description
BeforeDelete	All Outlook items	Fires before an item is deleted in Outlook. The item must be open in an Inspector window for this event to fire. If the user simply deletes the item from a view, this event does not fire. Synchronous events in Exchange 2000 are better for capturing delete events.

Setting Calendar Color with the *Appointment* Property

The Outlook Object Model does not have a way to query or set calendar color coding. However, you can use Collaboration Data Objects (CDO) to query and set the calendar color coding. You use the *Appointment* property set (*0220060000000000C000000000000046*); the property for the color is *0x8214*. The following quick sample shows you how to query this property using both CDO 1.21 and CDO for Exchange:

```
Dim oSession As New MAPI.Session
'CDO 1.21 Version
oSession.Logon
Dim oFolder As MAPI.Folder
Set oFolder = oSession.GetDefaultFolder(0)
Dim oItem As MAPI.AppointmentItem
Dim oMessages As MAPI.Messages

Set oItem = oFolder.Messages.GetFirst
MsgBox oItem.Fields.Item("0x8214", "0220060000000000C000000000000046")
'Values here will mimic the Outlook user interface
'0 = No color
'1 = 1st label (Important)
'2 = 2nd label (Business)
'3 = 3rd label (Personal)
'etc
oSession.Logoff

'CDO for Exchange version
Dim oAppt As New CDO.Appointment
strURL = "file://./backofficestorage/thomriznt5dom2.extest." & _
         "microsoft.com/mbx/thomriz/calendar/appt.eml"

oAppt.DataSource.Open strURL
'Propset is 00062002-0000-0000-C000-000000000046
'For CDO 1.21, this is transposed to 0220060000000000C000000000000046
'Property ID is 0x8214
MsgBox oAppt.Fields.Item("http://schemas.microsoft.com/mapi/id/" & _
    "{00062002-0000-0000-C000-000000000046}/0x00008214").Value
```

Programming Changes in Outlook 2003

The Outlook object model has changed in some major ways to support new functionality available through the Outlook 2003 user interface. The following sections examine these changes to the object model.

Application Object

The *Application* object has one new event called *NewMailEx*. One major complaint about the original *NewMail* event was that the event does not pass the items that are newly received. Instead, you have to troll the Inbox to figure out what items have been received since the last time your application was notified. To address this concern, the *NewMailEx* event passes a comma-delimited string of the EntryIDs for the new items received in your Inbox. This event doesn't work if you're working in the classic offline mode of Outlook or if Outlook is not running. When you restart Outlook, any new mail received after the startup of Outlook will fire the event, but any mail received while Outlook was closed will not fire it. If you need to capture every item coming into a mailbox, even if Outlook is closed, you should look at transport event sinks or store event sinks in Exchange Server. The following code shows how to use this new event:

```
Private Sub oApplication_NewMailEx(ByVal EntryIDCollection As String)
    'Try to retrieve the list of items that were just received
    'The list is a comma delimited collection of short-term EntryIDs
    Set oNamespace = oApplication.GetNamespace("MAPI")
    arrItems = Split(EntryIDCollection, ",")
    For i = LBound(arrItems) To UBound(arrItems)
        Set oItem = oNamespace.GetItemFromID(arrItems(i))
        MsgBox oItem.Subject
        Set oItem = Nothing
    Next
End Sub
```

Conflicts Collection, Conflict Item, and *AutoResolvedWinner*

Outlook 2003 features automatic resolution of conflicts using algorithms contained in Outlook. Outlook provides a *Conflicts* collection for every item type, such as *AppointmentItem* or *MailItem*, so you can determine whether an item is in conflict and what alternatives there are to the item. From the *Conflicts* collection, you can retrieve the Conflict item, if one exists. Conflict items are the losers of the automatic resolution in Outlook. The other way you can figure out the winner of a conflict in Outlook is to use the *AutoResolvedWinner* property, which is available on every item. This Boolean property is *True* if the item is the winner, *False* if the item is not the winner. Note that you cannot use *AutoResolvedWinner* in a Find or Restrict operation, nor can you use *SetColumns* with it because this property is a computed property. Instead, you have to manually scan a folder to determine whether any items have *AutoResolvedWinner* set to *True*.

You can use the *Item* property on the Conflict item to retrieve the item represented by the *Conflict* object. If you look at the *Type* property on the Conflict item, you will get the type of the item, not a conflict type. For example, in a conflict between appointment items, if you are looking at the loser of the conflict and you ask for the type, *Appointment* will be returned.

To replace a winner with an alternative item, you must delete the original item and move the other item to the folder where you want it to be. You must perform this operation programmatically because there is a hidden folder named Conflicts that contains all alternative versions of an item that is in conflict.

The following code shows how to use the new conflict features of the Outlook object model:

```
Set oApplication = GetObject("", "Outlook.Application")
Set oNamespace = oApplication.GetNamespace("MAPI")

Dim oCalendar As Outlook.MAPIFolder

'One way to find all conflicts in a folder
'is to scan the entire folder and look
'at the Conflicts collection
Set oCalendar = oNamespace.GetDefaultFolder(olFolderCalendar)
For Each oItem In oCalendar.Items
    Set oConflicts = oItem.Conflicts
    If oConflicts.Count > 0 Then
        MsgBox oItem.Subject & " has a conflict!"
        MsgBox "Displaying original item"
        oItem.Display
        i = 1
        For Each oConflict In oConflicts
            'Display each version
            MsgBox "Display conflict item #" & i
            oConflict.Item.Display
            i = i + 1
        Next
    End If
Next

'Another way is to search for True in the AutoResolvedWinner
'property
```

```
For Each oItem In oCalendar.Items
    If oItem.AutoResolvedWinner = True Then
        MsgBox oItem.Subject & " was the autoresolved winner!"
    End If
Next
End Sub
```

MeetingWorkspaceURL Property

To support the Windows SharePoint Services (WSS) integration features in Outlook 2003, the *AppointmentItem* and *MeetingItem* objects have a new read-only string property named *MeetingWorkspaceURL*, which corresponds to the URL of a shared WSS Web site used for planning and tracking the results of the meeting. Please note that you cannot use the Find, Restrict, or SetColumns methods with this property. The following code finds all items in a calendar that have a meeting workspace associated with them:

```
Set oApplication = GetObject("", "Outlook.Application")
Set oNamespace = oApplication.GetNamespace("MAPI")

Dim oCalendar As Outlook.MAPIFolder

'MeetingWorkspaceURL code
Set oCalendar = oNamespace.GetDefaultFolder(olFolderCalendar)
For Each oItem In oCalendar.Items
    If oItem.MeetingWorkspaceURL <> "" Then
        MsgBox oItem.Subject & " has a meeting workspace at: " & _
                oItem.MeetingWorkspaceURL
    End If
Next
```

ContactItem Object Changes

To support the addition of pictures to contacts, the *ContactItem* object has two new methods and a new property. The *AddPicture* method takes the path to a picture file to add to the contact. *HasPicture* is a Boolean property that returns *True* if the contact includes a picture or *False* if it does not. The *RemovePicture* method removes the picture from the contact. You must save the contact after making any changes to it, or else your changes will be lost. The following code demonstrates these methods and the property. (To test this code, be sure to update the names and picture path to values that are valid on your system.)

```
Set oApplication = GetObject("", "Outlook.Application")
Set oNamespace = oApplication.GetNamespace("MAPI")

'ContactItem Code
Dim oContacts As Outlook.MAPIFolder
Set oContacts = oNamespace.GetDefaultFolder(olFolderContacts)
```

```
'Create a new contact
Dim oContact As Outlook.ContactItem
Set oContact = oContacts.Items.Add
oContact.FirstName = "Tom"
oContact.LastName = "Rizzo"
'Add a picture
'This supports local paths and network paths
oContact.AddPicture "\\thomriznt52\f$\checkoutui.bmp"
MsgBox oContact.HasPicture
'Save the item
oContact.Save

For Each oItem In oContacts.Items
    If oItem.HasPicture = True Then
        MsgBox oItem.Subject & " has a picture!"
        'Remove the picture
        oItem.RemovePicture
        oItem.Save
    End If
Next
```

Explorer Object

With WSS integration, you can select WSS folders to add to your Outlook user interface. You can also select multiple calendar folders to display in the Outlook user interface. To support these capabilities, the *Explorer* object model has three additions. The first is the *Deselectfolder* method, which takes a *MAPIFolder* object. The *MAPIFolder* object should correspond to the WSS folder linked to Outlook or to an Outlook folder that is linked to the user interface, such as a calendar folder. You can usually find the linked SharePoint folders in the SharePoint Folders hierarchy in your folder list. This method will deselect the folder and remove it from the user interface.

The next addition is the *IsFolderSelected* method, which takes a *MAPIFolder* object and returns a Boolean value indicating whether the folder is selected in the user interface. The final addition is the *SelectFolder* method, which takes a *MAPIFolder* object and displays and selects the folder in the user interface. Here's some sample code:

```
'Explorer Code
'Get the WSS PST file in Outlook
Dim oFolder As Outlook.MAPIFolder
Dim oEventCalendar As Outlook.MAPIFolder
Dim oExplorer As Outlook.Explorer
Set oExplorer = oApplication.ActiveExplorer
'Get the Event Calendar folder
Set oEventCalendar = oNamespace.Folders("Mailbox - Thomas " & _
                     "Rizzo").Folders("Event Calendar")
```

```
If oExplorer.IsFolderSelected(oEventCalendar) Then
    'Deselect it
    oExplorer.DeselectFolder oEventCalendar
Else
    'Select it
    oExplorer.SelectFolder oEventCalendar
End If

Set oFolder = oNamespace.Folders("Mailbox - Thomas Rizzo")

For Each oFolder In oFolder.Folders
    'See if it's selected
    If oExplorer.IsFolderSelected(oFolder) Then
        MsgBox oFolder.Name & " is selected in the UI!"
    End If
Next
```

MailItem Object

To support some of the new features in Outlook, the *MailItem* object has been updated with some new properties. The first property is *EnableSharedAttachments*, which is Boolean. If you set this property to *True*, the Attachment Options pane (shown in Figure 6-9) will appear when a user attempts to add an attachment to a mail item. You can put attachments from Outlook into a shared workspace so all recipients can collaborate on the documents. If you specify *False*, this pane will not appear.

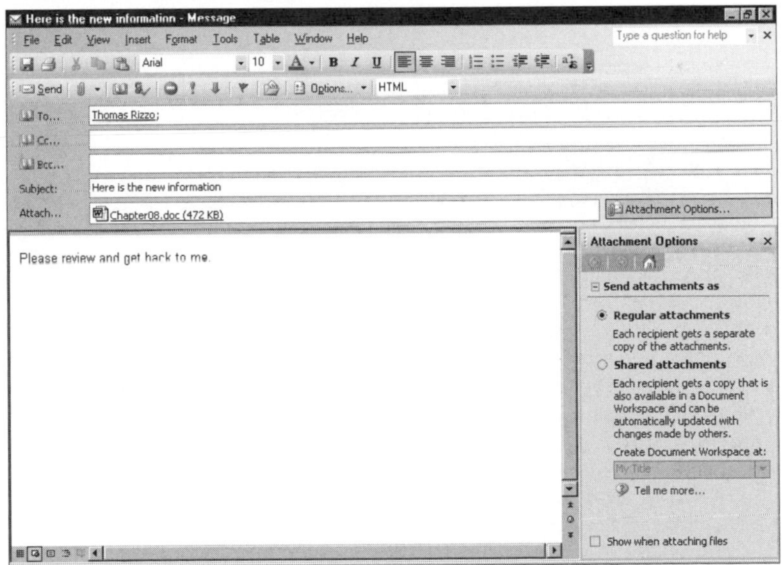

Figure 6-9 The Shared Attachment user interface in Outlook

The next property is the *FlagIcon* property. This property corresponds to the new quick-flag capabilities of Outlook, which let you specify a red, blue, green, or other color flag on your items.

To support the new IP fax features in Office, Outlook has two new fax properties. The *IsIPFax* property returns a Boolean specifying whether the item is an IPFax. The *HasCoverSheet* property returns a Boolean that specifies whether the fax has a cover sheet; if it does, the message body will display the cover sheet.

To support digital rights management (DRM) features, the *MailItem* object has some a new property called *Permission*. This property allows you to set the security on an Outlook item before sending it. The possible values are *olDoNotForward*, *olUnrestricted*, and *olTemplate*. The first one is self-explanatory. The second one, *olUnrestricted*, is the default and means that no restrictions are on the message. The final one, *olTemplate*, cannot be set as a value. This is the value when the received DRM protected message has been protected with an admin-defined template.

The final two properties solve one of the biggest pains in Outlook, which is retrieving the e-mail address and e-mail type of a sender without having to use CDO. Outlook now has the *SenderEmailAddress* string property and the *SenderEmailType* string property, which you can use to quickly retrieve address information about the sender of an e-mail message. These properties are also supported on the *MeetingItem* and *PostItem* objects.

The following code shows these additions in use in Outlook:

```
Dim oInbox As Outlook.MAPIFolder
Set oInbox = oNamespace.GetDefaultFolder(olFolderInbox)
Dim oMailItem As Outlook.MailItem
Set oMailItem = oInbox.Items.GetFirst

'Return the sender properties
MsgBox oMailItem.SenderEmailAddress & " type: " & _
       oMailItem.SenderEmailType

'Create a new mailitem and disable shared attachments
'And add a flag icon
Dim oNewItem As Outlook.MailItem
Set oNewItem = oApplication.CreateItem(olMailItem)
'Disable shared attachments
oNewItem.EnableSharedAttachments = False
'Add a flag icon
oNewItem.FlagIcon = olOrangeFlagIcon
'Display it and add an attachment manually
oNewItem.Display
```

MAPIFolder Object

To support WSS integration and the ability to show only unread item counts for a folder, the *MAPIFolder* object has two new properties. The first is *IsSharePointFolder*, a Boolean that is set to *True* if the folder is linked to a SharePoint folder and is set to *False* if the folder is not. The second property is *ShowItemCount*, which takes one of two values: *olShowTotalItemCount (2)* or *olShowUnreadItemCount (1)*. The following code illustrates the use of these properties:

```
'MAPIFolder Code for WSS Integration
Dim oMAPIFolder As Outlook.MAPIFolder
Set oMAPIFolder = oNamespace.GetDefaultFolder(olFolderInbox)
MsgBox oMAPIFolder.ShowItemCount
oMAPIFolder.ShowItemCount = olShowTotalItemCount

'Find all our SharePoint folders
'These are usually stored under the SharePoint Folders hierarchy
Dim oFolder As Outlook.MAPIFolder
Set oFolder = oNamespace.Folders("SharePoint Folders")
For Each oFolder In oFolder.Folders
    If oFolder.IsSharePointFolder Then
        MsgBox oFolder.Name & " is a SharePoint folder."
    End If
Next
```

MeetingItem Object

The *MeetingItem* object also supports the additions we've looked at for other objects. These include the *FlagIcon* property, the *MeetingWorkspaceURL* property, the *SenderEmailAddress* property, and the *SenderType* property.

Namespace Object

The *Namespace* object has a new method and a new property. The method, *AddStoreEx*, is an enhanced version of the *AddStore* method. It takes the path to a .pst file to add to Outlook; if that .pst file does not exist, Outlook creates it. The second new parameter to this method is the store type, which can be *olStoreANSI (3)*, *olStoreDefault (1)*, or *olStoreUnicode (2)*. Because Outlook now supports Unicode stores, this parameter had to be added to the method.

The new property of the *Namespace* object is the Exchange *ConnectionMode* property. (If you are running the beta of Outlook, you will see this as an older property called *ConnectionMode*. This property corresponds to Outlook's new online, low-bandwidth, cached, and offline modes. It returns the mode that Outlook is currently in, which can be *olNoExchange (0)*, *olOffline (100)*, *olDisconnected (200)*, *olConnectedHeaders (300)*, *olConnected (400)*, or *olOnline (500)*. The modes require some explaining. The *olNoExchange* mode is obvious—there is no Exchange Server. The *olOffline* mode means classic offline mode or the new cached Exchange mode. The *olDisconnected* mode is when you are using cached mode with a disconnected connection to your Exchange Server. *olConnectedHeaders* is returned if you are using cached Exchange mode but are in the Dialup/Slow Connection mode. The *olConnected* mode is when you are using cached Exchange mode in the LAN/Fast Connection mode. The *olOnline* mode is returned if you are using the classic online mode.

The following code shows how to use these additions to the *Namespace* object:

```
'Namespace Code

strText = ""
Select Case oNamespace.ConnectionMode
    Case olNoExchange:
        strText = "No Exchange Server!"
    Case olOffline:
        strText = "Offline"
    Case olDisconnected:
        strText = "Disconnected"
    Case olConnectedHeaders:
        strText = "Connected Headers"
    Case olConnected:
        strText = "Connected via LAN"
    Case olOnline:
        strText = "Online"
End Select

MsgBox "Current mode is " & oNamespace.ConnectionMode & " - " & strText

'Add a new unicode store
oNamespace.AddStoreEx "c:\mynewstore.pst", olStoreUnicode
```

One other change in the *Namespace* object is the addition of the *olFolderJunk* constant to the *GetDefaultFolder* and *GetSharedDefaultFolder* methods to support the new Junk e-mail folder.

PostItem Object

The *PostItem* object has two new properties, *SenderEmailAddress* and *SenderEmailType*.

Search Object

To support saved search folders, the *Search* object has a new *Save* method. This method takes a single parameter, which is the name of the search folder you want to create that contains the current search in the *Search* object. The following code creates a new search and saves the search as a search folder:

```
⋮
'Search Code
Dim oSearch As Outlook.Search
strFilter = "urn:schemas:mailheader:subject LIKE '%New Course Available%'"
strScope = "Inbox"
strTag = "SearchSubjects"

Set oSearch = oApplication.AdvancedSearch(strScope, strFilter, _
              True, strTag)
⋮

Private Sub oApplication_AdvancedSearchComplete( _
            ByVal SearchObject As Outlook.Search)
    MsgBox SearchObject.Tag & " returned " & SearchObject.Results.Count
    Dim oResults As Outlook.Results
    Set oResults = SearchObject.Results
    For Each oResult In oResults
        MsgBox oResult.Subject
    Next

    'Save the Search
    SearchObject.Save "My new subject search"
End Sub
```

Outlook Bar Changes

The object model of the Outlook Bar has not changed, but be aware that the object model works only with the Shortcuts portion of the Outlook Bar user interface. Therefore, you cannot change any part of the Outlook Bar user interface other than the shortcuts section. Also, if you have any code that leverages the Outlook bar object model, you should recheck it to be sure it works in Outlook 2003.

Other Common Outlook Development Tasks

After you start to create applications with Outlook, you might think of development tasks you want to accomplish that are beyond the standard Outlook object library in Outlook forms. We'll look next at three common development tasks in Outlook: automating Outlook from other applications, using CDO in Outlook applications, and programming the Rules Wizard.

Automating Outlook from Other Applications

Outlook supports automation, so you can access Outlook objects from other applications. To access Outlook objects, you typically set a reference to the Outlook object library. For example, to add a reference to the Outlook object library in Visual Basic, you choose References from the Tools menu. In the References dialog box, select the Microsoft Outlook 11.0 Object Library option. The following code sample shows how to use Visual Basic to automate Outlook to return the first Calendar appointment and display it. Notice that the Outlook constant *olFolderCalendar* can be used in Visual Basic and that replacing it with the actual value is not necessary, as it is in VBScript.

```
Private Sub Command1_Click()
    Set oOutlook = CreateObject("Outlook.Application")
    Set oNS = oOutlook.GetNameSpace("MAPI")
    Set oCalendar = oNS.GetDefaultFolder(olFolderCalendar)
    Set oItems = oCalendar.Items
    Set oFirst = oItems.GetFirst()
    oFirst.Display
End Sub
```

Using CDO in Outlook

Outlook provides an extensive object library with which you can develop custom applications, but sometimes you'll need to extend this environment by using other object libraries. The object library most commonly used to extend Outlook applications is CDO. CDO provides some functionality for dealing with data stored in Exchange Server that's beyond what is provided by the Outlook object library.

You'll need this additional functionality in the Account Tracking application, discussed in Chapter 8. One requirement for the application is that it keep track of the internal team assigned to work with a particular account. Keeping track of the team includes capturing the team's directory and e-mail information so other internal users who have questions about the account can send the team members e-mail. The easiest way for users to pick account team members is to display the address book. Outlook does not support displaying the address book and returning the individual that the user selected, but CDO does. To take advantage of the CDO functionality, we can extend the Account Tracking application to call the specific CDO functions, as shown here:

```
Sub FindAddress(FieldName, strCaption, iButtonText)
    On Error Resume Next

    Set oCDOSession = application.CreateObject("MAPI.Session")
    oCDOSession.Logon "","", False, False, 0
    txtCaption = strCaption

    If Not Err Then
        Set oRecip = oCDOSession.AddressBook (Nothing, txtCaption, _
        True, True, 1, iButtonText, "", "", 0)
    End If
```

```
    If Not Err Then
        item.UserProperties.Find(FieldName).value = oRecip(1).Name
    end if

    oCDOSession.Logoff
    oCDOSession = Nothing
End Sub
```

As you can see, to take advantage of CDO, you use the *CreateObject* method of the *Application* object, passing in the ProgID of CDO, which is MAPI.Session. Next you must log on to a session. Because Outlook already has an active session, the parameters passed to the CDO *Logon* method force CDO to use the already established Outlook session. From there, the application uses the CDO *AddressBook* method to bring up the address book with a specific caption and buttons, which enables the user of the application to select a person from the address book. The application then uses the Outlook object library to place the selection of the user in a custom Outlook property. The final task the application performs is to call the *Logoff* method of CDO and set the CDO object reference to *Nothing*. These two steps are important because you do not want stray objects left around after your application ends.

The integration of CDO in your Outlook applications does not stop there—you can also leverage the Outlook library in your CDO applications by using a similar technique. For more information on using the features of CDO in your Outlook application, see Chapter 11.

Installing CDO on Your Computer

Outlook can install CDO on a client computer if the user has not installed it. The following code automates the Windows Installer technology to load CDO on the local machine if CDO is not already installed:

```
Const msiInstallStateAbsent = 2
Const msiInstallStateLocal  = 3

If Not IsCDOInstalled Then
    ans = Msgbox("CDO is not installed.  Would you " & _
                 "like to install it?", vbYesNo)
    If ans = vbYes Then InstallCDO(msiInstallStateLocal)
Else
    Ans = Msgbox "CDO is already installed. Would you " & _
                 "like to remove it?", vbYesNo)
    If ans = vbYes Then InstallCDO(msiInstallStateAbsent)
End If

Function IsCDOInstalled()
    Dim testCDOobj
    On Error Resume Next
```

```
    Set testCDOobj = CreateObject("MAPI.Session")
    If Err.Number <> 0 Then
        IsCDOInstalled = False
    Else
        IsCDOInstalled = True
    End If

    If Not testCDOobj Is Nothing Then
        Set testCDOobj = Nothing
    End If
    Exit Function
End Function

Function InstallCDO(iInstallState)
    Dim blnSuccess
    Dim objInstaller, OL
    Dim strProductId, strFeatureName
    On Error Resume Next

    Set objInstaller = CreateObject("WindowsInstaller.Installer")
    Set OL = CreateObject("Outlook.Application")
    strProductId = OL.ProductCode
    strFeatureName = "OutlookCDO"

    If objInstaller.FeatureState(strProductId, strFeatureName) <> _
                                iInstallState Then
        objInstaller.ConfigureFeature strProductId, strFeatureName, _
                                iInstallState
        If Err.Number <> 0 Then
            blnSuccess = False
        Else
            blnSuccess = True
        End If
    Else
        blnSuccess = True
    End If

    Install = blnSuccess
End Function
```

Coding Rules in the Rules Wizard

In Outlook 2002 and later, you can call custom code as an action from the Rules Wizard. This feature allows you to perform more complex parsing of the items that meet the criteria you set in the Rules Wizard. The easiest way to use this feature is to write the code using VBA in Outlook.

Your VBA code must have two subroutines—one that accepts *MailItem* objects, and one that accepts *MeetingItem* objects—because Outlook will call one of these subroutines, depending on the type of item received. Remember that the Rules Wizard works only on your Inbox, so you cannot script for *AppointmentItem* objects. The following code shows how to use this new capability. Notice the subroutine names and parameters in the code. The subroutine name and arguments for your custom rule must be exactly the same as those shown.

```
Sub CustomMailMessageRule(Item As Outlook.MailItem)
    MsgBox "Mail message arrived: " & Item.Subject
End Sub

Sub CustomMeetingRequestRule(Item As Outlook.MeetingItem)
    MsgBox "Meeting request arrived: " & Item.Subject
End Sub
```

Summary

In this chapter, we learned about the power of the Outlook Object Model. In the next chapter, we'll see how you can take the Outlook Object Model and use it in Office COM Add-ins, which allows you to extend Outlook even further than Outlook forms solutions alone.

7

Office COM Add-Ins

When you develop Microsoft Office solutions, you probably want to extend existing Office applications by adding new functionality. In Microsoft Outlook 98, you can add new forms to your application's Outlook environment, but you cannot easily add new toolbars or program your application to respond to events other than form events such as *Item_Open* or *Item_Read*. To provide functionality beyond that of forms, you have to write an Exchange Client Extension, which involves strict requirements and coding practices, and any extensions have to be written in C/C++. With Outlook 98, a Microsoft Visual Basic or VBA developer is stuck either hacking a solution together or not enhancing the functionality at all.

Office 2000 and later includes support for COM add-ins. A COM add-in is a dynamic-link library (DLL) that can be used to add functionality to an Office application, and, as you can guess by the name, a COM add-in can be built using any COM or Microsoft .NET development tool, including Visual Basic, Visual C#, and Visual C++. Because COM add-ins are compatible with all Office products, you can design an add-in once and use it in several applications. For example, you can write a COM add-in that uses the CommandBar object model, which is shared across all the Office products, to customize the toolbars in your applications.

> **Note** The COM add-in I describe in this chapter can't be used across all the Office applications because it calls functionality that's specific to Outlook. However, the concepts behind building this COM add-in can be applied to any add-in designed for other Office applications.

COM add-ins are registered to be loaded by Office 2000 and later applications. Because COM add-ins are designed as in-process DLLs, they run in the same address space as the host application. One benefit of an in-process add-in is that it has efficient access to the object model of the host application, allowing the add-in to call methods and properties quickly or to receive events from the host application. One caution about running an add-in in-process is the danger of slowing down or even crashing the host application. Keep this in mind during development.

> **Note** This chapter shows how to build COM add-ins using Visual Basic and C#. The sample code includes a COM add-in built with Visual C++ for your reference.

When to Write a COM Add-In

You must consider a number of issues when deciding whether to develop a COM add-in. Some of the functionality COM add-ins provide in Outlook is similar to other Microsoft Exchange Server and Outlook development technologies, such as the Event Scripting Agent and Server Events in Exchange 2000 (discussed in Chapter 17). For this reason, I've provided three questions to help you determine whether to create a COM add-in or use another technology.

- **Do you need to receive events when the Outlook client is not running?** The life span of your COM add-in is controlled by Outlook. When the Outlook process is running, your COM add-in can run and receive events. When Outlook is not running, your add-in is also not running. If you need to receive events when the Outlook client is not running, consider using the Event Scripting Agent or Exchange Server Events; your agent will run on the server, so it will always receive events while the server is running. In Chapter 8, I'll examine a COM add-in that notifies users when an item in a folder changes—functionality that might be better implemented with the Event Scripting Agent or Exchange Server Events.
- **Is performance a big concern for your application?** If so, you should use an add-in because it is loaded in-process with Outlook. However, you must use defensive coding practices to prevent Outlook from crashing. Don't create an add-in that performs expensive lookups or data retrievals when starting because Outlook will wait for the add-in to finish these operations before continuing.

- **Is your application event-driven?** Outlook will fire a number of new events that your COM add-in can implement and handle. These events provide you with greater control over the Outlook user interface and Outlook data.

Developing a COM Add-In

If your answers to the three questions indicate that you should use a COM add-in, development is actually quite straightforward. Visual Basic has some features that can get you up and developing in a matter of minutes. In this section, I'll take a look at how to start developing COM add-ins, and then I'll review the features of the Outlook object model that you can employ in your COM add-ins.

Before you begin developing an add-in, you must create an ActiveX DLL project in Visual Basic (version 5.0 or later). After the project loads, select Microsoft Add-In Designer in the Project/References dialog box, as shown in Figure 7-1. This library contains the interfaces for your COM add-ins. (Another option is to use the add-in project; instead of selecting ActiveX DLL as your project type, select Add-in to open the Add-In Designer.)

In your Visual Basic code, you must type *Implements IDTExtensibility2* to see the *IDTExtensibility2* interface's events in the Procedure drop-down list in the Visual Basic code window. Figure 7-2 shows the code window with the *IDTExtensibility2* event procedures added.

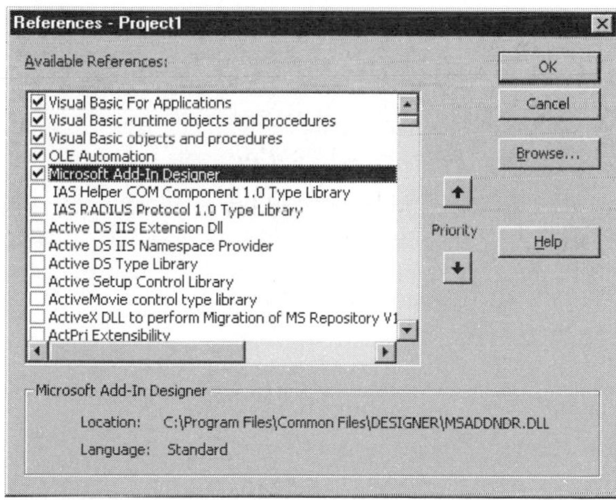

Figure 7-1 The Microsoft Add-In Designer in the Project/References dialog box

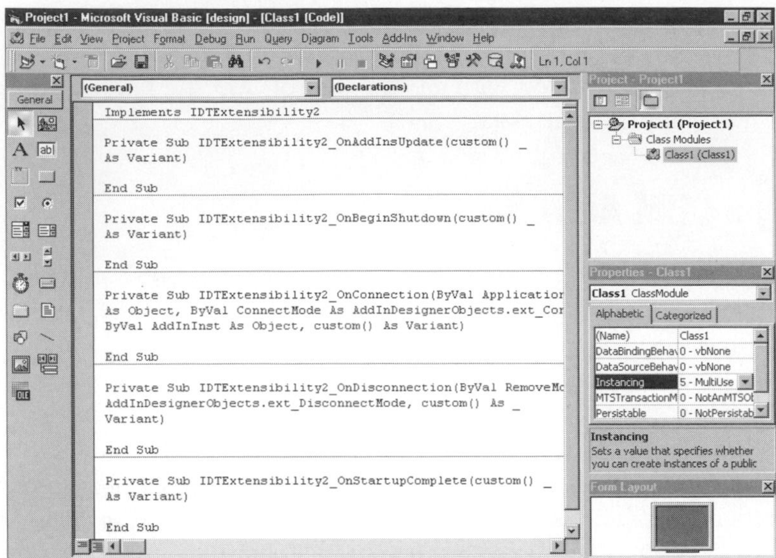

Figure 7-2 The Visual Basic 6.0 code window with the five event procedures for the *IDTExtensibility2* interface

The *IDTExtensibility2* Events

As you can see in Figure 7-2, *IDTExtensibility2* provides five events for you to use in your COM add-in: *OnConnection*, *OnDisconnection*, *OnStartupComplete*, *OnBeginShutdown*, and *OnAddInsUpdate*. Let's examine each of these events in detail.

OnConnection Event

The *OnConnection* event is called when your add-in is first loaded or a connection to it is established—for example, when Outlook starts or when the user chooses to load your COM add-in. The user can select your add-in in the COM Add-Ins dialog box in Outlook (as shown in Figure 7-3). You open this dialog box by choosing Options from the Tools menu, clicking on the Other tab, clicking the Advanced Options button, and clicking COM Add-Ins.

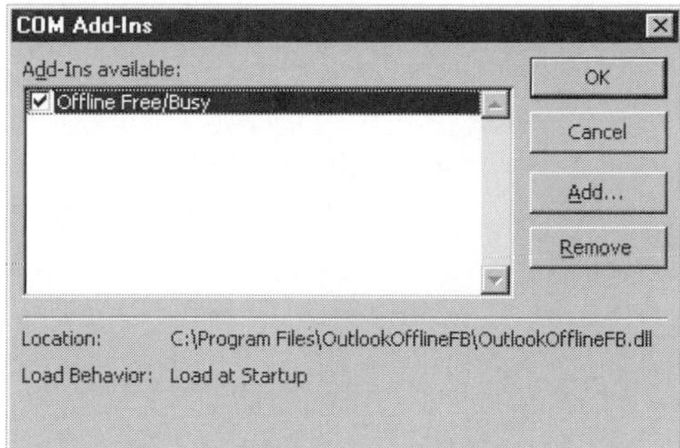

Figure 7-3 The COM Add-Ins dialog box, in which users add or remove COM add-ins

The *OnConnection* event procedure is a great place to grab and store the Outlook *Application* object for use in your code later. When an *OnConnection* event occurs, the *OnConnection* event procedure is passed the following four parameters: *Application*, *ConnectMode*, *AddInInst*, and *Custom()*. The *Application* parameter is a reference to the Outlook *Application* object. The *ConnectMode* parameter describes the way in which the COM add-in was loaded. The *ConnectMode* parameter is a *Long* data type that can be set to one of the following constants: *ext_cm_AfterStartup*, *ext_cm_CommandLine*, *ext_cm_External*, or *ext_cm_Startup*. The constants *ext_cm_CommandLine* and *ext_cm_External* do not apply to Office add-ins. The *ext_cm_AfterStartup* and *ext_cm_Startup* constants are subtly different from each other. The *ConnectMode* parameter is set to *ext_cm_AfterStartup* when the add-in is connected after Outlook starts or when the *Connect* property of the add-in is set to *True*. Usually, the *ConnectMode* parameter is set to *ext_cm_AfterStartup* when the user connects the add-in manually through the user interface. The *ConnectMode* parameter is set to *ext_cm_Startup* when your add-in is connected when Outlook starts up. The *AddInInst* parameter passes an object that refers to the current instance of your COM add-in. The *Custom* parameter is an array of *Variant* data types that can hold user-defined data for your add-in. For Office add-ins, this parameter should be ignored.

OnDisconnection Event

The *OnDisconnection* event occurs when your COM add-in is being disconnected from the application. The *OnDisconnection* event procedure is passed two parameters: *RemoveMode* and *Custom*. The *RemoveMode* parameter, which is a *Long* data type, specifies how your add-in was disconnected and can be set to *ext_dm_HostShutdown* or *ext_dm_UserClosed*. As you can guess by their names, *ext_dm_HostShutdown* indicates that the add-in is disconnected by the host shutting down, and *ext_dm_UserClosed* indicates either that a user is deselecting the add-in's check box in the COM Add-Ins dialog box or that the *Connect* property of the add-in is set to *False*.

The second parameter, *Custom*, is an array of *Variant* data types that can hold user-defined data for your add-in. For Office add-ins, this parameter should be ignored.

You use the *OnDisconnection* event to restore any changes made to the application or to perform general cleanup for your application. Be sure to destroy any *Inspector* or *Explorer* objects that you create because Outlook will not properly close if any instances of these objects still exist. The easiest way to do this is to check the *Explorers* and *Inspectors* collections to see if any of the objects exist.

Also note that in Outlook 2003, the Application's *Quit* event is fired earlier in the shutdown of Outlook. You can also use this event to destroy any references to Outlook objects that you have in your programs. However, because this applies only to Outlook 2003 and has not yet been back-ported to previous versions of Outlook, you might want to implement both options in your COM add-ins—attempt to destroy objects in the *Quit* event and also in *OnDisconnection*. Just be sure to have good error handling to catch any errors that occur in either event.

OnStartupComplete Event

If a COM add-in connects at the time the host application is started, the *OnStartupComplete* event fires when the host has completed all of its startup routines. The *OnStartupComplete* event does not fire if a user chooses to load the add-in from the COM Add-Ins dialog box after the application has already started. In that case, the *OnConnection* event fires. The *OnStartupComplete* event procedure takes one parameter, *Custom*, which you should ignore.

In the *OnStartupComplete* event procedure, you place code that interacts with the application and that should not be run until the application finishes loading. This event procedure is a good place to set some of your local and global variables to their corresponding Outlook objects. In the COM add-in example in Chapter 8, the *OnStartupComplete* event procedure searches the Outlook groups for a shortcut to the Account Tracking application and also has code to manipulate the command bars in the user interface.

OnBeginShutdown Event

The *OnBeginShutdown* event fires when the application is about to shut down; it is called before the *OnDisconnection* event. Even after *OnBeginShutdown* fires, you still have full access to the Outlook object model, so you can save your settings to the registry or a file, or save any changes to your objects, before your objects are unloaded.

> **Note** If you are using *Explorer* or *Inspector* objects in your COM add-in, listen for the *Close* event on these objects. When your application receives this event, it should destroy all open *Explorer* or *Inspector* objects because your Outlook COM add-in will not shut down correctly if any *Explorer* or *Inspector* objects are left open. (Chapter 6 covers the *Explorer* and *Inspector* objects.)

OnAddInsUpdate Event

The *OnAddInsUpdate* event fires when the list of COM add-ins is updated. When another add-in is connected or disconnected, this event occurs in any other connected COM add-in. You can use this event to ensure that any other add in that your add-in depends on is connected. Once the add-in that yours depends on is disconnected, you can disable your functionality or display a dialog box to warn the user to reconnect the other add-in. The *OnAddInsUpdate* event handler includes one parameter, *Custom*, which your application should ignore.

Registry Settings for COM Add-Ins

Now that you know which events fire for add-ins, you need to know how to register and load the add-ins. Outlook decides which add-ins to load on the basis of settings in the user's registry. If your add-in is not specified correctly in the registry, Outlook will not be able to load your add-in, nor will your add-in appear in the COM Add-Ins dialog box.

Registering Your Add-In

After you compile your add-in, you must register the add-in DLL for your add-in to work correctly. To do this, you use the Regsvr32 command and specify the path to your DLL. This registers your DLL under the HKEY_CLASSES_ROOT subtree in the registry. If you are deploying your add-in to multiple machines, you must figure out how to install your DLL on those machines. One way is to use logon scripts to copy and register the DLL. Another way is to deploy your add-in using the Visual Basic deployment and setup tools, an MSI, or Microsoft Systems Management Server (SMS).

After your COM add-in DLL is registered, you must add some settings to the registry on the local machine. These settings include the add-in's name, a description of the add-in, and the add-in's target application, initial load behavior, and connection state.

Before writing this information to the registry, you must decide how you want to deploy your add-in: you can either force all users to use your add-in or allow each user to decide whether to load it. The approach you use will determine where in the registry the information for your add-in must be written. If you want to ensure the add-in is always loaded and that every user on a machine has access to it, you must register it under the key:

```
\HKLM\Software\Microsoft\Office\<application>\AddIns
```

Installing your add-in here effectively locks down the COM Add-Ins dialog box because the user cannot unload add-ins that are registered here.

If you want to give your users the option to specify whether to load the add-in and to choose their own settings for the add-in, install your add-in under the key:

```
\HKCU\Software\Microsoft\Office\<application>\AddIns
```

This location allows per-user settings for the add-in. An example of a registered add-in under this key is shown in Figure 7-4.

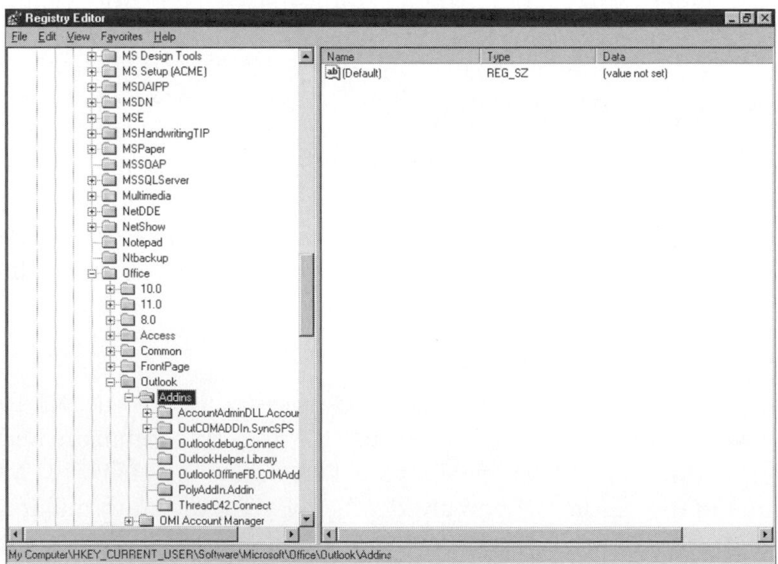

Figure 7-4 A registry key showing an add-in loaded under the key *\HKCU\Software\Microsoft\Office\Outlook\AddIns*

When you register your add-in under one of these registry keys, the information written to the key includes the following name/value pairs: *Description*, *FriendlyName*, and *LoadBehavior*. *Description* is a string type that provides a short description of the COM add-in. *FriendlyName* is a string that contains the name displayed in the COM Add-Ins dialog box. *LoadBehavior* is of type *DWORD*, where the value is an integer that specifies how to load your COM add-in. This integer can have a value of 0 for Disconnected, 1 for Connected, 2 for load on startup, 8 for load on demand, or 16 for connect first time. You can combine these values to create different types of load sequences. For example, if you assign the value 3 to *LoadBehavior*, the add-in will be loaded on startup as well as connected. If you assign 9 to the add-in, the add-in will be connected and demand-loaded when necessary, such as when the user clicks a button that uses code in the add-in.

The following code shows the content of a sample registry editor (.reg) file for a COM add-in:

```
REGEDIT4

[HKEY_CURRENT_USER\Software\Microsoft\Office\Outlook\
Addins\Sample.MyAddIn]
"FriendlyName"="My Sample Add-In"
"Description"="Sample Outlook COM Add-In"
"LoadBehavior"=dword:00000003
```

Trusting Your COM Add-Ins

You can specify whether to trust all installed COM add-ins on a machine by setting the *DWORD* value *DontTrustInstalledFiles* under the following registry key:

```
\HKCU\Software\Microsoft\Office\<version number>\Outlook\Security
```

By assigning 0 to *DontTrustInstalledFiles*, you specify that Outlook should trust all installed add-ins. A value of 1 specifies not to trust all add-ins. By default, Outlook trusts all files and installed add-ins. But this does not mean that Outlook will run all macros by default. Macros are different from COM add-ins. There is another setting for macros—the security level, which you can set to high, medium, or low. This setting controls whether signed, trusted macros are run.

Debugging COM Add-Ins

Debugging your add-in using Visual Basic 6.0 is easy. All you do is write your add-in, register it, set some breakpoints on the code statements you are interested in, and then run the add-in in the Visual Basic 6.0 development environment. In the Project Properties dialog box for your Visual Basic project (shown in Figure 7-5), you can set some debugging options. You can specify whether to wait for the component to be created by the host application or to have Visual Basic start an instance of the host application for you. I usually specify waiting for the components to be created by the host application. After Outlook starts and creates the COM add-in, the code in the add-in executes and stops on breakpoints it encounters. You can then step through your code in the Visual Basic Editor.

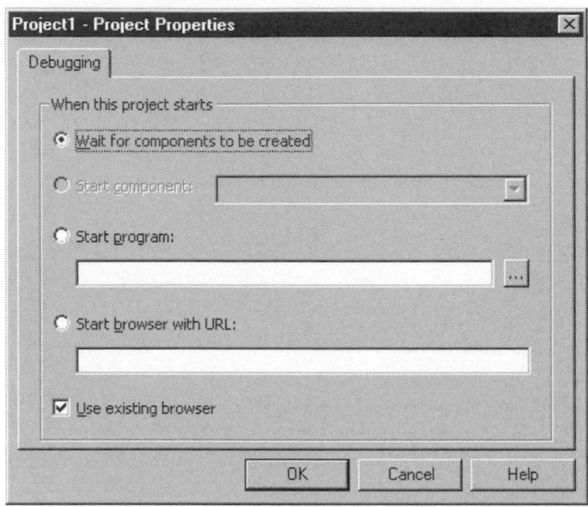

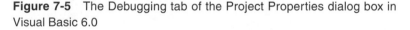

Figure 7-5 The Debugging tab of the Project Properties dialog box in Visual Basic 6.0

When you debug, be aware that message boxes in your add-in will appear in the Visual Basic development environment, not in Outlook. If Outlook stops responding, you should switch to Visual Basic to see whether a message box is visible and waiting for you to respond.

> **Important** In your COM add-ins, watch out for references to *Inspector* or *Explorer* objects in your code. If you do not properly destroy your variables, Outlook will exit but will stay in memory. Even if in your *OnBeginShutdown* procedure you set the variables holding references to these objects to *Nothing*, Outlook will still stay in memory. For this reason, the *Explorer* and *Inspector* objects both implement a *Close* event. You should add code, such as code that loops through the *Explorers* and *Inspectors* collections, to explicitly close each object to this event to destroy your references and check for any remaining *Explorer* or *Inspector* objects. If you find no *Inspector* objects and only one *Explorer* object, it's a sign that Outlook is properly shutting down.

Using COM Add-Ins from Custom Outlook Forms

You can leverage COM add-ins from Outlook forms in many ways. One of the best ways is to use them to add functionality that isn't easy to implement in Microsoft Visual Basic Scripting Edition (VBScript) or that might be very expensive to create. For example, you can create a CDO session in a COM add-in and then share that CDO session across multiple Outlook applications so each application does not have to create and destroy a CDO session. With VBScript, you can access the collections of COM add-ins available on your local machine and call public methods or set public properties on these add-ins. Furthermore, a COM add-in can provide a library of functions that you can use in all your custom Outlook forms.

Figure 7-6 shows a sample Outlook form that uses a COM add-in to launch other executable programs. Although VBScript doesn't support the *Shell* function, you can make use of the *Shell* function in your COM add-in.

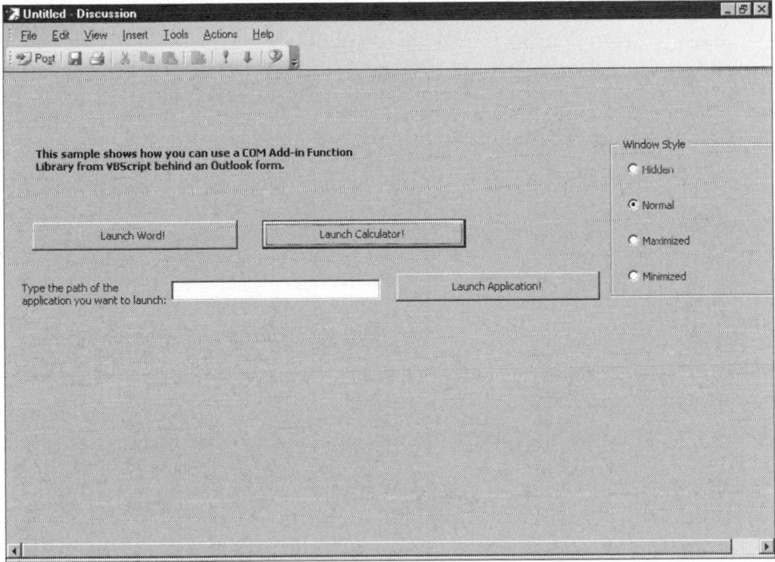

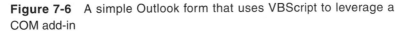

Figure 7-6 A simple Outlook form that uses VBScript to leverage a COM add-in

Take a look at the following code from the Outlook form shown in Figure 7-6. Notice that you can access the *COMAddins* collection to retrieve a list of the add-ins on your machine. You can then check whether the COM add-in you're interested in is loaded and connected in Outlook. To retrieve a COM add-in, you use the *Item* method on the collection and either pass in the index of your add-in in the collection or pass a string that specifies the ProgID of the add-in. Notice how I use the *GetObject* method with the ProgID of the COM add-in.

You might think that I could simply use the *Object* property of the COM add-in object that corresponds to my add-in. However, there is a known bug in Outlook that does not allow you to use this technique to get the COM add-in object. You should use the workaround in the code to make the COM add-in library work.

```
Dim oCOMAddinObj
Dim oCOMAddin

Sub cmdLaunchWord_Click
    Launch "winword"
End Sub

Sub cmdLaunchCalc_Click
    Launch "calc"
end sub

Sub cmdLaunchApp_Click
    Launch item.userproperties.find("strAppPath").value
end sub

Function Item_Open()
    'On error resume next
    Err.Clear
    'Try to get a reference to the COM add-in
    Set oCOMAddin = Application.COMAddIns.Item("OutlookHelper.Library")
    If err.number <> 0 Then
        MsgBox "There was an error retrieving a reference to the COM " _
               & "Add-in Helper Library!  Closing form!"
        Item_Open = False
        Exit Function
    End If
    'Check to see whether the COM add-in is connected
    If oCOMAddin.Connect = False Then
        MsgBox "You must connect the COM Add-in before using this app! "
        Item_Open = False
        Exit Function
    End If
    'Get the real COM add-in object
    'This doesn't work in Outlook!
    Set oCOMAddinObj = _
        Application.COMAddins.Item("OutlookHelper.Library").object
    'Workaround: use GetObject
    Set oCOMAddinObj = GetObject("","OutlookHelper.Library")
End Function

Sub Launch(strAppPath)
    'Get the Windows style
    iStyle = item.UserProperties.Find("strWindowsStyle").Value
    iError = oCOMAddinObj.CustomShell(strAppPath, iStyle)
    If iError = 0 then
       MsgBox "Error launching application!"
    End If
End Sub
```

In the next example, the add-in doesn't do much besides add a single public function named *CustomShell* that the user can call. This function leverages the *Shell* function in Visual Basic and allows you to shell out to another program. The function also provides a bit of error checking in case some bogus values get past the Outlook test form. If the add-in's *Shell* call is successful, it will return the ID of the shelled out executable; if not, it will return 0.

```
Implements IDTExtensibility2
Dim oApp As Outlook.Application   'Global Outlook Application Object

Private Sub IDTExtensibility2_OnAddInsUpdate(custom() As Variant)
    'Not used, but must be defined.
End Sub

Private Sub IDTExtensibility2_OnBeginShutdown(custom() As Variant)
    Set oApp = Nothing
End Sub

Private Sub IDTExtensibility2_OnConnection( _
    ByVal Application As Object, _
    ByVal ConnectMode As AddInDesignerObjects.ext_ConnectMode, _
    ByVal AddInInst As Object, custom() As Variant)

    Set oApp = Application
End Sub

Private Sub IDTExtensibility2_OnDisconnection( _
    ByVal RemoveMode As AddInDesignerObjects.ext_DisconnectMode, _
    custom() As Variant)
    'Not used, but must be defined.
End Sub

Private Sub IDTExtensibility2_OnStartupComplete(custom() As Variant)
    'Not used, but must be defined.
End Sub

Public Function CustomShell(strAppPath, iWindowStyle)
    If strAppPath = "" Then
        'Return back an error
        Err.Raise vbObjectError + 513, "Shell Function", "A blank " _
                 & "pathname was passed!"
        Exit Function
    Else
        'Check iWindowStyle
        If CInt(iWindowStyle) < 0 Or CInt(iWindowStyle) > 6 Then
            'Make it normal with focus
            iWindowStyle = vbNormalFocus
        End If
        'Try to execute the command and return the value
        iReturn = Shell(strAppPath, CInt(iWindowStyle))
        CustomShell = iReturn
    End If
End Function
```

Another way to fix this problem is to explicitly set the object reference for your COM add-in in Outlook's *OnConnection* event. The following is an example of how to use this workaround. You replace *YourAddin.Connect* with the ProgID of your COM add-in.

```
Private Sub IDTExtensibility2_OnConnection(ByVal Application As Object, _
    ByVal ConnectMode As AddInDesignerObjects.ext_ConnectMode, _
    ByVal AddInInst As Object, custom() As Variant)

    Application.COMAddIns.Item("YourAddin.Connect").Object = Me
End Sub
```

To reference the COM add-in object in your Outlook form, you use the following code:

```
Set myObj = Application.COMAddIns.Item("YourAddin.Connect").Object
```

Building COM Add-Ins Using .NET

> **Note** Before reading this section, you might want to read the section titled "Building Event Handlers in Visual Studio .NET" in Chapter 17, which covers overall COM interoperability issues with .NET.

Building a .NET application that requires you to interoperate with COM interfaces is similar to the event handler samples you saw earlier. The main differences between COM interoperability projects is that Visual Studio .NET sometimes does not import type libraries for you correctly in its automatic import capabilities. You might receive some strange and unexpected errors.

One of the best examples of Visual Studio .NET not importing a type library as it should is when you build a .NET COM add-in for Outlook. If you follow the standard steps shown earlier for event handler code and all you do is modify the code to work with the *IDTExtensibility2* interfaces and Outlook interfaces, you will run into problems. The problem is not with the *IDTExtensibility2* interfaces but with the way Visual Studio .NET imports Outlook interfaces. If you attempt to use any sort of events with the Outlook object model—for example, trying to capture *Explorer* or *Inspector* events—you will get a "No Interface" error. This error occurs because the type library was not imported correctly by Visual Studio .NET. Let's look in more detail at the process of importing a COM type library into .NET to uncover why these errors occur and how to fix them.

When you add a reference to a COM component in .NET, Visual Studio .NET imports the COM component as a type library and creates a .NET safe wrapper around that component's methods. This wrapper is usually an EXE or DLL assembly. For example, when you import the Outlook object library, Visual Studio .NET creates a file named Interop.Outlook.dll. To understand the information this file contains, you can use the IL disassembly tool (Ildasm.exe, which is part of the .NET Framework SDK) to view the file in a human-readable format.

To load the Outlook DLL into Ildasm, type **Ildasm.exe path\Interop.Outlook.dll**. You should see the interface shown in Figure 7-7. Ildasm shows not only the Microsoft Intermediate Language (MSIL) code but also namespaces, types, and interfaces.

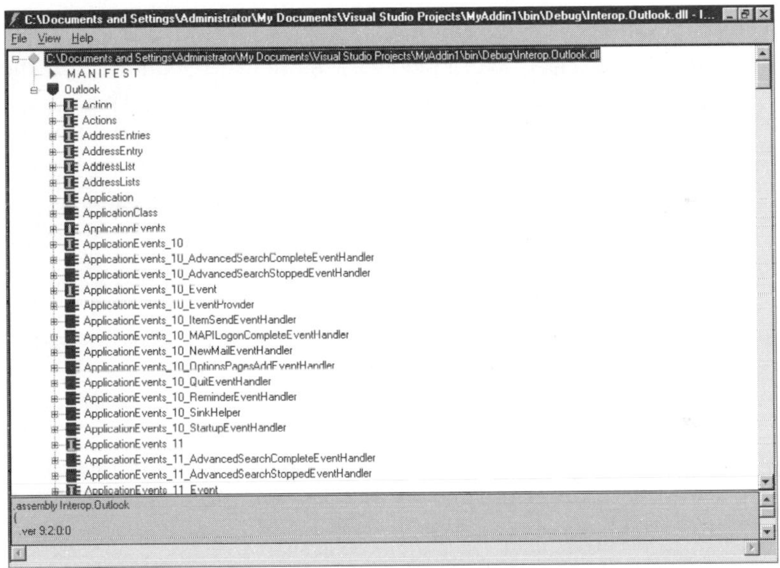

Figure 7-7 The Ildasm interface for the Outlook object model

Now let's find the Outlook *Application* events. If you look in the Ildasm tool, you will see the *ApplicationEvents_10* and *ApplicationEvents* interfaces if you're using Outlook 2002; in Outlook 2003, you should see *ApplicationEvents_11*. In those interfaces, you will see the standard Outlook *Application* events such as *NewMail* and *OptionsPagesAdd*. If you find the *ApplicationEvents_SinkHelper*, you will notice that this class is declared *private* in the first line, which states *.class private auto ansi sealed*. You must change all the *SinkHelper* classes to *public* in the IL file for Outlook events to work. The Ildasm tool does not allow you to modify the file, so you must use a text editor to do this.

After you modify the file, you must recompile the IL file. You do this using Ilasm.exe. You should pass the name of your IL file and the output file name and indicate that you want to compile the file as a DLL. The following is an example of compiling an Outlook IL file:

```
Ilasm.exe /dll /output=interop.outlook.dll /dll interop.outlook.il
```

Once the assembly is created, by running the command line just shown, you can use events successfully in the Outlook object model. If you continue to receive "No Interface Supported" errors, be sure to check your IL file again and recompile it. Also, you might want to set the *Copy Local* parameter for the interop DLL to *False*.

> **Note** To make it easier for you to get started using Outlook with Visual Studio .NET, I've included a sample that shows the modified Outlook interop assembly working within a program. This sample is in the OutlookEvents folder. You can take the Interop.Outlook.dll file from the bin directory of that sample and use it in your Outlook applications. Also, you can look at the Outlook.il file to see the correctly modified IL file that makes Outlook events work. Note that this is the Outlook 2002 IL—Outlook 2003 is in beta as of this writing. Be sure to use the Primary Interop Assembly (PIA) for Outlook 2003, which contains an already fixed Outlook interop DLL. This PIA ships with Outlook.

Visual Basic programmers can use the standard *WithEvents* keyword to implement Outlook events. Here's a quick example:

```
Public WithEvents oExplorer As Outlook.Explorer
Shared Sub oExplorer_SelectionChange() Handles oExplorer.SelectionChange
    MsgBox("Selection Changed")
End Sub
```

C# developers use different semantics to hook up events. Instead of *With Events*, you use the += operator to add an event handler for Outlook events. The following C# example shows how to add an event handler for Outlook events. The code assumes that the variable *application* contains a valid reference to an Outlook *Application* object.

```
outlookApp = (Outlook.Application) application;
outlookApp.Inspectors.NewInspector += new Outlook.InspectorsEvents_NewInspector
EventHandler (this.NewInspectorCallback);
public void NewInspectorCallback (Outlook.Inspector oInspector)
{
   try
   {
```

```
        //Your code goes here
    }
    catch (System.Exception e)
    {
        //Error handling here
    }
}
```

Tracing Errors

One important skill you need for writing .NET code—and especially COM add-ins—is the ability to trace errors through the stack trace in .NET. Both Visual Basic .NET and C# include the *System.Exception* class, which lets you trace error messages thrown by the .NET Framework at run time as well as through the stack trace. The following examples show both the error message and the stack trace in Visual Basic .NET and C# so you can track down where errors occur in your code.

```
'VB Example
On Error Resume Next
If Err.Number <> 0 Then
    Dim e As System.Exception = _
        Microsoft.VisualBasic.Information.Err.GetException()
    MsgBox(e.Message)
    MsgBox(e.StackTrace)
End if

//C# example
private debug_utils.logFileWriter _writer;
//
// Setup the log file writer
//

_writer = new debug_utils.logFileWriter ();
_writer.createNewLog = true;
_writer.logfileName = "c:\\error.log";

_writer.writeLine ("Starting up the addin");
try
{
   //Code goes here
}
catch (System.Exception e)
{
   __writer.writeLine ("Code failed: " + e.Message + "stack trace: " +
                       e.StackTrace);
}
```

Using the Extensibility Project for Your Add-In

The easiest way to create a COM add-in is to use the Visual Studio Shared Add-in Wizard. You can find this wizard under the Extensibility folder when you create a new project. Figure 7-8 shows the Shared Add-in Wizard template in the New Project dialog box in Visual Studio .NET. Figure 7-9 shows the user interface for the Visual Studio Add-in Wizard.

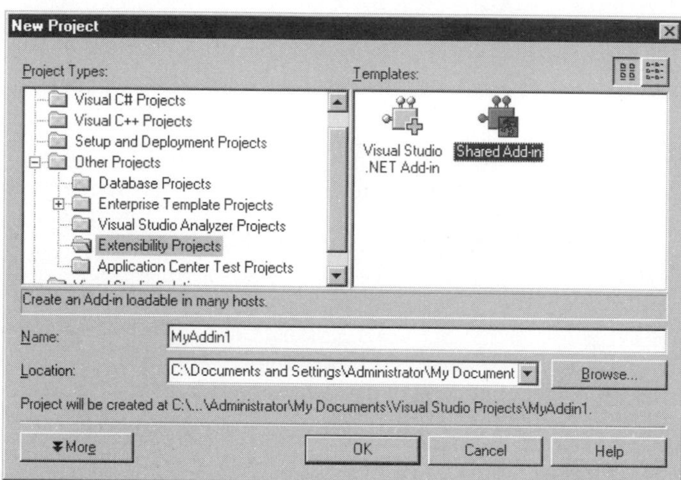

Figure 7-8 The Shared Add-In template in the New Project dialog box

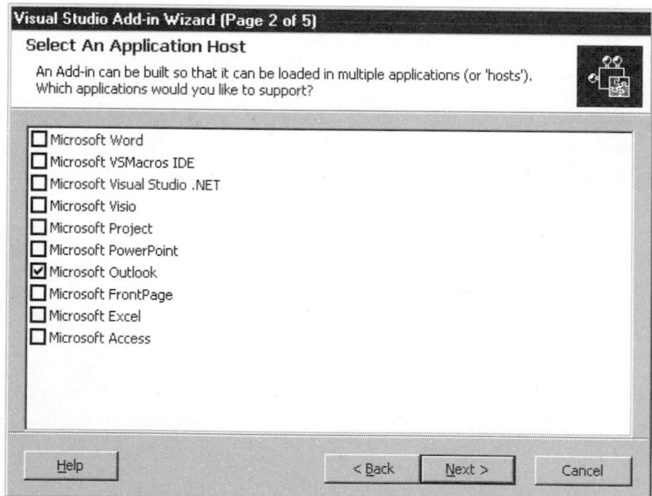

Figure 7-9 The interface for the Visual Studio Add-in Wizard

The wizard steps you through the process of creating an add-in by asking what language you want to use, the application hosts you want to target (for example, Outlook, Microsoft Word, or Visual Studio .NET), the friendly name and description of your add-in, and when you want to load the add-in. When you finish the wizard, it creates a project for you, fills out a stub of the add-in to implement the basic *IDTExtensibility2* interfaces, and adds a setup program that will automatically install and configure your application on the target machine as a COM add-in. The project that's created by default is shown in Figure 7-10. In the default project, you add your code to perform the functionality of your COM add-in.

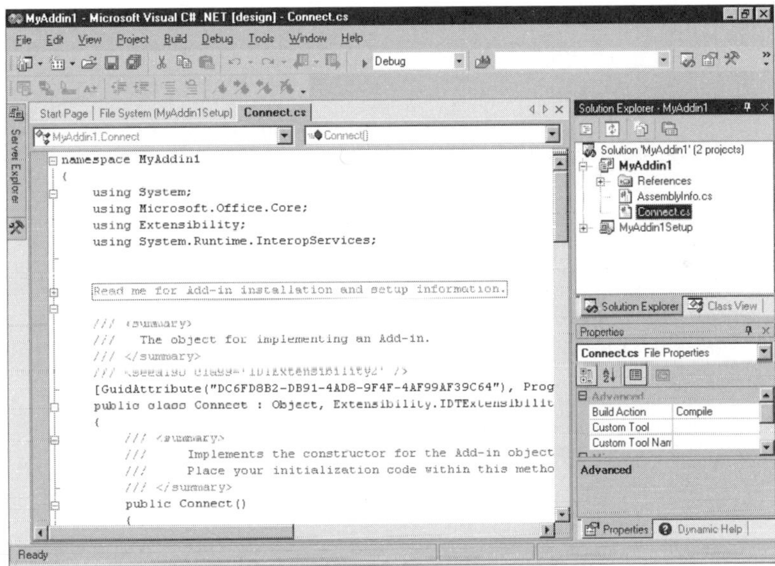

Figure 7-10 A default C# project created by the Visual Studio Add-in Wizard

An Add-In Example

To show you a simple example of an add-in, I created one that sends an e-mail message when Outlook starts up. You should note a couple of things in the code. First, in the *oConnection* subroutine, you must type cast the variable *oMailItem*, which is an *OutlookMailItem* object, to *Outlook._MailItem* before you can successfully call the *Send* method. You must do this because the word *Send* is ambiguous—it might relate to the *OutlookMailItem* object or the *Send* event on the Outlook *Items* collection. You must explicitly tell .NET that you want to call the *Send* method and are not implementing the *Send* event. Also notice the explicit garbage collection in the *OnDisconnection* event (which I'll discuss in more detail in the next section).

```
Imports System.Runtime.InteropServices
Imports Extensibility
Imports Outlook


<ProgId("DotNetAddin.OutComAddin"), _
 Guid("BCD79E56-29A5-42a2-8906-35C62FCFEC0F"), ComVisible(True)> _
Public Class DotNetCOMAddin
    Implements IDTExtensibility2

    Public oApplication As Outlook.Application
    Public oExplorer As Outlook.Explorer

    Public Sub OnBeginShutdown(ByRef custom As System.Array) _
        Implements Extensibility.IDTExtensibility2.OnBeginShutdown

        On Error Resume Next
        'Make sure to kill our references to our public variables
        'so Outlook can shut down
        Marshal.ReleaseComObject(oExplorer)
        Marshal.ReleaseComObject(oApplication)
        GC.WaitForPendingFinalizers()
        GC.Collect()
     CType(oApplication, Outlook._Application).Quit()
    End Sub

    Public Sub OnConnection(ByVal Application As Object, _
        ByVal ConnectMode As Extensibility.ext_ConnectMode, _
        ByVal AddInInst As Object, _
        ByRef custom As System.Array) _
        Implements Extensibility.IDTExtensibility2.OnConnection

        On Error Resume Next
        oApplication = CType(Application, Outlook.Application)
        'Send a new message telling the user we just connected
        Dim oMailItem As Outlook.MailItem = _
            oApplication.CreateItem(Outlook.OlItemType.olMailItem)
        oMailItem.To = oApplication.Session.CurrentUser.Address
        oMailItem.Subject = "OnConnection Called for .NET COM Add-in"
        oExplorer = oApplication.ActiveExplorer
        Dim oFolder As MAPIFolder = oExplorer.CurrentFolder
        Dim strOtherText As String = "Current Explorer: " & _
            oExplorer.Caption & " Number of items in " & oFolder.Name & _
            " is " & oFolder.Items.Count
            oMailItem.Body = "Outlook Version: " & oApplication.Version & _
            " " & "Current User: " & _
            oApplication.Session.CurrentUser.Name & strOtherText
        CType(oMailItem, Outlook._MailItem).Send()
    End Sub
```

```
    Public Sub OnDisconnection( _
        ByVal RemoveMode As Extensibility.ext_DisconnectMode, _
        ByRef custom As System.Array) _
        Implements Extensibility.IDTExtensibility2.OnDisconnection

    End Sub

    Public Sub OnStartupComplete(ByRef custom As System.Array) _
        Implements Extensibility.IDTExtensibility2.OnStartupComplete

        On Error Resume Next
        'Send a new message telling the user we just connected
        Dim oMailItem As Outlook.MailItem = _
            oApplication.CreateItem(Outlook.OlItemType.olMailItem)
        oMailItem.To = oApplication.Session.CurrentUser.Address
        oMailItem.Subject = "OnStartup Complete Called for .NET COM Add-in"
        oMailItem.Body = "Outlook Version: " & oApplication.Version & _
            " " & "Current User: " & oApplication.Session.CurrentUser.Name
        oMailItem.Save()
        CType(oMailItem, Outlook._MailItem).Send()
    End Sub

    Public Sub OnAddInsUpdate(ByRef custom As System.Array) _
        Implements Extensibility.IDTExtensibility2.OnAddInsUpdate
    End Sub
End Class
```

PropertyPage Extensions and .NET

PropertyPage extensions, which you will learn about in the next chapter, allow you to add custom pages to the property pages for folders or for the Options dialog box in Outlook. You can successfully create a PropertyPage extension using a .NET control that has COM interoperability enabled. However, you cannot get the parent of the control or use any of the advanced functionality of the PropertyPage extension because the .NET control does not exhibit the same interfaces as a true COM object. There is no real workaround for this problem, so if you want to use a .NET control in your PropertyPage, you should embed that control in a true COM control written in Visual Studio 6.0. However, if you are going to write the wrapper in Visual Studio 6.0, you might as well write the entire PropertyPage extension in that environment as well.

You can have a COM add-in written in .NET that calls a PropertyPage extension written in pure COM. That sort of mix and match works fine in Outlook.

Forcing Collection of Your Variables and Objects

One operation that can be difficult to grasp is the garbage collection environment that .NET introduces. If you've programmed with Visual Basic 6.0, you are used to Visual Basic controlling the lifetime of your variables and, when the variables go out of scope or are set to *Nothing*, having the variables immediately disappear.

This behavior does not occur in .NET. The .NET Framework destroys your references only on the next garbage collection cycle. For COM add-ins, this means that Outlook remains in memory until .NET garbage collection occurs, but this is not what you want.

To get around this situation, you can explicitly force garbage collection in your programs. As you can see in the sample add-in code presented earlier, you can explicitly control the lifetime of a COM object from your .NET application by using *Marshal.ReleaseCOMObject* and passing the COM object you want to release. This method decrements the reference count in the runtime callable wrapper (COM wrapper) for the COM object in .NET.

Next you call *GC.WaitForPendingFinalizers*. This method waits until all released objects have finished whatever functions they need to perform so they can be destroyed. Finally, you call *GC.Collect*, which forces garbage collection in .NET. This call allows .NET to reclaim the memory discarded by the released COM objects and allows Outlook to shut down cleanly. It's also good practice to call the *Quit* method on the *Application* object after forcing garbage collection to be sure that Outlook truly exits.

Working with Outlook Item Types and Common Properties

One gotcha you will find when you're working with the Outlook object model and .NET is that the Outlook *Items* collection allows heterogeneous item types in the collection. For this reason, you have to scroll through and check the type for each item. You must then declare the item as the correct type in .NET, such as *MailItem* or *PostItem*. To implement this type checking, you must produce a set of *If...Then* statements in your code.

Debugging Your .NET COM Add-In

Debugging in .NET is a bit different than in Visual Studio 6.0. In your .NET add-in, you set the debugging in your project so that Outlook will launch as an external application and then set your breakpoints in your code. Then you just run your program. Outlook will launch, and your breakpoint will be hit if your add-in loads correctly. You can add Outlook.exe as the external program to launch for your add-in under the Project Properties dialog box in Visual Studio .NET.

> **Note** Microsoft has released PIAs for Office 2002 and Office 2003 that fix a number of the problems described in this chapter. However, if you do not have these PIAs or you are running Outlook 2000, you can use the techniques described here to fix the Office interop assemblies. You should download the official PIAs for Office from *http://msdn.microsoft.com/office*. You must then reference these PIAs in your applications or place them in the Global Assembly Cache (GAC) for global use. You must also distribute the PIAs as part of your setup for client machines that will run your application. With Office 2003, the PIAs are part of the core Office setup.

VBA Support in Outlook

Outlook 2000 and later supports VBA. Now, you might be thinking that your Outlook forms already support VBA, but this is not the case. In fact, you still need to write VBScript behind your Outlook forms. VBA support in Outlook provides a way to customize the Outlook environment using the Outlook object model and all the events just discussed without using a separate development tool such as Visual Basic.

VBA Architecture

When you write your VBA applications in Outlook, you must contain your code in a VBA project. Each project is associated with a particular user, which means that different users on the same machine can customize Outlook differently using VBA. These projects can contain code modules or user forms. (User forms are different from Outlook forms.) To share information among these VBA projects, you must export your file and have the receiving user import your file into her VBA project.

Creating a VBA Application

The first step in creating a VBA application is to launch the Visual Basic Editor in Outlook. From the Tools menu, choose Macro. The Visual Basic Editor appears, as shown in Figure 7-11. You can use the editor to add class modules, code modules, and user forms, depending on the needs of your application. You can even write code that responds to Outlook events by declaring your variables using the *WithEvents* keyword.

The Outlook object model is automatically available to your VBA application. After you finish writing your macro in the editor, you can explicitly run it or create a button on your Outlook toolbar that runs the macro when clicked. Figure 7-12 shows a sample application that converts incoming mail to a specific message class using a VBA macro and the Outlook object model.

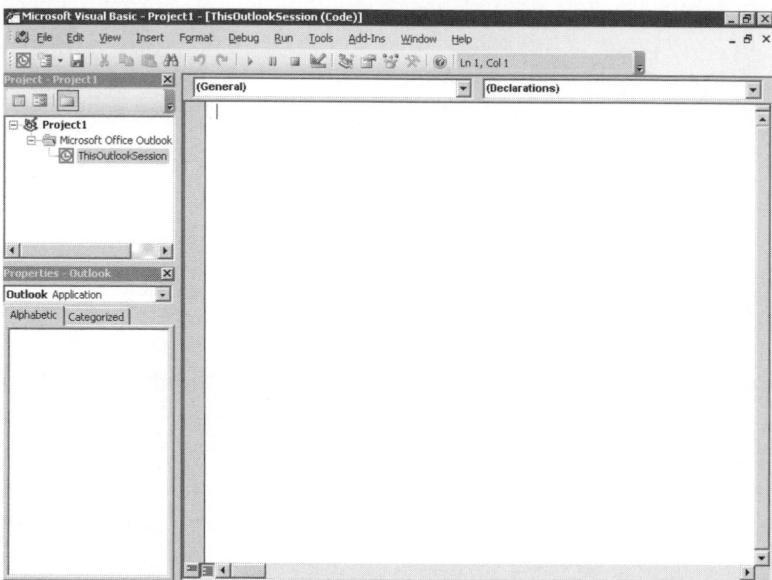

Figure 7-11 The Visual Basic Editor in Outlook

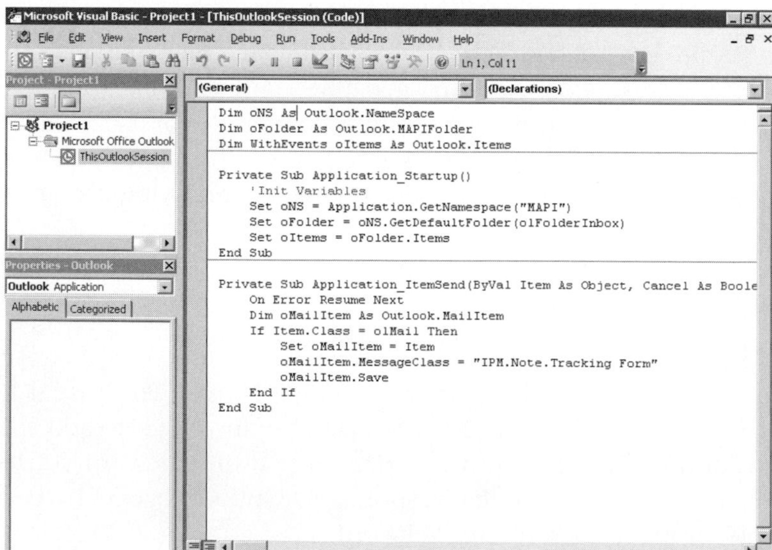

Figure 7-12 The sample mail conversion code in the Visual Basic Editor

Choosing What to Write: COM Add-In or VBA Program?

By now you must be wondering whether you should write VBA programs or COM add-ins to customize your Outlook environment. Both technologies have their merits, but if more than one user will run your program in an Outlook client, you should write a COM add-in. COM add-ins are easily distributed, and you can control a user's ability to run them.

If you want to customize only the Outlook client, writing a quick VBA program is easier than writing a full-blown COM add-in. To deploy your application in VBA, however, users must import the VBA file into their Outlook client, which is not the best deployment method. I predict that if you use COM add-ins, many users will install your application.

Summary

In this chapter, you learned how to build COM add-ins and use them to extend your Outlook applications. In the next chapter, we'll take what you have learned in the previous chapters on Outlook to create a rich, collaborative application that uses Outlook forms, views, folders, fields, and (of course) COM add-ins.

8

The Account Tracking Application

This chapter describes the Account Tracking application, an application for tracking contacts, team members, tasks, and revenue for different company accounts. It was developed using many of the techniques explained in previous chapters. The application is included with the book's sample files.

Overview of the Account Tracking Application

The Account Tracking application uses a customized Post form, a customized Contact form, the standard Task form, a customized Outlook Today page, a customized folder, and a database. (The use of the database is optional.) To create a new account, a user either installs the Account Tracking form in a forms library or uses the Create New Account hyperlink in the application's Outlook Today page. After the account is created, the user can create new contacts or new tasks for the account. The user can even track internal team members who service the account. The application also connects to a Microsoft Access database, which enables users to retrieve revenue information, but the application does not write back to the database. By studying this application, you can learn how to

- Customize a Post form and a Contact form in Microsoft Outlook.
- Use ActiveX controls on an Outlook form.
- Programmatically restrict items by using the Outlook object library.
- Automate other programs from an Outlook form.

- Connect a database to an Outlook form, and use a database as a data source for Outlook fields.
- Customize the Outlook Today page.
- Learn how to write COM Add-ins for Outlook.
- Learn how to use the Outlook View control and Outlook folder home pages.
- Call XML Web services from your Outlook applications.

After we review the features of the application, you'll learn how to set it up and examine the code that drives it.

The Account Tracking Folder

The primary way a user interacts with this application is to access data through the Account Tracking folder. This folder provides a number of views that enable users to quickly find the information they need. Although users can create their own data views for the folder, the application does provide some unique views by default. One view, called the Accounts view, lets a user see all accounts and related contacts and tasks in a threaded view. All associated tasks and contacts are threaded from the original form for the account, as shown in Figure 8-1.

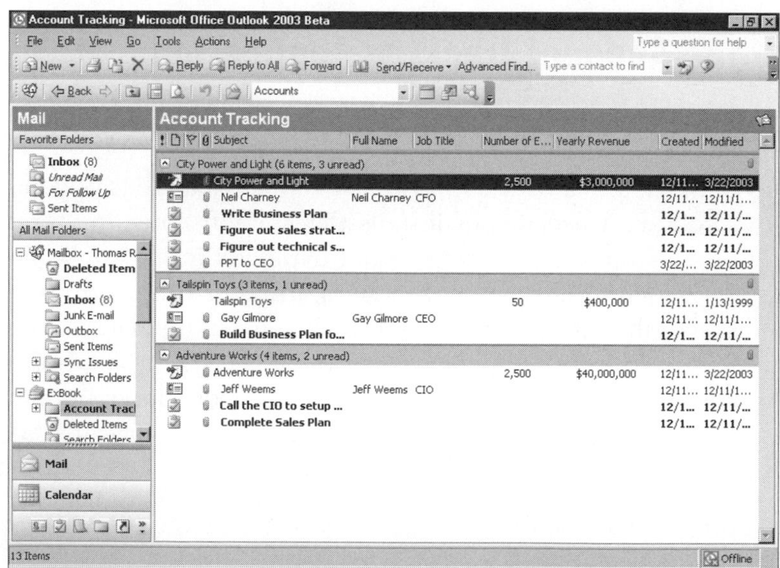

Figure 8-1 The Accounts view in the Account Tracking folder

Two other views use filters so the user can find only contacts or only tasks without looking at the other items in the folder. The Accounts-Color view uses conditional formatting to color-code accounts, contacts, and tasks.

Recall that Outlook supports multiple types of views, such as timeline and card views, in a single folder. Our Account Tracking folder offers these special types of views. Figure 8-2 shows the contacts for different accounts in a view named Account Contacts. This view allows users to print the contacts list so that it's portable—they can take it with them in paper-based planners.

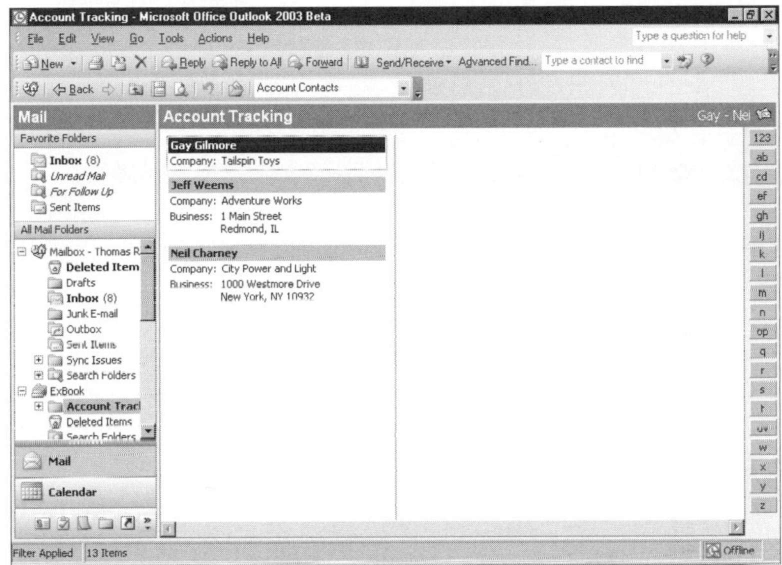

Figure 8-2 The Account Contacts view of the Account Tracking folder, which shows only the contacts for the different accounts.

The Account Tracking Form

Users employ the Account Tracking form to create a new account, contact, task, letter, NetMeeting, or some other new item. The form is accessed by double-clicking on an account or by choosing New Account Info from the Actions menu. Figure 8-3 shows the Account Tracking form. It consists of a customized Post form with multiple tabs and ActiveX controls.

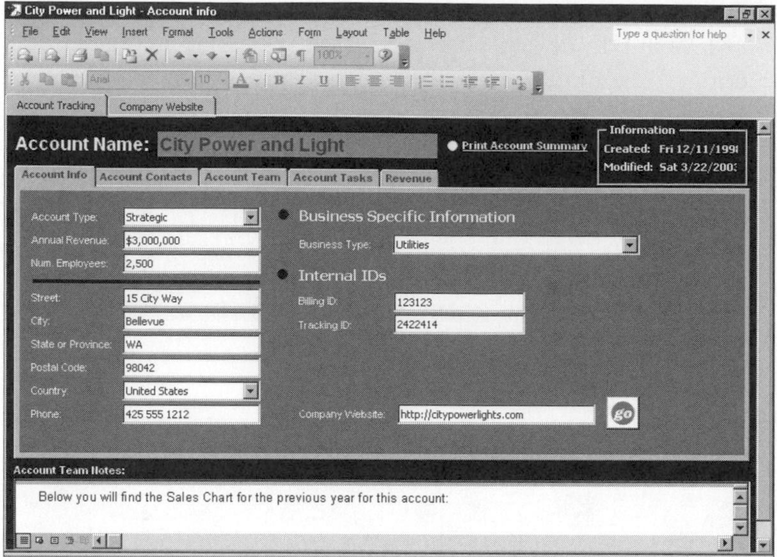

Figure 8-3 The Account Tracking form

Actions such as creating a task or a contact creates an item in the folder or launches a program such as Microsoft Word. Depending on the action invoked, a specific Outlook form might be displayed. This form is automatically posted into the folder as a reply to the original Account Tracking form, which allows the application to use the conversation topic and conversation index fields to create threaded views of the accounts, including their associated contacts and tasks. Figure 8-4 shows the Account Contact form, which is customized, and Figure 8-5 shows the Account Task form, which is a standard Outlook Task form.

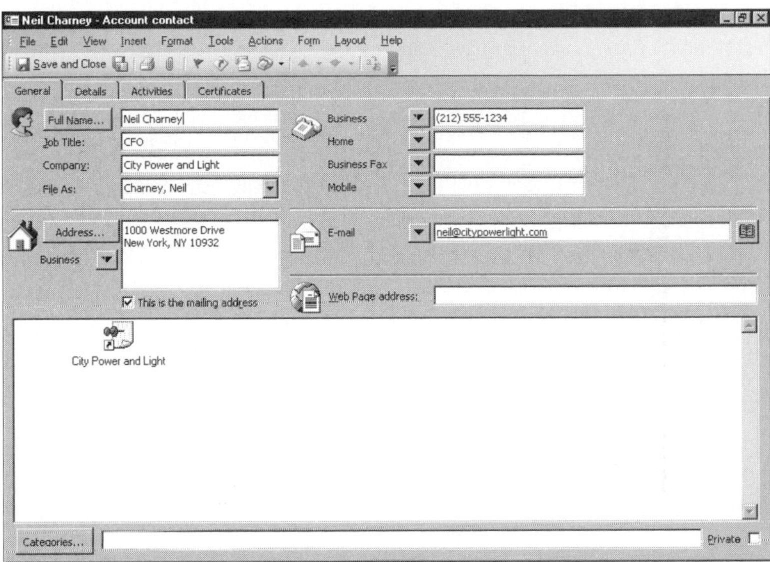

Figure 8-4 The Account Contact form, a customized version of the Outlook Contact form.

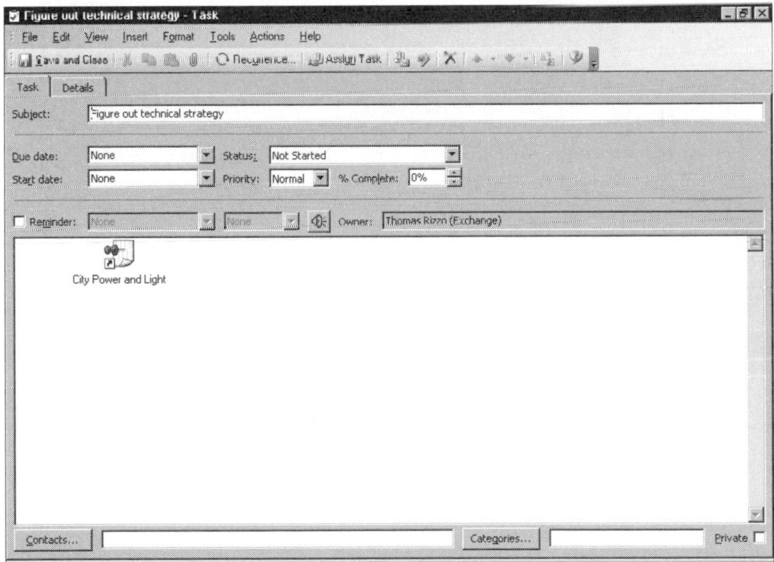

Figure 8-5 The Account Task form using the standard Outlook Task form.

The Account Tracking form includes an ActiveX control—the Microsoft Internet Explorer component—that is embedded on the Company Website tab of the form. Using this control, the user can browse an account's Web site by entering the site's address in the Company Website text box on the form's Account Info tab, as shown earlier in Figure 8-3, and then clicking the Go button. This control is automated by using the Microsoft Visual Basic Scripting Edition (VBScript) coder.

Optionally, the Account Tracking form can connect to a database using ActiveX Data Objects (ADO). The database can be used to retrieve financial information for the Revenue tab of the form. If information is pulled from the database, the Revenue tab will include Outlook formula fields that total the actual revenues and the quota for each product, as shown in Figure 8-6. If you want to use ADO.NET, you must encapsulate your code in a .NET control and provide that control to your Outlook form via COM interop. Outlook's VBScript does not natively support ADO.NET.

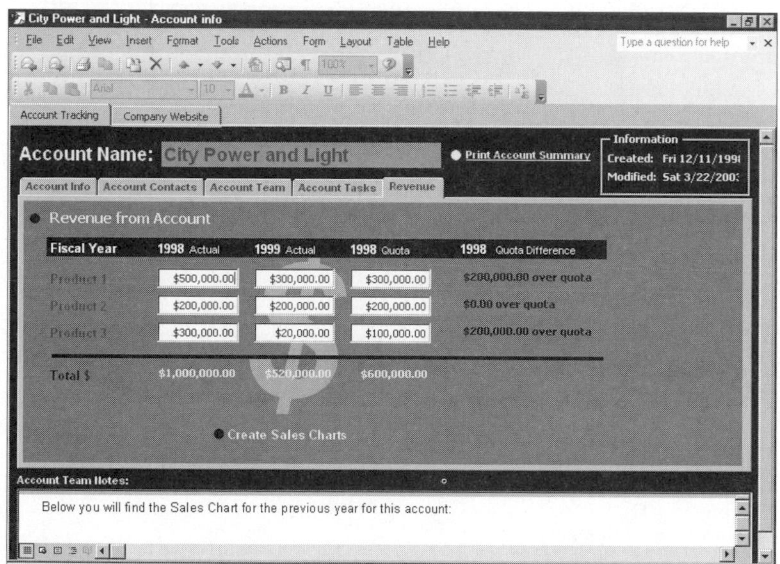

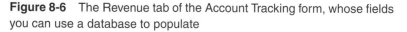

Figure 8-6 The Revenue tab of the Account Tracking form, whose fields you can use a database to populate

If the user has Microsoft Excel 2000 or later installed, the Account Tracking application can create reports and charts in Excel. If the user clicks on the Create Sales Charts link on the Revenue tab, Outlook will launch Excel and pass the numbers from the Revenue tab to the Excel chart, as shown in Figure 8-7. You implement this functionality by using VBScript in the form.

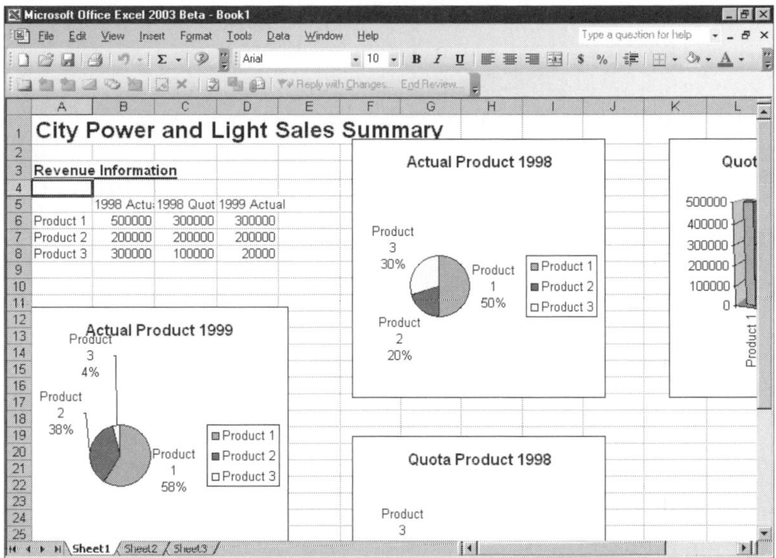

Figure 8-7 The user can click on the Create Sales Charts link on the Revenue tab to create Excel charts.

The final feature of the Account Tracking form is the use of Outlook events, such as *Item_Open* and *Item Close*, to set up the environment for the user and ensure that objects needed by the application are available. For example, when a user changes the address of an account using the Account Tracking form, the *Item_Close* event detects this and asks whether the user wants to update all the addresses for all contacts of that account. If the user answers yes, the application will find the account contacts and change the address of each, as long as the original address is the same as the account address.

Setting Up the Account Tracking Application

To install the Account Tracking application, you need a machine that has Outlook and at least one Microsoft Office application installed, preferably Excel. You must also have a user account on a Microsoft Exchange Server. We'll step through setting up the Account Tracking application next.

Copying the Account Tracking Folder

First you need to copy the Account Tracking folder from the .pst file included in the companion content to your Public Folders in Exchange. To do this, copy the ExBook.pst file to your local hard drive. Clear the read-only flag for this file.

In Outlook, choose Open from the File menu, and then select Outlook Data File. In the Open Outlook Data File dialog box, locate ExBook.pst on your hard drive, select it, and click OK. If you are prompted to convert a non-Unicode store to a Unicode store, accept the conversion. At this point, the file folder named ExBook should appear in your Outlook Folder List. Expand the ExBook file folder to display the Account Tracking folder. Hold down the Ctrl key, and drag and drop the Account Tracking folder to the location in the Public Folder tree where you want the folder to appear. (Pressing the Ctrl key makes a copy of the Account Tracking folder.)

> **Note** If you do not copy the Account Tracking folder from the ExBook.pst file folder to your Public Folders, the Assign Task To functionality will not work.

Copying the Product Sales Database

Included with the book's sample files is an Access database named Sales.mdb. The application can use this product sales database to retrieve sales and quota information for an account previously entered in the database. The default location for this database is in the root of your C drive. You can change the location by modifying some of the VBScript code in the Account Tracking form. By default, the application does not use the database, but you can change this setting in the VBScript for the form. To configure the Access database, follow these steps:

1. From the sample code, copy the file named Sales.mdb to your local hard drive and clear its read-only flag.
2. In the Outlook Public Folders list, select the Account Tracking folder you just copied.
3. Launch the Account Tracking form by choosing New Account Info from the Actions menu.
4. From the Tools menu, choose Forms, Design This Form.
5. From the Form menu, choose View Code.
6. If you want to use the sales database, in the Global Declaration section, change the line

   ```
   bUseDatabase = 0
   ```

to

```
bUseDatabase = 1
```

If you want to change the location of the database, find the *Item_Open* subroutine. Change the parameter in the line

```
InitializeDatabase "c:\sales.mdb"
```

to reflect the location of the database. For example, if the database is located on a file share, you should change the line to

```
InitializeDatabase "\\fileserver\fileshare\sales.mdb"
```

> **Note** Although an Access database is used in this sample application, you can also use a Microsoft SQL Server database.

7. Publish the form to save your changes by opening the Tools menu from the Account Tracking form, pointing to Forms, and then selecting Publish Form.

Setting Permissions on the Folder

After configuring the database, you must set permissions on the folder. You might want to give all users the ability to submit new items to the folder but give only the internal sales teams the ability to read and edit items in the folder. You might also want to create multiple folders for each internal sales team so that each team accesses only its accounts, contacts, and tasks. To set up permissions for the application, right-click on the Account Tracking folder in the folder list and choose Properties. Click on the Permissions tab, and use the menus to set the permissions for the users of the application. Consider using distribution lists to simplify setting permissions for teams of individuals.

Techniques Used in the Account Tracking Application

The Account Tracking application demonstrates many techniques that you can use in your Outlook applications. It shows how to connect databases to Outlook, for example, how to automate other applications from your Outlook application, and how to use the Outlook object library to modify the controls on your form at run time. Let's review some of the interesting techniques used in the Account Tracking application.

Setting Global Variables

The Account Tracking application uses global variables in VBScript to keep objects and variables in memory throughout the lifetime of the application. Global variables are also used to set the preferences for the application—for example, whether to use a database for the product sales information. The following code shows the global variables and global initializations:

```
'**********************************************
'Global Declarations
'**********************************************
Dim oRestrictedContactItems
Dim oRestrictedTaskItems
Dim oExcel
Dim oSheet
Dim ComposeMode
Dim bWebExists
Dim oDefaultPage
Dim oWebBrowser
Dim oCurrentFolder
Dim olstAssignTaskName
Dim oNameSpace
Dim oDatabase
Dim oDatabaseEngine
Dim bUseDatabase     'Used to tell the application to use an
                     'external DB
Dim txtAccountName
Dim txtOriginalStreet, txtOriginalCity, txtOriginalState
Dim txtOriginalPostalCode, txtOriginalCountry
Dim oExcelChart
bUseDatabase = 0     'Tells the application whether to use an Access
                     'database
                     'Set this to 1 to use a database, otherwise
                     'set it to 0.
ComposeMode = True   'Used to determine whether the application is in
                     'compose or read mode
bWebExists = False   'Used to determine whether the WebBrowser control
                     'was successfully created
```

Determining the Mode: The *Item_Read* Event

The *Item_Read* event is used to determine whether the user is creating a new account or reading an existing account from the folder. Determining the mode—compose mode or read mode—is important because during compose mode, the code for reading the database and updating the contact address should not be run. After the mode is determined, the code sets a global variable, *ComposeMode*, that is used throughout the application. Because the VBScript in an Outlook form runs whether an item is being composed or read, you can use the *Read* event and global variable approach to identify the application mode and have your application behave appropriately. The following code shows the *Item_Read* subroutine, which runs only when an item is being read:

```
'***********************************************
'Sub Item_Read
'
'This is the standard Read event for an Outlook form.
'It checks to see whether the user is in read or compose mode
'on the form.
'***********************************************
Sub Item_Read
    'Check to see if the application is in compose mode
    ComposeMode = False
End Sub
```

Initializing the Application: The *Item_Open* Event

The *Item_Open* event in the Account Tracking form is used to perform some application initialization, in this order:

1. It initializes the global variables used most commonly throughout the application, including the *Page* object for the default page of the form and the *NameSpace* object in Outlook.
2. It checks whether the *WebBrowser* control on the Company Website tab has been successfully created. If so, *Item_Open* enables a number of controls on the form by using the *Controls* collection.
3. It checks whether the user has filled in the internal account team. If so, it adds these users to the list box on the Account Tasks tab to make it easy for users to assign tasks to the account team members.
4. It stores the original information for the address of the company. This information is used later in the *Item_Close* event.
5. It initializes and opens the database using helper functions in the script.

The entire *Item_Open* subroutine is shown here:

```
'***********************************************
'Sub Item_Open
'
'This is the standard Outlook Open event. This subroutine
'sets some objects for use later in the app. Checks whether
'the WebBrowser control was successfully created and also checks
'to see whether there are names for the account team in the form.
'If the form is in compose mode, the subroutine selects the name of
'the account at the top of the form to draw the user's attention to
'that field.
'***********************************************
```

```
Sub Item_Open
    'Get the default page of the application to use later
    Set oDefaultPage = GetInspector.ModifiedFormPages( _
        "Account Tracking")
    Set oNameSpace = Application.GetNameSpace("MAPI")
    'Initialize the WebBrowser control
    Set oWebBrowser = GetInspector.ModifiedFormPages( _
        "Company Website").Controls("oWebBrowser")
    'Check to see if the browser was successfully created; if so,
    'enable the Go button for the company Web site and the
    'NetMeeting option
    If Err.Number = 0 Then
        bWebExists = True
        oDefaultPage.Controls("cmdGo").enabled = True
        oDefaultPage.Controls("cmdNetMeetingContact").Visible = True
        oDefaultPage.Controls("lblNetMeetingContact").Visible = True
        oDefaultPage.Controls("cmdNetMeetingContact").Enabled = True
        oDefaultPage.Controls("lblNetMeetingContact").Enabled = True
    End If
    'Get Current Folder
    Set oCurrentFolder = Application.ActiveExplorer.CurrentFolder
    Call cmdRefreshContactsList_Click
    Call cmdRefreshTasks_Click
    'Check to see if any users are assigned to the account team and
    'add them to assign task list
    Set olstAssignTaskName = oDefaultPage.Controls( _
        "lstAssignTaskName")
    CheckFor "txtAccountSalesRep"
    CheckFor "txtAccountSE"
    CheckFor "txtAccountConsultant"
    CheckFor "txtAccountSupportEngineer"
    CheckFor "txtAccountExecutive"

    If not(ComposeMode) Then
        txtOriginalStreet = _
            Item.UserProperties.Find("Account Street")
        txtOriginalCity = _
            Item.UserProperties.Find("Account City")
        txtOriginalState = _
            Item.UserProperties.Find("Account State")
        txtOriginalPostalCode = _
            Item.UserProperties.Find("Account Postal Code")
        txtOriginalCountry = _
            Item.UserProperties.Find("Account Country")
        oDefaultPage.Controls("lblDistrict").visible = True
        Set oDistrict = oDefaultPage.Controls("lstDistrict")
        oDistrict.visible = True
    End If

    If not(ComposeMode) and bUseDatabase Then
        txtAccountName = item.Subject
        'Initialize DB
        InitializeDatabase "c:\sales.mdb"
        GetDatabaseInfo "[1998 Actual]", "cur1998ActualProd1", _
```

```
            "cur1998ActualProd2","cur1998ActualProd3"
        GetDatabaseInfo "[1999 Actual]", "cur1999ActualProd1", _
            "cur1999ActualProd2","cur1999ActualProd3"
        GetDatabaseInfo "[1998 Quota]", "cur1998QuotaProd1", _
            "cur1998QuotaProd2","cur1998QuotaProd3"
    End If

    If ComposeMode Then
        oDefaultPage.txtName.SetFocus
        oDefaultPage.txtName.SelStart = 0
        oDefaultPage.txtName.SelLength = 11
    End If
End Sub
```

Connecting to the Sales Database: The *GetDatabaseInfo* Subroutine

If you have enabled a database for the sales information, the *GetDatabaseInfo* subroutine will be called to retrieve the sales information from the database and place this information into Outlook fields. This subroutine uses ADO to query the database and retrieve the sales information associated with accounts previously entered in the database. Once this information is placed in the form, Outlook formula fields determine whether the current sales of the product are exceeding the quota for the product. Outlook then displays how much the account team needs to sell to reach its quota or how much over quota the account team is. The following code shows the *GetDatabaseInfo* subroutine:

```
'***************************************************
'Sub GetDatabaseInfo
'
'This subroutine retrieves the Product revenue information
'from the database using the passed in tablename as well as
'field names and the current accountname from the open item.
'You can customize this subroutine to meet your specific needs
'***************************************************
Sub GetDatabaseInfo(TableName, FieldName1, FieldName2, FieldName3)
    On Error Resume Next
    strSQL = "Select Product1, Product2, Product3 FROM " & TableName & _
            " WHERE AccountName = '" & txtAccountName & "';"
    Set oRS = item.application.createobject("ADODB.Recordset")
    oRS.Open strSQL, oConnection
    If Err.Number <> 0 Then
        MsgBox Err.Description &  Err.Number & Chr(13) & _
            "OpenRecordset failed"
        Exit Sub
    End If
    oRS.MoveFirst

    Item.UserProperties.Find(FieldName1).Value = oRS.Fields(0)
    Item.UserProperties.Find(FieldName2).Value = oRS.Fields(1)
    Item.UserProperties.Find(FieldName3).Value = oRS.Fields(2)
End Sub
```

Displaying an Address Book Using CDO: The *FindAddress* Subroutine

Because Outlook does not natively support displaying an address book in its object library, you must extend the application by using the Collaboration Data Objects (CDO) library, which displays address books and returns the values selected by the user. To use CDO in the Account Tracking application, the VBScript code in the form has to create a CDO object by using the *CreateObject* method of the Outlook *Application* object. When the object is created, a subroutine starts a session using the CDO methods and displays an address book using the caption and button text, which are passed in as parameters. Then the subroutine stores the results selected by the user in a specific Outlook field, which is also passed in as a parameter. Finally, the subroutine logs out of the CDO session and destroys the CDO object. Figure 8-8 shows how the address book looks after you click one of the address book buttons on the Account Team tab.

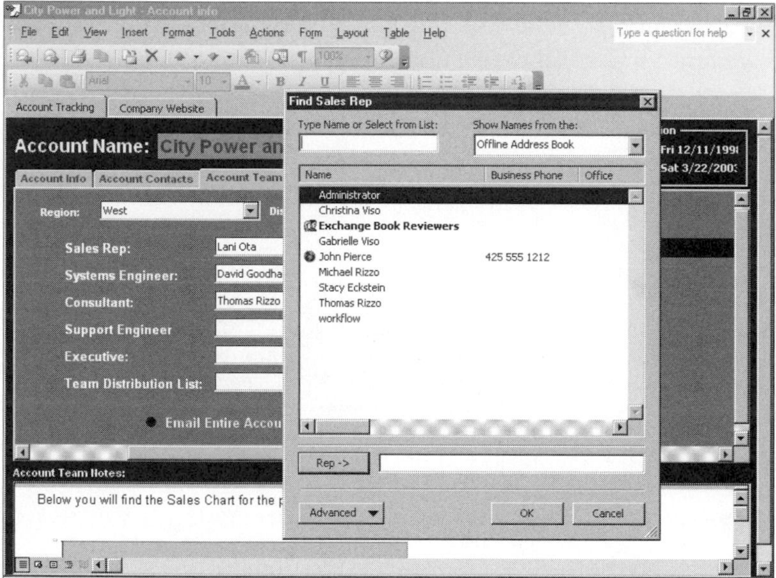

Figure 8-8 Displaying the address book in an Outlook form by using CDO

The following code shows how the address book is displayed using CDO:

```
'**********************************************
'Sub FindAddress
'
'This subroutine takes the Outlook field that stores
'the returned value and the caption for the dialog box as
'well as the button text for the dialog box, and then it
'displays the AddressBook dialog box by using CDO
'
```

```
'**********************************************
Sub FindAddress(FieldName, Caption, ButtonText)

    On Error Resume Next
    Set oCDOSession = application.CreateObject("MAPI.Session")
    oCDOSession.Logon "", "", False, False, 0
    txtCaption = Caption
    If Not err Then
        Set orecip = oCDOSession.addressbook (Nothing, txtCaption, _
            True, True, 1, ButtonText, "", "", 0)
    End If
    If Not err Then
        item.userproperties.find(FieldName).value = orecip(1).Name
    End If
    oCDOSession.logoff
    oCDOSession = Nothing
End Sub
```

Advanced CDO: Changing an Appointment Color

One topic that people always ask about is programming to more objects than the Outlook Object Model has. For example, the Outlook Object Model does not have a way to query or set calendar color coding. However, you can use CDO (which you will learn about in more detail in Chapter 11), to query and set the calendar color coding. You use the *Appointment* property set (*0220060000000000C000000000000046*); the property for the color is *0x8214*. The following quick sample shows how to query this property using both CDO 1.21 and CDO for Exchange. CDO for Exchange is covered in Chapter 15.

```
Dim oSession As New MAPI.Session
'CDO 1.21 Version
oSession.Logon
Dim oFolder As MAPI.Folder
Set oFolder = oSession.GetDefaultFolder(0)
Dim oItem As MAPI.AppointmentItem
Dim oMessages As MAPI.Messages

Set oItem = oFolder.Messages.GetFirst
MsgBox oItem.Fields.Item("0x8214", "0220060000000000C000000000000046")
'Values here will mimic the Outlook user interface
'0 = No color
'1 = 1st label (Important)
'2 = 2nd label (Business)
'3 = 3rd label (Personal)
'etc
oSession.Logoff

'CDO for Exchange version
Dim oAppt As New CDO.Appointment
```

```
strURL = "file://./backofficestorage/thomriznt5dom2.extest." & _
        "microsoft.com/mbx/thomriz/calendar/appt.eml"
oAppt.DataSource.Open strURL

'Propset is 00062002-0000-0000-C000-000000000046
'For CDO 1.21, this is transposed to 0220060000000000C000000000000046
'Property ID is 0x8214
MsgBox oAppt.Fields.Item("http://schemas.microsoft.com/mapi/id/" & _
    "{00062002-0000-0000-C000-000000000046}/0x00008214").Value
```

Creating Account Contacts: The *cmdAddAccountContact* Subroutine

After assigning personnel to the account team, the user can add new account contacts for the company. The application has a custom action that creates a reply in the folder by using the custom Account Contact form. Because you are using an action, the command for the action, Create New Account Contact, appears on shortcut menus. For example, if you right-click on an account item in Outlook, Create New Account Contact will be one of the choices. Using an action also makes it easy for Outlook to create a conversation thread for the account contact. Finally, using an action allows the application to attach the original item, in this case the account item, to the contact as a shortcut without any coding. The *cmdAddAccountContact* subroutine, shown in the following code snippet, executes the custom action by using the *Actions* collection on the account form. This code is similar to the *cmdAddTasks* subroutine, but instead of displaying an Account Contact form, it displays an Account Task form for the user to fill in.

```
'**********************************************
'Sub cmdAddAccountContact_Click
'
'This subroutine creates a new contact and displays
'the form for the new contact as a modal dialog box
'**********************************************
Sub cmdAddAccountContact_Click
    Item.Save
    Set AccountContactForm = item.Actions( _
        "Create New Account Contact").Execute
    AccountContactForm.Display(True)
    Call cmdRefreshContactsList_Click
End Sub
```

Refreshing the Contact List Box: The *cmdRefreshContactsList* Subroutine

When the form initially opens, or when a user adds or deletes contacts or tasks in the folder, the *ListBox* control that contains these items must be refreshed and filled with the most recent information from the folder. To do this, the application calls subroutines that restrict the folder based on the item type and on the account the item belongs to. The application then programmatically fills the list box with the correct information for the account. The list box is shown in Figure 8-9.

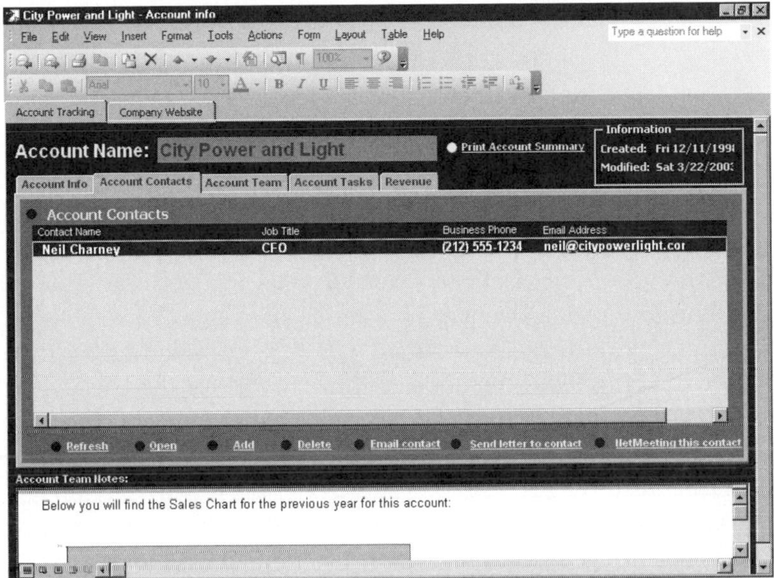

Figure 8-9 The Account Contacts list box for the Account Tracking application

The following code shows the *cmdRefreshContactsList* subroutine at work:

```
'**********************************************
'Sub cmdRefreshContactsList_Click
'
'This subroutine refreshes the list box of contacts by
'applying a restriction on the folder
'
'**********************************************
Sub cmdRefreshContactsList_Click
    'Initialize ListBox
    Set oListBox = oDefaultPage.Controls("lstContacts")
    oListBox.Clear
    oListBox.ColumnWidths = "0;172;140;80;120"

    'Create search criteria
    RestrictString = ""
    RestrictString = "[Message Class] = " & _
        """IPM.Contact.Account contact"" and [Conversation] = """ & _
        item.ConversationTopic & """"
    Set oRestrictedContactItems = _
        oCurrentFolder.Items.Restrict(RestrictString)
```

```
    For i = 0 to oRestrictedContactItems.Count - 1
        oListBox.AddItem
        oListBox.Column(1,i) = oRestrictedContactItems(i+1).FullName
        oListBox.Column(2,i) = oRestrictedContactItems(i+1).JobTitle
         oListBox.Column(3,i) = _
            oRestrictedContactItems(i+1).BusinessTelephoneNumber
        oListBox.Column(4,i) = _
            oRestrictedContactItems(i+1).Email1Address
    Next
End Sub
```

Performing Default Contact Actions: E-Mail, Letters, and NetMeeting

Because users will want to perform many actions for the account contacts they create, the Account Tracking application provides the most common actions as default controls on the Account Contacts tab. The user can click on the Email Contact link to e-mail a contact. This action uses the *CreateItem* method on the *Application* object to create an e-mail message, and then it uses the name of the selected contact to fill in the address information for the e-mail.

If Word is installed, the user can also send a letter to the contact by clicking on the Send Letter To Contact link. This action uses the *CommandBars* collection on Outlook forms to trigger toolbar actions. Then, by using the *FindControl* method and the *Execute* method of the *CommandBar* object, the application launches the New Letter To Contact command from the Actions menu for a contact. This, in turn, launches the Microsoft Word Letter Wizard, which uses the contact information to automatically populate the address information for the letter.

Finally, the user can start a Microsoft NetMeeting with the contact by clicking on the NetMeeting This Contact link. This action uses the WebBrowser control. If the WebBrowser control is available and the user launches the action, the application will use VBScript in Outlook to automate the WebBrowser control, which will start NetMeeting and connect the user to the Account contact using the NetMeeting client.

The following code shows the subroutines that enable the user to send an e-mail or a letter and to set up a NetMeeting:

```
'**********************************************
'Sub cmdEmailContact_Click
'
'This subroutine creates an e-mail message for the selected
'account contact. If no contact is selected, it displays an error.
'**********************************************
Sub cmdEmailContact_Click
    Set oListBox = oDefaultPage.Controls("lstContacts")
    If oListBox.ListIndex = -1 Then
        MsgBox "No selected account contact. Please select one.", _
            48, "Email Account Contact"
```

```
    Else
        Set oItem = oRestrictedContactItems(oListBox.ListIndex + 1)
        'Create an e-mail message
        Set oNewMessage = Application.CreateItem(0)
        oNewMessage.Recipients.Add oItem.Email1Address
        oNewMessage.Recipients.ResolveAll
        oNewMessage.Display
    End If
End Sub

'**************************************************
'Sub cmdSendLettertoContact_Click
'
'The following subroutine uses the commandbars
'property to automate the Contact form in Outlook
'to select the Send Letter To A Contact menu
'command. This in turn launches the Word Letter
'Wizard.
'**************************************************
Sub cmdSendLettertoContact_Click
    Set oListBox = oDefaultPage.Controls("lstContacts")
    If oListBox.ListIndex = -1 Then
        MsgBox "No selected account contact. Please select one.", _
            48, "Send letter to Account Contact"
    Else
        Set oItem = oRestrictedContactItems(oListBox.ListIndex + 1)
        oItem.Display
        oItem.GetInspector.CommandBars.FindControl(,2498).Execute
    End If
End Sub

'**************************************************
'Sub cmdNetMeetingContact_Click
'
'This subroutine checks the contact to see whether the
'NetMeeting information is filled in and, if so, it
'automates the WebBrowser control to use the NetMeeting
'callto: syntax to start a NetMeeting
'**************************************************
Sub cmdNetMeetingContact_Click
    Set oListBox = oDefaultPage.Controls("lstContacts")
    If oListBox.ListIndex = -1 Then
        MsgBox "No selected account contact.  Please select one.", _
            48, "NetMeeting Account Contact"
    Else
        Set oItem = oRestrictedContactItems(oListBox.ListIndex + 1)
        If oItem.NetMeetingAlias = "" Then
            MsgBox "The NetMeeting information is not filled" & _
                 " in for this contact.", 48, _
                "NetMeeting Account Contact"
            Exit Sub
        End If
        If oItem.NetMeetingServer = "" Then
            MsgBox "The NetMeeting information is not filled" & _
                " in for this contact.", 48, _
```

```
                "NetMeeting Account Contact"
            Exit Sub
        End If
        On Error Resume Next
        txtNetMeetingAddress = "callto:" & oItem.NetMeetingServer _
            & "/" & oItem.NetMeetingAlias
        oWebBrowser.Navigate txtNetMeetingAddress
        If err.number <> 0 Then
            MsgBox "NetMeeting is either not installed or not" & _
                " configured correctly.", 48, _
                "NetMeeting Account Contact"
            Exit Sub
        End If
    End If
End Sub
```

Automating Excel: The *cmdCreateSalesChart* and *cmdPrintAccountSummary* Subroutines

If a user has Excel installed, the Account Tracking application can automate Excel to create charts, as shown earlier in Figure 8-7. One way to begin creating the charts is to click on the Create Sales Chart control on the Revenue tab of the application. An even easier way to start this process is to use the shortcut menu in the Outlook window. For certain item types, you can right-click on an item and choose Create Account Sales Charts without opening the item. The application uses a custom action, the *Item_CustomAction* event, which it captures when the user selects the Create Account Sales Charts action. The application calls its own subroutine to handle the action rather than displaying a response form. The subroutine then creates sales charts by using VBScript to automate Excel. (Notice in the *Item_CustomAction* event procedure that I also try to create an action for printing an Excel account summary. Unfortunately, this action did not work from the shortcut menu.)

```
'*********************************************************
'Function Item_CustomAction
'
'This is the standard CustomAction event for an Outlook form.
'This event is captured so that the Create Account Sales Chart
'as well as the Print Account Summary actions can appear on the menu.
'However, these actions actually call VBScript functions. This
'is why these actions are canceled after the VBScript functions
'automate Excel to create the reports. Otherwise, a reply form
'would appear to the user.
'*********************************************************
Function Item_CustomAction(ByVal Action, ByVal ResponseItem)
   Select Case Action
      Case "Create Account Sales Charts"
         cmdCreateSalesChart_Click()
         'Disable the action so that a response form does not appear
         Item_CustomAction = False
```

```
      Case "Print Account Summary"
         cmdPrintAccountSummary_Click()
         Item_CustomAction = False
   End Select
End Function

'*************************************************
'Sub cmdCreateSalesChart_Click
'
'This subroutine responds to the Click event of the
'Create Sales Charts control. It automates Excel
'to create both a worksheet and embedded charts on that worksheet.
'You can modify this subroutine to meet your specific needs.
'*************************************************
Sub cmdCreateSalesChart_Click
    Set oExcel = Item.Application.CreateObject("Excel.Application")
    oExcel.Visible = True
    oExcel.Workbooks.Add
    Set oSheet = oExcel.Workbooks(1).Worksheets("Sheet1")
    'Set the title for the worksheet
    oSheet.Activate
    Set oSheetTitle = oSheet.Range("A1")

    oSheetTitle.Value = item.Subject & " Sales Summary"
    oSheetTitle.Font.Bold = -1
    oSheetTitle.Font.Size = 18
    oSheetTitle.Font.Name = "Arial"

    oExcel.Application.ActiveCell.Offset(2,0).Select
    oExcel.Application.ActiveCell.Value = "Revenue Information"
    oExcel.Application.ActiveCell.Font.Bold = -1
    oExcel.Application.ActiveCell.Font.Name= "Arial"
    oExcel.Application.ActiveCell.Font.Size = 11
    oExcel.Application.ActiveCell.Font.Underline = 2
    oExcel.Application.ActiveCell.Offset(1,0).Select

    oSheet.Range("A6").Value = "Product 1"
    oSheet.Range("A7").Value = "Product 2"
    oSheet.Range("A8").Value = "Product 3"

    oSheet.Range("B5").Value = "1998 Actual"
    oSheet.Range("B6").Value = item.userproperties( _
        "cur1998ActualProd1")
    oSheet.Range("B7").Value = item.userproperties( _
        "cur1998ActualProd2")
    oSheet.Range("B8").Value = item.userproperties( _
        "cur1998ActualProd3")

    oSheet.Range("C5").Value = "1998 Quota"
    oSheet.Range("C6").Value = item.userproperties( _
        "cur1998QuotaProd1")
    oSheet.Range("C7").Value = item.userproperties( _
        "cur1998QuotaProd2")
    oSheet.Range("C8").Value = item.userproperties( _
        "cur1998QuotaProd3")
```

```
    oSheet.Range("D5").Value = "1999 Actual"
    oSheet.Range("D6").Value = item.userproperties( _
        "cur1999ActualProd1")
    oSheet.Range("D7").Value = item.userproperties( _
        "cur1999ActualProd2")
    oSheet.Range("D8").Value = item.userproperties( _
        "cur1999ActualProd3")

    'Create charts
    Set oChart = oSheet.ChartObjects.Add(250, 20, 200, 200)
    oChart.Chart.ChartWizard oSheet.Range( _
        "a6:B8"),5,,2,1,,,"Actual Product 1998"
    Set oChart = oSheet.ChartObjects.Add(0, 150, 200, 200)
    oChart.Chart.ChartWizard oSheet.Range( _
        "a6:A8, D6:D8"),5,,2,1,,,"Actual Product 1999"
    Set oChart = oSheet.ChartObjects.Add(250, 250, 200, 200)
    oChart.Chart.ChartWizard oSheet.Range( _
        "a6:A8, C6:C8"),5,,2,1,,,"Quota Product 1998"
    Set oChart = oSheet.ChartObjects.Add(500, 20, 200, 200)
    oChart.Chart.ChartWizard oSheet.Range( _
        "a6:c8"),3,,2,1,,,"Quota vs Actual 1998"
    oSheet.ChartObjects(4).Chart.ChartType = 54
End Sub
```

When the user clicks on the Print Account Summary control on the Account Tracking tab, an account summary is created in Excel. The Excel Account Summary sheet is shown in Figure 8-10.

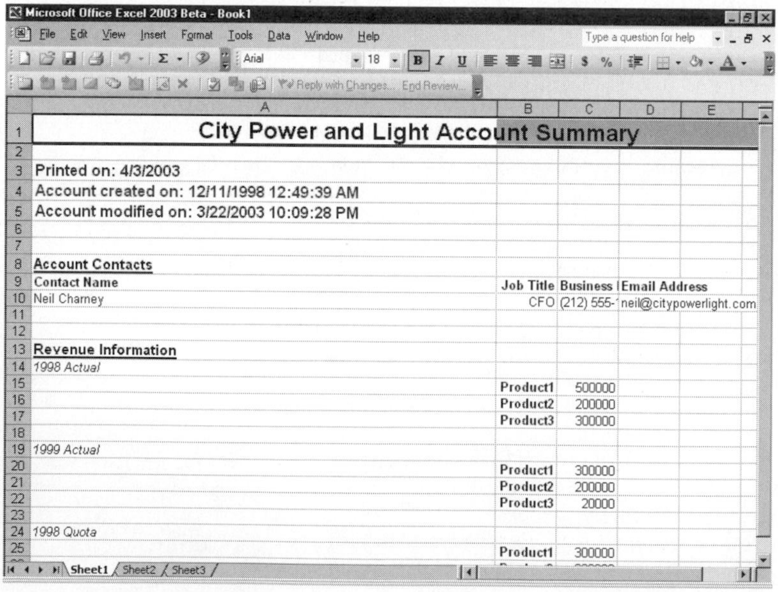

Figure 8-10 The Excel Account Summary sheet, which is programmatically created by the Account Tracking application

The code to create the Account Summary is shown here:

```
'**********************************************
'Sub cmdPrintAccountSummary_Click
'
'This subroutine calls the helper subroutine to
'print the Account Summary. You can replace the
'helper subroutine without having to replace the controls
'on the form.
'**********************************************
Sub cmdPrintAccountSummary_Click()
    CreateExcelSheet
End Sub

'**********************************************
'Sub ExcelPrintProductRevenue
'
'This subroutine is a helper subroutine that prints
'the passed-in product name as well as the current
'sales numbers. You can replace this subroutine
'with your own.
'**********************************************
Sub ExcelPrintProductRevenue(ByVal txtType, txtProd1, txtProd2, _
    txtProd3,curProd1,curProd2,curProd3)
    oExcel.Application.ActiveCell.Value = txtType
    oExcel.Application.ActiveCell.Font.Italic = -1
    oExcel.Application.ActiveCell.Offset(1,1).Value = txtProd1
    oExcel.Application.ActiveCell.Offset(1,1).Font.Bold = -1
    oExcel.Application.ActiveCell(2,3).Value = curProd1
    oExcel.Application.ActiveCell.Offset(2,1).Value = txtProd2
    oExcel.Application.ActiveCell.Offset(2,1).Font.Bold = -1
    oExcel.Application.ActiveCell(3,3).Value = curProd2
    oExcel.Application.ActiveCell.Offset(3,1).Value = txtProd3
    oExcel.Application.ActiveCell.Offset(3,1).Font.Bold = -1
    oExcel.Application.ActiveCell(4,3).Value = curProd3
End Sub

'**********************************************
'Sub CreateExcelSheet
'
'This subroutine automates Excel to create an Account
'Summary report. You can replace this subroutine
'with your own.
'**********************************************
Sub CreateExcelSheet
    Set oExcel = Item.Application.CreateObject("Excel.Application")
    oExcel.Visible = True
    oExcel.Workbooks.Add
    Set oSheet = oExcel.Workbooks(1).Worksheets("Sheet1")
    'Set the title for the worksheet
    oSheet.Activate
    Set oSheetTitle = oSheet.Range("A1")
```

```
oSheetTitle.Value = item.Subject & " Account Summary"
oSheetTitle.Font.Bold = -1
oSheetTitle.Font.Size = 18
oSheetTitle.Font.Name = "Arial"

'Put in the printout date
oSheet.Range("A3").Value = "Printed on: " & Date
oSheet.Range("A3").Font.Bold = -1
oSheet.Range("A3").Font.Name = "Arial"
oSheet.Range("A3").Font.Size = 12
oSheet.Range("A3").Font.Color = RGB(0,0,255)

'Put in the date the item was created
oSheet.Range("A4").Value = "Account created on: " & _
    item.CreationTime
oSheet.Range("A4").Font.Bold = -1
oSheet.Range("A4").Font.Name = "Arial"
oSheet.Range("A4").Font.Size = 12
oSheet.Range("A4").Font.Color = RGB(0,0,255)

'Put in the date the item was last modified
oSheet.Range("A5").Value = "Account modified on: " & _
    item.LastModificationTime
oSheet.Range("A5").Font.Bold = -1
oSheet.Range("A5").Font.Name = "Arial"
oSheet.Range("A5").Font.Size = 12
oSheet.Range("A5").Font.Color = RGB(0,0,255)
oSheet.Range("A7").Activate

'Retrieve contact information
oExcel.Application.ActiveCell.Offset(1,0).Select
oExcel.Application.ActiveCell.Value = "Account Contacts"
oExcel.Application.ActiveCell.Font.Bold = -1
oExcel.Application.ActiveCell.Font.Name= "Arial"
oExcel.Application.ActiveCell.Font.Size = 11
oExcel.Application.ActiveCell.Font.Underline = 2
oExcel.Application.ActiveCell.Offset(1,0).Select

'Refresh the contact listbox
cmdRefreshContactsList_Click
'Retrieve the data from the listbox
Set oPage = GetInspector.ModifiedFormPages("Account Tracking")
Set oListBox = oPage.lstContacts
If oListBox.ListCount > 0 Then
    oExcel.Application.ActiveCell.Value = "Contact Name"
    oExcel.Application.ActiveCell.Font.Bold = -1
    oExcel.Application.ActiveCell.Offset(0,1).Value = _
        "Job Title"
    oExcel.Application.ActiveCell.Offset(0,1).Font.Bold = -1
    oExcel.Application.ActiveCell.Offset(0,2).Value = _
        "Business Phone"
    oExcel.Application.ActiveCell.Offset(0,2).Font.Bold = -1
    oExcel.Application.ActiveCell.Offset(0,3).Value = _
```

```
            "Email Address"
        oExcel.Application.ActiveCell.Offset(0,3).Font.Bold = -1
        oExcel.Application.ActiveCell.Offset(1,0).Activate
        For intLB = 0 to oListBox.ListCount -1
            oExcel.Application.ActiveCell.Value = _
                oListBox.Column(1,intLB)
            oExcel.Application.ActiveCell.Offset(0,1).Value = _
                oListBox.Column(2,intLB)
            oExcel.Application.ActiveCell.Offset(0,2).Value = _
                oListBox.Column(3,intLB)
            oExcel.Application.ActiveCell.Offset(0,3).Value = _
                oListBox.Column(4,intLB)
            oExcel.Application.ActiveCell.Offset(1,0).Activate
        Next
    Else
        oExcel.Application.ActiveCell.Value = _
            "No contacts for this account"
    End If

    'Retrieve revenue information
    oExcel.Application.ActiveCell.Offset(2,0).Select
    oExcel.Application.ActiveCell.Value = "Revenue Information"
    oExcel.Application.ActiveCell.Font.Bold = -1
    oExcel.Application.ActiveCell.Font.Name= "Arial"
    oExcel.Application.ActiveCell.Font.Size = 11
    oExcel.Application.ActiveCell.Font.Underline = 2
    oExcel.Application.ActiveCell.Offset(1,0).Select
    'Retrieve the user properties for the revenue information
    Set ouserprop = item.userproperties

    ExcelPrintProductRevenue "1998 Actual","Product1","Product2", _
        "Product3",ouserprop("cur1998ActualProd1"), _
        ouserprop("cur1998ActualProd2"), _
        ouserprop("cur1998ActualProd3")
    oExcel.Application.ActiveCell.Offset(5,0).Select
    ExcelPrintProductRevenue "1999 Actual","Product1","Product2", _
        "Product3",ouserprop("cur1999ActualProd1"), _
        ouserprop("cur1999ActualProd2"), _
        ouserprop("cur1999ActualProd3")
    oExcel.Application.ActiveCell.Offset(5,0).Select
    ExcelPrintProductRevenue "1998 Quota","Product1","Product2", _
        "Product3",ouserprop("cur1998QuotaProd1"), _
        ouserprop("cur1998QuotaProd2"), _
        ouserprop("cur1998QuotaProd3")

    'Format the output
    oSheet.Columns("A:B").EntireColumn.AutoFit
    oSheet.Columns("B:B").HorizontalAlignment = -4152
    oSheet.Range("A1:F1").Select
    oSheet.Range("A1:F1").HorizontalAlignment=7
End Sub
```

Unloading the Application: The *Item_Close* Event

When the user is finished using the application, the *Item_Close* event for the application is invoked. In the event handler, the application checks to see whether the user has updated any account address information. If so, the application asks the user whether she wants to update all the contacts for that specific account in the folder. If the user answers yes, all the accounts are updated by using the properties of the standard Outlook contact. Figure 8-11 shows the message box that is displayed when the user changes the address in the Account Tracking form.

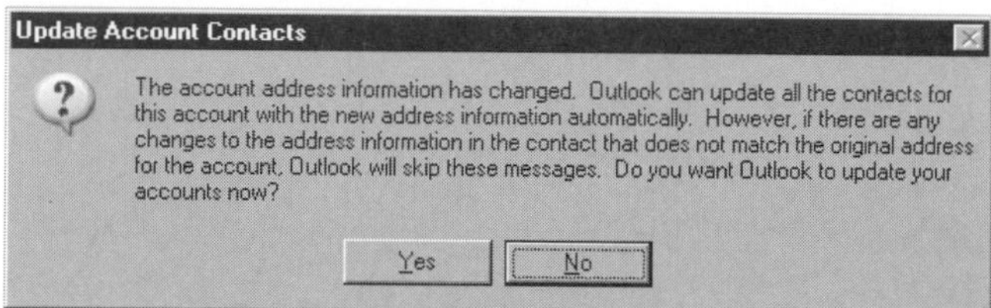

Figure 8-11 If the user wants to change the default address for each contact, this message box appears.

In the code that follows, notice that the *Save* method of the account contact is called only once after all the properties are changed. Outlook automatically parses the individual address properties, such as *BusinessAddressStreet*, *BusinessAddressCity*, and *BusinessAddressPostalCode*, to create the overall *BusinessAddress* property. If the code were to save the item after making a change in each property, Outlook would overwrite the previous changes when it parsed the individual properties to create the *BusinessAddress* property. Instead, a temporary variable, *boolSaveItem*, is used to notify the code at the end of the *If* statements whether the contact items being modified need to be saved. The *Item_Close* event handler also contains the code to destroy any database objects used in the application so they are not left in memory after the application closes. The following code shows the *Item_Close* event procedure:

```
'**********************************************
'Function Item_Close
'
'This function fires on the standard Outlook close
'event and prompts the user whether to update
'all contacts for the company if the user changed the
'master address for the company. This routine will
'update only the contacts that have the same text in
'the address fields as the original since users can
'change the address fields to reflect different
'locations or addresses for customers. This function
'also cleans up any open database objects that are left.
'**********************************************
```

```
Function Item_Close()
   boolSomethingDirty = 0         'False
   If not(ComposeMode) Then
      'Divided into multiple ifs to pinpoint changed property on
      'exit for faster performance when updating
      If oDefaultPage.Controls("txtStreet").Value <> _
      txtOriginalStreet Then
         boolStreetIsDirty = 1
         boolSomethingDirty = 1
       End If
      If oDefaultPage.Controls("txtCity").Value <> _
      txtOriginalCity Then
         boolCityIsDirty = 1
         boolSomethingDirty = 1
      End If
      If oDefaultPage.Controls("txtState").Value <> _
      txtOriginalState Then
         boolStateIsDirty = 1
         boolSomethingDirty = 1
      End If
      If oDefaultPage.Controls("txtPostalCode").Value <> _
      txtOriginalPostalCode Then
         boolPostalCodeIsDirty = 1
         boolSomethingDirty = 1
      End If
      If oDefaultPage.Controls("lstCountry").Value <> _
      txtOriginalCountry Then
         boolCountryIsDirty=1
         boolSomethingDirty = 1
      End If
      If boolSomethingDirty Then
         'Make sure the user wants to update all the
         'contact addresses
         intResponse = MsgBox("The account address " & _
            "information has changed. Outlook can update " & _
            "all the contacts for this account with " & _
            "the new address information automatically. " & _
            "However, if there are any changes to the " & _
            "address information in the contact that do " & _
            "not match the original address for the " & _
            "account, Outlook will skip these messages. Do " & _
            "you want Outlook to update your accounts now?", _
            292, "Update Account Contacts")
         If intResponse = 6 Then      'Yes
            For counter = 1 To oRestrictedContactItems.Count
               boolSaveItem = 0
               Set oItem = _
                  oRestrictedContactItems.Item(counter)
               If boolStreetIsDirty Then
                  If oItem.BusinessAddressStreet = _
                  txtOriginalStreet Then
                     oItem.BusinessAddressStreet = _
                     oDefaultPage.Controls("txtStreet").Value
```

```
                        boolSaveItem = 1
                    End If
                End If
                If boolCityIsDirty Then
                    If oItem.BusinessAddressCity = _
                    txtOriginalCity Then
                        oItem.BusinessAddressCity = _
                        oDefaultPage.Controls("txtCity").Value
                        boolSaveItem = 1
                    End If
                End If
                If boolStateIsDirty Then
                    If oItem.BusinessAddressState = _
                    txtOriginalState Then
                        oItem.BusinessAddressState = _
                        oDefaultPage.Controls("txtState").Value
                        boolSaveItem = 1
                    End If
                End If
                If boolPostalCodeIsDirty Then
                    If oItem.BusinessAddressPostalCode = _
                    txtOriginalPostalCode Then
                        oItem.BusinessAddressPostalCode = _
                            oDefaultPage.Controls( _
                            "txtPostalCode").Value
                        boolSaveItem = 1
                    End If
                End If
                If boolCountryIsDirty Then
                    If oItem.BusinessAddressCountry = _
                    txtOriginalCountry Then
                        oItem.BusinessAddressCountry = _
                        oDefaultPage.Controls("lstCountry").Value
                        boolSaveItem = 1
                    End If
                End If
                If boolSaveItem Then
                    'Make sure address information is only
                    'parsed once by Outlook
                    oItem.Save
                End If
            Next
        End If
    End If
End If
'Close the database If enabled
If ComposeMode=False and bUseDatabase Then
    oDatabase.Close
    Set oDatabaseEngine = Nothing
End If
End Function
```

Interacting with the Application Using Outlook Today

Users have a secondary way to interact with the Account Tracking application—through a customized Outlook Today page. Outlook Today, a feature that takes advantage of the HTML support in Outlook, allows users to view all their information in one HTML window rather than as separate modules. You can also customize Outlook Today's HTML code to display your Outlook or intranet information in a single window view.

When customized for the Account Tracking application, Outlook Today allows users to create new accounts, find account contacts, and open the Account Tracking folder to see how many accounts, tasks, and contacts it contains. The customized Outlook Today page is shown in Figure 8-12.

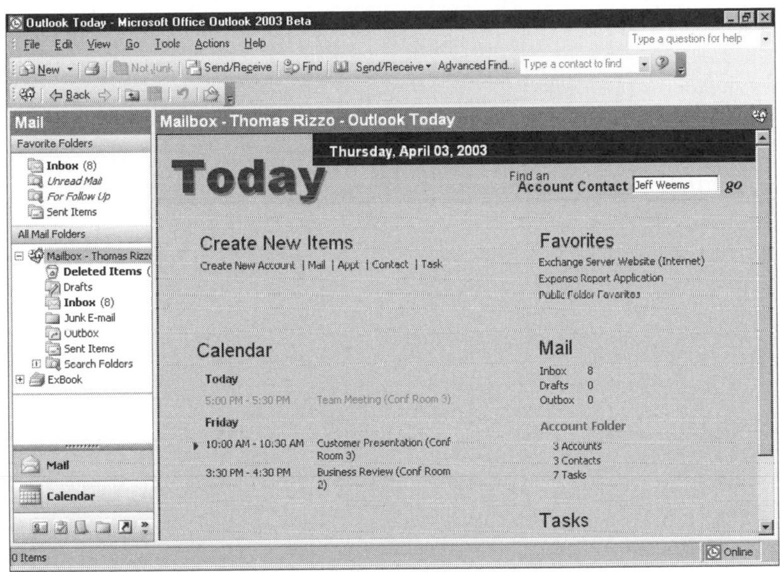

Figure 8-12 The customized Outlook Today page in the Account Tracking application

Viewing the Customized Outlook Today Page

The Outlook Today page in the Account Tracking application shows how to use your skills with VBScript and the Outlook object library in another medium, HTML. The code in the Outlook Today page uses the Outlook object library to count the number of items in the account folder and to search the folder for specific account contacts. The following code is taken from the Account.htm file, which is the Outlook Today page customized for the Account Tracking application:

```
<script language="VBScript">

'*****************************************************
'In-line code
'
'These lines of code are run when the browser reaches
'them while parsing the document. They set up the global
'variables that are needed throughout the application.
'*****************************************************
Set oApplication = window.external.OutlookApplication
Set oNS = oApplication.GetNameSpace("MAPI")

'Change this to your location for the Account Tracking Folder
Set oAccountFolder = oNS.Folders("ExBook").Folders("Account Tracking")

'*****************************************************
'Sub FindAccountContact
'
'This subroutine takes the name of the contact that the
'user types into the Outlook Today page and searches the
'contact folder for the contact. If the contact is
'found, it displays the contact. If the contact is not
'found, it displays a message box.
'*****************************************************
Sub FindAccountContact(ContactName)
   If ContactName <> "" Then
      boolFound = 0
      RestrictString = ""
      RestrictString = "[Message Class] = " _
         """IPM.Contact.Account contact"""
      Set oContacts = _
         oAccountFolder.Items.Restrict(RestrictString)
      For i = 1 To oContacts.Count
         Set oContact = oContacts.Item(i)
         If oContact.FullName = ContactName Then
            oContact.Display()
            boolFound = 1
            Exit For
         End If
      Next
      If boolFound = 0 Then
         MsgBox "No contact by that name was found",, _
            "Find Account Contact"
      End If
   End If
End Sub
'*****************************************************
'Sub CreateAccount
'
```

```
'This subroutine creates a new Account info form and
'displays it for the user to fill in
'*****************************************************
Sub CreateAccount()
   Set oAccount = oAccountFolder.Items.Add("IPM.Post.Account info")
   oAccount.Display()
End Sub

'*****************************************************
'Sub DisplayAccountFolder
'
'This subroutine finds and displays the Account Tracking
'folder in a separate Outlook window. The reason for this
'is to create a new Explorer object separate from the
'current Explorer object in Outlook Today.
'*****************************************************
Sub DisplayAccountFolder()
   'Change this location to your folder location
   Set oFolder = oNS.Folders("ExBook").Folders("Account Tracking")
   oFolder.Display()
End Sub

'*****************************************************
'Sub GetAccountFolderCounts
'
'This subroutine calculates how many accounts, contacts,
'and tasks are in the Account Tracking folder and
'displays this information
'*****************************************************
Sub GetAccountFolderCounts()
   RestrictString = ""
   RestrictString = "[Message Class] = ""IPM.Post.Account info"""
   Set oAccounts = oAccountFolder.Items.Restrict(RestrictString)
   oAcctCount = oAccounts.Count
   AccountCount.innerHTML = oAcctCount & " Accounts"

   RestrictString = ""
   RestrictString = "[Message Class] = " _
      """IPM.Contact.Account contact"""
   Set oContacts = oAccountFolder.Items.Restrict(RestrictString)
   oContactCount = oContacts.Count
   ContactCount.innerHTML = oContactCount & " Contacts"

   RestrictString = ""
   RestrictString = "[Message Class] = ""IPM.Task"""
   Set oTasks = oAccountFolder.Items.Restrict(RestrictString)
   oTasksCount = oTasks.Count
   TaskCount.innerHTML = oTasksCount & " Tasks"
End Sub
</script>
```

Setting Up the Outlook Today Page

You need to modify the Outlook Today page so it knows the location of the Account Tracking folder and also modify the registry to point Outlook at the customized Outlook Today page. If you want to deploy the customized Outlook Today page to users in your organization, consider writing a simple Visual Basic program that modifies their registries and points them to a Web server containing the Outlook Today page.

The following steps show how to modify the Outlook Today page and your registry for the Account Tracking application:

1. Open the file named Account.htm (included in the sample code) in a text editor such as Notepad.
2. Change the line

    ```
    Set oAccountFolder = oNS.Folders("ExBook").Folders( _
       "Account Tracking")
    ```

    so that it reflects the location of the Account Tracking folder. For example, if you copy the Account Tracking folder to the main tree of your Public Folder hierarchy, the code will look like this:

    ```
    Set oAccountFolder = oNS.Folders("Public Folders").Folders( _
       "All Public Folders").Folders("Account Tracking")
    ```

3. Modify the following line so that it shows the location where you copied the Account Tracking folder, whether it is in a .pst file or in your public folders:

    ```
    Set oFolder = oNS.Folders("ExBook").Folders(" _
       Account Tracking")
    ```

4. Save the file to your hard disk to keep your changes.

To modify the registry for the customized Outlook Today page, add the following key:

```
HKEY_CURRENT_USER\Software\Microsoft\Office\9.0\Outlook\Today
```

> **Note** If you are running Outlook 2000, change the 10.0 to 9.0 in the path. For Outlook 2003, change the 9.0 to 11.0 in the path.

Add a string value to the Today key named *Url*. For its value data, type the path to the Account.htm—for example, *file://C:\Account.htm*. Then click on the Outlook Today icon in Outlook to display your customized Outlook Today page. If you want to revert to the standard version of Outlook Today, just delete the *Url* string value.

Adding Folder Home Pages

Folder home pages enable you to link an HTML page to any folder in the Outlook environment. Folder home pages support offline viewing capabilities, so you can ask Outlook to synchronize an HTML file that is associated with an offline folder when a user synchronizes the folder. This ensures that your HTML page is available whether the user is working off line or on line. We will look at two folder home pages in this chapter, one of which uses the Outlook View control.

The process of associating a folder home page with a folder is easy. Outlook provides a user interface for this connection, as shown in Figure 8-13. You can access this Properties dialog box in Outlook by right-clicking on a folder and then choosing Properties.

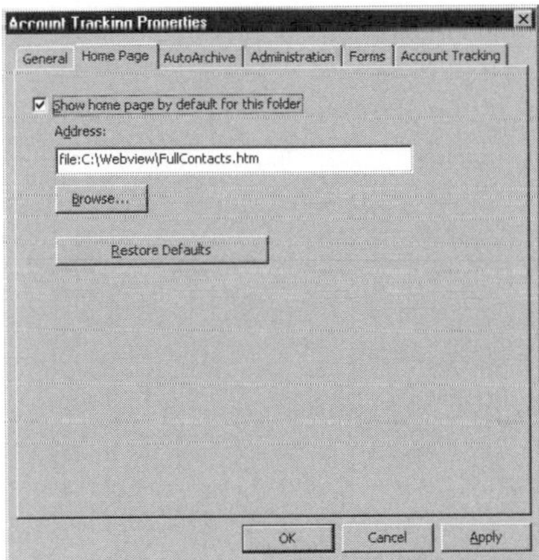

Figure 8-13 Configuring a folder home page for a folder

Because Outlook hosts Internet Explorer in-frame, when a user clicks on the folder, your folder home page can appear directly inside the Outlook client. Furthermore, you can make the folder home page the default view for a particular folder. In the Web pages for your folder home pages, you might want to include instructions for using the folder, a way to mail the folder owner, or a list of links related to that folder or other folders.

You can also add script to the folder home page to access the Outlook object model. Figure 8-14 shows the first example of a custom folder home page (Contacts.htm) for the Account Tracking application.

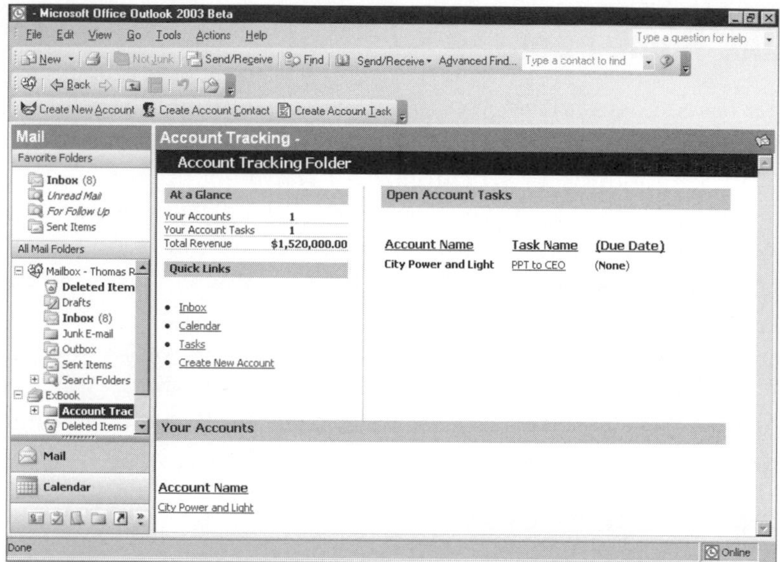

Figure 8-14 The folder home page (Contacts.htm) for the Account Tracking application

Setting Up the First Folder Home Page

To test the folder home pages, you need a machine that has Outlook with the Visual Basic Scripting Support and Collaboration Data Objects components installed. Follow these steps to set up the first folder home page:

1. If you haven't already set up the Account Tracking application, do so now (as explained in the section titled "Setting Up the Account Tracking Application" earlier in this chapter). If you want the application to create sales charts and print account summaries, install Excel.
2. If necessary, clear the read-only flag for the files contained in the Webview folder from the sample code.
3. Open the Webview\Contacts.htm file in Notepad.
4. Find the first occurrence of *oAccountFolder* and modify the path to the location of your Account Tracking folder.

5. Save Contacts.htm and close Notepad.
6. In Outlook, right-click on the Account Tracking folder and choose Properties.
7. In the Address text box of the Home Page tab, specify the location of the Contacts.htm file—for example, *file://C:\Webview\Contacts.htm*.
8. Select the Show Home Page By Default For This Folder option, and then click OK.
9. Click the Account Tracking folder in Outlook to display the folder home page. You will be prompted to allow access for an item to your address book. This prompt is triggered because the folder home page scans all the accounts to look for the current user as a team member on an account. This triggers the Outlook security dialog box.

Sample Script for the Folder Home Page

The following code shows the script for the folder home page (Contacts.htm) shown earlier in Figure 8-14:

```
<SCRIPT ID=clientEventHandlersVBS LANGUAGE=vbscript>
'*****************************************************
'In-line code
'
'These lines of code are run when the browser reaches
'them while parsing the document. They set up the global
'variables that are needed throughout the application.
'*****************************************************
Set oApplication = window.external.OutlookApplication
Set oNS = oApplication.GetNameSpace("MAPI")

'Change this to your location for the Account Tracking folder
Set oAccountFolder = oNS.Folders("Public Folders").Folders( _
   "All Public Folders").Folders("Account Tracking")

'Set some global vars for the EntryIDs
Dim arrTaskEntryIDs()
Dim oTasks    'Restricted collection of Tasks
Dim arrAccountEntryIDs()
Dim oAccounts    'Restricted collection of Accounts

'*****************************************************
'Sub CreateAccount
'
'This subroutine creates a new account info form and
'displays it for the user to fill in
'*****************************************************
```

```
Sub CreateAccount()
   Set oAccount = oAccountFolder.Items.Add("IPM.Post.Account info")
   oAccount.Display()
End Sub

'*****************************************************
'Sub GetTask(lEntryID)
'
'This subroutine gets the task that the user clicked on
'in the HTML page and displays it. An index into an
'array of EntryIDs is passed to this subroutine.
'*****************************************************
Sub GetTask(lEntryID)
   lTaskEntryID = arrTaskEntryIDs(lEntryID-1)
   For Each oItem In oTasks
      If oItem.EntryID = lTaskEntryID Then
         Set otmpTask = oItem
      End If
   Next
   otmpTask.Display()
End Sub

'*****************************************************
'Sub GetAccount(lEntryID)
'
'This subroutine gets the account that the user clicked on
'in the HTML page and displays it. An index into an
'array of EntryIDs is passed to this subroutine.
'*****************************************************
Sub GetAccount(lEntryID)
   lAccountEntryID = arrAccountEntryIDs(lEntryID-1)
   For Each oItem In oAccounts
      If oItem.EntryID = lAccountEntryID Then
         Set otmpAccount = oItem
      End If
   Next
   otmpAccount.Display()
End Sub

Sub Window_onLoad()
'***************************************************************
'All of the following lines are run when the HTML page is
'loaded
'***************************************************************
   'Put the name of the folder in the bar
   txtFolder.innerHTML = oAccountFolder.Name & " Folder"

'***************************************************************
'Figure out the account tasks for the current user
'***************************************************************
   RestrictString = ""
   RestrictString = "[Message Class] = ""IPM.Task""" & _
      " AND [Owner] = """ & oNS.CurrentUser.Name & """ AND _
```

```
        [Complete] = FALSE"
    Set oTasks = oAccountFolder.Items.Restrict(RestrictString)
    oTasksCount = oTasks.Count
    'Redim the EntryID array
    ReDim arrTaskEntryIDs(oTasksCount-1)
    strTaskList = "<TABLE Border=0 cellpadding=2 cellspacing=2 " & _
    "class='calendarinfo'><TR><TD><strong><Font Size=2><U>" & _
    "Account Name</u></STRONG></TD><TD>  </TD><TD>" & _
    "<STRONG><Font size=2><U>Task Name</U></FONT></STRONG>" & _
    "</TD><TD>  </TD><TD><STRONG><Font size=2><U>" & _
    "(Due Date)</U></FONT></strong></TD></TR>"
    'Count the tasks using counter
    counter = 1
    oTasks.Sort "[ConversationTopic]", False
    For Each oTask in oTasks
       boolOverDue = 0
       If oTask.DueDate = "1/1/4501" Then
          strDueDate = "None"
       Else
          strDueDate = oTask.DueDate
          'Check to see whether the task is overdue
          If DateDiff("d",CDate(strDueDate),Now) > 0 Then
             boolOverDue = 1
          End If
       End If
       If boolOverDue Then
          'Turn red
          strTaskList = strTaskList & "<TR><TD><FONT " & _
          "COLOR='#FF0000'><STRONG>" & oTask.ConversationTopic & _
          "</STRONG></FONT></TD><TD>  </TD><TD>" & _
          "<A HREF='' onclick=GetTask(" & counter & _
          ");window.event.returnValue=false>" & oTask.Subject & _
          "</a></TD><TD>  </TD><TD><FONT " & _
          "COLOR='#FF0000'>(<Strong>" & strDueDate & _
          "</Strong>)</FONT><BR></TD></TR>"
       Else
          strTaskList = strTaskList & "<TR><TD><STRONG>" & _
          oTask.ConversationTopic & "</STRONG></TD><TD>" & _
          "  </TD><TD><A HREF='' onclick=GetTask(" & _
          "counter & ");window.event.returnValue=false>" & _
          oTask.Subject & "</a></TD><TD>  </TD>" & _
          "<TD>(<Strong>" & strDueDate & "</Strong>)<BR></TD></TR>"
       End If
       arrTaskEntryIDs(counter-1) = oTask.EntryID
       counter = counter + 1
    Next
    TaskList.innerHTML = strTaskList & "</TABLE>"

'****************************************************************
'Figure out which accounts the current user is a team member of
'****************************************************************

    'Find accounts where this person is a team member.
```

```
'First restrict to only account items.
RestrictString = ""
RestrictString = "[Message Class] = "IPM.Post.Account info""
Set oAccounts = oAccountFolder.Items.Restrict(RestrictString)

'Now find accounts where this person is a team member
numFound = 0
strCurrentUser = oNS.CurrentUser.Name
numTotalRevenue = 0
strAccountHTML = "<table border=0 width=100% cellpadding=3 " & _
"cellspacing=0 ID='Home' style='DISPLAY: inline; " & _
"MARGIN-TOP: 12px'>"
strAccountHTML = strAccountHTML & "<TR><TD " & _
"class='calendarinfo'><STRONG><FONT SIZE=2><U>Account Name" & _
"</U></FONT></STRONG></TD></TR>"

RestrictString = ""
RestrictString = "[Message Class] = ""IPM.Post.Account info""" & _
" AND [txtAccountConsultant] = """ & strCurrentUser & _
""" OR [txtAccountExecutive] = """ & strCurrentUser & _
""" OR [txtAccountSalesRep] = """ & strCurrentUser & _
""" OR [txtAccountSE] = """ & strCurrentUser & _
""" OR [txtAccountSupportEngineer] = """ & strCurrentUser & """"

Set oAccounts = oAccountFolder.Items.Restrict(RestrictString)
numFound = oAccounts.Count
ReDim arrAccountEntryIDs(numFound)
counter = 1
For Each oAccount in oAccounts
   Set oUserProps = oAccount.UserProperties
   arrAccountEntryIDs(counter-1) = oAccount.EntryID
   'Get the total revenue for the account for 1998 and 1999.
   'Get the revenue and add it to the total.
   num1998Total = oUserProps.Find("form1998ActualTotal")
   num1999Total = oUserProps.Find("form1999ActualTotal")
   If num1998Total <> "Zero" Then
      numTotalRevenue = numTotalRevenue + num1998Total
   End If
   If num1999Total <> "Zero" Then
      numTotalRevenue = numTotalRevenue + num1999Total
   End If
   strAccountHTML = strAccountHTML & "<TR><TD " & _
   "class='calendarinfo'><A Href='' onclick=GetAccount(" & _
     "counter & ");window.event.returnValue=false>" & _
   oAccount.Subject & "</A></TD></TR>"
   counter = counter + 1
Next
numTotalRevenue = CCur(numTotalRevenue)
numTotalRevenue = FormatCurrency(numTotalRevenue)
TotalRevenue.innerHTML = "<STRONG>" & numTotalRevenue & _
  "</STRONG>"
strAccountHTML = strAccountHTML & "</TABLE>"
Accounts.innerHTML = strAccountHTML
```

```
   YourTasks.innerHTML = "<Strong>" & oTasksCount & "</Strong>"
   YourAccounts.innerHTML = "<STRONG>" & numFound & "</STRONG>"
End Sub    'Window_OnLoad
-->
</SCRIPT>
```

You can see that you need to follow a few critical steps to access the Outlook object model. The first step is to retrieve the Outlook *Application* object. To do this, you use the *Window.External.OutlookApplication* syntax. You can then retrieve the rest of the Outlook objects. For example, by calling the *ActiveExplorer* method on the *Application* object that's returned, you can retrieve the *Explorer* object that is hosting the folder home page.

The folder home page is a dynamic environment for viewing a folder, as illustrated by the folder home page used in the Account Tracking application. On the home page, the user is presented with a summary of her accounts, account revenue, and tasks. The home page allows you to restrict account tasks to the person currently viewing the folder. (You could create a similar view in Outlook, but you wouldn't be able to specify a filter for who can view the folder.) These account summaries are created by using the *Restrict* method on the Outlook *Items* collection for the folder. For the Tasks restriction, the code restricts only those messages in the folder that are tasks, and where the current user is the owner and the task status is incomplete. After receiving the restricted set, the code sorts the tasks by their conversation topics, which are the names of the accounts the tasks are for. The code loops through each task to see whether it has a due date. If it does, the code checks to see whether the task is past due. Then the code generates the HTML, which is placed in the Open Account Tasks list.

For the revenue summary, the code first finds all account items to tally a total. The code restricts the collection to all accounts for which the current user is a team member. Then the code loops through each account and retrieves the revenue, which is stored in the *UserProperties* collection as custom properties. Because the revenue properties are formula properties, they can contain text that indicates zero revenue from the account. To compensate for this, the code checks whether the value of the property is the string *"Zero"*. The code then builds a string for the restricted list of account names and prints out the account revenue. The string of account names is hyperlinked, as are the tasks, so that a user can quickly go to a specific account or task.

From the code sample, you can see how you can include the features of the Outlook object model, or any object model for that matter, inside the HTML page you create for your folders.

The Outlook View Control

Outlook 2000 included an add-on product named the Outlook View control. With Outlook 2002 and later, the Outlook View control ships as a core part of Outlook, so it is not necessary to download any separate controls to get it. The Outlook View control is an ActiveX wrapper around Outlook views such as Table, Calendar, Card, and Timeline. You can use this ActiveX control within a Web application, such as an Active Server Pages (ASP) application, or within your folder home page. This control saves you from having to rewrite significant portions of code to mimic Outlook functionality. Figure 8-15 shows the second folder home page example (FullContacts.htm), which hosts the View control.

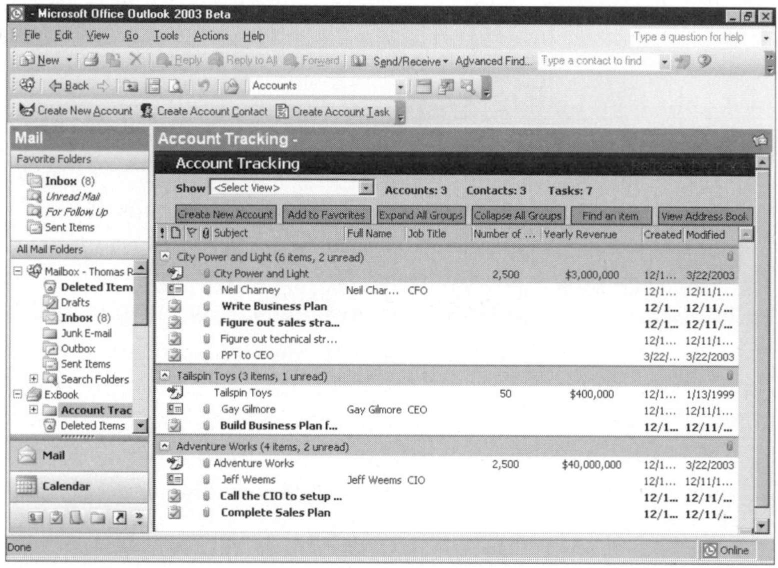

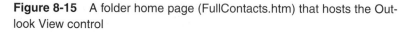

Figure 8-15 A folder home page (FullContacts.htm) that hosts the Outlook View control

The environment in which you place the View control determines the control's functionality. For example, when you place the View control in a folder home page, the control provides full access to the Outlook object model as well as automatic merging of menu commands with the Outlook container, as shown in Figure 8-16. In contrast, within a standalone Web page, the control does not allow access to any user data, nor does it provide access to the entire Outlook object model. This restriction prevents the control from downloading all the Outlook data when a user accesses the Web page. In either scenario, the View control does require Outlook to be installed on the machine. The control does not install Outlook for you.

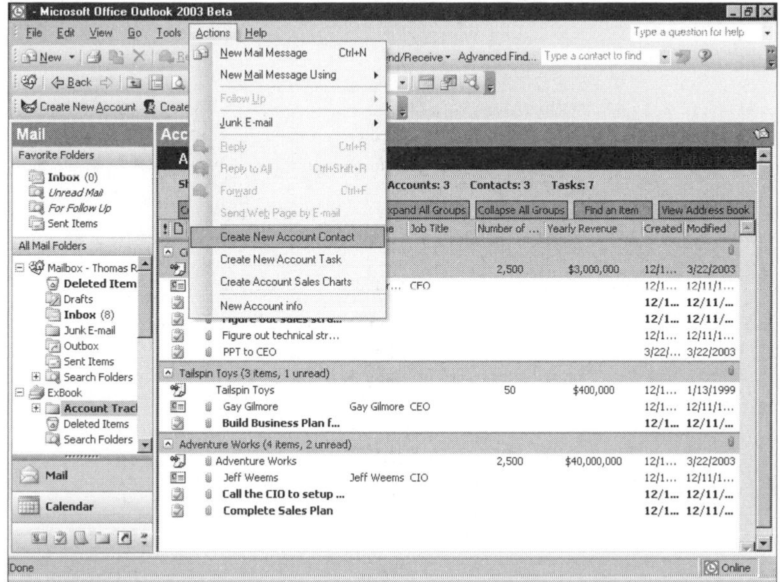

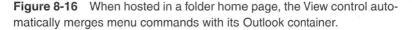

Figure 8-16 When hosted in a folder home page, the View control automatically merges menu commands with its Outlook container.

The View control allows you to programmatically change control properties so that you can place more than one control on a single page in your application. For example, you might want to show a side-by-side view of two calendars, or maybe a contacts list and all tasks associated with the currently selected contact. When multiple View controls are on a single page, the control with the focus determines the menu items available to the user.

Setting Up the Second Folder Home Page

Using a machine that has Outlook with Visual Basic Scripting Support and Collaboration Data Objects components installed, follow these steps to set up the second folder home page, which uses the Outlook View control:

1. In Outlook, right-click on the Account Tracking folder and choose Properties.
2. In the Address text box of the Home Page tab, specify the location of the FullContacts.htm file—for example, *file://C:\Webview\FullContacts.htm*—and click OK. (FullContacts.htm is included with the book's sample files.)
3. Click on the Account Tracking folder to display the folder home page.

The following section outlines how to add the View control to a Web page and program it.

Using the Outlook View Control

Adding a View control to your folder home page or Web page is actually quite easy. All you do is add the *OBJECT* tag to your page and give the control an ID that you will use in your program. For the Account Tracking folder home page, this *OBJECT* tag is inserted into the HTML page:

```
<OBJECT ID="oViewControl" WIDTH=100% HEIGHT=84%
style="border-bottom:1px silver solid"
CLASSID="CLSID:0006F063-0000-0000-C000-000000000046">
   <param NAME="Namespace" VALUE="MAPI">
   <param NAME="Folder" VALUE="">
   <param NAME="View" VALUE="Accounts">
</OBJECT>
```

This tag creates the View control object. Also notice the *param* tags—you can use these tags to pass parameters to the control. This example passes in *MAPI* for the *Namespace* parameter. It also passes in the folder, using a blank value so the control defaults to the folder that the user is currently looking at. Finally, it passes in, as a string, the default view we want in the control. The Accounts view is the default view for the Account Tracking folder.

After you insert the control, you can add code to the folder home page to grab the Outlook *Application* object, *Window.External.OutlookApplication*, using the technique you saw earlier. Because this script must be running in the Account Tracking folder (because this is the folder home page for that folder), I set a variable to the current folder so that I can use that variable later in the script.

After the folder variable is set, the code needs to accomplish one more task. Recall that the View control will bring up the default folder that the user is viewing. However, this folder might not be the Account Tracking folder. To ensure that the control displays the Account Tracking folder, the code finds the full path to the Account Tracking folder and passes this path as one of the control's properties, *Folder*. (For example, if the Account Tracking folder is a top-level folder in the Favorites folders, the path will be \\Public Folders\Favorites\Account Tracking\.) The code then fills in the total number of accounts, contacts, and tasks in the folder. The code for this process is shown here:

```
<SCRIPT ID=clientEventHandlersVBS LANGUAGE=vbscript>

'*****************************************************
'In-line code
'
'These lines of code are run when the browser reaches
'them while parsing the document. They set up the global
```

```
'variables that are needed throughout the application.
'*****************************************************

Set oApplication = window.external.OutlookApplication
Set oNS = oApplication.GetNamespace("MAPI")
Set oCurrentFolder = oApplication.activeExplorer.currentfolder
Set oAccountFolder = oCurrentFolder
'AvailWidth = document.body.clientWidth

'*****************************************************
'Function StrFullPath
'
'This function creates and returns the full path to the
'folder
'*****************************************************
Function StrFullPath()
   If oCurrentFolder Is Nothing Then
      strFolderName = ""
   End If
   Set olCollabFolder = oCurrentFolder
   strFolderName = ""
   Set olRoot = oCurrentFolder
   While (olRoot <> "Mapi")
      strFolderName = oCurrentFolder.Name & "\" & strFolderName
      Set olRoot = oCurrentFolder.Parent
      If olRoot <> "Mapi" Then
         Set oCurrentFolder = oCurrentFolder.Parent
      End If
   Wend
   strFullPath = "\\" & strFolderName
End Function

'*****************************************************
'Sub FillTotals()
'
'This subroutine gets the count for the different types
'of items in a folder, such as accounts, contacts, and
'tasks. It also fills in the HTML page with this
'information.
'*****************************************************
Sub FillTotals()
   RestrictString = ""
   RestrictString = "[Message Class] = ""IPM.Post.Account info"""
   Set oAccounts = oAccountFolder.Items.Restrict(RestrictString)
   oAcctCount = oAccounts.Count
   AccountTotal.innerHTML = "<STRONG>" & oAcctCount & "</STRONG>"
   RestrictString = ""
   RestrictString = _
      "[Message Class] = ""IPM.Contact.Account contact"""
   Set oContacts = oAccountFolder.Items.Restrict(RestrictString)
   oContactCount = oContacts.Count
   ContactTotal.innerHTML = "<STRONG>" & oContactCount & "</STRONG>"
   RestrictString = ""
```

```
    RestrictString = "[Message Class] = ""IPM.Task"""
    Set oTasks = oAccountFolder.Items.Restrict(RestrictString)
    oTasksCount = oTasks.Count
    TaskTotal.innerHTML = "<STRONG>" & oTasksCount & "</STRONG>"
End Sub

Fullpath = StrFullPath()
oViewControl.Folder = FullPath

'*****************************************************
'Sub Window_onLoad()
'
'This subroutine is called when the HTML page is loaded
'*****************************************************
Sub Window_onLoad()
    oViewControl.Folder = Fullpath
    'oViewControl.width = AvailWidth
    txtFolder.innerHTml = oAccountFolder.Name
    FillTotals()
End Sub
```

Now that some of the information for the HTML page is filled in, we need to add some buttons to the page to enable the user to call our subroutines that automate the View control. I've left out the HTML code that creates the buttons (you can look at this code in the FullContacts.htm file), but we will examine the automation code that drives the View control from these buttons.

The application provides six buttons and a drop-down list for changing the View control. The drop-down list enables the user to change the view of the control to one of the other views in the Outlook folder. Figure 8-17 shows another view of the Account Tracking folder home page.

The View control has no methods for creating new views, so the views must be predefined for the folder. To change the view by using code, you set the *View* property on the control to the name of the view you want. Because a fully functional Outlook application is running in the control, users can right-click on view columns to bring up the Field Chooser or customize the view directly in the page. The following code implements changing the views of the control:

```
'*****************************************************
'Sub WhatView_onChange
'
'This subroutine changes the view of the Outlook control
'depending on what the user picked in the drop-down list
'*****************************************************
Sub WhatView_onChange
    oViewControl.View = WhatView.Value
    window.Focus
End Sub
```

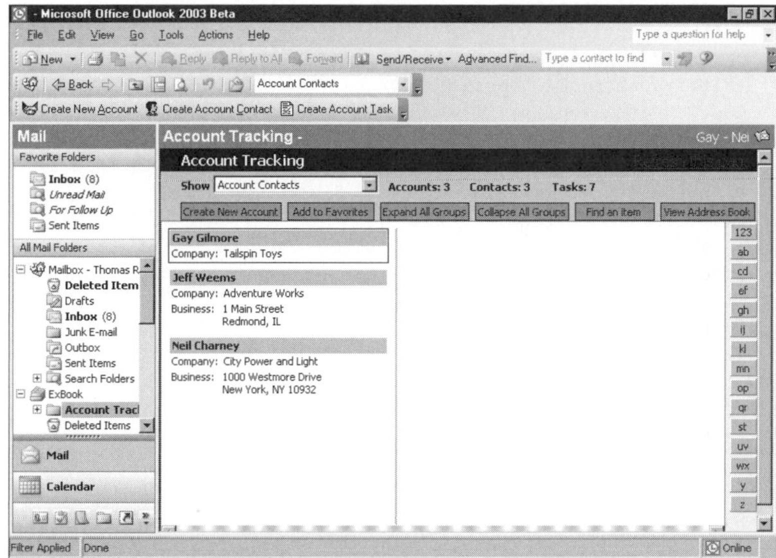

Figure 8-17 The folder home page for the Account Tracking application, which contains the Outlook View control

Implementing the functionality for the buttons is also pretty straightforward. Using the buttons, the user can create new accounts, expand groups, collapse groups, add a folder to a favorites list, find an item in a folder, and view the address book. Most of these actions are already contained in the View control as methods. For example, to view the address book, all the code has to do is call the *AddressBook* method on the View control. The same applies to adding the folder to the favorites—all the code has to do is call the *AddtoFavorites* method on the View control. Here's the code for the buttons:

```
'***************************************************
'Sub CreateAccount
'
'This subroutine creates a new account info form and
'displays it for the user to fill in
'***************************************************
Sub CreateAccount()
   Set oAccount = oAccountFolder.Items.Add("IPM.Post.Account info")
   oAccount.Display()
End Sub

'***************************************************
'Sub Actions_onClick(Action)
'
'This subroutine executes the correct action, such as
'finding an item, creating a new account, and so on,
'depending on what the user picked in the Web page.
'***************************************************
```

```
Sub Actions_onClick(Action)
   Select Case Action
      Case "AddressBook"
         oViewControl.AddressBook()
      Case "AddtoFavorites"
         oViewControl.AddtoFavorites()
      Case "ExpandAllGroups"
         oViewControl.ExpandAllGroups()
      Case "CollapseAllGroups"
         oViewControl.CollapseAllGroups()
      Case "AdvancedFind"
         oViewControl.AdvancedFind()
      Case "CreateAccount"
         CreateAccount()
   End Select
End Sub
```

You can also take advantage of other methods and properties in your applications that use the Outlook View control. To see a complete list of them, just add a reference to the Outlook View control in the Object Browser in VBA or Visual Basic. Most of the methods and properties are self-explanatory—for example, the *ReplyInFolder* and *ReplyAll* methods. Here are a few of the more interesting properties and methods for the View control that we haven't discussed yet:

- ***FlagItem* method** Opens a dialog box that flags an item with a reminder. This method will not work unless the user has selected a valid item in the View control, such as a PostItem.
- ***Categories* method** Opens the Categories dialog box, in which the user can select item categories. This is the same dialog box that appears when the Categories button is clicked in an Outlook form.
- ***CustomizeView* method** Opens a dialog box that lets a user select fields, the sort orders, the filters, the automatic formatting, and the grouping for the view. This is the same dialog box that appears when the user chooses Current View, Customize Current View from the View menu.
- ***ShowFields* method** Opens the Show Fields dialog box, where the user can quickly select fields for the View control to display for the current view.
- ***SynchFolder* method** Attempts to synchronize the current folder in the background. (I say *attempts* because your program might call this method only to find that the connection to the Exchange server is not available.) Consider creating a button on your HTML form so users can easily activate folder synchronization.

- ***Restriction* property** A powerful property that allows you to filter the items you want to display in your view. It takes the same string format as the *Restrict* method on the *Items* collection. For example, if you want to restrict the view so that only Task items appear, you pass to the *Restriction* property the following string: *[Message Class] = "IPM.Task"*. You can also pass your restriction as a parameter by using the following syntax when you create your View control:

  ```
  <param NAME=Restrict VALUE="[Message Class] = 'IPM.Task'">
  ```

  By using the *Restriction* property, you can place two View controls on a single page and have one view control show a restricted set of items on the basis of what the users select in the other View control.

View Control Changes in Outlook 2002

Unlike with previous versions of Outlook, Outlook 2002 includes the Outlook View control. You do not need to download additional components to get the View control on a machine. The Outlook 2002 View control offers some new functionality. For example, it provides direct view manipulation and supports a limited number of events. Table 8-1 lists the new properties of the Outlook 2002 View control.

> **Note** You cannot use the Outlook 2002 View control on a computer with only Outlook 2000. The Outlook View Control is the same between Outlook 2002 and 2003.

Table 8-1 New Properties of the Outlook 2002 View Control

Property	Description
EnableRowPersistence	A Boolean property that specifies whether the View control will remember the last row selected. It works only when hosted in Outlook. The default value is *False*.
Filter	A string property that applies a SQL-style filter to the view. For more information about the format of the filter, see Chapter 18. This property replaces the entire view with the results of the filter and persists the changes to the view.

Table 8-1 New Properties of the Outlook 2002 View Control

Property	Description
FilterAppend	A string property that is the filter to append to a view. The filter you apply is appended to the view filter as a logical AND statement. This property does not persist the changes to the view.
ItemCount	Returns the number of items in the folder currently displayed in the view.
Selection	Returns the Outlook *Selection* object, which refers to the items currently selected in the view.
ViewXML	Returns or sets the XML view descriptor used to render the view. For more information on view descriptors, see Chapter 18.

Table 8-2 describes the new events supported by the Outlook 2002 View control.

Table 8-2 New Events Supported by the Outlook 2002 View Control

Event	Description
Activate	Fires when the View control becomes the active element.
BeforeViewSwitch	A cancelable event that fires before the user switches to a new view in the control programmatically or through the user interface.
SelectionChange	Used in conjunction with the *Selection* property. This event fires when the selection changes in the control.
ViewSwitch	Fires after the user switches the view programmatically or through the user interface.

If the View control is hosted in a Web page, you should use it directly inside Outlook. This is the only way that code run within the control can access the Outlook object model. If you use Visual Basic or an Office Form to host the View control, you can always access the Outlook object model from the control. If you are hosting the control in a Web page outside Outlook, functionality such as the *View* property will not work; you must set the *View* property programmatically rather than attempt to set it as a parameter of the control in your HTML *object* tag.

The following samples show how to use some of the new properties and events in the View control. Notice that Boolean properties in Outlook filters take *0* as *False* and *1* as *True*. Also, you should host this application in an Outlook folder home page. If you host it in Internet Explorer, the View control will be locked down for security reasons. For example, many of the parameters you pass in the *object* tag will be ignored. You must script the values for the parameters, as shown here:

```
<html>

<head>
<title>Outlook 2003 View Control Sample</title>
</head>
<Script Language="vbscript">
    Sub Window_Onload()
        Set oApp = oViewControl.OutlookApplication
        If oApp is nothing Then
            MsgBox "This application does not work in IE directly!"
        End If
    End Sub

    Sub AppendFilter
        oViewControl.Filter = """urn:schemas:httpmail:read"" = 0"
        document.all.FilterAppend.disabled = True
    End Sub

    Sub NewFilter
        'Set the new filter

        oViewControl.Filter = " (""DAV:isfolder"" = False AND " & _
        """DAV:ishidden"" = False AND ""urn:schemas:httpmail:read"" = 0)"

        document.all.NewFilter.disabled = True
    End Sub

    Sub oViewControl_SelectionChange
        MsgBox "There are currently " & oViewControl.Selection.Count & _
               " item(s) selected in the view!"
    End Sub
</script>
<body>
<H1>Outlook .NET View Control Sample</H1>
<hr>
Click the buttons below to see the new properties and events of the Outlook .NE
T View Control in action.  Change selections to see the selectionchange event i
n action.
<p>
<input type=button id=NewFilter value="Use NewFilter (Only unread items will be
 shown)" onclick="NewFilter">
<BR>
<input type=button id=FilterAppend value="Use FilterAppend (Only unread items w
ill be shown)" onclick="AppendFilter"><BR>
<input type=button id=DisplayXML value="Display View XML"
onclick="vbscript:MsgBox oViewControl.ViewXML">
<object classid="clsid:0006F063-0000-0000-C000-000000000046" id="oViewControl"
```

```
width="774" height="489">
  <param name="folder" value="SPS Sync"
  <param name="Namespace" value="MAPI">
  <param name="Restriction" value="">
  <param name="DeferUpdate" value="0">
</object>
</p>
</body>
</html>
```

The Account Tracking COM Add-In

In this section, I'll describe a COM add-in for the Account Tracking application. COM add-ins allow you to extend Outlook in richer ways than when you use Outlook Forms. For more advanced functionality, such as showing property pages, we will use a COM add-in. We'll start by looking at how the COM add-in works and then delve into the code that implements it. The Account Tracking COM add-in includes the following features:

- A property page that allows users to set different options.
- On startup, checking for an Account Tracking group and a shortcut. If they do not exist, the add-in can create them.
- When creating the shortcut, enabling a folder home page for the Account Tracking folder.
- Custom buttons on the command bar.
- Notification to users via e-mail when new tasks or accounts are assigned to them.
- Notification to users via e-mail when changes to an account are made.

Compiling and Registering the COM Add-In

To set up the Account Tracking COM add-in, we first have to compile and register it. To compile it, you need a machine with Outlook and Visual Basic 6.0 installed. Follow these steps to compile the add-in:

1. Open the Account Admin folder from the sample.
2. Open AccountPP.vbp in Visual Basic 6.0.
3. Compile AccountPP.ocx. (This file is the ActiveX control property page. Compiling automatically registers it.)
4. Open AccountAdminDLL.vbp in Visual Basic 6.0.

5. Change the constant *STRFOLDERHOMEPAGEPATH* to the location of the FullContacts.htm file.

6. Search for the second occurrence of *oNS.Folders*, and change the statement

```
Set oFolder = oNS.Folders("Public Folders").Folders( _
   "All Public Folders").Folders("Account Tracking")
```

to the location of your Account Tracking folder.

7. Compile AccountAdminDLL.dll.

> **Note** You might need to specify the location of the AccountPP.ocx in the References dialog box. If AccountPP is displayed as MISSING in the References dialog box, deselect it, click OK to close the dialog box, open the References dialog box again, and browse for the location of AccountPP.ocx.

8. Double-click on AccountAdminDLL.reg to add the appropriate entries in the registry.

9. Launch Outlook.

10. From the Tools menu, choose Options. Click on the Other tab, click the Advanced Options button, and then click the COM Add-Ins button. In the COM Add-Ins dialog box, check that AccountAdmin is selected as an available add-in.

11. Log off, and close Outlook.

12. Restart Outlook.

Testing the COM Add-In

To test some of the COM add-in options, you have to turn them on using the Account Tracking tab, shown in Figure 8-18. This property page is the AccountPP control we compiled in Visual Basic 6.0. (Later in the chapter, we will examine how it is constructed.) To display this property page, choose Options from the Tools menu in Outlook and then click on the Account Tracking tab. Be sure all options are selected, and then click OK. (The Account Tracking tab is also available from the folder Properties dialog box, which you open by right-clicking on the Account Tracking folder and choosing Properties.)

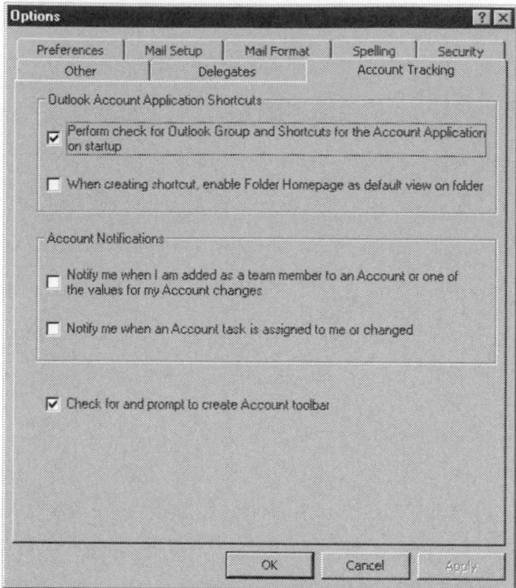

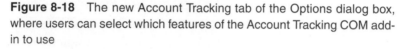

Figure 8-18 The new Account Tracking tab of the Options dialog box, where users can select which features of the Account Tracking COM add-in to use

The Account Tracking settings selected by the user in the Options dialog box or the Properties dialog box are automatically written to the registry so that the COM add-in can track the settings for each Outlook session. Figure 8-19 shows the registry with the user's settings for the COM add-in.

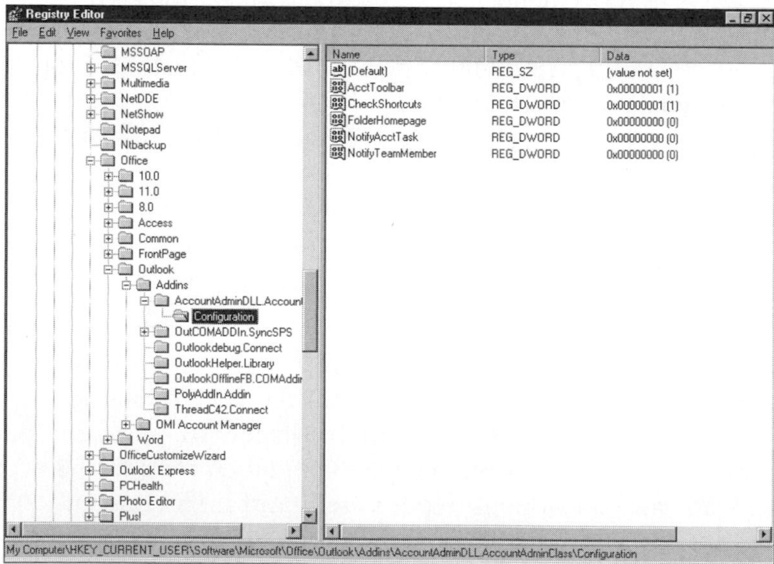

Figure 8-19 The registry settings for the Account Tracking COM add-in

Now that the COM add-in is set up and the options are turned on, let's see how the add-in works. Select the Account Tracking folder in Outlook, and then choose New Account Info from the Actions menu. Fill out the information for a new account. Be sure to add yourself as a team member, using your full name, on the Account Team tab. Then click on the Account Tasks tab and add a new task.

> **Note** If you don't have Outlook Visual Basic Scripting Support installed, a message will appear when you try to display New Account Info, indicating that scripting is not supported. You can install Outlook Visual Basic Scripting Support by rerunning setup for Office or choosing Change from the Add/Remove programs interface for Office.

If you left yourself as the task owner, after you add a new task the COM add-in should send two e-mail messages to your Inbox. The first message indicates that a new account has been created with you as a team member. The second message indicates that a task was assigned to you. Figure 8-20 shows an example of the second e-mail message.

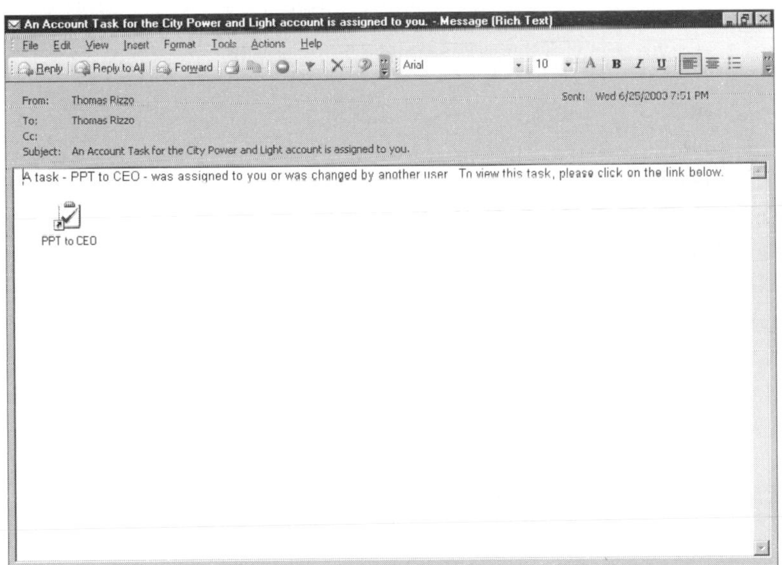

Figure 8-20 An e-mail notification stating that a task has been assigned to the current user or has changed

The COM add-in can notify a user when the user is added to the account team or, if the user is already a member of the account team, when the account information changes in the application. The information change notification can be triggered by changing the revenue of the account, the team members on the account, or the address of the account. Figure 8-21 shows the e-mail message that's sent to the user when his account changes.

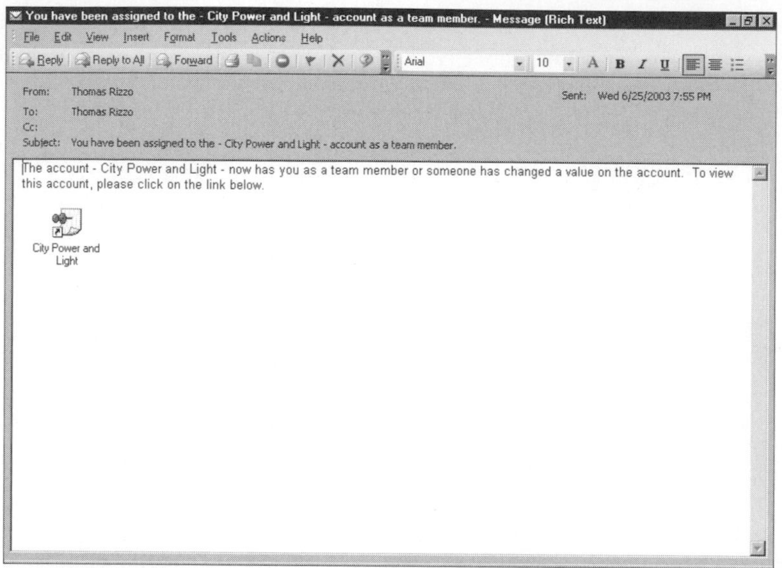

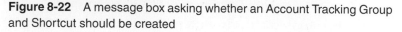

Figure 8-21 An e-mail notification stating that account information has changed

The Account Tracking COM add-in can also automatically search for an Account Tracking Outlook group and shortcut. This option was activated on the Account Tracking tab of the Options dialog box. When the user starts Outlook and an Account Tracking group or shortcut does not exist, the user is given the option to create a group or shortcut for the Account Tracking application, as shown in Figure 8-22. If the user clicks Yes, a new Account Tracking group and an Account Tracking shortcut are created on the Outlook Bar. If the Account Tracking Group dialog box is not displayed, try restarting Windows and opening Outlook.

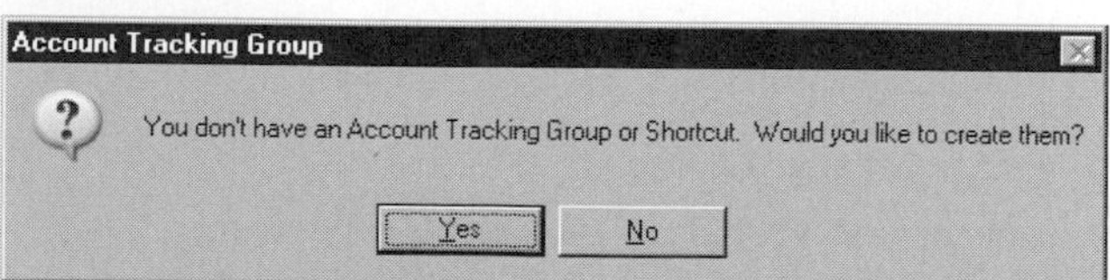

Figure 8-22 A message box asking whether an Account Tracking Group and Shortcut should be created

If the When Creating Shortcut Enable Folder Homepage As Default View On Folder option is selected on the Account Tracking tab, the folder home page will be set as the default view for the folder. For the Account Tracking application, the folder home page is FullContacts.htm, which was specified earlier in the AccountAdminDLL project.

The COM add-in includes a new command bar and command buttons designed specifically for the Account Tracking application. After you restart Outlook, the add-in should display the message box shown in Figure 8-23, which asks the user whether to create and display these new buttons. If the message box is not displayed, try clicking on the newly created Account Tracking shortcut in the Account Tracking group.

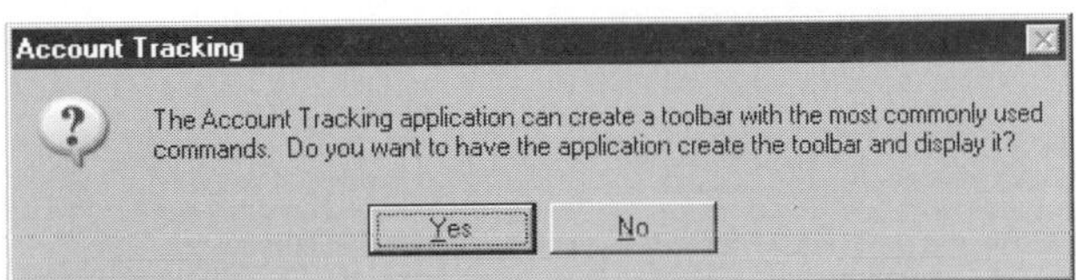

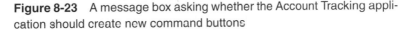

Figure 8-23 A message box asking whether the Account Tracking application should create new command buttons

The buttons make it easier for users to create new accounts, contacts, or tasks. Figure 8-24 shows the new command bar in Outlook. If these buttons are not displayed, right-click on the command bar and choose Account Tracking.

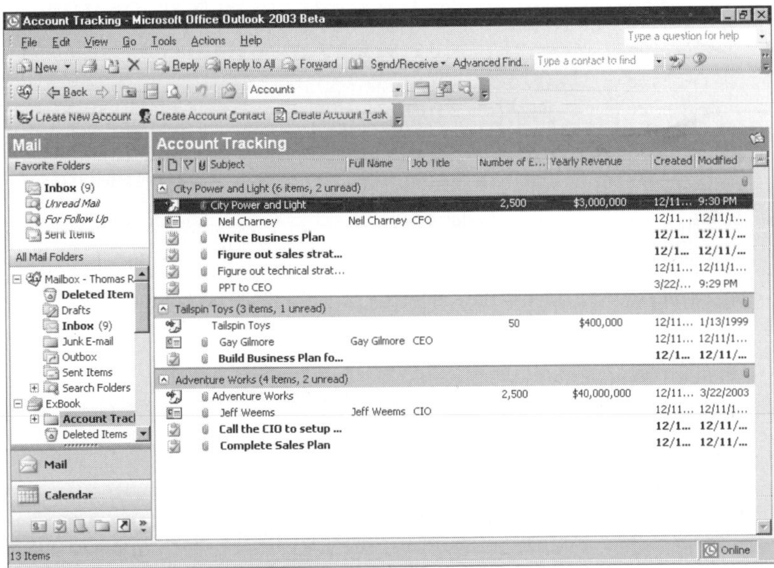

Figure 8-24 A command bar created programmatically by the COM add-in

Implementing the COM Add-In

Let's review our assumptions about the implementation of the Account Tracking COM add-in. To make the code easier to digest, we'll assume that users will always load the COM add-in at startup. For this reason, as you'll see, the *OnConnection* event for the COM add-in is pretty bare. Loading the add-in at startup calls the *OnConnection* and the *OnStartupComplete* events, so most of the code is included in the *OnStartupComplete* event for simplicity. If you want to be able to disconnect and reconnect the Account Tracking COM add-in, you must move some of the code from the *OnStartupComplete* event into a subroutine and then call that subroutine from both events. You must also revise the code to properly initialize some of the Outlook object variables.

The COM add-in options are stored in the registry. The registry path to these options is included in a code module with the add-in. To change the registry location for the COM add-in options, you simply change this path.

Searching for the Account Tracking Group and Shortcut

The first section of the code we'll examine searches for the Account Tracking group and shortcut on the Outlook Bar. As I mentioned earlier, this code runs only when the add-in is loaded and connected upon startup in Outlook. The main portion of this code is implemented in the *OnStartupComplete* event for the add-in. Remember that you must place *Implements IDTExtensibility2* in your project before you can create code for this event. The following code is from the general declarations and the *OnStartupComplete* event procedure:

```
Implements IDTExtensibility2

Dim WithEvents oApplication As Outlook.Application
Dim WithEvents oNS As Outlook.NameSpace
Dim WithEvents oItems As Outlook.Items
Dim oFolder As Outlook.MAPIFolder
Dim WithEvents oExplorer As Outlook.Explorer
Dim oCommandBar As Office.CommandBar
Dim WithEvents oCreateAccountBHandler As Office.CommandBarButton
Dim WithEvents oCreateAcctContactBHandler As Office.CommandBarButton
Dim WithEvents oCreateAcctTaskBHandler As Office.CommandBarButton
Dim oAcctItem As Outlook.PostItem
Dim oFolders As Outlook.Folders
Dim prefLookForShortcuts As Integer
Dim prefMakeFolderHomepage As Integer
Dim prefNotifyWhenNewMember As Integer
Dim prefNotifyWhenNewTask As Integer
Dim prefEnableAcctToolbar As Integer
Dim oNewPage As Object

Const STRFOLDERHOMEPAGEPATH = _
"file://C:\Webview\fullcontacts.htm"
Private Sub IDTExtensibility2_OnStartupComplete(custom() As Variant)
```

```
    On Error Resume Next
    Set oNS = oApplication.GetNamespace("MAPI")
    'Replace with your folder location.
    'This is for offline users since they must put the folder
    'in their Favorites folder.
    Set oFolder = oNS.Folders("Public Folders"). _
       Folders("Favorites").Folders("Account Tracking")
    If oFolder Is Nothing Then
       'You may prefer to add an EntryID here.
       Set oFolder = oNS.Folders("Public Folders").Folders( _
          "All Public Folders").Folders("Account Tracking")
    End If
    If oFolder Is Nothing Then
       Set oFolders = oNS.Folders("Public Folders").Folders( _
          "All Public Folders").Folders

       'The following code can be used if you want to search
       'the entire public folder hierarchy for the folder.
       'For performance reasons, this code is commented out.
'      If Not (oFolders Is Nothing) Then
'         Set otmpFolder = oFolders.GetFirst
'         Do While Not (otmpFolder Is Nothing)
'            ListFolders otmpFolder
'            If otmpFolder Is Nothing Then
'               Set otmpFolder = oFolders.GetNext
'            Else
'               Exit Do
'            End If
'         Loop
'      End If
'      If you do use this code, you need to uncomment the
'      ListFolders subroutine as well as add a check here
'      to see if oFolder is nothing after finishing.

       MsgBox "You have the Account Tracking COM add-in loaded" & _
              " but you have no Account Tracking folder. " & _
              "You may wish to unload the COM add-in.", _
              vbOKOnly + vbInformation, "Account Tracking COM add-in"
       Exit Sub
    End If
    Set oItems = oFolder.Items
    Set oExplorer = oApplication.ActiveExplorer
    'See if the user wants us to check for shortcuts
    If prefLookForShortcuts = 1 Then
       'The following code checks to see if the user has
       'an Outlook shortcut and group for the Account Tracking
       'application.
       Dim oPane As OutlookBarPane
       Dim oOLBarStorage As OutlookBarStorage
       Dim oOLBarGroups As OutlookBarGroups
       Dim oOLBarGroup As OutlookBarGroup
       Dim oOLBarShortcuts As OutlookBarShortcuts
       Dim oOLBarShortcut As OutlookBarShortcut
```

```
'Used if shortcut found with no group
Dim otmpOLAccountBarGroupIndex As Integer
Dim otmpOLBarGroup As OutlookBarGroup
Dim otmpOLShortcuts As OutlookBarShortcuts
Dim BarCounter As Integer
Dim ShortcutCounter As Integer
Set oPane = oExplorer.Panes("OutlookBar")
Set oOLBarStorage = oPane.Contents
Set oOLBarGroups = oOLBarStorage.Groups
boolFoundAcctGroup = 0
boolFoundAcctShortcut = 0
BarCounter = 1
For Each oOLBarGroup In oOLBarGroups
   'For debugging purposes
   'MsgBox "Group: " & oOLBarGroup.Name
   If oOLBarGroup.Name = "Account Tracking" Then
      boolFoundAcctGroup = BarCounter
   End If
   Set oOLBarShortcuts = oOLBarGroup.Shortcuts
   ShortcutCounter = 1
   For Each oOLBarShortcut In oOLBarShortcuts
      'For debugging purposes
      'MsgBox oOLBarShortcut.Name
      Err.Clear
      If IsObject(oOLBarShortcut.Target) Then
         'Check to see if this is the file target by
         'checking error.
         If oOLBarShortcut.Target.Name = _
         "Account Tracking" Then
            If Err.Number = -2147319765 Then
               'File Target
            ElseIf Err.Number = 0 Then
               'For Debugging purposes
               'MsgBox "Account Tracking Folder: " & _
                  oOLBarShortcut.Target.Name
                  boolFoundAcctShortcut = ShortcutCounter
                  otmpOLAccountBarGroupIndex = BarCounter
            End If
         End If
      Else
         'The target is a URL string
      End If
      ShortcutCounter = ShortcutCounter + 1
   Next
   BarCounter = BarCounter + 1
Next
'For debugging purposes
'MsgBox boolFoundAcctShortcut & boolFoundAcctGroup.
'Check to see whether shortcut exists without group.
If (boolFoundAcctShortcut <> 0) And _
(boolFoundAcctGroup = 0) Then
   'Check to see whether they want to remove the
   'shortcut and move it to a new group.
   Response = MsgBox("You have an Account " & _
```

```
            "Tracking shortcut without an Account " & _
            "Tracking group. Would you like to create a " & _
            "new Account Tracking group and move the " & _
            "Account Tracking shortcut there?", & _
            vbYesNo + vbQuestion, "Account Tracking")
        If Response = vbYes Then
            'Delete the old Account Tracking shortcut.
            'Get the Outlook Bar for the shortcut.
            Set otmpOLBarGroup = _
                oOLBarGroups.Item(otmpOLAccountBarGroupIndex)
            Set otmpOLShortcuts = otmpOLBarGroup.Shortcuts
            otmpOLShortcuts.Remove boolFoundAcctShortcut
            Dim otmp2OLBarGroup As OutlookBarGroup
            Dim otmp2OLShortcuts As OutlookBarShortcuts
            'Create a new Account Tracking group
            Set otmp2OLBarGroup = oOLBarGroups.Add( _
                "Account Tracking", oOLBarGroups.Count + 1)
            'For debugging purposes
            'MsgBox "Group: " & otmp2OLBarGroup.Name
            Set otmp2OLShortcuts = otmp2OLBarGroup.Shortcuts
            otmp2OLShortcuts.Add oFolder, "Account Tracking"
            'Check to see whether they want us to create a
            'Web view.
            If prefMakeFolderHomepage = 1 Then
                'Create the Web view
                oFolder.WebViewAllowNavigation = True
                oFolder.WebViewOn = True
                oFolder.WebViewURL = STRFOLDERHOMEPAGEPATH
            End If
        End If
        'Check to see whether group exists with no shortcut.
    ElseIf (boolFoundAcctShortcut = 0) And _
    (boolFoundAcctGroup <> 0) Then
        'See if user wants to add shortcut to group.
        Response = MsgBox("There is an Account " & _
            "Tracking Group without a shortcut to the " & _
            "Account Tracking folder. Do you want " & _
            "to add a shortcut to the Account Tracking " & _
            "folder in this group?", _
            vbYesNo + vbQuestion, "Account Tracking")
        If Response = vbYes Then
            Dim otmpOLGroup As OutlookBarGroup
            Set otmpOLGroup = oOLBarGroups.Item(boolFoundAcctGroup)
            'For debugging purposes
            'MsgBox otmpOLGroup.Name
            Set otmpOLShortcuts = otmpOLGroup.Shortcuts
            otmpOLShortcuts.Add oFolder, "Account Tracking"
            'Check to see whether user wants us to create a
            'Web view
            If prefMakeFolderHomepage = 1 Then
                'Create the Web view
                oFolder.WebViewAllowNavigation = True
                oFolder.WebViewOn = True
```

```
                oFolder.WebViewURL = STRFOLDERHOMEPAGEPATH
             End If
          End If
          'Check to see whether there is neither
       ElseIf (boolFoundAcctGroup = 0) And _
       (boolFoundAcctShortcut = 0) Then
          Response = MsgBox("You don't have an Account " & _
             "Tracking Group or Shortcut. Would you like to " & _
             "create them?", vbYesNo + vbQuestion, _
             "Account Tracking Group")
          If Response = vbYes Then
             Set otmpOLGroup = oOLBarGroups.Add( _
                "Account Tracking", oOLBarGroups.Count + 1)
             'For debugging purposes
             'MsgBox otmpOLGroup.Name
             Set otmpOLShortcuts = otmpOLGroup.Shortcuts
             otmpOLShortcuts.Add oFolder, "Account Tracking"
             'Check to see whether user wants us to create a
             'Web view
             If prefMakeFolderHomepage = 1 Then
                'Create the Web view
                oFolder.WebViewAllowNavigation = True
                oFolder.WebViewOn = True
                oFolder.WebViewURL = STRFOLDERHOMEPAGEPATH
             End If
          End If
          'There is one other scenario with an Account Tracking
          'shortcut and an Account Tracking group.
          'In this scenario, do nothing.
       End If
    End If
End Sub

Sub ListFolders(objFolder)
'   On Error Resume Next
'   If Not (objFolder Is Nothing) Then
'      'Check to see whether Account Tracking folder
'      If objFolder.Name = "Account Tracking" Then
'         Set oFolder = objFolder
'         Exit Sub
'      Else
'         'Check for child folders
'         Set objFolders = objFolder.Folders
'         Set objFolder = objFolders.GetFirst
'         Do While Not (objFolder Is Nothing)
'            ListFolders objFolder
'            Set objFolder = objFolders.GetNext
'         Loop
'      End If
'   End If
End Sub
```

The code first sets some of the application's variables to their correct values. The commented sections of the code show how to search for the Account Tracking public folder within the public folder hierarchy. Obviously, if the public folder hierarchy is large, completing the search can take a long time; you might decide not to implement the code. You can replace the code in the event with code that retrieves the Account Tracking folder by EntryID, which allows you to eliminate any hardcoded paths to the folder.

The code then checks to see whether the user wants to look for the Account Tracking group and shortcut. This configuration information is pulled from the registry, an operation that I'll explain shortly. If the user wants to search for the group and the shortcut, the code uses some of the new objects and collections in the Outlook object model.

The code grabs the *OutlookBar* pane from the current *Explorer* object. Then the code retrieves the *OutlookBarStorage* object for the contents of that pane, and it retrieves the *OutlookBarGroups* in the storage object. From there, the code uses a *For...Each* loop to find the Account Tracking group.

> **Note** You can replace the *For...Each* loop with a simpler version that uses the *Item* method on the *OutlookBarGroups* collection. By using the *Item* method, you can retrieve the group by name. But to show you how to use this collection, the code sample uses the *For...Each* loop.

In the *For...Each* loop, the code retrieves each shortcut in the group by using the *OutlookBarShortcuts* collection. It then loops through each shortcut, using the Account Tracking name to determine whether the target for that shortcut is the Account Tracking folder. You can also compare the EntryIDs of the target with the original folder we set earlier in the code. How you implement this is your choice.

In the *IDTExtensibility2_OnStartupComplete* procedure, you can see some error handling code. We have to make sure we do not error out on file system targets, which is a problem only with earlier versions of Outlook because Outlook 2003 has removed the file system functionality. This error-handling code skips file system targets.

Counters in the code let the application know the index of the Account Tracking group, as well as the index of the Account Tracking shortcut within that group if the shortcut exists. The code uses these counters to check a number of scenarios—for example, whether the group and the shortcut both exist. This checking scenario occurs when both counters are 0. The code also checks to see whether the shortcut exists, but not the group. If the shortcut exists, the code can create a new group, removing the existing shortcut and placing it in the new group. The code counts where the shortcut exists in a certain group, which simplifies removing the shortcut by using its index. If the group exists without a shortcut, the code can create a shortcut in the group and associate the shortcut with the folder.

The code also checks the option settings to see whether it should make the default view on the folder the folder home page. If the option that enables the folder home page (the option appears on the Account Tracking tab of the Options dialog box) is selected, the code uses the *WebViewAllowNavigation*, *WebViewOn*, and *WebViewURL* properties to set up the folder home page. *WebViewAllowNavigation* returns or sets the navigation mode for the folder if the user is viewing a folder home page. When this property is set to *True*, Outlook allows users to navigate using the Forward and Back buttons on the Microsoft Web Control. When this property is set to *False*, Outlook displays the folder home page in Native mode, which makes the Forward and Back buttons unavailable. If you set this property to *True*, the folder home page will provide more functionality for the user but will run a bit more slowly.

The *WebViewOn* property returns or sets the state of the folder home page. If you set this property to *True*, as the preceding code does, Outlook will display the folder home page as the default view for the folder.

The *WebViewURL* property returns or sets the string that identifies the URL for the folder home page. You can use any valid URL in this property, including a URL that begins with *file* or *http*. The application sets this property to a constant string, which is set in the declarations section of the program.

Using Events to Notify Users of Changes

The next section of the code we'll look at tracks when users add or change account or task items in the folder. The application does not track deleted items, and Outlook does not pass the deleted item in its *ItemRemove* event, which makes figuring out what was removed from the folder difficult.

To track additions and changes to items, the code declares the variable *oItems* as an *Outlook.Items* collection by using the *WithEvents* keyword. *WithEvents* lets you select the events you want to handle in the Visual Basic environment for the collection. The code for this application implements the *ItemAdd* and *ItemChange* events for the *Items* collection. Let's first review the *ItemAdd* event, shown here:

```
Private Sub oItems_ItemAdd(ByVal Item As Object)
   Dim oUser As Variant
   Dim oMail As Outlook.MailItem
   Dim oAttach As Outlook.Attachment
   Dim oItem As Outlook.TaskItem
```

```
Dim oAccountItem As Outlook.PostItem
Dim oUserProps As Outlook.UserProperties

oUser = oNS.CurrentUser.Name
 'Check to see what type of item was just created
If Item.Class = olTask Then
   'Check to see whether user wants notification
   If prefNotifyWhenNewTask = 1 Then
      'Transform into TaskItem
      Set oItem = Item
      'Check to see whether the current user is the owner
      If oItem.Owner = oUser Then
         'Send to the user a message with a link to the item
         Set oMail = oApplication.CreateItem(olMailItem)
         With oMail
            .To = oUser
            .Subject = "New Account Task for the " & _
               Item.ConversationTopic & _
               " account is assigned to you."
            .Body = "A new task - " & Item.Subject & _
               " - was assigned to you.  " & _
               "To view this task, please click" _
               & " on the link below."
         End With
         Set oAttach = oMail.Attachments.Add(Item, _
            olEmbeddeditem)
         oMail.Recipients.ResolveAll
         oMail.Send
      End If
   End If
ElseIf Item.MessageClass = "IPM.Post.Account info" Then
   'Check to see whether user wants notification
   If prefNotifyWhenNewMember = 1 Then
      Set oAccountItem = Item
      boolAccountMember = 0
      Set oUserProps = oAccountItem.UserProperties
      If oUserProps.Find("txtAccountConsultant") = oUser Then
         boolAccountMember = 1
      ElseIf oUserProps.Find("txtAccountExecutive") = _
         oUser Then
         boolAccountMember = 1
      ElseIf oUserProps.Find("txtAccountSalesRep") = _
         oUser Then
         boolAccountMember = 1
      ElseIf oUserProps.Find("txtAccountSE") = oUser Then
         boolAccountMember = 1
      ElseIf oUserProps.Find("txtAccountSupportEngineer") = _
      oUser Then
         boolAccountMember = 1
      End If
      If boolAccountMember = 1 Then
         'Send to the user a message with a link to the item
           Set oMail = oApplication.CreateItem(olMailItem)
```

```
            With oMail
               .To = oUser
               .Subject = "A New Account - " & _
                  Item.ConversationTopic & _
                  " - has been created with you as a " & _
                  "team member."
               .Body = "A new account - " & Item.Subject & _
                  " - was created with you as a team member." _
                  & " To view this account, please click" _
                  & " on the link below."
            End With
            Set oAttach = oMail.Attachments.Add(Item, _
               olEmbeddeditem)
            oMail.Recipients.ResolveAll
            oMail.Send
         End If
      End If
   End If
End Sub
```

The *oItems_ItemAdd* event procedure first retrieves the name of the current user. It then checks the class of the item that was added to the collection in the folder. If the item is a task, the code coerces the item into an *Outlook TaskItem* object before it attempts to call the methods and properties on that object type. If the current user is the owner of the new task, the application creates an e-mail message with the new task attached as a shortcut and then sends the e-mail to the user. The user receives the notification e-mail in the Inbox.

The code used to notify users of a new account in the folder is similar to the task code. However, instead of checking the owner property, the account code checks the item's custom properties, which correspond to the names of the team members for the account. If the user is found in one of these properties, the code sends an e-mail message to the user indicating that she has a new account for which she is a team member.

The only aspect of this subroutine and the next subroutine that you might want to change is the user who sends the item. In the current implementation, the user sends the update. You can change this functionality so that the public folder sends the message by giving your users Send On Behalf Of permissions in your Exchange Administrator program for the folder. You then either expose the folder in the address list so that it can be added to the From field, or you place the address of the folder in the From field. If you don't want the e-mail to come from the folder, you can create a mailbox to which you assign Send On Behalf Of permissions in the Exchange Administrator program.

To notify the user that she has been assigned an existing task or that a task for which she is the owner has changed, the code uses the *ItemChange* event for the *Items* collection. This event is also used to notify the user when she is added to an account team after the account is created or when an account for which she is a team member has been changed. The following code implements the *ItemChange* event:

```
Private Sub oItems_ItemChange(ByVal Item As Object)
   Dim oUser As Variant
   Dim oMail As Outlook.MailItem
   Dim oAttach As Outlook.Attachment
   Dim oTaskItem As Outlook.TaskItem
   Dim oAccountItem As Outlook.PostItem
   Dim oUserProps As Outlook.UserProperties

   'Since the event doesn't show us how the item changed,
   'we need to notify the user of the change but not what
   'specifically changed on the item

   oUser = oNS.CurrentUser.Name
   'Check to see what type of item was just created
   If Item.Class = olTask Then
      'Check to see whether the user wants to be notified
      If prefNotifyWhenNewTask = 1 Then

         'Transform into TaskItem
         Set oTaskItem = Item

         'Check to see whether the current user is the owner
         If oTaskItem.Owner = oUser Then
            'Send to the user a message with a link to the item
            Set oMail = oApplication.CreateItem(olMailItem)
            With oMail
               .To = oUser
               .Subject = "An Account Task for the " & _
                  Item.ConversationTopic & _
                  " account is assigned to you."
               .Body = "A task - " & Item.Subject & _
                  " - was assigned to you or was changed " & _
                  "by another user.  " _
                  & "To view this task, please click" _
                  & " on the link below."
            End With
            Set oAttach = oMail.Attachments.Add(Item, _
               olEmbeddeditem)
            oMail.Recipients.ResolveAll
            oMail.Send
         End If
      End If
   ElseIf Item.MessageClass = "IPM.Post.Account info" Then
      Set oAccountItem = Item
        boolAccountMember = 0
      Set oUserProps = oAccountItem.UserProperties
      If oUserProps.Find("txtAccountConsultant") = oUser Then
         boolAccountMember = 1
      ElseIf oUserProps.Find("txtAccountExecutive") = oUser Then
         boolAccountMember = 1
```

```
        ElseIf oUserProps.Find("txtAccountSalesRep") = oUser Then
           boolAccountMember = 1
        ElseIf oUserProps.Find("txtAccountSE") = oUser Then
           boolAccountMember = 1
        ElseIf oUserProps.Find("txtAccountSupportEngineer") = _
        oUser Then
           boolAccountMember = 1
        End If
        If boolAccountMember = 1 Then
           'Send to the user a message with a link to the item
           Set oMail = oApplication.CreateItem(olMailItem)
           With oMail
              .To = oUser
              .Subject = "You have been assigned to the - " & _
                 Item.ConversationTopic & _
                 " - account as a team member."
              .Body = "The account - " & Item.Subject & _
                 " now has you as a team member or someone " & _
                 "has changed a value " _
                 & "on the account. To view this account, " _
                 & "please click on the link below."
           End With
           Set oAttach = _
              oMail.Attachments.Add(Item, olEmbeddeditem)
           oMail.Recipients.ResolveAll
           oMail.Send
        End If
    End If
End Sub
```

The code that handles the *ItemChange* event is much like the code for *ItemAdd*, so I won't cover it in detail. The only difference between the two event handlers is the text of the message sent to the user. Because Outlook does not pass the property that was changed on the item as a parameter to *ItemChange*, the code can't know whether the user was assigned to an item or which property was changed. For this reason, the message text notifies the user only that a change to the item has occurred.

Adding and Handling Custom Command Bars and Buttons

The next section of code we'll look at adds a custom command bar and command buttons to the Outlook toolbar. It also provides event handlers for the buttons when users click them. The code for this functionality is shown here:

```
Private Sub oExplorer_BeforeFolderSwitch( _
    ByVal NewFolder As Object, Cancel As Boolean)
   'Add CommandBar buttons to the Outlook user interface for easy
   'creation
   Dim oTempFolder As Outlook.MAPIFolder
   Dim oCommandBars As Office.CommandBars
   Dim oCommandBar2 As Office.CommandBar
```

```
Dim oControls As Office.CommandBarControls
Dim oControl As Office.CommandBarButton
Dim otmpCommandBar As Office.CommandBar

'Make sure they want to do this
If prefEnableAcctToolbar = 1 Then
   'First check to see whether the folder is the
   'Account Tracking folder
   If Not (NewFolder Is Nothing) Then
      Set oTempFolder = NewFolder
      boolFoundCommandBar = 0
      'You might want to put in the EntryID here rather than
      'the name
      If oTempFolder.Name = "Account Tracking" Then
         'Check to see whether command bar already exists
         Set oCommandBars = _
            oApplication.ActiveExplorer.CommandBars
         For Each oCommandBar In oCommandBars
            If oCommandBar.Name = "Account Tracking" Then
               boolFoundCommandBar = 1
               Set otmpCommandBar = oCommandBar
               Exit For
            End If
         Next
         If boolFoundCommandBar = 0 Then
            'Need to create the command bar
            'Maybe add text box for searching for account
            'or contacts
            Response = MsgBox("The Account Tracking " & _
               "application can create a toolbar with " _
               & "the most commonly used commands. Do " & _
               you want to have the application create" _
               & " the toolbar and display it?", _
               vbYesNo + vbQuestion, "Account Tracking")
            If Response = vbYes Then
               'Create the command bar
               Set oCommandBar = oCommandBars.Add( _
                  "Account Tracking", Temporary:=False)
               Set oControls = oCommandBar.Controls
               'Create the buttons, and set the
               'event handler objects to the
               'buttons.
                 'Create the first button.
               Set oControl = oControls.Add( _
                  Type:=msoControlButton, ID:=1, _
                  Temporary:=False)
               oControl.Caption = "Create New &Account"
               oControl.FaceId = 609
               oControl.Style = msoButtonIconAndCaption
               Set oCreateAccountBHandler = oControl
               'Create the second button
               'Context menu
```

```
                Set oControl = oControls.Add( _
                   Type:=msoControlButton, ID:=1, _
                   Temporary:=False)
                oControl.Caption = "Create Account &Contact"
                oControl.FaceId = 607
                oControl.Style = msoButtonIconAndCaption
                Set oCreateAcctContactBHandler = oControl
                'Create the third button
                'Context menu
                Set oControl = oControls.Add( _
                   Type:=msoControlButton, ID:=1, _
                   Temporary:=False)
                oControl.Caption = "Create Account &Task"
                oControl.FaceId = 329
                oControl.Style = msoButtonIconAndCaption
                Set oCreateAcctTaskBHandler = oControl
                'Make the command bar visible
                oCommandBar.Visible = True
                oCommandBar.Position = msoBarTop
             End If
          Else
             'Account Tracking command bar already exists.
             'See if they want to do this.
             If prefEnableAcctToolbar = 1 Then
                'Check to see if visible; if not, make
                'visible
                Dim oCBControls As Office.CommandBarControls
                Dim oCBButton As Office.CommandBarButton
                If otmpCommandBar.Enabled = False Then
                   otmpCommandBar.Enabled = True
                End If
                If otmpCommandBar.Visible = False Then
                   otmpCommandBar.Visible = True
                End If
             End If
          End If
       Else
          'It's not the Account Tracking folder.
           'Look for the toolbar and disable it.
          On Error Resume Next
          Set oCommandBars = oApplication.ActiveExplorer. _
             CommandBars
          Set oCommandBar = oCommandBars("Account Tracking")
          oCommandBar.Enabled = False
       End If
    Else
       'It's a file system folder!
       'Disable toolbar.
       On Error Resume Next
       Set oCommandBars = _
          oApplication.ActiveExplorer.CommandBars
       Set oCommandBar = oCommandBars("Account Tracking")
       oCommandBar.Enabled = False
```

```
      End If
   End If
   Set oTempFolder = Nothing
   Set oCommandBars = Nothing
   Set oCommandBar = Nothing
   Set oControls = Nothing
   Set oControl = Nothing
End Sub
```

The application includes the Outlook *Explorer* object's *BeforeFolderSwitch* event, as shown in the preceding code. The *oExplorer_BeforeFolderSwitch* event procedure is passed, as a *MAPIFolder*, the folder that the user is trying to switch to. The code checks the folder's name to see whether it is the Account Tracking folder. You can also perform this comparison by using the EntryID of the folder.

If the folder is the Account Tracking folder, the code searches the *CommandBars* collection of the *Explorer* object to see whether an Account Tracking command bar exists. If the code finds the Account Tracking command bar, it simply makes the command bar visible. If the code doesn't find the Account Tracking command bar, it creates the command bar if the user selected to do so as a preference. The code adds a new *CommandBar* object to the *CommandBars* collection by passing the name of the command bar as well as the *Temporary* parameter. The *Temporary* parameter indicates that Outlook should persist the command bar between Outlook sessions. Then the code starts creating the buttons on the command bar.

To create the buttons, the code uses the *Controls* collection on the *CommandBar* object. The code then adds three button controls to the collection. The control type is identified with the *msoControlButton* constant. (You can create other types of controls on your command bars besides buttons—drop-down lists, combo boxes, and popups.) The code also passes an ID of 1 for all the controls; this value indicates that the control is a custom control and is not built in. The code passes the *Temporary* parameter and sets it to *False* so Outlook persists the buttons between sessions. The *Add* method returns an appropriate object for the type of control you specify, such as a *CommandBarButton*, a *CommandBarComboBox*, or *CommandBarPopup* object.

After the code receives the *CommandBarButton* object from the *Add* method on the *Controls* collection, it starts setting properties on the *CommandBarButton* object. The first property it sets is the *Caption* property, which is a string containing the caption text for the control. Notice that you can place an ampersand before one of the letters in the control caption to provide a shortcut key for the control. This *Caption* property is the default screen tip for the control.

The second property the code sets is *FaceId*, which specifies how the button face should look. Office has a number of built-in faces that you can use. If you want to use a custom face on your buttons, you must specify *0* for this property and copy your custom face to the Clipboard. Then you can use the *PasteFace* method on the *CommandBarButton* object to paste the face from the Clipboard onto your control.

The final property the code sets is the *Style* property. This property can have one of many values, such as the *msoButtonIconAndCaption* constant, which displays the button face as well as the caption text, or *msoButtonCaption*, which displays only the caption. To enhance usability of the buttons, the code displays both the icon and the caption. For a list of all the style values, refer to the general Office Help file.

After the new *CommandBarButtons* are created and set, they are assigned to other variables, for example *oCreateAccountBHandler*. If you take a look at the declarations section of the code, shown earlier in the chapter, you'll notice that *oCreateAccountBHandler* is declared as an *Office.CommandBarButton* using the *WithEvents* keyword. The *WithEvents* keyword specifies that *oCreateAccountBHandler* is used to respond to events for a *CommandBarButton*. The following code shows the event handlers for the three buttons on the Account Tracking command bar:

```
Private Sub oCreateAccountBHandler_Click(ByVal Ctrl As _
Office.CommandBarButton, CancelDefault As Boolean)
   Dim oAccount As Outlook.PostItem
   Set oAccount = oFolder.Items.Add("IPM.Post.Account info")
   oAccount.Display
End Sub

Private Sub oCreateAcctContactBHandler_Click(ByVal Ctrl As _
Office.CommandBarButton, CancelDefault As Boolean)
   Dim oSelection As Outlook.Selection

   On Error Resume Next
   boolFoundAccountItem = 0
   Set oSelection = oExplorer.Selection
   For Each oItem In oSelection
       If oItem.MessageClass = "IPM.Post.Account info" Then
         boolFoundAccountItem = boolFoundAccountItem + 1
         'Set the item found to a global variable just in case
         'it is the only one found
         Set oAcctItem = oItem
      End If
   Next
   If boolFoundAccountItem = 0 Then
      MsgBox "You have no account selected. Please select " & _
         "an account and try again.", _
         vbOKOnly + vbExclamation, "Create Contact"
      Exit Sub
```

```
   ElseIf boolFoundAccountItem > 1 Then
      MsgBox "You have more than one account selected. " & _
         "Please select only one account and try again.", _
         vbOKOnly + vbExclamation, "Create Contact"
      Exit Sub
   ElseIf boolFoundAccountItem = 1 Then
      Set AccountContactForm = oAcctItem.Actions( _
         "Create New Account Contact").Execute
      AccountContactForm.Display (True)
   End If
End Sub
Private Sub oCreateAcctTaskBHandler_Click( _
ByVal Ctrl As Office.CommandBarButton, CancelDefault As Boolean)
   On Error Resume Next
   boolFoundAccountItem = 0
   Set oSelection = oExplorer.Selection
   For Each oItem In oSelection
      If oItem.MessageClass = "IPM.Post.Account info" Then
         boolFoundAccountItem = boolFoundAccountItem + 1
         'Set the item found to a global variable just in case
         'it is the only one found
         Set oAcctItem = oItem
      End If
   Next

   If boolFoundAccountItem = 0 Then
      MsgBox "You have no account selected. Please select " & _
         "an account and try again.", _
         vbOKOnly + vbExclamation, "Create Contact"
      Exit Sub
   ElseIf boolFoundAccountItem > 1 Then
      MsgBox "You have more than one account selected. " & _
         "Please select only one account and try again.", _
         vbOKOnly + vbExclamation, "Create Contact"
      Exit Sub
   ElseIf boolFoundAccountItem = 1 Then
        Set AccountTaskForm = oAcctItem.Actions( _
         "Create New Account Task").Execute
      AccountTaskForm.Display (True)
   End If
End Sub

Private Function CheckSelection(strMessageClass) As Integer
   On Error Resume Next
   boolFoundAccountItem = 0
   Set oSelection = oExplorer.Selection
   For Each oItem In oSelection
      If oItem.MessageClass = strMessageClass Then
         boolFoundAccountItem = boolFoundAccountItem + 1
         'Set the item found to a global variable just in case
         'it is the only one found
         Set oAcctItem = oItem
      End If
```

```
    Next
    CheckSelection = boolFoundAccountItem
End Function
```

Notice that we use the standard Outlook object model to implement all three event handlers. The *oCreateAccountBHandler_Click* event handler is the simplest of the three because it only adds a new account form to the folder and displays this form to the user. The other two event handlers, *oCreateAcctContactBHandler_Click* and *oCreateAcctTaskBHandler_Click*, also use some of the features in the Outlook object model. Before a user can create either an account contact or a task, he must first select an account. The code for these handlers uses the *Selection* collection on the *Explorer* object to determine what the user has selected in the user interface.

The *oCreateAcctContactBHandler_Click* and *oCreateAcctTaskBHandler_Click* event handlers both loop through the collection of selected items to see whether any items are account items. Users can select multiple items in the user interface, so the code tracks how many account items it counts in the *Selection* collection. Both handlers set the last account item they see to a global variable just in case this account item is the only one in the selection. Because the add-in cannot guess for which account the user wants to create a new contact or task, the subroutines display error messages when the user has more than one account selected in the user interface. If no accounts are selected, the application displays an error message telling the user to select an account. If only one account is selected, the application calls the custom actions on the account form to create either a new account contact or a new task.

Adding Custom Property Pages and Storing User Settings

The final section of code implements the property pages that allow users to pick their custom settings for the application. We'll look at this code and also quickly look at how the registry is used to store these settings for the user. As you examine this code, you'll see some interesting objects implemented in Outlook—for example, the *PropertyPage* object, the *PropertyPageSite* object, and the *PropertyPages* collection object.

Custom property pages allow you to integrate your applications more tightly into the Outlook application. They also enable users to configure your application more easily because your customizations are part of the standard Outlook configuration pages. The following code implements the property page extension code in the COM add-in. Then we will look at the code for the ActiveX control, which creates the actual property page that appears.

```
Private Sub SetDefaultProps()
    oNewPage.prefLookForShortcuts = prefLookForShortcuts
    oNewPage.prefEnableAcctToolbar = prefEnableAcctToolbar
    oNewPage.prefMakeFolderHomepage = prefMakeFolderHomepage
```

```
    oNewPage.prefNotifyWhenNewMember = prefNotifyWhenNewMember
    oNewPage.prefNotifyWhenNewTask = prefNotifyWhenNewTask
End Sub

Private Sub oNS_OptionsPagesAdd(ByVal Pages As _
Outlook.PropertyPages, ByVal Folder As Outlook.MAPIFolder)
    If Folder.Name = "Account Tracking" Then
        'Add the Options page to the folder
        Set oNewPage = CreateObject("AccountPP.UCAdminPage")
        SetDefaultProps
        oNewPage.oAdminDLL = Me
        Pages.Add oNewPage
    End If
End Sub

Private Sub oApplication_OptionsPagesAdd(ByVal Pages As _
Outlook.PropertyPages)
    Set oNewPage = CreateObject("AccountPP.UCAdminPage")
    SetDefaultProps
    oNewPage.oAdminDLL = Me
    Pages.Add oNewPage
End Sub

Public Sub SetRegistryValues(prefShortcuts, prefAcctToolbar, _
prefFolderHomepage, prefNotifyMember, prefNotifyTask)
    'This subroutine is called by the Property page to have the
    'Options page persist its values
    boolSuccess = SetAppRegValue("CheckShortcuts", REG_DWORD, _
        prefShortcuts)
    boolSuccess = SetAppRegValue("AcctToolbar", REG_DWORD, _
        prefAcctToolbar)
    boolSuccess = SetAppRegValue("FolderHomepage", REG_DWORD, _
        prefFolderHomepage)
    boolSuccess = SetAppRegValue("NotifyTeamMember", REG_DWORD, _
          prefNotifyMember)
    boolSuccess = SetAppRegValue("NotifyAcctTask", REG_DWORD, _
        prefNotifyTask)
End Sub
```

In this code, two subroutines handle the *OptionsPagesAdd* event. The first subroutine uses the *NameSpace* object. The *OptionsPagesAdd* event fires for the *NameSpace* object when the user clicks on a folder in the namespace you are monitoring and then selects Properties. The *NameSpace OptionsPagesAdd* event procedure is passed two parameters: *Pages*, which is a collection of Outlook *PropertyPages*, and *Folder*, which is the folder the user is trying to retrieve properties for.

The second subroutine uses the Outlook *Application* object. The *OptionsPagesAdd* event fires the *Application* object when a user chooses Options from the Tools menu to configure the overall application settings for Outlook. Both *OptionsPagesAdd* event handlers call the same code because there is only one way to customize the Account Tracking application. However, for your add-ins, you can have two different property pages for these two different events if needed.

The first step both event handlers perform is to create an object. This object, an ActiveX control, is the actual property page that the subroutine will add to the *PropertyPages* collection. We'll look at the code for the control later in this chapter.

The next step the event handler performs is to set the default properties for the new property page. It does this by setting some of the variables on the control to the values that are currently stored in the add-in. All of these values are originally retrieved from the registry.

After all properties for the controls on the form are set, the code passes an add-in reference to the new property page. You might be wondering why it does this. The main reason is to allow the ActiveX control property page to call back into the add-in when a user makes a change and applies it. If the ActiveX control does not call back into the add-in, the add-in will not know that something has changed and will not behave as expected.

The final step in the code is to add the new page to the *PropertyPages* collection using the *Add* method of the collection. You can call this method in two ways. The first way, which is shown in the code, passes an object to the method so the object is displayed as a property page. The second way passes in the ProgID of the control as a string, which enables Outlook to create the control. If you use the second approach, you can also pass an optional string that is the caption for the property page. You'll see how to set the caption when we pass an ActiveX control later on.

Now that you know how to add our pages to the *PropertyPages* collection, we need to look at what the actual page should implement. The following code implements the ActiveX control, which is the property page extension. Figure 8-25 shows the interface for the control in Visual Basic 6.0 design mode.

```
Implements Outlook.PropertyPage
Private oSite As Outlook.PropertyPageSite
Dim m_prefLookForShortcuts As Integer
Dim m_prefMakeFolderHomepage As Integer
Dim m_prefNotifyWhenNewMember As Integer
Dim m_prefNotifyWhenNewTask As Integer
Dim m_prefEnableAcctToolbar As Integer
Dim m_fDirty As Boolean
Dim m_AdminDLL As Object
Private boolInitializing As Boolean
```

```
Private Sub SetDirty()
   If Not oSite Is Nothing Then
      m_fDirty = True
      oSite.OnStatusChange
   End If
End Sub

Public Sub RefreshControls()
   checkNotifyAccount.Value = m_prefNotifyWhenNewMember
   checkNotifyTask.Value = m_prefNotifyWhenNewTask
   checkPerformCheck.Value = m_prefLookForShortcuts
   CheckToolbar.Value = m_prefEnableAcctToolbar
   CheckWebShortcut.Value = m_prefMakeFolderHomepage
End Sub

Private Sub checkNotifyAccount_Click()
   If boolInitializing = False Then
      SetDirty
      m_prefNotifyWhenNewMember = checkNotifyAccount.Value
   End If
End Sub

Private Sub checkPerformCheck_Click()
   If boolInitializing = False Then
      SetDirty
      m_prefLookForShortcuts = checkPerformCheck.Value
   End If
End Sub

Private Sub checkNotifyTask_Click()
   If boolInitializing = False Then
      SetDirty
      m_prefNotifyWhenNewTask = checkNotifyTask.Value
   End If
End Sub

Private Sub CheckToolbar_Click()
   If boolInitializing = False Then
      SetDirty
      m_prefEnableAcctToolbar = CheckToolbar.Value
   End If
End Sub

Private Sub CheckWebShortcut_Click()
   If boolInitializing = False Then
      SetDirty
      m_prefMakeFolderHomepage = CheckWebShortcut.Value
   End If
End Sub
```

```
Private Sub PropertyPage_Apply()
   On Error GoTo PropertyPageApply_Err
   m_fDirty = False
   If Not m_AdminDLL Is Nothing Then
      m_AdminDLL.SetRegistryValues m_prefLookForShortcuts, _
         m_prefEnableAcctToolbar, m_prefMakeFolderHomepage, _
         m_prefNotifyWhenNewMember, m_prefNotifyWhenNewTask
      'Refresh the add-in DLL settings
      m_AdminDLL.CheckRegistryValues
   End If
   Exit Sub
PropertyPageApply_Err:
   MsgBox "Error in PropertyPage_Apply.  Err# " & Err.Number _
      & " and Err Description: " & Err.Description
End Sub

Private Property Get PropertyPage_Dirty() As Boolean
   PropertyPage_Dirty = m_fDirty
End Property

Private Sub PropertyPage_GetPageInfo(HelpFile As String, _
HelpContext As Long)
   HelpFile = "nothing.hlp"
   HelpContext = 102
End Sub

Private Sub UserControl_EnterFocus()
   boolInitializing = False
End Sub
Private Sub UserControl_Initialize()
   m_fDirty = False
   boolInitializing = True
End Sub

Private Sub UserControl_InitProperties()
   On Error Resume Next
   Set oSite = Parent
   RefreshControls
End Sub

Public Property Get prefLookForShortcuts() As Variant
   prefLookForShortcuts = m_prefLookForShortcuts
End Property

Public Property Let prefLookForShortcuts(ByVal vNewValue As Variant)
   m_prefLookForShortcuts = vNewValue
End Property
```

```
Public Property Get prefMakeFolderHomepage() As Variant
   prefMakeFolderHomepage = m_prefMakeFolderHomepage
End Property

Public Property Let prefMakeFolderHomepage( _
ByVal vNewValue As Variant)
   m_prefMakeFolderHomepage = vNewValue
End Property

Public Property Get prefNotifyWhenNewMember() As Variant
   prefNotifyWhenNewMember = m_prefNotifyWhenNewMember
End Property

Public Property Let prefNotifyWhenNewMember( _
ByVal vNewValue As Variant)
   m_prefNotifyWhenNewMember = vNewValue
End Property

Public Property Get prefNotifyWhenNewTask() As Variant
   prefNotifyWhenNewTask = m_prefNotifyWhenNewTask
End Property

Public Property Let prefNotifyWhenNewTask( _
ByVal vNewValue As Variant)
   m_prefNotifyWhenNewTask = vNewValue
End Property

Public Property Get prefEnableAcctToolbar() As Variant
   prefEnableAcctToolbar = m_prefEnableAcctToolbar
End Property

Public Property Let prefEnableAcctToolbar( _
ByVal vNewValue As Variant)
   m_prefEnableAcctToolbar = vNewValue
End Property

Public Property Get Caption() As Variant
   Caption = "Account Tracking"
End Property

Public Property Get oAdminDLL() As Variant

End Property

Public Property Let oAdminDLL(ByVal vNewValue As Variant)
   Set m_AdminDLL = vNewValue
End Property
```

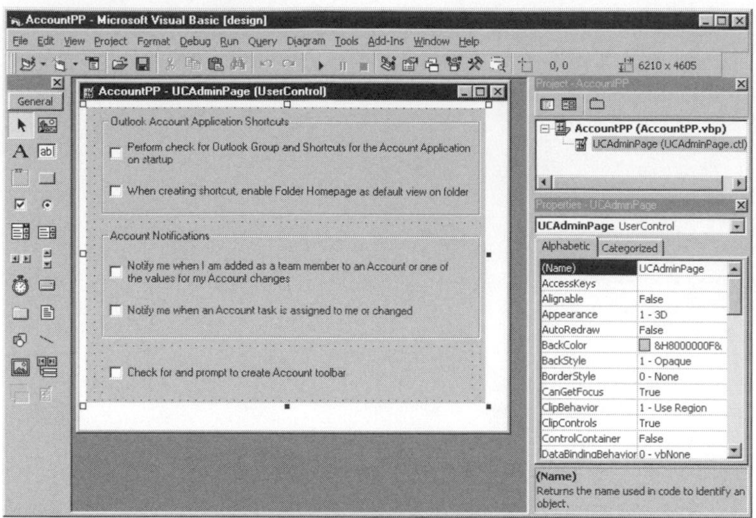

Figure 8-25 The ActiveX control that implements the property page extension in Visual Basic 6.0 design mode

As you can see from the preceding code, not much code is implemented in the extension. Property page extensions are actually pretty easy to write. You need to implement just a few important elements.

The first of these elements, which is at the top of the code, implements the *PropertyPage* interface. To implement this interface, you add a reference to the Outlook object model and then type **Implements Outlook.PropertyPage** in your declarations section. You can then select the methods and properties you need to implement for your property page. You must implement two methods, *GetPageInfo* and *Apply*, and one property, *Dirty*.

The *GetPageInfo* method is called by Outlook to retrieve help information about the property page for your users. In this method, you can set two parameters: *HelpFile* and *HelpContext*. *HelpFile* is a string that points to your help file. (The sample code points to a nonexistent help file.) The *HelpContext* parameter is a *Long* data type that specifies the context ID of the help topic associated with your property page.

The *Apply* method and the *Dirty* property work together with another method on the *Outlook PropertyPageSite* object, which we haven't discussed yet. The *PropertyPageSite* object, which in the sample code is declared in the declarations section, points to the container for your property page object. In this case, the container that holds the object is Outlook.

After you declare a variable to be a *PropertyPageSite*, you must initialize it. The best place to do this is in the intrinsic *InitProperties* event procedure of your ActiveX control. As you can see in the code, *oSite*, which is the *PropertyPageSite* variable, is set to the intrinsic *Parent* property of the ActiveX control. The *Parent* property in this case returns an *Outlook PropertyPageSite* object.

Now that you know how to retrieve the *PropertyPageSite*, we can continue looking at the *Apply* method and the *Dirty* property. When users make changes to your page, the code must be able tell Outlook that the page has become dirty and the Apply button should become active. To do this, you can keep a private variable that tracks whether the user has changed an option—in essence, a dirty flag. When the user changes an option, you set this flag to *True* and then call the *OnStatusChange* method of the *PropertyPageSite* object.

The *OnStatusChange* method, in turn, forces Outlook to try to retrieve the *Dirty* property for your property page. You can see this operation implemented in the *Property Get PropertyPage_Dirty* procedure. The code sets the *PropertyPage_Dirty* variable to the value of the private dirty flag, which should be *True*, and returns that value to Outlook. Once Outlook receives a *True* value, it enables the Apply button.

So what happens when the user clicks this newly enabled Apply button? Well, your *PropertyPage_Apply* subroutine is called. In this subroutine, you should take whatever steps are necessary to apply the changes and also set your private dirty flag back to *False*. You can see in the code for our property page that I set the dirty flag to *False* and then attempt to save the values the user selected back to the registry.

You might be wondering what the *m_AdminDLL* object in this subroutine is. It is the reference to the add-in, which we passed to the property page when we created it. Because the registry functions are already implemented in the add-in, the property page just calls back to the add-in. The *CheckRegistryValues* call forces the add-in to refresh its internal values with the new values the user has selected.

The *Apply* method is also called when there is a dirty setting in your property page and the user clicks OK in the Properties or Options dialog box. The *Apply* method is not called when the user clicks Cancel.

The only other element you must implement in your property page is its caption. To set the caption, you must add a property to your application. To do this, from the Tools menu, select Add Procedure and then select the settings for creating a new public property, as shown in Figure 8-26. After you add the *Caption* property procedure, choose Procedure Attributes from the Tools menu and select the property you just created from the drop-down list. Click the Advanced button, and then select the *Caption* procedure ID in the Procedure ID dialog box, as shown in Figure 8-27. By doing this, you associate your property with the identifier for the caption property on a control. Outlook will query this property ID for the caption for your property page. You then simply implement the code to set this property to the value you want for your caption. You can see an example of the *Caption* property procedure in the previous code.

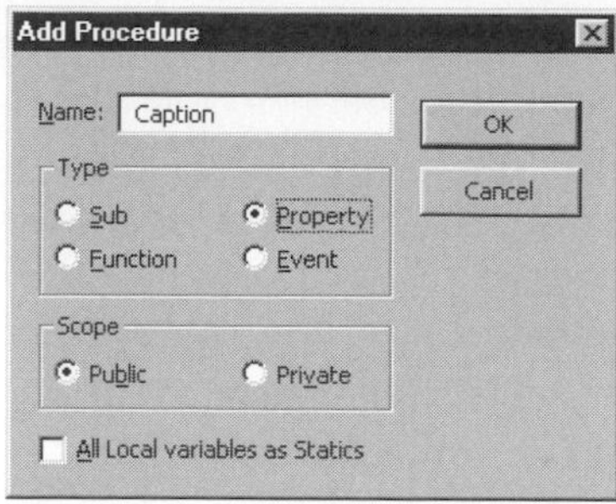

Figure 8-26 Creating a new property for the caption of your property page

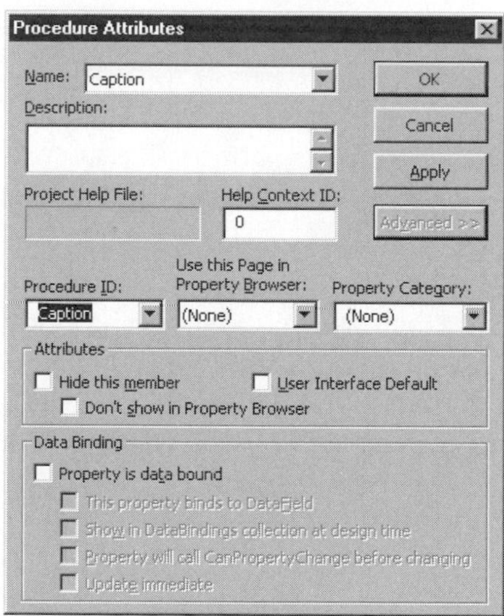

Figure 8-27 Setting the Caption Procedure ID for your property

Calling an XML Web Service from an Outlook Form

One feature you might want to take advantage of in your Outlook forms is the ability to call XML Web services. To do this, you should be familiar with the Visual Studio 6.0 SOAP toolkit. Because Outlook uses VBScript, the easiest way to call an XML Web service from an Outlook form is to use the COM component SOAP client that ships with the toolkit.

To show how to call a Web service, I've updated the Account Tracking application to use the free/busy XML Web service that you will learn about in Chapter 14. Before we can use the XML Web service, we must determine the SMTP address of the sales representative in the Account Team section of the Account Tracking application. To do this, we need to use CDO within Outlook. The CDO code for finding an SMTP address from a CDO *AddressEntry* object is shown next. Notice the use of the *PR_EMS_AB_PROXY_ADDRESSES* property, which contains the SMTP address as well as the X.400 and other addresses for the user.

```
Function FindSMTP(oAE)
    'Finds the SMTP address if the user
    On Error Resume Next
    Err.Clear
    EmailAddresses = oAE.Fields.Item(PR_EMS_AB_PROXY_ADDRESSES)
    Count = UBound(EmailAddresses)
    For i = LBound(EmailAddresses) To Count
        'Because there is probably SMTP, X.400, etc, find just SMTP
        If (instr(1,EmailAddresses(i),"SMTP:") = 1) Then
            'Strip out SMTP:
            strSMTP = mid(EmailAddresses(i),6)
            'Now, strip out everything up to the @ symbol
            AtSymbol = InStr(1,strSMTP,"@")
            If AtSymbol > 1 Then
                'Found it
                strSMTP = Mid(strSMTP, 1, ((AtSymbol)-1))
                'Figure out the properties from the address book
                FindSMTP = strSMTP
            End If
        End If
    Next
End Function
```

The next step is to call our Web service. We'll use the MSSOAP.SoapClient30 library to make the call. This client does the heavy lifting of wrapping our SOAP calls and our SOAP responses, plus it is a COM component, so no interop is required between .NET and COM in our code. The code initializes the SOAP client with pointers to the WSML and WSDL files for the free/busy Web service. Then the code gets the SMTP address of the user and calls the *GetFreeBusy* method on the Web service.

The code takes the response and passes it to the *CheckFB* function shown next. The *CheckFB* function takes the free/busy string returned by the Web service and parses the string to determine the sales rep availability over the next hour and returns it to the user.

```
Sub cmdLookupRepFreeBusy_Click
   On Error Resume Next
   Err.Clear

   If oDefaultPage.Controls("txtSalesRep").value = "" Then
      MsgBox "You must enter a value before checking free/busy"
      Exit Sub
   End If
   'Initialize the SOAP Client
   Set oSoapClient = CreateObject("MSSOAP.SoapClient30")
   oSoapClient.mssoapinit strWSDLLocation,,, strWSMLLocation
   Set oCDOSession = application.CreateObject("MAPI.Session")
   oCDOSession.Logon "", "", False, False, 0
   'Create a bogus message
   'Try to find the recipient in the address book by their
   'alias by sending a message
   Set otmpMessage = oCDOSession.Outbox.Messages.Add
   otmpMessage.Recipients.Add oDefaultPage.Controls("txtSalesRep").Value
   otmpMessage.Recipients.Resolve
   If otmpMessage.Recipients.Resolved <> True Then
      MsgBox "The name could not be resolved."
   Else
      'Get the SMTP address of the user
      Set orecip = otmpMessage.Recipients.Item(1)
      'Populate the other fields as necessary
      Set oAE = oCDOSession.GetAddressEntry(orecip.AddressEntry.ID)
      strSMTP = FindSMTP(oAE)
      Set otmpMessage = Nothing

      dNow = Now
      strStartDate = Month(dNow) & "/" & Day(dNow) & "/" & _
                     Year(dNow) & " 12:00 AM"

      strEndDate = Month(dNow) & "/" & Day(dNow) & "/" & _
                   Year(dNow) & " 11:59 PM"

      strServerResponse = oSoapClient.GetFreeBusy(strLDAPDirectory, _
                          strSMTP, strStartDate, strEndDate, "30")

      'Scroll through the response and add it to the listbox
      Dim arrResponse
      arrResponse = Split(strServerResponse, ",")
      For i = LBound(arrResponse) To UBound(arrResponse)
         'Get the full hour from the current time
         dNextStartDate = FormatDateTime(dNow, 2) & " " & _
                          FormatDateTime(Hour(dNow) & ":00", 3)

         'The end time should be the end of the day
         dNextEndDate = FormatDateTime(DateAdd("h",1,dNextStartDate),0)
         strFBResponse = CheckFB(arrResponse(i),strStartDate, _
                         dNextStartDate,dNextEndDate, "Sales Rep")
         oDefaultPage.Controls("lblSalesFreeBusy").Caption = strFBResponse
```

```
      Next
   End If
   Set otmpMessage = Nothing

   If Err.Number <> 0 Then
      MsgBox "There was an error in the free/busy checking routine."
      Err.Clear
   End If
End Sub

Function CheckFB(strFB, dFBStart, dStartTime, dEndTime, strUserName)
   'This function takes the starttime and the endtime for an appointment
   'and checks the free/busy for the user to see if the user
   'is free/busy/tenative
   'Returns back a string to insert into the label
   If Len(strFB) = 0 Then
      CheckFB = "Free/Busy information not available"
   Else
      'Grab Start time and figure out how far into the FB string the app
      'needs to go
      'Check to see if the appointment starts on the hour or half hour
      iMinute = Minute(TimeValue(Cdate(dStartTime)))
      If  iMinute <> 0 AND iMinute <> 30 Then
         'Figure out which side of the half hour the appt is on
         If iMinute < 30 Then
            'Move it back to the hour
            dStartTime = DateValue(dStartTime) & " " & _
                         Hour(dStartTime) & ":00"
         ElseIf iMinute > 30 Then
            'Move it ahead to the next hour
            'See if flips to next day
            dStartTime = DateAdd("h",1,dStartTime)
            dStartTime = DateValue(dStartTime) & " " & _
                         Hour(dStartTime) & ":00"
         End If

         dStartTime = FormatDateTime(dStartTime, 2) & " " & _
                      FormatDateTime(dStartTime, 3)
      End If

      'Since 1 day = 48 half-hour increments,
      'get the diff between start time
      'of appt and start time of F/B period
      Dim i30minDiffBeginEnd
      Dim i30minDiff

      i30minDiff = DateDiff("n",dFBStart,dStartTime)
      'Divide it by 30
      i30minDiff = i30minDiff/30
      'See if out of bounds due to flipping to next day
      If i30minDiff < Len(strFB) Then
         'Jump into the begin. middle or end of string
         'Figure out how many half-hour increments we need
```

```
'go to get the F/B
i30minDiffBeginEnd = DateDiff("n",dStartTime,dEndTime)
i30minDiffBeginEnd = i30minDiffBeginEnd / 30

'Jump into the string
iFree=0
iTenative = 0
iBusy = 0
iOOF = 0

Dim strText
For z=1 To i30minDiffBeginEnd
   tmpFB = mid(strFB,i30minDiff + z,1)

   Select Case tmpFB
      Case 0:
         iFree = iFree + 1
      Case 1:
         iTenative = iTenative + 1
      Case 2:
         iBusy = iBusy + 1
      Case 3:
         iOOF = iOOF + 1
   End Select
Next

If iFree=i30minDiffBeginEnd Then
   'Totally Free
   CheckFB = strUserName & " is free from " & _
             formatdatetime(dStartTime,3) & " to " & _
             formatdatetime(dEndTime,3) & "."
   Exit Function
End If

'This routine counts the timeslots but we do not need
'to display this.  Left in for your convenience.

If iTenative > 0 Then
   'strText = iTenative & " Tenative"
   strText = "Tenative"
End If
If iBusy > 0 Then
   'If strText <> "" Then
   '   strText = strText & ", " & iBusy & " Busy"
   'Else
   '   strText = iBusy & " Busy"
   'End If
   strText = "Busy"
End If
If iOOF > 0 tThen
   'If strText <> "" Then
   '   strText = strText & ", and " & iOOF & " Out-of-Office"
   'Else
```

```
            '   strText = iOOF & " Out-of-Office"
            'End If
            strText = "Out-of-Office"
         End If
         If strText = "" Then
            'Unknown!
            'Say it's free
            strText = strUserName & " calendar is showing free from " & _
                      formatdatetime(dStartTime,3) & " to " & _
                      formatdatetime(dEndTime,3) & "."
         End If
         CheckFB = strUserName & " calendar is showing " & strText & _
                   " " & formatdatetime(dStartTime,3) & _
                   " to " & formatdatetime(dEndTime,3) & "."
      Else
            'Longer than the string, say unknown
            CheckFB = "Free/Busy status is unknown."
      End If
   End If
End Function
```

The Offline Free/Busy Application

To give you a head start in building complex applications that use the development features in Outlook, I've included some applications with the companion content that are not covered in this chapter. One sample you might find particularly useful is the Offline Free/Busy application. By combining COM add-ins, ActiveX controls, and custom Outlook forms, this sample allows you to synchronize information about availability of users at different points in time (free/busy information) for all users in your organization. While working off line, users can also create meeting requests that query the free/busy information for other users. Figure 8-28 shows the property page you can use to set up the users you want to synchronize off line. Figure 8-29 shows the custom Outlook form and ActiveX control that allow you to work with the synchronized free/busy information.

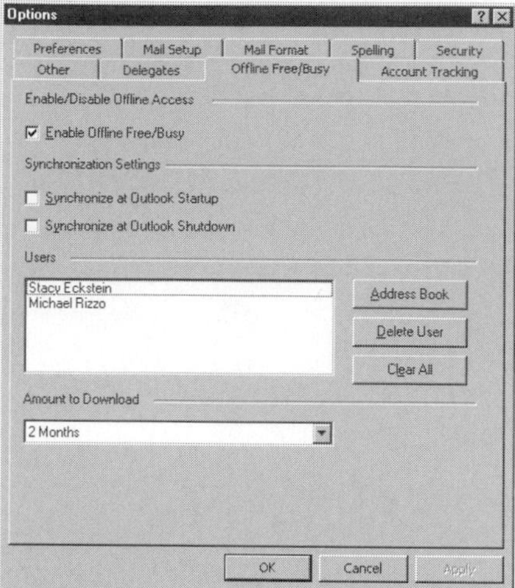

Figure 8-28 The property page of the Offline Free/Busy sample application

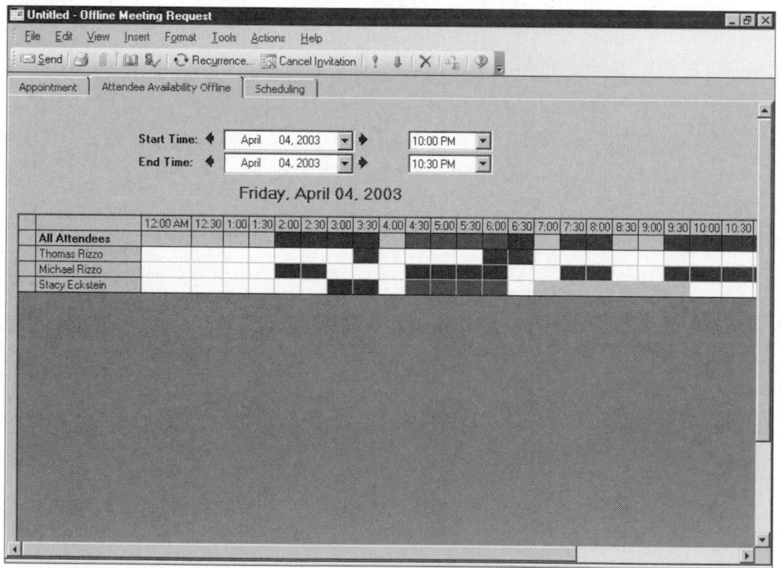

Figure 8-29 The custom Outlook form and ActiveX control that allow you to browse the availability of users while you work off line

Summary

In this chapter, you saw examples of using Outlook to build applications—from simple to complex—that use XML Web services. In the next chapter, you will learn about some of the other technologies you can use in Outlook and your broader Office applications, including smart tags and smart documents.

9

Developing Smart Tags and Smart Documents

Smart tags, which were introduced in Microsoft Office XP, allow developers to build solutions that can recognize data and provide additional functionality for that data. Smart tags recognize common terms, and based on that recognition, a program can perform actions associated with those terms. The best examples of smart tags are in Office. For example, when you type a stock symbol or a person's name in a Microsoft Word document, you might want to look up recent news about the stock or send the person an e-mail message. Before smart tags, you had to fire up your Web browser, go to a financial site, and look up the news about the company. Or to send e-mail, you had to start your e-mail client, type the person's e-mail address, and then send your message. The purple dotted lines under the text in Figure 9-1 show how recognized smart tags are indicated in Office.

The types of actions that can be performed on a smart tag are up to the developer and depend on the type of data. If the tag is a recognized Outlook contact, for example, you can send e-mail, schedule a meeting, or perform other standard Outlook functions. The smart tag icon that Office adds above the recognized term reveals a menu that shows the actions that you can perform. Figure 9-2 shows the action menu for a smart tag in Word.

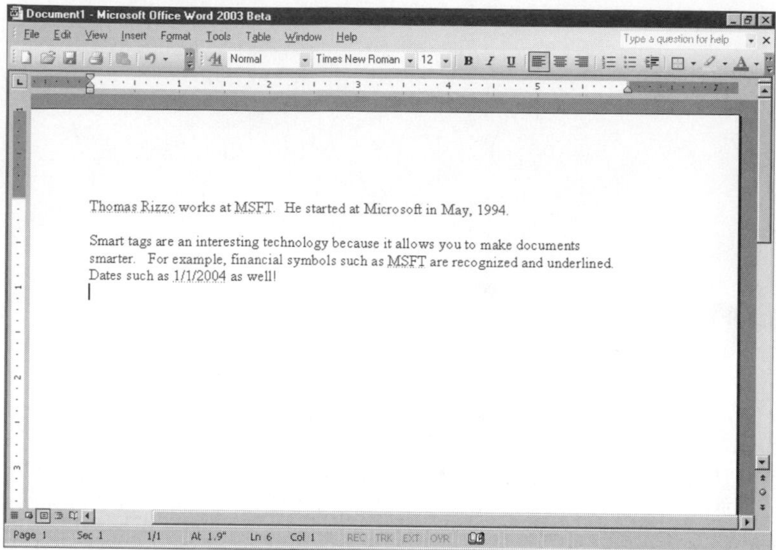

Figure 9-1 Recognized smart tag terms in Word 2003

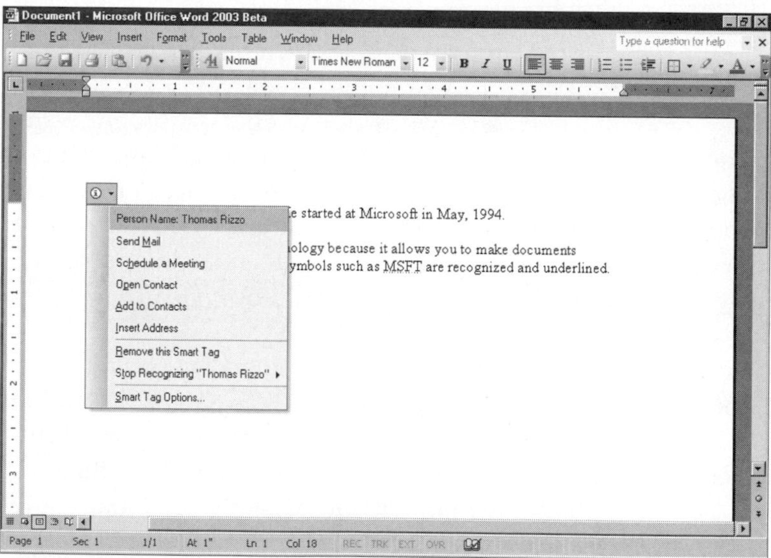

Figure 9-2 The action menu for a smart tag

Smart tags allow you to build dynamic applications that can recognize data and display a set of defined actions for that data. You can perform database lookups, create e-mail messages, or perform other functions based on the data and the action selected by the user.

In Office XP, only Word and Microsoft Excel support smart tags. In Office 2003, smart tag support has been expanded to include Microsoft PowerPoint and Microsoft Access. Outlook supports smart tags if you use Word as your e-mail editor. Smart tag support was removed from Microsoft Internet Explorer and Microsoft Windows XP because of customer feedback. Office installs a smart tag helper for Internet Explorer, which a program can leverage, but Internet Explorer does not support smart tags natively.

Smart Tag Architecture

You can think of smart tags as being made up of a recognizer component and an action component. The recognizer component checks to see whether any data passed to it is data that the smart tag should label and list actions for. If data passed to the recognizer is identified as a smart tag, the recognizer tells the hosting application that it should display the smart tag's actions for the item.

Recognizers work with actions, which are the verbs that the developer defines for their smart tags. The actions you implement can be anything that you can write in code. You can launch an application, add information to a database, or even send an e-mail or fax. You are not limited in the sorts of actions you can develop.

To get a clearer understanding of the smart tag architecture, look over Figure 9-3, which shows how smart tags relate to the Office applications. Notice that you need the Internet Explorer Binary Behavior, which comes with Office and can be freely distributed, for Internet Explorer to work with smart tags.

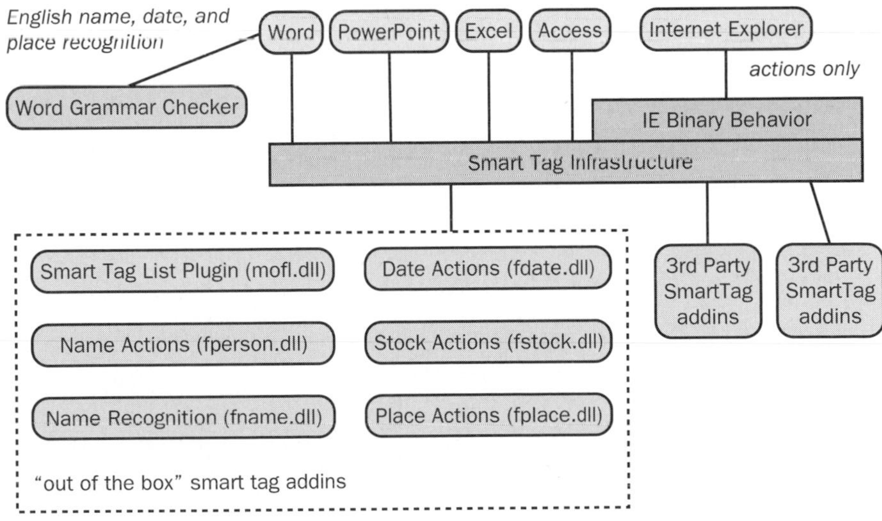

Figure 9-3 Smart tag architecture

Building Smart Tags

You can build smart tags in two ways. The first way does not require code. You simply provide a list of terms and associated actions to the Microsoft Office Smart Tag List (MOSTL) component. Using MOSTL limits your ability to dynamically recognize terms and perform actions, but you can set up update intervals for your smart tag lists and update them from a content source on your network. The second and more flexible way to build smart tags is by writing a COM component that implements the recognizer and action interfaces. This approach provides the most flexibility by enabling you to dynamically recognize terms and define actions. I'll describe how to build smart tags using code after describing MOSTL in more detail.

Using MOSTL

If you've ever enabled the MSN financial smart tag list, which enables a hyperlink to stock symbols, you have used MOSTL. This list is built as a smart tag list. To create a smart tag list for use with MOSTL, you create an XML file that contains your hit list and the actions associated with those hits. The following example from the MSN stock symbol smart tag list shows of the format of the XML file for MOSTL:

```
<FL:smarttaglist xmlns:FL="urn:schemas-microsoft-com:smarttags:list">
  <FL:name>MSN MoneyCentral Financial Symbols</FL:name>
  <FL:lcid>1033,0</FL:lcid>
  <FL:description>A list of stock ticker symbols for recognition, as well as a
set of actions that work with them.</FL:description>
  <FL:moreinfourl>http://office.microsoft.com</FL:moreinfourl>
  <FL:updateable>true</FL:updateable>
  <FL:autoupdate>true</FL:autoupdate>
  <FL:lastcheckpoint>100</FL:lastcheckpoint>
  <FL:lastupdate>5123942</FL:lastupdate>
  <FL:updateurl>http://office.microsoft.com/smarttags/stockupdate.xml</FL:upda
teurl>
  <FL:updatefrequency>20160</FL:updatefrequency>
  <FL:smarttag type="urn:schemas-microsoft-com:office:smarttags#stockticker">
    <FL:caption>Financial Symbol</FL:caption>
    <FL:terms>
      <FL:termfile><FL:filename>stocks.dat</FL:filename></FL:termfile>
    </FL:terms>
    <FL:actions>
      <FL:action id="LatestQuoteData">
        <FL:caption>Stock quote on MSN MoneyCentral</FL:caption>
        <FL:url>http://moneycentral.msn.com/redir/moneycentralredi
rect.asp?pageid=SmartTag_1&amp;Target=/scripts/web
quote.dll?ipage=qd%26Symbol={TEXT}</FL:url>
      </FL:action>
```

```
      <FL:action id="CompanyReportData">
        <FL:caption>Company report on MSN MoneyCentral</FL:caption>
        <FL:url>http://moneycentral.msn.com/redir/moneycentralredi
rect.asp?pageid=SmartTag_2&amp;Target=/investor/research/profile.asp?Sym
bol={TEXT}</FL:url>
      </FL:action>
      <FL:action id="RecentNews">
        <FL:caption>Recent news on MSN MoneyCentral</FL:caption>
        <FL:url>http://moneycentral.msn.com/redir/moneycentralredi
rect.asp?pageid=SmartTag_3&amp;Target=http://news.moneycentral.msn.com/ticker/
rcnews.asp?Symbol={TEXT}</FL:url>
      </FL:action>
    </FL:actions>
  </FL:smarttag>
</FL:smarttaglist>
```

As you can see in the XML, you must declare the *Smart Tag* namespace and use that namespace throughout your file. Table 9-1 describes the elements of the schema used in the XML file.

Table 9-1 Elements of the Smart Tag XML Schema

Element	Description
smarttaglist	The schema namespace declaration for the *Smart Tag* namespace. This tag is required.
name	The friendly name for the smart tag recognizer.
lcid	A comma-separated list of locale IDs that specify the languages of words that the list will identify.
description	A string that describes the smart tag.
Moreinfourl	The URL at which the user can get more information about the smart tag.
Updateable	A Boolean flag that indicates whether the list is updatable.
Autoupdate	A Boolean flag that specifies whether the list should update automatically.
Lastcheckpoint	An integer that specifies the version number for the smart tag list. If a newer version is available and *autoupdate* is set to *True*, the newer version will be downloaded.
Lastupdate	An integer that specifies when the last update occurred. It is specified in the number of minutes since 1970.
Updateurl	A string indicating the URL that the smart tag should check for any updates to the list.
Updatefrequency	An integer that specifies in minutes how often the smart tag should check for updates. If blank, 7 days (10080 minutes) is assumed.

Table 9-1 Elements of the Smart Tag XML Schema

Element	Description
smarttag	A smart tag type specified by a unique namespace. Smart tag types contain terms and actions.
Terms	The XML section that contains the term nodes for the smart tag.
Termfile	A link to a binary file that contains your terms. You will most likely use the *termlist* element. A *filename* subelement is required if *termfile* is used.
Termlist	A comma-separated list that contains your terms. To place quotation marks around terms, use three quotation marks—for example, *"""Tom"""* will appear as *"Tom"*.
Property	A name and value pair that you attach to the term if it is recognized. You can have only one property attached to any action.
Actions	The XML section that contains the action nodes for the smart tag.
Action	A particular action for the smart tag type. You must specify a unique ID for the action in the action element.
Caption	A string for the caption you want to display for the action.
url	A string that specifies the URL to call for the action. You can specify special terms in your *url* element, such as *{LCID}* to pass the locale ID and *{TEXT}* to pass the smart-tagged text. The MSN stock ticker list uses *{TEXT}* to pass the stock symbol name to a Web page to look up the company specified.

Creating and Storing Your XML Definitions

To create your XML smart tag list files, you can use any text editor. You can copy and modify an existing list, such as the MSN one, which makes creating the list easier and limits mistakes in your coding. The MSN list is located in the directory where you should save your XML definition files, which is *drive*:\Program Files\Common Files\Microsoft Shared\Smart Tag\Lists. Another possible location, if you want the list to roam with the user, is *drive*:\Documents and Settings*username*\Application Data\Microsoft\Smart Tag Lists. When you save your list, be sure to make the extension for the list .xml.

Updating a MOSTL List via a Web Server

If you fill in the schema elements for automatic updating and place a URL in the *updateurl* schema element, MOSTL will automatically update the smart tag list. For the smart tag list to be updated, you need to place an update file at the URL you specify. The following sample shows an update file:

```
<FLUP:smarttaglistupdate xmlns:FLUP="urn:schemas-microsoft-com:smarttags:list
update">
    <FLUP:checkpoint>400</FLUP:checkpoint>
    <FLUP:smarttaglistdefinition>new.xml</FLUP:smarttaglistdefinition>
 </FLUP:smarttaglistupdate>
```

You must link to this file from the *updateurl* element defined in the smart tag XML schema and set the *checkpoint* element in the update file to be greater than the *checkpoint* in the original file. If the smart tag list needs to be updated, MOSTL will grab the file listed in the *smarttaglistdefinition* element and download it to the client. The sample just shown, new.xml, is just a new smart tag list file that has the same format and schema elements as any smart tag list file. The downloaded filename becomes whatever the original list's filename was. For example, if new.xml is an update to original.xml, when new.xml is downloaded, it will be renamed original.xml and will replace the earlier original.xml.

Be sure that the *checkpoint* value you put in your update list XML file, shown in our example with a value of *400*, matches exactly the *checkpoint* value you put in your list definition file, which in this example is new.xml. Otherwise, your smart tag will always update or never update, depending on which *checkpoint* value is the greater of the two.

> **Note** Even though new file list definitions are downloaded automatically, Office XP applications do not refresh their smart tag lists until you shut down and restart those applications.

Writing Custom Smart Tags

MOSTL will not always meet the needs of your application. For example, if you need dynamic terms or dynamic action lists and you don't want to download and update a file every time the terms or actions change, MOSTL is not a good solution. To make smart tag development more extensible than MOSTL, Office XP and Office 2003 offer you the ability to write a COM component that can implement the smart tag interfaces for recognizers and actions. You can write your smart tag using any COM-compliant language, such as Visual Basic or Visual C++. We will look at Visual Basic examples in this chapter; the smart tag SDK, which is among the book's companion files, includes examples for Visual C++.

Building Custom Smart Tag Recognizers Using Visual Basic

When you build a custom smart tag recognizer, you should follow some general development guidelines. First, you should not implement any sort of visual user interface in the recognizers that you build, especially modal forms. This can cause unexpected behavior in the smart tag hosting application. Second, you should build your smart tags generically and not assume that Office applications will always be your client because other Microsoft applications or even third-party applications can add the capability to host smart tags.

One thing to note about building smart tag recognizers is that one recognizer can call multiple action DLLs and multiple recognizers can leverage a single action DLL.

The basic step in building a smart tag recognizer with Visual Basic is to build the recognizer and action DLLs as ActiveX DLLs. Your DLLs will leverage the Microsoft Smart Tags 1.0 type library, so you only need to implement the smart tag interfaces and the action functionality for your smart tag.

Creating the ActiveX DLL

If you are still using Visual Basic 6.0, your first step is to create an ActiveX DLL that contains both recognizer and action functionality. You could separate this functionality into two DLLs, but for this example we will use the same DLL. Next you add a reference to the smart tag type library, as shown in Figure 9-4.

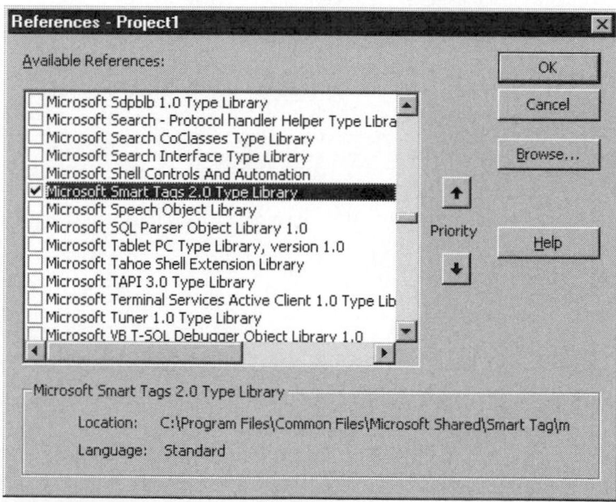

Figure 9-4 Adding a reference to the smart tag type library in Visual Basic 6.0

The next step is to implement the *ISmartTagRecognizer* interface. Table 9-2 lists the properties and method of the smart tag recognizer interface.

Table 9-2 Elements of the Smart Tag Recognizer Interface

Property	Description
Desc	A string that specifies what the smart tag does.
Name	A string that specifies the name of the smart tag. It's displayed as the caption for the smart tag in the Office user interface.
ProgID	A string that specifies the ProgID of the smart tag, such as *mysmarttag.recognizer*.
SmartTagCount	An integer value that specifies the number of smart tag types that this recognizer supports.
SmartTagDownloadURL	A string property that specifies a URL that allows the user to download the actions for the smart tag if they are not already on the system. This download can be performed by users when they choose the Check For New Actions menu command.
SmartTagName	A string that specifies the smart tag types that the recognizer supports. This string must be in the format *namespaceURI#tagname*, as in *myURI#Categories*.
Method	**Description**
Recognize	Recognizes the terms in the document. It passes four parameters. The first is a string that defines the text that should be recognized. The second is an enumeration of the data type for the text. For example, the enumeration can specify whether the text is sent a character at a time, is sent as a word, or is an Excel cell. Only paragraph and cell types are currently supported. The third parameter is the locale ID of the text. The final parameter is a *RecognizerSite* object (described later in this chapter) that allows you to interact with the smart tag host.

Before we examine the code used to create a recognizer, we need to look at two other types of objects that you will use with smart tags. The first is the *ISmartTagRecognizerSite* object, which you'll use to commit new smart tags to Word and Excel as well as to create property bags with which to pass arbitrary properties that you create between recognizers and actions. The second object is *ISmartTagProperties*, which is used in conjunction with the smart tag property bag you create with the *ISmartTagRecognizerSite* object. Table 9-3 describes the methods defined in the *ISmartTagRecognizerSite* interface. Table 9-4 describes the members of the *ISmartTagProperties* interface.

Table 9-3 Methods of the *ISmartTagRecognizerSite* Interface

Method	Description
CommitSmartTag	Creates a new smart tag in the host. You must pass four parameters to this method. The first is the smart tag type string, which must be in the format *namespaceURI#tag-name*. The second is an integer value that specifies the location at which to start the smart tag in the text. The underlining in Word for the smart tag begins at this location. The next parameter is an integer that specifies the number of characters the smart tag will span. The final parameter is a property bag object that you want to include with the smart tag.
GetNewPropertyBag	Returns an *ISmartTagProperties*-based object.

Table 9-4 Elements of the *ISmartTagProperties* Interface

Element	Description
Count	An integer that specifies the number of properties stored.
KeyFromIndex	Returns the key string corresponding to the integer index you pass.
Read	Gets the value corresponding to the key string you pass. If the key does not exist, this property returns *Null*.
ValueFromIndex	Returns the value string corresponding to the integer index you pass.
Write	Writes a key/value pair into the property bag. You must pass this method a key string and a value string.

Following is the smart tag recognizer code from our recognizer DLL that queries a setup of the Training application (presented later in the chapter) for the application categories you create. This code is written in the DLL for our smart tag. If the recognizer recognizes those categories in a document, it will tag the words as smart tags.

```
Implements SmartTagLib.ISmartTagRecognizer
'Declare path variables for the location where the Training Application
'and the Categories folder for the Training Application are
'installed. This path is used by the WebDAV query to figure out the
'categories for the application.
Dim strTrainingAppCategoriesURL As String
Dim strTrainingAppURL As String

'Recognized Categories
Private arrCategoriesRecognized As Variant
```

```
Private Sub Class_Initialize()
    'Lookup the training application categories so that we know
    'what to recognize.
    'Categories are stored as comma separated values in a
    'document called Categories.eml

    On Error Resume Next
    strTrainingAppCategoriesURL = _
        "http://thomriznt52/public/trainingst/Categories/Categories.EML"
    strTrainingAppURL = "http://thomriznt52/trainingst/"

    Set oXMLHTTP = CreateObject("microsoft.XMLHTTP")
    oXMLHTTP.Open "PROPFIND", strTrainingAppCategoriesURL, False
    oXMLHTTP.setRequestHeader "Content-type:", "text/xml"
    oXMLHTTP.setRequestHeader "translate", "f"
    strRequest = "<?xml version=""1.0"" encoding=""utf-8""?>" & _
                 "<a:propfind xmlns:a=""DAV:"">" & _
                 "<a:prop xmlns:m=""urn:schemas:httpmail:"">" & _
                 "<m:textdescription/></a:prop></a:propfind>"
    oXMLHTTP.send strRequest

    'Load up the result into an XMLDOM and parse out the
    'categories.
    Set oXMLDOM = CreateObject("microsoft.xmldom")
    oXMLDOM.async = False
    oXMLDOM.LoadXML oXMLHTTP.ResponseText
    Set CategoryNode = oXMLDOM.getelementsbytagname("d:textdescription")

    'Get the value from the node
    strCategories = CategoryNode.Item(0).nodeTypedValue
    arrCategoriesRecognized = Split(strCategories, ",")
End Sub

Private Property Get ISmartTagRecognizer_ProgId() As String
    ' Create a unique identifier for this recognizer
    ' that corresponds to the ProgID of this dll.

    ISmartTagRecognizer_ProgId = "STTrainingApp.Recognizer"
End Property

Private Property Get ISmartTagRecognizer_Name _
                    (ByVal LocaleID As Long) As String
    ' Add a short phrase that describes this recognizer that will be
    ' shown in the Tools > Autocorrect Option > Smart Tags
    ' dialog box in Word, Excel and PowerPoint.
    ISmartTagRecognizer_Name = "Training Application Category"
End Property

Private Property Get ISmartTagRecognizer_Desc _
                    (ByVal LocaleID As Long) As String
    ' Create a longer description of this recognizer.
    ISmartTagRecognizer_Desc = "Recognizes the Training" & _
        "Application Sample Application Categories"
End Property
```

```
Private Sub ISmartTagRecognizer_Recognize _
         (ByVal Text As String, _
          ByVal DataType As SmartTagLib.IF_TYPE, _
          ByVal LocaleID As Long, _
          ByVal RecognizerSite As SmartTagLib.ISmartTagRecognizerSite)

    Dim oPropBag As SmartTagLib.ISmartTagProperties
    Dim position As Integer
    Dim Length As Integer

    On Error Resume Next

    'Remove any question marks (??????)
    Length = Len(Text)
    If (Length > 0) Then
        position = InStr(1, Text, ChrW(-4))
    Else
        position = 0
    End If

    While (Length > 0 And position > 0)
        Mid$(Text, position, 1) = " "
        Length = Length - 1
        If (Length > 0) Then
            position = InStr(1, Text, ChrW(-4))
        Else
            position = 0
        End If
        position = InStr(1, Text, ChrW(-4))
    Wend
    Text = RTrim(Text)

    position = InStr(1, Text, ChrW(-4))
    If (position > 0) Then
        Length = Len(Text)
        Mid$(Text, position, (Length - position + 1)) = _
            Space$(Length - position + 1)
        Text = RTrim(Text)
    End If

    'Now trim off the carriage return at the end of the string
    'if there is one
    If (Right(Text, 1) = ChrW(13)) Then
        Text = Left(Text, Len(Text) - 1)
    End If

    'See if we match any of the terms returned by the Text property
    'UCASE both properties

    strUCASEText = UCase(Text)
    For i = LBound(arrCategoriesRecognized) To _
            UBound(arrCategoriesRecognized)
        iLoc = 1
```

```
        IndexLoc = InStr(1, strUCASEText, _
                        UCase(arrCategoriesRecognized(i)))
        Do While IndexLoc > 0
            'We found a match somewhere in the string
            'Since there could be multiple matches,
            'find all occurrences of the string.

            'Make sure there is a space after the phrase
            'so we're not at the beginning of a word
            strNextChar = " "
            'Figure out the end of the word by taking
            'the location and adding the length
            'of the term recognized.
            iEndOfWord = IndexLoc + Len(arrCategoriesRecognized(i))
            strNextChar = Mid(strUCASEText, iEndOfWord, 1)
            If strNextChar = "" Then
                strNextChar = " "
            End If

            'Make sure that a space precedes the beginning of
            'the phrase so we're not in the middle of the word.
            strPrevChar = " "
            strPrevChar = Mid(strUCASEText, IndexLoc - 1, 1)
            If strPrevChar = "" Then
                strPrevChar = " "
            End If
            If strPrevChar = " " And strNextChar = " " Then
                Err.Clear
                'Ask the recognizer site for a property bag.
                Set oPropBag = RecognizerSite.GetNewPropertyBag
                'Store the URL to the training site and
                'pass it to the action.
                oPropBag.Write "TrainingAppURL", strTrainingAppURL
                'Commit the Smart Tag
                RecognizerSite.CommitSmartTag "trainingapp#categories", _
                    IndexLoc, Len(arrCategoriesRecognized(i)), oPropBag
                Set oPropBag = Nothing
            End If
            IndexLoc = _
                InStr(IndexLoc + Len(arrCategoriesRecognized(i)), _
                strUCASEText, UCase(arrCategoriesRecognized(i)))
        Loop
    Next
End Sub

Private Property Get ISmartTagRecognizer_SmartTagCount() As Long
    'Specify the number of smart tag types this recognizer supports.
    '1 in this case.
    ISmartTagRecognizer_SmartTagCount = 1
End Property

Private Property Get ISmartTagRecognizer_SmartTagName _
                    (ByVal SmartTagID As Long) As String
```

```
    'Provide the name of the smart tag type supported.
    'SmartTag names are always in the format of namespaceURI#tagname.
    If (SmartTagID = 1) Then
        ISmartTagRecognizer_SmartTagName = "trainingapp#categories"
    End If
End Property

Private Property Get ISmartTagRecognizer_SmartTagDownloadURL _
                     (ByVal SmartTagID As Long) As String
    'For this particular smart tag type, there is a Web site
    'to support a smart tag download URL. Note that
    '"http://trainingapp" supplied below is a hypothetical
    'Web site used to demonstrate the Check for New Actions...
    'menu item.

    ISmartTagRecognizer_SmartTagDownloadURL = "http://trainingapp"
End Property
```

As you can see, the code sets up the ProgID, name, description, download URL, and other required properties to implement the *ISmartTagRecognizer* interface. During the initialization of the class, the application sends a WebDAV *PROPFIND* query to the server to retrieve the categories, which are stored as a comma-delimited string in a message in the categories folder.

The most important part of the code is in the *Recognize* subroutine. This routine is called by the smart tag host application. In Word, for example, the recognizer is called when the user presses the Spacebar, hits Return, or hits Tab. You might be wondering why the code removes question marks and carriage returns. For performance reasons, Word buffers user input by creating a memory allocation and filling the blank space in the memory allocation with the Unicode character FFFC. This character appears as question marks. The code in your *Recognize* subroutine must therefore remove these question marks at the end of the string and also in middle of strings because the character is used as a placeholder for images and/or OLE objects. The code then removes any carriage returns from the string at the end to make tokenizing the string easier.

The next step is to convert the incoming text to uppercase so the code doesn't run into case issues. The code then loops through the categories from the Training application, checking the text passed to see whether any of it matches a category. Notice that the code does not stop after a single recognition. It continues because the text passed to your application might be an entire sentence or a paragraph, which could contain multiple instances of the phrase. The code also checks before and after the recognized word for spaces or blank characters. It does this because a category might be common letters embedded in a word that has nothing to do with the Training application. For example, if one of the categories in the application is MIS, you do not want to have the application match on the word *mistakes*. The code stops this from happening.

This also means that categories must be single words with no spaces. You can code around this by looking for complete words, but the sample does not have this capability.

Next the code asks the *RecognizerSite* object to return a new property bag. This property bag contains name/value pairs that you can use to store and pass information to the actions for your smart tag, as you'll see in the action component later in this chapter. Once the property bag is returned, the application writes the key name and the key value to the property bag, which in this case is the URL to the Training application. The next step in the application is to commit the smart tag to the smart tag host. This operation is performed by calling the *CommitSmartTag* method.

All recognizers are stored in the registry under HKEY_CURRENT_USER \Software\Microsoft\Office\Common\Smart Tag\Recognizers\. Therefore, when you create a new recognizer, you must compile and register your DLL and then add either the ProgID or CLSID of your recognizer as a new key in this part of the registry. You should use the CLSID to register your component because registering it using the ProgID does not retain the user settings as to whether the user enabled or disabled the smart tag by using the AutoCorrect interface in Office between Office application sessions. This is a known bug with ProgID registrations. After you use the CLSID to register your component, you can try out your new recognizer in Word or Excel. Note, however, that when you work with smart tags, Excel matches entire cell values only, which means that if the entire cell value is not the value you recognize, the cell will not be tagged.

> **Note** Because Office runs recognition of smart tags on a background thread, it might take some time for Office applications to recognize your smart tags. Actions, on the other hand, are run in an active, foreground thread.

Now that we have a recognizer, we need to create a corresponding action for it. To do this, we can create another ActiveX DLL, or we can just add another module to our existing DLL. To create an action, all you do is implement the *ISmartTagAction* interface. This interface is very straightforward and is described in Table 9-5.

Table 9-5 Elements of the *ISmartTagAction* Interface

Element	Description
Desc	A string that specifies what the action does. You are passed the locale ID of the text being passed to your DLL so that you can localize the description.
Name	A string that specifies the name of the action.
ProgID	A string that specifies the ProgID of the action DLL.
SmartTagCaption	A string that specifies the caption to use for the action in the smart tag actions user interface. You are passed a smart tag ID and a locale ID. If your action is used by multiple smart tags, this method will be called with the recognizer's unique ID so you can customize the caption for each recognizer.
SmartTagCount	An integer that specifies the number of smart tag types supported by this DLL.
SmartTagName	A string value that specifies the smart tag types this DLL supports. This string must be in the format *namespaceURI#tagname*, as in *trainingapp#categories*.
VerbCaptionFromID	A string value that specifies the caption to use for your action in the action's drop-down list. This call passes three parameters. The first is the *VerbID*, which is the unique identifier for the verb. The second is the ProgID of the application. The third is the locale ID. You can disable actions by not setting this property for a particular action.
VerbCount	An integer that specifies the number of verbs this DLL supports.
VerbID	An integer property that is a unique identifier for your verbs. You are passed the smart tag name, such as *trainingapp#categories*, and a *verbindex* that is a unique identifier for your verb. The easiest way to handle this property is to pass back the *verbindex* passed to you as the value for this property.
VerbNameFromID	A string property that specifies a language-agnostic identifier for a verb. You are passed the *VerbID*.
InvokeVerb	A method that is called when a verb is invoked. It allows you to implement the functionality for that verb. The method is passed six parameters. The first is the *VerbID*. The second is the application name of the host, such as Word.Application.10. The third is an object that is the application-specific object responsible for calling the action. In Excel, this object is a *Cell* object, and in Word this object is a *Range* object. The next parameter is the property bag passed by the recognizer or by the action itself. The next parameter is the text of the smart tag. The final parameter is an XML representation of the smart tag.

The following code defines the actions for the recognizer we created earlier. This action DLL supports two verbs. Both verbs launch a new instance of Internet Explorer and take the user to the Web site that is passed from the recognizer to the action DLL in the property bag.

```
Implements ISmartTagAction

Private Property Get ISmartTagAction_ProgId() As String
    'Create a language-independent unique identifier
    'that corresponds to the ProgID of this DLL.
    ISmartTagAction_ProgId = "STTrainingApp.Actions"
End Property

Private Property Get ISmartTagAction_Name _
                    (ByVal LocaleID As Long) As String
    'Add a short phrase that describes this action provider DLL.
    ISmartTagAction_Name = "Training Application Actions"
End Property

Private Property Get ISmartTagAction_Desc _
                    (ByVal LocaleID As Long) As String
    'Create a longer description of this recognizer.
    ISmartTagAction_Desc = "Provides actions for " & _
                          "Training Application smart tag"
End Property

Private Property Get ISmartTagAction_SmartTagCount() As Long
    'How many smart tag types will this recognizer support?
    '1 in this case.
    ISmartTagAction_SmartTagCount = 1
End Property

Private Property Get ISmartTagAction_SmartTagName _
                    (ByVal SmartTagID As Long) As String
    If (SmartTagID = 1) Then
        ISmartTagAction_SmartTagName = "trainingapp#categories"
    End If
End Property

Private Property Get ISmartTagAction_SmartTagCaption _
                    (ByVal SmartTagID As Long, _
                     ByVal LocaleID As Long) As String
    'Specify the caption for smart tag(s) we support.
    ISmartTagAction_SmartTagCaption = "Categories"
End Property

Private Property Get ISmartTagAction_VerbCount _
                    (ByVal SmartTagName As String) As Long
    'For a given smart tag type, how many verbs do we support?
    If (SmartTagName = "trainingapp#categories") Then
        ISmartTagAction_VerbCount = 2
    End If
End Property
```

```
Private Property Get ISmartTagAction_VerbID _
                     (ByVal SmartTagName As String, _
                      ByVal VerbIndex As Long) As Long
    ISmartTagAction_VerbID = VerbIndex
End Property

Private Property Get ISmartTagAction_VerbCaptionFromID _
                     (ByVal VerbID As Long, _
                      ByVal ApplicationName As String, _
                      ByVal LocaleID As Long) As String
    Select Case VerbID
        Case 1
            ISmartTagAction_VerbCaptionFromID = _
                "View Training Application"
        Case 2
            'If we only wanted to support Excel
            'If ApplicationName = "Excel.Application.10" Then
            ISmartTagAction_VerbCaptionFromID = _
                "View Training Courses for this month"
            'End If
    End Select
End Property

Private Property Get ISmartTagAction_VerbNameFromID _
                     (ByVal VerbID As Long) As String
    Select Case VerbID
        Case 1
            ISmartTagAction_VerbNameFromID = "ViewTrainingApp"
        Case 2
            ISmartTagAction_VerbNameFromID = "ViewMonthCourses"
    End Select
End Property

Public Sub ISmartTagAction_InvokeVerb _
          (ByVal VerbID As Long, ByVal ApplicationName As String, _
           ByVal Target As Object, _
           ByVal Properties As SmartTagLib.ISmartTagProperties, _
           ByVal Text As String, ByVal XML As String)
    On Error Resume Next
    'If you want to retrieve the location of the text,
    'use the following code:
    'If ApplicationName = "Word.Application.10" Then
    '    Dim rWord As Word.Range
    '    Set rWord = Target
    'ElseIf ApplicationName = "Excel.Application.10" Then
    '    Dim rExcel As Excel.Range
    '    Dim oWorksheet As Excel.Worksheet
    '    Set rExcel = Target
    '    Set oWorksheet = rExcel.Worksheet
    'End If

    Select Case VerbID
        Case 1
            'Get the URL to the training app from the PropertyBag
```

```
                strTrainingURL = Properties.Read("TrainingAppURL")

                If strTrainingURL <> "" Then
                    Set oIE = CreateObject("InternetExplorer.Application")
                    If Right(strTrainingURL, 1) <> "/" Then
                        strTrainingURL = strTrainingURL & "/"
                    End If
                    oIE.Navigate2 (strTrainingURL)
                    oIE.Visible = True
                End If
            Case 2
                'Show the courses for this month
                'Get the URL to the training app from the PropertyBag
                strTrainingURL = Properties.Read("TrainingAppURL")

                If strTrainingURL <> "" Then
                    Set oIE = CreateObject("InternetExplorer.Application")
                    If Right(strTrainingURL, 1) <> "/" Then
                        strTrainingURL = strTrainingURL & "/"
                    End If
                    oIE.Navigate2 (strTrainingURL & _
                                   "calendar.asp?Date=Month&Command=Init")
                    oIE.Visible = True
                End If
        End Select
    End Sub
```

As you can see, the code is straightforward. The most interesting piece of the code is the *InvokeVerb* method, which actually performs the functionality for our actions. Figure 9-5 shows the recognizer and action DLL working in Word.

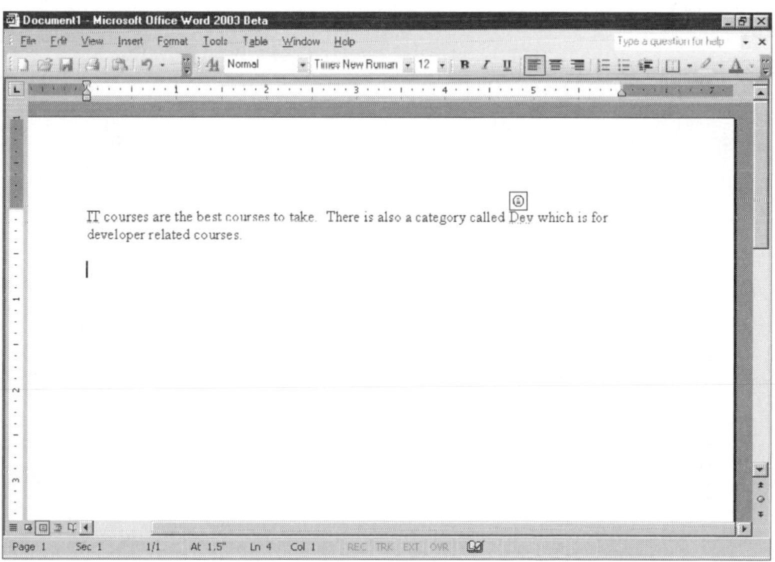

Figure 9-5 Our recognizer and action DLL working in Word

Testing Your Smart Tags

Sometimes, when you attempt to test your smart tag, you'll find that it doesn't seem to work. If you check your code over and over and can't find anything wrong with it, other settings in the system might be affecting your smart tag. The following are some troubleshooting actions you can take:

- Check the macro settings in the host application. If they are set too restrictively, such as with the High setting, your smart tag will be disabled.
- Close and restart the host applications after compiling. Changes in your smart tag are not picked up by the applications until all instances of Word, Excel, and Outlook are closed and restarted.
- If your smart tag crashes, Office will disable it. Check in the registry under the registration for your recognizer. If you see a *Status* subkey with a value of 1, your DLL crashed and has been disabled. If you see a value of 8, your DLL was disabled in Word. If you see a value of 16, your DLL was disabled in Excel. Delete the *Status* subkey and try again. If you see a value of 24 (8+16), the smart tag is disabled in both Word and Excel. For more values for this key, see the smart tag SDK.
- Your CLSID might have changed. If you registered your smart tag using ProgIDs, you do not have to worry about this. Be sure you are using Project Compatibility in Visual Basic when you create your DLLs.
- Your DLL might not be registered properly. Run Regsvr32 on your DLL file.

If none of these steps works, as a last resort you might have to unregister all your smart tags, unregister your DLLs, recompile your code to recreate the DLLs, and try again.

Debugging Your Smart Tags

If in your testing you find that your code is not working completely, you might need to kick your code into the Visual Basic debugger to fix the problems. Because smart tags are ActiveX DLLs, debugging them in Visual Basic is easy. You simply set a breakpoint in your code and then run the code in the Visual

Basic IDE. Select the option to wait for the component to be created. Then start a smart tag host application such as Word, be sure that your smart tag is enabled in Word, and type a term that will trip your break point in your recognizer. You can then use the standard debugging tools in Visual Basic to fix your code. Figure 9-6 shows a smart tag DLL in the debugger.

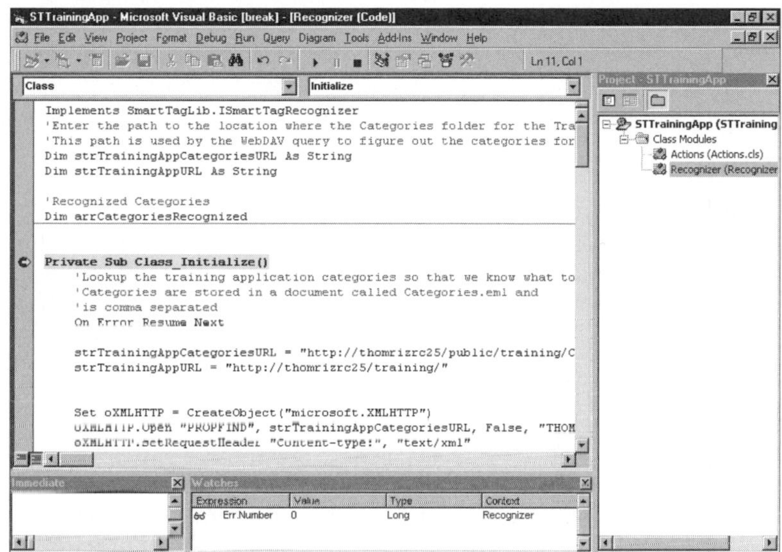

Figure 9-6 A smart tag DLL in the Visual Basic debugger

> **Note** When debugging a smart tag, you might find that terms that meet your criteria do not appear underlined in Word. Because Word runs the smart tag recognizer on a background thread, if your recognizer takes too long, as might be the case in stepping through a debugger, Word will invalidate the call to the recognizer and continue processing. If you then try to call *CommitSmartTag*, you will get an error because your recognizer has been invalidated and the purple underline will not appear. The only way to work around this issue is to debug using a document in which the smart tags are already tagged and trigger your code via a recheck of the smart tags in the document from the AutoCorrect menu command.

Deploying Your Smart Tags

Deploying your smart tags means getting your DLL and registrations onto the client machine. You can do this in a number of ways, such as by creating your own setup program, using the Visual Studio Installer, including your smart tag DLLs in a custom Office deployment package, or even using the Internet Component download component. Rather than describe each of these approaches in detail, I'll point you to the Smart Tag SDK in the book's companion content.

> **Note** You should read the smart tag security white paper included in the smart tag SDK to understand the security implications of smart tags. If possible, you should always digitally sign the DLLs that make up your smart tags.

Word and Excel Object Model Changes

To support smart tags in Word and Excel, the Word and Excel object models now have a *SmartTags* collection object that contains *SmartTag* objects. The most interesting aspect of these objects is that you can enumerate all the smart tags contained in your documents or spreadsheets by using the native object model of the smart tag host. Also, you can add your own smart tag to these applications by using their object models. See the Word and Excel documentation for more information on these two new objects.

Extending Existing Smart Tags in Office

At times, you might want to simply extend the actions of an existing recognizer in Office. For example, you might want to add the ability to look up a user's manager in Active Directory by adding your own action, called Lookup Manager, to the Person Names smart tag included with Office. Extending a smart tag's action list is easy. All you have to do is create a new action DLL. You don't need to create a new recognizer because the recognizer already exists. In your action DLL, you indicate that your action handles only smart tags of type *urn:schemas-microsoft-com:office:smarttags#PersonName*, which is the type emitted by the Person Names recognizer. Table 9-6 lists the smart tag types for the recognizers included with Office.

Table 9-6 Smart Tag Types for Built-In Office Recognizers

Smart Tag Type	Value
Person	*urn:schemas-microsoft-com:office:smarttags#PersonName*
Stock Ticker Symbol	*urn:schemas-microsoft-com:office:smarttags#stockticker*
Address	*urn:schemas-microsoft-com:office:smarttags#address*
Date	*urn:schemas-microsoft-com:office:smarttags#date*
Place	*urn:schemas-microsoft-com:office:smarttags#place*
Phone Number	*urn:schemas-microsoft-com:office:smarttags#phone*
Time	*urn:schemas-microsoft-com:office:smarttags#time*

The following code implements a skeleton for extending the Person Names recognizer with new actions:

```
Implements ISmartTagAction

Private Property Get ISmartTagAction_ProgId() As String
    'Create a language-independent unique identifier for this
    'action that corresponds to the ProgID of this DLL.
    ISmartTagAction_ProgId = "Extends.PersonNames"
End Property

Private Property Get ISmartTagAction_Name( _
                     ByVal LocaleID As Long) As String

    'Add a short phrase that describes this action provider DLL.
    ISmartTagAction_Name = "Extension to Person Names"
End Property

Private Property Get ISmartTagAction_Desc( _
                     ByVal LocaleID As Long) As String

    'Create a longer description of this recognizer.
    ISmartTagAction_Desc = "Provides actions for recognized names"
End Property

Private Property Get ISmartTagAction_SmartTagCount() As Long
    'How many smart tag types will this recognizer recognize?
    '1 in this case.
    ISmartTagAction_SmartTagCount = 1
End Property

Private Property Get ISmartTagAction_SmartTagName( _
                     ByVal SmartTagID As Long) As String
```

```
    If (SmartTagID = 1) Then
        ISmartTagAction_SmartTagName = _
            "urn:schemas-microsoft-com:office:smarttags#PersonName"
    End If
End Property

Private Property Get ISmartTagAction_SmartTagCaption( _
                     ByVal SmartTagID As Long, _
                     ByVal LocaleID As Long) As String

    'Action DLLs specify the caption for smart tags.
    ISmartTagAction_SmartTagCaption = "Custom Action"
End Property

Private Property Get ISmartTagAction_VerbCount( _
                     ByVal SmartTagName As String) As Long

    'For a given smart tag type, how many verbs do we support?
    If (SmartTagName = _
        "urn:schemas-microsoft-com:office:smarttags#PersonName") Then
        ISmartTagAction_VerbCount = 1
    End If
End Property

Private Property Get ISmartTagAction_VerbID( _
                     ByVal SmartTagName As String, _
                     ByVal VerbIndex As Long) As Long

    If (SmartTagName = _
        "urn:schemas-microsoft-com:office:smarttags#PersonName") Then
        ISmartTagAction_VerbID = VerbIndex
    End If
End Property

Private Property Get ISmartTagAction_VerbCaptionFromID( _
                     ByVal VerbID As Long, _
                     ByVal ApplicationName As String, _
                     ByVal LocaleID As Long) As String

    Select Case VerbID
        Case 1
            ISmartTagAction_VerbCaptionFromID = "Custom Action"
    End Select
End Property

Private Property Get ISmartTagAction_VerbNameFromID( _
                     ByVal VerbID As Long) As String

    Select Case VerbID
        Case 1
            ISmartTagAction_VerbNameFromID = "CustomAction"
    End Select
End Property
```

```
Public Sub ISmartTagAction_InvokeVerb( ByVal VerbID As Long, _
          ByVal ApplicationName As String, ByVal Target As Object, _
          ByVal Properties As SmartTagLib.ISmartTagProperties, _
          ByVal Text As String, ByVal XML As String)

    Select Case VerbID
        Case 1
            'Implement functionality here
    End Select
End Sub
```

Tagging HTML Documents

Internet Explorer does not support smart tags out of the box, but you can add custom markup to an HTML document to support smart tags on your Web pages. For this technique to work, you need to make sure that smart tag behavior for Internet Explorer is installed. (The IE smart tag behavior comes with Office.) The following HTML markup shows how to tag HTML documents with smart tags:

```
<HTML xmlns="http://www.w3.org/TR/REC html40"
 xmlns:o = "urn:schemas-microsoft-com:office:office"
 xmlns:categories = "trainingapp#categories">

 <HEAD>
  <TITLE>Smart Tag Sample</TITLE>
  <o:SmartTagType name="category"
   namespaceuri="trainingapp#categories"
   downloadurl="http://trainingapp">
  </o:SmartTagType>

  <OBJECT
   classid ="clsid:38481807-CA0E-42D2-BF39-B33AF135CC4D" id=ieooui>
  </OBJECT>

  <STYLE>
   categories\:* {BEHAVIOR: url(#ieooui)}
  </STYLE>
 </HEAD>

 <BODY>
  <categories:category>Developers</categories:category>
  develop on Office XP.
 </BODY>
</HTML>
```

In the code, you specify the XML namespace for Office and the namespace for your smart tag. Then you declare your smart tag element type. In this case, the element name is *category*, the namespace is *trainingapp#categories*, and a *downloadurl* is specified for any new actions. The next step is to declare an object tag for the IETag factory that enables Internet Explorer to label smart tags. Then you declare a behavior that uses the object you just declared for HTML elements of a certain type. The last step is actually to write your HTML and tag some elements as the specific type you declared in your behavior. Figure 9-7 shows Internet Explorer running the previous HTML page.

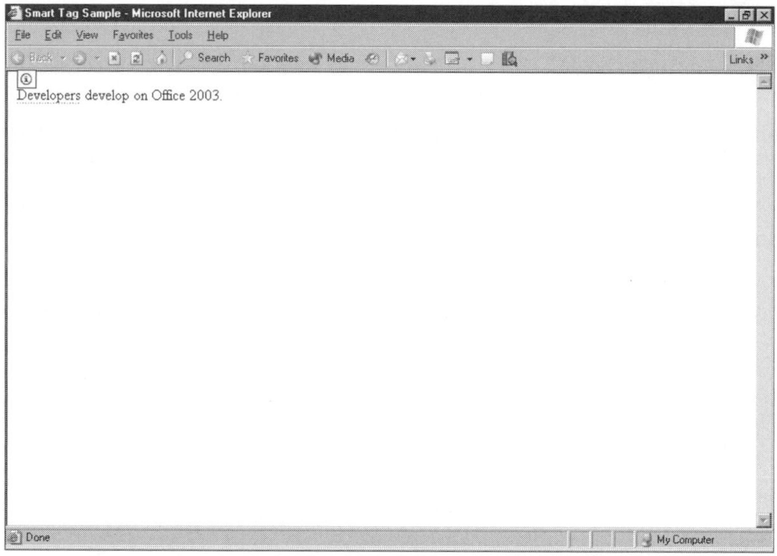

Figure 9-7 Internet Explorer showing smart tags

Building Smart Tags Using .NET

> **Note** You should read the white paper "Building Smart Tags in Microsoft Visual Basic .NET" at *http://msdn.microsoft.com/office* before reading this section. This section includes information adapted from that white paper and also provides additional details.

Building smart tags in .NET is similar to building COM add-ins. The chief difference is that .NET doesn't include a wizard for smart tags, as it does for COM add-ins. You have to create the necessary references, event handlers, and code manually to build your smart tag.

Because the process is so similar, I'll show you one completed smart tag, written in Visual Basic .NET, to help get you started. The code in this section is from the DotNet Smart Tag sample application. In Visual Basic .NET, you create a class library. The smart tag contains a recognizer that recognizes the word *Outlook* and a single action that displays in a message box the information recognized, such as the data type, locale ID, and the text. Here's the code for the recognizer:

```
Imports SmartTagLib
Imports System.Runtime.InteropServices

<ProgId("DotNetSmartTag.Recognizer"), _
GuidAttribute("8981FE26-D112-402e-9A01-06C8A2F01207"), _
ComVisible(True)> Public Class Recognizer
    Implements ISmartTagRecognizer

    <ComRegisterFunction()> Shared Sub Register( _
        ByVal RegKey As String)

        RegSmartTag(RegKey, True)
    End Sub

    <ComUnregisterFunction()> Shared Sub Unregister( _
        ByVal RegKey As String)

        RegSmartTag(RegKey, False)
    End Sub

    'Default Constructor with no arguments
    'Required for COM Interop
    Public Sub New()
    End Sub

    'A substantive description of what the recognizer does.
    Public ReadOnly Property Desc( _
        ByVal LocaleID As Integer) As String _
        Implements SmartTagLib.ISmartTagRecognizer.Desc

        Get
            Return "Sample DotNet Smart Tag"
        End Get
    End Property
```

```
'A short title reflecting what the recognizer does.
Public ReadOnly Property Name( _
    ByVal LocaleID As Integer) As String _
    Implements SmartTagLib.ISmartTagRecognizer.Name

    Get
        Return "DotNet Sample Smart Tag"
    End Get
End Property

'The COM ProgID of the Smart Tag
Public ReadOnly Property ProgId() As String _
    Implements SmartTagLib.ISmartTagRecognizer.ProgId

    Get
        Return "DotNetSmartTag.Recognizer"
    End Get
End Property

'Recognizes terms.
Public Sub Recognize(ByVal strRecText As String, _
    ByVal DataType As SmartTagLib.IF_TYPE, _
    ByVal LocaleID As Integer, _
    ByVal RecognizerSite As SmartTagLib.ISmartTagRecognizerSite) _
    Implements SmartTagLib.ISmartTagRecognizer.Recognize

    Dim position As Integer
    Dim lLength As Integer

    'Remove any ????
    lLength = Len(strRecText)
    If (lLength > 0) Then
        position = InStr(1, strRecText, ChrW(-4))
    Else
        position = 0
    End If

    While (lLength > 0 And position > 0)
        Mid$(strRecText, position, 1) = ""
        lLength = lLength - 1
        If (lLength > 0) Then
            position = InStr(1, strRecText, ChrW(-4))
        Else
            position = 0
        End If
        position = InStr(1, strRecText, ChrW(-4))
    End While

    strRecText = RTrim(strRecText)

    position = InStr(1, strRecText, ChrW(-4))
    If (position > 0) Then
        lLength = Len(strRecText)
        Mid$(strRecText, (lLength - position + 1)) = _
```

```
            Space$(lLength - position + 1)
        strRecText = RTrim(strRecText)
    End If

    If Right(strRecText, 1) = ChrW(13) Then
        strRecText = Left(strRecText, Len(strRecText) - 1)
    End If

    Dim intLocation As Integer = InStr(UCase(strRecText), _
                                       UCase("Outlook"), _
                                       CompareMethod.Binary)
    If intLocation > 0 Then
        Dim stPropBag As ISmartTagProperties = _
                          RecognizerSite.GetNewPropertyBag()
        Dim strPropType As String

        'Determine the data type (as a string)
        Select Case DataType
            Case IF_TYPE.IF_TYPE_CELL
                strPropType = "IF_TYPE_CELL"
            Case IF_TYPE.IF_TYPE_CHAR
                strPropType = "IF_TYPE_CHAR"
            Case IF_TYPE.IF_TYPE_PARA
                strPropType = "IF_TYPE_PARA"
            Case IF_TYPE.IF_TYPE_REGEXP
                strPropType = "IF_TYPE_REGEXP"
            Case IF_TYPE.IF_TYPE_SINGLE_WD
                strPropType = "IF_TYPE_SINGLE_WD"
        End Select

        'Add the data to the propbag
        stPropBag.Write("DataType", strPropType)
        'Add the text so the function can receive it
        stPropBag.Write("Text", strRecText)
        'Add the LocaleID
        stPropBag.Write("LocaleID", LocaleID)
        'Commit the SmartTag
        On Error Resume Next
        RecognizerSite.CommitSmartTag( _
            "urn:thomriz:com#DotNetSmartTag", _
            intLocation, 7, stPropBag)
    End If
End Sub

'The number of smart tag types that this recognizer supports
Public ReadOnly Property SmartTagCount() As Integer _
    Implements SmartTagLib.ISmartTagRecognizer.SmartTagCount

    Get
        Return 1
    End Get
End Property
```

```
    'We have no download URL, so return empty
    Public ReadOnly Property SmartTagDownloadURL( _
        ByVal SmartTagID As Integer) As String _
        Implements SmartTagLib.ISmartTagRecognizer.SmartTagDownloadURL

        Get
            Return ""
        End Get
    End Property

    'The unique IDs of smart tag types the recognizer supports.
    Public ReadOnly Property SmartTagName( _
        ByVal SmartTagID As Integer) As String _
        Implements SmartTagLib.ISmartTagRecognizer.SmartTagName

        Get
            Return "urn:thomriz:com#DotNetSmartTag"
        End Get
    End Property
End Class
```

Notice that the recognizer leverages the built-in COM interoperability features of the .NET platform. Otherwise, the recognizer looks like the standard recognizers we built using Visual Basic 6.0. The only difference is the register and unregister functions included for COM, which we will discuss in the next section. For the action, the code is as follows. (It is in a different class file.)

```
Imports SmartTagLib
Imports System.Runtime.InteropServices

<ProgId("DotNetSmartTag.Action"), _
GuidAttribute("A7253D8D-B8B0-4769-A8BB-65584AC3C9EF"), _
ComVisible(True)> _
Public Class Action
    Implements ISmartTagAction

    Public ReadOnly Property Desc( _
        ByVal LocaleID As Integer) As String _
        Implements SmartTagLib.ISmartTagAction.Desc

        Get
            Return "DotNet Smart Tag Action"
        End Get
    End Property

    Public Sub InvokeVerb(ByVal VerbID As Integer, _
        ByVal ApplicationName As String, _
        ByVal Target As Object, _
        ByVal Properties As SmartTagLib.ISmartTagProperties, _
        ByVal strText As String, ByVal Xml As String) _
        Implements SmartTagLib.ISmartTagAction.InvokeVerb

        Dim strMsg As String = strText
```

```
        Dim i As Short
        For i = 0 To Properties.Count - 1
            strMsg &= vbCrLf & Properties.KeyFromIndex(i)
            strMsg &= "=" & Properties.ValueFromIndex(i)
        Next
        MsgBox(strMsg, , "DotNet Smart Tag")
    End Sub

    Public ReadOnly Property Name( _
        ByVal LocaleID As Integer) As String _
        Implements SmartTagLib.ISmartTagAction.Name

        Get
            Return "DotNet Action"
        End Get
    End Property

    Public ReadOnly Property ProgId() As String _
        Implements SmartTagLib.ISmartTagAction.ProgId

        Get
            Return "DotNetSmartTag.Action"
        End Get
    End Property

    Public ReadOnly Property SmartTagCaption( _
        ByVal SmartTagID As Integer, _
        ByVal LocaleID As Integer) As String _
        Implements SmartTagLib.ISmartTagAction.SmartTagCaption

        Get
            Return "DotNet Smart Tag"
        End Get
    End Property

    Public ReadOnly Property SmartTagCount() As Integer _
        Implements SmartTagLib.ISmartTagAction.SmartTagCount

        Get
            Return 1
        End Get
    End Property

    Public ReadOnly Property SmartTagName( _
        ByVal SmartTagID As Integer) As String _
        Implements SmartTagLib.ISmartTagAction.SmartTagName

        Get
            Return "urn:thomriz:com#DotNetSmartTag"
        End Get
    End Property
```

```
    Public ReadOnly Property VerbCaptionFromID( _
        ByVal VerbID As Integer, _
        ByVal ApplicationName As String, _
        ByVal LocaleID As Integer) As String _
        Implements SmartTagLib.ISmartTagAction.VerbCaptionFromID

        Get
            Return "Show DotNet Smart Tag"
        End Get
    End Property

    Public ReadOnly Property VerbCount( _
        ByVal SmartTagName As String) As Integer _
        Implements SmartTagLib.ISmartTagAction.VerbCount

        Get
            Return 1
        End Get
    End Property

    Public ReadOnly Property VerbID( _
        ByVal SmartTagName As String, _
        ByVal VerbIndex As Integer) As Integer _
        Implements SmartTagLib.ISmartTagAction.VerbID

        Get
            Return 1
        End Get
    End Property

    Public ReadOnly Property VerbNameFromID( _
        ByVal VerbID As Integer) As String _
        Implements SmartTagLib.ISmartTagAction.VerbNameFromID

        Get
            Return "ShowTag"
        End Get
    End Property
End Class
```

Again, the code looks like a standard smart tag action except for the COM interoperability. Building smart tags with .NET is easy because .NET performs all the interoperability work for you.

Automatic Registration with Reflection

One useful function that the sample application called DotNet Smart Tag provides is a function for the smart tag to register itself as a smart tag in the registry when .NET registers the DLL for COM interoperability. You do this through

Reflection, which is the ability of your application to obtain information about itself or other components at run time. When .NET registers the DLL, the code contained in the recognizer's *Register* function fires and runs code that queries the component and places the information that's required to register the component as a smart tag recognizer in the registry. When the .NET component is unregistered, the opposite occurs, and the registry information is removed. The code for this functionality is shown in the following example and is explained more fully in the white paper cited at the beginning of this section.

```
Imports Microsoft.Win32
Imports System.Runtime.InteropServices
Imports System.Reflection
Imports System

Module FileRegistration
    'Registration flag so we know if this registration code
    'has already been executed.  (We only want it to run once.)
    Private fReg As Boolean = False

    Public Sub RegSmartTag( _
        ByVal RegKey As String, _
        ByVal Register As Boolean)

        If Not fReg Then
            OutputMsg("*****  Beginning SmartTag Registration *****")
            OutputMsg(vbTab & "Register=" & Register.ToString())
            OutputMsg("")

            'Main SmartTags Registry Key
            Dim rkeySmartTags As RegistryKey _
                = Registry.CurrentUser.OpenSubKey _
                ("Software\Microsoft\Office\Common\Smart Tag", True)

            'Actions Sub Key
            Dim rkeyActions As RegistryKey _
                = rkeySmartTags.OpenSubKey("Actions", True)

            'Recognizers Sub Key
            Dim rkeyRecognizers As RegistryKey _
                = rkeySmartTags.OpenSubKey("Recognizers", True)

            'Get the current assembly
            Dim reflAssembly As [Assembly] = _
                [Assembly].GetExecutingAssembly()

            'Get all public types for the assembly
            Dim reflTypes As Type() = reflAssembly.GetExportedTypes()
            Dim reflType As Type
```

```
            'Loop through the exported types.
            For Each reflType In reflTypes
                'Get the interfaces to look for the SmartTag interfaces.
                If reflType.IsClass Then  'Make sure that it's a class.
                    Dim reflInterfaces As Type() = _
                        reflType.GetInterfaces()
                    Dim reflInterface As Type

                    For Each reflInterface In reflInterfaces
                        Select Case reflInterface.Name
                            'SmartTag Action Interface
                            Case "ISmartTagAction"
                                HandleReg(reflType, rkeyActions, Register)

                            'SmartTag Recognizer Interface
                            Case "ISmartTagRecognizer"
                                HandleReg(reflType, _
                                          rkeyRecognizers, Register)
                        End Select
                    Next reflInterface
                End If
            Next reflType

            'Done.  Now clean up.
            reflTypes = Nothing
            reflAssembly = Nothing
            rkeyActions.Close()
            rkeyActions = Nothing
            rkeyRecognizers.Close()
            rkeyRecognizers = Nothing
            rkeySmartTags.Close()
            rkeySmartTags = Nothing

            fReg = True '<-- Set our shared variable to True

            OutputMsg("")
            OutputMsg("*****  Completed SmartTag Registration *****")
            OutputMsg("")
        End If
    End Sub

    Private Sub HandleReg( _
        ByVal sysType As Type, _
        ByVal RegKey As RegistryKey, _
        ByVal Register As Boolean)
        'Code to actually do the registration of the SmartTag.
        'INPUTS:
        '   sysType:  Type for the class that's getting registered.
        '   RegKey:   RegKey to register the class in.
        '             Should be the Actions or Recognizers Key.
        '   Register: True to register, False to Unregister.
```

```
    'Get the type of the GuidAttribute class.  We'll need this.
    Dim typGUIDAttr As Type = GetType(GuidAttribute)

    'Check to see if the GuidAttribute is defined on the class.
    If Attribute.IsDefined(sysType, typGUIDAttr) Then
        Dim attrValue As GuidAttribute

        'Get the GuidAttribute.
        attrValue = CType(Attribute.GetCustomAttribute( _
                        sysType, typGUIDAttr), GuidAttribute)

        'Get the string representation of the GUID.
        Dim strGuidVal As String = "{" & attrValue.Value & "}"

        If Register Then
            Try
                Dim newKey As RegistryKey _
                    = RegKey.CreateSubKey(strGuidVal)
                newKey.SetValue("Assembly", _
                                sysType.Assembly.FullName)
                newKey.SetValue("Type", sysType.FullName)
                OutputMsg(sysType.Name & _
                          " registered with SmartTags successfully")
            Catch
                OutputMsg("Failed to register " & _
                          sysType.Name & " with SmartTags")
                OutputMsg(Err.GetType.Name & ":" & Err.Description)
            End Try
        Else
            Try
                RegKey.DeleteSubKey(strGuidVal, False)
                OutputMsg(sysType.Name & _
                          " unregistered with SmartTags successfully")
            Catch
                OutputMsg("Failed to unregister " &
                          sysType.Name & " with SmartTags")
                OutputMsg(Err.GetType.Name & ":" & Err.Description)
            End Try
        End If
    Else
        'If we don't find the guid attribute,
        'write to the system console.
        OutputMsg("Could not register " & _
                  sysType.Name & " as SmartTag")
        OutputMsg("GUID Attribute not found on class")
    End If
End Sub

Private Sub OutputMsg(ByVal Msg As String)
    'Use DEBUG conditional compile constant to only output
```

```
        'when compiling the DEBUG version.
#If DEBUG Then
        System.Console.WriteLine(Msg)
#End If
    End Sub
End Module
```

Testing Your Smart Tag in .NET

When you test your smart tag, be sure to set macro security in your Office application to Medium—otherwise, the smart tag will not work. After you launch an Office application such as Word, you will then be prompted to enable or disable a DLL called mscoree.dll. If you are running Office 2003, you will not be prompted for .NET smart tags. This DLL is the DLL that contains the common language runtime (CLR). Be sure to enable this macro. You can then type the word *Outlook* wherever you want, and the smart tag should work as shown in Figure 9-8.

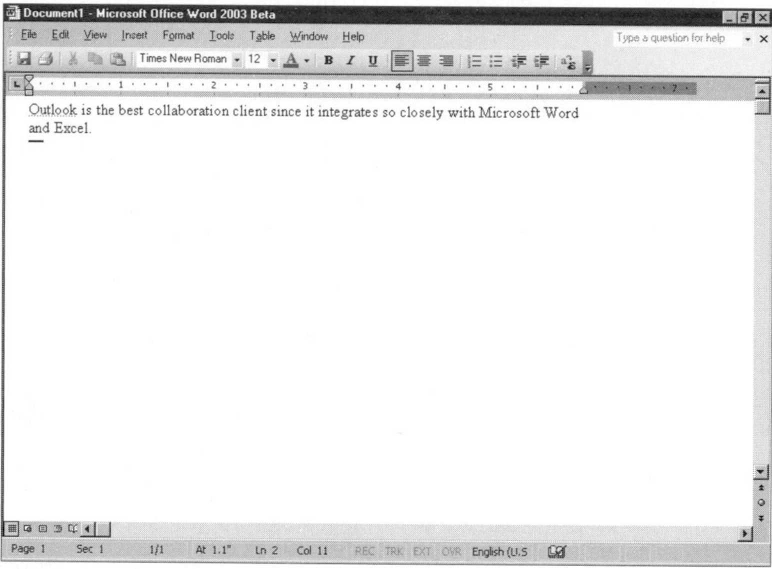

Figure 9-8 The .NET smart tag working in Word

Changes in Smart Tags in Office 2003

Smart tags have been significantly enhanced in Office 2003. First and foremost, PowerPoint, Access, and the new Research task panes feature in Office 2003 have smart tag support. Smart tags also have new object model capabilities. I'll describe the object model changes later in the chapter. First, we'll look at some of the other changes.

Universal Exception and Supplement Lists

If you've ever typed *MSN* into a Word document that has the financial symbol smart tag enabled, you know that Word recognizes MSN as a stock symbol. This behavior is probably not what you want on your client machines, so Office 2003 supports a universal exception list in which you specify terms that should never be recognized by certain smart tag recognizers. You can also turn off recognizers through the user interface, as shown in Figure 9-9.

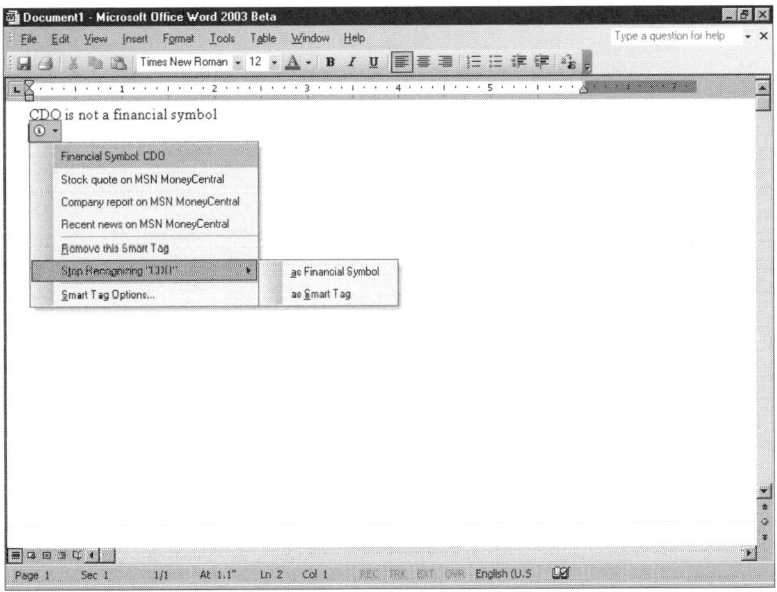

Figure 9-9 Turning off smart tag recognition through the Office interface

When you disable recognition through the user interface, a file named ignore.xml is created in the Documents and Settings*username*\\Application Data\\Microsoft\\Smart Tags\\Exceptions folder. You can create your own exception list and place it in Program Files\\Common Files\\Microsoft Shared\\Smart Tag\\Exceptions. You can direct Office to look in other directories for an exception list by creating a string value in the registry at HKCU\\Software\\Microsoft \\Office\\Common\\Smart Tag\\exceptionListDirectory. An exception list is simply an XML document that describes your exceptions. The following shows the format of an XML exception list. This exception list ignores CDO and MSN as stock symbols and ignores CDOEX as an overall smart tag.

```
<ST:smarttagsupplementallist xmlns:ST="urn:schemas-microsoft-com:smart-
tags:list">
    <ST:Item>
        <ST:String>Frank Murphy</ST:String>
        <ST:SmartTagTypeList>
            <ST:SmartTagType>
                urn:schemas-microsoft-com:office:smarttags#personname
            </ST:SmartTagType>
        </ST:SmartTagTypeList>
    </ST:Item>
    <ST:Item>
        <ST:String>ACME</ST:String>
        <ST:SmartTagTypeList>
            <ST:SmartTagType>
                urn:schemas-microsoft-com:office:smarttags#date
            </ST:SmartTagType>
        </ST:SmartTagTypeList>
    </ST:Item>
</ST:smarttagsupplementallist>
```

As you can see, you list the term and the recognizer that you want to have ignore the term as a smart tag. If you do not pass the recognizer in the *SmartTagType* node, all smart tags will ignore the term.

In addition to a universal exception list, you might want a universal supplemental list in case Office does not tag words that you know should be smart tags. For example, Office might not tag some names that you know are valid, which means you can't quickly send e-mail to these people because they are not recognized as smart tags. For example, if a name has a unique spelling or is a unique name, Office might not have it in its default list of names. To create a supplemental list, you use a format similar to the exception list. Instead of tagging the list as an exception, however, you tag it in the first node of the XML document as a supplemental list. You store your supplemental lists in the same directories as your exception lists. The following supplemental list adds Tom Rizzo as a person and ACME Corporation as a date to show you how you can add any sort of term to a recognizer:

```
<ST:smarttagsupplementallist xmlns:ST="urn:schemas-microsoft-com:smart-
tags:list">
    <ST:Item>
        <ST:String>Tom Rizzo</ST:String>
        <ST:SmartTagTypeList>
            <ST:SmartTagType>
                urn:schemas-microsoft-com:office:smarttags#personname
            </ST:SmartTagType>
        </ST:SmartTagTypeList>
    </ST:Item>
```

```
    <ST:Item>
        <ST:String>ACME</ST:String>
        <ST:SmartTagTypeList>
            <ST:SmartTagType>
                urn:schemas-microsoft-com:office:smarttags#date
            </ST:SmartTagType>
        </ST:SmartTagTypeList>
    </ST:Item>
</ST:smarttagsupplementallist>
```

MOSTL Improvements

Next I'll describe some of the improvements to MOSTL in Office 2003.

Localization Support

The first big improvement in MOSTL is support for localization. You can specify in any of the tags in MOSTL the LCID attribute and pass in a comma-delimited list of languages that are supported. If you specify an LCID in a parent element, all children elements will use that LCID. If no LCID is specified, all languages are assumed to be supported.

elementaction Tag

Another big improvement in MOSTL is the addition of the *elementaction* tag. Using this tag, you can add auto text for a smart tag or add XML fragments or documents. The following MOSTL file shows how to use the new *elementaction* capabilities.

```
<FL:smarttaglist xmlns:FL="urn:schemas-microsoft-com:smarttags:list">
  <FL:name>Sample</FL:name>
  <FL:lcid>1033</FL:lcid>
  <FL:description>A sample XML file that recognizes new elementaction</
FL:description>
  <FL:lastcheckpoint>100</FL:lastcheckpoint>
  <FL:lastupdate>5123942</FL:lastupdate>
  <FL:updateurl></FL:updateurl>
  <FL:updateable>false</FL:updateable>
  <FL:updatefrequency>10080</FL:updatefrequency>
  <FL:autoupdate>false</FL:autoupdate>
  <FL:smarttag type="urn:schemas-xml-com:document#fragment">
    <FL:caption>DocFrag Rec</FL:caption>
    <FL:terms>
      <FL:termlist>
        DocFrag
      </FL:termlist>
    </FL:terms>
    <FL:actions>
    <FL:action id="InsFrag">
      <FL:caption>Insert fragment</FL:caption>
```

```
        <FL:elementaction>
          <FL:insertdocfragment>c:\Lists\docfrag.xml</FL:insertdocfragment>
        </FL:elementaction>
    </FL:action>
    <FL:action id="InsXML">
      <FL:caption>Insert XML</FL:caption>
        <FL:elementaction>
          <FL:insertXML>"<contact>Tom Rizzo</contact>"</FL:insertXML>
        </FL:elementaction>
    </FL:action>

    <FL:action id="InsAutoText">
      <FL:caption>Insert AutoText</FL:caption>
        <FL:elementaction>
          <FL:insertautotextentry>Autotext:</FL:insertautotextentry>
        </FL:elementaction>
    </FL:action>

    </FL:actions>
  </FL:smarttag>
</FL:smarttaglist>
```

Cascading Menus

Another major improvement in MOSTL is support for cascading menus in smart tags. (You will see how to support cascading menus programmatically later in this chapter when we implement some custom actions.) MOSTL provides cascading menus by using a triple slash (///) in the caption property. The following sample MOSTL file displays cascading menus when you type the term *cascade* in a smart tag host. Figure 9-10 shows a cascading menu for a smart tag.

```
<FL:smarttaglist xmlns:FL="urn:schemas-microsoft-com:smarttags:list">
  <FL:name>Sample</FL:name>
  <FL:lcid>1033</FL:lcid>
  <FL:description>A sample XML file that recognizes cascade</FL:description>
  <FL:lastcheckpoint>100</FL:lastcheckpoint>
  <FL:lastupdate>5123942</FL:lastupdate>
  <FL:updateurl></FL:updateurl>
  <FL:updateable>false</FL:updateable>
  <FL:updatefrequency>10080</FL:updatefrequency>
  <FL:autoupdate>false</FL:autoupdate>
  <FL:smarttag type="urn:schemas-microsoft-com:office:smarttag#cascade">
    <FL:caption>Cascading Menus</FL:caption>
    <FL:terms>
      <FL:termlist>
        cascade
      </FL:termlist>
    </FL:terms>
    <FL:actions>
    <FL:action id="cascading">
      <FL:url>http://localhost/</FL:url>
```

```
                        <FL:caption>Cascade Menu///Home</FL:caption>
    </FL:action>
    <FL:action id="second menu">
      <FL:url>http://localhost/</FL:url>
                        <FL:caption>Cascade Menu///Option 2</FL:caption>
    </FL:action>
    <FL:action id="third menu">
      <FL:url>http://localhost/</FL:url>
                        <FL:caption>Cascade Menu///Option 3</FL:caption>
    </FL:action>
    <FL:action id="cascading2">
      <FL:url>http://localhost/</FL:url>
                        <FL:caption>Cascade Menu 2///Home</FL:caption>
    </FL:action>
    <FL:action id="second menu2">
      <FL:url>http://localhost/</FL:url>
                        <FL:caption>Cascade Menu 2///Option 2</FL:caption>
    </FL:action>
    <FL:action id="third menu2">
      <FL:url>http://localhost/</FL:url>
                        <FL:caption>Cascade Menu 2///Option 3</FL:caption>
    </FL:action>
    </FL:actions>
  </FL:smarttag>
</FL:smarttaglist>
```

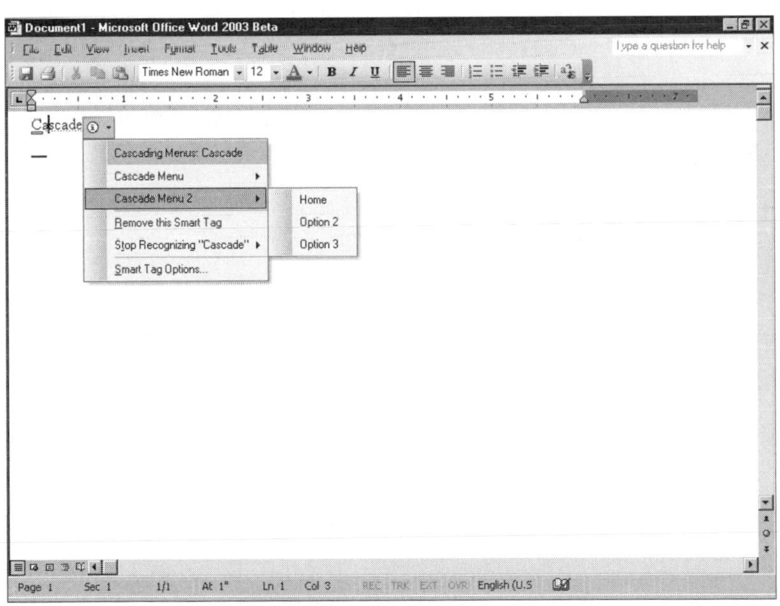

Figure 9-10 Cascading menus in smart tags

Running an Action on Recognition

MOSTL now has the ability to automatically run an action on recognition of a term. You might want to take advantage of this feature to launch a Web browser that points the user to a particular Web site when the user types a particular term in a document. The following sample shows how to use the *runAction* term to run an action on recognition. The sample launches the browser to the Microsoft Press Web site when you type the term *Exchange* or *Outlook*.

```
<FL:smarttaglist xmlns:FL="urn:schemas-microsoft-com:smarttags:list"
xmlns:o="http://schemas.microsoft.com/office/smarttags/2003/mostl">
  <FL:name>Sample</FL:name>
  <FL:lcid>1033</FL:lcid>
  <FL:description>A Sample RunAction</FL:description>
  <FL:lastcheckpoint>100</FL:lastcheckpoint>
  <FL:lastupdate>5123942</FL:lastupdate>
  <FL:updateurl></FL:updateurl>
  <FL:updateable>false</FL:updateable>
  <FL:updatefrequency>10080</FL:updatefrequency>
  <FL:autoupdate>false</FL:autoupdate>
  <FL:smarttag type="urn:schemas-ms-com:thomriz#auto">
    <FL:caption>Autoaction Recognizer</FL:caption>
    <FL:terms>
      <FL:termlistwithprops>
        <FL:prop o:runAction="MSPress"/>
        <FL:t>Exchange</FL:t>
        <FL:t>Outlook</FL:t>
      </FL:termlistwithprops>
    </FL:terms>
    <FL:actions>
    <FL:action id="MSPress">
      <FL:url>http://mspress.microsoft.com/</FL:url>
                        <FL:caption>MSPress website</FL:caption>
    </FL:action>
    </FL:actions>
  </FL:smarttag>
</FL:smarttaglist>
```

Property Page Support

Building on the previous sample, you can see how to add a property page to your smart tag via the new *PropertyPage* tag. This tag takes a URL where you provide more information about the smart tag. Unfortunately, you cannot provide customization of your smart tag from your Web application using this property unless your Web page writes out configuration information to a location and your smart tag can be configured dynamically. Figure 9-11 shows the new Properties button in Word.

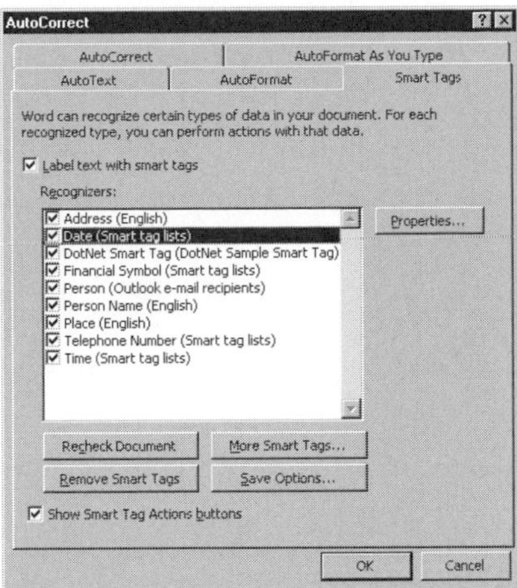

Figure 9-11 The new Properties button on the Smart Tags tab of the AutoCorrect dialog box in Word

```
<FL:smarttaglist xmlns:FL="urn:schemas-microsoft-com:smarttags:list"
xmlns:o="http://schemas.microsoft.com/office/smarttags/2003/mostl">
  <FL:name>Sample Proppage</FL:name>
  <FL:lcid>1033</FL:lcid>
  <FL:description>A Sample RunAction with Proppage</FL:description>
  <FL:lastcheckpoint>100</FL:lastcheckpoint>
  <FL:lastupdate>5123942</FL:lastupdate>
  <FL:updateurl></FL:updateurl>
  <FL:updateable>false</FL:updateable>
  <FL:updatefrequency>10080</FL:updatefrequency>
  <FL:autoupdate>false</FL:autoupdate>
  <FL:smarttag type="urn:schemas-ms-com:thomriz#autorunwithproppage">
    <FL:PropertyPage>http://localhost/myproppage</FL:PropertyPage>
    <FL:caption>Autoaction Recognizer with Proppage</FL:caption>
    <FL:terms>
      <FL:termlistwithprops>
        <FL:prop o:runAction="MSPress"/>
        <FL:t>Exchange</FL:t>
        <FL:t>Outlook</FL:t>
      </FL:termlistwithprops>
    </FL:terms>
    <FL:actions>
    <FL:action id="MSPress">
      <FL:url>http://mspress.microsoft.com/</FL:url>
                         <FL:caption>MSPress website</FL:caption>
    </FL:action>
    </FL:actions>
  </FL:smarttag>
</FL:smarttaglist>
```

New Types of Smart Tags: Expiring, Transitory, and Temporary

To support more diverse smart tag scenarios, Office includes three new types of smart tags. The first is an *expiring* smart tag. Say you have a term that you want recognized, but only for a limited time. For example, you might want to garner feedback on a document titled Charney v. Charney but you know that the feedback won't be valid after a certain date. You can add a property called *exp* to your term list. To this property you pass the year, month, day, hour, and minute (for example, 2003:10:01:10:00, which sets an expiration for the year 2003, month 10, day 01, hour 10, minute 00). The time is set in a 24-hour clock format. For example, you can pass just 2003:10:01, which expires the recognition of the term on October 1, 2003, right at midnight. The following sample expires the term *Charney v. Charney* using this new property:

```
<FL:smarttaglist xmlns:FL="urn:schemas-microsoft-com:smarttags:list"
xmlns:o="http://schemas.microsoft.com/office/smarttags/2003/mostl">
  <FL:name>Sample Expiry</FL:name>
  <FL:lcid>1033</FL:lcid>
  <FL:description>A Sample Expiry Action</FL:description>
  <FL:lastcheckpoint>100</FL:lastcheckpoint>
  <FL:lastupdate>5123942</FL:lastupdate>
  <FL:updateurl></FL:updateurl>
  <FL:updateable>false</FL:updateable>
  <FL:updatefrequency>10080</FL:updatefrequency>
  <FL:autoupdate>false</FL:autoupdate>
  <FL:smarttag type="urn:schemas-ms-com:sample#exp">
    <FL:caption>Expiring Recognizer</FL:caption>
    <FL:terms>
      <FL:termlistwithprops>
        <FL:prop o:exp="2002:12:04:13:14"/>
        <FL:t>Charney v. Charney</FL:t>
      </FL:termlistwithprops>
    </FL:terms>
    <FL:actions>
    <FL:action id="Legal">
      <FL:url>http://Legalnet</FL:url>
                      <FL:caption>LegalNet website</FL:caption>
    </FL:action>
    </FL:actions>
  </FL:smarttag>
</FL:smarttaglist>
```

The second new type of smart tag is the *transitory* smart tag, which is useful when a multiple word phrase is recognized as a smart tag and that the smart tag disappears as users type in the paragraph. For example, say you recognize the word *transitory* and also the phrase *transitory recognition*. If a user pauses long enough after typing *transitory* and then types *recognition*, both the word and the phrase will be smart tagged. You might prefer that the smart tag underlining disappear as soon as the user starts typing after the word *transitory* so the application can see whether the user is typing *recognition* or something else after *transitory*. To use transitory smart tags, you add the *ls*—short for lifespan—property to your *termlist* element, as shown in the following code:

```
<FL:smarttaglist xmlns:FL="urn:schemas-microsoft-com:smarttags:list"
xmlns:o="http://schemas.microsoft.com/office/smarttags/2003/mostl">
  <FL:name>Sample</FL:name>
  <FL:lcid>1033</FL:lcid>
  <FL:description>A Sample TransAction</FL:description>
  <FL:lastcheckpoint>100</FL:lastcheckpoint>
  <FL:lastupdate>5123942</FL:lastupdate>
  <FL:updateurl></FL:updateurl>
  <FL:updateable>false</FL:updateable>
  <FL:updatefrequency>10080</FL:updatefrequency>
  <FL:autoupdate>false</FL:autoupdate>
  <FL:smarttag type="urn:schemas-ms-com:thomriz#transitory">
    <FL:caption>Transitory recognizer</FL:caption>
    <FL:terms>
      <FL:termlistwithprops>
        <FL:prop o:ls="trans"/>
        <FL:t>Trans</FL:t>
        <FL:t>Trans Recognition</FL:t>
        <FL:t>Transitory</FL:t>
        <FL:t>Transitory Recognition</FL:t>
        <FL:t>Recognition</FL:t>
      </FL:termlistwithprops>
    </FL:terms>
    <FL:actions>
    <FL:action id="Link">
      <FL:url>http://Localhost</FL:url>
                    <FL:caption>Link to website</FL:caption>
    </FL:action>
    </FL:actions>
  </FL:smarttag>
</FL:smarttaglist>
```

The third new type of smart tag is the *temporary* smart tag. Regular smart tags can be saved and embedded in documents, but temporary smart tags cannot be saved, which stops people from accidentally sending sensitive information as a smart tag outside an organization. To make a temporary smart tag, you just add an *ls* property to your *termlist* and set that property to *temp*, as shown in the following code:

```
<FL:smarttaglist xmlns:FL="urn:schemas-microsoft-com:smarttags:list"
xmlns:o="http://schemas.microsoft.com/office/smarttags/2003/mostl">
  <FL:name>Sample</FL:name>
  <FL:lcid>1033</FL:lcid>
  <FL:description>A Sample TempAction</FL:description>
  <FL:lastcheckpoint>100</FL:lastcheckpoint>
  <FL:lastupdate>5123942</FL:lastupdate>
  <FL:updateurl></FL:updateurl>
```

```
  <FL:updateable>false</FL:updateable>
  <FL:updatefrequency>10080</FL:updatefrequency>
  <FL:autoupdate>false</FL:autoupdate>
  <FL:smarttag type="urn:schemas-ms-com:thomriz#temp">
    <FL:caption>Temporary recognizer</FL:caption>
    <FL:terms>
      <FL:termlistwithprops>
        <FL:prop o:ls="temp"/>
        <FL:t>Temp</FL:t>
      </FL:termlistwithprops>
    </FL:terms>
    <FL:actions>
    <FL:action id="Link">
      <FL:url>http://localhost</FL:url>
                      <FL:caption>Link to website</FL:caption>
    </FL:action>
    </FL:actions>
  </FL:smarttag>
</FL:smarttaglist>
```

Hiding the Smart Tag Underlining in the User Interface

Sometimes you might not want the smart tag underlining to appear in the user interface. Suppose you receive a large document with a section that is known to be a recognized term. Rather than have the entire section underlined in purple, you can hide the user interface for smart tags. The icon for the smart tag will appear, but the purple underline will not. You can set this option by using the *ShowSmartTagIndicator* tag and setting it to *False*. By default, or by setting this tag to *True*, the purple underline will appear. Here's a sample that uses this tag:

```
<FL:smarttaglist xmlns:FL="urn:schemas-microsoft-com:smarttags:list">
  <FL:name>NoUI</FL:name>
  <FL:lcid>1033,0</FL:lcid>
  <FL:description>This shows how to not show ST UI</FL:description>
  <FL:smarttag type="urn:schemas-microsoft-com:office:smarttags#NoUI">
    <FL:PropertyPage>http://office.microsoft.com</FL:PropertyPage>
    <FL:caption>NoUI Smart Tag</FL:caption>
    <FL:terms>
      <FL:termlist>NoUI</FL:termlist>
    </FL:terms>
    <FL:actions>
      <FL:action id="NoUIAction">
        <FL:caption>This is no UI</FL:caption>
        <FL:ShowSmartTagIndicator>False</FL:ShowSmartTagIndicator>
        <FL:url>http://noui</FL:url>
      </FL:action>
    </FL:actions>
  </FL:smarttag>
</FL:smarttaglist>
```

Regular Expression Support

A welcome improvement in MOSTL is the addition of regular expression/context-free grammar support. The regular expression support in MOSTL is similar to regular expressions in PERL. The regular expression rules are too complex to explain here, but you can find the PERL regular expression documentation at *http://www.perldoc.com/perl5.6/pod/perlre.html*. The date, phone, and time MOSTL files included with Office are good examples of how regular expressions are used in MOSTL. Here is another sample, which uses regular expressions to match *Customer ID: some number* or *Customer ID some number*. It passes the customer ID along with the query string to a Web page to look up the customer.

```
<FL:smarttaglist xmlns:FL="urn:schemas-microsoft-
com:smarttags:list" xmlns:o="urn:schemas-microsoft-com:office:office">
  <FL:name>Customer IDs</FL:name>
  <FL:lcid>1033,0</FL:lcid>
  <FL:description>
    Recognizes Customer IDs in format Customer ID: 123 or Customer ID 123
  </FL:description>
  <FL:moreinfourl>http://yourwebsite</FL:moreinfourl>
  <FL:updateable>false</FL:updateable>
  <FL:smarttag type="urn:schemas-microsoft-com:Customers#CustomerID">
    <FL:caption>Regular Expression for Customer IDs</FL:caption>
    <FL:re>
      <FL:exp>
        <FL:prop o:runAction="CustomerID:openInIE" CustomerID="$1" />
        Customer:*\s*ID*:*\s*(\d+)
      </FL:exp>
    </FL:re>
    <FL:actions>
      <FL:action id="CustomerID:openInIE">
        <FL:url>
          http://localhost/somepage.asp?CustomerID={PROP:CUSTOMERID}
        </FL:url>
        <FL:caption>&amp;CustomerID///Open &amp;Customer...</FL:caption>
      </FL:action>
    </FL:actions>
  </FL:smarttag>
</FL:smarttaglist>
```

You can also put the regular expression in an includes file, as the following code shows:

```
<FL:smarttag type="urn:schemas:Microsoft.com#myre>
    <FL:includefile>C:\myre\re.xml</FL:includefile>
⋮
```

Context-free grammar (CFG) is grammar that follows rules you set out in your MOSTL file. Because you can set a number of options for CFG, I'll refer you to the smart tag SDK. However, here is an example of CFG in a MOSTL file. This sample recognizes emoticons in your documents and links to an image.

```
<FL:smarttaglist xmlns:FL="urn:schemas-microsoft-com:smarttags:list">
  <FL:name>CFG Example emoticon</FL:name>
  <FL:lcid>1033</FL:lcid>
  <FL:description>This recognizer recognizes emoticons</FL:description>
  <FL:moreinfourl>http://microsoft.com</FL:moreinfourl>
  <FL:lastcheckpoint>1</FL:lastcheckpoint>
  <FL:lastupdate>4123942</FL:lastupdate>
  <FL:updateable>false</FL:updateable>
  <FL:updatefrequency>10080</FL:updatefrequency>
  <FL:autoupdate>false</FL:autoupdate>
  <FL:smarttag type="urn:schemas-microsoft-com:tools#smiley">
    <FL:caption>Emoticon Recognizer</FL:caption>
    <FL:cfg topRule="smiley">
      <FL:rule name="smiley">
        <FL:ruleref ref="eyes"/>
        <FL:ruleref ref="nose"/>
        <FL:ruleref ref="mouth"/>
      </FL:rule>

      <FL:rule name="eyes">
        <FL:l>
          <FL:p>:</FL:p>
          <FL:p>=</FL:p>
          <FL:p>8</FL:p>
          <FL:p>;</FL:p>
        </FL:l>
      </FL:rule>

      <FL:rule name="nose">
        <FL:o>
          <FL:l>
            <FL:p>-</FL:p>
            <FL:p>^</FL:p>
          </FL:l>
        </FL:o>
      </FL:rule>

      <FL:rule name="mouth">
        <FL:l>
          <FL:p>)</FL:p>
          <FL:p>|</FL:p>
          <FL:p>(</FL:p>
        </FL:l>
      </FL:rule>
    </FL:cfg>

    <FL:actions>
      <FL:action id="Smile!">
        <FL:url>http://localhost/smile.gif</FL:url>
        <FL:caption>Smile!</FL:caption>
      </FL:action>
    </FL:actions>
  </FL:smarttag>
</FL:smarttaglist>
```

Support for Arbitrary Properties in Items

The last enhancement to MOSTL that I'll discuss is the ability to add arbitrary properties to your items in a list of terms. The following MOSTL file shows how to do this using the *prop* tag:

```
<FL:smarttaglist xmlns:FL="urn:schemas-microsoft-com:smarttags:list"
xmlns:o="urn:schemas-microsoft-com:office:office">
  <FL:name>First Names</FL:name>
  <FL:lcid>1033,0</FL:lcid>
  <FL:description>Recognizes a few first names.</FL:description>
  <FL:updateable>false</FL:updateable>
  <FL:smarttag type="urn:schemas-microsoft-com:office:smarttags#firstName">
    <FL:caption>First Name</FL:caption>
    <FL:terms>
      <FL:termlistwithprops>
        <FL:prop RecognizedByMOSTLList="True" />
        <FL:t>Bob</FL:t>
        <FL:t>Sally</FL:t>
        <FL:t>Mary</FL:t>
      </FL:termlistwithprops>
    </FL:terms>
  </FL:smarttag>
</FL:smarttaglist>
```

Object Model Improvements for Smart Tags

In addition to the MOSTL improvements, version 2 of the smart tag object model has been upgraded. The main differences between version 1 and version 2 of the object model are additional capabilities using new interfaces. Version 2 is backward-compatible with version 1, so you can build version 1 smart tags using the new object model or upgrade existing smart tags to version 2 without breaking applications. The following sections describe the enhancements to the smart tag object model. All of the capabilities you saw in MOSTL files can be implemented in smart tag DLLs as well.

ISmartTagRecognizer2 Interface

Some additions to smart tags, such as property pages and better localization support, require updates to the recognizer interface. For this reason, version 2.0 of the library includes an *ISmartTagRecognizer2* interface. If you implement this interface in your smart tag, the smart tag will ignore an implementation of the *ISmartTagRecognizer* interface. Table 9-7 lists the changes in the *ISmartTagRecognizer2* interface

Table 9-7 Changes in the *ISmartTagRecognizer2* Interface

Method or Property	Description
DisplayPropertyPage	A method that takes the smart tag ID and the locale ID. In this method, you write code to display a property page for your smart tag so users can customize it or obtain more information about it.
PropertyPage	A Boolean property that takes the smart tag ID and locale ID and returns a value indicating whether the smart tag supports a property page. If you return *False*, the Properties dialog box in the Office applications for the smart tag will be disabled.
Recognize2	A method that recognizes the terms in the document. It passes six parameters. The first is a string that is the text that should be recognized. The second is an enumeration specifying the data type for the text. For example, the enumeration can specify whether the text is sent one character at a time or as a word, or is an Excel cell. The third parameter is the locale ID of the text. The fourth parameter is a *RecognizerSite2* object that allows you to interact with the smart tag host. (The *RecognizerSite2* object is described later in this chapter.) The fifth parameter is the name of the application as a string, such as *word.application.11*. The final parameter is the token list as an *ISmartTagTokenList* collection. This collection type is explained later in the chapter.
SmartTagInitalize	A method that is called when your smart tag is initializing for the first time. It takes the application name as a string. This method allows you to do any initialization work you need to do for your smart tag, such as loading data or initializing variables.

ISmartTagAction2 Interface

To support some of the enhancements for smart tag actions such as dynamic caption naming and hiding smart tag user interface indicators, you should use the new *ISmartTagAction2* interface for your action DLLs. Table 9-8 describes the elements of this interface.

Table 9-8 Elements of the *ISmartTagAction2* Interface

Element	Description
InvokeVerb2	A method that is called when a verb is invoked. The method allows you to implement the functionality for that verb. The method is passed seven parameters. The first is the VerbID. The second is the application name of the host, such as *word.application.11*. The third is an object that is the application-specific object responsible for calling the action. In Excel, this is a *Cell* object, and in Word, this is a *Range* object. The next parameter is the property bag passed by the recognizer or by the action itself. The next parameter is the text of the smart tag. The sixth parameter is an XML representation of the smart tag. The final parameter is the locale ID.
IsCaptionDynamic	A Boolean property used for dynamic smart tag action naming. For example, you might want to change the caption of an action on the basis of a number of factors. Smart tag hosts use this property to determine whether your action is dynamic. This property is passed the VerbID, the application name, and the locale ID. From these parameters, you can return *True* if your verb caption is dynamic or *False* if it is not.
ShowSmartTagIndicator	A Boolean property that specifies whether to show the smart tag underlining. This property is passed the VerbID, the application name, and the locale ID. Passing back *True* shows the underlining; *False* does not.
SmartTagInitialize	A method that allows you to do any initialization for your actions. The method is passed the application name as a string.
VerbCaptionFromID2	A string value that specifies the caption to use for your action in the Actions drop-down list. This call passes seven parameters. The first is the VerbID, which is identified by the VerbID that is the unique identifier for the verb. The second parameter is the application name of the smart tag host. The third parameter is the locale ID. The fourth parameter is the properties set by the recognizer as a *ISmartTagProperties* collection. The fifth parameter is the text recognized by the recognizer. The sixth parameter is the smart tag as an XML string. The seventh parameter is the target, such as an Excel *Cell* object or Word *Range* object.

ISmartRecognizerSite2 Interface

To support passing the new interfaces when you commit smart tags, the *ISmartTagRecognizerSite* interface has been updated to the *ISmartTagRecognizerSite2* interface. Table 9-9 explains the enhancements to this interface.

Table 9-9 Enhancements to the *ISmartTagRecognizerSite2* Interface

Method	Description
CommitSmartTag2	Creates a new smart tag in the host. You must pass four parameters to this method. The first is the smart tag type string, which must be in the format *namespaceURI#tag-name*. The second is an integer value that indicates the location at which to start the smart tag in the text. The underlining in Word for the smart tag will begin at this location. The next parameter is an integer that indicates the number of characters the smart tag will span. The final parameter is a property bag object that you want to include with the smart tag.

ISmartTagToken Interface

To support localization and easier word breaking, the smart tag 2.0 library can tokenize input so that you can implement multilingual smart tags. The *ISmartTagToken*, *ISmartTagTokenList*, and *ISmartTagTokenProperties* interfaces work together to support tokenization of input. Table 9-10 shows the *ISmartTagToken* interface's methods and properties, which represent an individual token of input.

Table 9-10 Elements of the *ISmartTagToken* Interface

Element	Description
Length	A long property that returns the length of the token.
Properties	An *ISmartTagTokenProperties* collection for arbitrary properties on the token.
Start	The position in the range of text at which the token started. This property is a long value.
Text	A string value that is the text of the token.

ISmartTagTokenList Collection

ISmartTagTokenList is a collection of *ISmartTagToken* objects. Table 9-11 lists the properties and methods for this collection.

Table 9-11 Elements of the *ISmartTagTokenList* Collection

Element	Description
Count	Returns the number of tokens in the list.
Item	Takes the index of the token as a number and returns the *ISmartTagToken* object that corresponds to that index.

ISmartTagTokenProperties Collection

The *ISmartTagTokenProperties* collection is a property bag for your tokens. It allows you to save arbitrary properties on your token for your application's custom use. Table 9-12 describes the elements of the *ISmartTagTokenProperties* collection.

Table 9-12 Elements of the *ISmartTagTokenProperties* Collection

Element	Description
Count	Returns the number of properties in the collection.
KeyFromIndex	Returns a string for the key of the specified property, based on a numbered index that you pass. For example, if you pass 1 to this method, the key is for the first custom property in the property bag.
Read	Passes the value associated with a specific key that you pass.
ValueFromIndex	Passes back the value of a property that's based on an index into the collection that you pass.

Reloading Recognizers and Actions Without Restarting

After installing a smart tag, the user must restart the smart tag host to use that smart tag. This is not ideal for the user experience. Also, users might not know that Outlook runs an instance of Word when they are editing e-mail, and they might not shut down Word completely. If they don't, the new smart tag won't load.

To solve this problem, we now have a *ReloadAll* method on the Word *Application* object's *SmartTagTypes* collection. This method reloads all smart tags in Word.

Deployment Improvements in Smart Tags

While you can still register smart tags under HKCU, you can now also register smart tags under HKLM using the same path—for example, HKLM\Software\Microsoft\Office\Common\Smart Tag. By registering under HKLM, you can make your smart tag available to all users of a computer rather than only the user who installed the smart tag. This registration option makes deploying a smart tag easier when multiple users work on a single machine. Plus, Office copies your smart tag registration from HKLM to HKCU automatically. You can then store customization data for your smart tag for individual users under HKCU.

Disabling Smart Tags for Individual Office Applications

Another addition to smart tag deployment is the ability to disable either a recognizer or an action DLL, depending on the Office application. You can even completely hide your actions or your recognizer in the user interface by setting some *DWORD* values in the registry keys where your action or recognizer is registered. For example, if you want to hide your smart tag from Word, you can find the CLSID for your recognizer and create a new *DWORD* value under that CLSID key. The name of the value should be *OpusApp*, which corresponds to Word's window frame name. You then put in a value of 2. If you simply want to disable your recognizer, you use a value of 1. A value of 0 means that the recognizer is visible and should be enabled.

As for actions, you can only disable or enable them. A *DWORD* value of 0 enables an action; a value of 1 disables the action. Table 9-13 lists the DWORD names for the Office applications.

Table 9-13 DWORD Names for Office Applications

DWORD	Description
IEFrame	Internet Explorer
OMain	Access
OpusApp	Word
PPFrameClass	PowerPoint
XLMain	Excel

For example, if you want to hide your smart tag from Word, disable it in Excel, and enable it in PowerPoint, you use the following DWORD key names with the following values:

```
OpusApp: 2
XLMain: 1
PPFrameClass: 0
```

Putting It All Together: Smart Tag Recognition Application

The book's companion files include a sample application that implements several of the new features for smart tags. This smart tag recognizes a number of terms and performs different smart tag actions based on those terms. For example, when you type *temporary*, a temporary smart tag is recognized. When you type *expire*, a smart tag is created that expires in 1 minute. When you type the application name in Word, Excel, or PowerPoint, a smart tag is created in that application. The example smart tag also shows how to use property pages and dynamic action naming. Here's the Visual Basic code for the recognizer DLL for the smart tag:

```
Implements SmartTagLib.ISmartTagRecognizer
Implements SmartTagLib.ISmartTagRecognizer2

Const smartTagType = "urn-schemas-microsoft-com#applicationName"

Private Property Get ISmartTagRecognizer_Desc( _
    ByVal LocaleID As Long) As String
    'Create a long description of this recognizer

    ISmartTagRecognizer_Desc = "Description of your recognizer goes here"
End Property

Private Property Get ISmartTagRecognizer_Name( _
    ByVal LocaleID As Long) As String
    'What is shown in the Tools | Autocorrect Option | Smart Tags
    'dialog box in Word, Excel and PowerPoint

    ISmartTagRecognizer_Name = "Application name recognizer"
End Property

Private Property Get ISmartTagRecognizer_ProgId() As String
'Unique identifier for this recognizer that corresponds
'to the ProgID of this DLL

    ISmartTagRecognizer_ProgId = "Smarttag.AllNewFeaturesRecog"
End Property

Private Sub ISmartTagRecognizer_Recognize( _
    ByVal Text As String, _
    ByVal DataType As SmartTagLib.IF_TYPE, _
    ByVal LocaleID As Long, _
    ByVal RecognizerSite As SmartTagLib.ISmartTagRecognizerSite)
    'This method should not be called since there is a
    'Recognize2 method in this recognizer DLL
End Sub

Private Property Get ISmartTagRecognizer_SmartTagCount() As Long
'The number of Smart Tag types this recognizer supports

    ISmartTagRecognizer_SmartTagCount = 1
End Property

Private Property Get ISmartTagRecognizer_SmartTagDownloadURL( _
    ByVal SmartTagID As Long) As String
```

```
    ISmartTagRecognizer_SmartTagDownloadURL = "http://smarttagweb"
End Property

Private Property Get ISmartTagRecognizer_SmartTagName( _
    ByVal SmartTagID As Long) As String
    'The name of the Smart Tag type supported

    If (SmartTagID = 1) Then
        ISmartTagRecognizer_SmartTagName = smartTagType
    End If
End Property

Private Sub ISmartTagRecognizer2_DisplayPropertyPage( _
    ByVal SmartTagID As Long, _
    ByVal LocaleID As Long)

    frmPropPage.Show vbModal
End Sub

Private Property Get ISmartTagRecognizer2_PropertyPage( _
    ByVal SmartTagID As Long, _
    ByVal LocaleID As Long) As Boolean

    ISmartTagRecognizer2_PropertyPage = True
End Property

Private Sub ISmartTagRecognizer2_Recognize2( _
    ByVal Text As String, _
    ByVal DataType As SmartTagLib.IF_TYPE, _
    ByVal LocaleID As Long, _
    ByVal RecognizerSite2 As SmartTagLib.ISmartTagRecognizerSite2, _
    ByVal ApplicationName As String, _
    ByVal TokenList As SmartTagLib.ISmartTagTokenList)

    Dim i As Long
    Dim sValue As String
    Dim lOffset As Long, lLength As Long
    Dim propbag As SmartTagLib.ISmartTagProperties
    Dim ShortAppName As String
    Dim endPos As Integer

    endPos = InStr(1, ApplicationName, ".")
    ShortAppName = LCase(Mid(ApplicationName, 1, endPos - 1))

    On Error GoTo Error_Handler

    If TokenList Is Nothing Then
        If LocaleID = 2052 Or LocaleID = 4100 Or LocaleID = 1028 Or _
           LocaleID = 3076 Or LocaleID = 5124 Or LocaleID = 1041 Or _
           LocaleID = 1042 Or LocaleID = 1054 Then
            MsgBox "TokenList is Nothing. This is a falure if " & _
                   "the word breaker for LocaleID = " & _
                   LocaleID & " is installed."
```

```
            Else
                MsgBox "TokenList is Nothing. It should have been " & _
                       "tokenized by the Western Language tokenizer " & _
                       "for LocaleID = " & LocaleID
            End If
        Else
            For i = 1 To TokenList.Count
                sValue = TokenList.Item(i).Text
                sValue = LCase(sValue)
                lOffset = TokenList.Item(i).Start
                lLength = TokenList.Item(i).Length
                Set propbag = RecognizerSite2.GetNewPropertyBag
                If LCase(sValue) = "recognize" Then
                    'Run action on recognize
                    propbag.Write "o:runAction", "launchCalc"
                    RecognizerSite2.CommitSmartTag2 smartTagType, _
                        lOffset, lLength, propbag
                ElseIf sValue = ShortAppName Then
                    'If the user types the app name such as Word
                    propbag.Write "sValue", sValue
                    propbag.Write "lOffset", Str(lOffset)
                    propbag.Write "lLength", Str(lLength)
                    RecognizerSite2.CommitSmartTag2 smartTagType, _
                        lOffset, lLength, propbag
                ElseIf LCase(sValue) = "expire" Then
                    'Get 1 minute from now to expire the smart tag
                    dDate = DateAdd("n", 1, Now)
                    dDate = Year(dDate) & ":" & Month(dDate) & _
                            ":" & Day(dDate) & ":" & Hour(dDate) & _
                            ":" & Minute(dDate)
                    propbag.Write "o:exp", dDate
                    RecognizerSite2.CommitSmartTag2 smartTagType, _
                        lOffset, lLength, propbag
                ElseIf LCase(sValue) = "temporary" Then
                    'Create a temporary smart tag
                    propbag.Write "o:ls", "temp"
                    RecognizerSite2.CommitSmartTag2 smartTagType, _
                        lOffset, lLength, propbag
                End If
            Next i
        End If

        Exit Sub

Error_Handler:
    MsgBox Err.Description
    Err.Clear
    Resume Next

End Sub

Private Sub ISmartTagRecognizer2_SmartTagInitialize( _
    ByVal ApplicationName As String)
```

```
    MsgBox "In ISmartTagRecognizer2_SmartTagInitialize. " & _
           "App name is " & ApplicationName
End Sub
```

The main points of interest in this code are in the property page implementation and the *Recognize2* method. The smart tag implements a property page and displays a Visual Basic form when a user clicks the Properties button in the smart tag user interface in the host application. Figure 9-12 shows the property page in Excel.

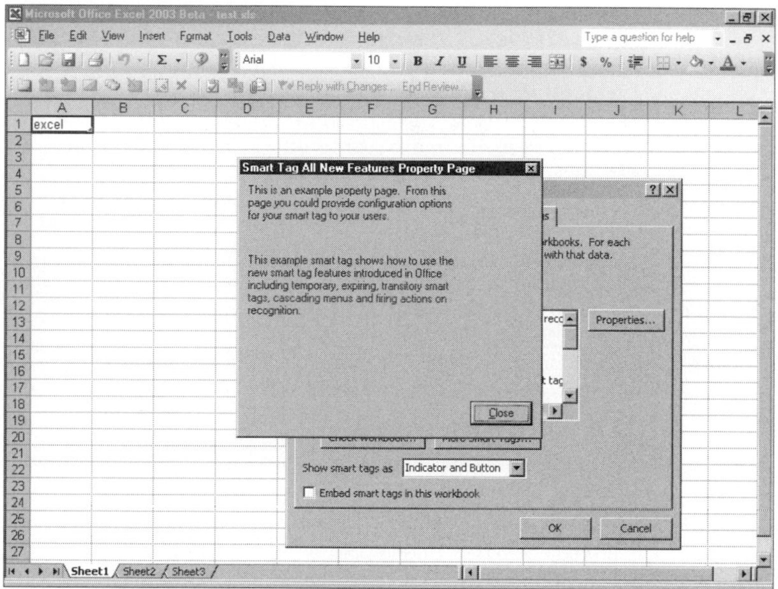

Figure 9-12 A Visual Basic property page form in Excel

The host application figures out that a property page is supported by inspecting the *ISmartTagRecognizer2_PropertyPage* Boolean property. The code returns *True*, which indicates that it supports a property page.

To show tokenizing the input, the *ISmartTagRecognizer2_Recognize2* method uses the new capabilities of that interface. You can see that the method goes through the token list returned by the smart tag host and recognizes which terms should be smart tagged. Then the method uses some of the new capabilities in smart tags—such as expiring, being temporary, or firing actions on recognition—as part of the sample.

The code for the action part of the DLL is shown here:

```
Implements ISmartTagAction
Implements ISmartTagAction2
```

```
Const smartTagType = "urn-schemas-microsoft-com#applicationName"

Private Property Get ISmartTagAction_Desc( _
    ByVal LocaleID As Long) As String
    'Description of Action DLL

    ISmartTagAction_Desc = _
        "This smart tag shows the new features of smart tags."
End Property

Private Sub ISmartTagAction_InvokeVerb( _
    ByVal VerbID As Long, _
    ByVal ApplicationName As String, _
    ByVal Target As Object, _
    ByVal Properties As SmartTagLib.ISmartTagProperties, _
    ByVal Text As String, _
    ByVal Xml As String)
    'This method shouldn't be called since we have an InvokeVerb2
End Sub

Private Property Get ISmartTagAction_Name( _
    ByVal LocaleID As Long) As String
    'Name of the Action DLL

    ISmartTagAction_Name = "All New Features Actions"
End Property

Private Property Get ISmartTagAction_ProgId() As String
    'ProgID of the Action DLL

    ISmartTagAction_ProgId = "Smarttag.AllNewFeaturesActions"
End Property

Private Property Get ISmartTagAction_SmartTagCaption( _
    ByVal SmartTagID As Long, _
    ByVal LocaleID As Long) As String
    'This will appear in the smart tag UI

    ISmartTagAction_SmartTagCaption = "All New Features Actions"
End Property

Private Property Get ISmartTagAction_SmartTagCount() As Long
    'Number of smart tag types this DLL supports

    ISmartTagAction_SmartTagCount = 1
End Property

Private Property Get ISmartTagAction_SmartTagName( _
    ByVal SmartTagID As Long) As String

    If (SmartTagID = 1) Then
        ISmartTagAction_SmartTagName = smartTagType
    End If
End Property
```

```
Private Property Get ISmartTagAction_VerbCaptionFromID( _
    ByVal VerbID As Long, _
    ByVal ApplicationName As String, _
    ByVal LocaleID As Long) As String

    If (VerbID = 1) Then
        ISmartTagAction_VerbCaptionFromID = _
            "&Dynamic actions unavailable"
    Else
        ISmartTagAction_VerbCaptionFromID = Null
    End If
End Property

Private Property Get ISmartTagAction_VerbCount( _
    ByVal SmartTagName As String) As Long
    'Specify the number of verbs supported for a given smart tag type

    If (SmartTagName = smartTagType) Then
        ISmartTagAction_VerbCount = 3
    End If
End Property

Private Property Get ISmartTagAction_VerbID( _
    ByVal SmartTagName As String, _
    ByVal VerbIndex As Long) As Long

    ISmartTagAction_VerbID = VerbIndex
End Property

Private Property Get ISmartTagAction_VerbNameFromID( _
    ByVal VerbID As Long) As String

    If (VerbID = 1) Then
        ISmartTagAction_VerbNameFromID = "action1"
    ElseIf (VerbID = 2) Then
        ISmartTagAction_VerbNameFromID = "action2"
    ElseIf (VerbID = 3) Then
        ISmartTagAction_VerbNameFromID = "launchCalc"
    End If
End Property

Private Sub ISmartTagAction2_InvokeVerb2( _
    ByVal VerbID As Long, _
    ByVal ApplicationName As String, _
    ByVal Target As Object, _
    ByVal Properties As SmartTagLib.ISmartTagProperties, _
    ByVal Text As String, _
    ByVal Xml As String, _
    ByVal LocaleID As Long)

    Dim sValue As String
    Dim sOffset As String
    Dim sLength As String
```

```
    If (VerbID = 1) Then
        sValue = Properties.Read("sValue")
        sOffset = Properties.Read("lOffset")
        sLength = Properties.Read("lLength")

        MsgBox "The token is " & sValue & Chr(13) & "Offset: " & _
               sOffset & Chr(13) & "Length: " & sLength
    ElseIf (VerbID = 2) Then
        MsgBox "Action #2"
    ElseIf (VerbID = 3) Then
        iRet = Shell("calc.exe", vbMaximizedFocus)
    End If
End Sub

Private Property Get ISmartTagAction2_IsCaptionDynamic( _
    ByVal VerbID As Long, _
    ByVal ApplicationName As String, _
    ByVal LocaleID As Long) As Boolean

    ISmartTagAction2_IsCaptionDynamic = True
End Property

Private Property Get ISmartTagAction2_ShowSmartTagIndicator( _
    ByVal VerbID As Long, _
    ByVal ApplicationName As String, _
    ByVal LocaleID As Long) As Boolean

    ISmartTagAction2_ShowSmartTagIndicator = True
End Property

Private Sub ISmartTagAction2_SmartTagInitialize( _
    ByVal ApplicationName As String)

    MsgBox "In ISmartTagAction2_SmartTagInitialize.  App is " & _
           ApplicationName
End Sub

Private Property Get ISmartTagAction2_VerbCaptionFromID2( _
    ByVal VerbID As Long, _
    ByVal ApplicationName As String, _
    ByVal LocaleID As Long, _
    ByVal Properties As SmartTagLib.ISmartTagProperties, _
    ByVal Text As String, _
    ByVal Xml As String, _
    ByVal Target As Object) As String

    If (VerbID = 1) Then
        If (LCase(Text) = "word") Then
            ISmartTagAction2_VerbCaptionFromID2 = "&Text is///word"
        Else
            ISmartTagAction2_VerbCaptionFromID2 = "&Text is not///word"
        End If
    ElseIf (VerbID = 2) Then
```

```
            If (LCase(ApplicationName) = "word.application.11") Then
                If (InStr(Target.paragraphs(1).range.Text, "the")) Then
                    ISmartTagAction2_VerbCaptionFromID2 = "Contains the"
                Else
                    'hide the action completely
                    ISmartTagAction2_VerbCaptionFromID2 = ""
                End If
            Else
                ISmartTagAction2_VerbCaptionFromID2 = "Not in Word"
            End If
        ElseIf (VerbID = 3) Then
            'No verb caption for firing on recognition
        Else
            ISmartTagAction2_VerbCaptionFromID2 = ""
        End If
    End Property
```

An interesting part of this code is the dynamic caption naming for the actions. If you look at *ISmartTagAction2_VerbCaptionFromID2*, you'll notice that this method supports getting the text that is recognized. Based on the text being passed, the application either changes the caption for the smart tag actions or hides the caption entirely by setting the property to ""

Smart Documents in Office 2003

Smart documents are a new technology in Office 2003. Smart documents build on the concepts of smart tags and enhance the user experience of working with document metaphors. For example, say you are designing an expense report in Excel. You might want relevant information to appear in the task pane in Office, depending on what the user is doing. You might also want to provide a Submit button in your application that is aware of context and is integrated into the task pane area. With smart documents, you can provide richer extensibility to Office-based solutions through standard XML or code that you write. In Office 2003, only Word and Excel support smart documents.

If you think about it, smart documents are the logical step beyond smart tags. While smart tags allow you to tag content in a document and associate actions, smart documents go one step further and allow you to customize the user interface and track interactions with the document. Because the two technologies are intertwined, you'll see many similarities between smart tags and smart documents. The smart document object model is actually part of the smart tag library.

To show you the benefits of a smart document solution, let's walk through building and deploying a review form in Word. Using the review form, a user enters her performance evaluation, and throughout the process, the smart document provides feedback. When the user finishes filling in the form, the smart document solution allows her to submit her review form through e-mail in Outlook. Our example is simple, so refer to the smart tag SDK for more information about building complex smart document solutions. Figure 9-13 shows the sample smart document solution.

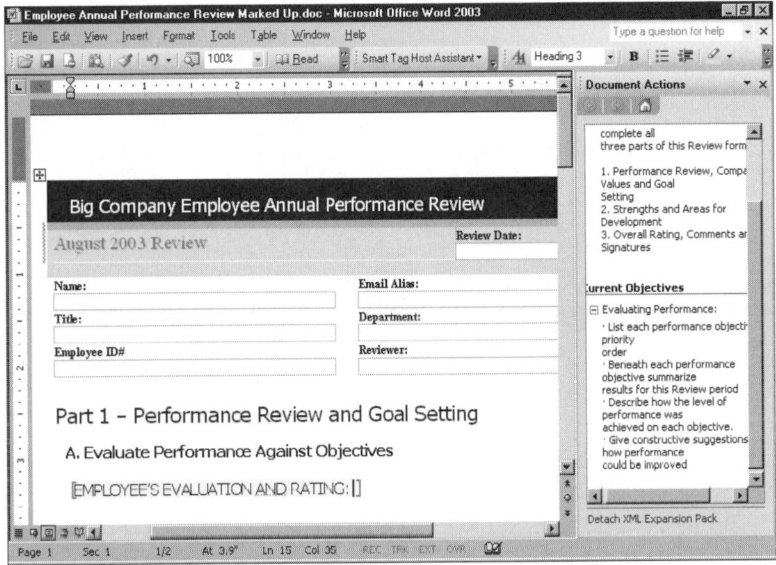

Figure 9-13 The Smart Document Review Form solution

The Parts of a Smart Document Solution

In the review form sample, the smart document solution includes a number of parts that we need to build. First we need the document, specifically a Word document for this example. Most documents that become smart documents have an XML schema (XSD) associated with them and are also marked up with XML tags. The markup allows you to apply your smart document logic to the document quite easily.

Next you need whatever support files your smart document requires. These support files might be ActiveX controls that you want to display in the document actions pane for your smart document, images, XML documents, or XSL stylesheets. You can also integrate smart documents with smart tags and COM add-ins to build more complex smart document solutions.

The final piece of a smart document solution is the manifest, or XML expansion pack file. A manifest file makes it easier to deploy smart document solutions. This file has an XML schema and is a description of your solution, with a list of the files needed for your solution and any actions to perform on those files. For example, if you create a DLL that needs to be deployed with your solution, you add the DLL to your manifest, and Office will copy the DLL from the location you specify and even register your DLL (using regsvr32). Furthermore, using a manifest file, you can deploy other files that are part of your smart document solution. Finally, the manifest can update your files if any changes are made. You'll learn more about manifest files later in this chapter.

Building a Smart Document Solution

Let's assume you already have a Word document that has an XML schema and has been marked up like the review form sample. To show you what XML markup looks like in Word, Figure 9-14 shows the review form with its XML structure displayed.

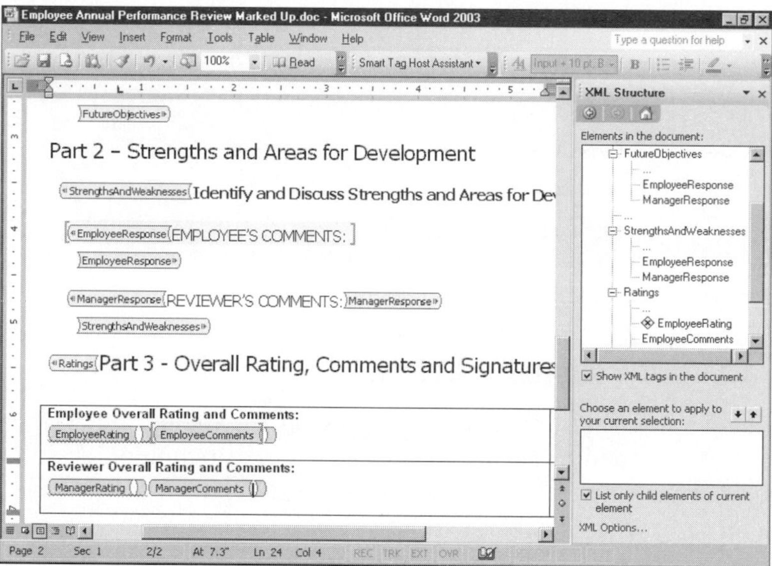

Figure 9-14 The review form sample XML markup in Word

The next step is to create a DLL that implements the *ISmartDocument* interface. This interface is part of the Smart Tags 2.0 Library. To implement the interface, you must implement a number of properties and functions that the interface requires. Table 9-14 lists the properties and functions you need to implement. As you can see, the implementation is similar to the implementation of a smart tag.

Table 9-14 Elements of the *ISmartDocument* Interface

Element	Description
Private Property Get ISmartDocument_ControlCaptionFromID(ByVal ControlID As Long, ByVal ApplicationName As String, ByVal LocaleID As Long, ByVal bstrText As String, ByVal bstrXML As String, ByVal Target As Object) As String	A property that specifies dynamic captions for the controls you create in your smart document solution.
Private Property Get ISmartDocument_ControlCount(ByVal SmartDocName As String) As Long	A property that specifies the number of controls supported by a specific smart document type.
Private Property Get ISmartDocument_ControlID(ByVal SmartDocName As String, ByVal ControlIndex As Long) As Long	A property that dynamically sets a unique control identifier for your smart document controls. The unique identifier ensures that controls do not have collisions when events fire for the controls.
Private Property Get ISmartDocument_ControlNameFromID(ByVal ControlID As Long) As String	A property that specifies a unique name for your control based on its unique ID.
Private Property Get ISmartDocument_ControlTypeFromID(ByVal ControlID As Long, ByVal ApplicationName As String, ByVal LocaleID As Long) As C_TYPE	A property that specifies the type of your control, based on your control ID. Examples include combo box, text box, radio group, image, label, and link.
Private Sub ISmartDocument_ImageClick(ByVal ControlID As Long, ByVal ApplicationName As String, ByVal Target As Object, ByVal Text As String, ByVal Xml As String, ByVal LocaleID As Long, ByVal XCoordinate As Long, ByVal YCoordinate As Long)	The first of the many *Click* events you'll see in the *ISmartDocument* interface. The *Click* event allows you to listen for your unique controls, based on their ID, and perform some action.
Private Sub ISmartDocument_InvokeControl (ByVal ControlID As Long, ByVal ApplicationName As String, ByVal Target As Object, ByVal Text As String, ByVal Xml As String, ByVal LocaleID As Long)	A method that works with the new document-fragments capabilities of smart documents. Document fragments are content that is either locally stored or remotely stored as XML document fragments. The difference between a label and a document fragment is that when a user clicks on a document fragment, it can be inserted into the document. This method is called when the user clicks on the document fragment.
Private Property Get ISmartDocument_IsControlDynamic(ByVal ControlID As Long, ByVal ApplicationName As String, ByVal LocaleID As Long) As Boolean	A property that specifies whether your control caption is dynamic.

Table 9-14 Elements of the *ISmartDocument* Interface

Element	Description
Private Sub ISmartDocument_OnCheckboxChange(ByVal ControlID As Long, ByVal Target As Object, ByVal Checked As Boolean)	A method that is called when a check box value changes for one of your check box controls.
Private Sub ISmartDocument_OnListOrComboSelectChange (ByVal ControlID As Long, ByVal Target As Object, ByVal Selected As Long, ByVal Value As String)	A method that is called when a list or combo box value is changed.
Private Sub ISmartDocument_OnPaneUpdateComplete(ByVal Document As Object)	A method that is called when the document actions pane is redrawn.
Private Sub ISmartDocument_OnRadioGroupSelectChange(By Val ControlID As Long, ByVal Target As Object, ByVal Selected As Long, ByVal Value As String)	A method that is called when the value of a radio group changes.
Private Sub ISmartDocument_OnTextboxContentChange(By Val ControlID As Long, ByVal Target As Object, ByVal Value As String)	A method that is called when the value in a text box changes.
Private Sub ISmartDocument_PopulateActiveXProps(ByVal ControlID As Long, ByVal ApplicationName As String, ByVal LocaleID As Long, ByVal Text As String, ByVal Xml As String, ByVal Target As Object, ByVal Props As SmartTagLib.ISmart-DocProperties, ByVal ActiveXPropBag As SmartTagLib.ISmartDocProperties)	The first of many populate methods for your controls, which are used to fill in the content of your controls. This method also allows you to customize your ActiveX controls. For example, you can specify the size of your control by writing *Props.Write "W", 150* for the width and *Props.Write "H", 200* for the height.
Private Sub ISmartDocument_PopulateCheckbox(ByVal ControlID As Long, ByVal ApplicationName As String, ByVal LocaleID As Long, ByVal Text As String, ByVal Xml As String, ByVal Target As Object, ByVal Props As SmartTagLib.ISmartDocProperties, Checked As Boolean)	A method for customizing or populating your check box controls.
Private Sub ISmartDocument_PopulateDocumentFragment(By Val ControlID As Long, ByVal ApplicationName As String, ByVal LocaleID As Long, ByVal Text As String, ByVal Xml As String, ByVal Target As Object, ByVal Props As SmartTagLib.ISmartDocProperties, DocumentFragment As String)	A method that populates your document fragment controls.

Table 9-14 Elements of the *ISmartDocument* Interface

Element	Description
Private Sub ISmartDocument_PopulateHelpContent(ByVal ControlID As Long, ByVal ApplicationName As String, ByVal LocaleID As Long, ByVal Text As String, ByVal Xml As String, ByVal Target As Object, ByVal Props As SmartTagLib.ISmartDocProperties, Content As String)	A method that populates your help controls.
Private Sub ISmartDocument_PopulateImage(ByVal ControlID As Long, ByVal ApplicationName As String, ByVal LocaleID As Long, ByVal Text As String, ByVal Xml As String, ByVal Target As Object, ByVal Props As SmartTagLib.ISmartDocProperties, ImageSrc As String)	A method that populates any image controls you have.
Private Sub ISmartDocument_PopulateListOrComboContent(ByVal ControlID As Long, ByVal ApplicationName As String, ByVal LocaleID As Long, ByVal Text As String, ByVal Xml As String, ByVal Target As Object, ByVal Props As SmartTagLib.ISmartDocProperties, List() As String, Count As Long, InitialSelected As Long)	A method that populates list or combo box controls.
Private Sub ISmartDocument_PopulateOther (ByVal ControlID As Long, ByVal ApplicationName As String, ByVal LocaleID As Long, ByVal Text As String, ByVal Xml As String, ByVal Target As Object, ByVal Props As SmartTagLib.ISmartDocProperties)	A method that applies to all controls that do not have a specific populate method. One example is a separator control.
Private Sub ISmartDocument_PopulateRadioGroup(ByVal ControlID As Long, ByVal ApplicationName As String, ByVal LocaleID As Long, ByVal Text As String, ByVal Xml As String, ByVal Target As Object, ByVal Props As SmartTagLib.ISmartDocProperties, List() As String, Count As Long, InitialSelected As Long)	A method that populates radio group controls.
Private Sub ISmartDocument_PopulateTextboxContent(ByVal ControlID As Long, ByVal ApplicationName As String, ByVal LocaleID As Long, ByVal Text As String, ByVal Xml As String, ByVal Target As Object, ByVal Props As SmartTagLib.ISmartDocProperties, Value As String)	A method that populates any text box content for your text box controls.

Table 9-14 Elements of the *ISmartDocument* Interface

Element	Description
Private Sub ISmartDocument_SmartDocInitialize(ByVal ApplicationName As String, ByVal Document As Object, ByVal SolutionPath As String, ByVal SolutionRegKeyRoot As String)	An important method that is called to initialize your smart document. You can then modify the document, store the *Document* object for your application, and determine where your solution files are installed.
Private Property Get ISmartDocument_SmartDocXmlTypeCaption (ByVal SmartDocID As Long, ByVal LocaleID As Long) As String	A property that specifies the captions for your XML tags in your document. These captions are shown in the document actions pane.
Private Property Get ISmartDocument_SmartDocXmlTypeCount() As Long	A property that specifies the number of XML types your document supports.
Private Property Get ISmartDocument_SmartDocXmlTypeName(ByVal SmartDocID As Long) As String	A property that specifies the names of the types of your XML tags, such as *http://schema/type*.

Now that you've seen the interfaces that need to be implemented, let's look at the code that implements the review form sample. We'll look at the initialization routine for the sample:

```
Private Sub ISmartDocument_SmartDocInitialize( _
    ByVal ApplicationName As String, _
    ByVal Document As Object, _
    ByVal SolutionPath As String, _
    ByVal SolutionRegKeyRoot As String)

    Dim oUnlockedNodes As Word.XMLNodes
    Dim oWordDocument As Word.Document
    Dim oWordRangeObject As Word.Range
    Dim initializeCounter As Integer
    Dim oXMLNode, oUserList As MSXML2.DOMDocument50
    Dim importName As Integer
    Dim boolHeader As Boolean
    Dim boolGoals As Boolean

    On Error GoTo ErV2

    'Turn on XML tags.
    ActiveDocument.Application.ActiveWindow.View.ShowXMLMarkup = 65535

    'Set up.
    Set oWordDocument = Document
```

```
Set oUserList = New MSXML2.DOMDocument50
Set oXMLNode = New MSXML2.DOMDocument50

'We need to set the path where our files are
'installed on the client machine.
FilesPath = SolutionPath & "\"

'Turn off the submittal button initially as well.
readyToSubmit = False

'To check if our employee has filled out the document,
'we'll use the state of the name field.
If oWordDocument.XMLNodes(1).SelectSingleNode(".//u:Name", _
    "xmlns:u='" & reviewFormURI & "'").Text = "" Then
    sWorkflowState = EmployeeState
Else
    sWorkflowState = ReviewerState
End If

Select Case sWorkflowState
    Case EmployeeState
        'First, we'll unlock the appropriate sections of the document.
        Set oUnlockedNodes = _
            oWordDocument.XMLNodes(1).SelectNodes( _
            ".//u:EmployeeResponse", _
            "xmlns:u='" & reviewFormURI & "'")

           initializeCounter - 0
        Do While initializeCounter < oUnlockedNodes.Count
            Set oWordRangeObject = _
                oUnlockedNodes(initializeCounter + 1).Range
            oWordRangeObject.MoveStart 1, -1
            oWordRangeObject.Editors.Add wdEditorEveryone
            oUnlockedNodes(initializeCounter + 1).PlaceholderText = _
                "[Fill in this information.]"
            initializeCounter = initializeCounter + 1
        Loop

        'Unlock the Employee Section of Company Values

        On Error Resume Next
        Set oUnlockedNodes = _
            oWordDocument.XMLNodes(1).SelectNodes(".//u:Employee", _
            "xmlns:u='" & reviewFormURI & "'")
        Dim oUnlockedNode As Word.XMLNode
        For Each oUnlockedNode In oUnlockedNodes
            Set oWordRangeObject = oUnlockedNode.Range
            oWordRangeObject.Editors.Add wdEditorEveryone
        Next
        On Error GoTo ErV2
```

```
'Also, unlock the employee comments.
Set oUnlockedNodes = _
    oWordDocument.XMLNodes(1).SelectNodes( _
    ".//u:EmployeeComments", "xmlns:u='" & _
    reviewFormURI & "'")

initializeCounter = 0
Do While initializeCounter < oUnlockedNodes.Count
    Set oWordRangeObject = _
        oUnlockedNodes(initializeCounter + 1).Range
    oWordRangeObject.MoveStart 1, -1
    oWordRangeObject.Editors.Add wdEditorEveryone
    oUnlockedNodes(initializeCounter + 1).PlaceholderText = _
        "[Fill in this information.]"
    initializeCounter = initializeCounter + 1
Loop

'This will populate the header fields:

boolHeader = MsgBox("Do you want to import the " & _
                    "personal information for the " & _
                    header automatically?", vbYesNo)

If (boolHeader = vbYes) Then
    'If you want to load from a file, use this code
    'oUserList.setProperty "SelectionNamespaces", _
    '    "xmlns:u='userNames'"
    'oUserList.async = False
    'oUserList.Load FilesPath & "userNames.xml"
    'oXMLNode.setProperty "SelectionNamespaces", _
    '    "xmlns:u='userNames'"
    'oXMLNode.async = False
    'oXMLNode.loadXML _
    'oUserList.SelectSingleNode(".//u:user").Xml
    'oWordDocument.XMLNodes(1).SelectSingleNode( _
    '    ".//u:Date", "xmlns:u='" & _
    '    reviewFormURI & "'").Range.Text = Date
    'oWordDocument.XMLNodes(1).SelectSingleNode( _
    '    ".//u:Name", "xmlns:u='" & _
    '    reviewFormURI & "'").Range.Text = _
    '    oXMLNode.SelectSingleNode(".//u:name").Text
    'oWordDocument.XMLNodes(1).SelectSingleNode( _
    '    ".//u:Alias", "xmlns:u='" & _
    '    reviewFormURI & "'").Range.Text = _
    '    oXMLNode.SelectSingleNode(".//u:alias").Text
    'oWordDocument.XMLNodes(1).SelectSingleNode( _
    '    ".//u:EmployeeID", "xmlns:u='" & _
    '    reviewFormURI & "'").Range.Text = _
    '    oXMLNode.SelectSingleNode(".//u:id").Text
    'oWordDocument.XMLNodes(1).SelectSingleNode( _
    '    ".//u:Title", "xmlns:u='" & _
```

```
'    reviewFormURI & "'").Range.Text = _
'    oXMLNode.SelectSingleNode(".//u:title").Text
'oWordDocument.XMLNodes(1).SelectSingleNode( _
'    ".//u:Reviewer", "xmlns:u='" & _
'    reviewFormURI & "'").Range.Text = _
'    oXMLNode.SelectSingleNode(".//u:managerAlias").Text
'oWordDocument.XMLNodes(1).SelectSingleNode( _
'    ".//u:Department", "xmlns:u='" & _
'    reviewFormURI & "'").Range.Text = _
'    oXMLNode.SelectSingleNode(".//u:department").Text

'Save the names to customize some of the SmartDoc pane.
'sReviewName = _
'    oWordDocument.XMLNodes(1).SelectSingleNode( _
'    ".//u:Name").Text
'sReviewerName = _
'    oWordDocument.XMLNodes(1).SelectSingleNode( _
'    ".//u:Reviewer").Text

  'Try to lookup info from the GAL
Dim oSession As New MAPI.Session
oSession.Logon "", "", True, True, 0, True

'Get the current user's name
Dim oWSHNetwork As Object
Set oWSHNetwork = CreateObject("WScript.Network")
Dim strUserName As String
strUserName = oWSHNetwork.UserName
Set oWSHNetwork = Nothing

Dim oMailItem As MAPI.Message
Dim oRecipients As MAPI.Recipients
Dim oRecipient As MAPI.Recipient

Set oMailItem = oSession.Outbox.Messages.Add
Set oRecipients = oMailItem.Recipients
Set oRecipient = oRecipients.Add(strUserName)
oRecipients.Resolve True

Dim oAE As MAPI.AddressEntry
Set oAE = oRecipient.AddressEntry

oWordDocument.XMLNodes(1).SelectSingleNode( _
    ".//u:Date", "xmlns:u='" & reviewFormURI & _
    "'").Range.Text = Date
oWordDocument.XMLNodes(1).SelectSingleNode( _
    ".//u:Name", "xmlns:u='" & reviewFormURI & _
    "'").Range.Text = strUserName
oWordDocument.XMLNodes(1).SelectSingleNode( _
    ".//u:Alias", "xmlns:u='" & reviewFormURI & _
```

```
                "'").Range.Text = oAE.Fields(&H3A00001E).Value
            oWordDocument.XMLNodes(1).SelectSingleNode( _
                ".//u:EmployeeID", "xmlns:u='" & reviewFormURI & _
                "'").Range.Text = "999999"
            oWordDocument.XMLNodes(1).SelectSingleNode( _
                ".//u:Title", "xmlns:u='" & reviewFormURI & _
                "'").Range.Text = oAE.Fields(&H3A17001E).Value
            oWordDocument.XMLNodes(1).SelectSingleNode( _
                ".//u:Reviewer", "xmlns:u='" & reviewFormURI & _
                "'").Range.Text = oAE.Manager.Name
            oWordDocument.XMLNodes(1).SelectSingleNode( _
                ".//u:Department", "xmlns:u='" & reviewFormURI & _
                "'").Range.Text = oAE.Fields(&H3A18001F).Value

            'Save the names to customize some of the SmartDoc pane.
            sReviewName = strUserName
            sReviewerName = oAE.Manager.Name

            'Discard CDO Stuff and logoff
            Set oAE = Nothing
            Set oMailItem = Nothing
            oSession.Logoff
            Set oSession = Nothing
        End If

        'This part will import the previous review's goals.
        boolGoals = MsgBox("Do you want to import your previous " & _
                           "review goals automatically?", vbYesNo)

        If (boolGoals = vbYes) Then
            Set oXMLNode = New MSXML2.DOMDocument50
            oXMLNode.Load FilesPath & "goals.xml"
            oWordDocument.XMLNodes(1).SelectSingleNode( _
                ".//u:CurrentObjectives//u:EmployeeResponse", _
                "xmlns:u='" & _
                reviewFormURI & "'").Range.InsertXML (oXMLNode.Xml)
        End If

        'Clean up.
        Set oXMLNode = Nothing
        Set oWordRangeObject = Nothing

    Case ReviewerState
        'First, we'll unlock appropriate sections of the document.
        Set oUnlockedNodes = oWordDocument.XMLNodes(1).SelectNodes( _
            ".//u:ManagerResponse", "xmlns:u='" & reviewFormURI & "'")

        initializeCounter = 0
        While initializeCounter < oUnlockedNodes.Count
            Set oWordRangeObject = _
                oUnlockedNodes(initializeCounter + 1).Range
            oWordRangeObject.MoveStart 1, -1
```

```
                oWordRangeObject.Editors.Add wdEditorEveryone
                oUnlockedNodes(initializeCounter + 1).PlaceholderText = _
                    "[Type Here]"
                initializeCounter = initializeCounter + 1
            Wend

            'Save the names to customize some of the SmartDoc pane.
            sReviewName = oWordDocument.XMLNodes(1).SelectSingleNode( _
                ".//u:Name", "xmlns:u='" & reviewFormURI & "'").Text
            sReviewerName = oWordDocument.XMLNodes(1).SelectSingleNode( _
                ".//u:Reviewer", "xmlns:u='" & reviewFormURI & "'").Text

            'Clean up.
            Set oWordRangeObject = Nothing
        End Select

    'Turn on XML tags.
    ActiveDocument.Application.ActiveWindow.View.ShowXMLMarkup = 0
    oWordDocument.Protect Password:="", NoReset:=False, _
        Type:=wdAllowOnlyReading

    Exit Sub

ErV2:
    MsgBox "ISmartDocument_SmartDocInitialize:" & Err.Description
    Resume Next

End Sub
```

The code does some work to unlock nodes in the document that employees should fill out to complete their review. The code also leverages Outlook to look up the user's header information—his alias, department, and manager's name, for example. The code can also import previous performance goals from the user's last review. The code then saves off some global variables to be used later in the application. Finally, the code locks down sections of the document that the user should not be able to modify.

Next, using the XML type information that we specify from our XML types in our document, Office can figure out which XML types should display the controls for our smart document. For example, we tell our smart document that we support different XML types as smart document types by using the *SmartDocXMLTypeName* and *SmartDocXMLTypeCount* properties. When Office hits an XML tag that's been designated as a smart document, it determines which controls should be loaded into the document actions pane and calls the populate methods for the controls that are loaded into the pane.

To figure out the controls, Office calls the *ControlCount* property and passes each of the XML tags from your document. If there is a nonzero number for this property in your code, Office knows that your XML tag has some smart document controls associated with it. Using the *ControlID* property, you assign unique control ID ranges to the controls in your smart document solution. Then, when the user clicks through your smart document, Office passes the ControlID to the ControlCaptionFromID (if your caption is dynamic) and to the correct populate method for your control.

Two special schema names you should be aware of are *yourschema-name#ActionPertainstoEntireSchema* and *http://schemas.microsoft.com/office/smartdocuments/2003#Default*. You should use these special schema tags for the smart document controls you want to display, regardless of the XML type the user has selected. You can think of these controls as global controls for your solution.

> **Note** Keep in mind that XML is case-sensitive. You might find that your solution does not work as you expect because of case issues in your XML schema or XML tags.

Deploying Your Smart Document Solution

To deploy your smart document solution, you can use the XML Expansion Pack technology included with Office. This is a text document with an XML schema that allows you to specify particular tags that will download, install, and update your smart document solutions. For the full breadth of XML tags that the XML Expansion Pack technology supports, see the smart tag SDK. Here is the XML Expansion Pack file for the review form sample:

```
<?xml  version="1.0" encoding="UTF-8" standalone="no"?>
<manifest xmlns=
  "http://schemas.microsoft.com/office/xmlexpansionpacks/2003">
  <version>1.11</version>
  <location>http://thomrizrc2:801/manifest.xml</location>
  <updateFrequency>20160</updateFrequency>
  <uri>http://thomrizrc2:801/</uri>
  <solution>
    <solutionID>ProgOutExchReviewFormSolution01</solutionID>
    <type>smartDocument</type>
    <alias lcid="1033">Review Form Solution</alias>
    <file>
      <type>solutionActionHandler</type>
      <version>1.0</version>
      <filePath>file:///C:/ReviewForm/SmartDoc/reviewform.dll</filePath>
      <CLSID>{29568A81-7FF3-4A28-8C4A-C30C98253079}</CLSID>
```

```
  <regsvr32/>
</file>
<file>
  <type>other</type>
  <version>1.0</version>
  <filePath>http://thomrizrc2:801/xml/usernames.xml</filePath>
</file>
<file>
  <type>other</type>
  <version>1.0</version>
  <filePath>http://thomrizrc2:801/docfragments/goals.xml</filePath>
</file>
<file>
  <type>other</type>
  <version>1.0</version>
  <filePath>
    http://thomrizrc2:801/docfragments/justification.xml
  </filePath>
</file>
<file>
  <type>other</type>
  <version>1.0</version>
  <filePath>http://thomrizrc2:801/helpfiles/intro.htm</filePath>
</file>
<file>
  <type>other</type>
  <version>1.0</version>
  <filePath>http://thomrizrc2:801/helpfiles/Part1BHelp.htm</filePath>
</file>
<file>
  <type>other</type>
  <version>1.0</version>
  <filePath>http://thomrizrc2:801/helpfiles/Part1CHelp.htm</filePath>
</file>
<file>
  <type>other</type>
  <version>1.0</version>
  <filePath>http://thomrizrc2:801/helpfiles/Part2AHelp.htm</filePath>
</file>
<file>
  <type>other</type>
  <version>1.0</version>
  <filePath>http://thomrizrc2:801/helpfiles/Part2Help.htm</filePath>
</file>
<file>
  <type>other</type>
  <version>1.0</version>
  <filePath>http://thomrizrc2:801/helpfiles/PartAHelp.htm</filePath>
</file>
<file>
  <type>other</type>
```

```
      <version>1.0</version>
      <filePath>http://thomrizrc2:801/helpfiles/rating25.htm</filePath>
    </file>
    <file>
      <type>other</type>
      <version>1.0</version>
      <filePath>http://thomrizrc2:801/helpfiles/rating30.htm</filePath>
    </file>
    <file>
      <type>other</type>
      <version>1.0</version>
      <filePath>http://thomrizrc2:801/helpfiles/rating35.htm</filePath>
    </file>
    <file>
      <type>other</type>
      <version>1.0</version>
      <filePath>http://thomrizrc2:801/helpfiles/rating40.htm</filePath>
    </file>
    <file>
      <type>other</type>
      <version>1.0</version>
      <filePath>http://thomrizrc2:801/helpfiles/rating45.htm</filePath>
    </file>
    <file>
      <type>other</type>
      <version>1.0</version>
      <filePath>http://thomrizrc2:801/helpfiles/rating50.htm</filePath>
    </file>
    <file>
      <type>other</type>
      <version>1.0</version>
      <filePath>http://thomrizrc2:801/images/hr.gif</filePath>
    </file>
  </solution>
  <solution>
    <solutionID>schema</solutionID>
    <type>schema</type>
    <alias lcid="1033">Review Form Schema</alias>
    <file>
      <type>schema</type>
      <version>1.0</version>
      <filePath>http://thomrizrc2:801/xml/review.xsd</filePath>
    </file>
  </solution>
</manifest>
```

As you can see in the XML, the file lists the version, location, and update frequency for the solution. It also lists the component of the solution, whether it is a DLL, such as the smart document action DLL included with the solution, or other files, such as the XML schema and images that need to be downloaded with the solution. When you use this type of file for your deployment, you can easily deploy smart documents across multiple desktops using Web technologies.

One interesting tag is the *<regsvr32/>* tag. You can have Office download and register the DLLs for you on the client machine. Also, XML Expansion Packs support tags that allow you to write to the registry and run solutions from the server.

To see how to deploy a solution that calls the XML Expansion Pack file, choose Templates And Add-Ins from the Tools menu in Word and click on the Solutions tab. Figure 9-15 shows the user interface for adding a solution manually.

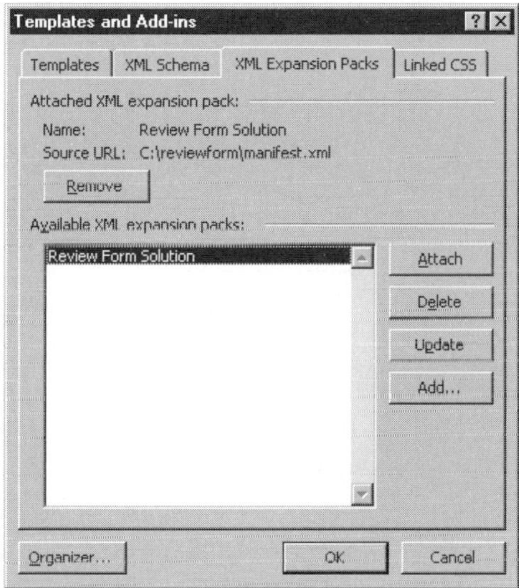

Figure 9-15 Adding a solution manually in Word

Another way to attach your solution to your documents is to add two custom properties to your documents as Office document properties. These two properties are *Solution URL* and *Solution ID*. *Solution URL* specifies the URL of the XML Expansion Pack file for your solution so Office can download and install the necessary components. *Solution ID* is a GUID, or unique identifier, that uniquely identifies a solution. Figure 9-16 shows these properties set in Word. Figure 9-17 shows the user interface that is displayed when a user opens an Office document with these custom properties set.

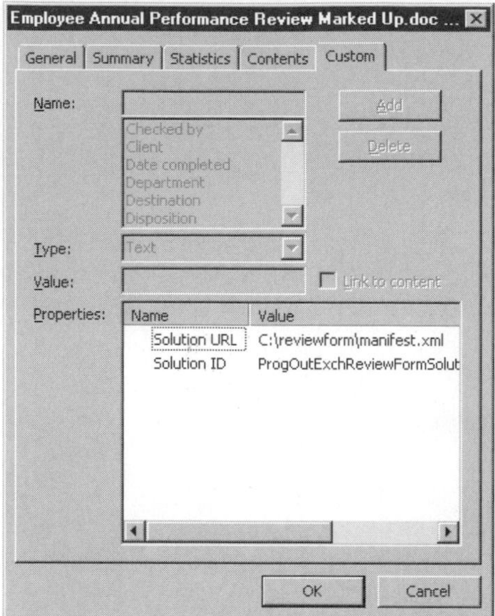

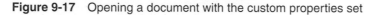

Figure 9-16 Setting the custom properties for a smart document solution in Word

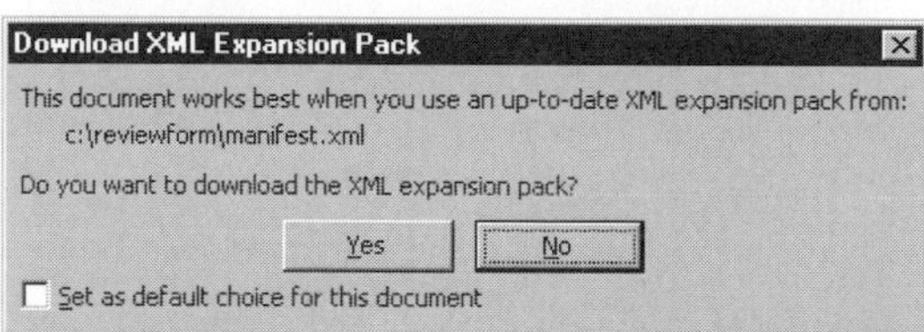

Figure 9-17 Opening a document with the custom properties set

By using these properties, you can easily deploy a smart document solution to your users.

MOSTL Support for Smart Documents

To support building smart documents without using DLLs, Office supports the smart document technology in MOSTL through some new tags. If you create your solution using MOSTL, however, you should still create an XML Expansion Pack file that deploys the MOSTL solution to your clients. The following is an example of a smart document solution that uses the new MOSTL tags:

```
<FL:smarttaglist xmlns:FL="urn:schemas-microsoft-com:smarttags:list">
  <FL:name>Sample MOSTL Smart Doc Solution</FL:name>
  <FL:lcid>1033</FL:lcid>
```

```
<FL:description>MOSTL description</FL:description>
<FL:moreinfourl></FL:moreinfourl>
<FL:lastcheckpoint></FL:lastcheckpoint>
<FL:lastupdate></FL:lastupdate>
<FL:updateurl></FL:updateurl>
<FL:downloadurl></FL:downloadurl>
<FL:updateable></FL:updateable>
<FL:updatefrequency></FL:updatefrequency>
<FL:autoupdate></FL:autoupdate>
<FL:smartdoc type=
  "http://schemas.microsoft.com/office/smartdocuments/2003#Default">
  <FL:caption>Default SmartDoc Action</FL:caption>
  <FL:actions>
  <FL:action id="defLink">
    <FL:actionType>Link</FL:actionType>
    <FL:caption>Microsoft Home Page</FL:caption>
    <FL:url>http://www.microsoft.com</FL:url>
  </FL:action>
  <FL:action id="defHelp">
    <FL:actionType>Help</FL:actionType>
    <FL:caption>Help Text</FL:caption>
    <FL:help>

    <html><body>Default Help</body></html>

    </FL:help>
  </FL:action>
  <FL:action id="defHelpURL">
    <FL:actionType>HelpURL</FL:actionType>
    <FL:caption>HelpURL text</FL:caption>
    <FL:help>
      http://localhost/
    </FL:help>
  </FL:action>
  <FL:action id="defSeparator">
    <FL:actionType>Separator</FL:actionType>
  </FL:action>
  <FL:action id="defButton">
    <FL:actionType>Button</FL:actionType>
    <FL:caption>Go to MSPress Homepage</FL:caption>
    <FL:url>http://mspress.microsoft.com</FL:url>
  </FL:action>
  <FL:action id="defLabel">
    <FL:actionType>Sample Label</FL:actionType>
    <FL:caption>This is sample label text</FL:caption>
  </FL:action>
  <FL:action id="defImage">
    <FL:actionType>Image</FL:actionType>
    <FL:caption>Sample Image</FL:caption>
    <FL:imageurl>
      http://localhost/pagerror.gif
    </FL:imageurl>
  </FL:action>
```

```
    </FL:actions>
  </FL:smartdoc>
</FL:smarttaglist>
```

This MOSTL file applies actions to the entire document and shows how to use the different control types for smart documents in MOSTL. Figure 9-18 shows the MOSTL solution in Word.

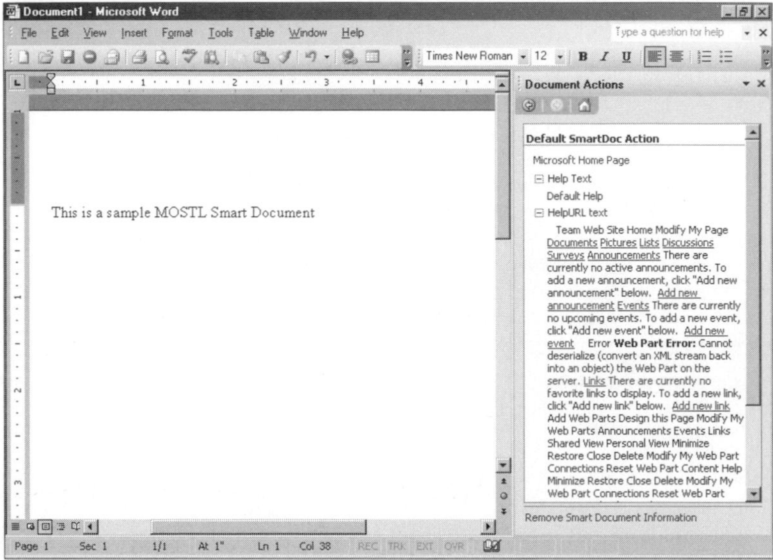

Figure 9-18 The MOSTL smart document solution running in Word

Which Office Solution Option Should I Use?

With all the new and different solution options available to you in Office, you might be wondering which option you should use to build your solutions. Each approach—using Outlook forms, COM add-ins, smart documents, or even Visual Studio .NET tools for Office—has different features and trade-offs. The key point is that you do not have to make a single choice. Many of the technologies work together. For example, you can build a solution that contains a COM add-in, smart tags, a smart document, and Outlook forms. The only issues you will run into are the different programming models, object libraries, and deployment mechanisms. Here are some suggestions for when to use each approach when building Office-based solutions:

- Outlook forms are the best choice when you are customizing built-in Outlook types and want to extend their functionality. For example, if you want to extend the contact form, you need to use Outlook forms. Outlook forms also provide off-line capabilities for your users.
- Use COM add-ins when you want to extend an Office application and you need a more powerful programming model than what Outlook forms provide. For example, if you are going to add new menus to Outlook or need to listen for Outlook application level events, a COM add-in is the technology you should use. COM add-ins can be written using native code in Visual Studio 6.0, or you can write managed add-ins with Visual Studio .NET. The only gotchas with COM add-ins involve deployment and updating.
- Smart tags are best if you want to provide context-sensitive actions in Office applications. These actions can be application independent in that they can work in Word, Excel, PowerPoint, Outlook, or Access. Smart tags are useful for tagging data that is meaningful to your users.
- Smart documents provide you with the power to customize the task pane to interact with XML-based documents in Word and Excel and to enhance your user's experiences with these documents. Smart documents can work in conjunction with other Office solution technologies, and they can even provide an easier deployment mechanism for a COM add-in if the add-in is included in your smart document solution.
- InfoPath is the best solution if you want to have your users fill in structured business forms that will have XML-based output that you want to integrate into your business processes. InfoPath is a new addition to Office that allows you to design rich forms that represent XML data. It works with Web services and provides a rich forms environment.
- Visual Studio .NET Windows Forms is another option for Office-based solutions. While Windows Forms is not integrated into the Office environment, you can use it to automate Office applications through the Office object models. Windows Forms is a good choice if you already know how to develop using Windows Forms and Office integration is not a key requirement in your solution.

- The Visual Studio .NET tools for Office are a good solution for Word and Excel if you want to harness the power of managed code in your applications. Using these tools, you can write managed Visual Basic .NET or Visual C# .NET code instead of VBA. For Outlook, you can use the Primary Interop Assemblies (PIAs) for Office to build managed add-ins.
- Finally, what about Web applications? Because many of the Office object models are not meant to be run in unattended environments such as server-side ASP or ASP.NET applications, you cannot really leverage the object models for Office in these environments. You can leverage the Office Web components and the Outlook View control in Web-based environments when they run in client-side Web browser code. For Web-based solutions, you should leverage CDO rather than the Outlook object model. Web-based applications provide one of the easiest deployment mechanisms for your applications, but they do not provide the offline capabilities that some of the other approaches provide.

Summary

You've had a whirlwind tour of what you can use in Office to build collaborative solutions. In the following chapters, we will turn our attention to the server—specifically, the development features of Microsoft Exchange Server—because most solutions require that the solution integrate with a server environment to share the information in the application.

Part III

Exchange Server Development

10

Web Fundamentals and Server Security

Security is a key issue with any application you build. Chapter 5 covered client security, and in this chapter I'll cover issues related to server security, focusing on security for Web-based applications. Most of the time, developers run into issues with authentication in their Web applications, and this in turn causes their Exchange applications to fail. This chapter will describe the basics of Active Server Pages (ASP) and authentication in ASP.

Active Server Pages and ASP.NET

In this section, we'll explore ASP technology. You should know about ASP for several reasons. First, most of your Collaboration Data Objects (CDO) or Active Directory Services Interface (ADSI) applications will run on the Web and use ASP. Second, most problems in Web applications stem from a lack of understanding of basic ASP concepts.

ASP Fundamentals

ASP pages are standard text files that contain HTML and script. The script can be written using any ActiveX scripting language, such as VBScript or JScript. The HTML files that most Web developers write differ from ASP files in two significant ways. First, instead of having an .htm or .html file extension, ASP files have an .asp file extension. When you include Microsoft Internet Information Services (IIS) as part of your installation, you also install an Internet Server Application Programming Interface (ISAPI) component that processes all files with an .asp extension. This ISAPI component parses the ASP file and executes the appropriate script. Second, the actual script is processed on the Web server. The processed results can include client-side scripting code, but for the most part the results are just simple HMTL. Returning only HTML is a big benefit: any modern Web browser can view the results of an ASP application.

Because ASP supports VBScript, you can easily move from developing Outlook forms to developing ASP pages. The only difference in the development process is that you should use the CDO library to write your ASP application rather than the Outlook object library because CDO is designed to be used in applications that will have multiple users and be run on a server.

The following code is an example of an ASP application. This example uses the VBScript function *Now* to print the date and time that the ASP application ran on the Web server.

```
<%@ LANGUAGE="VBSCRIPT"%>
<!DOCTYPE HTML PUBLIC "-//IETF//DTD HTML//EN">

<HTML>
<HEAD><TITLE>ASP Example</TITLE></HEAD>
<BODY>
<H1>I was created on <%=Now()%></H1>
</BODY>
</HTML>
```

As you can see, the syntax of the ASP script is a little different from the syntax for Outlook code. To tell the Web server that you want to run a script on the server, you must enclose the script in special characters: <% and %>. ASP supports placing your script directly in your HTML code—the script does not have to be in a separate section of the HTML file. If you run the same page on a server that does not have the proper ISAPI component for ASP, your code will look like only comments to that server. Also, with ASP.NET some changes have taken place. Your code is now separate from your HTML code to make coding easier.

Take a look at the first line of the code:

```
<%@ LANGUAGE="VBSCRIPT"%>
```

ASP assumes that the default language for server-side script is VBScript. If you replace *VBSCRIPT* with *JSCRIPT*, you can write server-side JScript code.

You might be wondering what the *<%=Now()%>* statement does in this example. The equal sign (=) indicates that the code should evaluate the expression, which in this case returns the current date and time. The equal sign in ASP is a shortcut for calling the *Write* method of the *Response* object.

Global.asa

If you've looked at the directories that contain .asp files, you might have noticed a file with the .asa extension: Global.asa. This is a special file in ASP applications that allows you to include code that executes when an application starts and ends and also when a session starts and ends. One thing to remember is that the Global.asa is an optional file for your Web applications. A skeleton Global.asa file is shown here:

```
<SCRIPT LANGUAGE="VBSCRIPT" RUNAT="Server">
   Sub Session_OnStart
      'Put your session startup code here
   End Sub
   Sub Session_OnEnd
      'Put your session termination code here
   End Sub
   Sub Application_OnStart
      'Put your application startup code here
   End Sub
   Sub Application_OnEnd
      'Put your application termination code here
   End Sub
</SCRIPT>
```

The Global.asa file contains stubs for your session and application start and end subroutines. To understand when these subroutines are called, you must understand what exactly constitutes a session and an application inside ASP.

When you browse Web pages, the Web server usually does not remember who you are or where you have been, and it does not store any values associated with you. One of the features of ASP is that it transforms the applications that you can build using the HTTP protocol from being stateless to being able to track the state of users. This ultimately lets you create global variables that are maintained for users throughout an application.

An ASP application consists of a virtual directory and associated files. But to understand when an ASP application starts and ends, you'll need a little bit more explanation of how ASP works. For your *Application_OnStart* subroutine to be called, the first user must request an .asp file from the virtual directory of your ASP application. The user can request an HTML file or another type of file from that directory, but these requests will not cause the *Application_OnStart* subroutine to be called. The user must explicitly request an ASP file. This is the only time this subroutine will be called, unless you restart the application. Restarting the application usually involves restarting the Web service.

You should use the *Application_OnStart* subroutine to initialize global variables across the lifetime of the Web application. A good example of a variable to initialize or set in your *Application_OnStart* subroutine is one that counts the number of users who have used your application. To improve performance, you should initialize the server components you are going to use for each user in the *Application_OnStart* subroutine. Figure 10-1 shows a Web browser sending a request to an ASP application for the first time.

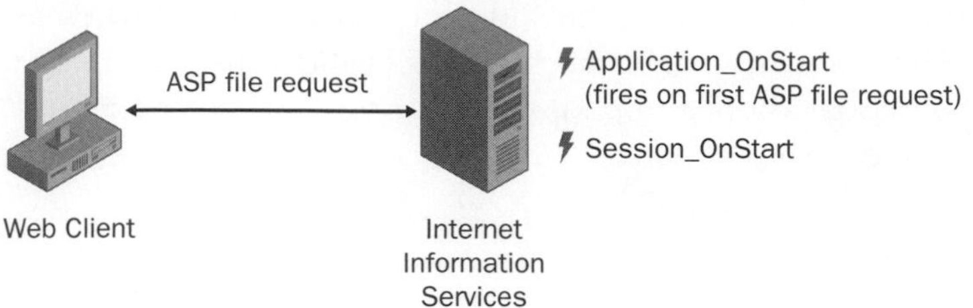

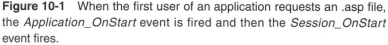

Figure 10-1 When the first user of an application requests an .asp file, the *Application_OnStart* event is fired and then the *Session_OnStart* event fires.

Unlike the *Application_OnStart* event, the *Session_OnStart* event is called for any user who makes an application file request. With ASP, each user of your application is considered to have a distinct session with the Web server. As a user browses Web pages in your ASP application, ASP implements and maintains state in a session by using cookies—whenever a user connects to your application, a file containing information (a cookie) is saved on the user's machine. When the session ends and the user closes his or her Web browser, the cookie is removed and the session is invalidated. If the user reconnects to your application, his machine receives a new cookie and a new session is started. For this reason, users of your application must support and accept cookies; otherwise, your ASP applications will not fully function. You can still use the server-side script of ASP, but you cannot maintain state information for any of your users. With ASP .NET, you can track state without cookies.

The *Session_OnStart* event is best used to initialize session variables for individual users. Session scope variables might include a connection to Exchange Server for an individual user and personalized information that a user sets in your application— for example, a user's preference for the background color of Web pages could be stored in a session variable. Each page the user accesses from your site during a session would be displayed with this background color. Figure 10-2 shows each Web browser starting a new session when accessing an ASP application.

The *Session_OnEnd* event is called when the session with the Web server ends. This end state can be reached in two ways:

- When the user has not requested or refreshed a Web page in the application for a specified amount of time
- By explicitly calling the *Abandon* method on the *Session* object

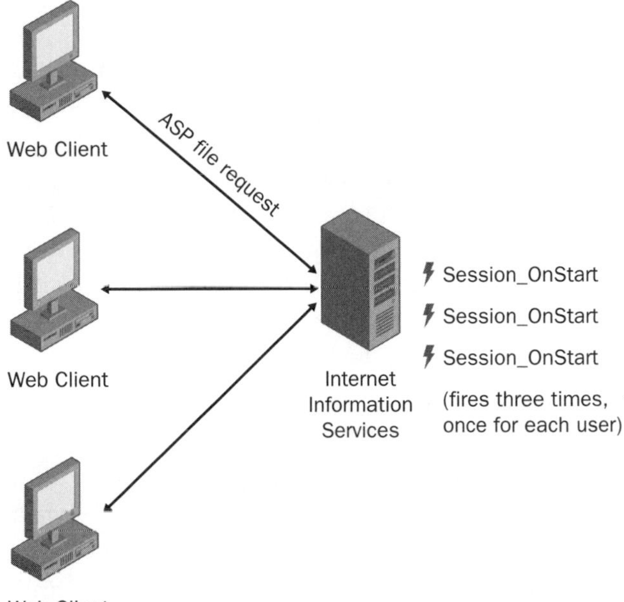

Figure 10-2 When a new user accesses your ASP application, the *Session_OnStart* event fires; *Application_OnStart* fires only when the first user accesses your application.

By default, IIS sets the timeout interval at 20 minutes. You can change this interval either through the administration program for IIS or by setting the *TimeOut* property on the intrinsic *Session* object in ASP. For example, to set a particular script timeout to 10 minutes, you would write the following code in your ASP application:

```
<% Session.TimeOut = 10 %>
```

The second way to reach the end state—by explicitly calling the *Abandon* method on the *Session* object—immediately ends the session and calls the *Session_OnEnd* event.

One final note about sessions: you have to be careful when you redirect people to other virtual directories in your application. Developers, including me, commonly make the mistake of redirecting users to another virtual root, forgetting that this is considered by ASP to be an application. When you do this, the session variables you establish in one application will not transfer to the other application unless you use the *Server.Transfer* method discussed later in this chapter. If you want to share session variables between two applications, you should place both applications in the same virtual directory in IIS or use *Server.Transfer*.

When a Web application ends, the *Application_OnEnd* event is called. You end a Web application in one of two ways: by shutting down the Web server or by stopping your application by using the Unload button in the IIS administrator. To use the Unload button, you must be running your Web application in a separate memory space. Be sure to save any application scope variables to a persistent medium, such as to your Exchange server or to a database, so that when your application restarts, the *Application_OnStart* event can reload the values. For example, you don't want a user-counter variable to restart at zero every time your application restarts. In this event handler, you should also destroy any server objects that you have created with an application scope, eliminating potential memory leaks on your server.

Global.asax File

With ASP.NET, you have a global.asax file rather than a global.asa file. While similar events to the ones we discussed earlier are available in ASP.NET, these events have new names, such as *Application_Sstart* and *Session_Start* rather than *Application_OnStart* and *Session_OnStart*. Also, there are some other events that the global.asa file does not contain but a global.asax can contain. Here is a list of the events that the global.asax file supports:

Event Name	Description
Application_Start	Fires when the first user hits your Web site.
Application_End	Fires when the last user in the site's session times out.
Application_Error	Fires when an unhandled error occurs in the application.
Session_Start	Fires when any new user hits your Web site.
Session_End	Fires when a user's session times out or ends.
Application_AcquireRequestState	Fires when ASP.NET acquires the current state (for example, session state) associated with the current request.
Application_AuthenticateRequest	Fires when a security module establishes the identity of the user.
Application_AuthorizeRequest	Fires when a security module verifies user authorization.
Application_BeginRequest	Fires when ASP.NET starts to process the request, before other per-request events.

Event Name	Description
Application_Disposed	Fires when ASP.NET completes the chain of execution when responding to a request.
Application_EndRequest	Fires as the last event during the processing of the request, after other pre-request events.
Application_PostRequestHandlerExecute	Fires right after the ASP.NET handler (a page or an XML Web service) finishes execution.
Application_PreRequestHandlerExecute	Fires just before ASP.NET begins executing a handler such as a page or an XML Web service.
Application_PreSendRequestContent	Fires just before ASP.NET sends content to the client.
Application_PreSendRequestHeaders	Fires just before ASP.NET sends HTTP headers to the client.
Application_ReleaseRequestState	Fires after ASP.NET finishes executing all request handlers. This event causes state modules to save the current state data.
Application_ResolveRequestCache	Fires after ASP.NET completes an authorization event to let the caching modules serve requests from the cache, bypassing execution of the handler (the page or Web service, for example).
Application_UpdateRequestCache	Fires after ASP.NET finishes executing a handler in order to let caching modules store responses that will be used to serve subsequent requests from the cache.

Built-In ASP Objects

The real power of ASP applications is that you can write server-side scripts and use their intrinsic objects. ASP and its built-in objects enable you to generate custom responses and maintain state information. We'll look next at the five built-in objects in ASP: *Application*, *Session*, *Request*, *Response*, and *Server*.

Application Object

The *Application* object is used to store global data related to an application that can be shared among all users. By using the methods and properties of this object in your application, you can create and set variables that have an application scope. To be sure that you do not run into concurrency issues when setting your application-level variables, as multiple users can be using the same application simultaneously, the *Application* object provides two methods: *Lock* and *Unlock*. These methods serialize the access to application-level variables so that only one client at a time can read or modify the values. The following example shows how to use the *Lock* and *Unlock* methods to increment a user-counter variable whenever a user accesses the application. The *Application* object maintains these variables in an internal collection. The example also shows how to set and retrieve application-level variables by using the *Application("VariableName")* syntax:

```
<HTML>
<HEAD>
<TITLE>Example: Application Object</TITLE>
</HEAD>
<BODY>
<%
   Application.Lock
   Application("NumVisitors") = Application"("NumVisitors") + 1
   Application.UnLock
%>
Welcome! You are visitor #<%=Application"(""NumVisitors")%>.
</BODY>
</HTML>
```

The *Application* object also contains two other collections in addition to the variables collection—*Contents* and *StaticObjects*. These collections allow you to browse through the application-level objects and variables you have created. You probably won't use either of these collections in your final application, but both of them provide great debugging functionality. For example, the *Contents* collection enables you to list the items that have been added to your application through a script command, and the *StaticObjects* collection enables you to list the items with an application scope that have been added using the *<OBJECT>* tag. By adding debugging code to your application at design time, when you run into application object problems, you can make ASP list the objects you've created with an application scope. The following code creates debugging code for the *Contents* and *StaticObjects* collections. The code output is shown in Figure 10-3. As you can see, objects and variables both can have an application scope.

```
<HTML>
<HEAD>
<TITLE>Debugging Application Objects</TITLE>
</HEAD>
<BODY>
<%
   'Create some application variables
   Application.Lock
   Set Application("oCDOSession") = _
       Server.CreateObject("MAPI.Session")
   Application("counter") = 10
   Application.UnLock
%>
<P>Objects from the Contents Collection<BR>
<%
```

```
   For each tempObj In Application.Contents
      response.write tempObj & "<BR>"
   Next
%>
<P>Objects from the StaticObjects Collection<BR>
<%
   For each tempObj In Application.StaticObjects
      response.write tempObj & "<BR>"
   Next
%>
</BODY>
</HTML>
```

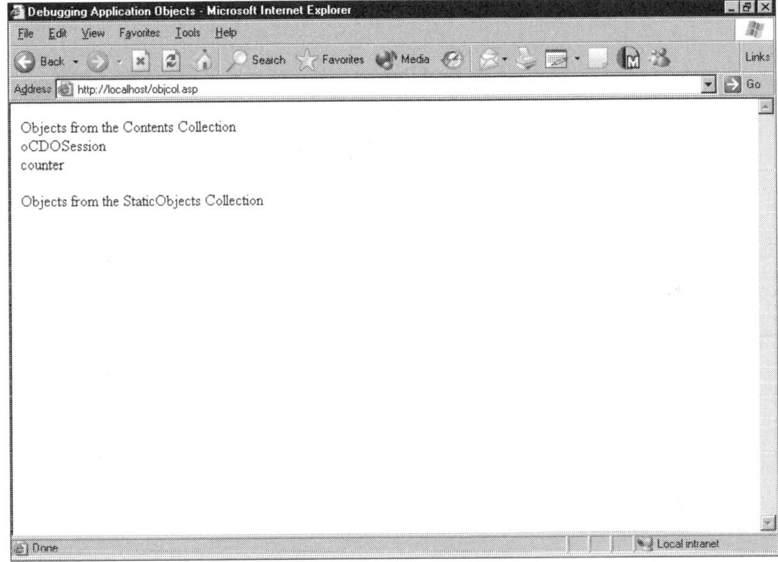

Figure 10-3 The debug output for the *Contents* and *StaticObjects* collections

Session Object

The *Session* object is one you'll use a lot in your Web applications. It holds the variables for individual users across the Web pages in your application. When you place a variable in the *Session* object, that variable is valid only for the current user and cannot be shared among users in the same way that an application variable can.

Like the *Application* object, the *Session* object contains the *Contents* and *StaticObjects* collections. You can create session variables in the same way you create application variables, by using the syntax *Session("VariableName")*.

The properties for the *Session* object include *CodePage*, *LCID*, *SessionID*, and *TimeOut*. The *CodePage* property represents the language code page that will be used to display the content for the HTML page, such as:

```
<% @LANGUAGE=VBSCRIPT CODEPAGE = 1252 %>
```

You can use the *LCID*, or locale identifier, property in conjunction with the *CodePage* property. The *LCID* property stores a standard international abbreviation that uniquely identifies a system-defined locale.

The *SessionID* property returns the unique session identifier for the current user. You should remember, however, that this ID is unique only during the lifetime of the ASP application. If you restart your Web server and therefore restart your Web applications, the Web server might generate the same IDs it already generated for the users before the Web application was restarted. For this reason, you should avoid storing these IDs and attempting to use them to uniquely identify a user of your application. If you always need to uniquely identify your users whenever they access your application, you should use globally unique identifiers (GUIDs) in cookies that are saved on the users' computers. You can also store their information in a SQL Server database and pull that information when they log on to the application.

The fourth property of the *Session* object is the *Timeout* property. This property enables you to change the timeout period associated with a particular ASP session. Remember that the timeout is set to 20 minutes by default. If you know that your application will be used for less than 20 minutes, you might want to decrease the duration of the timeout so that sessions end more quickly and resources are returned to the Web server at a faster rate.

The only method of the *Session* object is the *Abandon* method. As mentioned earlier, when you call this method, the user's session with the Web server as well as any associated objects and variables for that session are destroyed. If the user attempts to reconnect to the Web application, a new session starts on the server.

Request Object

The *Request* object allows you to access the information that was passed from the Web browser to your Web application. The *Request* object is crucial in ASP applications because it enables you to access user input for your server-side scripts. For example, suppose a user fills out an HTML form that you created. Once the user clicks the Submit button on the form, the *Request* object contains the form information that was passed to the server. By using the collections of the *Request* object, you can retrieve that information and your application can respond based on the user's input.

Request object collections

The *Request* object collections are created when the user submits a request to the Web server either by requesting an ASP file or by submitting an HTML form by clicking the Submit button. The three collections of the *Request* object that you'll primarily work with in your ASP applications are the *Form*, *QueryString*, and *ServerVariables* collections.

> **Note** For information on the other two *Response* object collections, *ClientCertificate* and *Cookies*, refer to the IIS documentation.

To understand when to use these collections, you first need to know about the different ways information can be passed from the Web browser to the Web server. Normally in your Web applications, you use HTML forms to gather input from the user so that you can use it in your calculations or store it in a data source. There are two main ways input is passed to the Web server from the client browser: the *Get* method and the *Post* method. The example that follows shows an HTML page that contains both methods on the same page.

```
<HTML>
<HEAD>
<TITLE>Forms Galore</TITLE>
<meta name="GENERATOR" content="Microsoft FrontPage">
</HEAD>
<BODY>
<form method="GET" action="getinfo.asp" name="GetForm">
   <p>What is your e-mail address?</p>
   <p><input type="text" name="email" size="20"></p>
   <p><input type="submit" value="Submit" name="GetSubmit"> </p>
</form>

<form method-"POST" action="getinfo.asp" name="PostForm">
   <p>What is your first name?</p>
   <p><input type="text" name="firstname" size="20"></p>
   <p><input type="submit" value="Submit" name="PostSubmit"> </p>
</form>
</BODY>
</HTML>
```

The *Action* attribute for each of the HTML forms specifies the same ASP file, getinfo.asp. The getinfo.asp file is shown here:

```
<HTML>
<HEAD>
<TITLE>Post and Get Methods Example</TITLE>
</HEAD>
</BODY>
<%txtRequestMethod = Request.ServerVariables("REQUEST_METHOD")%>
You selected to use the <B><%=txtRequestMethod%></B> Method.
<P><% if txtRequestMethod="GET" then %>
You entered your e-mail address as:
<B><%=Request.QueryString("email")%></B>
<% else %>
You entered your first name as: 
```

```
<B><%=Request.Form("firstname")%></B>
<% end if %>
</BODY>
</HTML>
```

This ASP code uses the *ServerVariables* collection of the *Request* object to check whether the form's *Request* method was a *Post* or *Get* method. Once the file determines which method was used, it displays the correct information for that particular type of form. Figure 10-4 shows a sample of the *Get* method.

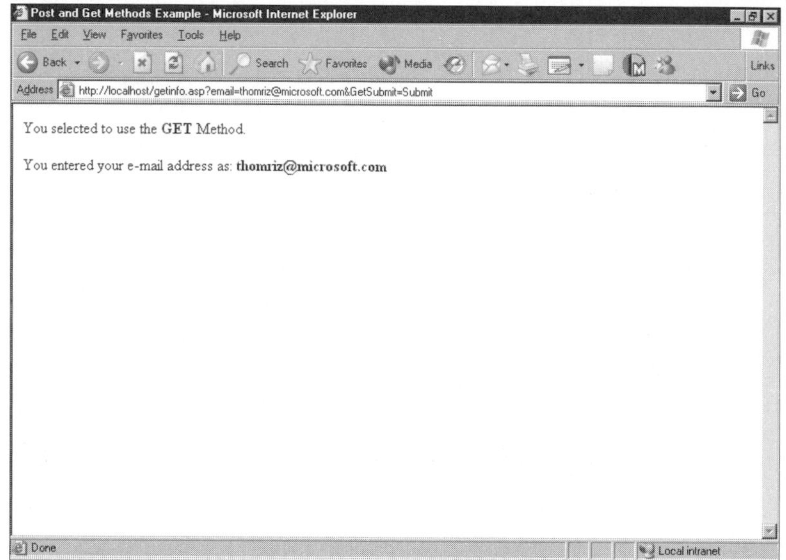

Figure 10-4 When a user types an e-mail address and submits the form, the *Get* method is used to pass the information to the *Request* object.

> **Note** You can also retrieve other server variables, such as *HTTP_USER_AGENT*, which returns information about which browser the client is using, and *LOGON_USER*, which represents the Windows account the user is currently logged on to. For a complete list of server variables, see the IIS documentation.

As you can see in Figure 10-4 with the *Get* method, the information from the form is actually appended to the URL—for example:

```
http://exserver/examples/getinfo.asp?email=thomriz@microsoft.com&GetSubmit=Sub-
mit
```

When data is appended to the URL using the *Get* method of a form, you use the *QueryString* collection of the *Request* object to retrieve the data. When using the *QueryString* collection, follow this format to retrieve the information:

```
Request.QueryString("VariableName")
```

Because the information passed to your application appears in the address of the user's browser, the user can see it, so you might want to restrict when you use the *Get* method. Instead, consider using the *Post* method.

The *Post* method places the form information inside the HTTP header, hiding the information from the client. However, when the *Post* method is used to submit form variables, you cannot use the *QueryString* collection. Instead, you need to use the *Forms* collection of the *Request* object. In the preceding example, the line

```
Request.Form("firstname")
```

retrieves the information the user typed into the First Name text box on the form. You can use this same syntax in your applications to retrieve information from an HTML form.

Response Object

The *Response* object is used to control the content that is returned to the client. For example, when you calculate a value on the server, you need a way to tell the ASP engine that you want to send the information back to the client. You do this by using the *Write* method of the *Response* object.

The *Write* method will be the most commonly used method in your ASP applications. Even though you have not seen any explicit statements using the *Response.Write* method in the examples, they are there. The syntax <%=*Variant*%> is equivalent to <% *Response.Write Variant* %>. The shorthand version makes it easier for you to put these statements in your code.

The *Response* object has a number of other collections, properties, and methods that you can use, such as the *Expires* property, which tells the Web browser how long to cache a particular page before it expires. If you do not want your clients to cache your Web pages, you would add the following line to your ASP files to cause your Web page to expire immediately on the user's local machine:

```
<% Response.Expires = 0 %>
```

The *Response* object allows you to buffer the output of your ASP page, which is useful if you want to hold back the output of your ASP code until the script completes its processing. The best example of when to use buffering is to capture errors in your code. For example, by turning on buffering using the command *Response.Buffer = True*, you can check throughout your ASP code whether an error has occurred. If one has, you can clear the buffer without sending its contents by using the *Response.Clear* method. You can then replace the output with new output, such as *Response.Write "An error has occurred. Please contact the administrator."* Finally, you can call the *Response.End* method, which sends the new contents of the buffer to the client and stops processing any further scripts in the page.

Server Object

The *Server* object provides you with utility methods and properties with which you can modify the information on your Web server. This object is used extensively in ASP applications because it contains both the *CreateObject* method and the *ScriptTimeout* property.

The *CreateObject* method allows you to create an object on the Web server by passing in the ProgID for the object. Let's look at an example. To create a CDO object, you would type this in your ASP file:

```
Set oSession = Server.CreateObject("MAPI.Session")
```

ASP creates an object and passes that object to your *oSession* variable. By default, when you do this on an ASP page, the object has page-level scope. This means that when ASP is done processing the current page, the object is destroyed. Therefore, you might want to create objects on a page and then store them by assigning them to either session variables or application variables, as shown in this code snippet:

```
<%
   Set oSession = Server.CreateObject("MAPI.Session")
   Set Session("oSession") = oSession
%>
```

As you learned earlier, an object that is assigned either a session or an application scope will be destroyed when either the session or the application ends, respectively. The one issue to watch out for with the *CreateObject* method and some objects is potential performance loss. You can instantiate almost every object on your Web server as an ASP object, but some objects are specifically designed to run in a server-based, multiuser environment such as CDO. When you instantiate an object that was not designed for an ASP environment, application performance might suffer if too many people hit the page containing that object at the same time.

The *ScriptTimeout* property of the *Server* object allows you to specify how long a script should run before it is terminated. By default, an ASP script can run for 90 seconds before it is terminated, but this interval might not be enough time to retrieve data from some data sources. By using the following syntax for this property, you can increase or decrease the amount of time the script will run before termination:

```
Server.ScriptTimeout = numseconds
```

Avoid increasing this number much beyond 90 seconds; users who are waiting for long periods of time might assume the page did not load correctly and might click their Stop and Refresh buttons continuously, flooding your Web server with requests.

With the *Server.Transfer* method, you can specify another ASP file to execute in a different ASP application without losing your existing variables in the calling ASP application. Use this method if you are going to transfer users from one virtual directory to another in IIS. Remember that different virtual directories are usually considered separate applications to IIS. For example, you might have two distinct applications on your IIS machine and you might need to move the user from one application to another but you do not want to lose the state information for the user in the transfer.

Server-Side Include Files

One powerful feature beyond the use of intrinsic objects in ASP is the ability to use server-side include files in your ASP files. Include files are just text files containing script or HTML that you want to add to your ASP page. Outlook Web Access relies heavily on server-side include files for common code libraries in its ASP files. Here are some examples of server-side include files:

```
<!-- #include file="library/vbsfunctions.inc" -->

<!-- #include virtual="/library/vbsfunctions.inc" -->
```

Using Type Libraries in ASP Applications

ASP uses VBScript, which does not use constants. Therefore, if you want to use globals or constants from a type library, you have to declare the constants yourself or import these constants into your application to use them throughout your code, which ASP allows you to do. The way you do this is by using the *METADATA* keyword in your applications. The following example shows the use of this keyword in your Global.asa file, which will make the constants available throughout your ASP application.

```
<!--METADATA TYPE="typelib" UUID="CD000000-8B95-11D1-82DB-00C04FB1625D"
    NAME="CDO for Exchange 2000 Type Library" -->
<!--METADATA TYPE="typelib" UUID="CD001000-8B95-11D1-82DB-00C04FB1625D"
    NAME="Microsoft CDO Workflow Objects for Microsoft Exchange"-->
<!--METADATA TYPE="typelib" UUID="25150F00-5734-11D2-A593-00C04F990D8A"
    NAME="Microsoft CDO for Exchange Management Library"-->
<!--METADATA TYPE="typelib" UUID="00000205-0000-0010-8000-00AA006D2EA4"
    NAME="ADODB Type Library" -->
```

Server Components

ASP can take advantage of built-in objects and also use server components to add functionality to your application. An example of two such components are Microsoft ActiveX Data Objects (ADO) and CDO. ADO allows you to connect to many types of databases; CDO allows you to connect to Exchange Server and other messaging servers. You can also write your own components using any COM-based development tool.

WebDAV Support

IIS also supports Web Distributed Authoring and Versioning (WebDAV). WebDAV is a set of extensions to HTTP that allows you to send to your Web server commands that will open, edit, move, search, or delete files. Exchange and SharePoint Portal Server (SPS) support WebDAV, so you'll learn more about it when I discuss Exchange and SPS in later chapters.

ASP Security

This section describes how ASP security works and how you should set up Windows to support the type of security you want for your Web applications.

When IIS is first installed, it creates a Windows user account named IUSR_*computername*, where *computername* corresponds to the current computer name. This account is assigned to the Guests account group, is given a random password, and is granted the right to log on locally. Whenever a user browses a Web page, this account attempts to access the page on behalf of the user. If the IUSR_*computername* account does not have the proper permissions to access the page, the request is rejected with a "401 Access Denied" error message. The Web server then informs the Web browser which authentication methods the Web server will support—either Basic authentication or Windows NT Challenge/Response authentication—depending on the settings defined on your IIS server.

Basic Authentication

Basic authentication is supported across all Web browsers. When the Web server informs the client that it supports Basic authentication, the Web browser displays a message box asking the user for a user name and password. Once the user types this information in, the Web server tries to invoke the request using the credentials that the user supplied rather than the IIS anonymous account. It is a good idea to pass in your domain name as well as the user name in the authentication dialog box in the Web browser, using the syntax *domain\username*.

Basic authentication, if used over Internet connections, can present some security concerns because the user name and password typed into the authentication dialog box is transmitted to the server as clear text. If you do use Basic authentication over Internet connections, use it in conjunction with Secure Sockets Layer (SSL). SSL will encrypt the connection between the Web browser and the Web server so that any information passed between the two cannot be viewed by unauthorized individuals.

For the Web server to impersonate the user whose name is typed into the authentication dialog box, the Web server must log on as that user. By default, Windows does not give regular users the Log On Locally right on the server computer. For this reason, you must grant the right to Log On Locally on the Web server to all users who you expect will use your Web application with Basic authentication. You do this is by granting all your domain users the Log On Locally right in the group policies for your domain controllers.

Digest Authentication

IIS supports the standard Digest authentication. Digest authentication is similar to Basic authentication, but Digest authentication does not send the user's password over the wire. Instead, Digest authentication uses a hashing algorithm to form a hexadecimal representation of a combination of user name, password, the requested resource, and the HTTP method.

Windows NT Challenge/Response Authentication

Windows NT Challenge/Response, or NTLM authentication, is the most secure form of authentication because the user name and password are not sent from the Web browser to the Web server. Instead an encrypted challenge/response handshake mechanism is used. Unlike Basic authentication, NTLM typically does not prompt the user for a name and password. The Windows NT security credentials of the Web user currently logged on are sent to IIS and are used to access the requested resource. IIS then changes to the context of the specified user and attempts to access the resource. If this fails, the user will be prompted for a user name and password.

> **Note** For Windows NT Challenge/Response to work correctly, the users you are trying to authenticate must have the Access This Computer From A Network right in the group policies for your domain. This is normally enabled for users by default.

A one-way encryption method is used, meaning the mechanism validates the user without sending the password to IIS. IIS doesn't know the user information and cannot use it to access other resources on other machines. Essentially, this is a problem of delegation. When IIS attempts to access a resource on another machine, the other machine will prompt IIS for user credentials. Since IIS does not have the password for the user, it cannot return the correct information to the other machine. For this reason, you cannot use the Windows NT Challenge/Response authentication method within a Web application that works with Exchange if the application is on a different server from your Exchange server. IIS cannot remotely send the authentication to the Exchange server when the Windows NT Challenge/Response method is used. You can solve this problem if you use the delegation features of Windows and IIS. However, delegation is quite powerful and should only be used if you understand the issues with it. Look at Microsoft Knowledge Base Article Q283201 for more information about delegation.

One more note about delegation is that Windows Server 2003 introduces a new type of delegation called *constrained delegation*. Constrained delegation allows you to delegate to only a certain application or service. Rather than allowing any type of delegation, constrained delegation lets you limit the service that the server can authenticate with on behalf of a user. You should look at these capabilities if you want your mid-tier application to authenticate a user against a back-end application and do not want to use basic authentication.

A second gotcha of the Windows NT Challenge/Response method is that you cannot use it over proxy connections for the same reasons just discussed. When setting up your Web server, consider NTLM's security advantages as well as its limitations.

A third gotcha for NTLM is that NTLM is supported only by Internet Explorer. This means that if you have a mixture of Web browser clients accessing your application, you might want to enable both Windows NT Challenge/Response and Basic authentication. If you enable only Windows NT Challenge/Response, when Netscape Navigator users attempt to access a secure resource or page, they'll receive a message denying them permission. With both security methods set up, if Windows NT Challenge/Response fails, Basic authentication will be used.

.NET Passport Authentication

Microsoft .NET Passport is a user-authentication service that permits single sign-in security, providing users with secure access to .NET Passport–enabled Web sites and services. Sites that support .NET Passport rely on the .NET Passport central server to authenticate users. However, the central server does not authorize or deny a specific user's access to individual .NET Passport sites. It is the responsibility of the Web site to control users' permissions. When you select this option, requests to IIS must contain valid .NET Passport credentials on either the query string or in the cookie. If IIS does not detect .NET Passport credentials, requests are redirected to the .NET Passport logon page.

ACLs

Another way to restrict access to your Web pages is by setting NTFS-level file permissions on your actual ASP files and directories. This will control which accounts have access to the files and the level of access they have. IIS respects the ACLs (Access Control Lists) on the files and will use the ACLs to attempt to verify users and their individual permissions on the files. Be careful when setting permissions on files, however, because if the permissions you set are too restrictive, users will not be able to use your application.

ASP.NET Authentication

Although ASP.NET builds on the authentication methods used in ASP, there are some differences. For example, ASP.NET natively supports forms-based authentication. Also, ASP.NET has more granular control when doing impersonation than ASP. This section will explore the enhancements in ASP.NET.

ASP.NET supports four types of authentication: None, Passport, Forms, and Windows. You can guess what None and Passport authentication are. Windows authentication is just standard IIS authentication. Forms authentication requires a bit more discussion.

Forms Authentication

With ASP.NET, you can perform HTML forms-based authentication rather than the standard IIS authentication, such as NTLM or Basic. With forms-based authentication, all unauthenticated requests are directed to a specified HTML form using client-side redirection. The user can then supply logon credentials and post the form back to the server. If the application authenticates the request using application-specific logic, such as looking up the user information in a database or other datasource, ASP.NET issues a cookie that contains the credentials or a key for reacquiring the client identity. Subsequent requests are issued with the cookie in the request headers, which means that subsequent authentications are unnecessary because the user is considered authenticated. In Chapter 13 you will learn how to use forms authentication with Active Directory as the authentication mechanism.

Impersonation in ASP.NET

With ASP.NET, impersonation is more granular, whereby you can have IIS authenticate the user. After that, IIS will pass the token of the user to ASP.NET. Using settings in the web.config file, you can have your ASP.NET application perform different types of impersonation. Here are the different types of impersonation that ASP.NET supports.

- Impersonation enabled with no user account identified. In this instance, ASP.NET will impersonate the token passed to it by IIS, which will be either an authenticated user or the anonymous Internet user account. Here is the code that will appear in your web.config file:

  ```
  <identity impersonate="true"/>
  ```

- Impersonation enabled but with a specific impersonation identity specified. In this instance, ASP.NET will impersonate the token generated using the configured identity. In this case the client token, if applicable, is not used. The code that should appear in your web.config file is the following:

  ```
  <identity impersonate="true" name="domain\user" password="pwd"/>
  ```

- Impersonation disabled is the default setting for backward compatibility with ASP. In this instance, the ASP.NET thread will run using the process token of the application worker process, which by default is the IIS system account, regardless of which combination of IIS and ASP.NET authentication have been used. Here is the code that should appear in your web.config file:

  ```
  <identity impersonate="false"/>
  ```

To figure out what account you are currently running under in your ASP.NET applications, you can use the following snippet of code.

```
System.Security.Principal.WindowsIdentity.GetCurrent().Name
```

ASP.NET Worker Account

The ASP.NET application worker process is called aspnet_wp.exe. You should run this process using an account with weaker privileges than the default System account. You will want to do this so that if your system is breached, the intruder does not have strong access to your system.

To run the ASP worker process using a specified account, add a *<processModel>* element to the root configuration file (machine.config), located in the \Windows\Microsoft.NET\Framework\<Version>\Config folder, as shown here:

```
<system.web>
  <processModel enable="true" username="domain\user" password="pwd"/>
</system.web>
```

In addition to specifying a particular user account, you can set the *username* attribute to one of two specially recognized values, *SYSTEM* and *MACHINE*. In both cases, the *password* attribute must be set to *AutoGenerate* because specific credentials are not required for these special accounts. The *SYSTEM* setting runs the worker process using the System account. The *SYSTEM* setting is the default for ASP.NET. The *MACHINE* value causes the worker process to run with a special account named with an ASPNET prefix. This account is similar to the IWAM_MACHINENAME account used by IIS for running instances of dllhost.exe when hosting regular ASP applications. The ASPNET account is created during .NET installation.

When you use CDO 1.21 with static profiles, one gotcha you need to remember is that information must be read from the registry for CDO 1.21 static profiles. This means that if you set the identity for the ASP.NET worker process to an identity that cannot read from the registry, you will get errors from CDO.

> **Note** The ASP.NET worker thread runs under a local machine account. By using a local machine account, when you attempt to debug an ASP.NET application on a domain or backup domain controller, you will get an error because all accounts are domain accounts, not local accounts. For this reason, you might not want to run your applications on a DC or you will have to enable the SYSTEM special user account.

Impersonating Users Through Code

There might be times when you want to impersonate a specific user programmatically. For example, you might only want to impersonate the authenticated user to run a certain section of code. The following code performs this functionality.

```
Dim impersonationContext As _
    System.Security.Principal.WindowsImpersonationContext
Dim currentWindowsIdentity As System.Security.Principal.WindowsIdentity

currentWindowsIdentity = CType(User.Identity, _
    System.Security.Principal.WindowsIdentity)
impersonationContext = currentWindowsIdentity.Impersonate()

'Insert your code that runs under the security context of the
'authenticating user here.

impersonationContext.Undo()
```

To authenticate a specific user for all requests to the server, you can use the Win32 API *LogonUser* method, just like you can with ASP. The following code, written for ASP.NET, logs on as a specific user. When you use the *LogonUser* method, you must know the username and password of the user. You can get this information by asking the user or by some other means.

```
<%@ Page Language="VB" %>
<%@ Import Namespace = "System.Web" %>
<%@ Import Namespace = "System.Web.Security" %>
<%@ Import Namespace = "System.Security.Principal" %>
<%@ Import Namespace = "System.Runtime.InteropServices" %>

<script runat=server>
Dim LOGON32_LOGON_INTERACTIVE As Integer  = 2
Dim LOGON32_PROVIDER_DEFAULT As Integer = 0

Dim oImpContext As WindowsImpersonationContext

Declare Auto Function LogonUser Lib "advapi32.dll" ( _
    ByVal lpszUsername As String, _
    ByVal lpszDomain As String, _
    ByVal lpszPassword As String, _
    ByVal dwLogonType As Integer, _
    ByVal dwLogonProvider As Integer, _
    ByRef phToken As IntPtr) As Integer
Declare Auto Function DuplicateToken Lib "advapi32.dll" ( _
    ByVal ExistingTokenHandle As IntPtr, _
    ImpersonationLevel As Integer, _
    ByRef DuplicateTokenHandle As IntPtr) As Integer

Public Sub Page_Load(s As Object, e As EventArgs)
    If ImpersonateUser("username", "domain", "password") Then
        'Run code that you want to run under the user context
         undoImpersonation()
    Else
        'Impersonation failed. Error should go here.
    End If
End Sub

Private Function ImpersonateUser( _
    userName As String, _
    domain As String, _
    password As String) As Boolean

    Dim tempWindowsIdentity As WindowsIdentity
    Dim token As IntPtr
    Dim tokenDuplicate As IntPtr

    If LogonUser(userName, domain, password, _
        LOGON32_LOGON_INTERACTIVE, LOGON32_PROVIDER_DEFAULT, _
        token) <> 0 Then
```

```
        If DuplicateToken(token, 2, tokenDuplicate) <> 0 Then
            tempWindowsIdentity = new WindowsIdentity(tokenDuplicate)
            oImpContext = tempWindowsIdentity.Impersonate()
            If oImpContext Is Nothing Then
               ImpersonateUser = False
            Else
               ImpersonateUser = True
            End If
        Else
           ImpersonateUser = False
        End If
    Else
        ImpersonateUser = False
    End If
End Function

Private Sub undoImpersonation()
    oImpContext.Undo()
End Sub
</script>
```

Summary

This chapter provided an overview of Web fundamentals and Web security, so we can dive right into programming against Exchange and Active Directory in the next chapters. Remember what you have read here because Web applications often fail due to security or configuration issues rather than coding or Exchange Server issues.

11

Collaboration Data Objects

As you saw in Chapter 10, you can use Microsoft Active Server Pages (ASP) or Microsoft ASP.NET to develop powerful Web applications that are not dependent on the capabilities of the browser. This power of ASP comes not from the built-in libraries of the ASP object model but from COM components that you call from your ASP programs. In this chapter and the next one, you'll learn about one of those COM components—Collaboration Data Objects (CDO)—which enables you to develop messaging and collaboration applications for the Web. You can use CDO for other purposes as well, such as in client-based or server based applications that you develop. In this chapter, you will learn what CDO is and how it compares to other technologies, what objects are in the CDO library, and how you can start developing ASP programs. In Chapter 12, you'll see a Microsoft Visual Basic application that takes advantage of this library.

What Is CDO?

CDO is an object library that exposes the interfaces of the Messaging Application Programming Interface (MAPI), but instead of requiring the C/C++ language as MAPI does, CDO can be programmed using any development tool that can reference COM objects, such as ASP, Visual Basic, Microsoft Visual C#, or Microsoft Visual C++.

CDO has had several incarnations; previous versions shipped with different names and functionality. For example, in Microsoft Exchange Server 4.0, CDO was named OLE Messaging, and in Exchange Server 5.0, it was named Active Messaging. With the advent of Exchange Server 5.5 and Microsoft Outlook 98, the library was renamed Collaboration Data Objects to better describe its services—CDO provides much more than messaging functionality. Even though the name has changed from version to version, CDO is backward compatible with applications that use a previous version of the object library. (As of this writing, the latest released versions of CDO are CDO for Microsoft Windows, CDO 1.21, and CDO for Exchange.)

CDO is actually divided into four dynamic link libraries (DLLs): CDO.dll and CDOHTML.dll for CDO 1.21, and CDOEX.dll and CDOEXM.dll for CDO for Exchange. We'll cover CDO 1.21 in this chapter and then look at CDO for Exchange in Chapters 15 and 18. CDO.dll contains the core collaborative functionality of CDO, such as functionality for sending messages, accessing the directory, and viewing free/busy calendar information. CDOHTML.dll is the CDO Rendering library. This library allows you to automatically convert information stored in Exchange Server to HTML by using custom views, colors, and formats. The CDO Rendering library is installed when you install OWA on your Web server. Throughout this chapter, you will learn how to use both CDO 1.21 libraries in your applications.

> **Note** You install CDO by installing Outlook on your machine or by installing Outlook Web Access (OWA) version 5.5 on your Web server. When you install CDO via Outlook, you do not get the CDO Rendering library. If you are using CDO 1.21 with Exchange 2000 or later, the CDO Rendering library will still work, but you should consider using some of the newer technologies included with Exchange, such as WSS Forms. Also, if you will be using CDO on your Web server and your Exchange Server is on a different server, you can get CDO by installing Exchange 5.5 OWA, Exchange 2000/2003 Server, or the Exchange administration program in Exchange 2003. Installing the Exchange administration program for Exchange 2000 does not install CDO, but Exchange 2003 does. Also, you should not install a secure version of CDO, such as the CDO that comes with Outlook, on the server because any Outlook security prompts will not work in a non-UI environment such as server-side code in ASP or ASP.NET. If you find that you are getting logon or unexplained errors using CDO, make sure you do not have a secure version of CDO on the machine by checking to see if Outlook is on the machine.

CDO and the Outlook Object Library

CDO and the Outlook object library are complementary technologies. The Account Tracking application discussed in Chapter 8 illustrates how to use the

CDO library in conjunction with the Outlook object library. You might be wondering when to use each library. To make a decision, you should consider security criteria such as where the application will run and what type of information it will access. As you develop applications, you will find that deciding between the Outlook library and the CDO library will almost never be simple. You can use the Outlook object library to do the following:

- Access special information stored in Outlook, such as Tasks and Journal items, that CDO does not support
- Open another user's information, such as the Calendar or Inbox
- Sort or filter complex Outlook properties

You can use the CDO library to do the following:

- Render objects or data into HTML
- Create multiuser server-based applications
- Access detailed information stored in the directory or display address books for users to pick from

CDO and CDO for Windows

When you install Microsoft Internet Information Services (IIS), you have the option to install a Simple Mail Transfer Protocol (SMTP) component and a Network News Transfer Protocol (NNTP) component on your Web server. These components are subsets, functionally, of the CDO library named Collaboration Data Objects for Windows (CDOSYS). The CDO for Windows library allows you to quickly build applications that do not require the complete functionality of CDO. For example, if on your web page you want to create a simple way for users to send comments through e-mail, you should use the CDO for Windows object library rather than CDO. If your application requires looking up a user in a directory server, however, you should use the advanced functionality of the full CDO library. Another difference between CDO and CDO for Windows is that CDO for Windows uses only SMTP and NNTP to communicate with a server. The use of these protocols to talk with the server limits the functionality that CDO for Windows library can provide. With that said, you should use the CDO for Windows library to do the following:

- Send unauthenticated e-mail from a Web page
- Send bulk mailings via e-mail
- Support Mime HTML (MHTML)

You should use the CDO 1.21 library to do the following:

- Use authenticated or anonymous access to information, but not anonymous e-mails
- Access or create calendaring information
- Access a directory and its information

Which CDO Should I Use Where?

With all the versions of CDO, you might get confused about which CDO you can use where and which version to use with which version of Exchange Server or Outlook. Table 11-1 can help you decide.

Table 11-1 CDO Version Reference

Application Usage	Outlook Object Model	CDO 1.21s (secure version installed via Outlook)	CDO 1.21 (server version via Exchange Server or OWA)	CDO for Exchange 2000
Client-Side Application (Outlook form, Visual Basic application)	Yes	Yes	Yes	No (not remotable)
Web Server Application	No	No (security dialog boxes cause problems in Web applications)	Yes	Yes (if Web server is on same server as Exchange 2003)
Windows Service	No	No (security dialog box problems)	Yes	Yes
Access Exchange 5.5 Data	Yes	Yes	Yes	No
Access Exchange 2003 Data	Yes	Yes	Yes	Yes

CDO and .NET

One thing to watch for with CDO is that certain versions of the CDO library are not supported in a .NET environment. For example, as of this writing, CDO 1.21

is not supported by Microsoft if you use it via COM interop from Visual Studio .NET. CDO for Exchange, CDO for Exchange Management, Web Distributed Authoring and Versioning (WebDAV), Windows Management Instrumentation (WMI), Collaboration Data Objects (CDO) for Windows, and the OLEDB provider for Exchange are supported in .NET. You should check Microsoft Knowledge Base article 813349 regularly because support policies can change without notice. With that said, I've worked extensively with CDO 1.21 using .NET and have samples that use .NET in this book. In my testing, CDO 1.21 seems to work fine with just a few little quirks in the .NET environment. However, you should judge for yourself whether using .NET and CDO 1.21 will meet the needs of your project and whether its lack of official support is acceptable. You can always go back to Visual Studio 6.0 and not use .NET if you find it unacceptable.

Overview of the CDO 1.21 Library

The CDO library is a hierarchical library consisting of objects and collections. As you read the chapter, you'll find that some collections have the same name as others even though they contain different objects. However, the information that each collection accesses is specific to the object the collection refers to.

In the CDO library, the *Session* object is at the highest-level and contains all of the other CDO objects and collections. This makes sense because you need some type of session, either an Exchange Server session or an offline session, to start accessing information stored in an Exchange Server database. Figure 11-1 shows the hierarchy of the CDO library, which begins with the *Session* object. All other objects are created as children of the CDO *Session* object.

> **Note** If you're familiar with ActiveX Data Objects (ADO), it might be helpful to know that the *Session* object is similar to the ADO *Connection* object. However, do not confuse the *Session* object in ASP with the *Session* object in CDO. They are entirely different objects.

As you can see from Figure 11-1, the CDO library is quite logical in its layout of collections and objects. Below the *Session* object are the major collections and objects of the CDO library, such as the *InfoStores* collection, which contains the data stores for your application, and the *AddressLists* collection, which contains the address entries your application can use. Below these major collections are other collections, such as the *Folders* collection, which contains the folders for a particular *InfoStore*, and the *Messages* collection, which contains the messages for a particular folder. The CDO library is one of the most approachable Microsoft object libraries; it allows you to quickly build powerful collaborative applications.

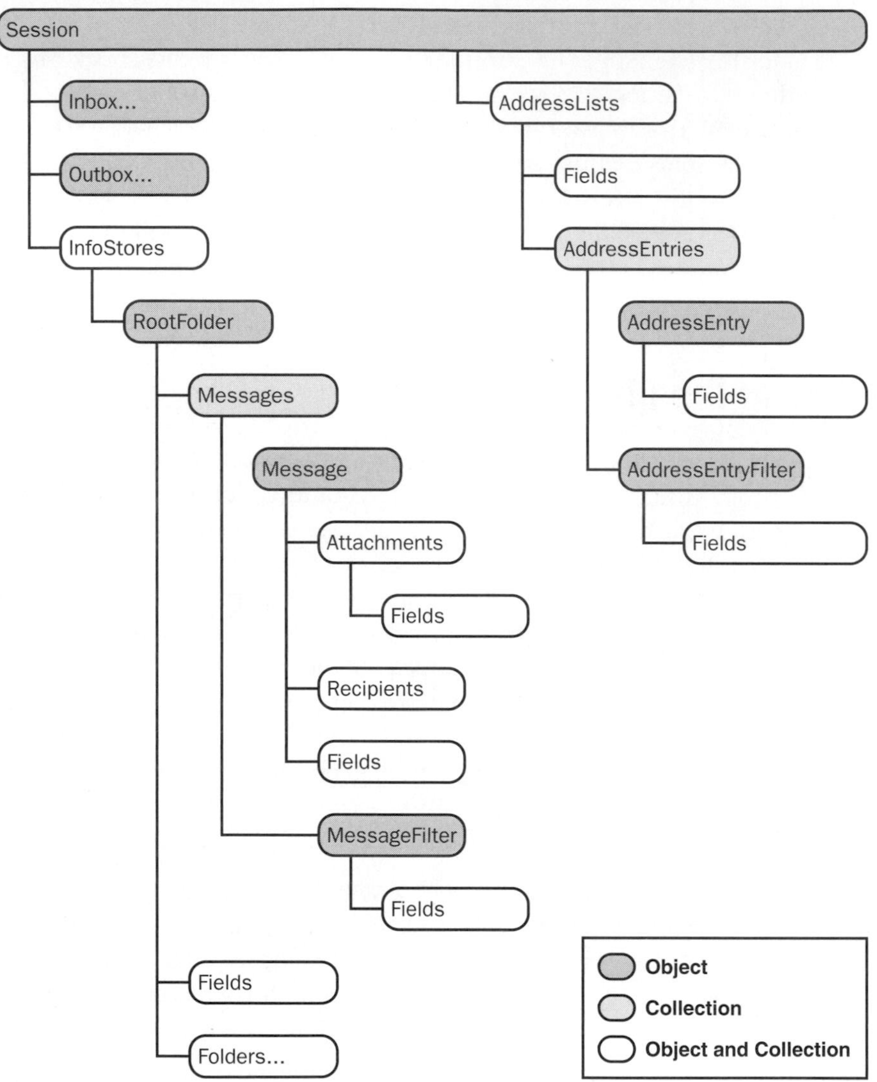

Figure 11-1 The CDO library hierarchy

Getting Help with the CDO Library

This chapter provides an overview of the CDO library, but you might also want to look at the CDO help file, which provides useful information as well as code samples. The CDO Windows Help file (cdo.hlp) is on the Exchange Server CD and the Outlook CD. The CDO compiled HTML Help file (cdo.chm) is available with the companion content for this book. It is also available as part of the Platform Software Development Kit (SDK) section of the MSDN Library, which you can access online at *http://msdn.microsoft.com/library*. Also refer to Chapter 12, which contains some tips and tricks for building CDO applications.

Background for the Four Sample CDO Applications

The easiest way to learn any new object library is to look at the objects in action, so the rest of this chapter shows you two sample applications that demonstrate different technologies in the CDO library: a Helpdesk application and a Calendar of Events application. Chapter 12 shows you two advanced samples: an Intranet News application and a CDO Visual Basic application. From these four samples, you will learn how to use the CDO library in your applications and become aware of the technical considerations that arise when you build CDO applications. All of these applications are written using Visual Basic and use either ASP or Windows Forms. You will need a version of Visual Studio 6.0 if you want the best experience in modifying the applications. Before we dive into the details of the sample applications, we'll first look at the necessary Exchange Server logon step.

Using the CDO *Session* Object

Whether you build CDO applications by using ASP or some other development tool, the most important point to remember is that you cannot create any other objects in the CDO library if you do not first successfully create a *Session* object. Furthermore, you cannot access any data in Exchange Server unless you successfully log on to the server using the *Session* object. Before we can look at the code in the CDO applications, you must understand how to log on to an Exchange server by using the *Session* object.

The *Session* object is the top-level object in the CDO hierarchy. It contains sessionwide settings and properties that return top-level objects. When you use the *CreateObject* method in your applications, you use the ProgID of the *Session* object—*MAPI.Session*—to create a CDO object. With one exception, CDO does not allow you to access any other objects in the library until you have successfully logged on using the *Logon* method of the *Session* object. The exception is the *SetLocaleIDs* method, which sets the *Locale* and *CodePage* IDs for the user.

Using the *Logon* Method

The *Logon* method takes a number of parameters, as shown in the following code; the parameter you use depends on the needs of your application:

```
objSession.Logon( [ProfileName] [, ProfilePassword] [, ShowDialog]
[, NewSession] [, ParentWindow] [, NoMail] [, ProfileInfo] )
```

The two common ways to log on to a CDO session are by passing in a MAPI profile name and by passing in the specific information CDO needs to dynamically generate a profile. Dynamically generated profiles are the preferred method when you build ASP applications with CDO. Because ASP pages cannot remotely access the profiles on a client's machine, CDO has no way to pull information from one of those profiles.

Authenticated Logon Using a Profile

To log on using a profile, you pass the profile name as the first parameter, *ProfileName*, to the *Logon* method. If you don't know which profile name to use, set the *ShowDialog* parameter to *True*, and CDO will prompt the user to pick a profile. The second parameter, *ProfilePassword*, specifies the profile password. You can leave this parameter blank and set the *ShowDialog* parameter to *True*, and CDO will prompt the user for a password. By setting the *NewSession* parameter to *False*, you can have CDO take advantage of an existing MAPI session, eliminating the overhead of creating a new MAPI session on the user's machine. The following code snippet shows how to use the *Logon* method with a profile named *MS Outlook Settings*:

```
oSession.Logon ProfileName:="MS Outlook Settings", _
   showDialog:=True, NewSession:=True
```

Authenticated Logon Using a Dynamically Generated Profile

If your application is running in an environment in which profiles or the ability to prompt a user for a profile are not available, CDO allows you to dynamically generate a profile for the user by passing the user's server name and mailbox name to the *Logon* method. To get this information, you can have your application prompt the user for his server name and mailbox name. Alternatively, CDO can pull the default Exchange Server name from the registry by using the *ConfigParameter* properties in the CDO Rendering library, which you will learn about later in this chapter. For now, the code sample assumes that you know the name of at least one Exchange server in your organization. The following code shows how to log on to CDO using a dynamically generated profile:

```
strServer = "Exchange Server Name"
strMailbox = "User Alias Name (Not Display Name)"
strProfileInfo = strServer + vbLf + strMailbox
oSession.Logon "", "", False, True, 0, True, strProfileInfo
'Check for a valid logon
set oInbox = oSession.GetInbox

If Err.number <> 0 Then  'Not Successful
    oSession.Logoff
    Response.Write "Logon Unsuccessful!"
End If
```

> **Note** For the user's mailbox name, don't use the display name, such as *Thomas Rizzo*. Instead, use the alias of the user, such as *thomriz*. Also, when you use the *ProfileInfo* parameter, try to access an item in a CDO message store, such as the first message in the Inbox, because the *Logon* method will return success even if the parameters in *ProfileInfo* are incorrect. If an attempt to access items returns an error, the user was not successfully logged on. If you find that the alias has multiple overlaps, such as *Rizzo* and *Rizzoti*, and you must log on *Rizzo*, you can instead use the SMTP address of the user to log on to CDO.

Anonymous Access

CDO also allows users to anonymously access the Exchange Server public folder store as well as the Exchange Server directory. Anonymous access must be enabled by the administrator of the Exchange Server system. Also, the administrator or developer can control which folders and which directory entries the anonymous user can see by setting some options in the Exchange Administrator program. These options are discussed in more detail throughout this chapter.

To use anonymous access, you must pass the distinguished name of the Exchange server and the Anon account in the *ProfileInfo* parameter. You do this by using the following format:

```
server distinguished name & vbLf & vbLf & "anon"
```

The server's distinguished name takes this form:

```
/o=enterprise/ou=site/cn=Configuration/cn=Servers/cn=server
```

The *enterprise* parameter corresponds to the Exchange Server organization, and the *site* parameter corresponds to the Exchange Server site you want to access. The following code shows you how to log on using anonymous access:

```
strProfileInfo = "/o=" & "Your Exchange Org" & "/ou=" & _
    "Your Site" & "/cn=Configuration/cn=Servers/cn=" & _
    "Your Server" & vbLF & vbLF & "anon"
oSession.Logon "", "", False, True, 0, True, strProfileInfo
If Err.number <> 0 Then
    oSession.Logoff
    response.Write "Logon Unsuccessful!"
End If
```

Note Anonymous access does not work with Exchange 2000 or 2003. For the sample applications to work, you must add some entries to the registry that a clean install of Exchange 2000 or 2003 does not include. The entries to add under the *HKLM\SYSTEM\CurrentControlSet\Services\MSExchangeWEB\Parameters* key are:

Server
The name of your Exchange Server
Enterprise
The name of your enterprise, such as First Organization
Site
The name of your site, such as First Administrative Group

You should avoid Anonymous Access with CDO 1.21 unless you have upgraded from Exchange 5.5 or have a mixed-mode environment with Exchange 5.5. A clean installation of Exchange will not include the necessary registry settings.

The Helpdesk Application

Now that you know how to successfully log on to the Exchange Server, let's take a look at our first sample application, the Helpdesk application. This is a Web-based application that allows users to submit new help requests. Helpdesk technicians can, in turn, use their Web browser to view and answer help requests as well as schedule meetings to go on site to solve the users' problems. The technicians can use different views for the help tickets stored in the system to quickly see who the ticket is from, when it was sent, and its status. (A help ticket for the Helpdesk application is shown in Figure 11-2.) When browsing help tickets, the technicians are presented with machine configuration information from a Microsoft Access database, which makes it easier for them to determine whether the issue is related to hardware, software, or a user error.

This application is the most complex of all the sample applications in this book, but the code is easy to follow and shows you how to use many of the objects in the CDO library. There are actually two versions of the application among the book's sample files. The version you use will depend on the Web browser you want to target. One version implements a user interface for the help tickets by using Dynamic HTML (DHTML). The other version uses HTML tables. A screen from the non-DHTML version is shown in Figure 11-3.

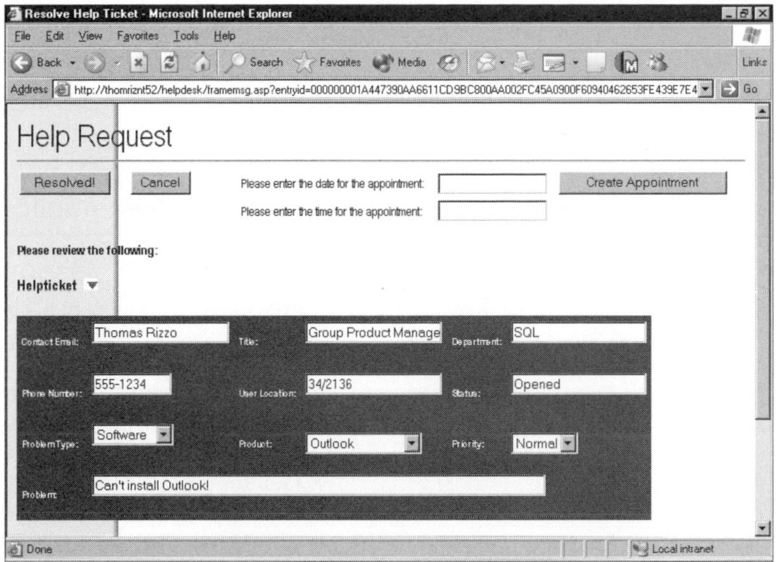

Figure 11-2 A help ticket in the Dynamic HTML version of the Helpdesk application

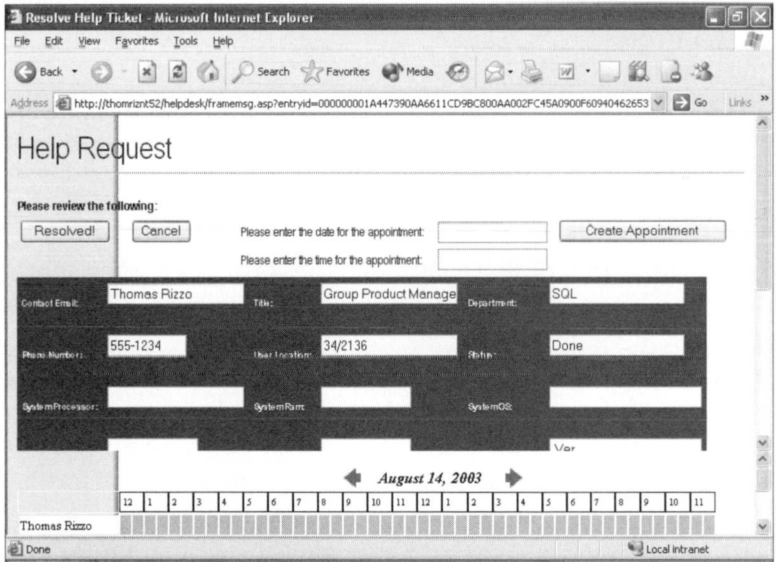

Figure 11-3 The non-DHTML version of a help ticket

Setting Up the Application

Before you can install the application, you must have a Windows 2000 or later server and a client with certain software installed. Table 11-2 outlines the installation requirements.

Table 11-2 Installation Requirements for the Helpdesk Application

Required Software	Installation Notes
Exchange Server 5.5 with the latest service pack or Exchange 2000/2003 with the latest service pack	OWA must be installed for Exchange 5.5. Exchange 2003 installs OWA by default.
IIS 3.0 or later with ASP	IIS 5.0 is recommended.
CDO library (cdo.dll) and CDO Rendering library	Exchange Server installs CDO 1.21. For CDO Rendering on a clean Exchange 2003 install, you must install OWA from Exchange 5.5 on the machine to get CDOHTML.
ActiveX Data Objects	
Access 97 or later (optional)	Install Access if you want to use the database access feature. Access 2000 or beyond is recommended.
For the client:	
A Web browser or Outlook	For the Web browser, Internet Explorer 5.0 or later is recommended. You can run the client software on the same machine or on a separate machine.

To use the Helpdesk application, you must have some e-mail users. You can either select currently set up e-mail users or add new ones using the Exchange Administrator program. Be sure to fill in the directory information for your users; this information should include their office locations, phone numbers, titles, and departments. The Helpdesk application dynamically retrieves this information using the CDO library. If the information is not available in the directory, the application displays the text "None specified" for these fields.

To install the application, copy the Helpdesk folder from the companion content to the Web server where you want to run the application. If you are going to use a browser that does not support DHTML, such as Microsoft Internet Explorer 3.0, copy the three .asp files from the Nondhtml subfolder to the Helpdesk folder, overwriting the current files. These files will replace the DHTML versions of the Helpdesk with the HTML versions.

Start the IIS administration program. The user interface you see will depend on what version of IIS you have. Create a virtual directory that points to the location where you copied the helpdesk files, and then name the virtual directory *helpdesk*. You can use the URL *http://<yourservername>/helpdesk* to access your helpdesk.

Included with the helpdesk files is a sample Access database (smsdata.mdb) that allows the application to query for system information about the current user. To use this database, you must set up a system Data Source Name (DSN) for it on the server machine by using the Data Sources (ODBC) administrative tool in Control Panel. Point the system DSN at the smsdata.mdb file, and name the DSN *Helpdesk*. Open smsdata.mdb in Access, and edit the UserID fields for all three tables to reflect the display names of the users you have in Exchange.

Launch Outlook. (You can launch it on any machine because you will create a public folder for the help tickets; the only requirement is that the Exchange server with which the IIS server communicates can access that public folder.) Create a new public folder under All Public Folders. Name the folder *Helpdesk*, and select Task Items as the default item type for the folder.

> **Note** You must install the Helpdesk folder under All Public Folders or the application will not work. If you cannot install the application there, you can modify the code contained in the Helpdesk application so it looks for the folder in another location, or you can retrieve the folder by using its EntryID. You can use a tool such as MDBVUE (which is included with Exchange Server) to look up the EntryID of a folder.

Among the Helpdesk files, you will find a file named helpdesk.fdm. This is a form definition file that you will use to import the correct fields needed by the Helpdesk application. In this case, the form is a Help Request task form with multiple custom fields.

To install the Help Request form, you must import this file into the Helpdesk public folder. To do this, right-click on the Helpdesk public folder and choose Properties. Click on the Forms tab, and click Manage to display the Forms Manager dialog box, as shown in Figure 11-4.

In the Forms Manager dialog box, click Install to display the Open dialog box. Select the All Files option from the Files Of Type drop-down list so Outlook does not search only for files with a .cfg extension. Locate and double-click on the helpdesk.fdm file to display the Form Properties dialog box. Click

Cancel, and then click Close and OK. When you have the Helpdesk public folder selected, you should see a new item on the Actions menu named New Helpdesk Request.

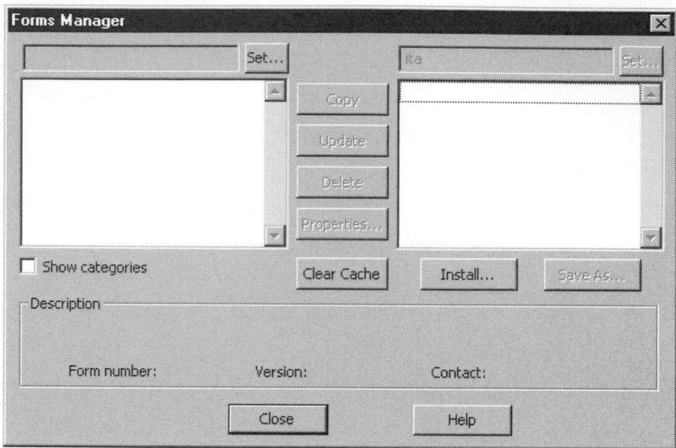

Figure 11-4 The Forms Manager dialog box

You must create some views in the Outlook client that will be available to the Web browser client. This is one of the powerful features of CDO. These views will include some of the custom fields from the Help Request form you just installed. Using the Define Views dialog box and the information in Table 11-3, create the helpdesk, from, and status views for the Helpdesk public folder. (For information about creating views, see the section titled "Views" in Chapter 3.)

Table 11-3 Information for Creating Helpdesk, From, and Status Views

View	Type	Fields	Group By
Helpdesk	Table	Flag, From User (select from Help Request form), Received, Subject (select from All Mail Fields)	None
From	Table	Flag (select from Help Request form), Received, Subject (select from All Mail Fields)	From User, in ascending order
Status	Table	From User (select from Help Request form), Received, Subject (select from All Mail Fields)	Flag, in ascending order

Using the Properties dialog box in Outlook for the Helpdesk public folder, set the permissions for your users. Give regular users who will submit help tickets Create Items permission. Give technicians who can submit, view, and resolve help tickets Create Items and Read Items permissions. Figure 11-5 shows a sample permissions setup for the Helpdesk folder. As you will see, the application checks the permissions of the current user for the Helpdesk folder to determine whether the user is a technician or just a regular user. If you do not give yourself at least Read Items permissions, you will not be able to see the menu item View Current Help Tickets in the Helpdesk application.

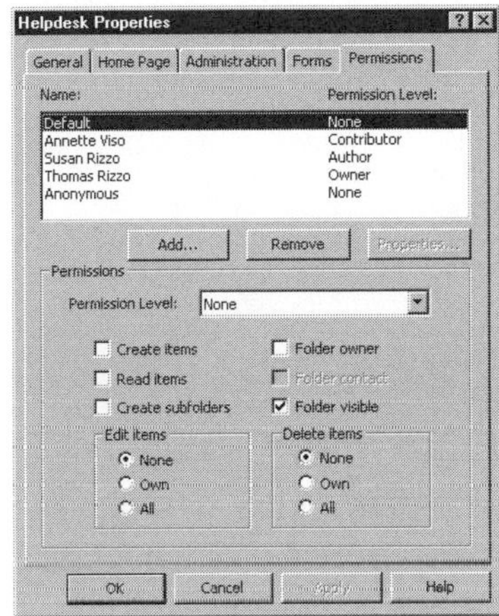

Figure 11-5 The Permissions tab of the Properties dialog box for the Helpdesk public folder

You're finished setting up the application. Try connecting your browser to *http://<yourservername>/helpdesk* to access the application.

Helpdesk CDO *Session* Considerations

You must be aware of certain issues when you build ASP-based applications with CDO (like the Helpdesk application). Recall from Chapter 10 that the ASP *Session* object, which is created when a new user connects to your Web application, maintains the user state for Web applications. ASP, in turn, runs the *Session_OnStart* subroutine in the Global.asa file. When a user's session times out or the user abandons the session, ASP runs the *Session_OnEnd* subroutine in the Global.asa file. This might seem simple enough, but the most common problem developers run into with CDO applications is that they don't put the correct code in the *Session_OnStart* and *Session_OnEnd* subroutines in the Global.asa. If you do not put the correct code in these subroutines, you might get an ASP 0115 error, which indicates that a trappable error has occurred in an external object. Your ASP application will cease working until you restart the Web server. To help you better understand what you need to do as a CDO developer, and to help you avoid this error in your application, let me explain in more detail exactly what happens when a user logs on and off an Exchange server in a CDO ASP application. I'll do this by showing you the Global.asa file from the Helpdesk application:

```
<SCRIPT LANGUAGE=VBScript RUNAT=Server>
Sub Application_OnStart
   On Error Resume Next
   Set objRenderApp = Server.CreateObject("AMHTML.Application")
   If Err = 0 Then
      Set Application("RenderApplication") = objRenderApp
   Else
      Application("startupFatal") = Err.Number
      Application("startupFatalDescription") = _
         "Failed to create application object<br>" & _
         Err.Description
   End If
   Application("hImp") = 0
   'Load the configuration information from the registry
   objRenderApp.LoadConfiguration 1, _
      "HKEY_LOCAL_MACHINE\System\CurrentControlSet\" & _
      "Services\MSExchangeWeb\Parameters"
   Application("ServerName") = objRenderApp.ConfigParameter("Server")
   Err.Clear
End Sub

Sub Application_OnEnd
   Set Application("RenderApplication") = Nothing
End Sub

Sub Session_OnStart
   On Error Resume Next
   'This is a handle to the security context.
   'It will be set to the correct value when a
   'CDO session is created.
   Session("hImp") = 0
   Set Session("AMSession") = Nothing
End Sub
'While calling the Session_OnEnd event, IIS doesn't call us in
'the right security context.
'Workaround: current security context is stored in Session
'object and then gets restored in Session_OnEnd event handler.
'
'All CDO and CDO Rendering library objects stored in the
'Session object need to be explicitly set to Nothing between
'the two objRenderApp.Impersonate calls below.
Sub Session_OnEnd
   On Error Resume Next
   set objRenderApp = Application("RenderApplication")
   fRevert = FALSE
   hImp = Session("hImp")
   If Not IsEmpty(hImp) Then
      fRevert = objRenderApp.Impersonate(hImp)
   End If
```

```
    'Do our cleanup. Set all CDO and CDOHTML objects inside
    'the session to Nothing.
    'The CDO session is a little special because we need to do
    'the Logoff on it.
    Set objOMSession = Session("AMSession")
    If Not objOMSession Is Nothing Then
       Set Session("AMSession") = Nothing
       objOMSession.Logoff
       Set objOMSession = Nothing
    End If
    If (fRevert) Then
       objRenderApp.Impersonate(0)
    End If
End Sub
</SCRIPT>
```

Note If you are running a clean install of Exchange 2000 or 2003 and have not upgraded your machine from Exchange 5.5, some of the techniques shown here will not work because Exchange 2000 does not create certain registry entries in the same way as Exchange 5.5. For example, retrieving the server name using the *RenderingApplication* object's *ConfigParameter* code will not work. You can get around this by using the Window Scripting Host *Network* object's *ComputerName* property or some other method.

The *Application_OnStart* subroutine is run only once, when the first user connects to the application. As you can see in the code, the first step is to create a new *Application* object from the CDO Rendering library. The ProgID for the CDO Rendering *Application* object is *AMHTML.Application*. The *Application* object is stored in an application-level variable so you can avoid having to create multiple *AMHTML* objects. Your application will perform better if you create the *AMHTML* object once and then use it throughout all user sessions.

Note CDO was formerly named Active Messaging, so you will see both *CDO* and *AM* used throughout the CDO library. Consider any objects that are prefixed with *AM* to be CDO objects.

The *Application_OnStart* subroutine initializes some variables and then uses a method of the *Application* object to retrieve the name of the Exchange server from the Web server's registry. This method allows portability of the code. You don't have to hardcode the name of the Exchange server; the Helpdesk application pulls the information from the registry. If you do not want to use the registry and instead want to retrieve the server information using code, you can use the Windows Scripting Host *Network* object:

```
Set wshNetwork = Server.CreateObject("WScript.Network")
MsgBox "Computer Name = " & wshNetwork.ComputerName
```

After the first user connects and *Application_OnStart* is finished running, ASP runs the *Session_OnStart* subroutine for all users. *Session_OnStart* clears a session variable named *hImp*, which is a handle to the security context for the current user. Remember that when a user first browses a Web page in IIS, she is running in the security context of the IUSR_*servername* account. This account is useful for browsing Web pages anonymously, but it is not useful for accessing Exchange Server objects and information because it has no implicit permissions on Exchange Server objects. So when you build an authenticated CDO application, you must force IIS to challenge the current user for her Microsoft Windows credentials. IIS and CDO can use the Windows security context for that user to attempt a logon to the Exchange server. The following code, taken from the Logon.inc file of the Helpdesk application, checks the *http* variables to make sure the current user is authenticated by the Web server using the user's Windows credentials. In the Helpdesk application, this section of code is called by every ASP page, just in case the user's ASP session has timed out.

```
Public Function BAuthenticateUser
    On Error Resume Next
    'Response.Write("In BAuthenticateUser<br>")
    BAuthenticateUser = False
    bstrAT = Request.ServerVariables("AUTH_TYPE")
    vbTextCompare = 1
    bstrAuthTypesSupported = "BasicNTLMDPAMBS_BASICNegotiate"

    If (InStr(1, bstrAuthTypesSupported, bstrAT, vbTextCompare) < 2) Then
        Response.Buffer = TRUE
        Response.Status = ("401 Unauthorized")
        Response.AddHeader "WWW.Authenticate", "Basic"
        Response.End
    Else
        BAuthenticateUser = True
    End If
End Function
```

This function searches the *AUTH_TYPE* server variable to see whether *Basic*, *NTLM*, or *Negotiate* is contained anywhere in the string. If none of these is found, the user is unauthenticated and the script sends back a "401 Unauthorized" response and a header that will force the browser to challenge the user for credentials. Note that *Negotiate* was introduced with Windows 2000 and

Internet Explorer 5.0. It allows the client to negotiate the authentication that it will use with the server.

Once the user is authenticated, you must save her security context as a *Session* variable. You must do this because IIS uses multiple threads of execution and you cannot be guaranteed that the thread that tries to destroy the session when the user logs off will be the same thread used to create the session. In the *Session_OnEnd* subroutine, the script checks to see whether *hImp* is not empty, which would imply that it is a valid handle. If *hImp* is not empty, *hImp* is used to specify the Windows NT security context to impersonate. Once the CDO and CDO Rendering objects are set to *Nothing* and the session is logged off, the CDO Rendering *Application* object reverts from the authenticated thread to the unauthenticated thread by calling the *Impersonate* method, with *0* as the parameter.

As we step through the Helpdesk application, you will see that every page in the application checks to see whether the ASP session, and therefore the CDO session, has been abandoned or has timed out. If the session has been abandoned or has timed out, the application redirects the user to the logon page so she can restart her ASP and CDO sessions. Figure 11-6 shows the logon page.

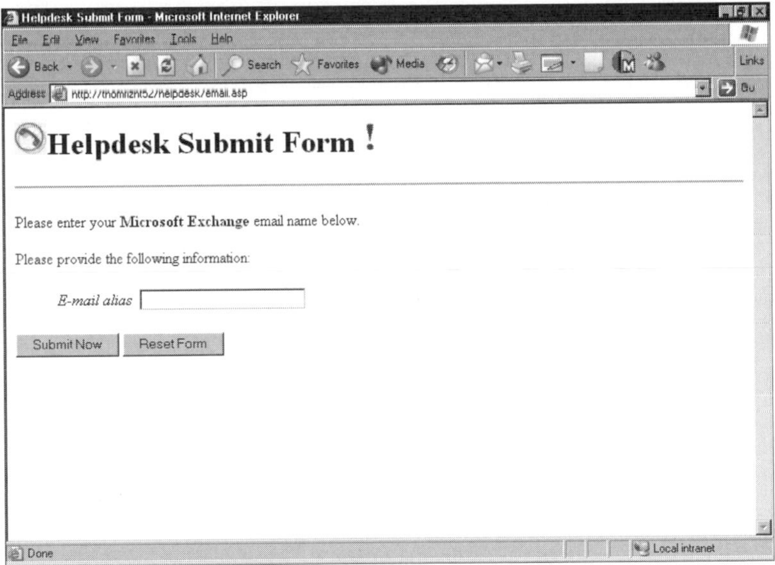

Figure 11-6 The logon page for the Helpdesk application

Logging On to the Helpdesk

You've seen that the Global.asa and Logon.inc files both help to authenticate users and maintain sessions. However, we have not yet discussed how you actually use the *Logon* method of the CDO *Session* object in the Helpdesk application to create a valid session with the Exchange server. The *Logon* method must be called before you attempt to access any other CDO objects. The script that implements user logons is contained in the Logon.inc file, shown here:

```
<%
'logon.inc. VBScript methods to create and check an
'ActiveMessaging session

'============================
'ReportError
'============================
Function ReportError(bstrContext)
    ReportError= False
    If Err.Number <> 0 Then
        Response.Write( "Error: " & bstrContext & " : " & _
            Err.Number & ": " & Err.Description & "<br>")
        Err.Clear
        ReportError= True
    End If
End Function

'============================
'BauthenticateUser
'
'Ensures user is authenticated. Note that this implies that
'Basic authentication is enabled on the IIS server.
'============================
Public Function BAuthenticateUser
    On Error Resume Next
    'Response.Write("In BAuthenticateUser<br>")
    BAuthenticateUser = False
    bstrAT = Request.ServerVariables("AUTH_TYPE")
    vbTextCompare = 1
 bstrAuthTypesSupported = "_BasicNTLMDPAMBS_BASICNegotiate"

    If (InStr(1, bstrAuthTypesSupported, bstrAT, vbTextCompare) < 2) Then
        Response.Buffer = TRUE
        Response.Status = ("401 Unauthorized")
        Response.AddHeader "WWW.Authenticate", "Basic"
        Response.End
    Else
        BAuthenticateUser = True
    End If
End Function

'============================
'CheckAMSession
'
'Checks for and returns the AM session in the Session object.
'If not found, calls NoSession.
'Call this before emitting any HTML or any redirects,
```

```
'authentication, and so on.
'Returns True if session exists or can be created.
'=============================
Public Function CheckAMSession()
    On Error Resume Next
    'Response.Write("In GetSession<br>")
    Dim amSession
    CheckAMSession= False
    Set amSession= Session("AMSession")
    If amSession Is Nothing Then
        NoSession
        amSession= Session("AMSession")
    End If
    If Not amSession Is Nothing Then
        CheckAMSession = True
    End If
End Function

'=============================
'NoSession
'
'Called when the AM session can not be found.
'Either creates a session or gets more info from the user.
'Returns only if the session was created.
'=============================
Sub NoSession()
    On Error Resume Next

    Dim bstrMailbox
    Dim bstrServer
    Dim bstrProfileInfo
    Dim objAMSession1
    Dim objRenderApp
    Dim objInbox

    bstrServer = ""
    bstrServer = Application("ServerName")
    'REPLACE "MYSERVERNAME" WITH YOUR ACTUAL SERVER NAME
    'bstrServer = "MYSERVERNAME"
    If bstrServer = "" Then
        response.write "Server Name is empty. Please check logon.inc " & _
        "and replace the line 'bstrServerName = ""MYSERVERNAME"" " & _
        "with your Exchange server name and uncomment the line. " & _
        "For example, if your server's name is SERVER then this " & _
        "line should read bstrServer = ""Server"""
        response.end
    Else
        If Session("mailbox") Is Nothing Then
            bstrMailbox = Request.QueryString("Contact_Email")
        Else
            bstrMailbox = Session("mailbox")
        End If
        'must be authenticated to successfully logon
```

```
        BAuthenticateUser

        Err.Clear
        Set objAMSession1 = Server.CreateObject("MAPI.Session")
        If Not ReportError("create MAPI.Session") Then
            Set objRenderApp = Application("RenderApplication")

            'Construct the ActiveMessaging profile from the
            'server and mailbox name
            bstrProfileInfo = bstrServer + vbLf + bstrMailbox
            Err.Clear
            objAMSession1.Logon "", "", False, True, 0, True, _
                bstrProfileInfo

            If Not ReportError( "CDO Logon") Then
                'To ensure that we are really logged on,
                'we need to try retrieving some data.
                Err.Clear
                Set objInbox = objAMSession1.Inbox


                'The logon is no good.  We'll do a little cleanup here.
                If Err.number <> 0 Then
                    objAMSession1.Logoff
                    Set objAMSession1 = Nothing
%>
<META HTTP-EQUIV="REFRESH" CONTENT="0; URL=email.asp"; TARGET="_top">
<%
                    'Response.Redirect "default.htm"
                End If

                'This will be retrieved back up in CheckSession
                'Note that if the logon failed this is set to 'Nothing'
                Set Session("AMSession") = objAMSession1
                'Need this to recreate the proper security
                'context in Session_OnEnd
                Session("hImp") = objRenderApp.ImpID
            End If    'objAMSession1.Logon
        End If   'Server.CreateObject()
    End If    'bstrServerName
End Sub
```

The first function called on every ASP page in the Helpdesk application is the *CheckAMSession* function, which checks to see whether the user already has a valid CDO *Session* object with the Exchange server. If this function does not find a valid object, it calls the *NoSession* subroutine to log the user on to CDO.

In the *NoSession* subroutine, the variable *bstrServer* is set to the Exchange server name, which is pulled from the registry in the Global.asa file. (Again, retrieving the Exchange server name from the registry allows the code to be ported to any Web server or Exchange server.) If the script cannot find the server name, it will return an error to the user. The script then checks to see whether the ASP *Session* variable named *mailbox* contains a valid mailbox alias name. If this variable is empty, the script attempts to grab the mailbox name from the URL that was passed to the Web server by the logon screen of the application.

The *BAuthenticateUser* function is called to ensure that the user is logged on to Windows NT correctly before the code attempts the CDO *Session Logon* method. After the CDO object is created, its *Logon* method is called. The variable *bstrProfileInfo* is set so CDO can dynamically create a profile for the user. The script calls the *Logon* method, and if that method returns no errors, the script tries to retrieve the Inbox for the user. You should follow similar steps in your applications because the *Logon* method can return successfully when called with dynamic profiles, even when the server or mailbox name is not valid. If you do not try to retrieve information from the server directly and assume that the *Session* object is valid because the method returned successfully, you will run into many problems.

If the code cannot retrieve the user's Inbox, it logs off and redirects the user to the logon page. If it can retrieve the Inbox, it stores the handle to the security context for this user in the *hImp* session variable.

Accessing Folders in the Helpdesk

You don't have much of a Helpdesk application if your users can't enter information and your technicians can't retrieve information. This Helpdesk application uses a public folder to store and retrieve information about ticket status. CDO provides access to public folders through its *InfoStores* collection, which contains all the different stores or databases that CDO can access. For example, with the *InfoStores* collection, you can access not only public folders and server-based mailboxes but also personal folders stored in .pst files or offline replicated folders stored in .ost files. Of course, to enable CDO to access some of these infostores, you must run your CDO application on the client machine. Figure 11-7 shows the *InfoStores* collection with some of its child objects.

In the Helpdesk application, the *InfoStores* collection is used to find the public folder store. The following code from default.asp uses a *For Each...Next* statement to loop through the *InfoStores* collection and retrieve each store in the collection. Each store is checked to see whether the store name corresponds to the public folder store. If a corresponding store name is found, the *For...Each* statement is exited.

```
Set objInfoStoresColl = objOMSession.InfoStores
For Each objInfoStore In objInfoStoresColl
    If objInfoStore.Name = "Public Folders" Then
        Exit For
    End If
Next
```

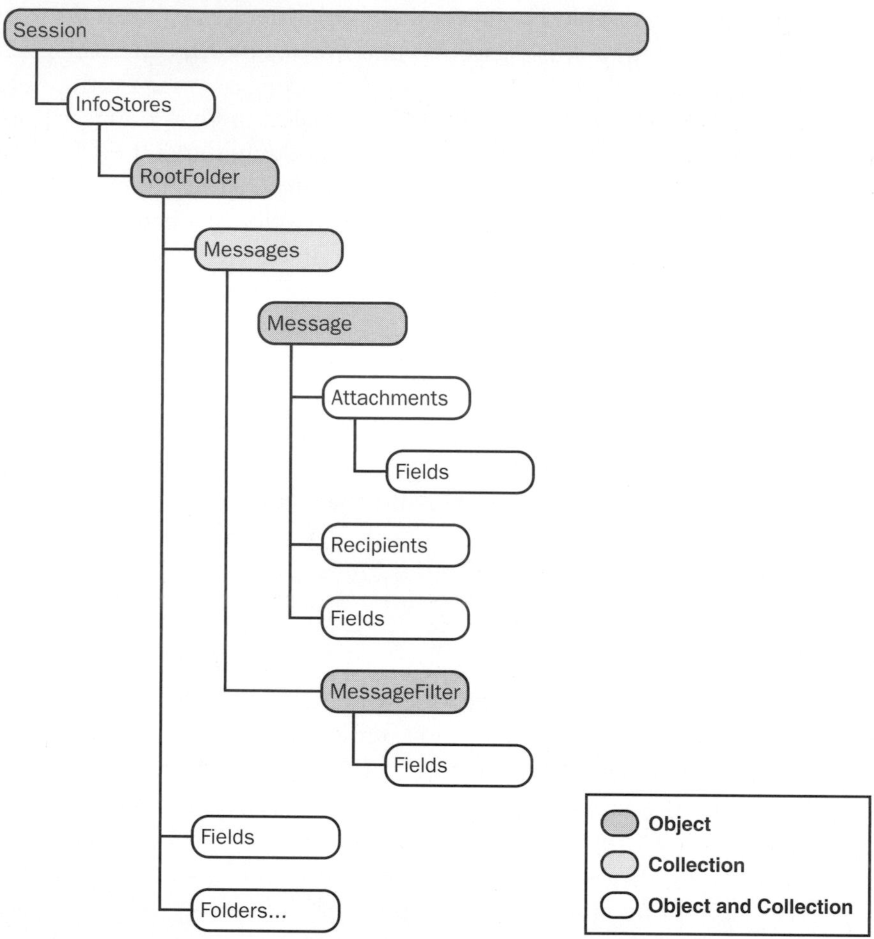

Figure 11-7 The InfoStores collection in CDO, which is used to access data stored in Exchange Server

Now that the application has the correct infostore, the correct set of folders must be accessed in that infostore. The *InfoStore* object in CDO has a *RootFolder* property that returns a *Folder* object representing the root of all the folders. For your mailbox and public folder stores, the *RootFolder* property returns a *Folder* object named *IPM_Subtree*. By using that *Folder* object, you can traverse all folders in your mailbox or top-level public folders. However, there's one caveat with this property: you cannot use the *RootFolder* property to access public folders if your application is running as a Windows NT service. Instead, you must use the *Fields* collection on the *InfoStores* object with the specific property tag *PR_IPM_PUBLIC_FOLDERS_ENTRYID* (*&H66310102*). Once you retrieve the EntryID for the root public folder from the *Fields* collection, you can use the *GetFolder* method to actually retrieve the root public folder. (An EntryID is like a globally unique identifier, or GUID, in that it uniquely identifies the folder in the Exchange Server database.) After retrieving the root folder, you can use the *Folders* collection of the root public folder to retrieve the root folder's subfolders. The following code, taken from default.asp, shows the *GetFolder* method in action. It retrieves the folders in the public folder tree and then iterates through the top-level folders as it searches for the Helpdesk folder.

```
'This is the EntryID for the root public folder
bstrPublicRootID = objInfoStore.Fields.Item(&H66310102).Value

Set myrootfolder = objOMSession.GetFolder(bstrPublicRootID, _
    objInfoStore.ID)
'Now get the Folders collection below the root
Set myfoldercollect = myrootfolder.Folders
Set recursefolder = myfoldercollect.GetFirst()
'Recurse it until we get the folder we are looking for
Do While recursefolder.Name <> "Helpdesk"
    Set recursefolder = myfoldercollect.GetNext()
Loop

If Err.Number <> 0 Then
    response.Write "Could not find Helpdesk folder " & _
                   "under All Public Folders."
    response.End
End If
Set objFolder = recursefolder
Set Session("HelpdeskFolder") = recursefolder
Session("InfoStoreID") = objInfoStore.ID
```

Once the code finds the Helpdesk folder, it stores the CDO *Folder* object that corresponds to the Helpdesk folder as well as the unique identifier for the public folder *InfoStore* object because, from a performance standpoint, recursing the *InfoStores* and *Folders* collection in every ASP page in the Helpdesk application to find this information is expensive. Because we now have this information available across the entire session, the other pages will use the *Session* object for the folder whenever access to the Helpdesk folder is required.

Implementing Helpdesk Folder Security

When a user logs on to the Helpdesk application, the options displayed depend on the user's folder permissions. For example, if a user accesses the application and he has only Create Items permission for the Helpdesk folder, the ASP displays only the Submit A Help Ticket and Logoff options, as shown in Figure 11-8. However, if a technician who has Read Items and Create Items permissions for the Helpdesk folder logs on to the application, the ASP displays an additional option—View Current Help Tickets, as shown in Figure 11-9.

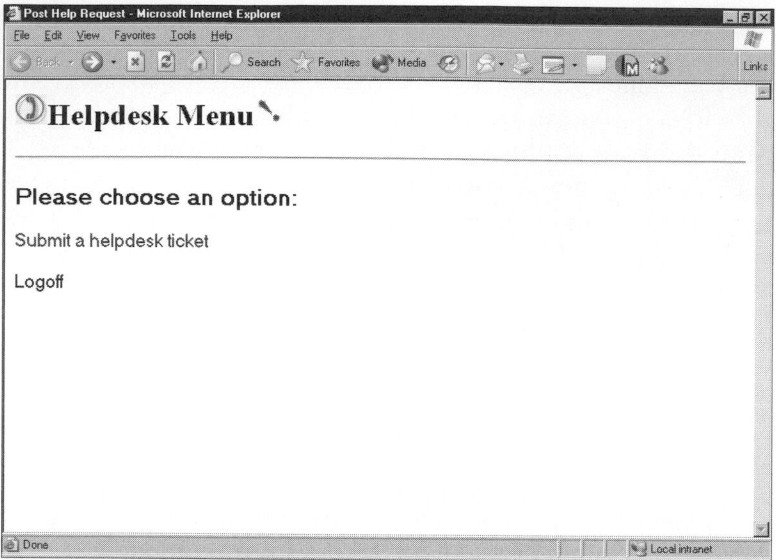

Figure 11-8 The Helpdesk Menu page, where the user who logged on has Create Items permissions for the Helpdesk folder

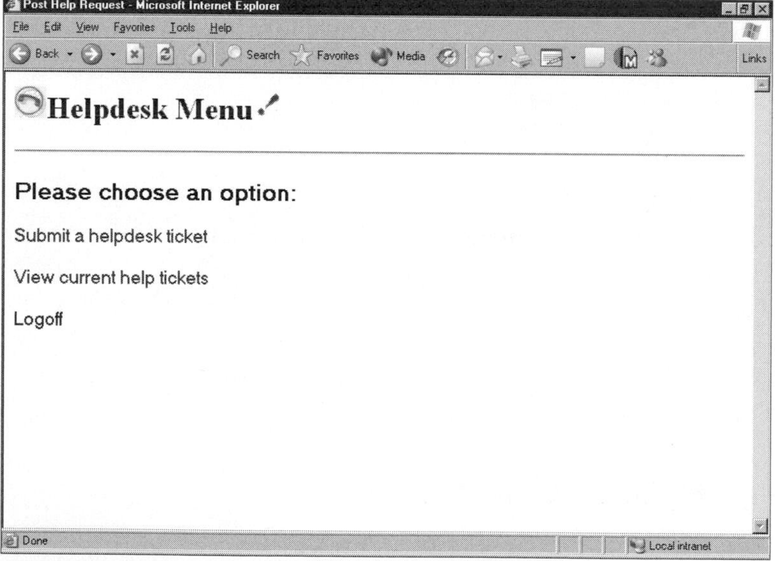

Figure 11-9 The Helpdesk Menu page, where the user logged on is a technician and has Create Items and Read Items permissions for the Helpdesk folder

This functionality is implemented in CDO by using the *Fields* collection on the *Folder* object. The *Fields* collection, a common collection across many of the objects in CDO, allows you to access specific properties stored for an object that CDO does not have an explicit object or property for. With the *Fields* collection, you can pass a unique identifier that corresponds to the properties you want to retrieve. In the next section of Helpdesk code, which is from the default.asp file, we pass in the unique identifier for the MAPI property *ActMsgPR_ACCESS* (*&H0FF4003*), which contains a bitmask of flags corresponding to the user's permissions level for the current *Folder* object. The code then performs a logical *AND* on the returned value from the *Fields* collection by using the known bitmask of the MAPI_ACCESS_READ permission. If the result does not equal zero, the user can read items in the folder, and the ASP will display the View Current Help Tickets link on the helpdesk menu.

```
<h2>Please choose an option:</h2>
<a href="default1.asp">Submit a help ticket</a><P>

<%
'Check permissions on the folder to see whether the user has
'Read access. If the user does, the user must be a technician,
'so display the ability to view help tickets.
nAccess = objFolder.Fields.Item(ActMsgPR_ACCESS)
bCanPost = nAccess And MAPI_ACCESS_READ
If bCanPost <> 0 Then
%>
<a href="render.asp">View current help tickets</a>
<% End If %>
<P>
<a href="logoff.asp">Logoff</a>
```

You can pass many types of identifiers to the *Fields* collection. The Helpdesk application does not use the *CdoPR_CONTAINER_CLASS* (*&H3613001E*) property, but it demonstrates the type of information you can access through the *Fields* collection on CDO objects. It contains the message class of the default type of item contained in the folder. For example, if in Outlook you set the default item type for a Public Folder as contacts, the *CdoPR_CONTAINER_CLASS* property will contain *IPF.Contact*. How do you change the default item type in a folder programmatically through CDO? By using the *Fields* collection on a folder and this property, as shown in the next bit of sample code, the code changes the default item type of a folder to tasks. For example, if you decide you want to change the default content in the folder, you can avoid the trouble of creating a new folder, moving all the data, resetting permissions, and performing other administrative tasks by changing the default type of the folder. The code uses the *InfoStores* collection to retrieve the mailbox of the user. It then retrieves the root folder of the mailbox by using the *RootFolder* property. From that root folder, it retrieves the contacts folder in the mailbox. The next line of code uses the *Fields* collection on the folder to set a property that corresponds to the default item type for the folder. Finally, to make the default item-type change permanent, the *Update* method of the *Folder* object is called, committing the changes to the server.

```
Set oStore = oSession.InfoStores("Mailbox - Thomas Rizzo (Exchange)")
Set oFolder = oStore.RootFolder.Folders("Contacts")
MsgBox "Before Update: " & oFolder.Fields(&H3613001E)
oFolder.Fields(&H3613001E) = "IPF.Tasks"
oFolder.Update
MsgBox "After Update: " & oFolder.Fields(&H3613001E)
```

> **Note** For the complete list of the identifiers you can use with the *Fields* collection in your applications, refer to cdo.chm on the companion Web site. On the Contents tab, look in the Appendixes section for the MAPI Property Tags document.

Retrieving User Directory Information

If the user chooses Submit A Help Ticket from the Helpdesk menu, the file default1.asp is called. This ASP file displays a Help Request form, which is shown in Figure 11-10.

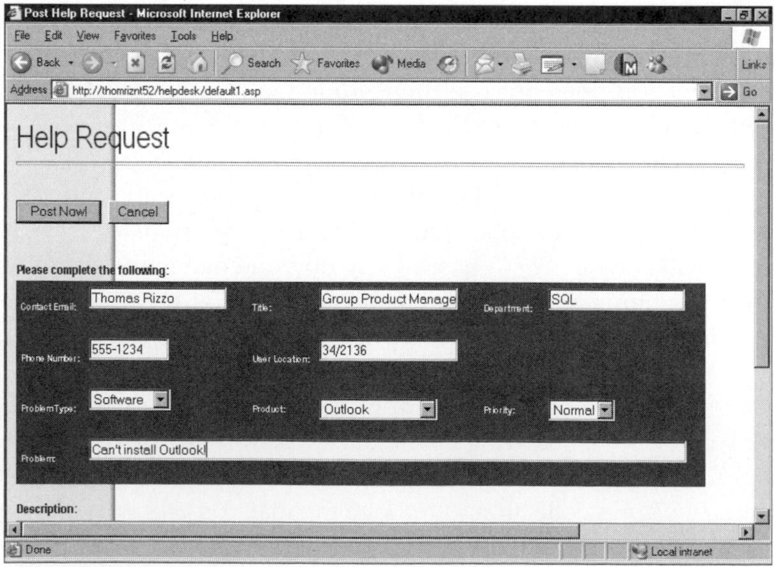

Figure 11-10 The Help Request form allows users to post information to the Helpdesk application.

As you can see in Figure 11-10, some information about the user is already entered in the Help Request form. This information is dynamically pulled from the Exchange Server directory to help users save time when filling out requests. The enabling technology for this dynamic lookup primarily involves two CDO objects, the *Recipient* object and the *AddressEntry* object. A diagram illustrating the hierarchy of these two objects is shown in Figure 11-11.

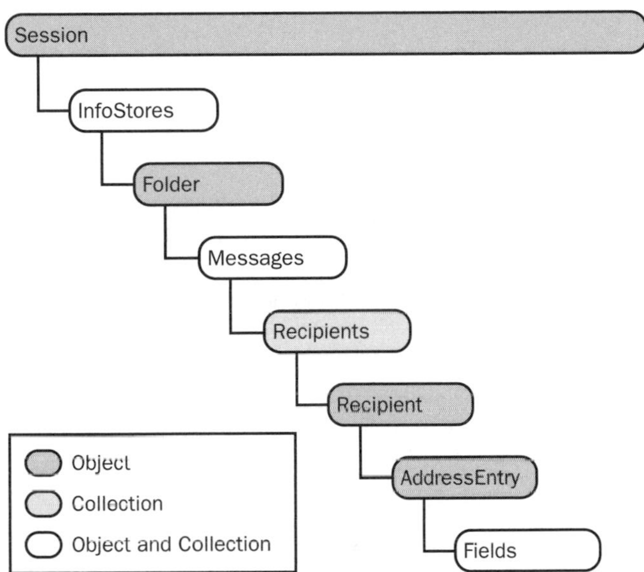

Figure 11-11 The Recipients collection and the Recipient object in CDO

The *Recipient* object represents a recipient of a message. You might wonder why a *Recipient* object is used to retrieve directory information from Exchange Server. There are two primary reasons. The first is that CDO does not explicitly support querying for directory information without first retrieving the *AddressEntry* object for the given user. The second is that adding the name of the user to a message as a *Recipient* and then using the *Resolve* method of the *Recipient* object is probably the easiest way to retrieve the *AddressEntry* object for a particular user. After resolving the name, you can call the *AddressEntry* property on the resolved *Recipient* object to retrieve the corresponding *AddressEntry* object. Just be sure to destroy the temporary objects you created for the *Message* and *Recipient* objects. The *AddressEntries* collection and *AddressEntry* object in CDO are shown in Figure 11-12.

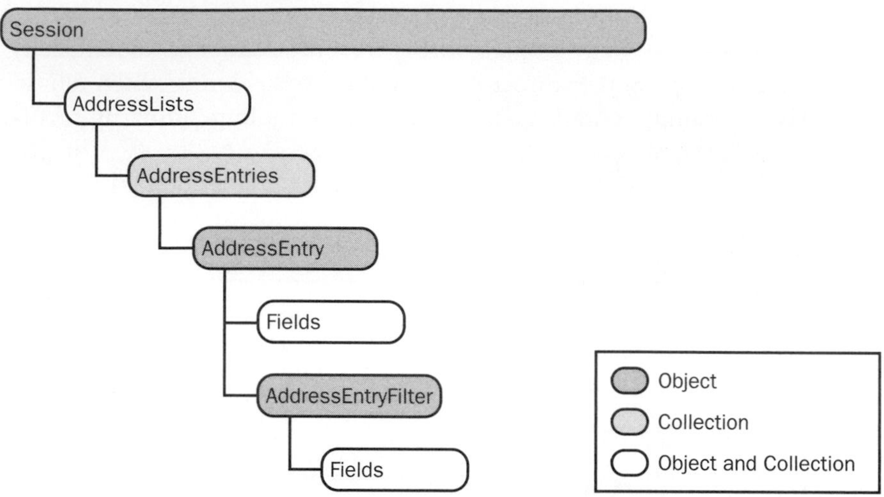

Figure 11-12 The AddressEntries collection and AddressEntry object in CDO

The *AddressEntry* object contains the directory and address information for a user in the Exchange Server system. You can use the built-in properties of this object to access the e-mail address information for a particular user, but to access directory information (department, office location, and phone number), you must use the *Fields* collection of the *AddressEntry* object with MAPI property tags. The following code sample, which is taken from default1.asp, shows you how the Helpdesk application implements directory lookup for users:

```
Set objmessage = objOMSession.Outbox.Messages.Add
'Create the recipient
Set objonerecip = objmessage.Recipients.Add
'Retrieve the e-mail address from the previous HTML form
objonerecip.Name = Session("mailbox")
'Resolve the name against the Exchange Server directory
objonerecip.Resolve
'You can add code to handle unresolved names here
'Get the address entry so that we can pull out template information
Set myaddentry = objonerecip.AddressEntry
Set myfields = myaddentry.Fields
'The numbers in parentheses are the hard-coded IDs for department,
'title, and so on
Set mydept = myfields.Item(974651422).value
Set mytitle = myfields.Item(974585886).value
Set myworkphone = myfields.Item(973602846).value
Set myoffice = myfields.Item(974716958).value
If mydept = "" Then
    mydept = "None specified"
End If
If mytitle = "" Then
```

```
    mytitle = "None specified"
End If
If myworkphone = "" Then
    myworkphone = "None specified"
End If
If myoffice = "" Then
    myoffice = "None specified"
End If
Set objmessage = Nothing
Set objonerecip = Nothing
```

This code first adds a new message to the Outbox of the user by calling the *Add* method on the Outbox folder. Then it adds a new *Recipient* object to the message. Because the ASP session contains the display name of the current user, this value is passed in as the *Name* property for the recipient. The code then calls the *Resolve* method on the *Recipient* object to make CDO check for ambiguous names in the directory. Once the user is resolved, the *AddressEntry* object for the user is retrieved using the *AddressEntry* property of the *Recipient* object.

From there, the *Fields* collection of the *AddressEntry* object is retrieved. The code then uses some MAPI property identifiers to retrieve specific information from the directory. If the information is unavailable in the directory, the code specifies that the value for the variables be *None specified*. To make sure the temporary *Message* and *Recipient* objects are released from memory, the code sets both objects to *Nothing*.

Posting Information in the Helpdesk

Once the user fills in the help ticket information, such as a problem description, he clicks the Post Now! button on the HTML form. The action of this HTML form sends the user information to another ASP file named posthelp.asp. The posthelp.asp file uses the CDO library to post this information to the Helpdesk public folder by creating a new *Message* object in the folder. The hierarchy for the *Message* object and its parent collection, *Messages*, is shown in Figure 11-13.

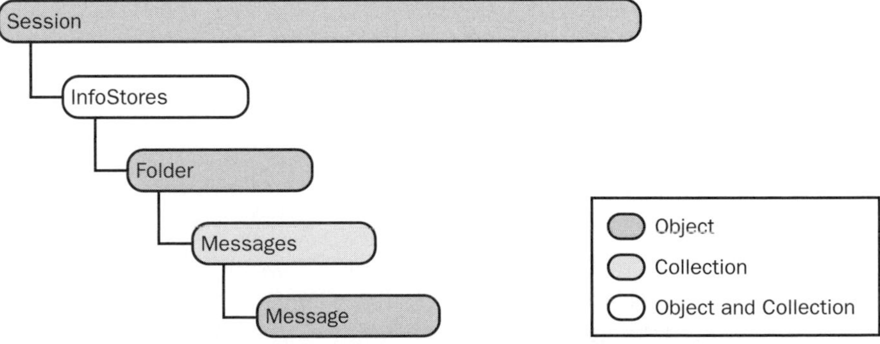

Figure 11-13 The Messages collection and the Message object in CDO

The *Messages* collection is accessed by calling the *Messages* property on a *Folder* object. The *Messages* collection consists of *Message* objects, which you can manipulate to change items in folders or to create new items. To add a new message to a folder, you use the *Add* method of the *Messages* collection—essentially, it adds a new item to the collection. The type of message created depends on which folder you are calling the *Add* method in. For example, if you call the *Add* method in your Inbox, CDO will return a new *Message* object. If you call the *Add* method in your Calendar folder, CDO will return a new *AppointmentItem* object.

After adding a new item to the collection, you can set the properties for the item and then call the *Send* or *Update* method, depending on the type of item you created. If you used the *Add* method in your Outbox, you should call the *Send* method because e-mail messages are created in the Outbox. In the Helpdesk application, the script calls the *Update* method because the application does not e-mail new help tickets into the folder but rather posts them into the folder. The following script from posthelp.asp posts the information from the HTML form into the public folder:

```
Set objFolder = Session("HelpdeskFolder")
Set recursefolder = objFolder
'Add a new message to the public folder
Set oMessage = recursefolder.Messages.Add
'Set the message properties
oMessage.Subject = Request("Subject")
oMessage.Sent = True
oMessage.Unread = True
oMessage.TimeSent = Now
oMessage.TimeReceived = Now
oMessage.Type = "IPM.Task.Help Request"
oMessage.Importance = Request("Priority")
oMessage.Fields.Add "From User", 8, Request.Form("Contact_Email")
oMessage.Fields.Add "Description", 8, Request("Description")
oMessage.Fields.Add "Problem Type", 8, Request("Type")
oMessage.Fields.Add "Product", 8, Request("Product")
oMessage.Fields.Add "Phone", 8, Request("Phone")
oMessage.Fields.Add "User Location", 8, Request("Location")
oMessage.Fields.Add "Flag", 8, "Opened"
'Set the conversation properties
oMessage.ConversationTopic = oMessage.Subject
oMessage.ConversationIndex = objOMSession.CreateConversationIndex
'Post the message
oMessage.Submitted = FALSE
oMessage.Update
Set oMessage = Nothing
```

As you can see in the code, some properties on the new *Message* object, such as *Sent*, *Unread*, *TimeSent*, *TimeReceived*, and *Submitted*, are explicitly set. These properties must be set because when you post an item into a public folder as the Helpdesk does, the underlying messaging system does not set these properties for you. They must be set before you call the *Update* method on the *Message* object for posted items; otherwise, you will receive an error.

The *Sent* property is a Boolean that determines whether the message has been sent through the system. Because we are posting information directly into the folder, we must set this property explicitly to *True* before calling the *Update* method. The *Submitted* property is also a Boolean that must be set to *True* before we call the *Update* method. The *Submitted* property determines whether the item has been submitted into the messaging subsystem.

The *TimeReceived* and *TimeSent* properties contain dates that tell the user when the message was received by the folder and when the user sent the message. You should set both of these properties to the current date and time before posting the item to the folder. The easiest way to do this is to assign them to the value returned by the *Now* function.

The *Unread* property is a Boolean that represents whether the current user has read the item. This property is not set automatically by CDO when you post an item into a public folder. For this reason, you must set this property to *False* before posting your item into the public folder.

Now that we have set the required properties to successfully post a message into a public folder, we can use some of the other properties on the *Message* object to implement the functionality of our application. Notice in the script that the *Type* property is set to *IPM.Task.Help Request*. The *Type* property corresponds to the message class of the item. When this property is set to a custom message class, Outlook and OWA users can use a custom form that handles that message class to open the item in the folder.

The *Importance* property in the script is set to the importance level that the user selected in the Priority drop-down list in the HTML form. This property has three possible values: *CdoLow (0)*, *CdoNormal (1)*, and *CdoHigh (2)*. Setting *Importance* to *CdoLow (0)* has the same effect as adding the down arrow icon to an e-mail message in Outlook; *CdoHigh (2)* has the same effect as the exclamation point icon in Outlook.

The *Subject* property is set to whatever the user typed in the Problem text box of the Helpdesk form. It is rendered as a hyperlink later in the application so that from their Web browser, technicians can click on a specific problem and drill down to the specifics about the help ticket and the user who submitted it.

You use the *Fields* collection of the *Message* object in the script to add custom fields to the item programmatically—a powerful technique, because any items you create in CDO can use your fields. These custom properties, or fields, are then accessible from Outlook. Because the Exchange Server database is a semistructured database, you can even change or add new properties to the items in a folder without worrying about breaking a schema. This means that in your application, every item and its properties can have a different schema. Your application can dynamically add new properties to items depending on the input of the user.

The way you add new custom properties to an item is by using the *Add* method of the *Fields* collection. This is the syntax for the *Add* method:

```
Set objField = objFieldsColl.Add (Name, Class [, Value] [, PropsetID])
```

> **Note** Exchange Server is a semistructured database; Microsoft SQL Server is completely structured. With SQL Server, you must define your schema before you can start adding data, and the schema is usually fixed. With Exchange Server, every message can be different. For example, one message might have 0 attachments and another might have 15 attachments. Exchange Server is designed to efficiently handle this varying data.

Passing the last two parameters to this method and catching the value returned by this method are optional. You can see in the preceding script that the code does not set an object variable to the return value of this function.

The first parameter that the *Add* method takes is the name of the custom property. This name is limited to 120 characters; if you attempt to exceed this limit, CDO will return an error. The second parameter is the class, or data type, that you want to store in the property. The *class* parameter should pass one of the following values: *vbArray (8192)*, *vbBlob (65)*, *vbBoolean (11)*, *vbCurrency (6)*, *vbDataObject (13)*, *vbDate (7)*, *vbDouble (5)*, *vbEmpty (0)*, *vbInteger (2)*, *vbLong (3)*, *vbNull (1)*, *vbSingle (4)*, *vbString (8)*, or *vbVariant (12)*. The data type you will use most often in your applications is *vbString (8)*. As you can see in the Helpdesk script, all custom properties on the posted item use the string data type.

The third parameter, which is optional, is the value for the property. Usually you should pass this parameter to the method so you do not have to write extra code to initialize the custom property with the value.

The fourth and final parameter is *PropsetID*. This parameter is a GUID that uniquely identifies the MAPI property set to which the custom field should belong. In your applications, you will almost always use the default property set, which is assumed if you omit the *PropsetID* parameter. Only if you are developing a custom MAPI application that uses its own property sets will you ever need to set *PropsetID*.

In addition to adding new custom properties, the script sets the *ConversationTopic* and *ConversationIndex* properties for the help ticket before posting it into the folder. These properties are used by both CDO and Outlook to allow you to create threaded views of information in your folders. Your users might want to create these types of views in your applications, so you should set these properties in your code.

The *ConversationTopic* property is a string that describes the subject of the conversation. All the items in the same conversation have the same property value, and because *ConversationTopic* corresponds to the overall subject of the conversation, the most logical value for it is the *Subject* property of your message.

The *ConversationIndex* property is a hexadecimal string that represents the relationship between items in the same conversation. CDO and Outlook use this property to determine which items are replies to other items and how to thread these items in a view. Because you do not want multiple messages with the same index, CDO provides a method for generating unique conversation index values—the *CreateConversationIndex* method on the CDO *Session* object. As you can see in the Helpdesk code, all you need to do is call *CreateConversationIndex* and assign its value to the *ConversationIndex* property for your item.

After setting all these properties, the script calls the *Update* method on the *Message* object, and a new help ticket is created in the folder. If you do not call the *Update* method, CDO will not commit your changes to the public folder.

Rendering the List of Helpdesk Tickets

When you create a Web application, one of the hardest parts to design is the user interface. You have to worry about using HTML tables to line up content, and you have to make sure these tables have the correct format and spacing to appear properly in a browser. The beauty of CDO is that you do not have to worry about the user interface. The CDO library has a companion library, the CDO Rendering library, which provides objects that automatically convert Exchange Server information to an HTML format in a preset layout. Figure 11-14 shows the relationships among the objects and collections of the CDO Rendering library.

The CDO Rendering library can not only render simple types of information such as your Inbox, but it can also leverage any custom table views you create in Outlook. For example, you can use the CDO Rendering library to render your Inbox as HTML, grouping messages by sender. The CDO Rendering library provides this functionality with a minimal amount of coding, as you will see. Plus, the formats that the library uses to render information to HTML are customizable, so if you want to change the color or the font of items to meet particular criteria or contain particular properties, you can easily do this by using the Rendering library objects. Figure 11-15 shows an HTML view of help tickets in a folder, created using the CDO Rendering library.

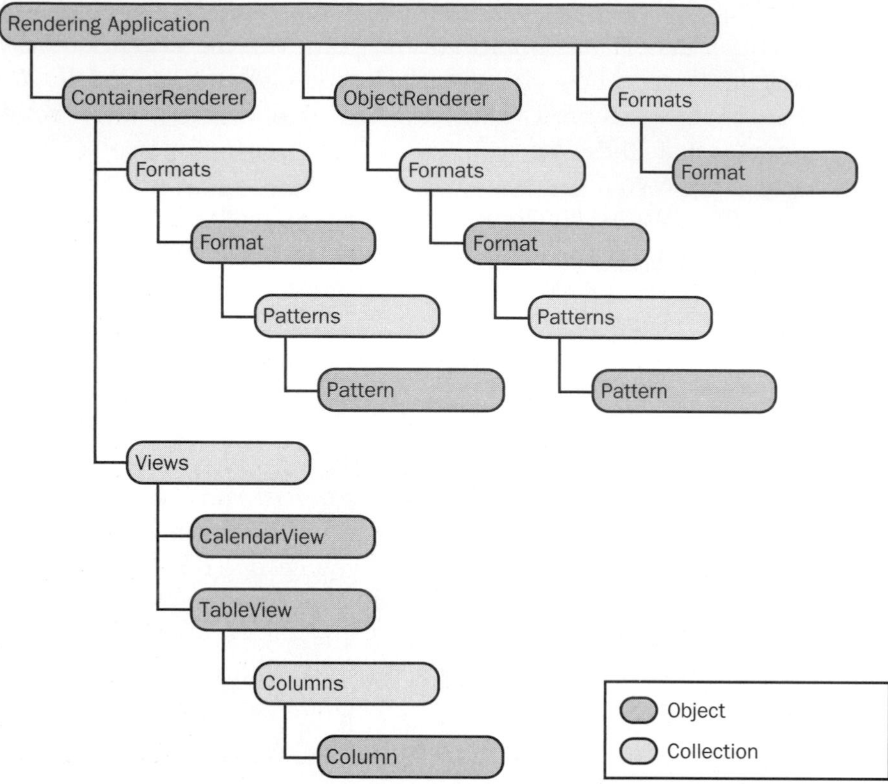

Figure 11-14 The CDO Rendering library

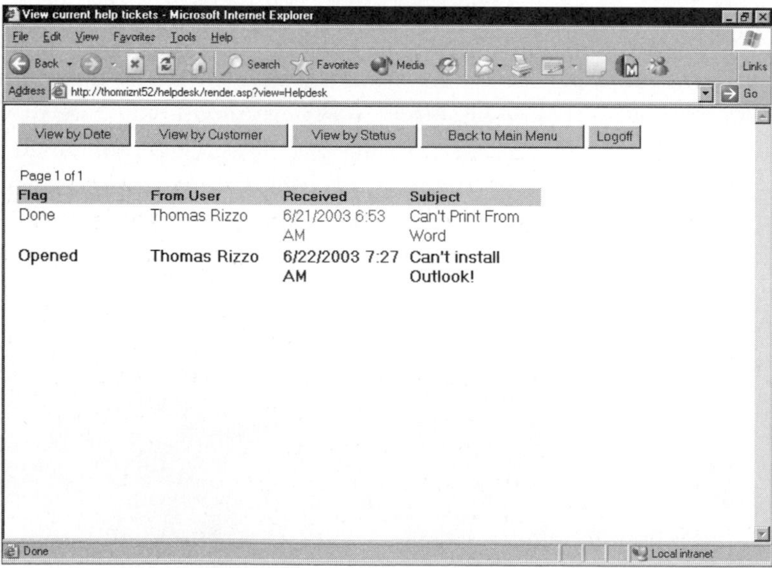

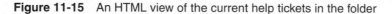

Figure 11-15 An HTML view of the current help tickets in the folder

Similar to the *Session* object in the CDO library, the *RenderingApplication* object of the CDO Rendering library is the parent object of all other objects in the library. To create a *RenderingApplication* object, you use the *CreateObject* method and pass the ProgID of the CDO Rendering library, which is *AMHTML.Application*. In the Helpdesk application, the *RenderingApplication* object is created in the Global.asa file and given application scope in ASP so all sessions in the Helpdesk application can create individual objects from the global *RenderingApplication* object. This is a good practice to use in your CDO ASP applications.

The *RenderingApplication* object contains a number of properties, such as the code page or virtual root, that you can set and use throughout all the rendering objects created from the *RenderingApplication* object. When you first create your *RenderingApplication* object, most of the properties on the object will be filled in with default values. Most of these default values do not need to be changed unless you are developing completely customized applications that cannot use the defaults.

The most important property and the two most important methods of the *RenderingApplication* object to learn about are the *ConfigParameter* property, the *CreateRenderer* method, and the *LoadConfiguration* method. You'll use these in almost all of your ASP CDO applications. The *LoadConfiguration* method and the *ConfigParameter* property work together to tell the CDO Rendering library where to pull configuration information from—such as the registry or the Exchange Server directory. This location information is used to retrieve specific configuration data from the selected data source. In the Global.asa file for the Helpdesk application, the name of the Exchange server that CDO communicates with is retrieved by using the *LoadConfiguration* method and the *ConfigParameter* property. The *ConfigParameter* property can retrieve other types of configuration parameters, such as whether anonymous access is enabled on the Exchange server, the organization and site names for the Exchange Server directory, and whether the http protocol is even enabled on the Exchange server.

The *CreateRenderer* method creates a new rendering object, which is attached to the current *RenderingApplication* object. This method takes an integer argument that specifies the type of rendering object to create. The value for this integer parameter can be *CdoClassContainerRenderer (3)* or *CdoClassObjectRenderer (2)*. In your applications, use the object renderer to render only specific properties on items, such as the subject or the text of the item. You should use the container renderer to render rows of information, such as all the messages in a folder.

In the render.asp file for the Helpdesk application, the following script first gets the global *RenderingApplication* object and then calls the *CreateRenderer* method to create a container renderer. The application uses a container renderer to display all the items in the Helpdesk folder rather than specific properties on a specific item.

```
'Create Rendering Application
Set objRenderApp = Application("RenderApplication")
'Create Container Renderer id=3
Set objrenderer = objRenderApp.CreateRenderer(3)
```

The application then sets the *DataSource* property for the container renderer to the *Messages* collection in the Helpdesk folder. With any type of rendering object, you must set the *DataSource* property because it tells the rendering object what data to actually convert to HTML. The container renderer can accept an *AddressEntries*, *Folders*, *Messages*, or *Recipients* collection as its data source.

```
Set oMsgCol = objFolder.Messages
'Set the data source for the Rendering object to the
'helpdesk public folder
objrenderer.DataSource = oMsgCol
```

The next step in the code figures out whether the application passed along a custom Outlook view name with the query string. If it did, the script uses that custom view name as the default view for the rendering object. This is an important point. You can use custom Outlook views as views in your rendering objects. This means you do not have to create views on the fly in your CDO applications and can instead create views in Outlook and then leverage them in your application. The rendering object supports views that contain sorting, grouping, and filtering—support that will save you many hours of coding custom views.

If the application did not pass a view name with the query string, the default view named Helpdesk is used to render the tickets in the folder, as shown in the following code:

```
'Get the requested view from the query string
requestedview = Request.QueryString("view")
'Get the Folder Views collection
Set objviews = objrenderer.Views
'If there is no selected view, set it to Helpdesk view
'created in Outlook
If requestedview = "" Then
    requestedview = "Helpdesk"
End If
'Search the Views collection until you find the view
i=1
```

```
Do While objviews.item(i).Name <> requestedview
    i=i+1
    If err.number <> 0 Then
        response.write "The Outlook views were not created. " & _
        "Please create the views according to the setup instructions."
        response.end
    End If
Loop
Set objview = objviews.Item(i)
```

The next step in setting up the container renderer is to enable a hyperlink on a field in the view so technicians can click on the hyperlink to retrieve the information contained in the ticket. If you do not include this step in your CDO applications, the rendering objects will return HTML without any clickable links. To create hyperlinks, you must first select the column in the view for which you want to create the hyperlink. In the Helpdesk application, the third column in the view is always used to create the hyperlink. You access the third column by using the *Columns* collection and the *Column* object of the *TableView* object that is represented by the custom Outlook view. The *Column* object has a property named *RenderUsing* that allows you to specify the HTML code to use when rendering that specific column. You specify not only the HTML but also substitution tokens within percent signs in the *RenderUsing* property, which CDO replaces with actual values when rendering the information to the Web browser. The two most commonly used substitution tokens are *%obj%* and *%value%*.

You use the *%obj%* token when you want to place the unique identifier for the item as a string in your HTML. This token is used in the Helpdesk application so the hyperlink on the third column passes the unique identifier for the ticket to the next ASP file, framemsg.asp. You use the *%value%* token when you want to place the actual value of the property into the HTML returned by the rendering object. The Helpdesk application uses this token to display the actual third-column property value in the view. For the Helpdesk view, this property value is the subject of the message. The following code shows you how to use both of these substitution tokens as well as the *RenderUsing* property and *Column* object:

```
Set objcolumns = objview.Columns
Set objcolumn = objcolumns.Item(3)
'Change the column renderer so that it renders the subject field
'as an ahref with the entry ID of the message
objcolumn.RenderUsing = _
    "<a href='framemsg.asp?entryid=%obj%'>%value%</a>"
```

The final step in enabling the container renderer is to set the *CurrentView* property as the custom view just modified by the application. To do this, the application sets the *CurrentView* property equal to the *TableView* object we just modified, as shown in the following code:

```
'Set the current view equal to the view just selected
objrenderer.CurrentView = objview
```

To actually render the information to HTML and return it to the browser, you must call the *Render* method on your *ContainerRenderer* object. The *Render* method takes four parameters. The first parameter is a *Long* data type that determines the style that the data should be rendered in. This parameter has two possible values—*CdoFolderContents (1)* and *CdoFolderHierarchy (2)*:

- *CdoFolderContents* is used to render the actual contents of the data source and not the child objects.
- *CdoFolderHierarchy* is used to render child folders for a *Folders* collection. If you want to build an HTML page that displays a folder hierarchy for users to scroll through, you use the *CdoFolderHierarchy* style.

The second parameter, which is optional, is also a *Long* data type and specifies the page number at which rendering should begin. In the CDO Rendering library, you can have CDO automatically break up the content of a data source into data pages so that when the HTML is rendered by the library, the length of the resulting HTML table is not massive. By default, CDO breaks the content at every 25 rows in the HTML table. It does this to enhance the performance of your application as well as to make it easier for users to read the information. You can change the default number of rows rendered by setting the *RowsPerPage* property on the *ContainerRenderer* object.

The third parameter is for internal use only by the CDO Rendering library. You should always pass *0* as its value. The final parameter is the *Active Server Response* object to which you want to send the HTML output from the *Render* method. This parameter should always be *Response* if you want to render the information to the browser.

When you have large amounts of information to render, you should be aware that CDO does not automatically generate a way to navigate rows on multiple pages, nor does it tell you whether you need to render multiple pages of information. Therefore, in your application, you must provide navigation elements if the number of rows in the table is larger than the value of the *RowsPerPage* property. You also must remember which page the user is currently rendering as well as the total number of pages. If the number of help tickets exceeds the *RowsPerPage* property, the render.asp file for the Helpdesk application will display graphical navigation arrows as well as text indicating the current page of information. When a user clicks on the Next Page or Previous Page arrow, the current page variable is either incremented or decremented, and this value is sent with the query string. The ASP script retrieves the value and renders the correct content on the page. If there are no previous or next pages, the graphical navigation elements are not displayed. The following code from render.asp handles viewing help tickets on multiple pages:

```
'Calculate total number of pages
intMessageCount = oMsgCol.Count
numrows = objRenderer.RowsPerPage
intPages = (intMessageCount - 1) \ numrows
intPages = intPages + 1
intCurPage = CInt(Request.QueryString("curpage"))
If intCurPage > intPages or intCurPage < 1 Then
    'Initialize it
    intCurPage = 1
ElseIf intMessageCount < 1 Then
   intCurPage = 1
End If

<% If intCurPage <> 1 Then %>
<a href=
"render.asp?view=<%=requestedview%>&curpage=<%=intCurPage-1%>">
<img src = "left.gif" Align="Middle" border=0 Alt="Previous Page"></a>
<% End If %>
  Page <%=intCurPage%> of <%=intPages%> 
<% If intCurPage <> intPages Then %>
<a href="render.asp?view=<% response.Write requestedView %>
&curpage=<%=intCurPage+1%>">
<img src = "right.gif" Align="Middle" border=0 Alt="Next Page"></a>
<% End If %>
<table border="0" width="65%">
   <tr>
      <td><% objRenderer.Render 1,intCurPage,0,Response %></td>
   </tr>
</table>
```

Notice how you can easily calculate the total number of pages you need to render to completely show all the information in your application. Take the number of messages minus 1, integer-divide that number by the number of rows per page set for the *ContainerRenderer* object, and then add 1 to that value. Therefore, if the number of messages is less than or equal to the number of rows per page, the integer division will return 0. This value will be incremented by 1, indicating that there is one page of information.

Rendering the Actual Help Ticket

When the technician clicks on one of the hyperlinks in the rendered list of help tickets, the application calls another ASP file, message.asp, to render the actual ticket for the technician, as shown in Figure 11-16. The technician can then view a number of different items for the ticket, resolve the ticket, or schedule a meeting with the customer who submitted the ticket.

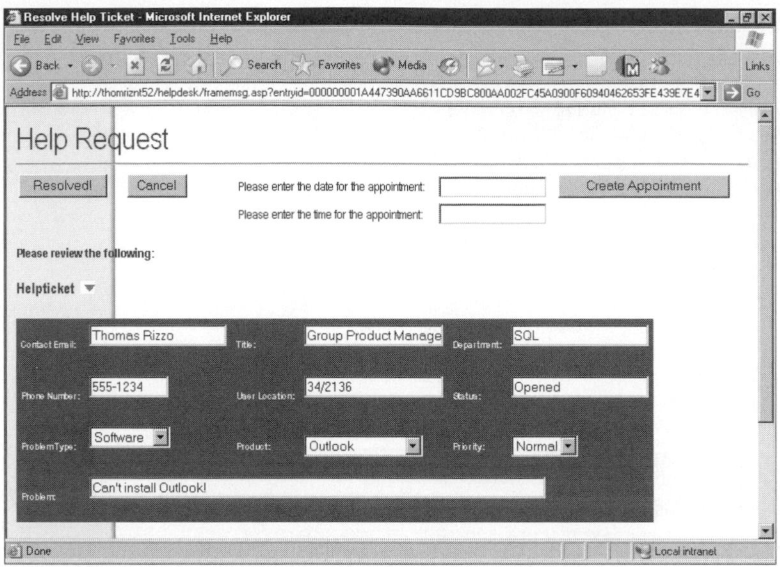

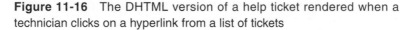

Figure 11-16 The DHTML version of a help ticket rendered when a technician clicks on a hyperlink from a list of tickets

The Helpdesk application uses DHTML to simplify navigating information contained in a ticket. It also uses ADO and queries an Access database to pull out the relevant information about the user's machine. This portion of the application shows you how you can combine CDO and ADO to make rich Web applications that access information from two types of data sources: Exchange Server and an ODBC/OLEDB database.

In the code for the help ticket page, the EntryID of the help ticket link that the user clicked on is retrieved from the *Request.QueryString* collection. The script then calls the *GetMessage* method of the CDO *Session* object to retrieve the message from the Exchange Server database. The *GetMessage* method is an easy and fast way to retrieve information from Exchange Server if you know the unique EntryID for the desired message. If you do not know the EntryID, you must search the folder where the message is stored or use a *MessageFilter* object to filter out only your message. The *MessageFilter* object is discussed in the Calendar of Events application later in this chapter.

The script then sets the *Unread* property of the message to *False* and calls the *Update* method of the *Message* object to save that property back to the database. Because CDO does not automatically update the *Unread* property for you, you must set it in code. After the code sets *Unread*, when the technician goes back to the table of tickets in the folder, the code displays all messages read by the technician as nonbold tickets. This functionality of not bolding read messages is provided automatically by the *Rendering* objects and ultimately makes your application easier to use. Also, the Exchange Server database maintains a per-user *Unread* property so each technician will receive different read and unread messages in the folder according to what each has actually read. The VBScript code for this functionality is shown here:

```
'Get the EntryID for the message from the query string
Set objMessageID = Request.QueryString("entryid")
'Get the message by its ID
Set oMessage = objOMSession.GetMessage(objMessageID, _
    Session("InfoStoreID"))
'Set the message as read
oMessage.Unread = FALSE
'Update the message in the folder
oMessage.Update
```

The application then pulls out the status of the ticket, either *Opened* or *Done*, and also the name of the user who submitted the ticket. An ADO *Connection* object is created, and a connection to the Access database is established by the application. In ADO, you can specify values for the *Open* method on the *Connection* object to determine which OLE DB data source you want to open. In this case, the DSN name *Helpdesk*, which we created earlier on the machine, is passed as the parameter for the *Open* method. Once the connection is established, three queries are executed against three database tables to figure out the machine configuration for the current user. We accomplish this by using the name of the user retrieved from the help ticket. These queries use the *Execute* method of the ADO *Connection* object. This information is used later in the form. The following code shows the ADO connection and queries. (For more information about ADO and its object library, visit the Microsoft Web site at *http://www.microsoft.com/data*.)

```
'Start the ADO connection
On Error Resume Next
Set Conn = Server.CreateObject("ADODB.Connection")
Conn.Open "Helpdesk"
Set RS = Conn.Execute( _
    "SELECT SystemChipType, SystemChipSpeed, SystemChipCount, " & _
    "SystemOS, SystemRAM FROM tblMachine " & _
    "WHERE Userid like '" & objuser & "';")
Set RSIP = Conn.Execute( _
    "SELECT CompName, IPAddress FROM tblNetwork " & _
    "WHERE Userid like '" & objuser & "';")
Set RSSoft = Conn.Execute( _
    "SELECT SoftwareName, SoftwareVersion FROM tblSoftware " & _
    "WHERE Userid like '" & objuser & "';")
```

The script retrieves the user information from the Exchange Server directory and stores it in variables. (You saw this code earlier when we discussed submitting a help ticket.) Then the body of the actual ticket is displayed using DHTML. The DHTML code includes some JavaScript to allow the user to dynamically expand or collapse the different sections of the help ticket, such as system information or the description of the problem.

Creating the Calendar Information

One interesting section in the body of the HTML is the drop-down section of calendar information, shown in Figure 11-17. This section allows technicians to view the free/busy information for the user and for themselves at the bottom of the help ticket page. With this information, the technician can quickly find time slots that are open for both the technician and the user.

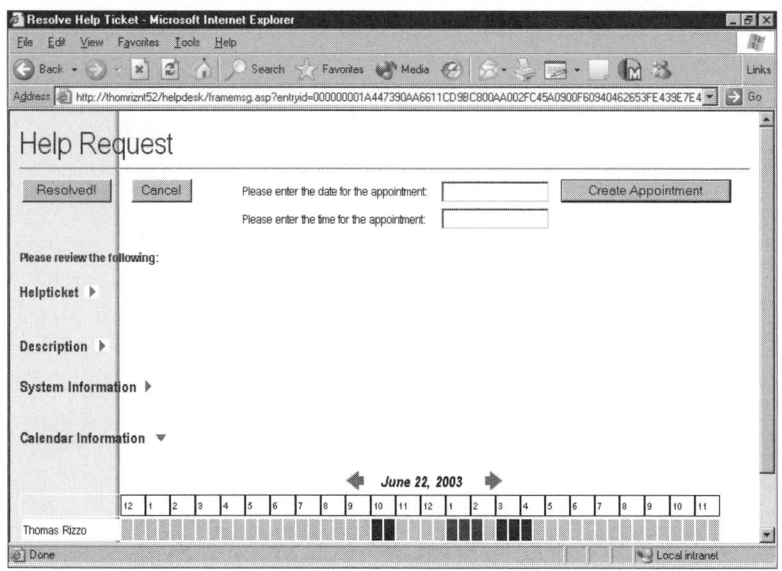

Figure 11-17 The help ticket showing the calendar information

> **Note** To obtain up-to-the-minute calendar information for a user on the Help Request page, you might have to adjust the calendar settings in Outlook. By default, Outlook updates the calendar free/busy information on the server every 15 minutes. You can decrease this time in Outlook by choosing Options from the Tools menu, clicking Calendar Options, and then clicking Free/Busy Options. If you do decrease this, you should remember that this will cause more network traffic in your system.

This calendar information is created by using the calendaring functionality of the CDO library. The code for the drop-down section is shown here:

```
<%
bcGrayM = "#c0c0c0" 'gray
bcGrayD = "#909090"
buildmonth = Request.QueryString("m")
buildday = Request.QueryString("d")
buildyear = Request.QueryString("y")
builddate = buildmonth & "/" & buildday & "/" & buildyear
dtCurrentDay =  DateValue(builddate)
arrBGColors= _
    Array(bcGrayM, "#99ccff", "#0000ff", "#940080", "#ff0000")
Dim MeetingPlanner(2)
%>
<B><FONT STYLE="ARIAL NARROW" SIZE=3><SPAN style="cursor:hand"
CLASS=ex TITLE="Calendar Information"
ID="CalInfo" onclick="checkExpand()" myArrow=4>Calendar Information
</SPAN></FONT></B>
<IMG WIDTH=15 HEIGHT=13 SRC="addarrow.gif" ID="imgArrow4"><P>

<TABLE ID = "CalInfoChild" style="display:none" BORDER = 0>
<TR>
<td nowrap=nowrap width="355" align="right">
<A href="message.asp?entryid=<%response.write objMessageID%>
&m=<%=Month(dtCurrentDay-1)%>&d=<%=Day(dtCurrentDay-1)%>
&y=<%=Year(dtCurrentDay-1)%>" target="main">
<img src="left.gif" border=0 alt="Previous Day"></a></td>
<td nowrap=nowrap width="10"></TD>
<td nowrap=nowrap border=0><i><b>
<%=MonthName(Month(dtCurrentDay)) & " " & Day(dtCurrentDay) & _
", " & Year(dtCurrentDay)%></b></i></TD>
<td nowrap=nowrap border=0 width="10"></td>
<td nowrap=nowrap width="20" align="right">
<A href="message.asp?entryid=<%response.write objMessageID%>
&m=<%=Month(dtCurrentDay+1)%>&d=<%=Day(dtCurrentDay+1)%>
&y=<%=Year(dtCurrentDay+1)%>" target="main">
<img src="right.gif" border=0 alt="Next Day"></a></td>
</Table>

<table ID = "CalInfoChild2" style="display:none" cols=50
bordercolor=#FFFFFF border=1 cellspacing=0 cellpadding=0>
<tr>
<td nowrap=nowrap width="102">
<td colspan=2> </td>
<% For idx = 0 to 23 %>
<td bordercolor=#000000 colspan=2 align=left width="24">
<font size=-2%> <%= CStr((((idx + 11) Mod 12) + 1))%>
</font></td>
<% Next %>
</tr>
</TABLE>
```

```
<%
'Loop from 3 to 4
For x = 3 to 4
   If x = 3 Then
       Set objRecip = objOMSession.CurrentUser
   Else
       set objRecip = objonerecip
   End If
   'Initialize the string
   aFB = ""
   aFB = objRecip.GetFreeBusy( dtCurrentDay, dtCurrentDay+1, _
       30, true)
   szFreeBusy = aFB
%>
   <table ID = "CalInfoChild<%=x%>" style="display:none" Border=0>
   <tr bordercolor=#000000>
   <td nowrap=nowrap bgcolor="#ffffff" width="100"><font size=-1>
   <%= objRecip.Name %><br></font></td>
<%
    If Len(szFreeBusy) = 0 Then
%>
      <TD><font size=2>Free/Busy Information is not available
      </font></TD>
<%
    Else
        For idy = 1 to 48
            sCell= Mid( szFreeBusy, idy, 1)
%>
         <td bgcolor=<%= arrBGColors(CInt(sCell)) %> width="9">
          </td>
<%
        Next 'idy
    End If
Next 'x
%>
</table>
<TABLE ID="CalInfoChild5" style="display:none" border=0>
<TR>
<td nowrap=nowrap width="100"><b>Legend:</b></TD>
<TD bgcolor=<%= arrBGColors(1) %>>  </TD>
<TD> Tentative </TD>
<TD bgcolor=<%= arrBGColors(2) %>>  </TD>
<TD> Busy </TD>
<TD bgcolor=<%= arrBGColors(3) %>>  </TD>
<TD> Out of Office </TD>
</TABLE>
```

First the code tries to retrieve, from the query string, the day, month, and year values passed by the application. When the user first clicks on a hyperlink from the list of help tickets, these date values are filled with the current day, month, and year from the Web server machine. The code then builds a date from the values, such as 10/12/2003, so the string containing the date value can be used as a parameter to the *DateValue* function in VBScript. This function returns a *Variant* of the subtype *Date* so you can use it in the rest of the code.

The application then builds an array of information. This array, named *arrBGColors*, comprises background colors used to render the free/busy information to the Web browser. These colors correspond to the Outlook colors for rendering calendar information, such as blue for busy slots, light blue for tentative slots, and purple for out-of-office slots. You'll understand why we place these colors into an array when we look at the *GetFreeBusy* method in CDO and see how the values are returned from this method and parsed by the application.

The next step in the code is to render the navigation elements to move to the previous or next day in the calendar and also to display the date the technician is viewing. The navigation elements to move to the next and previous days are implemented using hyperlinks, which pass the next or previous date, broken up into day, month, and year, across the query string to message.asp. To retrieve the day, month, and year from the *dtCurrentDay* variable, which has the form 12/31/2003, the VBScript functions *Day*, *Month*, and *Year* are used.

The code then uses a *For...Next* loop from 0 through 23 to draw a table that creates the time values across the top of the free/busy information. Starting at 12 A.M., the code draws table elements until 11:30 P.M. the same day. Adding 11 to the current index of the loop, using the *Mod* operator to return the remainder when divided by 12, and then adding 1 to that value produces the correct identifiers for the time slots. The code uses the *CStr* function to convert the number returned by the formula to a string value.

The next portion of the code uses the calendaring features of CDO. Figure 11-18 shows some of the calendar-related objects in the CDO library. The CDO library provides extensive support for building calendaring applications: the Helpdesk application shows how to use the *GetFreeBusy* method and the meeting request functionality of CDO, and the Calendar of Events application, which we'll examine later in this chapter, shows appointment filtering and rendering of calendars using the Rendering library.

A *For...Next* loop is used to loop through the code twice. The loop starts at the number 3 and continues through the number 4. The loop does not start at the number 1 because the index of the loop is used to create unique *<DIV>* elements in the HTML code so the JavaScript *checkExpand* function can find the tables using them. Because this code is fairly generic, you can use it in other applications that render tens or hundreds of blocks of free/busy information for users rather than blocks for only two users. All you do is change the ending point of the loop and pass in the targeted users' free/busy information as an array of names.

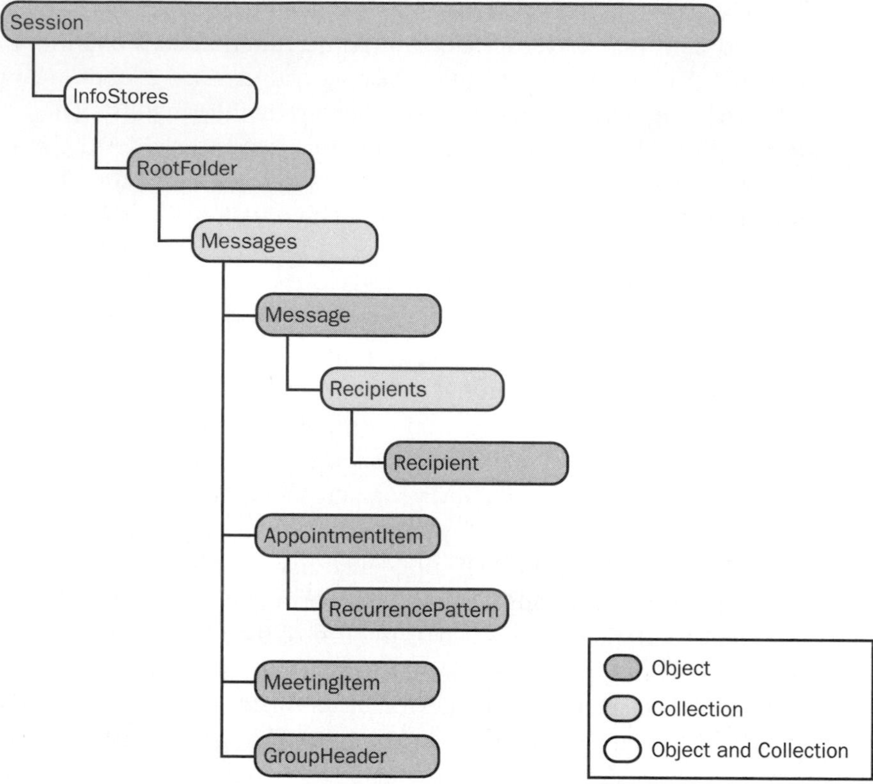

Figure 11-18 The calendar-related objects of the CDO library

The code uses the *GetFreeBusy* method of the CDO *Recipient* object to return the free/busy calendaring information for the current user, which is retrieved using the *CurrentUser* property on the CDO *Session* object, and the name of the person who submitted the help ticket, which is stored in the *Recipient* object named *objonerecip*. The *GetFreeBusy* method in CDO is exactly the same as the *GetFreeBusy* method in the Outlook object library. You must pass the following four parameters to this method:

- The start time of the first slot you want to retrieve.
- The end time of the last slot you want to retrieve.
- The interval, in minutes, of each of the slots.
- A Boolean specifying whether you want to have CDO return full formatting for the slots. Full formatting will inform you of the exact nature of busy slots: *CdoFree (0)*, *CdoTentative (1)*, *CdoBusy (2)*, or *CdoOutOfOffice (3)*. If you do not enable full formatting, CDO will return *0* for free and *1* for busy.

For *GetFreeBusy*, CDO returns the most committed value in the time slots. This means that if a user has overlapping appointments in the slot and one is tentative and the other is out-of-office, CDO returns the out-of-office value. CDO does not return "free" for time slots unless the entire time slot is free. Be careful when you work with free/busy information far beyond the current date. By default, free/busy information is published only two months past the current date. If you query beyond the published information for free/busy, CDO will return free slots even though the user might have appointments during those slots. You can ask your Outlook users to change the number of months to a maximum of 12 months past the current date for free/busy information if you need longer term information. They can change this number of months in Outlook by choosing Options from the Tools menu, clicking Calendar Options, and clicking Free/Busy Options.

The return value for this method returns a string of numbers that correspond to the free/busy status of the user for all the time slots you specified. Your code must then parse the string and make a graphical representation of this information in your application.

The Helpdesk application parses this string by first looking at the length to make sure it's not zero, which would mean there is no free/busy information for the user. It then uses a *For...Next* loop and the VBScript *Mid* function to retrieve each character from the string and display the free/busy status for the user in an HTML table. Notice in the code that the value from the retrieved free/busy status interval is used as an index for the *arrBGColors* array of colors we created earlier: *CdoFree (0)* displays light gray, *CdoTentative (1)* displays light blue, *CdoBusy (2)* displays blue, and *CdoOutOfOffice (3)* displays purple. The *For...Next* loop ranges from 1 through 48 because we specified 30 minutes as the interval for the time slots in the call to the *GetFreeBusy* method. If you calculate the number of 30-minute intervals from 12 A.M. to 11:30 P.M., the result turns out to be 48.

Creating a Meeting with the User

Once a technician finds time slots in the Calendar Information section of a help ticket that are open for both the technician and the user, she can schedule a meeting with the user to troubleshoot on site. She can schedule a meeting by first typing the date and time for the appointment in the text boxes at the top of the help ticket, as shown in Figure 11-19.

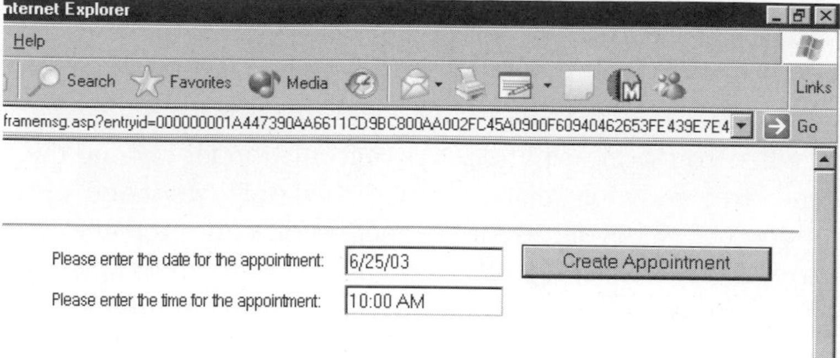

Figure 11-19 The help ticket with the date and time for an appointment filled in

When a technician types a date and a time and then clicks Create Appointment, createcal.asp is called by the application to create the actual meeting request, as shown in this code:

```
<%
'Convert the passed-in date to a vbDate
Set querydate = Request.Form("Date")
apptdate = CDate(querydate)
Set querytime = Request.Form("Time")
appttime = TimeValue(querytime)
compdatime = apptdate & " " & appttime
compdatime = CDate(compdatime)

'Add a new message to the user's calendar
Set calfolder = objOMSession.GetDefaultFolder(0)
Set CalRequest = calfolder.messages.add

'Set the message properties
CalRequest.Subject = oMessage.Subject
CalRequest.StartTime = compdatime
CalRequest.EndTime = DateAdd("n", 90, CalRequest.StartTime)
CalRequest.Location = myoffice
CalRequest.ResponseRequested = TRUE
set meetingrecip = CalRequest.Recipients.Add
meetingrecip.Name = objUser
meetingrecip.Resolve
CalRequest.ReminderSet = True
CalRequest.ReminderMinutesBeforeStart = 30
CalRequest.MeetingStatus = 1
CalRequest.Send
If Err.Number = 0 Then
    response.write "<SCRIPT LANGUAGE = 'JavaScript'>"
    response.write
        "window.alert('Meeting successfully created!');"
    response.write "</SCRIPT>"
```

```
Else
    response.write "<SCRIPT LANGUAGE = 'JavaScript'>"
    response.write "window.alert('Error: " & Err.Number & " " &
        Err.Description &"');"
    response.write "</SCRIPT>"
End If
%>
```

First the code converts the passed-in date to a *Date* data type and the passed-in time to a *Date*. Then it combines the two and converts the results to a *Date* so the date can be passed to the CDO property *StartTime* to indicate the start time of the appointment. The code uses the *GetDefaultFolder* method of the CDO *Session* object to retrieve the calendar folder of the technician. The *GetDefaultFolder* method in CDO is similar to the *GetDefaultFolder* method in the Outlook object library, but be careful when you use them because the values for the constants that represent the folders are different in the two libraries.

By using the *Add* method on the *Messages* collection in the calendar folder, CDO automatically adds a new *AppointmentItem* object to the collection. The code then sets the properties for this new *AppointmentItem* object to turn it into a *MeetingItem* object, which is sent to the user.

To create a meeting request in CDO, you must set some specific properties on the *AppointmentItem* object to turn it into a *MeetingItem* object. First you need to add some recipients to the inherited *Message* object by creating a *Recipient* object in the *Recipients* collection. In the Helpdesk application, the name of the person who submitted the help ticket is added and resolved against the address book as a recipient for the *MeetingItem* object.

You then set the *MeetingStatus* property to *CdoMeeting (1)* for the *AppointmentItem* object you created so the current user—the technician—is set as the meeting organizer in the *Organizer* property. The *MeetingStatus* property can take other values as well:

- *CdoNonMeeting (0)*, the default, which tells CDO that the appointment being organized is a regular appointment and does not represent a meeting.
- *CdoMeetingCanceled (5)*, which indicates that the meeting organizer has canceled the meeting.

Although the ability to cancel a meeting is not included in the Helpdesk application, here is some information about it. To cancel a meeting, you call the *Send* method again on the object to send the cancellation to all attendees. Also, be sure to set the object that holds the meeting to *Nothing*. If you are the organizer of the canceled meeting and Outlook is the main calendar store for your users, you must also call the *Delete* method on the *Message* object that is the parent of the *MeetingItem* object you just canceled. If you do not do this, you might get unexpected results when you work with the folder and its contents in the future.

You should also set the *ResponseRequested* property. This property takes a Boolean that tells CDO whether the meeting organizer wants responses to the meeting request. You should set this property to *False* only if you want to send out an FYI meeting request, which adds the item to a user's calendar but does not need to track whether the user has accepted or rejected the item. For example, you can set the property to *False* if you are sending out meeting requests for all the holidays in a year but do not actually care which holidays your users decide to accept on their calendars.

The preceding script sets some general properties for the appointment item, such as the *Subject*, which is the problem contained in the ticket. It also sets the *StartTime* and *EndTime* properties of the appointment so the *EndTime* is 90 minutes after the *StartTime*. The *Location* property is set to the office location for the user, which is pulled from the Exchange Server directory. The *ReminderSet* and *ReminderMinutesBeforeStart* properties are set to *True* and 30 minutes before the appointment, respectively, to make sure both parties remember that they need to meet.

The final step when you create any meeting request is to call the *Send* method on the *MeetingItem* object, which sends the request to the recipients you invited to the meeting. If any of the properties you set are incorrect or empty, CDO will return an error after calling *Send*. For this reason, the code checks the *Err* object in VBScript. Depending on whether an error occurred, the JavaScript client code will display a success message or an error message. Figure 11-20 shows the success message. If a property is empty, such as the *Office* property for an Exchange user, the error message "Error 448: Named argument not found" is displayed.

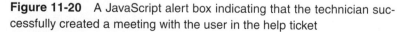

Figure 11-20 A JavaScript alert box indicating that the technician successfully created a meeting with the user in the help ticket

After the meeting request is sent, the user can use any client to accept or decline the meeting request. You can even send meeting requests to users over the Internet; as long as they are using Outlook or OWA, they can view and accept or decline meeting requests. You cannot, however, view the free/busy information of users on different systems. Figure 11-21 shows the scheduled meeting in the user's Outlook calendar.

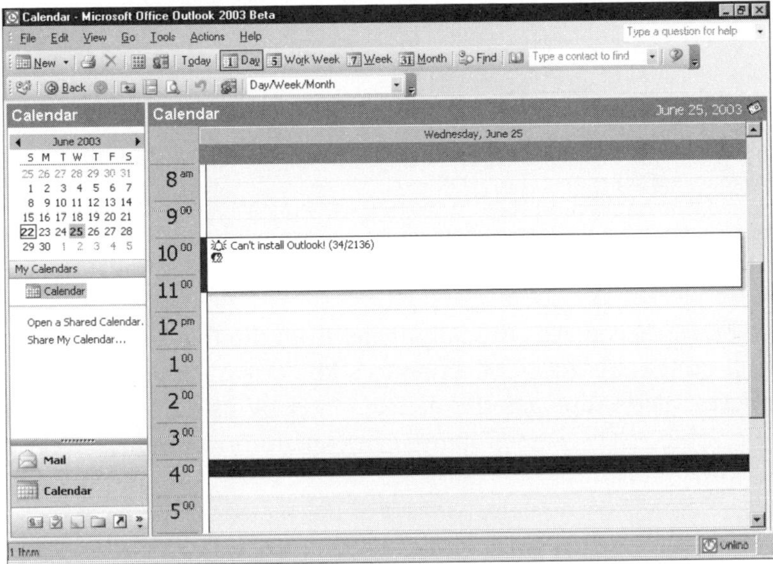

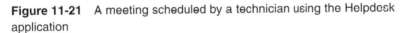

Figure 11-21 A meeting scheduled by a technician using the Helpdesk application

Resolving the Help Ticket

The technician can mark a help ticket as resolved. Resolving a help ticket consists of setting the status of the ticket to *Done* and sending an e-mail message to the user who submitted the ticket explaining that the issue has been resolved. The code that resolves the help ticket is in the resolved.asp file. This code shows you how to update fields on a message and also how to send e-mail messages using the CDO library:

```
<%
If InStr(Request.Form("Action"), "Resol") then
    Set objFolder = Session("HelpdeskFolder")
    Set recursefolder = objFolder

    Set objMessageID = Request.QueryString("entryid")
    Set oMessage = objOMSession.GetMessage(objMessageID, _
        Session("InfoStoreID"))
    'Retrieve the message flag and set it
    Set msgstatus = oMessage.Fields("Flag")
    msgstatusid = msgstatus.ID
    oMessage.Fields(msgstatusid) = "Done"
    oMessage.Update
```

```
    'Send a resolved message to the user stating that the
    'problem was resolved
    Set objNewMsg = objOMSession.Outbox.Messages.Add
    objNewMsg.Text = "Your problem: " & oMessage.Subject & _
        " was resolved on " & Now & chr(10) & chr(10) & _
        "Please see the helpdesk FAQ at " & _
        "http://exserver/faq/ for commonly asked questions."
    objNewMsg.Subject = "Resolved: " & oMessage.Subject
    Set objonerecip = objNewMsg.recipients.add
    objonerecip.Name = oMessage.Fields("From User")
    objonerecip.Resolve
    'Send the message without showing a dialog box
    objNewMsg.Send showDialog=False
End If
%>
```

The script retrieves the help ticket from the folder and then uses the *Add* method on the *Messages* collection to add a new message to the Outbox of the technician. The script sets the message text by using the *Text* property of the *Message* object. The *Text* property can contain only plain text. It does not support formatted text.

The code then sets the *Subject* of the message and adds recipients to the *Recipients* collection. The recipient for this message is the user who submitted the ticket. The code uses the *Resolve* method of the *Message* object to make sure there are no ambiguous recipients on the message. Finally, it calls the *Send* method to send the message to the user. Figure 11-22 shows a sample of the e-mail received by the user.

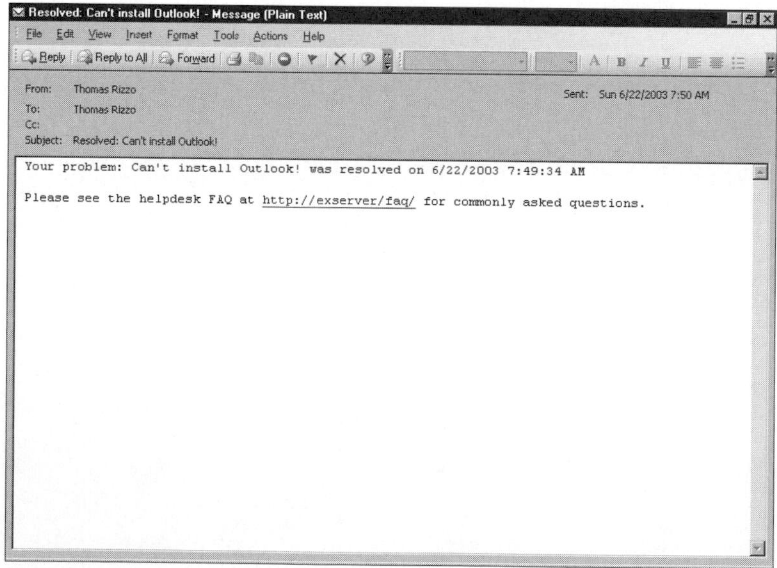

Figure 11-22 An e-mail message sent to the user by the technician, indicating that the problem has been solved

The Calendar of Events Application

The Helpdesk application showed you a little bit about the calendaring functionality in the CDO library; the Calendar of Events application demonstrates the full power of CDO calendaring. The idea behind the Calendar of Events application is to allow a corporation to publish, either internally or externally, a calendar of corporate events. The application is based on Exchange Server and Outlook, so it is rich enough to support permissions for the creator or modifier of the calendar content and easy enough for users to add new content by employing familiar tools.

The Calendar of Events application shows how to create publicly accessible calendars, use message filters in the CDO library, and use more objects in the CDO Rendering library. You will also see some of the current limitations in the CDO library and learn about ways to work around these limitations, particularly the limitations of not supporting public folder calendars and not being able to filter by category when you use appointment items.

The monthly results page for the application is shown in Figure 11-23. As you can see, the application is Web-based, but users can take advantage of Outlook's calendaring features to create the contents for the Web-based calendar. The application dynamically connects and retrieves the information that Outlook users create in the Exchange Server database and exposes it to Web clients. Outlook users can also use their Outlook client to retrieve calendar information, as shown in Figure 11-24.

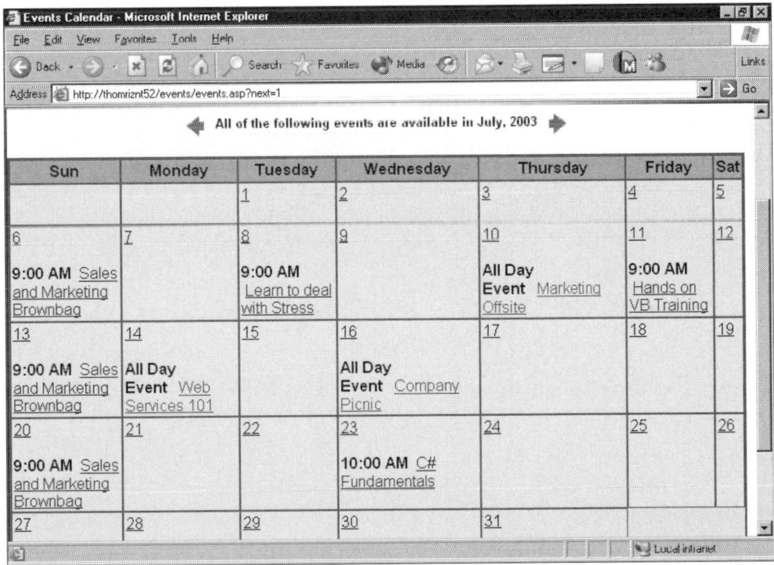

Figure 11-23 The monthly view of the Calendar of Events in HTML

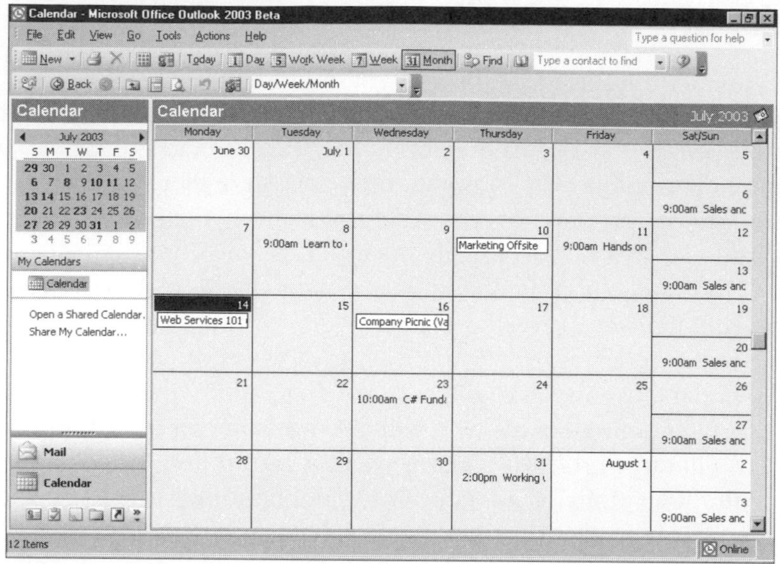

Figure 11-24 A monthly view in Outlook of the source calendar for the Calendar of Events application

Setting Up the Application

Before you can install the Calendar of Events application, you must have a Windows NT 4.0 Server or a Windows 2000/2003 Server and a client with certain software installed. Table 11-4 outlines the installation requirements.

Table 11-4 Installation Requirements for the Calendar of Events Application

Required Software	Installation Notes
Exchange Server 5.5 with the latest service pack or Exchange 2000/2003 with the latest service pack	OWA must be installed for Exchange 5.5. Exchange 2003 installs OWA by default.
IIS 3.0 or later with ASP	IIS 5.0 is recommended.
CDO library (cdo.dll) and CDO Rendering library	Exchange Server installs CDO 1.21. For CDO Rendering on a clean Exchange 2003 install, you must install OWA from Exchange 5.5 on the machine to get CDOHTML.
Client Requirements	
A Web browser or Outlook	You can run the client software on the same machine or on a separate machine.

To install the application, copy the Calendar Of Events folder from the sample files to the location on your Web server from which you want to run the application.

Start the IIS administration program. Create a virtual directory that points to the location where you copied the Calendar Of Events files, and name the virtual directory *events*. Enable Execute permissions on the virtual directory. This step allows you to use the URL *http://<yourservername>/events* to access your Events Calendar.

Create a new user in the Active Directory with a display name of *Events Calendar* and an alias of *events*. Make sure to create a mailbox for this user. Set the mailbox rights for the user under the *Exchange Advanced* tab for the user in Active Directory so that the IIS anonymous user account (IUSR_*servername*) has *Full mailbox access* rights. Also, add your own account to have *Full mailbox access* rights as well.

> **Note** Your anonymous IIS user account should be a domain account or should at least be assigned as the owner of a mailbox in Exchange Server. Normally, the account that IIS uses to log users on to your Web pages anonymously is named IUSR_*servername*. The Calendar of Events application uses this account when starting an ASP session to automatically log on to the Exchange server without prompting for credentials. You will see how this works when we step through the application. If the IIS anonymous user account is not a domain account or cannot be assigned as an owner of a mailbox in Exchange Server, change the account so that it can be assigned Owner permissions.

If you use a different alias name for the Events Calendar mailbox, you must modify the Global.asa file. Open the Global.asa file in the Calendar Of Events folder on your IIS server. Find the line

```
Application("MailboxName") = "events"
```

and change the name to the alias name of the Events Calendar mailbox you created.

The application includes a file named cats.inc. Because the application allows you to filter events based on Outlook categories, you might want to change cats.inc to reflect the categories that are important to your application. If you do change the categories, you must specify the total number of categories you want to filter on.

The following code is from the sample application:

```
<% NumberofCats = 5
Dim strCategories(5)
strCategories(1) = "Business"
strCategories(2) = "Competitive"
strCategories(3) = "Presentations"
strCategories(4) = "Hands-On Training"
strCategories(5) = "Social"
%>
```

To change the values for your categories, modify the *NumberofCats* integer to be the total number of categories. Then change the *Dim strCategories (5)* statement to reflect the number of categories, thereby enabling VBScript to create an array of the category names. Now type the name of the category as a string argument in one of the cells of the array.

If you specified a name for the virtual root that is different from */events*, find the file named virtroot.inc, open it, and change the virtual root to match the one you created for the application.

Create a profile for Outlook that connects to the Events Calendar mailbox you created. You can create a new profile by opening the Mail applet in Control Panel and clicking Show Profiles. On the General tab, you can add a new profile. You can also create a new profile by clicking the New button in the Choose Profile dialog box when you start Outlook. If this dialog box does not automatically appear when you start Outlook, choose the Mail applet again and under Show Profiles, select the Prompt For A Profile To Be Used option.

With Outlook opened to the Events Calendar mailbox, right-click on the Calendar folder, choose Properties, and click on the Permissions tab. Set permissions for the users in your organization who need to create and edit appointments in the calendar. You do not have to set the Default permissions on the folder, so you can restrict the access permissions for each user in the organization and enable permissions for creating and deleting items without giving permissions to everyone with access to the calendar. This step will allow Outlook users with the proper permissions to view and possibly edit the calendar for the Events Calendar mailbox. To open the Calendar folder for the Events Calendar mailbox, other users can choose Open from the File menu in Outlook and then select Other User's Folder. In the Open Other User's Folder dialog box, they can select and open the Calendar folder. You're finished. You can now add events to the Outlook calendar for the Events Calendar mailbox and then test the viewing of those events from the URL *http://<yourservername>/events*.

CDO Sessions

The Calendar of Events application uses the Global.asa file of the Helpdesk application with a few changes. The file is modified primarily because CDO

1.21 does not support accessing calendars in public folders or delegated calendars. Just a quick note, though: CDO for Exchange 2000/2003 does support this capability, but not with an Exchange 5.5 Server. It supports it only on an Exchange 2000 Server.

With CDO 1.21, you can access calendars only when you are the primary Windows account owner of the mailbox. With ASP, you can get around this limitation by assigning the anonymous IIS user account as the primary owner of a mailbox, thereby making all users who browse your Web page automatically log on to CDO using this mailbox as their default.

Because IIS uses the security context of this anonymous user account to browse web pages anonymously, you do not have to prompt users for security credentials to enable them to log on to the mailbox, as we had to in the Helpdesk application. Instead, all you do is add a CDO logon to the *Session_OnStart* subroutine in your Global.asa. This logon method forces every new Web user to log on to the Exchange server using the mailbox you created as well as the security credentials of the anonymous user account in IIS. The Global.asa code for the Calendar of Events application is shown here:

```
<SCRIPT LANGUAGE="VBScript" RUNAT="Server">

Sub Application_OnStart
    On Error Resume Next
    Set objRenderApp = Server.CreateObject("AMHTML.Application")
    If Err = 0 Then
        Set Application("RenderApplication") = objRenderApp
    Else
        Application("startupFatal") = Err.Number
        Application("startupFatalDescription") = _
            "Failed to create application object<br>" & _
            Err.Description
    End If

    Application("hImp") = Empty
    'Load the configuration information from the registry
    objRenderApp.LoadConfiguration 1, _
        "HKEY_LOCAL_MACHINE\System\CurrentControlSet\Services\" & _
        "MSExchangeWeb\Parameters"

 'Uncomment the following line and
 'Please enter your Exchange servername here
 'Application("ServerName") = "myserver"

 Application("ServerName") = objRenderApp.ConfigParameter("Server")
    Application("MailboxName") = "events"
    Err.Clear
End Sub

Sub Application_OnEnd
    Set Application("RenderApplication") = Nothing
End Sub
```

```
Sub Session_OnStart

    Set objRenderApp = Application("RenderApplication")
    hOldImp = objRenderApp.ImpID
    Set Session("AMSession") = Nothing
    Set objOMSession = Server.CreateObject("MAPI.Session")
    bstrProfileInfo = Application("ServerName") + vbLF + _
        Application("MailboxName")
    objOMSession.Logon "", "", False, True, 0, True, bstrProfileInfo
    set Session("AMSession") = objOMSession
    'This is a handle to the security context.
    'It will be set to the correct value when the CDO session is created.
    Session("hImp") = objRenderApp.ImpID
End Sub

'While calling the Session_OnEnd event, IIS doesn't call us in
'the right security context.
'Workaround: current security context is stored in Session
'(look at logon.asp) and then gets restored in Session_OnEnd
'event handler.
'
'All CDO and CDOHTML objects stored in the Session object
'need to be explicitly set to Nothing between the two
'objRenderApp.Impersonate calls below.
Sub Session_OnEnd
    On Error Resume Next
    Set objRenderApp = Application("RenderApplication")
    hImp = Session("hImp")
    If Not IsEmpty(hImp) Then
        objRenderApp.Impersonate(hImp)
    End If
    'Do our cleanup. Set all CDO and CDOHTML objects inside
    'the session to Nothing.
    'The CDO session is a little special because we need to do
    'the Logoff on it.
    Set objOMSession = Session("AMSession")
    If Not objOMSession Is Nothing Then
        Set Session("AMSession") = Nothing
        objOMSession.Logoff
        Set objOMSession = Nothing
    End If
End Sub
</SCRIPT>
```

Because all users of the application will access the same mailbox, you might wonder why the code for logging on to the Exchange server is in the *Session_OnStart* subroutine and not in the *Application_OnStart* subroutine. The main reason for creating a new session for each user to the same mailbox is to improve the performance of the application. If the application did not do this, all users would use the same CDO session to connect to the Exchange server.

Prompting the User for Input

After a CDO session has been created for the user but before the user can start viewing the calendar, the application must ask which appointment types and month the user wants to view in the calendar. To do this, the application presents a search page with options to select the month, year, and event categories, as shown in Figure 11-25.

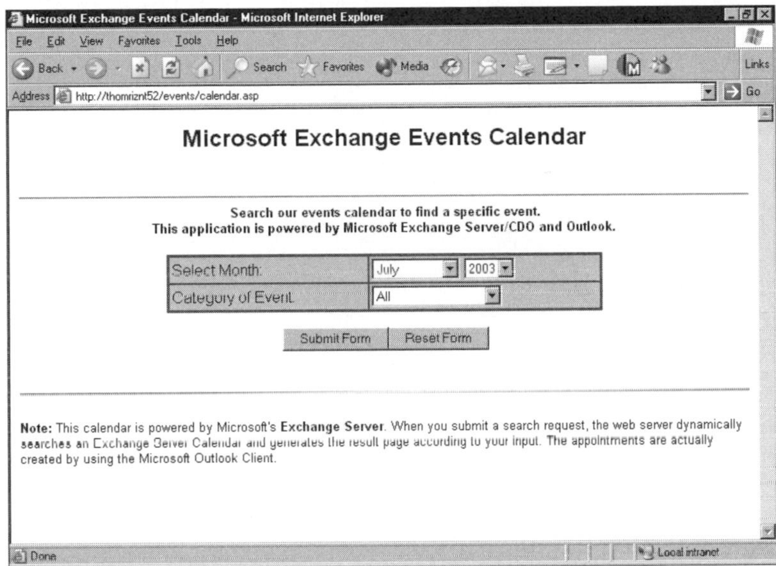

Figure 11-25 From the search page of the Events Calendar, the user can select the month, year, and event categories to search for.

The next section of code is for the search page shown in Figure 11-25. Notice how the code figures out the current month on the Web server machine and uses it as the default value in the Select Month drop-down list. Using the current year as the point of reference, the code dynamically generates the previous year and next year in the Year drop-down list. This page also uses a hidden control on the HTML form that will indicate to the next ASP page, Events.asp, that the user originated from the current page.

The HTML page does not have to check whether a valid ASP session exists for the current user because the page does not use any CDO code. The CDO logon code is handled in the *Session_OnStart* procedure, so when the user's session has timed out, he is automatically logged on again when he refreshes the screen or moves to a different page. Here is the code for the search page:

```
<!--#include file="cats.inc"-->
<Title>Microsoft Exchange Events Calendar</Title>
<center>
```

```
<p><b><FONT FACE="Arial, Helvetica" SIZE=5>
Microsoft Exchange Events Calendar</font></b></P>
<BR>
<HR>
<FONT FACE="Arial, Helvetica" SIZE=2>
<b>Search our Events Calendar to find a specific event. <BR>
This application is powered
by Microsoft Exchange Server/CDO and Outlook.</b>
<FORM METHOD=POST ACTION="events.asp">
<TABLE BORDER=2 Width=60% Bordercolor="008000" cellpadding="2"
cellspacing="0" borderdarkercolor="008000" bgcolor="#FFCC00"
borderlightcolor="008000">

<%
'***********************************
'Figure out the month
'***********************************
%>
   <TR>
   <TD>Select Month:</TD>
   <TD>
   <SELECT NAME="month" SIZE=1>
   <%
   Dim MonthArray(12)
   MonthArray(1)="January"
   MonthArray(2)="February"
   MonthArray(3)="March"
   MonthArray(4)="April"
   MonthArray(5)="May"
   MonthArray(6)="June"
   MonthArray(7)="July"
   MonthArray(8)="August"
   MonthArray(9)="September"
   MonthArray(10)="October"
   MonthArray(11)="November"
   MonthArray(12)="December" %>

    <% For i = 1 To 12 %>
      <% If month(now) = i Then %>
         <OPTION Selected Value = <%=i%>> <%= MonthArray(i) %>
      <% Else %>
         <OPTION Value = <%=i%>> <%= MonthArray(i) %>
      <% End If %>
   <% Next %>
   </SELECT>

<%
'***********************************
'Figure out the year
'***********************************
%>
   <SELECT NAME="year" SIZE=1>
```

```
<% 'Figure out the current year, and go back and ahead 1 year %>
<% yearprevious = DateAdd("yyyy",-1,date) %>
   <OPTION> <% Response.Write Year(yearprevious) %>
   <OPTION SELECTED> <% Response.Write Year(date) %>
<% yearnext = DateAdd("yyyy",1,date) %>
<OPTION> <% Response.Write Year(yearnext) %>
   </SELECT>
   </TD></TR>

<%
'****************************************
'Figure out the categories
'****************************************
%>

   <TR>
   <TD>Category of Event:</TD>
   <TD><SELECT NAME="Type" SIZE=1>
      <OPTION SELECTED>All
      <% For c = 1 Ro NumberofCats
         Response.Write "<OPTION>" & strCategories(c)
      Next
      %>
   </SELECT>
   </TD></TR>
</TABLE>

<%
'****************************************
'Create a hidden field so that we know the
'request came from calendar.asp
'****************************************
%>
  <INPUT TYPE=HIDDEN NAME="fromcalendar" VALUE="fromcalendar"><BR>
<INPUT TYPE=SUBMIT VALUE="Submit Form"><INPUT TYPE-RESET
VALUE="Reset Form">
</FORM>
<br>
<HR>
</center>
</font>
<BR>
<FONT FACE="Arial, Helvetica" SIZE=2>
<P><b>Note:</b> This calendar is powered by Microsoft
<b>Exchange Server</b>.
When you submit a search request, the Web server dynamically
searches an Exchange Server calendar and generates the
result page according to your input. The appointments are
actually created by using the Microsoft Outlook client.
</font>
</BODY>
</HTML>
```

Displaying Calendar Views

When the user clicks the Submit Form button on the HTML form, the application passes the entered information to the next ASP page in the application, Events.asp. This page creates a monthly view of the information stored in the Events Calendar, as shown in Figure 11-26.

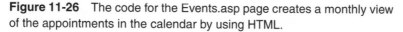

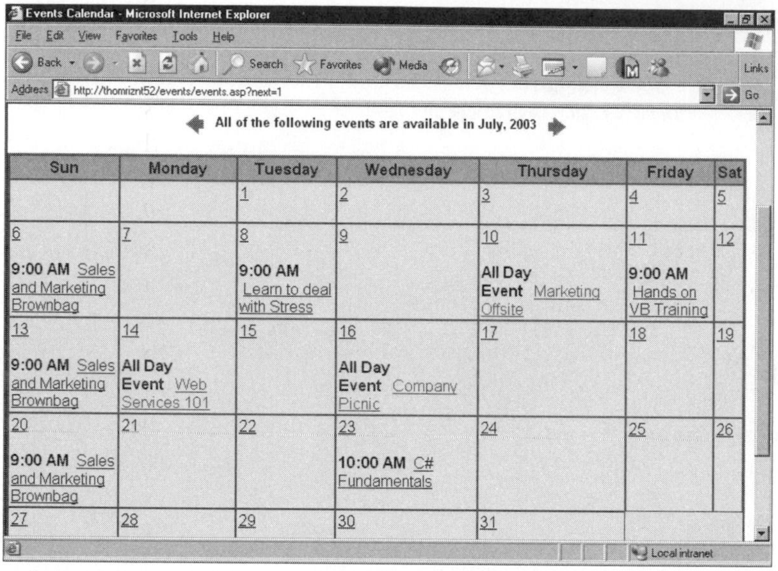

Figure 11-26 The code for the Events.asp page creates a monthly view of the appointments in the calendar by using HTML.

Because the CDO Rendering library does not natively support monthly calendar views, the page in Figure 11-26 creates a monthly view using only HTML tables and data from the Events Calendar. However, the CDO Rendering library does support daily and weekly views of calendars. Therefore, when the user selects to view all events in the calendar, the application renders the calendar day numbers as hyperlinks from which the user can drill down into either daily views of the calendar day or weekly views of the events for the entire calendar week. Weekly views are available only when the user clicks on the hyperlink for Sunday. Daily views are available on all other calendar days. Both view types are generated by the CDO Rendering library.

This page also stores values for the month, day, and year in ASP session scope variables so the application can remember the values in other pages. Storing these values also enables the application to create filters on the appointments contained in the calendar folder so that only the appointments for the specified month appear in the calendar. Let's take a look at the application and associated CDO objects in more detail.

Filtering Events from the Calendar

So that only certain events appear in the calendar, the application uses the *MessageFilter* object in the CDO library. This object is available in any *Messages* collection and allows you to specify the criteria that messages must meet before they are added to the collection. When you instantiate a new *Messages* collection, by default a *MessageFilter* object is created without filters on the content.

The *MessageFilter* object allows you to filter on built-in and custom properties for message objects in the *Messages* collection. However, you should note one caveat with the *MessageFilter* object: if the collection contains *AppointmentItem* objects (as a calendar folder does), the *MessageFilter* object offers only a limited subset of its functionality. This subset is the ability to filter on the start and end times for the items in the collection. For this reason, in the source code for the Events.asp file, you'll notice a *MessageFilter* object that uses the month selected by the user as the input for the filter's start and end times. You will also notice that custom VBScript code searches through the filtered set of appointments to figure out which appointments actually have the category the user selected. This functionality is implemented as custom VBScript because the *MessageFilter* object lacks this functionality for appointments. The following code creates and sets the *MessageFilter* object for the events calendar:

```
<%
'*****************************************************************
'Filter all appointments except the requested month's appointments
'*****************************************************************
'Get the Calendar folder
Set Session("objFolder") = objOMSession.GetDefaultFolder(0)
Set objFolder = Session("objFolder")
Set objAppointment = objFolder.Messages.GetFirst()
Set objAppointments = objFolder.Messages
Set objMsgFilt = objAppointments.Filter

'Calculate the start and end dates based on the month the
'user selected
StartDate = EventMonth & "/" & "1" & "/" & EventYear
EndDate = EventMonth & "/" & "1" & "/" & EventYear
EndDate = DateAdd("m",1,EndDate)
objMsgFilt.Fields(ActMsgPR_START_DATE) = EndDate
objMsgFilt.Fields(ActMsgPR_END_DATE) = StartDate

Set Session("objAppointments") = objAppointments
Session("LastDayofMonth") = iLastDay
%>
```

As the preceding code illustrates, the first step in creating a filter is retrieving the *Messages* collection you want to apply the filter to. Because the *MessageFilter* object is a child of the *Messages* collection, you must retrieve it by using the *Filter* property on the *Messages* collection. If the collection you are filtering does not contain appointments, you can create your filter by setting the properties on the *MessageFilter* object.

Because we are retrieving the calendar folder for the events calendar mailbox, we must specify properties for the start and end times by using the *Fields* collection of the *MessageFilter* object. The specific identifiers for these two properties are *&H00600040* for the start date and *&H00610040* for the end date. (These identifiers are defined in the file Amprops.inc, which is included with the Calendar of Events files in the companion content.) To create the filter, all you do is set these identifiers in the *Fields* collection to your values.

Be careful when you set these properties—they don't work the way you might expect. For example, you might think that you specify a value for the start date by entering the first day for the filter, which would make CDO return every appointment starting from the day you specified and moving forward in time. However, the way the code is implemented in the library, the *MessageFilter* object actually returns any appointments that start on that day or occurred *before* that date. For the end date, the filter returns any appointments that end on the date or occur *after* that date. Therefore, in the Calendar of Events application, the first day of the month selected by the user is specified as the start date value for the filter, and the first day of the next month after the month selected by the user is specified for the end date value. These values return all appointments in the specified month.

Now that we have all the appointments in the month, we must manually filter them by the category the user specified. For example, if the user specifies only hands-on training events, we must provide a subroutine to filter and print only hands-on training events. The next snippet of code does this. It uses the *For Each... Next* statement in VBScript to scroll through the filtered *Messages* collection we created. While the code loops through the collection, it checks to see whether the current appointment starts on the current day. If the appointment does start on the current day, the code checks to see whether the user selected a specific category. If the user did select a category, the code loops through the categories on the *AppointmentItem* object, checking to see whether the object contains the specified category. If the category is found, the application prints out the appointment. If the category is not found, the code moves to the next appointment in the collection.

You might have noticed a variable in the code named *AlreadyPrinted*. I added this variable to help you enable the application to support users who specify multiple categories to search on. Imagine that you have an event that is marked for the Business and Hands-On Training categories. If you allow users to specify both search categories such that any event categorized as either Hands-On Training or Business is identified, you will run into problems with duplicate printing of events because the values for appointment categories added in Outlook are not guaranteed to be in a particular order. The *Categories* field for one appointment might have the values *Business, Hands-On Training, Competitive*, while another might contain the same values but in a different order: *Hands-On Training, Competitive, Business.* When this is the case, both events will print.

The code uses a *For Each...Next* loop to scroll through the categories collection. After it finds the targeted category value and prints the item on the calendar, the code changes the *AlreadyPrinted* variable to *True*. Therefore, if this item meets other subsequent categories the user selected, it won't be duplicated on the calendar. Why does the code use a variable rather than contain an *Exit For* statement? I used a variable because it offers more flexibility if you want to change the code to perform other functionality. However, an *Exit For* statement would work just as well in this case. Here's the code that filters the appointment categories:

```
<%
'*****************************************************
'Check to see whether event should be written
'*****************************************************
%>
<%

AlreadyPrinted = FALSE
For Each objappointment In objAppointments
    StartTime = objappointment.StartTime
    'Check the day of the message
    oDay = DAY(StartTime)
    'Figure out friendly start time
    If Hour(StartTime) = 12 Then  '12:00 PM
        If Minute(StartTime) = 0 Then '0 minutes
            dStartTime = "12:00 PM"
        Else
            dStartTime = "12:" & Minute(StartTime) & " PM"
        End If
    ElseIf Hour(StartTime) > 12 Then
        If Hour(StartTime) > 11 Then  'PM
            If Minute(StartTime) = 0 Then '0 minutes
                dStartTime = (Hour(StartTime)-12) & ":00 PM"
            Else
                dStartTime = (Hour(StartTime)-12) & ":" & _
                Minute(StartTime) & " PM"
            End If
        End If
    Else
        If Hour(StartTime) = 0 Then '12 AM
            If Minute(StartTime) = 0 Then '0 minutes
                dStartTime = "12:00 AM"
            Else
                dStartTime = "12:" & Minute(StartTime) & " AM"
            End If
        Else
            If Minute(StartTime) = 0 Then '0 minutes
                dStartTime = Hour(StartTime) & ":00 AM"
            Else
```

```
                dStartTime = Hour(StartTime) & ":" & _
                Minute(StartTime) & " AM"
            End If
        End If
    End If 'Friendly start time

    If oDay = (i-iDayMarker) Then
        'Check the categories if AllBit = 0
        If AllBit = 1 Then
            'Check to see if all-day event
            If objappointment.AllDayEvent = True Then
                response.write "<B>All Day Event" & _
                "   </B><A HREF='details.asp?id=" & _
                objappointment.id & _
                "' style='color: rgb(255,0,0)'>" & _
                objappointment.Subject & "</a><BR>"
            Else
                response.write "<B>" & dStartTime & _
                "</B>  <A HREF='details.asp?id=" & _
                objappointment.id & _
                "' style='color: rgb(0,0,255)'>" & _
                objappointment.Subject & "</a><BR>"
            End If
        Else
            'Check categories!
            If IsEmpty(objappointment.Categories) Then
                'No categories
            Else
                For Each category In objappointment.Categories
                    If InStr(category,EventType) Then
                        If Not(AlreadyPrinted) Then
                            If objAppointment.AllDayEvent = True Then
                                response.write _
                                "<B>All Day Event" & _
                                "   " & _
                                dStartTime & "</B>  " & _
                                <A HREF='details.asp?id=" & _
                                objappointment.id & "' style" & _
                                "='color: rgb(255,0,0)'>" & _
                                objappointment.Subject & _
                                "</a><BR>"
                            Else
                                response.write "<B>" & _
                                dStartTime & "</B>  <A " & _
                                HREF='details.asp?id=" & _
                                objappointment.id & "' style" & _
                                "='color: rgb(0,0,255)'>" & _
                                objappointment.Subject & _
                                "</a><BR>"
                            End If
                            AlreadyPrinted = TRUE
                        End If 'Not Already Printed
                    End If 'Categories Match
                Next
```

```
            End If 'Check categories
        End If 'All Bit
    End If 'oDay
    AlreadyPrinted = FALSE 'Reset Already Printed
Next
Set objappointment = Nothing
n=1
%>
```

Displaying a Weekly View

When the user is not filtering by category and clicks on the hyperlink for any Sunday in the calendar, a weekly view appears showing events for the current week, as illustrated in Figure 11-27.

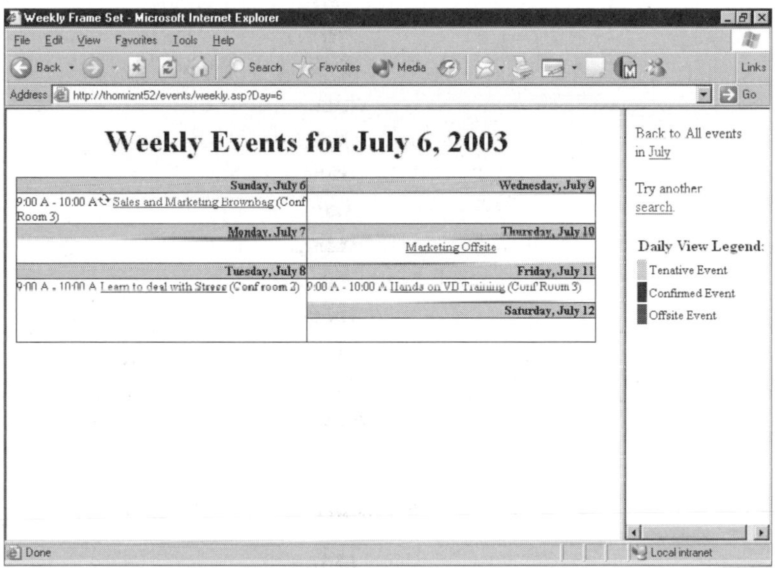

Figure 11-27 The weekly view in the Events Calendar

The weekly view is implemented in the Events Calendar by using the CDO Rendering library. You could create your own weekly view, but it is much easier to leverage the CDO Rendering library and customize the way it renders the view using the library's objects. The CDO Rendering library offers rich object support for customizing what it renders.

As illustrated in the Helpdesk application, the way to get started with the CDO Rendering library in an application is to create a container or an object renderer by using the *CreateRenderer* method on the *RenderingApplication* object. The Calendar of Events application creates a container renderer because the items rendered by the application are contained in a calendar folder. However, unlike the Helpdesk application, which uses *TableView* objects to render its data, the Calendar of Events application uses *CalendarView* objects. The

Calendar of Events application also customizes the patterns and formats of the *CalendarView* object to specify the graphics to be used when rendering information. The placement of the *CalendarView* object in the CDO Rendering library is shown in Figure 11-28. Most of the properties of the *CalendarView* object are filled in by default when you instantiate the object, so you don't have to set these properties unless you want to customize the way CDO renders the information into HTML.

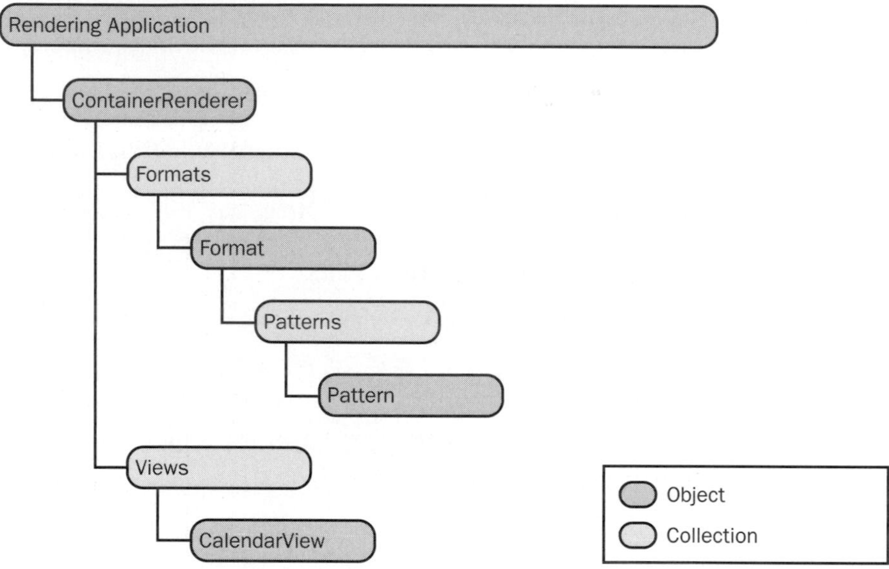

Figure 11-28 The CDO CalendarView object is a child object of the Views collection in the CDO Rendering library.

As in the Helpdesk application, we need to set a data source to be rendered. In this case, the data source is the filtered set of appointments we created for the calendar. To instantiate a *CalendarView* object, we retrieve from our data source a view from the *Views* collection. The daily view always has an index of 1 in the *Views* collection, so the code grabs the daily view for the calendar using this index instead of scrolling through all the views in the collection. As you will see later, the daily view is morphed into a weekly view by using the *Mode* property for the *CalendarView* object.

Once we have a *CalendarView* object, we can manipulate the *Format* and *Pattern* objects of the *ContainerRenderer* object to add custom HTML rendering. The *Format* object controls how a particular property is rendered by the CDO Rendering library. For example, you can pass to the *Formats* collection either the ID of a built-in property or the name of a custom property to create a custom HTML format for that property when the property is rendered by the library. This code shows an example from the weeklyview.asp file:

```
'Sensitivity
Set objFormat = oCalContRenderer.Formats.Add( _
    ActMsgPR_SENSITIVITY, Null)
```

After adding the format, you can retrieve the *Patterns* collection on the *Format* object to specify how a particular value for a property should be formatted. In the previous example, if the sensitivity of the appointment in the calendar is set to *Private*, an image of a key is placed before the text of the appointment. You can make the patterns more complex because the values for the patterns will accept any legal HTML tags.

You can specify a default pattern for the *Pattern* objects if a particular property does not contain one of your values. To the *Patterns* collection, just add a *Pattern* object that takes the asterisk character (*) as its value. You then specify the HTML tags CDO should use to render the unspecified value types. The code for both specified and unspecified values is shown here:

```
Set objPatterns = objFormat.Patterns
bstrHTML = bstrImgSrc + _
    "/images/private.gif WIDTH=13 HEIGHT=13 BORDER=0>"
objPatterns.Add 1, bstrHTML   'personal
objPatterns.Add 2, bstrHTML   'private
objPatterns.Add 3, bstrHTML   'confidential
objPatterns.Add "*", ""       'normal
```

The following code shows you the other *Format* and *Pattern* object settings for the weekly view in the Calendar of Events application:

```
'Recurring
Set objFormat = oCalContRenderer.Formats.Add( _
    AmPidTag_IsRecurring, Null)
Set objPatterns = objFormat.Patterns
objPatterns.Add 0, ""
bstrHTML = bstrImgSrc + _
    "/images/recur.gif WIDTH=13 HEIGHT=13 BORDER=0>"
objPatterns.Add "*", bstrHTML

'Meeting status
Set objFormat = oCalContRenderer.Formats.Add( _
    AmPidTag_ApptStateFlags, Null)
Set objPatterns = objFormat.Patterns
objPatterns.Add 0, ""
bstrHTML = bstrImgSrc + _
    "/images/meeting.gif WIDTH=12 HEIGHT=13 BORDER=0>"
objPatterns.Add "*", bstrHTML

'Location
Set objFormat = oCalContRenderer.Formats.Add( )
    AmPidTag_Location, Null)
Set objPatterns = objFormat.Patterns
objPatterns.Add "",  ""
objPatterns.Add "*", "(%value%)"
```

After you set your *Format* and *Pattern* objects, you can customize the way CDO renders the HTML tables it creates. The properties you need to manipulate the *ContainerRenderer* object are *TablePrefix*, *TableSuffix*, *RowPrefix*, *RowSuffix*, *CellPattern*, and *LinkPattern*. The following code is taken from weeklyview.asp, which sets these properties:

```
oCalContRenderer.TablePrefix = _
    "<table columns=%columns% border=0 cellpadding=0 cellspacing=1 " & _
    "WIDTH=100% HEIGHT=10% bgcolor='#000000'>" & Chr(10)
oCalContRenderer.TableSuffix = "</table>" & Chr(10)
oCalContRenderer.RowPrefix = "<tr>" & Chr(10)
oCalContRenderer.RowSuffix = "</tr>" & Chr(10)
oCalContRenderer.CellPattern = "<font size=2>%value%</font>"
oCalContRenderer.LinkPattern = "<a href='details.asp?id=%obj%' " & _
    "target='_top'>%value%</a>"
```

The *TablePrefix* property allows you to customize the HTML table that CDO renders before CDO creates a separate table for the actual item content in the data source. By customizing *TablePrefix*, you can add custom HTML tags before CDO renders any content to the browser. This property works in conjunction with the *TableSuffix* property, which specifies what to render at the end of the HTML table created by the *TablePrefix* property.

The *RowPrefix* property allows you to customize the HTML that appears at the beginning of each HTML table row. You can use this property to change the way the row is rendered—for example, modifying the height, width, or alignment of the items in the row. *RowSuffix* specifies the HTML that should appear after the row and is used in conjunction with *RowPrefix*.

The *CellPattern* property specifies the HTML for every cell in each table row that you render. In the code for the Calendar of Events application, the *CellPattern* property is set to a font size of 2 and is set to display the value contained in the appointment. This property does not affect any hyperlinked values in your cell, and CDO always generates a link for exactly one cell in each row. So you use *CellPattern* in conjunction with *LinkPattern* to create fully functional table rows because the *LinkPattern* property affects only the hyperlink cell in your table. As you can see in the code, the application sets the *LinkPattern* property for the hyperlinked cells so the hyperlink points at the details.asp file, and it passes the EntryID that corresponds to the current appointment clicked on by the user to this ASP by using the *%obj%* token. It also dynamically prints out the subject of the appointment by using the *%value%* token.

The final section of the code sets some options on the *ContainerRenderer* object, such as the start and end times for the business day, and the time zone for the appointment dates and times. This section also morphs the daily view into a weekly view by setting the *Mode* property for the *CalendarView* object to *CdoModeCalendarWeekly (1)* rather than *CdoModeCalendarDaily (0)*. The code then calls the *RenderAppointments* method on the *CalendarView* object, which takes as its arguments the starting date for rendering information and the output stream used to send the generated HTML. Normally for the output stream parameter, you would type *Response*, which tells CDO to render the HTML to the *Response* object of the ASP object library. The following code implements this functionality for the Calendar of Events application:

```
oCalContRenderer.TimeZone = objOMSession.GetOption("TimeZone")
'Set Sunday as first day of week
oCalContRenderer.FirstDayOfWeek = 7
oCalContRenderer.Is24HourClock = _
    objOMSession.GetOption("Is24HourClock")
oCalContRenderer.BusinessDayStartTime = _
    objOMSession.GetOption("BusinessDayStartTime")
oCalContRenderer.BusinessDayEndTime = _
    objOMSession.GetOption("BusinessDayEndTime")
oCalContRenderer.BusinessDays = _
    objOMSession.GetOption("BusinessDays")
oCalView.NumberOfUnits = 1
curDay = CDate(curDay)
oCalView.Mode = 1
oCalView.RenderAppointments curDate,Response
```

Displaying a Daily View

When the user is not filtering by category and clicks on the hyperlink for any day in the calendar week except Sunday, a daily view appears, as shown in Figure 11-29.

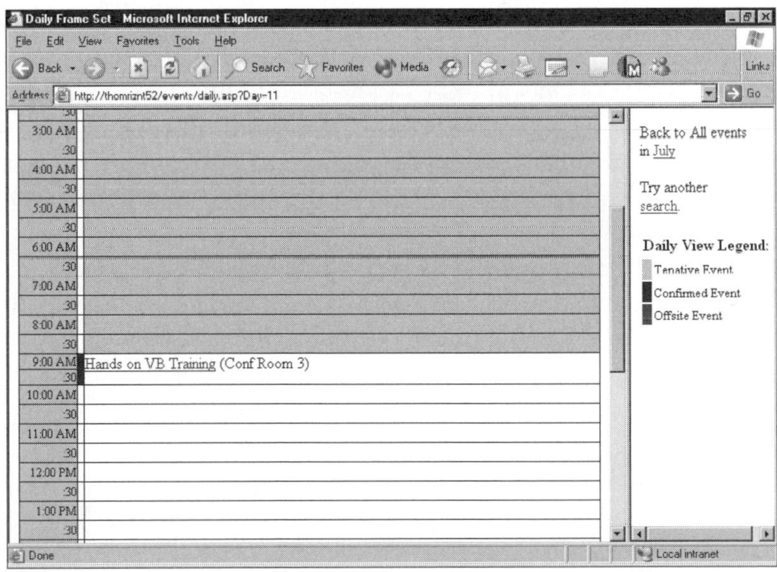

Figure 11-29 The daily view for the Calendar of Events application allows users to see more details about the events on a specific day.

The code for rendering the daily view in the file dailyview.asp is the same as the code for rendering a weekly view except for two main differences. First, we keep the daily view as the view in the *Mode* property for the *CalendarView* object rather than change it, as we did in the weekly view rendering code. Second, we must explicitly render all-day events separately from appointments in the view. In the weekly view mode, CDO automatically renders all-day events.

The way to render events separately from appointments in a daily view is to explicitly call the *RenderEvents* method on the *CalendarView* object before calling the *RenderAppointments* method. The *RenderEvents* method takes the same parameters as the *RenderAppointments* method, which includes the date for which you want to render the events and the output stream that will place the HTML code created by the method. The following code shows how to render both events and appointments using *RenderEvents* and *RenderAppointments*:

```
oCalView.RenderEvents curDate,Response
oCalView.RenderAppointments curDate,Response
```

Displaying the Details of an Event

When a user clicks on any hyperlink (from monthly, weekly, or daily view) to get the details for an event, details.asp is called. This ASP page displays details about the event so a user can find the event location and obtain any supporting materials. The ASP page also automatically supports rendering and viewing attachments because it uses the CDO Rendering library to display the text describing the event. The user interface for this page is shown in Figure 11-30.

The code in the details.asp page is pretty straightforward, but it shows you how to use other objects in the CDO Rendering library, such as the *ObjectRenderer* object. The *ObjectRenderer* object (as opposed to the *ContainerRenderer* object) is used because you are displaying properties from an individual CDO object, such as an appointment. You should use the *ContainerRenderer* object only if you are rendering a collection of items, such as all the messages in your Inbox. Figure 11-31 shows the *ObjectRenderer* object hierarchy.

To create an *ObjectRenderer* object, all you do is pass the constant *CdoClassObjectRenderer (2)* to the *CreaterRenderer* method of the *RenderingApplication* object. (There are a lot of "renders" in that last sentence!) Here is the code from details.asp:

```
'Create an ObjectRenderer
set objObjRenderer = objRenderApp.CreateRenderer(2)
```

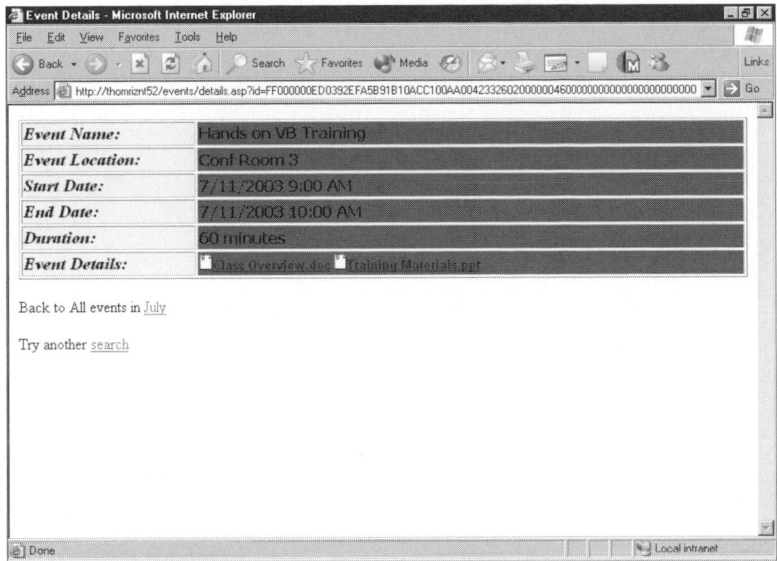

Figure 11-30 The Details page for an event in the Calendar of Events application can render rich text as well as hyperlinks because it uses the CDO Rendering library.

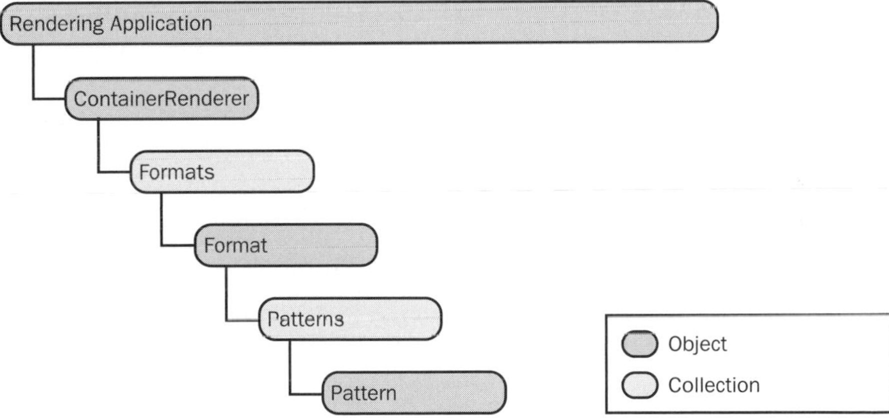

Figure 11-31 The ObjectRenderer object in the CDO Rendering library is used to display properties of individual items rather than of collections.

After creating the *ObjectRenderer*, we must set the *DataSource* property for it. This property is the same as the *DataSource* property for a *ContainerRenderer* object except for one fundamental difference: the *ObjectRenderer* object can take only individual items as its data source, such as an *AddressEntry*, an *AppointmentItem*, or a *Message* object.

Now that the data source is set, we can start using some of the methods on the *ObjectRenderer* object. To render the details of the event, we need to render individual properties off the *AppointmentItem* object, such as name, location, and details. The *ObjectRenderer* object has a method, *RenderProperty*, that allows you to render individual properties off the object. The *RenderProperty* method takes three arguments:

- The property ID for built-in properties, or the name of the property if it is a custom property that you want to render
- A reserved argument, for which you should always pass *0* as the value
- The output stream, to pass the HTML that the CDO Rendering library generates

Normally, you would type *Response* for this argument to return the HTML to the browser. The following code is taken from details.asp. It shows how *RenderProperty* renders the different properties on an *AppointmentItem* object:

```
<table border="1" width="100%">
<tr>
   <td width="24%" bgcolor="#FFFF80"><big><em><strong>
   Event Name:</strong></em></big></td>
   <td width="76%" bgcolor="#8000FF"><strong><font face="Tahoma">
   <% objObjRenderer.RenderProperty ActMsgPR_SUBJECT, 0, Response %>
   </font></strong> </td>
</tr>
<tr>
   <td width="24%" bgcolor="#FFFF80"><big><em><strong>
   Event Location:</strong></em></big></td>
   <td width="76%" bgcolor="#8000FF"><strong><font face="Tahoma">
   <%
   If objEvent.Location = "" Then
       response.write "None specified"
   Else
      objObjRenderer.RenderProperty AmPidTag_Location, 0, _
      Response
   End If
   %>
   </font></strong></td>
</tr>
<tr>
   <td width="24%" bgcolor="#FFFF80"><big><em><strong>
   Start Date:</strong></em></big></td>
   <td width="76%" bgcolor="#8000FF"><strong><font face="Tahoma">
   <% objObjRenderer.RenderProperty AmPidTag_ApptStartWhole, 0, _
   Response %>
   </font></strong></td>
```

```
</tr>
<tr>
   <td width="24%" bgcolor="#FFFF80"><big><em><strong>
   End Date:</strong></em></big></td>
   <td width="76%" bgcolor="#8000FF"><strong><font face="Tahoma">
   <% objObjRenderer.RenderProperty AmPidTag_ApptEndWhole, 0, _
   Response %>
   </font></strong></td>
</tr>
<tr>
   <td width="24%" bgcolor="#FFFF80"><big><em>
   <strong>Duration:</strong></em></big></td>
   <td width="76%" bgcolor="#8000FF"><strong><font face="Tahoma">
   <% objObjRenderer.RenderProperty AmPidTag_ApptDuration, 0, _
   Response %>
   minutes</font></strong></td>
</tr>

<tr>
   <td width="24%" bgcolor="#FFFF80"><big><em><strong>
   Event Details:</strong></em></big></td>
   <td width="76%" bgcolor="#8000FF"><strong><font face="Tahoma">
   <%
   If objEvent.Text = "" Then
      response.write "None specified"
   Else
      objObjRenderer.RenderProperty ActMsgPR_RTF_COMPRESSED, _
      0, Response
   End If
   %>
   </font></strong></td>
</tr>
</table>
```

Most of the properties are pretty straightforward, but one of them requires careful handling when rendering because it is quite powerful and can easily cause problems if you do not handle the output correctly. This property is the last one rendered by the application, *ActMsgPR_RTF_COMPRESSED*. It is the message body for the item. When you use the *RenderProperty* method with this property, the CDO Rendering library automatically converts the rich-text formatting in the message to HTML. This is a powerful feature and one of the primary reasons you should use the CDO Rendering library to display the body of an item.

However, one aspect of this method to watch out for is that in addition to converting the body of an item, the method also converts the attachments in the item to hyperlinks. This is useful and makes your application very powerful, but CDO defaults the hyperlinks it creates to retrieve a file named read.asp in the Exchange virtual root on the IIS server. Remember how IIS defines ASP applications—by virtual root. Now can you see the inherent problem? When the user clicks on this default hyperlink, IIS starts a new ASP application under the Exchange virtual root. This causes the Outlook Web Access logon screen to appear because ASP applications cannot share session and application states, and OWA has no idea that the user has already been authenticated with the Calendar of Events application. Furthermore, if the user enters her security credentials, the attachment will not appear in the browser; instead, OWA will open the user's Inbox—not the desired functionality.

To fix this problem, we must first change the default virtual root of *RenderingApplication*, which is the Exchange virtual root. To do this, we use the *VirtualRoot* property on the *RenderingApplication*. The *VirtualRoot* property takes a string argument that sets the beginning of the URL when you render items. In this case, we need to change the *VirtualRoot* property to point to the virtual root we set in our virtroot.inc file. The following code does this:

```
'Change the virtual root for the rendering application
Set objRenderApp = Application("RenderApplication")
objRenderApp.VirtualRoot = virtroot
```

The next problem we have to resolve is what file to use for the read.asp file that *RenderingApplication* is creating a hyperlink to. Well, OWA happens to provide a read.asp file that renders attachments you click on in its browser window. The OWA read.asp automatically downloads and opens the attachment on the user's machine. In addition, the read.asp file launches the application in place in the browser if the user's browser supports this option. Otherwise, the read.asp file prompts the user to download and view the file.

To add the OWA read.asp to the Calendar of Events application, you must modify some code. The main modification has to be done to session and local variable names because the default read.asp for OWA uses different variable names from those in the Calendar of Events application. The code that checks for a valid session must also be modified because the two applications use different types of session-checking code.

The way attachments are rendered to the browser is the same for both applications. First, the application parses the query string, which contains an *att* variable. This variable contains the attachment record key, which is a unique identifier used to retrieve, from the *Attachments* collection of the *Message* object, the particular attachment the user clicked on. Once this attachment is retrieved, the application figures out the attachment's filename so that when the user chooses to save the file after bringing it up, the browser uses the same filename as the filename of the original item. Finally, the application adds a header to the *Response* object, which tells the browser that it is going to send data to the browser. Then the application uses the *RenderProperty* method of *ObjectRenderer* to stream the binary data of the attachment to the browser. Once the data is streamed down, the attachment opens. The following code implements this functionality:

```
szAttach = Request.QueryString("att")
nPos = InStr(1, szAttach, "-", 0)
```

```
nPos = InStr(nPos+1, szAttach, "-", 0)
nPos2 = InStr(nPos+1, szAttach, "-", 0)
If nPos2 = 0 Then
    nPos2 = Len(szAttach)+1
End If

szRecordKey = Mid(szAttach, nPos+1, nPos2-(nPos+1))
szAttachName = Mid(szAttach, nPos2+1)
szObj = Request.QueryString("obj")
Set objOneMsg = Session("szObj")
If objOneMsg Is Nothing Then
    Set objOneMsg = OpenMessage(szObj)
    If objOneMsg Is Nothing Then
        ReportError1 L_errCannotGetMessageObj_ErrorMessage
    ElseIf objOneMsg.ID = "" Then
        ReportError1 L_errMessageDeleted_ErrorMessage
    End If
End If

Set objAttach = objOneMsg.Attachments.Item(szRecordKey)
If objAttach Is Nothing Then
    ReportError1 L_errFailGettingAttachment_ErrorMessage
End If
bstrFileName = ""
bstrFileName=  objAttach.Fields(ActMsgPR_ATTACH_LONG_FILENAME)
If bstrFileName = "" Then
    bstrFileName =  objAttach.Fields(ActMsgPR_ATTACH_FILENAME)
End If
'For short filename compatibility, add these lines
'If bstrFileName = "" then
'    bstrFileName = objAttach.Name
'End If

Response.Addheader "Content-Disposition", "attachment;filename=" & _
    bstrFileName
Set objRenderAtt = GetMessageRenderer
objRenderAtt.DataSource = objAttach
objRenderAtt.RenderProperty ActMsgPR_ATTACH_DATA_BIN, 0,Response
```

Summary

This chapter covered the basics of CDO 1.21 and how to build applications with this object library. CDO makes building collaborative applications easier on Exchange Server through its intuitive object model and rich functionality. In the next chapter, you will see how to build advanced functionality with CDO.

12

Advanced CDO Topics and Tips

In this chapter, I will cover some advanced CDO topics, such as working with property sets from Microsoft Outlook, and offer tips for working with CDO. I will also explain how to program against CDO from the Microsoft .NET environment.

The CDO Visual Basic Application

We will look at an application built using Microsoft Visual Basic that allows users to log on to their Exchange servers using CDO, query the server for other users, and retrieve information about those users. This application shows how to program CDO with Visual Basic, which is different from programming CDO with VBScript and Microsoft Active Server Pages (ASP). It also shows how to use the *AddressEntryFilter* object. Figure 12-1 shows the application in action.

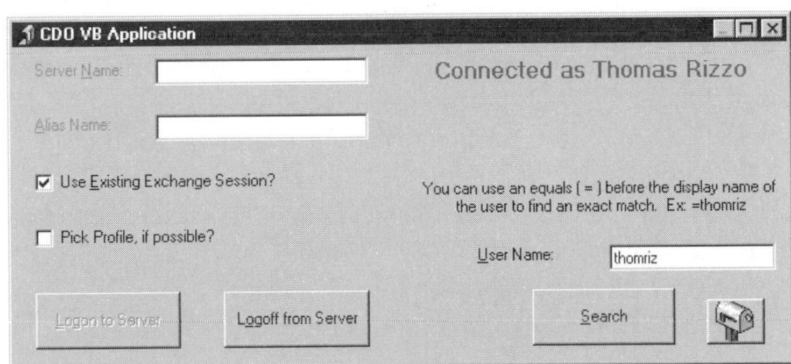

Figure 12-1 The CDO Visual Basic application

Setting Up the Application

Before you can install the application, you must have a client with Outlook installed and a Microsoft Windows 2000 server with the following software installed:

- Exchange Server 2000 or later (with the latest service pack recommended)
- CDO library (cdo.dll)

To install the CDO Visual Basic application, run the Setup.exe file in the CDO VB folder (included with the book's companion content) and follow the instructions.

Programming CDO with Visual Basic

The main difference between programming CDO with VBScript and ASP and programming CDO with Visual Basic is that Visual Basic allows you to use early binding of objects in the CDO library. By declaring your variables as a specific type of object, the variables will be bound early. For example, in Visual Basic, you can use the *Dim* statement to declare a variable as a CDO *Session* object by using the following statement:

```
Dim oSession as MAPI.Session
```

Once you declare a variable, you can take advantage of some of the powerful features of the Visual Basic development environment, such as Auto List Members, which lists the available properties and methods for an object, and Auto Quick Info, which displays the syntax for a statement. For example, if in the code window you start typing the name of the *oSession* variable and then the dot operator (.), Visual Basic will automatically display the properties and methods for the CDO *Session* object. Also, using early binding allows your application to execute faster because the binding takes place at compile time rather than at run time. VBScript and ASP cannot use early binding and therefore always default to late binding when creating objects.

To use CDO in Visual Basic, you add a reference to the CDO library. You can then declare variables of a specific CDO type in your code, and the CDO objects will appear in the Visual Basic Object Browser. You use the Object Browser to view information about libraries, such as properties, methods, events, constants, classes, and other information.

To add the reference to the CDO library, in Visual Basic choose References from the Project menu. Scroll down until you find Microsoft CDO 1.21 Library, and add a check mark next to it. If you want to add a reference to the

CDO Rendering library, add a check mark next to Collaborative Data Objects Rendering Library 1.2. Click OK. Now you can take advantage of early binding with your CDO objects, and the CDO library will be available in the Visual Basic Object Browser. Most of the time, you will not use the CDO Rendering library in your client-based applications. Instead, you will use this library in your Web-based applications.

Logging On the User

As you know, you cannot create any other objects in the CDO library without first creating a CDO *Session* object and successfully logging on with that *Session* object. Because we are developing a Visual Basic application, we don't have to worry about a Global.asa file or authenticating the user—CDO uses the Windows NT credentials of the user who is currently logged on. This makes logging on much easier for users, as you can see in the following authenticated logon code:

```
Dim oRecipients As MAPI.Recipients
Dim oRecipient As MAPI.Recipient
Dim oInfoStores As MAPI.InfoStores
Dim oInfoStore As MAPI.InfoStore
Dim oInbox As MAPI.Folder
Dim boolUseCurrentSession, boolLogonDialog
Private Sub cmdLogon_Click()
    On Error Resume Next
    Err.Clear
    'Check to see whether user wants to use a current session.
    'If so, piggyback on that session.
    If boolUseCurrentSession = 0 Then
        If (txtServerName.Text <> "") And (txtAliasName.Text <> "") Then
            strProfileInfo = txtServerName & vbLf & txtAliasName
            oSession.Logon NewSession:=True, NoMail:=False, _
                showDialog:=boolLogonDialog, ProfileInfo:=strProfileInfo
            strConnectedServer = " to " & txtServerName.Text
        Else
            MsgBox "You need to enter a value in the " & _
                "Server or Alias name.", vbOKOnly + vbExclamation, _
                "CDO Logon"
            Exit Sub
        End If
    Else
        oSession.Logon NewSession:=False, showDialog:=boolLogonDialog
        strConnectedServer = ""
    End If
```

```
    If (Err.Number <> 0) Or _
        (oSession.CurrentUser.Name = "Unknown") Then
        'Not a good logon; log off and exit
        oSession.Logoff
        MsgBox "Logon error!", vbOKOnly + vbExclamation, "CDO Logon"
        Exit Sub
    End If

    'Check store state to see whether online or offline
    Set oInbox = oSession.Inbox
    strStoreID = oInbox.StoreID
    Set oInfoStore = oSession.GetInfoStore(strStoreID)
    If oInfoStore.Fields(&H6632000B).Value = True Then
        strConnectedServer = "Offline"
    End If

    'Enable other buttons on the form
    cmdLogoff.Enabled = True
    cmdLogon.Enabled = False
    txtUserName.Enabled = True
    cmdSearch.Enabled = True
    cmdViewAB.Enabled = True
    lblUserName.Enabled = True
    'Change the label to indicate status
    lblConnected.Caption = "Connected" & strConnectedServer _
        & " as " & oSession.CurrentUser.Name
End Sub
```

To support early binding, a number of variables are declared as specific CDO object types. The code tries to log on to the Exchange server by using the CDO *Logon* method. Unlike the ASP code you saw earlier, in this code we can use existing sessions between the client and the Exchange server rather than always creating new sessions. The user can enable this functionality by selecting the Use Existing Exchange Session check box (as shown earlier in Figure 12-1). The existing session, typically an Outlook client session, is used by CDO to connect to the Exchange server.

After the user logs on, the code finds the *InfoStore* object associated with the user's mailbox. The *Fields* collection on *InfoStore* is used to look up a specific property, *PR_STORE_OFFLINE* (*&H6632000B*), which contains either *True* or *False*. *True* indicates that the current *InfoStore* is an offline replica. The value for this property is used in the status text, which indicates the connection state of the user, as shown in Figure 12-2.

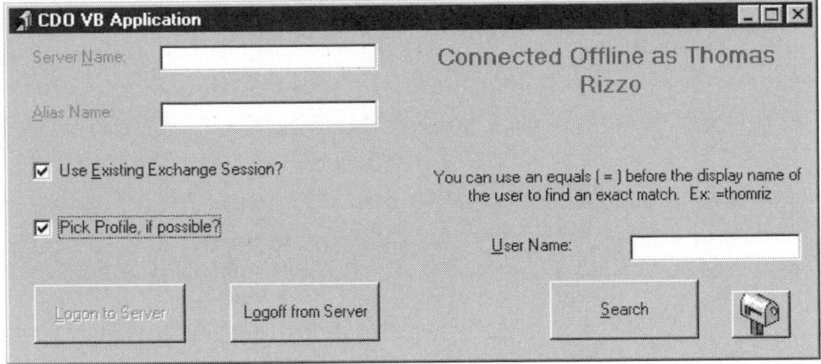

Figure 12-2 If the user is working off line, the connection status message will display this information.

Finding the Details of the Specific User

After logging on, the user can type a name in the User Name text box. The application uses this name to search the directory or distribution list. The search is implemented by using the *AddressEntryFilter* object in the CDO library. This object is similar to the *MessageFilter* object, which we examined in the Calendar of Events application in Chapter 11. The only difference is that the *AddressEntryFilter* object is used with objects in the directory and the *MessageFilter* object is used with messages in a folder. Following is the code that searches for the user by using the *AddressEntryFilter* object and displays the results:

```
Private Sub cmdSearch_Click()
    On Error Resume Next
    'The On Error is to handle the user canceling the
    'details dialog box
    Err.Clear
    If txtUserName.Text = "" Then
        MsgBox "No User Specified", vbOKOnly + vbExclamation, _
            "User Search"
        Exit Sub
    Else
       Set oAddressList = oSession.GetAddressList(CdoAddressListGAL)
       Set oAddressEntries = oAddressList.AddressEntries
       Set oAddEntryFilter = oAddressEntries.Filter
       oAddEntryFilter.Name = txtUserName.Text
       If oAddressEntries.Count < 1 Then
           MsgBox "No entries found", vbOKOnly, "Search"
       ElseIf oAddressEntries.Count > 1 Then
           MsgBox "Ambiguous entries found", vbOKOnly, "Search"
       Else
           Set oAddressEntry = oAddressEntries.GetFirst
           oAddressEntry.Details
       End If
    End If
End Sub
```

This code gets the Global Address List (GAL), either off line or on line, by using the *GetAddressList* method on the *Session* object. It then instantiates an *AddressEntryFilter* object by using the *Filter* property on the *AddressEntries* collection. To specify the condition for the filter, the *Name* property on the *AddressEntryFilter* object is set to the name typed in by the user. This name can be either the user's display name, such as *Thomas Rizzo (Exchange)*, or the alias of the user, such as *thomriz*. CDO also supports direct matches when you place the equal sign (=) before your text, as in *=Thomas Rizzo*.

Once the filter is set, the code retrieves the count of the newly restricted *AddressEntries* collection to determine how many *AddressEntry* objects were returned. If more than one *AddressEntry* object was returned, the code displays an ambiguous name error to notify the user that more specific criteria is needed. If less than one *AddressEntry* object is returned, the code displays that no entries meet the criteria of the user. If exactly one *AddressEntry* object is returned, the code uses the *Details* method of the *AddressEntry* object to display the information about the directory object, as shown in Figure 12-3. You can see not only the name and alias of the user but also organizational information, such as the user's manager.

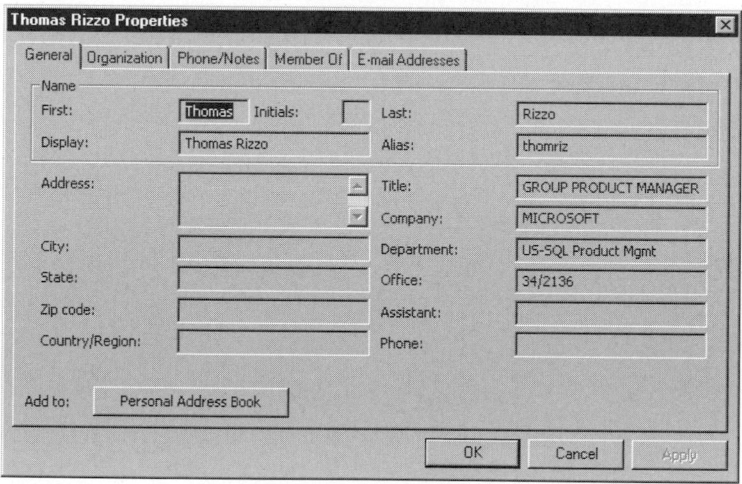

Figure 12-3 The details page of an *AddressEntry* object

Finally, a subroutine is included to handle the run-time error thrown by CDO when the user clicks Cancel in the Properties dialog box displayed by the *Details* method.

CDO Tips and Pitfalls

The CDO library is powerful and approachable, but you can run into problems if you aren't careful when writing your code. This section introduces some tips and tricks you should use and some pitfalls you should avoid. Many of the pitfalls I mention are from personal experience—they are quite frustrating, so I recommend that you read this section before attempting to write any CDO code.

Avoid the *GetNext* Trap

Let's jump right in! Look at the following code and try to figure out what is wrong:

```
MsgBox oSession.Inbox.Messages.GetFirst.Subject
For Counter = 2 To oSession.Inbox.Messages.Count
    MsgBox oSession.Inbox.Messages.GetNext.Subject
Next
```

The same subject will appear in your message box as many times as the number of messages in your Inbox. Despite what the code looks like, it won't recurse through your Inbox because if you don't explicitly assign an object to a variable, CDO will create needed temporary objects for each statement and then discard the object after the statement. This means you will instantiate a new object every time you loop in the *For...Next* loop. Each new object does not maintain the state of the previous temporary object, so the object will always point to the first message in the collection. So you should set explicit variables to refer to a collection to get the desired functionality. The following listing shows the rewritten code, which behaves as expected:

```
Set oMessages = oSession.Inbox.Messages
Set oMessage = oMessages.GetFirst
MsgBox oMessage.Subject
For Counter = 2 To oMessages.Count
    Set oMessage = oMessages.GetNext
    MsgBox oMessage.Subject
Next
```

Avoid Temporary Objects if Possible

Whenever possible, avoid the use of temporary objects, as demonstrated in the previous section. But don't spend a lot of time scouring your code to get rid of temporary objects unless you are a major offender of this rule. Sometimes you'll want to use temporary objects to represent the different CDO objects rather than declare variables. However, using temporary objects should be an exception and not a rule in your coding practices.

Use Early Binding with Visual Basic

To improve the performance of your Visual Basic CDO applications, always try to use early binding by declaring your CDO variables as specific CDO objects. Not only will it be easier to write your code because Visual Basic can perform type checking and help you finish statements in your code, but your users will thank you for the application's improved performance.

Use *With* Statements

You use the dot operator to set a property, call a method, or access another object. Essentially, each dot represents additional code that must be executed. If you can reduce the number of dot operators in your code, you can improve performance of your application. One way to do this is by using *With* statements. For example, consider the following code snippet, which has no *With* statements and is inefficient in terms of both performance and readability:

```
MsgBox "Text: " & oSession.Inbox.Messages.GetFirst.Text
MsgBox "Subj: " & oSession.Inbox.Messages.GetFirst.Subject
```

Now consider the next bit of code, which does use the *With* statement. This code executes faster:

```
With oSession.Inbox.Messages.GetFirst
    MsgBox "Text: " & .Text
    MsgBox "Subj: " & .Subject
End With
```

The rule of thumb is to think of dots in your code as expensive.

Avoid the Dreaded ASP 0115 Error

For writing CDO applications using ASP, the best tip I can give you is that you should use the code from this book to handle your logons and logoffs from CDO and ASP sessions. The most common pitfall that new and even experienced CDO developers run into when writing ASP applications is forgetting to insert the correct impersonation code into Global.asa, which properly destroys the CDO and ASP sessions. When a user attempts to access your Web application after Microsoft Internet Information Services (IIS) attempts to use the wrong context to destroy these objects, the application returns the ASP 0115 error, which means that a trappable error has occurred in an external object.

Avoid the MAPIE_FailOneProvider and CDOE_FailOneProvider Errors

In your ASP applications, you should also avoid the CDOE_FailOneProvider and MAPIE_FailOneProvider errors, which occur when you try to access the root folder of the Public Folder *InfoStore* object or a folder in the mailbox of a specific user. Many developers run into these errors, especially those who are new to ASP programming. The most common cause of these errors is not changing the security context that IIS uses to access the Exchange server so that the Web user will be authenticated via Windows Challenge/Response authentication or Basic authentication. The Web user will therefore try to access the root of the Public Folder store or a user's mailbox using the Windows credentials of the anonymous IIS user account. This anonymous account often doesn't have security permissions to access the Exchange server. When this is the case, CDO returns CDOE_FailOneProvider or MAPIE_FailOneProvider to indicate an error in accessing the information.

The easiest way to solve this problem is to use the logon and logoff code from the examples in this book. These examples, especially the Helpdesk application, authenticate users by prompting them for their Windows credentials before attempting to access any Exchange Server information.

Learn Your Properties and Their IDs Well

As you have seen, many of the objects in the CDO library support the *Fields* property. This property returns a *Fields* collection, which allows you to find custom and built-in properties using identifiers supplied by either Exchange Server or MAPI. These Exchange Server and MAPI properties are powerful yet elusive. They allow you to perform operations on Exchange Server and Outlook items in situations where CDO does not provide objects. For example, in the Helpdesk application, user information is pulled out of the *AddressEntry* property by using the unique identifiers for department name, office location, and other properties. If you did not know that these properties existed, you would think that their information was inaccessible from CDO because CDO does not provide explicit objects for them.

Another scenario that illustrates why these unique properties are valuable is when you set up folders to work off line. Documentation on this process is hard to find, but MAPI provides a property called *PR_OFFLINE_FLAGS* (*&H663D0003*), which contains a zero (0) if the folder is not currently set to synchronize off line and a 1 if it is. By using this property, you can programmatically set any folder in the mailbox of a user to synchronize off line—the user does not have to set synchronization manually through Outlook. If this field does not already exist in the *Fields* collection, you must add it to the collection by using the *Add* method.

The best place to find the information about the properties you can use with the *Fields* collection is in the CDO help file under "MAPI Property Tags" or in the Messaging and Collaboration section of the MSDN Library under "Collaboration Data Objects," "CDO 1.2.1," "SDK Documentation," "CDO 1.2.1," and then "Appendixes." MSDN contains both the MAPI property tags and the Exchange Server property tags. These properties can provide new functionality to your applications even though CDO might not provide explicit objects for this functionality.

Learn to Love MDBVUE

If you have never used the MDBVUE tool, you should get familiar with it. MDBVUE is included on the Exchange Server CDs. It uses MAPI and allows you to look at the internals of your Exchange Server such as property IDs and detailed MAPI information. Note that the property IDs you get back when you use MDBVUE are machine specific. This means you cannot take the property ID returned for the IM address of an Outlook contact and use it on another machine. Instead, you have to use the full property set ID and property ID, which we will discuss in the next section.

Dealing with Outlook Property Sets in CDO

You might have to deal with using Outlook MAPI property identifiers and property sets in your CDO code. For example, because CDO 1.21 does not natively support contacts, you must use Outlook contact properties in CDO using the *Fields* collection. When you access MAPI properties using CDO 1.21, you must transpose the propset ID. The companion content includes a saved version of the main Web page from that site, which has the list of all the MAPI Outlook properties along with sample code.

When you look at properties in MAPI, you will see that your properties are made up of a property set and a property ID. This is how Outlook and Exchange look up the properties in their own schemas or in your custom schemas. A section of the property range called the public strings section is visible to all applications. Outlook does not create all of its properties in this area. Instead, it creates properties in private property set identifiers. For this reason, if you are going to work with Outlook or Exchange properties that CDO does not have an object for, you must use property set identifiers with the correct property identifier.

An example might make this clearer. You might at some point want to work with Outlook contacts or tasks from CDO. However, CDO does not have a contact or task object. You can use the property sets and property IDs of contacts and tasks to work with these objects. All of the properties used in this example are on the Web for you to download. The following sample shows how to use the *SetNamespace* method in CDO to set the right property set and also how to read and write properties into Outlook. You can also pass the property set identifier as one of the arguments to the *Fields* collection, which is also shown in the example.

```
Const AMPidTag_BusinessAddress = "0x801B"
Const AMPidTag_HomeAddress = "0x801A"
Private Sub Command1_Click()

'On Error Resume Next
Set oSession = CreateObject("MAPI.Session")
oSession.Logon "", "", False, False, 0, True

'Contact Example
Set oContactFldr = oSession.GetDefaultFolder(5)
Set oContacts = oContactFldr.Messages
Set oContact = oContacts.GetFirst
Set oFields = oContact.Fields
'Set the namespace to the correct Propset for Contacts
oFields.SetNamespace "0420060000000000C000000000000046"
strBusinessAddress = oFields(AMPidTag_BusinessAddress).Value
strHomeAddress = oFields(AMPidTag_HomeAddress).Value
MsgBox "Contact Name: " & oContact.Subject & vbLf _
    & "Contact Home Address: " & vbLf _
    & strHomeAddress & vbLf & "Contact Business Address: " & vbLf _
    & strBusinessAddress

'Task Example
Set oTaskFldr = oSession.GetDefaultFolder(8)
Set oTasks = oTaskFldr.Messages
Set oTask = oTasks.GetFirst
Set oFields = oTask.Fields
'Use the fields collection to pass the property set
strStartDate = oFields.Item("0x8104", _
                "0320060000000000C000000000000046").Value
'Use the other format as well
strEndDate = oFields.Item("{0320060000000000C000000000000046}0x8105").Value
'Set the namespace to Tasks
oFields.SetNamespace "0320060000000000C000000000000046"
boolCompleted = CBool(oFields.Item("0x810F").Value)
MsgBox "Task Name: " & oTask.Subject & vbLf _
    & "Task Start Date: " & vbLf _
    & strStartDate & vbLf & "Task End Date: " & vbLf _
    & strEndDate & vbLf & "Task Completed: " & boolCompleted
End Sub
```

Remember that Outlook does more than just set properties on items. For example, when you change the home city for a contact in Outlook, Outlook has code that takes the change and puts it into the home address property (which is a combination of street, city, state, and Zip code). If you write code in CDO that uses Outlook properties but does not populate all the properties that Outlook expects, you can cause Outlook to malfunction. For this reason, when you're using the properties described earlier, you should test your code thoroughly with Outlook. Another way to figure out what properties Outlook expects is to perform the actions in Outlook and look at what happens in the MAPI properties using MDBVUE.

A CDO 1.21 .NET Sample Application

To show you how to use some of the existing COM interfaces in your .NET applications, I'll show you a simple application (in both Visual Basic .NET and Visual C#) that uses the CDO 1.21 object model.

The application creates a new CDO session, logs on, queries the user's inbox to display some information, and then sends an e-mail from the user's account. Here it is in Visual Basic:

```
Imports MAPI
Public Class Form1
    Inherits System.Windows.Forms.Form

#Region " Windows Form Designer generated code "
⋮
#End Region

    Dim oSession As New MAPI.Session()
    Private Sub cmdLogon_Click(ByVal sender As System.Object, _
        ByVal e As System.EventArgs) Handles cmdLogon.Click
        Err.Clear()
        'Attempt to Logon
        'Check to make sure server and user alias are filled in
        If txtExServer.Text = "" Then
            MsgBox("You must enter a server name!")
            Exit Sub
        End If

        If txtAlias.Text = "" Then
            MsgBox("You must enter an alias!")
            Exit Sub
        End If

        Try
            'Attempt to logon
            oSession.Logon("", "", True, True, 0, True, _
```

```
            txtExServer.Text & vbLf & txtAlias.Text)
        'Get the Inbox
        Dim oInbox As MAPI.Folder = oSession.GetDefaultFolder( _
            MAPI.CdoDefaultFolderTypes.CdoDefaultFolderInbox)
        Dim oMessages As MAPI.Messages = oInbox.Messages
        lblInbox.Text = "There are "
        lblInbox.Text &= oMessages.Count & " items in your inbox."
        MsgBox("Logon successful.")
    Catch
        'Some error has occurred!
        Dim oException As System.Exception
        oException = Err.GetException
        MsgBox("ERROR: " & Err.Number & " " & Err.Description & _
            " Line number: " & Err.Erl & " Stack dump: " & _
            oException.StackTrace)
    End Try
End Sub

Private Sub cmdSend_Click(ByVal sender As System.Object, _
    ByVal e As System.EventArgs) Handles cmdSend.Click
    Try
        If txtTo.Text = "" Then
            MsgBox("You must enter a To address!")
            Exit Sub
        End If

        If txtSubject.Text = "" Then
            MsgBox("Please enter a subject.")
            Exit Sub
        End If

        If txtBody.Text = "" Then
            MsgBox("Please enter a body.")
            Exit Sub
        End If

        'Send the message
        Dim oMessage As MAPI.Message
        Dim oOutbox As MAPI.Folder
        oOutbox = oSession.GetDefaultFolder( _
            MAPI.CdoDefaultFolderTypes.CdoDefaultFolderOutbox)
        oMessage = oOutbox.Messages.Add()
        Dim oRecips As MAPI.Recipients
        oRecips = oMessage.Recipients
        Dim oRecip As MAPI.Recipient = oRecips.Add(txtTo.Text, , _
            MAPI.CdoRecipientType.CdoTo)
        oMessage.Subject = txtSubject.Text
        oMessage.Text = txtBody.Text

        'Resolve the recipients
        oRecips.Resolve(True)
        If oRecips.Resolved <> True Then
            MsgBox("You must resolve the recipients!")
```

```
                Exit Sub
            End If
            oMessage.Send(True)
        Catch
            'Some error has occurred!
            Dim oException As System.Exception
            oException = Err.GetException
            MsgBox("ERROR: " & Err.Number & " " & Err.Description & _
                " Line number: " & Err.Erl & " Stack dump: " & _
                oException.StackTrace)
        End Try
    End Sub
End Class
```

The C# sample has the same functionality as the Visual Basic version. You need to know a couple of things about programming with C# to be successful programming against CDO 1.21. First, you must declare the default threading for your application to be a single-threaded apartment (STA). You do this by using the *[STAThread]* attribute. This is what CDO expects your application threading model to be. If you skip this step, you will probably get a MAPI_E_UNKNOWN error.

Second, you must pass *Missing.Value* for any optional object arguments in the method calls in CDO. Otherwise, C# will throw a compilation error because it will not be able to find CDO function prototypes that match your calls. Be sure to include the *System.Reflection* namespace to take advantage of the *Missing.Value* statement.

Besides these two differences and the difference in language semantics between Visual Basic and C#, the code is pretty much the same. Here is the C# version:

```
using System;
using System.Drawing;
using System.Collections;
using System.ComponentModel;
using System.Windows.Forms;
using System.Data;
using System.Reflection;

namespace CDO121CSharp
{
    /// <summary>
    /// Summary description for Form1.
    /// </summary>
    public class frmMain : System.Windows.Forms.Form
    {
        private System.Windows.Forms.Button cmdGo;
        /// <summary>
        /// Required designer variable.
        /// </summary>
        private System.ComponentModel.Container components = null;
```

```
public frmMain()
{
    //
    // Required for Windows Form Designer support
    //
    InitializeComponent();

    //
    // TODO: Add any constructor code after
    // InitializeComponent call
    //
}

/// <summary>
/// Clean up any resources being used.
/// </summary>
protected override void Dispose( bool disposing )
{
    if( disposing )
    {
        if (components != null)
        {
            components.Dispose();
        }
    }
    base.Dispose( disposing );
}

#region Windows Form Designer generated code
/// <summary>
/// Required method for Designer support - do not modify
/// the contents of this method with the code editor.
/// </summary>
. . .
#endregion

/// <summary>
/// The main entry point for the application.
/// </summary>
[STAThread]
static void Main()
{
    Application.Run(new frmMain());
}

private void cmdGo_Click(object sender, System.EventArgs e)
{
    // Class variables
    MAPI.Session oSession;
    string strExchangeServer = "thomrizwin2k";
    string strUserName = "thomriz";
```

```
                    // Establish a new Session
                    oSession = new MAPI.Session();

                    // Connect to the Exchange Server and establish
                    try
                        {
                            oSession.Logon( Missing.Value, Missing.Value,
                                false, true, -1, true, strExchangeServer +
                                "\n" + strUserName);
                            MessageBox.Show("Logon Successful!");

                            MAPI.Folder oInbox =
                                MAPI.Folder)oSession.GetDefaultFolder(
                                MAPI.CdoDefaultFolderTypes.CdoDefaultFolderInbox);
                            MAPI.Messages oMessages =
                                (MAPI.Messages)oInbox.Messages;
                            MessageBox.Show("There are " + oMessages.Count +
                                " items in your inbox!");

                            //Send a new message
                            MAPI.Folder oOutBox =
                                (MAPI.Folder)oSession.GetDefaultFolder(
                                MAPI.CdoDefaultFolderTypes.CdoDefaultFolderOutbox);
                            MAPI.Messages oOutMessages =
                                (MAPI.Messages)oOutBox.Messages;
                            MAPI.Message oMsg =
                                (MAPI.Message)oOutMessages.Add(Missing.Value,
                                Missing.Value,Missing.Value,Missing.Value);
                            MAPI.Recipients oRecips =
                                (MAPI.Recipients)oMsg.Recipients;
                            MAPI.Recipient oRecip =
                                (MAPI.Recipient)oRecips.Add("Thomas Rizzo",
                                Missing.Value,Missing.Value,Missing.Value);
                            oRecips.Resolve(true);
                            oMsg.Subject = "New Test Message";
                            oMsg.Text = "Test 123";
                            oMsg.Send(Missing.Value,Missing.Value,Missing.Value);

                        }
                        catch (System.Exception oException)
                        {
                            throw new Exception(
                                "Could not logon to Exchange Server " +
                                strExchangeServer, oException);
                        }
                }
            }
        }
```

> **Note** To use ASP.NET with CDO 1.21, you must have the nonsecure version of CDO 1.21 on your server machines by installing Exchange or Outlook Web Access (OWA) on the server. (The version of CDO that ships with Outlook is secure, so it will not work.) This is the only way to get CDO 1.21 on the machine. You can get CDO 1.21 installed on your Web server with the administration-tools-only installation of Exchange. You will not run into issues when an ASP.NET application that uses CDO 1.21 and your Exchange server are on the same machine. However, if they are on separate machines, you might get a MAPI_E_FAILONEPROVIDER error or a MAPI_E_LOGON_FAILED error. Removing the secure CDO installation and installing a server-side version of CDO should fix this problem. Also, with ASP.NET the worker thread does not have access to the Windows file directory; if you use dynamic profiles with CDO, you might get errors. To fix this problem, follow the steps in Microsoft Knowledge Base Article Q166599.

Summary

CDO 1.21 provides a powerful environment in which you can build applications against Exchange Server. You can do advanced Exchange applications using some of the tips and tricks highlighted in this chapter. In the next chapter, we will look at how you can use Active Directory Services Interface (ADSI) to program against Exchange data stored in the Active Directory. This tool allows you to integrate rich directory information into your Exchange applications.

13

Programming Exchange Server Using ADSI

Messaging and communication technologies are not the only technologies you need for building a collaborative application. Having a robust directory is also a key requirement, whether you're building a simple messaging application or a full-blown workflow system. A directory holds communication information such as e-mail addresses and phone numbers as well as organizational and hierarchical information such as managers and direct reports. It also stores facility and personal information, such as building locations, cost centers, and pictures of users.

The ability to retrieve this range of information is important for the application and beneficial to any organization. Recall our Collaboration Data Objects (CDO) Helpdesk application in Chapter 11, which used a directory to obtain a user's personal information. Because Microsoft Exchange Server, through Active Directory, supports an extensible directory, you can add your own fields to the directory to store the type of custom information we've retrieved in our sample applications.

What Is ADSI?

You've seen one way to access the directory—by using the CDO library. CDO provides a set of objects that allow you to query information stored in the Exchange Server directory under the AddressEntry section of the CDO hierarchy. Another way to access Exchange Server information stored in Active Directory is to use Microsoft Active Directory Services Interfaces (ADSI).

ADSI is a set of COM interfaces that allow you to manipulate objects in different directories, including Exchange Server 5.5 and Active Directory. ADSI supports such protocols as Lightweight Directory Access Protocol (LDAP), NetWare Directory Services (NDS), and Microsoft Windows NT Directory Services (NTDS). The advantage of ADSI is that its design isn't based on a specific directory's API, which makes it flexible in the type and number of directories it can work with. Also, ADSI can be used with multiple programming languages, such as Microsoft Visual Basic, Microsoft Visual Basic Scripting Edition (VBScript), Java, and Microsoft Visual C++.

Accessing the Directory: CDO or ADSI?

The big question is how to access the information provided by Active Directory. CDO offers you a limited subset of features—it can access only the properties that have corresponding Messaging API (MAPI) unique IDs. Therefore, if CDO provides access to the directory properties that you need in your application, you should use it for directory access. Using CDO has the benefit of allowing you to write your application using a familiar object library, and you do not have to write to a second object library, which can save debugging time.

Another way to access Active Directory is by using the ADSI object library, which gives you more flexibility. Using ADSI, you can access not only the properties used by CDO but also other properties stored in Active Directory—for example, configuration information, such as which protocols are enabled on the Exchange Server, user information, and computer information.

Design Goals of the ADSI Object Library

The ADSI library is the strategic library for accessing directory objects and information from Microsoft, whether this information is in Exchange Server or in Active Directory. When designing ADSI, Microsoft had three primary goals in mind. First, ADSI had to be based on COM-compatible providers to access directory information. In a provider-based model, the client interacts with the COM interfaces exposed by the ADSI library, and the installed providers convert the calls in the interfaces into function calls that access the targeted directory provider. The provider model allows the same calls to be used in an ADSI client application to access any type of directory with an ADSI provider. ADSI ships with four primary directory providers: a Microsoft Windows NT directory provider for Windows NT 4.0, a Novell NDS provider, a Novell NetWare Binding provider for NetWare versions before 4.*x*, and an LDAP provider. You can also write your own provider because the ADSI provider architecture is extensible. We will focus on the built-in LDAP provider in this chapter because it supports accessing and updating Active Directory.

Microsoft's second goal for ADSI was to allow developers to use any COM-based or .NET-based development tool with the object library, including Visual Basic, Visual C#, Visual C++, Java, VBScript, and JavaScript. You can decide which tool is the best for creating your ADSI Exchange Server applications. In this chapter, I use VBScript and Microsoft Active Server Pages (ASP) to create a Web-based administrator program for Exchange Server. However, this application could easily have been written in Visual Basic or Visual C#. Near the end of this chapter, you'll find information on .NET and Web services support for ADSI.

The third goal of ADSI was to provide a single directory API as a replacement for multiple directory APIs. With Exchange Server, you can use CDO to access information stored in Active Directory. With Active Directory, you can use LDAP functions to access information stored in Active Directory. However, depending on your application, it might be easier to write to a single set of interfaces and use different providers for these directory services rather than learn two or three different APIs. With ADSI, you need to learn only one API to use a multitude of directory services.

ADSI Object Library Architecture

The ADSI object library is a very approachable object library. Although it does not contain many objects, you can perform many functions with the objects in the library. The only potential difficulty in using the ADSI object library is understanding how to access the objects in your applications using distinguished pathnames. At first, these pathnames can be a little intimidating, but after you experiment with ADSI and its objects, you will understand how to exploit the power of these paths. We'll discuss creating paths later in this chapter in the section titled "Creating Paths to Active Directory Objects and Attributes."

In the ADSI architecture, every element in a directory service, such as the Exchange Server configuration information, is represented by an ADSI object. The interfaces supported by the ADSI object are determined by the underlying functionality of the directory object. For example, a mailbox in Exchange Server, which does not contain directory objects under it, supports the *IADs* interface. In contrast, a container in Active Directory, which can hold objects such as mailboxes, distribution lists, and other containers under it, implements the *IADsContainer* interface. Because the requirements for a directory object that contains other directory objects extend beyond those for a single directory object, ADSI provides more methods and properties, through extra interfaces, for them.

IADs and *IADsContainer* Interfaces

The primary interfaces you will use when working with ADSI objects are the *IADs* interface and the *IADsContainer* interface. The *IADs* interface is required for all ADSI objects. It provides properties that describe the object—in essence, the metadata of the object—and methods that allow you to manage the actual directory information that the object contains. ADSI stores this directory information in a property cache, which gives you a mechanism to batch changes or additions to a specific object in a temporary location and then burst this information to the directory service in one call. This property cache is useful because some programming languages, such as Visual Basic, do not provide native batching mechanisms, and without a property cache, every change you make to an ADSI object is put over the wire, decreasing the performance of your application.

The property cache is useful, but only if you remember to use it! The most common mistake new ADSI developers make is not calling the specific ADSI method *SetInfo* to flush the cache and submit object modifications to the directory. If you exit your application and do not call this method then the changes you make will not be persisted in the directory. The second most common mistake new ADSI developers make is not calling the *GetInfo* method to refresh the cache after making changes. The *SetInfo* method does not automatically refresh the cache for you.

In addition to supporting the *GetInfo* and *SetInfo* methods, the *IADs* interface supports the *Get*, *GetEx*, *GetInfoEx*, *Put*, and *PutEx* methods. *Get* and *Put* do exactly what their names imply: *Get* retrieves a specific property from the directory, and *Put* saves the value for a specific property in the property cache. The versions of these methods with the *Ex* suffix allow you to get or put a multivalue property. A multivalue property can contain multiple values of the same type. The best example of a multivalue property in Active Directory is the *reports* property. Because one person can have many direct reports, the *reports* property in the directory is a multivalue property—multiple direct report names can be stored in a single property for the directory object named reports. To access this property from ADSI, you must use the *GetEx* method. *GetInfoEx* is provided so that you can specify which properties to refresh in the property cache and avoid having to reload the entire cache from the underlying directory service.

The properties that the *IADs* interface implements are *Name*, *AdsPath*, *GUID*, *Class*, *Schema*, and *Parent*. (For our purposes, the *Schema* and *Parent* properties are not as important as the other four, so this discussion will focus on

Name, *AdsPath*, *GUID*, and *Class*.) The *Name* property returns the relative name of the object. The *AdsPath* property returns the path to the object. In Exchange Server, this is the LDAP query string that is used to access the object. The *GUID* property returns the GUID of the object from the underlying directory. The *Class* property is important because it returns the schema class name of the object. This property and its return value will get a bit more attention in the next section.

IADsContainer Interface

As mentioned earlier, if a directory object contains other objects, the directory object is considered a container. In ADSI, a container implements not only the *IADs* interface but also the *IADsContainer* interface. The *IADsContainer* interface provides methods to traverse the child objects in the container as well as modify the container's properties. As you will see in the sample applications in this chapter, you can use the *For...Each* construct in Visual Basic or VBScript to easily loop through all the child objects below a container object and retrieve individual properties from each child object. By traversing the individual objects under the container, you can easily build a hierarchical view of the information stored in Active Directory.

Other ADSI Interfaces

Covering the other ADSI interfaces is beyond the scope of this book, but you should know that ADSI provides a powerful feature set so you can build not only directory applications that work with Exchange Server but also applications that work with other directory services. For example, ADSI defines an *IADsComputer* interface that lets you store information about a computer in a directory service. ADSI also defines interfaces such as *IADsPrintQueue* and *IADsPrintJob*, which enable you to list printers available in the directory service and store specifics about the actual print jobs taking place on those print queues. For guidance on finding more information on the other types of ADSI interfaces, refer to the "Getting Help with ADSI" section later in this chapter.

Exchange Server Object Classes

You should be aware of some important classes in Exchange Server when you develop your applications:

- ***container*** Identifies the object as a container for other objects in the directory.

- ***group*** Corresponds to distribution lists in the Exchange Server directory.
- ***person*** An abstract class that represents any object that can receive mail so other objects, such as distribution lists, can inherit some attributes from the class. Because the *person* class is an abstract class, you can never create an explicit object from it.
- ***organizationalPerson*** Represents recipients in the directory.
- ***contact*** Corresponds to a custom recipient in the directory.

Creating Paths to Active Directory Objects and Attributes

The first step in developing any ADSI application that accesses Active Directory is creating a valid instance of ADSI and passing this instance a valid path to the object you want to access. When you write Java, Visual Basic, VBScript, or Visual Basic for Applications (VBA) applications, the easiest way to create a valid instance of the ADSI library is to use the *GetObject(AdsPath)* syntax. The *AdsPath* parameter contains a valid ADSI path to a specific object. For example, to access a specific container object named *Users*, using a specific server named *DirServer* and in a specific domain named *Microsoft.com*, you pass in the following *AdsPath* to the *GetObject* method:

```
LDAP://DirServer/cn=Users, dc=Microsoft, dc=com
```

The *LDAP* at the beginning of the path specifies the ADSI provider to use. If you want to simply set an object variable to a specific ADSI provider without attempting to open an object, you can also use the *GetObject(ADSIProvider)* syntax. For example, the following sets the *oIADs* variable to the LDAP provider:

```
oIADs = GetObject("LDAP:")
```

To specify a different provider, you can replace the LDAP string with *WinNT* or *NDS*. To access a specific recipient in a specific container on the DirServer server, you use the following *AdsPath*:

```
LDAP://DirServer/cn=RecipientName, cn=RecipientContainer,
dc=Microsoft, dc=com
```

As you can see from the examples, the syntax for creating a valid path follows this structure:

```
LDAP://DirectoryServer/cn=Bottommost object,
cn=next level of object, dc=domain1, dc=domain2
```

The sample application in this chapter shows examples of how to use this syntax to query different parts of Active Directory.

> **Note** Do not mix cases in your identifiers when you create paths (for example, CN=*users* or dc=*microsoft*. If you do, you will get an error from ADSI.

ADSI vs. CDO for Exchange Management

This chapter shows examples that use ADSI. However, CDO for Exchange Management and even CDO for Exchange also support working with Active Directory. How do you decide which object library to use in your application? Most times, if you are just querying the directory, you should stick with just ADSI. However, if you are creating mailboxes, mail-enabling users, creating users, or implementing other sorts of Exchange administrative functions, you will want to leverage both libraries. CDO makes it easy to turn an Active Directory object into a CDO object by using type casting. You should learn both object models because you'll probably use both in your applications.

What Is *RootDSE*?

Most times, you will not hardcode the name of your directory server but will use serverless binding instead. Serverless binding allows you to connect to your Active Directory infrastructure without knowing the name of any servers in that domain. To connect to the Active Directory infrastructure, you use the LDAP *rootDSE* mechanism. The following is the *AdsPath* that connects to a directory server in the user's current domain:

```
LDAP://rootDSE
```

From *rootDSE*, you can retrieve properties that describe the domain, such as the default naming context, the name of the server, the current time, and the supported LDAP version. The following Visual Basic sample shows some of the more common properties you can retrieve using *rootDSE*. See the ADSI documentation for the complete list of properties.

```
Set orootDSE = GetObject("LDAP://rootDSE")
MsgBox orootDSE.get("currentTime")
MsgBox orootDSE.get("defaultNamingContext")
```

```
MsgBox orootDSE.get("RootDomainNamingContext")
MsgBox orootDSE.get("ServerName")
MsgBox orootDSE.get("DnsHostName")
```

Mailbox-Enabled vs. Mail-Enabled

The most basic difference between mailbox-enabled and mail-enabled users in Exchange is that mail-enabled users have a valid e-mail address in the system but might not have a local mailbox on the Exchange server. A mailbox-enabled user has both a valid e-mail address and a local Exchange Server mailbox in the system. You can think of mail-enabled recipients as custom recipients from Exchange 5.5.

A Sample ADSI Application

The best way to learn about using ADSI to program with the Exchange Server directory is to examine a sample application. I developed one that demonstrates how to create custom recipients, query distribution lists, and query for recipient directory information such as user's names, addresses, and phone numbers.

Setting Up the Application

Before you can install the application, you must have a Windows 2000 Server and a client with the software listed in Table 13-1 installed.

Table 13-1 Installation Requirements for the ADSI Application

Minimum Software Requirements	Installation Notes
Exchange Server 2000 or later	
Microsoft Internet Information Services (IIS) 5.0 or later with ASP	
ADSI 2.0 or later	Active Directory Client Extensions (ADSI 2.5) is available as a free download from *http://www.microsoft.com/adsi*. Windows 2000 and 2003 install ADSI 2.5 by default.
Microsoft ActiveX Data Objects (ADO)	IIS 5.0 installs ADO by default. Visual Basic 6.0 installs ADO 2.0. For more information on ADO, go to *http:/www.microsoft.com/data/*.

Table 13-1 Installation Requirements for the ADSI Application

Minimum Software Requirements	Installation Notes
For the client:	
Microsoft Internet Explorer 4.0 or later	You can run the client software on the same machine or on a separate machine.

To install the ADSI application, first copy the ADSI folder from the companion content to the Web server where you want to run the application. Start the IIS administration program. Create a virtual directory that points to the location where you copied the ADSI files, and name the virtual directory *adsi*. Be sure to turn off anonymous access to the virtual directory and enable either NTLM or Basic authentication. You should be able to use the following URL to access your ADSI application: *http://<yourservername>/adsi*.

The first page displayed in the ADSI application is the logon page, as shown in Figure 13-1. Once a user enters logon information and verifies the dynamically generated Exchange Server information, the application presents a menu of available administrative options for the user, as shown in Figure 13-2.

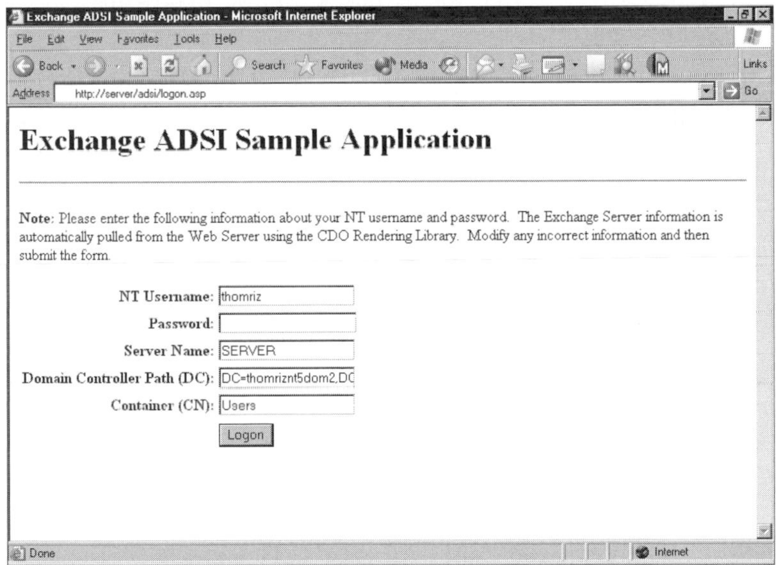

Figure 13-1 The logon page for the ADSI application

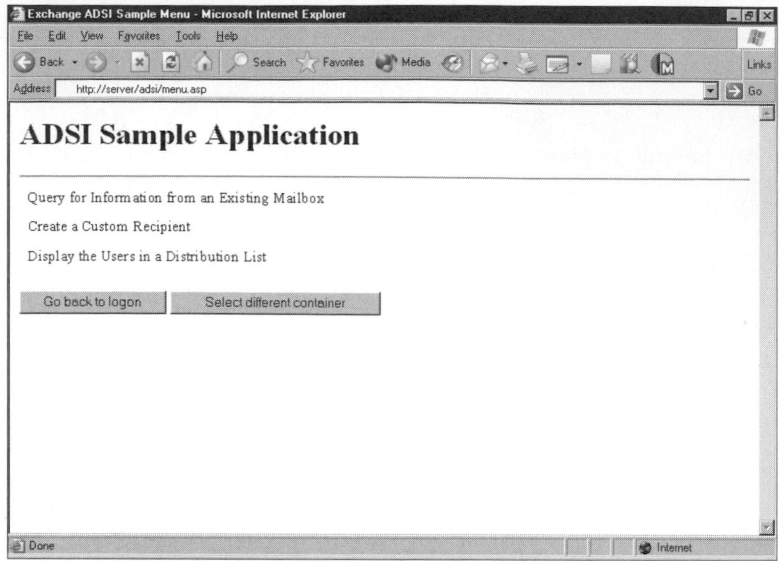

Figure 13-2 The main menu of the ADSI application

Now let's step through the actual code that makes up these menu items and see how to use the ADSI object library with an Exchange Server directory.

Logging On to ADSI

The most common operation in the code for the menu items is the object binding code for ADSI. This binding code is dispersed throughout all the code modules in the application rather than being centralized and performed only once. This makes it easier for you to browse the code and understand exactly what is happening.

To bind successfully to an object in the Exchange Server directory using ADSI when you don't want to pass a path directly to the *GetObject* function, you must use the *GetObject* method to set an object variable to the ADSI library and then call the *OpenDSObject* method. The *OpenDSObject* method takes four parameters:

- ***AdsPath*** The path of the object you want to bind to. You saw how to create this path earlier in the chapter.
- **The Windows username** This is used to attempt authentication against the directory service.

- **The password for the Windows username you specify**
- **A flag that specifies the binding option to use** The *&H00000001* flag specifies use of secure authentication, *&H00000010* specifies use of encryption, and *&H00000200* specifies use of server binding if you pass the name of a server in your LDAP path instead of using *rootDSE*. There are also other flags you can use in ADSI. See the Platform SDK for information about them.

Depending on the provider used, the flags that specify the binding option might or might not be supported. On the LDAP provider, if you set the secure authentication and the encryption flags and pass in a user name and a password, ADSI will perform a simple bind over Secure Sockets Layer (SSL) sessions, which is a secure authentication over a secure channel. The sample application does not use *OpenDSObject* for most of its operations; instead, it uses *GetObject* and passes the directory path in *GetObject*. If you use *OpenDSObject* and do not use either of those flags, a *0* will be passed in as the value for the final parameter to indicate that no encryption and no secure authentication should be used.

The following code shows how to set an object variable to the LDAP provider and log on using the *OpenDSObject* method, as well as how to use the *GetObject* method with a path:

```
Set oIADs = GetObject("LDAP:")
oIADs.OpenDSObject(AdsPath, UserName, Password, 0)
Set oIADs2 = GetObject("LDAP://servername")
```

Querying for Information from an Existing Mailbox

The ADSI application also shows how to query for information from an existing Exchange Server mailbox. The user interface, shown in Figure 13-3, allows the user to type the first name of the user to find the mailbox.

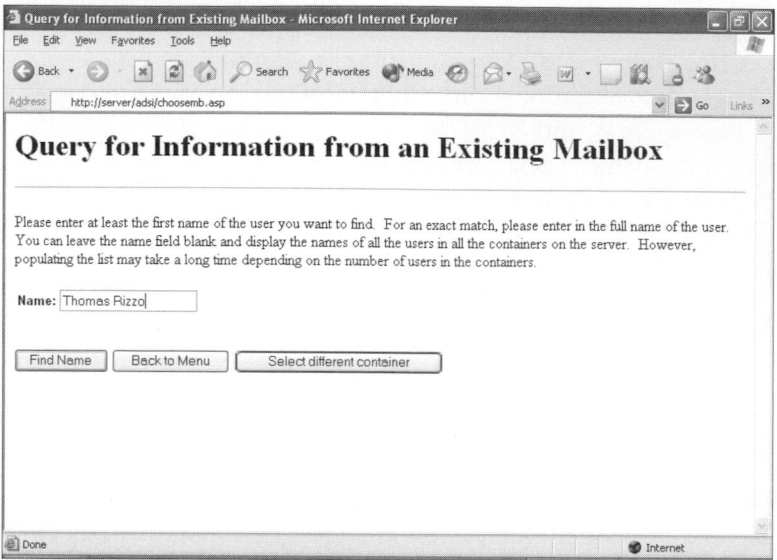

Figure 13-3 The user can type the first name of the user in the directory to locate the mailbox.

After the user types a name, the application uses ADO to query the directory service using LDAP. You might wonder why ADO is used rather than the *OpenDSObject* method you saw earlier. The reason is that if you use the *OpenDSObject* method, the user must know the exact name of the desired object in the directory. ADO is more forgiving; the user can simply type a portion of the first name. Also, users often do not know the alias of users they are querying, so forcing them to type aliases does not make sense. The code to create the ADO object and perform the query is shown here:

```
bstrSearchCriteria = Request.Form("UserName")
bstrServer = Session("Server")
'Create an ADO object
Set ADOconn = CreateObject("ADODB.Connection")
If Err.Number = 0 Then
    ADOconn.Provider = "ADSDSOObject"
    ADOconn.Open "ADs Provider"
    'Create a query using ADO to find all users across all containers
    bstrADOQueryString = "<LDAP://" + bstrServer & _
        ">;(&(objectClass=organizationalPerson)(cn=" & _
        bstrSearchCriteria & "*));cn,adspath;subtree"
    Set objRS = ADOconn.Execute(bstrADOQueryString)
    If Err.Number = 0 Then
        If objRS.RecordCount > 0 Then %>
            <p>Please select one of the following names from the
            list of names.</p>
            <p><em><strong>Returned Names:</strong></em></p>
            <SELECT NAME='MailboxPath'>
```

```
            <%
            'Builds the select control of the queried records
            While Not objRS.EOF
                bstrSelectStatement = bstrSelectStatement & _
                    "<OPTION VALUE='" & objRS.Fields(iCN).Value & _
                    "'>" & objRS.Fields(iADSPATH)
                objRS.MoveNext
            Wend
            Response.Write bstrSelectStatement & "</SELECT>"
        Else %>
            <B><I>No entries match your search criteria.
            Try again using a different value.</I></B>
            <%
        End If
    Else
        If Hex(Err.Number) = 80070044 Then
            Response.Write "<FONT FACE='Arial, Helvetica' " & _
                "SIZE=2>Error " & Hex(Err.Number) & _
                ":  Too many entries match your search " & _
                "criteria!</FONT>"
            Err.Clear
        Else
        %>
        <SCRIPT LANGUAGE="JavaScript">
            alert("Error Number: <%=Hex(Err.Number)%> \n
                Error Description: <%=Err.Description%>")
            history.back()
        </SCRIPT>
        <%
        Err.Clear
        End If
    End If
Else
    %>
    <SCRIPT LANGUAGE="JavaScript">
        alert("Error Number: <%=Hex(Err.Number)%> \nError Description:
            <%=Err.Description%>")
        history.back()
    </SCRIPT>
    <%
    Err.Clear
End If
%>
```

This code creates an ADO *Connection* object and sets the *Provider* property to *ADSDSOObject*, which specifies the LDAP provider for ADSI. You can specify any string for the connection string argument to the *Open* method of the ADO *Connection* object. In this case, the application specifies *ADs Provider* as the argument. The code then creates an LDAP query, which consists of four elements separated by semicolons. This is the format:

```
<LDAP://server/adsidn>;ldapfilter;attributescsv;scope
```

The *server* argument specifies the name or the IP address of the server where the directory is hosted. The *adsidn* argument specifies the distinguished name in the directory where we want to start our query. You should pass in a correctly formed path, which you saw how to create earlier in the chapter. The *filter* parameter specifies the LDAP filter string to use. In this case, the LDAP filter states that the object class must be *organizationalPerson* and the name of the object must match the letters typed by the user. The next argument, *attributescsv*, is a list of attribute names, separated by commas, that you want returned for each row in the recordset. In our application, we want the name of the person and the *AdsPath* to the object that corresponds to that person returned so we can place this information in the HTML form, as shown in Figure 13-4. The final argument, *scope*, informs the directory service how deeply in the hierarchy to search for the information being queried. The *scope* argument can be one of three values: *base*, *onelevel*, or *subtree*. We want to query for all mailboxes that match our specified criteria across all recipient containers in the directory, so we specified *subtree* for this argument. The *subtree* argument causes the directory service to search for the information in every *subtree* under the starting object. The *base* argument searches only the currently specified object, and *onelevel* searches one level below the current object in the hierarchy.

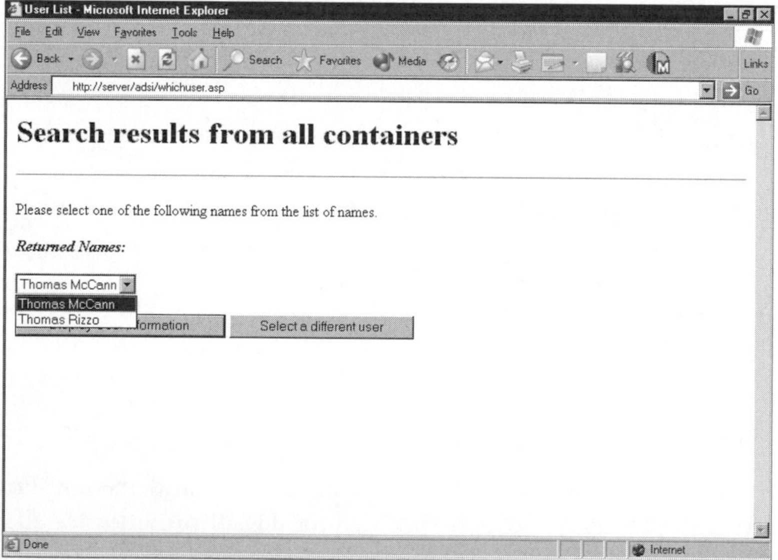

Figure 13-4 After the query runs, the HTML form is populated with the corresponding records so a user can select the person she wants more information about.

If the query successfully returns records that match the filter, the code uses the standard ADO methods to scroll through the recordset and place the records in the HTML form.

After the user selects the name of the person she wants more information about in the HTML form, the application opens the directory object for that person and retrieves information such as the address, phone number, manager, and direct reports. This information is represented using a DHTML tabbed dialog box in the browser, as shown in Figure 13-5.

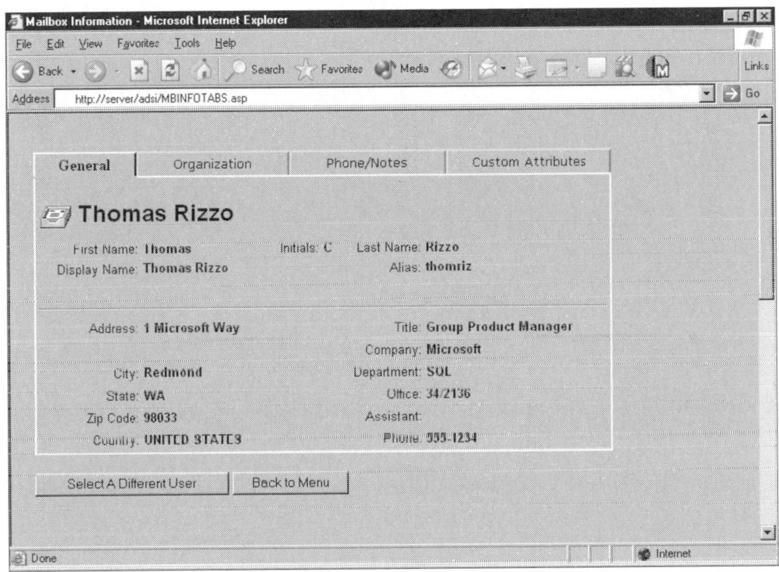

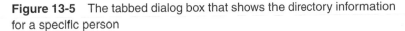

Figure 13-5 The tabbed dialog box that shows the directory information for a specific person

The next section of code retrieves the information about the specific person from the directory. I intentionally left out some of the DHTML code from the listing to highlight how ADSI is used in the code. Also, only a portion of the ADSI code is shown here because the structure of the code throughout this part of the application is similar. Only the specific properties retrieved from the directory using ADSI are different. The full code is included with the companion content.

```
On Error Resume Next

If Request.QueryString("Path") = "" Then
    bstrMailboxPath = Request.Form("MailboxPath")
Else
    bstrMailboxPath = Request.Querystring("Path")
```

```
End If
bstrServer = Session("Server")

Set objIADs = GetObject(bstrMailboxPath)
⋮

<TR>
<TD VALIGN=MIDDLE ALIGN=RIGHT><FONT FACE="Arial, Helvetica" SIZE=2>
First Name:</TD>
<TD VALIGN=TOP><FONT FACE="Arial, Helvetica" SIZE=2><B><%=Server.HTMLEn-
code(objIADs.Get("givenName"))%></B></FONT>
</TD>

<TD VALIGN=MIDDLE ALIGN=RIGHT><FONT FACE="Arial, Helvetica" SIZE=2>
Initials:</TD>
<TD VALIGN=TOP><FONT FACE="Arial, Helvetica" SIZE=2><B><%=Server.HTMLEn-
code(objIADs.Get("initials"))%></B></FONT>
</TD>

<TD VALIGN=MIDDLE ALIGN=RIGHT><FONT FACE="Arial, Helvetica" SIZE=2>
Last Name:</TD>
<TD VALIGN=TOP><FONT FACE="Arial, Helvetica" SIZE=2><B><%=Server.HTMLEn-
code(objIADs.Get("sn"))%></B></FONT></TD>
</TR>

<TR>
<TD VALIGN=MIDDLE ALIGN=RIGHT><FONT FACE="Arial, Helvetica" SIZE=2>
Display Name:</TD>
<TD VALIGN=TOP><FONT FACE="Arial, Helvetica" SIZE=2><B><%=Server.HTMLEn-
code(objIADs.Get("cn"))%></B></FONT></TD>
<TD> </TD>
<TD> </TD>
<TD VALIGN=MIDDLE ALIGN=RIGHT><FONT FACE="Arial, Helvetica" SIZE=2>
Alias:</TD>
<TD VALIGN=TOP><FONT FACE="Arial, Helvetica" SIZE=2><B><%=Server.HTMLEn-
code(objIADs.Get("mailNickname"))%></B></FONT>
</TD>
</TR>

<TR>
<td width="100%" colspan="10"> <hr>
</TD>
</TR>

<TR>
<TD VALIGN=TOP ALIGN=RIGHT><FONT FACE="Arial, Helvetica" SIZE=2>
Address:</FONT></TD>
<TD VALIGN=TOP><FONT FACE="Arial, Helvetica" SIZE=2><B><%=Server.HTMLEn-
code(objIADs.Get("streetAddress"))%></B></FONT>
</TD>

<TD> </TD>
<TD> </TD>
```

```
<TD ALIGN=RIGHT><FONT FACE="Arial, Helvetica" SIZE=2>Title:</FONT></TD>
<TD ALIGN=LEFT><FONT FACE="Arial, Helvetica"
SIZE=2><B><%=Server.HTMLEncode(objIADs.Get("title"))%></B></FONT></TD>
</TR>

<TR>
<TD> </TD>
<TD> </TD>
<TD> </TD>
<TD> </TD>

<TD ALIGN=RIGHT><FONT FACE="Arial, Helvetica" SIZE=2>Company:</FONT>
</TD>
<TD><FONT FACE="Arial, Helvetica" SIZE=2><B><%=Server.HTMLEn-
code(objIADs.Get("Company"))%></B></FONT>
</TD>
</TR>

<TR><TD ALIGN=RIGHT><FONT FACE="Arial, Helvetica" SIZE=2>City:</FONT>
</TD>
<TD VALIGN=TOP><FONT FACE="Arial, Helvetica" SIZE=2><B><%=Server.HTMLEn-
code(objIADs.Get("l"))%></B></FONT></TD>

<TD> </TD>
<TD> </TD>

<TD ALIGN=RIGHT><FONT FACE="Arial, Helvetica" SIZE=2>Department:</FONT>
</TD>
<TD><FONT FACE="Arial, Helvetica" SIZE=2><B><%=Server.HTMLEn-
code(objIADs.Get("department"))%></B></FONT>
</TD>

</TR>

<TR>
<TD ALIGN=RIGHT><FONT FACE="Arial, Helvetica" SIZE=2>State:</FONT></TD>
<TD><FONT FACE="Arial, Helvetica" SIZE=2><B><%=Server.HTMLEn-
code(objIADs.Get("st"))%></B></FONT></TD>

<TD> </TD>
<TD> </TD>

<TD ALIGN=RIGHT><FONT FACE="Arial, Helvetica" SIZE=2>Office:</FONT></TD>
<TD><FONT FACE="Arial, Helvetica" SIZE=2><B>
<%=Server.HTMLEncode(objIADs.Get("physicalDeliveryOfficeName"))%>
</B></FONT></TD>
</TR>

<TR>
<TD ALIGN=RIGHT><FONT FACE="Arial, Helvetica" SIZE=2>Zip Code:</FONT>
</TD>
<TD><FONT FACE="Arial, Helvetica" SIZE=2><B>
<%=Server.HTMLEncode(objIADs.Get("postalCode"))%></B></FONT></TD>
```

```
<TD> </TD>
<TD> </TD>

<TD ALIGN=RIGHT><FONT FACE="Arial, Helvetica" SIZE=2>Assistant:</FONT>
</TD>
<TD><FONT FACE="Arial, Helvetica" SIZE=2><B>
<%=Server.HTMLEncode(objIADs.Get("secretary"))%></B></FONT></TD>
</TR>

<TR><TD ALIGN=RIGHT><FONT FACE="Arial, Helvetica" SIZE=2>Country:</FONT>
</TD>
<TD><FONT FACE="Arial, Helvetica" SIZE=2><B>
<%=Server.HTMLEncode(objIADs.Get("co"))%></B></FONT></TD>

<TD> </TD>
<TD> </TD>

<TD ALIGN=RIGHT><FONT FACE="Arial, Helvetica" SIZE=2>Phone:</FONT></TD>
<TD><FONT FACE="Arial, Helvetica" SIZE=2><B>
<%=Server.HTMLEncode(objIADs.Get("telephoneNumber"))%></B></FONT></TD>
</TR>
</TABLE>
</DIV>
```

The mailbox that the user wants to query is passed to the ASP page. Using the *GetObject* method, the code opens the mailbox in the Exchange Server directory and sets an object variable, *objIADs*, to that mailbox. Throughout much of the remaining code, the *Get* method of the *objIADs* object is used to retrieve specific attributes on the mailbox.

The most interesting pieces of code besides the code for retrieving attributes include those that retrieve the person's manager and direct reports from the directory. In the application, the manager's name is displayed as a hyperlink on the Organization tab so users can quickly look up the manager's directory information. The person's direct reports are also displayed as hyperlinks on the Organization tab so users can look at the direct report's directory information as well. Figure 13-6 shows a sample of these hyperlinks.

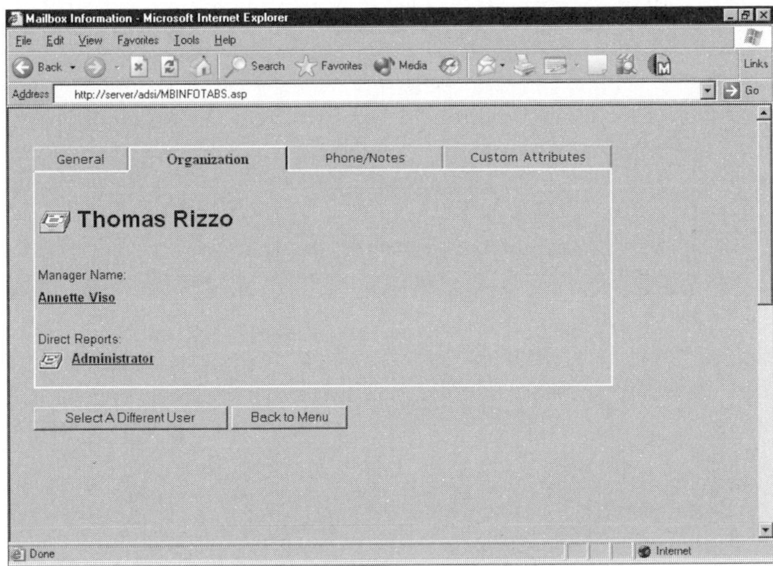

Figure 13-6 The Organization tab for a queried mailbox displays the manager and direct reports as hyperlinks.

The following code implements the hyperlink functionality:

```
<TABLE border=0>
<TR>
<TD ALIGN=LEFT NoWrap><FONT FACE="Arial, Helvetica" SIZE=2>
Manager Name:</FONT></TD>
<TR> </TR>
<%
    strManager = objIADs.Get("manager")
    strManagerPath = "LDAP://" & Session("Server") & "/" & strManager
    Set oIADsManager = GetObject(strManagerPath)
    strManagercn = Server.HTMLEncode(oIADsManager.Get("cn"))
%>
<TR>
<TD><FONT FACE="Arial, Helvetica" SIZE=2><B>
<A Href='MBINFOTABS.ASP?Path=<%=strManagerPath%>'><%=strManagercn%></A>
</B></FONT></TD>
</TR>
<TR><TD> </TD></TR>
<TR><TD ALIGN=LEFT><FONT FACE="Arial, Helvetica" SIZE=2>Direct Reports:</
FONT></TD></TR>

<%
    Err.clear
    strReports = objIADs.GetEx("directReports")
    If lBound(strReports) <0 Then
%>
```

```
    <TR><TD><FONT FACE="Arial, Helvetica" SIZE=2><B> 
 No Direct Reports Found
 </B></FONT></TD></TR>
<%
    Else
        For i = LBound(strReports) To UBound(strReports)
            'Get each DS object to return the friendly name
            strDirectPath = "LDAP://" & Session("Server") & _
                "/" & strReports(i)
            Set oIADsReports = GetObject(strDirectPath)
            strReportscn = Server.HTMLEncode(oIADsReports.Get("cn"))
%>
            <TR><TD><FONT FACE="Arial, Helvetica" SIZE=2><B>
            <img src="mailboxs.jpg" ALIGN="Middle"> 
   <A Href='MBINFOTABS.ASP?Path=<%=strDirectPath%>'>
                <%=strReportscn%></A>
            </B></FONT></TD></TR>
<%
        Next
    End If
%>
</TR>
</TABLE>
```

When you retrieve the manager property from the Exchange Server directory, the directory returns the distinguished name of the manager. To retrieve the display name of the manager, the code uses the distinguished name to create a full *AdsPath* to the directory object that corresponds to the manager. Then the code opens that object and retrieves the display name of the manager.

To retrieve the direct reports, the code uses the *GetEx* method in ADSI. (Recall that the *reports* attribute is a multivalued property. You must use *GetEx* when you retrieve multivalued properties from Active Directory.) The *GetEx* code returns an array of distinguished names for all of the person's direct reports. The code loops through each direct report in the array and displays as a hyperlink an image and the full name of each direct report.

Creating a Custom Recipient

Creating a custom recipient is straightforward. A custom recipient has *contact* as the object class, and you must set the *targetAddress* property of the custom recipient, which specifies the actual e-mail address of the recipient.

The following code creates a custom recipient using ADSI:

```
On Error Resume Next
Err.Clear
smtp = Request.Form("SMTP")
fn = Request.Form("FN")
ln = Request.Form("LN")
```

```
dn = Request.Form("DN")
al = Request.Form("AL")

Set oIADs = GetObject("LDAP:")
bstr1 = "LDAP://" + Session("Server") + "/CN=" + Session("CN") + _
    "," + Session("DC")
bstr2 = Session("bstr2")
bstr3 = Session("bstr3")

Set oContainer = GetObject(bstr1)
Set oIADs = oContainer.Create("contact", "cn=" + CStr(dn))

oIADs.Put "mail", CStr(SMTP)
oIADs.Put "targetAddress", CStr(SMTP)

oIADs.Put "givenName", CStr(fn)
oIADs.Put "sn", CStr(ln)
oIADs.Put "displayName", CStr(dn)
oIADs.SetInfo
```

Displaying the Members of a Distribution List

The sample application allows you to display the members of a distribution list in an HTML table, as shown in Figure 13-7. This table is generated by using a *For...Each* construct to scroll through the collection returned by the *Members* method of the *IADsGroup* interface. After retrieving the object that corresponds to each member, the code checks the object class and displays the correct identifier for each member, such as mailbox, distribution list, or custom recipient. Remember that distribution lists can hold different types of objects. The code that displays the members of a distribution list is shown here:

```
<HTML>
<HEAD>
<TITLE>Display Users in a DL</TITLE>
</HEAD>
<BODY>
<h1>The members of this DL are:</h1>

<hr>

<form METHOD="POST" NAME="INFO" ACTION="">
<input TYPE="button" VALUE="Back to Main Menu"
  OnClick='window.location="menu.asp";'>
  <input TYPE="button" VALUE="Select different container" OnClick='window.loca-
tion="logon.asp?diffcont=1";'>
</FORM>
<P>
<TABLE BORDER=1 bgcolor="#79AA86">
<%
```

```
Dim oIADs
Dim MyContainer
Dim objRecipients
Dim item
On Error Resume Next
Err.Clear
strDLName = Request.Form ("DLSELECT")

Set oIADs = GetObject("LDAP:")
bstr1 = strDLName
bstr2 = Session("bstr2")
bstr3 = Session("bstr3")

Set objDL = GetObject(bstr1)

Response.Write "<TR><TD><B>Class</TD><TD><B>Display Name</TD><TD><B>Alias</
TD><TD><B>Directory Name</TD></TR>"

For Each item In objDL.Members
    Set objitem =  GetObject(item.ADSPath)
    strClass = objitem.Get("class")
    Select Case strClass
        Case "organizationalPerson"
            Response.Write "<TD>MailBox</TD><TD>" & objitem.Get("cn") & _
                           "</TD><TD>" & objitem.Mail & "</TD><TD>" & _
                           objitem.Name & "</TD></TR>"
        Case "person"
            Response.Write "<TD>Custom Recipient</TD><TD>" & _
                           objitem.Get("cn") & "</TD><TD>" & _
                           objitem.Get("mailNickname") & "</TD><TD>" & _
                           objitem.Name & "</TD></TR>"
        Case "group"
            Response.Write "<TD>Distribution List</TD><TD>" & _
                           objitem.Get("cn") & "</TD><TD>" & _
                           objitem.Get("mailNickname") & "</TD><TD>" & _
                           objitem.Name & "</TD></TR>"
        Case Else
            Response.Write "<TD>" & item.Class & "</TD><TD>" & _
                           objitem.Get("cn") & "</TD><TD>" & _
                           objitem.get("mailNickname") & "</TD><TD>" & _
                           objitem.Name & "</TD></TR>"
        End Select
Next
%>
</TABLE>
```

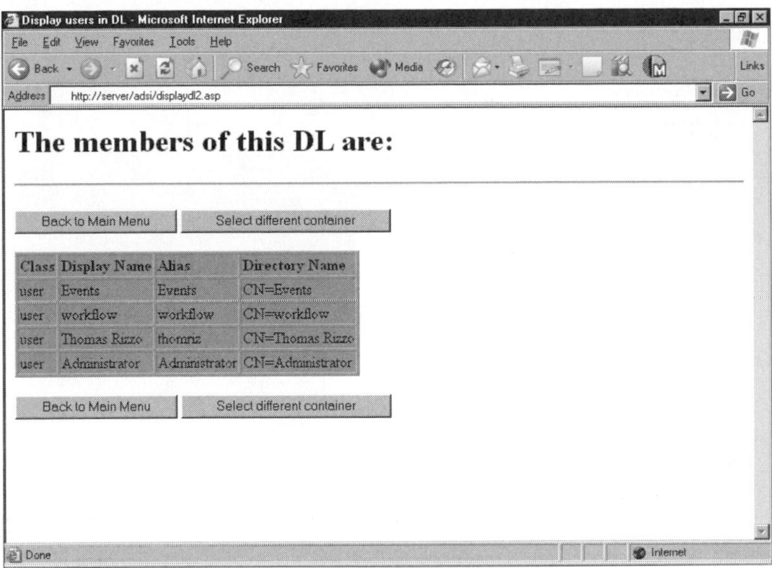

Figure 13-7 An HTML table of the members in a specific distribution list

> **Note** By default, Active Directory returns only 100 results, so you might want to increase the number of results returned for LDAP queries. If you are using ADO with the Active Directory OLEDB provider, you can do this by increasing the *PageSize* property.

The Org Chart Sample Application

To show you another example of how to use your ADSI skills against the Active Directory, I created a simple Web-based application that draws an organizational chart. Figure 13-8 shows the application's logon page, where the user can type the name of a person and execute an ASP page that sets the correct credentials for the directory and then calls the organizational chart ASP program.

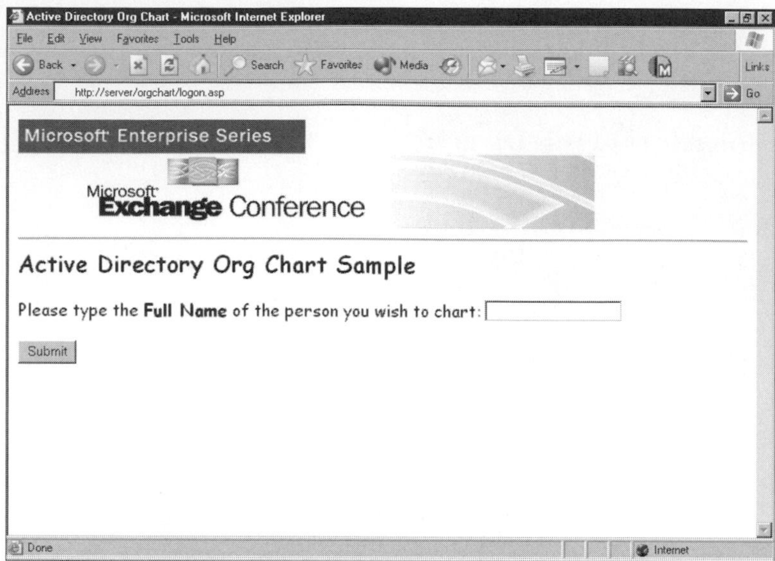

Figure 13-8 The logon page for the ADSI Org Chart application

ADSI makes working with Active Directory and Exchange Server information easy. The code for the query follows.

```
<%
'Get information from Active Directory

Set oIADs = GetObject("LDAP:")
bstr1 = "LDAP://" + Session("Server") + "/cn=" + strUser + ",cn=" + _
        Session("cn") + ",dc=" + Session("Domain") + ",dc=" + _
        Session("DC") + ",dc=" + Session("OU") + ",dc=" + Session("o")


bstr2 = Session("bstr2")
bstr3 = Session("bstr3")


Set objIADs = oIADs.OpenDSObject(bstr1, bstr2, bstr3, 0)
'Response.Write objIADs.Get("manager")
'Get the current person's information
strDisplayName = objIADs.Get("displayName")
strOffice = objIADs.Get("physicalDeliveryOfficeName")
strTelephone = objIADs.Get("telephoneNumber")
strTitle = objIADs.Get("title")
strcn = objIADs.Get("cn")
'Try to retrieve the Mail property
strmail = ""
strmail = objIADs.Get("mail")
If strmail = "" Then
```

```
    'Try getting mailNickname
    strmail = objIADs.Get("mailNickname")
End If
'Response.Write "strcn= " & strcn
strManager = objIADs.Get("manager")
'Response.Write strManager
strManagerPath = "LDAP://" & Session("Server") & "/" & strManager
'Response.Write strManagerPath
set oIADsManager = oIADS.OpenDSObject(strManagerPath,bstr2,bstr3,0)
strManagercn = oIADsManager.Get("cn")
'Try to retrieve the Mail property
strManagerMail = ""
strManagerMail = oIADsManager.Get("mail")
If strManagerMail = "" Then
    strManagerMail = oIADsManager.Get("mailNickname")
End If
'Response.Write "mcn=" & strManagercn
strManagerOffice = oIADsManager.Get("physicalDeliveryOfficeName")
strManagerTelephone = oIADsManager.Get("telephoneNumber")
strManagerTitle = oIADsManager.Get("title")
strManagerDisplayName = oIADsManager.Get("displayName")
strReports = objIADs.GetEx("directReports")
%>

<!DOCTYPE HTML PUBLIC "-//IETF//DTD HTML 3.2//EN">
<HTML>
<HEAD>
<Title>Web Org-Chart (java version)</Title>
</HEAD>
<center><font face=Verdana size=6><B>From Active

Directory</B></center></font>
<p align="CENTER">

<applet
   codebase="java"
   code=JOrgChart.class
   id=JOrgChart
   width=480
   <% if UBound(strReports) = LBound(strReports) then
         iHeight = 0
      else
         iHeight = UBound(strReports)
      end if
   %>
   height=<%=(Int(iHeight/2)+3)*65%>>
   <param name=HostName value="<% =ROOTURL %>?Alias=">
   <param name=Root value="<%=strManagerDisplayName%>?
            <%=strManagerMail%>?
            <%=EmptyToNA(strManagerTitle)%>?
            <%=EmptyToNA(strManagerOffice)%>?
            <%=EmptyToNA(strManagerTelephone)%>">
   <param name=L1Node
```

```
value="<%=strDisplayName%>?<%=strMail%>?<%=EmptyToNA(strTitle)%>?<%=Empty

ToNA(strOffice)%>?<%=EmptyToNA(strTelephone)%>">
<%
   For i = LBound(strReports) To UBound(strReports)

      strLogonName = left(strReports(i),(instr(1,strReports(i),",")-1))

         'Get each DS object to return the friendly name
         strDirectPath = "LDAP://" & Session("Server") &
                         "/" & strReports(i)
         set oIADsReports = oIADs.OpenDSObject(strDirectPath, bstr2,bstr3,0)
         strReportscn = oIADsReports.Get("cn")
         'Try to get the mail address
         strReportsMail = ""
         strReportsMail = oIADsReports.Get("mail")
         If strReportsMail = "" Then
            strReportsMail = oIADsReports.Get("mailNickname")
         End If
         strReportsOffice = oIADsReports.Get("physicalDeliveryOfficeName")
         strReportsTelephone = oIADsReports.Get("telephoneNumber")
         strReportsTitle = oIADsReports.Get("title")
         strReportsDisplayName = oIADsReports.Get("displayName")
%>
   <param name=L2Node<%=i%> value="<%=strReportsDisplayName%>?
            <%=strReportsMail%>?
            <%=EmptyToNA(strReportsTitle)%>?
            <%=EmptyToNA(strReportsOffice)%>?


<%=EmptyToNA(strReportsTelephone)%>">
<%
   Next
%>

</applet>
</p>
<P>
<B>Select a different alias by clicking <a href="logon.asp">here.</B>
</BODY>
```

Getting Help with ADSI

This chapter's examples show the most common features you will want to program using ADSI with Active Directory, but ADSI offers a lot more functionality.

If you want to learn more about ADSI and Active Directory, I recommend that you review the ADSI information in the MSDN Library. Also, to make it easier to visualize the relationships among the objects in the Active Directory hierarchy, you can use the program named Active Directory Browser (adsvw.exe), which is included with the companion files. This program draws out the hierarchy of any directory service using ADSI and allows you to query and browse the objects and properties contained in a specific directory, as shown in Figure 13-9. This program is an invaluable tool for helping you discover the objects and attributes contained in Active Directory.

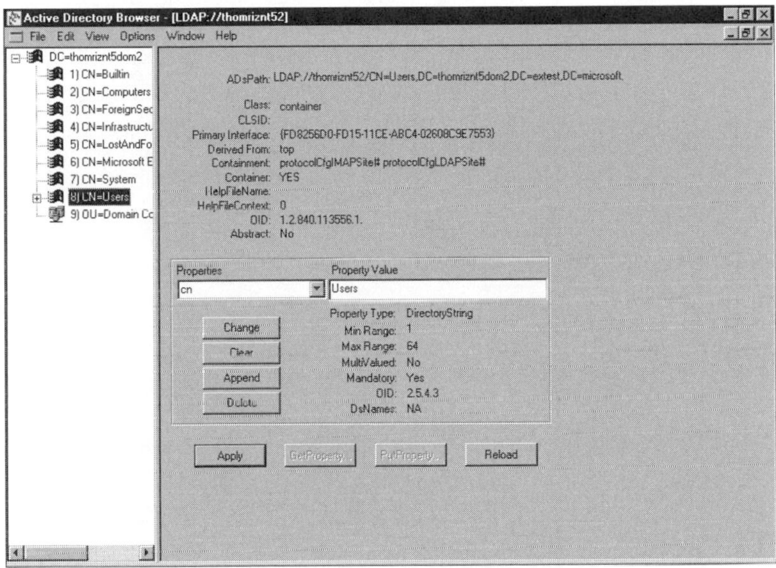

Figure 13-9 The Active Directory Browser program, which graphically displays the relationships and attributes of the objects contained in any directory that you can connect to using ADSI

LDP

The LDP tool, which is included in the Windows 2000 Resource Kit, provides a graphical, low-level interface for LDAP operations such as *Bind*, *Search*, *Modify*, and *Delete*. You can use LDP with any LDAP-compliant directory, such as Active Directory or the Exchange Server 5.5 directory. Figures 13-10 and 13-11 show the LDP tool working with Active Directory.

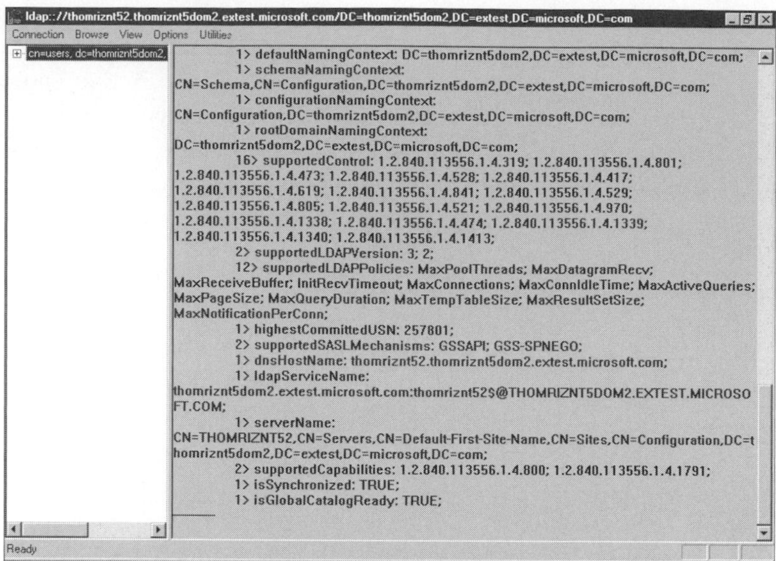

Figure 13-10 LDP at work, connecting to Active Directory

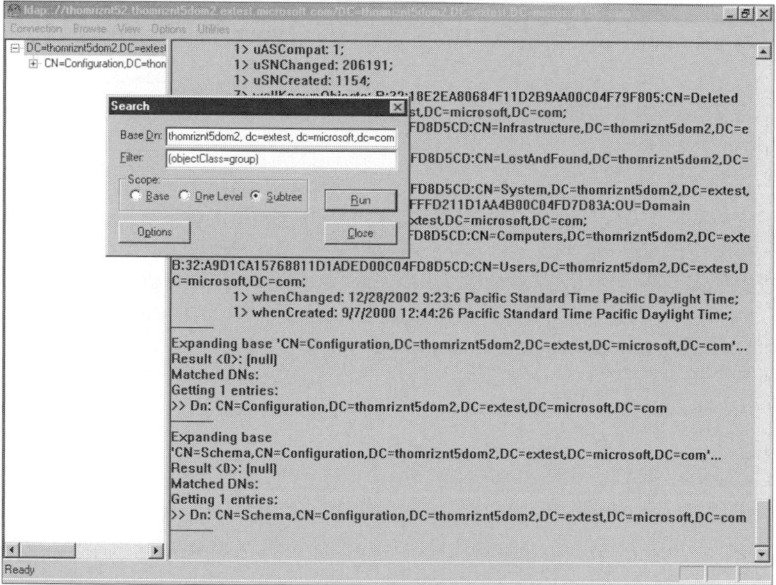

Figure 13-11 Using LDP to search for distribution lists in Active Directory

ADSI Edit

ADSI Edit is a Microsoft Management Console (MMC) snap-in that allows you low-level access to Active Directory by using ADSI interfaces. You can use this tool, shown in Figure 13-12, to browse and modify information in Active Directory.

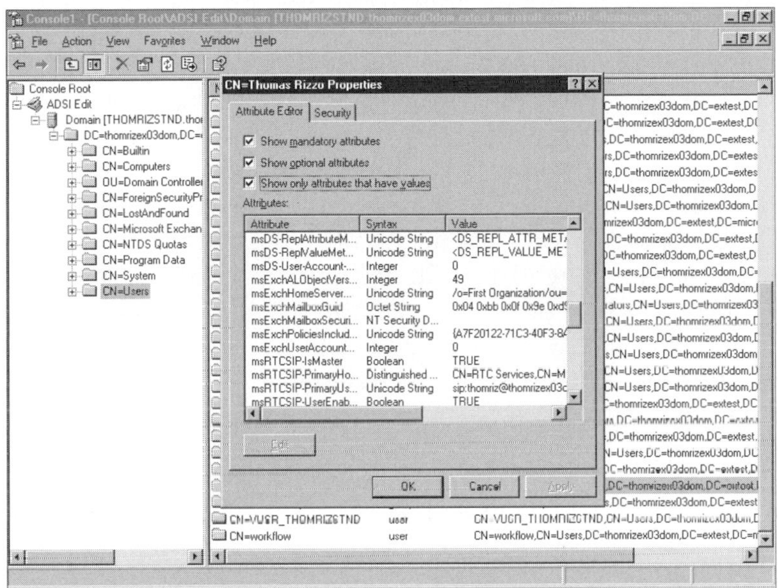

Figure 13-12 ADSI Edit working with Active Directory

ADSI Support in .NET

To support programming against ADSI in managed code, the .NET Framework provides the *System.DirectoryServices* namespace. Rather than forcing you to write legacy code to COM interfaces, which would degrade performance, the *System.DirectoryServices* namespace is implemented as all managed code, although COM versions of ADSI still work inside of .NET. If you need to maintain legacy applications, you should still write to the COM interfaces. However, for any new development that you want to perform using .NET, you should leverage the *System.DirectoryServices* namespace.

The .NET Framework SDK includes the complete documentation for this namespace. I'll cover just a subset of the functionality of this namespace next. We will look at three tasks that you will commonly perform with this namespace against Active Directory: searching, reading entries, and writing entries. Please note that the *DirectoryServices* namespace works with more than just the LDAP provider and Active Directory. You can also use it with IIS, NDS, and WinNT providers.

Searching Active Directory Using the *DirectoryServices* Namespace

You will primarily use two classes in the *DirectoryServices* namespace: *DirectoryEntry* and *DirectorySearcher*. The *DirectoryEntry* class is for accessing a node in the directory; we'll discuss it when we look at reading and writing entries in the directory. The *DirectorySearcher* class is used to search the directory. The result it returns is a .NET collection, which you can iterate through.

The first thing you do with the *DirectorySearcher* class is to construct a new object of that class. The constructor for the class takes an optional argument—the search base where the search will start. If you do not specify the search base, the search base will default to the domain. You can specify the search base at a later point using the *SearchRoot* property.

Next, you specify a search scope. The search scope can be *Base* (this level only), *OneLevel* (first-level children), or *Subtree* (entire subtree below the base). You set the search scope using the *SearchScope* property on the instance of your *DirectorySearch* class.

Next you specify the LDAP filter you want to use to search the directory. Here are some examples of filters:

- **(objectClass=*)** All objects
- **(sn=n*)** All objects where the surname starts with *n*
- **(&(objectCategory=Person)(objectClass=user))** All users
- **(&(objectCategory=Person)(mail=*))** All users with e-mail addresses
- **(|(department=100)(department=200))** All objects in department 100 or 200

The next step is to specify the properties to load by using the *PropertiesToLoad* collection's *Add* method. If you do not specify the properties to load, ADSI will load all properties for the returned objects.

You can optionally specify the page size, size limit, server time limit, and other properties. The page size is useful if you believe that a large number of results will be returned. Instead of dumping all the results back, ADSI will return pages of results based on the size you specify.

The final step before getting your results is to perform the search by calling the *FindAll* method. This method performs the search and returns a collection of all objects that meet your criteria. The key thing about the results that are returned is that they are read-only. If you want to modify a result, you should request its associated *DirectoryEntry* object by using the *GetDirectoryEntry* method on the returned result object. You can access any of the properties that are returned in your results using the notation *object.Properties("property-name").Item(0)*.

The following code, from the WinForms sample that's included with the companion files, shows how to use the *DirectorySearch* class:

```
On Error Resume Next
If txtLDAPPath.Text <> "" Then
    Dim oRoot As New _
        System.DirectoryServices.DirectoryEntry(txtLDAPPath.Text)
    Dim strAlias As String
    strAlias = txtAlias.Text

    Dim oSearcher As New _
        System.DirectoryServices.DirectorySearcher(oRoot)
    'Can change search base using SearchRoot
    'oSearcher.SearchRoot = "NewSearchBase"
    'Set the search to subtree to search entire tree
    oSearcher.SearchScope = DirectoryServices.SearchScope.Subtree
    oSearcher.Filter = "(mailNickname=" + strAlias + ")"
    oSearcher.PropertiesToLoad.Add("cn")
    oSearcher.PropertiesToLoad.Add("title")
    oSearcher.PropertiesToLoad.Add("department")
    oSearcher.PropertiesToLoad.Add("physicalDeliveryOfficeName")
    oSearcher.PropertiesToLoad.Add("telephoneNumber")

    Dim oResults As System.DirectoryServices.SearchResultCollection
    oResults = oSearcher.FindAll()

    Dim oResult As System.DirectoryServices.SearchResult
    For Each oResult In oResults
        MsgBox(oResult.Path)
        MsgBox(oResult.Properties("cn").Item(0))
        MsgBox(oResult.Properties("title").Item(0))
        MsgBox(oResult.Properties("department").Item(0))
        MsgBox(oResult.Properties("physicalDeliveryOfficeName").Item(0))
        MsgBox(oResult.Properties("telephoneNumber").Item(0))
        'You can get the Directory Entry by calling
        Dim oEntry As System.DirectoryServices.DirectoryEntry = _
            oResult.GetDirectoryEntry
        MsgBox(oEntry.Path)
    Next oResult
Else
    MsgBox("You must enter an LDAP path!", vbOKOnly + vbExclamation)
End If
```

Reading and Writing Entries

Instead of searching for entries in the directory, if you know the path of the entry you want to view, you can use the *DirectoryEntry* class. This class allows you to create, read, write, rename, move, enumerate, or delete children in the directory. The first thing to do when you create your *DirectoryEntry* instance is to either pass the path to the constructor of the directory object you want to open or pass nothing to the constructor. If you pass nothing to the constructor, the Active Directory Locator Service will help you find the right directory server to work with.

You can also navigate through the directory hierarchy by using the *DirectoryEntry* class. You can get the parent of the current node by using the *Parent* property. You can get the children by using the *Children* property, which returns a collection containing the children. If you want to find a specific child, you can use the *Find* method and pass along the directory identifier you want to use to find the specified child, such as *cn=Username.*

The *DirectoryEntry* object also provides access to the properties contained in the directory object it is associated with. You can use the *Properties* collection to view specific properties contained in the directory object. Because this is a collection, it can hold a single value or multiple values. When you use the *Value* property on the *Properties* collection, this is the same thing as asking for the first element in the collection, such as *object.Properties.Item(0).value.*

Sometimes you might want to modify a property. To do this, you just set the property to the new value. If you simply want to add a value, use the *AddRange* method. Be sure to call *CommitChanges* after modifying the properties.

To add an entry, you just call the *Add* method and pass the name of the new entry and the schema class name for the new entry. This method returns a *DirectoryEntry* object. Set the appropriate mandatory properties according to the directory service you are using, and then call *CommitChanges.*

To remove an entry, you just call the *Remove* method and pass the name of the child you want to remove. If you want to remove an entire tree, call the *DeleteTree* method.

The following sample shows you how to use the *DirectoryEntry* object to read and write directory properties:

```
Try
    Dim oDE As New _
        System.DirectoryServices.DirectoryEntry(txtLDAPPath.Text)
    'You could also use either of these:
    'Dim oDE As New _
    '    System.DirectoryServices.DirectoryEntry(txtLDAPPath.Text, _
    '    "username", "password")
    'Dim oDE As New _
```

```
    '    System.DirectoryServices.DirectoryEntry(txtLDAPPath.Text, _
    '    "", "", System.DirectoryServices.AuthenticationTypes.Secure)

    'Msgbox some properties
    MsgBox(oDE.Properties("cn").Value)
    MsgBox(oDE.Properties("title").Value)

    'Get the children
    Dim oDEChildren As System.DirectoryServices.DirectoryEntries
    oDEChildren = oDE.Children()

    Dim oDEChild As System.DirectoryServices.DirectoryEntry
    For Each oDEChild In oDEChildren
        MsgBox(oDEChild.Properties("cn").Value)
    Next

    'You can also find specific children using Find()
    'Find a user with cn=Thomas Rizzo
    Dim oTRDE As System.DirectoryServices.DirectoryEntry = _
        oDEChildren.Find("CN=Thomas Rizzo")
    MsgBox(oTRDE.Properties("cn").Value)
    'Modify a property
    oTRDE.Properties("title").Value = "King of the World!"
    'Need to commit changes!
    oTRDE.CommitChanges()

    'Example: Create a new entry
    Dim oBGDE As System.DirectoryServices.DirectoryEntry = _
        oDEChildren.Add("CN=Bill Gates", "user")
    'Set the appropriate mandatory properties defined by the
    'directory service
    oBGDE.Properties("X").Value = "y"
    'Call CommitChanges
    oBGDE.CommitChanges()
Catch
    MsgBox("There was an error.  " & Err.Number & " " & Err.Description)
End Try
```

Calling Native ADSI Interfaces

Not all ADSI functions are exposed via *System.DirectoryServices*. This means that sometimes you might need to call directly to the previous version of ADSI. You don't have to include both libraries in your application, however—the *DirectoryEntry* class provides an *Invoke* method that allows you to call the non-managed version of ADSI to perform your function. For example, *Directory-Entry* does not expose the *SetPassword* method, but ADSI does. Using the

Invoke method, as shown in the following code, you can call the *SetPassword* method in ADSI:

```
Dim oDE As New System.DirectoryServices.DirectoryEntry(txtLDAPPath.Text)
'Need to pass a param array with the call for any parameters
'to the ADSI call
Try
    Dim oObject(0) As Object
    oObject(0) = "NewPassword"
    oDE.Invoke("SetPassword", oObject)
Catch
    MsgBox("Error! " & Err.Number & " " & Err.Description)
End Try
```

Disposing of Connections

When you work with the *DirectoryServices* namespace, connections to the directory are cached if you are accessing the same server with the same username, password, and port number. If you no longer need the connection, you should implicitly call the *Dispose* method to close the connection and free the resources used by the connection.

Authenticating Against Active Directory Using Forms-Based Authentication

When you work with the *DirectoryServices* library, you might want to use .NET forms-based authentication and allow your program to pass a username and a password for authentication against Active Directory. The following C# code shows how to do this:

```
public bool IsUserValid(String uid, String pwd)
{
   DirectoryEntry entry = new DirectoryEntry(_path, uid, pwd,
      AuthenticationTypes.Delegation);

   try
   {
      //Bind to the native AdsObject to force authentication.
      Object obj = entry.NativeObject;
   }
   catch (System.Runtime.InteropServices.COMException e)
   {
      //Something happened. You will need to write code to see if it is
      //an Access Denied e.ErrorCode or something else.
      throw new Exception(ex.Message);
   }
   return true;
}
```

A More Complex Sample Application

The companion files include a more complex sample application. It is a console application that can expose the groups that a computer or a user is a member of. This code shows a number of techniques for using the DirectoryServices library. First is the use of the *schemafilter* property, which allows you to filter containers based on schemas of objects in the container. Second is the use of the *Invoke* method to call a native method on Active Directory. Here is the code from the sample application:

```
using System;
using System.DirectoryServices;
using System.Reflection;
using System.Collections;

namespace ADSI_Console_App
{
   /// <summary>
   /// Summary description for Class1.
   /// </summary>
   class Class1
   {
      /// <summary>
      /// The main entry point for the application.
      /// </summary>
      [STAThread]
      static void Main(string[] args)
      {
         try
         {
            //Replace thomriznt5dom2 with your domain
            GroupsMembers("WinNT://thomriznt5dom2/thomriznt52,computer");
            // groups in computer
            UserGroups("LDAP://
CN=Thomas Rizzo,CN=Users,DC=thomriznt5dom2,DC=extest,DC=microsoft,DC=com");
            // local groups member
            UserGroups("WinNT://thomriznt5dom2/thomriz,user");
            // local groups member
         }
         catch (Exception e)
         {
            Console.WriteLine("*** Exception: " + e);
         }
         return;
      }

      // ----------------------------------------
      // Get all members for groups in given root.
      static void GroupsMembers(string root_name)
      {
```

```
    Console.WriteLine("");
    Console.WriteLine(" --- Groups Members in: " + root_name);

    DirectoryEntry entryMachine = new DirectoryEntry(root_name);
    entryMachine.Children.SchemaFilter.Add("group");

    int kg = 0;
    foreach ( DirectoryEntry grp in entryMachine.Children )
    {
        Console.WriteLine("group: " + grp.Name);
        object members = grp.Invoke("Members");
        // IADsGroup method call

        if ( ++kg > 12 ) break;   // stop long output
        foreach ( object member in (IEnumerable)members)
        {
            try
            {
                DirectoryEntry memberEntry = new DirectoryEntry(member);
                // 'member' is an IAds ptr object
                Console.WriteLine("   member = " + memberEntry .Name);
            }
            catch (System.Runtime.InteropServices.COMException e)
            {
                Console.WriteLine("   !!! Bad Member. Hr: 0x" +
                Convert.ToString(e.ErrorCode,16) + " - " + e.Message);
            }
        }
    }
    Console.WriteLine("----");
}

// ----------------------------------------
// Get all groups which a user is member of.
static void UserGroups(string user_name)
{
    Console.WriteLine("");
    Console.WriteLine("--- User: " + user_name +
        " is the member of: ");

    DirectoryEntry entryUser = new DirectoryEntry(user_name);


    object groups = entryUser.Invoke("Groups");
    // IADsUser method call

    foreach ( object group in (IEnumerable)groups)
    {
        DirectoryEntry groupEntry  = new DirectoryEntry(group);
        // 'group' is an IAds ptr object
        Console.WriteLine("  group = " + groupEntry.Name);
    }
```

```
            Console.WriteLine(" --- ");
        }
    }
}
```

Directory Services Markup Language

Directory Services Markup Language (DSML) provides a means of representing directory structural information and directory operations as an XML document. DSML was created to allow XML-based enterprise applications to leverage profile and resource information from a directory in their native XML environment. DSML allows XML and directories to work together because it is based on standards such as XML, SOAP, and HTTP. It is approved by the Organization for the Advancement of Structural Information Standards (OASIS). DSML can run on Windows 2000 or Windows Server 2003.

DSML in Windows includes the following components:

- **SOAP listener component** This component intercepts DSMLv2 requests and sends back corresponding DSMLv2 responses.
- **Support for equivalent LDAP operations** This service performs equivalent LDAP operations such as *addRequest*, *modifyRequest*, and *searchRequest*. It also supports advanced operations such as LDAP controls and extended requests.
- **Session support** DSML was designed and based on the request/response protocol; DSML Services for Windows allows users to keep the state between requests by specifying the session ID in the SOAP header. This is useful for some LDAP control operations that might span multiple requests, such as a page-size control when browsing through a directory.
- **IIS security support** This service supports all IIS security configurations, including integrated Windows authentication, Basic authentication, Basic authentication over SSL, and Digest authentication.
- **Connection pooling** This service manages incoming requests and promotes scalability by sharing connections from a common pool.
- **Multiple configuration options** DSML supports many different configuration options to optimize performance, including the ability to customize ports, virtual directories, connections, timeouts, and other configuration parameters.

Working with DSML

DSML is SOAP-based, so you send your requests using a SOAP envelope with a LDAP payload; you get back a SOAP envelope with the response payload. We won't go through all the supported schema and methods in DSML in this section—you should look at the DSML documentation. Instead, we will look at some of the most common operations with DSML that you will implement with ADSI.

Basic DSML Payloads

The following SOAP envelope contains a blank DSML request to the server:

```
<se:Envelope xmlns:se="http://schemas.xmlsoap.org/soap/envelope/">
   <se:Body xmlns="urn:oasis:names:tc:DSML:2:0:core">
      <batchRequest/>
   </se:Body>
</se:Envelope>
```

As you can see in the request, you pass in the DSML namespace and then pass in a *batchRequest* element. *batchRequest* elements are different from *authRequest* elements and other request types. *batchRequest* elements are queries or modifications to the server. You can send multiple commands in a *batchRequest* and have the server process them in parallel or sequentially.

When you send this request, you get the following response from the DSML server (formatted for clarity):

```
<soap:Envelope
   xmlns:soap=http://schemas.xmlsoap.org/soap/envelope/
   xmlns:xsi="http://www.w3.org/2001/XMLSchema-instance"
   xmlns:xsd="http://www.w3.org/2001/XMLSchema"
   xmlns:soapenc="http://schemas.xmlsoap.org/soap/encoding/">
   <soap:Body>
      <batchResponse
         xmlns="urn:oasis:names:tc:DSML:2:0:core"
         xmlns:xsd="http://www.w3.org/2001/XMLSchema"
         xmlns:xsi="http://www.w3.org/2001/XMLSchema-instance">
      </batchResponse>
   </soap:Body>
</soap:Envelope>
```

This response contains a *batchResponse* element, which includes any response from the server for your *batchRequest*.

All of this is over HTTP, so you can leverage *XMLHTTP*, *ServerXMLHTTP*, or, in .NET, the *WebRequest* class to send and receive your DSML requests and responses.

DSML Samples

The following samples show some of the basic operations you can perform with DSML, along with the SOAP requests that perform the operations. To run these samples, get the sample DSML query application from the DSML SDK. These samples use XMLHTTP to send and receive its HTTP commands.

Reading an Object from Active Directory

The following request includes a *searchRequest* object, which searches Active Directory. The filter in the request is on the *objectclass*. In this case, the response will be all attributes on the object specified in the DN for the search request.

```
<se:Envelope xmlns:se="http://schemas.xmlsoap.org/soap/envelope/">
   <se:Body xmlns="urn:oasis:names:tc:DSML:2:0:core">
      <batchRequest>
         <searchRequestdn="cn=thomas rizzo,cn=users, dc=thomriznt5dom2,
         dc=extest,dc=microsoft,dc=com" scope="baseObject"
derefAliases="neverDerefAliases" sizeLimit="1000">
            <filter>
               <present name="objectclass"/>
            </filter>
         </searchRequest>
      </batchRequest>
   </se:Body>
</se:Envelope>
```

Adding an Object

To add an object, you use the *addRequest* element in your payload. The following example adds a new OU to your Active Directory. You can see the use of the *attr* element for setting attributes.

```
<se:Envelope xmlns:se="http://schemas.xmlsoap.org/soap/envelope/">
   <se:Body xmlns="urn:oasis:names:tc:DSML:2:0:core">
      <batchRequest xmlns="urn:oasis:names:tc:DSML:2:0:core"
      xmlns:xsd="http://www.w3.org/2001/XMLSchema">
         <addRequest dn="ou=MyNewOU,dc=thomriznt5dom2,dc=extest,
         dc=microsoft,dc=com">
            <attr name="objectClass">
            <value>organizationalUnit</value>
            </attr>
         </addRequest>
      </batchRequest>
   </se:Body>
</se:Envelope>
```

Modifying Objects

To modify an object, you send a *modifyRequest* element and also a modification element, which includes the name of the attribute you want to modify and the type of modification, which can be add, replace, or delete. The following example changes the OU description we created in the previous example and also replaces the telephone number for a user:

```
<se:Envelope xmlns:se="http://schemas.xmlsoap.org/soap/envelope/">
   <se:Body xmlns="urn:oasis:names:tc:DSML:2:0:core">
      <batchRequest>
         <modifyRequest dn="ou=MyNewOU,dc=thomriznt5dom2,dc=extest,
         dc=microsoft,dc=com">
            <modification name="description" operation="replace">
               <value>This is a sample OU</value>
            </modification>
         </modifyRequest>
         <modifyRequest dn="cn=Thomas Rizzo,cn=Users,dc=thomriznt5dom2,
         dc=extest,dc=microsoft,dc=com">
            <modification name="telephoneNumber" operation="replace">
               <value>555-1234</value>
            </modification>
         </modifyRequest>
      </batchRequest>
   </se:Body>
</se:Envelope>
```

Deleting Objects

To delete an object, you send a *delRequest* to the server with the DN of the object you want to delete. The following deletes the OU we created earlier:

```
<se:Envelope xmlns:se="http://schemas.xmlsoap.org/soap/envelope/">
   <se:Body xmlns="urn:oasis:names:tc:DSML:2:0:core">
      <batchRequest>
         <delRequest dn="ou=MyNewOU,dc=thomriznt5dom2,dc=extest,dc=microsoft,
         dc=com"/>
      </batchRequest>
   </se:Body>
</se:Envelope>
```

Performing Simple Searches

To perform a simple search, you send a *searchRequest* element. As part of this XML structure, you must pass a filter, which is the filter that Active Directory will filter the responses on. Also, you can pass an attribute structure that will be the set of attributes from Active Directory that you want returned in your response.

```
<se:Envelope xmlns:se="http://schemas.xmlsoap.org/soap/envelope/">
   <se:Body xmlns="urn:oasis:names:tc:DSML:2:0:core">
      <batchRequest>
         <searchRequest dn="cn=users,dc=thomriznt5dom2,dc=extest,dc=microsoft,
         dc=com" scope="singleLevel" derefAliases="neverDerefAliases"
         sizeLimit="1000">
            <filter>
               <present name="objectclass"/>
            </filter>
```

```
            <attributes>
               <attribute name="name"/>
               <attribute name="description"/>
               <attribute name="whenCreated"/>
               <attribute name="sAMAccountName"/>
            </attributes>
         </searchRequest>
      </batchRequest>
   </se:Body>
</se:Envelope>
```

Performing Advanced Searches

You can perform more advanced searches using the *searchRequest* structure. The following example shows searching for all contacts with a last name that starts with *R*. You can do equality or substring searches, and you can use *not* elements to negate search terms in your searches. Finally, you can also use matching rules that are defined in LDAP.

```
<se:Envelope xmlns:se="http://schemas.xmlsoap.org/soap/envelope/">
   <se:Body xmlns="urn:oasis:names:tc:DSML:2:0:core">
      <batchRequest>
         <searchRequest dn="cn=users,dc=thomriznt5dom2,dc=extest,dc=microsoft,
         dc=com" scope="wholeSubtree" derefAliases="neverDerefAliases"
         sizeLimit="10">
            <filter>
               <and>
                  <equalityMatch name="objectCategory">
                     <value>contact</value>
                  </equalityMatch>
                  <substrings name="sn">
                     <initial>R</initial>
                  </substrings>
               </and>
            </filter>
            <attributes>
               <attribute name="name"/>
               <attribute name="dn"/>
            </attributes>
         </searchRequest>
      </batchRequest>
   </se:Body>
</se:Envelope>
```

Session Support

The final topic we will look at for DSML is session support. You might want to maintain authentication or responses across multiple, separate requests. You can begin, use, and end a session using DSML. The following code begins a session:

```
<se:Envelope xmlns:se="http://schemas.xmlsoap.org/soap/envelope/" se:encoding-
Style="http://schemas.xmlsoap.org/soap/encoding/">
```

```
   <se:Header>
      <ad:BeginSession xmlns:ad="urn:schema-microsoft-com:activedirec-
tory:dsmlv2" se:mustUnderstand="1"/>
   </se:Header>
   <se:Body xmlns="urn:oasis:names:tc:DSML:2:0:core">
      <batchRequest xmlns="urn:oasis:names:tc:DSML:2:0:core" xmlns:xsd="http:
//www.w3.org/2001/XMLSchema" xmlns:xsi="http://www.w3.org/2001/XMLSchema-
instance"/>
   </se:Body>
</se:Envelope>
```

In the response to the *BeginSession* request, you get a *SessionID*. In your subsequent requests to the server, you should pass a header that specifies the *SessionID* as part of a *Session* element, as shown here:

```
<se:Envelope xmlns:se="http://schemas.xmlsoap.org/soap/envelope/" se:encoding-
Style="http://schemas.xmlsoap.org/soap/encoding/">
   <se:Header>
      <ad:Session xmlns:ad="urn:schema-microsoft-com:activedirectory:dsmlv2"
ad:SessionID="duZ0kbF+buULEdIlWR3S6P29" se:mustUnderstand="1"/>
   </se:Header>
   <se:Body xmlns="urn:oasis:names:tc:DSML:2:0:core">
      <batchRequest xmlns="urn:oasis:names:tc:DSML:2:0:core" xmlns:xsd="http:
//www.w3.org/2001/XMLSchema" xmlns:xsi="http://www.w3.org/2001/XMLSchema-
instance"/>
   </se:Body>
</se:Envelope>
```

To end your session, you must pass an *EndSession* header with the *SessionID* of the session you want to end:

```
<se:Envelope xmlns:se="http://schemas.xmlsoap.org/soap/envelope/" se:encoding-
Style="http://schemas.xmlsoap.org/soap/encoding/">
   <se:Header>
      <ad:EndSession xmlns:ad="urn:schema-microsoft-com:activedirec-
tory:dsmlv2" ad:SessionID="duZ0kbF+buULEdIlWR3S6P29" se:mustUnderstand="1"/>
   </se:Header>
   <se:Body xmlns="urn:oasis:names:tc:DSML:2:0:core">
      <batchRequest xmlns="urn:oasis:names:tc:DSML:2:0:core" xmlns:xsd="http:
//www.w3.org/2001/XMLSchema" xmlns:xsi="http://www.w3.org/2001/XMLSchema-
instance"/>
   </se:Body>
</se:Envelope>
```

Summary

This chapter showed you how to program Active Directory using ADSI and DSML. Using these technologies, you can use Active Directory to create and query objects in Active Directory. Combining Active Directory with the other Microsoft collaboration technologies allows you to build richer applications that have a replicated and powerful directory service that your applications can use.

14

Web Services and Exchange

XML Web services allow you to expose programmable services to other applications or programmers. You can build XML Web services in two ways. The first way is by using Microsoft Visual Studio 6.0 and the SOAP Toolkit. The second way is to use Visual Studio .NET, which has built-in support for building and consuming Web services. This section will look at both techniques—you can decide which way is best for your needs.

Building a Web Service Using Visual Studio 6.0 and the SOAP Toolkit

To build a Web service using Visual Studio 6.0 and the SOAP Toolkit, you must first download and install the SOAP Toolkit from *http://msdn.microsoft.com/soap*. Using the toolkit, building a Web service is easy—you simply create the DLL that will implement your functionality. The Toolkit takes your DLL and creates a Web Services Definition Language (WSDL) file that contains the description of the methods, their parameters, and their return values for the DLL that implements your Web service. For our example, we will implement a free/busy lookup Web service. The following code for our free/busy lookup DLL was written using Visual Basic. Notice that the DLL exposes a public function as the main entry point that other applications can call:

```
Public Function GetFreeBusy(strDirURL As String, _
                            strUserNames As String, _
                            strStartDate As String, _
```

```
                                strEndDate As String, _
                                strInterval As String) As String
On Error Resume Next
'This function looks up free/busy information for users.
'User names must be email addresses separated by commas.
'The return value is a string of freebusy values for
'the users, separated by commas.

'Make sure a directory URL was passed
If strDirURL = "" Then
    GetFreeBusy = "You must pass a directory URL " & _
                  "in the format LDAP://directory"
    Exit Function
End If

If Not (IsDate(strStartDate)) Then
    'Not a date
    GetFreeBusy = "Start Date is not a valid date!"
    Exit Function
End If

If Not (IsDate(strEndDate)) Then
    'Not a date
    GetFreeBusy = "End Date is not a valid date!"
    Exit Function
End If

If Not (IsNumeric(strInterval)) Then
    GetFreeBusy = "You must enter a number for the interval."
    Exit Function
ElseIf CInt(strInterval) <= 0 Then
    GetFreeBusy = "You must enter a positive number for the interval."
    Exit Function
End If

'Make sure that user names were passed
arrUserNames = Split(strUserNames, ",")
If UBound(arrUserNames) < 0 Then
    'No usernames passed.  Error and exit.
    GetFreeBusy = "There were no user names passed."
    Exit Function
End If

'Start building the string array for the free/busy info
strFreeBusy = ""
For x = LBound(arrUserNames) To UBound(arrUserNames)
    If strFreeBusy = "" Then
        strFreeBusy = strFreeBusy & PrivGetFreeBusy(arrUserNames(x), _
                      strDirURL, strStartDate, strEndDate, strInterval)
    Else
        strFreeBusy = strFreeBusy & "," & _
                      PrivGetFreeBusy(arrUserNames(x), strDirURL, _
                      strStartDate, strEndDate, strInterval)
    End If
```

```
    Next

    GetFreeBusy = strFreeBusy
End Function

Private Function PrivGetFreeBusy(strUserName as String, _
                                   strDirURL as String, _
                                   strStartDate as String, _
                                   strEndDate as String, _
                                   strInterval as String) As String
    On Error Resume Next
    Dim oAddressee As CDO.Addressee
    Set oAddressee = CreateObject("CDO.Addressee")
    oAddressee.EmailAddress = strUserName
    bFound = oAddressee.CheckName(strDirURL)
    If bFound = False Then
        PrivGetFreeBusy = "Could not resolve username: " & strUserName
        Exit Function
    End If

    'Get the freebusy information
    PrivGetFreeBusy = oAddressee.GetFreeBusy(strStartDate, strEndDate, _
                                               strInterval)
    Set oAddressee = Nothing
End Function
```

Next you generate a Web Service Description Language (WSDL) file and a Web Services Meta Language (WSML) file for your DLL. The WSDL file is an XML file that is a contract between the client and the server. It describes the format that the client should send to the server to call the Web service. The WSDL file for the free/busy Web service is shown here:

```
<?xml version='1.0' encoding='UTF-8' ?>
<!-- Generated 12/10/01 by Microsoft SOAP Toolkit WSDL File Generator,
Version 1.02.813.0 -->
<definitions  name ='VS6FB'   targetNamespace = 'http://tempuri.org/wsdl/'
   xmlns:wsdlns='http://tempuri.org/wsdl/'
   xmlns:typens='http://tempuri.org/type'
   xmlns:soap='http://schemas.xmlsoap.org/wsdl/soap/'
   xmlns:xsd='http://www.w3.org/2001/XMLSchema'
   xmlns:stk='http://schemas.microsoft.com/soap-toolkit/wsdl-extension'
   xmlns='http://schemas.xmlsoap.org/wsdl/'>
   <types>
      <schema targetNamespace='http://tempuri.org/type'
         xmlns='http://www.w3.org/2001/XMLSchema'
         xmlns:SOAP-ENC='http://schemas.xmlsoap.org/soap/encoding/'
         xmlns:wsdl='http://schemas.xmlsoap.org/wsdl/'
         elementFormDefault='qualified'>
      </schema>
   </types>
   <message name='FreeBusy.GetFreeBusy'>
      <part name='strDirURL' type='xsd:string'/>
      <part name='strUserNames' type='xsd:string'/>
```

```
        <part name='strStartDate' type='xsd:string'/>
        <part name='strEndDate' type='xsd:string'/>
        <part name='strInterval' type='xsd:string'/>
    </message>
    <message name='FreeBusy.GetFreeBusyResponse'>
        <part name='Result' type='xsd:string'/>
        <part name='strDirURL' type='xsd:string'/>
        <part name='strUserNames' type='xsd:string'/>
        <part name='strStartDate' type='xsd:string'/>
        <part name='strEndDate' type='xsd:string'/>
        <part name='strInterval' type='xsd:string'/>
    </message>
    <portType name='FreeBusySoapPort'>
        <operation name='GetFreeBusy' parameterOrder=
        'strDirURL strUserNames strStartDate strEndDate strInterval'>
            <input message='wsdlns:FreeBusy.GetFreeBusy' />
            <output message='wsdlns:FreeBusy.GetFreeBusyResponse' />
        </operation>
    </portType>
    <binding name='FreeBusySoapBinding' type='wsdlns:FreeBusySoapPort' >
        <stk:binding preferredEncoding='UTF-8'/>
        <soap:binding style='rpc'
        transport='http://schemas.xmlsoap.org/soap/http' />
        <operation name='GetFreeBusy' >
            <soap:operation
            soapAction='http://tempuri.org/action/FreeBusy.GetFreeBusy' />
            <input>
                <soap:body use='encoded'
                namespace='http://tempuri.org/message/'
                encodingStyle='http://schemas.xmlsoap.org/soap/encoding/' />
            </input>
            <output>
                <soap:body use='encoded'
                namespace='http://tempuri.org/message/'
                encodingStyle='http://schemas.xmlsoap.org/soap/encoding/' />
            </output>
        </operation>
    </binding>
    <service name='VS6FB' >
        <port name='FreeBusySoapPort' binding='wsdlns:FreeBusySoapBinding' >
            <soap:address location='http://thomriznt52/vs6fb/VS6FB.WSDL' />
        </port>
    </service>
</definitions>
```

SOAP also requires a server-based WSML file, which provides the information that maps the operations of the service (as described in the WSDL file) to specific methods of the COM object. The WSML file determines which COM object and method should be used to service any requests. The WSML file for the sample is shown here:

```
<?xml version='1.0' encoding='UTF-8' ?>
<!-- Generated 12/10/01 by Microsoft SOAP Toolkit WSDL File Generator,
```

```
Version 1.02.813.0 -->
<servicemapping name='VS6FB'>
   <service name='VS6FB'>
      <using PROGID='ExchWS.FreeBusy' cachable='0' ID='FreeBusyObject' />
      <port name='FreeBusySoapPort'>
         <operation name='GetFreeBusy'>
            <execute uses='FreeBusyObject' method='GetFreeBusy'
            dispID='1610809344'>
               <parameter callIndex='1' name='strDirURL'
               elementName='strDirURL' />
               <parameter callIndex='2' name='strUserNames'
               elementName='strUserNames' />
               <parameter callIndex='3' name='strStartDate'
               elementName='strStartDate' />
               <parameter callIndex='4' name='strEndDate'
               elementName='strEndDate' />
               <parameter callIndex='5' name='strInterval'
               elementName='strInterval' />
               <parameter callIndex='-1' name='retval'
               elementName='Result' />
            </execute>
         </operation>
      </port>
   </service>
</servicemapping>
```

You might wonder how to go about generating these files. Well, you could attempt to generate the files by hand, but a much simpler and less error-prone approach is to use the WSDL generator tool from the SOAP Toolkit (shown in Figure 14-1).

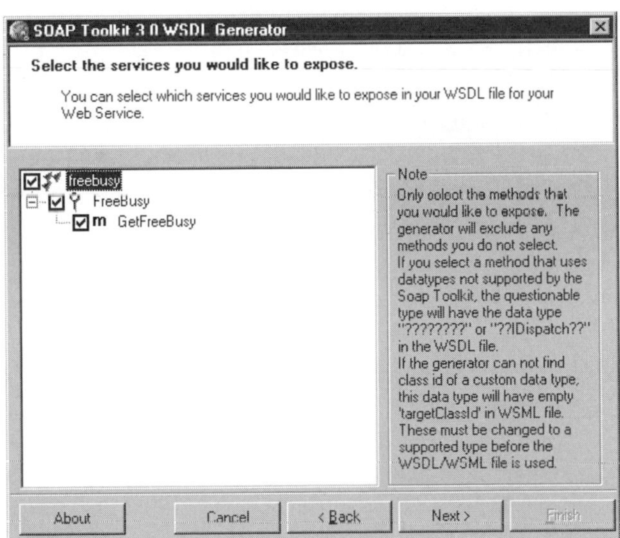

Figure 14-1 The WSDL generator tool from the SOAP Toolkit

This tool outputs the files you need to create and call your Web service. The only other thing you need to do is test the service. The sample includes a consumer of the Web service. It is just a simple Visual Basic application that allows you to specify users, dates, the directory server, and the free/busy interval to use. The sample is shown in Figure 14-2.

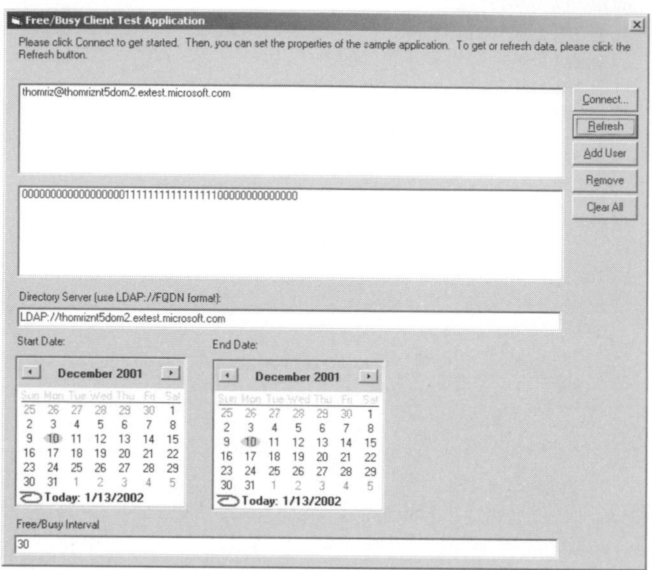

Figure 14-2 The free/busy Web service consumer application

The consumer application uses the Microsoft SOAP Type Library and its *SOAPClient* object to talk to the Web service. The *SOAPClient* object makes it easy to connect to and call methods on a Web service. As you can see in the following code from the consumer application, the *SOAPClient* object has an *MSSOAPINIT* method that takes a WSDL file and a WSML file as arguments. If the method can successfully open these files from the Web service, the *SOAPClient* object will be initialized and can be used against the Web service. The *SOAPClient* object can then call Web service methods directly, and you can retrieve any failures or errors through the *SOAPClient* object as well.

```
Option Explicit

Private mSoapClient As SoapClient
Dim strServerResponse As String

Private Sub cmdConnect_Click()
    On Error GoTo ErrorHandler
```

```
    'See if there are any users
    Dim NewSoapClient As New SoapClient
    Dim WSDL As String
    Dim WSML As String

    If frmConnect.Connect(Me, WSDL, WSML) Then
        Me.MousePointer = vbHourglass
        NewSoapClient.mssoapinit WSDL, , , WSML
        Set mSoapClient = NewSoapClient
        cmdRefresh.Enabled = True
        Me.MousePointer = vbNormal
    End If

    Exit Sub

ErrorHandler:

    Me.MousePointer = vbDefault

    If NewSoapClient.faultstring <> "" Then
        MsgBox "Connect failed. " & NewSoapClient.faultstring, _
                vbExclamation
    Else
        MsgBox "Connect failed. " & Err.Description, vbExclamation
    End If

    Err.Clear
End Sub

Private Sub cmdRefresh_Click()
    On Error GoTo ErrorHandler

    listResponse.Clear
    'Make sure the end date is not before the start date
    If DateDiff("d", monthStart.Value, monthEnd.Value) < 0 Then
        MsgBox "The end date must be after the start date!", _
                vbOKOnly + vbExclamation
        Exit Sub
    End If

    'Make sure interval is a #
    If Not (IsNumeric(txtInterval.Text)) Then
        MsgBox "You must enter a number for the interval.", _
                vbOKOnly + vbExclamation
        Exit Sub
    ElseIf CInt(txtInterval.Text) < 0 Then
        MsgBox "You must enter a number greater than zero.", _
                vbOKOnly + vbExclamation
        Exit Sub
    End If

    'Make sure there is a directory server
    If txtDirServer.Text = "" Then
```

```
        MsgBox "You must enter a directory server!", _
               vbOKOnly + vbExclamation
        Exit Sub
    End If

    Me.MousePointer = vbHourglass

    Dim strStartDate as String
    Dim strEndDate as String
    Dim strSMTPAddresses as String
    'Figure out start and end date
    strStartDate = monthStart.Value & " 12:00 AM"
    strEndDate = monthEnd.Value & " 11:59 PM"

    'Get the SMTP Addresses
    If listUsers.ListCount > 0 Then
        'Scroll through each user and separate with commas
        Dim i
        For i = 0 To listUsers.ListCount - 1
            If i = 0 Then
                strSMTPAddresses = listUsers.List(i)
            Else
                strSMTPAddresses = strSMTPAddresses & ", " & _
                                   listUsers.List(i)
            End If
        Next
    Else
        MsgBox "You must enter users in order to query the server!", _
               vbOKOnly + vbExclamation
        Me.MousePointer = vbNormal
        Exit Sub
    End If

    'Get the Response
    strServerResponse = mSoapClient.GetFreeBusy(txtDirServer.Text, _
                        strSMTPAddresses, strStartDate, strEndDate, _
                        txtInterval.Text)

    'Loop through the response and add it to the listbox
    Dim arrResponse
    arrResponse = Split(strServerResponse, ",")
    For i = LBound(arrResponse) To UBound(arrResponse)
        listResponse.AddItem arrResponse(i)
    Next

    Me.MousePointer = vbDefault
    Exit Sub

ErrorHandler:

    Me.MousePointer = vbDefault
    If mSoapClient.faultstring <> "" Then
        MsgBox "Could not refresh application. " & _
```

```
            mSoapClient.faultstring, vbExclamation
    Else
        MsgBox "Could not refresh application. " & Err.Description
    End If

    Err.Clear
End Sub
```

Building a Web Service Using Visual Studio .NET

As you saw with the Visual Studio 6.0 example, building and consuming a Web service is pretty straightforward. Visual Studio .NET makes it even easier to work with Web services because it has built-in tools that can add references to existing Web services and built-in methods for building Web services. To get started with our Visual Studio .NET example, we'll migrate our Visual Basic 6.0 Web service to Visual Basic .NET.

To be honest, the migration is not all that difficult. The only change to the underlying code will be the code for generating the Web service. To create the Visual Studio .NET Web service, you just select the ASP.NET Web service under the Visual Basic projects in Visual Studio .NET, as shown in Figure 14-3. (You can also create Web services using C#, as you'll see in the next section.)

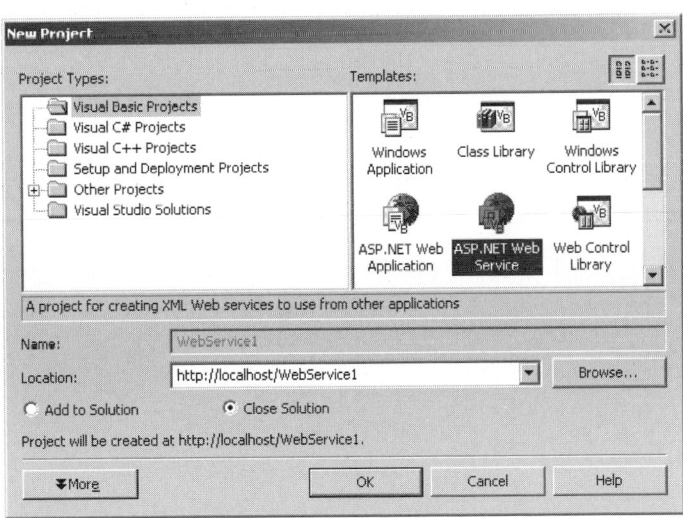

Figure 14-3 Creating a Visual Basic .NET Web service project

Visual Studio .NET creates a stub of a sample HelloWorld service, which you can use as a starting point. Notice in the following code that the *System.Web.Services* namespace is imported and the *WebService* and *WebMethod* attributes are added to our application. The rest of the code is the same as in our Visual Studio 6.0 service, so I've left some of it out.

```
Imports System.Web.Services

<WebService(Namespace := "http://tempuri.org/")> _
Public Class Service1
    Inherits System.Web.Services.WebService


    ' WEB SERVICE EXAMPLE
    ' The HelloWorld() example service returns the string Hello World.
    ' To build, uncomment the following lines then save and build the
    ' project.
    ' To test this web service, ensure that the .asmx file is the
    ' start page and press F5.
    '
    '<WebMethod()> Public Function HelloWorld() As String
    '    HelloWorld = "Hello World"
    ' End Function
    <WebMethod()> Public Function GetFreeBusy(ByVal strDirURL As String, _
    ByVal strUserNames As String, ByVal strStartDate As String, ByVal _
    strEndDate As String, ByVal strInterval As String) As String
        ⋮
    End Function

    Private Function PrivGetFreeBusy(ByVal strUserName as String, _
                                  ByVal strDirURL as String, _
                                  ByVal strStartDate as String, _
                                  ByVal strEndDate as String, _
                                  ByVal strInterval as String) as String
        ⋮
    End Function

End Class
```

To test the .NET version of our Web service, all we do is make sure our .asmx file is the start page for our application and then run the application. Visual Studio .NET will then launch our application. Figure 14-4 shows the test page for our Web service. We can fill in the parameters and try the service to see if it works.

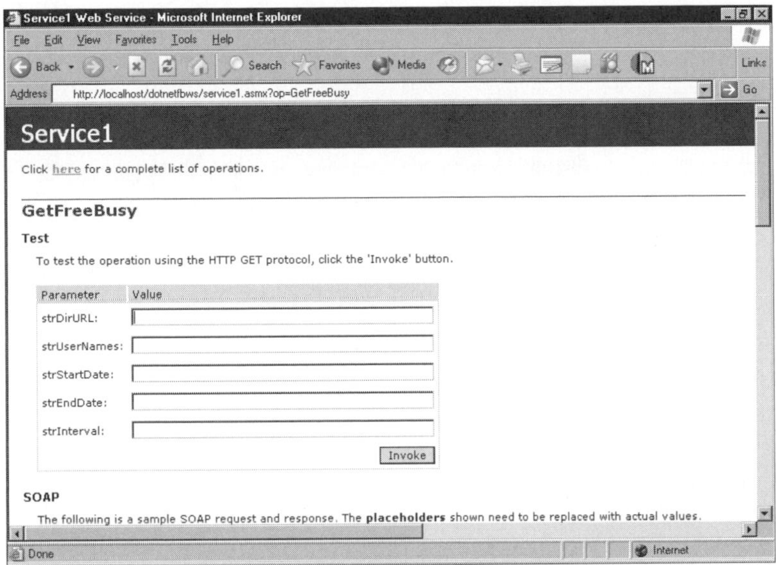

Figure 14-4 Testing the Web service

Building a Web Service Using C#

To give you a sense of programming in C#, we'll also build the free/busy Web service in that language. The difference between the Visual Basic and C# Web services is that the C# Web service uses Outlook Web Access (OWA) to return free/busy information rather than using Collaboration Data Objects (CDO); the C# service also has multiple methods. The C# Web service can return the free/busy information in three ways:

- As the raw XML returned by OWA
- As XML that the code formats, which makes the return value easier to understand
- As an ADO.NET dataset

We'll explore each option in detail.

Returning Raw Free/Busy Information

The first method of the Web service simply returns the raw XML free/busy information from the server. A typical response to this method looks like this:

```
<?xml version="1.0" encoding="utf-8" ?>
<string xmlns="http://tempuri.org/
```

```
"><a:response xmlns:a="WM"> <a:recipients> <a:item><a:displayname>All Attendees
</a:displayname><a:type>1</
a:type><a:fbdata>000000000000000000000000000000000000000000000000</a:fbdata></
a:item><a:item><a:displayname>Thomas Rizzo</
a:displayname><a:email type="SMTP">thomriz@thomrizex2kdom.extest.microsoft.com<
/a:email><a:type>1</
a:type><a:fbdata>000000000000000000000000000000000000000000000000</a:fbdata></
a:item> </a:recipients> </a:response></string>
```

Before we look at the code for this portion of the Web service, we'll first look at how the overall Web service is implemented in C#. As you will see, C# is different from Visual Basic in its syntax and is closer to C or C++. The first thing we need to do is add references to the object libraries we will be using. In Visual Basic, we would use the *imports* keyword. In C#, we use the *using* keyword, as shown here:

```
using System;
using System.Collections;
using System.Configuration;
using System.ComponentModel;
using System.Data;
using System.Diagnostics;
using System.Web;
using System.Web.Services;
using System.Xml;
using System.Xml.Serialization;
using System.Xml.XPath;
using System.Net;
using System.IO;
using System.Text;
using System.Windows.Forms;    // For SystemInformation.ComputerName API
```

Next we need to declare our namespace, our class, and any classes we inherit from. Because this is a Web service, our class will be based on the *System.Web.Services.Webservice* class. We then initialize some variables that we will use throughout the application: the domain, username, password, and timezone information. The designer then places some implemented code into the application for us.

```
namespace FreeBusyService
{
   /// <summary>
   /// Summary description for Service1.
   /// </summary>
   public class Service1 : System.Web.Services.WebService
   {
      static String serverName = "";
      static String domain = "THOMRIZEX2KDOM";
      static String userName = "thomriz";
      static String password = "password";
      static String TimeString = "T00:00:00-07:00";
```

```
public Service1()
{
   //CODEGEN: This call is required by the ASP.NET
   //Web Services Designer
   InitializeComponent();
}

#region Component Designer generated code

//Required by the Web Services Designer
private IContainer components = null;

/// <summary>
/// Required method for Designer support - do not modify
/// the contents of this method with the code editor.
/// </summary>
private void InitializeComponent()
{
}

/// <summary>
/// Clean up any resources being used.
/// </summary>
protected override void Dispose(bool disposing)
{
   if(disposing && components != null)
   {
      components.Dispose();
   }
   base.Dispose(disposing);
}

#endregion
```

Next we implement our methods. As with Visual Basic, we use the *WebMethod* attribute to expose any of our methods as Web service methods. Here is the code for the raw free/busy method:

```
[WebMethod]
public string GetFreeBusyRaw(string SMTPAddress, string FBDate)
{
   String retXml = "<response>There was a problem getting the " +
                   "Free/Busy data</response>";

   try
   {
      string StartDateTimeString = "";
      string EndDateTimeString = "";

      try
      {
```

```
    DateTime startDate = DateTime.Parse(FBDate);
    StartDateTimeString = startDate.Year.ToString("####") +
       "-" + startDate.Month.ToString("0#") + "-" +
       startDate.Day.ToString("0#") + TimeString;

    DateTime endDate = startDate.AddDays(1);
    EndDateTimeString = endDate.Year.ToString("####") + "-" +
       endDate.Month.ToString("0#") + "-" +
       endDate.Day.ToString("0#") + TimeString;
}
catch (Exception e)
{
    Console.WriteLine(e.ToString());
    retXml = "<response>The string wasn't recognized as a " +
             "valid DateTime string</response>";
    goto cleanup;
}

serverName = SystemInformation.ComputerName;
String getURL = "http://" +
    serverName +
    "/public/?Cmd=freebusy&start=" +
    StartDateTimeString +
    "&end=" +
    EndDateTimeString +
    "&interval=30&u=SMTP:" +
    SMTPAddress;

// Create an HTTP GET Request
HttpWebRequest request =
    (HttpWebRequest)WebRequest.Create(new Uri(getURL));

// Put the proper credentials on the request
NetworkCredential credentials =
    new NetworkCredential(userName, password, domain);
request.Credentials = credentials;

// Set the user-agent headers
request.UserAgent = "Mozilla/4.0 (compatible; MSIE 5.01; " +
                    "Windows NT)";

// Execute the Get request and get the response in a stream
WebResponse results = request.GetResponse();
Stream responseStream = results.GetResponseStream();

StringBuilder responseString = new StringBuilder();
Byte[] read = new Byte[512];
int bytes = responseStream.Read(read, 0, 512);

while (bytes > 0)
{
    responseString.Append(System.Text.Encoding.ASCII.GetString
                          (read, 0, bytes));
```

```
            bytes = responseStream.Read(read, 0, 512);
         }

         if (responseString.Length != 0)
         {
            retXml = responseString.ToString();
         }
         responseStream.Close();
      }
      catch (Exception e)
      {
         return e.ToString();
      }

      cleanup:
         return retXml;
   }
```

The code first takes the date entered by the user of the Web service and parses it. Then it uses the inherent date/time functions in C# to turn the date into a format that OWA will understand, which is *YYYY-MM-DDTHH:MM:SS-TZ*. The code then adds a day to the date for the free/busy query.

To make our query, the code needs to know which server to query OWA on. The code assumes it is running on an Exchange server, so it uses the *SystemInformation* class to retrieve the current computer's name. You can change this code to query another server if you want.

The code then generates the URL to pass to OWA that will return the free/busy information. As you can see, OWA requires the start date, the end date, the interval, and the SMTP address of the user to get the free/busy information.

Now that we have our URL, we need a way to call the URL via HTTP. You should get familiar with the *HTTPWebRequest* and *HTTPWebResponse* classes because you will use them for any HTTP calls you make, including WebDAV calls to Microsoft Exchange or Microsoft SharePoint Portal Server (SPS). I can't cover all the properties and methods that these classes support, but we will use a lot of the properties and methods that you should know to get started programming with .NET and WebDAV.

The first thing we need to do with the *HTTPWebRequest* class is to create an instance of the class. We do this by calling the *Create* method on the *WebRequest* class and pass in either a string that is a valid URL or a URI object that contains a valid URL. Because *HTTPWebRequest* inherits from *WebRequest*, the code just typecasts the returned *WebRequest* object into an *HTTPWebRequest* object.

Next we need to set the right credentials on our HTTP calls so they are not rejected by the server. To do this, we create a new instance of the *NetworkCredential* class, passing the username, password, and domain of the network credential we want to create to the constructor of the class. You can also pass the default credentials of the user currently logged-in or the user who is being impersonated. In ASP.NET, this is usually the anonymous IIS user. To use the default credentials, we can change the code to the following:

```
request.Credentials = System.Net.CredentialCache.DefaultCredentials;
```

For the sake of simplicity, we'll have the code pass the username and password. In production code, you might want to be able to control and cache credentials that are sent to the server. For example, if Basic authentication is enabled on the server, the credential code will send the username and password in clear text. To control the protocol and username/password combination, to store multiple credentials to different resources, or to cache credentials so you do not have to re-create them on every call, you should use the *CredentialCache* class. Using this class, you can store multiple credentials that will be used with different authentication types. This class has an *Add* method that you can leverage to specify the URI of the resource that the credential applies to, the authentication type (such as Basic or NTLM), and the network credential to use. We can use the following code to use the *CredentialCache* class with the Negotiate authentication type only:

```
CredentialCache cache = new CredentialCache();
Cache.Add(new Uri(proxyinstance.Url), "Negotiate" ,
        new System.Net.NetworkCredential(username, password, domain))
request.Credentials = cache;
```

Once we set our credentials, we must set some properties on our *HTTPWebRequest* so OWA will think we are a normal Web client making the request and will generate the XML response we need. We do this by using the *User-Agent* property on our request object. The *HTTPWebRequest* object has a number of properties that map to the standard HTTP headers that you can set, such as the Accept header, the Content-Type header, and the User-Agent header.

Once we set the header, we're done setting up our request object. To make the actual call to the Web server, we need to call the *GetResponse* method on our request object. This method returns a *WebResponse* object. If the request is unsuccessful, we can get the *WebException* object to see what went wrong.

The *WebResponse* object returns any headers in the response, the content type of the response, and a stream interface to the response from the server. By passing back a stream, you can use the methods on the *Stream* class to read and write to the stream.

We need to pass back the raw free/busy XML data as a string, so we must convert the stream returned to us to a string. To do this, we use the new *StringBuilder* class, which provides methods for creating, appending, removing, replacing, and inserting characters into the string. In the code, we create a new instance of an array of bytes, which we will use to read our string into. If the stream is more than the 512 bytes we originally passed, we append the next set of bytes, which are converted to an ASCII string, to our existing string. Then, if the string is actually nonzero in length, which means that we received a response, this string is passed back as the return value for the method.

Returning Data in XML Format

It might be more useful for the consumer of our Web service to receive XML data that corresponds to the free/busy information for the user rather than the raw XML returned back by OWA. To generate our XML response, we'll use some of the new XML capabilities of the .NET Framework. In particular, we'll use the *XmlTextReader*, *XmlTextWriter*, and *XmlDocument* classes.

The *XmlTextReader* class provides a fast, noncached, forward-only access method to XML data. The good thing about the *XmlTextReader* class is that it works interchangeably with the *XmlDocument* class. You can pass an *XmlTextReader* to an *XmlDocument* object. As you can guess, the *XmlDocument* class is the .NET implementation of the *XMLDOM*. The *XmlTextWriter* also allows you to write XML documents to multiple output types, such as a file, the console, or a stream. It's a fast way to generate streams or files that contain XML data.

The following is the code for the free/busy method that returns XML rather than raw free/busy data:

```
//WEB SERVICE EXAMPLE
        [WebMethod]
        public String GetFreeBusyXml(string SMTPAddress, string FBDate)
        {
            String retXml = "<response>There was a problem getting the Free/
Busy data</response>";
            XmlDocument resultDoc = null;

            try
            {
                // Get the free/busy data from the server
                String responseString = GetFreeBusyRaw(SMTPAddress, FBDate);

                // Now convert the return value to a byte array to feed
                // into a memory stream
                Byte[] read = Encoding.GetEncoding(1252).GetBytes
                              (responseString);

                // Load the XmlDocument object with the results for parsing
                MemoryStream stream = new MemoryStream(read);
                XmlTextReader reader = new XmlTextReader(stream);
                XmlDocument xmlDoc = new XmlDocument();
                xmlDoc.Load(reader);
                XPathDocument xmlPath = new XPathDocument(reader);
```

```
String displayName = "DN";
String smtpAddress = "SMTP";
String type = "1";
String fbData = "10101";

XmlNodeList xmlNodes = xmlDoc.GetElementsByTagName("*");

for(int i=0;i < xmlNodes.Count;i++)
{
    XmlNode xmlCurrentNode = xmlNodes[i];
    if (xmlCurrentNode.Name == "a:displayname")
    {
        displayName = xmlCurrentNode.InnerText;
    }
    else if (xmlCurrentNode.Name == "a:email")
    {
        smtpAddress = xmlCurrentNode.InnerText;
    }
    else if (xmlCurrentNode.Name == "a:type")
    {
        type = xmlCurrentNode.InnerText;
    }
    else if (xmlCurrentNode.Name == "a:fbdata")
    {
        fbData = xmlCurrentNode.InnerText;
    }
}



StringBuilder dataString = new StringBuilder();

// Build the result XML
dataString.Append("<?xml version=\"1.0\
                  "?>\n<fbresponse>\n<person>");
dataString.Append("<displayname>" + displayName +
                  "</displayname>");
dataString.Append("<email type=\"SMTP\">" + smtpAddress +
                  "</email>");
dataString.Append(MakeFBDataNode(FBDate, fbData));
dataString.Append("</person>\n</fbresponse>");

// Now convert the return value to a byte array to feed
// into a memory stream
Byte[] output = Encoding.GetEncoding(1252).GetBytes
               (dataString.ToString());

// Load the XmlDocument object with the results for parsing
MemoryStream outputStream = new MemoryStream(output);
XmlTextReader outputReader = new XmlTextReader(outputStream);
```

```
                resultDoc = new XmlDocument();
                resultDoc.Load(outputReader);

                MemoryStream writeStream = new MemoryStream
                                           (output.Length * 2 );
                XmlTextWriter outputWriter = new XmlTextWriter(writeStream,
                                             Encoding.GetEncoding(1252));
                outputWriter.Formatting = Formatting.Indented;

                resultDoc.WriteTo(outputWriter);
                outputWriter.Flush();

                retXml = System.Text.Encoding.ASCII.GetString
                         (writeStream.GetBuffer(), 0, (int)writeStream.Length);

            }
            catch (Exception e)
            {
                return e.ToString();
            }
            return retXml;
        }

private String MakeFBDataNode(string FBDate, string FBData)
        {
            String dateString;
            StringBuilder retXml = new StringBuilder();

            DateTime DTDate = new DateTime();
            try
            {
                DTDate = DateTime.Parse(FBDate);
                dateString = DTDate.Month.ToString("0#") + "/" +
                    DTDate.Day.ToString("0#") + "/" +
                    DTDate.Year.ToString("####");
            }
            catch (Exception e)
            {
                dateString = "Bad Date Format";
            }

            retXml.Append( "<fbdata date=\"" + dateString + "\">" );

            DateTime TimeVar = new DateTime(DTDate.Year, DTDate.Month,
                                  DTDate.Day, 0, 0, 0);

            for (int index = 0; index < FBData.Length; index++)
            {
                retXml.Append("<timeslot>");
```

```
            retXml.Append("<starttime>");
            retXml.Append(TimeVar.ToShortTimeString());
            retXml.Append("</starttime>");

            retXml.Append("<endtime>");
            retXml.Append(TimeVar.AddMinutes(30).ToShortTimeString());
            retXml.Append("</endtime>");

            retXml.Append("<fbstatus>");
            switch ( FBData[index] )
            {
                case '0':
                    retXml.Append("Free");
                    break;
                case '1':
                    retXml.Append("Tentative");
                    break;
                case '2':
                    retXml.Append("Busy");
                    break;
                case '3':
                    retXml.Append("Out Of Office");
                    break;
                default:
                    retXml.Append("Data Not Available");
                    break;
            }
            retXml.Append("</fbstatus>");

            retXml.Append("</timeslot>");

            TimeVar = TimeVar.AddMinutes(30);
        }

        retXml.Append( "</fbdata>" );
        return retXml.ToString();
    }
```

Here is an example of the formatted XML returned by this method:


```
<?xml version="1.0" encoding="utf-8" ?>
  <string xmlns="http://tempuri.org/
"><?xml version="1.0"?> <fbresponse> <person> <displayname>Thomas Rizzo</
displayname> <email type="SMTP">thomriz@thomrizex2kdom.extest.microsoft.com</
email> <fbdata date="01/04/2002"> <timeslot> <starttime>12:00 AM</
starttime> <endtime>12:30 AM</endtime> <fbstatus>Free</fbstatus> </
timeslot> <timeslot> <starttime>12:30 AM</starttime> <endtime>1:00 AM</
endtime> <fbstatus>Free</fbstatus> </timeslot> <timeslot> <starttime>1:00 AM</
starttime> <endtime>1:30 AM</endtime> <fbstatus>Free</fbstatus> </
timeslot> <timeslot> <starttime>1:30 AM</starttime> <endtime>2:00 AM</
endtime> <fbstatus>Free</fbstatus> </timeslot> <timeslot> <starttime>2:00 AM</
starttime> <endtime>2:30 AM</endtime> <fbstatus>Free</fbstatus> </
timeslot> <timeslot> <starttime>2:30 AM</starttime> <endtime>3:00 AM</
```

```
endtime> <fbstatus>Free</fbstatus> </timeslot> <timeslot> <starttime>3:00 AM</
starttime> <endtime>3:30 AM</endtime> <fbstatus>Free</fbstatus> </
timeslot> <timeslot> <starttime>3:30 AM</starttime> <endtime>4:00 AM</
endtime> <fbstatus>Free</fbstatus> </timeslot> <timeslot> <starttime>4:00 AM</
starttime> <endtime>4:30 AM</endtime> <fbstatus>Free</fbstatus> </
timeslot> <timeslot> <starttime>4:30 AM</starttime> <endtime>5:00 AM</
endtime> <fbstatus>Free</fbstatus> </timeslot> <timeslot> <starttime>5:00 AM</
starttime> <endtime>5:30 AM</endtime> <fbstatus>Free</fbstatus> </
timeslot> <timeslot> <starttime>5:30 AM</starttime> <endtime>6:00 AM</
endtime> <fbstatus>Free</fbstatus> </timeslot> <timeslot> <starttime>6:00 AM</
starttime> <endtime>6:30 AM</endtime> <fbstatus>Free</fbstatus> </
timeslot> <timeslot> <starttime>6:30 AM</starttime> <endtime>7:00 AM</
endtime> <fbstatus>Free</fbstatus> </timeslot> <timeslot> <starttime>7:00 AM</
starttime> <endtime>7:30 AM</endtime> <fbstatus>Free</fbstatus> </
timeslot> <timeslot> <starttime>7:30 AM</starttime> <endtime>8:00 AM</
endtime> <fbstatus>Free</fbstatus> </timeslot> <timeslot> <starttime>8:00 AM</
starttime> <endtime>8:30 AM</endtime> <fbstatus>Free</fbstatus> </
timeslot> <timeslot> <starttime>8:30 AM</starttime> <endtime>9:00 AM</
endtime> <fbstatus>Free</fbstatus> </timeslot> <timeslot> <starttime>9:00 AM</
starttime> <endtime>9:30 AM</endtime> <fbstatus>Free</fbstatus> </
timeslot> <timeslot> <starttime>9:30 AM</starttime> <endtime>10:00 AM</
endtime> <fbstatus>Free</fbstatus> </timeslot> <timeslot> <starttime>10:00 AM</
starttime> <endtime>10:30 AM</endtime> <fbstatus>Busy</fbstatus> </
timeslot> <timeslot> <starttime>10:30 AM</starttime> <endtime>11:00 AM</
endtime> <fbstatus>Busy</fbstatus> </timeslot> <timeslot> <starttime>11:00 AM</
starttime> <endtime>11:30 AM</endtime> <fbstatus>Busy</fbstatus> </
timeslot> <timeslot> <starttime>11:30 AM</starttime> <endtime>12:00 PM</
endtime> <fbstatus>Free</fbstatus> </timeslot> <timeslot> <starttime>12:00 PM</
starttime> <endtime>12:30 PM</endtime> <fbstatus>Free</fbstatus> </
timeslot> <timeslot> <starttime>12:30 PM</starttime> <endtime>1:00 PM</
endtime> <fbstatus>Out Of Office</fbstatus> </
timeslot> <timeslot> <starttime>1:00 PM</starttime> <endtime>1:30 PM</
endtime> <fbstatus>Out Of Office</fbstatus> </
timeslot> <timeslot> <starttime>1:30 PM</starttime> <endtime>2:00 PM</
endtime> <fbstatus>Out Of Office</fbstatus> </
timeslot> <timeslot> <starttime>2:00 PM</starttime> <endtime>2:30 PM</
endtime> <fbstatus>Free</fbstatus> </timeslot> <timeslot> <starttime>2:30 PM</
starttime> <endtime>3:00 PM</endtime> <fbstatus>Tentative</fbstatus> </
timeslot> <timeslot> <starttime>3:00 PM</starttime> <endtime>3:30 PM</
endtime> <fbstatus>Tentative</fbstatus> </
timeslot> <timeslot> <starttime>3:30 PM</starttime> <endtime>4:00 PM</
endtime> <fbstatus>Tentative</fbstatus> </
timeslot> <timeslot> <starttime>4:00 PM</starttime> <endtime>4:30 PM</
endtime> <fbstatus>Free</fbstatus> </timeslot> <timeslot> <starttime>4:30 PM</
starttime> <endtime>5:00 PM</endtime> <fbstatus>Free</fbstatus> </
timeslot> <timeslot> <starttime>5:00 PM</starttime> <endtime>5:30 PM</
endtime> <fbstatus>Free</fbstatus> </timeslot> <timeslot> <starttime>5:30 PM</
starttime> <endtime>6:00 PM</endtime> <fbstatus>Free</fbstatus> </
timeslot> <timeslot> <starttime>6:00 PM</starttime> <endtime>6:30 PM</
endtime> <fbstatus>Free</fbstatus> </timeslot> <timeslot> <starttime>6:30 PM</
starttime> <endtime>7:00 PM</endtime> <fbstatus>Free</fbstatus> </
timeslot> <timeslot> <starttime>7:00 PM</starttime> <endtime>7:30 PM</
endtime> <fbstatus>Free</fbstatus> </timeslot> <timeslot> <starttime>7:30 PM</
```

```
starttime> <endtime>8:00 PM</endtime> <fbstatus>Free</fbstatus> </
timeslot> <timeslot> <starttime>8:00 PM</starttime> <endtime>8:30 PM</
endtime> <fbstatus>Free</fbstatus> </timeslot> <timeslot> <starttime>8:30 PM</
starttime> <endtime>9:00 PM</endtime> <fbstatus>Free</fbstatus> </
timeslot> <timeslot> <starttime>9:00 PM</starttime> <endtime>9:30 PM</
endtime> <fbstatus>Free</fbstatus> </timeslot> <timeslot> <starttime>9:30 PM</
starttime> <endtime>10:00 PM</endtime> <fbstatus>Free</fbstatus> </
timeslot> <timeslot> <starttime>10:00 PM</starttime> <endtime>10:30 PM</
endtime> <fbstatus>Free</fbstatus> </timeslot> <timeslot> <starttime>10:30 PM</
starttime> <endtime>11:00 PM</endtime> <fbstatus>Free</fbstatus> </
timeslot> <timeslot> <starttime>11:00 PM</starttime> <endtime>11:30 PM</
endtime> <fbstatus>Free</fbstatus> </timeslot> <timeslot> <starttime>11:30 PM</
starttime> <endtime>12:00 AM</endtime> <fbstatus>Free</fbstatus> </timeslot> </
fbdata> </person> </fbresponse></string>
```

The code first calls the free/busy raw method to get the raw version of the free/busy information to convert to XML. It loads the string returned into a byte array so the code can load the byte array into a stream object, and then it loads the stream object into an *XmlTextReader*. Next the code creates a new *XmlDocument* object and loads the *XmlTextReader* into the *XmlDocument*. We now have an *XmlDocument* filled with the raw XML data that was returned.

To give you an example of how to load an *XPathDocument* object with the XML data, the code includes a line that loads the *XmlTextReader* into a new instance of the *XPathDocument* class. With the *XPathDocument* class, you can transform the XML document using XSLT or query the document using XPath.

Next the code uses the XML DOM to scroll through the returned free/busy XML document from OWA. The code finds the corresponding free/busy information for the user and loads that information into some variables.

The code then creates a new string using the *StringBuilder* class, which will contain the formatted XML that we need to send back from the service. As part of the construction of the XML, the *MakeFBDataNode* function is called. This function takes the data passed to it and creates the timeslot nodes for the formatted XML response.

The code goes through a number of additional steps to create an *XmlTextWriter*. The XmlTextWriter formats the XML by indenting the child objects by setting the *Formatting* property to *Formatting.Indented*. At the end of the code, the method sends back the text version of the formatted XML.

Returning an ADO.NET *DataSet*

If you have not looked at the data access features of .NET, you should. .NET includes a new set of data access functionality and classes called ADO.NET. Even though ADO.NET sounds similar to ADO, the two object models are very different. You can still use ADO via the COM interoperability layer in .NET. You'll see a sample of using ADO later in this chapter.

ADO.NET includes a number of new objects, such as the *DataSet*, *DataReader*, and *DataAdapter* objects. A *DataSet* is an in-memory representation of data from a relational or hierarchical datasource. You can put data from an SQL Server into a *DataSet* or put XML data into a *DataSet*. The *DataSet* will maintain the relations and constraints that you assign to that data. You can even pass an ADO *Recordset* to a *DataSet*, and it will import the records, as you'll see later in this chapter.

Note that the *DataSet* will not automatically write back the changed or updated data to the data source unless the *DataSet* is connected to or related to a *DataAdapter*, which is similar to an OLEDB data adapter. Unfortunately, neither the EXOLEDB nor the MSDAIPP providers are fully supported via the managed OLEDB providers with .NET. EXOLEDB does support the OLEDB .NET data provider for read-only operations against Exchange or SharePoint. However, the OLEDB .NET data provider expects command syntax such as *UPDATE* or *INSERT* in order to update data rather than cursors, which EXOLEDB supports. You cannot modify data in Exchange from the OLEDB .NET provider. The following code snippet shows how to use the OLEDB .NET data adapter against Exchange in Visual Basic:

```
On Error Resume Next
Dim conn As New OleDb.OleDbConnection("Provider=Exoledb.datasource; " & _
    "Data Source=file://./backofficestorage/thomriznt5dom2.extest." & _
    "microsoft.com/public folders/folder/")

Dim query As String = "SELECT ""urn:schemas:httpmail:subject"" FROM " & _
    "SCOPE('shallow traversal of "file://./backofficestorage/" & _
    "thomriznt5dom2.extest.microsoft.com/public folders/folder/""')"

Dim oCmd As New System.Data.OleDb.OleDbCommand(query, conn)
conn.Open()
Dim oOLEDBReader As System.Data.OleDb.OleDbDataReader
oOLEDBReader = oCmd.ExecuteReader
While oOLEDBReader.Read()
    MsgBox(oOLEDBReader.GetString(0))
End While
```

This effectively means you cannot use the included .NET *DataAdapter* objects with Exchange or SPS. Instead, you can use the non-.NET version of ADO to access your collaborative data or you can use WebDAV and XML with the .NET data access features. You can also write your own data adapter by using WebDAV and XML.

To show you how to use a *DataSet* with XML, the Web service also returns the results as an ADO.NET *DataSet* filled with XML data. The following is the code in the service that creates and returns the *Dataset*:

```
[WebMethod]
public DataSet GetFreeBusyDataSet(string SMTPAddress, string FBDate)
{
    DataSet resultSet = null;

    try
    {
        // Get the free/busy data from the server
        String responseString = GetFreeBusyXml(SMTPAddress, FBDate);

        // Now convert the return value to a byte array to feed
        // into a memory stream
        Byte[] output = Encoding.GetEncoding(1252).GetBytes
                        (responseString);

        // Load the XmlDocument object with the results for parsing
        MemoryStream outputStream = new MemoryStream(output);
        XmlTextReader outputReader = new XmlTextReader(outputStream);

        XmlDataDocument resultDoc = new XmlDataDocument();
        resultDoc.DataSet.ReadXml(outputReader);
        resultSet = resultDoc.DataSet;
    }
    catch(Exception e)
    {
        return resultSet;
    }
    return resultSet;
}
```

The first thing the code does is leverage our existing XML formatted free/busy function to get back the free/busy information for the user. Next it loads a stream with the XML output. That stream is then loaded into an *XmlTextReader*. Then an *XmlDataDocument* is loaded with the *XmlTextReader*. An *XmlDataDocument* extends the standard *XmlDocument* class and allows you to load relational or XML data into the class. The *XmlDataDocument* is closely related to the *Dataset* class and has a *Dataset* property, which returns a *Dataset* that represents the XML data in the *XmlDataDocument*. The *Dataset* returned by this property is returned to the caller of the Web service.

Consuming the Web Service from .NET

You could test the functionality of the *Dataset* component of the Web service by using the simple Web service test utility that launches when you run your application, but the sample files include a test application that shows how to call all the functions of the Web service. The main interface for the test application is shown in Figure 14-5.

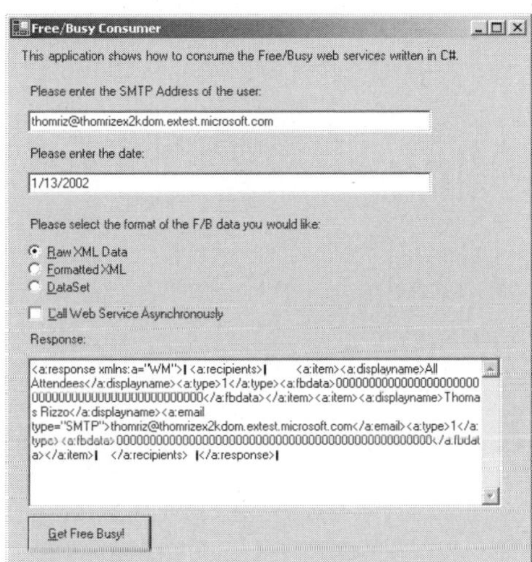

Figure 14-5 The .NET test application for the free/busy Web service

One thing the test application shows is how to add a reference to a Web service in your Visual Studio .NET applications. To add a reference to any Web service, you choose the Add Web Reference command from the Project menu. You will see the interface shown in Figure 14-6, which allows you to browse Web sites for Web services or query UDDI to find a Web service.

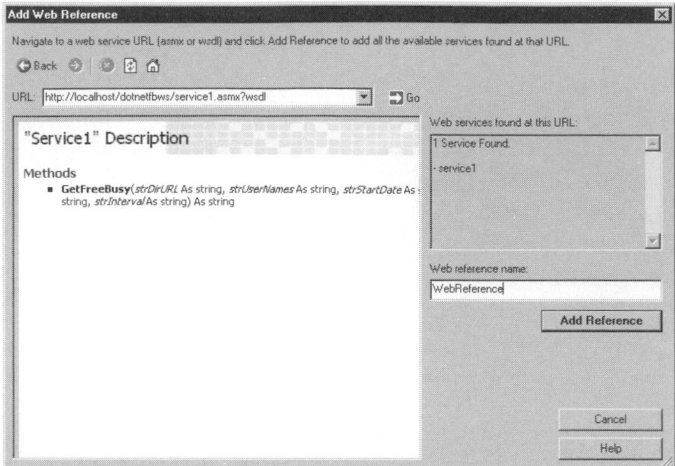

Figure 14-6 The Add Web Reference interface

When you add your Web reference, you can browse the contract information or documentation for the Web service before adding a reference. Browsing the documentation for our free/busy service shows the default page you saw earlier when we tested our Web service, as shown in Figure 14-7.

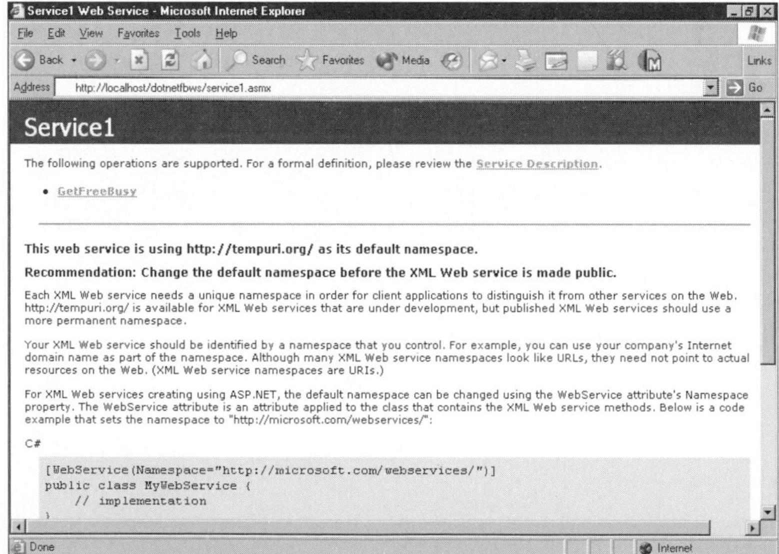

Figure 14-7 Browsing the documentation for the free/busy Web service

Once the reference is added, you will see the Web service as part of the Web References section in Solution Explorer in Visual Studio .NET. You can now initialize a variable as an instance of the Web service and use the IntelliSense features of Visual Studio .NET to have autocompletion and function information available for the functions of the Web service.

Calling the Web Service

The following code from the consumer application calls the Web service:

```
Private Sub frmMain_Load(ByVal sender As System.Object, _
    ByVal e As System.EventArgs) Handles MyBase.Load

    'Fill the date with the current date
    txtDate.Text = Month(Now) & "/" & DatePart(DateInterval.Day, Now) & _
                   "/" & Year(Now)
End Sub

Private Sub cmdGetFB_Click(ByVal sender As System.Object, _
    ByVal e As System.EventArgs) Handles cmdGetFB.Click

    On Error Resume Next
    'Validate some values
    If txtSMTPAddress.Text = "" Then
        MsgBox("You must enter a valid SMTP Address!", _
               MsgBoxStyle.Critical + MsgBoxStyle.OKOnly)
        Exit Sub
    End If

    If (txtDate.Text = "") Or Not (IsDate(CDate(txtDate.Text))) Then
        MsgBox("You must enter a valid Date!", _
               MsgBoxStyle.Critical + MsgBoxStyle.OKOnly)
        Exit Sub
    End If

    'Figure out which version of the web service we need to call
    Dim oWS As New localhost.Service1()
    If RadioRaw.Checked = True Then
        'Need to just get the raw data
        'See if we need to call asynchronously
        If checkAsync.Checked = True Then
            'Async
            Dim olocalhost As localhost.Service1 = _
                New localhost.Service1()
            Dim oCB As AsyncCallback
            oCB = New AsyncCallback(AddressOf frmMain.RawCallBack)
            Dim ar As IAsyncResult = oWS.BeginGetFreeBusyRaw(_
                txtSMTPAddress.Text, txtDate.Text, oCB, olocalhost)
        Else
            'Sync
            DataGrid1.Visible = False
```

```
                txtResponse.Visible = True
                txtResponse.Text = oWS.GetFreeBusyRaw(txtSMTPAddress.Text, _
                                                      txtDate.Text)
            End If
        ElseIf RadioFormatted.Checked = True Then
            'Get Formatted
            DataGrid1.Visible = False
            txtResponse.Visible = True
            txtResponse.Text = oWS.GetFreeBusyXml(txtSMTPAddress.Text, _
                                                  txtDate.Text)
        ElseIf RadioDataSet.Checked = True Then
            'Get Dataset
            Dim oDataSet1 As New DataSet()
            oDataSet1 = oWS.GetFreeBusyDataSet(txtSMTPAddress.Text, _
                                               txtDate.Text)
            DataGrid1.SetDataBinding(oDataSet1, "")
            txtResponse.Visible = False
            DataGrid1.Visible = True
        End If
    End Sub

    Public Shared Sub RawCallBack(ByVal ar As IAsyncResult)
        Dim oFinishService As localhost.Service1 = ar.AsyncState
        Dim results As String

        ' Get the completed results.
        results = oFinishService.EndGetFreeBusyRaw(ar)
        MsgBox("The results from the async call were: " & results)
    End Sub

    Private Sub RadioFormatted_CheckedChanged(ByVal sender As System.Object, _
        ByVal e As System.EventArgs) Handles RadioFormatted.CheckedChanged

        If RadioFormatted.Checked = True Then
            checkAsync.Enabled = False
        End If
    End Sub

    Private Sub RadioRaw_CheckedChanged(ByVal sender As System.Object, _
        ByVal e As System.EventArgs) Handles RadioRaw.CheckedChanged

        If RadioRaw.Checked = True Then
            checkAsync.Enabled = True
        End If
    End Sub

    Private Sub RadioDataSet_CheckedChanged(ByVal sender As System.Object, _
        ByVal e As System.EventArgs) Handles RadioDataSet.CheckedChanged

        If RadioDataSet.Checked = True Then
            checkAsync.Enabled = False
        End If
    End Sub
```

The first thing you will notice in the *cmdGetFB_Click* subroutine is that the variable *oWS* is initialized to our Web service. When you call the functions of a Web service, you have two options for calling the Web service. You can either call the function synchronously and your application will wait for the Web service response before continuing, or you can call the Web service asynchronously.

There is no special code in our Web service that makes the calls asynchronous or synchronous. Instead, when Visual Studio .NET generates the WSDL file for our Web service, it generates the standard synchronous and asynchronous versions of the methods in our class.

The caller does have to write some special code, however, to be able to call the Web service asynchronously. You will notice that the first thing the asynchronous version does is create a new *AsyncCallback* object. When you call asynchronous methods in .NET, you must pass a delegate that .NET can call when the asynchronous method completes. To pass this function, when the constructor for the *AsyncCallback* object is called, the code passes the address of the callback function called *RawCallBack*. It then calls the asynchronous version of the method, which normally starts with *begin*, as in *begingetfreebusyraw*.

When the Web service completes and calls the *RawCallBack* function, it passes an *IAsyncResult* object. The *IAsyncResult* object contains the status of an asynchronous operation. This object has a property called *AsyncState*, which contains the results of the asynchronous operation. The object also has another property called *IsCompleted*, which we can check to see if the asynchronous operation completed. Because we are using a callback function, we'll assume that the operation completed when we get the callback.

The next step is to get the completed results. To do this, we call the *EndGetFreeBusyRaw* method on our Web service and pass it our *IAsyncResult* object. The code simply writes out the results of the Web service. By using an asynchronous call, our code could have continued processing some other code while making the call to the Web service.

The next part of the code to note is the part that works with the *DataGrid* object to display our *DataSet* returned from the Web service. A *DataGrid* object is a new control similar to the *FlexGrid* in Visual Studio 6.0. The *DataGrid* allows you to display data in a scrollable grid. What makes the *DataGrid* useful is that it works directly with a *DataSet*. Using the *SetDataBinding* method, you can pass a *DataSet* as the table for the *DataGrid* to bind to. The *DataGrid* then inherits the column names and schema from the passed *DataSet* and displays the information from the *DataSet*, as shown in Figure 14-8.

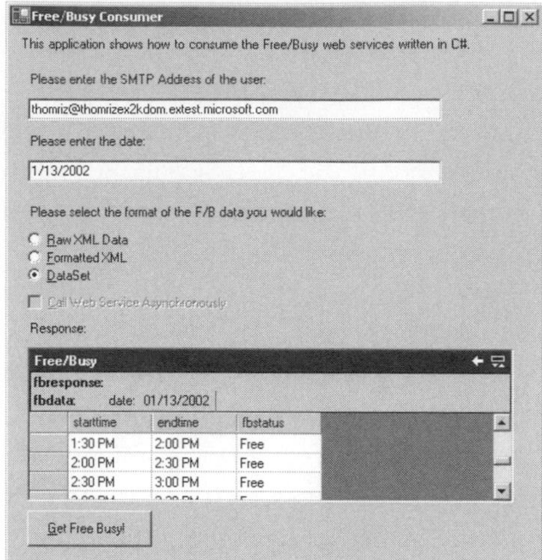

Figure 14-8 Displaying a *Dataset* in a *Datagrid* control

Summary

Visual Studio makes it easy to build Web services, whether those Web services access information in Exchange or other datastores. You can expose your collaborative information using Web services, allowing other applications to get or set data in your application. This is what makes Web services so powerful: a programming model that works across many products and many platforms. When you build your applications on Exchange, you should evaluate whether exposing most of the functionality from your application through Web services makes sense. Web services provide great benefits with very little additional coding.

15

The Training Application

You might remember the Training application from the second edition of this book. This comprehensive solution showed how to build an application that uses some of the features in Microsoft Exchange. Rather than force readers to learn an entirely new application, this edition has expanded and reworked the Training application for Exchange 2003. The application demonstrates how to build applications against Exchange 2003 using technologies such as XML, server events, workflow, instant messaging, calendaring, and other Exchange technologies. An addition, we will look at a number of samples of Microsoft .NET applications built using Exchange. Table 15-1 describes the new features in the expanded Training application.

Table 15-1 New Features in the Training Application

Feature	Description
Automated security settings	The Exchange Software Development Kit (SDK) has a security module that shows you how to set permissions using Web Distributed Authoring and Versioning (WebDAV) or ActiveX Data Objects (ADO). The sample uses some of that code to set permissions for the folders in the application and shows how to use the security module in your own applications that need to set or get security settings. Security is discussed in more detail in Chapter 17.
Messenger support for instant messaging (IM)	With the removal of IM technologies from Exchange and the release of the Microsoft Office Live Communications Server 2003, the application has been updated to take advantage of the new server and the Messenger IM client. Office Live Communications technologies are covered in Chapter 19.

Table 15-1 New Features in the Training Application

Feature	Description
Ability to create new storage groups	To show how to create new storage groups and storage databases using Collaboration Data Objects (CDO) for Exchange Management, the sample application allows you to browse and create new places to store the application's data.
Ability to run Web files directly from Exchange	Exchange supports the ability to access Web files directly rather than from the file system. The updated sample supports setting up Exchange virtual directories and running Web files directly from Exchange Server.
Web Storage System (WSS) Forms support	The sample supports WSS Forms, which you will learn about in Chapter 20.
RichEdit control support	The sample's support for the Outlook Web Access (OWA) RichEdit control allows you to type rich text in your browser for course descriptions. You can use the same technology in your own Web applications.
Treeview control support	The sample supports OWA's treeview control so that you can easily display a list of Exchange folders without having to write all the code yourself.
Free/busy lookup for students and conference rooms	The sample has added support for free/busy lookup through the OWA freebusy command (which is covered later in this chapter).
Support for on-demand courses	Using WSS Forms file upload technologies, the sample supports the ability to upload videos and course materials directly through the browser.
Exchange Conferencing Server support	The sample supports Exchange Conferencing Server so that you can schedule virtual classes. This topic is covered in Chapter 19.
SharePoint Portal Server (SPS) support	The sample supports SPS 2001. The application can run on that product and can also use its document management and portal capabilities. These additional capabilities are provided through SPS folders and the built-in Web parts in the sample application.

The Training application manages an internal training program site and provides a Web interface through which students and instructors can register for, critique, and discuss training courses. I created a setup program that makes it easier to get the application started and shows how to perform some administrative functions for Exchange Server 2003. The setup program also shows how to perform COM+, Microsoft Internet Information Services (IIS), and Active Directory administrative tasks.

Before examining the code and technologies used in the Training application, we'll discuss exactly what the application does. That way, when we cover each of the application's implementation sections, you'll understand what each section does within the context of the entire application.

Setting Up the Training Application

When you launch the setup program for the Training application, the first thing you see is the Microsoft Visual Basic interface for the setup program (as shown in Figure 15-1).

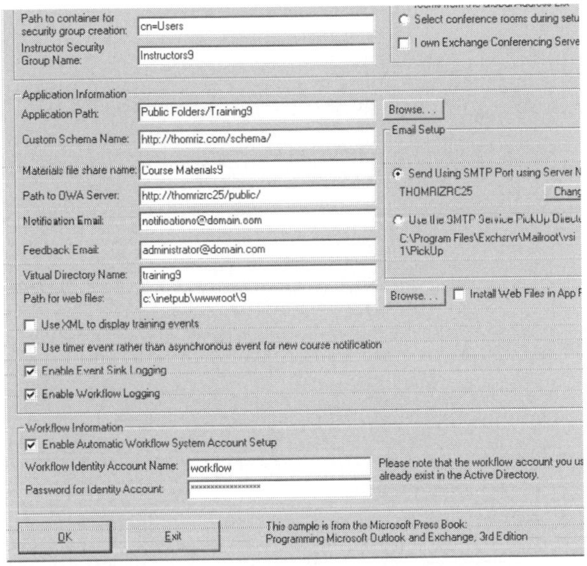

Figure 15-1 The user interface for the setup program, which requires you to specify where to place the Training application

The setup program takes the information you provide and sets up the application; you don't have to perform any extra steps. The setup program does the following:

- Detects whether you're running Exchange or SharePoint. The rest of this list assumes that you are running Exchange. As mentioned earlier, the application can run on both Exchange and SharePoint.
- Establishes an ADO connection to the Exchange Server so the *Connection* object can be used throughout the setup process and certain parts of the setup can be transacted and rolled back.

- Creates the Exchange Server folders.
- Creates the custom schema, including custom content classes and properties.
- Creates messages in the Emails folder, which contains the HTML templates for the notification e-mails sent by the application.
- Prompts the user for which categories to create for training events and stores those categories in the Configuration folder.
- Creates a security group in Active Directory that will contain the users who are instructors for the application.
- Creates the IIS virtual directory and copies the Web files to it.
- Creates a Windows file share for the course materials.
- Copies and registers the event dynamic link libraries (DLLs).
- Registers the event DLL files as a COM+ application.
- Creates the event registrations for the application that will handle new course notification, survey notification, and survey result compilation.
- Imports, registers, and enables the workflow process definition.
- Creates the event registrations for the workflow process.
- Installs Web Storage System forms for file upload and course material viewing.
- Sets the default security on the application folders.

The setup program completes other tasks as well, but I won't detail those that are unrelated to Exchange Server or are noncritical application deployment steps, such as creating virtual directories in IIS using Active Directory Services Interfaces (ADSI). To learn more about such steps, you can look at the source code for the setup program, which is among the book's sample files.

> **Note** You must run the setup program directly on your Exchange server. You must also be an administrator of both the Windows and Exchange Server systems.

Using the Training Application

After you run the setup program, you can start using the Training application. The application uses a series of public folders that store all the application's information. Figure 15-2 shows the application's folder hierarchy. As you can see, the types of folders range from standard message folders to contact folders and calendar folders.

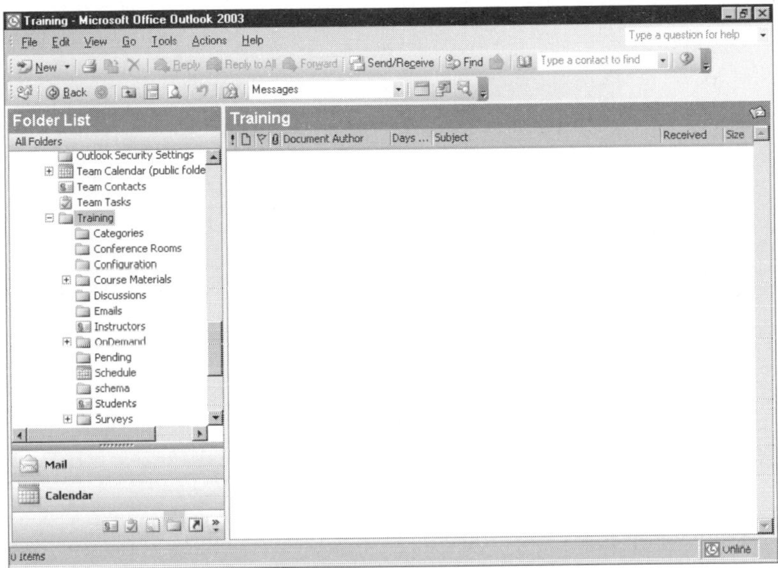

Figure 15-2 The folder hierarchy for the Training application as it appears in Microsoft Outlook

The classes are contained in the Schedule folder, while student information and instructor information are contained in their respective contact folders. The application interface is the default training page, which is different for instructors and for students. The instructor home page is shown in Figure 15-3.

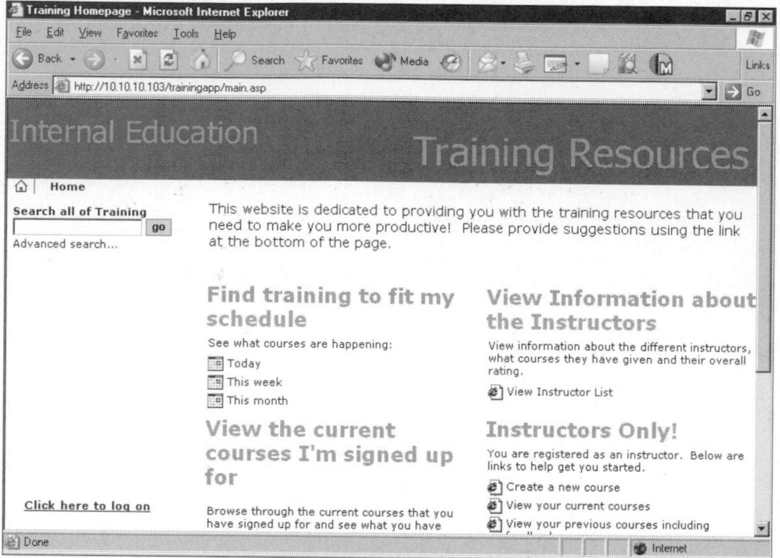

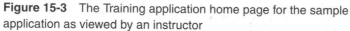

Figure 15-3 The Training application home page for the sample application as viewed by an instructor

From the home page, you can retrieve the schedule of classes, view information about instructors, change your notification preferences, or, if you are an instructor, create a new course. The application determines whether you are an instructor by using Windows 2000 security groups. The application searches the instructor security group you specify in the setup program and checks to see whether the user accessing the application is a member of that security group. If the user is a member of that security group, the instructor-specific content will appear on the Web page. Figure 15-4 shows the Instructors Properties dialog box as it appears when you display the group's properties in Active Directory Users And Computers.

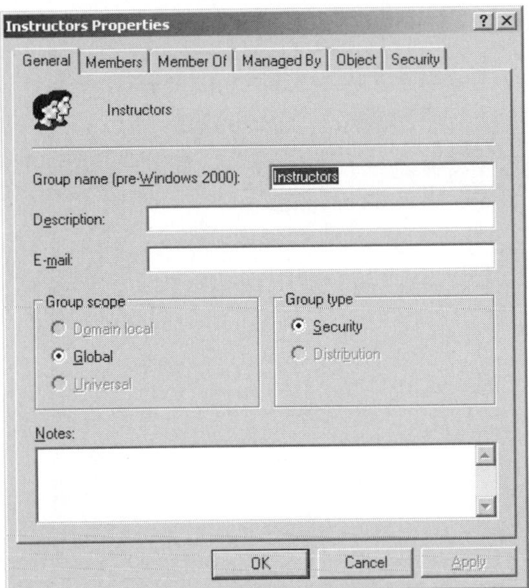

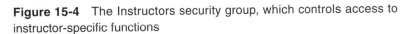

Figure 15-4 The Instructors security group, which controls access to instructor-specific functions

Note that the Training application creates its folders in the Public Folder hierarchy. I coded the application in this way so you can see the folders in Outlook. However, if I were to actually deploy this application, I would not create the folders in the Public Folder hierarchy because the hierarchy is Web based. Instead, I would create a new top-level hierarchy, not visible by Outlook, to contain my application. This would enable me to conduct deep searches of the folders using ADO and would prevent access to the application from Outlook.

Creating a Course

The application allows an instructor to create courses and register students for them. When an instructor creates a course, the application asks her whether she wants to create a file share for course materials or a discussion group for the course. This functionality demonstrates how to use the Installable File System (IFS) components of the Web Storage System through the file share capabilities, and it illustrates the reusability of OWA. Figure 15-5 shows a course listing that contains links to both the course materials and a discussion group for the course.

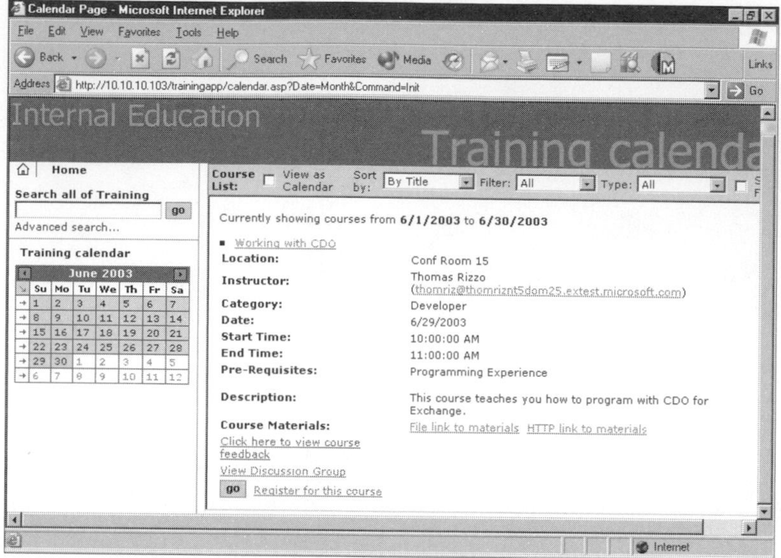

Figure 15-5 A course listing that uses both IFS and OWA extensibility in an Exchange Server application

After an instructor creates a course, an asynchronous or timer event (depending on which you specified in the setup program) fires in the Schedule folder. This event checks to see whether any students have asked to be notified when new training is available in the specific course category. As the application administrator, you must specify these categories—for example, *Developer*, *End User*, and *IT*. If the application locates students who need to be notified about the training, it sends the students an HTML-formatted message, as shown in Figure 15-6.

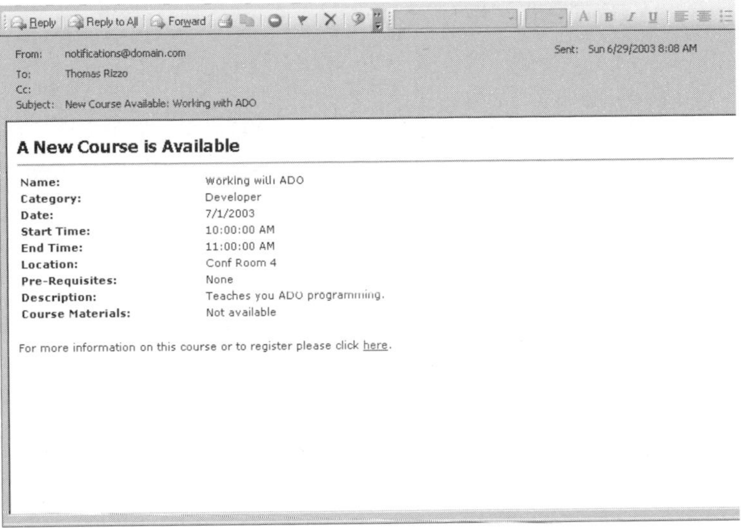

Figure 15-6 An HTML-formatted message sent to students who want to be notified about new training events

The notification preferences of each student are stored on their respective contact record in the Students folder. Students can change their preferences for notification through the application's Web interface, as shown in Figure 15-7.

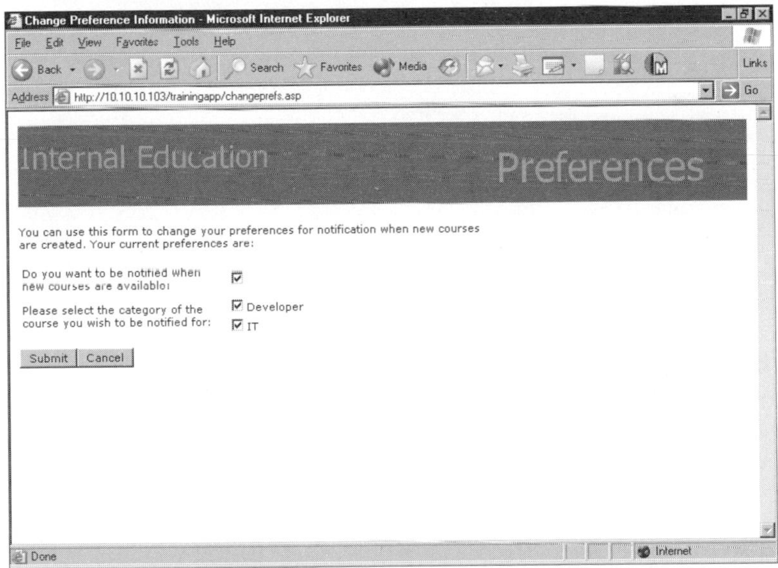

Figure 15-7 The Web page for changing course availability notifications

Browsing Available Courses

The application provides two ways for students to browse through the available courses in the Schedule folder. First, a student can specify date ranges from a Date Picker control and view the courses in a simple list. The student can then re-sort the list by title, date, or category. The page containing this simple list is shown in Figure 15-8.

> **Note** You can generate the simple list page shown in Figure 15-8 in two ways. One way is to use ADO inside ASP pages. The other technique involves using the *XMLHTTP* component of Microsoft Internet Explorer and requesting XML data from the Exchange server. The Training application then renders that XML data locally, thereby eliminating a round-trip to the server if the user wants to re-sort the list of classes.

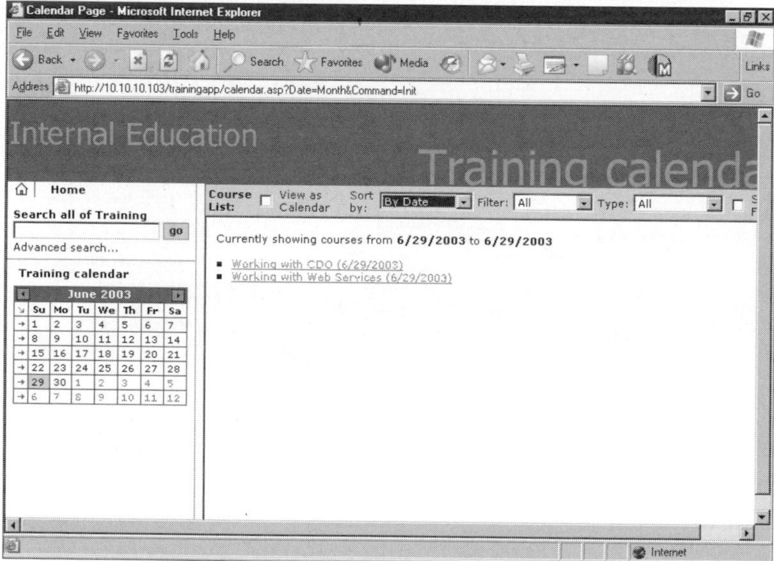

Figure 15-8 The page showing a simple list of courses for a specific date range

The second way that students can browse through the available courses leverages the extensibility of OWA. By passing OWA-specific parameters (which are covered in more detail in Chapter 20), you can make OWA display information. Figure 15-9 shows how the Training application employs the rich calendar views of OWA to display the schedule of courses.

When a user double-clicks on one of the calendar items in the view, the application displays a custom Web Storage System form instead of displaying the standard OWA appointment form. The ability to replace OWA forms with your own is a powerful one. Figure 15-10 shows the Web Storage System form displayed when a user clicks on a training event in the calendar.

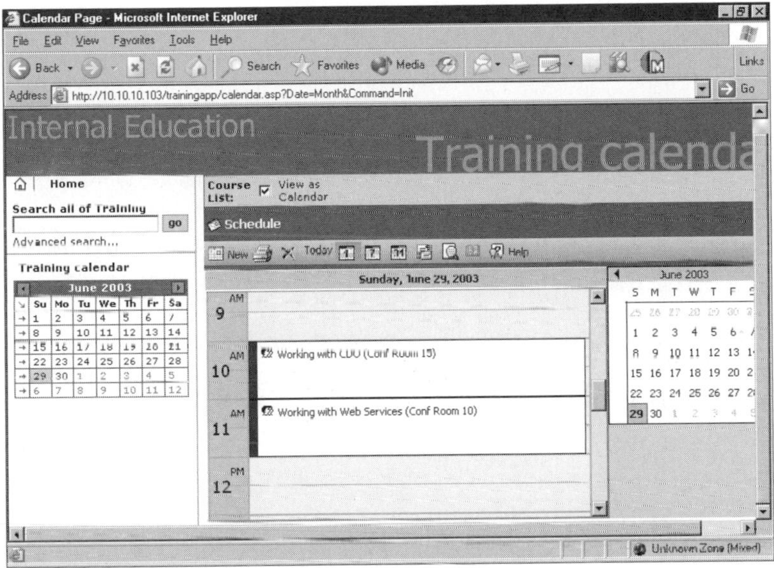

Figure 15-9 Using OWA and the calendar view to display a list of available courses

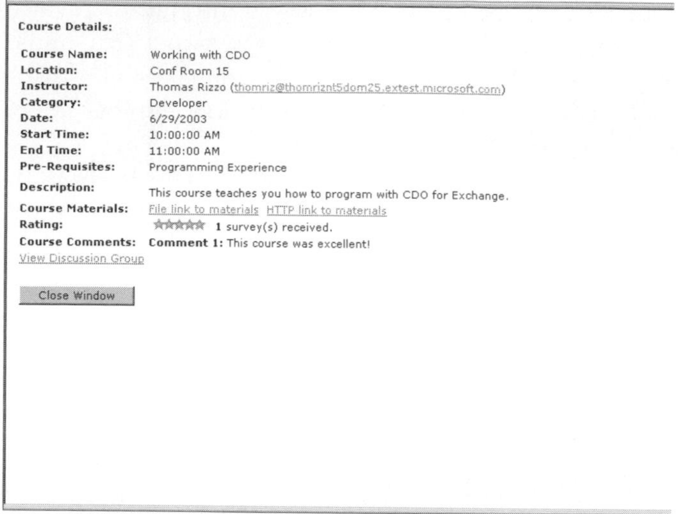

Figure 15-10 The Web Storage System form that is displayed when a user clicks on an item in the Training application's calendar

Searching for a Course

The Training application also offers students and instructors two ways to quickly find course information: quick search and advanced search. Both types of search eventually follow the same code path, but the advanced search provides a more powerful interface for specifying search options. Figure 15-11 shows the Advanced Search page of the Training application. The search capabilities can take advantage of the built-in content indexing of Exchange Server if you enable content indexing. You'll learn about content indexing later in this chapter.

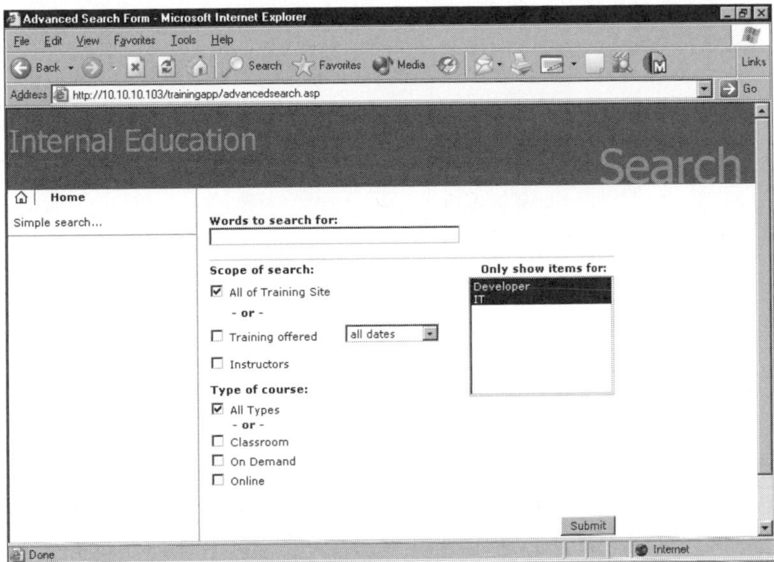

Figure 15-11 The Advanced Search page of the Training application

Obtaining Approval for Registration

The Training application uses the built-in workflow engine and the graphical Workflow Designer of Exchange Server. If an instructor specifies that a course requires approval, the application starts a workflow process when a student attempts to register for the course. The application sends an e-mail to the student's manager, who can then approve the student for the course. If the manager rejects the request or doesn't approve it in time, the student can't take the course.

Figure 15-12 shows the workflow process in the Workflow Designer for Exchange Server. Figure 15-13 shows the e-mail that the manager receives when an approval is required for a student to take a course.

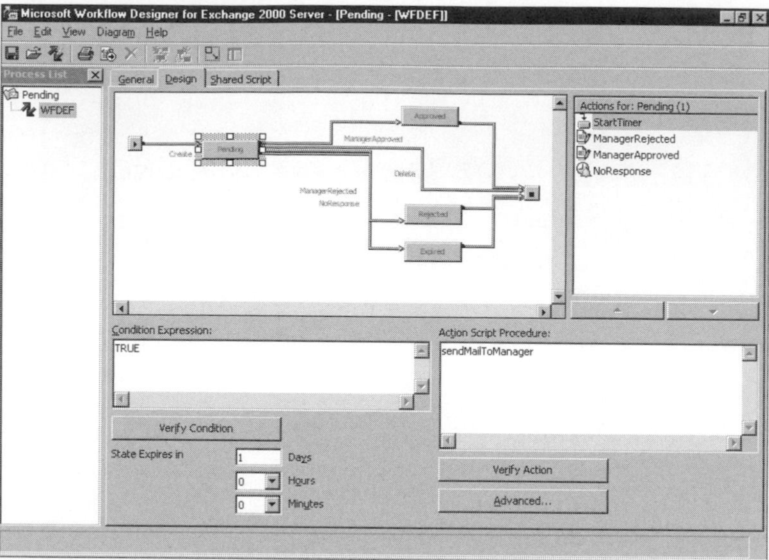

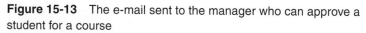

Figure 15-12 The workflow process shown in the Workflow Designer for Exchange Server

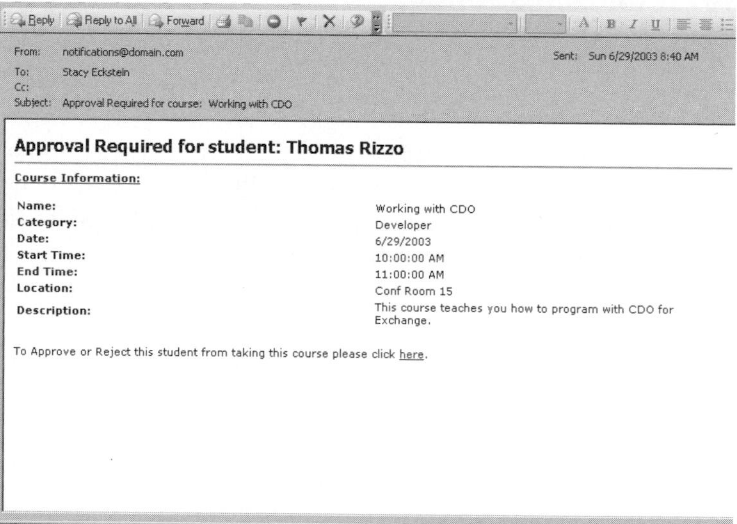

Figure 15-13 The e-mail sent to the manager who can approve a student for a course

Implementing Surveys

The Training application also provides a survey component. A timer-based event fires on the Exchange server every night to implement the course survey component. This event checks to see whether any courses have been completed on that day. If a course has been completed, the timer agent e-mails a notice to the students who were registered for the course, as shown in Figure 15-14. The students can then click on a link in the e-mail message and fill out a survey to rate both the course and the instructor. The application checks to make sure that students don't fill out multiple surveys for either the course or the instructor. Figure 15-15 shows a survey form for a course.

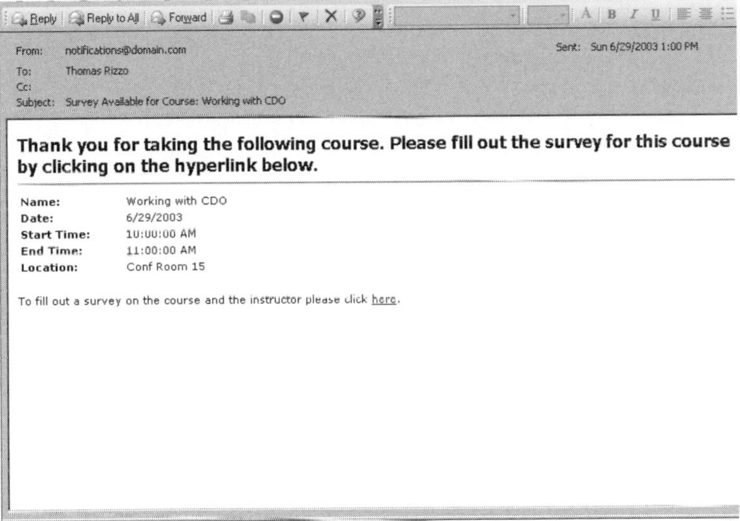

Figure 15-14 The e-mail notice that a survey is available for a course

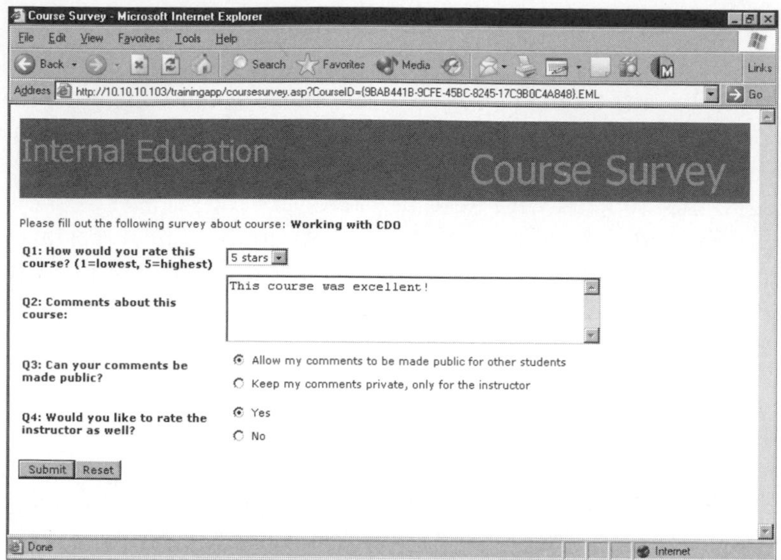

Figure 15-15 A survey for a course that the student can fill out

After the student fills out the survey, the survey is saved into one of the Surveys folders, depending on whether the survey is a course survey or an instructor survey. The survey agent collates all surveys received for the course and the instructor and determines an overall rating for each. The agent also takes any comments from users and adds them to the course or the instructor rating. Figure 15-16 shows how the final results look after the agent completes its processing. Other students can then view ratings and comments about the instructor or the course.

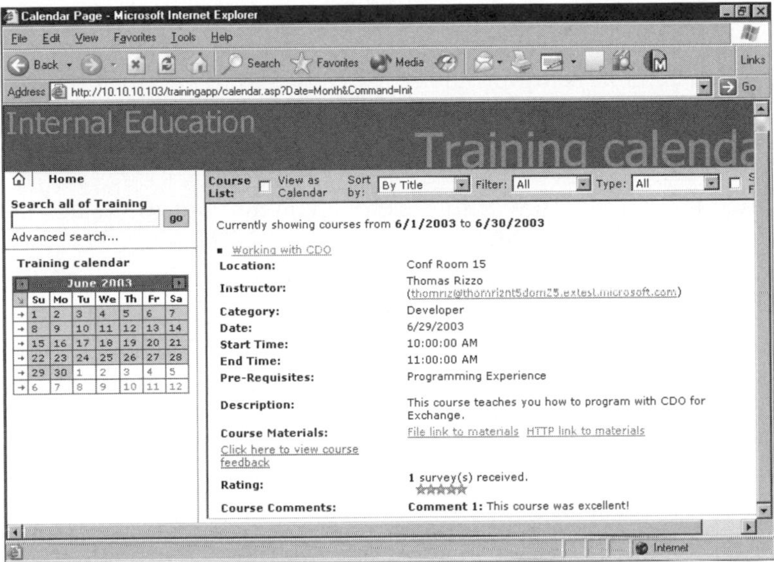

Figure 15-16 Ratings and comments shown in the main views for both the instructor and the course. Here we see the ratings for a course.

Now that you've had a quick overview of the Training application, let's look at how the application was actually built. We'll look at the technologies used and examine some code snippets from both the setup program and the application itself.

The Wonderful World of Schemas

Your first consideration when building an Exchange Server application is whether to use the schema support that's built into the product. As mentioned earlier, Exchange Server allows you to create schemas for your applications—which means you can define classes of items, such as *myproject* or *mycontact*. On those classes of items, you can have default sets of properties, such as *myname* or *mylocation*.

You don't have to create schemas in order to use built-in or custom properties on items in Exchange Server. For example, you can append new properties to an item by using ADO and store that item in Exchange Server. You must create a custom schema if you want to reuse your properties across multiple items rather than with a single, one-off item. Also, if you want your users to easily discover your properties, you must use a schema. You can access your properties through ADO when you run a SQL *SELECT* statement against your application, or it can be with the Web Storage System forms you create. The Training application uses many custom properties across many items, so it creates schemas in its setup program. We'll discuss that part of the program next.

Overview of the Exchange Server Schemas

You need to know a few things before you attempt to create schemas. First, Exchange Server ships with some schemas already in place for the default items it understands, such as messages, documents, appointments, and contacts. The schemas for these items are stored in a hidden folder in your Exchange server. You can view this hidden folder by writing a simple program or by looking at the folder through the MDBVUE utility. Figure 15-17 shows how to view the Schema folder using MDBVUE.

> **Note** You'll find the Schema folder under the Public Folders tree in the non-ipm subtree. This folder contains XML files that define the Exchange Server schemas. Exchange Server supports defining schemas through XML, but in the setup program for the Training application, I used ADO to create my schema definitions.

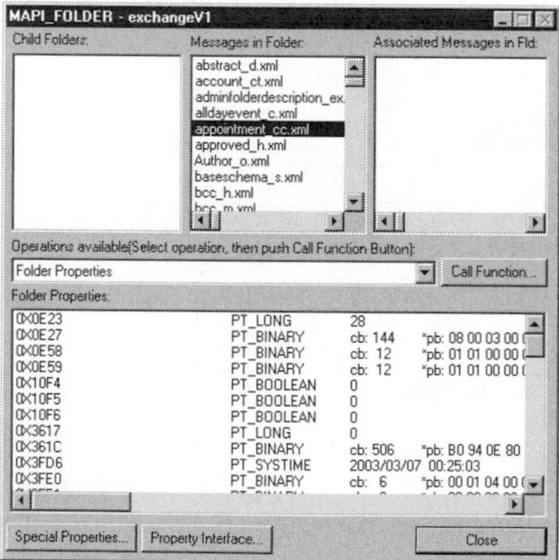

Figure 15-17 MDBVUE browsing the hidden Schema folder for Exchange Server.

Second, you should understand the idea of a content class as part of the base Exchange Server schema. For example, a message has a content class of *urn:content-classes:message*. Content classes are groupings of properties that define a certain type of item. If you set the content class of a particular item to *message*, the item will receive all the properties from your schema that are associated with the *message* content class.

If you're coming from the Exchange Server 5.5 development environment, you might be wondering how the content class and the message class are related. They actually have no explicit relationship; you can have a content class that's entirely independent from a message class. If you need to support Outlook or previous versions of OWA, just be sure to explicitly set both the content class and the message class in your application. Don't worry about the custom properties in your content class. Exchange Server makes those available in the *PS_PUBLIC_STRINGS* namespace in MAPI so that Outlook or any MAPI application can retrieve those custom properties.

> **Note** Outlook supports field names of up to 32 characters in its Field Chooser. If you create a property with a name longer than 32 characters, you might not be able to retrieve it from Outlook. Also, Outlook does not automatically recognize new properties added via ADO or CDO. To get these properties to display properly in Outlook, create a new field in Outlook with the same name as the field you created using ADO or CDO. Then add this new property to your Outlook view to check whether the property value is correctly displayed.

Creating Custom Content Classes

The first step when you create a custom content class is to decide what to call it. Be sure the name you select for your content class doesn't clash with other content class definitions. After you name your content class, you'll want to think about the properties contained in it. Exchange Server supports a wide range of built-in content classes, so you can inherit your content class from an existing one. For example, the Training application has training events. These events require properties that already exist on the appointment content class. However, the training events also need some extra properties that will exist on all training event items. Using inheritance, the Training application inherits the properties from both the appointment content class and the item content class.

Exchange Server supports multiple inheritance for content classes. Here are the default content classes that Exchange Server supports:

- *urn:content-classes:appointment*
- *urn:content-classes:calendarfolder*
- *urn:content-classes:calendarmessage*
- *urn:content-classes:contactfolder*
- *urn:content-classes:contentclassdef*
- *urn:content-classes:document*
- *urn:content-classes:dsn*
- *urn:content-classes:folder*
- *urn:content-classes:freebusy*
- *urn:content-classes:item*
- *urn:content-classes:journalfolder*
- *urn:content-classes:mailfolder*
- *urn:content-classes:mdn*
- *urn:content-classes:message*
- *urn:content-classes:notefolder*
- *urn:content-classes:object*
- *urn:content-classes:person*
- *urn:content-classes:propertydef*
- *urn:content-classes:recallmessage*
- *urn:content-classes:recallreport*
- *urn:content-classes:taskfolder*

Once you figure out which content classes you want to inherit from, you'll need to create some property definitions for your content class. Property definitions describe the name, type, value, and special characteristics of the properties you want in your content class. Be aware that a property definition you create can be used across multiple content classes. You'll see this in the Training application, in which both instructors and training events share survey result property definitions.

Let's look at some code from the setup program that creates the property definitions for a training event. We'll then examine exactly what's happening in the code.

```
:
CreateSchemaPropDef "instructoremail", "string", False, True, _
                    False, CStr("")
CreateSchemaPropDef "prereqs", "string", False, True, False, CStr("")
CreateSchemaPropDef "seats", "string", False, True, False, CStr("")
CreateSchemaPropDef "authorization", "string", False, True, False, _
                    CStr("")
CreateSchemaPropDef "category", "string", False, True, False, CStr("")
CreateSchemaPropDef "surveycount", "string", False, True, False, CStr("")
CreateSchemaPropDef "discussionurl", "string", False, True, False, _
                    CStr("")
CreateSchemaPropDef "materialsfilepath", "string", False, True, _
                    False, CStr("")
CreateSchemaPropDef "materialshttppath", "string", False, True, _
                    False, CStr("")
:

Private Sub CreateSchemaPropDef(strName, strType, bMultiValued, _
                            bIndexed, bReadOnly, varDefaultValue)
    Dim rec As New ADODB.Record
    With rec
        .Open strAppSchemaFolder & "/" & strName, , adModeReadWrite, _
              adCreateNonCollection + adCreateOverwrite

        'Create new property definition
        .Fields("DAV:contentclass") = "urn:content-classes:propertydef"

        'Give it a name
        .Fields("urn:schemas-microsoft-com:xml-data#name").Value = _
                strSchema & strName

        'Set the data type for the property
        .Fields("urn:schemas-microsoft-com:datatypes#type").Value = _
                strType

        'Set the other fields for the property
        .Fields("urn:schemas-microsoft-com:" & _
                "exch-data:ismultivalued").Value = bMultiValued
        .Fields("urn:schemas-microsoft-com:" & _
                "exch-data:isindexed").Value = bIndexed
        .Fields("urn:schemas-microsoft-com:" & _
                "exch-data:isreadonly").Value = bReadOnly
        .Fields("urn:schemas-microsoft-com:" & _
                "exch-data:default").Value = varDefaultValue
        .Fields.Update
        .Close
    End With
End Sub
```

This code creates a new item for my property definition in the Schema folder for the Training application. I recommend that you avoid modifying the built-in schemas for Exchange Server unless absolutely necessary (if you wanted a new property on all default messages, for example). Instead, you can inherit from them. Create a Schema subfolder for your applications and place your property and content class definitions in it.

> **Note** You must create property definition names in a unique namespace. The setup program asks you what schema namespace you want to use. By default, you should include your Internet domain name, if you have one, because it's guaranteed to be unique. For example, a good namespace might be *http://yourdomainname/schema/*. You can then append to that namespace the names of the custom properties for your application.
>
> You should also be aware that property names are case sensitive. I recommend lowercasing your entire property name to make your coding easier.

Once the new item is created, the code sets the content class property in the *DAV* namespace to *urn:content-classes:propertydef*. Exchange Server defines a number of new namespaces for properties, such as *DAV*, *http://schemas.microsoft.com/exchange/*, or *urn:schemas-microsoft-com:office:office*. The code then sets the *urn:schemas-microsoft-com:xml-data#name* property to the fully qualified name of the property. Next the code sets the data type, which can be one of a number of values. The most common ones you'll use are *String*, *Float*, *Boolean*, *DateTime*, *i2*, *i4*, *i8*, *Uuid*, *Int*, and *Bin.base64*. You should always use the most suitable data types in your application.

Once the data type is set, you can set other values for your properties. One such value is the *ismultivalued* property. By setting this property to *True*, you tell the Web Storage System that the property supports multiple values of the data type you specified. When you work with multivalue properties, you should set and get the values by using arrays. Examples of built-in multivalue properties are *urn:schemas-microsoft-com:xml-data#element* and *urn:schemas-microsoft-com:xml-data#extends*, which are properties on the content class definition item. We'll discuss creating a content class definition item shortly.

Another property you can set is the *isindexed* property. This property has nothing to do with content indexing (which we'll look at later); instead, it corresponds to the Exchange Server database index. If you set this property to

True, Exchange Server will create an index for the property so that sorting, grouping, and other operations on it execute quickly. One caveat about using *isindexed*: if you are concerned about the load on your Exchange server, don't set this property to *True* for all your properties. Instead, just determine which properties you really need indexing on, and set this property to *True* for those properties. To create the index for your custom properties, you must issue the *CREATE INDEX* command in ADO. You'll learn more about this command and ADO access to Exchange Server later in this chapter.

The next property you can set is the *isreadonly* property. You don't have to set this property because only properties provided by the Web Storage System can be set to read-only. However, I threw in this property just to expose you to it. You can query the value of this property from your applications to see whether a Web Storage System property is read-only.

The final property you'll want to set is the *default* property. This property specifies what default value, if any, your property should have when it's created by the application or the user. You don't have to set this property, but you should do so in order to initialize your properties to a default value.

Once the code finishes setting these properties using ADO, a call to the *Update* method of the *Fields* collection is required. When I cover ADO support in Exchange Server later in the chapter, we'll discuss the use of transactions with ADO and Exchange Server. I highly recommend that you use transactions where appropriate in your application in case you receive an error while processing your ADO commands. You can then roll back the transaction rather than leave your application's data in an inconsistent state. Although the previous code segment doesn't show it, the entire schema creation process is wrapped in a local OLE DB transaction.

Creating Content Class Definition Items

Now that we've created the custom property definitions for our content class, we need to create a content class definition in our schema. To do this, we create an item in the Schema folder that has the correct content class and properties set so that Exchange Server knows we want to create a custom content class. The following code shows how to create a definition of a custom content class:

```
⋮
arrTrainingEventProps = BuildSchemaArray(Array("instructoremail", _
    "prereqs", "seats", "authorization", "category", "surveycount", _
    "discussionurl", "materialsfilepath", "materialshttppath", _
    "publiccomments", "overallscore"))
CreateContentClass "trainingevent", _
    "urn:content-classes:trainingevent", _
    Array("urn:content-classes:item", "urn:content-classes:appointment"), _
```

```
    arrTrainingEventProps
⋮

Private Function BuildSchemaArray(arrProperties)
    Dim tmpArray()
    For i = LBound(arrProperties) To UBound(arrProperties)
        ReDim Preserve tmpArray(i)
        tmpArray(i) = strSchema & arrProperties(i)
    Next
    BuildSchemaArray = tmpArray
End Function

Private Sub CreateContentClass(strItemName, strContentClassName, _
                                arrExtends, arrFields)
    Dim rec As New ADODB.Record
    With rec
        'Create item in application Schema folder
        .Open strAppSchemaFolder & "/" & strItemName, , adModeReadWrite, _
              adCreateNonCollection + adCreateOverwrite
        '
        'Create new content class definition
        '
        .Fields("DAV:contentclass") = _
                "urn:content-classes:contentclassdef"

        'Name the content class
        .Fields("urn:schemas-microsoft-com:xml-data#name").Value = _
                strContentClassName

        'Enter what other content classes this one extends
        .Fields("urn:schemas-microsoft-com:xml-data#extends").Value = _
                arrExtends

        'Enter the fields that exist on the content class
        .Fields("urn:schemas-microsoft-com:xml-data#element") = arrFields

        'Save change
        .Fields.Update
        .Close
    End With
End Sub
```

The code first calls the function *BuildSchemaArray* to create an array containing the custom schema properties that the new content class will contain. This is an example of how to create values for a multivalue property.

Once the array is built, the code calls the *CreateContentClass* subroutine, which creates a new item in the Schema folder using ADO. The code sets the content class of the item to *urn:content-classes:contentclassdef*, which tells Exchange Server that this is a new content class definition item. The code then sets the name of the new content class definition to the name passed to the subroutine. In this example, the content class name is *urn:content-class:trainingevent*.

The code sets the *extends* property next. This multivalue string property contains a list of all the other content classes that this content class inherits from. A content class can either have no inheritance or can inherit from one or more content classes. What you want to accomplish in your application and which properties you need on your custom content class will dictate which content classes you inherit from. Because the *trainingevent* content class is so similar to the *appointment* content class in terms of properties required, the code inherits from the *appointment* content class. The code also inherits from the *item* content class, which most other content classes inherit from.

Finally, the code sets the *element* property. This is a multivalue property that should contain all the custom fields that your content class implements. Once this property is set, you can call the *Update* method on the ADO *Fields* collection to write the data to Exchange Server.

You can also use XML to create content class definitions and property definitions. If you create a correctly structured XML document and place it into the schema folder for your application, Exchange Server will allow you to use these new content classes and properties. The following example shows what two XML files—one for the content class definition and one for the property definition—look like in XML:

```
This XML file is for the content class definition
<?xml version="1.0"?>
<Schema
    name='ExchangeSchema'
    xmlns="urn:schemas-microsoft-com:xml-data"
    xmlns:d="DAV:" xmlns:ex="http://schemas.microsoft.com/exchange/"
    xmlns:cc="urn:content-classes:"
    xmlns:dt="urn:schemas-microsoft-com:datatypes"
    xmlns:s="urn:schemas-microsoft-com:exch-data:"
    xmlns:m="urn:schemas:httpmail:"
    xmlns:h="urn:schemas:mailheader:" xmlns:cs="http://customschemaname/">
    <ElementType name="cs:customprop" d:contentclass="cc:contentclassdef">
        <extends type="cc:item"/>
        <element type="cs:mycustompropname"/>
    </ElementType>
</Schema>

This XML file is for the property definition
<?xml version="1.0"?>
<Schema
    name='ExchangeSchema'
    xmlns="urn:schemas-microsoft-com:xml-data"
    xmlns:d="DAV:" xmlns:cc="urn:content-classes:"
```

```
    xmlns:dt="urn:schemas-microsoft-com:datatypes"
    xmlns:s="urn:schemas-microsoft-com:exch-data:"
    xmlns:m="urn:schemas:httpmail:" xmlns:cs="http://customschemaname/">
    <ElementType
        name="cs:PNAC"
        dt:type="string"
        s:ismultivalued="0"
        d:contentclass="cc:propertydef"
        s:isindexed="1"
        s:isreadonly="0"
        s:isrequired="0"
        s:isvisible="1">
    </ElementType>
</Schema>
```

The *expected-content-class* Property

You must take a few more steps when you use custom schemas. First you must set the property *urn:schemas-microsoft-com:exch-data:expected-content-class* on the folders for your application. This multivalue property tells Exchange Server what content classes to expect in the folder. This property can specify multiple content classes. The query processor in Exchange Server uses this list of expected content classes when you issue a *SELECT ** statement in the folder to determine which properties—besides the built-in schema ones—the query should return.

You should try to limit your use of *SELECT ** statements because the query processor has to retrieve every built-in and custom property in your content class, which can take a long time. If you know the specific properties you need to retrieve as part of your result set, you should specify them in your query. Here's an example of setting the *expected-content-class* property in code:

```
oFolderRecord.Fields _
  ("urn:schemas-microsoft-com:exch-data:expected-content-class").Value = _
   Array("urn:content-classes:appointment", _
   "urn:content-classes:mycontentclass")
```

The *schema-collection-ref* Property

In addition to setting the expected content class property, you need to set the *urn:schemas-microsoft-com:exch-data:schema-collection-ref* property on your application's folders. This property contains a URL that links to the first folder in which you want the Exchange server to look for schema definition items. In your custom applications, you set this property to the Schema subfolder. When we discuss using ADO with Exchange Server later in the chapter, you'll see how to determine the URL that will be the value of this property. If you do not set this property on your folders, Exchange Server will default to its built-in Schema folder in the non-ipm subtree. You can also use the ##SCHEMAURI## macro, which we will discuss later in this chapter. Here is an example of setting this property in code:

```
oFolderRecord.Fields _
  ("urn:schemas-microsoft-com:exch-data:schema-collection-ref").Value = _
   "file://./backofficestorage/domain/public folders/myapp/schema"
```

The *baseSchema* Property

You have one final task to perform to make your application's schema work well: setting the *urn:schemas-microsoft-com:exch-data:baseschema* property on your schema subfolder. This multivalue property provides URLs that Exchange Server will search if it doesn't find schema definitions in your schema subfolder. The server will search the set of URLs you provide in the order they're set in the property. So if Exchange Server finds the correct schema definition, it will stop searching subsequent URLs. By setting the *schema-collection-ref* property for your folders, you can have Exchange Server search your schema folder first and then search the built-in schema folder. The following is an example of setting this property:

```
strBaseSchemaFolder = _
    "file://./backofficestorage/domainname/public folders/" & _
    "non_ipm_subtree/schema/"
'Or you can use ##SCHEMAURI## discussed below
strBaseSchemaURI = "http://server/virtdir/##SCHEMAURI##/microsoft/ExchangeV1"
With oSchemaFolder
    .Fields("urn:schemas-microsoft-com:exch-data:baseschema") = _
            Array (strBaseSchemaFolder)
   .Fields.Update
End With
```

Using the ##SCHEMAURI## Macro

When working with global schema, such as the schema located at *http://server/public//non_ipm_subtree/schema/*, you should use the ##SCHEMAURI## convention to point at the schema. A number of problems can arise if you use hard-coded schema paths. First, accessibility is nondiscoverable. If you point your base schema to *http://server/public/non_ipm_subtree/schema/* while in a non-MAPI top-level hierarchy (TLH), rather than the Public Folders hierarchy, you will get an error because Exchange does not support crossing database boundaries. Your non-MAPI TLH is in a separate database from your MAPI TLH.

Also, when new versions of the schema are installed, such as with Microsoft SharePoint Portal Server 2001, which extends the Exchange schema with new properties and content classes, having a single schema folder does not provide for a scalable environment. Finally, if you create a virtual root that points to the middle of a folder hierarchy (such as a virtual root called Foo) and the root points directly to a folder called Bar in the third level of the folder hierarchy, you cannot point to the base schema folder if you did not create a virtual root that points at the root of the TLH.

##SCHEMAURI## is a macro that is expanded by the Web Storage System when you make a request for a schema lookup; you can use this macro instead of hardcoding the path to a base schema folder. Because Exchange supports versioned schema folders, you will see multiple schema folders depending on which applications you install on the server. If you install Exchange and SPS 2001 on the same machine, there will be multiple versioned schemas because SPS extends the Exchange schema, as mentioned earlier. Here are some examples of uses of ##SCHEMAURI##:

- *http://server/public/##SCHEMAURI##* is the location of the root for the base schema introduced in Exchange 2000 and is equivalent to the old path *http://server/public/non_ipm_subtree.*
- *http://server/public/##SCHEMAURI##/microsoft/ExchangeV1* is the location of the schema folder corresponding to the Exchange 2000 version of the schema and is equivalent to *http://server/public /non_ipm_subtree/schema/.*
- *http://server/sharepoint portal server/##SCHEMAURI##/microsoft /TahoeV1* is the location of the schema folder corresponding to the SPS 2001 version of the schema.
- *http://server/public/##SCHEMAURI##/default* is an empty folder made available to add any non-Microsoft schemas and to create subfolders of custom schemas.

> **Note** The ##SCHEMAURI## will not be supported in the private store (mailboxes) on Exchange.

If you are building an application on Exchange, I recommend using the macro instead of the *non_imp_subtree* way of accessing schemas because this new macro will be the default location to perform schema discovery. In the case of SPS, the *non_ipm_subtree* will be inaccessible, and you should always use ##SCHEMAURI##.

If you are using a non-MAPI TLH, you must replace *public* with the vroot that points to your non-MAPI TLH or use relative URL paths. The ##SCHEMAURI## needs to know which TLH to search to find the base schema. You can also use the ##SCHEMAURI## in setting your *SCR* and *baseschema* properties. An example might make this clearer. The Training application has been updated to take advantage of the new ##SCHEMAURI## code. The following code generates the schema properties for the application using this new macro:

```
'Figure out base schema folder
'Schema folders are stored in each folder tree
'Pull it off the path entered by the user
strBaseSchemaFolder = "http://" & strServerName & "/" & strRootFolder _
                    & "##schemauri##/microsoft/ExchangeV1"
With oSchemaFolder
    .Fields("urn:schemas-microsoft-com:exch-data:baseschema") = _
                    Array(strBaseSchemaFolder)
    .Fields.Update
End With
```

The code points to the ExchangeV1 schema folder because it uses only content classes and properties from that schema. SPS installs this schema folder as well as its own schema folder. The Training application will work on either Exchange or SPS because it uses the default Exchange base schema, which is available on both systems.

You can also use relative paths when you set the base schema or schema collection reference properties, which means the following path is valid as well:

```
urn:schemas.microsoft.com:exch-data:baseschema =  _
    Array("/##SCHEMAURI##/microsoft/ExchangeV1)
```

Global Schema Definitions

You can also create database-wide properties, content classes, and form registrations by adding these items to the global schema folder. Here *global* means the default schema folder for each public folder TLH because schemas are per TLH, not per server. An example is the schema folder for the default public folders root, *http://server/public/##SCHEMAURI##/microsoft/ExchangeV1*. This folder contains the default content classes and properties for that TLH (such as those added by Exchange 2003). One word of caution: working with the global schema can adversely affect your server's health and performance if you extend the global schema incorrectly.

Through code, the use of XML files, or tools, you can add new definitions to the global schema folder, and you can create your own schema folders (for example, *http://server/public/##SHEMAURI##/default/myfolder*). Create new property definition items, set the *isindexed* attribute to *TRUE*, and store the item in a global schema folder.

Besides using ADO and Web Distributed Authoring and Versioning (WebDAV) to create the new definitions, you can also extend the global schema via XML. This is the way the schema is initially populated by Exchange Server itself. If you look in the Exchange Server directory under the schema directory, you will see a number of files with an .xml extension. These are the XML files used to populate the Exchange schema using a system event. If you want to use the same method, take the following steps:

1. Create XML files to define your content classes, property definitions, or form registrations. (When you create the properties, remember to set the *isindexed* flag to *1*, which is *Boolean* true.) You can find great examples of these XML files in the Schema directory mentioned earlier.
2. Copy your new XML files to the Exchange 2003 global schema folder (for example, *http://server/public/##SCHEMAURI##/microsoft/ExchangeV1*).

Once the items are stored in the schema folder, an *OnSyncSave* store event will kick off EXSCHEMA.EXE. This process will promote the XML documents to schema definition items.

Using ADO and OLE DB with Exchange Server

Windows ships with OLE DB and ADO, and Exchange Server includes the OLE DB 2.5 and later provider for Exchange Server. If you've done any development with Microsoft SQL Server, you know how easy to use and powerful the ADO object model is. The OLE DB provider in Exchange Server, called EXOLEDB, capitalizes on this ease and power. In this section, we'll take a quick look at some of the features in ADO. Then, using the Training application, we'll examine how to build ADO applications with Exchange Server.

Note that the OLE DB provider should be used with Exchange Server only on the server side. Do not attempt to use the provider remotely from client-side applications, including using the new version of CDO on the client side. For applications that require client-side interaction, you can leverage WebDAV or previous versions of CDO or the Outlook object model.

ADO Features

Two major enhancements of ADO in version 2.5 and beyond should be of interest to Exchange Server developers: URL binding support, and *Record* and *Stream* support. These enhancements enable ADO to work so easily with the type of data stored in an Exchange Server application, for two reasons:

- Exchange Server is best at storing semistructured data rather than structured, relational data.
- Exchange Server supports URL addressing for every record in the Exchange Server database.

URL Binding Support

One of the most annoying things about the earlier versions of ADO is all the setup work required to open a data source connection. You have to create a *Connection* object, set the properties on that object, and then issue a query and retrieve your recordset from the data source. Recent versions of ADO let you bypass all that setup work. You simply provide a URL for the data you want to retrieve, and OLE DB sets up all the connections and manages all the security for you. Here is an example of binding directly to an Exchange Server resource with this new URL support:

```
'You can achieve the binding like this:
Set oRec = CreateObject("ADODB.Record")
oRec.Open "http://server/public/myfolder/myitem", , _
         adReadWrite, adOpenIfExists

'Or with one statement, like this:
oRec.Open "file://./backofficestorage/domain/" & _
         "public folders/myfolder/myitem", , adReadWrite, _
         adOpenIfExists
```

Notice that I don't have to create a *Connection* object. OLE DB does this automatically. The technology that makes this URL binding work is the new Root Binder in OLE DB. The Exchange Server OLE DB provider and other OLE DB providers register themselves with the Root Binder, specifying which types of URLs they support. For example, the Exchange Server OLE DB provider registers for the URL *"file://./backofficestorage"*. Using the file protocol, you can access mailboxes and Public Folders via *"file://./backofficestorage/defaultSMTP domain/public folders/myfolder"*.

> **Note** Notice that the *file:// URL* format requires passing a domain as part of the path, as in *file://./backofficestorage/microsoft.com/public*. This domain is usually the same as your Windows domain name. However, the real value for the domain is pulled from the default SMTP policy that you set in Exchange. If this policy uses a different addressing scheme than your Windows domain, the two will not match up. If you want to get a domain programmatically, the address you'll want will be stored in the following Active Directory object as the *gatewayProxy* property. You can use ADSI to read this property.

```
LDAP://server/CN=Default Policy,CN=Recipient Policies,
     CN=First Organization,CN=Microsoft Exchange,CN=Services,
     CN=Configuration,DC=domain,DC=com
```

Be aware that EXOLEDB does not register for the URLs that begin with *http://*. However, the Microsoft OLE DB Provider for Internet Publishing does. Therefore, if you want to use *http://* in the URLs to connect to Exchange Server data, you must explicitly specify that you want to use the EXOLEDB provider. To do so, you can create or grab an explicit *Connection* object that sets the provider to EXOLEDB and then use that object in your ADO methods. To work with Exchange Server using the EXOLEDB provider and *http://* URLs, the code will look like this:

```
Set oConnection = CreateObject("ADODB.Connection")
'Open a connection to the Exchange server by using a throw-away record
Set oThrowAwayRec = CreateObject("ADODB.Record")
oThrowAwayRec.Open "http://server/public/"
set oConnection = oThrowAwayRec.ActiveConnection
oConnection.Provider = "EXOLEDB.DataSource"
Set oRec = CreateObject("ADODB.Record")
oRec.Open "http://server/public/myfolder/myitem", _
        oConnection, adReadWrite, adOpenIfExists
```

> **Note** You can create the *Connection* object in other ways as well. Keep in mind that if you want to use *http://* URLs, you have to be sure the provider is EXOLEDB. Also, to get at Public Folders, you do not use Public Folders in the *http://* URL as you do with the *File://* URL. Instead, Exchange automatically creates a public virtual directory that points at your Public Folders. If you create other top-level hierarchies and you are going to access folders using the *http://* URL, you should create virtual directories that point at the hierarchy that contains those folders.

If you plan to use OLE DB transactions in your code, you might want to continue to explicitly create *Connection* objects. In ADO, you accomplish this by using the *BeginTrans*, *CommitTrans*, and *RollbackTrans* methods.

Because you'll be using URLs extensively with Exchange Server, you should commit one property to memory quickly: *DAV:href*, which is available on every item in Exchange Server. This property contains the URL to the associated item, making it easy for you to retrieve the URL and pass it to procedures or functions in your application.

Record and *Stream* Support

Previous versions of ADO allowed you to create only recordsets. Yet ADO enables you to create records and streams. Creating recordsets is useful for relational data sources because recordsets are very "rectangular," which means the data in the data sources will be uniform. However, nonrelational data sources such as Exchange Server are not very rectangular in nature. In fact, one row in an Exchange Server database could have many more or many fewer columns than the next row because Exchange Server provides flexible schema support even within a table (or folder, as it's called in Exchange Server). This is why the ability to create records and streams of information is a welcome addition to ADO.

***Record* object** In previous versions of ADO, if you wanted to open a single row, you had to create an entire recordset to contain that single row. However, with its record support, recent ADO allows you to pass the URL to a unique item in Exchange Server, and without requiring you to create a *Connection* or *RecordSet* object, ADO opens that item into your *Record* object. You can then use the properties and methods of the *Record* object to manipulate the data. You'll see the *Record* object used extensively throughout the code samples for the Training application shown later in the chapter.

***Stream* object** You can use the *Stream* object to manipulate streams of data, either text or binary. An Exchange Server message is a good example of a stream. When you retrieve the stream of a message, you're given the entire message, its headers, and its content as serialized data. You can then manipulate the data using the methods on the *Stream* object. In Chapter 17, when we look at how to set up the workflow process definition programmatically, you'll see an excellent example of working with streams.

Putting ADO to Work with Exchange Server

You'll mainly use ADO to access data in Exchange Server. Exchange Server supports the major features of ADO, including the ability to perform queries with clauses such as *WHERE* or *ORDER BY*. However, there is one major restriction on issuing SQL queries against Exchange Server: Exchange Server does not provide *JOIN* support, so you cannot join two Exchange Server folders into a single recordset.

SELECT Statement

Exchange Server supports SQL *SELECT* statements. Here is the basic format of a *SELECT* statement:

```
SELECT * | select-list
  FROM SCOPE(resource-list)
  [WHERE search-condition]
  [order-by-clause]
```

You should avoid using *SELECT ** if possible. Instead, pass in the property list that you want to retrieve from Exchange Server as part of your *SELECT* statement. An example of retrieving a specific set of properties from Exchange Server is shown here. Notice that you must place property names in quotes in order to retrieve them.

```
'Build the SQL statement
strURL = "file://./backofficestorage/domain/public folders/myfolder/"
strSQL = "SELECT ""urn:schemas:httpmail:subject"" " & _
    "FROM scope('shallow traversal of """ & strURL & _
    """') WHERE ""DAV:iscollection"" = false AND ""DAV:ishidden"" = false"

'Create a new RecordSet object
Set rst = New RecordSet
With rst
    'Open RecordSet based on the SQL string
    .Open strSQL
End With

If rst.BOF And rst.EOF Then
    Debug.Print "No Records!"
    End
End If

rst.MoveFirst
Do Until rst.EOF
Debug.Print rst.Fields("urn:schemas:httpmail:subject").value
    rst.MoveNext
Loop
```

You'll notice that the *SELECT* statement contains a *SCOPE* clause and a *WHERE* clause. The *SCOPE* clause identifies the resource at which you want the search to begin, such as the URL of a folder. Exchange Server supports deep and shallow traversals of the scope. A deep traversal of the URL means that Exchange Server searches not only the specified folder but also all its subfolders. As you'd expect, a shallow traversal means that Exchange Server searches only the specified folder.

> **Note** Deep traversals are not supported in the MAPI Public Folder top-level hierarchy (TLH), but shallow traversals are. Deep traversals are supported in other TLHs and in Mailbox folders, however. If your application requires deep traversals, this is something you should take into consideration.

Using the *SCOPE* clause, you can request multiple folders as long as the traversal is the same for all the folders. For example, you might want to perform deep traversals of multiple folders that do not have a parent-child relationship. This means that a single-level deep traversal will not search all the folders. Using the *SCOPE* clause, you can specify multiple URLs to search. The following example searches multiple folders using a shallow traversal. Note, however, that your traversal must be the same for all URLs and that this technique will not work in the Public Folder hierarchy.

```
'Build the SQL statement
strURL = "file://./backofficestorage/domain/myTLH/myfolder/Events/"
strURL2 = "file://./backofficestorage/domain/myTLH/myfolder/Students/"

strSQL = "SELECT ""urn:schemas:httpmail:subject"" " & _
         "FROM SCOPE('shallow traversal of """ & strURL & _
         """", 'shallow traversal of """ & strURL2 & _
         """") WHERE ""DAV:iscollection"" = false AND " & _
         """DAV:ishidden"" = false"
```

The *SCOPE* clause is optional. If you do not specify the clause, the shallow traversal is used. When you have a *SCOPE* clause without a traversal, the default traversal is the deep traversal. The following example illustrates this:

```
'Build the SQL statement
strURL = "file://./backofficestorage/domain/myTLH/myfolder/Events/"

'Shallow traversal is used
strSQL = "SELECT ""urn:schemas:httpmail:subject"" " & _
         "FROM """ & strURL & """"

'Deep traversal is used
strSQL = "SELECT ""urn:schemas:httpmail:subject"" " & _
         "FROM SCOPE('""" & strURL & """')"
```

The *WHERE* clause in your Exchange Server queries can be as complex or as simple as you want. The previous examples simply check whether the items are collections, which is really a check to see whether the items are folders or whether they are hidden. If either of these checks is true, the item is not returned from the query.

The Training application uses some complex *WHERE* clauses in its searches. For example, the following SQL statement is from the application's showcourses.asp file, which shows the available courses a student can take:

```
Function TurnintoISO(dDate,strType)
    'Format should be "yyyy-mm-ddThh:mm:ssZ"
    strISO = Year(dDate) & "-"
    If Month(dDate)<10 Then
        strISO = strISO & "0" & Month(dDate) & "-"
    Else
        strISO = strISO & Month(dDate) & "-"
    End If

    If Day(dDate)<10 Then
        strISO = strISO & "0" & Day(dDate) & "T"
    Else
        strISO = strISO & Day(dDate) & "T"
    End If

    If strType = "End" Then
        'Make it 23:59:59 PM on the day
        strISO = strISO & "23:59:59Z"
    Else
        'Make it first thing in the morning 00:00:01
        strISO = strISO & "00:00:01Z"
    End If

    TurnintoISO = strISO
End Function

:
'Figure out the sort order from a QueryString variable
If Request.QueryString("SortBy") = "" Then
    strSortBy = """urn:schemas:mailheader:subject"""
ElseIf Request.QueryString("SortBy") = "0" Then
    strSortBy = """urn:schemas:mailheader:subject"""
ElseIf Request.QueryString("SortBy") = "1" Then
    strSortBy = """urn:schemas:calendar:dtstart"""
ElseIf Request.QueryString("SortBy") = "2" Then
    strSortBy = """" & strSchema & "category""," & _
                """urn:schemas:mailheader:subject"""
Else
    strSortBy = """urn:schemas:mailheader:subject"""
End If
```

```
'Figure out the date to show from QueryString
If Request.QueryString("DateStart") = "" Then
    dDateStart = Date
Else
    dDateStart = CDate(Request.QueryString("DateStart"))
End If

If Request.QueryString("DateEnd") = "" Then
    dDateEnd = Date
Else
    dDateEnd = CDate(Request.QueryString("DateEnd"))
End If

'Put this date into an ISO format
dISODateEnd = TurnintoISO(dDateEnd,"End")
dISODateStart = TurnintoISO(dDateStart,"Start")

'Build the SQL statement
strSQL = "Select ""urn:schemas:mailheader:subject""," & _
    """DAV:href"",""urn:schemas:calendar:dtstart""," & _
    """urn:schemas:calendar:dtend"" FROM scope('shallow traversal of """ & _
    strScheduleFolderPath & _
    """') WHERE (""DAV:iscollection"" = false) AND " & _
    "(""DAV:ishidden"" = false) " & _
    "AND (""urn:schemas:calendar:dtstart"" >= " & _
    "CAST(""" & dISODateStart & """ as 'dateTime'))" & _
    "AND (""urn:schemas:calendar:dtstart"" <= " & _
    "CAST(""" & dISODateEnd & """ as 'dateTime'))" & _
    "ORDER BY " & strSortBy
:
```

Notice that the *SELECT* statement uses the *CAST* clause to cast the date specified from the URL to the ASP page into a *dateTime* data type. This is necessary if you plan to compare dates in your SQL statements. You'll also need to use the *CAST* clause to set the correct data types for multivalue properties. The format for a multivalue string is *CAST("Properties" as 'mv.string')*. Use the *CAST* clause for your custom properties that are not strings, including custom *Boolean* properties. Otherwise, Exchange will evaluate your custom properties as strings.

> **Note** Missing *CAST* clauses are one of the biggest gotchas when you're working with custom properties. When you try to select your property or query on the property, things might not work as expected. Be sure to *CAST* all your custom properties except string properties.

You'll also notice that the *Date* data type must be formatted into a standard ISO8601 format, such as *yyyy-mm-ddThh:mm:ssZ*. Exchange Server stores all dates in Universal Time Coordinate (UTC) format and expects your date queries to use the ISO8601 format. Therefore, when you work with ADO, all dates are returned as UTC dates rather than in the client's local time zone. If you want time-zone conversion performed for you automatically, you must use CDO instead.

Performance Considerations with Query Scope

When shallow traversal queries are scoped to a single folder, Exchange Server automatically caches results of that shallow traversal query. These cached results are saved in a search folder that is kept up-to-date with changes in the folder to which the query is scoped. As a result of this cache, if the query is repeated, the results are available again without requiring a repeat of the entire query. By default, Exchange limits the number of search folders that it keeps per folder to 11, and it limits the time it keeps a search folder since it was last used to 8 days. It does this because there is an additional cost to maintain the search folder when changes occur to the scoped folder. If you want to increase the number of cached views beyond 11, you should modify the property *http://schemas.microsoft.com/mapi/proptag/xe680003* on the desired folder. Just set this property to the number of cached views you want for the folder. Remember, though, that each cached view takes resources, so be careful not to set this number too high for multiple folders.

You can also change the default value of 11 views per folder on a databasewide basis by setting the *MsExchMaxCachedViews* parameter in Microsoft Active Directory. You can find this property on the *AD* object for the database by using ADSI Edit.

In the case of searches, to take advantage of a cached view, the search must exactly match the search on which the cached view was created. The searches must match each other, down to the order in which the expressions are listed in the *WHERE* clause. If the expressions are not listed in exactly the same way, Exchange will create a new search rather than search the cached results.

Increasing the number of cached views on a given folder also results in a small additional performance cost of about 5 percent for each additional cached view when you add, update, or remove items from the folder if the item in question satisfies the restriction on the view. The cost is much less if the changed item does not satisfy the restriction.

Hierarchical Traversal

When you do a deep traversal search in which you only want to search against folder (such as nonmessage and nondocument) resources, an application can improve the performance of the search by specifying that the search uses hierarchical traversal rather than deep traversal. For example, both of the following searches return the same results, but the first returns much faster and uses fewer server resources than the second because the first uses the hierarchical traversal rather than a deep traversal, which looks at every item in the database:

```
"SELECT "DAV:displayname" from scope('HIERARCHICAL TRAVERSAL OF
"http://myserver/public"')

"SELECT "DAV:displayname" from scope('DEEP TRAVERSAL OF
"http://myserver/public"') WHERE "DAV:iscollection" = true
```

ORDER BY Clause

Exchange Server supports the *ORDER BY* clause. The next code sample, taken from the Training application, shows how to use *ORDER BY*. Exchange Server lets you sort your records by multiple columns in both ascending and descending order. In the Training application, for example, the user can sort the list of courses by subject, by date, or by category and then by date. You can specify a list of properties in your *ORDER BY* clause. If you do not specify a sorting order for your property, the default sorting order is ascending. To specify ascending or descending order, use *ASC* or *DESC*, respectively.

```
'Figure out the sort order from a querystring variable
If Request.QueryString("SortBy") = "" Then
    strSortBy = """urn:schemas:mailheader:subject"""
ElseIf Request.QueryString("SortBy") = "0" Then
    strSortBy = """urn:schemas:mailheader:subject"""
ElseIf Request.QueryString("SortBy") = "1" Then
    strSortBy = """urn:schemas:calendar:dtstart"""
ElseIf Request.QueryString("SortBy") = "2" Then
    strSortBy = """" & strSchema & "category""," & _
                """urn:schemas:mailheader:subject"""
Else
   strSortBy = """urn:schemas:mailheader:subject"""
End If

'This will eventually become part of the overall SELECT
'statement, such as:
'SELECT prop FROM URL WHERE condition
'ORDER BY strSortBy
```

LIKE Predicate

Exchange Server supports the *LIKE* predicate, which allows you to perform queries using pattern matching of wildcard characters. The format of the *LIKE* predicate follows:

```
SELECT Select_List | *
    FROM_Clause
    [WHERE Column_Reference [NOT] LIKE 'String_Pattern']
    [ORDER_BY_Clause]
```

You can specify any column you want, as long as its data type is compatible with the string pattern specified. Table 15-2 shows the wildcard characters you can use.

Table 15-2 Wildcard Characters You Can Use with the *LIKE* Predicate

Wildcard Name	Character	Description
Percent	%	Matches one or more characters
Underscore	_	Matches exactly one character
Square brackets	[ ]	Matches any single character in the range or set that you specify in the brackets
Caret	^	Matches any single character not within the range

The following code is taken from the search page for the Training application. This code uses the % wildcard to perform a full-text search on certain properties to see whether they contain a substring of the search criteria specified in strText:

```
strFullText = " AND (""urn:schemas:mailheader:subject"" LIKE '%" _
   & strText & "%' OR ""urn:schemas:httpmail:textdescription"" " & _
   "LIKE '%" & strText & "%' OR ""urn:schemas:calendar:location"" " & _
   "LIKE '%" & strText & "%' OR """ & strSchema & _
   "instructoremail"" LIKE '%" & strText & "%' OR " & _
   " """ & strSchema & "prereqs"" LIKE '%" & strText & "%')"
```

Be aware that the *LIKE* predicate uses the Exchange Server query processor. This is different than the *CONTAINS* and *FREETEXT* statements, which we'll examine when we look at content indexing. Both *CONTAINS* and *FREETEXT* require you to turn on content indexing before you can use them in your SQL statement. The *LIKE* predicate is not as fast as *CONTAINS* or *FREETEXT* because the Exchange Server query processor must search each item to see whether one of its columns contains the value you specified.

GROUP BY Predicate

Exchange Server supports the *GROUP BY* predicate, allowing you to group all rows that have the same value into a single row. This is useful when you want to obtain distinct counts based on a specific value. For example, you can use *GROUP BY* to count the number of people listed in your Inbox who sent you e-mail. Instead of having to scroll through your Inbox and count all the From addresses, you can use the *GROUP BY* statement, as shown here:

```
strURL = "file://./backofficestorage/domain/mbx/mailbox/inbox/"

'Build the SQL statement
strSQL = "Select ""urn:schemas:mailheader:from"" " & _
    "From scope('shallow traversal of """ & strURL & _
    """') GROUP BY ""urn:schemas:mailheader:from"""
Set conn = New ADODB.Connection
With conn
    .Provider = "exoledb.datasource"
    .Open strURL
End With

'Create a new RecordSet object
Set rst = New RecordSet
With rst
    'Open RecordSet based on the SQL string
    .Open strSQL, conn
End With

If rst.BOF And rst.EOF Then
    Msgbox "No values found!"
    End
End If

iCount = 0
rst.MoveFirst
Do Until rst.EOF
    iCount = iCount + 1
    strFrom = rst.Fields("urn:schemas:mailheader:from").Value
    Debug.Print "From: " & strFrom
    rst.MoveNext
Loop
Debug.Print "There are " & iCount & _
   " distinct FROM addresses in your inbox."
```

Here is the output from this code sample:

```
From: "System Administrator"
   <postmaster@thomriznt5dom.extest.microsoft.com>
From: "Thomas Rizzo" <thomriz@thomriznt5dom.extest.microsoft.com>
From: <notifications@domain.com>
There are 3 distinct FROM addresses in your Inbox.
```

CREATE INDEX Predicate

You might be wondering how you actually force Exchange Server to create a database index on the properties for which you set the *isindexed* property to *True*. One way is to specify a *SELECT ** statement on the folder. The preferred way is to use the *CREATE INDEX* statement. Here is the format for this statement:

```
CREATE INDEX * ON scopeURL (*)
```

A command that uses this statement looks like this:

```
CREATE INDEX * ON
   file://./backofficestorage/domain/public folders/my folder/ (*)
```

Note that the scope of this statement is the folder, so if you have multiple application folders, you should run the statement multiple times with the different scopes. One issue to note is that the index created by Exchange is kept permanently, so you need to issue this statement only once per folder. You cannot explicitly name or delete the index. Creating the index should give your applications faster performance. This index is different from the full-text index, which we'll discuss in the next chapter.

Property-level indexes help the performance only of searches that use the indexed property in the *WHERE* clause of the search. For example, if an index has been created on *myFolder* for the property *myProp1*, the following search will yield a performance gain:

```
SELECT DAV:displayname from scope('DEEP TRAVERSAL OF
"http://myserver/public/myFolder"') WHERE "myProp1" = 'foo'
```

If the restriction is more complicated, however, the addition of a single index might not be sufficient, depending on how efficiently the query can be evaluated. For example, the following restriction benefits from the index on *myProp1* because Exchange can evaluate the first clause of the restriction by using the index and then apply the second part of the restriction against those results.

```
WHERE "myProp1" = 'foo' and "myProp2" = 'bar'
```

You will not see improved performance for the following restriction because while the first half of the restriction can be evaluated efficiently, the second half must be evaluated by looking at every item because there is no index on *myProp2*. To evaluate this efficiently, indexes on both properties are required.

```
WHERE "myProp1" = 'foo' or "myProp2" = 'bar'
```

With the use of property-level indexes, applications experience a performance decrease of about 1 percent per index when you insert or update items in the folders that have had indexes created or remove items from those folders. This decrease is due to the cost of updating the index information for that folder to reflect the update operation. To maximize application performance you should create indexes only on properties that are frequently searched against.

Aliasing Column Names

To make it easier for you to work with the long schema names that Exchange Server provides, the Exchange Server OLE DB provider supports aliasing column names. This means you can give friendly names to the column names of the schema in your *SELECT* statements. The following is an example of such aliasing:

```
strURL = "file://./backofficestorage/domain/mbx/thomriz/inbox/"

'Build the SQL statement
strSQL = "Select ""urn:schemas:mailheader:from"" AS " & _
         "EmailFrom From scope('shallow traversal of """ & strURL & _
         """') ORDER BY EmailFrom"

'Create a new RecordSet object
Set rst = New RecordSet
With rst
    'Open RecordSet based on the SQL string
    .Open strSQL
End With

If rst.BOF And rst.EOF Then
    End
End If

rst.MoveFirst
Do Until rst.EOF
Debug.Print "From: " & rst.Fields("EmailFrom").Value
    rst.MoveNext
Loop
```

As you'll notice in the code, aliasing requires you to use the *AS* keyword and then the name of the alias you want for the column. You'll also notice that aliasing is supported in the *ORDER BY* clause. However, it is not supported in the *WHERE* or *GROUP BY* clauses. Also, aliasing is supported when you use the *Fields* collection. This makes it easy to create short, memorable aliases for the schema names in your applications.

> **Note** Aliasing works only for a specific *SELECT* statement; it is not global in nature.

> **Note** Exchange Server does not support the following SQL statements: *SET*, *DISTINCT*, *DELETE*, *INSERT*, *UPDATE*, *CONVERT*, *DATASOURCE*, *CREATE VIEW*, *COUNT*, *SUM*, *AVG*, *MIN*, and *MAX*. Also, Exchange Server does not support *JOIN*.

Content Indexing and Using CI from ADO

Exchange Server provides built-in support for content indexing. If you plan to use Exchange Server as a repository for a large amount of information, or if you think that your users will require advanced search features, you should consider using content indexing. While content indexing can index the standard properties such as the From, Subject, and Message text fields, you can also use content indexing to search for text in attachments on items. Content indexing supports indexing attachments in different formats, such as Office and HTML documents, as well as standard text attachments. The only caveat for content indexing is the requirement for higher processor and disk resources due to the indexing overhead. To keep this overhead within reasonable limits, you can schedule incremental crawls of the data sources for content indexing through the Exchange System Manager, shown in Figure 15-18.

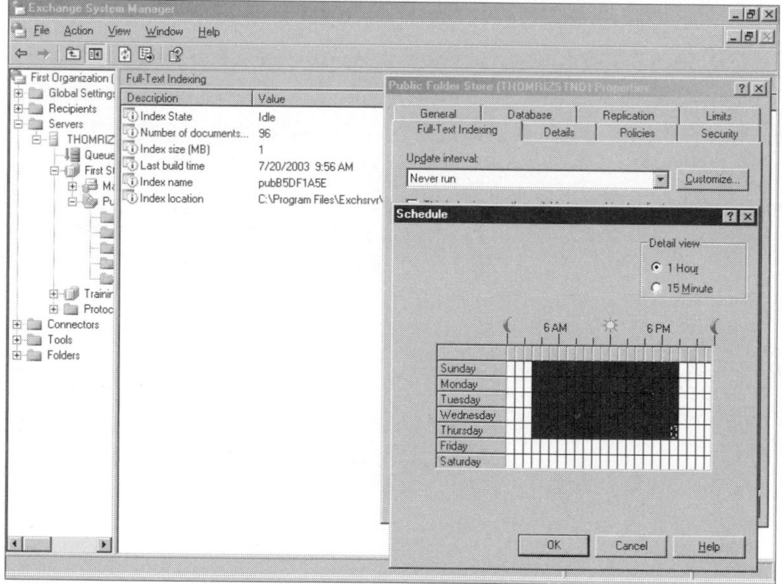

Figure 15-18 Using the Exchange System Manager to schedule Content Indexing.

If you have SharePoint Portal Server in your environment, you will want to leverage that technology to search Exchange and other data sources in a single search, because Exchange can only index and search Exchange information, while SharePoint can search many data sources, including Exchange, Lotus Notes, Web sites, and file shares. The one advantage Exchange content indexing has over SharePoint is that SharePoint can index only Exchange public folders, while Exchange can index and search user's mailboxes as well. For more information on SharePoint and programming search in SharePoint, please refer to the online chapters for this book on the Microsoft Press Web site.

With content indexing, you can perform quick queries against a full-text index inside your Exchange Server applications. Using the full-text index is as easy as generating a SQL query that uses the *CONTAINS* or *FREETEXT* predicate. You cannot use these predicates, however, unless you turn on content indexing for your Exchange server. Be aware that content indexing operates on a per-store basis, which means there is no top-level index that allows you to search across stores. Let's see how a SQL query containing the *CONTAINS* or *FREETEXT* predicate looks.

CONTAINS Predicate

The *CONTAINS* predicate allows you to perform text-matching operations against the full-text index. With *CONTAINS*, you can perform simple queries, such as "Show me all items that contain the word *Bob* in the subject," as well as complex queries with weighting on the terms they contain. (You can use a weighted query to indicate relative importance of the terms you search for.) The following code snippet shows several ways you can use the *CONTAINS* predicate. The code includes a simple version of *CONTAINS*; it also shows how to use the *NEAR* keyword, prefix matching, linguistic matching (such as drive, driving, and so on), and weighted queries. For more information on this pred icate, please refer to the Microsoft Developer Network (MSDN) at *http://msdn.microsoft.com*.

```
'Contains Bob
strSQL = "SELECT ""urn:schemas:httpmail:subject"" FROM " _
       & "SCOPE('SHALLOW TRAVERSAL OF """ & strURL _
       & """') WHERE CONTAINS(""urn:schemas:httpmail:subject"",' ""Bob"" ')"

'Contains Bob AND Cool, could also be OR
strSQL = "SELECT ""urn:schemas:httpmail:subject"" FROM " _
       & "SCOPE('SHALLOW TRAVERSAL OF """ & strURL _
       & """') WHERE CONTAINS(""urn:schemas:httpmail:subject"",' ""Bob"" " _
       & "AND ""Cool""')"

'Word prefix match
strSQL = "SELECT ""urn:schemas:httpmail:subject"" FROM " _
       & "SCOPE('SHALLOW TRAVERSAL OF """ & strURL _
       & """') WHERE CONTAINS(""urn:schemas:httpmail:subject"",' ""*Bob*"" ')"

'Linguistic matching
strSQL = "SELECT ""urn:schemas:httpmail:subject"" FROM " _
       & "SCOPE('SHALLOW TRAVERSAL OF """ & strURL _
       & """') WHERE CONTAINS('FORMSOF(INFLECTIONAL,""drive"") ')"
```

```
'Bob NEAR cool, where ~ is same as NEAR (within 50 words)
strSQL = "SELECT ""urn:schemas:httpmail:subject"" FROM " _
       & "SCOPE('SHALLOW TRAVERSAL OF """ & strURL _
       & """') WHERE CONTAINS(""urn:schemas:httpmail:subject""," _
       & "'""Bob"" ~ ""cool""')"

'Weighted Match
strSQL = "SELECT ""urn:schemas:httpmail:subject"" FROM " _
       & "SCOPE('SHALLOW TRAVERSAL OF """ & strURL _
       & """') WHERE CONTAINS(""urn:schemas:httpmail:subject""," _
       & "'ISABOUT (""Bob"" WEIGHT(0.9), ""Cool"" WEIGHT(0.1))')"
```

FREETEXT Predicate

You can use the *FREETEXT* predicate to search columns based on the meaning of the search words rather than the exact wording. When you use *FREETEXT*, the query engine breaks the string you specify into a number of search terms, assigns weights to the terms, and then attempts to find a match. The following code performs a search for the meaning "best server on the planet." I have in my Inbox a message with the subject "Exchange Server is the best server in the world," and the search finds that message even though the wording is slightly different.

> **Note** You can use the *AND*, *OR*, and *FREETEXT* predicates together.
>
> ```
> 'FREETEXT
> strSQL = "SELECT ""urn:schemas:httpmail:subject"" FROM " _
>        & "SCOPE('SHALLOW TRAVERSAL OF """ & strURL _
>        & """') WHERE FREETEXT(""urn:schemas:httpmail:subject""," _
>        & "'best server on the planet')"
> ```

Working with Ranking

When you use content indexing with a query, you might want to retrieve the rank value of a document compared to the search terms in your query. The search engine will assign a rank of 0 to 1000 to your items based on how well they match the query. In your SQL *SELECT* statement, you can request the rank property by adding the *urn:schemas.microsoft.com:fulltextqueryinfo:rank* property. You can use the *ORDER BY* predicate with this property to sort the items returned by the query based on their relevance to the search terms. Also, you can force Exchange to coerce the values for the rank by using clause weighting or rank coercion.

The idea of clause weighting is similar to that of weighted columns, which you saw in an earlier example. The difference is that instead of applying the weight to only the column, you apply the weight to the entire search term using the *RANK BY* predicate. This predicate takes a number of options, such as *WEIGHT* and *COERCION*.

The next example demonstrates clause ranking, so it uses the *WEIGHT* option. This option takes a decimal value from 0 through 1 plus up to three digits past the decimal, as in 0.832. Using the technique of clause weighting, you can assign certain search terms a fraction of the weight that other search terms have. The following example searches all properties on the items for the term *transportation* and the terms *heavy* and *trains*. As you can see by the ranking, if the search engine finds only *transportation*, it should rank that item at one-quarter the value of an item containing *heavy trains*. When you use weighting in this manner, the search engine applies weighting to the terms in the preprocessing stage.

```
StrSQL = "Select ""urn:schemas:httpmail:subject"", " _
       & """urn:schemas.microsoft.com:fulltextqueryinfo:rank"" FROM " _
       & "scope('shallow traversal of ""file://./backofficestorage/" _
       & "thomriznt5dom.extest.microsoft.com/apps/items/""') WHERE " _
       & "CONTAINS(*,'""transportation""') RANK BY WEIGHT(0.25) OR " _
       & "CONTAINS(*,'""heavy trains""') RANK BY WEIGHT(1.0)"
```

Coercion, especially rank coercion, is a post-processing concept in which, after the search engine finds matches for the search terms, your application can tell the search to recalculate the rank according to your specifications. Coercion is best illustrated with an example. Suppose you are searching for a document that contains the word *Exchange*. If the word *Exchange* is in a particular property that you think will make the item containing the word particularly relevant, such as the *subject* property, you can coerce the search engine into giving the item you are searching for a very high ranking. If the search engine finds an item with the word *Exchange* in another property (that is, a property other than the *subject* property), you can have the search engine read just the ranking so the items containing *Exchange* found in the other properties are ranked lower than those found in the *subject* property.

You can perform coercion using one of two approaches. One approach is absolute coercion, in which you assign an absolute value, such as *500*, to the items that meet your criteria for coercion. But what if you have more complex scenarios and absolute coercion will not meet your needs? For example, say you want items with the word *Exchange* in the *subject* property to be ranked from 900 through 1000. (Remember that the rank can range from 0 through 1000.) Using a coercion formula—the second approach—you can tell the search engine to assign the coerced rank of these items according to the formula 900 + the uncoerced rank × 0.1. For the items containing the word *Exchange* in a property different from *subject*, you can coerce the rank to be in the range of 0 through 900 by making the coerced rank equal to the uncoerced rank multiplied by 0.9.

Using a coercion formula requires that your users know which columns they should have the search engine rank higher when their search criterion involves those columns. You can implement some logic in your application to take a shot at defining which columns should be coerced as ranking higher if search terms are found in those columns. The following code shows using both absolute coercion and a coercion formula for the example we just looked at:

```
'Use absolute coercion
'1000 - Exchange in Subject
'500 - Exchange anywhere else
StrSQL = "SELECT ""urn:schemas:httpmail:subject""," _
       & """urn:schemas.microsoft.com:fulltextqueryinfo:rank"" FROM " _
       & "SCOPE('SHALLOW TRAVERSAL OF ""file://./backofficestorage/" _
       & "thomriznt5dom.extest.microsoft.com/apps/items/""') WHERE " _
       & "CONTAINS(""urn:schemas:httpmail:subject"",'""Exchange""') " _
       & "RANK BY COERCION(ABSOLUTE,1000) OR CONTAINS(*,'""Exchange""') " _
       & "RANK BY COERCION(ABSOLUTE,500)"

'Use coercion formula
'900 - 1000 - Exchange in Subject using MULTIPLY and ADD
'0 - 900 - Exchange anywhere else using MULTIPLY
'MULTIPLY takes a decimal number from 0 to 1, with 3 digits after
'the decimal
'ADD takes an integer
'You cannot go above 1000
StrSQL = "SELECT ""urn:schemas:httpmail:subject""," _
       & """urn:schemas.microsoft.com:fulltextqueryinfo:rank"" FROM " _
       & "SCOPE('SHALLOW TRAVERSAL OF ""file://./backofficestorage/" _
       & "thomriznt5dom.extest.microsoft.com/apps/items/""') WHERE " _
       & "(CONTAINS(""urn:schemas:httpmail:subject"",'""Exchange""') " _
       & "RANK BY COERCION(MULTIPLY,0.1)) RANK BY COERCION(ADD,900) OR " _
       & "CONTAINS(*,'""Exchange""') RANK BY COERCION(MULTIPLY,0.9)"
```

Indexing Default Properties

The content indexing engine by default indexes a certain set of built-in properties, which are listed in Table 15-3. Note that there is currently no simple way to tell the engine to index your custom properties, such as setting a *fulltext-indexed* property in your schema. The only way to ensure that your custom properties are full-text indexed is to create a text file, such as *http://thomriz.com/schema/myprop*, that contains the fully qualified names for your properties on separate lines. You then need to locate the following registry key:

HKLM\Software\Microsoft\Search\1.0

If the registry key does not already exist, add a key under 1.0 with the name *ExchangeParameters*. If the *ExchangeParameters* key does not already exist, add a string value under *ExchangeParameters* with the name *SchemaTextFilePathName*. The *SchemaTextFilePathName* string should contain the path to the text file of properties, such as C:\Exchsrvr\fulltextprops.txt.

Table 15-3 Built-In Properties Indexed by the Content Indexing Engine by Default

MAPI Property	*urn:schemas:httpmail* Property
PR_SUBJECT, PR_SUBJECT_W	*urn:schemas:httpmail:subject*
PR_BODY, PR_BODY_W	*urn:schemas:httpmail:textdescription*
PR_SENDER_NAME, PR_SENDER_NAME_W	*urn:schemas:httpmail:textdescription*
PR_SENDER_NAME_W	*urn:schemas:httpmail:sendername*
PR_SENT_REPRESENTING_NAME, PR_SENT_REPRESENTING_NAME_W	*urn:schemas:httpmail:fromname*
PR_DISPLAY_TO, PR_DISPLAY_TO_W	*urn:schemas:httpmail:displayto*
PR_DISPLAY_CC, PR_DISPLAY_CC_W	*urn:schemas:httpmail:displaycc*
PR_DISPLAY_BCC, PR_DISPLAY_BCC_W	*urn:schemas:httpmail:displaybcc*
PR_SENDER_EMAIL_ADDRESS, PR_SENDER_EMAIL_ADDRESS_W	*urn:schemas:httpmail:senderemail*

You can use the following code, taken from the Training application, when you turn on content indexing for the application. In the Training application, I've commented out this code since you may not have content indexing enabled on the store where you install the application. To see this code in action, remove my comment characters. The following listing shows the code in activated state:

```
'Uses CONTAINS instead of LIKE
'**************************** BEGIN
strCategoryText = "CONTAINS (""" & strSchema & "category"","

If strCategories = "all" Then

    arrCategories = Session("arrCategories")
```

```
        'Select the first one
        'Generate the rest
        strCategoriesSQL = strCategoryText
        For i = LBound(arrCategories) To UBound(arrCategories)
            If i = LBound(arrCategories) Then
                'First one, start the '
                strCategoriesSQL = strCategoryText & "'""" & arrCategories(i)
                If LBound(arrCategories) = UBound(arrCategories) Then
                    'Only one, end the statement
                    strCategoriesSQL = strCategoriesSQL & """')"
                Else
                    strCategoriesSQL = strCategoriesSQL & """ OR "
                End If
            ElseIf (i < UBound(arrCategories) AND i > LBound(arrCategories)) Then
                    strCategoriesSQL = strCategoriesSQL & """" _
                                     & arrCategories(i) & """ OR "
            Else
                'It's the last one, drop the OR
                If Right(arrCategories(i),1) = chr(10) Then
                    'Must be a carriage return/linefeed
                    arrCategories(i) = Mid(arrCategories(i), _
                                           1,(len(arrCategories(i))-2))
                End If
                strCategoriesSQL = strCategoriesSQL & """" _
                                 & Trim(Cstr(arrCategories(i))) & """')"
            End If
        Next
    Else
        'Need to create the category search string
        'Grab the querystring value which should be separated by $
        strCats = Request.QueryString("Categories")
        arrCats = Split(strCats,"$")

        'Always going to be at least one
        For i = LBound(arrCats) to UBound(arrCats)
            If i = LBound(arrCats) Then
                'First one, start the '
                strCategoriesSQL = strCategoryText & "'""" & arrCats(i)
                If LBound(arrCats) = UBound(arrCats) Then
                    'Only one, end the statement
                    strCategoriesSQL = strCategoriesSQL & """')"
                Else
                    strCategoriesSQL = strCategoriesSQL & """ OR "
                End If
            ElseIf (i < UBound(arrCats) AND i > LBound(arrCats)) Then
                strCategoriesSQL = strCategoriesSQL & """" & arrCats(i) _
                                 & """ OR "
            Else
                'It's the last one, drop the OR
                If Right(arrCats(i),1) = chr(10) Then
                    'Must be a carriage return/linefeed
                    arrCats(i) = Mid(arrCats(i), 1, (len(arrCats(i))-2))
                End If
```

```
            strCategoriesSQL = strCategoriesSQL & """" _
                             & Trim(Cstr(arrCats(i))) & """')"
        End If
    Next
End If
'************************************** END
```

Common Tasks Performed Using ADO

This section describes the eight most common tasks you'll perform when using ADO with Exchange Server: creating folders, creating items, deleting folders or items, copying folders or items, moving folders or items, working with the *Fields* collection, working with recordsets, and handling errors.

Creating New Folders

To create a new folder using ADO, you must construct the URL to the folder and then use the *Open* method on the ADO *Record* object with the parameter *adCreateCollection*. The following code, taken from the setup program of the Training application, creates the application folders by using ADO:

```
Private Sub CreateFolder(strFolderPath, strFolderName, _
                         strExpectedContentClass, strMAPIFolderClass)
    Dim oFolderRecord As New ADODB.Record
    oFolderRecord.Open strFolderPath & strFolderName, _
                       oConnection, adModeReadWrite, adCreateCollection
    oFolderRecord.Fields("urn:schemas-microsoft-com:exch-data:" & _
                         "expected-content-class").Value = _
                         Array("urn:content-classes:" & _
                         strExpectedContentClass)
    'Set the Schema collection reference to our schema folder
    'even though it may not exist yet
    oFolderRecord.Fields("urn:schemas-microsoft-com:exch-data:" & _
                         "schema-collection-ref").Value = _
                         strFolderPath & "schema"
    oFolderRecord.Fields("DAV:contentclass").Value = _
                         "urn:content-classes:folder"
    'Set the PR_CONTAINER_CLASS
    'so that Outlook displays it correctly
    oFolderRecord.Fields("http://schemas.microsoft.com/mapi/proptag/" & _
                         PR_CONTAINER_CLASS).Value = strMAPIFolderClass
    oFolderRecord.Fields.Update
    oFolderRecord.Close
End Sub

Private Sub CreateFolders()
    On Error GoTo errHandler
    'Create all the folders in a local OLE DB transaction
    'so that all are created or none are created
    oConnection.BeginTrans
    'Create the root folder first
```

```
    Dim oRecord As New ADODB.Record
    oRecord.Open strExchangeServerFilePath & txtFolderPath, _
                 oConnection, adModeReadWrite, adCreateCollection
    oRecord.Fields("DAV:contentclass").value = _
                   "urn:content-classes:folder"
    oRecord.Fields("http://schemas.microsoft.com/mapi/proptag/" & _
                   PR_CONTAINER_CLASS).Value = "IPF.Note"
    strPath = oRecord.Fields("DAV:href")
    oRecord.Close
    strPath = strPath & "/"
    CreateFolder strPath, "Categories", "message", "IPF.Note"
    CreateFolder strPath, "Configuration", "message", "IPF.Note"
    CreateFolder strPath, "Course Materials", "message", "IPF.Note"
    CreateFolder strPath, "Discussions", "message", "IPF.Note"
    CreateFolder strPath, "Emails", "message", "IPF.Note"
    CreateFolder strPath, "Instructors", "instructor", "IPF.Contact"
    CreateFolder strPath, "Pending", "message", "IPF.Note"
    CreateFolder strPath, "Schedule", "trainingevent", "IPF.Appointment"
    CreateFolder strPath, "schema", "message", "IPF.Note"
    CreateFolder strPath, "Students", "student", "IPF.Contact"
    CreateFolder strPath, "Surveys", "message", "IPF.Note"
    CreateFolder strPath, "Surveys\Courses", "survey", "IPF.Note"
    CreateFolder strPath, "Surveys\Instructors", "survey", "IPF.Note"
    If Err.Number = 0 Then
        oConnection.CommitTrans
    End If
    Exit Sub

errHandler:
    MsgBox "Error in CreateFolders.  Error " & Err.Number & " " & _
        Err.Description
    oConnection.RollbackTrans
End Sub
```

Notice that the code is wrapped in an OLE DB transaction. The *CreateFolder* subroutine takes the full URL to the new folder to be created, creates a new *Record* object, and calls the *Open* method on that object with the URL. The *Open* method takes several parameters. The syntax for the *Open* method is shown here:

```
Open Source, ActiveConnection, Mode, CreateOptions, Options, _
    UserName, Password
```

To create the folder, you pass the *Mode* parameter the value *adReadWrite*, and you pass the *CreateOptions* parameter the value *adCreateCollection*. Exchange 2000 does not support passing a username and password.

If you're using schemas, you can set the *expected-content-class* and *schema-collection-ref* fields on the folder. You should set the content class of the folder to *urn:content-classes:folder*. Also, if you plan to display the folder in Outlook, you must set the *PR_CONTAINER_CLASS* property in the MAPI namespace, which is *"http://schemas.microsoft.com/mapi/proptag/"*. You should pass the unique hex identifier to the property you're interested in without the leading 0. For example, 0x00212 would be *x00212*. If you don't want to set the MAPI property yourself, you can set *http://schemas.microsoft.com/exchange/outlookfolderclass* to *IPF.Note* or another value.

If you're trying to access custom properties you created in Outlook via ADO, you must use a slightly different format. The following code shows how to get a custom property, called *MyProp*, that you set through MAPI. This property can be created using MAPI itself, CDO, or Outlook. The long GUID that you see in the code is the ID for the *PS_PUBLIC_STRINGS* property set, where public properties are created in MAPI.

```
strSQL = "Select ""http://schemas.microsoft.com/mapi/string/" & _
    "{00020329-0000-0000-c000-000000000046}/MyProp"" AS MAPIProp" & _
    " From scope('shallow traversal of """ & strURL & """')"

'Create a new RecordSet object
Set rst = New RecordSet
With rst
    'Open RecordSet based on the SQL string
    .Open strSQL
End With

If rst.BOF And rst.EOF Then
    End
End If

rst.MoveFirst
Do Until rst.EOF
    Debug.Print "MyProp: " & rst.Fields("MAPIProp").Value
    rst.MoveNext
Loop
```

Note that this format is not the only format you can use to query for MAPI properties. One format requires that you know the propset ID and the hexadecimal value for the property, and it is illustrated in the next bit of code. The other two formats are easier to use, but you can use the one I just described to access properties in your own namespaces beyond the public strings namespace.

```
http://schemas.microsoft.com/mapi/id/{propset GUID}/value

Example:

http://schemas.microsoft.com/mapi/id/{3f0a69e0-7f56-11d2-b536-
00aa00bbb6e6}/0x001E1232
```

> **Note** Sometimes you must preface your MAPI properties with a 0, as in *0x001E1232*. If you do not include the leading 0, the property might not return a value.

Creating New Items

Creating new items in Exchange Server using ADO is similar to creating folders using ADO. The only difference is that you pass as the *CreateOptions* parameter the value *adCreateNonCollection*. Other than that, it's pretty much the same code. The following code from the setup program of the Training application shows how to create a new item. The code creates e-mail messages for different notifications for the application, such as a new course or an authorization requirement. This makes the application fairly easy to configure, depending on which settings you specify. Note that I set the MAPI property tag for the message class. You can also set the property *http://schemas.microsoft.com/exchange/outlookmessageclass* to the correct message class for your item.

```
Private Sub CreateEmailTemplates()
    On Error GoTo errHandler:

    oConnection.BeginTrans
    'Open the Emails folder
    Dim oRec As New ADODB.Record
    oRec.Open strPath & "Emails", oConnection, adModeReadWrite, _
              adFailIfNotExists

    'Create a new post in the folder by using ADO
    Dim oEmail As New ADODB.Record
    oEmail.Open strPath & "Emails/New Discussion Group Email", _
               oConnection, adModeReadWrite, adCreateNonCollection

    'Open the text file on the hard drive
    'and read the data

    Open App.Path & "\discussionemail.txt" For Input As #1
    Dim strMessage
    Do While Not EOF(1)
        Input #1, strLine
        strMessage = strMessage & strLine
    Loop
    Close #1

    oEmail.Fields("urn:schemas:httpmail:textdescription").Value = _
                 strMessage
    oEmail.Fields("DAV:contentclass") = "urn:content-classes:message"
    oEmail.Fields("http://schemas.microsoft.com/mapi/proptag/" & _
```

```
                PR_MESSAGE_CLASS).Value = "IPM.Post"
oEmail.Fields.Update
oEmail.Close

oEmail.Open strPath & "Emails/ " & _
            "Survey Email", oConnection, adModeReadWrite, _
            adCreateNonCollection

'Open the text file on the hard drive
'and read the data

Open App.Path & "\surveyemail.txt" For Input As #1
strMessage = ""
Do While Not EOF(1)
    Input #1, strLine
    strMessage = strMessage & strLine
Loop
Close #1

oEmail.Fields("urn:schemas:httpmail:textdescription").Value = _
              strMessage
oEmail.Fields("DAV:contentclass") = "urn:content-classes:message"
oEmail.Fields("http://schemas.microsoft.com/mapi/proptag/" & _
              PR_MESSAGE_CLASS).Value = "IPM.Post"
oEmail.Fields.Update
oEmail.Close


oEmail.Open strPath & "Emails\New Course Email", oConnection, _
            adModeReadWrite, adCreateNonCollection

'Open the text file on the hard drive
'and read the data

Open App.Path & "\courseemail.txt" For Input As #1
strMessage = ""
Do While Not EOF(1)
    Input #1, strLine
    strMessage = strMessage & strLine
Loop
Close #1

oEmail.Fields("urn:schemas:httpmail:textdescription").Value = _
              strMessage
oEmail.Fields("DAV:contentclass") = "urn:content-classes:message"
oEmail.Fields("http://schemas.microsoft.com/mapi/proptag/" & _
              PR_MESSAGE_CLASS).Value = "IPM.Post"
oEmail.Fields.Update
oEmail.Close

'Create a new post in the folder by using ADO
oEmail.Open strPath & "Emails/WorkflowMessage", oConnection, _
            adModeReadWrite, adCreateNonCollection
```

```
    'Open the text file on the hard drive
    'and read the data

    Open App.Path & "\workflowmessage.txt" For Input As #1
    strMessage = ""
    Do While Not EOF(1)
        Input #1, strLine
        strMessage = strMessage & strLine
    Loop
    Close #1

    oEmail.Fields("urn:schemas:httpmail:textdescription").Value = _
                  strMessage
    oEmail.Fields("DAV:contentclass") = "urn:content-classes:message"
    oEmail.Fields("http://schemas.microsoft.com/mapi/proptag/" & _
                  PR_MESSAGE_CLASS).Value = "IPM.Post"
    oEmail.Fields.Update
    oEmail.Close

    oRec.Close

    If Err.Number = 0 Then
        oConnection.CommitTrans
    End If

    Exit Sub

errHandler:
    MsgBox "Error in CreateEmailTemplates.  Error " & Err.Number & _
           " " & Err.Description
    oConnection.RollbackTrans
    End
End Sub
```

When you create items using ADO, you must watch out for conflicting names. Check to see whether you receive an error when you try to create an item or folder. If so, pick a different name or add a random number to the end of the name. The following code shows you how to do this:

```
On Error Resume Next
Set rec = Server.CreateObject("ADODB.Record")
With rec
    .Open strStudentsFolderPath & "/" & strName, , 3, 0
    If err.number = &H80040e98 Then
    'Already exists; try to open with a random name!
        err.clear
        Randomize
        iRandom = Int((50000 * Rnd)+1)
        .Open strScheduleFolderPath & "/" & strName & iRandom,,3,0
    End If
End With
```

Deleting Folders or Items

To delete a folder or an item, you can use the *DeleteRecord* method on an ADO *Record* object. If you delete a folder, all items in the folder will also be deleted. The following code shows you how to delete a folder called MyFolder:

```
Set Rec = CreateObject("ADODB.Record")
'This URL is for a public folder
strURL = "file://./backofficestorage/" & DomainName & "/" & strFolderPath

Rec.Open strURL
Rec.DeleteRecord
'Or you could do
'Rec.DeleteRecord strURL
Rec.Close
```

If you want to delete items using a recordset instead of the *Record* object, you can use the *Delete* method of the *RecordSet* object. The following example deletes all items in a folder:

```
'Create a query with a WHERE clause to delete only items
strQ = "SELECT * FROM scope('shallow traversal of " & Chr(34) & _
       strURL & Chr(34) & "')"
strQ = strQ & " WHERE ""DAV:isfolder"" = FALSE"

'Open the RecordSet
Rs.Open strQ
Rs.MoveFirst

Do Until Rs.EOF
    'Delete current record (row); 1 is parameter for adAffectCurrent
    Rs.Delete 1
    Rs.MoveNext
Loop
```

Copying Folders or Items

To copy folders or items, you use the *CopyRecord* method on the *Record* object. If you copy a folder, all items and subfolders will be copied as well. Note that you cannot copy folders or items between Exchange Server databases. Therefore, you cannot copy between private or public databases because they reside in different Exchange Server databases. However, you can create a new item in the separate database, copy the properties from the original item to the new item, and save the new item. The *creator*, *creation time*, and other properties on the item will not be the same as those of the original item, however. The following code copies an item named *MyItem* from one folder to another:

```
Set Rec = CreateObject("ADODB.Record")
strURL = "file://./backofficestorage/" & DomainName & "/" & _
         strPath & "/MyItem"
Rec.Open strURL
```

```
Rec.CopyRecord ,"file://./backofficestorage/" & DomainName & _
               "/" & strDestination
```

Moving Folders or Items

To move items, you can call the *MoveRecord* method. Moving has the same restrictions as copying in that you cannot move between Exchange Server stores. Moving a folder moves all the items in the folder as well. The following code sample moves an item:

```
Set Rec = CreateObject("ADODB.Record")
Rec.Open URLFrom, , adModeReadWrite
NewURL = Rec.MoveRecord(URLFrom, URLTo, "","", adMoveOverWrite)
```

This is the syntax for the *MoveRecord* method:

```
URL = MoveRecord (Source, Destination, UserName, Password, Options, Async)
```

This method typically returns the *Destination* parameter, which is the string value of the destination the item was moved to. The *Options* parameter allows you to provide options for the move. The most common option you'll provide is the *adMoveOverWrite* option.

Using the *Fields* Collection

You've already seen how to get properties using the *Fields* collection in ADO. You might want to set properties on an item or folder using the *Fields* collection. If you do so, remember that the property is available only on the specified item rather than on every item in the folder. Adding new fields using the *Fields* collection is not like adding custom schemas. When you add to the *Fields* collection, your properties are not included when a *SELECT ** statement is issued. Unlike schemas, new properties added to the *Fields* collection cannot be shared among multiple items in a folder unless you explicitly create the property on every item. With schemas, you can set the content class of your items to be of a particular type, and those items will implement the properties you specified in your schemas.

The *Fields* collection supports the *Append* method, which allows you to add custom fields to a recordset or a *Record* object. Here is the syntax for the *Append* method:

```
fields.Append Name, Type, DefinedSize, Attrib, FieldValue
```

The *Type* parameter specifies the data type of the field. This parameter can have one of many different values; however, you'll probably use *adWChar*, *adBStr*, *adDate*, *adInteger*, or *adBoolean*.

The *DefinedSize* parameter specifies the size of the new field. Normally, you would leave this parameter blank because ADO will base the size of the new field on the data type you specify.

The *Attrib* parameter allows you specify attributes of the field—for example, whether the field is nullable or contains fixed-length data. Normally, you would leave this parameter blank, too, unless your field really needs special handling.

The final parameter is a value for the field. ADO allows you to simply assign the value to the field right in its parameter rather than having to create the field and then use another line of code to set the value.

The following code shows you how to add new fields to a record:

```
'Assumes oNewRecord is a new item in Exchange Server
oNewRecord.Fields.Append "MyNewProp",adInteger,,,12
oNewRecord.Fields.Update
```

Notice how the code calls the *Update* method on the *Fields* collection. If you do not call the *Update* method, your changes won't be saved to Exchange Server—which means your new field won't be added to the item. Also, if you suspect that the values for your fields might have changed while you were working with your data, you can call the *ReSync* method to have ADO requery Exchange Server for the latest values for your data.

Working with Recordsets Using ADO

To efficiently work with the *RecordSet* object, you need to know about some of its methods. For example, you need to know how to scroll through records in the recordset as well as detect the end of the recordset.

The first thing you will want to know about your recordset after you have Exchange perform a query for you is the number of items returned in the recordset. ADO provides a *RecordCount* property on the *RecordSet* object so you can know how many records are contained in the recordset. This number depends on the cursor type you use for your recordset. Table 15-4 lists the cursor types and how they affect the *RecordCount* property.

Table 15-4 Cursor Types and How They Affect the *RecordCount* Property

Cursor Type	Description	Recordset Count Returned
Dynamic	A dynamic collection of records that is the most flexible of all cursors. Additions, changes, and deletions by you or other users are immediately visible. You can scroll forward or backward through the records.	–1
Keyset	Like a dynamic cursor except you cannot see the records added by other users. You cannot access the records that other users delete.	–1

Table 15-4 Cursor Types and How They Affect the *RecordCount* Property

Cursor Type	Description	Recordset Count Returned
Static	A copy of the records. Additions, changes, and deletions by other users are not reflected, but any type of movement is allowed.	Actual number
Forward Only	Similar to a static cursor except you can only scroll forward through the records. This is the default type of cursor created.	Actual number

Using the *RecordCount* property's value, you can decide whether you need to scroll through the records if any were returned. To make scrolling the records easy in a recordset, ADO provides the *BOF* and *EOF* properties on a *RecordSet* object. *BOF* is a *Boolean* value that, if *True*, indicates that the current record position is before the first record—in effect, it indicates that you are at the beginning of the recordset. *EOF* is a *Boolean* value that, if *True*, indicates that the current record position is after the last record in the recordset. To make sure you do not read beyond the end or the beginning of your recordset, you can use these two properties while scrolling forward or backward through the recordset.

To actually scroll through the recordset, you use the *MoveFirst*, *MoveNext*, *MoveLast*, and *MovePrevious* methods of the *RecordSet* object. Depending on the cursor type you specify, these methods will provide you with differing degrees of usability. The method names are pretty self-explanatory. *MoveFirst* moves you to the first record, *MoveNext* moves you to the next record, if it exists (and returns an *Error* object if it doesn't), *MoveLast* moves you to the last record, and *MovePrevious* moves you to the previous record.

Querying for MAPI Entry IDs

There is a special case you have to worry about when you query for MAPI entry IDs in your ADO code. First, the property name for the *entryid* property is *http://schemas.microsoft.com/mapi/proptag/x0fff0102*. Second, once you try to retrieve this property, you will find that the property is a byte array. You must write some code that constructs the string-based *entryid* from this byte array. Once you create the string-based *entryid*, you can pass it to CDO 1.21 or the Outlook object model to have those APIs retrieve the item as well. The following example shows you how to perform the steps:

```
Dim Rec As New ADODB.Record
Dim Rs As New ADODB.RecordSet
Dim strUrl As String
Dim strSQL As String
```

```
strUrl = "file://./backofficestorage/domain.com/mbx/thomriz/inbox/"

Rec.Open strUrl
Set Rs.ActiveConnection = Rec.ActiveConnection

strSQL = "select ""DAV:href"", " & _
         """http://schemas.microsoft.com/mapi/proptag/x0fff0102"" " & _
         "from scope('shallow traversal of """ & strUrl & """') "

Rs.Source = strSQL
Rs.Open

Dim arrEntryID As Variant
Dim i As Integer

arrEntryID = _
  Rs.Fields("http://schemas.microsoft.com/mapi/proptag/x0fff0102").Value
For i = 0 To UBound(arrEntryID)
    strEntryID = strEntryID & Right("0" & Hex(arrEntryID(i)), 2)
Next

Rs.Close
Rec.Close
```

Working with Attachments in ADO

Exchange has some properties that make it easier to work with attachments in ADO, rather than CDO. They are listed in Table 15-5. Every item in Exchange exposes these properties.

Table 15-5 Properties for Attachments in ADO

Property	Description
http://schemas.microsoft.com/exchange/attachlist	An array that contains the URLs to all attachments in an item
http://schemas.microsoft.com/exchange/attachcontenttype	An array that contains all the content types, such as *application/msword* or *application/msexcel* for all attachments on an item
http://schemas.microsoft.com/exchange/attachname	An array that contains the friendly display name for all attachments on an item

The three properties work together. For example, if you want to know the name, type, and URL of the third attachment on your item, you can grab all three properties and go into the third entry in each array to get the values. Be aware, though, that these properties return only top-level attachments. If you have attachments embedded in attachments, you must open up the item using the correct CDO object for the type of item to get at the embedded attachments. Also, these properties are supported only on items, not folders (as you would expect) or freedocs (embedded items such as Word documents stored directly in Exchange that cannot have attachments). You must retrieve these properties from the *Fields* collection for the item. The following code shows how to use these properties with the ADO *Record* object:

```
Dim oRecord as new ADODB.Record
oRecord.Open "file://./backofficestorage/domain/ " _
           & "Public Folders/myFolder/myworddoc.doc"
arrAttachURLs = oRecord.Fields("http://schemas.microsoft.com/" & _
                              "exchange/attachlist").value
arrAttachNames = oRecord.Fields("http://schemas.microsoft.com/" & _
                              "exchange/attachname").value
arrAttachContentTypes = oRecord.Fields("http://schemas.microsoft.com/" & _
                              "exchange/attachcontenttype").value
For i=LBOUND(arrAttachURLs) To UBOUND(arrAttachURLs)
    MsgBox "The name of the attachment is: " & arrAttachNames(i)
    MsgBox "The content type of the attachment is: " _
         & arrAttachContentTypes(i)
    MsgBox "The URL to the attachment is: " & arrAttachURLs(i)
Next
```

Note These attachment properties are available only via EXOLEDB and ADO. You cannot retrieve them using WebDAV. With WebDAV, you should use the *X-MS-ENUMATTS* command to retrieve attachment information; we will discuss this in the next chapter.

Handling Errors in ADO

You must always be prepared to handle errors in your code. ADO provides built-in error-handling capabilities through its *Errors* collection on the *Connection* object. The *Errors* collection contains *Error* objects, which have three properties of interest to Exchange developers:

- ***Description*** The default property for the *Error* object. This is a string representation of the error text.
- ***Number*** A long integer that contains the number associated with the error. You can look at the *ErrorValueEnum* constants in ADO to see whether this number matches one of the ADO-defined errors.

- ***Source*** A string that contains the name of the object that raised the error.

You can use the *Errors* collection in your error handling to scroll through all the *Error* objects in the collection. When you find the errors, you can take action on them. For example, you can roll back a transaction, which we'll see shortly, or print an error message for the user.

Using OLE DB Transactions

The Exchange Server OLE DB provider supports local OLE DB transactions. This allows you to treat your ADO operations as transactions when you work with Exchange Server. If for some reason an operation fails during the transaction, you can roll back the entire transaction without leaving your Exchange Server application in an inconsistent state. Because Exchange Server transactions are different from SQL Server ones, there are a few things you need to know.

First, as you would expect, for the transactions to work you must perform all your ADO operations on the same connection to the Exchange server. Therefore, when you use the methods of the *Record* or *RecordSet* object, always pass as a parameter the *Connection* object that you created at the beginning of the transaction.

Second, transactions in Exchange Server are not supported across Exchange Server stores. This means transactions will not work if performed on folders or items located in different Exchange Server stores. The most common example of different Exchange Server stores are the private store and the public store.

Finally, Exchange Server does not support distributed transactions with SQL Server. You cannot wrap in a single transaction ADO commands between the two databases, nor can you use the distributed transaction coordinator with both databases. Therefore, you should use local transactions in each database and perform all your SQL Server work before doing your Exchange Server work. That way, you guarantee that the SQL Server transactions go through, and you don't have to worry about rolling back your Exchange Server transactions.

You work with a transaction by using one ADO *Connection* object. On this object, you must first call the *BeginTrans* method, which starts a transaction. When your ADO methods are complete, you call the *CommitTrans* method, which attempts to commit the transaction to the Exchange database. If you find that an error occurred during your ADO calls, you can use the *RollBackTrans* method to roll back the entire transaction. The following example, taken from the Training application setup program, shows you how to use these methods:

```
Private Sub CreateCategoryMessage()
    On Error GoTo errHandler:

    oConnection.BeginTrans
    'Open the Categories folder
    Dim oRec As New ADODB.Record
    oRec.Open strPath & "Categories", oConnection, adModeReadWrite, _
             adFailIfNotExists

    'Create a new post in the folder by using ADO
    Dim oEmail As New ADODB.Record
    oEmail.Open strPath & "Categories\Categories", oConnection, _
               adModeReadWrite, adCreateNonCollection
    oEmail.Fields("urn:schemas:httpmail:textdescription").Value = _
                 strCategories
    oEmail.Fields("http://schemas.microsoft.com/mapi/proptag/" & _
                 PR_MESSAGE_CLASS).Value = "IPM.Post"
    oEmail.Fields.Update
    oEmail.Close

    oRec.Close


    If Err.Number = 0 Then
        oConnection.CommitTrans
    End If


    Exit Sub
errHandler:
    MsgBox "Error in CreateEmailTemplates.  Error " & Err.Number & _
          " " & Err.Description
    oConnection.RollbackTrans
    End
End Sub
```

Best Practices When Using ADO

I suggest three best practices for working with ADO and Exchange Server. First, learn your Exchange Server properties well. When you work with ADO, you need to remember all the different properties in all the different namespaces that Exchange Server provides. The most common ones you will work with are listed here. For the full list of properties, refer to the Exchange Server SDK.

- *DAV:href*
- *DAV:contentclass*
- *DAV:displayname*
- *DAV:iscollection*

- *DAV:isfolder*
- *DAV:ishidden*
- *DAV:isreadonly*
- *urn:schemas-microsoft-com:office:office#Author*
- *urn:schemas-microsoft-com:office:office#Category*
- *urn:schemas-microsoft-com:office:office#Comments*
- *urn:schemas:httpmail:to*
- *urn:schemas:httpmail:subject*
- *urn:schemas:httpmail:cc*
- *urn:schemas:httpmail:bcc*
- *urn:schemas:httpmail:hasattachment*
- *urn:schemas:httpmail:from*

The second best practice is to use transactions wherever appropriate. There are a number of reasons for this. First, using transactions allows you to roll back the Exchange Server database to the original state in case of an error. Second, using transactions is key when you work with events to eliminate erroneous event firing. If you create an item in the database using ADO, Exchange Server will fire an event. If you then update the fields after creating the item, Exchange Server will fire another event. You don't want this to happen; you want only one event to fire. (The problem of multiple events firing can be a tough one to debug.) When you use transactions, the information is entered into the Exchange Server database only when the transaction is committed, thereby causing only one event to fire.

The third best practice for working with ADO is to reuse existing connections. Creating new connections to the Exchange Server database taxes your computer's resources because Exchange Server needs to keep open the connections you create. Therefore, you should reuse the same *Connection* object in a session variable—especially if you're writing ASP applications.

Calling COM Components from .NET

Before I explain how to work with CDO or the other object models in Exchange, we need to look at Component Object Model (COM) interoperability in .NET because you will be calling objects through this interoperability layer. This section describes what COM interoperability is and how it works. We will look at using ADO against Exchange Server as an example of COM interoperability.

You will often call COM components such as CDO, Knowledge Management Collaboration Data Objects (PKMCDO), or ADO from Visual Studio .NET. Visual Studio .NET makes it easy to integrate COM components into your .NET applications by providing seamless interoperability between the managed code environment in .NET and the unmanaged code environment in COM. We will look at calling COM components from .NET and what really happens under the covers when you do this.

COM differs from the .NET Framework in a couple of ways. First, clients of COM objects must manage the lifetime of those objects. Meanwhile, the .NET Framework, through its garbage collection and memory allocation support, manages the lifetime of all objects in its environment.

Second, COM clients discover the services of the COM object they are working with by requesting an interface that provides the service and getting back a pointer to that interface if the service exists. .NET objects expose the description of the functionality of the object through reflection, which leverages assemblies that describe the object and its properties and methods.

Finally, COM uses pointers that assume that the object will remain in the same memory location. The .NET Framework can move objects around in memory at run time for performance reasons, and the framework will dynamically update all references to the object when it is moved.

So, to interoperate with COM, the .NET Framework must bridge the gaps between the .NET and COM runtime environments. To do this, .NET leverages runtime callable wrappers (RCWs) and COM callable wrappers (CCWs). All the wrappers do is expose the expected interfaces from .NET to COM and also marshal any calls and parameters between COM and the .NET runtime.

The RCW is what allows your .NET application to call a COM component. This wrapper abstracts and manages the calls and makes sure you do not have to code to the differences between COM and .NET.

The CCW reverses the process. It allows COM objects to call a method on a .NET object. As a result, the COM object will have no idea that its calls are actually going to a .NET component. The wrapper simulates all the necessary COM interfaces to interoperate between the COM and .NET environments.

To start taking advantage of calling COM components from your .NET applications, all you need to do is add a reference to the COM component. The easiest way to do this is by choosing Add Reference from the Project menu in Visual Studio .NET. In the Add Reference dialog box (shown in Figure 15-19), select your COM component and click Select.

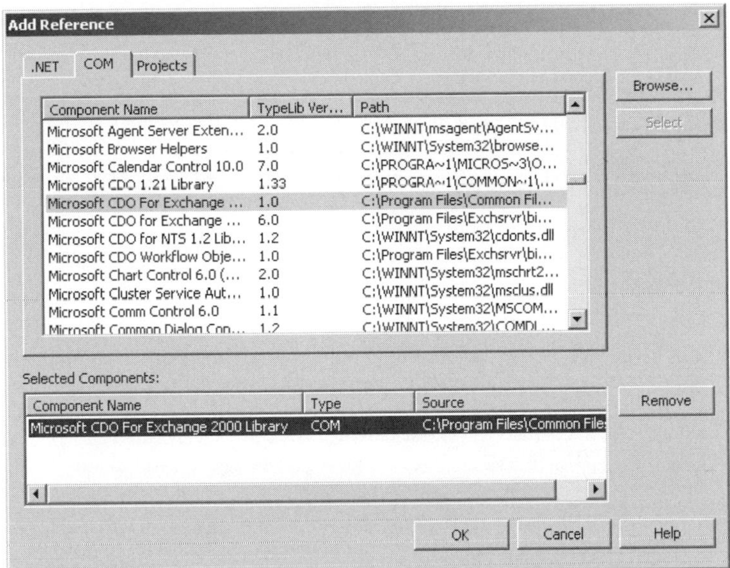

Figure 15-19 Adding a reference to a COM component from .NET

What really happens under the covers is that Visual Studio .NET scans the type library for the COM object and creates an interop .NET assembly for your COM component. If you look at the files included with your project, you will see the new files that Visual Studio .NET creates for working with the COM component.

If you want to manually import a COM component, you can use the type library importer tool included with the .NET Framework. This is a command-line tool that offers the same functionality as Visual Studio .NET. The tool has the filename tlbimp.exe. Most times, you will just use Visual Studio .NET to automatically import the type library.

Of course, you can go the other way and export your .NET object to COM. We covered this functionality when we built a COM add-in for .NET in Chapter 7.

Once you add your reference, you can call the COM interfaces for the COM component in the same way you would for any .NET component. The sample in Figure 15-20 shows an application that uses the COM version of ADO.

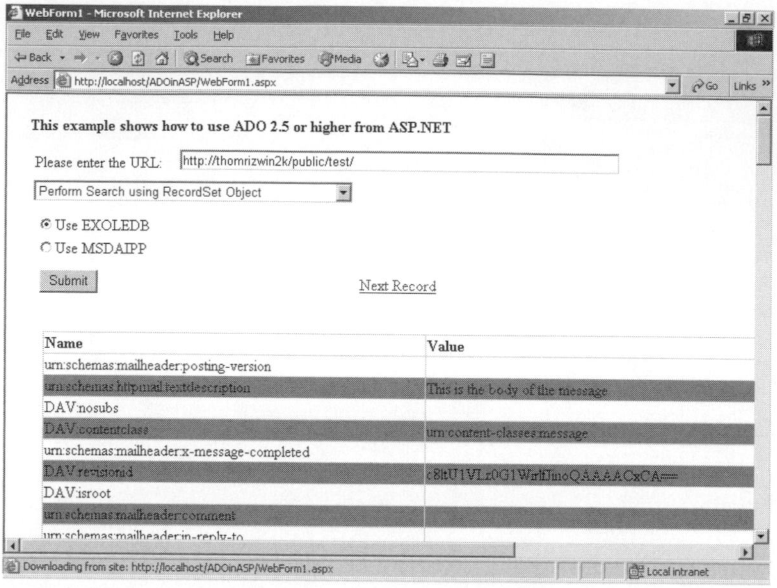

Figure 15-20 The COM interoperability sample application

Note that the original ASP architecture used a single-threaded apartment (STA) model, whereas the new ASP.NET engine uses a multi-threaded apartment (MTA) architecture for better performance. As a result, before your ASP .NET applications can use legacy ADO code, you must tell ASP .NET to use the STA model. To do so, you use the ASPCOMPAT directive. You will want to use this directive with any COM interoperability objects that you use in ASP.NET, such as CDO 1.21 or CDO for Exchange.

```
<%@ Page Language="VB" ASPCompat="True" %>
```

Otherwise, you can call your ADO code just as you did in Visual Studio 6.0. The following is the relevant code from the sample application shown using Visual Basic .NET:

```
Private Sub Submit1_ServerClick(ByVal sender As System.Object, _
                                ByVal e As System.EventArgs) _
                                Handles Submit1.ServerClick
    'See what the user selected
    If dropdownCommand.SelectedIndex = 0 Then
        linkNext.Visible = False
        'Retrieve properties using Record Object
        Dim oRecord As New ADODB.Record()
        'Figure out the type of connection to use
        oConnection = GetConnection()
        If Not (oConnection Is Nothing) Then
            'Open the item
```

```
            oRecord.Open(txtURL.Text, oConnection)
            'Create a datasource to fill our datagrid
            DataGrid1.DataSource = CreateDataSource(oRecord)
            DataGrid1.DataBind()
            oRecord.Close()
            oConnection.Close()
        Else
            lblError.Text = "There was an error.  " & _
                            "There is no valid Connection object."
        End If
    ElseIf dropdownCommand.SelectedIndex = 1 Then
        'Perform Search
        'Figure out the type of connection to use
        oConnection = GetConnection()
        If Not (oConnection Is Nothing) Then
            'Create a simple search to use to show how it works
            Dim strQuery As String = "SELECT * FROM SCOPE('SHALLOW " & _
                                "TRAVERSAL OF """ & txtURL.Text & """')"
            oRS.Open(strQuery, oConnection)

            'Another way would be to populate one-way an OLEDB data
            'adapter with an ADO RecordSet object as shown below
            'Dim myDA As System.Data.OleDb.OleDbDataAdapter = _
            '    New System.Data.OleDb.OleDbDataAdapter()
            'Dim myDS As DataSet = New DataSet()
            'myDA.Fill(myDS, oRS, "MyTable")
            'DataGrid1.DataSource = myDS

            DataGrid1.DataSource = CreateDataSource(oRS)
            DataGrid1.DataBind()
            linkNext.Visible = True
            Session("oRS") = oRS
            Session("oConnection") = oConnection
        Else
            lblError.Text = "There was an error.  " & _
                            "There is no valid Connection object."
        End If
    ElseIf dropdownCommand.SelectedIndex = 2 Then
        'Create item using Record object
        Try
            linkNext.Visible = False
            Dim oRecord As New ADODB.Record()
            oConnection = GetConnection()
            If Not (oConnection Is Nothing) Then
                'Open the item
                oRecord.Open(txtURL.Text, oConnection, _
                    ADODB.ConnectModeEnum.adModeReadWrite, _
                    ADODB.RecordCreateOptionsEnum.adCreateNonCollection)

                oRecord.Fields("urn:schemas:httpmail:subject").Value = _
                    "Test Message"
                oRecord.Fields("urn:schemas:" & _
                                "httpmail:textdescription").Value = _
```

```
                                "This is a test message!"
                    oRecord.Fields("http://schemas.microsoft.com/" & _
                                "exchange/outlookmessageclass").Value = _
                                "IPM.Post"
                    oRecord.Fields("DAV:contentclass").Value = _
                                "urn:content-classes:message"
                    oRecord.Fields.Update()
                    lblError.Text = "Successfully created item at " & _
                                oRecord.Fields("DAV:href").Value
                    oRecord.Close()
                    oConnection.Close()
                Else
                    lblError.Text = "There was an error.  " & _
                                "There is no valid Connection object."
                End If
            Catch
                lblError.Text = "There was an error. Error#" & Err.Number & _
                            " Description: " & Err.Description
            End Try
        End If
    End Sub

    Private Function GetConnection() As ADODB.Connection
        'Try to create the connection based off the type
        'specified by the user and also using the URL
        Dim oConnection As New ADODB.Connection()
        Try
            'Detect connection type
            If radioMethod.SelectedIndex = 0 Then
                'Use EXOLEDB
                oConnection.Provider = "EXOLEDB.DataSource "
            Else
                'Use MSDAIPP
                oConnection.Provider = "MSDAIPP.DSO"
            End If

            oConnection.Open(txtURL.Text)
            GetConnection = oConnection
        Catch
            'Some error occured, maybe bad URL
            'Return back an empty object
            GetConnection = Nothing
        End Try
    End Function

    Function CreateDataSource(ByVal oRecord As Object) As ICollection
        On Error Resume Next
        Dim dt As New DataTable()
        Dim dr As DataRow

        dt.Columns.Add(New DataColumn("Name"))
        dt.Columns.Add(New DataColumn("Value"))
```

```
    Dim oField As ADODB.Field
    For Each oField In oRecord.Fields
        dr = dt.NewRow()
        dr(0) = oField.Name
        dr(1) = oField.Value
        dt.Rows.Add(dr)
    Next

    Dim dv As New DataView(dt)
    Return dv
End Function


Private Sub linkNext_Click(ByVal sender As System.Object, _
                           ByVal e As System.EventArgs) _
                           Handles linkNext.Click
    'Scroll to the next item
    oRS = Session("oRS")
    oConnection = Session("oConnection")
    If Not (oRS.EOF) Then
        oRS.MoveNext()
        DataGrid1.DataSource = CreateDataSource(oRS)
        DataGrid1.DataBind()
    End If
End Sub
```

The ADO code in the sample is self-explanatory—it is standard ADO code that you've seen before. The interesting part of the sample is the code that shows the returned data in a .NET *DataGrid* object and the code that shows the interoperability between a .NET *DataSet* and an ADO *RecordSet* or *Record* object.

Filling the *DataGrid* with ADO information is very straightforward. First, we need to get a *DataView* object that contains the data we want to display in our *DataGrid*. We do this by creating a *DataTable* object in the *CreateDataSource* function. A *DataTable* is a single table of in-memory data. The *CreateDataSource* function creates a new *DataTable*, manually adds new columns to the table, and then fills in the rows and columns with the information from our ADO *RecordSet*. The last step in the function is to create a new *DataView* on the *DataTable* and return that *DataView* to the caller of the function.

Once the main code gets back the *DataView* object, it sets the *DataSource* property of the *DataGrid* to the new *DataView*. The code then calls the *DataBind* method on the *DataGrid* object to bind the table to the grid control. The *DataGrid* is now populated with the data from our ADO *RecordSet*. Be sure to close all the connections to your databases when you use the COM version of ADO—otherwise, those connections will remain open until the next garbage collection pass in the .NET Framework.

To fill a *DataSet* with an ADO *RecordSet* or *Record* is even easier. To allow this, the OLE DB .NET Data provider overloads the *Fill* method of the *OleDb-*

DataAdapter to allow this method to accept an ADO *RecordSet* or *Record* object. This is only a one-way operation, however. Your code must manually handle any updates to the *DataSet* after it has been filled. The *OleDbDataAdapter* will not handle making changes back through ADO to the source database.

Now that you've seen how to interoperate with ADO as a COM component, you can imagine how you can start using CDO, PKMCDO, or other COM object libraries in your .NET applications. To start taking advantage of these other libraries, you just need to add a reference to them from your Visual Studio .NET projects.

CDO for Exchange Server

Exchange Server contains a version of CDO called CDO for Exchange. This version of CDO builds on OLE DB, which means that its object model is different from that of previous versions. For example, instead of having navigational objects, such as *InfoStore*, the new version of CDO relies on ADO for record navigation. Therefore, if you want to query Exchange Server for a specific set of records, you must rely on ADO. However, if you want to perform collaborative functions on those records, you need to use CDO. You can retrieve items using ADO and then open and process each item using CDO.

CDO adds collaborative functionality above and beyond that provided by ADO. If you need to create recurring meetings, ADO won't be very helpful—for example, you would have to determine which properties to set to make an appointment recur on the third Tuesday of every month. With CDO, however, you set some properties, save the appointment, and suddenly you have a recurring meeting. CDO does all the hardcoding for you behind the scenes.

CDO and ADO were designed to work together. Both object models have the same *Fields* collection. Furthermore, CDO objects can be bound directly to ADO objects. This allows you to use the same connection with the Exchange server.

CDO Design Goals

Microsoft had a number of design goals in mind for the CDO object library. First, as just discussed, integrating with and extending ADO was key. Second, having learned from previous versions of the CDO object model, the CDO design team knew the model needed to be dual-interfaced so that different development environments, such as Visual Basic, Microsoft Visual C++, and ASP, could take advantage of it. The third goal was to have CDO adhere to Internet standards. Internet standards are now critical to CDO because it uses vCard, iCal, Lightweight Directory Access Protocol (LDAP), Multipurpose Internet Mail Extensions (MIME), MIME Encapsulation of Aggregate HTML Documents (MHTML), Simple Mail Transfer Protocol (SMTP), and Network News Transfer Protocol (NNTP). The final and probably most important design goal for CDO was to make the developer's job easier by providing a rich set of objects on top of OLE DB for building collaborative applications.

CDO for Windows

You might have seen CDO for Windows. Consider this object model the little brother of CDO for Exchange Server. CDO for Windows provides SMTP and NNTP support. It also provides support for protocol events such as SMTP events. However, CDO for Windows does not provide mailbox support or public folder support. CDO for Exchange Server provides these features and extends CDO for Windows. If you get started with CDO for Windows, you'll have a working knowledge of the basics of CDO for Exchange Server.

The CDO Object Model

The CDO object model consists of five main components. I say *components* rather than *objects* because the CDO object model contains dozens of objects. The five main components are messaging, calendaring, contacts, workflow, and management. We'll cover the most common tasks you'll perform with the CDO library in each of these areas. I won't cover the specific properties and methods of these components in great detail, however; the Exchange Server SDK provides extensive documentation on this subject.

Frequently Used Objects in CDO

You'll commonly work with two objects, the *Configuration* object and the *DataSource* object, on all CDO objects you use in your applications. Before we look at the most typical CDO functionality you'll use, let's examine these two objects.

Configuration Object

The *Configuration* object allows you to customize the parameters CDO uses and the way CDO works. For example, using the *Configuration* object, you can set the e-mail address of the message sender, set which proxy server to use, set the username and password if you require authentication via SMTP or NNTP, or select other configuration options. The following code, taken from the workflow process, sets the sender e-mail address for a meeting request to the notification address you specified in the setup program of the Training application:

```
'Create a throwaway appointment
set oAppt = CreateObject("CDO.Appointment")
set oConfig = CreateObject("CDO.Configuration")
strNotificationAddress = GetWorkflowSessionField("notificationaddress")
oConfig.Fields("http://schemas.microsoft.com/cdo/" & _
    "configuration/sendemailaddress") = strNotificationAddress
oConfig.Fields.Update
oAppt.Configuration = oConfig
```

As you can see, you use the *Fields* collection on the CDO *Configuration* object to set your properties. All the properties you can set are contained in the *"http://schemas.microsoft.com/cdo/configuration"* namespace.

Another common use for the *Configuration* object is to set the time zone for viewing appointments from Exchange Server. Remember that Exchange Server stores dates in UTC format. Any dates you retrieve through ADO are returned in UTC. However, you can use CDO to change UTC dates to local time zone dates for the client. Sometimes you might want to use a different time zone in your application than the one originally detected by CDO. The *Configuration* object allows you to do this. The following code changes the time zone to Mountain:

```
Dim objAppt As New CDO.Appointment
Dim objConfig As New CDO.Configuration
objConfig.Fields(cdoTimeZoneID) =  cdoMountain
objAppt.Configuration = objConfig
```

DataSource Object

The *DataSource* object provides access from CDO objects to data sources, such as the Web Storage System or Active Directory. You can use the *DataSource* object to open items from or save items to data sources from CDO. You should become familiar with six methods on the *DataSource* object: *Open*, *OpenObject*, *Save*, *SaveTo*, *SaveToContainer*, and *SaveToObject*.

***Open* method** The *DataSource* object's *Open* method is similar to the *Open* method on the ADO *Record* object. The only difference is that ADO can create items using the *Open* method, and CDO cannot. Here is the syntax for the *Open* method:

```
Open(ByVal SourceURL as String,
     ByVal ActiveConnection as Object,
     [ByVal Mode as ConnectModeEnum],
     [ByVal CreateOptions as RecordCreateOptionsEnum],
```

```
    [ByVal Options as RecordOpenOptionsEnum],
    [ByVal UserName as String],
    [ByVal Password as String])
```

Here is a code example that uses the *Open* method in conjunction with an ADO *RecordSet*:

```
Dim rs as New RecordSet
Dim msg as New Message

fldr = "file://./backofficestorage/domain/MBX/user/inbox"

rs.Open "Select * from " & _
    "scope('shallow traversal of " & _
    fldr & "')" & _
    "where urn:schemas:mailheader:subject = 'hello'"
rs.MoveFirst
msg.DataSource.Open rs("DAV:href"),rs.ActiveConnection
```

***OpenObject* method** You can use the *OpenObject* method to open data from another object rather than from a data source such as Exchange Server. A common use for *OpenObject* is to open an embedded message in another message. This is the syntax for *OpenObject*:

```
OpenObject(ByVal Source as Object, ByVal InterfaceName as String)
```

The following code opens an embedded message within another message. The code assumes that you already retrieved the object that represents the embedded message in a variable named *oBodyPart*.

```
oDataSource.OpenObject oBodyPart, "IBodyPart"
```

***Save* method** The *Save* method writes back data to the currently opened data source. This method is so simple that we won't even look at a code sample. You should, however, call this method if you change any values that need to be written back. You should also be sure to open the data source with the read/write flags; otherwise, you will receive an error.

***SaveTo* method** The *SaveTo* method allows you to save an item to a URL you specify. As you will see momentarily, this method differs from the *SaveToContainer* method, which doesn't let you specify a URL to the item that you want to create. Instead, the *SaveToContainer* method lets you specify the URL to the container where you want to save the item. When you use *SaveToContainer*, CDO generates a GUID to identify your item. This is actually quite useful because you do not have to worry about conflicting URLs when you save items. The syntax for the *SaveTo* method is shown here, along with a code sample:

```
SaveTo(ByVal SourceURL as String,
       ByVal ActiveConnection as Object,
       [ByVal Mode as ConnectModeEnum],
       [ByVal CreateOptions as RecordCreateOptionsEnum],
       [ByVal Options as RecordOpenOptionsEnum],
       [ByVal UserName as String],
       [ByVal Password as String])

'Assume oMsg is a valid message
Set oDataSource = oMsg

oDataSource.SaveTo "PATHTOFOLDER/myitem.eml", _
                   MyCONN, _
                   adModeReadWrite, _
                   adCreateOverwrite
```

***SaveToContainer* method** The *SaveToContainer* method, as just discussed, saves the item to a container you specify and assigns a GUID as the identifier for the item. Here is the syntax for the *SaveToContainer* method, along with a code sample taken from the Training application that saves a new course to the schedule folder:

```
SaveToContainer(ByVal ContainerURL as String,
                ByVal ActiveConnection as Object,
                [ByVal Mode as ConnectModeEnum],
                [ByVal CreateOptions as RecordCreateOptionsEnum],
                [ByVal Options as RecordOpenOptionsEnum],
                [ByVal UserName as String],
                [ByVal Password as String])

With iAppt
    .Fields("DAV:contentclass").Value = _
           "urn:content-classes:trainingevent"
    .Fields(strSchema & "instructoremail").Value = _
           Cstr(Request.Form("email"))
    .Fields(strSchema & "prereqs").Value = CStr(Request.Form("prereqs"))
    .Fields(strSchema & "seats").Value = CStr(Request.Form("seats"))
    .Fields(strSchema & "authorization").Value = _
           Cstr(Request.Form("authorization"))
    .Fields(strSchema & "category").Value = cStr(Request.Form("category"))
    .Fields("http://schemas.microsoft.com/mapi/proptag/" & _
           "x001A001E").Value = "IPM.Appointment"
    .Fields.Update
End With

iAppt.DataSource.SaveToContainer strScheduleFolderPath
```

***SaveToObject* method** The *SaveToObject* method allows you to save data to a run-time object rather than to a data source. *SaveToObject* works the same way as the *OpenObject* method, except that you're saving information rather than opening it.

CDO Messaging Tasks

In this section, we'll look at some of the most common CDO messaging tasks you can perform. But first you need to know how MIME works because CDO leverages MIME to read and store content.

The MIME specification divides a message body into parts separated by boundary tags. This enables a mail reader to discern where the logical breaks between parts occur. The message body parts can contain child parts or data. MIME body parts can have one of two content types: singular parts or multiple parts. The nice thing about CDO is that unless you really want to, you don't have to deal with the MIME stream itself; CDO provides an easy object model to manipulate MIME. By supporting MIME, CDO allows you to send complex messages, such as embedded messages, as well as messages that contain HTML pages. The following is an example of a MIME message:

```
From: "Thomas Rizzo" <thomriz@microsoft.com>
To: "Stacy" <stacy@test.com >
Subject: Text and HTML Message
Date: Tue, 7 Mar 2003 3:32:48 -0700
MIME-Version: 1.0
Content-Type: multipart/alternative; boundary="----=_123"
------=_ 123
Content-Type: text/plain; charset="iso 8859 1"
Content-Transfer-Encoding: quoted-printable
This is a multipart/alternative text & html message.
 ------=_ 123
Content-Type: text/html; charset="iso-8859-1"
Content-Transfer-Encoding: quoted-printable
<HTML>
<BODY>This is a multipart/alternative text &amp; html message.</FONT>
</BODY></HTML>
------=_123--
```

Now we're ready to discuss the various CDO messaging tasks.

Sending a Standard Message

Sending an e-mail using CDO is straightforward. You simply create the CDO message object, address the message, set the subject and body, and then send the message. We'll look at some of the more complex tasks you can perform with CDO messages in a moment. The code for sending a simple message is shown here:

```
set oMsg = createobject("CDO.message")
oMsg.To = "stacy@test.com"
oMsg.From = "bob@test.com"
oMsg.Subject = "Hello world!"
oMsg.AutoGenerateTextBody = True
oMsg.MimeFormatted = True
```

```
oMsg.HTMLBody = "<HTML><BODY>This is HTML!</BODY></HTML>"
oMsg.Send
```

Sending an MHTML Message

In addition to sending a simple HTML message, CDO allows you to send a message with an entire Web page embedded in it. The MHTML standard enables you to take HTML content, convert it into MIME, and embed it in an e-mail message. In CDO, creating an MHTML message is as easy as calling a single method, *CreateMHTMLBody*. This method takes as parameters the URL of the Web resource you want to embed; flags that specify any content you don't want to embed, such as sounds or images; and if the Web site that you're embedding requires authentication, a username and password. The following code embeds the Microsoft Exchange Web site into an e-mail and mails it:

```
Set oMsg = CreateObject("CDO.Message")
oMsg.To = "test@test.com"
oMsg.Subject = "Exchange Web site"
oMsg.CreateMHTMLBody "http://www.microsoft.com/exchange"
oMsg.Send
```

Adding an Attachment

CDO makes adding attachments easy, too. CDO supports an *AddAttachment* method, which takes as a parameter a URL for the resource you want to add, and if that resource requires authentication, a username and password. If successful, CDO will return to you the MIME body part that corresponds to the new attachment. Here is code that adds an attachment:

```
Dim oMsg as New CDO.Message
Dim oBp as CDO.IBodyPart
Set oBp = oMsg.AddAttachment("http://www.microsoft.com/myfile")
Set oBp = iMsg.AddAttachment("c:\docs\my.doc")
Set oBp = iMsg.AddAttachment("file://mypublicshare/docs/mydoc.doc")
iMsg.Send
```

Adding Mail Headers

You can now access mail headers directly from CDO. Most of the properties that you'll want to access in the mail header are already exposed as top-level properties in CDO. For example, you could look in the mail header to see who a message is from and who it will be sent to. However, CDO already has two properties that perform this service for you: *From* and *To*. You might instead want to access the mail headers for a message you're having a problem with if CDO doesn't provide an object for the header you're interested in or if you want to get and set custom headers. The following code sets some built-in and custom headers in an e-mail message:

```
Dim oMsg as New CDO.Message
Dim oFlds as ADODB.Fields
Set oFlds = oMsg.Fields

With oFlds
    .Item("urn:schemas:httpmail:to") = "test@test.com"
    .Item("urn:schemas:httpmail:from") = "stacy@test.com"
    .Item("urn:schemas:mailheader:mycustomheader") = "test"
    .Update
End With
```

> **Note** When you work with the *BCC* property, you need to know about an important workaround. If you attempt to use the *Configuration* object with *CdoSendUsingExchange*, you will not be able to send the message. If you need to add users to the *BCC* property, you should instead set the *CdoSendUsingMethod* method on the CDO *Configuration* object to *CdoSendUsingPort*. Then add information about your server and the port (normally port 25) for connecting to that server to send SMTP mail.

Sending a Message with Custom Properties

If you modify the properties on a message and you want those custom properties to travel with the item, you must use the *CdoSendUsingExchange* option for the CDO *Configuration* object. If you do not use this option, all the custom properties on your messages will be lost.

Resolving Addresses

Before adding addresses to the *To*, *CC*, or *BCC* properties on a CDO *Message* object, you might want to resolve the address against a directory or the Contacts folder to make sure the address is correct. The way to resolve addresses is to use the CDO *Addressee* object. This object has a number of properties, such as *DisplayName* and *EmailAddress*, which you can fill out to try and resolve an address. The names of these properties provide a clue to what values should go in them. Once you create the *Addressee* object and fill in one of the two properties just described, you can call the *CheckName* method, which takes either an LDAP path to your Active Directory or the file path to a Contacts folder contained in Exchange Server.

If the address can be resolved without ambiguous names, you can use some other properties on the *Addressee* object to get more information about the person. For example, the *DirURL* property returns either the Active Directory path or the file path to a contact, depending on whether you are validating the address against Active Directory or the Contacts folder. You can also call the *Resolved-Status* property, which will contain *0* for unresolved, *1* for resolved, or *2* for ambiguous. If you get an ambiguous address, you can use the *AmbiguousNames* property to return the *Addressees* collection, which is made up of *Addressee* objects that are ambiguous with respect to your current *Addressee* object.

The following sample shows how to use the properties and methods just described:

```
Dim oAddressee As New CDO.Addressee

'Use the Display Name
oAddressee.DisplayName = "Thomas Rizzo"

'Use the Active Directory

oAddressee.CheckName "LDAP://thomriznt5srv"
If oAddressee.ResolvedStatus = 1 Then
    'Resolved
    MsgBox oAddressee.DirURL & vblf & oAddressee.EmailAddress
End If

'Use the E-mail Address
Dim oAddressee2 As New CDO.Addressee
oAddressee2.EmailAddress = "thomriz@thomriznt5dom.microsoft.com"

'Use a Contact folder
oAddressee2.CheckName "file://./backofficestorage/" & _
    "thomriznt5dom.microsoft.com/public folders/contacts"
If oAddressee2.ResolvedStatus = 2 Then
    'Ambiguous
    Set oAddressees = oAddressee2.AmbiguousNames
    For Each otmpAddressee In oAddressees
        'Scroll through the ambiguous addressees
        MsgBox otmpAddressee.EmailAddress
    Next
End If
```

CDO Calendaring Tasks

The new version of CDO provides some invaluable calendaring features. For example, if you have the correct permissions, you can open other users' calendars and perform operations on those calendars. Also, you can use public folder calendars. Plus, CDO directly supports iCalendar, which allows you to send meeting requests in a standard format that other clients can understand. The following sections discuss the most common tasks you'll perform with the CDO calendaring component.

Creating Appointments

Creating appointments using CDO is easy. You create a new CDO *Appointment* object, specify some properties, and use the *DataSource* interface on the *Appointment* object to save the appointment into a folder. This process is shown in the following sample:

```
Dim oAppt As New Appointment
sCalendarURL = "file://./backofficestorage/thomriz.com/MBX/User/Calendar/"

'Set the appointment properties
oAppt.StartTime = #2/14/2003 12:30:00 PM#
oAppt.EndTime = #2/14/2003 1:30:00 PM#
oAppt.Subject = "Shop for Valentine's Day present!"
oAppt.Location = "Gift Store"
oAppt.TextBody = "Don't forget this year!!!!"

'Save the appointment
oAppt.DataSource.SaveToContainer sCalendarURL
```

Creating Meeting Requests and Checking Free/Busy Information

You can create a meeting request by creating an appointment and then adding the names of the desired attendees. When generating a meeting request, you can also retrieve the free/busy information for all attendees. The following code creates a meeting request, finds the first available slot of free/busy time for an attendee, and sends the meeting request to the attendee:

```
Dim oAppt As New CDO.Appointment
Dim oAttendee As CDO.Attendee
Dim oAddressee As New CDO.Addressee

oAddressee.EmailAddress = "bobw@thomriznt5dom.extest.microsoft.com"
'Check the address against the local directory
'You could also specify any LDAP path
oAddressee.CheckName ("LDAP://thomriznt5dom.extest.microsoft.com")

If oAddressee.ResolvedStatus = cdoResolved Then
    'Create an hour meeting sometime on March 7th
    'Get the free/busy information.
    strFB = oAddressee.GetFreeBusy(CDate("3/7/2003 9:00:00 AM"), _
            CDate("3/7/2003 5:00:00 PM"), 60)
    'Returns a string of 0,1,2,3
    '0 - Free, 1 - Tenative, 2 - Busy, 3 - OOF, 4 - No F/B data
    'Find the first free spot by looking for 0
    bFoundFB = False
    For i = 1 To 8
        'Look for a free spot
        If Mid(strFB, i, 1) = 0 Then
            dStart = DateAdd("h", i, CDate("3/7/2003 8:00 AM"))
            dEnd = DateAdd("h", 1, dStart)
            bFoundFB = True
```

```
            Exit For
        End If
    Next

    If bFoundFB = True Then
        Dim oConfig As New CDO.Configuration
        oConfig.Fields("http://schemas.microsoft.com/cdo/" & _
                       "configuration/sendemailaddress") = _
                       "thomriz@thomriznt5dom.extest.microsoft.com"
        oConfig.Fields("http://schemas.microsoft.com/cdo/" & _
                       "configuration/calendarlocation") = _
                       "file://./backofficestorage/" & _
                       "thomriznt5dom.extest.microsoft.com/" & _
                       "MBX/thomriz/calendar"
        oConfig.Fields.Update

        oAppt.Configuration = oConfig
        oAppt.StartTime = dStart
        oAppt.EndTime = dEnd
        oAppt.Subject = "Meeting"
        oAppt.Location = "Your office"
        oAppt.TextBody = "Meeting with you!"
        Set oAttendee = oAppt.Attendees.Add
        oAttendee.Address = oAddressee.EmailAddress
        oAttendee.Role = cdoRequiredParticipant
        Set oCalMsg = oAppt.CreateRequest
        oCalMsg.Message.Send

        strCalendarURL = "file://./backofficestorage/" & _
                         "thomriznt5dom.extest.microsoft.com/" & _
                         "MBX/thomriz/calendar"
        'Save to organizer calendar
        oAppt.DataSource.SaveToContainer strCalendarURL
    End If
End If
```

Notice that the code uses the *Addressee* object. This object allows you to create and resolve addresses using LDAP with a directory server. Once the attendee is resolved, the free/busy information is retrieved for the attendee by using the *GetFreeBusy* method. This method takes the start time, the end time, and the interval in minutes that you want to break the free/busy information into.

The code then checks for the first time when the attendee is free. Next it creates an appointment, fills out the appropriate fields, and then calls the *CreateRequest* method. This method returns a *CalendarMessage* object. You can then call the contained *Message* object's methods, such as *Send*. Finally, the code saves the appointment to the calendar.

Another Way to Check Free/Busy Information

In addition to using CDO to check the free/busy information for a user on the server, you can leverage HTTP to access that information. Exchange Server provides a special URL that Outlook Web Access uses to check a user's free/busy data. The nice thing about this technique is that you are not limited by where your code runs. Because CDO requires you to run your code on the Exchange server, you can use this approach with the *XMLHTTP* or *ServerXMLHTTP* objects (discussed in the next chapter). The server will return XML that contains the overall free/busy status of all attendees aggregated and the individual free/busy status for each attendee. Then you must write code to parse the XML and display, calculate, or perform whatever functionality your application requires. Here is the URL you need to pass to the server to use this technique:

```
http://SERVER/public/?Cmd=freebusy&start=ISOFORMATTEDDATE&end=ISOFORMATTED-
DATE&interval=30&u=SMTP:user@user.com
```

As you can see, you go into the public vroot and pass a *Cmd* of *freebusy*. With that *Cmd*, you must pass the start date and time as a specially formatted ISO string such as *yyyy-mm-ddThh:mm:ssTZOffset*. For example, *2003-10-12T06:00:00-08:00* is a valid start and end date. You then specify an interval such as 30 or 60. This interval can be any interval you want. Exchange will return the free/busy information for the users who are using that interval as the default. Finally, you specify the SMTP address of the users you want to retrieve using the format *u=SMTP:smtpaddressofuser*. To return multiple users, pass in *multiple u=SMTP:smtpaddressofuser* parameters in your query. The following XML code is returned with a query of two people using the following URL:

```
http://server/public/?Cmd=freebusy&start=2003-06-11T00:00:00-08:00&end=2003-06-
12T00:00:00-08:00&interval=10&u=SMTP:thomriz@domain.com&u=jwierer@domain.com
```

```
<a:response xmlns:a="WM">
 <a:recipients>
 <a:item>
  <a:displayname>All Attendees</a:displayname>
  <a:type>1</a:type>
  <a:fbdata>0000000000000000000000000000000000002222222222220002222220000002222
22222222000000000000222222222000000000000000000000000000000000000000000000000</
a:fbdata>
  </a:item>
<a:item>
  <a:displayname>Thomas Rizzo</a:displayname>
  <a:email type="SMTP">thomriz@domain.com</a:email>
  <a:type>1</a:type>
  <a:fbdata>0000000000000000000000000000000000002222221111110002222220000002222
22222222000000000000222222222000000000000000000000000000000000000000000000000</
a:fbdata>
  </a:item>
```

```
 <a:item>
  <a:displayname>Jeff Wierer</a:displayname>
  <a:email type="SMTP">jwierer@domain.com</a:email>
  <a:type>1</a:type>
  <a:fbdata>0000000000000000000000000000000000000000002222220002222220000000001
1111100000000000000011122222200000000000000000000000000000000000000000000000000</
a:fbdata>
  </a:item>
  </a:recipients>
  </a:response>
```

As you can see from the XML returned, an all attendees row is returned, which is the aggregate of all the free/busy information. Then individual item rows are returned for each user containing the displayname, e-mail address, type, and free/busy data. From this, you need to write code that will parse the XML and return whatever user interface or functionality your application requires. The following sample code shows you how to format a request, send that request using the *XMLHTTP* object, get back a response, and then parse that response using the XMLDOM:

```
⋮
Dim oXMLHTTP As New MSXML2.XMLHTTP30
dtCurrentDay = Date
dStartDate = dtCurrentDay
dEndDate = dtCurrentDay + 1
dISODateStartFB = TurnintoUTCFB(DateValue(dStartDate), _
                    FormatDateTime(TimeValue(dStartDate), 4))
dISODateEndFB = TurnintoUTCFB(DateValue(dEndDate), _
                  FormatDateTime(TimeValue(dEndDate), 4))

strURL = "http://server/public/?Cmd=freebusy&start=" & _
         dISODateStartFB & "&end=" & dISODateEndFB & _
         "&interval=30&u=SMTP:thomriz@domain.com&u=SMTP:user@domain.com"

oXMLHTTP.Open "GET", strURL, False
oXMLHTTP.setRequestHeader "Content-type", "text/xml"
oXMLHTTP.setRequestHeader "translate", "t"
oXMLHTTP.setRequestHeader "user-agent", _
                          "Mozilla/4.0 (compatible; MSIE 5.01; Windows NT)"
oXMLHTTP.Send ("")

Set objXML = CreateObject("MSXML.DOMDocument")
objXML.loadXML oXMLHTTP.ResponseText

bGetFBForThisNode = False
Set objnodelist = objXML.getElementsByTagName("*")
For i = 0 To (objnodelist.length - 1)
    Set objnode = objnodelist.nextNode
    If objnode.nodeName = "a:email" Then
        'Check to see if the current user
        If UCase(objnode.Text) = UCase("thomriz@domain.com") Then
```

```
            bGetFBForThisNode = True
        End If
    End If
    If bGetFBForThisNode = True Then
        If objnode.nodeName = "a:fbdata" Then
            'Get the FB
            aFB = CStr(objnode.Text)
        End If
    End If
Next

Function TurnintoUTCFB(dDate, strTime)
    'Format should be "yyyy-mm-ddThh:mm:ssTZOffset"
    strUTC = Year(dDate) & "-"

    If Month(dDate) < 10 Then
        strUTC = strUTC & "0" & Month(dDate) & "-"
    Else
        strUTC = strUTC & Month(dDate) & "-"
    End If

    If Day(dDate) < 10 Then
        strUTC = strUTC & "0" & Day(dDate) & "T"
    Else
        strUTC = strUTC & Day(dDate) & "T"
    End If

    If Mid(strTime, 3, 1) <> ":" Then
        'Must be X not 0X
        strUTC = strUTC & "0" & strTime & ":00"
    Else
        strUTC = strUTC & strTime & ":00"
    End If

    'Add the timezone difference
    iDiff = -8
    If Len(iDiff) = 2 Then
        'It's -8 or +8, not -08 or +08, add a zero
        iDiff = Left(iDiff, 1) & "0" & Right(iDiff, 1)
    End If

    strUTC = strUTC & iDiff & ":00"

    TurnintoUTCFB = strUTC
End Function
```

Creating Recurring Meeting Requests

To create a recurring meeting request, you simply add a *RecurrencePattern* object to the appointment and set some properties on it. If you want to get more complex, you can add an *Exception* object to the *RecurrencePattern* object to specify that a certain date be excluded from the meeting request. The following code shows how to create a simple recurring meeting request:

```
Dim oAppt As New CDO.Appointment
Dim oAttendee As CDO.Attendee
Dim oAddressee As New CDO.Addressee
Dim oRP As CDO.IRecurrencePattern

oAddressee.EmailAddress = "bobw@thomriznt5dom.extest.microsoft.com"
'Check the address against the local directory.
'You could also specify any LDAP path.
oAddressee.CheckName ("LDAP://thomriznt5dom.extest.microsoft.com")


If oAddressee.ResolvedStatus = cdoResolved Then
    Dim oConfig As New CDO.Configuration
    oConfig.Fields("http://schemas.microsoft.com/cdo/" & _
                   "configuration/sendemailaddress") = _
                   "thomriz@thomriznt5dom.extest.microsoft.com"
    oConfig.Fields("http://schemas.microsoft.com/cdo/" & _
                   "configuration/calendarlocation") = _
                   "file://./backofficestorage/" & _
                   "thomriznt5dom.extest.microsoft.com/" & _
                   "MBX/thomriz/calendar"
    oConfig.Fields.Update

    oAppt.Configuration = oConfig
    oAppt.StartTime = dStart
    oAppt.EndTime = dEnd
    oAppt.Subject = "Meeting"
    oAppt.Location = "Your office"
    oAppt.TextBody = "Meeting with you!"
    Set oRP = oAppt.RecurrencePatterns.Add("ADD")
    'Make it weekly
    oRP.Frequency = cdoWeekly
    oRP.Interval = 1
    oRP.Instances = 10

    Set oAttendee = oAppt.Attendees.Add
    oAttendee.Address = oAddressee.EmailAddress
    oAttendee.Role = cdoRequiredParticipant
    Set oCalMsg = oAppt.CreateRequest
    oCalMsg.Message.Send

     strCalendarURL = "file://./backofficestorage/" & _
         "thomriznt5dom.extest.microsoft.com/MBX/thomriz/calendar"
    'Save to organizer calendar
    oAppt.DataSource.SaveToContainer strCalendarURL
End If
```

The code creates the *RecurrencePattern* object by using the *RecurrencePatterns* collection on the *Appointment* object. The *Add* method of this collection has only two values that you can pass to its parameter: *ADD* and *DELETE*. Once the new *RecurrencePattern* object has been added to the collection, the code sets the properties on the object to make the recurrence weekly, specifying only 10 recurrences. If you do not specify the instances, CDO will make the meeting recur indefinitely.

Creating Exceptions

You can create exceptions to your recurring meetings or appointments by using the CDO exceptions and the *Exception* object. I'll show a simple example of adding a single exception to a recurring appointment, but you can do more complex operations with the CDO *Exception* object. The following code sample uses the CDO *Exceptions* collection to add a new exception to a recurring meeting. You can also delete and modify exceptions using the CDO *Exceptions* collection.

```
Set oException = oAppt.Exceptions.Add("Add")
oException.StartTime = "5/2/2003 10:00 AM"
oException.EndTime = "5/2/2003 11:00 AM"
```

Responding to a Meeting Request

You can use CDO calendaring to accept, decline, or mark as tentative a meeting request. This operation is quite easy, so I'll just show you the code. This code sample assumes that the meeting request you want to process is in your Inbox and is already assigned to the *oAppt* object:

```
Set oMsg = oAppt.Accept
'You can then modify the response message by modifying oMsg
oMsg.Message.Send
'Save the appointment to your calendar
oAppt.DataSource.SaveTo URLTOYOURCALENDAR
```

Opening Other Users' Mailbox Folders

To open another user's folder or folders, all you need to do is pass the path to that folder to a *Record* object or to a query that returns an ADO recordset. The following example opens up Neil Charney's Calendar folder. To open another user's folder, you must have permissions on that user's folders.

```
Dim oRecord as New ADODB.Record
oRecord.Open "file://./backofficestorage/domain/MBX/neilc/calendar/"
```

Working with Time Zones

One of the first issues you have to deal with when working with CDO calendaring functionality, and even when working with ADO, is the storage of dates in UTC format in Exchange. CDO offsets the UTC date to the local time zone specified in the CDO *Configuration* object. If you do not explicitly set a time zone, CDO will use the time zone of the machine. This functionality is different from how ADO handles time zones; ADO does no offset at all and returns the date in UTC format. You can run into some strange debugging issues if you forget this fact—if you create event registrations or calendar appointments using ADO and then look at those items through CDO, you will see different dates.

Time zones play an important role in the Training application when setup creates event registrations for the survey and creates course notification events. To use ADO to create the event registrations so the events fire daily at 10 P.M. local time on the server, the application has to figure out the offset from 10 P.M. local time to UTC time. The following code does this by leveraging CDO to create an appointment at 10 P.M. local time. The code then retrieves that appointment using ADO, which returns the start time for the appointment at UTC time, not at 10 P.M. local time. The code then figures out the offset between UTC and local time on the server by using the *DateDiff* function. This information is used by the application event handlers to make sure the ADO query to find all items created in the last 24 hours finds those items with the correct date and time. You must figure out the UTC offset because Exchange stores the creation dates of items in UTC. Otherwise, you will not really be querying for items created in the past 24 hours in local time.

```
'Figure out start time for timer events.
'Since the start time needs to be UTC, we need to figure
'out the local server time and then figure out the UTC
'time to tell the event to fire so that it is 10 PM.

Dim oAppt As CDO.Appointment
Set oAppt = CreateObject("CDO.Appointment")
oAppt.Subject = "Delete me"
If DateDiff("n", Now, Date & " 10:00 PM") < 60 Then
    If DateDiff("n", Now, DateAdd("h", 1, Date & " 10:00 PM")) <= 60 Then
        'We're passing 10 PM for the current day
        dDate = DateAdd("d", 1, Date)
    Else
        dDate = Date
    End If
Else
    dDate = Date
End If

oAppt.StartTime = DateValue(dDate) & " 10:00 PM"
oAppt.EndTime = DateAdd("n", 60, oAppt.StartTime)
strTime = TimeValue(oAppt.StartTime)

'Dump the appt into the root folder
oAppt.DataSource.SaveToContainer strPath
strdeletehref = oAppt.Fields("DAV:href").Value
Set oAppt = Nothing
'Get it back
```

```
Dim oDeleteRecord As New ADODB.Record
oDeleteRecord.Open strdeletehref, , adModeReadWrite
strNow = oDeleteRecord.Fields("urn:schemas:calendar:dtstart").Value

'Figure out the offset from UTC to the local time zone.
'This is needed for the survey notification event handler
'so that it knows how much to offset its query for items created
'during the current day.
strDate = oDeleteRecord.Fields("urn:schemas:calendar:dtstart").Value

strLocDate = dDate & " " & strTime
iDiff = DateDiff("h", strDate, strLocDate)

'Delete it
oDeleteRecord.DeleteRecord
```

CDO Contact Tasks

CDO implements a *Person* object for working with contacts in both the Exchange Server store and Active Directory. Using this object, you can create and query contact objects in Exchange Server and Active Directory. CDO handles all the property mapping between Exchange Server and Active Directory. The CDO *Person* object is very straightforward, so instead of telling you all the properties you can set on this object, I'll just show you some code samples.

Creating a Contact in Exchange Server

Creating a contact in Exchange Server is as easy as creating a CDO *Person* object, setting several properties, and then calling *SaveToContainer*. The following code shows these steps:

```
Dim oPerson As New CDO.Person
strContactURL = "file://./backofficestorage/thomriznt5dom." & _
                "extest.microsoft.com/public folders/group contacts/"
oPerson.FirstName = "Thomas"
oPerson.LastName = "Rizzo"
oPerson.Company = "Microsoft"
oPerson.WorkStreet = "1 Microsoft Way"
oPerson.WorkCity = "Redmond"
oPerson.WorkState = "WA"
oPerson.WorkPostalCode = "98052"
oPerson.Email = "thomriz@microsoft.com"
oPerson.WorkPhone = "425 555 1212"
oPerson.Email2 = "test@test.com"

'Save the Person object to the folder
oPerson.DataSource.SaveToContainer strContactURL
```

Creating a Contact in Active Directory

Creating a contact in Active Directory is similar to creating a contact in an Exchange Server folder. The only difference is that you provide an LDAP URL rather than a file URL, as shown here:

```
strContactURL = "LDAP://thomriznt5srv/cn=tomrizzo,cn=users," & _
                "dc=extest,dc=microsoft,dc=com"
oPerson.FirstName = "Thomas"
oPerson.LastName = "Rizzo"
oPerson.Company = "Microsoft"
oPerson.WorkStreet = "1 Microsoft Way"
oPerson.WorkCity = "Redmond"
oPerson.WorkState = "WA"
oPerson.WorkPostalCode = "98052"
oPerson.Email = "thomriz@microsoft.com"
oPerson.WorkPhone = "425 555 1212"
oPerson.Email2 = "test@test.com"

'Save the Person object to the folder
oPerson.DataSource.SaveToContainer strContactURL
```

Saving Your Contact as a vCard

CDO allows you to access or create vCard information for your contacts. vCard is a standard way of describing contact information on the Internet. CDO vCard support allows you to send or save your contacts to any compliant vCard system. You get the vCard information by using the *GetVCardStream* method, which returns the information about a contact in vCard format to an ADO *Stream* object. The following code uses the *GetVCardStream* method to retrieve the vCard information and print it to the screen for a contact:

```
Dim oPerson as New CDO.Person
oPerson.DataSource.Open "file://./backofficestorage/domain/folder/name.eml"
oPerson.GetVCardStream.SaveToFile "c:\vcard.txt"
```

The output from running the preceding code, which is contained in the text file vcard.txt, is shown here:

```
BEGIN:VCARD
VERSION:2.1
N:Rizzo;Thomas
FN:Thomas Rizzo
ORG:Microsoft Corporation
TITLE:Product Manager
NOTE;ENCODING=QUOTED-PRINTABLE:=0D=0A
TEL;WORK;VOICE:(425) 555-1212
ADR;WORK:;;1 Microsoft Way;Redmond;WA;98052;United States of America
LABEL;WORK;ENCODING=QUOTED-
PRINTABLE:1 Microsoft Way=0D=0ARedmond, WA 98052=0D=0AUnited States of America
URL:
URL:http://www.microsoft.com/exchange
```

```
EMAIL;PREF;INTERNET:thomriz@microsoft.com
REV:20030410T033803Z
END:VCARD
```

Interoperating with Outlook Properties

The good thing about CDO for Exchange is that it automatically sets some of the properties that enable seamless Outlook integration, such as making contacts that you create automatically appear in Outlook address books. However, there are some contact properties that CDO cannot set, and you have to resort to the MAPI equivalents to set these properties. One of these properties is the IM address property on a contact. The MAPI property set for contact items in Outlook is *00062004-0000-0000-C000-000000000046*. If you're using CDO 1.21, you must transpose this property, as in *0420060000000000C000000000000046*. Please check Knowledge Base article 298401 for more information. The property identifier for the IM address property is *0x8062*. The following code creates a new contact and uses the *Fields* collection of the CDO *Person* object to set the IM address of the contact:

```
Dim oContact As New CDO.Person
strURL = "file://./backofficestorage/thomriznt5dom2." & _
         "extest.microsoft.com/public folders/contacts/"
oContact.FirstName = "Tom"
oContact.LastName = "Rizzo"
oContact.Email = "thomriz@microsoft.com"
oContact.FileAs = "Rizzo, Tom"
'Set the IM Address
'Propset is 00062004-0000-0000-C000-000000000046
'For CDO 1.21, this is transposed to 0420060000000000C000000000000046
'Property ID is 0x8062
oContact.Fields.Item("http://schemas.microsoft.com/" & _
                     "mapi/id/{00062004-0000-0000-C000-" & _
                     "000000000046}/0x00008062").Value = _
                     "thomriz@microsoft.com"
oContact.Fields.Update
oContact.DataSource.SaveToContainer strURL
```

CDO Folder Tasks

CDO provides a *Folder* object that allows you to create or access folders contained in the Exchange database. Using this object, you can retrieve the number of read and unread items contained in the folder. You will interact most with the *Folder* object's properties, which include the following: *Configuration*, *ContentClass*, *DataSource*, *Description*, *DisplayName*, *EmailAddress*, *Fields*, *HasSubFolders*, *ItemCount*, *UnreadItemCount*, and *VisibleCount*.

Most of these properties are straightforward. The only one that really needs explaining is the *VisibleCount* property. This property is the total number of hidden items in the folder. Hidden items are created in the associated Contents table. These items can be created by setting the *DAV:ishidden* property to *True*.

Creating a Folder

To create a folder using the CDO *Folder* object, you first create a CDO *Folder* object and then use the *DataSource* property to save the folder. The following example shows you how to create a folder using CDO:

```
Dim oFolder As New CDO.Folder

oFolder.Description = "This is my folder"
oFolder.ContentClass = "urn:content-classes:contactfolder"
oFolder.Fields("http://schemas.microsoft.com/exchange" & _
            "/outlookfolderclass") = "IPF.Contact"
oFolder.Fields.Update
oFolder.DataSource.SaveTo "file://./backofficestorage/" & _
    "thomriznt5dom.extest.microsoft.com/public folders/my contact folder"
```

Mail-Enabling Folders

With the addition of new top-level hierarchies, Exchange Server does not, by default, mail-enable folders in the new hierarchies. You can mail-enable the folders either through the administrative UI or programmatically. The latter approach is quite easy. All you do is use the *IMailRecipient* interface from the CDO for Exchange Management library. To retrieve the interface, you set a variable to the *IMailRecipient* interface. Then you set the value of that variable to be your CDO folder. Call the *MailEnable* method on the folder, and then make the changes to the properties on the *IMailRecipient* interface. For example, you might set up the alias, establish the SMTP e-mail address, and decide whether the new address should be hidden from the address book. Once you finish setting the properties, you can just save the folder back to the Exchange database. Remember that you will need to open the folder in the read/write mode using the CDO *Folder* object, as shown in the following code:

```
Dim oFolder As New CDO.Folder
Dim oRecip As CDOEXM.IMailRecipient

oFolder.DataSource.Open "file://./backofficestorage/thomriznt5dom." & _
                        "extest.microsoft.com/public folders/" & _
                        "my contact folder", , adModeReadWrite
Set oRecip = oFolder
oRecip.MailEnable
oRecip.SMTPEmail = "contacts@domain.com"
oRecip.HideFromAddressBook = False
oRecip.Alias = "My Contacts Folder"
oFolder.DataSource.Save
```

What About Tasks?

As you might have noticed, there is no CDO task object. However, for simple task functions such as creating, modifying, or deleting tasks, you can use task schema properties to perform these operations. You can attempt to code task recurrence and task assignment, but this is much harder and can easily break Outlook if done incorrectly. For this reason, these functions are not shown in the following code because they are complex and prone to breaking Outlook:

```
'Core Task Properties
Const cdoTaskStartDate = "http://schemas.microsoft.com/mapi/id/" & _
    "{00062003-0000-0000-C000-000000000046}/0x00008104" 'PT_SYSTIME
Const cdoTaskDueDate = "http://schemas.microsoft.com/mapi/id/" & _
    "{00062003-0000-0000-C000-000000000046}/0x00008105" 'PT_SYSTIME
Const cdoTaskPercentComplete = "http://schemas.microsoft.com/mapi/id/" & _
    "{00062003-0000-0000-C000-000000000046}/0x00008102" 'PT_DOUBLE
Const cdoTaskComplete = "http://schemas.microsoft.com/mapi/id/" & _
    "{00062003-0000-0000-C000-000000000046}/0x0000811c" 'PT_BOOLEAN
Const cdoTaskDateCompleted = "http://schemas.microsoft.com/mapi/id/" & _
    "{00062003-0000-0000-C000-000000000046}/0x0000810f" 'PT_SYSTIME
Const cdoTaskStatus = "http://schemas.microsoft.com/mapi/id/" & _
    "{00062003-0000-0000-C000-000000000046}/0x00008101" 'PT_LONG
Const cdoTaskState = "http://schemas.microsoft.com/mapi/id/" & _
    "{00062003-0000-0000-C000-000000000046}/0x00008113" 'PT_LONG
Const cdoTaskActualEffort = "http://schemas.microsoft.com/mapi/id/" & _
    "{00062003-0000-0000-C000-000000000046}/0x00008110" 'PT_LONG
Const cdoTaskEstimatedEffort = "http://schemas.microsoft.com/mapi/id/" & _
    "{00062003-0000-0000-C000-000000000046}/0x00008111" 'PT_LONG
Const cdoTaskMode = "http://schemas.microsoft.com/mapi/id/" & _
    "{00062003-0000-0000-C000-000000000046}/0x00008518" 'PT_LONG

'Common Props
Const cdoBillingInformation = "http://schemas.microsoft.com/mapi/id/" & _
    "{00062008-0000-0000-C000-000000000046}/0x00008535" 'PT_UNICODE
Const cdoCompanies = "http://schemas.microsoft.com/mapi/id/" & _
    "{00062008-0000-0000-C000-000000000046}/0x00008539" 'PT_MV_UNICODE
Const cdoMileage = "http://schemas.microsoft.com/mapi/id/" & _
    "{00062008-0000-0000-C000-000000000046}/0x00008534" 'PT_UNICODE

'Reminder Props
Const cdoReminderDelta = "http://schemas.microsoft.com/mapi/id/" & _
    "{00062008-0000-0000-C000-000000000046}/0x00008501" 'PT_LONG
Const cdoReminderNextTime = "http://schemas.microsoft.com/mapi/id/" & _
    "{00062008-0000-0000-C000-000000000046}/0x00008560" 'PT_SYSTIME
Const cdoReminderTime = "http://schemas.microsoft.com/mapi/id/" & _
    "{00062008-0000-0000-C000-000000000046}/0x00008502" 'PT_SYSTIME
Const cdoReminderSet = "http://schemas.microsoft.com/mapi/id/" & _
    "{00062008-0000-0000-C000-000000000046}/0x00008503" 'PT_BOOLEAN

Private Sub Form_Load()
    Dim TaskItem As New ADODB.Record
```

```
    'Modify this URL to point to an item in your task folder
    TaskItem.Open "file://./backofficestorage/domain.com/MBX/users/" & _
                  "tasks/mytask.eml", , adModeReadWrite, adCreateOverwrite
    TaskItem.Fields.Item("DAV:contentclass") = "urn:content-classes:task"
    TaskItem.Fields.Item("http://schemas.microsoft.com/exchange/" & _
                         "outlookmessageclass").Value = "IPM.Task"

    'Set core Task props
    TaskItem.Fields.Item(cdoTaskStartDate).Value = Now
    TaskItem.Fields.Item(cdoTaskDueDate).Value = Now
    TaskItem.Fields.Item(cdoTaskActualEffort).Value = 36000 'Minutes.
    TaskItem.Fields.Item(cdoTaskEstimatedEffort).Value = 72000 'Minutes.

    'Set additional Props
    TaskItem.Fields.Item("urn:schemas-microsoft-com:office:office" & _
                         "#Keywords").Value = Array("my tasks", "Exchange")
    TaskItem.Fields.Item("urn:schemas:httpmail:textdescription").Value = _
                         "Description goes here!!"
    TaskItem.Fields.Item("urn:schemas:httpmail:subject").Value = _
                         "Tasks Rock!!"
    TaskItem.Fields.Item(cdoBillingInformation).Value = _
                         "Microsoft Corporation"
    TaskItem.Fields.Item(cdoCompanies).Value = Array("Expedia", "Microsoft")
    TaskItem.Fields.Item(cdoMileage).Value = "120"
    TaskItem.Fields.Append cdoTaskState, adInteger, , , 1
    TaskItem.Fields.Update

    'Set the PercentComplete and Task Status together for Unassigned Tasks
    'TaskItem.Fields.Append cdoTaskPercentComplete, adDouble, , , "0.0"
    'TaskItem.Fields.Append cdoTaskStatus, adInteger, , , 0
    'TaskItem.Fields.Update
    'MsgBox "The Task Status is Unassigned!"

    'Set the PercentComplete and Task Status together when updating
    'Task Status
    'TaskItem.Fields.Append cdoTaskPercentComplete, adDouble, , , "0.5"
    'TaskItem.Fields.Append cdoTaskStatus, adInteger, , , 1
    'TaskItem.Fields.Update
    'MsgBox "The Task Status was Updated!"

    'Set the PercentComplete, Task Status, Task Complete and
    'TaskDateCompleted together
    'TaskItem.Fields.Append cdoTaskPercentComplete, adDouble, , , "1.0"
    'TaskItem.Fields.Append cdoTaskStatus, adInteger, , , 2
    'TaskItem.Fields.Item(cdoTaskComplete).Value = True
    'TaskItem.Fields.Item(cdoTaskDateCompleted).Value = Now
    'TaskItem.Fields.Update
    'MsgBox "The Task Status was Updated!"

    TaskItem.Close
End Sub
```

Interoperability Between CDO 1.21 and CDO for Exchange

Sometimes you might want to get the entry ID of a message using CDO for Exchange and pass that entry ID to CDO 1.21 to open the message via CDO. You can use the MAPI property identifier for the *entryID* property to retrieve the entry ID via CDO or ADO. The following code shows how to retrieve the entry ID using CDO for Exchange and then pass that property to CDO 1.21:

```
strMsgURL = "file://./backofficestorage/thomriznt5dom2.extest." & _
            "microsoft.com/public folders/folder/message.eml"
Set objCDOEXMsg = CreateObject("CDO.Message")
objCDOEXMsg.DataSource.Open strMsgURL

'Convert the byte array in MAPI property PR_ENTRYID to a string.
strIDProp = "http://schemas.microsoft.com/mapi/proptag/0x0fff0102"
byteArray = objCDOEXMsg.Fields(strIDProp).Value

For Each singleByte In byteArray
    byteString = Hex(singleByte)
    If Len(byteString) < 2 Then
        byteString = "0" & byteString
    End If
    strEntryID = strEntryID & byteString
Next

Set objCDOEXMsg = Nothing

'Log on via CDO 1.21.
Set objSession = CreateObject("MAPI.Session")
objSession.Logon
'Get the message based on the message entry ID.
Set objMsg = objSession.GetMessage(strEntryID)
MsgBox "Message Subject: " & objMsg.Subject

objSession.Logoff
```

Note One question developers always ask about CDO is how to programmatically send encrypted and/or digitally signed mail. Rather than cover this in detail here, I'll just tell you that you can do this by programming to the cryptography APIs in Windows. The secure mail sample application, which you can find on the companion content for this book, shows you how to do this with CDO for Exchange.

A CDO for Exchange .NET Sample Application

Using CDO for Exchange with .NET is straightforward. You just add your references to the CDO library and then start coding. The following sample connects to a public folder and creates a new post in the folder. Then it creates a new appointment in the user's mailbox. It is shown in Visual Basic .NET.

```
Public Class Form1
    Inherits System.Windows.Forms.Form

#Region " Windows Form Designer generated code "
⋮
#End Region

    Private Sub cmdGo_Click(ByVal sender As System.Object, _
                            ByVal e As System.EventArgs) _
                            Handles cmdGo.Click
        'Show how to use CDO for Exchange with VB.NET
        'Open a public folder
        'Create a new post in the public folder

        Dim strURL As String = "http://thomrizwin2k/public/test/"
        Dim strMailBoxURL As String = _
            "http://thomrizwin2k/exchange/thomriz/calendar/"

        Dim oFolder As New CDO.Folder()
        'To make sure we use EXOLEDB, pass a new connection object to
        'the open call
        Dim oConnection As New ADODB.Connection()
        oConnection.Provider = "EXOLEDB.DataSource "
        oConnection.ConnectionString = strURL
        oConnection.Open()
        oFolder.DataSource.Open(strURL, oConnection, _
            ADODB.ConnectModeEnum.adModeReadWrite)
        MsgBox(oFolder.DisplayName & " has " & oFolder.ItemCount & " items.")

        'Add a new item to the folder
        Dim oItem As New CDO.Item()
        oItem.ContentClass = "urn:content-classes:message"
        oItem.Fields("urn:schemas:httpmail:subject").Value = "My New Post"
        oItem.Fields("urn:schemas:httpmail:textdescription").Value = _
                    "New Message Body"
        oItem.Fields("http://schemas.microsoft.com/exchange/" & _
                    "outlookmessageclass").Value = "IPM.Post"
        oItem.Fields.Update()
        oItem.DataSource.SaveToContainer(strURL, oConnection)

        'Create a new appointment as well
        Dim oAppt As New CDO.Appointment()
```

```
        'Need to create a new Connection object to the
        'mailbox store
        Dim oConnectionMailbox As New ADODB.Connection()
        oConnectionMailbox.Provider = "EXOLEDB.DataSource "
        oConnectionMailbox.ConnectionString = strMailBoxURL
        oConnectionMailbox.Open()

        oAppt.Subject = "My New Appointment"
        oAppt.StartTime = "1/23/2003 10:00 AM"
        oAppt.EndTime = "1/23/2003 11:00 AM"
        oAppt.Location = "Building 34"
        oAppt.TextBody = "This is the body of an appointment."
        oAppt.Fields("http://schemas.microsoft.com/exchange/" & _
                    "outlookmessageclass").Value = "IPM.Appointment"
        oAppt.Fields.Update()
        oAppt.DataSource.SaveToContainer(strMailBoxURL, oConnectionMailbox)

        oConnection.Close()
        oConnectionMailbox.Close()

    End Sub
End Class
```

Here is a scaled-down C# version of the sample:

```
using System;
using System.Drawing;
using System.Collections;
using System.ComponentModel;
using System.Windows.Forms;
using System.Data;
using CDO;

namespace CDOEx2kCSharp
{
    /// <summary>
    /// Summary description for Form1.
    /// </summary>
    public class Form1 : System.Windows.Forms.Form
    {
        private System.Windows.Forms.Button cmdGo;
        /// <summary>
        /// Required designer variable.
        /// </summary>
        private System.ComponentModel.Container components = null;

        public Form1()
        {
            //
            // Required for Windows Form Designer support
            //
            InitializeComponent();
```

```
        //
        // TODO: Add any constructor code after InitializeComponent call
        //
    }

    /// <summary>
    /// Clean up any resources being used.
    /// </summary>
    protected override void Dispose( bool disposing )
    {
        if( disposing )
        {
            if (components != null)
            {
                components.Dispose();
            }
        }
        base.Dispose( disposing );
    }

    #region Windows Form Designer generated code
    . . .
    #endregion

    /// <summary>
    /// The main entry point for the application.
    /// </summary>
     [STAThread]
    static void Main()
    {
        Application.Run(new Form1());
    }

    private void cmdGo_Click(object sender, System.EventArgs e)
    {
        string strURL = "http://thomrizwin2k/public/test";

        CDO.Folder oFolder = new CDO.Folder();
        ADODB.Connection oConnection = new ADODB.Connection();
        oConnection.Provider = "EXOLEDB.DataSource ";
        oConnection.ConnectionString = strURL;
        oConnection.Open(oConnection.ConnectionString,"","",0);
        oFolder.DataSource.Open(strURL, oConnection,
                    ADODB.ConnectModeEnum.adModeReadWrite,
                    ADODB.RecordCreateOptionsEnum.adFailIfNotExists,
                    ADODB.RecordOpenOptionsEnum.adOpenSource, "", "");
        MessageBox.Show(oFolder.DisplayName + " has "
                     + oFolder.ItemCount + " items.");

        //Add a new item
        CDO.Item oItem = new CDO.ItemClass();
        oItem.ContentClass = "urn:content-classes:message";
        oItem.Fields["urn:schemas:httpmail:subject"].Value =
```

```
                                                 "My New C# Post";
            oItem.Fields["urn:schemas:httpmail:textdescription"].Value =
                                                 "New Message Body";
            oItem.Fields["http://schemas.microsoft.com/"
                    + "exchange/outlookmessageclass"].Value = "IPM.Post";
            oItem.Fields.Update();
            oItem.DataSource.SaveToContainer(strURL, oConnection,
                         ADODB.ConnectModeEnum.adModeReadWrite,
                         ADODB.RecordCreateOptionsEnum.adCreateNonCollection,
                         ADODB.RecordOpenOptionsEnum.adOpenSource, "", "");
            oConnection.Close();
        }
    }
}
```

Summary

This chapter started you off on the long road to Exchange development. You will find that most of your server-side development in Exchange uses ADO or CDO for Exchange. In the next chapters, we will explore events, workflow, and instant messaging capabilities and how to use them in your applications.

16

Exchange Server and XML

Extensible Markup Language (XML) has been one of the biggest buzzwords in the industry. XML provides an easy way to describe data and share it among applications. XML is finding its way into many applications such as Microsoft Office. If you have not learned about XML yet, you need to. Technologies such as XML Web services, Microsoft Biztalk Server, Microsoft Exchange Server, and Microsoft SQL Server all have XML support. Exchange Server 2000 directly supports XML, and Exchange Server 2003 continues this tradition. Regardless which version you use, you can use XML to get and set data in Exchange information stores directly.

I won't try to cover all aspects of XML in this chapter—Microsoft Press publishes many good books on the topic. Instead, I'll discuss how to get, set, search, and format using Extensible Stylesheet Language (XSL) and XML data in Exchange Server. Because XML-based messaging solutions are typically used to access existing data, I will focus on querying for data and won't cover how to create complex XML documents from scratch.

The *HTTPWebRequest* Class

If you are programming from Microsoft .NET, you will want to use the *HTTPWebRequest* class, which allows you to send Web Distributed Authoring and Versioning (WebDAV) commands to Exchange Server. We covered this class extensively in Chapter 14, so here I will cover the other components you can use to program against WebDAV with Exchange, as well as details about WebDAV itself.

The XMLHTTP Component

You can retrieve XML data from Exchange in a number of ways. We looked at one way—using XML Web services—in Chapter 14. Another approach uses the WebDAV protocol. WebDAV is an extension to HTTP, which specifies how to perform file processing. Using WebDAV commands, you can lock a resource, get a property, or change a property, and because WebDAV is an HTTP extension, it can even work through firewalls and proxy servers.

You might be wondering how to use a protocol such as WebDAV within your Web applications. Microsoft Internet Explorer 5.0 and later ship with a component called XMLHTTP for working with the WebDAV protocol. In Internet Explorer 6.0, this component is part of the Microsoft XML Core Services (MSXML). If you use Internet Explorer 6.0, be sure to get the most recent patches as outlined in Microsoft Security Bulletin MS02-008.

With the XMLHTTP component (shown in Figure 16-1), you must still send correctly formatted WebDAV requests. However, the XMLHTTP component simplifies this. You should use this component only on the client side because that's the environment it was built for. If you're writing code on the Exchange server, you should write to the server version of XMLHTTP (called ServerXMLHTTP), Collaboration Data Objects for Exchange (CDOEX), or ActiveX Data Objects (ADO).

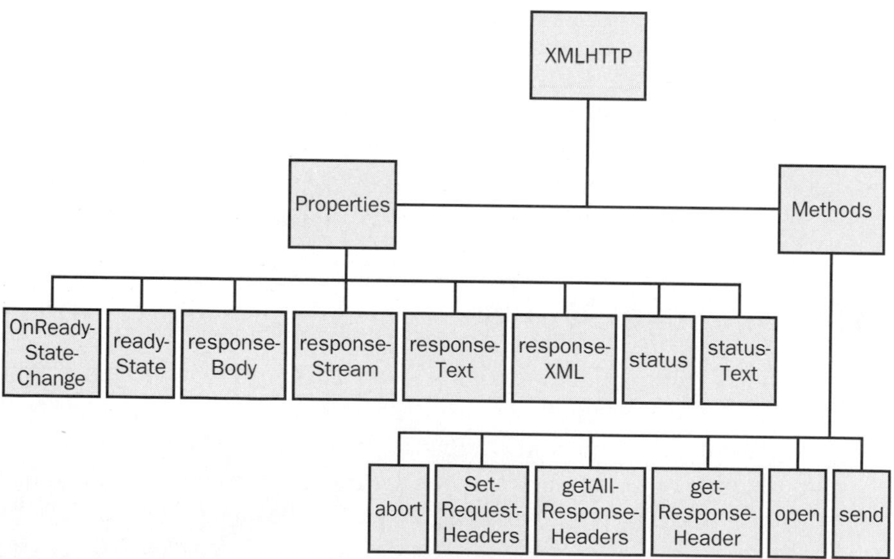

Figure 16-1 Properties and methods of the XMLHTTP component

We'll look at the most important properties and methods of the XMLHTTP component so you can use them in your client applications. These properties and methods are *Abort*, *OnReadyStateChange*, *Open*, *ReadyState*, *responseBody*, *responseStream*, *responseText*, *responseXML*, *Send*, *SetRequestHeader*, *Status*, and *StatusText*. All other properties and methods of XMLHTTP are fully documented by Microsoft Developer Network (MSDN) at *http://msdn.microsoft.com*.

Open Method

The first method you'll probably use with the XMLHTTP component is the *Open* method. This method takes five parameters: *Method*, *URL*, *Async*, *User*, and *Password*. The *Method* parameter specifies which HTTP method to use, such as *GET*, *POST*, *PROPPATH*, or *SEARCH*. The *URL* parameter represents the absolute Uniform Resource Locator (URL) to the resource—for example, *http://myserver/exchange/alias/inbox*. The *Async* parameter is a Boolean that specifies whether the call is asynchronous. If set to *True*, which is the default, the call returns immediately. Finally, you can use the *User* and *Password* parameters to pass the username and password with which you want the component to access secured sites. The following JavaScript code example, taken from the coursexml.asp file in the Training application (included among the book's sample content), shows how to create an XMLHTTP object and use the *Open* method:

```
request = new ActiveXObject("Microsoft.XMLHTTP");

//Example propfind
//request.open("PROPFIND", strURL, true);

request.open("SEARCH", strURL, true);
```

SetRequestHeader Method

The *SetRequestHeader* method allows you to specify the name and value for an HTTP header. The most common headers you will set are Depth header and Content-Type header. A Depth header, defined in Request for Comments (RFC) 2518, specifies how deep in a hierarchy the request applies. For example, setting the Depth header to *"1, noroot"* means that the method will be applied to all the children of the specified URL but not to the URL itself. If you do not specify a depth, Exchange will default to an infinite depth. A Content-Type header, defined in RFC 1049, specifies the structure of the message body you plan to send to the server. The following code snippet shows how to use this method:

```
//For propfind you can select a depth
//request.setRequestHeader("Depth", "1,noroot");

request.setRequestHeader("Content-Type", "text/xml");
```

ReadyState Property

The *ReadyState* property contains the state of the request object. Table 16-1 lists the five possible values.

Table 16-1 Values of the *ReadyState* Property

Value	Description
UNINITIALIZED	The object has been created, but the *Open* method has not been called.
LOADING	The object has been created, but the *Send* method has not been called.
LOADED	The *Send* method has been called, but the response is not yet available.
INTERACTIVE	The object is not yet fully loaded, but the user can already interact with it. Partial results can be viewed in the browser.
COMPLETED	All data has been received and can be viewed in the browser.

OnReadyStateChange Property

The *OnReadyStateChange* property allows you to specify which event handler to call when the *ReadyState* property changes. The following code sets the function to be called to *dostatechange*. You'll see what *dostatechange* does in a moment, when we look at the *responseXML* property.

```
request.onreadystatechange = dostatechange;
```

Send Method

As you would guess, the *Send* method sends the request to the server. You specify the request as a string parameter to this method. The following code sends the body of our request. You'll see what this body looks like later in the chapter, when we examine WebDAV requests.

```
request.send(body);
```

responseBody, *responseStream*, *responseText*, and *responseXML* Properties

The *responseBody*, *responseStream*, *responseText*, and *responseXML* properties allow you to retrieve the response in each type of format. You'll most often use *responseText* and *responseXML* in your applications. The *responseStream* property returns the response as an *IStream* object. The *responseText* property returns the XML response as a text string. The *responseXML* property returns the response as an XML document parsed by the MSXML parser, which means you'll receive an object that you can format using XSL or you can call methods on objects in the XMLDOM to interact with the data. You'll use these properties in the event handler you specified for the *onreadystatechange* property. The following JavaScript code (interlaced with server-side code for *dDateStart* and *dDateEnd*) gets the XML response and formats it via XSL:

```
thexml = request.responseXML;
datediv.innerHTML = "<B>Showing Courses from <%=dDateStart%> "
                  + "to <%=dDateEnd%></B><BR>";

//Check for empty body
if (thexml.selectSingleNode("a:multistatus/a:response") == null)
{
    msgdiv.innerHTML = "<B>No courses found.</B>";
    request = null;
    return;
}

//For debugging purposes
//alert(request.responseText);
msgdiv.innerHTML = thexml.transformNode(reportXSL.documentElement);
```

Status and *StatusText* Properties

The *Status* and *StatusText* properties contain status information about the request. *Status* contains the HTTP status returned by the request. This is an integer that corresponds to an HTTP status code. *StatusText* returns a string that represents the status returned by the request. The following code checks to see whether the *Status* property has a value of 207, which indicates that the request was successful. If *Status* does not have a value of 207, the code will print out the values of the *Status* and *StatusText* properties as an error.

```
if(request.status != 207)
{
    msgdiv.innerText = "Error, status = " + request.status + " "
                     + request.statusText;
    msgdiv.style.fontFamily = "verdana"
}
```

Abort Method

The *Abort* method cancels the current HTTP request and restores the XMLHTTP component to the *UNINITIALIZED* state. (See Table 16-1, shown earlier.)

ServerXMLHTTP Object

In MSXML 3.0, Microsoft introduced a new *ServerXMLHTTP* object. You should use this object in server-side code, such as in an Active Server Pages (ASP) application. The XMLHTTP component is great for building client-side applications that can be programmed via JavaScript or VBScript inside of Internet Explorer, but it is fundamentally built on the WinInet library and the WinInet library was not designed to support multiple clients. WinInet has some inherent scalability issues and provides features that are not critical for server applications, such as offline support.

The *ServerXMLHTTP* object's methods and properties are similar to those of the *XMLHTTP* object. *ServerXMLHTTP* is backward-compatible with XMLHTTP, so changing your code to use it is as easy as changing the ProgID you pass to your *CreateObject* function. The ProgID for *ServerXMLHTTP* is *MSXML2.ServerXMLHTTP*. *ServerXMLHTTP* adds four new methods to the collection of standard XMLHTTP methods and properties it inherits. These new methods are *getOption*, *setOption*, *waitForResponse*, and *setTimeouts*.

The *getOption* method allows you to determine how *ServerXMLHTTP* handles Unicode URLs. This method returns one of four values: *SXH_OPTION_URL_CODEPAGE (0)*, *SXH_OPTION_ESPACE_PERCENT_IN_URL (1)*, *SXH_OPTION_IGNORE_SERVER_SSL_CERT_ERROR_FLAGS (2)*, and *SXH_OPTION_SELECT_CLIENT_SSL_CERT (3)*. The first value means that a client can override the default codepage used to convert a Unicode URL to a single-byte representation. The second value tells *ServerXMLHTTP* that when it escapes ANSI characters in the URL (for example, a space in a URL becomes *%20*), *ServerXMLHTTP* should also escape the % character itself. The third and fourth values deal with SSL certificates. You can ignore SSL errors and also tell *ServerXMLHTTP* which client certificate to use explicitly.

setOption is used in conjunction with *getOption*. When you call *setOption*, you pass one of the enumerated values we already discussed for *getOption* to set that particular option for *ServerXMLHTTP*.

The *waitForResponse* method is an interesting feature. When you use *XMLHTTP* with an asynchronous call, you must continuously check the *readyState* property to see if the current state of the *XMLHTTP* object has changed. With *waitForResponse*, you can specify how long in seconds to wait for the asynchronous send operation to complete. If the send is successful, you will get back a *True* value. If the send call ends in a timeout, this method will return *False*. The request will not be aborted—you can keep waiting for the send operation to complete by simply calling *waitForResponse* again. The following VBScript example calls a *GET* on a URL and waits 500 seconds for it to complete:

```
Set oXMLHTTP = CreateObject("MSXML2.ServerXMLHTTP")
oXMLHTTP.Open "GET", "http://<server>/public/myitem.eml", True
oXMLHTTP.Send
Do While oXMLHTTP.readyState <> 4
    oXMLHTTP.waitForResponse 500
Loop
```

The *setTimeouts* method allows you to specify how long *ServerXMLHTTP* should wait to resolve the domain name, establish the connection to the server, send data, and then receive a response. The values you pass are in milliseconds—for example, a value of 1000 means 1 second. You can pass 0 to set the timeout to infinite. The following VBScript example waits 1 second for resolving, 2 seconds for connecting, 3 seconds for sending, and 4 seconds for receiving a response:

```
Set oXMLHTTP = CreateObject("MSXML2.ServerXMLHTTP")
oXMLHTTP.setTimeOuts 1000, 2000, 3000, 4000
oXMLHTTP.Open "GET", http://myserver/public/item.eml, false
oXMLHTTP.Send
```

WinHTTP Proxy Configuration Utility

When you work with *ServerXMLHTTP*, you need to use the WinHTTP Proxy Configuration utility (Proxycfg.exe) to access your HTTP servers through a proxy server. Proxycfg.exe updates the registry with your proxy configurations, so you must have local administrative rights on the machine before running the program. Proxycfg.exe settings are machine specific, not user specific. Note that WinHTTP proxy settings are different from Internet Explorer proxy settings. Changing your proxy settings in Internet Explorer will not affect ServerXMLHTTP.

Table 16-2 lists the parameters that Proxycfg.exe supports.

Table 16-2 WinHTTP Proxy Configuration Parameters

Parameter	Description	Example
-d	Specifies that all HTTP and HTTPS servers should be accessed directly, without a proxy.	`Proxycfg -d`
-p proxy-server-list optional-bypass-list	Lists the proxy servers to use and an optional host list that should be accessed by bypassing the proxy servers.	The following example accesses all hosts using myproxy or myhttpsproxy, except hosts without a period in their name, local hosts, or any host in the microsoft.com domain. `Proxycfg -p "http=myproxy https=myhttsproxy" "<local>;*.microsoft.com"`
-u	Imports the Internet Explorer proxy settings. Autodiscovery and configuration script–based proxy settings are not supported.	`Proxycfg -u`

WebDAV Commands

Now that you know about the object model of *XMLHTTP* and *ServerXMLHTTP*, which allows you to send WebDAV commands to the Exchange server, you're probably wondering what these commands are. WebDAV supports a number of commands, including *MKCOL*, *PROPPATCH*, *PROPFIND*, *DELETE*, *MOVE*, *COPY*, *SEARCH*, *LOCK*, *UNLOCK*, *SUBSCRIBE*, and *POLL*. Each of these commands serves a distinctive purpose in your applications. For example, *MKCOL* allows you to create a collection (or a folder) on your server. *PROPPATCH* and *PROPFIND* allow you to set and get properties on resources, respectively. If you are interested in details about these individual commands, take a look at RFC 2518. For now, let's look at some typical tasks you can perform with WebDAV using each of these commands.

> **Note** Some of the commands also support batch methods. These batch methods allow you to perform an action against multiple resources in a single call. For example, if you need to *PROPPATCH* a property onto 300 items, such as changing a shared value across the 300 items with a new value, you need 300 different *PROPPATCH* commands unless you use the batch version of *PROPPATCH*, which allows you to pass multiple URLs with one call. The batch methods are *BCOPY*, *BDELETE*, *BMOVE*, *BPROPFIND*, and *BPROPPATCH*. They are similar to their nonbatch counterparts; see the Exchange SDK (included with the book's companion content) for more information on batch methods.

Creating Folders

To create a folder using WebDAV, you issue the *MKCOL* command and pass the URL of the new folder that you want to create. If the creation is successful, you'll receive a *Status* of *201* and *StatusText* of *Created*. The following JavaScript code uses *XMLHTTP* to create a new folder (as shown in Figure 16-2):

```
<HTML>
<BODY>

<SCRIPT LANGUAGE=javascript>
<!---
    //Remember to escape any special characters in your URLs
    var strURL = "http://localhost/public/my%20new%20folder/";
    var request = new ActiveXObject("Microsoft.XMLHTTP");
    request.open("MKCOL", strURL, false);
    request.send();
    alert(request.status + " " + request.statustext);
//-->
</SCRIPT>

</BODY>
</HTML>
```

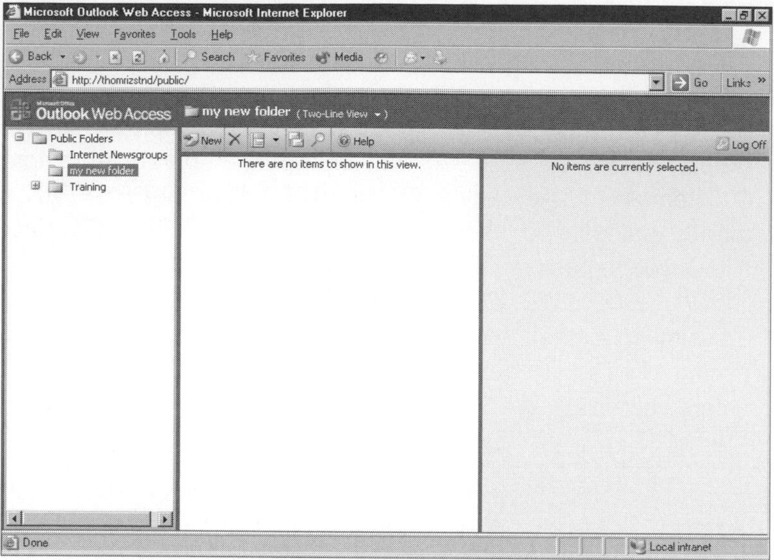

Figure 16-2 A folder created via WebDAV and XMLHTTP

Creating Items

To create an item, you use the HTTP *PUT* method and pass to it the URL of the new item you want to create. If you are successful, you'll get a *Status* of *201* and *StatusText* of *Created*. The following JavaScript code creates a new post in the public folder we created earlier (as shown in Figure 16-3):

```
<HTML>
<BODY>

<SCRIPT LANGUAGE=javascript>
<!--
    var strURL =
        "http://localhost/public/my%20new%20folder/my%20new%20 item.eml";
    var request = new ActiveXObject("Microsoft.XMLHTTP");
    request.open("PUT", strURL, false);
    request.setRequestHeader("Translate", "f");
    request.send();
    alert(request.status + " " + request.statustext);
//-->
</SCRIPT>

</BODY>
</HTML>
```

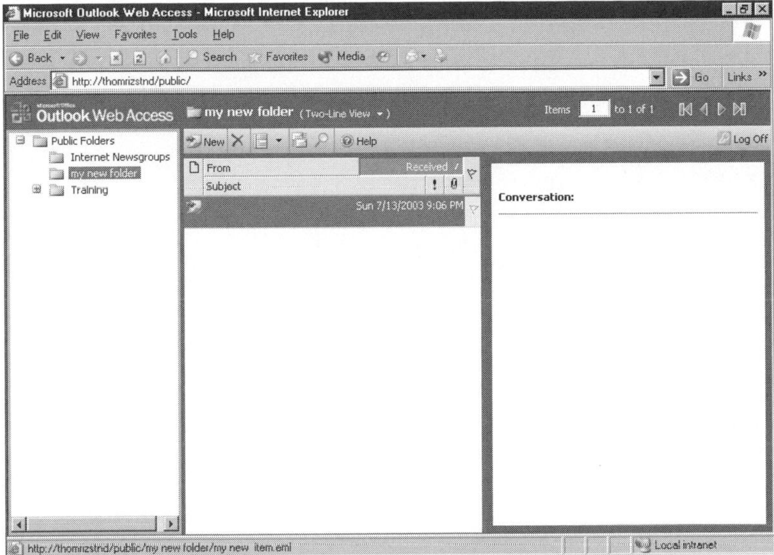

Figure 16-3 Creating an item in a public folder via WebDAV and XMLHTTP

Copying Folders and Items

To copy both items and folders, you use the *COPY* command. This command takes as a parameter the source URL of the item to be copied. As part of your request headers, you must specify the destination URL for the copied item. If you are copying a folder, all the contents of that folder will be copied as well. The following JavaScript code copies the newly created folder and item from the earlier example into another folder. If you are successful, you should receive a *Status* value of *201*.

```
<HTML>
<BODY>

<SCRIPT LANGUAGE=javascript>
<!--
    var strSourceURL = "http://localhost/public/my%20new%20folder/";
    var strDestURL = "http://localhost/public/my%20new%20folder%202/";
    var request = new ActiveXObject("Microsoft.XMLHTTP");
    request.open("COPY", strSourceURL, false);
    request.setRequestHeader("Destination", strDestURL);
    request.send();
    alert(request.status + " " + request.statustext);
//-->
</SCRIPT>

</BODY>
</HTML>
```

Moving Folders and Items

Moving folders is as easy as copying them. All you do is change the command from *COPY* to *MOVE*. The following JavaScript code shows how to move a folder:

```
<HTML>
<BODY>

<SCRIPT LANGUAGE=javascript>
<!--
    var strSourceURL = "http://localhost/public/my%20new%20folder/";
    var strDestURL = "http://localhost/public/my%20new%20folder%203/";
    var request = new ActiveXObject("Microsoft.XMLHTTP");
    request.open("MOVE", strSourceURL, false);
    request.setRequestHeader("Destination", strDestURL);
    request.send();
    alert(request.status + " " + request.statustext);
//-->
</SCRIPT>

</BODY>
</HTML>
```

To rename a folder, you use *MOVE* but create the Allow-Rename header and set it to *t* for *true*, as shown in the following line of code:

```
request.setRequestHeader("Allow-Rename", "t");
```

Deleting Items and Folders

To delete items or folders, you use the *DELETE* command and pass to it the URL of the item to be deleted. If you are successful, you'll receive a *Status* of *200* and *StatusText* of *OK*. The following code deletes a folder:

```
<HTML>
<BODY>

<SCRIPT LANGUAGE=javascript>
<!--
    var strURL = "http://localhost/public/my%20new%20folder%203/";
    var request = new ActiveXObject("Microsoft.XMLHTTP");
    request.open("DELETE", strURL, false);
    request.send();
    alert(request.status + " " + request.statustext);
//-->
</SCRIPT>

</BODY>
</HTML>
```

Setting Properties

To set properties, you use the *PROPPATCH* command. To use this command, you must create an XML document to send that lists the properties you want updated. You can generate this XML document in a number of ways. The two easiest ways are to use XMLDOM or to simply generate the XML yourself by using JavaScript code. The following JavaScript example generates the XML directly and sends it to the server to update the properties (as shown in Figure 16-4):

```
<HTML>
<BODY>

<SCRIPT LANGUAGE=javascript>
<!--
    var strURL =
        "http://localhost/public/my%20new%20folder%202/my%20new%20item.eml";
    request = new ActiveXObject("Microsoft.XMLHTTP");
    request.open("PROPPATCH", strURL, false);
    request.setRequestHeader("Content-Type", "text/xml");

    proplist  = "<M:subject>My New Message</M:subject>";
    proplist = proplist +
              "<M:textdescription>This is my body</M:textdescription>";

    body = "<?xml version='1.0'?>";
    body += "<D:propertyupdate xmlns:D='DAV:' "
    body += "xmlns:M='urn:schemas:httpmail:'>";
    body += "<D:set><D:prop>";
    body += proplist;
    body += "</D:prop></D:set>";
    body += "</D:propertyupdate>";

    request.send(body);
    alert(request.status + " " + request.statustext);

//-->
</SCRIPT>

</BODY>
</HTML>
```

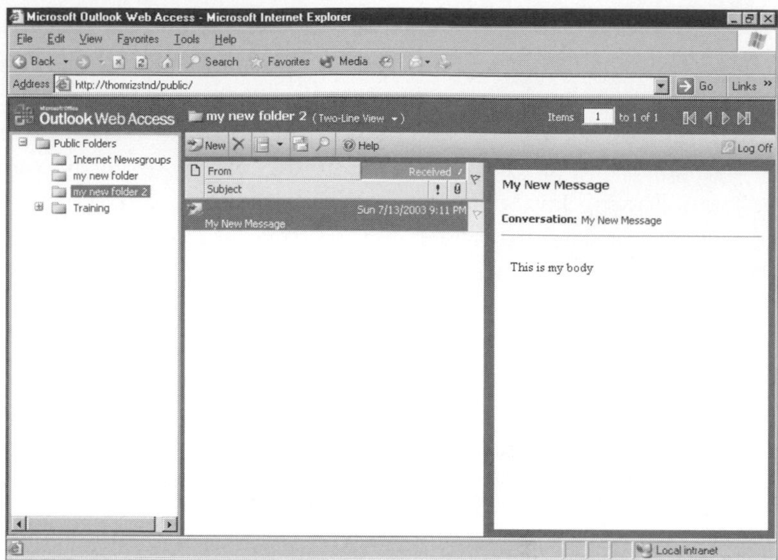

Figure 16-4 Updating subject line and message body via WebDAV and XMLHTTP

Working with Multivalue Properties

You might be wondering how you can work with multivalue properties using WebDAV. To set a multivalue property, you wrap your values for the property between XML tags. The following example shows an XML file that can be used to set a multivalue property using WebDAV:

```
<?xml version="1.0"?>
<a:propertyupdate xmlns:a="DAV:"
        xmlns:d="urn:schemas-microsoft-com:exch-data:"
        xmlns:b="urn:uuid:c2f41010-65b3-11d1-a29f-00aa00c14882/"
        xmlns:c="xml:">
  <a:set>
    <a:prop>
      <d:expected-content-class b:dt="mv.string">
             <c:v>urn:content-classes:message</c:v>
             <c:v>urn:content-classes:myclass1</c:v>
             <c:v>urn:content-classes:item</c:v>
      </d:expected-content-class>
    </a:prop>
  </a:set>
</a:propertyupdate>
```

The following code takes this XML data (saved in a file called c:\body.xml) and uses it to perform the actual work using WebDAV. Your security settings might require explicit permissions to instantiate the *FileSystemObject*. Be sure to click Yes in the corresponding Internet Explorer dialog box. *207 Multi-Status* indicates a successful operation.

```
<HTML>
<BODY>

<script language="JavaScript">

    var strURL =
        "http://localhost/public/my%20new%20folder%202/my%20new%20item.eml/";
    request = new ActiveXObject("Microsoft.XMLHTTP");
    request.open("PROPPATCH", strURL, false);
    request.setRequestHeader("Content-Type", "text/xml");

    //Use the following lines to read the XML from a file called body.xml
    //instead of having to compose a lengthy and error-prone string variable.
    var TristateFalse = 0;
    var ForReading = 1;
    oActiveXObject = new ActiveXObject("Scripting.FileSystemObject");
    file = oActiveXObject.GetFile("c:\\body.xml");
    text = file.OpenAsTextStream(ForReading, TristateFalse);

    body = text.ReadAll();
    text.Close();
    //End of reading XML

    request.send(body);
    alert(request.status + " " + request.statustext);


//-->
</SCRIPT>

</BODY>
</HTML>
```

When you retrieve a multivalue property, if you are trying to load the XML result set from WebDAV into an *XMLDOMDocument* object, be sure to set the *validateonparse* property to *false*. The *XMLDOMDocument* object does not see the multivalue properties returned as valid XML; setting this property to *false* prevents unnecessary trouble.

Retrieving Properties

To retrieve properties, you use the *PROPFIND* command. *PROPFIND* can request a single property, all properties with values, or just all the property names. When you work with *PROPFIND*, you must set the Depth header value to the depth you want the request's scope to be. The depth value can be *0*, which indicates only the entity in the URL specified; *1*, which signifies the target URL and any of its immediate children; or *Infinity*, which indicates the target URL, its children, and its children's children, all the way down to the leaves of the tree. Also, you must send an XML document that specifies the property list you want to retrieve from the resource. The following code requests some WebDAV properties from a messaging object in a public folder:

```
<HTML>
<BODY>
<TEXTAREA rows=10 style="width:100%" id=textarea1 name=textarea1>

</TEXTAREA>
<SCRIPT LANGUAGE=javascript>
<!--
    var strURL =
        "http://localhost/public/my%20new%20folder%202/my%20new%20item.eml/";

    request = new ActiveXObject("Microsoft.XMLHTTP");
    request.open("PROPFIND", strURL, false);
    request.setRequestHeader("Depth", "1,noroot");
    request.setRequestHeader("Content-Type", "text/xml");

    proplist = "<D:iscollection/><D:displayname/>"
             + "<D:getlastmodified/><D:creationdate/>";

    body = "<?xml version='1.0'?>";
    body += "<D:propfind xmlns:D='DAV:'>";
    body += "<D:prop>";
    body += proplist;
    body += "</D:prop>";
    body += "</D:propfind>";

    request.send(body);

    alert(request.status + " " + request.statustext);
    textarea1.value = request.responseText;

//-->
</SCRIPT>

</BODY>
</HTML>
```

The returned XML stream that is placed into the *TEXTAREA* is shown in Figure 16-5. Notice that it is a multi-status response.

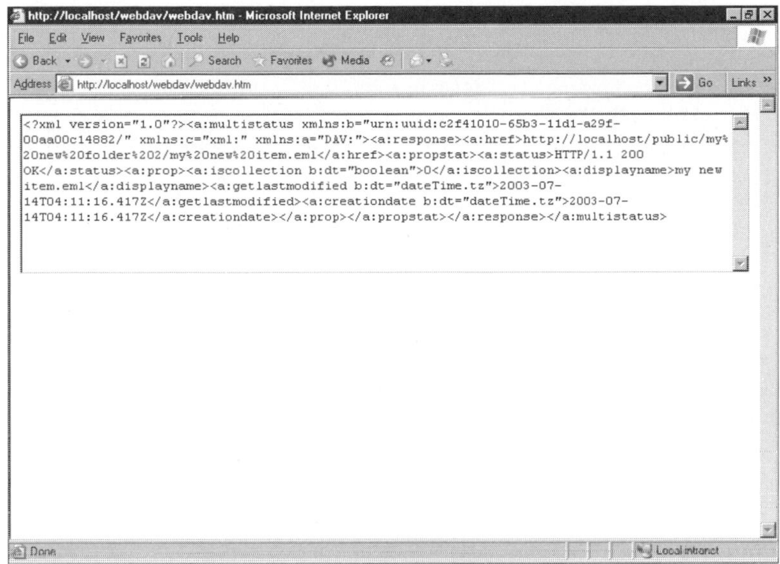

Figure 16-5 An XML stream obtained via WebDAV and XMLHTTP

To retrieve all properties in the *DAV* namespace, you issue the following WebDAV command:

```
<?xml version="1.0" ?>
<D:propfind xmlns:D="DAV:">
    <D:allprop/>
</D:propfind>
```

To retrieve all the properties for the *DAV* namespace and also the *Exchange* namespace, you send the following command. The *DAV* and *Exchange* namespaces contain the DAV and Exchange properties (such as *DAV:href* or *http://schemas.microsoft.com/exchange/contentexpiryagelimit*).

```
<?xml version="1.0"?>
<a:propfind xmlns:a="DAV:" xmlns:e="http://schemas.microsoft.com/exchange/">
  <a:allprop>
    <e:allprop>
    </e:allprop>
  </a:allprop>
</a:propfind>
```

Sometimes you might want to exclude certain properties from being returned in your *PROPFIND*. To do this, you can use the exclude and include extensions to WebDAV. You use these extensions to list the properties you want to include or exclude. The following sample shows a *PROPFIND* request that excludes some Messaging Application Programming Interface (MAPI) properties while including other properties:

```
<?xml version="1.0"?>
<a:propfind xmlns:a="DAV:"
        xmlns:b="urn:uuid:c2f41010-65b3-11d1-a29f-00aa00c14882/"
        xmlns:c="xml:"
        xmlns:d="http://schemas.microsoft.com/exchange/"
        xmlns:e="urn:schemas:httpmail:"
        xmlns:f="http://schemas.microsoft.com/mapi/proptag/"
        xmlns:g="urn:schemas-microsoft-com:exch-data:">
    <a:allprop>
      <a:exclude>
        <e:htmldescription/>
        <f:x0079001e/>
        <f:x66590102/>
      </>
      <a:include>
        <f:x65e00102/>
        <e:msgfolderroot/>
        <e:inbox/>
        <e:outbox/>
        <e:deleteditems/>
        <e:sentitems/>
        <e:sendmsg/>
        <e:calendar/>
        <e:tasks/>
        <e:journal/>
        <e:contacts/>
        <e:notes/>
        <e:drafts/>
        <g:schema-uri/>
        <e:hasattachment/>
      </>
    </a:allprop>
</a:propfind>
```

Deleting Properties

Sometimes you might find it necessary to delete properties from an item. You can do this by passing a *propertyupdate* command with a remove node and a node that contains the property you want to remove. If you work with XMLHTTP, open the resource as if you want to set a property, and set the Content-Type header as follows:

```
    request.open("PROPPATCH", strURL, false);
    request.setRequestHeader("Content-Type", "text/xml");
```

You can then use the following WebDAV command to remove the *DAV:comment* property, as in this example:

```
<?xml version="1.0"?>
<a:propertyupdate xmlns:a="DAV:">
   <a:remove>
      <a:prop>
         <a:comment/>
       </>
   </>
</>
```

Locking a Resource

You might want to lock a resource, such as a file or a collection, so that no other process can access it. You can acquire an exclusive or shared lock on a resource. Each lock has a timeout, affording you a precise window of opportunity to make your changes before the lock expires. If a lock does expire, you can always request another lock on the resource from the server. The following code requests an exclusive write lock on a message object in a public folder. The XML body requests exclusive access to the *DAV:owner* property, and the lock will remain in effect for 3000 seconds. If another application tries to modify the message object, it will receive an XML document that contains a *lockdiscovery* property, which contains the *owner* property of the person who currently has a lock on the resource. The application can use this property to request that the current lock owner disable the lock or notify the application when the lock is released.

```
<HTML>
<BODY>
<TEXTAREA rows=10 style="width:100%" id=textarea1 name=textarea1>

</TEXTAREA>
<SCRIPT LANGUAGE=javascript>
<!--

    var strURL =
        "http://localhost/public/my%20new%20folder%202/my%20new%20item.eml/";
    request = new ActiveXObject("Microsoft.XMLHTTP");
    request.open("LOCK", strURL, false);
    request.setRequestHeader("Content-Type", "text/xml");
    request.setRequestHeader("Timeout", "Second-3000");

    body = "<?xml version='1.0'?>";
    body += " <a:lockinfo xmlns:a='DAV:'>"
    body += "<a:lockscope><a:exclusive /></a:lockscope>";
    body += "<a:locktype><a:write /></a:locktype>";
```

```
        body += "<a:owner><a:href>mailto:thomriz</a:href>";
        body += "</a:owner></a:lockinfo>";

        request.send(body);
        alert(request.status + " " + request.statustext);
        textarea1.value = request.responseText;

//-->
</SCRIPT>

</BODY>
</HTML>
```

After this request is sent to the server, the response shown in Figure 16-6 will be received:

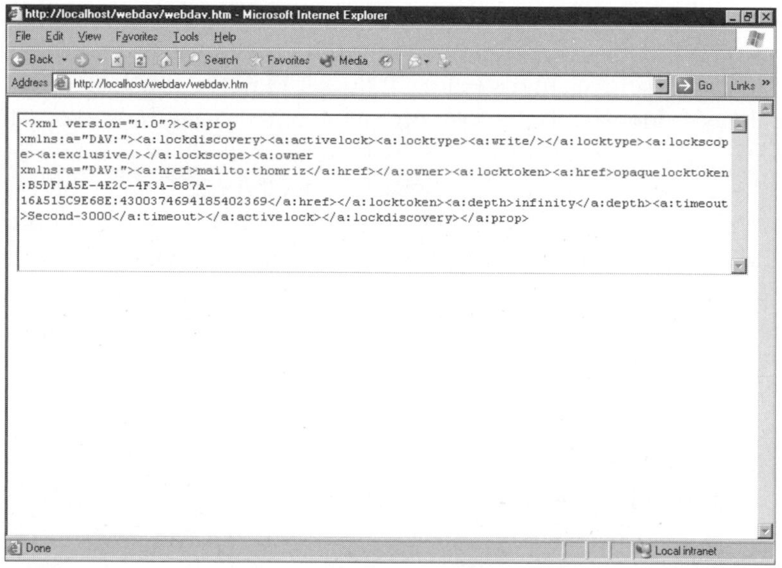

Figure 16-6 A WebDAV response containing the *locktoken* property

If the lock is successful, you'll receive a *Status* of *200 OK*, along with the XML just shown. The most important property to be aware of is the *locktoken* property. This property uniquely identifies your lock and must be used in future requests. Because HTTP is stateless, you must pass this lock token with your future requests so the server knows who is attempting to write to the resource. You'll also need this property for the *PUT*, *PROPPATCH*, and other requests you send, and to unlock the file.

> **Note** If the resource is already locked when you try to lock it, you will receive a *Status* of *423 Locked.*

Transactions with Locks

Sometimes you might need to not only lock a resource, but also have a single atomic transaction across that lock token. Once you lock the resource, you can pass the lock token of the resource to subsequent WebDAV commands and have all of those commands constitute a single transaction when you unlock the resource. To use transactions, you pass the transaction XML element as part of your lock, as shown in the following code. Also, on all subsequent WebDAV commands that you want as part of the transaction, you must pass a Transaction header with the lock token included in the header. Note that transactions can only have a depth of 0. Notice in the code that when the WebDAV *UNLOCK* command is used to unlock the resource, you must tell the server whether to commit or abort the transactions. To show how you can program WebDAV from Visual Basic, the following code is written in Visual Basic. It also shows an example of using early binding in Visual Basic to the MSXML library, which you need to add as a reference in your Visual Basic application.

```
Private Sub Command1_Click()
    Dim oXMLHTTP As New MSXML2.XMLHTTP30

    strURL =
        "http://localhost/public/my%20new%20folder%202/my%20new%20item.eml/"

    oXMLHTTP.Open "LOCK", strURL, False

    oXMLHTTP.setRequestHeader "Content-Type", "text/xml"
    oXMLHTTP.setRequestHeader "Depth", "0"
    oXMLHTTP.setRequestHeader "Timeout", "Second 45"

    body = "<?xml version='1.0'?>"
    body = body & "<a:lockinfo xmlns:a='DAV:'>"
    body = body & "<a:lockscope><a:local /></a:lockscope>"
    body = body & "<a:locktype><a:transaction><a:groupoperation/>"
    body = body & "</a:transaction></a:locktype>"
    body = body & "<a:owner><a:href>mailto:thomriz</a:href>"
    body = body & "</a:owner></a:lockinfo>"

    oXMLHTTP.Send body
    MsgBox "Status: " & oXMLHTTP.Status & vbNewLine & oXMLHTTP.ResponseText
```

```
'Get the OpaqueLockToken to be used later
'when sending a proppatch in a transaction
Dim xmldom As MSXML2.DOMDocument
Set xmldom = oXMLHTTP.responseXML
Dim oDomElement As MSXML2.IXMLDOMNodeList

Set oDomElement = xmldom.getElementsByTagName("a:locktoken")
Set oDomElementChild = oDomElement.nextNode
strLockToken = oDomElementChild.Text
MsgBox strLockToken

oXMLHTTP.Open "PROPPATCH", strURL, False
oXMLHTTP.setRequestHeader "Content-Type", "text/xml"

'Pass the Transaction header so Exchange knows this is part
'of a transaction
oXMLHTTP.setRequestHeader "Transaction", "<" & strLockToken & ">"

proplist = "<M:textdescription>This is my body</M:textdescription>"

body = "<?xml version='1.0'?>"
body = body & "<D:propertyupdate xmlns:D='DAV:' "
body = body & "xmlns:M='urn:schemas:httpmail:'>"
body = body & "<D:set><D:prop>"
body = body & proplist
body = body & "</D:prop></D:set>"
body = body & "</D:propertyupdate>"

oXMLHTTP.Send body
MsgBox "Status: " & oXMLHTTP.Status & vbNewLine & oXMLHTTP.ResponseText


'Send another proppatch to show atomic transaction

oXMLHTTP.Open "PROPPATCH", strURL, False
oXMLHTTP.setRequestHeader "Content-Type", "text/xml"

'Send the Transaction header
oXMLHTTP.setRequestHeader "Transaction", "<" & strLockToken & ">"

proplist = "<M:subject>My New Message</M:subject>"

body = "<?xml version='1.0'?>"
body = body & "<D:propertyupdate xmlns:D='DAV:' "
body = body & "xmlns:M='urn:schemas:httpmail:'>"
body = body & "<D:set><D:prop>"
body = body & proplist
body = body & "</D:prop></D:set>"
body = body & "</D:propertyupdate>"

oXMLHTTP.Send body
MsgBox "Status: " & oXMLHTTP.Status & vbNewLine & oXMLHTTP.ResponseText
```

```
    'Unlock the resource by passing a commit element as part of our
    'transactionstatus if we want to abort, we should pass abort

    oXMLHTTP.Open "UNLOCK", strURL, False

    oXMLHTTP.setRequestHeader "Content-Type", "text/xml"
    oXMLHTTP.setRequestHeader "Lock-Token", "<" & strLockToken & ">"

    'Commit the transaction
    body = "<?xml version='1.0'?>"
    body = body & "<D:transactioninfo xmlns:D='DAV:'><D:transactionstatus>"
    body = body & "<D:commit/></D:transactionstatus></D:transactioninfo>"

    'If we wanted to abort, we would use the following
    'body = "<?xml version='1.0'?><D:transactioninfo xmlns:D='DAV:'>"
    'body = body & "<D:transactionstatus><D:abort/>"
    'body = body & "</D:transactionstatus></D:transactioninfo>"

    oXMLHTTP.Send body

    MsgBox "Status: " & oXMLHTTP.Status & vbNewLine & oXMLHTTP.ResponseText
End Sub
```

Unlocking a Resource

Unlocking a resource is easy if you have a unique lock token. You simply send the *UNLOCK* command to the server and add a header that contains your lock token. If you are successful, the server will return a *Status* of *204 No Content*. This means that the command completed successfully but the server had no text to return except the status. The following JavaScript code uses a specific lock token to unlock a resource. You must replace the lock token in the code with a specific lock token from your own application. Otherwise, the code will return error 412 (precondition failed).

```
<HTML>
<BODY>
<SCRIPT LANGUAGE=javascript>
<!--

    var strURL =
        "http://localhost/public/my%20new%20folder%202/my%20new%20item.eml/";
    request = new ActiveXObject("Microsoft.XMLHTTP");
    request.open("UNLOCK", strURL, false);
    request.setRequestHeader("Lock-Token",
          "<opaquelocktoken:9641CB50-729A-4966-B904-"
        + "6F55773AA5B7:10582347518064984065>");
   request.send();
   alert(request.status + " " + request.statustext);
```

```
//-->
</SCRIPT>

</BODY>
</HTML>
```

Subscribing to a Resource

You can use WebDAV to subscribe to a resource. As a subscriber, you can receive notification about changes to a resource in one of two ways: you can have the server inform you when the resource changes or you can poll the server for any changes to the resource. To create a subscription, you use the *SUBSCRIBE* command and pass the URL you want to subscribe to, as in the following example. You can listen for different types of notifications (such as deletes, updates, or moves) by specifying the Notification-Type header. See the Exchange SDK for full documentation on the *SUBSCRIBE* command. This JavaScript example also sets the timeout for a subscription.

```
<HTML>
<BODY>
<SCRIPT LANGUAGE=javascript>
<!--

    var strURL =
        "http://localhost/public/my%20new%20folder%202/my%20new%20item.eml/";
    request = new ActiveXObject("Microsoft.XMLHTTP");
    request.open("SUBSCRIBE", strURL, false);
    request.setRequestHeader("Subscription-Lifetime", 1000);
 request.SetRequestHeader("Notification-Type","update");

    request.send();
    alert(request.status + " " + request.statustext);

//-->
</SCRIPT>

</BODY>
</HTML>
```

If your subscription is successful, the server will return a *Subscription-id*, which you should keep because you'll need to pass it when you later poll the server or unsubscribe from the resource.

Polling the Server

To poll the server to see whether any of the resources you've subscribed to have changed, you use the *POLL* command. This command requires that you pass the *Subscription-id* that the *SUBSCRIBE* command gave you when you subscribed to the resource. The following code checks whether anything has changed on a resource. If not, the server will return a *204* status code. In addition to polling, you can listen on a TCP/IP port for a UDP notification of changes. See the full code in the sample application (in the companion content that accompanies this book) called UDP Notification to learn how to use this technique.

```
<HTML>
<BODY>
<SCRIPT LANGUAGE=javascript>
<!--

    var strURL =
        "http://localhost/public/my%20new%20folder%202/my%20new%20item.eml/";
    request = new ActiveXObject("Microsoft.XMLHTTP");
    request.open("POLL", strURL, false);
    //Replace <SomeID> with a Subscription ID from another request
    request.setRequestHeader("Subscription-id", "<SomeID>");

    request.send();
    alert(request.status + " " + request.statustext);

//-->
</SCRIPT>

</BODY>
</HTML>
```

Querying with WebDAV *SEARCH*

One neat thing you can do with WebDAV is to perform SQL syntax queries against Exchange Server and have your results formatted as XML. Having your query returned to the client as XML is a powerful capability. Most important is the ability of XML data to represent hierarchical relationships. This is significantly different from ADO and relational data models, which represent relationships with a single flat virtual table. Representing hierarchical relationships with XML saves memory space and reduces the data transmission overhead. Furthermore, XML allows you to perform client-side formatting with XSL, and because the XML is already on the client, you can quickly re-sort the data. The following code is taken from the coursexml.asp file in the Training application. The code sends a *SEARCH* request to the Exchange server and receives the data from the server as XML.

```
request = new ActiveXObject("Microsoft.XMLHTTP");

//Example propfind
//request.open("PROPFIND", URLSchedule, true);

request.open("SEARCH", URLSchedule, true);
```

```
//For propfind you can select a depth
//request.setRequestHeader("Depth", "1,noroot");
request.setRequestHeader("Content-Type", "text/xml");

proplist = "<D:iscollection/><D:displayname/>";
proplist += "<D:getlastmodified/><D:creationdate/>";
proplist += "<C:instructoremail/><CAL:location/><O:";
proplist += "<O:Manager/><O:Title/><H:Subject/>

//You can also do a propfind to find specific properties
//body = "<?xml version='1.0'?>";
//body += "<D:propfind xmlns:D='DAV: '
//xmlns:O='urn:schemas-microsoft-com:office:office'
//xmlns:C='<%=strSchema%>' xmlns:CAL='urn:schemas:calendar:'
//xmlns:H='urn:schemas:httpmail:'>";

body = "<searchrequest xmlns='DAV:'>";
body += "<sql>";
body += "SELECT \"strSchemamaterialshttppath\" as materialshttppath,";
body += "\"<%=strSchema%>overallscore\" as ";
body += "overallscore,\"<%=strSchema%>rating\" as rating,";
body += "\"<%=strSchema%>materialsfilepath\" as ";
body += "materialsfilepath,\"<%=strSchema%>surveycount\" as surveycount, ";
body += "\"<%=strSchema%>discussionurl\" as ";
body += "discussionurl,\"<%=strSchema%>prereqs\" as prereqs, ";
body += "\"urn:schemas:httpmail:textdescription\" as ";
body += "description,\"<%=strSchema%>category\" as category, ";
body += "\"urn:schemas:calendar:dtstart\" as ";
body += "starttime, \"urn:schemas:calendar:dtend\" as endtime, ";
body += "\"DAV:iscollection\" as iscollection,\"DAV:href\" as href,";
body += "\"urn:schemas:httpmail:subject\" as ";
body += "subject,\"urn:schemas:calendar:location\" as ";
body += "location, \"<%=strSchema%>instructoremail\" as ";
body += "instructoremail FROM scope('shallow traversal of ";
body += "\"<%=strURLToSchedule%>\"') where ";
body += "\"DAV:ishidden\" = false AND \"DAV:isfolder\" = false";

//Add date restriction
body += " AND \"urn:schemas:calendar:dtstart\" &gt;&eq;";
body += " CAST(\"<%=dISODateStart%>\" as 'dateTime')";
body += " AND \"urn:schemas:calendar:dtstart\" &lt;&eq;";
body += " CAST(\"<%=dISODateEnd%>\" as 'dateTime')";
body += "</sql>";
body += "</searchrequest>";

body += "</sql>";
body += "</searchrequest>";

//For debugging
//alert(body);

//Propfind example
//body += "<D:prop>";
//body += proplist;
```

```
//body += "</D:prop>";
//body += "</D:propfind>";

request.onreadystatechange = dostatechange;
msgdiv.innerHTML = "<font face='verdana' size='+1'>Loading...</font>";
request.send(body);
```

The *SELECT* statement in this code uses column aliasing, which makes the data easier to format using XSL. You'll see how to use XSL to format the XML data returned shortly. The following code shows the raw XML data returned from this query, illustrating how custom and built-in schemas can be queried and returned with XML:


```
<?xml version="1.0"?><a:multistatus xmlns:b="urn:uuid:c2f41010-65b3-11d1-
a29f-00aa00c14882/" xmlns:c="xml:" xmlns:d="urn:schemas-microsoft-com:
office:office" xmlns:a="DAV:"><a:response><a:href>http://thomriznt5srv/
public/140/Training/Schedule/{8C35C44B-68EB-4651-AC3E-5C475923A7A1}
.EML</a:href><a:propstat><a:status>HTTP/1.1 200 OK</a:status><a:prop>
<materialshttppath>http://thomriznt5srv/public/140/Training/Course
Materials/Leveraging XML in Exchange 2000/?Cmd=contents&amp;View=Messages
</materialshttppath><materialsfilepath>file://THOMRIZNT5SRV/Course
Materials140/Leveraging XML in Exchange 2000</materialsfilepath>
<discussionurl>http://thomriznt5srv/public/140/Training/Discussions/
Leveraging XML in Exchange 2000/?Cmd=contents&amp;View=By Conversation
Topic</discussionurl><prereqs>fejio</prereqs><description>fjeoj
</description><category>dev</category><starttime b:dt="dateTime.tz">
2000-03-08T21:00:00.000Z</starttime><endtime b:dt="dateTime.tz">2000-03-
 08T23:00:00.000Z</endtime><iscollection b:dt="boolean">0</iscollection>
<href>http://thomriznt5srv/public/140/Training/Schedule/{8C35C44B-68EB-
4651-AC3E-5C475923A7A1}.EML</href><subject>Leveraging XML in Exchange
2000</subject><location>43</location><instructoremail>thomriz@thomriznt
5dom.extest.microsoft.com</instructoremail></a:prop></a:propstat>
<a:propstat><a:status>HTTP/1.1 404 Resource Not Found</a:status><a:prop>
<overallscore/><rating/><surveycount/></a:prop></a:propstat></a:response>
<a:response><a:href>http://thomriznt5srv/public/140/Training/Schedule/
{75BD5A83-09E7-47B7-A9F1-A75DD62F5BA7}.EML</a:href><a:propstat>
<a:status>HTTP/1.1 200 OK</a:status><a:prop><prereqs>fjoi</prereqs>
<description>fei</description><category>dev</category><starttime
b:dt="dateTime.tz">2000-03-08T18:00:00.000Z</starttime><endtime
b:dt="dateTime.tz">2000-03-08T19:00:00.000Z</endtime><iscollection
b:dt="boolean">0</iscollection><href>http://thomriznt5srv/public/140/
Training/Schedule/{75BD5A83-09E7-47B7-A9F1-A75DD62F5BA7}.EML
</href><subject>CDO and You</subject><location>43</location>
<instructoremail>thomriz@thomriznt5dom.extest.microsoft.com</
instructoremail></a:prop></a:propstat><a:propstat><a:status>HTTP/
1.1 404 Resource Not Found</a:status><a:prop><materialshttppath/>
<overallscore/><rating/><materialsfilepath/><surveycount/><discussionurl/>
</a:prop></a:propstat></a:response></a:multistatus>
```


Sending E-Mail Through WebDAV

You can use WebDAV to submit e-mail that is to be sent through Exchange by using a special Uniform Resource Identifier (URI), called the Exchange Mail

Submission URI. You can retrieve this URI by getting the property *urn:schemas:httpmail:sendmsg* off the person's private mailbox folder. Before you can submit mail using this URI, you must be logged on as the user, have the user's credentials, or have send-on-behalf permissions for the user. You either write an RFC 821 stream to the item's stream using a WebDAV *PUT* or ADO *Stream* object, or you write to properties on the item and have Exchange automatically create the stream for you. If you write to the properties, you cannot add attachments or send complex MIME messages. For this reason, you should stick to the first approach.

The following code shows how to submit a message using the mail submission URI using WebDAV. (See Figure 16-7.) Note that if you want the item saved in the user's Sent Items folder, you must pass a header called Saveinsent with a value of *t* for *true*.

```
Private Sub Command1_Click()
    Dim strSubURL As String
    Dim strAlias As String
    Dim strUserName As String
    Dim strPassWord As String
    Dim strExchSvrName As String
    Dim strFrom As String
    Dim strTo As String
    Dim strSubject As String
    Dim strBody As String
    Dim bResult As Boolean

    ' Exchange Server Name.
    strExchSvrName = "Server"
    ' Alias of the sender.
    strAlias = "alias"

    ' User Name of the sender.
    strUserName = "DOMAIN\username"
    ' Password of the sender.
    strPassWord = "password"
    ' Email address of the sender.
    strFrom = "alias@domain.com"
    ' Email address of recipient.
    strTo = "alias@domain.com"
    ' Subject of the mail.
    strSubject = "My Subject"
    ' Text body of the mail.
    strBody = "Textbody"

    strSubURL = FindSubmissionURL(strExchSvrName, strAlias, strUserName, _
                              strPassWord)

    If strSubURL <> "" Then
        bResult = False
```

```
        bResult = SendMail(strSubURL, strFrom, strTo, strSubject, strBody, _
                           strUserName, strPassWord)
        If bResult Then
            MsgBox "Mail has been successfully sent via WebDAV!"
        End If
    End If

End Sub

Function FindSubmissionURL(strExchSvr, strAlias, strUserName, _
                           strPassWord) As String

    Dim query As String
    Dim strURL As String
    Dim xmlRoot As IXMLDOMElement
    Dim xmlNode As IXMLDOMNode
    Dim baseName As String

    Dim xmlReq As MSXML2.XMLHTTP
    Dim xmldom As MSXML2.DOMDocument
    Dim xmlAttr As MSXML2.IXMLDOMAttribute

    ' Find the mail submission URI by doing a PROPFIND

    Set xmlReq = CreateObject("Microsoft.XMLHTTP")

    strURL = "http://" & strExchSvr & "/exchange/" & strAlias
    xmlReq.Open "PROPFIND", strURL, False, strUserName, strPassWord
    xmlReq.setRequestHeader "Content-Type", "text/xml"
    xmlReq.setRequestHeader "Depth", "0"

    query = "<?xml version='1.0'?>"
    query = query + "<a:propfind xmlns:a='DAV:'>"
    query = query + "<a:prop xmlns:m='urn:schemas:httpmail:'>"
    query = query + "<m:sendmsg/>"
    query = query + "</a:prop>"
    query = query + "</a:propfind>"

    xmlReq.send (query)

    If (xmlReq.Status >= 200 And xmlReq.Status < 300) Then
        MsgBox "Found URI! " & " Status = " & xmlReq.Status & ": " _
               & xmlReq.statusText

        Set xmldom = xmlReq.responseXML

        Set xmlRoot = xmldom.documentElement
        For Each xmlAttr In xmlRoot.Attributes
            If xmlAttr.Text = "urn:schemas:httpmail:" Then
                baseName = xmlAttr.baseName
                Exit For
            End If
        Next
```

```
            Set xmlNode = xmlRoot.selectSingleNode("//" & baseName & ":sendmsg")
            FindSubmissionURL = xmlNode.Text

        Else
            MsgBox "Failed to find mail submission URL"
            FindSubmissionURL = ""
        End If

ErrExit:
    Set xmlReq = Nothing
    Set xmldom = Nothing
    Set xmlRoot = Nothing
    Set xmlNode = Nothing
    Set xmlAttr = Nothing
    Exit Function
ErrHandler:
    MsgBox Err.Number & ": " & Err.Description
    FindSubmissionURL = ""
End Function


Function SendMail(strSubURL, strFrom, strTo, strSubject, strBody, _
                  strUserName, strPassWord) As Boolean

    On Error GoTo ErrHandler

    Dim xmlReq As MSXML2.XMLHTTP
    Dim strText

    ' Construct the text of the PUT request.
    strText = "From: " & strFrom & vbNewLine & _
              "To: " & strTo & vbNewLine & _
              "Subject: " & strSubject & vbNewLine & _
              "Date: " & Now & _
              "X-Mailer: test mailer" & vbNewLine & _
              "MIME-Version: 1.0" & vbNewLine & _
              "Content-Type: text/plain;" & vbNewLine & _
              "Charset = ""iso-8859-1""" & vbNewLine & _
              "Content-Transfer-Encoding: 7bit" & vbNewLine & _
              vbNewLine & _
              strBody

    ' Create the DAV PUT request to create the message body
    Set xmlReq = CreateObject("Microsoft.XMLHTTP")
    xmlReq.Open "PUT", strSubURL, False, strUserName, strPassWord
    If strText <> "" Then
        xmlReq.setRequestHeader "Content-Type", "message/rfc822"
        xmlReq.send strText
    End If

    'Process the results.
    If (xmlReq.Status >= 200 And xmlReq.Status < 300) Then
        MsgBox "Success!   " & "PUT Results = " & xmlReq.Status & _
```

```
                ": " & xmlReq.statusText
            SendMail = True
        ElseIf xmlReq.Status = 401 Then
            MsgBox "You don't have permission to do the job! " & _
                "Please check your permissions on this item."
            SendMail = False
        Else
            MsgBox "Request Failed.  Results = " & xmlReq.Status & _
                ": " & objRequest.statusText
            SendMail = False
        End If
    ErrExit:
        Set xmlReq = Nothing
        Exit Function
    ErrHandler:
        MsgBox Err.Number & ": " & Err.Description
        SendMail = False
    End Function
```

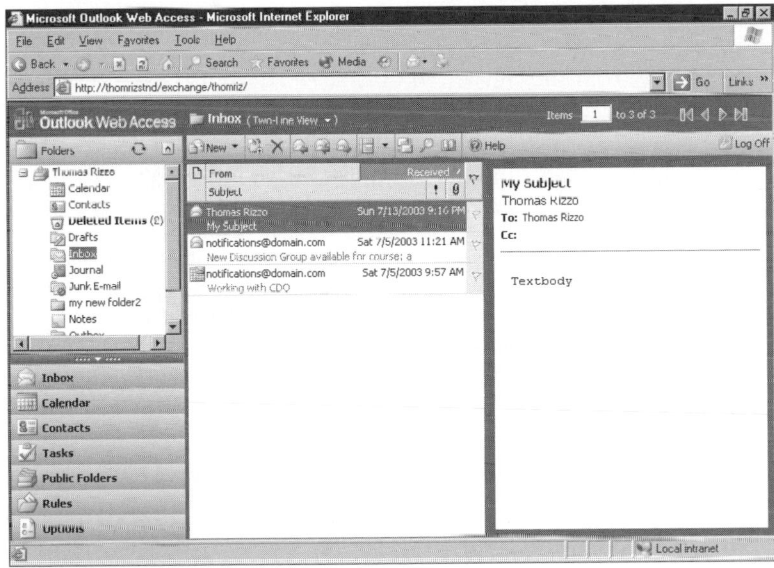

Figure 16-7 Sending a message via WebDAV and HTTPXML

WebDAV XML Elements

In the Exchange SDK, which is included in the companion content, you should look at the WebDAV XML elements section. We have covered many of these elements in this chapter, such as the response, lock, target, and other elements that can be passed to WebDAV requests and responses, but not all of them. You should browse the elements section of the SDK if you plan to work extensively with WebDAV and Exchange.

Working with Attachments in WebDAV

Exchange supports an extension to the WebDAV commands that allows you to enumerate attachments on a message. This WebDAV command is called *X-MS-ENUMATTS*. You send it like a normal WebDAV command such as *PROPPATCH* or *PROPFIND*. The following code shows how to use this command and shows a typical response from the server. In the response, you will see the filename, size, and the application type. These are the most interesting properties in the response to look at.

```
Dim oXMLHTTP As New MSXML2.XMLHTTP30

strURL = "http://localhost/public/my%20new%20folder%202/my%20new%20item.eml"
oXMLHTTP.Open "X-MS-ENUMATTS", strURL, False
oXMLHTTP.Send ""
```

Response from the Server (*oXMLHTTP.responseText*):


```
<?xml version="1.0"?><a:multistatus xmlns:b="urn:uuid:c2f41010-65b3-11d1-a29f-
00aa00c14882/" xmlns:f="http://schemas.microsoft.com/mapi/
" xmlns:e="urn:schemas:httpmail:" xmlns:c="xml:" xmlns:d="http://sche-
mas.microsoft.com/mapi/proptag/" xmlns:g="http://schemas.microsoft.com/
exchange/" xmlns:j="urn:schemas-microsoft-com:office:office" xmlns:h="http://
schemas.microsoft.com/repl/
" xmlns:i="urn:schemas:contacts:" xmlns:a="DAV:"><a:response><a:href>http://
thomriznt52/public/folder/message.eml/document%20upload.doc</a:href><a:prop-
stat><a:status>HTTP/1.1 200 OK</a:status><a:prop><d:x3704001e>docume~1.doc</
d:x3704001e><d:x666c000b b:dt="boolean">0</
d:x666c000b><d:x37050003 b:dt="int">1</
d:x37050003><d:x68100102 b:dt="bin.base64">AAAAAAAAAAAAAAAAAAA=</
d:x68100102><e:attachmentfilename>document upload.doc</
e:attachmentfilename><d:x0e200003 b:dt="int">149056</
d:x0e200003><d:x3703001e>doc</d:x3703001e><d:x370b0003 b:dt="int">-1</
d:x370b0003><d:x3f880014 b:dt="i8">-7903522676918976511</
d:x3f880014><d:x3716001e>attachment</
d:x3716001e><d:x0ff90102 b:dt="bin.base64">ze+uqDfel0ySCYYOCU1KaA==</
d:x0ff90102><d:x0e210003 b:dt="int">0</d:x0e210003><i:cn>document upload.doc</
i:cn><d:x370e001e>application/msword</d:x370e001e></a:prop></a:prop-
stat><a:propstat><a:status>HTTP/1.1 200 OK</a:status><a:prop><d:x0e12000d/
><d:x0e13000d/></a:prop></a:propstat></a:response><a:response><a:href>http://
thomriznt52/public/folder/message.eml/extensions.txt</a:href><a:prop-
stat><a:status>HTTP/1.1 200 OK</a:status><a:prop><d:x3704001e>extens~1.txt</
d:x3704001e><d:x666c000b b:dt="boolean">0</
d:x666c000b><d:x37050003 b:dt="int">1</
d:x37050003><d:x68100102 b:dt="bin.base64">AAAAAAAAAAAAAAAAAAA=</
d:x68100102><e:attachmentfilename>extensions.txt</
e:attachmentfilename><d:x0e200003 b:dt="int">648</
```

```
d:x0e200003><d:x3703001e>txt</d:x3703001e><d:x370b0003 b:dt="int">-1</
d:x370b0003><d:x3f880014 b:dt="i8">-7759407488843120639</
d:x3f880014><d:x3716001e>attachment</
d:x3716001e><d:x0ff90102 b:dt="bin.base64">v5Z//1J3jUi7FoO3muigAg==</
d:x0ff90102><d:x0e210003 b:dt="

int">1</d:x0e210003><i:cn>extensions.txt</i:cn><d:x370e001e>text/plain</
d:x370e001e></a:prop></a:propstat><a:propstat><a:status>HTTP/1.1 200 OK</a:sta-
tus><a:prop><d:x0e12000d/><d:x0e13000d/></a:prop></a:propstat></a:response></
a:multistatus>
```


Other Resources

Additional WebDAV functionality includes the ability to create contacts, appointments, and meeting requests. It is nice that you can do this through WebDAV because WebDAV is remotable, unlike ADO with the EXOLEDB provider. However, you do need to be careful when you create appointments and contacts with WebDAV because of time zone and Outlook interoperability issues. You might want to simply use CDO for Exchange to create your appointments and contacts, if you can. CDO for Exchange includes all the necessary Outlook interoperability and time zone conversion code, but, as ADO, it isn't remotable. If you are still interested in using WebDAV for this purpose, check out the Microsoft Knowledge Base at *http://support.microsoft.com*, which includes a host of articles about creating Exchange items using WebDAV (such as articles 296126, 309699, and 291171). Also, if you want to remotely create contacts, appointments, or mail messages and want to harness the power of CDO, you can create a XML Web service on your Exchange Server and call that from your mid-tier or client applications.

WebDAV Headers

You have seen some WebDAV headers in the previous examples, such as Destination and Depth. Two other WebDAV headers you should be aware of are Translate and Overwrite.

The Translate header takes a value of *t* or *f*, for *true* or *false*. Specifying *t* tells Exchange to translate the returned contents into a renderable format for the client to read. In most cases, if you are dealing with native Exchange types such as e-mail messages, appointments, or contacts, the default rendering will be done by Outlook Web Access (OWA). This means that instead of getting back an XML document containing the data you requested, you will instead receive the HTML stream that OWA generates—as if OWA were rendering the item into a browser. This is probably not what you want. As a best practice, you might want to set the Translate header in your code to always be *f* when you issue a *GET* command and you want the item's stream content back rather than a rendering of the item. For example, if you issue a *GET* against an e-mail message with translate equal to *f*, you will get back the stream of the message formatted using rfc822 rather than the HTML that OWA would use to render the e-mail message to the browser.

The overwrite header takes a value of *t* or *f* as well. This header is used with the *MOVE* and *COPY* operations; it specifies whether the destination resource should be overwritten if it exists. If you do not specify this header, it will default to *t*. You should be careful because this might not be the behavior you want. You might instead want to fail if the destination resource already exists. If you set this header to *f* and the resource exists, you will get back a *402* (*Precondition Failed*) error from Microsoft Internet Information Services (IIS).

MSXML and Namespaces

Starting with MSXML 3.0, you might find that the returned information from Exchange cannot be parsed because MSXML has removed support for the data type namespace that Exchange 2000 and 2003 returns, which is *urn:uuid:c2f41010-65b3-11d1-a29f-00aa00c14882/*. MSXML uses the new data type namespace, *urn:schemas-microsoft-com:datatypes*. You will also find that Exchange 2000 and 2003 return some property names beginning with 0, such as *0x12345678*. This is invalid XML.

To work around these errors, you must replace the data type namespace returned by Exchange (and also Microsoft SharePoint Portal Server 2001), and you must remove any invalid XML that starts with 0. Also, if you are using the XMLDOM, you should set the *validateOnParse* property to *false* so MSXML will not attempt to validate all the XML nodes while parsing through the document. The following code shows how to perform all these steps:

```
Set request = CreateObject("Microsoft.XMLHTTP")

request.Open "PROPFIND", _
            "http://localhost/public/my%20new%20folder%202/" _
& "my%20new%20item.eml"

request.setRequestHeader "Content-Type", "text/xml"
request.setRequestHeader "Translate", "f"

body = "<?xml version=""1.0"" encoding=""utf-8""?>" _
    + "<a:propfind xmlns:a=""DAV:""><allprop/></a:propfind>"

request.send body
```

```
Dim oXMLDOM As New MSXML.DOMDocument
strXML = request.responseText

'Replace the UUID stuff with urn:uuid:c2f41010-65b3-11d1-a29f-00aa00c14882/
strXML = Replace(strXML, "urn:uuid:c2f41010-65b3-11d1-a29f-00aa00c14882/", _
                 "urn:schemas-microsoft-com:datatypes")
strXML = Replace(strXML, "0x", "x")

oXMLDOM.validateOnParse = False
oXMLDOM.loadXML strXML
```

Another way to work with and manipulate namespaces is by using the *NamespaceManager* object included with MSXML. The namespace manager allows you to push and pop namespaces for your current local context. The following code sets the prefix of the *urn:schemas:httpmail:* namespace to *d*.

```
oNSManager.declarePrefix "d", "urn:schemas:httpmail:"
```

Another option you have with MSXML is to have the MSXML parser remap the prefixes to ones that you define. For example, the following code sets the prefixes for the *DAV* and *office* namespaces:

```
oXMLDOM.SetProperty "SelectionNamespaces", "xmlns:d='DAV:'" & Space(1) _
    & "xmlns : o = 'urn: schemas -microsoft - com: office: office'"
```

You can then use the following code to retrieve your properties:

```
Set oNodeList = oXMLDOM.selectNodes("d:propstat/d:prop/o:Title")
```

You can also use *SetProperty* to specify using XPath syntax over the default XSL Transformations (XSLT) syntax in your node selection, if that is what you prefer. The following code does this:

```
oXMLDOM.SetProperty("SelectionLanguage", "XPath")
```

A WebDAV Sample: Creating Tasks

To show you how to use WebDAV in a little more detail, the following code creates a task programmatically using WebDAV. (See Figure 16-8.) To learn how to create, modify, or delete a contact using WebDAV, see the Microsoft Knowledge Base article 296126.

```
strPropSet = "<?xml version='1.0'?>" _
    & "<d:propertyupdate xmlns:d='DAV:' " _
    & "xmlns:e='http://schemas.microsoft.com/exchange/' " _
    & "xmlns:b='urn:uuid:c2f41010-65b3-11d1-a29f-00aa00c14882/' " _
    & "xmlns:f='urn:schemas:mailheader:' " _
    & "xmlns:g='urn:schemas:httpmail:' " _
    & "xmlns:h='http://schemas.microsoft.com/mapi/id/" _
    & "{00062003-0000-0000-C000-000000000046}/'><d:set><d:prop>" _
```

```
        & "<d:contentclass>urn:content-classes:task</d:contentclass>" _
        & "<e:outlookmessageclass>IPM.Task</e:outlookmessageclass>" _
        & "<f:subject>This is a test-task</f:subject>" _
        & "<g:textdescription>Body-Text goes here</g:textdescription>" _
        & "<h:0x00008102 b:dt='float'>.25</h:0x00008102>" _
        & "<h:0x00008101 b:dt='int'>1</h:0x00008101>" _
        & "</d:prop></d:set></d:propertyupdate>"
        '8102 is % Task Complete
        '8101 is Task Status - Not started, In progress, etc.

    With New XMLHTTP
        strURL = "http://server/Exchange/user/tasks/testtask.eml"

        .open "PROPPATCH", strURL, False, "username", "userpassword"
        .setRequestHeader "Content-Type:", "text/xml"
        .setRequestHeader "Translate", "f"
        .send strPropSet

        If Not (.Status >= 200 And .Status < 300) Then
            MsgBox .Status & " " & .statusText
        End If
    End With
```

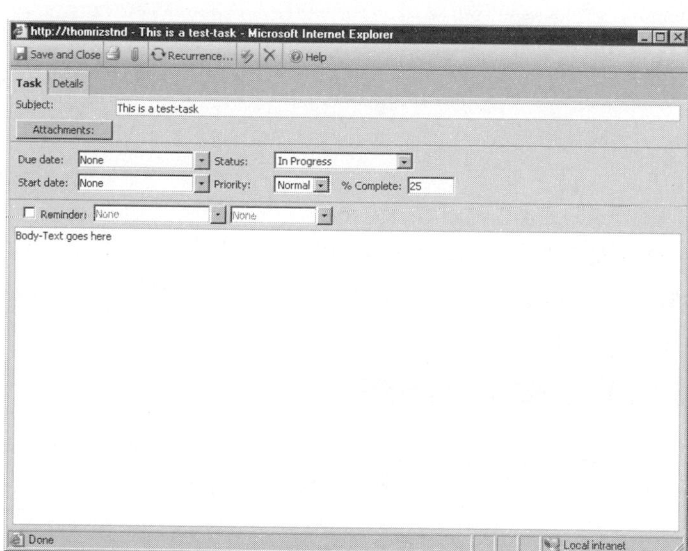

Figure 16-8 Creating a task item via WebDAV and XMLHTTP

Persisted Search Folders

When you use WebDAV, you can use the WebDAV search methods that we looked at earlier. Exchange 2000 and later provide the ability to create persisted search folders when using WebDAV. These search folders are like standard folders in that you can use a URL to access them and query them. You can create search folders in any of your application hierarchies. You cannot, however, create search folders in the MAPI All Public Folders hierarchy. Also, you cannot create search folders using ADO.

Search folders allow you to offload to the server the task of finding new items that meet your SQL search criteria. For example, imagine you have an application that spans 10 folders under the root folder. In each folder, you need to find all the items with a specific property, such as items whose content classes are a certain type—say, *urn:content-classes:mycc*. Rather than querying Exchange every time you need to find items that meet this criterion, you can create a top-level search folder. This search folder will asynchronously add links to new items that meet the criterion (or criteria) you specified in the search folder. Your application can query the search folder rather than perform a deep traversal of all the application folders. Plus, Exchange stores and dynamically updates search results without requiring clients to be connected or requery the Exchange database. Search performance should be much greater with a search folder.

Creating a Search Folder

To create a search folder, all you do is issue an *MKCOL* command. This command also specifies a *DAV:searchrequest* property that contains the SQL statement you want the search folder to perform. The following JavaScript example shows how to create a search folder:

```
function SearchFolderCreate(folderURL, SQLQuery)
{
    var oXMLHTTP;
    oXMLHTTP = new ActiveXObject("Microsoft.XMLHTTP");

    oXMLHTTP.Open("MKCOL", folderURL, false);
    strR = "<?xml version='1.0'?>";
    strR += "<d:propertyupdate xmlns:d='DAV:'>";
    strR += "<d:set><d:prop><d:searchrequest><d:sql>" + SQLQuery + "</d:sql>";
    strR += "</d:searchrequest></d:prop></d:set></d:propertyupdate>";
    oXMLHTTP.SetRequestHeader("Content-Type:", "text/xml");

    oXMLHTTP.send(strR);

    if(!Req.Status == "207")
    { // Multistatus response
        alert("An error has occurred!! ");
    }
}
```

If the command is successful, the server will return a *207 Multi-Status* response. Here is an example of a *SELECT* statement that selects all items that are not hidden or are folders in a public folder tree outside of the MAPI folder tree. You can use this statement as the query in the creation of your search folder.

```
var SQLQuery = "SELECT \"DAV:displayname\" FROM Scope('deep traversal of";
SQLQuery += "\"http://server/newtree/\"') WHERE \"DAV:ishidden\" = false";
SQLQuery = "AND \"DAV:isfolder\" = false";
```

Search folders are just like regular folders in that they contain properties, but they are different in that they contain properties unique to them. Table 16-3 lists the special properties for search folders.

Table 16-3 Properties Unique to Search Folders

Property	Description
DAV:resourcetype	Has a value of *<DAV:collection/><DAV:searchresults/>* if the folder is a search folder.
DAV:searchrequest	Contains the original SQL query for the persisted search. You cannot change this property. If you need to modify your search, you must delete your search folder and re-create it, or create a new search folder.
DAV:searchtype	Set to *dynamic* by the Web Storage System.

Searching a Persisted Search Folder

To query your search folder, all you do is use the WebDAV *Search* or *PropFind* method (described earlier) and then specify the search folder URL. Optionally, you can specify a Range header in your Search queries to return a certain number of rows. For example, you can specify that you want only the first 10 rows or the last 10 rows. The following examples show how to use the Range header with XMLHTTP.

```
Set Req = CreateObject("Microsoft.XMLHTTP")
   . . .
'Rows 10-20 and 40-50
Req.setRequestHeader "Range", "rows=10-20,40-50"
'Last 10 rows
Req.setRequestHeader "Range", "rows=-10"
'From Row 10 to the end of the resultset
Req.setRequestHeader "Range", "rows=10-"
'Rows 1-10 and the last 10 rows
Req.setRequestHeader " Range", "rows=1-10,-10"
```

Using ADO to Retrieve XML Data from Exchange Server

You can retrieve XML data from Exchange Server in a number of other ways. One way is to generate the XML data yourself by using ADO. For example, you can generate an XML document for your data and simply plug in values for the properties from the ADO *Fields* collection. It's not too pretty or easy a technique, but it works.

Another way you can retrieve XML data from Exchange Server is to leverage the XML persistence feature in ADO. ADO allows you to both load and save data in an XML format. The XML format must, however, adhere to the structure expected by ADO. To save data as XML, you just call the *Save* method of the *RecordSet* object and pass in a location and *adPersistXML (1)*.

The cool thing about using ADO with XML is that ADO can persist to the file system or directly to the ASP *Response* object. This means you can either save your *RecordSet* to an XML file or blast the data to the browser in ASP applications. You can also reload a *RecordSet* from a correctly formatted XML document. We'll cover that feature later when we talk about deploying the workflow portion of the Training application. The following XML document comes from the Training application data saved by ADO's XML features:

```
<xml xmlns:s='uuid:BDC6E3F0-6DA3-11d1-A2A3-00AA00C14882'
    xmlns:dt='uuid:C2F41010-65B3-11d1-A29F-00AA00C14882'
    xmlns:rs='urn:schemas-microsoft-com:rowset'
    xmlns:z='#RowsetSchema'>
<s:Schema id='RowsetSchema'>
   <s:ElementType name='row' content='eltOnly' rs:updatable='true'>
      <s:AttributeType name='c0' rs:name='urn:schemas:mailheader:subject'
         rs:number='1' rs:nullable='true' rs:write='true'>
         <s:datatype dt:type='string' dt:maxLength='32768'/>
       </s:AttributeType>
      <s:AttributeType name='c1' rs:name='DAV:href' rs:number='2'
         rs:nullable='true'>
         <s:datatype dt:type='string' dt:maxLength='32768'/>
      </s:AttributeType>
      <s:AttributeType name='c2' rs:name='urn:schemas:calendar:dtstart'
         rs:number='3' rs:nullable='true' rs:write='true'>
         <s:datatype dt:type='dateTime' rs:dbtype='filetime'
            dt:maxLength='16' rs:precision='19' rs:fixedlength='true'/>
      </s:AttributeType>
      <s:AttributeType name='c3' rs:name='urn:schemas:calendar:dtend'
         rs:number='4' rs:nullable='true' rs:write='true'>
         <s:datatype dt:type='dateTime' rs:dbtype='filetime'
            dt:maxLength='16' rs:precision='19' rs:fixedlength='true'/>
      </s:AttributeType>
      <s:extends type='rs:rowbase'/>
   </s:ElementType>
</s:Schema>
```

```
<rs:data>
   <z:row c0='CDO and You' c1='file://./backofficestorage/
      thomriznt5dom.extest.microsoft.com/Public Folders/140/Training/
      Schedule/{75BD5A83-09E7-47B7-A9F1-A75DD62F5BA7}.EML'
      c2='2000-03-08T18:00:00' c3='2000-03-08T19:00:00'/>
   <z:row c0='Leveraging XML in Exchange 2000' c1=
      'file://./backofficestorage/thomriznt5dom.extest.microsoft.com/
         Public Folders/140/Training/Schedule/{8C35C44B-68EB-4651-AC3E-
         5C475923A7A1}.EML'
       c2='2000-03-08T21:00:00' c3='2000-03-08T23:00:00'/>
</rs:data>
</xml>
```

Using XSL to Format XML

Now that we've retrieved our XML data from Exchange Server, you're probably wondering how to display this data in our application. This is where XSL comes in. XML provides a great way to describe data, but it doesn't provide a way to display data. And HTML provides a great way to display data but doesn't provide a good way to describe data. XSL bridges the gap between XML and HTML so you can support rich descriptions of data while also supporting rich viewing of that data.

The following code, taken from coursexml.asp in the Training application, shows how to use XSL to format the XML data returned from Exchange Server. (See Figure 16-9.) I don't have room to cover everything XSL allows you to do, but I will point out the major tasks you can perform with XSL. This code should help you get started.

```
<SCRIPT LANGUAGE="javascript">
    var thexml;
    function Resort()
    {
        var strProp = document.all.SortByProp.innerText;
        //Call sortfield
        sortfield(strProp);
    }
</SCRIPT>
<LABEL ID="SortByProp" style="display:none"
    onpropertychange="javascript:Resort()"></LABEL>
<DIV id="datediv"></DIV>
<BR>
<DIV id=msgdiv></DIV>

<xml id=reportXSL>
<xsl:template
    xmlns:xsl="uri:xsl"
    xmlns:d="DAV:"
    xmlns:o="urn:schemas-microsoft-com:office:office"
```

```
    xmlns:c="<%=strSchema%>"
    xmlns:h="urn:schemas:httpmail:"
    xmlns:cal="urn:schemas:calendar:">

<xsl:script>
function getMyDate(objThis, szDateFormatString, szTimeFormatSTring)
{
    var m_objDate = new Date();
    var m_x=0;
    var gszDateString = "";

    var szDate   = objThis.text;
    var szSubStr = szDate.substring(5,7);

    if(szSubStr.charAt(0) == "0")
    {
        szSubStr = szSubStr.charAt(1);
    }
    m_objDate.setUTCFullYear(szDate.substring(0,4));      //Set Year
    m_objDate.setUTCMonth(Number(szSubStr)-1);            //Set Month
    m_objDate.setUTCDate(szDate.substring(8,10));         //Set Date
    m_objDate.setUTCHours(szDate.substring(11,13));       //Set Hours
    m_objDate.setUTCMinutes(szDate.substring(14,16));     //Set Minutes
    m_objDate.setUTCSeconds(szDate.substring(17,19));     //Set Seconds

    var iNumHours = m_objDate.getHours();
    var szFormattedTime = formatTime(m_objDate.getVarDate(),
                                     szTimeFormatSTring);
    var szFormattedDate = formatDate(m_objDate.getVarDate(),
                                     szDateFormatString);
    gszDateString = szFormattedDate.substring(0,szFormattedDate.length-1)
                    + " " + szFormattedTime;

    return (gszDateString);
}
</xsl:script>

<table id="XMLTable">
<TBODY>
    xsl:for-each select="d:multistatus/d:response"
        order-by="<%=Request.QueryString("SortBy")%>">
    <xsl:if test="d:propstat/d:prop/href[.!='']">
    <xsl:if test="d:propstat/d:prop/iscollection[.='0']">
    <xsl:if test="d:propstat/d:prop/subject[.!='']">
    <TR><TD>
        <LI>
            <A HREF='detaildrop.asp' title='Click to view more information
                about this course.' onclick="vbscript:ExpandCollapse()">
                <xsl:attribute name="ID"><xsl:value-of
                select="d:propstat/d:prop/href" /></xsl:attribute>
                <xsl:value-of select="d:propstat/d:prop/subject" />
            </A>
        </LI>
    </TD></TR>
```

```
<TABLE style="display: none"><xsl:attribute name="ID">Details
    <xsl:value-of select="d:propstat/d:prop/href"/>
    </xsl:attribute>
    <TR><TD>
        <B>Location:</B></TD><TD>
        <xsl:value-of select="d:propstat/d:prop/location" />
    </TD></TR>
    <TR><TD><B>Instructor:</B></TD><TD>

        <!--turn into mailto-->
        <A><xsl:attribute name="href">mailto:<xsl:value-of select=
           "d:propstat/d:prop/instructoremail" /></xsl:attribute>
           <xsl:value-of select="d:propstat/d:prop/instructoremail" />
             </A>
    </TD></TR>
    <TR><TD><B>Category:</B></TD><TD>
        <xsl:value-of select="d:propstat/d:prop/category" />
    </TD></TR>

        <!--convert to the correct timezone -->
    <TR><TD><B>Start Time:</B></TD><TD>
        <xsl:for-each select="d:propstat/d:prop/starttime">
           <xsl:eval>getMyDate(this,"MM-dd-yyyy",
           "h:mm tt")</xsl:eval></xsl:for-each>
    </TD></TR>
    <TR><TD><B>End Time:</B></TD><TD>
        <xsl:for-each select="d:propstat/d:prop/endtime">
           <xsl:eval>getMyDate(this,"MM-dd-yyyy","h:mm tt")
           </xsl:eval></xsl:for-each>
    </TD></TR>
    <TR><TD><B>Prerequisites:</B></TD><TD>
        <xsl:value-of select="d:propstat/d:prop/prereqs" />
    </TD></TR>
    <TR><TD><B>Description:</B></TD><TD>
        <xsl:value-of select="d:propstat/d:prop/description" />
    </TD></TR>
        <xsl:if test="d:propstat/d:prop/materialsfilepath[.!='']">
    <TR><TD><B>Course Materials:</B></TD>
        <TD>
            <A href=""><xsl:attribute name="onclick">
                javascript:window.open('<xsl:value-of select=
                "d:propstat/d:prop/materialsfilepath" />');
                window.event.returnValue=false;</xsl:attribute>
                File link to materials
            </A>
             
            <A href=""><xsl:attribute name="onclick">
                javascript:window.open('<xsl:value-of select=
                "d:propstat/d:prop/materialshttppath" />');
                window.event.returnValue=false;</xsl:attribute>
                HTTP link to materials
            </A>
    </TD></TR>
    </xsl:if>
```

```
                <xsl:if test="d:propstat/d:prop/discussionurl[.!='']">
                <TR><TD>
                    <A style="color: olive" href="" title="Click here to
                        view the discussion for this course.">
                        <xsl:attribute name="onclick">
                        javascript:window.open('<xsl:value-of select=
                        "d:propstat/d:prop/discussionurl" />');
                        window.event.returnValue=false;</xsl:attribute>
                        View Discussion Group
                    </A>
                </TD></TR>
                </xsl:if>
                <TR><TD>
                    <xsl:choose>
                    <xsl:when test="d:propstat/d:prop/starttime[. &lt;
                         '<%=TurnIntoIso(Date(),"end")%> ']">
                         <!--Course has already taken place work -->
                         <B>This course has already taken place.</B>
                    </xsl:when>
                    <xsl:otherwise>
                         <A style="color: olive" href="" title="Click here
                             to register for this course."><xsl:attribute
                             name="onclick">javascript:window.
                             open('register.asp?FullCourseURL=<xsl:value-of
                             select="d:propstat/d:prop/href" />');
                             window.event.returnValue=false;</xsl:attribute>
                             Register for this course
                         </A>
                    </xsl:otherwise>
                    </xsl:choose>
                </TD></TR>
                <TR><TD><BR></BR>
                </TD></TR>
            </TABLE>
            </xsl:if>
            </xsl:if>
            </xsl:if>
            </xsl:for-each>
</TBODY>
</table>
</xsl:template>
</xml>

<script language="javascript">

var URLSchedule ="<%=strURLToSchedule%>";

function sortfield(sortby)
{
    thenode =
        reportXSL.selectSingleNode("xsl:template/table/TBODY/xsl:for-each");
    thenode.setAttribute("order-by", sortby);
    if (thexml.selectSingleNode("a:multistatus/a:response") == null)
```

```
    {
        msgdiv.innerHTML = "<B>No courses found.</B>";
    }
    else
    {
        msgdiv.innerHTML = thexml.transformNode(reportXSL.documentElement);
    }
}
```

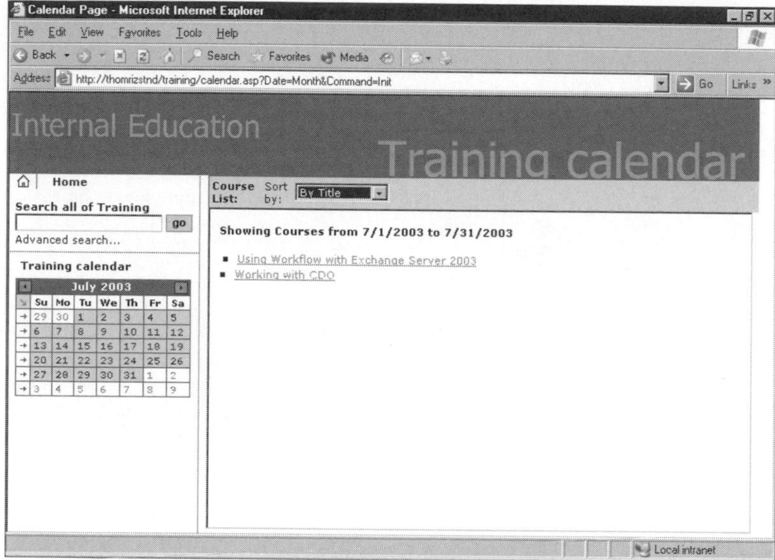

Figure 16-9 XML data formatted via XSL

You'll notice that the code contains an XSL template that combines XSL commands with HTML. The template also contains embedded JavaScript that allows the XSL to transform the XML data into correctly formatted HTML.

XSL Elements

Let's take a look at some of the most frequently used XSL elements.

XSL *Value-of*

Value-of is one of the XSL elements you'll use the most. It places the value of the node you specify as part of the element. Here is an example of this element, taken from the code in the previous section:

```
<xsl:value-of select="d:propstat/d:prop/category" />
```

XSL *If*

As you can guess by the name, the *If* element implements simple, conditional logic. You can pass in the *Language* parameter for this element to indicate the scripting language you want to use to evaluate script in your condition testing. The *Test* parameter is the actual condition you want to test for. The following code checks to see whether the subject of the item returned is not empty. You can test for multiple conditions by using the *Choose*, *When*, and *Otherwise* elements (discussed next).

```
<xsl:if test="d:propstat/d:prop/subject[.!='']">
```

XSL *Choose*, *When*, and *Otherwise*

You use the *Choose*, *When*, and *Otherwise* elements together when you require more complex conditional testing. You can use these three elements to implement an *If…ElseIf…Else* structure. The following code checks to see whether the start time of the course is less than the current time, which would mean the course has already taken place. If the start time is after the current time, a registration link is created for the course.

```
<xsl:choose>
<xsl:when test="d:propstat/d:prop/starttime[. &lt;
    '<%=TurnIntoIso(Date(),"end")%>']">
    <!--Course has already taken place work -->
    <B>This course has already taken place.</B>
</xsl:when>

//Another xsl:when could go here

<xsl:otherwise>
    <A style="color: olive" href=""
    title="Click here to register for this course.">
    <xsl:attribute name="onclick">
    javascript:window.open('register.asp?FullCourseURL=<xsl:value-of
    select="d:propstat/d:prop/href" />');
    window.event.returnValue=false;</xsl:attribute>
    Register for this course
</A>
</xsl:otherwise>
</xsl:choose>
```

XSL *Attribute*

Notice the use of the XSL *Attribute* element in the previous code example. This element allows you to put an attribute on an HTML element inside your XSL template. You should do this if, as part of your HTML element, you want to evaluate another XSL element as the HTML element's value. In the previous example, the *onclick* attribute is added to the hyperlink (*A*) element in the HTML. The *href* to the item is added as the value for the *onclick* attribute by using the XSL *Value-of* element.

XSL *For-Each*

The XSL *For-Each* element is similar to the Visual Basic *For Each...Next* loop. The *For-Each* element allows you to apply a template to an element. The best example of how you can use this element can be found in the first *For-Each* element that appears in the previous section's code. This *For-Each* element uses a *Select* clause and pattern matching to select only the response nodes in the XML. Furthermore, this example uses the *Order-by* criteria to support sorting the data by a specific node in the XML. The code example from the previous section follows:

```
<xsl:for-each select="d:multistatus/d:response"
    order-by="<%=Request.QueryString("SortBy")%>">
```

XSL *Script* and XSL *Eval*

> **Note** The *<xsl:script>* namespace is a Microsoft extension to XSLT. If you are using later versions of the Microsoft XML parser, use the *<msxml:script>* namespace rather than the *<xsl:script>* namespace, as in *<msxsl:script language="javascript" implements-prefix="user"> </msxsl:script>*.

You'll probably want to use the XSL *Script* and *Eval* elements together in your template. The *Script* element allows you to specify a global script that the rest of your XSL template can call. You can pass the *Script* element a *Language* parameter that specifies the scripting language, such as JavaScript, for your script code.

The *Eval* element evaluates a script expression and generates a text string. You'll usually need to call a script you defined by using the *Script* element in your *Eval* element and have that script return a text value. You can, however, place inline script in the *Eval* element as well. The following code gets the date of a given training course object and correctly formats it using the *Script* and *Eval* elements:

```
<xsl:script>
function getMyDate(objThis, szDateFormatString, szTimeFormatSTring)
{
    var m_objDate = new Date();
    var m_x = 0;
    var gszDateString = "";
    var szDate = objThis.text;
    var szSubStr = szDate.substring(5,7);

    if(szSubStr.charAt(0) == "0")
    {
        szSubStr = szSubStr.charAt(1);
    }
    m_objDate.setUTCFullYear(szDate.substring(0,4));   //Set Year
    m_objDate.setUTCMonth(Number(szSubStr)-1);         //Set Month
    m_objDate.setUTCDate(szDate.substring(8,10));      //Set Date
    m_objDate.setUTCHours(szDate.substring(11,13));    //Set Hours
    m_objDate.setUTCMinutes(szDate.substring(14,16)); //Set Minutes
    m_objDate.setUTCSeconds(szDate.substring(17,19)); //Set Seconds

    var iNumHours = m_objDate.getHours();
    var szFormattedTime = formatTime(m_objDate.getVarDate(),
                                     szTimeFormatSTring);
    var szFormattedDate = formatDate(m_objDate.getVarDate(),
                                     szDateFormatString);

    gszDateString = szFormattedDate.substring(0,szFormattedDate.length-1)
                 + " " + szFormattedTime;

    return (gszDateString);
}

</xsl:script>
. . .
                <!--convert to the correct time zone -->
                <TR><TD><B>Start Time:</B></TD><TD>

                <xsl:for-each select="d:propstat/d:prop/starttime">
                   <xsl:eval>getMyDate(this,"MM-dd-yyyy","h:mm tt")
                   </xsl:eval></xsl:for-each>

                </TD></TR>
                <TR><TD><B>End Time:</B></TD><TD>

                <xsl:for-each select="d:propstat/d:prop/endtime">
                   <xsl:eval>getMyDate(this,"MM-dd-yyyy","h:mm tt")
                   </xsl:eval></xsl:for-each>

                </TD></TR>
. . .
```

I've barely begun to scratch the surface of XSL, but this overview should help you get started in transforming your XML using XSL. XSL is still evolving and has not been formally defined in an RFC. The best resource I have found on XSL is the MSDN library at *http://msdn.microsoft.com/*. Also check out the Web Workshop section in the Platform SDK. Not only does it include lots of documentation on XML, it includes a wealth of information on XSL. Last but not least, you might want to check out the Web site of the World Wide Web Consortium (W3C).

> **Note** I won't examine the XML Document Object Model (XMLDOM) in any detail here, but it's important for you to know about it. The XMLDOM provides a programmatic way for you to get, change, and create XML nodes in an XML document. Using the XMLDOM, you can display the data returned to you from WebDAV and avoid using XSL. However, the XMLDOM will most likely be slower than XSL because you have to traverse through all the elements in the XML document and print them out using script. XSL is implemented by Internet Explorer natively, so you pass your XSL template to Internet Explorer and it transforms the XML document using your XSL template.

Calling WebDAV Using *HTTPWebRequest* in .NET

As a cutting-edge programmer, you might be wondering how you call WebDAV from .NET. The .NET Framework includes the *HTTPWebRequest* and *HTTPWebResponse* classes, which allow you to make WebDAV calls to the server. The easiest way to learn how to use these classes is to see a sample application. Figure 16-10 shows a WebDAV client sample application. This application shows how to do *PROPPATCH*, *PROPFIND*, and searches using these classes.

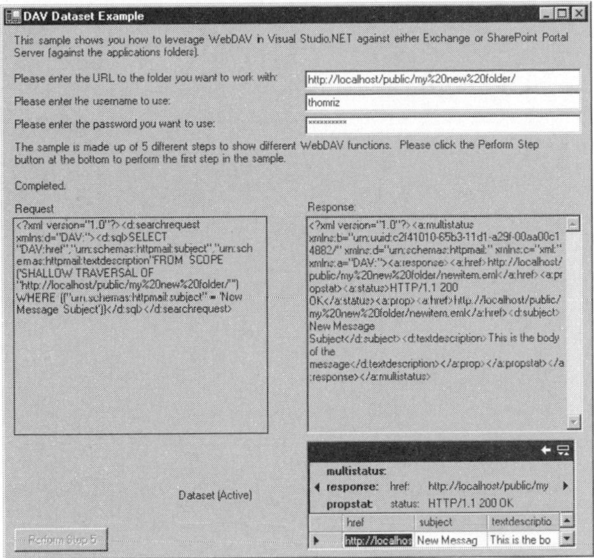

Figure 16-10 The WebDAV .NET sample application

The following is the code from the sample application:

```
Imports System.Net
Imports System.IO
Imports System.Xml
Public Class Form1
    Inherits System.Windows.Forms.Form
    Dim iCurStep = 1
    Dim strURL As String = ""
    Dim bFailed As Boolean
    Dim responsestring As String = ""
    'This sample shows how to leverage the httpwebrequest
    'and httpwebresponse objects against Exchange or SPS
    '5 things are shown
    '1: Creating an item
    '2: Using a proppatch
    '3: Using a propfind
    '4: Performing a search
    '5: Loading that search into a dataset

#Region " Windows Form Designer generated code "
. . .
#End Region

    Private Sub txtPerformStep_Click(ByVal sender As System.Object, _
                                     ByVal e As System.EventArgs) _
                                     Handles cmdPerformStep.Click
        'Check the current step
        If iCurStep = 1 Then
```

```
            'Check the URL of the folder
            If txtURL.Text = "" Then
                MsgBox("You must enter a valid URL!", _
                       MsgBoxStyle.Exclamation + MsgBoxStyle.OKOnly)
                Exit Sub
            Else
                'perform the step: Create the item
                Try
                    If Microsoft.VisualBasic.Right(txtURL.Text, 1) = "/" Then
                        strURL = txtURL.Text
                    Else
                        strURL = txtURL.Text & "/"
                    End If
                    lblRequest.Text = "PUT " & strURL
                    bFailed = False
                    bFailed = CallWebRequest(strURL & "newitem.eml", "PUT", _
                                     "message/rfc822", "", "Subject: Test")
                    If bFailed Then
                        MsgBox("Web request failed!")
                        Exit Sub
                    End If
                    iCurStep = 2
                    lblCurrentStep.Text = "Step 2: Perform a Proppatch"
                    cmdPerformStep.Text = "Perform Step 2"
                Catch
                    MsgBox("Error on the 1st step. Error#:" & Err.Number _
                           & " Description: " & Err.Description)
                    Exit Sub
                End Try
            End If
        ElseIf iCurStep = 2 Then
            Try
                Dim strXML As String
                strXML = "<?xml version=""1.0""?>" _
                       & "<D:propertyupdate xmlns:D=""DAV:"" " _
                       & "xmlns:M=""urn:schemas:httpmail:"">"
                strXML += "<D:set><D:prop><M:subject>New Message " _
                       & "Subject</M:subject><M:textdescription>" _
                       & "This is the body of the message</M:textdescription>"
                strXML += "</D:prop></D:set></D:propertyupdate>"
                lblRequest.Text = strXML
                bFailed = False
                bFailed = CallWebRequest(strURL & "newitem.eml", _
                                     "PROPPATCH", "text/xml", "", strXML)
                If bFailed Then
                    MsgBox("Web request failed!")
                    Exit Sub
                End If
                iCurStep = 3
                lblCurrentStep.Text = "Step 3: Perform Propfind"
                cmdPerformStep.Text = "Perform Step " & iCurStep
            Catch
                MsgBox("Error on the 2nd step. Error#:" & Err.Number _
```

```
                & " Description: " & Err.Description)
        End Try
    ElseIf iCurStep = 3 Then
        Try
            Dim strXML As String
            strXML = "<?xml version=""1.0""?>" _
                   & "<D:propfind xmlns:D=""DAV:"">"
            strXML += "<D:prop><D:displayname/>" _
                   & "<D:getlastmodified/><D:creationdate/>"
            strXML += "</D:prop></D:propfind>"
            lblRequest.Text = strXML
            bFailed = False
            bFailed = CallWebRequest(strURL & "newitem.eml", "PROPFIND", _
                                    "text/xml", "1,noroot", strXML)
            If bFailed Then
                MsgBox("Web request failed!")
                Exit Sub
            End If
            iCurStep = 4
            lblCurrentStep.Text = "Step 4: Perform a search"
            cmdPerformStep.Text = "Perform Step " & iCurStep
        Catch
            MsgBox("Error on the 3rd step. Error#:" & Err.Number _
                   & " Description: " & Err.Description)
        End Try
    ElseIf iCurStep = 4 Then
        Try
            Dim strXML As String
            Dim strSQL As String = "SELECT ""DAV:href"", "
            strSQL += """urn:schemas:httpmail:subject"""
            strSQL += "FROM SCOPE('SHALLOW TRAVERSAL OF """ & strURL
            strSQL += """') WHERE ((""urn:schemas:httpmail:subject"" = '"
            strSQL += "New Message Subject'))"
            strXML = "<?xml version=""1.0""?>"
            strXML += "<d:searchrequest xmlns:d=""DAV:"">"
            strXML += "<d:sql>" & strSQL & "</d:sql>"
            strXML += "</d:searchrequest>"
            lblRequest.Text = strXML
            bFailed = False
            bFailed = CallWebRequest(strURL, "SEARCH", "text/xml",
                                    "1", strXML)
            If bFailed Then
                MsgBox("Web request failed!")
                Exit Sub
            End If
            iCurStep = 5
            lblCurrentStep.Text = "Step 5: Load a search " _
                                & "into a Dataset object"
            cmdPerformStep.Text = "Perform Step " & iCurStep
        Catch
            MsgBox("Error on the 4th step. Error#:" & Err.Number _
                   & " Description: " & Err.Description)
        End Try
```

```
        ElseIf iCurStep = 5 Then
            Try
                Dim strXML As String
                Dim strSQL As String = "SELECT ""DAV:href"", "
                strSQL += """urn:schemas:httpmail:subject"", "
                strSQL += """urn:schemas:httpmail:textdescription"""
                strSQL += "FROM SCOPE('SHALLOW TRAVERSAL OF """ & strURL
                strSQL += """') WHERE ((""urn:schemas:httpmail:subject"" = '"
                strSQL += "New Message Subject'))"
                strXML = "<?xml version=""1.0""?>"
                strXML += "<d:searchrequest xmlns:d=""DAV:"">"
                strXML += "<d:sql>" & strSQL & "</d:sql>"
                strXML += "</d:searchrequest>"
                lblRequest.Text = strXML
                bFailed = False
                bFailed = CallWebRequest(strURL, "SEARCH", "text/xml", _
                                         "1", strXML)
                If bFailed Then
                    MsgBox("Web request failed!")
                    Exit Sub
                End If
                Dim output As Byte() = System.Text.Encoding.GetEncoding( _
                                           1252).GetBytes(responsestring)

                'Load the XmlDocument object with the results for parsing
                Dim outputStream As MemoryStream = New MemoryStream(output)
                Dim outputReader As XmlTextReader = _
                                            New XmlTextReader(outputStream)

                Dim resultdoc As XmlDataDocument = New XmlDataDocument()
                resultdoc.DataSet.ReadXml(outputReader)
                Dim resultSet As New Data.DataSet()
                resultSet = resultdoc.DataSet
                DataGrid1.SetDataBinding(resultSet, "")
                Label7.Text = "Dataset (Active)"
                lblCurrentStep.Text = "Completed."
                cmdPerformStep.Enabled = False
            Catch
                MsgBox("Error on the 5th step. Error#:" & Err.Number _
                       & " Description: " & Err.Description)
            End Try
        End If
    End Sub
    Public Function CallWebRequest(ByVal strURL, ByVal strMethod, _
                                   ByVal strContentType, ByVal strDepthHeader, _
                                   ByVal strXML) As Boolean
        Try
            Dim oHTTPRequest As HttpWebRequest = _
                      CType(WebRequest.Create(strURL), HttpWebRequest)
            oHTTPRequest.PreAuthenticate = True
            oHTTPRequest.Credentials = _
                      New NetworkCredential(txtUserName.Text, txtPassword.Text)
            oHTTPRequest.Method = strMethod
```

```
            oHTTPRequest.Headers.Add("Translate", "f")
            If strDepthHeader <> "" Then
                oHTTPRequest.Headers.Add("Depth", strDepthHeader)
            End If
            oHTTPRequest.ContentType = strContentType
            oHTTPRequest.ContentLength = strXML.Length
            Dim byteXML() As Byte = _
                     System.Text.Encoding.ASCII.GetBytes(strXML)
            Dim oStream As Stream = oHTTPRequest.GetRequestStream
            oStream.Write(byteXML, 0, byteXML.Length)
            oStream.Close()
            Dim oHTTPResponse As HttpWebResponse = oHTTPRequest.GetResponse()
            Dim oReader As StreamReader
            oReader = New StreamReader(oHTTPResponse.GetResponseStream, _
                                 System.Text.Encoding.ASCII)
            txtResponse.Text = oReader.ReadToEnd
            responsestring = txtResponse.Text
            CallWebRequest = False
        Catch
            MsgBox("Error! Error#:" & Err.Number & " Description: " _
                   & Err.Description)
            CallWebRequest = True
        End Try
    End Function
End Class
```

The first thing to notice in the code is that all the WebDAV commands are the same commands we used with the XMLHTTP component. You can make the same calls using the HTTPWebRequest component.

Next, notice that the meat of the code is contained in the *CallWebRequest* function. This is the function that takes the WebDAV command and sends it to the server. Let's step through this code and examine what it does.

The first section of the code creates a new *HTTPWebRequest* object that points at the URL passed to the function. We need to typecast the standard *WebRequest* object that is returned by the *WebRequest Create* method to an *HTTPWebRequest* object.

Next the code sets the *PreAuthenticate* property to *True*. This setting means that when we make our request to the server, .NET will include the WWW-Authenticate header and pass our credentials to the Web server. This frees the application from having to request the credentials from the user.

Next the code sets the credentials to the specified username and password to impersonate for the request. Immediately after that the code also sets the WebDAV method to use, such as *PROPFIND* or *PROPPATCH*. Then the code sets some headers, such as the Translate header and the Depth header. The code also sets the Content-Type and Content-Length headers.

The next section of code is very important. This is the section where we actually set the body of our request that we will send to the server. Note that the

ContentLength property must be set before you call any of the code that follows that property. First the code loads the body of the request into a byte array. The reason for this is so we can load the byte array into the stream, which is returned by the *GetRequestStream* method on the *HTTPWebRequest* object. Then, to make our WebDAV call to the server, we need to call the *Write* method on the stream, passing in our byte array, the offset of which is zero in this case, and finally the number of bytes to write, which is the length of our byte array.

The next section of code uses the *HTTPWebResponse* to get the HTTP response back from the server. First, to get the response, the code calls the *GetResponse* method on the *HTTPWebRequest* object. Because the contents of the response are returned in an *HTTPWebResponse* object and that object requires us to use a stream to read that response, the code creates a new *StreamReader* object. Then the code reads the stream from the *HTTPWebResponse* into the *StreamReader* and uses the *ReadToEnd* method to write out the text of the response to the screen.

That is all you need to do to leverage WebDAV from your .NET applications. The other interesting part of the code is where the response is loaded into a dataset. This code is similar to the code we saw in the free/busy Web service consumer application in Chapter 14, so I won't cover the code here.

Summary

As you have seen in this chapter, Exchange Server supports XML extensively. Now that you have seen ADO and WebDAV, we can move to more advanced topics, such as server events, workflow, and security programming. The techniques and technologies you have learned in this chapter are the foundation for the chapters that follow.

17

Server Events, Workflow, and Security

The ability to capture and program events in Microsoft Exchange Server 2003 opens up a world of possibilities for the applications you write. For example, you might want to add some workflow to your applications or validate items before they are put into the server. Because the events are on the server side, it doesn't matter which client puts items into the database—the events will fire and your code will run. For example, if a user drags and drops a Microsoft Word document into Exchange Server using the new file system capabilities, your events will fire.

The Simple Mail Transport Protocol (SMTP) service of Microsoft Internet Information Services (IIS) offers two types of events: protocol events and transport events. Because Exchange 2000 and Exchange 2003 are built on the SMTP service in IIS, Exchange not only provides Exchange-specific events through its Information Store service but also inherits transport and protocol events. In fact, Exchange relies on those events extensively to extend the standard SMTP service with Exchange-specific functionality. We will discuss transport and protocol events after we discuss Exchange Server events.

Exchange Server Events

In this section, we will look at the events that Exchange fires—specifically, synchronous, asynchronous, and system events. You register for synchronous events using an event registration. That event registration points to an event handler, which is the code you write that handles the firing of the event and performs the correct actions.

Synchronous events are events that fire after the item is saved. Exchange Server not only supports synchronous events but also adds them. They are called before the item is committed to the database. With synchronous events, your application can look at the item and then either accept it or prevent it from being committed into Exchange Server. However, remember that your event source is blocked while your event code runs. A good rule of thumb is try to make your events asynchronous if you can and make them synchronous only if you really require synchronous events. For example, if you need to check an item and stop it from being committed unless it meets certain requirements, you should use synchronous events. If you are just sending a notification to users that a new item was posted, asynchronous events will work.

Events are fired when items are moved, copied, created, or deleted in Exchange Server. The scope of these events is limited to a folder, and you can write event handlers that use ActiveX Data Objects (ADO) or OLE Database (OLE DB), depending on the programming language you use. You can write your event handlers in Visual Basic Script (VBScript), Microsoft Visual Basic, or Microsoft Visual C++. I'll concentrate on Visual Basic in this discussion. I recommend that you write your event handlers in this language unless your language of choice is Visual C++. We will look at building event handlers using Microsoft .NET later in this chapter.

I don't recommend writing event handlers in VBScript because it's harder to do and harder to debug. However, using scripts can be helpful at times. For example, if you do not have the permissions required to register Component Object Model (COM) components on the server, scripts might be a good alternative. Also, if you are used to the Exchange 5.5 model of writing events—which is VBScript-based—you will already be familiar with VBScript events in Exchange 2003. But use VBScript events as your last resort. As mentioned earlier, it's not as rich an experience to write and debug your event handlers in VBScript as in full-featured programming languages such as Visual C++.

The Firing Order of Events

When an item is saved into Exchange Server, the types of events are fired in a fixed order in the system. This firing order is important to understand because multiple entities can be working on the items in your folders, which can make it look as if your application isn't working. Synchronous events fire first, followed by any server-side folder rules you have created using Outlook or Outlook Web Access (OWA), and finally asynchronous events. As you might have guessed, these events follow one another. For instance, if your synchronous event aborts the item from being saved, the rules and asynchronous events will not be notified of the item. Furthermore, if any events that are higher up in the chain move or delete an item, the other events should be prepared to not have access to the item. For example (and this is just good coding practice), if your asynchronous events are expecting to open the item and some other synchronous event or folder rule has moved the item, you should have error code in your event handler to handle this situation.

System events, such as timer-based events or store startup/shutdown, fire only at specific times that you set or when you perform a certain action. For example, if you shut down Exchange, the shutdown event will fire so that you can capture that the Information Store service is shutting down.

Security Requirements

You should know about security requirements before you write your event handlers because security will affect how you register your event handlers and what user context your event handlers will run under. First, you must be a folder owner to register an event handler in a folder. Also, Exchange Server provides an extra security precaution in the form of the *ICreateRegistration* interface. This interface is called when you attempt to register a component to handle events in your folder. Using *ICreateRegistration*, the component developer can prohibit you from registering the event handler.

Second, if you're writing COM components to implement your event handlers, you must have the required access permissions to install components on the Exchange server. Exchange Server does not support instantiating and running remote components via Distributed COM (DCOM) as event handlers. Nothing can stop you from calling remote components or Web services in your event handler, but you must remember that the Exchange OLE DB (EXOLEDB) provider is not remotable—the code has to run on the same server the data is on. You can, however, use DCOM to connect to another component residing on another server that accesses data on that server. Plus, for remote access you can use XML Web services or Web Distributed Authoring and Versioning (WebDAV), both discussed in earlier chapters, to get access to remote data from your event handlers. Getting the security contexts to support this is the hard part. If you use COM+ applications (which we'll talk about shortly), you can have your components run in a specific security context, which makes deployment easier.

Synchronous Events

Synchronous event handlers are called twice by Exchange Server. The first time, the event handler is called before the item is committed to the Exchange Server database. The second time the event handler is called, the item has been either committed or aborted. On the first pass, the item is read/write. You can modify properties or copy the item somewhere else. However, on the second pass, after the transaction has been committed, the item is read-only. Be aware that the item is not a true item in the database on the first pass. Because the item is not yet committed, you shouldn't grab any properties that might change in the future (between the time you access the item and the time it is committed). For example, the URL to the item is not valid on the first pass, nor is the EntryID, because the item is not yet in the database. Many factors can change the URL or EntryID, so you shouldn't query or save the item during the first pass.

In synchronous events, your event handler runs in the context of a local OLE DB transaction. Therefore, any changes you make to the item will not trigger other events. However, you must realize that the work performed in your event handler can be discarded if another event handler rejects the item from being committed. All the event handlers that act on an item in a folder must commit in order for the action to occur. If any event handler rejects the transaction, the action will not occur. If your event handler has already run, it will be called a second time and will be notified that the action has been aborted. Your event handler can then perform any necessary cleanup.

For example, let's say you have two event handlers registered in a folder for the *OnSyncSave* event, which is one of the synchronous events in Exchange. One of the event handlers opens the item and saves attachments to another location. The other event handler validates data in the item before allowing it to commit. Based on the priority you set for your event handlers, if the validation occurs after you copy the attachments, the validation might fail and the transaction for saving the item might be aborted. Now, any good developer would obviously make validation precede the other events. However, because multiple developers can register event handlers (as long as they meet the security requirements mentioned earlier), other event handlers can abort transactions. In this case, your event handler for copying the attachments will be notified that the transaction was aborted, and you should clean up your work by deleting the attachments from the other location.

You also should be aware that synchronous event handlers, while running, are the only processes that can access an item. Exchange Server blocks any other threads, processes, or applications from accessing that item while your event handler is running and working on it. This is critical because if you write an inefficient event handler, you can degrade the performance of other applications and Exchange Server. For example, if your event handler takes 10 seconds to run, each time an Outlook user saves an item in a folder that triggers your event handler, Outlook will show an hourglass for 10 seconds. Therefore, if you can use asynchronous events to implement your functionality, you should do so. If the Outlook scenario were to use an asynchronous event, Outlook would return immediately and allow the user to continue working. However, asynchronous events also have limiting factors, which I will cover shortly.

Synchronous events are expensive for Exchange Server to perform. The server must stop its processing on the item, call your event handler, wait, and then figure out whether to commit or abort the transaction for the item based on your event handler. All this creates temporary copies of the item before committing and forces the Exchange Server threads to wait, which affects performance.

Continuing with the Outlook scenario, if you abort the transaction, different clients will display different error messages. For example, Outlook will probably display an error message stating that the item couldn't be saved. A custom application will display just a general error that the operation failed. You cannot show user interface elements in your event handlers because they are running on the server. Instead, you must find a way to notify your users that they submitted the item incorrectly or that the action they're trying to perform is not allowed. You can perform this notification via e-mail or another method.

Exchange Server supports two synchronous events: *OnSyncSave* and *OnSyncDelete*. As you can guess from their names, these events support save and delete operations, respectively. However, both events are called as part of move and copy operations, too. For example, if you move an item from one folder to another, a save event will be fired in the new folder and a delete event will be fired in the old folder. If either is aborted, the move will not occur. With a copy, you get a save event in the location where the copy is supposed to be placed. You should know that the *OnSyncDelete* event is not called on an item when the item's parent folder is moved or deleted. Also, *OnSyncDelete* can distinguish between hard and soft deletes. A hard delete is a deletion in which the item is completely removed from the Exchange database. A soft delete is a deletion in which the item is moved into the dumpster. (An analogy would be the Deleted Items subfolder for every folder.) A user can recover an item from the dumpster using the interface in Outlook or OWA. You are notified of the deletion type by the flags that are passed to the *OnSyncDelete* event.

OnSyncSave is not called for items in a folder when the parent folder for the items is being moved or copied and an event registration exists for the parent folder. The event is called, however, for the parent folder; you can then abort the transaction if you don't want the items moved or copied.

You might be asking yourself, "If only save and delete are supported, how do I get notified of a change?" If a user makes a change to an item (such as modifying the subject or any property) and saves the item, you will receive the *OnSyncSave* event. The flags that are passed to the event will notify you that the item has been modified. However, you will not receive notification of which property the user changed in the item. You must scan the item to see what changed. To do this, you must have an original copy of the item, which you can obtain by copying the item in your event handler to another folder. I admit, though, that this approach isn't very practical if the number of copied items is large. In this situation, Microsoft SQL Server 2000 might provide a more suitable repository.

When you register your event handler, if you do not specify criteria for the types of items for which you want to receive events, Exchange Server will notify you of all new items being put into the folder. Folders store some surprising items that you might not expect to handle in your event handler. For example, when someone publishes a form or adds a field to a folder in Outlook, a hidden item is added to the folder. We discussed hidden items in folders in Chapter 11, when we discussed CDO 1.21 and how it can access hidden items. Hidden items trigger an event. You should set the criteria for your event registration (which we'll discuss later) so that only the items your event handler is interested in can trigger events.

Asynchronous Events

Exchange Server 2000 supports two asynchronous events, *OnSave* and *OnDelete*. These asynchronous events are called after a transaction has been committed to the database (such as items being created or deleted), and they fire in no particular order. Although these events are guaranteed to be called, another process or user might delete or move the item before the event handler even sees it. Exchange Server doesn't guarantee when it will call your event handler, but usually your event handler is called as soon as the item is committed to the Exchange Server database. Furthermore, as mentioned, if multiple asynchronous event handlers are registered for a single folder, Exchange does not guarantee the order in which the event handlers are called. Again, you should use asynchronous events rather than synchronous events whenever possible. If you need a guaranteed firing order, use synchronous events with the *priority* property, which we will discuss later in the chapter.

System Events

The three system events of Exchange Server are *OnMDBStartup*, *OnMDBShutdown*, and *OnTimer*. *OnMDBStartup* and *OnMDBShutdown* are called whenever an Exchange Server store starts or shuts down. This is useful for event handlers that want to scan the database or perform some sort of activity whenever the database starts or shuts down. Because these two events are asynchronous, Exchange Server doesn't wait for your event handler to finish before continuing execution of starting or shutting down Exchange.

The *OnTimer* event fires according to your configured parameters. For example, you can have a timer event fire every five minutes, daily, weekly, or monthly. It all depends on the requirements of your application. We'll look at how the sample Training application (introduced in Chapter 15) uses timer events for notification about new courses and student surveys for courses that already have taken place.

Registering an Event Handler

I'm going to go about this a little bit backward. Writing event handlers involves working with registration parameters, so I'll discuss the registration process first. That way, things will be clearer to you when we talk about writing actual event handlers later in this section.

Registering an event handler is quite easy. Exchange Server 2003 provides a script program called regevent.vbs, which allows you to pass some parameters to the program. The regevent.vbs program registers events of any event type you specify. Besides using regevent.vbs, you can create event registration items for your applications by simply creating new items in Exchange using ADO. In the setup program for the Training application, the three event handlers for the application are registered automatically using ADO. We'll look at the code for this registration at the end of this section.

Event Registration Properties

When you register events, you must set some criteria to tell Exchange Server what events you're interested in, what the ProgID or script location of the event handler is, and so on. Table 17-1 shows the criteria to register an event handler. All these properties are contained in the *http://schemas.microsoft.com/exchange/events/* namespace.

Table 17-1 Criteria Required by Exchange Server 2003 for Registering an Event Handler

Property	Required?
criteria	No
enabled	No
eventmethod	Yes
matchscope	No
priority	No
scripturl	Yes (for script event handlers only)
sinkclass	Yes

Table 17-1 Criteria Required by Exchange Server 2003 for Registering an Event Handler

Property	Required?
timerexpirytime	No (for timer events only)
timerinterval	Yes (for timer events only)
timerstarttime	Yes (for timer events only)

***criteria* property** The *criteria* property allows you to specify a SQL *WHERE* clause that will act as a filter for your event handler so that the handler is called only when items meet your criteria. This property allows you to avoid being called for items that you're not interested in. For example, the Training application uses the following criteria so that it doesn't get called when hidden items or folders are created:

```
WHERE "DAV:ishidden" = false AND "DAV:isfolder" = false
```

You can use *AND*, *OR*, *NOT*, or *EXISTS* as part of your *WHERE* clause. *CONTAINS* and *FREETEXT* are not supported, however. Also, if you plan to check custom schemas, you must explicitly cast your custom property to the right data type. For example, if you want to make sure that your event handler is called only in an application in which a property on items submitted is greater than 100, you set the *criteria* property for your event registration to the following value:

```
"WHERE CAST($"MySchema/MyNumber"$ AS 'i4') > 100"
```

Notice that the `$` character is used to avoid using double quotation marks.

> **Note** For the *OnDelete* asynchronous event, you cannot use the *criteria* property because *OnDelete* events are fired for all items.

***enabled* property** The *enabled* property is a *Boolean* property that allows you to specify whether your event handler is enabled. Rather than deleting an event registration, if you plan to reuse it in the future, you can set this property to *False*.

***eventmethod* property** The *eventmethod* property is a multi-value string that specifies the types of events you are interested in receiving, such as *OnSyncSave* and *OnDelete*. You can register for event methods of the same type within the same event registration. For example, one event registration can be used for *OnSyncSave*, *OnSyncDelete*, *OnSave*, or *OnDelete* but cannot include *OnTimer*. You must register *OnTimer* and the other system events separately. However, your event handler COM component can implement the interfaces for all the events.

***matchscope* property** The *matchscope* property allows you to specify the scope of the event. The value for this property can be *any*, *fldonly*, *deep*, *exact*, or *shallow*. You use only the value *any* with database-wide events. The scope of the *exact* value is a specific item. This is similar to *shallow*, which fires for items only in the exact folder you specify. The *fldonly* value will notify you only of changes to the folder itself, such as modifications to a property on the folder. The *deep* value notifies you of changes in the current folder as well as any items in subfolders. If you set the property to *deep*, even new subfolders and items created in them will trigger your event handler. However, keep in mind that system events do not support this property.

***priority* property** The *priority* property is an integer property that indicates the priority of your event handler compared with other event handlers. The number can range from *0* to *0xFFFFFFFF*. By default, your event handler is registered with a value of *0x0000FFFF (65,535)*. This property is valid only for synchronous events and tells the system the order in which you want these events to fire. If you give two synchronous events the same priority, it is undetermined which one will get called first. When you register your event handlers, you might want to check to see whether other event registrations exist in the folder. If they do, check their priority before registering your event handler.

***scripturl* property** When you write script for your event handler, the *scripturl* property holds the URL to the script file. Exchange Server supports the *file://* and *http://* URL formats in this property. The script file can reside in a folder in Exchange Server or in another location accessible via a URL, as long as the location is on the same machine as the Exchange server. Note that when you use script handlers, you must specify *ExOleDB.ScriptEventSink* for the *sinkclass* property in addition to filling out the *scripturl* property. Remember, though, that script event handlers should be your last resort.

***sinkclass* property** The *sinkclass* property holds the CLSID or the ProgID of your event handler. Exchange Server then instantiates the object when an event is triggered. By default, Exchange Server caches your object so it doesn't have to instantiate the object multiple times.

***timerstarttime* property** The *timerstarttime* property specifies the date and time to start notifying your event handler of *OnTimer* events. If you do not specify this property, Exchange Server will start notifying your handler immediately.

Note that this value can be affected by Exchange storing date and time values as Universal Time Coordinate (UTC) values. You should therefore set the UTC time, not the local time, when you want your timer event to start firing. For example, the Training application setup program must create the event registration for survey notifications. The survey notification event handler should be called at 10 P.M. local time every night. To create the correct *timerstarttime* property value, the setup program has to figure out what 10 P.M. local time is in UTC. Then it must register to be notified at the correct UTC time, which Exchange will convert to 10 P.M. local time for the server machine's time zone.

***timerexpirytime* property** The *timerexpirytime* property is an integer property that specifies the number of minutes after the *timerstarttime* property that the event handler should stop receiving *OnTimer* notifications. If you don't specify this property, your event handler will never stop receiving notifications. Obviously, this property is valid only for *OnTimer* event registrations.

***timerinterval* property** The *timerinterval* property is an integer property that specifies the number of minutes to wait to notify your event handler of another *OnTimer* event. If you do not set this property, Exchange Server will call your event handler only once after the creation of your registration item for the *OnTimer* event.

> **Note** Before you dive into creating the event registration item, note that events will not fire on a user's outbox or sent items folders. Even if you register global events or events directly on either of these folders, events will still not fire. If you want to put a footer on every mail message, which is the main reason people try to put an event on the Outbox, use a transport event handler instead. See Microsoft Knowledge Base article 297274 for more information on this limitation.

Creating an Event Registration Item

The easiest way to register your event handler with Exchange Server is to use ADO to create an event registration item in the Exchange Server database and set the properties we just discussed on that item. Be aware that when you create your event registration item, you should do it in the context of an OLE DB transaction. Why? Because Exchange Server uses an asynchronous event handler to listen for and track your requests for registering an event handler. The built-in Exchange Server event registration event handler looks for items with a special content class, *urn:content-class:storeeventreg*. The event handler then takes those items, scans the properties, and performs its magic, making the items valid event registrations. This magic includes turning the item into an invisible message item in the folder by making it part of the associated contents table. This table is the same place that views, forms, and rules are stored in.

If you don't use OLE DB transactions, you might trigger the built-in Exchange Server event handler when you first attempt to create your registration item using ADO and set the *DAV:contentclass* property to *urn:content-class:storeeventreg*. If this happens and you haven't yet set the properties for your registration item, the event handler will think that your event registration item is invalid. By using an OLE DB transaction and atomically creating and setting your properties at the same time, you avoid this problem.

The following code, taken from the setup program for the Training application, shows how easy it is to create an event registration item:

```
. . .

'Create the Survey Notification Event Registration
    'Timer event
    strNow = Now
    arrRequired = GenerateRequiredEventArray("", "ontimer", _
        "EventSink.SurveyNotify", "", "" )
    arrOptional = GenerateOptionalEventArray("", "", "", "", _
        1440, strNow, "")
    CreateEvtRegistration oConnection, strPath & _
        "Schedule/surveynotification", arrRequired, arrOptional, False

. . .

'Event Registration Helper Sub
Sub CreateEvtRegistration(cn, strEventRegPath, arrRequiredParameters, _
                          Optional arrOptionalParameters, Optional bWorkflow)
                          On Error GoTo errHandler

    'Create the event registration.
    'cn - Connection to Exchange Server database for transaction purposes
    'strEventRegPath - Full file path to the event item
    'arrRequiredParameters - Required parameters for all event registrations
    'arrOptionalParameters - Optional parameters such as criteria

    Const propcontentclass = "DAV:contentclass"
    Const propScope = "http://schemas.microsoft.com/exchange/events/Scope"
    Dim propname As String

    Dim rEvent As New ADODB.Record

    cn.BeginTrans
    rEvent.Open strEventRegPath, cn, 3, _
        adReadWrite + adCreateOverwrite + adCreateNonCollection
```

```
        'Set the properties in the item
        With rEvent.Fields
            .Item(propcontentclass) = "urn:content-class:storeeventreg"

            'Scroll through and commit required parameters.
            'Scroll through and commit optional parameters.
            If IsArray(arrRequiredParameters) Then
                For i = LBound(arrRequiredParameters, 1) To _
                                                 UBound(arrRequiredParameters, 1)
                    'Use Dimension 1 since the second dimension should
                    'always be the same
                    If Not (IsEmpty(arrRequiredParameters(i, 0))) Then
                        .Item(arrRequiredParameters(i, 0)) = _
                                                 arrRequiredParameters(i, 1)
                    End If
                Next
            End If

            If IsArray(arrOptionalParameters) Then
                For i = LBound(arrOptionalParameters, 1) To _
                                                 UBound(arrOptionalParameters, 1)
                     'Use Dimension 1 since the second dimension should always
                     'be the same
                    If Not (IsEmpty(arrOptionalParameters(i, 0))) Then
                        .Item(arrOptionalParameters(i, 0)) = _
                                                 arrOptionalParameters(i, 1)
                    End If
                Next
            End If

            'Add custom properties that the event sink can use to
            'determine the context of this event registration

            If bWorkflow = False Then
                strConfigurationFolderPath = strPath & "Configuration/"
                 'Hard-code this one property so that we can always find it!
                propname = "http://thomriz.com/schema/configurationfolderpath"
                 'For a case switch in the event sink
                .Append propname, adVariant, , , strConfigurationFolderPath
            End If

            .Update  'Get the ADO object current

        End With
        cn.CommitTrans

        Exit Sub

    errHandler:
        MsgBox "Error in CreateEvtRegistration.  Error " & Err.Number & " " _
              & Err.Description
        End
    End Sub
```

```
Function GenerateRequiredEventArray(strCriteria, strEventMethod, _
                                    strSinkClass, strScriptURL, strSinkList)

    Const propCriteria = _
        "http://schemas.microsoft.com/exchange/events/Criteria"
    Const propEventMethod = _
         "http://schemas.microsoft.com/exchange/events/EventMethod"
    Const propSinkClass = _
         "http://schemas.microsoft.com/exchange/events/SinkClass"

    Const propScriptURL = _
         "http://schemas.microsoft.com/exchange/events/ScriptUrl"
    Const propSinkList = _
         "http://schemas.microsoft.com/exchange/events/SinkList"

    'Generate the array by checking the passed arguments.
    'Note dynamic arrays only support redimensioning the last dimension.
    'This causes a problem, so dimension an array and fill in blanks if
    'necessary.
    'Flip-flop value - propname
    Dim arrRequired(4, 1)
    iArrayCount = 0
    If strCriteria <> "" Then
        arrRequired(iArrayCount, 0) = propCriteria
        arrRequired(iArrayCount, 1) = strCriteria
        iArrayCount = iArrayCount + 1
    End If
    If strEventMethod <> "" Then
        arrRequired(iArrayCount, 0) = propEventMethod
        arrRequired(iArrayCount, 1) = strEventMethod
        iArrayCount = iArrayCount + 1
    End If
    If strSinkClass <> "" Then
        arrRequired(iArrayCount, 0) = propSinkClass
        arrRequired(iArrayCount, 1) = strSinkClass
        iArrayCount = iArrayCount + 1
    End If
    If strScriptURL <> "" Then
        arrRequired(iArrayCount, 0) = propScriptURL
        arrRequired(iArrayCount, 1) = strScriptURL
        iArrayCount = iArrayCount + 1
    End If
    If strSinkList <> "" Then
        arrRequired(iArrayCount, 0) = propSinkList
        arrRequired(iArrayCount, 1) = strSinkList
        iArrayCount = iArrayCount + 1
    End If
    GenerateRequiredEventArray = arrRequired

End Function
```

```
Function GenerateOptionalEventArray(bEnabled, strMatchScope, lPriority, _
                                    bReplicateReg, iTimerInterval, _
                                    iTimerStart, iTimerStop)

    Const propEnabled = _
         "http://schemas.microsoft.com/exchange/events/Enabled"
    Const propMatchScope = _
         "http://schemas.microsoft.com/exchange/events/MatchScope"
    Const propPriority = _
        "http://schemas.microsoft.com/exchange/events/Priority"
    Const propReplicateEventReg = _
        "http://schemas.microsoft.com/exchange/events/ReplicateEventReg"
    Const propTimerInterval = _
        "http://schemas.microsoft.com/exchange/events/TimerInterval"
    Const propTimerStartTime = _
        "http://schemas.microsoft.com/exchange/events/TimerStartTime"
    Const propTimerExpiryTime = _
        "http://schemas.microsoft.com/exchange/events/TimerExpiryTime"

    Dim arrOptional(6, 1)
    iArrayCount = 0
    If bEnabled <> "" Then
        arrOptional(iArrayCount, 0) = propEnabled
        arrOptional(iArrayCount, 1) = bEnabled
        iArrayCount = iArrayCount + 1
    End If
    If strMatchScope <> "" Then
        arrOptional(iArrayCount, 0) = propMatchScope
        arrOptional(iArrayCount, 1) = strMatchScope
        iArrayCount = iArrayCount + 1
    End If
    If lPriority <> "" Then
        arrOptional(iArrayCount, 0) = propPriority
        arrOptional(iArrayCount, 1) = lPriority
        iArrayCount = iArrayCount + 1
    End If
    If bReplicateReg <> "" Then
        arrOptional(iArrayCount, 0) = propReplicateEventReg
        arrOptional(iArrayCount, 1) = bReplicateReg
        iArrayCount = iArrayCount + 1
    End If
    If iTimerInterval <> "" Then
        arrOptional(iArrayCount, 0) = propTimerInterval
        arrOptional(iArrayCount, 1) = iTimerInterval
        iArrayCount = iArrayCount + 1
    End If
    If iTimerStart <> "" Then
        arrOptional(iArrayCount, 0) = propTimerStartTime
        arrOptional(iArrayCount, 1) = iTimerStart
        iArrayCount = iArrayCount + 1
    End If
    If iTimerStop <> "" Then
        arrOptional(iArrayCount, 0) = propTimerStopTime
```

```
        arrOptional(iArrayCount, 1) = iTimerStop
        iArrayCount = iArrayCount + 1
    End If

    GenerateOptionalEventArray = arrOptional

End Function
```

As you can see in the code, ADO is used to create an event registration item. The *Fields* collection is used to fill in the properties needed to make the item a valid event registration, and the item is saved to Exchange Server. Although this application uses events in public folders, you can register and fire events from private folders as well. You need the proper security for your event handler to access the user's information and manipulate that information (if necessary).

You can also use WebDAV to create event registration items. To download a sample that does this, see Microsoft Knowledge Base article 306046.

> **Note** Terminal Server does not work with event registrations. This means you cannot use Terminal Server to remotely connect to your Exchange Server and register an event. Instead, you should either run your registration script directly on the server, use Exchange Explorer (which is part of the Exchange SDK) to register your event handler, or use WebDAV to remotely create an event registration.

Registering a Database-Wide Event

In addition to scoping your event handlers to just one folder, you can scope them to the entire store or messaging database (MDB). However, you cannot scope your event handler to the entire server (all MDBs at once). All types of event registrations are per individual MDB only. To create an MDB-wide event registration, you must change the value for the *matchscope* property and the location in which you put your registration item. Note that only synchronous events such as *OnSyncSave* and *OnSyncDelete* are supported in global events. If you attempt to register asynchronous events as global, the registration will fail. Also, note that global events will not fire on the sent items or outbox folders in user's mailboxes, so unfortunately you can't process outgoing messages in this way.

You should specify *any* as the value of the *matchscope* property to indicate that any scope is valid for notifying your event handler. All other properties can stay the same, based on the type of event you're registering for.

As just mentioned, the location in which you put the registration item will change. Instead of throwing the item into the folder where you want the scope of the event notifications to begin, you must place the registration item in the GlobalEvents folder. This folder is located in Public Folders in the non-IPM subtree in a folder called StoreEvents{*<MDBGUID>*}, where *<MDBGUID>* is the unique identifier for the MDB. The easiest way to retrieve the Globally Unique Identifier (GUID) of the MDB is to use the *StoreGUIDFromURL* method in EXOLEDB. The following code shows how to use this method:

```
set oStoreGUID=CreateObject("Exoledb.StoreGuidFromUrl")
'Get the GUID
strguid = oStoreGUID.StoreGuidFromUrl("<Path to GlobalEvents folder>")
```

A valid path to save your registration item to would look something like this:

```
file://./backofficestorage/ADMIN/domain/public folders/non_ipm_subtree/
StoreEvents{915c615a-6353-4d1d-9ff2-8bd0e3f54bcd}/GlobalEvents/

File://./backofficestorage/ADMIN/domain/MBX
/SystemMailbox{19bb5c7c-3904-4581-9e3c-32e3945881de}/StoreEvents/GlobalEvents
```

Only the Administrator account, which is a member of the Domain Administrators group, or users in the Exchange Administrators role in Active Directory can register global events. It is not enough to be a member of the Administrators group or the Exchange Servers group (due to heightened security around global events and the impact they can have on system performance). Use global events sparingly because every action in the Exchange database where a global event is registered will fire an event and call your handler.

> **Note** For more information on database-wide events, see Microsoft Knowledge Base article 306989.

Using the *ICreateRegistration* Interface

If you're writing event handlers that you think other developers will register for, or if you want to protect your application event handlers, you can implement the *ICreateRegistration* interface. For example, if you write your event handler and save it on a server and you think other users will try to create event registrations in their own applications that will use your event handler object, you should consider using the *ICreateRegistration* interface. This interface is called whenever a user tries to register for your event handler. *ICreateRegistration* passes you the event registration information, including the registration item for the particular user. You can grab information from this item, or you can retrieve from the item information about the user who's trying to register for your event handler. You can then decide whether to permit or reject the user's registration.

To implement this interface, you must add an *Implements ICreateRegistration* line to your Visual Basic code and put your validation code in the *ICreateRegistration_Register* function.

Writing an Event Handler

The code samples containing event handlers that you'll see in this section are taken from the Training application. All these event handlers are written in Visual Basic. When you write Visual Basic event handlers, you first should create an ActiveX DLL. In addition, be sure to add references to the various object libraries your application might need to access. You will definitely need a reference to the EXOLEDB type library; libraries such as ADO 2.5 and later and Microsoft Collaboration Data Objects (CDO) for Exchange Server also might come in handy.

Once you add the references, you must use the *Implements* keyword. Depending on the type of event handler you plan to write, you'll need to implement the *IExStoreSyncEvents*, *IExStoreAsyncEvents*, or *IExStoreSystemEvents* interface. You can implement all three in a single DLL if you want.

Next you must implement the subroutines for the events you're interested in. The following code, taken from the course notification event handler, shows the *OnSave* and *OnTimer* events being implemented. I won't list all the code for the implementation of these two events because I mainly want to show you the parameters that are passed your functions.

```
Implements IExStoreAsyncEvents
Implements IExStoreSystemEvents
Const strHTMLMsgSubject = "New Course Email"

Dim oEventRegistration         'Global that holds the event
                               'registration record
Dim bShowPreviousDay           'Global that holds whether to show
                               'new courses only
                               'From previous day, just in case timer
                               'event runs after midnight
Dim oRecord As ADODB.Record    'Global record to hold item that
                               'triggered event
Dim strHTMLBody                'Global string that holds HTML message body

'Add Discussion group, file, and http link notification as part of
'the message.
'Update HTML message to incorporate file and http link, as well as
'discussion group.
```

```
Private Sub IExStoreAsyncEvents_OnDelete(ByVal pEventInfo As _
                                         Exoledb.IExStoreEventInfo, _
                                         ByVal bstrURLItem As String, _
                                         ByVal lFlags As Long)
    'Not implemented
End Sub

Private Sub IExStoreAsyncEvents_OnSave(ByVal pEventInfo As _
                                       Exoledb.IExStoreEventInfo, _
                                       ByVal bstrURLItem As String, _
                                       ByVal lFlags As Long)
    If (lFlags And EVT_NEW_ITEM) > 0 Then
        'New item put in.
        'Get the ADO Record object for the item.
        'Set oRecord = dispInfo.EventRecord
        Set oRecord = CreateObject("ADODB.Record")
        oRecord.Open bstrURLItem
        'Check to see whether the item happened very recently.
        'If it did, just exit since the training event is
        'probably having its survey information updated by
        'a user. Don't notify people of old training events.
        If DateDiff("d", Now, _
                oRecord.Fields("urn:schemas:calendar:dtstart").Value) > 0 Then
            'It's OK; event happens in future.
            'Load the global settings.
            LoadAppSettings oRecord, pEventInfo
            If bEventLogging Then
                App.LogEvent "Event Notification OnSave event called for " _
                             & "training event.  Path: " & bstrURLItem
            End If
            strCategory = GetCourseCategory(oRecord)
            QueryPreferences strCategory
        End If
    End If
End Sub

Private Sub IExStoreSystemEvents_OnMDBShutDown(ByVal bstrMDBGuid As String, _
                                               ByVal lFlags As Long)
    'Not implemented
End Sub

Private Sub IExStoreSystemEvents_OnMDBStartUp(ByVal bstrMDBGuid As String, _
                                              ByVal bstrMDBName As String, _
                                              ByVal lFlags As Long)
    'Not implemented
End Sub

Private Sub IExStoreSystemEvents_OnTimer(ByVal bstrURLItem As String, _
                                         ByVal lFlags As Long)
    On Error Resume Next

    Dim rec As ADODB.Record
    Dim rst As ADODB.RecordSet
    Dim conn As ADODB.Connection
```

```
Set oBindingRecord = Nothing
'Get the registration
Set oBindingRecord = CreateObject("ADODB.Record")
oBindingRecord.Open bstrURLItem

On Error GoTo 0
If Err.Number = 0 Then
    'Could retrieve the item
    LoadAppSettings oBindingRecord

    If bEventLogging Then
        App.LogEvent "Event Notification: OnTimer event called at " & Now
    End If
    'Get the folder in which the timer is running.
    'This is never used since we know the folder already.
    'However, this shows you how to retrieve the folder if you need to.
    strFolder = oBindingRecord.Fields.Item("DAV:parentname")
    'Figure out all the courses created in the current 24 hours or
    'previous 24 hours
    curDate = Date
    If bShowPreviousDay Then
        'Subtract a day
        curDate = DateAdd("d", -1, curDate)
    End If
    dISODateStart = TurnintoISO(curDate, "Start")
    dISODateEnd = TurnintoISO(curDate, "End")

    strSQL = "Select ""urn:schemas:mailheader:subject"", " _
           & """DAV:href"",""urn:schemas:calendar:dtstart"", " _
           & """urn:schemas:calendar:dtend"" FROM scope('shallow " _
           & "traversal of """ & strScheduleFolderPath _
           & """') WHERE (""DAV:iscollection"" = false) AND " _
           & "(""DAV:ishidden"" = false) " _
           & "AND (""urn:schemas:calendar:dtstart"" >= CAST(""" _
           & dISODateStart & """ as 'dateTime'))" _
           & "AND (""urn:schemas:calendar:dtstart"" <= CAST(""" _
           & dISODateEnd & """ as 'dateTime'))"

    Set conn = CreateObject("ADODB.Connection")
    Set rst = CreateObject("ADODB.RecordSet")
    Set oRecord = CreateObject("ADODB.Record")

    With conn
        .Provider = "EXOLEDB.Datasource"
        .Open strScheduleFolderPath
    End With

    'Create a new RecordSet object

    With rst
        'Open RecordSet based on the SQL string
        .Open strSQL, conn, adOpenKeyset
    End With
```

```
        Dim iAppt As CDO.Appointment

        If Not (rst.BOF And rst.EOF) Then
            Set iAppt = CreateObject("CDO.Appointment")
            'On Error Resume Next
            rst.MoveFirst
            Do Until rst.EOF
                'Set oRecord to the current item in the RecordSet
                On Error Resume Next
                oRecord.Close
                Err.Clear
                On Error GoTo 0
                oRecord.Open rst.Fields("DAV:href").Value, conn
                strCategory = GetCourseCategory(oRecord)
                QueryPreferences strCategory

                rst.MoveNext
            Loop
            rst.Close

            Set iAppt = Nothing
            Set rst = Nothing
            Set rec = Nothing
            Set conn = Nothing
        Else
            If bEventLogging Then
                App.LogEvent "Event Notification: No students need to be " _
                          & "notified of training event."
            End If
        End If
    End If
End Sub
```

As you can see in the code, your application is passed different parameters for the different events. However, all events have some common parameters. For example, you are always passed a URL to the item that triggered the event. For system events such as *OnTimer*, this is the event registration item itself. If you need to, you can add custom properties to the event registration item so that when your *OnTimer* event handler is called, you can retrieve that custom property.

I use this trick in the Training application. When I register the *OnTimer* event handler for the application's workflow process, I add a custom property that is the full URL to the application's configuration folder. Because you can customize where the application is installed, you must tell the workflow process where to look for the customization information that you select during setup. Because I've added an extra property, I can grab it in my workflow code, get the configuration message contained in the folder the property specifies, and determine the value for the customized fields in the application, such as which e-mail address to send notification messages from. We discussed custom properties in Chapter 15.

For nontimer events, the URL you receive is the path to the item that's triggering the event. You can then retrieve the item and look at its properties.

An event handler also receives a parameter called *lFlags*. This parameter corresponds to flags that tell you exactly what's happening to the item. For example, one of the flags, *EVT_NEW_ITEM*, tells you that the item triggering the event is a new item rather than an item that already existed in the folder and had some properties changed. You should use a bitwise *AND* with the *lFlags* parameter and one of the identifiers from Table 17-2 to determine the values of flags in the *lFlags* parameter. The flag names are included in the EXOLEDB type library, so you will want to add a reference to this library and use the friendly names of the flags from this library.

> **Note** Not all flags are supported by all events. For example, the delete flags are supported only by the delete events.

When you use server events in addition to the flags and the URL, you receive a *pEventInfo* variable of type *Exoledb.IExStoreEventInfo*. You should set this variable to another variable of type *Exoledb.IExStoreDispEventInfo*, which is the *IDispatch* version of the interface. From this interface, you can control the transaction state for the event handler for synchronous events and get more information about the context of the event. Table 17-3 lists the elements you retrieve and call on the *IExStoreDispEventInfo* interface. Also check out the Exchange SDK for more information on these parameters.

Table 17-2 Flag Values for the *lFlags* Parameter

Flag	Description
EVT_NEW_ITEM	The item being saved is new rather than an existing, modified item.
EVT_IS_COLLECTION	The item being saved is a collection (folder).
EVT_REPLICATED_ITEM	The item being saved is the result of a replication event, which occurs when the item is replicated using Exchange Server replication.
EVT_IS_DELIVERED	The item being saved is the result of a message delivery.

Table 17-2 Flag Values for the *lFlags* Parameter

Flag	Description
EVT_SOFTDELETE	A soft delete has occurred. (The item has been moved to the dumpster.)
EVT_HARDDELETE	A hard delete has occurred. (The item has been removed from the store.)
EVT_INITNEW	This is the first time the event handler has been called, so you can perform any necessary initialization procedures. Your event handler is passed this flag only once during its lifetime.
EVT_MOVE	The event is the result of a move operation.
EVT_COPY	The event is the result of a copy operation.
EVT_SYNC_BEGIN	The event handler is being called in the begin phase of a synchronous event. This is the point at which you can abort the item being saved into the database. Also, the URL you receive for the item is invalid at this point because the item is not yet in the database.
EVT_SYNC_COMMITTED	The event handler is being called in the commit phase of a synchronous event, after the transaction has been committed to the database.
EVT_SYNC_ABORTED	A synchronous event has been aborted.
EVT_INVALID_URL	The URL passed to the event handler is invalid.
EVT_INVALID_SOURCE_URL	The source URL could not be obtained during a move operation.
EVT_ERROR	Some error occurred in the event.

Table 17-3 Elements of the *IExStoreDispEventInfo* Interface

Element	Description
AbortChange	Aborts the transaction in which the event is currently executing. Exchange Server will not commit the item to its database. You pass a long value, which specifies the error code you want returned.
EventBinding	Returns as an object the registration item for the event handler. You can use the returned object to retrieve the custom properties that you set on the event registration item.
EventConnection	Specifies the ADO *Connection* object under which the event is executing.
EventRecord	Specifies the ADO *Record* object bound to the item that triggered the event.
SourceURL	Specifies the original source URL in an *OnSyncSave* event. This property is valid only for a move operation.

Table 17-3 Elements of the *IExStoreDispEventInfo* Interface

Element	Description
StoreGUID	Specifies the GUID for the MDB where the item that triggered the event is located.
UserGUID	Specifies the GUID for the user that triggered the event. You can use this in conjunction with the Win32 APIs to look up the user's name.
UserSID	Specifies the Security Identifier (SID) of the user who triggered the event.
Data	This property allows you to save in-memory data between the begin and commit or abort phase of a synchronous event. This property is useful for passing to your event sink the variables between the different calls in a transaction; you don't have to save those variables to Exchange or to disk.

Creating COM+ Applications

If you plan to write your event handlers in Visual Basic, you should definitely install your DLLs as COM+ applications. There are a number of reasons for doing this. First, Exchange Server won't let you try to run an event handler for synchronous events that are not COM+ enabled. Second, if your event handler has problems, wrapping it into a COM+ application isolates it and allows you to shut it down without affecting other parts of the system. Finally, by making your DLLs COM+ applications, you can take advantage of COM+ roles and security.

This last point is key—it allows you to retrieve the SID of the user who is triggering the event. Using the COM+ Services Type Library and the SID, you can employ COM+ roles-based security. For example, you can use the *IsSecurityEnabled* function to check whether COM+ security is enabled. You can also use the *IsUserInRole* function to see whether the user is in a particular role. For more information on COM+ security issues, refer to the Platform SDK on the Microsoft Developer Network (MSDN) at *http://msdn.microsoft.com*.

The Training application places its event handlers into a COM+ application. The application's setup program deploys the COM+ application with the built-in COM+ deployment tools. When you export your COM+ application from the COM+ user interface, as shown in Figure 17-1, COM+ creates a Windows Installer file. You can then run this file if you want to install the COM+ application on your computer.

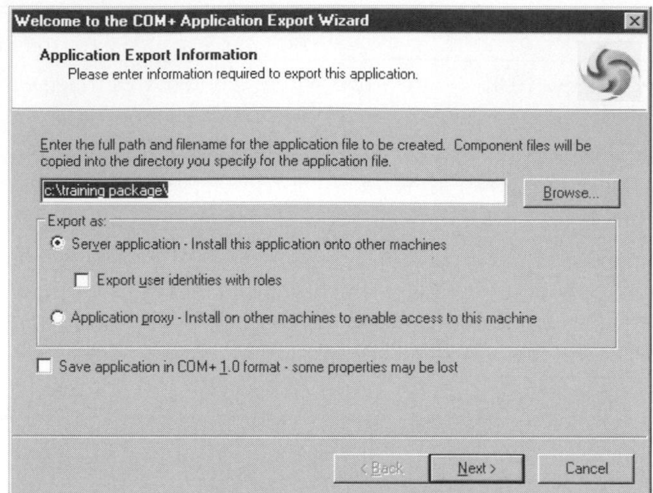

Figure 17-1 Exporting the COM+ application for the Training sample

Advanced Information for Your Event Handlers

In your event handlers, you might want to work with some advanced information, such as security information, provided by the *EventInfo* structure, such as *UserGUID* and *UserSID*. To do so, you must know some special information about Active Directory and ways to work with GUID structures in Visual Basic. The value of working with these properties is that in your event handlers, you can look up the user who is firing the event in Active Directory to pull out their username or e-mail address. You can also obtain group membership information. Groups are especially useful if you want to allow only certain users to perform certain actions in your application. Please note that some properties, such as *UserGUID* and *UserSID*, are available only from synchronous events.

When you work with the *UserGUID* and *UserSID* properties, the first thing to know is that these properties are provided only with synchronous events, not asynchronous events. What is actually returned to you with the *UserGUID* property is a string containing a GUID:

```
{F4CFFA65-82C2-46C4-994D-B6FAF28B10D3}
```

This is a 32-character (not including the dashes or brackets) string of hex numbers. You might think that all you need to do to find the user who owns this GUID in Active Directory is remove the extra characters (such as dashes and brackets) and then just run a query against Active Directory. Unfortunately, this is not the case. You might also assume that the *objectGUID* property in Active Directory is the property that maps to the *UserGUID* property that is passed to you. Again, this is not true. The steps you need to go through to find the user might seem complex at first, but after you implement them once, you'll find that they are easy to carry out. Plus, you can reuse this code after the first implementation.

The first step in the process is to realize that the value for *UserGUID* actually maps to the *msExchMailboxGuid* attribute in Active Directory, not the *objectGUID* attribute. Figure 17-2 shows what Active Directory contains for a sample *msExchMailboxGuid* using the Active Directory Services Interface (ADSI) Edit tool, which we discussed in Chapter 13 and which is available on the Windows Server CD as part of the support tools.

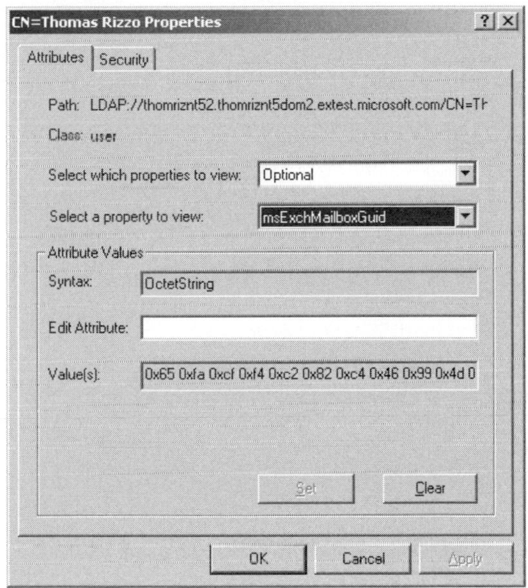

Figure 17-2 ADSI Edit showing the value for a sample *msExchMailboxGuid*

The numbers in the figure are shown here with the *0x* removed from each number:

```
65FACFF4C282C446994DB6FAF28B10D3
```

You might wonder how the first number we saw earlier relates to this number. If you were to take the first number that the event handler passes to you and try to query Active Directory using this number against *msExchMailboxGuid*, you would get no results from the query because the two numbers are ordered completely differently. If you look closely at the two numbers, they are the same characters, but in a different order.

Changing the order of the *UserGUID* property is, as you can guess, the second step. You strip all the brackets and dashes from the string, and then you walk eight characters into the string because the first eight characters must be reversed in two-character pairs. For the example we're using, *F4CFFA65* must become *65FACFF4*, which is the first eight characters of the property from the Active Directory value. Then the same process must be done for the next four characters and the next four characters after that. The key thing is that you cannot flip all eight characters at once because you need to keep the ordering of the characters intact to match the GUID in Active Directory. For example, *82C246C4* needs to become *C282C446*. Finally, you need to append the remaining 16 characters in their existing order.

This is a pretty easy process, but if you did not know that you need to do this to get the right string format for your GUID, you'd get very frustrated trying to figure out how to work with the *UserGUID* property to find out which user triggered your event. To help you with this, I've taken all these steps and created some simple Visual Basic functions that do this work for you. All you do is pass the *UserGUID* value to this function, and it will pull out the dashes and brackets from this value, perform the steps we just discussed, and return the correctly formatted GUID string for you to use to query against Active Directory:

```
Function ReverseGUID(strGUID)
    strnewGUID = strGUID
    'Take away the { and - from the GUID
    strnewGUID = Replace(strnewGUID, "{", "")
    strnewGUID = Replace(strnewGUID, "-", "")
    strnewGUID = Replace(strnewGUID, "}", "")

    'Count in 8 characters to the middle of the 32 character string
    strTempGUID = Left(strnewGUID, 8)

    'Begin to flip around the GUID by pulling out
    '2 character pairs in reverse order
    strFirstEightGUID = ""
    strFirstEightGUID = GetGUIDinReverseOrder(strTempGUID)

    'Count in character from character 9 another 4
    strTempGUID = Mid(strnewGUID, 9, 4)

    'Flip around this
    strMiddleFourGUID = ""
    strMiddleFourGUID = GetGUIDinReverseOrder(strTempGUID)
```

```
    'Get the last four and flip them
    strTempGUID = Mid(strnewGUID, 13, 4)
    strLastFourGUID = ""
    strLastFourGUID = GetGUIDinReverseOrder(strTempGUID)

    'Get the last 16 characters in the GUID
    strOriginalSixteenGUID = Mid(strnewGUID, 17, 16)

    'Combine to create the new GUID
    strnewGUID = strFirstEightGUID & strMiddleFourGUID _
               & strLastFourGUID & strOriginalSixteenGUID

    'Return back the value
    ReverseGUID = strnewGUID
End Function

Function GetGUIDinReverseOrder(strTempGUID)
    strTmp = ""
    'Take the GUID and start parsing from the back
    'to the front in 2 character pairs
    For i = (Len(strTempGUID) - 1) To 1 Step -2
        strTmp = strTmp & Mid(strTempGUID, i, 2)
    Next
    GetGUIDinReverseOrder = strTmp
End Function
```

Now that we have the correctly formatted GUID, we need to query Active Directory. In Chapter 13, you learned how to use ADO with the *ADsDSOObject* provider. We'll use this same provider to perform our GUID search against Active Directory. Another interesting twist here is that when you work with GUIDs and Active Directory, to query for a GUID by passing a string, you must prepend a slash (\) before every two-character pair in your string that represents the GUID. So, for our example, our string *65FACFF4C282C446994DB6FAF28B10D3* needs to become *\65\FA\CF\F4\C2\82\C4\46\99\4D\B6\FA\F2\8B\10\D3*. Again, I have a Visual Basic function for you that makes this easy. The following code adds the slashes to our GUID string and then queries Active Directory using ADSI to find the user whose *msExchMailboxGuid* matches the string we're passing in:

```
Function FindByGUID(strGUID, domain)
    'Find the user's object
    Dim usr
    Set con = CreateObject("ADODB.Connection")
    con.provider = "ADsDSOObject"
    con.Open "ADs Provider"
    'Take the strGUID and every 2 spaces add a \
    strGUID = AddSlashes(strGUID)
    strSQL = "<LDAP://" & domain _
           & ">;(&(objectClass=user)(msExchMailboxGuid=" _
           & strGUID & "));cn,adspath,userPrincipalName;subtree"
    Set rs = con.Execute(strSQL)
```

```
    If rs.RecordCount > 1 Or rs.RecordCount = 0 Then
        'Return back nothing
        Set FindByGUID = Nothing
        Exit Function
    End If
    Do While Not rs.EOF
        Set usr = GetObject(rs.Fields("AdsPath").Value)
        rs.MoveNext
    Loop
    Set FindByGUID = usr
End Function

Function AddSlashes(strGUID)
    'GUID should be 32 characters
    iNumofSlashes = (Len(strGUID) \ 2)
    'Add the slashes
    For i = 1 To (Len(strGUID) + iNumofSlashes) Step 3
        strGUID = Left(strGUID, i - 1) & "\" & Mid(strGUID, i)
    Next
    AddSlashes = strGUID
End Function
```

The function *FindByGUID* takes the string GUID and the fully qualified domain name that you want to search. If it successfully finds one user that matches that GUID, it will return the corresponding *IADs* object that corresponds to the type of object the query matches. For users, this object will be the *IADsUser* object. From the *IADsUser* object, you can use the *cn* or *mail* property to return the username or e-mail address of the user causing the event. If you are interested in checking group membership information, use the *IADsUser* object's *Groups* method to obtain a collection of ADSI group objects to which this user belongs.

Besides using the GUID to identify the user in Active Directory, you can also use the SID passed to you in the *UserSID* property. The *UserSID* property has its own set of quirks when you work from Visual Basic, just as the *UserGUID* property does. The *UserSID* property that is passed to your event handler is a variant array of bytes. This array of bytes is a set of decimal numbers that make up the user's SID. If you use ADSI Edit and look at the *objectSID* property that the *UserSID* corresponds to, you will see the following value with the extra characters removed:

```
010500000000000515000000be043e32e7cbdd7da837d66558040000
```

If you take the array values for the *UserSID* property and just combine the values together, you will get the following string:

```
1500000521000190462502312032211251685521410188400
```

As you can see, our version of the SID is very different from and shorter than the version in Active Directory. What we actually need to do is take the values in the array returned by Exchange, pad values that are less than 16 (or hex 10) with a leading zero, and then convert the value into hex. Then the SID we create will exactly match the SID in Active Directory. The following function performs these steps:

```
Function GetSID(arrSID)
    'The SID is provided as an array of values, put into a useful
    'version for ADSI
    strSID = ""
    For i = LBound(arrSID) To UBound(arrSID)
        If arrSID(i) < 16 Then
            'Need to pad a 0 in front of the hex #
            strPAD = "0"
        Else
            strPAD = ""
        End If
        strSID = strSID & strPAD & CStr(Hex(arrSID(i)))
    Next
    GetSID = strSID
End Function
```

The next step before we can query Active Directory is to add a slash before every two characters in the string so our query will work. We can use the same *AddSlashes* function that you saw earlier with *UserGUID*. Then we can query Active Directory. The following function queries Active Directory using the SID value we created against the *objectSID* value in Active Directory. It returns an *ADSI* object that corresponds to the Active Directory user object found.

```
Function FindBySID(strSID, domain)
    'Find the user's object
    Dim usr
    Set con = CreateObject("ADODB.Connection")
    con.provider = "ADsDSOObject"
    con.Open "ADs Provider"
    strSQL = "<LDAP://" & domain & ">;(&(objectClass=user)(objectSid=" _
           & strSID & "));cn,adspath,userPrincipalName;subtree"
    Set rs = con.Execute(strSQL)
    If rs.RecordCount > 1 Or rs.RecordCount = 0 Then
        'Return back nothing
        Set FindBySID = Nothing
        Exit Function
    End If
    Do While Not rs.EOF
        Set usr = GetObject(rs.Fields("AdsPath").Value)
        rs.MoveNext
    Loop
    Set FindBySID = usr
End Function
```

Another way you can quickly look up the user information from the SID is by using the Win32 API function *LookupAccountSID*. This function takes the name of the server you want to use to look up the SID, the SID itself, a variable that the function can pass the username into, the size of the variable for the username, a variable that the function can pass the domain name into, the size of the domain name, and finally a variable that the function uses to pass back a value for the *SID_NAME_USE* enumeration type that identifies the SID type (such as user, group, or computer). With this technique, you do not have to modify the SID returned by Exchange. Instead, you just pass the *UserSID* information to the function:

```
Private Declare Function LookupAccountSid Lib "advapi32.dll" Alias _
    "LookupAccountSidA" (ByVal lpSystemName As String, _
                         Sid As Any, _
                         ByVal name As String, _
                         cbName As Long, _
                         ByVal ReferencedDomainName As String, _
                         cbReferencedDomainName As Long, _
                         peUse As Integer _
                         ) As Long
'
' Lookup a SID and return the account name as a string
'
Private Function LookupNameOfSid(ByVal Sid As Variant) As String
    On Error Resume Next

    Dim Sidbytes() As Byte ' The byte array in the variant as
                           ' returned by DispEvtInfo.UserSid
    Sidbytes = Sid ' get the byte array from the Sid Variant
                   ' which is an array of bytes (vartype 8209)

    Dim result As Long
    Dim userName As String
    Dim cbUserName As Long
    Dim domainName As String
    Dim cbDomainName As Long
    Dim peUse As Integer

    ' Pass in the SID to get the user name and domain
    userName = Space(255)
    domainName = Space(255)
    cbUserName = 255
    cbDomainName = 255
    result = LookupAccountSid(vbNullString, Sidbytes(0), userName, _
                              cbUserName, domainName, cbDomainName, peUse)

    If result Then 'Strip the Null characters from the returned strings
        domainName = Left(domainName, InStr(domainName, Chr(0)) - 1)
        userName = Left(userName, InStr(userName, Chr(0)) - 1)
        LookupNameOfSid = domainName & "\" & userName
```

```
    Else
        LookupNameOfSid = "Error calling LookupAccountSID: " & result
    End If


End Function
```

One more GUID value that you need to be aware of is the *StoreGUID* value (in synchronous events), which is the same as the *bstrMDBGUID* variable passed to *OnMDBStartup* and *OnMDBShutdown* events. The *StoreGUID* property is not available to asynchronous events. If you look at the *StoreGUID* property that is given to you, it will look conspicuously like the *UserGUID* property in format. This means that the steps we used to transform the *UserGUID* value into a valid string value for Active Directory are exactly the same steps you use to transform the *StoreGUID* property.

The only difference is that we do not need to put a slash before every two characters because we're not going to query Active Directory for the object that corresponds to the database that the event is firing in—the GUID value we finally get can be used with ADSI directly to open the object using the *GC://<GUID=guidvalue>* format. You cannot use this technique with *UserGUID* because, as you saw earlier, *UserGUID* does not map to *objectGUID* but to *msExchMailboxGuid*. I won't repeat the code for the GUID formatting process here; however, the following code shows how to take the GUID you get back from those functions and open the Active Directory object:

```
Function OpenADObject(strGUID)
    On Error Resume Next

    'Use GUID binding of AD to open the AD object for the folder
    strGUID = LCase(strGUID)
    guidADsPath = "GC://<GUID=" & strGUID & ">"
    Set oDS = GetObject(guidADsPath)
    If Err.Number <> 0 Then
        'Return back nothing
        Set OpenADObject = Nothing
    Else
        Set OpenADObject = oDS
    End If
End Function
```

You might want to use this functionality to detect the database where the event is taking place. For the database shutdown and startup events, you might want to get the Active Directory object to query for certain properties of the database, such as the name, location of database files, or any other property stored in Active Directory for the database.

Debugging an Event Handler

When you set up the Training application, it asks whether you want to enable event handler debugging. Debugging your event handler is easy if you use COM+ applications. All you need to do to debug your event handler is set the identity of your COM+ application so that it uses the built-in interactive user option in COM+, add some breakpoints to your Visual Basic event handler, and then put the Visual Basic event handler in run mode by pressing F5 in Visual Basic. You can then take advantage of all the great Visual Basic debugging features. Figure 17-3 shows an example of an event handler in the Visual Basic debugger.

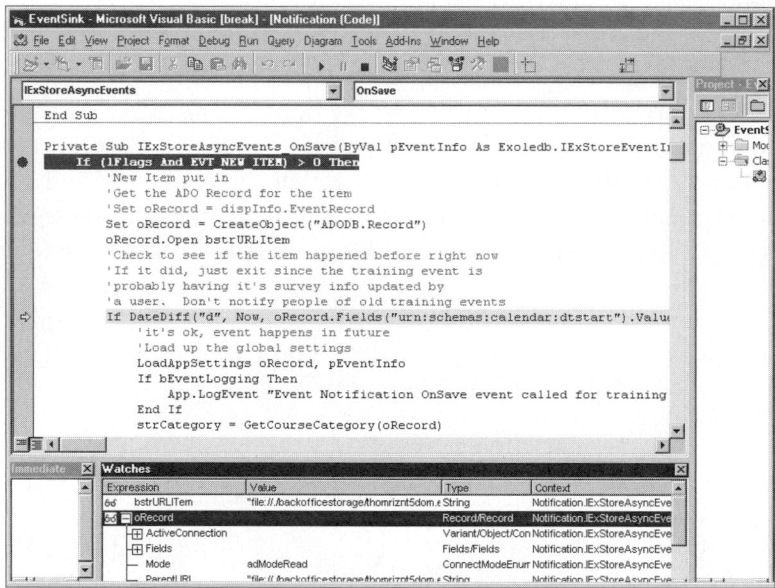

Figure 17-3 One of the Training application event handlers in the Visual Basic debugger

In addition to using the debugger, you can use the Visual Basic *LogEvent* method on the *App* object. Using this method, you can have Visual Basic place entries into the Windows event log. This is the sort of debugging that the Training application uses. Figure 17-4 shows an entry from the event log for one of the Training application's event handlers.

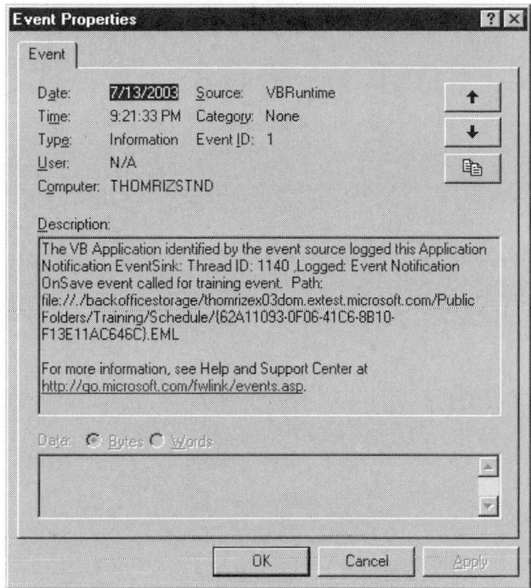

Figure 17-4 A message posted by Visual Basic into an event handler's log

Building Event Handlers in Visual Studio .NET

To write event handlers in .NET, you have to build a .NET component that is callable from COM. This is a bit harder than using COM from .NET because you have to do some special work to make sure your .NET component is exposed correctly to COM and you also need to set up your Visual Studio .NET project to enable COM interoperability.

Many of the programming interfaces today are built on COM, so COM interoperability is an important topic. You need this capability to build event handlers, COM add-ins, and smart tags. However, once you learn how to build one of these types of applications, building the other types is easy because they all require the same initial steps to set up COM interoperability.

To show you how to build a .NET COM–compatible component, we'll build an event handler in .NET for Exchange or SharePoint Portal Server (SPS) 2001. The great thing about using .NET to build your components is that you get all the advanced features of .NET, such as Visual Basic .NET, C#, the .NET Framework, and the common language runtime (CLR).

The first thing you do when you build any .NET project that will correspond to a COM DLL is to use the class library project. The choice of programming language is up to you. For this example, I'll use Visual Basic .NET. We'll look at a C# example later in this chapter.

Next you add a reference to whatever COM libraries you need to work with in your application. For an event handler, we need to add a reference to EXOLEDB and implement the interfaces for asynchronous or synchronous events contained there. As you learned in Chapter 15, when you add the reference, Visual Studio .NET imports that library and creates a .NET-compatible assembly for interoperability. Figure 17-5 shows adding a reference to the EXOLEDB type library.

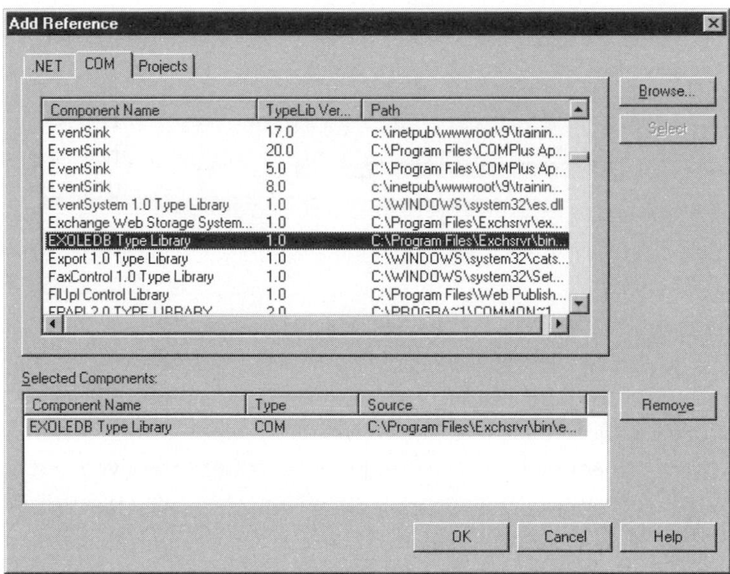

Figure 17-5 Adding a reference to the EXOLEDB type library

Next we can start coding our application. We'll be working with interfaces from EXOLEDB, so we'll want to use the import mechanism to make it easy to reference those in our application. This step is not necessary, but it will simplify our variable and type declarations. We also want to import the *System.Runtime.InteropServices* namespace because it includes useful classes for interacting with COM. The import statements are shown here:

```
Imports Exoledb
Imports System.Runtime.InteropServices
```

Next we need to declare our class. When Visual Basic .NET created our project, it created a default class for us called *Class1*. We can change the name of this class to whatever name we want. For this example, we'll change the class name to *ExchangeEventSink*. Next we need to tell the class that it implements whatever event interfaces we will listen for. In this case, we'll implement asynchronous events, so we will add the following line of code:

```
Implements Exoledb.IExStoreAsyncEvents
```

The next step is to make sure that our .NET component can interoperate with COM. To do this, we need to add some attributes to the class that the COM interop services will use. The three main attributes we need to add are *ProgID*, *GuidAttribute*, and *COMVisible*. The *ProgID* attribute lets you specify the COM ProgID that your .NET component will use.

GuidAttribute lets you specify the GUID to be used for your class ID. The easiest way to generate this GUID is to use the Create GUID command from the Tools menu. You should select the fourth option, which is to create the GUID in the Registry Format (which is {xxxxxxxxx-xx … xxx}). Click the Copy button, and then click the Exit button. When you paste the GUID, remove the curly braces. Neither this attribute nor the *ProgID* attribute are required for COM interoperability, but they make it easier for you to control the ProgID and GUID used for your component.

The final attribute, *COMIsVisible*, allows you to either make all your public classes visible to COM (by putting this attribute in your AssemblyInfo.vb file) or make individual classes visible. We'll need only this individual class to be visible, so we will use this attribute only with our one class.

Finally, because COM will call our class, we need to create a default constructor for the class that takes no arguments.

If you need to do some work when COM creates your object, you can modify the default constructor for your class. We're not doing any work on the construction, so we'll just leave the default constructor.

When you add all these attributes and the default constructor, your code should look something like this:

```
<ProgId("DotNetES.EventSink"), _
    Guid("7E303074-88B9-4be8-8C16-AC0CD8195CA4"), _
    ComVisible(True)> _
Public Class ExchangeEventSink
    Implements Exoledb.IExStoreAsyncEvents

    Public Sub New()

    End Sub
End Class
```

Next we can implement our functionality for our event sink, as we did in Visual Basic 6.0. The easiest way to do this is to select the functions in the *IExStoreAsyncEvents* interface from the drop-down menus at the top of the Integrated Development Environment (IDE) in Visual Studio .NET. Here is the complete code that implements the *OnSave* and *OnDelete* events using Visual Basic .NET:

```
Imports System.Runtime.InteropServices
Imports Exoledb

<ProgId("DotNetES.EventSink"), _
    Guid("7E303074-88B9-4be8-8C16-AC0CD8195CA4"), _
    ComVisible(True)> _
Public Class ExchangeEventSink
    Implements Exoledb.IExStoreAsyncEvents

    Dim strToAddress As String = _
        "thomriz@thomrizex2kdom.extest.microsoft.com"
    Dim strFromAddress As String = _
        "thomriz@thomrizex2kdom.extest.microsoft.com"

    Public Sub OnDelete(ByVal pEventInfo As Exoledb.IExStoreEventInfo, _
                   ByVal bstrURLItem As String, ByVal lFlags As Integer) _
                   Implements Exoledb.IExStoreAsyncEvents.OnDelete
        'Create a simple email to send
     'System.Web.Mail is covered in Chapter 20
        Dim oMailMessage As New System.Web.Mail.MailMessage()
        oMailMessage.To = strToAddress
        oMailMessage.From = strFromAddress
        oMailMessage.Subject = "OnDelete Event Sink!"
        oMailMessage.Body = "This event was fired at " & Now() _
                            & " Url: " & bstrURLItem
        Dim oSMTPMail As System.Web.Mail.SmtpMail
        oSMTPMail.Send(oMailMessage)
    End Sub

    Public Sub OnSave(ByVal pEventInfo As Exoledb.IExStoreEventInfo, _
                  ByVal bstrURLItem As String, ByVal lFlags As Integer) _
                  Implements Exoledb.IExStoreAsyncEvents.OnSave
        'Create a simple email to send
        On Error Resume Next
        Dim oMailMessage As New System.Web.Mail.MailMessage()
        Dim pNewEventInfo As Exoledb.IExStoreDispEventInfo
        Dim oRecord As ADODB.Record
        pNewEventInfo = CType(pEventInfo, Exoledb.IExStoreDispEventInfo)
        oRecord = pNewEventInfo.EventRecord
        oMailMessage.To = strToAddress
        oMailMessage.From = strFromAddress
        oMailMessage.Subject = "OnSave Event Sink!"
        Dim strMessageText As String = "Errors: " & Err.Number _
            & Err.Description & " This event was fired at " & Now() _
```

```
            & " Url: " & bstrURLItem & vbLf & "ADO Record Subject: " _
            & oRecord.Fields("urn:schemas:httpmail:subject").Value _
            & vbLf & "Flags: " & lFlags
        oMailMessage.Body = strMessageText
        Dim oSMTPMail As System.Web.Mail.SmtpMail
        oSMTPMail.Send(oMailMessage)
    End Sub
End Class
```

All the code does is send a simple e-mail message to a user when the event happens. The key code that you want to look at is in *OnSave*. You will notice the use of *IExStoreDispEventInfo*. This is the dispatch interface to get the event item as an ADO *Record* object as well as provide other Exchange event functions. In Visual Basic 6.0, you can just *Dim* a variable as this type and pass it the *pEventInfo* variable, which is an *IExStoreEventInfo* object, and Visual Basic 6.0 will automatically convert the types. With Visual Basic .NET, you need to do an explicit type conversion using the *CType* function to convert between the two types. Once you do that, the dispatch interfaces work the same as they do in Visual Basic 6.0.

The next step is to make sure that when we build our application, Visual Studio .NET registers our assembly with COM. To do this, we right-click on our project in Solution Explorer and choose Properties. Then select the Configuration Properties folder. Under the Build section, make sure that Register For COM Interop is enabled. The interface for performing these steps is shown in Figure 17-6.

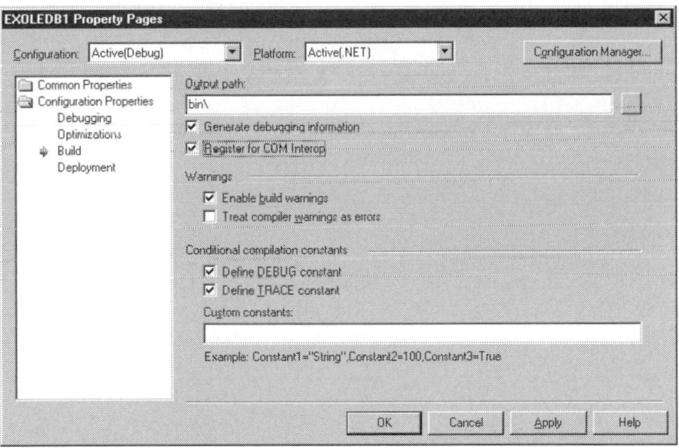

Figure 17-6 Registering for COM interoperability in Visual Studio .NET

Finally, if you want to debug your application, you need to tell Visual Studio .NET what application to start in order to start debugging. Unlike with Visual Basic 6.0, you cannot just wait for your component to be created. When you work with event sinks, you need to cause some action to occur that will trigger the sink. Outlook will probably be the primary interface to create or delete items that will fire your sink, so you need to register Outlook as the application to launch to start debugging. To do this, right-click on the project in Solution Explorer and choose Properties again. Expand the Configuration Properties folder and click on Debugging. In the Start Action area, click Start External Program and type the path to Outlook on your system. This is shown in Figure 17-7.

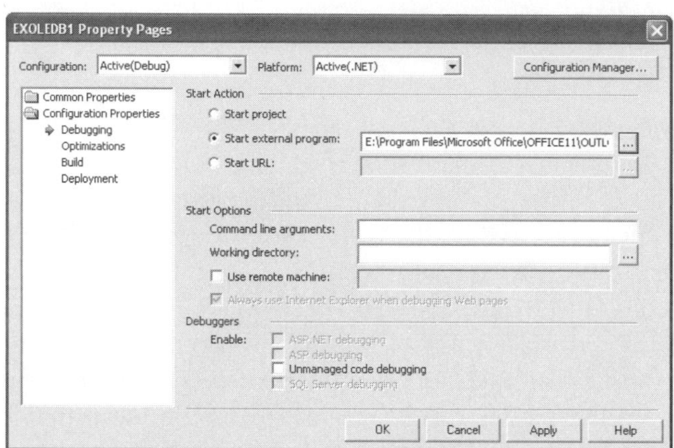

Figure 17-7 Setting Outlook as the program to launch to start debugging

Building More Than One Handler in a Single File

With Exchange Server, you can implement only one type of event handler (synchronous, asynchronous, or system) in a single COM component. With Visual Basic 6.0, you can implement only a single class in a single file. In other words, if you need multiple event handlers, you must implement them in separate component libraries. With Visual Basic .NET, you can implement multiple classes in a single file. With the power you have in Visual Basic .NET with multiple classes and the ability to control COM interoperability and interfaces, you can create a single file with all the different event handlers you need. For COM interoperability, all you do is specify a different ProgID and GUID for your new classes. The following code is included with the asynchronous event handler in the same file but implements synchronous event handling:

```
<ProgId("DotNetES.SyncEventSink"), _
    Guid("4D40EE77-6C7E-462e-8868-9893E1A1CDFB"), _
    ComVisible(True)> _
```

```
Public Class ExchangeSyncEventSink
    Implements Exoledb.IExStoreSyncEvents

    Dim strToAddress As String = _
        "thomriz@thomrizex2kdom.extest.microsoft.com"
    Dim strFromAddress As String = _
        "thomriz@thomrizex2kdom.extest.microsoft.com"

    Public Sub OnSyncDelete(ByVal pEventInfo As Exoledb.IExStoreEventInfo, _
                            ByVal bstrURLItem As String, _
                            ByVal lFlags As Integer) _
                            Implements Exoledb.IExStoreSyncEvents.OnSyncDelete

    End Sub

    Public Sub OnSyncSave(ByVal pEventInfo As Exoledb.IExStoreEventInfo, _
                          ByVal bstrURLItem As String, _
                          ByVal lFlags As Integer) _
                          Implements Exoledb.IExStoreSyncEvents.OnSyncSave
        'Create a simple email to send
        On Error Resume Next
        Dim oMailMessage As New System.Web.Mail.MailMessage()
        Dim pNewEventInfo As Exoledb.IExStoreDispEventInfo
        Dim oRecord As ADODB.Record
        pNewEventInfo = CType(pEventInfo, Exoledb.IExStoreDispEventInfo)
        oRecord = pNewEventInfo.EventRecord
        oMailMessage.To = strToAddress
        oMailMessage.From = strFromAddress
        oMailMessage.Subject = "OnSyncSave Event Sink!"
        Dim strMessageText As String = "Errors: " & Err.Number _
            & Err.Description & " This event was fired at " & Now() _
            & " Url: " & bstrURLItem & vbLf & "ADO Record Subject: " _
            & oRecord.Fields("urn:schemas:httpmail:subject").Value _
            & vbLf & "Flags: " & lFlags
        oMailMessage.Body = strMessageText
        Dim oSMTPMail As System.Web.Mail.SmtpMail
        oSMTPMail.Send(oMailMessage)

        'If you wanted to abort the transaction,
        'you can use the following code
        'pNewEventInfo.AbortChange()
    End Sub
End Class
```

Finishing Touches

Once you have compiled and built your new COM components and have had Visual Studio .NET register them, all you need to do is to register these new components in COM+, just like you would with your Visual Basic 6.0 components. Figure 17-8 shows registering one of our new .NET components with COM+.

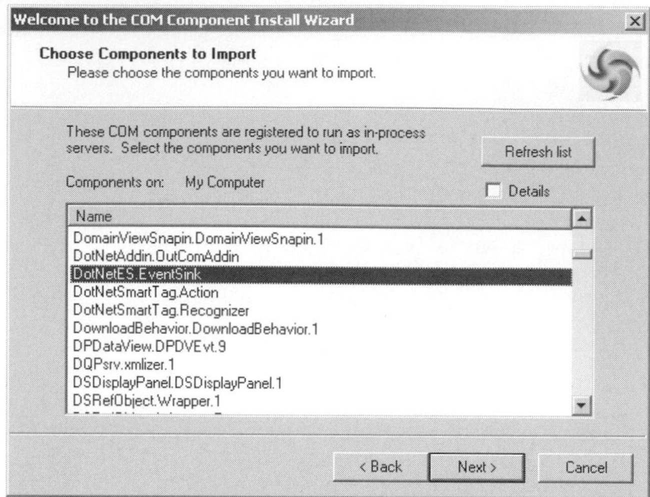

Figure 17-8 Registering a .NET COM interoperability component with COM+

The last step is to create a registration in Exchange, as you would for a Visual Basic 6.0 component, to tell Exchange what component to call when an event occurs. You can do this using the Event Registration Wizard in Exchange Explorer included in the Exchange SDK.

To test your application, all you do is try to create, modify, or delete items in the folder where you registered for events.

A C# Example

To give you an idea of what the same type of event handler would look like in C#, I created a C# example for the code. You will notice similar semantics in C#, such as specifying the GUID and ProgID as well registering for COM interoperability as part of the project. The only major difference between the Visual Basic code and the C# code is the semantic differences between the languages in terms of type-casting and statement declaration.

```
using System;
using System.Runtime.InteropServices;
using Exoledb;
using System.Web.Mail;

namespace ExEventSinkCSharp
{

    /// <summary>
    /// This sample shows implementing an Event Sink using C#
```

```
    /// </summary>
    ///
    [GuidAttribute("38F89F18-5293-4774-8F72-41C40733DB1E"),

    ProgIdAttribute("ExEventSink.CSharp")]
    public class ExEventSink : Object, Exoledb.IExStoreAsyncEvents
    {
        string strToAddress = "thomriz@thomrizex2kdom.extest.microsoft.com";
        string strFromAddress = "thomriz@thomrizex2kdom.extest.microsoft.com";

        public ExEventSink()
        {
            //
            // TODO: Add constructor logic here
            //
        }

        public void OnSave(Exoledb.IExStoreEventInfo pEventInfo,
                           string bstrURLItem, int lFlags)
        {
            /// Implements OnSave
            ///
            /// Send a simple email to the user
            ///
            System.Web.Mail.MailMessage oMailMessage =
                new System.Web.Mail.MailMessage();
            oMailMessage.To = strToAddress;
            oMailMessage.From = strFromAddress;
            oMailMessage.Subject = "OnSave Event Fired (C#)";
            /// Get the EventInfo and convert it so we can use it
            ///
            Exoledb.IExStoreDispEventInfo pNewEventInfo =

                (Exoledb.IExStoreDispEventInfo)pEventInfo;
            /// Get something off the new variable
            ///
            ADODB.Record oRecord = new ADODB.Record();
            oRecord = (ADODB.Record)pNewEventInfo.EventRecord;

            oMailMessage.Body = "This event was fired "

                + DateTime.Now.ToString() + " URL to item: "
                + oRecord.Fields["DAV:href"].Value + " Flags: " + lFlags;
            System.Web.Mail.SmtpMail.Send(oMailMessage);
        }

        public void OnDelete(Exoledb.IExStoreEventInfo pEventInfo,
                             string bstrURLItem, int lFlags)
        {
            /// Implements OnDelete
        }
    }
}
```

Transport and Protocol Events

Besides programming to database events, you can also write to events at the transport and protocol event level. Before we discuss writing to these events, I want to point out that I highly recommend that you write to these events using C++, although you can use languages compatible with .NET as well if you have to. The reason for this is that with certain events, specifically transport events, your event handler will process every message that goes through the system, both internally and externally delivered. This means poorly written code or code written with an interpreted language such as a scripting language can seriously affect the performance of your Exchange servers. For this reason, only a single event is exposed to non-C++ developers such as script or Visual Basic developers. I'll describe this event as well as the architecture for the overall transport and protocol event architecture. You can write more complex event handlers using C++ (because of the numerous transport and protocol events), but that topic is beyond the scope of this book. The Exchange SDK has good documentation on this topic and also has new information on writing managed code event handlers. The SDK even includes a Primary Interop Assembly for transport and protocol events that you can download.

Transport and Protocol Event Architecture

Figure 17-9 depicts where and when transport and protocol events occur. As you can see, transport events occur when communication between client and server takes place over that protocol. For example, when an Internet-based client or a remote SMTP system starts a new SMTP session with an Exchange server, the server fires a new event that tells you a new SMTP command is inbound. You can then capture that command and perform whatever processing you need. Transport events occur when messages flow through the system, whether they need to be locally or remotely delivered.

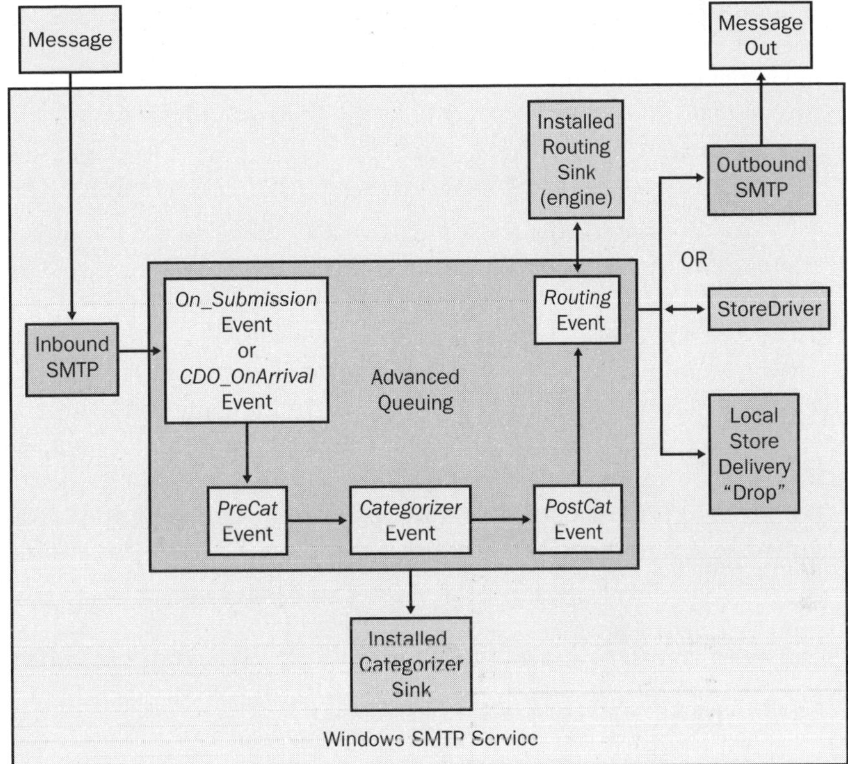

Figure 17-9 The relationship between transport and protocol events

We will discuss only event handlers that you can write in Visual Basic or VBScript, so we need to look at the transport events. Figure 17-10 depicts the architecture for transport events.

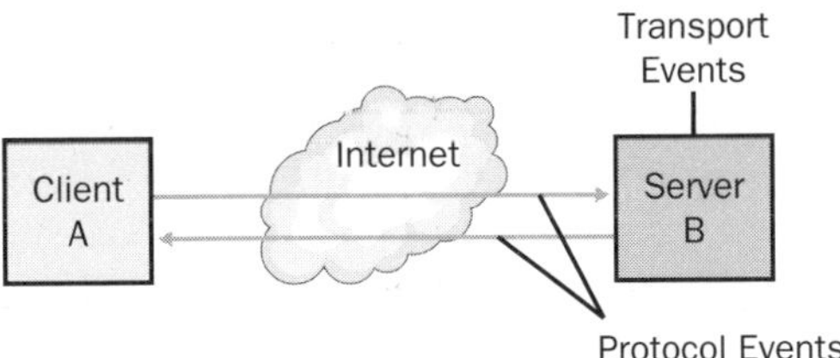

Figure 17-10 The system flow for transport events

You will notice a *CDO_OnArrival* event. This event is a CDO wrapper around the *OnArrival* event so that programmers using Visual Basic or a scripting language can handle this event. This event fires when an e- mail message is received at the server. The event has the following definition:

```
Sub ISMTPOnArrival_OnArrival(ByVal Msg As CDO.Message, _
                             EventStatus As CDO.CdoEventStatus)
```

You are passed the message as a CDO message, and you need to set the *EventStatus* to one of two values: *CdoRunNextSink (0)* or *CdoSkipRemainingSinks (1)*. Depending on what you do in your code, you will either allow lower-priority event sinks to run or you will stop them from running. The following example shows how you can write to the CDO *OnArrival* event using Visual Basic. With Visual Basic, you should implement the *IsCacheable* interface so the SMTP service will cache your DLL into memory and will not have to load it from disk. With scripting languages, this is not the case, so you do not have to implement this interface because the script will always be interpreted by the server. The following example just writes out information about the message to a text file:

```
Implements CDO.ISMTPOnArrival
Implements IEventIsCacheable

Private Sub IEventIsCacheable_IsCacheable()
    'Just implement the interface so we're cached
End Sub

Private Sub ISMTPOnArrival_OnArrival(ByVal Msg As CDO.Message, _
                                     EventStatus As CDO.CdoEventStatus)

    Dim ofs As New Scripting.FileSystemObject
    Dim oFile As Scripting.TextStream
    Set oFile = ofs.OpenTextFile("c:\MsgLog.txt", ForAppending, True )
    oFile.Write "From: " & Msg.From & vbCrLf
    oFile.Write "To: " & Msg.To & vbCrLf
    oFile.Write "Subject: " & Msg.Subject & vbCrLf & vbCrLf
    oFile.Write Msg.TextBody & vbCrLf & vbCrLf
    oFile.Close
    EventStatus = cdoRunNextSink
End Sub
```

Registering Your Event Handler

As with database events, you must register with the system that you want to handle the *OnArrival* event. The difference between database event registrations and transport event registrations is that the latter are stored in the IIS metabase and database event registrations are stored in the Exchange information store. Therefore, you must write to the metabase to create your transport or protocol event registrations. Luckily, you find a program called smtpreg.vbs (or nntpreg.vbs for NNTP events) in the Exchange SDK. This file includes code to register, enumerate, and unregister your event handlers. You can also pass protocol rules so that your event handler is not called for every message sent to the server, just specific messages. Be sure to put your protocol rules in quotes on the command line. To get the best information about the .vbs files, just run them and pass along the command line a */?* command. The following code registers an event handler for the *OnArrival* CDO event on the first SMTP virtual server in IIS for a DLL called MyEventHandler.MySink to process every e-mail message coming into the system:

```
cscript smtpreg.vbs /
add 1 onarrival MyDisplayName MyEventHandler.MySink  "mail from=*"
```

Advanced Considerations

If you have never heard about the Transport Neutral Encapsulation Format (TNEF), you might want to conduct some research on it before you write event handlers. When you send mail between internal servers in an Exchange organization via Outlook or OWA, all mail, including the body, attachments, and custom properties, is stored in TNEF. Therefore, if you register an event handler for the *OnArrival* event and you get one of these messages, you will not be able to look at the body or the attachments because they are TNEF encoded. So, here's a best practice. If you need to modify the body or attachments of mail sent entirely within your system, you can write to the database events we discussed earlier. These events pass the right content to you—you do not have to worry about the original format that the content came in (whether it was Multipurpose Internet Mail Extensions [MIME] or TNEF).

If you want to process e-mails and want to affect the content of the messages, your best bet is to run your transport event handlers on your border SMTP servers. Mail coming in from or going out to other systems will probably not be in TNEF, but rather MIME or plain text. CDO can parse the format, and your event handler can modify the content of the messages.

For the not faint of heart, there are TNEF APIs that you can use to decode and encode TNEF. MSDN has a TNEF decoder sample, but it's written entirely in C++; if it does not meet your needs, you would have to rewrite portions of it.

Workflow Capabilities

Exchange Server allows you to build applications that model and automate business processes. You can hardcode a workflow process by using server events and Visual Basic, but the built-in workflow engine—Workflow Designer—and CDO workflow objects of Exchange Server simplify this development task by providing specialized workflow tools.

With these tools, you can build database workflows and e-mail workflows on Exchange Server. You can also enable the user to connect directly to the data or to an application that directly touches the data to update state information in the workflow. The Training application is a database workflow. When a manager approves a user to take a course, an ASP page updates a property on the pending approval message to the student, which in turn triggers the workflow engine to change the state of the pending approval message to *Approved*. This change of state causes the application to register the student for the course and then notify the student. Database workflows are great if your users have direct access to the process instances of the workflow, and, in effect, to the items undergoing the workflow process, so that they can update the state.

In e-mail workflows, instead of having the user directly interact with the data, notifications and data copies are sent to the user via e-mail. The user can then perform an action, such as approve or edit the data, and return it to the application via e-mail. The Exchange Server workflow engine directs the e-mail to the correct process instance in your workflow folder, and you can update your process instance accordingly. This style of workflow is useful if you can't guarantee that users have direct access to your data or if you want to provide an easy transmission method for data and approval. Most users understand and have ready access to Outlook e-mail, so this solution works well for business processes that extend beyond a corporation and over the Internet. Note that to use e-mail-style workflow, you must be running Outlook on your client.

Workflow in Exchange Server

Exchange Server uses four main components to implement workflow: CDO for Workflow (CDOWF), server event sinks (handlers), action tables, and script files. The workflow engine in Exchange Server is stored in CDOWF. This engine works in conjunction with the other components to evaluate and maintain the workflow state, such as *Approved* or *Rejected*. CDOWF also provides the object model you can use to interact with the engine to change states or validate workflow properties.

The workflow engine works in conjunction with the action table, which is basically a finite state machine that describes transitions between states in the workflow. Table 17-4 shows an example of an action table based on the Training application. In this action table, a request for approval of user's enrollment is e-mailed to the user's manager, and the workflow engine waits 15 minutes for a response. If a response isn't received from the manager within 15 minutes, the engine e-mails the user that the request was not processed. If the manager approves the course request, the engine registers the user and sends an e-mail that tells the user of the approval.

Table 17-4 A Simple Action Table Based on the Training Application

State	New State	Event Type	Condition	Action	Expiration Interval
	Created	*OnCreate*	*CheckValidity*	*SendMailtoManager*	
	Created	*OnEnter*	*True*		15 minutes
Created	Approved	*OnChange*	*ApprovalStateofItem*	*RegisterUserSend-MailtoUser*	
Created	NoResponse	*OnExpiry*	*True*	*SendNoResponseto-User*	

To determine what changes have been made to workflow items and to evaluate whether they are valid according to the action table, the workflow engine implements both synchronous and *OnTimer* event handlers. When you drop a new document into a folder in which a workflow process is enabled, the *Workflow* event handler in that folder fires before the item is committed to the Exchange Server database. If workflow is enabled, the event handler creates the process instance for your item in the folder and determines the initial state of the item. If a user changes that item, the event handler checks the change against the valid state changes in the action table. If the state change is not valid, it is not committed to Exchange Server. If the time expires for a specific state and there is a state transition for that event in the action table, the *OnTimer* event will move the workflow item to the next state. Figure 17-11 shows the *Workflow* event handler that's installed by default as a COM+ application.

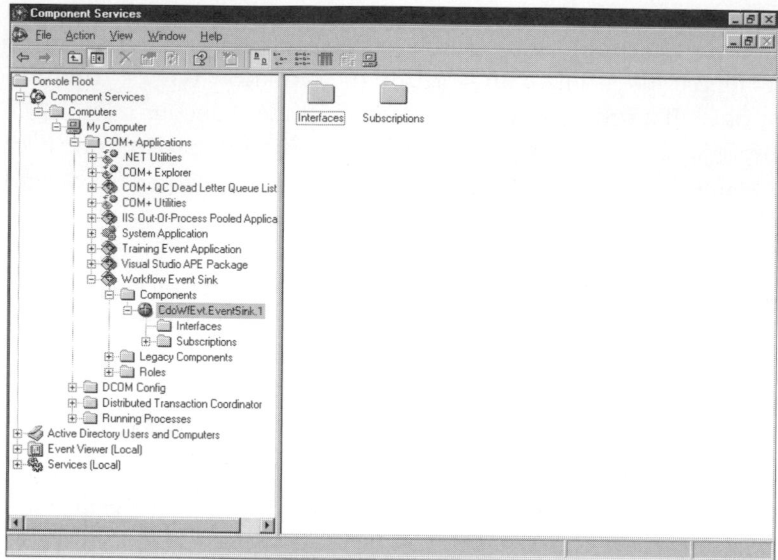

Figure 17-11 The *Workflow* event handler that's installed as a COM+ application

The script file is used in conjunction with CDOWF, the server event handlers, and the action tables. Your script implements the conditions for the state transitions and the actions that occur at the time of those transitions. For example, to check the validity of an item before posting it in the workflow folder, you write script to check the necessary properties and return to the workflow engine a *Boolean* that indicates whether the item is valid. You must use condition functions in your script. If a condition is valid, for example, you might want to send an e-mail to the user who needs to approve the item. You have to write script for the action portion of your workflow in order to send the e-mail.

Developing Workflow Applications

Enough talk about what workflow is—let's look at how to write a workflow application with Exchange Server. In this section, I'll concentrate on the Workflow Designer for Exchange because it makes creating workflow applications easier. Everything we'll discuss in this section can be performed programmatically using CDOWF.

Setting Up the Workflow Environment

To start writing workflow applications, you first need to set up the workflow environment for Exchange Server. I won't go into the gory details of how to set up all the accounts and infrastructure. You can find all this information in the Exchange SDK, in a section called "Adding the Workflow System Account." Essentially, you need to create an account and make it your default workflow system account.

Next you need to add yourself to the Can Register Workflow role for the Workflow Event Sink COM+ application. This role lists all the users or groups that can actually register for the event handlers we discussed earlier. Figure 17-12 shows this COM+ application with the roles populated.

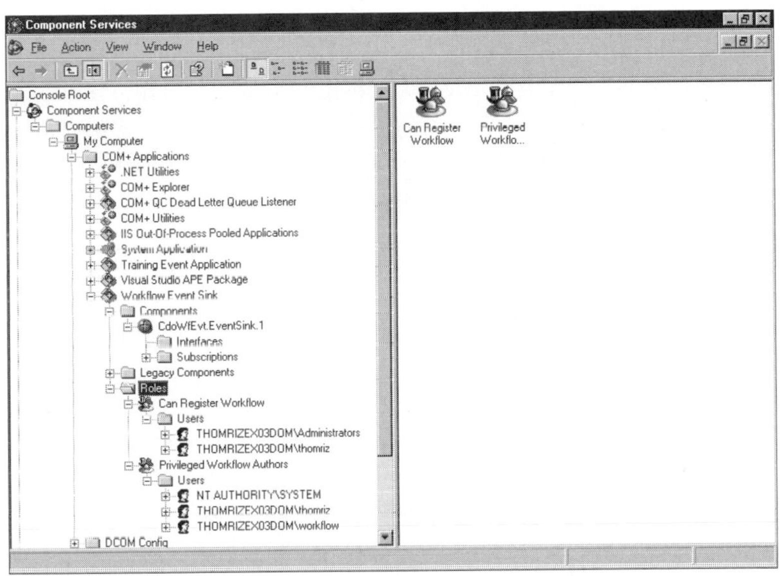

Figure 17-12 The Can Register Workflow role populated with users and groups

If necessary, you also should add yourself to the Privileged Workflow Authors role. If you are not in this role, your workflow scripts will be sandboxed. In other words, they will only be able to modify the item undergoing workflow, send notification mail, or write to the workflow audit trail. They will not be able create objects at all. If you add yourself to the Privileged Workflow

Authors role, you'll be able to create objects and access other items you have permissions for in Exchange Server.

> **Note** If you are a privileged workflow author, you will be running under the workflow system account you initially specified. Also, Exchange supports ad hoc workflows. This means that items coming into the folder where workflow is enabled must already have a workflow definition on them. Only restricted mode workflows can be run as ad hoc. You cannot allow ad hoc workflows and enable privileged mode.

Using the Workflow Designer

As mentioned earlier, the Workflow Designer for Exchange makes building and deploying your workflow applications easier. Its graphical user interface (GUI) simplifies the process of visualizing your workflow while automating the process of creating the event handler registrations and action tables in your workflow-enabled folders.

I won't cover all the GUI elements of the Workflow Designer; you can find that information easily in the Exchange Server documentation, or you can just read the Workflow Designer screen. However, I will cover three important elements that make up your workflow in the designer: states, actions, and script. The states are the boxes in the GUI that indicate whether your workflow is pending, approved, rejected, or expired. The actions provide the transitions between the states. These actions, which I'll detail momentarily, can be found in your action table and include *OnEnter*, *OnExit*, and *OnCreate*, among others. The script implements the condition checking and the actions.

The states in the Workflow Designer are not very interesting because they don't perform any task; they only serve as a destination for the workflow item to move to during the workflow process. Therefore, your only concern with states should be that your scripts allow you to check which state the workflow item is in, to see whether it's being approved or rejected or placed in any other state you specify.

Actions are among the most important aspects of the Workflow Designer because they are associated with the transitions between states. These transitions define how the work in your workflow is performed. Figure 17-13 shows how to create actions in the Workflow Designer.

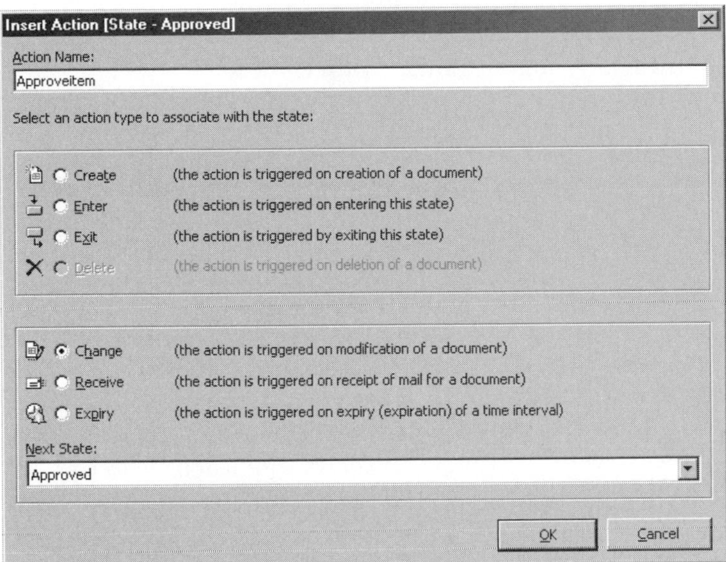

Figure 17-13 Creating actions in the Workflow Designer

Table 17-5 describes the actions in the Workflow Designer. Be aware that some actions, such as the *OnChange* action, can appear multiple times on a state. But each time it appears for the same state, it must have different conditions that make the action valid for a workflow item. For example, one condition might check changes to the subject line and another might check changes to the message body.

Table 17-5 Actions of the Workflow Designer

Workflow Designer	Action Table	Description
Create	*OnCreate*	An item was created. You must have at least one *Create* action in your workflow, otherwise, no items can be created in the folder.
Enter	*OnEnter*	This action manages the time used by the *Expiry* action. As soon as the state is entered using this action, the timer is started for the expiration interval you set. Entry into states is implicitly allowed, so you don't have to add this action to every state. You will normally use this action for timer-based workflow requirements only.
Exit	*OnExit*	The state is transitioning to a new state.

Table 17-5 Actions of the Workflow Designer

Workflow Designer	Action Table	Description
Delete	*OnDelete*	The document is deleted. If you do not have a *Delete* action, workflow items cannot be deleted. If that's the case, Exchange Server will return an error if an application or user attempts to delete an item.
Change	*OnChange*	The document is modified. You can have multiple *Change* actions on a single state. If you have no *Change* actions, documents cannot be modified.
Receive	*OnReceive*	The workflow has received an e-mail message that correlates to a workflow item. This action allows your workflow to respond to e-mail.
Expiry	*OnExpiry*	The document has passed its time limit for the current state. This action is useful for time-based tasks, such as reminder notifications to managers to approve workflow items.

The following code is the XML representation of a real action table generated by the Workflow Designer. Notice the action and state names in the XML code. You'll see how to use XML action tables to simplify deploying workflow processes later in the chapter.

```
<xml xmlns:s='uuid:BDC6E3F0-6DA3-11d1-A2A3-00AA00C14882'
                    xmlns:dt='uuid:C2F41010-65B3-11d1-A29F-00AA00C14882'
                    xmlns:rs='urn:schemas-microsoft-com:rowset'
                    xmlns:z='#RowsetSchema'>
<s:Schema id='RowsetSchema'>
    <s:ElementType name='row' content='eltOnly' rs:updatable='true'>
        <s:AttributeType name='ID' rs:number='1' rs:write='true'>
            <s:datatype dt:type='string' dt:maxLength='4294967295'
                rs:precision='0' rs:long='true' rs:maybenull='false'/>
        </s:AttributeType>
        <s:AttributeType name='Caption' rs:number='2' rs:write='true'>
            <s:datatype dt:type='string' dt:maxLength='4294967295'
                rs:precision='0' rs:long='true' rs:maybenull='false'/>
        </s:AttributeType>
        <s:AttributeType name='State' rs:number='3' rs:write='true'>
            <s:datatype dt:type='string' dt:maxLength='4294967295'
                rs:precision='0' rs:long='true' rs:maybenull='false'/>
        </s:AttributeType>
        <s:AttributeType name='NewState' rs:number='4' rs:write='true'>
            <s:datatype dt:type='string' dt:maxLength='4294967295'
               rs:precision='0' rs:long='true' rs:maybenull='false'/>
```

```
        </s:AttributeType>
        <s:AttributeType name='EventType' rs:number='5' rs:write='true'>
            <s:datatype dt:type='string' dt:maxLength='4294967295'
                rs:precision='0' rs:long='true' rs:maybenull='false'/>
        </s:AttributeType>
        <s:AttributeType name='Condition' rs:number='6' rs:write='true'>
            <s:datatype dt:type='string' dt:maxLength='4294967295'
                rs:precision='0' rs:long='true' rs:maybenull='false'/>
        </s:AttributeType>
        <s:AttributeType name='Action' rs:number='7' rs:write='true'>
            <s:datatype dt:type='string' dt:maxLength='4294967295'
                rs:precision='0' rs:long='true' rs:maybenull='false'/>
        </s:AttributeType>
        <s:AttributeType name='ExpiryInterval' rs:number='8' rs:write='true'>
            <s:datatype dt:type='string' dt:maxLength='4294967295'
                rs:precision='0' rs:long='true' rs:maybenull='false'/>
        </s:AttributeType>
        <s:AttributeType name='RowACL' rs:number='9' rs:write='true'>
            <s:datatype dt:type='string' dt:maxLength='4294967295'
                rs:precision='0' rs:long='true' rs:maybenull='false'/>
        </s:AttributeType>
        <s:AttributeType name='TransitionACL' rs:number='10' rs:write='true'>
            <s:datatype dt:type='string' dt:maxLength='4294967295'
                rs:precision='0' rs:long='true' rs:maybenull='false'/>
        </s:AttributeType>
        <s:AttributeType name='DesignToolFields' rs:number='11'
                                                            rs:write='true'>
            <s:datatype dt:type='string' dt:maxLength='4294967295'
                rs:precision='0' rs:long='true' rs:maybenull='false'/>
        </s:AttributeType>
        <s:AttributeType name='CompensatingAction' rs:number='12'
                                                            rs:write='true'>
            <s:datatype dt:type='string' dt:maxLength='4294967295'
                rs:precision='0' rs:long='true' rs:maybenull='false'/>
        </s:AttributeType>
        <s:AttributeType name='Flags' rs:number='13' rs:write='true'>
            <s:datatype dt:type='string' dt:maxLength='4294967295'
                rs:precision='0' rs:long='true' rs:maybenull='false'/>
        </s:AttributeType>
        <s:AttributeType name='EvaluationOrder' rs:number='14'
                                                            rs:write='true'>
            <s:datatype dt:type='string' dt:maxLength='4294967295'
                rs:precision='0' rs:long='true' rs:maybenull='false'/>
        </s:AttributeType>
        <s:extends type='rs:rowbase'/>
    </s:ElementType>
</s:Schema>
<rs:data>
    <rs:insert>
        <z:row ID='1' Caption='Create' State='' NewState='Pending'
            EventType='OnCreate' Condition='TRUE' Action=''
            ExpiryInterval='0' RowACL='' TransitionACL=''
```

```
        DesignToolFields='-1:1:' CompensatingAction='' Flags='0'
        EvaluationOrder='1000'/>
    <z:row ID='2' Caption='Delete' State='Pending' NewState=''
        EventType='OnDelete' Condition='true' Action=''
        ExpiryInterval='0' RowACL='' TransitionACL=''
        DesignToolFields='1:-2:' CompensatingAction='' Flags='0'
        EvaluationOrder='7000'/>
    <z:row ID='3' Caption='StartTimer' State='' NewState='Pending'
        EventType='OnEnter' Condition='TRUE' Action='sendMailToManager'
        ExpiryInterval='15' RowACL='' TransitionACL=''
        DesignToolFields='0:1:' CompensatingAction='' Flags='0'
        EvaluationOrder=''/>
    <z:row ID='5' Caption='ManagerApproved' State='Pending'
        NewState='Approved' EventType='OnChange'
        Condition='WorkflowSession.Fields
        (&#x22;http://thomriz.com/schema/approvalstatus&#x22;).value =
        &#x22;Approved&#x22;'
        Action='strCourseName = GetCourseName
        strStudentEmail = GetStudentEmail
        strManagerEmail = GetManagerEmail
        strBody = &#x22;Your manager approved you for the course:
        &#x22; &#x26; strCourseName
        sendMail strBody,strStudentEmail &#x26; &#x22;,&#x22; &#x26;
        strManagerEmail,&#x22;Approved for course: &#x22; &#x26;
        strCourseName
        addregistration
        sendcalendarmessage'
        ExpiryInterval='0' RowACL='' TransitionACL='' DesignToolFields=
        '1:3:' CompensatingAction='' Flags='0' EvaluationOrder='3001'/>
    <z:row ID='6' Caption='ManagerRejected' State='Pending'
        NewState='Rejected' EventType='OnChange'
        Condition='WorkflowSession.Fields
        (&#x22;http://thomriz.com/schema/approvalstatus&#x22;).value =
        &#x22;Rejected&#x22;'
        Action='strCourseName = GetCourseName
        strStudentEmail = GetStudentEmail
        strManagerEmail = GetManagerEmail
        strBody = &#x22;Your manager rejected you for the course: &#x22;
        &#x26; strCourseName
        sendMail strBody,strStudentEmail &#x26; &#x22;,&#x22; &#x26;
        strManagerEmail,&#x22;Rejected for course: &#x22; &#x26;
        strCourseName '
        ExpiryInterval='0' RowACL='' TransitionACL='' DesignToolFields=
        '1:2:' CompensatingAction='' Flags='0' EvaluationOrder='3000'/>
    <z:row ID='7' Caption='NoResponse' State='Pending' NewState='Expired'
        EventType='OnExpiry' Condition='TRUE'
        Action='strCourseName = GetCourseName
        strStudentEmail = GetStudentEmail
        strManagerEmail = GetManagerEmail
```

```
            strBody = &#x22;Your manager did not approve your attending
            of the course: &#x22; &#x26;
            strCourseName &#x26; &#x22; in enough time.  You will not
            be registered for this course.&#x22;
            sendMail strBody, strStudentEmail &#x26; &#x22;,&#x22; &#x26;
            strManagerEmail, &#x22;Approval not received for course:
            &#x22; &#x26; strCourseName '
            ExpiryInterval='0' RowACL='' TransitionACL='' DesignToolFields=
            '1:4:' CompensatingAction='' Flags='0' EvaluationOrder='5000'/>
        <z:row ID='8' Caption='' State='Rejected' NewState=''
            EventType='OnDelete' Condition='TRUE' Action='' ExpiryInterval=''
            RowACL='' TransitionACL='' DesignToolFields='2:-2:'
            CompensatingAction='' Flags='0' EvaluationOrder='7001'/>
        <z:row ID='10' Caption='' State='Approved' NewState=''
            EventType='OnDelete' Condition='TRUE' Action='' ExpiryInterval=''
            RowACL='' TransitionACL='' DesignToolFields='3:-2:'
            CompensatingAction='' Flags='0' EvaluationOrder='7002'/>
        <z:row ID='11' Caption='' State='Expired' NewState=''
            EventType='OnDelete' Condition='TRUE' Action='' ExpiryInterval=''
            RowACL='' TransitionACL='' DesignToolFields='4:-2:'
            CompensatingAction='' Flags='0' EvaluationOrder='7003'/>
    </rs:insert>
</rs:data>
</xml>
```

Instead of using the Workflow Designer to create your workflow process, you could programmatically create your action table by using just ADO and CDOWF. However, in most cases, you'll want to take advantage of the Workflow Designer and generate your action tables to XML, as shown in the preceding example. You can then import the XML action table into ADO and use that data to programmatically generate your workflow process.

Creating Event Scripts

We have a workflow engine, event handlers, and an action table, but we don't have a true workflow application yet. The real foundation of the workflow application is the VBScript code you write for the actions in your action table. Whether you want to send a message, change a property, or update an item, you need to implement this action in your script. Writing your workflow script is pretty straightforward; you'll probably call ADO or CDO to perform functions in Exchange Server. The Workflow Designer includes a script editor, shown in Figure 17-14.

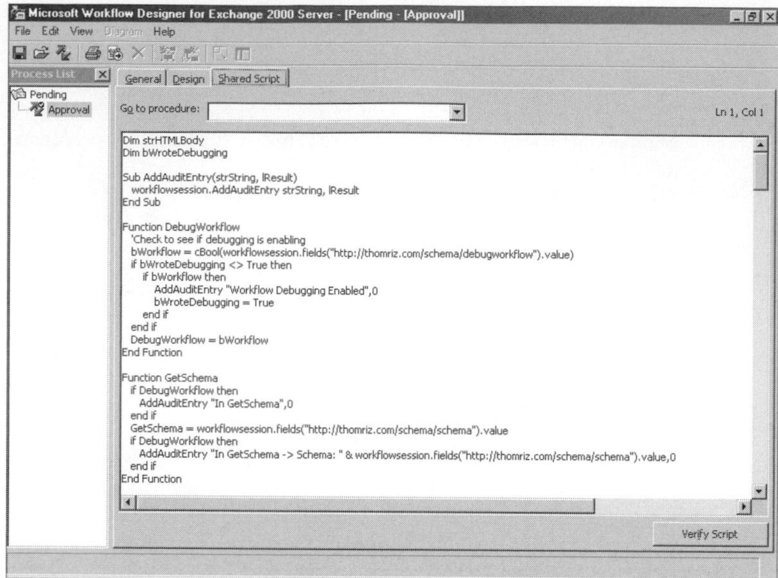

Figure 17-14 The script editor built into the Workflow Designer

You don't have to use the Workflow Designer script editor to write your scripts. You can use another editor, such as Microsoft Visual Studio .NET, and save the scripts to a common location or even implement the handlers for your actions using COM components. You can then point the Workflow Designer, or a workflow process you programmatically create, to a common script file. The following script file is used in the Training application to implement the workflow process:

```
Dim strHTMLBody
Dim bWroteDebugging

Sub AddAuditEntry(strString, lResult)
    WorkflowSession.AddAuditEntry strString, lResult
End Sub

Function DebugWorkflow()
    'Check to see whether debugging is enabled
    bWorkflow = cBool(WorkflowSession.Fields( _
                      "http://thomriz.com/schema/debugworkflow").value)
    If bWroteDebugging <> True Then
        If bWorkflow Then
            AddAuditEntry "Workflow Debugging Enabled", 0
            bWroteDebugging = True
        End If
    End If
```

```
    DebugWorkflow = bWorkflow
End Function

Function GetSchema()
    If DebugWorkflow Then
        AddAuditEntry "In GetSchema", 0
    End If
    GetSchema = _
        WorkflowSession.Fields("http://thomriz.com/schema/schema").value
    If DebugWorkflow Then
        AddAuditEntry "In GetSchema -> Schema: " & _
            WorkflowSession.Fields("http://thomriz.com/schema/schema").value,0
    End If
End Function

Function GetWorkflowSessionField(strField)
    If DebugWorkflow Then
        AddAuditEntry "In GetWorkflowSessionField -> Value: " & strField, 0
    End If
    GetWorkflowSessionField = _
        WorkflowSession.Fields("http://thomriz.com/schema/" & strField).value
End Function

Function GetCourse(bReadOnly)
    If DebugWorkflow Then
        AddAuditEntry "In GetCourse", 0
    End If
    Set oRec = CreateObject("ADODB.Record")
    If DebugWorkflow Then
        AddAuditEntry "Course URL: " & WorkflowSession.Fields( _
            "http://thomriz.com/schema/fullcourseurl").value, 0
    End If
    If bReadOnly Then
        iAccess = 1
    Else
        iAccess = 3
    End If
    oRec.Open WorkflowSession.Fields("http://thomriz.com/sche" & _
        "ma/fullcourseurl").value, WorkflowSession.ActiveConnection, iAccess
    If DebugWorkflow Then
        AddAuditEntry "In GetCourse -> CourseName: " _
            & oRec.Fields("urn:schemas:httpmail:subject").value, 0
    End If
    Set GetCourse = oRec
End Function

Function GetCourseName()
    'Returns the name of the course
    Set oRec = GetCourse(True)
    If DebugWorkflow Then
        AddAuditEntry "In GetCourseName -> CourseName = " _
            & oRec.Fields("urn:schemas:httpmail:subject").value, 0
    End If
```

```
    GetCourseName = oRec.Fields("urn:schemas:httpmail:subject").value
End Function

Sub ReplaceString(strToken, strReplacement)
    'Take the token and replace it in the global strHTMLBody
    strHTMLBody = Replace(strHTMLBody, strToken, strReplacement)
End Sub

Function GenerateHTMLBody()
    'Generates the HTML to send in the message.
    'Retrieve the message containing the HTML.
    'The HTML template must always be called WorkflowMessage.
    If DebugWorkflow Then
      AddAuditEntry "In GenerateHTMLBody", 0
    End If
    strHTMLBody = ""

    'Build the SQL statement.
    'Query for the e-mail message.
    strEmailsFolderPath = GetWorkflowSessionField("stremailsfolderpath")
    strSQL = "SELECT ""urn:schemas:httpmail:textdescription"" FROM " _
           & "SCOPE('SHALLOW TRAVERSAL OF """ & strEmailsFolderPath _
           & """') WHERE ""DAV:iscollection"" = false AND " _
           & """DAV:ishidden"" = false AND " _
           & """urn:schemas:httpmail:subject"" LIKE '%WorkflowMessage%'"

    'Create a new RecordSet object
    Set rst = CreateObject("ADODB.RecordSet")
    With rst
        'Open RecordSet based on the SQL string
        .Open strSQL, WorkflowSession.ActiveConnection
    End With

    If rst.BOF And rst.EOF Then
        GenerateHTMLBody = ""
        Exit Function
    End If

    'On Error Resume Next
    rst.MoveFirst
    strHTMLBody = rst.Fields("urn:schemas:httpmail:textdescription").Value

    'Get the course
    Set oCourse = GetCourse(True)
    'Load it into CDO Appointment
    Set iAppt = CreateObject("CDO.Appointment")
    iAppt.DataSource.Open oCourse.Fields("DAV:href").value, _
                          WorkflowSession.ActiveConnection, 1

    strSchema = GetSchema
    'Replace the tokens with real values
    ReplaceString "%StudentName%", _
                  GetWorkflowSessionField("strStudentFullname")
```

```
    ReplaceString "%Name%", _
                  iAppt.Fields("urn:schemas:httpmail:subject").Value
    ReplaceString "%Category%", iAppt.Fields(strSchema & "category").Value
    strDate = Month(iAppt.StartTime) & "/" & Day(iAppt.StartTime) & "/" _
            & Year(iAppt.StartTime)
   ReplaceString "%Date%", strDate
    ReplaceString "%StartTime%", TimeValue(iAppt.StartTime)
    ReplaceString "%EndTime%", TimeValue(iAppt.EndTime)
    ReplaceString "%Location%", iAppt.Location
    ReplaceString "%Description%", iAppt.TextBody

    strHTTPURL = GetWorkflowSessionField("strRootDirectory") _
               & "workflow.asp?CourseID=" & iAppt.Fields("DAV:href") _
               & "&student=" & GetWorkflowSessionField("fullStudentURL")
    ReplaceString "%URLLink%", strHTTPURL

    If strHTMLBody <> "" Then
        GenerateHTMLBody = strHTMLBody
    Else
        GenerateHTMLBody = ""
    End If

    rst.Close
    Set rst = Nothing
End Function

Sub sendMail(strMsg, strAddress, strSubject)
    set msg = createobject("CDO.Message")
    msg.To = strAddress
    msg.From = GetWorkflowSessionField("NotificationAddress")
    msg.Subject = strSubject
    msg.TextBody = strMsg
    If DebugWorkflow Then
        AddAuditEntry "In SendMail: Address -> " & strAddress & vblf _
            & "Subject -> " & strSubject & vblf & "Message: " & strMsg, 0
    End If
    msg.Send
End sub

Function GetStudentEmail()
    If DebugWorkflow Then
        AddAuditEntry "In GetStudentEmail", 0
    End If
    GetStudentEmail = GetWorkflowSessionField("StudentEmail")
End Function

Function GetManagerEmail()
    If DebugWorkflow Then
        AddAuditEntry "In GetManagerEmail", 0
    End If
    GetManagerEmail = GetWorkflowSessionField("ManagerEmail")
End Function
```

```
Sub SendMailToManager()
    'Get the manager's e-mail
    strManagerEmail = GetWorkflowSessionField("ManagerEmail")
    If DebugWorkflow Then
        AddAuditEntry "In SendMailToManager -> Manager: " & strManagerEmail, 0
    End If
    set oMsg = CreateObject("CDO.Message")
    set oRecord = GetCourse(True)
    oMsg.To = strManagerEmail
    oMsg.From = GetWorkflowSessionField("NotificationAddress")
    oMsg.Subject = "Approval Required for course:  " _
                 & oRecord.Fields("urn:schemas:httpmail:subject").value
    oMsg.AutoGenerateTextBody = True
    oMsg.MimeFormatted = True
    oMsg.HTMLBody = GenerateHTMLBody
    oMsg.Send
End Sub

Function GetStudent(bReadOnly)
    If DebugWorkflow Then
        AddAuditEntry "In GetStudent",0
    End If
    Set oRec = CreateObject("ADODB.Record")
    If DebugWorkflow Then
        AddAuditEntry "Student URL: " & WorkflowSession.Fields( _
            "http://thomriz.com/schema/fullstudenturl").value, 0
    End If
    If bReadOnly Then
        iAccess = 1
    Else
        iAccess = 3
    End If
    oRec.Open WorkflowSession.Fields("http://thomriz.com/sche" _
                                & "ma/fullstudenturl").value, _
                                WorkflowSession.ActiveConnection, iAccess
    If DebugWorkflow Then
        AddAuditEntry "In GetStudent -> StudentName: " _
            & oRec.Fields("urn:schemas:httpmail:subject").value, 0
    End If
    Set GetStudent = oRec
End Function

Sub addRegistration()
    Set oRecord = GetStudent(False)
    strSchema = GetSchema
    strCourseURL = GetWorkflowSessionField("shortCourseURL")
    oRecord.Fields(strSchema & "registrations") = oRecord.Fields(strSchema _
                                                & "registrations") _
                                                & strCourseURL & ","
    oRecord.Fields.Update
    oRecord.Close
    Set oRecord = Nothing
End Sub
```

```
Sub sendCalendarMessage()
    If DebugWorkflow Then
        AddAuditEntry "In SendCalendarMessage", 0
    End If
    'Get the original appointment
    Set oOriginalAppt = CreateObject("CDO.Appointment")
    oOriginalAppt.Datasource.Open GetWorkflowSessionField("fullCourseURL"), _
                              WorkflowSession.ActiveConnection, 1

    'Create a throwaway appointment
    Set oAppt = CreateObject("CDO.Appointment")
    set oConfig = CreateObject("CDO.Configuration")
    strNotificationAddress = GetWorkflowSessionField("NotificationAddress")
    oConfig.Fields("http://schemas.microsoft.com/cdo/config" _
                & "uration/sendemailaddress") = strNotificationAddress
    oConfig.Fields.Update

    oAppt.Configuration = oConfig

    oAppt.StartTime = oOriginalAppt.StartTime
    oAppt.EndTime = oOriginalAppt.EndTime
    oAppt.Subject = "Course: " & oOriginalAppt.Subject
    oAppt.Location = oOriginalAppt.Location
    strSchema = GetSchema
    oAppt.TextBody = "The Instructor is " _
                & oOriginalAppt.Fields(strSchema & "instructoremail").Value
    'Don't ask for a response since we don't care if they accept or decline
    oAppt.ResponseRequested = False

    Set oAttendee = oAppt.Attendees.Add
    strEmail = GetStudentEmail

    oAttendee.Address = strEmail
    oAttendee.Role = 0

    Set oMtg = oAppt.CreateRequest
    oMtg.Message.Send

End Sub
```

This script uses ADO and CDO to perform its functions. However, another object is at work in the script: *WorkflowSession*. This intrinsic object (which you don't have to create) is passed to your script by the workflow engine. It allows you to access properties on the process instance as well as the audit trail specified for the workflow. Table 17-6 shows the most important properties and methods of this object. For more information on the properties and methods, refer to the Exchange Platform SDK.

Table 17-6 Properties and Methods of the *WorkflowSession* Object

Property or Method	Description
ActiveConnection	A property that returns an ADO *Connection* object. You should use this *Connection* object in your script's ADO and CDO functions, especially if you want them to take part in transactions.
AddAuditEntry	A method that allows you to add an audit entry to the selected audit entry provider of the workflow process. You pass a string and a long value to specify what the entry should say and the custom result you want for the value. By default, Exchange Server ships with one audit trail provider, which writes to the Windows Event Log. You can create custom audit trail providers by creating COM components that implement the *IAuditTrail* interface.
DeleteReceivedMessage	A method that deletes the received e-mail, if one exists, for the workflow item. You usually call it in the *Receive* action.
DeleteWorkflowItem	A method that deletes the workflow item.
Domain	A property that returns the domain of the server. This property works in conjunction with the *Server* property to make it easier for you to generate *file://* or *http://* URLs.
ErrorDescription	A property used in conjunction with the *ErrorNumber* property. *ErrorDescription* contains a description of the error to report to the audit trail provider.
ErrorNumber	A property that holds the number of the errors to report to the client and the audit trail provider.
Fields	A property that returns the ADO *Fields* collection for the workflow item. Using *Fields*, you can access built-in and custom schemas on the workflow item.
GetNewWorkflowMessage	A method that creates and returns a new *WorkflowMessage* object. The object allows you to send e-mail messages from restricted workflows because you cannot create a CDO *Message* object in a restricted workflow. Also, the CDO message is created in the context of the workflow transaction so if the state transition fails, the e-mail created using this method never gets sent.
GetUserProperty	A method that gets an Active Directory attribute off an Active Directory object.

Table 17-6 Properties and Methods of the *WorkflowSession* Object

Property or Method	Description
IsUserInRole	A method that checks to see whether a user is in a folder role. You pass to this method the user's e-mail address and the name of the role. The method returns a *Boolean* indicating whether that user is in that particular folder role. A folder role is a grouping of users who perform a particular function that you define for the folder. The roles are stored on the folder, so to implement roles-based workflow, you do not need permissions to modify or add properties to Active Directory.
ItemAuthors	A property that contains a collection representing a list of all users with authoring ability on the workflow item. Exchange Server supports item-level permissions, so you might want to set such permissions on workflow items.
ItemReaders	A property that contains a collection of users who should have Reader permissions on the workflow item.
Properties	A property that returns an *ISessionProps* interface so you can add properties you need persisted for a single session that lasts for one *ProcessInstance* transition. Here's a good example of using this property: Suppose you have multiple actions that need to be evaluated to make a state transition. You do not want each action to check multiple times whether a certain property on the item already exists as part of the evaluation criteria. So you use this property to cache the value and share the value between multiple condition scripts.
ReceivedMessage	A property that returns the e-mail message that was received in correlation to a workflow item.
Sender	A property that contains the SMTP address of the person who initiated the state transition.
Server	A property that contains the name of the server and is used in conjunction with the *Domain* property.
StateFrom	A property that contains the name of the state before the current process transition.
StateTo	A property that holds the name of the state after the current transition.
TrackingTable	Used with e-mail workflows, this property contains a *RecordSet* object that has a number of properties relating to the current workflow item. Refer to the Exchange Platform SDK for more information on this property.

The *GetUserProperty* method is very useful. It takes three parameters. The first is the distinguished name of the object in Active Directory, which can be either the Active Directory path to the object or the unique e-mail address of the object. The second parameter is the Active Directory attribute you want to get off the object. The third parameter works in conjunction with the first and tells CDO whether the first parameter is an Active Directory path (*1*) or an e-mail address (*0*). Probably the most common use for this method is to retrieve the manager of the owner of the item that is undergoing the workflow to get approval. You retrieve the manager by getting the *manager* property off the current user's Active Directory object. You can get the e-mail address of the current user by using the *WorkflowSession.Sender* property. You can then retrieve the *mail* property from the manager's Active Directory object. The *manager* property returns to you the Active Directory path to the manager. The following example illustrates this scenario:

```
With WorkflowSession
    strUserAddress = "username@company.com"
    mgrDN = .GetUserProperty(strUserAddress, "manager", 0)
    strUserMgrEmail = .GetUserProperty(mgrDN, "mail", 1)
End With
```

Two other properties in Table 17-6, *ItemAuthors* and *ItemReaders*, also demand more explanation. *ItemAuthors* is a collection used to specify per-item modify and delete permissions. If you add any users to this collection, only those users can modify or delete the item as well as read it. If you remove all users from this collection, the default permissions on the folder apply.

With *ItemReaders*, you can specify per-item read access. If you add users to this collection, only those users can read or view the item, but they cannot necessarily modify the item. This means that even when other users query, know the URL of the item, or try to retrieve a specific property on the item, they cannot modify the item unless they are in the *ItemReaders* collection. When you clear the collection, default folder permissions will apply.

Both *ItemAuthors* and *ItemReaders* return an *IMembers* interface. This interface supports one property and three methods: the *Count* property, and the *Add*, *Clear*, and *Delete* methods. *Count* returns the number of members in the collection. *Add* adds a new member by taking two parameters, *Name* and *Type*. *Name* must be a string that specifies the e-mail address of the user or a role. Exchange supports the string literals *"Role 1"* through *"Role 16"* for adding roles. The *Type* parameter is an integer that specifies the type of user you are adding, whether it is an e-mail address (*0*) or a role (*1*). The *Clear* method clears all members from the collection. Finally, the *Delete* method deletes a member from the collection. You must pass a numbered index into the collection or a string that uniquely identifies a member of the collection. This string can be a role name such as "*Role 1*" or the e-mail address of the user you want to remove from the collection. The following example shows how to add two different users to the *ItemAuthors* and *ItemReaders* collections on a workflow item:

```
strAddress = "user@domain.com"
WorkflowSession.ItemAuthors.Add strAddress, 0  'cdowfEmailAddress
strAddress = "user2@domain.com"
WorkflowSession.ItemReaders.Add strAddress, 0  'cdowfEmailAddress
```

Compensating Actions

Even though you do not want state transitions to fail because of intermittent computer issues or people attempting transitions when they do not have permissions to, these situations can occur. The Workflow Designer gives you the ability to run compensating actions if a state transition fails. The compensating action is VBScript code. A good example of using a compensating action is when you update a SQL database in the beginning of your state transition—for some reason, the state transition fails. You can use the compensating script to undo your changes to the SQL server since the state transition failure. Figure 17-15 shows where to set your compensating actions. Compensating actions are not required. There is no need to create them unless you need to for your application.

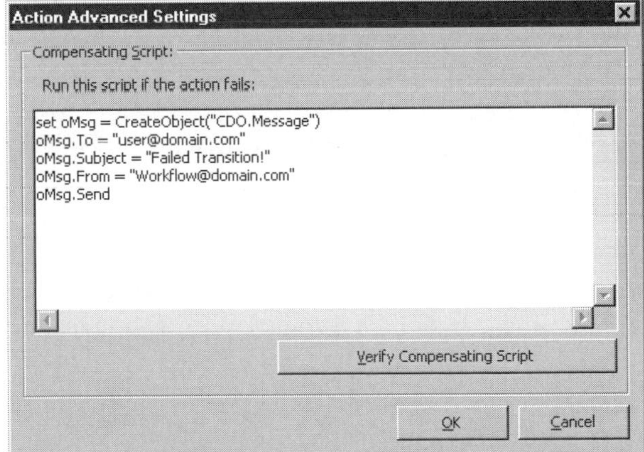

Figure 17-15 A compensating script in the Workflow Designer

Mapping URLs Using the EXOLEDB *URLMAPPER*

One other requirement of your workflow might be to change the inherent file-based URL that you receive in your workflow to an HTTP URL that you can e-mail to the end user to open the work item. The file URL will look something like *file://./backofficestorage/yourdomain/public folders/folder/myitem.eml*. Microsoft Internet Explorer cannot use this URL to browse to the item. You could manually convert the item file URL to an HTTP URL, but the OLE DB provider for the Web Storage System provides this capability as a core part of its functionality in an object called *URLMAPPER*. The *URLMAPPER* can take file URLs and map them to HTTP, and vice versa.

The methods of *URLMAPPER* are shown in Table 17-7.

Table 17-7 Methods of the *URLMAPPER* Object

Method	Description
ExoledbFileURLtoFilePath	Takes a file URL in the form *file://./backofficestorage/yourdomain* and changes it to a file path. You can then turn the file path into an HTTP URL by using the *FilePathtoHTTPURLs* method.
FilePathtoEXOLEDBFileURL	Takes a file path in the form *\\.\backofficestorage\domain\folder\folder* and converts it to *file://./backofficestorage/domain/folder/folder* so you can use the path with EXOLEDB.
FilePathtoHTTPURLs	Takes a file path and returns a variant array that contains all combinations of the HTTP URL, including *http://server/foldertree/folder/item*, *https://server/foldertree/folder/item*, *http://server/exadmin/folder/item*, and *https://server/exadmin/folder/item*.
HttpURLtoFilePath	Takes an HTTP URL to an item and converts it to a file path.

Therefore, to convert the standard file URL that is passed to you via the workflow engine, you can use the *URLMAPPER*. The following code converts the URL to an HTTP URL and sends it to the user who just submitted the item:

```
Sub URLMAPPER
    strURL = WorkflowSession.Fields("DAV:href").value
    set oMapper = CreateObject("Exoledb.UrlMapper")
    strFilePath = oMapper.ExoledbFileUrlToFilePath(strURL)
    arrHTTP = oMapper.FilePathtoHTTPURLs(strFilePath)

    set oMsg = CreateObject("CDO.Message")
    oMsg.From = "Workflow"
    oMsg.To = WorkflowSession.Sender
    oMsg.Subject = "HTTP URLs"
```

```
    For i = LBound(arrHTTP) To UBound(arrHTTP)
        'Strip out the https and exadmin URLS
        If InStr(1, arrHTTP(i), "https") =  0 Then
            'Not HTTPS, check for exadmin
            If InStr(1, arrHTTP(i), "exadmin") = 0 Then
                'Not exadmin, send it to the user
                strText = "The URL of the item is: " & arrHTTP(i)
                Exit For
            End If
        End If
    Next
    oMsg.TextBody = strText
    oMsg.Send
End Sub
```

A couple of things about *URLMAPPER*. First, you must be running in privileged mode to use it because you need to use *CreateObject* to create the component. Using *CreateObject* in your script requires privileged mode. Second, on a creation event, the URL for an item does not exist because the workflow engine uses synchronous events. This means that before the item is even committed to the database, your code will be running against that item. An item might already exist in the folder where the application is trying to place the new item. No two items in the Exchange database can have the same URL. Exchange will append a number to the URL, as in *myitem-2.eml*. For this reason, pulling the URL of the item and using it with *URLMAPPER* to determine the HTTP URL in order to send this URL in an e-mail is not recommended in *Create* events. Most times, the URL you can get for the item is probably the final URL, but if it is not, your application might show unexpected results.

One neat thing you can do to get around the privileged mode requirement for URL mapping is to use the workflow session object to retrieve the *IExOLEDBURLMapper* interface. To do this, you use the following code in your workflows:

```
Function GetHTTPUrl()
    On Error Resume Next
    Dim oMap, strFileURL
    strFileURL = WorkflowSession.Fields("DAV:href").Value
    Set oMap = WorkflowSession.Properties.Get("IExoledbUrlMapper")
    GetHTTPUrl = oMap.FilePathtoHttpUrls( _
                        oMap.exoledbFileUrlToFilePath(cstr(strFileURL)))(0)
    Set oMap = Nothing
End Function
```

Transactions

You might be wondering how you can use ADO and OLE DB transactions inside of your workflow code. The Web Storage System supports transactions, which you can use to make sure that all your code commits to the Web Storage System or rolls back. One thing to note is that transactions are supported across a single ADO connection. So, if you have multiple ADO connections, you will have multiple transactions. For this reason, you should use a single ADO *Connection* if you want a single transaction context. You can either use the built-in *WorkflowSession ActiveConnection* property and its transaction context or create your own new *Connection* object with your own transaction context. Let's take a look at the pros and cons of these two approaches.

When you use the built-in *WorkflowSession ActiveConnection* object's transactions, you can do all of your work in a transacted state. This means that if you use ADO to add a new item or delete an item, if the state transition fails, all of your work will be rolled back. This is a great benefit. However, there is one drawback. Connections in the Web Storage System are per database. This means that if you want to connect to another database and perform work, you must set up a new *Connection* object. This new *Connection* object will have its own transaction context. Therefore, any work you do over the new connection will not be in the transaction context, and the rest of the *WorkflowSession* commands you perform over this *Connection* object will not be rolled back in the case of a transition failure.

The benefit of creating a new *Connection* object and its own transaction context is that you might want to commit your transaction before the state transition is complete. Because the workflow engine will not commit your transaction until the state transition is complete, you cannot commit your commands before the state transition is complete. Both concepts might be made clearer with some sample code.

The following code shows how you can use the built-in *WorkflowSession* transaction context. The first example sends an e-mail using CDO for Exchange and does this on the transaction context of the *WorkflowSession*. If something were to happen so that the state transition did not occur, the e-mail would not be sent.

```
Sub SendEmail(strAddress,strSubject,strBody)
    'Create a CDO Message Object
    'You could also use the WorkflowSession object
    'GetNewWorkflowMessage method
    'However, this is to show explicit transaction use.

    'Create a new CDO Configuration object
    'so we can set the ActiveConnection
    Set oConfig = CreateObject("CDO.Configuration")
    oConfig.Fields("http://schemas.microsoft.com/cdo/configuration" _
              & "/activeconnection") = WorkflowSession.ActiveConnection
```

```
    Set oMessage = CreateObject("CDO.Message")
    oMessage.Configuration = oConfig
    oMessage.Sender = "workflow"
    oMessage.To = strAddress
    oMessage.Subject = strSubject
    oMessage.TextBody = strBody
    oMessage.Send

End Sub
```

The next example shows how to create your own transaction using the ADO *Connection* object. Here an item is created in a separate folder, but the transaction is rolled back so it never occurs. When you build applications, you should attempt to use the built-in transaction context because it provides the best way to roll back if errors occur.

```
Sub PostMessage(strPath)
    'Create a new ADO connection to the workitem
    Set oConn = CreateObject("ADODB.Connection")
    oConn.Provider = "Exoledb.Datasource"
    oConn.Open "URL=" & WorkflowSession.fields("DAV:href").value

    oConn.BeginTrans
    Set oRecord = CreateObject("ADODB.Record")
    'Open a new item in the folder as read/write
    oRecord.Open strPath, oConn, 3, 0
    oConn.RollbackTrans
End Sub
```

E-Mail-Based Workflow

Besides supporting database-style workflow in which the user interacts with the work item directly through an application to manipulate data, the Web Storage System also supports e-mail-style workflow, with some special requirements. First, the folder you are sending from must be mail-enabled—otherwise, the folder cannot receive any e-mail responses. You mail-enable a folder through the Exchange System Manager or through the CDO for Exchange Management objects. By default, top-level folders in the default Public Folder hierarchy are mail-enabled. However, folders in other folder trees are not mail-enabled. Second, the Windows account you use for the workflow event sink to run under must have a mailbox on the local Exchange server. Finally, you cannot send e-mail on an *OnCreate* action and have the workflow engine correlate and track that e-mail back onto your workflow process. If you need to do this, you must advance the workflow from an *OnCreate* event and get an *OnChange* event to fire, from which you send your workflow message. The following example creates a workflow CDO message and sends it to a user:

```
Sub CreateWFMessage()
    set oWFMsg = WorkflowSession.GetNewWorkflowMessage
    With oWFMsg
        .From = WorkflowSession.Sender
        .To = WorkflowSession.Sender
        .Subject = "Workflow Message"
        .TextBody = WorkflowSession.StateFrom & " -> " _
                  & WorkflowSession.StateTo
        .Fields("http://schemas.microsoft.com/exchange/" _
              & "outlookmessageclass").value = "IPM.Note.Workflow"
        .Fields.Update
        .SendWorkflowMessage 2 'cdowfAdd (not strict)
    End With
End Sub
```

E-mail-based workflow is supported only by clients that understand how to send back MAPI-based messages because custom properties need to be set on the reply message. For example, you must set the *workflowmessageid* and *parentprocessinstance* on your reply so the workflow engine knows to correlate the e-mail response rather than create an entirely new work item. The easiest way to add these properties to your responses is to use a custom Outlook or Web application that adds these properties. If you are going to use a custom Outlook form, you add code such as the following to your Outlook form to take the original properties from the e-mail sent by the workflow engine and add the needed properties to the response. If the code does not work for you, you might need to use CDO 1.21 in your Outlook form to add these custom properties to the item. The Outlook object model sometimes does not work correctly with these properties, but CDO 1.21 does. (The Outlook object model is covered in Chapter 6, and CDO is covered in Chapter 11.)

```
Sub Item_Reply(ByVal Response)
    set CurrentProp = Response.UserProperties.Add( "http://" _
                      & "schemas.microsoft.com/cdo/workflow/" _
                      & "parentprocinstance", 1)
    CurrentProp.Value = Item.UserProperties("http://" _
                      & "schemas.microsoft.com/cdo/workflow/" _
                      & "parentprocinstance").Value
    set CurrentProp = Response.UserProperties.Add ("http://" _
                      & "schemas.microsoft.com/cdo/workflow/" _
                      & "workflowmessageid", 1)
    CurrentProp.Value = Item.UserProperties("http://" _
                      & "schemas.microsoft.com/cdo/workflow/" _
                      & "workflowmessageid").Value
End Sub
```

The workflow engine, when you use the *SendWorkflowMessage* method, automatically adds the properties shown in the previous code to the outgoing message. When you receive the response back to the folder, you must tell the workflow engine to correlate the response back onto the work item. You can have the engine automatically do this for you by setting the *http://schemas.microsoft.com/cdo/workflow/response* in your custom form. If you do not set this property, you must update the *TrackingTable* in your workflow yourself. The *TrackingTable* is a record that the workflow engine keeps for each response. It contains standard properties for each response, such as date, state, e-mail address, and the tracking ID. It also contains custom fields that you can use for your custom data called *custom0* to *custom9*. The following code manually updates the *TrackingTable* for a response:

```
With WorkflowSession
    .TrackingTable.Fields("custom0") = .TrackingTable.Fields("custom0") _
                                     & vbCrLf &.ReceivedMessage.TextBody

    .TrackingTable.Fields.Update
End With
```

> **Note** You can debug your workflow solutions by using either the audit trail provider included with Exchange or script debugging. To enable script debugging, you must either select the script debugging option in the Workflow Designer or set to *True* the property on your workflow's event handler registration called *http://schemas.microsoft.com/cdo/workflow/enabledebug*. For the debugger to work, you must make sure that just-in-time (JIT) debugging is enabled in Windows. You can do this by modifying a key in the registry under HKCU/Software/Microsoft/Windows Script Host/Settings/ActiveDebugging and setting it to *1*.

Displaying Workflow States Using XMLDOM

You might want to graphically show or provide a text list of all the states in a workflow, and then perhaps display a list of current work items and finally display the state that the current work item is in. Retrieving and displaying the list of states—or, for that matter, doing this with state transitions or other workflow elements—is just a matter of retrieving the .wfd file for the workflow, which is stored in the folder. Then you just parse the XML that is contained in that file, looking for the specific XML elements you are interested in. The following code finds all row nodes in the XML that correspond to the different states in the workflow:

```
Function StateExist(strState, strStateArray) As Boolean
    Dim i, lo, hi As Integer

    StateExist = False
    lo = LBound(strStateArray)
    hi = UBound(strStateArray)
    For i = lo To hi
        If strStateArray(i) = strState Then
            StateExist = True
            Exit Function
        End If
    Next
End Function

Sub PopulateStates()
    ' Return all defined actions from specified workflow definition
    Dim cnn As ADODB.Connection
    Dim rec As ADODB.Record
    Dim fld As ADODB.Field
    Dim urlResource, urlFolder 'As String
    Dim xmlDoc As MSXML.DOMDocument
    Dim nodelist As MSXML.IXMLDOMNodeList
    Dim n As MSXML.IXMLDOMNode
    Dim strStateArray() As String
    Dim strState As String
    Dim intNrStates As Integer

    ReDim strStateArray(0)

    urlFolder = "http://thomriznt52/public/workflow/showstates/"
    urlResource = "showwfstate.wfd"

    ' Open the resource
    Set cnn = CreateObject("ADODB.Connection")
    With cnn
        .Provider = "Exoledb.Datasource"
        .Open urlFolder
    End With

    Set rec = CreateObject("ADODB.Record")
    rec.Open urlResource, cnn, adModeRead, adOpenIfExists

    ' Get the action table as XML
    Set fld = rec.Fields("http://schemas.microsoft.com/" _
            & "cdo/workflow/actiontable")

    Set xmlDoc = CreateObject("MSXML2.DOMDocument")
    xmlDoc.validateOnParse = False
```

```
    ' Load the Action Table
    xmlDoc.loadXML fld.Value

    ' Get the row node instances
    Set nodelist = xmlDoc.documentElement.selectNodes("//z:row")

    ' Return the name of each state and remove duplicates
    intNrStates = 0
    For Each n In nodelist
        strState = n.Attributes.getNamedItem("NewState").Text
        If strState <> "" And ((intNrStates = 0) Or _
                          Not StateExist(strState, strStateArray)) Then
            intNrStates = intNrStates + 1
            ReDim Preserve strStateArray(intNrStates - 1)
            strStateArray(intNrStates - 1) = strState
            strStateList = strStateList & " " & strStateArray(intNrStates - 1)
        End If
    Next

    MsgBox "The states are: " & strStateList
    ' Clean up
    rec.Close
    cnn.Close
    Set rec = Nothing
    Set fld = Nothing
    Set cnn = Nothing
    Set xmlDoc = Nothing
    Set nodelist = Nothing
    Set n = Nothing
End Sub

Private Sub Command1_Click()
    PopulateStates
End Sub
```

Deploying Workflow Solutions

Once you've drawn out your process, implemented your conditions and actions, and written your script, the next step is to deploy your workflow process to a folder. The Workflow Designer makes this step easy because you can save the workflow process into any folder in which you have permissions to create a workflow. Figure 17-16 shows how to select a public folder via the Save Workflow Process To Folder dialog box in the Workflow Designer.

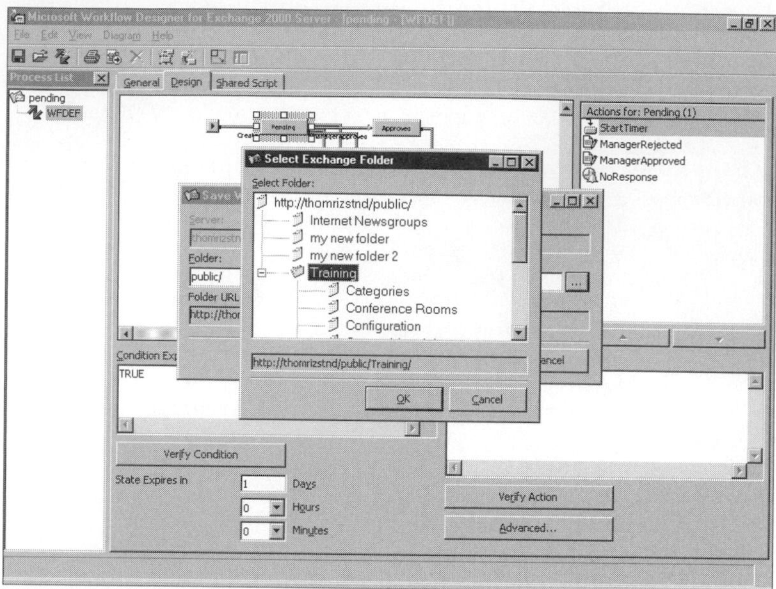

Figure 17-16 The Save Workflow Process To Folder dialog box makes it easy to deploy workflow solutions.

In some cases, you might need to programmatically deploy your solutions. Unfortunately, the Workflow Designer doesn't have an object model that you can automate to use the Save Workflow Process To Folder feature. Instead, you have to write some code to deploy your workflow process. If you do so, you should first use the Workflow Designer to export to XML the action table for your workflow process.

The following code, taken from the Training application setup program, shows how to deploy your workflow application programmatically. You'll notice the following steps in the code:

1. Create your common script file (if necessary).
2. Create a workflow *ProcessDefinition* object.
3. In the *ProcessDefinition* object, add your action table by creating a new *RecordSet* object and using the XML features of ADO to load the XML version of the action table that the Workflow Designer saved for you.
4. As part of creating your *ProcessDefinition* object, select your audit trail provider, set the location of your common script file, and set the mode that the workflow process should run under (restricted or privileged).

5. Save the *ProcessDefinition* object into the folder.

6. Create the event registration items for the *OnSyncSave*, *OnSync-Delete*, and *OnTimer* events. On the server events registration item for *OnSyncSave* and *OnSyncDelete*, set the properties in the *http://schemas.microsoft.com/cdo/workflow/* namespace—for example, the pointer to the default process definition for the folder, whether ad hoc workflows are allowed in the folder, whether to enable script debugging, and whether to log successful state transitions to the audit trail provider.

```
Private Sub AddWorkflowProcess()
    Dim oRS As New ADODB.RecordSet
    Dim oPD As New CDOWF.ProcessDefinition

    On Error GoTo errHandler

    'Add the common script file
    Dim oScriptRec As New ADODB.Record
    Dim oStream As New ADODB.Stream
    'Load the script file
    Dim fso As New Scripting.FileSystemObject
    Dim ofile As TextStream

    Set ofile = fso.OpenTextFile(App.Path & "\commonscript.txt")

    strCommonScript = ofile.ReadAll

    oScriptRec.Open strPath & "/Pending/commonscript", oConnection, _
                    adModeReadWrite, adCreateNonCollection
    oStream.Open oScriptRec, adModeReadWrite, adOpenStreamFromRecord
    With oStream
        .Charset = "unicode"
        .Type = adTypeText
        .Position = 0
        .SetEOS
        .WriteText strCommonScript
        .Position = 0
        .Flush
        .Close
    End With
    strScriptURL = oScriptRec.Fields("DAV:href").Value

    'Load the action table
    oRS.Open App.Path & "\actiontable.xml"
    With oPD
        .ActionTable = oRS
        .AuditTrailProvider = "CDOWF.AuditTrailEventLog"
        .CommonScriptURL = strScriptURL
        .Mode = cdowfPrivilegedMode
```

```
            .Fields("DAV:ishidden") = True
        End With

        oPD.DataSource.SaveTo strPath & "/Pending/WFDEF", oConnection, _
                              adModeReadWrite, adCreateNonCollection

        strPDHREF = oPD.Fields("DAV:href").Value

        'Create the event registrations

        'First create the timer event
        arrRequired = GenerateRequiredEventArray("", "ontimer", _
                      "CdoWfEvt.EventSink.1", "","")
        strNow = Now
        arrOptional = GenerateOptionalEventArray("", "", "", "", 15, _
                                                   strNow, "")

        CreateEvtRegistration oConnection, strPath & "Pending/timer", _
                              arrRequired, arrOptional, True

        'Create the OnSyncSave and onSyncDelete registration
        arrRequired = GenerateRequiredEventArray("WHERE ""DAV:ishidden"" = " _
                                      & "false AND ""DAV:isfolder"" = false", _
                                      "onsyncsave;onsyncdelete", _
                                      "CdoWfEvt.EventSink.1", "", "")
        'Create a new array and add some further properties for workflow
        Dim arrWorkflowRequired(6, 1)
        For i = LBound(arrRequired) To UBound(arrRequired)
            arrWorkflowRequired(i, 0) = arrRequired(i, 0)
            arrWorkflowRequired(i, 1) = arrRequired(i, 1)
        Next
        'Add workflow properties
        arrWorkflowRequired(3, 0) = _
            "http://schemas.microsoft.com/cdo/workflow/defaultprocdefinition"
        arrWorkflowRequired(3, 1) = strPDHREF
        arrWorkflowRequired(4, 0) = _
            "http://schemas.microsoft.com/cdo/workflow/adhocflows"
        arrWorkflowRequired(4, 1) = 0
        arrWorkflowRequired(5, 0) = _
            "http://schemas.microsoft.com/cdo/workflow/enabledebug"
        arrWorkflowRequired(5, 1) = False
        arrWorkflowRequired(6, 0) = _
            "http://schemas.microsoft.com/cdo/workflow/disablesuccessentries"
        arrWorkflowRequired(6, 1) = False   'Enable success entries

        CreateEvtRegistration oConnection, strPath & "Pending/workflowreg", _
                              arrWorkflowRequired, arrWorkflowOptional, True
        Exit Sub
    errHandler:
        MsgBox "Error in AddWorkflowProcess.  Error " & Err.Number & " " & _
               Err.Description
        End
    End Sub
```

Workflow Security and Deployment Gotchas

One gotcha you should be aware of when you deploy workflow solutions is a feature that can trip you up if you don't understand it. The workflow event handlers have two COM+ roles that they implement, which you saw earlier: *CanRegisterWorkflow* and *PrivilegedWorkflowAuthors*. If you don't understand what these roles are used for and how the workflow engine uses them, you might run into some issues. This section outlines how these two roles and the workflow engine work together.

The *CanRegisterWorkflow* role is used when someone attempts to register for the *Workflow* event handler. The *Workflow* event handler implements *ICreateRegistration*, so when someone attempts to register for the *Workflow* event handler, the event handler is called to verify whether it wants to allow the registration to go through. The *Workflow* event handler calls the COM+ method *IsUserInRole(CanRegisterWorkflow)* to determine whether the user attempting the registration is authorized to do so. If this call returns *True*, the *Workflow* event handler allows the registration to go through.

The *PrivilegedWorkflowAuthors* role is used to ensure that any executable workflow code to be run in Privileged mode has not been tampered with by an unauthorized person. Here's the scenario: User A has privileged permissions and registers a new workflow that contains a script to run in privileged mode. User B is allowed to write only sandboxed workflows, but he does have write access to user A's script file. User B later inserts malicious script into these workflow files, knowing it will be run in Privileged mode because User A has privileged workflow permissions.

To prevent this, at run time, the *Workflow* event sink checks to see which user last modified and saved the process definition, the script, and the event handler registration item. For each of these SIDs, the event sink calls COM+ *IsUserInRole(PrivilegedWorkflowAuthors)*. If any of these documents were last modified by a nonprivileged person, the workflow engine knows that the files were tampered with. The workflow engine immediately stops execution and logs a security error.

So, if you want to run privileged mode workflows, you must make sure that the account used to save all the critical documents, such as the process definition, scripts, and event registrations, is a member of the *PrivilegedWorkflowAuthors* role.

The Workflow Designer in Office XP Developer

To help you more quickly develop workflow applications, Microsoft has introduced a new version of the Workflow Designer in Office XP Developer Edition.

The new version of the Workflow Designer adds some new productivity enhancements for building workflow applications, and it can still import and modify your existing workflows built using the previous version of the Workflow Designer. Figure 17-17 shows the new interface for the Workflow Designer.

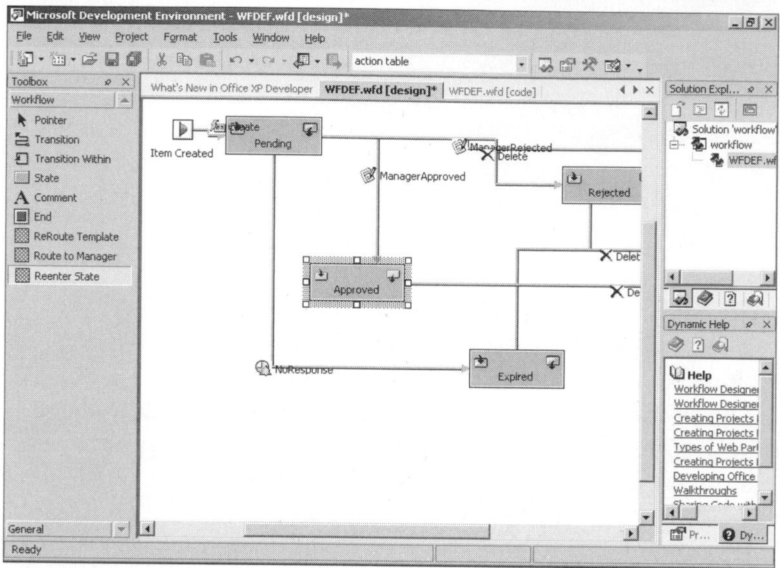

Figure 17-17 The new Workflow Designer in Office XP Developer

The first thing you will notice about the new designer is that the interface looks like the Visual Studio .NET interface. The Office XP Developer team took the Visual Studio .NET shell and used it as the basis for their new version. This means you get all the new shell enhancements that Visual Studio .NET supports. It does not mean that you get all the new features of Visual Studio .NET (such as C# and Web services development). You simply get used to the Visual Studio .NET shell by using Office XP Developer. If you want the Visual Studio .NET feature set, you have to buy Visual Studio .NET.

The new Workflow Designer has no new events or object models, but it has new security fixes and new functionality, such as the URLMapper support in workflows and development feature enhancements. We'll look at some of these enhancements next.

Coding Enhancements

One of the most exciting changes to the designer is that you now get a real coding environment instead of the Notepad-like environment in the previous version. With this version, you have color coding of your code, which makes it much easier to read through the code and understand where your functions and subs are, as well as your comments.

The code editor also supports autocompletion of your statements and IntelliSense. IntelliSense works just like in Visual Basic. When you start typing code, the IDE tries to help you complete that code or display parameter information when you type a function. You can also show class definitions and comments when you hover your cursor over a function. An example of code completion is when you type the word *WorkflowSession* in your code. The code editor displays the available methods and properties for the *WorkflowSession* object so you can quickly select one. An example of displaying parameters is when you type the *InStr* function. As soon as you type the parentheses for that function, the code editor displays the necessary parameters for the function as a tooltip.

Another new feature in the Visual Studio .NET shell used by Office XP Developer is code outlining. You can select multiple lines of code and collapse that code. If you want to see the code again, you can expand that section of code. This feature makes it much easier to read your code by allowing you to collapse code that you are not currently interested in. These and many other features make using the code editor much more efficient.

Enhanced Design Environment

Beyond making the code editor easier to use, Office XP Developer also has an enhanced Workflow Designer user interface. The new development environment offers drag-and-drop creation of all the different workflow primitives, such as states, transitions, and comments. When you double-click on any of these primitives, you are automatically launched into the code editor to modify the code for that primitive. For example, if you double-click on a state, the designer will automatically create the stub for the *OnEnter* event in your code and place you in the middle of that stub so you can write your specific handler code for that event. The previous version did not do this.

The designer toolbox, which is part of the development environment, also supports templatized workflows. This means that if you have a common element or elements that you use in multiple workflows, you can select those elements and drop them on the designer toolbox. Then you can just drag and drop the new toolbox item onto a new workflow and suddenly you will have the elements you added to the template. This makes it easier to reuse your common workflow states and transitions. Plus, it allows you to build up a rich toolbox from which you can quickly create workflows by leveraging common workflow templates.

A Seamless Upgrade

One nice thing about the workflow designer in Office Developer XP is that you can import your workflows that you built using the previous version of the designer. The new designer asks you if you want to translate the previous version's format into the new version's. It also migrates your code from the previous version to the new version. With this feature, you can quickly get your previous workflow designs into the new tool.

Some New Concepts

You will have to get used to some new concepts in the new designer. First and foremost is that the condition expression and action script procedure windows are gone. These windows have been replaced by functions that get called in your script code. For example, say you have an action called *Change1*. Previously, you would write your condition expression in the condition expression window, as in this example:

```
WorkflowSession.Fields("http://thomriz.com/schema/" _
                       & "approvalstatus").value = "Rejected"
```

Then you would write your action script procedure in the action script procedure window, as in this example:

```
strCourseName = GetCourseName
strStudentEmail = GetStudentEmail
strManagerEmail = GetManagerEmail
strBody = "Your manager rejected you for the course: " & strCourseName
sendMail strBody,strStudentEmail & "," _
         & strManagerEmail,"Rejected for course: " & strCourseName
```

With the new designer, you instead create functions and subs for both of these events. For example, your condition expression becomes a *Validate* function, such as *Change1_OnChangeValidate*. You must specify what makes this function *true*, and if the function is *true*, the *OnChange* sub for the element will be called. The *OnChangeValidate* function for *Change1* is shown here:

```
Function Change1_OnChangeValidate()
    bRetVal = CBOOL(WorkflowSession.Fields("http://thomriz.com/schema/" _
                    & "approvalstatus").value = "Rejected")
    Change1_OnChangeValidate = bRetVal
End Function
```

Your action script procedure becomes an *OnChange* sub, such as *Change1_OnChange*, as shown here:

```
Sub Change1_OnChange()
    strCourseName = GetCourseName
```

```
    strStudentEmail = GetStudentEmail
    strManagerEmail = GetManagerEmail
    strBody = "Your manager rejected you for the course: " & strCourseName
    sendMail strBody, strStudentEmail & "," & strManagerEmail, _
             "Rejected for course: " & strCourseName
End Sub
```

Finally, if you have a compensating action for *Change1*—so that if your code or an external component fails and the state of the workflow needs to be rolled back—you must implement an *OnChangeRollback* sub. In the previous version, you would implement a compensating action. The *OnChangeRollback* sub is shown here:

```
Sub Change1_OnChangeRollback
    WorkflowSession.AddAuditEntry "Failed!!!"
End Sub
```

Exchange Server and Security

Exchange 2000 Server and Exchange Server 2003 offer the ability to set permissions not only at the folder level but also at the item and property levels for documents or other objects contained in the Exchange information store. This means that you can secure your applications even further when data is stored in a single folder. We'll discuss the security features in Exchange and look at a Web application that allows you to try out these security features.

> **Note** If you set item-level security in Exchange 2000 or 2003 and the item is replicated to an Exchange 5.5 server, your security will not be enforced because Exchange 5.5 does not support item-level security.

Security Features

Exchange Server supports native Windows security descriptors. Using these descriptors, you can allow or deny access to an item or the item's properties, grant this access using Windows security identifiers, and access and set permissions by viewing and modifying the descriptor in an XML format from WebDAV or ADO/OLE DB (which we discussed in Chapter 16). By providing you with an XML representation of the security descriptor, Exchange makes it easy for you to work with security settings; you do not have to learn Windows API programming to change permissions. Furthermore, the technology in Exchange takes your XML descriptor and turns it into the correct binary representation of the descriptor in the Exchange database. You can access the XML-formatted descriptor by querying for the *http://schemas.microsoft.com/exchange/security/descriptor* property. The following code is an example of what is returned on an item when you query for this property from ADO:

```
'ADO code
Dim oRecord As New ADODB.Record
oRecord.Open "file://./backofficestorage/domain/apps/items/exchange.eml"
strSec = oRecord.Fields( _
           "http://schemas.microsoft.com/exchange/security/descriptor").value
```

Following are the XML results:

```
<S:security_descriptor
    xmlns:S="http://schemas.microsoft.com/security/"
    xmlns:D="urn:uuid:c2f41010-65b3-11d1-a29f-00aa00c14882/"
    D:dt="microsoft.security_descriptor">
 <S:revision>1</S:revision>
 <S:owner S:defaulted="0">
  <S:sid>
   <S:string_sid>S-1-5-21-1659004503-152049171-1202660629-1110</S:string_sid>
   <S:nt4_compatible_name>THOMRIZNT5DOM\thomriz</S:nt4_compatible_name>
   <S:user_principal_name>thomriz@thomriznt5dom.extest.microsoft.com
   </S:userprincipal_name>
   <S:display_name>Thomas Rizzo</S:display_name>
  </S:sid>
 </S:owner>
 <S:primary_group S:defaulted="0">
  <S:sid>
   <S:string_sid>S-1-5-21-1659004503-152049171-1202660629-513</S:string_sid>
   <S:nt4_compatible_name>THOMRIZNT5DOM\Domain Users</S:nt4_compatible_name>
  </S:sid>
 </S:primary_group>
 <S:dacl S:defaulted="1" S:protected="0" S:autoinherited="1">
  <S:revision>2</S:revision>
  <S:effective_aces>
   <S:access_allowed_ace S:inherited="1">
    <S:access_mask>1fcfff</S:access_mask>
    <S:sid>
     <S:string_sid>S-1-5-21-1659004503-152049171-1202660629-1110
     </S:string_sid>
     <S:nt4_compatible_name>THOMRIZNT5DOM\thomriz</S:nt4_compatible_name>
     <S:user_principal_name>thomriz@thomriznt5dom.extest.microsoft.com
     </S:user_principal_name>
     <S:display_name>Thomas Rizzo</S:display_name>
    </S:sid>
   </S:access_allowed_ace>
   <S:access_allowed_ace S:inherited="1">
    <S:access_mask>1fcfff</S:access_mask>
    <S:sid>
     <S:string_sid>S-1-5-21-1659004503-152049171-1202660629-1105
     </S:string_sid>
```

```
    <S:nt4_compatible_name>THOMRIZNT5DOM\Domain EXServers
    </S:nt4_compatible_name>
   </S:sid>
  </S:access_allowed_ace>
  <S:access_allowed_ace S:inherited="1">
   <S:access_mask>1fcfff</S:access_mask>
   <S:sid>
    <S:string_sid>S-1-5-21-1659004503-152049171-1202660629-500
    </S:string_sid>
    <S:nt4_compatible_name>THOMRIZNT5DOM\Administrator
    </S:nt4_compatible_name>
    <S:display_name>Administrator</S:display_name>
   </S:sid>
  </S:access_allowed_ace>
  <S:access_allowed_ace S:inherited="1">
   <S:access_mask>1fcfff</S:access_mask>
   <S:sid>
    <S:string_sid>S-1-5-21-1659004503-152049171-1202660629-519
    </S:string_sid>
    <S:nt4_compatible_name>THOMRIZNT5DOM\Enterprise Admins
    </S:nt4_compatible_name>
   </S:sid>
  </S:access_allowed_ace>
  <S:access_allowed_ace S:inherited="1">
   <S:access_mask>1fcfff</S:access_mask>
   <S:sid>
    <S:string_sid>S-1-5-21-1659004503-152049171-1202660629-512
    </S:string_sid>
    <S:nt4_compatible_name>THOMRIZNT5DOM\Domain Admins
    </S:nt4_compatible_name>
   </S:sid>
  </S:access_allowed_ace>
  <S:access_allowed_ace S:inherited="1">
   <S:access_mask>12088f</S:access_mask>
   <S:sid>
    <S:string_sid>S-1-1-0</S:string_sid>
    <S:nt4_compatible_name>\Everyone</S:nt4_compatible_name>
   </S:sid>
  </S:access_allowed_ace>
 </S:effective_aces>
 </S:dacl>
</S:security_descriptor>
```

This XML code is for a nonfolder security descriptor—specifically, an item. A folder security descriptor is a bit different, but as you can see in the XML structure shown in the code, a security descriptor is made up of a Discretionary Access Control List (DACL), which in turn is made up of Access Control Entries (ACEs). Each ACE in the DACL either grants or denies a trustee a certain set of rights to the object. The access mask, which you see defined in the XML, describes the set of rights that are granted or denied to a user. Access masks are

32-bit numbers in which the upper 16 bits describe generic rights and the lower 16 bits describe object-specific rights.

Some quick points about what you see in the XML that is returned. The *defaulted* flag tells whether the DACL was a default DACL. For example, on item creation, a default DACL was used rather than someone specifying it. This affects how inherited ACEs are treated in the DACL. The *protected* flag specifies whether the DACL of the security descriptor will inherit any aces from its parent. It gets changed by an application program or when you deselect the Allow Inheritable Permissions From The Parent To Propagate check box in the Security Settings dialog box. If you want to set up custom security on your folder and not inherit from your parent, you set the *protected* flag to 1 for your DACL. This causes all inherited ACEs to be ignored. The *autoinherited* flag specifies whether the DACL can have ACEs automatically propagated to child objects. The primary group tag is for POSIX compatibility.

We need to discuss three other blocks: *effective_aces*, *subcontainer_inheritable*, and *subitem_inheritable*. The descriptor section for *effective_aces* applies to the item in question, and *subcontainer_inheritable* applies to subfolders and is present only in the security descriptor for folders. The *subitems_inheritable* section applies to items and messages and is present only in the security descriptor of a folder. When a folder or item is created, by default it gets the permissions that appear in the subcontainer/subitem block of the security descriptor of its parent folder. If the *no_propagate_inherit* attribute is set in the ACE, it applies only to the immediate sublevel and will not appear in the *subcontainer_inheritable* block of the new folder.

A quick comment about working with security in Exchange. How you create the format for your security descriptor will depend on whether you are working in a MAPI public folder top-level hierarchy (TLH) or a non-MAPI TLH. A MAPI TLH requires that you create your security descriptor using the MAPI canonical format. This is what clients, such as Outlook, expect to see; the importance of this requirement cannot be overemphasized. If you create your security descriptor using the Windows canonical format, you will break Outlook! It is also possible to lock yourself out from being able to modify existing items or folders. Therefore, you must be very careful when you work with security descriptors. I highly recommend that you just take advantage of the Security Module that ships with the Exchange SDK. It understands how to correctly create both MAPI and Windows canonical formats and includes code to make sure you don't do any harm when working with security descriptors. You can find more information on the Security Module later in this chapter.

Note You might be wondering whether you should ever go through the M: drive to set security for your applications. In Exchange 2003, the M: drive is turned off by default, and you should try to keep it that way. However, if you turn the M: drive on, there are some security issues you should know about. For example, if you are working in non-MAPI folder trees—which are essentially not in the MAPI-based public folder hierarchy—you can use this method to set your security. If you are in the MAPI TLH and set security using Windows Explorer through the M: drive, you will break MAPI client applications such as Outlook and affect their ability to view and set permissions. This is because Windows Explorer formats the ACLs as Windows canonical and not MAPI canonical. In other words, do not set permissions using the M: drive for MAPI folders.

Tables 17-8, 17-9, and 17-10 describe the kinds of access rights you can have: standard access rights, access rights on folders, and access rights on non-folders (items), respectively. You can combine values in each table and put them into the access mask to create the correct security descriptor for the user.

If you were to create an access mask with all the properties in Table 17-8, the value would be *0x1F0000*.

Table 17-8 Standard Rights (Non-Exchange, Windows)

Access Right	Value (Hex)	Description
fsdrightDelete	*0x00010000*	Delete
fsdrightReadControl	*0x00020000*	Read access to security descriptor and owner
fsdrightWriteSD	*0x00040000*	Write DACL permissions
fsdrightWriteOwner	*0x00080000*	Used to assign write owner
fsdrightSynchronize	*0x00100000*	Used to synchronize access to the object

If a user were to have all rights in Table 17-9, the value of the mask would be *0xCFFF*.

Table 17-9 Folder Rights

Access Right	Value (Hex)	Description
fsdrightListContents	*0x00000001*	Right to list contents of the directory.
fsdrightCreateItem	*0x00000002*	Right to add a file to the folder.
fsdrightCreateContainer	*0x00000004*	Right to add a subfolder.
fsdrightReadProperty	*0x00000008*	Right to read extended attributes.
fsdrightWriteProperty	*0x00000010*	Right to write extended attributes.
fsdrightReadAttributes	*0x00000080*	Right to read file attributes. Currently unused.
fsdrightWriteAttributes	*0x00000100*	Right to change file attributes. Currently unused.
fsdrightWriteOwnProperty	*0x00000200*	Right to modify own items (Exchange-specific property).
fsdrightDeleteOwnItem	*0x00000400*	Right to delete own items.
fsdrightViewItem	*0x00000800*	Right to view items (Exchange-specific property).
fsdrightOwner	*0x00004000*	Owner of the folder. Provided for backward compatibility.
fsdrightContact	*0x00008000*	Contact for the folder. Provided for backward compatibility.

If a user were to have all the rights in Table 17-10, the value would be *0x0FBF*.

Table 17-10 Item Rights

Access Right	Value (Hex)	Description
fsdrightReadBody	*0x00000001*	Right to read data from a file.
fsdrightWriteBody	*0x00000002*	Right to write data to a file.
fsdrightAppendMessage	*0x00000004*	Same as *fsdrightWriteBody*. Not currently used.
fsdrightReadProperty	*0x00000008*	Right to read extended attributes.
fsdrightWriteProperty	*0x00000010*	Right to write extended attributes.
fsdrightExecute	*0x00000020*	Right to execute a file. Currently not used.

Table 17-10 Item Rights

Access Right	Value (Hex)	Description
fsdrightReadAttributes	*0x00000080*	Right to read file attributes.
fsdrightWriteAttributes	*0x00000100*	Right to change file attributes.
fsdrightWriteOwnProperty	*0x00000200*	Right to modify own item (Exchange-specific property).
fsdrightDeleteOwnItem	*0x00000400*	Right to delete own item (Exchange-specific property).
fsdrightViewItem	*0x00000800*	Right to view item (Exchange-specific property).

In the preceding XML code example, you can have an *access_allowed_ace*, which contains the access mask for the rights you will allow for the user on the item or folder. You can also have an *access_denied_ace*, which specifies an access mask that contains the rights you will deny for the user on the folder or item. If the user has all rights, as in the preceding XML example, the access mask will be *0x1FCFFF*, which means all rights from the three previous tables are granted to the user. Creating the access mask is just a matter of adding together the hexadecimal values from the tables and creating the ACE for the user. We'll see an example on how to create an ACE later in this chapter using the XMLDOM.

Before we drill down into a sample application, you need to know that there are certain rights the user needs in order to access the security descriptor: *fsdrightReadControl*, *fsdrightWriteSD*, and *fsdrightWriteOwner*.

A Sample Security Application

The security sample application included with the book's companion content makes using the XML security descriptor much easier. It is a Web application that leverages XMLDOM, XSL, and WebDAV to show you how to work with and set the XML security descriptors in Exchange. Figure 17-18 shows the main interface for the security application.

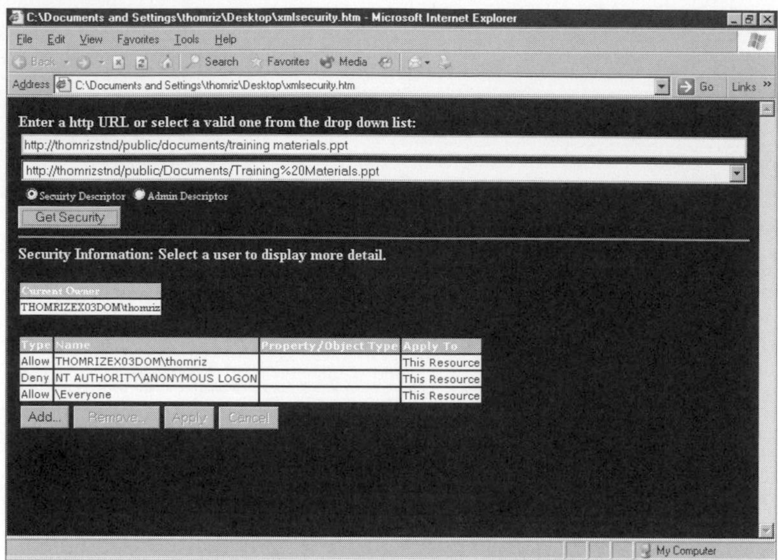

Figure 17-18 The main interface for the security application

One task to try when you work with the security application is restricting who can view items in an Exchange folder. The next bit of code shows how to do this. As you can see in Figure 17-19, the user can view the document named Training Materials. However, after applying the setting that denies this user access to the document, as shown in Figure 17-20, the user can no longer see the specific document but can see all the other documents contained in the folder. The figure shows what the user sees after you apply the security change.

The application works by combining XMLDOM, XSL, and WebDAV to get, display, and set item-level and property-level security in Exchange. As you can see from the following code snippet, when you click the OK button to retrieve the security for an object in Exchange, the application does a *PROPFIND* on the *http://schemas.microsoft.com/exchange/security/descriptor* property. The application then uses XSL to display the HTML that you see in the browser.

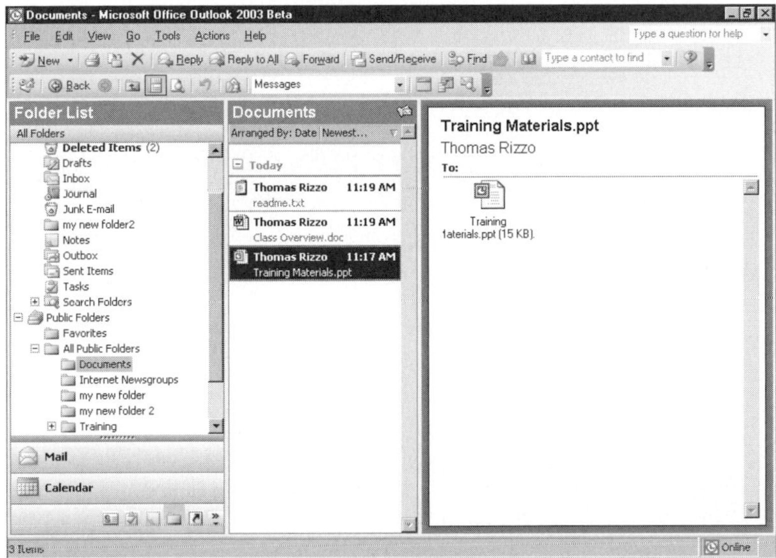

Figure 17-19 Before you apply the security settings, the user can view the full list of documents.

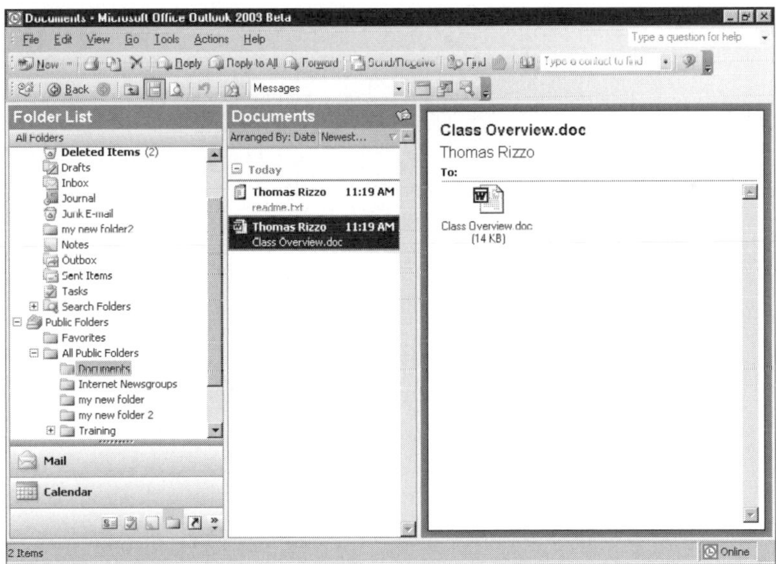

Figure 17-20 After you apply the security settings, the user can no longer view the restricted files.

```
function cmdGetSec.onclick()
{
    var strReqBody = "";

    if(txtUrl.value == "")
    {
        alert("Please Enter or select a valid URL.");
        return;
    }

    strReqBody = "<?xml version=\"1.0\" encoding=\"utf-8\"?>"
        + "<propfind xmlns=\"DAV:\">"
        + "<prop xmlns:r=\"http://schemas.microsoft.com/exchange/security/\">"
        + "   <r:descriptor/>"
        + "</prop>"
        + "</propfind>";

    DAVRequest.open("PROPFIND", txtUrl.value, false);
    DAVRequest.setRequestHeader("Content-Type", "text/xml");
    DAVRequest.setRequestHeader("Depth", "0");
    DAVRequest.setRequestHeader("Translate", "f");
    DAVRequest.send(strReqBody);

    if(chkMultiStatusForErr(DAVRequest) >= 0)
    {
        xmlResponse = DAVRequest.responseXml;
        perm_entries_dest.innerHTML =
            xmlResponse.transformNode(xslPerm_Entries);
            ace_entries_dest.innerHTML = "<div/>";
            ace_edit_dest.innerHTML = "<div/>";
            add_dest.innerHTML = "<DIV/>";

        xmlResponse.transformNodeToObject(xslAceEntries.documentElement,
            xmlAceEntries);

        HiLitePermsTable();
        propfindForResources();

        cmdAdd.disabled = false;
        cmdRemove.disabled = true;
        cmdAceApply.disabled = true;
        cmdAceCancel.disabled = true;

        strOwner = owner.innerText;
    }
}
```

To add a new ACE, all the application does is take your entered data and turn it into a new XML node that it adds to the XML security descriptor. To do this, the application fills in the required properties to correctly generate a new

ACE, such as a Windows-compatible name, the access mask, as well as the ACE type. The code that does the XML work is shown here:

```
function addAce(strUserName, strMask, strPropName, strApplyTo, _
                strRoleProp, strRoleScope, fbAllow)
{
    //   Basic variable declarations.
    var baseNode      = null;
    var nodeFirstAce  = null;
    var nodeSubNode   = null;
    var nodeNewNode   = null;
    var nOrder        = 0;

    nOrder = getAceOrder(strUserName, null, strPropName, strApplyTo,
                         strRoleProp, strRoleScope, fbAllow);

    while(nOrder > -1)
    {
        removeAce(nOrder);
        nOrder = getAceOrder(strUserName, strMask, strPropName, strApplyTo,
                             strRoleProp, strRoleScope, fbAllow);
    }

    //   Establish the base node.
    baseNode = xmlAceEntries.documentElement;

    //   Create the ace node.
    nodeNewNode = xmlAceEntries.createNode(1, "ace", "");

    //   Add the NT4_Compatible_Name sub node.
    nodeSubNode = xmlAceEntries.createNode(1, "NT4_Compatible_Name", "");
    nodeSubNode.text = strUserName;
    nodeNewNode.appendChild(nodeSubNode);

    //   Add the Access_Mask sub node.
    nodeSubNode = xmlAceEntries.createNode(1, "Access_Mask", "");
    nodeSubNode.text = strMask;
    nodeNewNode.appendChild(nodeSubNode);

    //   Add the Ace_Type sub node.
    nodeSubNode = xmlAceEntries.createNode(1, "Ace_Type", "");

    nodeSubNode.text = getAceType(strPropName, fbAllow);

    nodeNewNode.appendChild(nodeSubNode);

    //   Add the Apply_To sub node.
    nodeSubNode = xmlAceEntries.createNode(1, "Apply_To", "");
    nodeSubNode.text = strApplyTo;
    nodeNewNode.appendChild(nodeSubNode);
```

```
    //   Add the Property_Name sub node.
    nodeSubNode = xmlAceEntries.createNode(1, "Property_Name", "");
    nodeSubNode.text = strPropName;
    nodeNewNode.appendChild(nodeSubNode);

    if(strRoleScope != null && strRoleScope != "")
    {
        nodeSubNode = xmlAceEntries.createNode(1, "Role_Scope", "");
        nodeSubNode.text = strRoleScope;
        nodeNewNode.appendChild(nodeSubNode);
    }

    if(strRoleProp != null && strRoleProp != "")
    {
        nodeSubNode = xmlAceEntries.createNode(1, "Role_Property", "");
        nodeSubNode.text = strRoleProp;
        nodeNewNode.appendChild(nodeSubNode);
    }

    baseNode = xmlAceEntries.documentElement;
    baseNode.appendChild(nodeNewNode);

    refreshAceList();
}
```

To set the security, the application does a *PROPPATCH* to the same property but with the new security descriptor formatted as XML and the new security added as XML nodes:

```
function cmdAceApply.onclick()
{
    var xmldomAce = new ActiveXObject("Microsoft.XMLDOM");
    var xmlAccessMaskNode = null;
    var xmlAceTypeNodes = null;
    var xmlAceTypeNode = null;
    var xmlUserNameNode = null;
    var xmlApplyToNode = null;
    var xmlPropNode = null;

    cmdAceApply.disabled = true;
    cmdAceCancel.disabled = true;

    addAcesOutstandingAcesToXML();

    xmlAceEntries.transformNodeToObject(xslProppatch.documentElement,
                                        xmldomProppatch);

    DAVRequest.open("PROPPATCH", txtUrl.value, false);
    DAVRequest.setRequestHeader("Content-Type", "text/xml");
    DAVRequest.setRequestHeader("Translate", "f");
    DAVRequest.send(xmldomProppatch);
```

```
    if(chkMultiStatusForErr(DAVRequest) >= 0)
    {
        HiLitePermsTable();

        if(nCurrentAce > -1)
        {
            xmldomAce.loadXML(
                xmlAceEntries.childNodes(0).childNodes(nCurrentAce).xml);
            ace_entries_dest.innerHTML =
                xmldomAce.transformNode(xslDips_ACE_Info);
            ace_edit_dest.innerHTML =
                xmldomAce.transformNode(xslACE_Edit.documentElement);

            perm_entries_dest.innerHTML =
                xmldomProppatch.transformNode(xslPerm_Entries);
            HiLiteRow(thetable, nCurrentAce+1);
        }
    }

    cmdGetSec.onclick();

    return "";
}
```

Working with Roles

Exchange offers 16 folder-based roles named, coincidentally, *Role1* through *Role16*. By offering folder-based roles, you can set up roles per application and you do not need to modify Active Directory to create your roles. This gives workflow developers (or any developers, for that matter) the flexibility for using roles without requiring Active Directory permissions. The code for creating roles is beyond the scope of this chapter, but there is an excellent whitepaper on the Microsoft Exchange Developer Center at *http://msdn.microsoft.com/exchange*. The sample files for the book include Visual C++ code to work with and create folder-based roles. Also included is the compiled C++ code in a DLL so you can create roles without having to compile the source. The following code uses the DLL to create a new role and add users to that role:

```
Dim strDomain As String
strDomain = "YOURDOMAIN"
Dim strURL As String
Dim rec As ADODB.Record
Dim fld As ADODB.Field
Dim rol As Role
Dim sidAdmin As Sid
Dim sidUser1 As Sid
Dim sidUser2 As Sid
```

```
Dim varRole As Variant
Dim isid As Long

'Open a record and get access to PR_XMT_SECURITY_ROLE_1
strURL = "file://./backofficestorage/" & strDomain _
      & "/public folders/NewFolder"
Set rec = New ADODB.Record
rec.Open strURL, , adModeReadWrite

'Create some sid's
Set sidAdmin = New Sid
sidAdmin.NT4CompatibleName = "Administrator"
Set sidUser1 = New Sid
sidUser1.NT4CompatibleName = "thomriz"
Set sidUser2 = New Sid
sidUser2.NT4CompatibleName = "user1"

'Create a role object with these sid's as members
Set rol = New Role
rol.Add sidAdmin
rol.Add sidUser1
rol.Add sidUser2
varRole = rol.OpaqueData

'Set as value for role property
rec.Fields.Append "http://schemas.microsoft.com/mapi/proptag/x3D250102", _
                  adVarBinary, Len(varRole), , varRole
rec.Fields.Update
rec.Close
Set rec = Nothing

'Reopen
Set rec = New ADODB.Record
rec.Open "file://./backofficestorage/" & strDomain _
        & "/public folders/NewFolder"
Set fld = rec.Fields("http://schemas.microsoft.com/" _
        & "mapi/proptag/x3D250102")

'Get the role object
Set rol = New Role
rol.OpaqueData = fld.Value

'Display what's there
Debug.Print rol.Count
For isid = 0 To rol.Count - 1
    Dim sidT As Sid

    Set sidT = rol.Member(isid)
    Debug.Print sidT.NT4CompatibleName
Next isid
```

Unfortunately, you cannot currently rename the 16 built-in roles. When you work with the workflow engine, you normally work with roles using the *ItemAuthors* and *ItemReaders* collections, which we discussed earlier. Therefore, you need to know what the different roles were used for in your application. One way to determine this is to use some form of lookup in your code. For example, you can store the role name in a multivalue property in the corresponding index in the array of values.

Once you have roles established in your workflow applications, using them is very straightforward. Instead of passing usernames to the workflow functions, you can pass roles. The following example uses *Role1*, which corresponds to an approver's role in the workflow. It sets the *ItemAuthors* collection to *Role1* and clears the *ItemReaders* collection. It also uses the *IsUserInRole* function to see if the person attempting to approve the item is in the *Role1* role. If she is not, the state transition will fail.

```
Sub SetItemAuthors()
    WorkflowSession.ItemAuthors.Add "Role1", 1
End Sub

Sub SetItemReaders()
    'Clear the collection
    WorkflowSession.ItemReaders.Clear
    WorkflowSession.ItemReaders.Add "Role1", 1
End Sub

Function CheckRole(strName, strRole)
    CheckRole = WorkflowSession.IsUserInRole(strName, strRole)
End Function
```

As you can see in the code, it is easy to use roles once you know how. The DLL makes it easy to create roles for your applications that you can leverage and makes management of the membership of roles easy. Plus, with the built-in support for roles in the workflow engine, you should take advantage of roles when it makes sense for your applications—such as when you do not have write permissions to Active Directory.

The Exchange SDK Application Security Module

Many developers requested the ability to set and get permissions on items and folders in the Exchange information store. Security can be complex and hard to understand, so the Application Security Module included with the SDK is especially valuable. The module is installed when you install the Exchange SDK. You can find it in the SDK directory under the Samples/Security folder. The module includes a set of JavaScript and ASP pages that allow you to access and modify the XML security descriptor in both Exchange and SPS 2001. The module can modify permissions either by using the XMLHTTP component on the client or by using ADO on the server. It's up to the application developer to decide which mode to use. I recommend the server-side version if you want the broadest range of browser support. The XMLHTTP component is supported only by Internet Explorer.

Besides providing code to update security descriptors, the module includes an interesting sample application that shows how to use the object model for the module. You can modify this sample application for use in your own applications. The application has an interface similar to the permissions property page in Outlook.

To work with the sample, you just create a new virtual directory. Copy the security files into that new virtual directory and then point your browser to the start.asp page in the virtual directory. If you want to take just the security module files and use them in your application, take the files listed in Table 17-11.

Table 17-11 Application Security Module Files

File	Description
Security.js	Defines the properties and methods for the *DACL* and *Entity* objects
LoadSaveDACL.js	Contains properties and methods for loading and saving a DACL
CustomLoadSaveDacl.js	Contains properties and methods for loading and saving a DACL for a non–Internet Explorer browser
Daclstrutil.js	Contains functions for converting DACLs to XML strings and vice versa for non–Internet Explorer browsers

To work with these files in ASP, you just use the *#include* directive to include the server-side JavaScript files with the rest of your ASP code. The following code snippet shows how to do this:

```
<%@ Language=javascript%>
<script language="javascript" runat=server src="loadsavedacl.js"></script>
<script language="javascript" runat=server src="security.js"></script>
```

The security module contains an object model that consists mainly of an *Entity* object, which is a security principal (a user, usually) and that security principal's SIDs, and a *DACL* object, which contains one or more entity objects.

You need to know some caveats about the security module, however. First, it cannot change permissions on inherited ACEs. This means that if a user's permissions are inherited from the parent folder, you cannot modify these permissions. Second, the module is written in JavaScript, so if you're using Visual Basic, you have to do some work to load the Internet Explorer control in a form in Visual Basic so you can run code that calls the security module. The Training application setup program does exactly this, as you will see later in this chapter. Also, with the code written in JavaScript, you must make JavaScript the default language for your ASP pages, which means you have to write the rest of your code in JavaScript. If you are like me and prefer to write most of your server-side ASP code in VBScript, this can make working with the security module a bit hard.

If these shortcomings don't affect you, the security module makes the task of working with security easy. We'll look next at the object model for the security module and then at how to perform common security programming tasks using the module.

Entity Object

As mentioned earlier, the security module is made up of *Entity* and *DACL* objects. Table 17-12 lists the methods of the *Entity* object.

Table 17-12 Methods of the *Entity* Object

Method	Description
ClearByTemplate	Clears a specified DACL from an entity based on a template. You must pass a *DACL* object used as the template and a string value of an entity to try to match in the template. This name can be an Exchange 5.5 template name such as "Owner", "Author", or "Editor", or a domain\username string.
HasMask	Returns a *Boolean* that specifies whether the entity has specific rights to the object. You must pass the masks to test for which is a string value.
HasMaskByTemplate	Returns a *Boolean* and checks to see if an entity has specific rights to an object by comparing the entity rights with a template you specify. You must pass the name of the entity to try to match, such as "Owner", "Editor", or a domain\username. Then you must pass a *DACL* object to be used as the template to compare with the *Entity* object.
HasMaskofEntity	Used to determine whether one entity has the same mask as another entity. You must pass to this method the other *Entity* object. This method returns a *Boolean*. You can use this method to see if a user has a specific predefined role, such as "Owner" or "Author".

Table 17-12 Methods of the *Entity* Object

Method	Description
IsEqualMask	Returns a *Boolean* that specifies whether the entity has exactly the same specified mask. You must pass the bitmask to test the entity against.
IsEqualTo	Returns a *Boolean* that specifies whether the two entities match exactly. You must pass to this method the second entity to try and test for a match.
MakeEqualToTemplate	Sets the masks in the entity equal to the masks of a template you specify. You must pass a *DACL* object to use as a template and the name of an entity to match in the *DACL* object. The module will then set the masks of the entity to match the entity it finds in the *DACL* template.
SetByTemplate	Adds masks to an *Entity* object from a template. You must specify the *DACL* object to use as a template and the name of the entity in the *DACL* template to add to your specified entity.

Table 17-13 lists the properties of the *Entity* object.

Table 17-13 Properties of the *Entity* Object

Property	Description
DisplayName	The display name of the security entity specified by the *Entity* object. This name is pulled from Active Directory and is usually the friendly name of the user or group.
Inherited	A *Boolean* property that specifies whether the security descriptor for the entity is inherited from the parent folder.
Masks	The access masks for the entity returned as a hexadecimal number.
NT4Name	The domain and username for the security principal. Note that all the strings used to denote domain and username are double-slashed with the security module, as in *domain**username*.
SID	Returns the SID for the security principal.
SIDType	Returns the type of SID, such as user, group, domain, alias, or well_known_group.

DACL Object

Now that you've seen the methods and properties of the *Entity* object, let's look at the methods and properties for the *DACL* object. Table 17-14 lists the methods of the *DACL* object. I've grouped some similar operations together in the table to make it easier for you to understand how they can be used interchangeably.

Table 17-14 Methods of the *DACL* Object

Method	Description
AddEmptySecurityEntity	Adds a new *Entity* object to the *DACL* object's *Entities* collection. You must pass the *SIDType*, such as user, group, domain, alias, well_known_group, deleted_account, invalid, unknown, or computer. You must also pass the *SID* of the entity. Next you must pass the domain and username of the user. Then you must pass the display name of the security principal. Finally, you can optionally pass a *Boolean* that specifies whether the entity is inherited.
AddEntity	Copies the *Entity* object you pass into the *Entities* collection for the *DACL* object.
AddSecurityEntity	The same as the *AddEmptySecurityEntity* except that before the optional *Boolean* inherited parameter, there is a required masks parameter, which is an array of hexadecimal numbers you pass to specify the access mask for the new entity.
AddSimpleSecurityEntity	Adds a new entity to the *DACL* object without requiring the *SIDType*, *SID*, and display name. You will most commonly use this method to add new entities. You must pass the domain\username of the security principal and access mask as parameters to this method.
ClearByTemplate	Removes a specific access mask from a specific entity in the *DACL* object. You must pass the entity name to match as *domain\username*. You must then pass a *DACL* object to use as a template. Finally, you must pass the name of the entity in the *DACL* template to search for.
CopyUserMasks	Copies the access masks of one entity to another in the *DACL* object. You must pass the domain\username of the security principal or a predefined role such as "Author" as the source whose masks are copied. Then you must pass the domain\username or predefined role as the target where the masks are to be copied.

Table 17-14 Methods of the *DACL* Object

Method	Description
CreateSecurityDACL	Creates a *DACL* object from an item's XML security descriptor. This is the first method you call when you work with the security module. You can pass *SECURITY_ON_SERVER* or *SECURITY_ON_CLIENT* to this method. Server security is enabled by default.
GetAllByEqualMask, *GetAllByMask*, *GetAllBySIDType*	These methods are similar. You must pass access masks for the first two methods, and you must pass a SID type for the third method. These methods return an array of index values for all entities that match your specified parameters.
GetEntityByIndex	Returns an *Entity* object by the index you specify, which must be an integer. Note that the *Entities* collection is zero-based.
Load	Creates a *DACL* object from an item. You must pass the URL to the item as a parameter. You can also optionally pass the username and password as parameters to access the item. If you do not pass a username or password, the application will use the credentials of the currently logged on user to attempt to access the item.
MakeEqualToTemplate	Sets the masks in an entity in a *DACL* object to be equal to the masks in the specified entity. You must pass a string that specifies the entity in the original *DACL* object. Then you must pass another *DACL* object to use as a template. Finally, you must pass a string that is the name of the entity in the *DACL* template to find, retrieve its access mask, and copy that access mask to the specified entity in the first parameter.
ModifyByTemplate	Performs an action you specify on the masks in a *DACL* object that match any of the masks you specify in a template *DACL* object. You must specify the name of the entity to match in the *DACL* template, the *DACL* template itself, and the string name of the entity to find in the *DACL* template. Finally, you must pass the action, such as *Make*, *Set*, or *Clear*. *Make* sets the masks of the specified DACL to the masks of the template DACL. *Set* does a bitwise *OR* of the masks. *Clear* deletes the masks.
RemoveByDisplayName, *RemoveByIndex*, *RemoveByNT4Name*, *RemoveBySID*	Each of these methods removes an *Entity* object from a DACL based on the parameter you pass. The last words of the method indicate what the parameter should be. For example, for *RemoveByDisplayName*, you must pass the display name of the entity to remove.

Table 17-14 Methods of the *DACL* Object

Method	Description
RemoveInheritedEntities	This method takes no parameters and removes the inherited entities from the DACL's *Entities* collection.
Save	Saves the DACL. You can optionally pass a username and a password as parameters to this method.
SaveTo	Saves the DACL to the item specified by the URL you pass as a string to this method.
SearchForIndexByDisplayName, *SearchForIndexByMask*, *SearchForIndexByNT4Name*, *SearchForIndexBySID*, *SearchForIndexBySIDType*	Each of these methods searches for and returns an index of an entity based on the last words in its name. You must pass a different parameter depending on the search criteria for each different method. For example, the *SearchForIndexByDisplayName* method takes a display name and returns the index of the entity, if any, that matches that display name in the DACL's *Entities* collection.
SearchForObjectByDisplayName, *SearchForObjectByMask*, *SearchForObjectByNT4Name*, *SearchForObjectBySID*, *SearchForObjectBySIDType*	Each of these methods returns the *Entity* object that matches the criteria specified by the last words in the method name. For example, *SearchForObjectByDisplayName* takes the display name of the entity to search for; if it finds the entity, the method returns the *Entity* object that matches that display name.
SetProtected	A *Boolean* method. A value of *True* means the application will prevent DACLs from inheriting ACEs. The method makes copies of all inherited ACEs. If you need to make changes to inherited principals, you must use this method to copy them first to break the inheritance because the module cannot modify inherited permissions. You can then explicitly set your permissions on that principal.
SetByTemplate	Sets the masks of the *DACL* object from a template. You must specify the domain\username of a security principal. Then you must specify the *DACL* object to use as a template. Finally, you must specify the name of the entity to find in the template *DACL* object to apply to the original DACL.

Table 17-15 lists the properties of the *DACL* object.

Table 17-15 Properties of the *DACL* Object

Property	Description
Count	Returns the number of entities in the DACL.
Entities	Returns an array of *Entity* objects that the *DACL* object contains.
IsFolder	A *Boolean* that returns *True* if the DACL points to an item that is a folder and *False* if the DACL points to an item that is really an item and not a collection.
IsProtected	A *Boolean* that returns *True* if the *DACL* object does not inherit any ACEs from its parent.
Loc	Specifies the location where the *DACL* object was created. This can be client (*1*) or server (*0*).
URL	Specifies the URL to the item from which the *DACL* object was instantiated.

Access Mask Templates

The security module includes access mask templates that make it easier to set permissions or find users or groups that match these templates. The four key templates are *DACLLegacyRoles*, *DACLLegacyMetaRights*, *DACLWebStorageItem*, and *DACLWebStorageFolder*. *DACLLegacyRoles* specifies the access masks for MAPI-based roles, such as "Owner", "Publishing Editor", or "Reviewer". Instead of you having to figure out the specific bitmask to pass to set permissions for a user as "Owner", you can just use the *DACLLegacyRoles* template. We'll look at how to do this later in the following section.

The *DACLLegacyMetaRights* template specifies the MAPI permissions that make up the legacy roles. This template includes access masks for such permissions as Create Items, Read Items, Folder Owner, Edit All, Edit Own, Edit None, and the other permissions you see in the Permission property page for folders in Outlook.

The *DACLWebStorageItem* and *DACLWebStorageFolder* templates contain the access masks for working with Exchange items and folders. These access masks are used when you work with non-MAPI folders or items contained in non-MAPI folders.

To give you a better idea of what these access mask templates look like, here's some code from the security module that creates these access mask templates. These templates can simplify your coding tremendously, as you'll soon see.

```
function DaclLegacyRoles()
{
    // This section initializes the legacy roles (aka MapiRoles)
```

```
    // Note that the SIDs are empty as they are irrelevant for this object
    var daclLegacyRoles = CreateSecurityDACL();

    daclLegacyRoles.URL =
        "Legacy roles, from the MAPI security dialog in Exchange 5.5";
    daclLegacyRoles.AddSimpleSecurityEntity("None",
        [0x1208a9, 0xdc916, 0x1208a9, 0xdc916, 0x0, 0x1f0fbf]);
    daclLegacyRoles.AddSimpleSecurityEntity("Owner",
        [0x1fc9bf, 0x0, 0x1fc9bf, 0x0, 0x1f0fbf, 0x0]);
    daclLegacyRoles.AddSimpleSecurityEntity("Publishing Editor",
        [0x1208af, 0xdc910, 0x1208af, 0xdc910, 0x1f0fbf, 0x0]);
    daclLegacyRoles.AddSimpleSecurityEntity("Editor",
        [0x1208ab, 0xdc914, 0x1208ab, 0xdc914, 0x1f0fbf, 0x0]);
    daclLegacyRoles.AddSimpleSecurityEntity("Publishing Author",
        [0x1208af, 0xdc910, 0x1208af, 0xdc910, 0x120ea9, 0x1f0716]);
    daclLegacyRoles.AddSimpleSecurityEntity("Author",
        [0x1208ab, 0xdc914, 0x1208ab, 0xdc914, 0x120ea9, 0x1f0716]);
    daclLegacyRoles.AddSimpleSecurityEntity("Non-Editing Author",
        [0x1208ab, 0xdc914, 0x1208ab, 0xdc914, 0x120ca9, 0x1f0716]);
    daclLegacyRoles.AddSimpleSecurityEntity("Reviewer",
        [0x1208a9, 0xdc916, 0x1208a9, 0xdc916, 0x1208a9, 0x1f0716]);
    daclLegacyRoles.AddSimpleSecurityEntity("Contributor",
        [0x1208ab, 0xdc914, 0x1208ab, 0xdc914, 0x0, 0x1f0fbf]);

    daclLegacyRoles.MakeDaclReadOnly();
    return daclLegacyRoles;
}
```

Programming Tasks

Now that you've seen all the objects with their properties and methods, let's step through some common programming scenarios that use the methods and properties from the security module.

Instantiating the Security Module

The first thing you typically need to do is instantiate the model itself. If you do not want to use the sample application included with the SDK that shows permissions for a particular folder or item using an interface similar to Outlook and instead want to add the security module functions to an existing Web application using your own interface, you must copy the files LoadSave-DACL.js and Security.js to your Web application—assuming, of course, that you want server-side security. If you want client-side security, your best bet is to copy over most of the files from the security folder in the SDK because you will need to detect the browser type coming in—client-side security is supported only in Internet Explorer. Netscape and other non-Microsoft browsers must use server-side security.

The next step after getting the files into your application is to add code to your Web page to use the security module. You must include the two JavaScript files in your Web page. Use the following ASP code to do this:

```
<%@ Language=javascript%>
<script language="javascript" runat=server src="loadsavedacl.js"></script>
<script language="javascript" runat=server src="security.js"></script>
```

Specifying Where the Security Code Should Run

The next task after adding the JavaScript files is to create a DACL. When you create a DACL, you must specify where the security code should run—the server or the client. You use the *CreateSecurityDACL* method we spoke about earlier to do this. The following code shows how to create the DACL on both the server and the client:

```
var objDacl = CreateSecurityDACL(SECURITY_ON_SERVER());
var objDacl = CreateSecurityDACL(SECURITY_ON_CLIENT());
```

The next step is to open the item you want to get or set security on. This item can be a folder or an item in Exchange. You use the *Load* method to do this, and you pass the URL (based on either *http://* or *file://*) to this method. The following code shows an example of using the *Load* method:

```
// Load the security descriptor in dacl object.
var objLoadResult = objDacl.Load(itemURL);
if(objLoadResult.number != 0)
{
    bError=true;
    return(false);
}
```

Listing User Permissions

Now that you've seen how to instantiate and load a DACL, we can start doing interesting things with that DACL. The first thing you will want to do is list user permissions. This is easy to do using the security module methods. The following code retrieves the entities for the DACL using the *Entities* property on the *DACL* object, which returns the *Entities* collection. Then the code loops through all the entities and prints out their properties. Figure 17-21 shows the results from the following code:

```
function ListPermissions(itemURL)
{
    var objDacl = CreateSecurityDACL(SECURITY_ON_SERVER());
    var objResult;

    // Load the security descriptor in dacl object.
    var objLoadResult = objDacl.Load(itemURL);
    if(objLoadResult.number != 0)
    {
        bError=true;
        return(false);
    }

    //Show the information about the DACL
    Response.Write("Below is the information about the DACL:<BR>");
    Response.Write("<TABLE>");
    Response.Write("<TR><TD>URL:</TD><TD>" + objDacl.URL + "</TD></TR>");
    Response.Write("<TR><TD>IsProtected:</TD><TD>"
                + objDacl.IsProtected() + "</TD></TR>");
    Response.Write("<TR><TD>Number of Entities:</TD><TD>"
                + objDacl.Count + "</TD></TR>");
    Response.Write("</TABLE>");

    Response.Write("<BR>");
    Response.Write("Entities for the folder:<BR>");
    Response.Write("<TABLE>");

    //Retrieve all the entities for the DACL
    var objEntities = objDacl.Entities
    for (i=0;i<objDacl.Count;i++)
    {
        Response.Write("<TR><TD><B>Entity #" + i + "</B></TD></TR>");
        Response.Write("<TR><TD>Name:</TD><TD>"
                    + objEntities[i].DisplayName + "</TD></TR>");
        Response.Write("<TR><TD>Inherited:</TD><TD>"
                    + objEntities[i].Inherited + "</TD></TR>");
        Response.Write("<TR><TD>Masks:</TD><TD>"
                    + objEntities[i].Masks + "</TD></TR>");
        Response.Write("<TR><TD>NT4 Name:</TD><TD>"
                    + objEntities[i].NT4Name + "</TD></TR>");
        Response.Write("<TR><TD>SID:</TD><TD>"
                    + objEntities[i].SID + "</TD></TR>");
        Response.Write("<TR><TD>SID Type:</TD><TD>"
                    + objEntities[i].SIDType + "</TD></TR>");

        Response.Write("<TR><TD> </TD></TR>");
    }
}
```

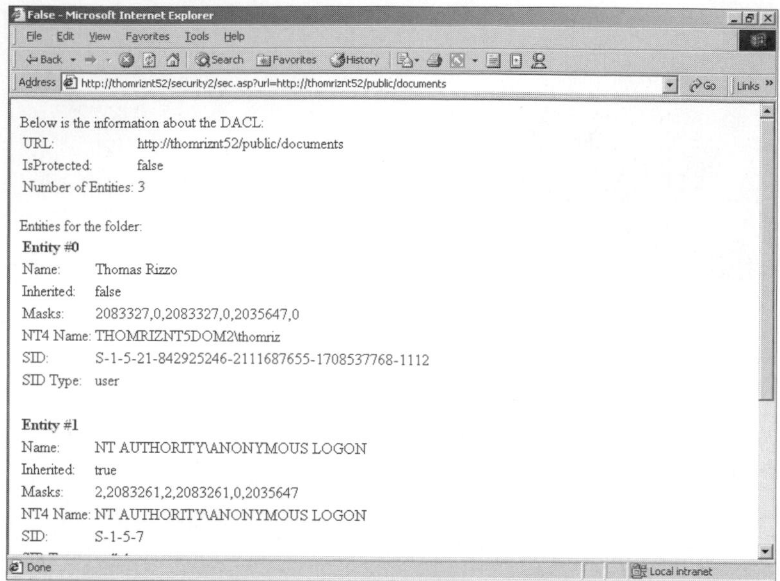

Figure 17-21 Results showing the permissions for an item

Setting and Changing Permissions for a User or Group

The next thing you might want to do with the security module is to set or change permissions—such as adding a new user or group to the folder or changing permissions for existing users or groups. The easiest way to add new users or groups is to use the *AddSimpleSecurityEntity* method and pass the access mask that you want the new security principal to have. Remember that folders and items have different types of security you can set. For this reason, the sample code you will see checks to see if you are trying to modify permissions for a folder or item.

Changing permissions is relatively easy. You can just use the access mask templates included with the security module. You can use the *SetByTemplate* method to find the appropriate access mask and then modify the user's existing access mask to be the new access mask.

However, before you do any of this, you must do a couple of things so you do not run into problems. First and foremost—and I cannot stress this enough—you must make sure the Web application requires authentication before you attempt to use the security module. If you allow anonymous access to your Web application, you will get an access denied error when you try to save your DACL because the module uses the current security credentials of the logged on Web user. With anonymous access enabled, this is the IIS anonymous account, which has no permissions to even see Exchange data, let alone modify security permissions. Remove anonymous access.

Second, you must check that the security principal does not already exist. You can do this by using one of the *SearchForObjectByXXXX* methods, where *XXXX* can be the Windows NT 4.0 name, the SID, or the display name. If the *Entity* object already exists for the user, just modify it rather than creating a new one.

Third, be sure to escape any names that contain slashes (\). For example, when you pass the Windows NT 4.0 name of a user using domain\username, you must pass it as *domain\\username* because JavaScript will interpret the backslash in domain\username as *\u*.

The following code shows how to add and change existing permissions on an item or a folder:

```
function AddNewPermissions(NT4User, itemURL)
{
    var objDacl = CreateSecurityDACL(SECURITY_ON_SERVER());
    var objResult;

    // Load the security descriptor in dacl object.
    var objLoadResult = objDacl.Load(itemURL);
    if(objLoadResult.number != 0)
    {
        bError=true;
        return(false);
    }

    //Search for the user to make sure
    //they are not already in the Entities collection
    var entityUser = objDacl.SearchForObjectByNT4Name(NT4User);
    if (!entityUser)
    {
        bNotFound=true;
        //Add new permissions
        //You can add new permissions using the built-in MASKS
        //or by creating your own mask
        //We will create our own mask here
        //Check whether it's a folder or not.
        //Permissions will be different for the two.
        if (objDacl.isFolder)
        {
            //It is a folder, load the right Access Mask Template for a folder
            var daclWSFolderTemplate = DaclWebStorageFolder();
            //Create and add a new entity for the user
            //Set create container (create subfolder) for the user
            var objResult = objDacl.AddSimpleSecurityEntity(NT4User,
                [0x0004, 0x0004, 0x0004, 0x0004, 0x0000, 0x0000]);
            if (objResult.number!=0)
            {
```

```
                Response.Write("Error adding user!");
                bError=true;
                return(false);
            }
        }
        else
        {
            //It is an item, load the Access Mask Template for an item
            var daclWSItemTemplate = DaclWebStorageItem();
            //Add permissions to allow the user to Delete items
            var objResult = objDacl.AddSimpleSecurityEntity(NT4User,
                [0x10000, 0x10000, 0x10000, 0x10000, 0x10000, 0x10000]);
            if (objResult.number!=0)
            {
                Response.Write("Error adding user!");
                bError=true;
                return(false);
            }
        }
    }
    else
    {
        //User already exists, just change permissions
        Response.Write("User already exists!");
        if (objDacl.isFolder)
        {
            //It is a folder, load the right Access Mask Template for a folder
            var daclWSFolderTemplate = DaclWebStorageFolder();
            //Change the user's permissions
            //Set create container (create subfolder) for the user
            var objResult = entityUser.SetByTemplate(daclWSFolderTemplate,
                                                "Folder Create container");
            if (objResult.number!=0)
            {
                Response.Write("Error modifying permissions user!");
                bError=true;
                return(false);
            }
        }
        else
        {
            //It is an item, load the Access Mask Template for an item
            var daclWSItemTemplate = DaclWebStorageItem();
            //Add permissions to allow the user to Delete items
            var objResult = entityUser.SetByTemplate(daclWSFolderTemplate,
                                                "Delete");
            if (objResult.number!=0)
            {
                Response.Write("Error adding user!");
                bError=true;
                return(false);
            }
```

```
        }
    }

    //Try to save the changes
    //Save the DACL on the item
    objResult = objDacl.Save();
    if(objResult.number != 0)
    {
        Response.Write("<b>Failed to Save DACL: "
                     + objResult.description + "</b><br>");
       return(objResult.number);
    }
}
```

Deleting Permissions

You might want to remove permissions for a user. To do this, you can use the *Remove* methods on the *DACL* object, such as *RemoveByNT4Name* or *RemoveByDisplayName*. The following sample deletes a user's permissions from an item.

```
function DeletePermissions(NT4User, itemURL)
{
    var objDacl = CreateSecurityDACL(SECURITY_ON_SERVER());
    var objResult;

    // Load the security descriptor in dacl object.
    var objLoadResult = objDacl.Load(itemURL);
    if(objLoadResult.number != 0)
    {
        bError=true;
        return(false);
    }

    //Try to delete the user
    var objResult = objDacl.RemoveByNT4Name(NT4User);
    if (objResult.number != 0)
    {
        Response.Write("<b>Failed to RemoveByDisplayName: " + objResult.number
                     + " " + objResult.description + "</b><br>");
        return(objResult.number);
     }

    //Save the DACL on the item
    objResult = objDacl.Save();
    if (objResult.number != 0)
    {
        Response.Write("<b>Failed to Save DACL: " +objResult.number + " "
                     + objResult.description + "</b><br>");
        return(objResult.number);
    }
}
```

Setting MAPI Permissions

One thing you might want to do in your folders is set the permissions using MAPI role names, such as "Editor", "Author", or "Reviewer". Setting permissions using these MAPI roles is supported in any type of Exchange folder. The security module will perform the right translations between MAPI folders and non-MAPI folders. The following code sets permissions on a folder to allow Everyone to be an "Editor".

```
var o;
//Notice how Everyone is \\Everyone
o = setMAPIPermissions("\\Everyone", strURL, "Editor");

function setMAPIPermissions(NT4User, itemURL, MAPIRole)
{
    var objDacl = CreateSecurityDACL(SECURITY_ON_SERVER());
    var objResult;

    // Load the security descriptor in dacl object.
    var objLoadResult = objDacl.Load(itemURL);
    if(objLoadResult.number != 0)
    {
        bError=true;
        return(false);
    }

    // Get the legacy DACL template
    var objDLR = DaclLegacyRoles();

    //get user entity from the first URL
    var entityUser = objDacl.SearchForObjectByNT4Name(NT4User);
    if (!entityUser)
    {
        bError=true;
        return(false);
    }

    var objResult = entityUser.SetByTemplate(objDLR, MAPIRole);
    if (objResult.number != 0)
    {
        bError=true;
        return(false);
    }

    objResult = objDacl.Save();
    if (objResult.number != 0)
    {
        bError=true;
        return(false);
    }
}
```

Removing Inherited ACLs

You might also want to modify an inherited ACL. The security module cannot do this, so you must break the inheritance of the ACL and then set your permission explicitly on the new noninherited entity. For example, if you try to run the MAPI permissions code shown earlier on the Everyone group, this is usually an inherited entity. You must first use the *SetProtected* method and pass *True* to it. *SetProtected* will copy all inherited entities and disable inheritance. Then you can set the ACLs on the formerly inherited entities.

Finding Entities

You've seen how to find entities in the previous samples, but it is important to know that you can find entities using multiple types of searches. For example, you can use the *SearchForIndexByXXXX* method, where *XXXX* can be the display name, the Windows NT 4.0 name, or another parameter. This method returns the index of the entity in the *Entities* collection if the entity exists. You can also use the *SearchForObjectByXXXX* method, where *XXXX* can also be the display name, the Windows NT 4.0 name, or another parameter. This method returns the *Entity* object if it is found in the *Entities* collection.

Using the Security Module from Visual Basic

You can use the security module from a Visual Basic application. The Training sample application does this in its setup program. Certain folders need certain permissions set for course instructors, so the Training setup program uses the security module to set permissions on these folders from its Visual Basic setup program. Admittedly, the security module is not the easiest tool to use from anything other than Web pages. However, the Visual Basic setup program embeds an Internet Explorer browser control into a Visual Basic form to call a Web page that in turn calls the security module. It is very roundabout. However, this is easier than trying to figure out all the idiosyncrasies involved with setting permissions in MAPI folders or non MAPI folders, with all the ACL formatting and error checking involved.

If you want to mimic what the setup program does, I recommend that you look at both the security Visual Basic form that I created and the Sec.asp file. You'll find a good snippet of code in the form that shows the folder trees for Exchange in the setup program to show how you can find the default Web site for a server, copy a Web file to that Web site, and then call that file. This saves you from having to create a virtual directory in IIS, copy your file there, call your ASP page, delete the ASP file, and delete the virtual directory. Use this technique only if you do not have an existing virtual directory and you do not want to code to create a new virtual directory just to run your security ASP file.

Summary

Events, workflow, and security are all important to the Exchange and Outlook developer. They will help you program against other Exchange technologies, such as CDO and WebDAV. In the next chapter, we will turn our focus to programming applications that manage Exchange using the object models of both Exchange via CDO for Exchange Management (CDOEXM or EMO) and Windows via Windows Management Instrumentation (WMI).

18

CDO for Exchange Management and Windows Management Instrumentation

CDO for Exchange Management (CDOEXM), as its name implies, makes it easier for you to programmatically manage your Microsoft Exchange environment. The object model is straightforward and allows you to query and set administrative options on your Exchange server. With CDOEXM, you can create mailbox databases, mailboxes, storage groups, and public folder databases as well as new public folder top-level hierarchies (TLHs).

The Training application (introduced in Chapter 15) makes heavy use of CDOEXM in its setup program to figure out what sort of server you are running on and to allow you to create new storage groups, folder hierarchies, and folder databases. Figure 18-1 shows the interface in the Training application setup program that allows you to do this. You will notice that this interface also uses the Outlook Web Access (OWA) folder list control. You'll learn in Chapter 20 how to use that control as well as other controls included with OWA.

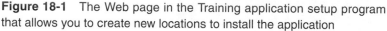

Figure 18-1 The Web page in the Training application setup program that allows you to create new locations to install the application

In addition to using CDOEXM to manage your Exchange infrastructure, you can also use the Windows Management Instrumentation (WMI) providers that ship with Exchange. WMI is the Microsoft implementation of Web-Based Enterprise Management (WBEM), which is an industry initiative to develop a standard technology for accessing management information in an enterprise environment. WMI uses the Common Information Model (CIM) industry standard to represent systems, applications, networks, devices, and other managed components.

The CDOEXM Object Model

Figure 18-2 depicts the object model for CDOEXM. CDOEXM does not have many methods and properties, so the object model is easy to learn. The methods and properties make the most common administrative tasks easy to automate. To add a reference to CDOEXM in Microsoft Visual Basic, you just need to include the Microsoft CDO for Exchange Management Library (CDOEXM.DLL). You get this library wherever you install Exchange Server or the Exchange System Manager. The code can run either client-side or server-side as long as you have this object library on your machine.

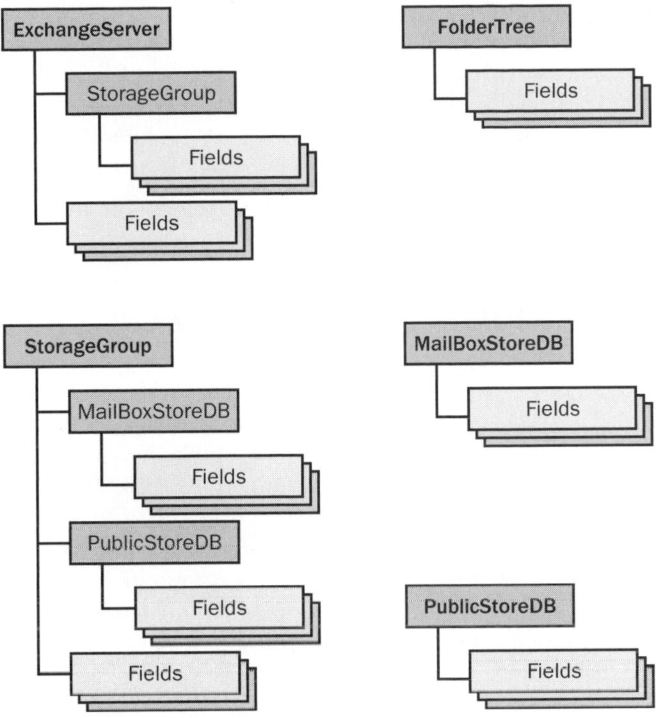

Figure 18-2 The CDOEXM object model

What About ADSI?

CDOEXM and Active Directory Services Interfaces (ADSI) are tightly interwoven. You do not use CDOEXM to create Windows accounts in Active Directory—you use ADSI. However, to mailbox-enable those Windows accounts, you can use CDOEXM. To access advanced properties in Active Directory, you also use ADSI. If you are going to use CDOEXM, you should be proficient with ADSI as well. Also, you should know the ADSI tools, such as ADSI Edit and LDP (which we discussed in Chapter 13), because they will help you investigate and configure Active Directory settings. One word of caution, though: do not try to set Exchange settings in Active Directory yourself for complex operations such as creating storage groups. Use CDOEXM to do the work because certain properties and processes must be implemented to ensure that the system does not become unstable or is not forced into an inconsistent state.

Accessing Exchange Server Information

When you write code, you'll generally want to understand what kind of information about an Exchange server you can access programmatically. CDOEXM provides the *ExchangeServer* object, which has properties that return the version number, storage groups, and directory server that the Exchange server uses. Table 18-1 lists the properties of the *ExchangeServer* object. This object has no methods.

Table 18-1 Properties of the *ExchangeServer* Object

Property	Description
DataSource	Retrieves the *IDataSource2* interface. From this interface, you can open a connection to an Exchange server by passing the name of the server to the *Open* method of the *DataSource* object.
DaysBeforeLogFileRemoval	Specifies the number of days before Exchange Server log files will be removed from the server. Please refer to the Exchange Server documentation for the types of log files that Exchange Server uses.
DirectoryServer	Returns the fully qualified domain name (FQDN) of the Active Directory domain controller that the Exchange server communicates with. This is a read-only property.
ExchangeVersion	Returns the version of Exchange Server that is running. An example of output from this property is *Version 6.5 (Build 6944)* for the Release to Manufacturer (RTM) version of Exchange 2003.
Fields	Returns the *Fields* collection. The fields you get back are mostly fields from Active Directory such as *heuristics*, *whenCreated*, *whenChanged*, and *objectClass*.
MessageTrackingEnabled	A *Boolean* that specifies whether message tracking is enabled on the Exchange server. For more information on message tracking, refer to the Exchange Server documentation.
Name	Returns the name of the Exchange server. This is a read-only property.
ServerType	Returns a *CDOEXMServerType* enumeration. There are only two types: *CDOEXMBackEnd* and *CDOEXMFront-End*. Front-End (FE) and Back-End (BE) Exchange servers are discussed in detail in the Exchange documentation.

Table 18-1 Properties of the *ExchangeServer* Object

Property	Description
StorageGroups	Returns an array that lists the Active Directory path to all storage groups on the server. You can then use these Active Directory paths with the *StorageGroup* object to open a specific storage group.
SubjectLogging	A *Boolean* that specifies whether subject logging is enabled.

The sample file named EMOSample.vbp, which you can find in the book's companion content, makes this clearer. Figure 18-3 shows the user interface for the sample.

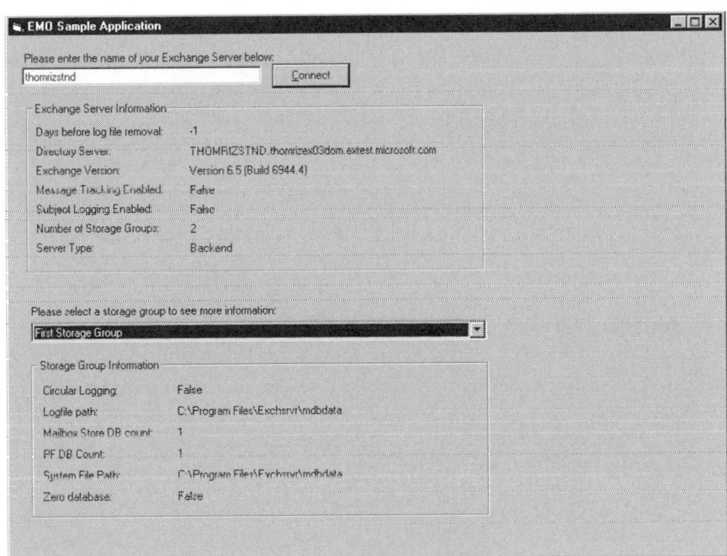

Figure 18-3 The CDOEXM sample application

Here is some of the code from the sample that uses the *ExchangeServer* object to determine server-specific information:

```
Dim oExchangeServer As New CDOEXM.ExchangeServer
Dim arrSGs() As CDOEXM.StorageGroup

Private Sub cmdConnect_Click()
    On Error GoTo errHandler:
    If txtExServerName.Text = "" Then
        MsgBox "You must enter a name in the Exchange Server name box!", _
               vbCritical + vbOKOnly
```

```
        Exit Sub
    End If

    If Right(txtExServerName.Text, 7) = "LDAP://" Then
        'Remove the LDAP
        txtExServerName.Text = Mid(txtExServerName.Text, 8)
    End If

    'Try to connect
    oExchangeServer.DataSource.Open txtExServerName.Text

    'Try to fill in Exchange Server info
    FillInExchangeServerInfo

    'Retrieve the storage groups
    FillInStorageGroups

    Exit Sub
errHandler:
    MsgBox "There was an error in cmdConnect_Click(). Error#" _
         & Err.Number & " Description:" & Err.Description, _
           vbCritical + vbOKOnly
    End
End Sub

Sub FillInExchangeServerInfo()
    On Error GoTo errHandler
    lblLogRemoval.Caption = oExchangeServer.DaysBeforeLogFileRemoval
    lblDirServer.Caption = oExchangeServer.DirectoryServer
    lblVersion.Caption = oExchangeServer.ExchangeVersion
    lblMsgTracking.Caption = oExchangeServer.MessageTrackingEnabled
    lblSubjectLogging.Caption = oExchangeServer.SubjectLoggingEnabled
    lblSGCount.Caption = UBound(oExchangeServer.StorageGroups) + 1
    If oExchangeServer.ServerType = cdoexmBackEnd Then
        lblServerType.Caption = "Backend"
    Else
        lblServerType.Caption = "Frontend"
    End If

    Exit Sub
errHandler:
    MsgBox "There was an error in FillInExchangeServerInfo. Error#" _
         & Err.Number & " Description:" & Err.Description, _
         vbCritical + vbOKOnly
End Sub
```

Working with Storage Groups

The *StorageGroup* object allows you to work with storage groups. From this interface, you can retrieve the log file paths for the database, figure out how many databases and what types of databases are in the storage group, and create new storage groups. Table 18-2 lists the methods and properties of the *StorageGroup* object.

Table 18-2 Methods and Properties of the *StorageGroup* Object

Method or Property	Description
CircularLogging	A *Boolean* property that specifies whether new log entries will overwrite the oldest log entries in the file.
DataSource	Returns the *IDataSource2* interface. From this interface, you can use the *Open* method to open a storage group by passing the Active Directory path to the storage group, or you can use the *SaveTo* method to create a new storage group. You can also use the *Delete* method to delete a storage group.
Fields	Returns the ADO *Fields* collection for the storage group. Most of the interesting properties are already directly exposed by the *StorageGroup* object, so the *Fields* collection is not that interesting.
LogFilePath	A string that specifies where the database transaction log files are stored.
MailboxStoreDBs	An array of strings that contains the Active Directory path to any mailbox databases in the storage group. You can then use the *Open* method of the *DataSource* property on the *MailboxStoreDB* object to open the mailbox database.
Name	Specifies the name of the storage group.
PublicStoreDBs	An array of strings that contains the Active Directory path to any public folder databases in the storage group. You can then use the *Open* method of the *DataSource* property on the *PublicStoreDB* object to open the mailbox database.
SystemFilePath	A string that specifies where database system files are stored.
Zerodatabase	A *Boolean* that specifies whether deleted database pages will be overwritten with zeroes when you back up the server.
MoveLogFiles	A method that takes a string that specifies the new path to move the transaction log files to.
MoveSystemFiles	A method that takes a string that specifies the new path to move the database system files to.

The *StorageGroup* object is straightforward. The following code shows how to use this interface. The following code from the EMOSample application opens a *StorageGroup* object and queries for the properties of the storage group.

```
Sub FillInStorageGroups()
    On Error GoTo errHandler
```

```
    'Scroll through the array of storage groups and
    'open each one into a SG object
    arrEXSG = oExchangeServer.StorageGroups
    Dim oTmpSG As CDOEXM.StorageGroup
    ReDim arrSGs(UBound(arrEXSG))
    For i = LBound(arrEXSG) To UBound(arrEXSG)
        Set oTmpSG = CreateObject("CDOEXM.StorageGroup")
        oTmpSG.DataSource.Open "LDAP://" & arrEXSG(i)
        Set arrSGs(i) = oTmpSG
        'Fill in the combo box
        comboSG.AddItem oTmpSG.Name
        Set oTmpSG = Nothing
    Next

    comboSG.ListIndex = 0

    Exit Sub
errHandler:
    MsgBox "There was an error in FillInStorageGroups. Error#" & Err.Number _
         & " Description:" & Err.Description, vbCritical + vbOKOnly
End Sub

Sub FillInSGInfo(iIndex)
    lblCL.Caption     = arrSGs(iIndex).CircularLogging
    lblLFPath.Caption = arrSGs(iIndex).LogFilePath
    lblMBDB.Caption   = UBound(arrSGs(iIndex).MailboxStoreDBs) + 1
    lblPFDB.Caption   = UBound(arrSGs(iIndex).PublicStoreDBs) + 1
    lblZeroDB.Caption = arrSGs(iIndex).ZeroDatabase
    lblSFPath.Caption = arrSGs(iIndex).SystemFilePath
End Sub
```

Creating New Storage Groups

To create a new storage group in your system, all you do is figure out the right Active Directory path to pass to the *SaveTo* method of the *DataSource* object on the *StorageGroup* object. This is not difficult, but the path will be long because the location where Exchange Server stores its information in Active Directory is buried a couple of layers deep in the hierarchy. Here's an example path to a storage group reference in Active Directory:

```
CN=First Storage Group,CN=InformationStore,CN=SERVERNAME,CN=Servers,CN=First Ad
ministrative Group,CN=Administrative Groups,CN=First Organization,CN=Microsoft
Exchange,CN=Services,CN=Configuration,DC=DOMAIN,DC=com
```

As you can see, storage groups are stored under Services, then Exchange, then your organization, then the administrative group, then the server, and finally the information store. Figure 18-4 shows this storage group object in ADSI Edit.

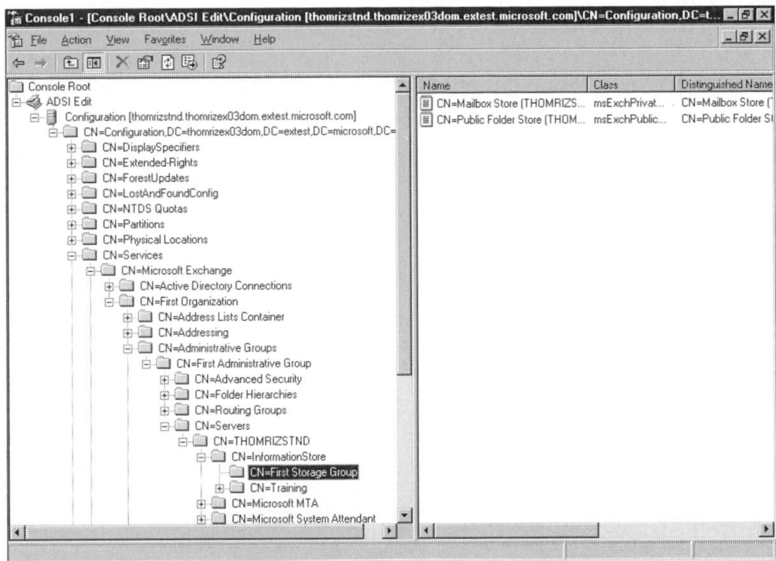

Figure 18-4 The location of storage group objects in Active Directory

To create a new storage group, you just create a new *StorageGroup* object, generate the correct Active Directory path, and add a *CN=MyStorageGroup* name at the beginning. The following code creates a new storage group called MyNewSG using CDOEXM:

```
Dim oNewSG As New CDOEXM.StorageGroup
    oNewSG.DataSource.SaveTo "LDAP://server/CN=MyNewSG,CN=InformationStore," _
        & "CN=SERVERNAME,CN=Servers,CN=First Administrative Group," _
        & "CN=Administrative Groups,CN=First Organization,CN=Microsoft " _
        & "Exchange, CN=Services,CN=Configuration,DC=DOMAIN, ,DC=com"
```

If you do not want to hardcode the path, you can just grab an existing storage group from the *ExchangeServer* object and parse it to get the path. The following code from the Training application does this:

```
'cut out the Storage Group name from the URL
strTemp = oCDOEXMServer.StorageGroups(0)
strTemp = Mid(strTemp, InStr(2, UCase(strTemp), "CN"))
' Build the URL to the StorageGroup
strSGURL = "LDAP://" & oCDOEXMServer.DirectoryServer & "/CN=" _
         & strFolderStoreName & "," & strTemp
```

A blank storage group is an interesting beginning to your application. You'll see later in the chapter how to create a new mailbox or public folder databases in a storage group. You'll also learn how to create a folder tree. Finally, you'll see how to create a new mailbox.

Deleting Storage Groups

Deleting empty storage groups is no problem. You just open the storage group that you want to delete by using the *Open* method of the *DataSource* object on the *StorageGroup* object. If you find any databases in the storage group, delete them—you cannot delete a storage group that contains any databases. Then call the *Delete* method of the *DataSource* object, as shown in the following code:

```
Dim oNewSG As New CDOEXM.StorageGroup
oNewSG.DataSource.Open "LDAP://SERVER/CN=MyNewSG,CN=InformationStore," _
    & "CN=SERVERNAME,CN=Servers,CN=First Administrative Group," _
    & "CN=Administrative Groups,CN=First Organization," _
    & "CN=Microsoft Exchange,CN=Services,CN=Configuration,DC=DOMAIN,DC=com"
oNewSG.DataSource.Delete
```

Working with Folder Trees

Before we talk about working with databases, let's briefly discuss how to work with public folders. If you don't plan to do anything with public folders, you can skip this section.

To create a new public folder database, you first create a new public folder tree that the database will be associated with. By having a separate tree, you can associate different databases with different public folder trees. This gives you the flexibility to build many different hierarchies of public folders for your applications. Mailbox databases do not have this requirement.

To work with folder trees, you use the *FolderTree* object. This interface has just three unique properties beyond the *DataSource*, *Fields*, and *Name* properties you saw earlier. These properties are listed in Table 18-3.

Table 18-3 Properties of the *FolderTree* Interface

Property	Description
RootFolderURL	Specifies the URL to the root folder in the tree. Do not expect this to be the URL to use for your applications. For example, the public folders *RootFolderURL* value is *http://SERVER/ExAdmin/domain.com/Public%20Folders*.
StoreDBs	A string array of Active Directory paths of other public store databases that contain replicas of this folder tree.
TreeType	An enumeration that specifies the type of folder tree. The three possible values are *cdoexmGeneralPurpose* (a non-MAPI public folder tree), *cdoexmMAPI*, and *cdoexmNNTPOnly*.

Creating a New Folder Tree

To create a new folder, you create a new *FolderTree* object. You set the name property on that object, and then you figure out the right Active Directory path to save your folder tree to, using the *Save* method of the *FolderTree* object's *DataSource* object. A typical path for a folder tree differs from that for a storage group. Here is an example path for the public folders folder tree. You would also use this path to open a folder tree.

```
LDAP://SERVER/
CN=Public Folders,CN=Folder Hierarchies,CN=First Administrative Group,CN=Admini
strative Groups,CN=First Organization,CN=Microsoft Exchange,CN=Services,CN=Conf
iguration,DC=DOMAIN,DC=com
```

The following code creates a new folder tree called MyNewFT. Note that you must use the *SaveTo* method and save to the Folder Hierarchies container as well as add a *CN=MyNewFT* to the path.

```
Dim oNewSG As New CDOEXM.FolderTree
oNewSG.Name = "MyNewFT"
oNewSG.DataSource.SaveTo "LDAP://SERVER/CN=MyNewFT,CN=Folder Hierarchies," _
    & "CN=First Administrative Group,CN=Administrative Groups," _
    & "CN=First Organization,CN=Microsoft Exchange," _
    & "CN=Services,CN=Configuration,DC=DOMAIN,DC=com"
```

Deleting a Folder Tree

To delete a folder tree, you open the folder tree and then call the *Delete* method on the *DataSource* object for the *FolderTree* object. You cannot orphan public folder databases, so you must first delete the database or disassociate the database with the folder tree before attempting to delete the folder tree. The following code deletes the folder tree we created earlier:

```
Dim oNewSG As New CDOEXM.FolderTree
oNewSG.DataSource.Open "LDAP://SERVER/CN=MyNewFT,CN=Folder Hierarchies," _
    & "CN=First Administrative Group,CN=Administrative Groups," _
    & "CN=First Organization,CN=Microsoft Exchange," _
    & "CN=Services,CN=Configuration,DC=DOMAIN,DC=com"
oNewSG.DataSource.Delete
```

Working with Public Folder Databases

You can work with two types of databases in Exchange: mailbox databases and public folder databases. We'll look at public folder databases first. When you work with public folder databases, you use the *PublicStoreDB* object. Table 18-4 lists the properties and methods of this interface.

Table 18-4 Properties and Methods of the *PublicStoreDB* Object

Element	Description
DataSource	Returns the *IDataSource2* interface. From this interface, you can use the *Open* method to open a public folder database by passing the Active Directory path to the database or use the *SaveTo* method to create a new public folder database. You can also use the *Delete* method to delete the public folder database.
DaysBeforeGarbageCollection	Returns or sets the number of days before deleted items in the database will be permanently deleted. See the Exchange Server documentation for more information on garbage collection.
DaysBeforeItemExpiration	Returns or sets the number of days before items and folders will expire in the database.
DBPath	A read-only property that returns the file path to the database file. This file will end with the .edb extension.
Enabled	A *Boolean* property that specifies whether the database will be mounted at startup. A value of *True* means that the database will be mounted.
Fields	Returns the ADO *Fields* collection for the object.
FolderTree	A string property that returns or sets the Active Directory path to the folder tree associated with the public folder database.
GarbageCollectOnlyAfterBackup	A *Boolean* that specifies whether items that have not been backed up will be permanently deleted from the database. A value of *True* means that items cannot be deleted until they are backed up.
HardLimit	A property that specifies the size in kilobytes beyond which posting will be disabled.
ItemSizeLimit	A property that specifies the maximum allowable size (in kilobytes) of an item in the database.
Name	Specifies the name of the database.
SLVPath	A read-only string property that returns the path to the streaming file database. The streaming file database contains data stored in its Internet content format. For more information about the database architecture of Exchange Server, see the product documentation.

Table 18-4 Properties and Methods of the *PublicStoreDB* Object

Element	Description
Status	A read-only property that returns a *CDOEXMStoreDB-Status* enumeration value that specifies whether the database is mounted. The enumeration contains four values: *cdoexmOnline*, *cdoexmOffline*, *cdoexm-Mounting*, and *cdoexmDismounting*.
StoreQuota	A property that specifies or returns the maximum size (in kilobytes) of the database.
Dismount	A method that dismounts the database. It takes an optional property that specifies the amount of time in seconds that the system will attempt to dismount the database.
Mount	A method that mounts the database. It takes an optional property that specifies the amount of time in seconds that the system will attempt to mount the database.
MoveDataFiles	A method that moves the data files for the database. It takes three parameters. The first is the new path for the database file. The second is the new path for the streaming files. The final parameter is optional and is a flags parameter reserved for future use.

Creating a New Public Folder Database

To create a new public folder database, you must have created your folder tree. You then create the Active Directory path to your public folder database. Next you create a *PublicFolderDB* object. Then you set the *FolderTree* property to the folder tree you created. Next you call the *SaveTo* method on the *Public FolderDB* object with the Active Directory path. If you want to mount the database, you can then call the *Mount* method on the *PublicFolderDB* object. The following code shows how to create a new public folder database called MyNewPFDB. The folder tree MyNewFT must already exist.

```
Dim oPFDB As New CDOEXM.PublicStoreDB

oPFDB.FolderTree = "LDAP://SERVER/CN=MyNewFT,CN=Folder Hierarchies," _
    & "CN=First Administrative Group,CN=Administrative Groups," _
    & "CN=First Organization,CN=Microsoft Exchange," _
    & "CN=Services,CN=Configuration,DC=DOMAIN,DC=com"

oPFDB.DataSource.SaveTo "LDAP://SERVER/CN=MyNewPFDB,CN=MyNewSG," _
    & "CN=InformationStore,CN=SERVER,CN=Servers,CN=First Administrative " _
    & "Group,CN=Administrative Groups,CN=First Organization," _
```

```
    & "CN=Microsoft Exchange,CN=Services,CN=Configuration," _
    & "DC=DOMAIN,DC=microsoft,DC=com"
oPFDB.Mount
```

Deleting Public Folder Databases

To delete a public folder database, you first open the database by passing the Active Directory path to the database, and then you call the *Open* method on the *DataSource* object for the *PublicFolderDB* object. Next you call the *Delete* method on the *DataSource* object. The following code deletes the MyNew-PFDB database:

```
Dim oPFDB As New CDOEXM.PublicStoreDB
oPFDB.DataSource.Open "LDAP://SERVER/CN=MyNewPFDB,CN=MyNewSG," _
    & "CN=InformationStore,CN=SERVER,CN=Servers,CN=First Administrative " _
    & "Group,CN=Administrative Groups,CN=First Organization," _
    & "CN=Microsoft Exchange,CN=Services,CN=Configuration," _
    & "DC=DOMAIN,DC=microsoft,DC=com"
oPFDB.DataSource.Delete
```

Creating Exchange Server Virtual Directories

When you create virtual directory entries in Internet Information Services (IIS) that point to Web files or folders that are stored in an Exchange database, IIS does not automatically add the proper Exchange ISAPI extension called Davex.dll to the virtual directory. This happens because you must create an Exchange virtual directory. If you just create a new virtual directory through Microsoft Internet Information Services (IIS), the virtual directory information will be stored in the IIS metabase, not in Active Directory. Exchange Server replicates information stored in Active Directory to the IIS metabase for creation of Exchange virtual directories. Therefore, the easiest way for you to create Exchange virtual directories programmatically is by creating them in Active Directory to begin with. Then you do not have to worry about creating the pointer to the Exchange Internet Server Application Programming Interface (ISAPI) yourself. If you want a graphical tool for creating Exchange virtual directories, use the Exchange System Manager.

Figure 18-5 shows the Exchange System Manager interface for creating a new Exchange virtual directory.

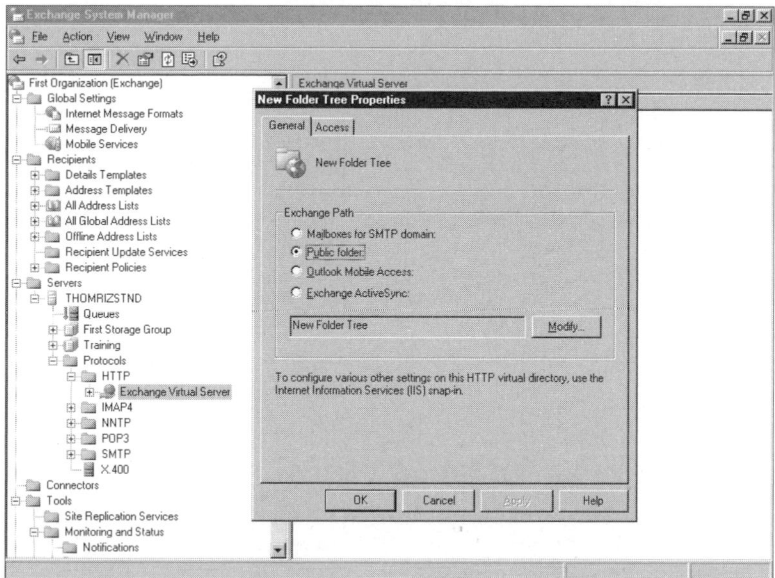

Figure 18-5 Creating an Exchange virtual directory in the Exchange System Manager

To programmatically create the entries in Active Directory using ADSI, you must get the container called 1 under the HTTP protocols section under the Microsoft Exchange section in Active Directory. Then you must create a new entry of class *msExchProtocolCfgHTTPVirtualDirectory* and set its properties appropriately. The following code from the Training application does this:

```
Function SetNewWeb(strComputerName, strFolderName, strDomainName,_
                   strVirDirName, bAddTrainingApp)
    On Error Resume Next
    Dim iServer     As New CDOEXM.ExchangeServer
    Dim strFHname   As String
    Dim NewWeb      As IADsContainer
    Dim ExchFolder  As Object

    Dim ADCont      As IADsContainer

    Result = True

    'Create an Exchange Virtual Directory so that OWA
    'is the default view for the virtual directory

    iServer.DataSource.Open strComputerName
    Result = Result And GetFolderTreeURL(strComputerName, strFHname)
```

```
    WriteLog "Getting Object: LDAP://" & iServer.DirectoryServer _
           & "/CN=1,CN=HTTP,CN=Protocols," & _
           Mid(iServer.DataSource.SourceURL, _
               InStr(1, iServer.DataSource.SourceURL, "CN="))

    Set ADCont = GetObject("LDAP://" & iServer.DirectoryServer _
                         & "/CN=1,CN=HTTP,CN=Protocols," _
                         & Mid(iServer.DataSource.SourceURL, _
                               InStr(1, iServer.DataSource.SourceURL, "CN=")))

    Set NewWeb = ADCont.Create("msExchProtocolCfgHTTPVirtualDirectory", _
                               "CN=" & strVirDirName)

    NewWeb.Put "HTTPPubGAL", CBool(0)
    'NewWeb.Put "anonymousAccount", "IUSR_MSEX2K"
    If bAddTrainingApp Then
        strFolderName = strFolderName & "\trainingapplication"
    End If
    NewWeb.Put "folderPathname", CStr(strFolderName)
    'Allow Write access in Access Flags so user can create folders
    NewWeb.Put "msExchAccessFlags", CInt(535)
    NewWeb.Put "msExchAuthenticationFlags", CInt(6)
    NewWeb.Put "msExchBasicAuthenticationDomain", CStr(strDomainName)
    NewWeb.Put "msExchDefaultLogonDomain", CStr(strDomainName)
    NewWeb.Put "msExchDirBrowseFlags", -1073741794
    NewWeb.Put "msExchLogonMethod", CInt(3)
    NewWeb.Put "msExchLogType", CInt(0)
    NewWeb.Put "msExchServerAutoStart", CBool(True)
    NewWeb.Put "msExchServerRole", CInt(0)
    NewWeb.Put "name", CStr(strVirDirName)
    NewWeb.SetInfo
    If Err <> 0 Then
        If Err.Number <> &H80071392 Then 'If virtual dir exists
                                         'no need to raise an error
            MsgBox "Error creating virtual directory for " _
                   & strFolderName, vbInformation + vbOKOnly, App.Title
            WriteLog "Error creating virtual directory " & strVirDirName _
                   & " for folder tree " & strFolderName
            SetNewWeb = -1
        End If
    Else
        SetNewWeb = 0
    End If

    Set iServer = Nothing

End Function
```

Table 18-5 lists the properties you must set (except those that are always the same value, such as *msExchLogonMethod*).

Table 18-5 Required Properties for Exchange Virtual Directories

Property	Description
anonymousAccount	Specifies the Windows account that IIS will use to authenticate users when they are accessing the Web site anonymously.
folderPathname	Specifies the relative folder path. For example, a folder path to a folder called Helpdesk under Public Folders would be specified as *Public Folders\Helpdesk*.
msExchAccessFlags	An integer that specifies the access flag for the virtual directory. You can combine the following values to get different levels of access: ■ Read access (*1*) ■ Write access (*2*) ■ Script source access (*16*) ■ Execute permissions for scripts (*512*) ■ Execute permissions for scripts and executables (*516*) For example, if you want read access to your virtual directory and you want to execute scripts, you can specify the value 513 for this property.
msExchAuthenticationFlags	Specifies whether Anonymous, Basic, and/or Integrated Windows Authentication is allowed for the virtual directory. These are the values: ■ Anonymous (*1*) ■ Basic (*2*) ■ Integrated Windows Authentication (*4*) ■ Digest Authentication (*16*) For example, if you want all authentication methods, you can pass 7 as the value for this property. Remember, though, that IIS restricts machine hops when you use NTLM authentication, and this can affect what security mode you use in an FE/BE configuration. You should use Basic Authentication over SSL in that scenario.
msExchBasicAuthenticationDomain	If you're using Basic Authentication, you can specify the default Windows domain to try to validate the username and password against. If you do not specify this property, IIS will use the default domain on the server on which IIS is running.

Table 18-5 Required Properties for Exchange Virtual Directories

Property	Description
msExchDefaultLogonDomain	Specifies the default domain to try Exchange Server authentication against. This property is used when a client does not specify a domain to log onto in the browser logon box.
msExchDirBrowseFlags	If you want to enable directory browsing, which allows users to look at the items in your folders pointed to by the IIS virtual directory, you must specify *–1073741794* for this property. If you want to disallow directory browsing, you must specify *1073741854*.

Any future changes you make to the virtual directory should be made through the Exchange System Manager and not through the IIS tools because those changes will not be replicated back into Active Directory. If you do make changes in the IIS tools and Exchange replicates the changes from Active Directory, the changes you make with the IIS tools might be overwritten and lost.

Working with Mailbox Databases

To work with a mailbox database, you use the *MailboxStoreDB* object. This object is similar in its properties to the *PublicStoreDB* object, and the methods are exactly the same. Table 18-6 lists the properties of this object that are different from those of the *PublicStoreDB* object.

Table 18-6 Properties of the *MailboxStoreDB* Object

Property	Description
OfflineAddressList	A string that specifies an Active Directory path to the offline address list for mailboxes stored in this database.
OverQuotaLimit	Specifies the size limit (in kilobytes) for mailboxes in this database. If this limit is exceeded, the user cannot send mail.
PublicStoreDB	A string that specifies the Active Directory path to the default public folder database for this mailbox.

Creating Mailbox Databases

To create a mailbox database, you just create a *MailboxStoreDB* object, create an Active Directory path to the new database, and call the *SaveTo* method on the *DataSource* object for the *MailboxStoreDB* object. If you want, you can then call the *Mount* method to mount the new database. The following code creates a new mailbox database called *MyNewMailboxDB*:

```
Dim oMB As New CDOEXM.MailboxStoreDB
oMB.DataSource.SaveTo "LDAP://SERVER/CN=MyNewMailboxDB," _
    & "CN=First Storage Group,CN=InformationStore,CN=SERVER," _
    & "CN=Servers,CN=First Administrative Group," _
    & "CN=Administrative Groups,CN=First Organization," _
    & "CN=Microsoft Exchange,CN=Services,CN=Configuration,DC=DOMAIN,DC=com"
oMB.Mount
```

Deleting a Mailbox Database

Before you can delete a mailbox database, you must first be sure that there are no active mailboxes on that database. You can do this by moving all the mailboxes to a new mailbox database or by mail-disabling any of the users in the database. To delete the mailbox database, you just open the database using the *Open* method on the *DataSource* object for the *MailboxStoreDB* object, and then you call the *Delete* method.

Creating New Mailboxes

Before you create a new mailbox, you should probably create a new user in Active Directory. The easiest way to create a new user programmatically is to use ADSI. Then you can create a new mailbox for that new user.

To create a new user using ADSI, you retrieve the container where you want to add the user. In the simplest case, this is the Users container. Then you create a new object in that container of the user class. You must set some properties, such as first name, last name, and account name. Then you call the *SetInfo* method to save the information into Active Directory.

The next step is to set the *MailboxStore* object you created to the *IADsUser* object you just created for the new user. This aggregates the *MailboxStore* object onto the *IADsUser* object. Then you can call the *CreateMailbox* method over the *MailboxStore* object. You pass the Active Directory path to the mailbox database where the new mailbox will be created. You then call the *SetInfo* method again to make sure the changes CDOEXM has made to the *IADsUser* object are saved back to Active Directory. The following code does all of this:

```
Dim objUser As IADsUser
Dim objContainer As IADsContainer
Dim objMailbox As CDOEXM.IMailboxStore
Dim recipname As String, recip As String

recip = "CN=New User"
```

```
' get the container
Set objContainer = GetObject("LDAP://CN=users,DC=thomriznt5dom2," _
                             & "DC=extest,DC=microsoft,DC=com")

' create a recipient
Set objUser = objContainer.Create("User", recip)
objUser.Put "samAccountName", "newuser"
objUser.Put "sn", "User"
objUser.Put "givenName", "New"
objUser.Put "userPrincipalName", "newuser"

objUser.SetInfo
objUser.SetPassword "password"
objUser.AccountDisabled = False

Set objMailbox = objUser

'Create a mailbox for the recipient
'You cannot create a mailbox using ADSI, so use CDOEXM

objMailbox.CreateMailbox "LDAP://thomriznt52.thomriznt5dom2.extest." _
    & "microsoft.com/CN=Mailbox Store (THOMRIZNT52)," _
    & "CN=First Storage Group,CN=InformationStore,CN=THOMRIZNT52," _
    & "CN=Servers,CN=First Administrative Group," _
    & "CN=Administrative Groups,CN=First Organization," _
    & "CN=Microsoft Exchange,CN=Services,CN=Configuration," _
    & "DC=thomriznt5dom2,DC=extest,DC=microsoft,DC=com"
objUser.SetInfo
```

Using the *MailboxStore* object, you can also delete and move mailboxes as well as set properties on the mailbox. Table 18-7 lists the properties and methods of the *MailboxStore* object.

Table 18-7 Properties and Methods of the *MailboxStore* Object

Property	Description
DaysBeforeGarbageCollection	Specifies the number of days that deleted mail will be retained before it is permanently deleted.
Delegates	Contains an array of string values that are the URLs of the other users who have access to this mailbox.
EnableStoreDefaults	A *Boolean* that specifies whether to use the database defaults for storage limits. A value of *True* means that the default limits will be used.
GarbageCollectOnlyAfterBackup	Specifies whether items can be permanently deleted only after the mailbox has been backed up.
HardLimit	Specifies the size (in kilobytes) beyond which the user can no longer send and receive mail.

Table 18-7 Properties and Methods of the *MailboxStore* Object

Property	Description
HomeMDB	Specifies the Active Directory path to the mailbox store for the recipient.
OverQuotaLimit	Specifies a size limit (in kilobytes) of a mailbox. If this limit is exceeded, sending mail is disabled.
OverrideStoreGarbageCollection	Specifies whether this mailbox should use the garbage collection properties set on this mailbox or the properties set on the database.
RecipientLimit	An integer that specifies the maximum number of recipients this user can send a single e-mail to.
StoreQuota	Specifies the maximum size (in kilobytes) of the mailbox.
Method	**Description**
CreateMailbox	Takes the path to the mailbox database where you will create a new mailbox.
DeleteMailbox	Deletes the mailbox.
MoveMailbox	Moves the mailbox to a new mailbox database. You must specify as a parameter the Active Directory path of the new mailbox database where you want to move the mailbox.

To access a mailbox, you use both ADSI and the *MailboxStore* object. The following code opens a user in Active Directory and retrieves the *MailboxStore*-related object for that user:

```
Dim oMB As CDOEXM.IMailboxStore
Dim objUser As ActiveDs.IADsUser

Set objUser = GetObject("LDAP://CN=new user,CN=users," _
                        & "DC=thomriznt5dom2,DC=extest,DC=microsoft,DC=com")
Set oMB = objUser
```

The Recipient Update Service

Before any object can become truly mailbox- or mail-enabled in the system, you must run a component of Exchange called the Recipient Update Service (RUS). The RUS populates a number of properties, such as the proxy address of the new user. The RUS can take seconds or hours to run, but you configure how often it runs through the Exchange System Manager. It runs asynchronously, so it will not fire on new mailbox creation. The following code sets the RUS to start processing immediately by setting the *msExchReplicateNow* attribute to *true*. Because the RUS is asynchronous, it will not run that very second, but this code can significantly reduce the time you have to wait for the RUS to run.

```
strDomainName = "domain"
strDomain = "DC=domain,DC=com"
strServer = "MyServer"
'Kick off the Recipient Update Service
' >>>> ToDo:  Make sure the following string is correct by finding the RUS for
'             your domain via ADSIEdit.
strRUS = "CN=Recipient Update Service (" & strDomainName _
       & "),CN=Recipient Update Services," _
       & "CN=Address Lists Container,CN=Microsoft," _
       & "CN=Microsoft Exchange,CN=Services," _
       & "CN=Configuration," & strDomain
set objRUS = GetObject("LDAP://" & strServer & "/" & strRUS)
objRUS.Put "msExchReplicateNow", True
objRUS.SetInfo
```

Combining CDOEXM and CDO for Exchange

One of the most common programming tasks you will perform is to combine CDOEXM with CDO for Exchange (CDOEX). Some of the objects in CDOEX expose interfaces that you can use to retrieve certain CDOEXM interfaces. For example, the *Person* object in CDOEX also implements the *IMailboxStore* interface, so if the CDOEX *Person* object you are working with has a mailbox, you can retrieve the *IMailboxStore* interface for that person by using the *GetInterface* method on the *Person* object or by forcing CDOEX to do this for you by setting a *MailboxStore* object equal to a CDOEX *Person* object. An example is shown here:

```
Dim oPerson As CDO.Person
Dim oMailbox As CDOEXM.IMailboxStore

Set oPerson = CreateObject("CDO.Person")
oPerson.DataSource.Open "mailto:thomriz@thomriznt5dom2.extest.microsoft.com"

'Set oMailbox = oPerson.GetInterface("IMailboxStore")
'Or you could coerce CDOEX to do it for you
Set oMailbox = oPerson

MsgBox oMailbox.RecipientLimit
```

Working with Mailbox Rights

To programmatically modify the permissions on your Exchange mailboxes, you can use the new *MailboxRights* property on the *IExchangeMailbox* interface in Exchange 2000 Service Pack 2 and later. This is a read/write property that can take an ADSI security descriptor. The following code uses this new property to set full control permissions for another user on a mailbox. You need the ADSI security DLL from the ADSI Resource Kit to run this code.

```
Dim SecurityDescriptor As IADsSecurityDescriptor
Dim Dacl As IADsAccessControlList
Dim newace As New AccessControlEntry
Dim objUser As CDOEXM.IExchangeMailbox
Dim objMailboxSD As IADsSecurityDescriptor

Set objUser = GetObject("LDAP://domain.com/CN=users," _
                     & "CN=users,DC=domain,DC=com")

Set objMailboxSD = objUser.MailboxRights

Set Dacl = objMailboxSD.DiscretionaryAcl

For Each obj In Dacl
    Debug.Print "Trustee:", obj.Trustee
    Debug.Print "AccessMask:", obj.AccessMask
    Debug.Print "AceFlags:", obj.AceFlags
    Debug.Print "AceType:", obj.AceType
Next

'AceTypes:
'ADS_ACETYPE_ACCESS_DENIED = 1
'ADS_ACETYPE_ACCESS_ALLOWED = 0
newace.AceType = ADS_ACETYPE_ACCESS_ALLOWED

'Inheritance Flags
'CONTAINER_INHERIT_ACE = 2
newace.AceFlags = 2

'Set the AccessMask from ADSI
'ADS_RIGHT_DELETE = 0x10000,
'ADS_RIGHT_READ_CONTROL = 0x20000,
'ADS_RIGHT_WRITE_DAC = 0x40000,
'ADS_RIGHT_WRITE_OWNER = 0x80000,
'ADS_RIGHT_SYNCHRONIZE = 0x100000,
'ADS_RIGHT_ACCESS_SYSTEM_SECURITY = 0x1000000,
'ADS_RIGHT_GENERIC_READ = 0x80000000,
'ADS_RIGHT_GENERIC_WRITE = 0x40000000,
'ADS_RIGHT_GENERIC_EXECUTE = 0x20000000,
'ADS_RIGHT_GENERIC_ALL = 0x10000000,
'ADS_RIGHT_DS_CREATE_CHILD = 0x1,
'ADS_RIGHT_DS_DELETE_CHILD = 0x2,
'ADS_RIGHT_ACTRL_DS_LIST = 0x4,
'ADS_RIGHT_DS_SELF = 0x8,
'ADS_RIGHT_DS_READ_PROP = 0x10,
'ADS_RIGHT_DS_WRITE_PROP = 0x20,
'ADS_RIGHT_DS_DELETE_TREE = 0x40,
'ADS_RIGHT_DS_LIST_OBJECT = 0x80,
'ADS_RIGHT_DS_CONTROL_ACCESS = 0x100
```

```
'Exchange permissions correspond to
Const ACE_MB_FULL_ACCESS = &h1
Const ACE_MB_DELETE_STORAGE = &h10000
Const ACE_MB_READ_PERMISSIONS = &h20000
Const ACE_MB_CHANGE_PERMISSIONS = &h40000
Const ACE_MB_TAKE_OWNERSHIP = &h80000
newace.AccessMask = 983041

'Set a valid user account
newace.Trustee = "domain\user"

'Add the ACE to the DACL
Dacl.AddAce newace

'Set changed DACL to Object
objMailboxSD.DiscretionaryAcl = Dacl

   'Set the MailboxRights property
objUser.MailboxRights = Array(objMailboxSD)

objUser.SetInfo
```

Programming CDOEXM with Visual Studio .NET

You can also leverage CDOEXM from Visual Studio .NET by using COM interoperability. The following code shows how to create a new mailbox by using the *DirectoryEntry* class in the .NET Framework for ADSI and by using CDOEXM:

```
using System;
//You need to add references to CDOEXM and System.DirectoryServices for this
//to work
using CDOEXM;
using System.DirectoryServices;

namespace MBSample
{
    class Class1
    {
        [STAThread]
        static void Main(string[] args)
        {
            string defaultDC = "DC=domain,DC=com";
            string alias = "thomriz";
            string fullName = "Tom Rizzo";
            string password = "password1234";
            string domainName = "domain.com";
            string homeMDB = "CN=Mailbox Store (Server),CN= Storage Group,"
                    + "CN=InformationStore,CN= Server,CN=Servers,"
                    + "CN=Your Administrative Group,CN=Administrative Groups,"
```

```
                + "CN=Your Org,CN=Microsoft Exchange,CN=Services,"
                + "CN=Configuration,DC=domain,DC=Com";

            DirectoryEntry container, user;
            CDOEXM.IMailboxStore mailbox;

            //Create a new user in the "users" container
            //Set the sAMAccountName and the password
            container = new DirectoryEntry("LDAP://CN=users," + defaultDC);
            user = container.Children.Add("CN=" + fullName, "user");
            user.Properties["sAMAccountName"].Add(alias);
            user.CommitChanges();
            user.Invoke("SetPassword", new object[]{password});

            //Enable the new user:
            //ADS_UF_NORMAL_ACCOUNT = 0x200
            user.Properties["userAccountControl"].Value = 0x200;
            user.CommitChanges();

            //Obtain IMailboxStore interface
            //Create the mailbox
            //commit the changes
            mailbox = (IMailboxStore)user.NativeObject;
            mailbox.CreateMailbox(homeMDB);
            user.CommitChanges();

            return;
        }
    }
}
```

Windows Management Instrumentation

Besides using CDOEXM to manage your Exchange infrastructure, you can also use the WMI providers that ship with Exchange.

Table 18-8 WMI Classes Available in Exchange 2000

Class	Description
ExchangeLink	Contains information about message-handling links between servers. This class can contain zero or more *ExchangeQueue* objects.
ExchangeQueue	Contains information about the dynamic queues that are created to transfer messages between mail servers.

Table 18-8 WMI Classes Available in Exchange 2000

Class	Description
ExchangeConnectorState	Provides information about a connector and its current state.
ExchangeServerState	Provides information about your Exchange server and its current status.
ExchangeClusterResource	Provides information about a clustered resource in an Exchange clustered environment.
Exchange_DSAccessDC	Provides information about the domain controllers available to the Exchange *DSAccess* component.
Exchange_MessageTrackingEntry	Provides information about events that have happened to a message as it goes through the Exchange system.

Exchange 2003 adds a large number of new classes and some additional capabilities to existing WMI classes (such as *ExchangeLink*). Table 18-9 lists the new classes. I won't cover all of them in detail—just the new classes that you are most likely to use in your applications.

Table 18-9 WMI Classes Available in Exchange 2003

Class	Description
Exchange_FolderTree	Contains information about folder tree hierarchies in Exchange.
Exchange_Link	Contains information about links between servers. Provides more capabilities than the *ExchangeLink* class.
Exchange_Logon	Contains logon information for the Exchange server, such as last logon time, client version used, and open message count.
Exchange_Mailbox	Contains mailbox information for a user, including total size of the mailbox, last logon time, and storage limit information.
Exchange_PublicFolder	Contains information about public folders in the system.
Exchange_Queue	Contains information about Exchange queues.
Exchange_QueueCacheReloadEvent	Contains information about the last time the queue updated its data.
Exchange_QueueData	Contains information about a queue that is available in XML format.

Table 18-9 WMI Classes Available in Exchange 2003

Class	Description
Exchange_QueuedMessage	Contains information about a queued message.
Exchange_QueuedSMTPMessage	Contains information about a queued SMTP message.
Exchange_QueuedX400Message	Contains information about a queue's X400 message.
Exchange_QueueSMTPVirtualServer	Enables or disables SMTP virtual servers.
Exchange_QueueVirtualServer	Contains information about Exchange virtual servers.
Exchange_QueueVirtualX400Server	Contains information about a virtual X400 server.
Exchange_ScheduleInterval	Sets the schedule interval for your server.
Exchange_Server	Contains information about your Exchange server, such as whether the server is a front-end server, and the Exchange version number.
Exchange_SMTPLink	Contains information about an Exchange SMTP link.
Exchange_SMTPQueue	Contains information about Exchange SMTP queues.
Exchange_X400Link	Contains information about X400 links.
Exchange_X400Queue	Contains information about X400 queues.

Besides the Exchange WMI providers and classes, other providers and classes ship with other software products and Windows. Table 18-10 describes some of these other WMI providers.

Table 18-10 Other WMI Providers

Provider	Description
Event Log Provider	Provides information, notification, and access to the Windows Event Log.
Performance Monitor Provider	Provides notification and access to performance monitor data.

Table 18-10 Other WMI Providers

Provider	Description
Registry Event Provider	Provides notifications when changes happen in the registry.
Registry Provider	Provides access to registry information.
SNMP Provider	Provides access and notification from Simple Network Management Protocol (SNMP) devices.

Exchange WMI Classes

The Exchange WMI classes are well documented in the SDK, so I won't go into detail on each one. Instead, I'll show how to code to these classes from an application. I'll highlight some of the key properties for the classes. The SDK is included with the book's sample files, so you can browse through the details of each class there.

The Exchange WMI classes are located in the WMI namespace *\\.\root\cimv2\Applications\Exchange*. You can access WMI in two ways. If you are used to standard programming, the easiest way is to use *CreateObject*. The following code creates the WMI locator that allows you to connect to a local or remote WMI namespace. It then calls the *ConnectServer* method of the WMI locator and passes the name of the server and the namespace to connect to. Finally, the code uses the *InstancesOf* method to retrieve an instance of a couple of the Exchange classes.

```
strConnectServer = "thomriznt52"
Set objLocator = CreateObject("WbemScripting.SWbemLocator")
Set objService = objLocator.ConnectServer(strConnectServer, _
                                    "root/cimv2/applications/exchange")
Set Clusters = objService.InstancesOf("ExchangeClusterResource")
Set ExchangeLinks = objService.InstancesOf("ExchangeLinks")
Set ExchangeServerState = objService.InstancesOf("ExchangeServerState")
```

The other way to get the WMI objects is the same way you retrieve ADSI objects—using the *GetObject* method. The following code accomplishes the same thing as the previous code:

```
Set Clusters = GetObject("winmgmts:{impersonationLevel=" _
                & "impersonate}!/root/cimv2/applications/exchange" _
                ).InstancesOf("ExchangeClusterResource")
Set ExchangeLinks = GetObject("winmgmts:{impersonationLevel= " _
                & "impersonate}!/root/cimv2/applications/exchange" _
                ).InstancesOf("ExchangeLinks")
Set ExchangeServerState = GetObject("winmgmts:{impersonationLevel=" _
                & "impersonate}!/root/cimv2/applications/exchange" _
                ).InstancesOf("ExchangeServerState")
```

Notice that instead of using *LDAP://* in the *GetObject* call, we use *winmgmts:* to specify WMI. No matter which method you use, the same classes are returned. I prefer using the *winmgmts:* method.

Once you get the classes, retrieving properties from the WMI classes is straightforward. First you have to determine the number of instances in the class if the class has multiple instances. (For example, *Win32_Processor* might have multiple instances if the machine has multiple processors.) To do this, you can use the *count* property on the class that is returned or you can use a *For..Each* loop to loop through each instance.

Once you have an instance, you can retrieve or set properties on that instance. To retrieve a property, you specify the property just as you would for any other type of object you program against. The following example displays information about your Exchange server by using the *ExchangeServerState* class:

```
strConnectServer = "thomriznt52"
Set objLocator = CreateObject("WbemScripting.SWbemLocator")
Set objService = objLocator.ConnectServer(strConnectServer, _
                                    "root/cimv2/applications/exchange")
Set ExchangeServerState = objService.InstancesOf("ExchangeServerState")
For Each ExchangeServer In ExchangeServerState
    MsgBox "Exchange Server Name: " & ExchangeServer.Name
    MsgBox "Exchange Server State: " & ExchangeServer.ServerStateString
    MsgBox "Exchange Server State: " & ExchangeServer.ServerStateString
    MsgBox "Exchange Server CPU State: " & ExchangeServer.CPUStateString
    MsgBox "Exchange Server Disks State: " & ExchangeServer.DisksStateString
    MsgBox "Exchange Server Services State: " _
          & ExchangeServer.ServicesStateString
Next
```

WMI Query Language (WQL)

WMI provides a SQL query language for querying WMI providers for specific criteria. Rather than having to write looping code, you can use this query language to search for information in WMI. WQL, as you can see in the following example, is similar to SQL. Also, you only need to call the *ExecQuery* method on WMI to execute your queries. I'll cover only data queries here, but you can also create event and schema queries in WMI. These types of queries allow you to look for specific system events or query on specific schemas in WMI. The following example finds out whether the services on the Exchange Server are OK:

```
Set oExServer = GetObject("winmgmts:{impersonationLevel=" _
                         & "impersonate}!/root/cimv2/applications/exchange" _
                         ).ExecQuery("SELECT * FROM ExchangeServerState " _
                         & "WHERE ServicesState = 0 OR ServicesState =  2 " _
                         & "OR ServicesState = 3")
```

This is just a quick look at what you can do with Exchange Server and WMI; you should learn more about WMI in general on your own. WMI provides a universal way to access not only Exchange Server management information but also a host of Windows and other Microsoft product information. It is a general-use Application Programming Interface (API) that is very useful if you are writing programs to manage Windows-based servers. (See the WMI section in MSDN for more information.)

The Antivirus API

I want to mention the Antivirus API (AVAPI)—also called the Virus Scanning API (VS API)—so you know that it exists and that independent software vendors (ISVs) can write to it. I don't expect non-antivirus software vendors to write to this API—or even care about it. But as a developer, you can use the performance counters and logging that the API provides to display information in your applications about successful scans, number of quarantined messages, loading and unloading of vendor DLLs, and the number of detected viruses.

Summary

In this chapter, we looked at developing solutions that manage Exchange. In the next chapter, we will turn our attention to the real-time collaboration technologies you can use in your Exchange applications, including Exchange Server Conferencing Server, the Live Communications Server 2003, and the Windows Messenger client. These technologies can make your application more interactive and provide information for smarter workflows or online interaction information.

19

Real-Time Collaboration

One important enhancement to Microsoft Exchange Server is the addition of real-time collaboration capabilities. With the addition of Microsoft Exchange Conferencing Server and Instant Messaging (IM) to Exchange 2000 Server, you can quickly build real-time collaborative applications.

With Microsoft Exchange Server 2003, IM moves to the new conferencing technologies of Microsoft Office Live Communications Server 2003—previously code-named Greenwich—which are built on a different protocol from the IM system in Exchange 2000. Later in this chapter, I will cover the MSN Messenger object model and the Live Communications Server technologies. (I've updated the IM content from the second edition of this book to focus primarily on Live Communications Server rather than Exchange Server IM.)

> **Note** "Microsoft Office Live Communications Server 2003" (Live Communications Server) is the final release name for Microsoft's new conferencing technology. During beta phases it was called "Real-Time Communications Server 2003" (RTC). Although some of the code in this chapter uses "RTC," the name does not affect how the code operates.

Instant Messaging

IM consists of two main features. The first is collaboration through instant messages, whiteboarding, voice communication, or application sharing. Instant messages differ from e-mail in that they pop up on the receiving user's screen immediately after the message is sent—there is no delay. They also differ from e-mail in that a user can block another user from sending an instant message. The only way you can "block" people from sending you e-mail is by automatically deleting the message or marking the user as an unsolicited e-mailer.

The second and perhaps the more interesting feature is the ability to track and display "presence" information about specified contacts. For example, a user can track her team—she can track whether team members are online, away from their computers, and so on. A user can also track the availability and status of virtual teams across the Internet. This is where the real power of presence technology lies.

As I mentioned, IM is now included with the new Live Communications Server from Microsoft. This server relies on Windows Server 2003 for its core components. The Live Communications Server IM infrastructure uses Active Directory and allows the user to extend the services she can offer and develop in the Microsoft environment. Furthermore, the Windows Messenger Service client can be installed on workstations so users in an organization can leverage IM technology.

You might wonder how MSN Messenger and Windows Messenger differ. Windows Messenger is a superset of MSN Messenger and supports technologies such as Live Communications Server and the older Exchange Server IM server. MSN Messenger supports only the .NET Messenger Service, which is hosted by Microsoft. For corporate environments, you should use Windows Messenger.

You can take advantage of IM features in your collaborative Exchange applications by integrating IM, presence technology, or both. A number of APIs from Microsoft make the process of integrating IM in your applications easy. In this chapter, we will look at these APIs, which include the Windows Messenger APIs and the Live Communications Client API.

Before we look at the details of these APIs, take a look at the updated main page of the Training application, shown in Figure 19-1, which has IM functionality added. In the sample, students can see which instructors are on line.

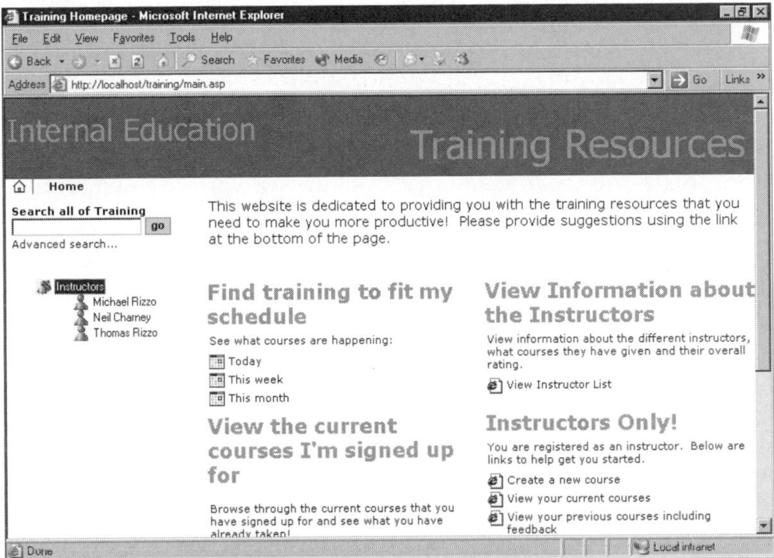

Figure 19-1 The updated Training application main page with IM technology added

The Windows Messenger APIs

With the release of the Messenger APIs to the Microsoft Developer Network (MSDN), you can develop applications that leverage the capabilities of Windows Messenger. The Messenger APIs are similar to the Exchange IM control APIs. In fact, many of the events and methods have the same or similar names. The main difference between the Exchange IM and Messenger object models is that Exchange IM supports only the Rendezvous Protocol (RVP), while Messenger supports a number of protocols, including RVP and the Session Initiation Protocol (SIP). Also, Messenger does not ship a control with a user interface; you have to build your own interface for your Messenger applications.

To show you how to use the Messenger library, I built a simple ActiveX control that uses the library. This control can be hosted in the Training application instead of the Exchange IM control.

You start working with Messenger by using the Messenger API type library, which allows you to listen for events occurring within Messenger and also enumerate groups, contacts, and other Messenger lists. At the core of the Messenger object library is the *Messenger.UIAutomation* object. This is the object you must create to use the other objects in the object library. The following code from the custom control initializes a variable to this object and also sets up Visual Basic to listen for events from the object model:

```
Dim WithEvents oMessenger As Messenger

Private Sub UserControl_Initialize()
    'Initalize the treeview control and Messenger control
    'See if the user is logged on
    On Error GoTo errHandler
    TreeViewContacts.ImageList = ImageListContacts
    TreeViewContacts.Scroll = True
    Set oMessenger = CreateObject("Messenger.UIAutomation.1")
    If oMessenger.MyStatus = MISTATUS_OFFLINE _
                         Or oMessenger.MyStatus = MISTATUS_UNKNOWN Then
        Dim oNode As Node
        Set oNode = TreeViewContacts.Nodes.Add(, 1, "NodeRoot", _
                                          "Click here to logon", 3)
        oNode.Bold = True
        oNode.Selected = True
        SetStatus oMessenger.MyStatus
    Else
        SetStatus oMessenger.MyStatus
        'Parse through the groups and add info to the tree
        DrawTree
    End If

    Exit Sub
errHandler:
    MsgBox "There was an error initializing the control.  Error# " _
         & Err.Number & " Description: " & Err.Description
    UserControl.Enabled = False
End Sub
```

Once you create this object, you can access some of the other objects, such as the *Groups* collection and its child object the *Contacts* collection. The following code taken from the control shows how to enumerate groups and contacts and display them. Notice that you can use *for...each* to loop through each collection.

```
Sub DrawTree()
    On Error Resume Next
    'Clear the tree
    TreeViewContacts.Nodes.Clear
    'Scroll through all lists in Messenger and
    'draw out the contacts on the list.
```

```
    Dim oGroups As MessengerAPI.IMessengerGroups
    Dim oGroup As MessengerAPI.IMessengerGroup
    Set oGroups = oMessenger.MyGroups
    For Each oGroup In oGroups
        'Create a root node for each group
        Set oTestNode = TreeViewContacts.Nodes.Add(, 1, oGroup.Name, _
                                               oGroup.Name, 6)
        'Scroll through all contacts in the list and add them
        Dim oContacts As MessengerAPI.IMessengerContacts
        Set oContacts = oGroup.Contacts
        Dim oContact As MessengerAPI.IMessengerContact
        For Each oContact In oContacts
            'Add the contact to the group
            'Generate random number to add to key
            'just in case more than one key exists already
            Randomize
            RndInt = Int((500 * Rnd) + 1)
            TreeViewContacts.Nodes.Add oGroup.Name, 4, _
                                    oContact.SigninName & " " _
                                    & RndInt, oContact.FriendlyName, _
                                    GetStatusImageIndex(CInt(oContact.Status))
            oTestNode.Sorted = True
        Next
    Next
End Sub
```

The final interesting part of the Messenger API concerns events. Messenger fires events for groups being added or deleted through the user interface, contacts being added or deleted through the user interface, status changes, or even sign-in and sign-out actions. All the events are documented in the SDK. Here is some of the event code in the custom control:

```
Private Sub SetStatus(iStatus As Integer)
    Dim txtStatus As String
    txtStatus = ""
    Select Case iStatus
        Case 1
            txtStatus = "Offline"
        Case 2
            txtStatus = "Online"
        Case 6
            txtStatus = "Appear Offline"
        Case 10
            txtStatus = "Busy"
        Case 14
            txtStatus = "Be Right Back"
        Case 18
            txtStatus = "Away"
        Case 34
            txtStatus = "Away"
        Case 50
            txtStatus = "On the Phone"
```

```
        Case 66
            txtStatus = "Out to Lunch"
    End Select
    lblStatus.Caption = txtStatus
End Sub

Private Sub oMessenger_OnMyStatusChange(ByVal hr As Long, _
                                  ByVal mMyStatus As MessengerAPI.MISTATUS)
    SetStatus CInt(mMyStatus)
End Sub

Private Sub oMessenger_OnSignin(ByVal hr As Long)
    On Error Resume Next
    'Change the root node if successful
    If hr = 0 Then
        DrawTree
    End If
End Sub

Private Sub oMessenger_OnSignout()
    On Error Resume Next
    TreeViewContacts.Nodes.Clear
    Set oNode = TreeViewContacts.Nodes.Add(, 1, "NodeRoot", _
                                         "Click here to logon", 3)
    oNode.Bold = True
    oNode.Selected = True

    'Change back the root node
    TreeViewContacts.Nodes.Item("NodeRoot").Text = "Click here to logon"
End Sub
```

We've taken just a quick look at the Messenger object model. The object model also supports adding custom add-ins to Messenger and other functionality. Be sure to browse through the sample control included with the companion files and also browse through the Messenger SDK.

Microsoft Office Live Communications Server 2003

Microsoft Office Live Communications Server 2003 replaces the Exchange IM server. With Live Communications Server, you administer your users through Active Directory, just as you do with Exchange, and you can easily enable or disable Live Communications Server for users through the Active Directory graphical management interface, as shown in Figure 19-2.

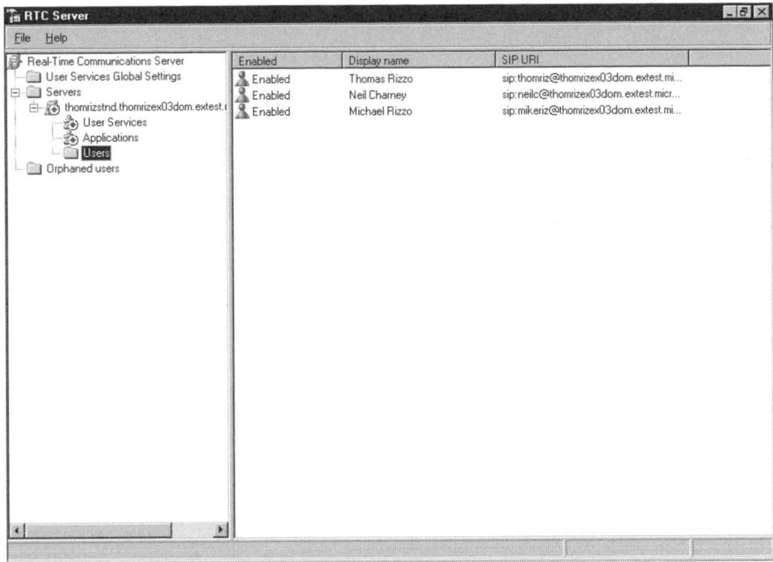

Figure 19-2 The user interface to enable or disable RTC for users in Active Directory

Once you enable a user for Live Communications, the Server will fill in properties for the user in Active Directory, such as *msRTCSIP-PrimaryHomeServer*, *msRTCSIP-PrimaryUserAddress*, and *msRTCSIP-UserEnabled*. You can query for these properties using Active Directory Service Interfaces (ADSI), which you learned about in Chapter 13.

Live Communications Server uses SIP and the related SIP for Instant Messaging and Presence Leveraging Extensions (SIMPLE). Live Communications Server allows users to register the presence information with the server and query for other users' presence information. The SIP and SIMPLE standards are owned by the Internet Engineering Task Force (IETF).

The most common way to program against Live Communications Server is by using the Windows Messenger library or the Live Communications Client API. If you are running on client platforms other than Windows XP, you should use the Messenger API because that client is supported on other platforms. The Live Communications Client API is supported on other platforms, but with limited capabilities. However, if you have Windows XP, you can leverage the Live Communications Client Library, which is integrated directly with Windows XP.

I will show you the basics of using the Live Communications Client API, but you can find full documentation of this rich object model on MSDN. You should refer to this documentation to build more advanced Live Communications Client Library applications. Furthermore, if you want to build server-side Live Communications Server applications, you should install the server and its companion SDK to learn how to build extensions to the server for your particular application.

The Live Communications Client Library

The Live Communications Client Library is a COM-based library. In the library, the main objects are the *Client, Session, Participant, Buddy, Watcher*, and *Profile* objects. The *Client* object is used to set up the *Session* object with the correct settings. The *Session* object allows you to create a session with another user, answer a session from another user, or terminate a session. The *Participant* object contains all the information about a session participant.

The *Buddy* and *Watcher* objects work together to provide presence querying and details information. Using these objects, you can look for the presence of people in your buddy list. You can also listen for when others add you to their buddy list and request the status of your presence information.

Finally, the *Profile* object is used to maintain your client provisioning information, such as your server, your display name, your logon alias, and other information about the current user's profile.

Building Your First Live Communications Client Application

The sample code we will look at is written in Visual Basic. When you program against the Live Communications Client Library, you must add a reference to the Live Communications Core 1.0 Library (also known as RTC Core 1.0 Library), which contains the objects we want. Figure 19-3 shows this step in Visual Basic. You can also use the Live Communications Client Library from .NET, using the COM interoperability mode of .NET.

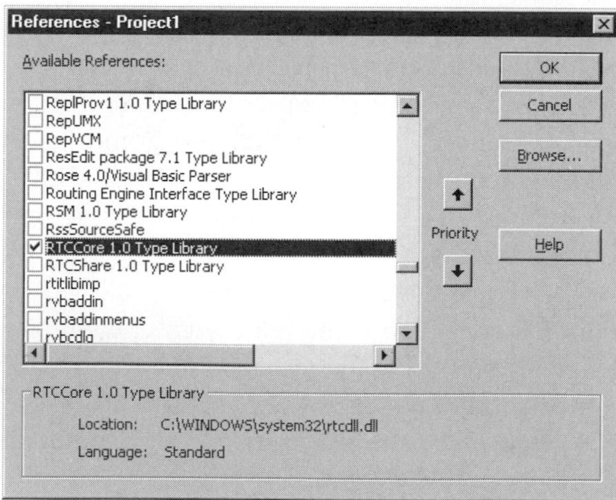

Figure 19-3 Adding a reference to the Live Communications Core 1.0 Library in Visual Basic

The next step is to start your coding. With the Live Communications Client Library, you must initialize the object library before attempting to program against it. You do this by calling the *Initialize* method on the Live Communications *Client* object. Once you initialize the library, you can display personal information about the currently logged on user or send instant messages to other users. The following Visual Basic code shows how to use the Real Communications Client Library:

```
Dim WithEvents oRTCClient As RTCClient

Private Sub Command1_Click()
    Dim oRTCClient As New RTCClient
    Dim strDestURI As String        '(for example, someone@example.com)
    Dim strDestName As String       '(for example, Neil Charney)
    Dim strMsgHeader As String      '(specify message header)
    Dim strMsg As String            '(specify message)
    Dim lCookie As Long             '(Application-provided cookie used for
                                    ' pairing the notifications with the
                                    ' messages sent)
    Dim oParticipant As IRTCParticipant
    Dim oSession As IRTCSession

    Set oRTCClient = New RTCClient

    'Initalize the client
    oRTCClient.Initialize

    'Put out some basic information
    MsgBox ("Username: " & oRTCClient.LocalUserName & vbLf _
            & "URI: " & oRTCClient.LocalUserURI)

    oRTCClient.ListenForIncomingSessions = RTCLM_DYNAMIC

    strDestURI = "thomriz@thomrizex03dom.extest.microsoft.com"
    strDestName = "Thomas Rizzo"

    'Create an IM session.
    Set oSession = oRTCClient.CreateSession(RTCST_IM, vbNullString, _
                                            Nothing, 0)

    'Add a participant to the IM session.
    Set oParticipant = oSession.AddParticipant(strDestURI, strDestName)

    strMsg = "Test!"
    strMsgHeader = "MIME-Version: 1.0\r\nContent-Type: text/plain; " _
                 & "charset=UTF-8\r\n\r\n"

    'Send a message.
    oSession.SendMessage strMsgHeader, strMsg, lCookie

End Sub
```

```
Private Sub oRTCClient_Event(ByVal RTCEvent As RTCCORELib.RTC_EVENT, _
                             ByVal pEvent As Object)
    If RTCEvent = RTCE_PARTICIPANT_STATE_CHANGE Then
        MsgBox "Participant changed state!"
    Else
        MsgBox "Event raised: " & RTCEvent
    End If
End Sub
```

Microsoft Exchange Conferencing Server

Beyond IM, Exchange Server also offers the ability to perform real-time audio and video conferencing as well as data sharing through Exchange Conferencing Server. This platform, which is an additional server that works with Exchange, adds a server component to the NetMeeting environment so you can host more users and schedule your meetings without requiring a client organizer PC and so administrators can control how much bandwidth and how many real-time meetings can take place on their network.

You can use Outlook or a Web interface for scheduling and listing your real-time conferences. The Web interface also introduces an additional object model that you can use to schedule real-time conferences from your own applications. Figure 19-4 shows this Web interface.

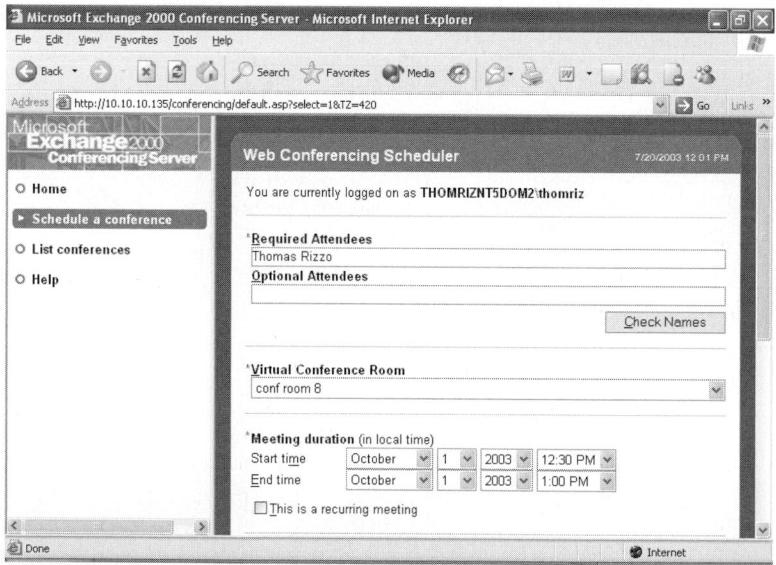

Figure 19-4 The Web interface for scheduling real-time conferences

Beyond scheduling from the Web, users can also browse for real-time conferences from the Web. Both scheduling and browsing rely on ASP, so you can look at the source code behind the pages to learn more about how they work. Figure 19-5 shows the interface for browsing real-time conferences.

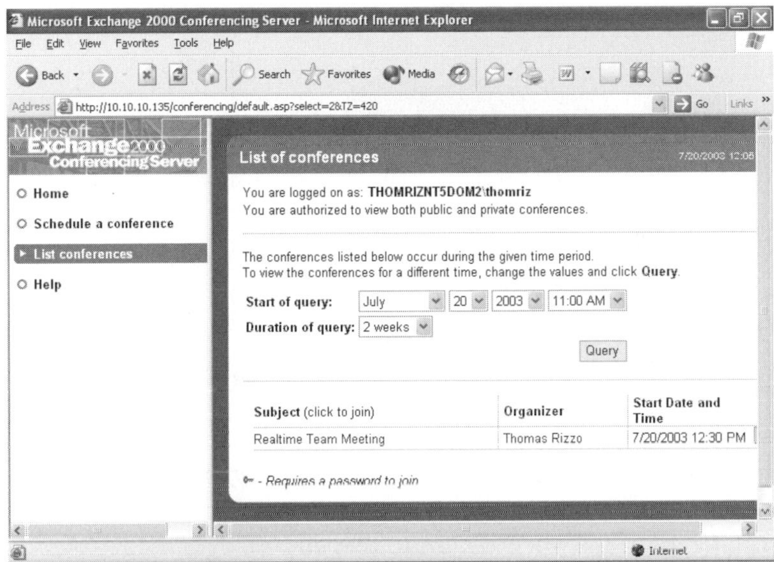

Figure 19-5 Browsing for real-time conferences

Finding Real-Time Resources in Active Directory

To show how to use Exchange Conferencing Server as part of an application, the Training application has the ability to schedule classes as online classes. You must have Exchange Conferencing Server somewhere in your environment to take advantage of this ability. The first step in scheduling an online class is to find the list of online classrooms that are available. Figure 19-6 shows the interface for searching Active Directory from the Training application to find real-time resources.

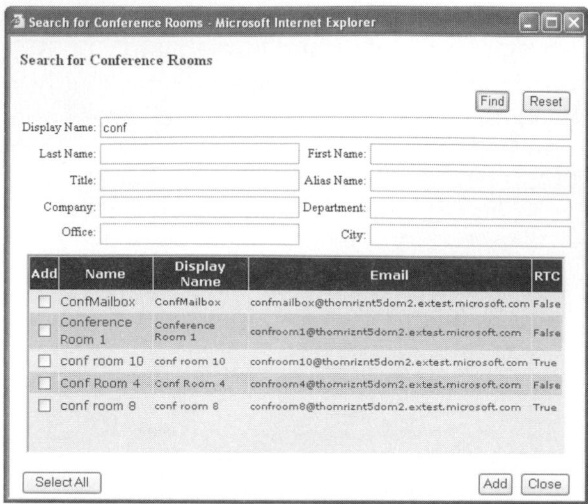

Figure 19-6 The Web page for searching for real-time resources

Exchange Conferencing Server labels its resources with a special globally unique identifier (GUID) in the *msExchResourceGUID* Active Directory property so that the application can find real-time resources. This GUID is *{A1C12B06-B01B-11d2-85EB-00C04FA376EB}*. If you perform an ADSI search using that GUID, you will find all Exchange Conferencing Server resources on your network. All Exchange Conferencing Server resources are created as users with mailboxes stored inside of Exchange so that the online conference room can generate free/busy information and you can use Outlook direct booking, which allows Outlook to schedule a conference directly in the conference room's calendar.

Figuring Out Free/Busy Information for a Conference Room

Once we find the online conference room we're looking for, we must check the free/busy information for that conference room. The Training application can view the free/busy information for any room or person. A real-time conference room is exactly the same as a regular mailbox, so we can just use Collaboration Data Objects (CDO) or WebDAV to query for the free/busy information for that room. The application also takes an extra step while it is querying the free/busy information to find out whether the mailbox it is querying is a conferencing mailbox or a regular mailbox. The user interface for querying for free/busy information is shown in Figure 19-7. Note that the Training application can use either server-side CDO or WebDAV to query for free/busy information. This means that free/busy lookup works whether the Exchange server is on the same machine or a different machine from the application. (For example, the Training application might be running on a Microsoft SharePoint Portal Server [SPS] 2001 server, which is discussed in the companion material posted on the book's Web site.)

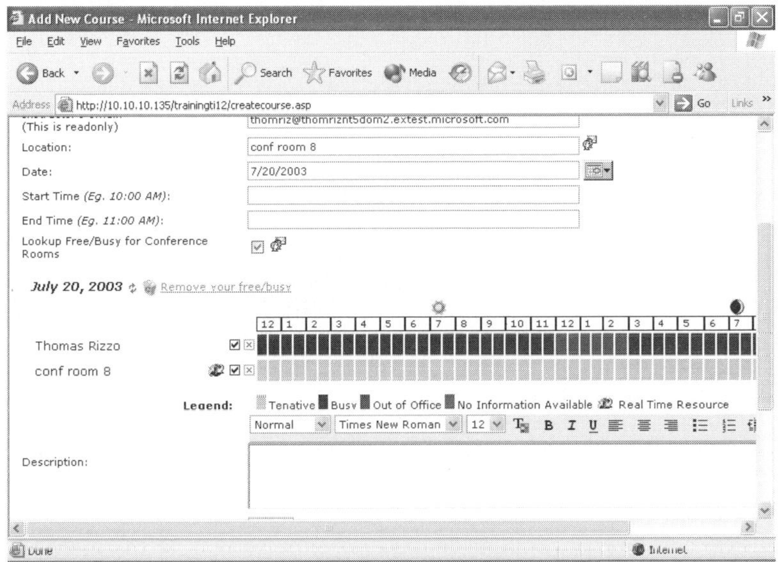

Figure 19-7 The free/busy lookup user interface

Scheduling an Online Conference via CDO

Once we know that the instructor wants to schedule an online conference, we can schedule the online event in a number of ways. The most straightforward and easiest way is to just use CDO to send a meeting request to the corresponding conferencing mailbox as an attendee. An event sink sitting on the conferencing server will capture the meeting request and respond to the organizer with the URL that should be sent to all attendees. This is different from direct booking in Outlook, in which the URL is automatically placed in the appointment in each attendee's calendar. The e-mail that is sent by the conferencing server is shown in Figure 19-8.

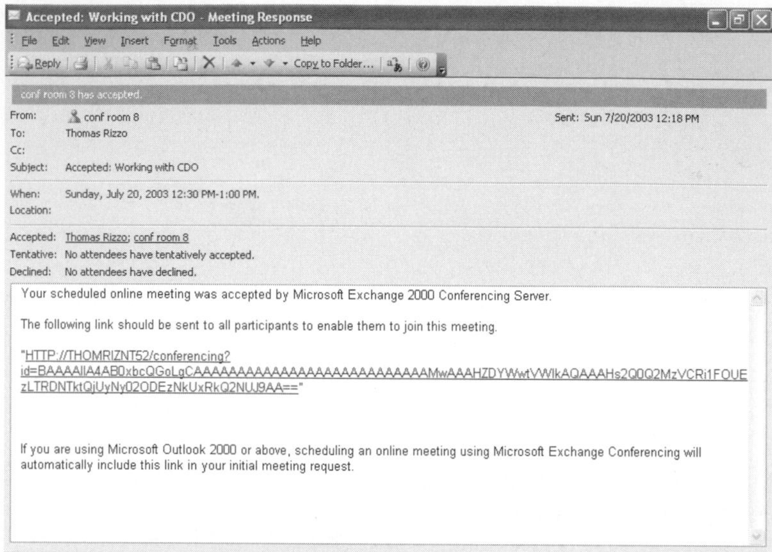

Figure 19-8 The e-mail sent by the conferencing server when scheduling a conference using CDO

The code to schedule a real-time conference via CDO is shown here:

```
Dim oConfig As New CDO.Configuration

oConfig.Fields(cdoSendEmailAddress) = "thomriz@mydomain.com"
oConfig.Fields(cdoMailboxURL) = "http://myserver/exchange/thomriz"
oConfig.Fields.Update

'Create new Appointment
Dim oAppt As New CDO.Appointment
oAppt.Configuration = oConfig
oAppt.Subject = "New Virtual Meeting"
oAppt.StartTime = "11/9/2003 10:00 AM"
oAppt.EndTime = "11/9/2003 11:00 AM"
oAppt.Attendees.Add "lylecu@mydomain.com"

Dim oAttendee As CDO.Attendee
Set oAttendee = oAppt.Attendees.Add("realtimeconf@mydomain.com")
oAppt.Resources = "realtimeconf@mydomain.com"

Dim oCalRequest As CDO.CalendarMessage
Set oCalRequest = oAppt.CreateRequest
oCalRequest.Message.Send
```

Scheduling an Online Conference via *ConferenceLocatorManager*

Exchange Conferencing Server includes an object that you can call to schedule real-time conferences from your applications: the *XConfLoc.ConferenceLocatorManager* object. This is the same object that the ASP pages from Exchange Conferencing Server use. The reason you should use this object rather than CDO to schedule and cancel your conferences is that CDO is not remotable—your code must run directly on the server. This implies that if you have an Exchange Conferencing server that is different from the Exchange server where the conferencing mailbox is located, you have to write the code to use Distributed COM (DCOM) to create a CDO session on that remote server to cancel or schedule the conference. The Exchange Conferencing Server object does all of this for you under the covers.

The *XConfLoc.ConferenceLocatorManager* object is contained in the file xconfloc.exe under the Microsoft Exchange Conferencing Server directory. You can install Exchange Conferencing Server on servers that do not even have Exchange Server on them. This means that you can set up pure Exchange Conferencing servers. Be sure that you have the latest Service Pack for Exchange Conferencing Server on these servers before you attempt to use this object.

The *XConfLoc.ConferenceLocatorManager* object provides a number of classes. The only class I'll cover is the *IScheduler* class.

> **Note** Much of this code is modeled after the online scheduling ASP code that Exchange Conferencing Server itself uses; however, this class is undocumented, so you use this code at your own risk. The following code could stop working or could change at any point if Microsoft changes the API.

To schedule an online resource, the *IScheduler* interface gives you a *Send* method. You pass the domain user in the form *domain\user* to *TO* recipients, the *CC* recipients, the SMTP address of the online conference room (the conferencing mailbox), the start date of the meeting, the end date of the meeting, a *Boolean* that specifies whether the meeting is recurring, the subject of the meeting, the body of the meeting request, whether the meeting is private, the password (if there is one) to join the meeting, and a variable (which is the URL to the meeting) that will be filled by the method call. Note that the start and end times must be in Universal Time Coordinate (UTC) offset format. A code example will make this easier to understand. Here is the code from the Training application to schedule a real-time course:

```
On Error Resume Next

'Try to create the conference locator from SP1
Set ConfLocatorManager = CreateObject("XCONFLOC.ConferenceLocatorManager")
If Err.Number = 0 Then
    Call ConfLocatorManager.GetInterface("IID_IScheduler", Scheduler)
    'Get the Auth User from the server variables

    strDOMAINUSER = Request.ServerVariables("LOGON_USER")

    set oADInfo = Server.CreateObject("ADSystemInfo")
    strDomainName = oADInfo.DomainShortName

    'see if Logonuser has the domain name as well
    iRevSlash = InStr(1,strDOMAINUSER,"\")
    If iRevSlash = 0 Then
        'Add the domain at the beginning
        strDOMAINUSER = strDomainName & "\" & strDOMAINUSER
    End If

    strEmail = Session("UserEmail")
    strConfRoomSMTP = Request.Form("confroomSMTP")

    'Turn the start time and end time into UTC
    'Figure out offset from UTC for this timezone

    dDate = Now
    'Break out Date / Time

    dCurDate = Month(dDate) & "/" & Day(dDate) & "/" & Year(dDate)
    dHour = Hour(dDate)
    If Len(dHour) = 1 Then
        dHour = "0" & Hour(dDate)
    End If

    dMinute = Minute(dDate)
    If Len(dMinute) = 1 Then
        dMinute = "0" & Minute(dDate)
    End If

    dCurTime = dHour & ":" & dMinute

    iTimeZoneOffset = getUTCOffset(dCurDate,dCurTime)
    'iTimeZoneOffset is in minutes

    dStartDate = CDate(Request.Form("date") & " " _
                & Request.Form("starttime"))

    dateStartTime = DateAdd("n", iTimeZoneOffset, dStartDate)
```

```
    dEndDate = CDate(Request.Form("date") & " " & Request.Form("endtime"))
    dateEndTime = DateAdd("n", iTimeZoneOffset,dEndDate)

    strSubject = Cstr(Request.Form("title"))
    strBody = Cstr(Request.Form("description"))

    'Don't make it private so other students can join in and
    'see the course
    vbPrivate = false

    'Don't support recurring meetings
    bIsRecurring = ""

    strURL = ""

    'Add the instructor as a To recipient
    strToRecips = Session("UserEmail")

    'Book the resource
    'Response.Write "<P>" & strDOMAINUSER & strToRecips & strCcRecips _
                  & strConfRoomSMTP & dateStartTime & dateEndTime _
                  & bIsRecurring & strSubject & strBody & vbPrivate _
                  & strDecodedPassword & strURL
    'Response.End

    Err.Clear

    CALL Scheduler.Send(strDOMAINUSER, strToRecips, strCcRecips, _
                        strConfRoomSMTP, dateStartTime, dateEndTime, _
                        bIsRecurring, strSubject, strBody, vbPrivate, _
                        strDecodedPassword, strURL)
    Err.Clear     'Clear all errors since conf server in beta
                  'throws error even if successful.
    If Err.Number <> 0 Then
        bConfSendError = True
    End If

    If strURL <> "" Then
        'We got back the conference URL, store it on the item
        iAppt.Fields(strSchema & "httppathonlineconference").Value = strURL
        iAppt.Fields.Update
    End If
<script language=javascript runat=server>

    function GetUTCOffset(dDate, dTime)
    {
        var s;
        //Take the date and figure out the UTC offset from it
        var dValue = dDate + " " + dTime;
        var d = new Date(dValue);
        s = d.getTimezoneOffset();
        return(s);
    }
</script>
```

Canceling an Online Conference via *ConferenceLocatorManager*

Canceling an online conference is easy. All you do is call the *Delete* method on the *Scheduler* object. You pass in the username in the form *domain\username*, the SMTP of the online resource, the ID of the meeting (which can be obtained from the URL to the meeting), and whether the meeting is recurring. The following code example shows these steps:

```
'Try to create the conference locator from SP1
On Error Resume Next
Set ConfLocatorManager = CreateObject("XCONFLOC.ConferenceLocatorManager")
If Err.Number = 0 Then
    Call ConfLocatorManager.GetInterface("IID_IScheduler", Scheduler)
    'Get the Auth User from the server variables

    strDOMAINUSER = Request.ServerVariables("LOGON_USER")

    Set oADInfo = Server.CreateObject("ADSystemInfo")
    strDomainName = oADInfo.DomainShortName

    'see if Logonuser has the domain name as well
    iRevSlash = InStr(1,strDOMAINUSER,"\")
    If iRevSlash = 0 Then
        'Add the domain at the beginning
        strDOMAINUSER = strDomainName & "\" & strDOMAINUSER
    End If

    'Get SMTP Address of the resource
    strSMTPAddress = iAppt.Fields(strSchema & "confroomsmtp").Value

    'Get the meeting ID
    'Parse the online http address in reverse to id=
    strMeetingURL = iAppt.Fields(strSchema _
                            & "httppathonlineconference").Value

    iResult = instrrev(strMeetingURL,"?id=")
    txtMeetingID = Mid(strMeetingURL,iResult+4)

    fRecurring = False
    CALL Scheduler.Delete(strDOMAINUSER, strSMTPAddress, _
                        txtMeetingID, fRecurring)
End If
```

Listing Online Conferences via *ConferenceLocatorManager*

The final function you will probably perform with Exchange Conferencing Server is listing all the available conferences to your users. The easiest way to do this is to use the list.asp file that comes with Exchange Conferencing Server (Service Pack 1 or later). You can place this file in an IFRAME in your Web application to list the available conferences. However, if you want to do custom work to display the available conferences, you must use *GetProfilesByTime2* from the *IConferenceLocator2* interface. You must pass the meeting ID (if you are looking for a particular conference), the username in the form *domain\username*, the start time and end time to query for (in UTC offset, not in the local time zone), and a variable that will hold a collection of conference profiles that are returned. The returned conference profiles correspond to the *IConferenceProfiles* interface, which you can find in the Exchange Conference Management Service 1.0 Type Library (xconfmgr.exe). The following code makes this clearer:

```
'Try to create the conference locator from SP1 or later
On Error Resume Next

Set ConfLocatorManager = CreateObject("XCONFLOC.ConferenceLocatorManager")
If Err.Number = 0 Then
    Call ConfLocatorManager.GetInterface("IID_IConferenceLocator2", _
                                         ConfLocator2)
    'Get the Auth User from the server variables
    strDOMAINUSER = Request.ServerVariables("LOGON_USER")

    set oADInfo = Server.CreateObject("ADSystemInfo")
    strDomainName = oADInfo.DomainShortName

    'see if Logonuser has the domain name as well
    iRevSlash = InStr(1, strDOMAINUSER, "\")
    If iRevSlash = 0 Then
        'Add the domain at the beginning
        strDOMAINUSER = strDomainName & "\" & strDOMAINUSER
    End If

    CALL ConfLocator2.GetProfilesByTim2("", strDOMAINUSER, _
                                        dateStart, dateEnd, confProfiles)

    For Each confProfile In confProfiles
        'Retrieve the subject using the UserProperty method
        Response.Write "Name: " & confProfile.UserProperty(PR_SUBJECT, _
                                                           MAPI_RESOURCE)
        Response.Write "Start time: " & confProfile.StartTime
        Response.Write "End time: " & confProfile.EndTime
        Response.Write "Organizer: " & confProfile.Organizer
        Response.Write "Is Recurring: " & confProfile.IsRecurring
        Response.Write "Meeting ID: " & confProfile.MeetingID
    Next
End If
```

Summary

This chapter gave you an introduction to the world of real-time collaboration. Using real-time collaboration, you can add exciting capabilities to your applications and also leverage new functionality such as the ability to detect presence information in your applications. The next chapter will look at the forms technology in Exchange and how to use some built-in OWA capabilities to quickly build collaborative Exchange applications.

20

Web Storage System Forms, Outlook Web Access, and *System.Web.Mail*

So far we have seen how you can program custom applications using the Application Programming Interfaces (APIs) in Exchange Server. Now we will turn our attention to taking advantage of some of the technologies in Exchange that will speed up your development and do not require as much coding as the examples we have seen in previous chapters. The technologies we will look at are Web Storage System (WSS) Forms, Outlook Web Access (OWA), and *System.Web.Mail*. They are very closely related, since you can use Web Storage System Forms to replace the default forms in Outlook Web Access. Plus, you can use Outlook Web Access controls in your Web Storage System Forms. Let's dive in, starting with OWA first.

Reusing Outlook Web Access

One of the great things about the Web Storage System and Outlook Web Access is that it lets you customize the client without advanced programming by either using WSS Forms, which we'll look at momentarily, or simply, adding some parameters to the URL you pass to OWA. In this section, we'll take a quick look at the most important parameters you can pass to OWA to implement the functionality you want. Table 20-1 lists these parameters.

Table 20-1 Most Common Parameters for Customizing OWA

Command	Supported Parameters	Description
Cmd=	*Navbar*	Displays only the left-hand navigation of OWA, including the Outlook bar, Outlook icons, and the folder list.
	Contents	Displays only the right-hand contents of OWA without the navigation bar.
	New	Creates a new item in the folder.
	Options	Displays the Options page.
	Open	Opens an item for reading. Be careful because e-mail messages end in *.eml*. If you pass just the subject of the e-mail message without the trailing .eml, OWA will not be able to find the item. A page-not-found error will then be returned.
	Preview	Works with an item in Exchange to display the preview pane rendition of the item.
	Edit	Opens an item for editing.
	Reply, *ReplyAll*, *Forward*	Performs the specific operation on the item.
	SaveItem	Saves the item. Used most commonly with WSS Forms.
View=	A string that specifies a view in the folder—for example, *"By Conversation Topic"*, *"Daily"*, or *"Monthly"*	Shows the items in the folder using the view you specify. The view name is case sensitive.
M=	A number that corresponds to a month	The month value you want to display. Only use this parameter with a calendar folder.
D=	A number that corresponds to a day	The day value you want to display. Only use this parameter with a calendar folder.
Y=	A number that corresponds to a year	The year value you want to display. Only use this parameter with a calendar folder.

The Training application takes advantage of the *Cmd=Contents*, the *View=*, and the date semantics, as in *M=*, *D=*, and *Y=*. For example, this URL from the Training application shows a calendar-type public folder with a monthly view, without the navigation bar (see Figure 20-1): *http://<server>/<pfpath>/?Cmd=Contents&View=Monthly&D=15&M=4&Y=2003*.

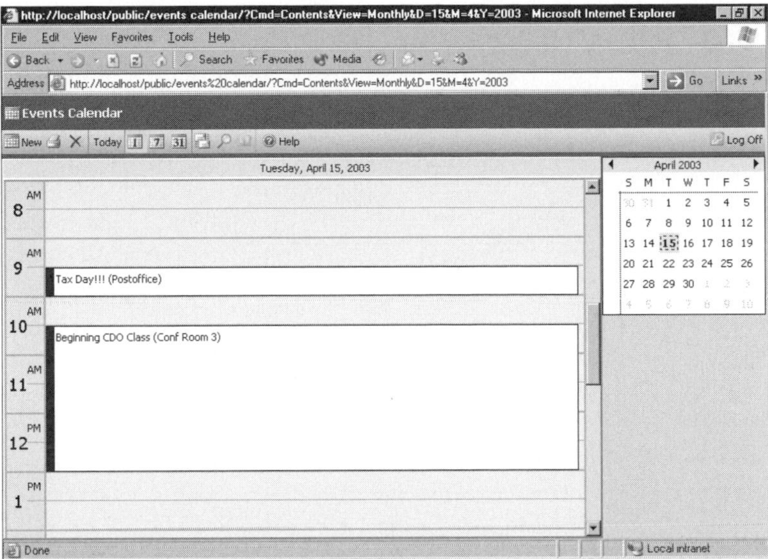

Figure 20-1 Showing a calendar-type public folder without the navigation bar

You can take these URL parameters and use them as hyperlinks or even as sources for frames within your applications. This extensibility of OWA allows you to quickly add Web pages, such as calendaring pages, without having to write a single line of code.

OWA Web Controls

Before we look at samples and tools for using WSS Forms, we need to look at two controls offered by OWA that you can use in your applications: the rich edit control and the folder tree control. These controls are similar to the view control in that they are implemented as Hypertext Markup Language (HTML) Components (HTCs). The Training application shows how to use both of these controls.

Rich Edit Control

The rich edit control allows users to format text right inside the browser—for example, by bolding or underlining or selecting fonts. This control is supported only by Internet Explorer (IE) 5.0 and later. The control is useful when you want to allow users to enter or display rich text. Figure 20-2 shows the rich edit control in action in the Training application.

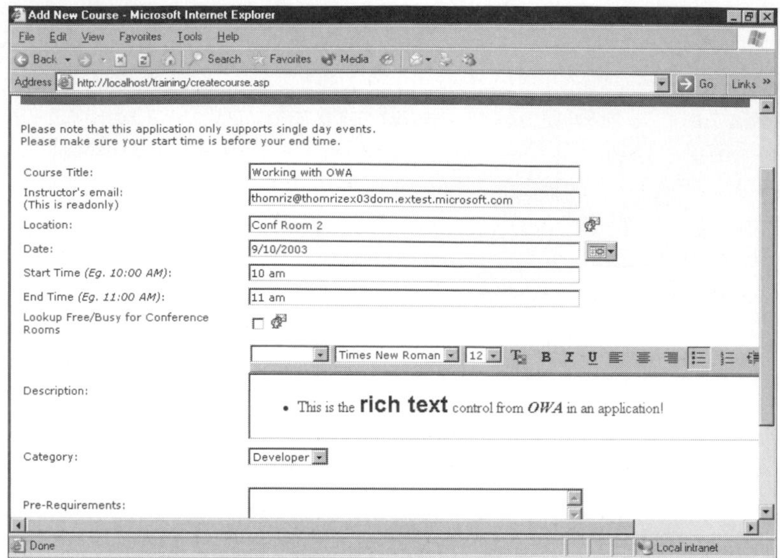

Figure 20-2 The OWA rich edit control inside the Training application

The control itself is implemented as an HTC, just like the view control. To use the control inside a Web page, you include a style that points to the HTC for the control. This HTC is stored with the view control in the controls section of the /exchweb virtual directory as richedit.htc. The first step for using the rich edit control is to add a style to your page that defines the control and its name. The following code is from createcourse.asp in the Training application. It defines *htmledit* as a behavior that is implemented by richedit.htc.

```
<style>
  .htmledit { BEHAVIOR:url("/exchweb/controls/richedit.htc"); }
</style>
```

Next you add a *textarea* to your form that you want rich-text enabled, as shown in the following code:

```
<TEXTAREA class="htmledit" cols=41 name=description id=description
    rows=10 style="HEIGHT: 100px; WIDTH: 600px"
    tooltips="Paragraph Styles;Font Names;Font Size;Font
        Color;Bold;Italic;Underline;Align Left;Center;Align
        Right;Bullets;Numbered List;Decrease Indent;Increase Indent"
    headerStyleNames="Normal;Heading 1;Heading 2;Heading 3;
        Heading 4;Heading 5;Heading 6;Address;Formatted"
    fonts="Arial:Arial;Courier:Courier;Roman:Roman;System:System;
        Times New Roman:Times New Roman;Verdana:Verdana"
    imagePath="/exchweb/img/" textformat="text">
</TEXTAREA>
```

As you can see in the definition of the *TEXTAREA*, we declared the class as *htmledit* in order to use the rich text control. Then we set the *tooltips*, *headerStyleNames*, and *imagePath* properties. These are all properties found in the richedit.htc file. You will generally keep the standard properties and values shown in the previous code to enable your rich text control.

Once you include the rich text control, you can easily take the contents of the control and save them as the text for your item. You should be aware of a couple of things about how the control saves messages. First and foremost, the control returns HTML, not text, because it needs a way to retain the formatting you select in the control. Second, the HTML it returns contains special characters such as spaces and the greater-than and less-than signs in encoded form. You must be aware of this if you plan to redisplay the entered text in an *IFRAME* without using the rich text control to render the contents. Let's look at an example. The following is some sample text entered into the rich text control and saved into the body of an item:

```
<!DOCTYPE HTML PUBLIC "-//W3C//DTD HTML 4.0 Transitional//EN">
<HTML>
  <HEAD>
    <META http-equiv=Content-Type content="text/html; charset=unicode">
    <META content="MSHTML 5.50.4134.600" name=GENERATOR>
  </HEAD>
  <BODY>
    <PRE>This is some sample multi-space
         &amp;nbsp;&amp;nbsp;&amp;nbsp;&amp;nbsp; text
         <FONT face=System>Some Formatting This is a greater &amp;gt;
         this is a less &amp;lt;&amp;nbsp;</FONT>
    </PRE>
  </BODY>
</HTML>
```

In the HTML, single spaces are fine. However, when you put in multiple spaces, the control writes in * *. If you do a greater-than or less-than, the control will write *>* or *<*, respectively. When you try to use the Active Server Pages (ASP) object's *Response.Write* method natively with the text returned with these special characters, instead of getting multiple spaces or a greater-than or less-than, you will get the actual * *. This is usually not what you want. You could fix this problem by allowing the rendering of the text to be done by the rich text control again. However, if you are presenting a read-only interface, this can confuse the user because it looks like the user should be able to modify the contents.

Instead, you should write a bit of shim code to modify the HTML that you stored from the rich text control to replace *&* with just *&* to turn * * into the correct HTML for a space, which is * *. This is an easy piece of code and is used in showcourses.asp to render the rich text descriptions of the courses that an instructor enters. The ASP code in the sample to correct this problem is shown here:

```
<TR>
  <TD>
    <B>Description:</B>
  </TD>
  <TD>
    <%
      iAppt.TextBody = replace(iAppt.TextBody,"&amp;","&")
      Response.write iAppt.TextBody
    %>
  </TD>
</TR>
```

Now you've got an easy way to add rich text editing to your dynamic Web applications without much coding at all.

Folder Tree Control

If you have ever used OWA, you've seen the folder tree that appears in the folder list for OWA. This folder tree mimics the folder tree in Outlook. There might be occasions when you want to display a folder tree but do not want to write your own HTML or ActiveX control to do this. In this case, you can use the folder tree control that is included with OWA. This control is also an HTC and is stored in the controls directory under the /exchweb virtual directory. The file is called Exchangetree.htc. Figure 20-3 shows the folder tree in action for the setup program for the Training application. The folder tree allows you to select where you want to install the application. It also allows you to add new folder sub trees to the folder tree and create new folders within the folder tree (if you have the required permissions). The folder tree uses Web Distributed Authoring and Versioning (WebDAV) under the covers to perform all of its operations and is entirely asynchronous, which forces you to listen for some callbacks from the control, as you will see in the code.

Figure 20-3 The folder tree control in the Training application in foldertree.asp

As in the two previous examples with the view and rich edit controls, when you work with HTCs you must add a tag to your HTML page to identify that you want the HTC available. Also, you must look through Exchangetree.htc for all the properties, methods, and events the control supports. I use only a limited subset of these interfaces—the common ones—for the sample application, and I do not have room to document all of the interfaces here, so you are better off looking at the control itself because most of the interfaces are straightforward to work with.

First we need to add a tag to our Web page to identify the HTC, as shown here:

```
<?XML:NAMESPACE PREFIX="WM"/>
<STYLE>
  WM\:TreeView { BEHAVIOR:url(/exchweb/controls/ExchangeTree.htc) }
</STYLE>
```

Just as in the previous two samples, you must then add the actual control to your Web page and pass the default properties you want to specify for the control and the events that your code will handle from the control. The following code from foldertree.asp shows how to do this:

```
<WM:TreeView id="objTree" style=''
    onPickFolder = "objTree_OnPickFolder()"
```

```
    onAddHierarchy = "objTree_OnAddHierarchy()"
    imagePath = "/exchweb/img/"
/>
```

In the code, the *TreeView* control is added and given an ID of *objTree*. The code registers for two events—*onPickFolder*, which is fired when a user picks a folder, and *onAddHierarchy*, which is called when a new folder tree is successfully added to the control. When you work with the control, you should use some of its methods, such as *AddHierarchy*, *CreateFolder*, *MoveFolder*, *CopyFolder*, or *RenameFolder* (to name a few). The full list of methods, properties, and events are in the HTC itself.

The next thing you must do with the control is to listen for the HTML *window* object's *onload* event. In this event, you must load whatever the default folder tree is for your user or application. Otherwise, the tree control will not know what to render by default. The following code implements this functionality. I'm using the folder tree control for a specific purpose, so I pass a parameter (*strDefaultTree*) along the URL, which is the path to the default tree to render such as http://server/public.

```
function window.onload()
{
    var strDefaultTree = "<%=Request.Querystring("strDefaultTree")%>";
    objTree.addHierarchy(strDefaultTree, true);
}
```

Next you just use the methods and write your event handlers for the control. The following snippet of code shows how to use the *AddHierarchy* and *CreateFolder* methods:

```
function addFolderTree()
{
    window.event.returnValue = false;
    var strFolderTreePath = "";
    strFolderTreePath =
        prompt("Please enter the path to the Folder Tree:","http://");
    if (strFolderTreePath == "")
    {
        alert("You must enter a valid path!");
        return;
    }
    else if (strFolderTreePath == null)
    {
        return;
    }
    else
    {
        //Add the folder tree to the hierarchy
        objTree.addHierarchy(strFolderTreePath, false);
    }
}
```

```
function createFolder()
{
    window.event.returnValue = false;
    //Get the globally selected node
    if (strURLSelectedFolder == "")
    {
        alert("You must select a folder first!");
        return;
    }
    else
    {
        var strFolderName =
            prompt("Please type a name for the folder", "New Folder");
        if(strFolderName == "")
        {
            alert("You must enter a valid folder name!");
            return;
        }
        else if(strFolderName == null)
        {
            return;
        }
        else
        {
            objTree.createFolder(strURLSelectedFolder, strFolderName,
                                 "urn:content-classes:folder");
        }
    }
}
```

The *addHierarchy* method takes three parameters, of which the last two are optional. Looking through the JavaScript code for the function, the first parameter is the URL to the folder tree that you want to render. The second is a *Boolean* that specifies whether the tree should be expanded by default. A value of *false* will make the tree not expanded by default. The final parameter is an optional display name for the folder tree.

The *createFolder* method takes as its first parameter the URL of the parent folder in which you want to create the folder as a subfolder. The second parameter is the new folder name. The final parameter is the content class of the new folder. The control will attempt to create the new folder, and if successful, it will refresh with the new folder in its proper location.

You can also listen for events. The two events we registered for in the sample were *onAddHierarchy* and *onPickFolder*. The control calls the code when these events occur. As you can guess by their names, the *onAddHierarchy* event handler is called when a new hierarchy is added to the control, and the *onPick-*

Folder event is called when a user picks a folder. The following is the event handler code for both of these events:

```
function objTree_OnPickFolder()
{
    //alert(event.URL);
    strURLSelectedFolder = event.URL;
}

function objTree_OnAddHierarchy()
{
    //LastRenderedURL contains the URL to the last hierarchy
    //rendered by the control
    if(event.LastRenderedURL==document.all.cmdText.innerText)
    {
        //Just rendered out the correct URL, stop trying to render it
        document.all.cmdTextComplete.innerText = "True";
        //Hide the status text
        document.all.AddingFolderTree.style.display = "none";
    }
}
```

The *onPickFolder* code just sets a global variable to the URL of the folder that the user picked so that the rest of the code in the application can know that information. The *onAddHierarchy* code checks to see if the last URL that was rendered by the control is equal to the URL that the user wants to add to the control. If it is not, the code displays a nice message stating that it's loading the hierarchy you selected. Once the hierarchy is loaded and it is the last rendered URL, the code removes that message from the Web page because the folder tree is visible.

One event that I do not use but you should look at is the *onContextMenu* event. You can find more information about this control in the article "Customizing Microsoft Outlook Web Access" on the Microsoft Technet Web site. This event is called to display the custom right-click shortcut menus in OWA. You can customize these shortcut menus to add your own commands. I warn you that this is not for the faint of heart. It involves using another HTC called dropmenu.htc. The following code adds the necessary reference to this HTC to our Web page:

```
<?XML:NAMESPACE PREFIX="WM"/>
<STYLE>
  WM\:DROPMENU { BEHAVIOR:url(/exchweb/controls/dropmenu.htc); }
</STYLE>
<LINK rel=stylesheet type=text/css href="/exchweb/controls/navbar.css">
```

The next step is to define your drop-down menu using the XML format that OWA understands, as in this example:

```
<WM:DROPMENU id=idDropMenu class="nbDropMenu"
    HOLDSTYLE=false
    menuName="itemMenu"
    style="font-family: arial; font-size:24">
  <WM:MENUROW>
    <WM:MENUITEM type="default">
      <WM:MENUITEMIMG/>
      <WM:MENUITEMCAPTION>My custom dropdown</WM:MENUITEMCAPTION>
      <WM:MENUITEMSCRIPT>
        MyJavaScriptHere();AnotherJavaScriptFunction();
    </WM:MENUITEMSCRIPT>
    </WM:MENUITEM>
  </WM:MENUROW>
  <WM:MENUDIVIDER/>
  <WM:MENUROW>
    <WM:MENUITEM type="default">
      <WM:MENUITEMIMG/>
      <WM:MENUITEMCAPTION>My custom dropdown2</WM:MENUITEMCAPTION>
      <WM:MENUITEMSCRIPT>
        CustomJavaScript();YetAnotherJavaScriptFunction();
    </WM:MENUITEMSCRIPT>
    </WM:MENUITEM>
  </WM:MENUROW>
</WM:DROPMENU>
```

Next we add to our folder tree definition that we want to also handle the *oncontextmenu* event. Here's the folder tree definition from before with this new event handler added:

```
<WM:TreeView id="objTree" style=''
    onPickFolder = "objTree_OnPickFolder()"
    onAddHierarchy = "objTree_OnAddHierarchy()"
    imagePath = "/exchweb/img/"
    oncontextmenu="myContextMenu()"
/>
```

Finally, we need to implement the *myContextMenu* function. The code for this is simple. It just calls the *menuShow* method, which shows our custom menu.

```
function myContextMenu()
{
    // make our menu visible
    idDropMenu.menuShow(true);

    // Don't let the browser bubble up the right click
    event.returnValue = false;
}
```

Web Storage System Forms

As shown in the beginning of this chapter, OWA provides a neat extensibility model in the form of querystring parameters added to the URL, yet one of the key requirements for customizing OWA is the ability to replace the default forms that it displays for items contained in the information store with custom forms. Imagine that you create an ASP application that stores information in Exchange Server, and suppose that you want to provide your users with a customized interface to access your application's content. In this scenario, you would most likely want to replace the default OWA forms with your application's forms. That's why Exchange Server supports WSS Forms and a WSS Forms Registry.

WSS Forms Architecture

Before we write code that uses WSS Forms, let's look at the architecture of WSS Forms so you will understand why you have to do certain things to get WSS Forms Registry going.

First and foremost, you must understand that WSS Forms and the WSS Forms Registry are implemented as Internet Server Application Program Interface (ISAPI) extensions. WSS Forms live in a DLL called exwform.dll, which is at *http://server/exchweb/bin/exwform.dll*. When you create a form registration that leverages the WSS Forms Renderer, which is part of that DLL, the WSS Forms Registry DLL calls exwform.dll to render your data. For the WSS Forms Registry, you will find that this DLL lives in an ISAPI extension called davex.dll. If you look at the configuration in the Internet Information Services (IIS) Manager under any Exchange virtual directory, you will see davex.dll in the list of ISAPI DLLs. To see the configuration, create a new application name for your virtual directory in IIS by clicking the Create button and then click the Configuration button. Davex.dll is registered to parse every HTTP request coming into a virtual directory that points at an Exchange datasource. This is so the DLL can look in the WSS Forms Registry to see whether the data that the user or application is requesting has a form registered to display the data. This is also how the WSS Forms Registry can detect the type of browser and language that is requesting the data. All of these headers are passed by the browser to IIS, which passes that data to the ISAPI davex.dll.

If you use the WSS Forms Renderer and the data requested has a WSS Form associated with it, the renderer will use the EXOLEDB provider to read the HTML form specified in the form registration's *FormURL* property. (This is why WSS Forms must live inside the Exchange database.) It will then parse that form for any special markup that specifies data binding, as you'll see shortly.

The renderer will then request the required databound properties against the data item specified in the form registration's *DataURL* property. The values it retrieves will be formatted according to the formats you specified in your form, and any necessary time zone conversions will be performed. The renderer will then combine the data and the HTML form and return the new combined form to the client that made the request. The renderer does all the heavy lifting for you. It actively goes out and combines your marked up HTML form with the data from Exchange.

Creating a WSS Form

Because WSS Forms can be ASP forms or simply HTML forms, you don't need a custom tool to create them. Instead, you can simply use common HTML development tools such as Microsoft FrontPage, Microsoft Visual Studio .NET, or Microsoft Visual Notepad.

When you create WSS Forms, you have two choices for rendering (that is, emitting HTML data to the browser). You can simply use an ASP file and generate all the code and HTML yourself without getting any help from Exchange Server, or you can use HTML forms and the WSS Forms Renderer. The first approach requires you to program with Collaboration Data Objects (CDO), ActiveX Data Objects (ADO), or ServerXMLHTTP and WebDAV. The latter does not require you to write any code.

Using ASP Forms

The Training application uses the first approach of creating a WSS Form because of the flexibility that ASP provides. When a user chooses OWA as the interface to the Events Calendar page and opens an item from the calendar, Exchange Server checks the WSS Forms Registry and determines that an ASP page is registered for the calendar. Instead of displaying the default calendar form, Exchange Server hands over execution of the application to the ASP application and passes it some parameters within the URL. As part of the URL, Exchange Server passes the *DataURL* parameter. The *DataURL* parameter is the full path to the item that the user requested from Exchange Server. By using the value in this *DataURL* parameter, you can open the item via CDO, ADO or ServerXMLHTTP if you are programming an XML-based server-to-server solution and perform the necessary operations for your application. The following code is taken from eventwsform.asp, which is the ASP file called in the Training application, and Figure 20-4 shows the resulting Web page as displayed in the user's browser:

```
'Figure out display from a querystring variable
set rec = Server.CreateObject("ADODB.Record")
```

```
strFullURL = request.QueryString("DataURL")
set oConnection = Server.CreateObject("ADODB.Connection")
oConnection.ConnectionString = strFullURL
oConnection.Provider = "ExOledb.Datasource"
oConnection.Open
rec.Open strFullURL,oConnection

Response.Write "<B>Course Details:</B><BR><BR>"

'Open the connection
set iAppt = Server.CreateObject("CDO.Appointment")

Dim strhref

'Load the appointment into CDO
'Response.Write strhref
strhref = rec.Fields("DAV:href")
iAppt.DataSource.Open strhref, oConnection, 1
. . . .
```

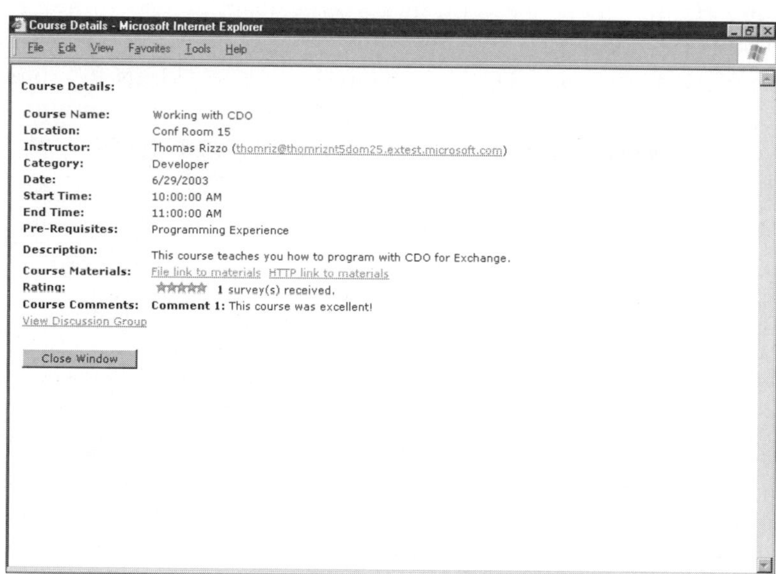

Figure 20-4 An example of an ASP-based WSS Form.

Using HTML Forms

Creating an HTML form that supports data binding is easy with Exchange Server and WSS Forms. By using some special HTML markup, you can turn ordinary HTML elements into data-bound elements. The markup you'll need to implement consists of two attributes to set. First you must set the *name* attribute of the HTML element as the schema name that you want to bind to the element—

for example, *urn:schemas:httpmail:subject*. The second attribute you need to set on the HTML element is named *class*. You must always set this attribute to a value of *field* to tell the WSS Forms Renderer that this is a data-bound field. The following HTML sets a text box to suddenly be data-bound to a WSS field named *myprop*:

```
My Prop: <input type="text" name="urn:schemas:myschema:myprop" class="field">
```

You also receive the *DataURL* parameter as you would in an ASP WSS Form. Using *DataURL*, you can set the action of your form to post the data back to the URL from which the data was retrieved. The following code permits a user submitting a form to have that form post back to Exchange Server and then redirect the Web page to the application's default page:

```
<form class="form" method="post"
    actionspec="%DataURL%?Cmd=SaveItem&Redir=%DataURL%/../">
```

That's it. As you can see, creating a WSS data-bound HTML form is pretty simple.

Registering a WSS Form

Now that you've created a WSS Form, you need to tell Exchange Server what to do with it. For example, you might want your form to replace another form. Or you might want your form to process commands sent to a specific server. To tell Exchange Server how to use your form, you must add a form registration to your application. A form registration is just another item in the Exchange Server database; however, it contains some special properties, which we'll examine momentarily. Normally, you will want to save your form registrations in the schema folder for your applications, which is typically the same place you store your custom content classes and properties.

The following code shows how to register a form using ADO and results in a form like that in Figure 20-5. This particular registration displays the custom form whenever a user browses to the folder over HTTP, either by typing a URL in Internet Explorer or by browsing through the folders of OWA and selecting a folder.

```
Set oRec = CreateObject("ADODB.Record")
oRec.Open "default.reg", oCon, 3, 0

oRec.Fields("DAV:contentclass") = _
    "urn:schemas-microsoft-com:office:forms#registration"
oRec.Fields("urn:schemas-microsoft-com:office:forms#contentclass") = _
    "urn:content-classes:folder"
oRec.Fields("urn:schemas-microsoft-com:office:forms#request")= "GET"
oRec.Fields("urn:schemas-microsoft-com:office:forms#cmd") = "*"
oRec.Fields("urn:schemas-microsoft-com:office:forms#formurl") = "default.htm"
```

```
oRec.Fields("urn:schemas-microsoft-com:office:forms#executeurl") = _
    "/exchweb/bin/exwform.dll"
oRec.Fields("urn:schemas-microsoft-com:office:forms#executeparameters") = ""
oRec.Fields("urn:schemas-microsoft-com:office:forms#contentstate") = "*"
oRec.Fields("urn:schemas-microsoft-com:office:forms#platform") = "WINNT"
oRec.Fields("urn:schemas-microsoft-com:office:forms#browser") = "*"
oRec.Fields("urn:schemas-microsoft-com:office:forms#majorver") = "*"
oRec.Fields("urn:schemas-microsoft-com:office:forms#minorver") = "*"
oRec.Fields("urn:schemas-microsoft-com:office:forms#version") = ""
oRec.Fields("urn:schemas-microsoft-com:office:forms#messagestate") = "*"
oRec.Fields("urn:schemas-microsoft-com:office:forms#language") = "*"
oRec.Fields.Update

oRec.Close
```

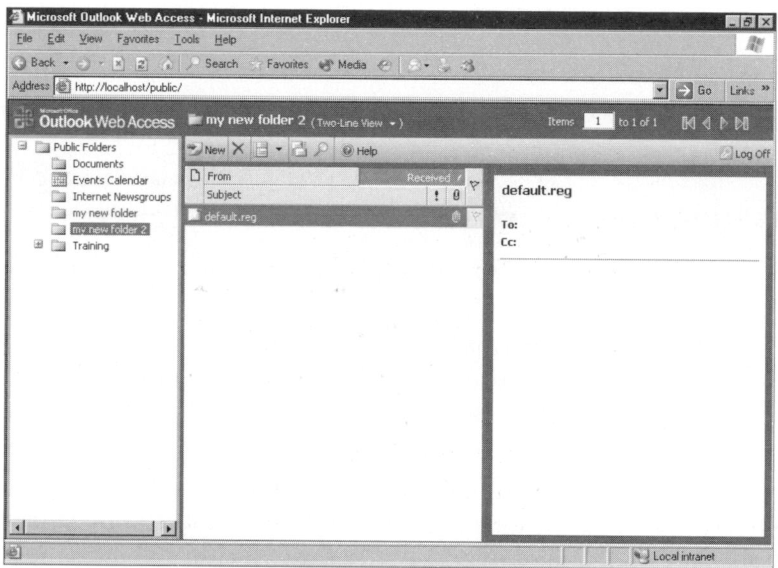

Figure 20-5 A form registration item for a WSS Form

The code simply creates a new item in Exchange Server (see Figure 20-5). It sets the content class of the item to *urn:schemas-microsoft-com:office:forms#registration*, which tells Exchange Server that the item is a form registration object. Then the code sets some properties that tell Exchange Server which commands and requests the form should handle, what languages the form should be used for, and which type the form is. You can have multiple form registrations in a single folder that target similar types of requests but display different forms based on the criteria you set, such as browser, language, or content state. Table 20-2 describes these properties in more detail. Be aware that, when appropriate, properties can support wildcards that allow all values.

Table 20-2 Form Registration Properties

Property	Description
urn:schemas-microsoft-com:office:forms#browser	Indicates the type of browser. This property is useful if you want different forms for different browsers. For example, you can detect a cell phone microbrowser that is making a request and return an appropriate version of the form for that type of browser.
urn:schemas-microsoft-com:office:forms#cmd	Corresponds to a URL querystring *Cmd* parameter, such as *Myurl/?Cmd=Contents*. You can also set this property to custom commands that you implement and register. For example, you can have a parameter named *NewEvent*, which you register for when the URL contains *Myurl/?Cmd=NewEvent*.
urn:schemas-microsoft-com:office:forms#contentclass	Specifies the content class the form is registered for. You can specify a built-in content class or a custom one.
urn:schemas:microsoft-com:office:forms#contentstate	Checks the form against the *urn:schemas:microsoft-com:office:forms#contentstate* property. You can set this property to any value you want. For example, you can set *contentstate* to *approved* and have a form display the item differently depending on whether the *contentstate* property is *approved* or *not approved*.
urn:schemas-microsoft-com:office:forms#executeparameters	Specifies the parameters to pass to the form rendering engine.
urn:schemas-microsoft-com:office:forms#executeurl	Specifies the URL from which to execute the form. If you're using the built-in renderer, this URL will be */exchweb/bin/exwform.dll*. If you're using ASP, you'll want to use the URL of your ASP page as this value because ASP applications don't need the help of exwform.dll for processing.
urn:schemas-microsoft-com:office:forms#formurl	Specifies the URL to the form that should be used to render the data.
urn:schemas-microsoft-com:office:forms#language	Specifies the language of the browser client for which the form should be rendered. This property can be any language code that is valid for HTTP headers.
urn:schemas-microsoft-com:office:forms#majorver	The browser major version.
urn:schemas-microsoft-com:office:forms#messagestate	The message state (such as *read* or *submitted*).
urn:schemas-microsoft-com:office:forms#minorver	The browser minor version.

Table 20-2 Form Registration Properties

Property	Description
urn:schemas-microsoft-com:office:forms#platform	Specifies the platform of the browser, such as WINNT or UNIX.
urn:schemas-microsoft-com:office:forms#request	Specifies whether the form is the default for a *GET* or *POST* request.

Since WSS Forms build on Web technologies, you can send custom querystring parameters to the form. These parameters allow you to specify custom commands or pass custom variables to your WSS Form.

I already showed an example of registering a form by using the built-in WSS Forms Renderer, so I'll also show an example of a registration that uses an ASP page. This code is taken from the setup program for the Training application. Notice that the *FormURL* and *ExecuteURL* parameters differ from the version that we used to register a form based on the WSS Forms Renderer (exwform.dll).

```
'Create the registration in the schema folder
Set oRec = CreateObject("ADODB.Record")
oRec.Open strPath & "schema/webstoreform.reg", oConnection, 3, 0

oRec.Fields("DAV:contentclass") = _
    "urn:schemas-microsoft-com:office:forms#registration"
oRec.Fields("urn:schemas-microsoft-com:office:forms#contentclass") = _
    "urn:content-classes:appointment"
oRec.Fields("urn:schemas-microsoft-com:office:forms#request") = "GET"
oRec.Fields("urn:schemas-microsoft-com:office:forms#cmd") = "*"

'Put full URL to Web Store forms
oRec.Fields("urn:schemas-microsoft-com:office:forms#formurl") = _
    strHTTPURL & "/eventwsform.asp"
oRec.Fields("urn:schemas-microsoft-com:office:forms#executeurl") = _
    strHTTPURL & "/eventwsform.asp"
oRec.Fields("urn:schemas-microsoft-com:office:forms#executeparameters") = ""
oRec.Fields("urn:schemas-microsoft-com:office:forms#contentstate") = "*"
oRec.Fields("urn:schemas-microsoft-com:office:forms#platform") = "WINNT"
oRec.Fields("urn:schemas-microsoft-com:office:forms#browser") = "*"
oRec.Fields("urn:schemas-microsoft-com:office:forms#majorver") = "*"
oRec.Fields("urn:schemas-microsoft-com:office:forms#minorver") = "*"
oRec.Fields("urn:schemas-microsoft-com:office:forms#version") = ""
oRec.Fields("urn:schemas-microsoft-com:office:forms#messagestate") = "*"
oRec.Fields("urn:schemas-microsoft-com:office:forms#language") = "*"

oRec.Fields.Update
oRec.Close
```

Another way to register a new form for a folder is by using the *DAV:defaultdocument* property. This property takes a string that specifies the Web page to open when the user browses to the folder by using OWA. Instead of displaying the contents of the folder when this property is set, OWA displays the custom form. You can easily set this property by using ADO or WebDAV.

Registering WSS Forms Globally

You might want to register a WSS Form globally so that no matter which folder the user is in, the WSS Form appears. For example, you might want to globally replace the standard OWA compose form. When you work with global forms, the forms are registered per store, not per server, so if you have multiple databases on a single server, you must perform multiple registrations. If you run into permissions problems, make sure the system mailbox on your Exchange server has permissions to the folder where you are attempting to place your global form registration. The following code shows how to register WSS Forms globally in Exchange:

```
'NOTE: Search for ToDo and when appropriate modify
'the line of code below the ToDo comment

'remember EXOLEDB is covered in Chapter 17
Set igetSG = CreateObject("Exoledb.StoreGuidFromUrl.1")

'Get the guid for the registration process:
'ToDo: Replace Anystoreitem with a proper Exchange URL. Any store item in the '
store will get you the store url. It might be something like: "user1/inbox"
Guid = igetSG.StoreGuidFromUrl("http://<servername>/exchange/Anystoreitem")

'ToDo: Uncomment the lines below if registering the form in the Private Store
'regURL = "http://<servername>/exchange/SystemMailbox" & Guid

'ToDO: Uncomment the line below if registering the form in a Non-MAPI TLH
'regURL = "http://<servername>/vroot"

'ToDO: Uncomment the line below if registering the form in a MAPI TLH
'regURL = "http://<servername>/exadmin/admin/domain.com/public%20folders"

If Trim(regURL) = "" Then
    Exit Sub
End If

'Fill the Default Schema folder with form registrations

Set oCon = CreateObject("ADODB.Connection")
oCon.ConnectionString = regURL +  "/##SchemaURI##/microsoft/exchangeV1"
oCon.Provider = "ExOledb.Datasource"
```

```
oCon.Open

'---------------------------------------------------
'Register the default page for the folder
Set oRec = CreateObject("ADODB.Record")

oRec.Open "CustomFormReg.reg", oCon, 3, 0

oRec.Fields("DAV:contentclass") = _
    "urn:schemas-microsoft-com:office:forms#registration"

'ToDo: Change content class to the desired content class
oRec.Fields("urn:schemas-microsoft-com:office:forms#contentclass") = _
    "urn:content-classes:message"
oRec.Fields("urn:schemas-microsoft-com:office:forms#cmd") = "open"

'ToDo: Change to appropriate url form
oRec.Fields("urn:schemas-microsoft-com:office:forms#formurl") = _
    "http://<servername>/public/pf/form.asp"

'ToDo: Change to appropriate url for your form
oRec.Fields("urn:schemas-microsoft-com:office:forms#executeurl") = _
    "http://servername/public/pf/form.asp"

oRec.Fields.Update
oRec.Close

'Further instructions
MsgBox "Copy Form.ASP into the folder that is referenced when setting the " _
     & "urn:schemas-microsoft-com:office:forms#formurl. " _
     & "Enable script execution on the directory."
```

Web Storage System Forms—The Renderer

Beyond providing easy URLs to work with and a rich forms registry, Web Storage System Forms also allow you to perform no-code data binding, database lookups to populate controls, and built-in document upload as standalone documents or as attachments, and they provide an easy way to create views by using an XML view descriptor. We will look at all of these features in Web Storage System Forms and discuss when to use Web Storage System Forms technology and when to roll your own using ASP forms. These features are provided by the WSS Forms Renderer.

Note If you are going to work with Web Storage System Forms using ASP pages in the public vroot for Public Folders, be sure to enable Script execution in the Microsoft Internet Information Service (IIS) Services Manager. Otherwise, you will receive the standard IIS "unauthorized to view this page in your browser" error.

Also, when you use WSS Forms, you need to enable freedocs support via the registry on your server. You will want to add a DWORD value *HKEY_LOCAL_MACHINE\SYSTEM\CurrentControlSet\Services\MSExchangeWEB\OWA\EnableFreedocs*. Set the DWORD to one of the following values:

- 0: (or key not present): Freedocs are inaccessible (default value)
- 1: Freedocs are accessible only when accessed from a back-end server
- 2: Freedocs are accessible only when accessed from a back-end server or a front-end server that is listed in AcceptedAttachmentFrontEnds entry.
- 3: Freedocs are allowed (no restrictions)

The default behavior (Freedocs are inaccessible in public folders) will cause workflow applications that request Freedocs, such as a Web Forms application using the exwform.dll renderer, to not function correctly. You will receive a *403* error which is a forbidden error.

Registering Your WSS Forms to Use the Renderer

If you want to use the WSS Forms Renderer and not build your own ASP pages that do data binding via EXOLEDB or another method, you must change your form registrations slightly. You have to change your *ExecuteURL* to */exchweb/bin/exwform.dll* so the renderer will be the DLL that is executed when the form is loaded. Also, you have to change your *FormURL* and *DataURL* to point to your HTML form and the Exchange item that you want to render, respectively. The HTML form you pass can be just a simple HTML form with no server-side or client-side script, or it can be a full-blown ASP page that contains both server-side and client-side script. With ASP forms you can still use HTML binding, but you can also add more complex scripts and code than you can in a pure HTML form. It is up to you how complex you make your forms. However, you can use the built-in renderer and view capabilities in WSS Forms in either case, as you will see.

WSS Forms Data Binding

The WSS Forms Renderer provides the ability to perform automatic data binding, whether you are creating new items, displaying items, or updating existing items. To provide a no-code solution, the WSS Forms Renderer uses some special HTML markup to specify that you want an HTML element data-bound to a particular field in your Exchange data. This special markup uses HTML element *class=field* and sets the *Name* of the HTML element to the full property name that you want to data-bind to. For example, the following HTML binds the subject of a message to a text box on the form:

```
<input type="text" name="urn:schemas:httpmail:subject" class="field">
```

Depending on the type of HTML element you bind to an item in Exchange, you will get different results. For example, the previous example binds a text box to a single-value string in Exchange. However, you can bind the same text box to a multivalue string. Using a comma or a semi-colon as your delimiter, you can post multiple values for your multivalue string back to Exchange. Check boxes and radio buttons are also supported as data-bound fields. If a value from the data-bound field matches the value in the check box or radio button group, that HTML element is checked or selected. Finally, you can also data-bind other types of HTML elements, such as *DIVs, SPANs,* anchors, and even *IMG* (image) tags.

Let's take a look at a slightly more complex form in HTML:

```
<HTML>
  <body>
    <form method="POST" class="form" name="theform"
                                 actionspec="%DataURL%?cmd=contents">
        <H1>My list</H1>
        <BR>
        Read only:
        <input type="checkbox" name="DAV:isreadonly" class="field"
                                 form="theform" value="ON">
        <p>
        Hidden: <br><input type="radio" name="DAV:ishidden" value="1
                                 class="field" form="theform">True<BR>
        <input type="radio" name="DAV:ishidden" value="0" class="field"
                                 form="theform">False
        <p>
        Friendly name: <DIV name="DAV:displayname" class="field"
                                 form="theform"> </DIV><p>
        Expiration date:
        <input type="text" name="urn:schemas:httpmail:expiry-date"
```

```
                                    class="field" form="theform" size="20"
                                    wsformat="dddd, MMMM d, yyyy"><p>
        Keywords:
        <select size="1"
             name="urn:schemas-microsoft-com:office:office#Keywords"
             class="field" form="theform">
            <option value="option1">Option 1 </option>
            <option value="option2">Option 2 </option>
        </select>
        <p>
        Content state: <textarea rows="2" cols="20"
             name="http://schemas.microsoft.com/exchange/contentstate"
             class="field" form="theform"></textarea>
        <p>
        <input type="hidden" name="DAV:contentclass" value="My_list"
                                    form="theform">
        <BR>
        <input type="submit" value="Submit" name="B1"><input type="reset"
                                    value="Reset" name="B2">
        <input type="hidden"
             name="http://schemas.microsoft.com/exchange/nosave/hintforurl"
             value="DAV:isreadonly">
    </form>
  </body>
</html>
```

The first thing you might notice is the *ActionSpec* attribute on the form. The WSS Forms Renderer takes the *ActionSpec* attribute and uses it as a template to create the *Action* attribute. The *Action* attribute is what occurs after the form is posted. In this example, you see *%DataURL%?Cmd=contents*. The macro *%DataURL%* is one of the macros you can use in your WSS Forms. It is automatically expanded by the renderer into the URL to the data item in Exchange. The macros you can use are shown in Table 20-3.

Table 20-3 Macros Used with WSS Forms

Macro	Description
%FormURL%	The URL to the form being rendered. This can either be a relative or absolute URL, depending on how you registered the form in your form registration.
%FormContainer%	This is the URL to the folder containing the form being rendered.
%DataURL%	This is the URL to the data item being rendered in the form.
%DataContainer%	This is the URL to the folder containing the data item being rendered.

Creating New Items

One of the most common tasks you will do using WSS Forms is to create new items. To create a new item, you just create a form registration for the folder where you want to create your new item. Be sure to make the *ExecuteParameters* property in your registration equal to *CreateNew*. This instructs the WSS Forms Renderer to create a new item rather than update the properties of the folder itself. If you do this, you will notice two things. First, after you create and submit the item, the item is automatically displayed back in the browser. Second, the display name of the item is a long, nasty GUID. Solving both of these problems is easy with WSS Forms.

For the first problem, you will want to use the Redir token. This token is part of your *ExecuteParameters* property—or you can put it right into your *ActionSpec* attribute in your form. For example, the following *ExecuteParameter* property for a form registration specifies that a new item should be created and then the browser should be redirected to a specific folder:

```
ExecuteParameter: cmd=CreateNew&Redir=http://server/public/myfolder/
```

To fix the second problem, the WSS Forms technology provides a way for you to give hints to the renderer on what you want the name of the item to be. You must specify a field on the form to use as the hint—you do this by adding the *http://schemas.microsoft.com/exchange/nosave/hintforurl* property on your form. For example, the following HTML specifies the subject of the message to be the hint for the URL. If another item has the same subject, Exchange will add a numbered suffix to the end, as in *mymessage-1.eml*.

```
<input type="text" name="urn:schemas:httpmail:subject" value="test">
<input type="hidden"
    name="http://schemas.microsoft.com/exchange/nosave/hintforurl"
    value="urn:schemas:httpmail:subject">
```

Updating Items

The WSS Forms Renderer will automatically update an item if a user modifies any of the values. Just be sure to use the *Redir* token (which we discussed earlier) to redirect your users to a folder view or another page. Otherwise, they will be stuck viewing the same item over and over again.

Formatting Fields

When working with your fields, you might want to change the way the data is formatted when displayed in the browser. For example, you might want to show a date as a long date or show just the time portion of a date/time field. Instead of forcing you to write code to perform this formatting, the WSS Forms Renderer allows you to add a special attribute to your HTML fields called *wsformat*. For the *wsformat*, you pass a format string that specifies the type of data that should be rendered for that field and how you want the data to appear. Table 20-4 lists the format strings, data types, and examples for each format string.

Table 20-4 Format Strings for WSS Forms

Format String	Data Type	Example
""	String, Multi-valued String	Unformatted text
"#,#"	Integer, Real	1,2345 –1,2345
"#,#.0"	Integer, Real	1,234.5 –1,234.5
"#,#.00"	Integer, Real	1,234.56 –1,234.56
""	Date/Time	10/1/2001 3:15:43 PM
"M/d/yyyy || h:mm:ss tt"	Date/Time	10/1/2001 3:15:43 PM
"MMMM d, yyyy"	Date/Time	October 1, 2001
"d-MMM-yy"	Date/Time	1-Oct-01
"M/d/yyyy"	Date/Time	10/1/2001
"MMMM yy"	Date/Time	October 01
"M/yyyy"	Date/Time	10/2001
"h:mm tt"	Date/Time	3:15 PM
"h:mm"	Date/Time	3:15

The following example shows how to use the *wsformat* attribute:

```
<input type="text" name="urn:schemas:httpmail:expiry-date"
       class="field" form="theform" size="39"
       wsformat="M/d/yyyy|| h:mm:ss tt">
```

The XML View Descriptor, which we'll discuss later in the chapter, also uses these format strings.

Dynamic Database Lookups

When you work with the HTML *SELECT* element, you can have the WSS Forms Renderer look up the values for the element using another folder in Exchange. You can thus avoid hardcoding values into your *SELECT* elements. This solution also lets you avoid writing code to do this dynamic population. Instead, as you've seen with the rest of the WSS Forms technology, you only have to do some simple HTML markup. For example, say you have a folder called Options that contains items with the options you want to display dynamically in a drop-down list on your HTML form. Let's say the subject of the message is what you want to display for the option in the user interface and that the text of the message is what you really want the value of the option to be when selected and posted to the server. To accomplish your dynamic lookup using WSS Forms, you provide the following HTML:

```
<select size="1" name="urn:schemas-microsoft-com:office:office#Keywords"
        class="field" form="theform"
        values="urn:schemas:httpmail:subject"
        valuesfolder="/public/options"
        optionvalues="urn:schemas:httpmail:textdescription">
```

Now imagine that the Options folder is filled with three messages: Green, Orange, and Blue. Green and Blue have no text and Orange has "This is text" as its text body. When the WSS Forms Renderer displays your drop-down list, this is the HTML it will send to the browser:

```
<select size="1" name="urn:schemas-microsoft-com:office:office#Keywords"
        form="theform"
        values="urn:schemas:httpmail:subject"
        valuesfolder="/public/options"
        optionvalues="urn:schemas:httpmail:textdescription">
    <option value="This is text">Orange</option>
    <option value=" ">Green</option>
    <option value=" ">Blue</option>
</select>
```

Okay. Let's get a little bit more complicated. You might be wondering how to filter which items are returned from the folder that contains your options. Well, you can optionally pass *filtersrc* and *orderby* values that tell the WSS Forms Renderer the SQL *WHERE* filter you want to use and the *ORDER BY* clause to use, respectively. In our example, say we want to filter only by a certain value such as *Orange* in the subject and you want those items to be sorted in ascending order by subject. This is what our new form HTML would look like for our *SELECT* element:

```
<select size="1" name="urn:schemas-microsoft-com:office:office#Keywords"
        class="field" form="theform"
        values="urn:schemas:httpmail:subject"
        valuesfolder="/public/options"
        optionvalues="urn:schemas:httpmail:textdescription"
        filtersrc="&quot;urn:schemas:httpmail:subject&quot; ='Orange'"
        orderby="&quot;urn:schemas:httpmail:subject&quot; ASC">
```

Notice that you have to quote your *WHERE* and *ORDER BY* clauses using the HTML *"*. Otherwise, you will get errors from the renderer because your SQL clauses will be formatted incorrectly. Also note that if you have any existing hardcoded *OPTION* elements in your *SELECT* element, they will first be rendered by WSS Forms and then your dynamic options will be placed in the *SELECT* element. Table 20-5 lists the parameters you can use with a *SELECT* element to make it a dynamically populated element.

Table 20-5 Parameters for the *SELECT* Element

Parameter	Required?	Description
Values	Yes	Specifies the property with the value to insert for the display name for the *OPTION* element in your *SELECT* element
valuesfolder	Yes	Specifies the URL to the folder from which the WSS Forms Renderer should pull data to populate the *SELECT* element
Filtersrc	No	Specifies the *WHERE* clause to apply to the items contained in your *valuesfolder* parameter
optionvalues	No	Specifies the property to use as the value for each of the *OPTION* elements in your *SELECT* element
orderby	No	An *ORDER BY* clause to apply to the items contained in your *valuesfolder* parameter

Document and Attachment Upload

One common task you will perform with mail messages or documents is uploading attachments or a document directly. To make this functionality easier for you, the WSS Forms Renderer includes the ability to upload a document as a freedoc or attachment on an item. You therefore do not have to buy or create an upload component to upload files using a browser to your Exchange Server.

The first type of upload we will look at is document upload. This type of upload places the document directly in the folder as a standalone document and not as an attachment to an item. Using this method, you can quickly have users upload their documents to a document repository application or some other type of document-centric application. When the user clicks on the document in a user interface such as Microsoft Outlook or OWA, the document will open directly. Also, if the document uploaded is a Microsoft Office document, Exchange will promote all the Office document properties, such as author, number of words, last saved time, and edit time to fields in the database. This means that you can sort, group, and filter as well as add these Office document properties to your views.

The only caveat about property promotion is that it is only property promotion. Exchange does not demote the properties back into the document if you change those properties using ADO or WebDAV. The only way to get new values into your Office document properties is to use the object model or user interface of the Office application that created the document. When you place the document in Exchange again, those new values will be promoted.

You implement document upload by setting the encoding type of your HTML *FORM* element to be *multipart/form-data* and by placing a HTML *INPUT* element on your form that specifies the *FILE* type for that *INPUT* element. When you use the *FILE* type, the browser will automatically display a browse button so a user can browse his local drive for the file path rather than having to manually type the file path into the input box. Be sure to name your *FILE INPUT* element *DOCUMENTBODY*. This tells the WSS Forms Renderer that the file being uploaded should be placed into Exchange as a standalone document.

An example will make this clearer. The Training application uses the document upload capabilities of WSS Forms in two places. First, instructors can tape a class in Audio Video Interleave (AVI), Windows Media, or Quicktime format and upload that recording as an on-demand version of the class for students that could not attend a class. This means that any student can view this on-demand version from any computer at any time. To place the on-demand version into Exchange and associate the file with the course, the Training application uses the WSS Forms document upload capabilities. Figure 20-6 shows the user interface for uploading an on-demand version of a course.

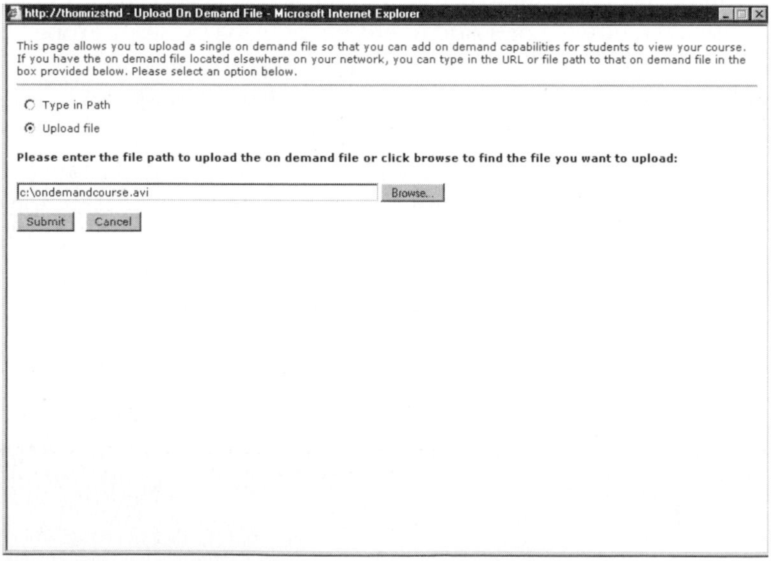

Figure 20-6 Uploading an on-demand version of a course using the WSS Form document upload

A more interesting example is uploading course materials for a course. If instructors want to make the course materials available, they can use the file share that the application creates. However, the more common way to upload course materials is by using a Web browser. Again, the application uses the document upload capabilities of WSS Forms. As Figure 20-7 shows, the course materials portion also uses the new WSS view control to display the list of course materials in the folder. You'll see how to create views using this control later in the chapter.

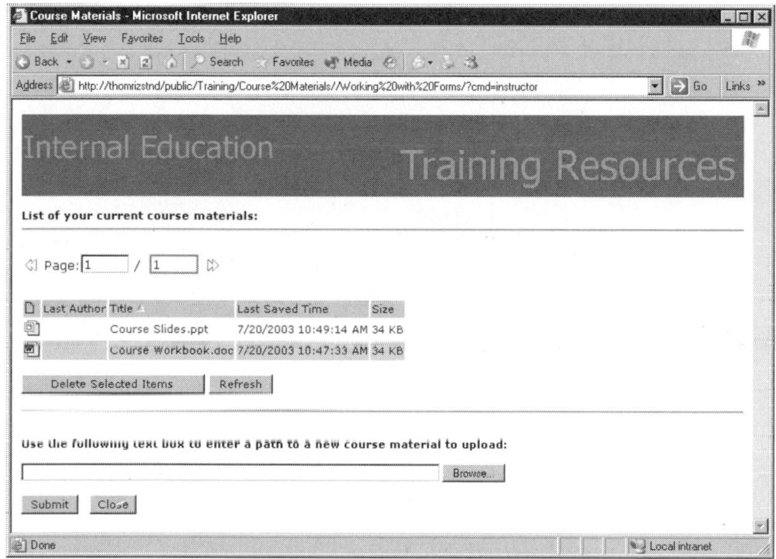

Figure 20-7 Uploading course materials in the Training application

Here is some of the code from the course materials page in the Training application:

```
<form enctype="multipart/form-data" id="theForm1" name="theform1"
      method="post" class="form" actionspec="./">
    <B>Use the following text box to enter a path to a new course material
       to upload:
    </B><BR><BR>
    <input type=file value="Add new course material" class=field
           id=doc name="DOCUMENTBODY" size=70>
    <BR><BR>
    <input type="submit" id="submitfilepathbutton" value="Submit"
           onclick="VBScript:ValidateUpload">  
    <input type="button" id="cancel" value="Close"
           onclick="javascript:window.close();">
</form>
<script language="VBScript">
    Sub ValidateUpload()
```

```
        'Make sure that there is something in the path!
        If document.all.doc.value = "" Then
            MsgBox "You must enter a valid path in the text box!"
            window.event.returnValue = false
        End If
    End Sub
</script>
```

In the code, you can see an HTML form that has its *enctype* set to *multipart /form-data*. Also, the form contains an *INPUT* element on the file type with the name equal to *DOCUMENTBODY* to specify that the file should be uploaded as a standalone document. That's all you need to do to get started with document upload using WSS Forms. Note, however, that your form must reside in Exchange and the document must be uploaded to Exchange. You cannot use this technique for forms that run outside of Exchange folders, nor can you upload documents that upload into non-Exchange sources such as the file system.

Also note that a form cannot have multiple *DOCUMENTBODY* inputs. Also, if you mix and match document upload with attachment upload in the same form, the attachment will be ignored and the document upload will win.

Attachment Upload Support

WSS Forms supports placing multiple documents into a single item. As part of its attachment support, WSS Forms provides three key services: the ability to upload attachments, the ability to delete attachments, and the ability to render an attachment well (described shortly) that allows your application to list and select attachments.

Uploading Attachments

Attachment upload is similar to document upload in that you set your form encoding to *multipart/form-data* and you use the *FILE* input type. The main difference is that instead of naming your *FILE* input type *DOCUMENTBODY*, you name it *ATTACHMENT*. Unlike document upload, attachment upload supports multiple *FILE* inputs in a single form. All files will be attached to the same item in Exchange. To distinguish between multiple attachments, Exchange adds the name of the original file to the item and creates a unique URL for each attachment. For example, if you upload an attachment from c:\my documents\mydocument.doc, the name of the attachment will be mydocument.doc. The URL to the attachment might then be something like *http://server/public /documents/item.eml/1_multipart_xF8FF_2_mydocument.doc*.

The following code shows an example of adding attachment upload to your form:

```
<form method="POST" enctype="multipart/form-data" class="form"
      name="theform" actionspec="%dataurl%?cmd=contents">
    <Input type="file" name="ATTACHMENT" size="20" class="field"
          form="theform">
</form>
```

Attachment Wells

Now that we've uploaded an attachment to an item, we need a way to display not only that attachment but any attachments in the item. You don't have to write code to do this because WSS Forms includes the ability to display an attachment well. An attachment well is just an interface that allows the user to work with the attachment collection for the item. It is optional for your applications. The attachment well can list the attachments in both read-only and editable form, provide hyperlinks to the attachments so the user can open them, and provide an interface so the user can select attachments for deletion. The interface is also customizable.

You add an attachment well to your form by simply creating a *DIV* element and naming the *CLASS* of that *DIV attachmentWell*. When WSS Forms renders that *DIV*, it generates an HTML 3.2 table containing the attachments on the form. This HTML table can contain different elements in its cells, depending on the formatting options you select for the attachment well. Table 20-6 lists the attachment well attributes you can specify.

Table 20-6 Attachment Well Attributes

Attribute	Description
Cols	Specifies how many attachments to list in a single row before starting a new row. The default value is 1.
Spacing	Specifies the spacing between attachments. This attribute directly corresponds to the *CellSpacing* attribute of your HTML table. The default value is 15.
IncludeDelete	If this attribute is set to 1, the renderer will insert a check box into the cell to allow the user to select the attachment for deletion. The default value is 0, which means that deletion is not enabled by default.

Table 20-6 Attachment Well Attributes

Attribute	Description
Icon	If this is set to *small*, the renderer will insert an *IMG* tag into the cell for the small icon for the file type. The renderer uses the icon images included with OWA. If you set this property to *large*, the renderer will insert an *IMG* tag to a large icon for the specified file. If you specify anything besides these two values, the renderer will assume that you are specifying the URL to a custom icon for the attachment. This URL can be absolute or relative. By default, no image is displayed in the attachment well.
IncludeLink	If this is set to *1*, a hyperlink to the attachment will be added for the user to open the attachment. A value of *0* means that no hyperlink is added. The default value is *1*.
AttachStyle	Specifies the HTML style element for the *TD* element for the table row. For example, a value of *color:blue* turns into the HTML *style="color:blue"*.
AttachClass	Sets the Cascading Style Sheet (CSS) *class* for the *TD* element for the table row. For example, a value of *mycustomclass* turns into the HTML *class="mycustomclass"*.
Target	Specifies the HTML target for the attachment link. For example, you can specify *_blank* to open in a new window or *_self* to open in the same window.

The following are examples of markups that use the attributes specified in the table. Figure 20-8 shows an HTML page with an attachment well in action.

- **Read-only attachment well** *<DIV Class="AttachmentWell">*
- **Read/write attachment well** *<DIV Class="AttachmentWell" Icon="Small" IncludeDelete="1">*
- **Read/write attachment well that opens the attachment in a new window** *<DIV Class="AttachmentWell" Icon="Small" IncludeDelete="1" Target="_blank">*

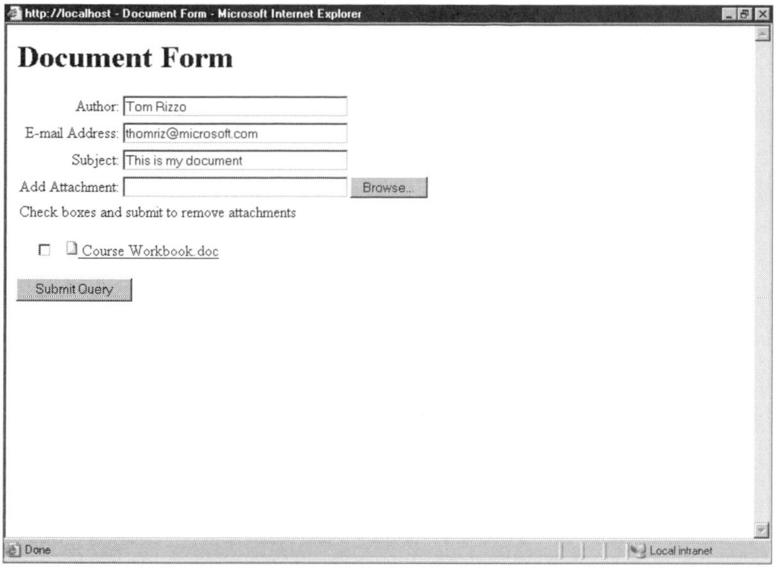

Figure 20-8 A rendered attachment well for an item in Exchange

Deleting an Attachment

If you look at the rendered code for the attachment well when you specify a value of *1* for *IncludeDelete*, you will see that for each attachment there is a check box named *http://schemas.microsoft.com/exchange/nosave/deleteattach*, which is the URL to the attachment. You delete an attachment by selecting this check box. When the form is posted back to the server, WSS Forms will look through the data to see if the check box is selected for the attachment; if it is, it will open the item and delete the attachment whose URL corresponds to the check box name. Using the attachment well is the easiest way to delete an attachment. You can also manually add the correct HTML elements to your own form.

WSS Form Views and the XML View Descriptor

If you want to display a list of items for a folder inside your Web application, you don't have to write the code for this functionality. WSS Forms lets you place a view control inside your HTML pages that you can customize via parameters to display the items in your folder. This view control is similar to the view control you see in OWA. The view control also supports rich clients such as Internet Explorer 5.0 and later (which can use DHTML and XML) as well as HTML 3.2 clients such as Internet Explorer 4.0 or Opera. The key thing is that you do not have to know what type of browser is attempting to access the view. The view control automatically detects the browser and displays either a rich view for rich clients or an HTML 3.2 view for HTML 3.2 clients. Also, the view control has built-in grouping and sorting capabilities, and you can filter based on queries and customize the user interface.

Adding a View to a Web Page

The first thing you'll want to do when you add a view to your Web page manually is to declare an XML namespace in your HTML. You can do this by adding the line *<HTML XMLNS:wf>*. Next you specify a *WF:VIEW* tag as follows:

```
<style>
  @media all {
    WF\:VIEW { BEHAVIOR:url("exchweb/controls/wfview.htc") }
  }
</style>
```

As you can see, the view control is actually an HTC. HTCs are script-based components. For example, wfview.htc, which is usually located where you installed Exchange Server (*drive*:/program files/exchsrvr/exchweb/controls/), contains code that declares properties, methods, and events for the HTC and some script that implements those properties, methods, and events.

The next step is to actually insert the view. You do this by dropping a *WF:VIEW* tag into your code. The following code shows all of these elements combined to display a simple view:

```
<html XMLNS:WF>
<STYLE>
  @media all {
    WF\:VIEW { behavior:url(/exchweb/controls/wfview.htc) }
  }
</STYLE>
<WF:VIEW id="FolderView1"
         style="width: 100%; height: 80%"
         URL="%DataURL%"
         viewDescriptor="FolderView1_XML"
         linkspecSingleClick="%DataURL%"
         targetSingleClick="_self">
```

You might notice in the *WF:VIEW* tag that the *viewDescriptor* property points at *FolderView1_XML*. The *viewDescriptor* property tells the view control where to pull the XML view descriptor that specifies the columns, sorting, and grouping that is contained in the view. This view descriptor can be an XML island in the Web page or can contain an absolute or relative URL to a file that contains the XML view descriptor.

Before we drill into the specific XML tags contained in the view descriptor, you need to be aware of two issues. First, if you look at the *WF:VIEW* tag, you might notice some parameters such as *style*, *URL*, and *targetSingleClick*. It makes no difference whether you specify these parameters in the *WF:VIEW* tag or as part of the XML view descriptor. Second, the XML view descriptor is shared between Exchange and Outlook. Outlook can expose and set its views using the XML view descriptor.

XML View Descriptor Format

The XML view descriptor format has four kinds of tags: primary, column, group by and sort by, and formatting tags. The primary tags are the ones that really affect the general settings of the view control. One example of a primary tag is the *filter* tag. You can specify the overall SQL *WHERE* clause to filter the items in the view by using the primary *filter* tag.

Column tags, on the other hand, affect only the column in which the tag is specified. Column tags can change the style, user interface, or functionality of the column. Also, you use column tags to specify properties from the items you want to display in the view. You should learn all about column tags because they are the primary means of getting the view control to display your data.

Group by and sort by tags are optional tags that specify whether there is grouping or sorting for the overall view. They are not required to render a view.

Formatting tags affect the overall rendering of your view. You can specify formatting for alternate rows to provide a unique user interface, header styles, or other styles to customize the view control.

Primary Tags

Table 20-7 lists the primary tags.

Table 20-7 Primary Tags

Tag	Description
boldUnreadItems	A value of *1* (the default) specifies that unread items are in bold. A value of *0* does not bold unread items.
filter	Specifies the SQL *WHERE* clause to use to filter the items contained in the view. Note that the *WHERE* clause must be properly escaped for XML. This means that operators such as < and > must become *<* or *>*.

Table 20-7 Primary Tags

Tag	Description
highlightrowstyle	Specifies the CSS text for style attributes on a selected row in a view. The default value is *background–color:HIGHLIGHT;color:HIGHLIGHTTEXT*. You can change this style to make the selected rows appear in yellow or green or whatever user interface styles you want.
imagepath	Specifies the URL path from which the view control will pull the image. The default value is */exchweb/img*, which is where OWA pulls its images from.
linkSpec	Specifies the URL that the view control will use as the link for items in the view. The default value is *%DataURL%?cmd=open*, which will be replaced with the exact URL to each item with the open parameter as the command.
linkSpecSingleClick	Specifies the macro that is the URL to use when an item is clicked. The default value is *%DataURL%?cmd=preview*. This value will be replaced with the URL to the data item with the preview command along the querystring. When the values in the *linkSpecSingleClick* and *linkSpec* tags are the same, click and double-click have the same effect.
page	Specifies which page in the view to show. If the page does not exist, the view control will show the first page or the page that the user was already viewing.
rowsPerPage	Specifies as an integer the number of rows to show in the view for each page. If you specify a value of *0* for this tag, the entire result set will be shown.
scope	Specifies a specific SQL *FROM* clause in case you need to do a custom *SCOPE* or traversal in your query. The default value for this tag is a shallow traversal of the current folder. If you specify the *searchSubfolders* tag, this tag is ignored.
searchSubfolders	A value of *1* indicates that you want to do a deep traversal. A value of *0* specifies a shallow traversal. Remember that you cannot do a deep traversal in the MAPI Public Folder tree.
shadowrowstyle	Specifies the CSS style text for the selected rows in a view when the view does not have the focus. The default value is *background–color:THREEDFACE*.
sortascicon	Specifies the icon to use for the column heading when sorting in ascending order in that column. The default value is */exchweb/img/view-sortup.gif*.
sortdescicon	The opposite of the *sortascicon* tag. It specifies the icon to use when sorting the view in a descending order. The default value is */exchweb/img/view-sortdown.gif*.

Table 20-7 Primary Tags

Tag	Description
target	Specifies where HTML links should open from the view, such as *_self* or *_blank*. You will normally want to set this to *_blank* to make items open in a new browser. If you specify *targetSingleClick*, you do not have to specify this tag.
targetSingleClick	Specifies where HTML links should open from the view when a user clicks on an item or link. You will normally want to set this tag to *_blank* to have the view control open the item in a new browser window.
view	A required root element of the view descriptor. Every view descriptor has a view tag. The rest of your tags are placed between the *<view>...</view>* tags.
viewDescriptorURL	Specifies the location of an external view descriptor. All the standard WSS Forms macros are supported in this URL, including *%DataURL%*, *%DataContainer*, *%FormURL%*, and *%FormContainer%*.
viewDescriptor	Specifies the location of an internal view descriptor. This is normally an XML data island. If you specify both the *viewDescriptor* and *viewDescriptorURL* properties, the *viewDescriptor* property will be used.
Xslpassthrough	Used in conjunction with the *customxsl* tags in the column tags. This tag specifies valid XSL that you can use to transform data from Exchange before displaying that data in the view. You will see an example of XSL passthrough later in this chapter.

Let's look at an XML view descriptor that uses primary tags. The following view descriptor has a filter and opens the item in a new browser window when you click the item:

```
<WF:VIEW id="FolderView1" viewDescriptor="FolderView1_XML">
    <XML id="FolderView1_XML">
        <view>
            <style>width: 100%; height: 80%</style>
            <URL>%DataURL%</URL>
            <linkspecSingleClick>%DataURL%</linkspecSingleClick>
            <targetSingleClick>_blank</targetSingleClick>
            <filter>
                "DAV:ishidden" = false AND "DAV:isfolder" = false
                AND "DAV:contentclass" = 'My_list'
            </filter>
            <viewstyle></viewstyle>
            <headerstyle>background-color:#C0C0C0</headerstyle>
            <rowstyle></rowstyle>
            <searchSubfolders>0</searchSubfolders>
```

```
        </view>
    </XML>
</WF:VIEW>
```

Column Tags

The only problem with the view descriptor you just saw is that it is blank. This is because the view has no column tags. Column tags specify the actual data columns to place in the view. Table 20-8 lists the column tags.

Table 20-8 Column Tags

Tag	Description
Bitmap	A value of *1* means that an *IMG* element will be created with the *SRC* attribute pointing to the contents of the property specified in the *prop* tag. Do not specify the *checkbox* tag with this tag because the results are undefined. The default value is *0*.
Boolfalseicon	Specifies the absolute or relative URL to an image when your property is a *Boolean* that is *false*.
Booltrueicon	Specifies the absolute or relative URL to an image when your property is a *Boolean* that is *true*.
Checkbox	A value of *1* means that the column will be a set of check boxes that the user can select or deselect.
Column	The root element for all your columns. All the rest of the column tags must be children between your *<column>… </column>* tags.
customxsl	Specifies the name of the XSL passthrough block to be used to format the data for this column.
Format	Specifies the format string to use for numeric and date data. The format strings you can use were described earlier in the chapter.
Groupbycolumn	Specifies that the current column should be grouped in the view. This tag is useful only for HTML 3.2 views.
Headerstyle	Specifies the HTML style you want to apply to the header for the column.
Heading	Specifies the string you want displayed for the column heading.
Multivalued	A value of *1* tells the view control that your multivalue property is comma delimited. The default value is *0* (not comma delimited).
name	Associates check boxes with the column. Useful only when you have check boxes in your view.

Table 20-8 Column Tags

Tag	Description
Prop	Specifies the property to be displayed in the column. For example, to show the subject of the message, you set this property to *urn:schemas:httpmail:subject*.
Sortable	A value of 1 tells the view that your column can be sorted by the user.
Style	Specifies the HTML style to be applied to every column.
Type	Specifies the type of property, such as string.
Visible	Specifies whether to show the column. A value of 1 makes the column visible, and 0 makes the column invisible. This is useful if you want dynamic views and when you use URL overrides (as discussed later in the chapter).

The following is the earlier view descriptor but with column tags added:

```
<WF:VIEW id="FolderView1" viewDescriptor="FolderView1_XML">
    <XML id="FolderView1_XML">
        <view>
            <style>width: 100%; height: 80%</style>
            <URL>%DataURL%</URL>
            <linkspecSingleClick>%DataURL%</linkspecSingleClick>
            <targetSingleClick>_blank</targetSingleClick>
            <column>
                <heading>Read only</heading>
                <prop>DAV:isreadonly</prop>
                <headerstyle>width: 33%</headerstyle>
                <style>width: 33%</style>
                <format></format>
                <sortable>1</sortable>
                <visible>1</visible>
                <checkbox>0</checkbox>
                <bitmap>0</bitmap>
            </column>
            <column>
                <heading>Hidden</heading>
                <prop>DAV:ishidden</prop>
                <headerstyle></headerstyle>
                <style></style>
                <format></format>
                <sortable>1</sortable>
                <visible>1</visible>
                <checkbox>0</checkbox>
                <bitmap>0</bitmap>
            </column>
            <column>
                <heading>Friendly name</heading>
```

```
        <prop>DAV:displayname</prop>
        <headerstyle></headerstyle>
        <style></style>
        <format></format>
        <sortable>1</sortable>
        <visible>1</visible>
        <checkbox>0</checkbox>
        <bitmap>0</bitmap>
    </column>
    <column>
        <heading>Content state</heading>
        <prop>
            http://schemas.microsoft.com/exchange/contentstate
        </prop>
        <headerstyle></headerstyle>
        <style></style>
        <format></format>
        <sortable>1</sortable>
        <visible>1</visible>
        <checkbox>0</checkbox>
        <bitmap>0</bitmap>
    </column>
    <column>
        <heading>Expiration date</heading>
        <prop>urn:schemas:httpmail:expiry-date</prop>
        <headerstyle></headerstyle>
        <style></style>
        <format>M/d/yyyy|| h:mm:ss tt</format>
        <sortable>1</sortable>
        <visible>1</visible>
        <checkbox>0</checkbox>
        <bitmap>0</bitmap>
    </column>
    <column>
        <heading>Keywords</heading>
        <prop>
            urn:schemas-microsoft-com:office:office#Keywords
        </prop>
        <headerstyle></headerstyle>
        <style></style>
        <format></format>
        <sortable>1</sortable>
        <visible>1</visible>
        <checkbox>0</checkbox>
        <bitmap>0</bitmap>
    </column>
    <column>
        <heading>Has attachments</heading>
        <prop>urn:schemas:httpmail:hasattachment</prop>
        <headerstyle></headerstyle>
        <style></style>
```

```
                <format></format>
                <sortable>1</sortable>
                <visible>1</visible>
                <checkbox>0</checkbox>
                <bitmap>0</bitmap>
            </column>
            <filter>
                "DAV:ishidden" = false AND "DAV:isfolder" = false
                AND "DAV:contentclass" = 'My_list'
            </filter>
            <viewstyle></viewstyle>
            <headerstyle>background-color:#C0C0C0</headerstyle>
            <rowstyle></rowstyle>
            <searchSubfolders>0</searchSubfolders>
        </view>
    </XML>
</WF:VIEW>
```

Group By and Sort By Tags

Group by and sort by tags specify whether there is grouping or sorting in the view. These tags are summarized in Table 20-9.

Table 20-9 Group By and Sort By Tags

Tag	Description
Countlabel	Specifies the label to use to display the number of items in the grouping. For example, if three items are in the grouping and you set this tag to *Number of Items*, the view control will display *Number of Items: 3* in its user interface.
Groupby	Specifies the grouping for your view. You use the *Order* tag to specify the property to group by and in what order to group multiple properties.
Heading	Specifies the string to prepend to the group by column heading in your view. This is usually the friendly name of the property you are grouping by.
Order	Used in conjunction with *Groupby* and *Orderby* to specify the properties to group or sort by and the order in which to perform each of those operations on the specified properties.
Orderby	The container tag for specifying a sort order in your view.
Prop	Specifies the name of the property, such as *urn:schemas:httpmail:subject*.
Style	Specifies the HTML style to apply to the header rows of a grouped view. You can specify any style that is valid for a *<TR>* tag.

Table 20-9 Group By and Sort By Tags

Tag	Description
Sort	Specifies how to sort a column. The possible values are *ASC* and *DESC*.
Unreadlabel	If this tag is present, the unread count for the grouped items is displayed in the header for the grouping. You specify the string that should appear before the number of unread items—usually *Unread*.

The following example shows how to use group by and sort by tags:

```
<view>
. . .
<groupby>
    <order>
        <heading>Friendly name</heading>
        <prop>DAV:displayname</prop>
        <headerstyle></headerstyle>
        <style></style>
        <format></format>
        <sortable>1</sortable>
        <visible>1</visible>
        <checkbox>0</checkbox>
        <bitmap>0</bitmap>
        <countlabel>Count</countlabel>
        <unreadlabel>Unread</unreadlabel>
        <sort>ASC</sort>
        </order>
    </groupby>
. . .
</view>
```

Formatting Tags

You might want to apply some general formatting to your view, such as making alternating rows different colors (as you can in Microsoft Excel). To do general formatting, you use the formatting tags, which are listed in Table 20-10.

Table 20-10 Formatting Tags

Tag	Description
Altrowstyle	Specifies the HTML style for all the odd rows in your view. You can specify a different color for the odd rows.
Headerstyle	Specifies the HTML style to apply to all your headings in the view.

Table 20-10 Formatting Tags

Tag	Description
Rowstyle	Specifies the HTML style to apply to all your rows in your view.
Viewstyle	Specifies the HTML style to apply to the overall HTML <*TABLE*> that makes up your view.

The following example uses these tags to create a highly customized view:

```
<view>
. . .
    <viewstyle>width:100%; </viewstyle>
    <headerstyle>background-color:#c0c0c0;CURSOR: hand</headerstyle>
    <rowstyle></rowstyle>
    <altrowstyle>background-color:lightblue</altrowstyle>
. . .
</view>
```

Methods, Properties, and Events of the View Control

Beyond the tags we just covered, the view control has some extra methods and properties. If you look through the HTC code for the control, you will find these methods, properties, and events. For example, to use script in your Web page to refresh the control, delete the selected items in the control, listen for selection change events, or even add page navigation to the control, you need to use these methods, properties, or events. I cannot adequately describe each and every one, but I will highlight the key tasks you'll want to perform with them.

Deleting Selected Items and Refreshing the View Control

If you look through the actual code in wfview.htc, you will see some properties and methods, including the *deleteItems* and *Refresh* methods. When called from your client-side script, the methods delete the items selected in the view and refresh the view, respectively. They are valid only for the rich view control that is in Internet Explorer 5.0 and later, not for the HTML 3.2 rendering of the view control. The following code from the Training application shows how to get the reference to the view control on the page and how to use both methods:

```
<WF:VIEW id="view1"
         style=""
         URL=""
         onReady="viewload()"
         viewDescriptor="FolderView1_XML"
         linkspec="%DataURL%"
         target="_blank"
         rowsPerPage="15">
```

```
<XML id="FolderView1_XML">
    <view>
        <column>
            <heading>Icon</heading>
            <prop>
              http://schemas.microsoft.com/exchange/outlookmessageclass
            </prop>
            <headerstyle></headerstyle>
            <style>cursor:hand</style>
            <format></format>
            <sortable>1</sortable>
            <visible>1</visible>
            <checkbox>0</checkbox>
            <bitmap>1</bitmap>
        </column>
        <column>
            <heading>Last Author</heading>
            <prop>
                urn:schemas-microsoft-com:office:office#LastAuthor
            </prop>
            <headerstyle></headerstyle>
            <style>cursor:hand</style>
            <format></format>
            <sortable>1</sortable>
            <visible>1</visible>
            <checkbox>0</checkbox>
            <bitmap>0</bitmap>
        </column>
        <column>
            <heading>Title</heading>
            <prop>urn:schemas:httpmail:subject</prop>
            <headerstyle></headerstyle>
            <style>cursor:hand</style>
            <format></format>
            <sortable>1</sortable>
            <visible>1</visible>
            <checkbox>0</checkbox>
            <bitmap>0</bitmap>
        </column>
        <column>
            <heading>Last Saved Time</heading>
            <prop>DAV:getlastmodified</prop>
            <headerstyle></headerstyle>
            <style>cursor:hand</style>
            <format></format>
            <sortable>1</sortable>
            <visible>1</visible>
            <checkbox>0</checkbox>
            <bitmap>0</bitmap>
        </column>
        <column>
            <heading>Size</heading>
            <prop>
```

```
                http://schemas.microsoft.com/mapi/proptag/x0e080003
            </prop>
            <headerstyle></headerstyle>
            <style>cursor:hand</style>
            <format></format>
            <sortable>1</sortable>
            <visible>1</visible>
            <checkbox>0</checkbox>
            <bitmap>0</bitmap>
        </column>
        <filter>
            "DAV:ishidden" = false AND "DAV:isfolder" = false
        </filter>
        <viewstyle></viewstyle>
        <headerstyle>
            background-color:#c0c0c0;CURSOR: hand
        </headerstyle>
        <altrowstyle>background-color:lightblue</altrowstyle>
        <rowstyle>background-color:FFFFFF</rowstyle>
        <searchSubfolders>0</searchSubfolders>
        <orderby>
            <order>
                <prop>urn:schemas:httpmail:subject</prop>
                <sort>ASC</sort>
            </order>
        </orderby>
    </view>
  </XML>
</WF:VIEW>
<BR>
<input type-button value="Delete Selected Items"
       onclick="javascript:document.all.view1.deleteItems()">
<input type=button value="Refresh"
       onclick="javascript:document.all.view1.refresh()"
       id=button2 name=button2>
```

As you can see, the client-side HTML just listens for an *onclick* event for two buttons on the form. Then some client-side JavaScript is called that gets the view element, which is called *view1* from its ID, and calls the methods on the component.

Adding Navigation to Your Page

By default, when you add paging to your view via the *rowsperpage* property, the view control does not provide a way to navigate to new pages. You must provide this capability if multiple pages of data need to be displayed. Luckily, some methods and properties make adding navigation easy. The sample from the Training application has all the script you need to add navigation to your application. You use the *pageCount* property, which specifies the total number of pages of data. You also use the *nextPage* and *previousPage* methods, which move the control to the next and previous page, respectively. The following code from the sample application shows how to implement navigation paging in your view:

```
<form class="form" name=viewform method="POST" action="">
    <IMG id=idPageControl_PrevPage onclick="GoToPreviousPage()"
         title="Previous Page" src="../resources/view-prevpage.gif"
         style="CURSOR: hand; HEIGHT: 20px; POSITION: relative;
                WIDTH: 20px">
    <FONT face=verdana id=idPageControl_PageText size=2
          style="POSITION: relative;COLOR:#000000; TOP: -5px">
    Page:<INPUT id=idPageControl_PageNumInput onkeydown="changePage()"
                style="FONT-FAMILY: verdana; FONT-SIZE: 12px;
                       POSITION: relative; WIDTH: 50px">
    /  
    <INPUT id=idPageControl_PageMaxInput readOnly
           style="BACKGROUND-COLOR: #FFFFFF;
                  BORDER-BOTTOM-COLOR: appworkspace;
                  BORDER-BOTTOM-STYLE: solid;
                  BORDER-LEFT-COLOR: appworkspace;
                  BORDER-LEFT-STYLE: solid;
                  BORDER-RIGHT-COLOR: appworkspace;
                  BORDER-RIGHT-STYLE: solid;
                  BORDER-TOP-COLOR: appworkspace;
                  BORDER-TOP-STYLE: solid; COLOR: #000000;
                  FONT-FAMILY: verdana; FONT-SIZE: 12px;
                  POSITION: relative; WIDTH: 50px">
    </FONT>
    <IMG id=idPageControl_NextPage onclick="GoToNextPage()"
         title="Next Page" src="../resources/view-nextpage.gif"
         style="CURSOR: hand; HEIGHT: 20px; POSITION: relative;
                WIDTH: 20px">
</form>
<script language="javascript">
    //View behavior Navigation script
    function GoToNextPage()
    {
        currentPage =
            document.forms["viewform"]["idPageControl_PageNumInput"];
        pageCount =
            document.forms["viewform"]["idPageControl_PageMaxInput"];
        if (view1.pageCount != "0")
        {
            if ( currentPage.value != view1.pageCount)
            {
                view1.nextPage()
                currentPage.value++;
                pageCount.value = view1.pageCount;
            }
        }
    }
```

```
    function GoToPreviousPage()
    {
        currentPage =
            document.forms["viewform"]["idPageControl_PageNumInput"];
        pageCount =
            document.forms["viewform"]["idPageControl_PageMaxInput"];
        if ( currentPage.value != "1")
        {
            view1.previousPage()
            currentPage.value--;
            pageCount.value = view1.pageCount;
        }
    }

    function viewload()
    {
        currentPage =
            document.forms["viewform"]["idPageControl_PageNumInput"];
        pageCount =
            document.forms["viewform"]["idPageControl_PageMaxInput"];

        currentPage.value = "1";

        if(view1.pageCount == "0")
        {
            pageCount.value = "1";
        }
        else
        {
            pageCount.value = view1.pageCount;
        }
    }

    function changePage()
    {
        currentPage =
            document.forms["viewform"]["idPageControl_PageNumInput"];
        pageCount =
            document.forms["viewform"]["idPageControl_PageMaxInput"];
        if (event.keyCode == 13)
        {
            view1.page = currentPage.value;
            pageCount.value = view1.pageCount;
        }
        event.cancelBubble = true;
    }
</script>
```

The code contains an HTML form that has buttons for next and previous pages as well as listings for the current page and the total amount of pages. The script is called when you click one of these buttons, type a number to change to a different page, or reload the view. The script has validation code that makes sure you are not trying to go to pages in the view that do not exist.

Listening for Selection Change Events

Events are a powerful way to make your code aware of the changes happening in the control. However, you must look through the source code to find the events, which include *onReady*, *onRefresh*, *onBeforeDelete*, and *onError*. You can see the events denoted in the source code with the identifier *PUBLIC:EVENT*. Once you figure out which event you want to listen for, you must register some client-side code to be called when that event occurs.

The *onSelectionChange* event from wfview.htc can be useful if you want to know which item the user is currently selecting in the view. You can then populate data in a form from that item or do a database lookup based on that item's data.

To register client-side code to be called when this event occurs, you add a line to your view declaration. The following view declaration registers a client-side script called *FolderView1_OnSelectionChange* to be called when the *onSelectionChange* event occurs for the view control:

```
<WF:VIEW id="FolderView1"
         style="width: 100%; height: 80%"
         URL="%DataURL%"
         viewDescriptor="FolderView1_XML"
         RowsPerPage="10"
         page=1
         linkspec="%DataURL%"
         target="_blank"
         onSelectionChange = "FolderView1_OnSelectionChange">
```

To register for *onReady* or *onError*, you just add another line to the declaration just like the *onSelectionChange* line. You must then write the script that implements *FolderView1_OnSelectionChange*. However, I recommend that you always look at the source code that fires the event in wfview.htc. The event-firing code usually passes you an event object that contains valuable properties about the object firing the event. The following code from wfview.htc shows that the fire code for *onSelectionChange* passes an event object that specifies whether multiple items were selected in the *multipleItems* property, the HTML element that was selected as *srcElement*, and the selected item's URL in *selectedURL*:

```
function mf_fireOnSelectionChange(objRow, b_wasSelected)
{
    var f_MultipleItems = "NONE";
    if(null != objRow && "true" == objRow.isGroupHeader)
    {
        return;
    }
```

```
    var objSelectedItems = this.all("selected");
    if (null != objSelectedItems)
    {
        if(null != objSelectedItems.length)
        {
            switch(objSelectedItems.length)
            {
                case 0:     f_MultipleItems = "NONE"; break;
                case 1:     f_MultipleItems = "SINGLE"; break;
                default: f_MultipleItems = "MULTIPLE"; break;
            }
        }
        else
        {
            f_MultipleItems = "SINGLE";
        }
    }
    var objEvent = createEventObject();
    objEvent.type        = "SelectionChange";
    objEvent.srcElement    = this;
    objEvent.selectedURL= (null == objRow) ? null : objRow._href;
    objEvent.selected    = b_wasSelected;
    objEvent.multipleItems = f_MultipleItems;
    _ideventonSelectionChange.fire(objEvent);
}
```

We can now effectively write our event handler. We'll simply have the code *MsgBox* out the selected URL and whether multiple items were selected in the view.

```
<script language=VBScript>
    Sub FolderView1_OnSelectionChange()
        MsgBox window.event.selectedURL
        MsgBox window.event.multipleItems
    End Sub
</script>
<script language=Javascript>
    Function FolderView1_OnSelectionChange()
    {
        alert(window.event.selectedURL);
        alert(window.event.multipleItems);
    }
</script>
```

That's all you need to do to figure out which events the control offers, register for those events, and then write your handler for the events.

Using an External View Descriptor

Rather than having to hardcode a view descriptor into your Web page, you can point the control at a location from which to retrieve the XML view descriptor. The view descriptor file must be on the computer that's running the Web Storage System.

Using XSL Passthrough

You might want to apply your own custom formats, calculations, or other sorts of custom processing to data. When you use the view control, you can use the *xslpassthrough* and *customxsl* properties to customize how the control displays or calculates data by providing your own custom XSL scripts that process individual columns before displaying them in the view. For example, you might want a numeric rating column that is displayed as a graphic with stars (which is common for rating systems on the Internet) rather than showing a numeric rating. You can use the *xslpassthrough* property to create calculated columns in your views; however, this property is supported only in Internet Explorer 5.0 and later.

To use *xslpassthrough*, you perform a couple of steps in your view descriptor. First you add the XSL namespace to your view definition. You will see this step in the upcoming sample code. Then you define an *xslpassthrough* block containing a unique name. This block will contain the XSL markup that you want to implement. You can think of the *xslpassthrough* block as similar to an XSL stylesheet. Finally, you find the column where you want to run your custom XSL when it is displayed. You can do this by adding a *customxsl* tag that contains the name of the *xslpassthrough* block you want to call.

The following code shows all of these steps. It displays a calculated icon (such as the graphic with stars mentioned earlier) for a column rather than the number that would normally appear in the column.

```
<WF:VIEW id="FolderView1"
        style="width: 100%; height: 80%"
        URL="%DataURL%"
        viewDescriptor="FolderView1_XML"
        linkspecSingleClick="%DataURL%"
        targetSingleClick="_self">
    <XML id="FolderView1_XML">
        <view xmlns:xsl="http://www.w3.org/TR/WD-xsl">
            <column>
                <heading>myinteger</heading>
                <prop>myinteger</prop>
                <headerstyle></headerstyle>
                <style></style>
                <format></format>
                <sortable>1</sortable>
                <visible>1</visible>
                <checkbox>0</checkbox>
                <bitmap>0</bitmap>
```

```
    <customxsl>calcrating</customxsl>
</column>
<column>
    <heading>Friendly name</heading>
    <prop>DAV:displayname</prop>
    <headerstyle></headerstyle>
    <style></style>
    <format></format>
    <sortable>1</sortable>
    <visible>1</visible>
    <checkbox>0</checkbox>
    <bitmap>0</bitmap>
</column>
<filter>
    "DAV:ishidden" = false AND "DAV:isfolder" = false
     AND "DAV:contentclass" = 'My_list'
</filter>
<viewstyle></viewstyle>
<headerstyle>background-color:#C0C0C0</headerstyle>
<rowstyle></rowstyle>
<searchSubfolders>0</searchSubfolders>
<xslpassthrough name="calcrating">

    <xsl:choose>
        <xsl:when test="prop1[. = 1]">
            <DIV>
                <IMG SRC="../images/1star.gif">
                    <xsl:attribute name="alt">
                    <xsl:value-of select="prop1"/>
                    </xsl:attribute>
                </IMG>
            </DIV>
        </xsl:when>
        <xsl:when test="prop1[. = 2]">
            <DIV>
                <IMG SRC="../images/2stars.gif">
                    <xsl:attribute name="alt">
                    <xsl:value-of select="prop1"/>
                    </xsl:attribute>
                </IMG>
            </DIV>
        </xsl:when>
        <xsl:when test="prop1[. = 3]">
            <DIV>
                <IMG SRC="../images/3stars.gif">
                    <xsl:attribute name="alt">
                    <xsl:value-of select="prop1"/>
                    </xsl:attribute>
                </IMG>
            </DIV>
        </xsl:when>
        <xsl:otherwise>
            <DIV>
```

```
                        <IMG SRC="../images/4stars.gif">
                            <xsl:attribute name="alt">
                            <xsl:value-of select="prop1"/>
                            </xsl:attribute>
                        </IMG>
                    </DIV>
                </xsl:otherwise>
            </xsl:choose>
        </xslpassthrough>
    </view>
  </XML>
</WF:VIEW>
```

You might be wondering where the value *prop1* came from in the XSL *value-of* statement. You have to look at the *SELECT* statement that the view control creates to understand this. Here is the *SELECT* statement for the previous view:

```
SELECT "myinteger" As prop1, "DAV:displayname" As prop2, "urn:schemas:http-
mail:read" As read, "http://schemas.microsoft.com/exchange/outlookmessage-
class" As messageclass, "DAV:href" As davhref FROM SCOPE('SHALLOW TRAVERSAL OF
""') WHERE "DAV:ishidden" = false AND "DAV:isfolder" = false AND "DAV:content-
class" = 'My_list'
```

As you can see from the *SELECT* statement, your columns are aliased into *propX*, where *X* is the location of your property in the column order. Therefore, *prop1* refers to the *myinteger* property. Once you know this, creating the XSL code for the *xslpassthrough* property is straightforward. You can have multiple *xslpassthrough* blocks to implement different functionality for different columns in your application. Also, note that you can access different column values in your XSL by just specifying a different property name in your XSL code. This means you can add columns together to create a calculated column in your view.

Working with URL Overrides

In some cases, you might want to change the *SELECT* statement that you created in your view by using the *filter* tag. For example, you might want to add hyperlinks to your Web page to allow users to sort by a particular column or filter by a dynamic property (such as who the user is). To allow you to dynamically modify any property of the view control, the control supports the ability to pass along URL overrides of the properties of the control. You can also use script to override any of the properties of the control.

To use URL overrides, you just append certain keywords to the URL of the Web page that contains the view control. Here is the syntax for using URL overrides:

```
http://URL/?view.<viewid>.<property>=<value>&<property>=<value>
```

For example, if you want to append a new filter to the existing filter used in the SQL *SELECT* statement for your view, you can use the *filterappend* property in your URL and specify the additional SQL *WHERE* clause parameter you want to add. In the following URL, we will create a filtered view to display only those items where the display name is a certain value and sort the view in ascending order of importance. In this example, the ID of the view is named *folderview1* in our *wf:view* definition.

```
http://server/public/myapp/?view.folderview1.filterappend="DAV:dis-
playname"='myvalue.eml'&view.folderview1.sort="importance;ASC"
```

Besides exact matches, you can use other predicates such as the *LIKE* predicate. The following URL appends a filter to find all items that begin with the character *t*:

```
http://server/public/myapp/?view.folderview1.filterappend="DAV:displayname"
  LIKE 't%'
```

Below is the escape character encoded version of the URL.

```
http://server/public/myapp/?view.folderview1.filterappend="DAV:dis-
playname"%20LIKE%20't%25'
```

You can change any of the view control properties. Remember that if you are going to append filters, you must cast any values that are not *String* or *Boolean*. The following example shows a URL with the correct casting to query on an integer value:

```
http://server/public/myapp/?view.folderview1.filterappend="myinteger"=CAST("2"
as "i8")&view.folderview1.sort="importance;ASC"
```

The WSS Forms Object Model

Besides being able to just use the WSS Forms Renderer technology from HTML pages where you include special markup, you can also use WSS Forms from ASP pages because WSS Forms provides an object model that you can program against. Using ASP pages offers greater control over the way the forms are validated and rendered. For example, you might want to validate the data in the form on the server, and if an error occurs, you can display a message and point the user to the error. Using just the WSS Forms Renderer does not allow you to do this, but using WSS Forms in ASP pages does. Figure 20-9 depicts the object model for WSS Forms.

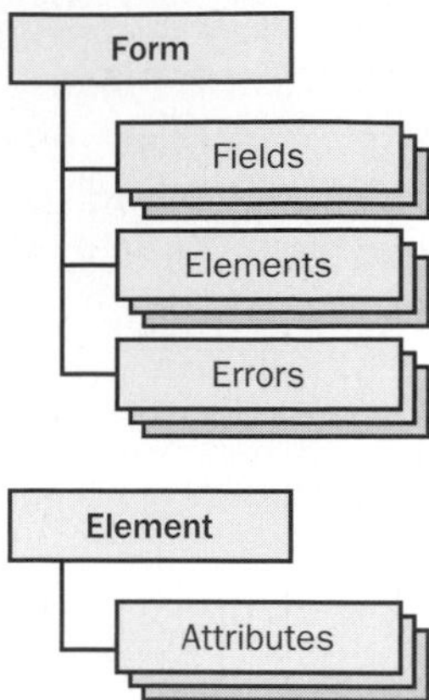

Figure 20-9 The WSS Forms object model

The main object in the object model is the *Form* object. The ProgID that you use to create this object in your ASP pages is *WSS.Form*. Table 20-11 lists the properties of the WSS *Form* object.

Table 20-11 Properties of the WSS *Form* Object

Property	Description
CodePage	The codepage for the form.
DataURL	Returns the URL to the item if it exists in Exchange.
Elements	Returns the *Elements* collection, which contains all the HTML elements on the page that are identified with a *name* or *id* attribute.
Errors	Returns the *Errors* collection, which contains all the errors that occur when you attempt to set values in the *Fields* collection.
Fields	Returns the ADO *Fields* collection for the item.
HasErrors	A *Boolean* that specifies whether there are any errors on the form. These errors can be application generated, such as when error strings are set on data in the item, or they can be generated by WSS Forms.
IsNew	A *Boolean* that returns *true* if the item is a new item.
LCID	Returns the locale identifier for the form.

Table 20-12 lists the methods of the WSS *Form* object.

Table 20-12 Methods of the WSS *Form* Object

Method	Description
Render	Renders the form, including any data-bound fields or views. You should call this method after all the work in your ASP is done because any ASP code after this method is ignored. You can use the WSS Form object model to perform any processing of items after your ASP code. This method can take two optional parameters. The first, *bCallResponseEnd*, is a *Boolean* that specifies whether to call the ASP *Response* object's *End* method. The default value is *True*. The other optional parameter, *bReturnError*, specifies whether any error information should be returned.
Update	Updates the *Fields* collection for the form. You can pass two optional parameters. The first is a string called *bstrURL*, which can be the URL to the item that you want updated. You will usually pass a blank string. The second parameter is a *Boolean* called *bOverwrite*, which specifies whether the existing data can be overwritten.

FormElements Collection and *FormElement* Object

When you use the *Elements* collection on the WSS *Form* object, you get back a *FormElements* collection. This collection contains all of the HTML elements in your form. You can use this collection to change the attributes of the element or the value of the element or to mark the element as having an error. The collection does not really have any special methods and properties, so we will jump right to the *FormElement* object. The *FormElements* collection has the standard *Count* and *Item* methods. For the *Item* method, you can pass either the numeric index or a string for which the object model will try to find a matching HTML element with an *id* or *name* attribute that matches that string.

The *FormElement* object allows you to query or modify HTML elements in your form. Table 20-13 lists the properties of the *FormElement* object.

Table 20-13 Properties of the *FormElement* Object

Property	Description
Attributes	Returns the *FormAttributes* collection.
EndTag	Returns a *Boolean* that is *true* if the element has a matching end tag.
ErrorString	A string that can specify any HTML you want to place after the element. You usually use this to display error strings if your validation script finds an error in the form. You'll see this property used in an upcoming example.
InnerText	A string that can specify any HTML you want between the opening and closing tag of the element.

Table 20-13 Properties of the *FormElement* Object

Property	Description
TagMarkup	Returns a string that is the entire opening tag of the element. For example, a hyperlink might return the following: `<A href="mylink.asp" style="color:blue">`
TagName	Returns the HTML element tag name (such as *DIV*).
Value	Returns the value from the *Fields* collection that is bound to the element.
Visible	A *Boolean* that controls whether the element is visible when the form is rendered.

FormAttributes Collection

The *FormAttributes* collection is part of the *FormElement* object. This is a collection of HTML attributes for the element. For example, an attribute for an *<A>* HTML element can be *id*, *name*, *href* or *style*. Using this collection, you can browse, add, or delete attributes on the HTML elements in your form. Table 20-14 lists the properties and methods of this collection.

Table 20-14 Properties and Methods of the *FormAttributes* Collection

Property	Description
Count	Returns the number of attributes.
Item	Retrieves an attribute by name or index number.
Method	**Description**
Add	Adds a new attribute. You must pass a string that is the name of the new attribute. You can then pass two optional parameters. The first specifies whether the attribute has a name only. The second specifies the value of the new attribute.
Delete	Deletes an attribute from the collection. You must pass the index of the attribute.

FormAttribute Object

From the *FormAttributes* collection you can get a *FormAttribute* object. This object is a single attribute on your HTML element. Table 20-15 lists the properties of this object.

Table 20-15 Properties of the *FormAttribute* Object

Property	Description
Name	Specifies the name of the attribute.
Value	Specifies the value of the attribute.
NameOnly	A *Boolean* that returns *false* if the attribute has a value.

FormErrors Collection

The *FormErrors* collection contains any errors after the form was submitted to the server. You can check this collection before calling the *Update* method as well to see if any errors are lingering in the form. Table 20-16 lists the properties of this collection.

Table 20-16 Properties of the *FormErrors* Collection

Name	Description
Count	Returns the number of *Error* objects in the collection.
Item	Retrieves a *FormError* using its index.

FormError Object

The *FormError* object allows you to programmatically access the properties and values for an error. Table 20-17 lists the properties of this object.

Table 20-17 Properties of the *FormError* Object

Property	Description
Description	Returns a description of the error.
File	Returns the source file where the error occurred.
Line	Returns the line number where the error occurred.
Name	Returns the name of the error.
Number	Returns the number of the error.
Source	Returns the actual source code that caused the error.
Value	Returns the value of the error.

Putting It All Together

Now that you've seen all the objects, methods, and properties of WSS Forms, let's look at a sample that puts everything together. The following sample uses the object model to hide fields when the item is new and to set fields when the item is posted. If a certain field is not filled in—in this case, the subject—when the user attempts to post an item, an error will be displayed in red next to the field, telling the user to fill in the field. This example just shows you how to get started with WSS Forms.

```
<HTML>
<%

    Set oForm = Server.CreateObject("WSS.Form")

    If (Request.ServerVariables("REQUEST_METHOD") = "POST") Then
        If (oForm.IsNew) Then
            If oForm.Elements("urn:schemas:httpmail:subject").Value="" Then
                oForm.Elements( _
                    "urn:schemas:httpmail:subject" _
                    ).ErrorString = "<DIV style=color:red " _
                                  & "id=subjecterror><B> You must enter " _
                                  & "a value for the subject!</B></DIV>"
            End If
            If oForm.HasErrors = True Then
                oForm.Elements("ItemInfo").Visible = False
            End If

            oForm.Fields("Status").Value = "NotApproved"
            oForm.Update()
        End If
    End If

    If (Request.ServerVariables("REQUEST_METHOD") = "GET") Then
        If (oForm.IsNew) Then
            oForm.Elements("ItemInfo").Visible = False
        End If
    End If

    oForm.Render()
%>

<HEAD>
    <title>Sample Page</title>
</HEAD>
<BODY>
    <form class="form"  method="POST" actionspec="%DataURL%"
          name="theform1" name="theform1">

        <span id="ItemInfo">
            Created: <span class="field" name="DAV:creationdate"></span>
```

```
            <br>
            Last Modified:
            <span class="field" name="DAV:getlastmodified"></span>
            <br>
    </span>
    <p>
    Subject:
    <input type="text" class="field" name="urn:schemas:httpmail:subject"
           size="20">
    <p>
    Status:
    <select class="field" name="Status" >
        <option value="NotApproved" selected>Not Approved
        <option value="Approved">Approved
        <option value="InProgress">In Progress
        <option value="Completed">Completed
    </select>
    <br>
    Description:
    <br>
    <textarea class=""field"  name="Description" rows="4" cols="30"
              rows="1" cols="20" form="theform1">
    </textarea>
    <p>
    <input type="submit" size="20" form="theform1">
    <input type="hidden"
           name="http://schemas.microsoft.com/exchange/nosave/hintforurl"
           value="urn:schemas:httpmail:subject">
    <input type="hidden" name="DAV:contentclass" value="SampleItem">
</form>

</BODY>
</HTML>
```

Remember that if you want to use ASP or ASP .NET as your rendering engine to modify your *ExecuteURL* in your form registration, do not use */exchweb/bin/exwform.dll*—instead, point to your ASP or ASP .NET file.

ASP/ASP.NET vs. WSS Forms

From the previous section, you can see that using ASP forms gives you a lot of flexibility in writing code that uses WSS Forms. However, it's easier to write code using just the renderer and pure HTML forms. Fortunately, you don't have to choose one or the other. You can intermix pure HTML forms with the special WSS Form markup with ASP or ASP .NET forms, which provide more complex functionality. In ASP or ASP .NET, you can use the WSS Form object model. Either approach will make writing Exchange applications a lot easier.

The *System.Web.Mail* Namespace

To make it easy for your .NET applications to send SMTP mail, the .NET Framework includes the *System.Web.Mail* namespace. The classes in this namespace are not as feature rich as CDO 1.21 or CDO for Exchange. The main difference between *System.Web.Mail* and CDO is that if you need to send just e-mail, use *System.Web.Mail* in your .NET applications. If you need to do complex collaborative applications that use calendaring or more advanced features of Exchange, use CDO in your .NET applications.

When working with this namespace, make sure to add a reference to the *System.Web* namespace. This namespace leverages the Collaboration Data Objects for Windows (CDOSYS) messaging component. Using this namespace, you can quickly construct plain text or HTML mail messages with or without attachments. The namespace includes three main classes: *MailMessage*, *MailAttachment*, and *SmtpMail*.

MailMessage Class

This class provides the methods and properties to construct an e-mail message. As you would suspect, this class supports the standard properties that an e-mail message needs such as *From*, *To*, *Cc*, *Bcc*, *Priority*, *Attachments*, *Fields*, and *Body* formatting properties. The sample application below will show you how to use the *MailMessage* class.

MailAttachment Class

This class provides the methods and properties for constructing e-mail attachments. By default, attachments are UUEncoded. This class is straightforward and the most common property you will use in the class is the *Filename* property. This property should be set to the path to the attachment you want to create in the instance of your class. The constructor for this class can also take a string argument. If you pass the path to the file you want to attach when you construct the object, you will achieve the same effect as setting the *Filename* property. You can have multiple instances of this class in order to add multiple attachments to a mail message. Once you have created your instances, you will want to use the *Add* method on the *Attachments* collection on the *MailMessage* class to add those attachments.

SMTPMail Class

This class provides the properties and methods for sending your mail messages via SMTP. This class allows you to set the SMTP server you want to use to send the message using the *SMTPServer* property. The class also has a *Send* method that you can use to send the message.

Sample Application

Since the *System.Web.Mail* namespace and classes in the namespace are very straightforward, a sample application is the best way to demonstrate how to use the classes and their properties and methods. Figure 20-10 shows the sample application. The application is a simple e-mail program written in Visual Basic that sends a message either as HTML or as plain text with an optional single attachment. The sample also shows how to use the *FileDialog* control to allow you to select the attachment you want to add.

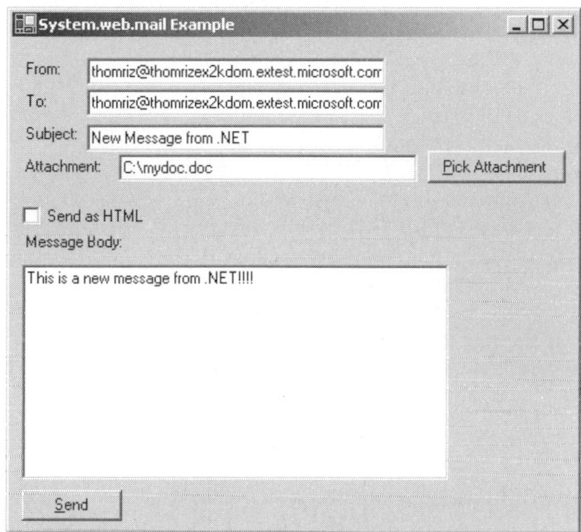

Figure 20-10 The sample e-mail application

```
Private Sub cmdSelectAttachment_Click(ByVal sender As System.Object,
                                      ByVal e As System.EventArgs)
                                      Handles cmdSelectAttachment.Click
    OpenFileDialog1.CheckFileExists = True
    OpenFileDialog1.CheckPathExists = True
    OpenFileDialog1.Multiselect = False
    Dim dialogresult As DialogResult = OpenFileDialog1.ShowDialog
    If dialogresult = dialogresult.OK Then
        'Get the file path
        txtAttachment.Text = OpenFileDialog1.FileName
    End If
End Sub

Private Sub cmdSend_Click(ByVal sender As System.Object,
                          ByVal e As System.EventArgs)
                          Handles cmdSend.Click
    On Error Resume Next
    'Check the values
    If txtFrom.Text = "" Then
```

```
        MsgBox("You must fill in the from field!")
        Exit Sub
    ElseIf txtTo.Text = "" Then
        MsgBox("You must fill in the to field!")
        Exit Sub
    End If
    Dim oMailMessage As New System.Web.Mail.MailMessage()
    'See if we need to send as HTML
    If checkSendAsHTML.Checked = True Then
        oMailMessage.BodyFormat = Web.Mail.MailFormat.Html
    End If
    oMailMessage.To = txtTo.Text()
    oMailMessage.From = txtFrom.Text()
    oMailMessage.Subject = txtSubject.Text()
    oMailMessage.Body = txtBody.Text()
    'See if there is an attachment
    If txtAttachment.Text <> "" Then
        'Add the attachment
        Dim oMailAttachment As New _
                    System.Web.Mail.MailAttachment(txtAttachment.Text())
        oMailMessage.Attachments.Add(oMailAttachment)
    End If

    Dim oSMTPMail As System.Web.Mail.SmtpMail
    oSMTPMail.Send(oMailMessage)
End Sub
```

Conclusion

It has been a long journey through the many collaborative development technologies you can use with Exchange and Outlook. You have learned how rich an environment Exchange and Outlook offer. You can provide applications that meet the needs of your users, whether those needs require Windows or Web technologies.

With the introduction of Windows SharePoint Services and the newest version of SharePoint Portal Server, the world of collaboration on the Microsoft platform has grown tremendously. For this reason, be sure to look at the companion material posted on this book's Web site. There you will find not only the samples used in this book but also additional chapters on both Exchange and Outlook development. Also, there are chapters on developing using the SharePoint family of products and technologies that were not included in this edition of the printed book.

Index

Symbols

A

B

C

D

E

G

H

M

O

P

Q

R

S

T

U

V

W

X

Y

Z

Thomas Rizzo

Thomas Rizzo is a group product manager in the SQL Server product group. Before working on SQL Server, Tom worked in the Exchange Server group for five years, where his focus was getting customers to use the platform confidently. Prior to moving to Microsoft's corporate product teams, Tom worked as a systems engineer for the Microsoft office in Washington, D.C. He holds a degree from Georgetown University.

The manuscript for this book was prepared and galleyed using Microsoft Word. Pages were composed by Microsoft Press using Adobe FrameMaker+SGML for Windows, with text in Garamond and display type in Helvetica Condensed. Composed pages were delivered to the printer as electronic prepress files.

Cover Designer:	Methodologie, Inc.
Interior Graphic Designer:	James D. Kramer
Principal Compositor:	Dan Latimer
Interior Artist:	Joel Panchot
Principal Proofreader:	Ina Chang
Indexer:	Seth Maslin

In-depth technical information and tools for Microsoft Windows Server 2003

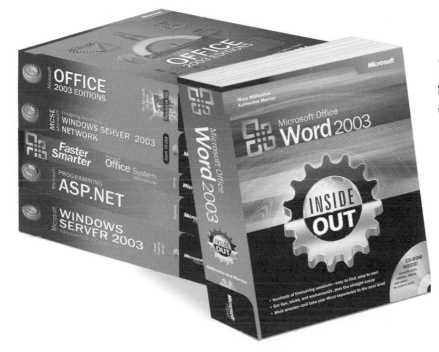

Get a **Free**

e-mail newsletter, updates, special offers, links to related books, and more when you

register online!

Register your Microsoft Press® title on our Web site and you'll get a FREE subscription to our e-mail newsletter, *Microsoft Press Book Connections.* You'll find out about newly released and upcoming books and learning tools, online events, software downloads, special offers and coupons for Microsoft Press customers, and information about major Microsoft® product releases. You can also read useful additional information about all the titles we publish, such as detailed book descriptions, tables of contents and indexes, sample chapters, links to related books and book series, author biographies, and reviews by other customers.

Registration is easy. Just visit this Web page and fill in your information:

http://www.microsoft.com/mspress/register

Microsoft®

Proof of Purchase

Use this page as proof of purchase if participating in a promotion or rebate offer on this title. Proof of purchase must be used in conjunction with other proof(s) of payment such as your dated sales receipt—see offer details.

Programming Microsoft® Outlook® and Microsoft Exchange 2003, Third Edition

0-7356-1464-4

____

CUSTOMER NAME

Microsoft Press, PO Box 97017, Redmond, WA 98073-9830